LEARNSMART ADVANTAGE WORKS

LEARNSMART®

A	B	C	D	
30.5%	33.5%	22.6%	8.7%	4.7%

A	B	C	D	
19.3%	38.6%	28.0%	9.6%	4.5%

Without LearnSmart

More C students **earn B's**

*Study: 690 students / 6 institutions

Over 20%
more students pass the class with LearnSmart

*A&P Research Study

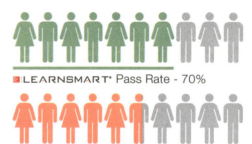

LEARNSMART® Pass Rate - 70%

Without LearnSmart Pass Rate - 57%

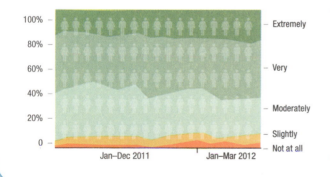

100% — Extremely
80%
60% — Very
40%
20% — Moderately
0 — Slightly
— Not at all

Jan–Dec 2011   Jan–Mar 2012

More than 60%
of all students agreed LearnSmart was a very or extremely helpful learning tool

*Based on 750,000 student survey responses

> *AVAILABLE*
ON-THE-GO

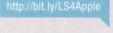

How do you rank against your peers?

What you know (green) and what you still need to review (yellow), based on your answers.

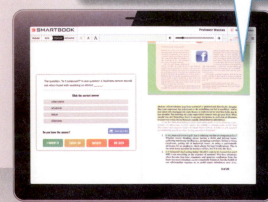

Let's see how confident you are on the questions.

COMPARE AND CHOOSE WHAT'S RIGHT FOR YOU

	BOOK	LEARNSMART	ASSIGNMENTS	
connect	✓	✓	✓	LearnSmart, assignments, and SmartBook—all in one digital product for maximum savings!
connect Looseleaf	✓	✓	✓	Pop the pages into your own binder or carry just the pages you need.
connect Bound Book	✓	✓	✓	The #1 Student Choice!
SMARTBOOK® Access Code	✓	✓		The first and only book that adapts to you!
LEARNSMART® ADVANTAGE Access Code		✓		The smartest way to get from a B to an A.
create™	✓	✓	✓	Check with your instructor about a custom option for your course.

> Buy directly from the source at http://shop.mheducation.com.

Corporate Finance

The McGraw-Hill/Irwin Series in Finance, Insurance, and Real Estate

Stephen A. Ross
Franco Modigliani Professor of Finance and Economics Sloan School of Management
Massachusetts Institute of Technology
Consulting Editor

FINANCIAL MANAGEMENT

Block, Hirt, and Danielsen
Foundations of Financial Management
Fifteenth Edition

Brealey, Myers, and Allen
Principles of Corporate Finance
Eleventh Edition

Brealey, Myers, and Allen
Principles of Corporate Finance, Concise
Second Edition

Brealey, Myers, and Marcus
Fundamentals of Corporate Finance
Eighth Edition

Brooks
FinGame Online 5.0

Bruner
Case Studies in Finance: Managing for Corporate Value Creation
Seventh Edition

Cornett, Adair, and Nofsinger
Finance: Applications and Theory
Third Edition

Cornett, Adair, and Nofsinger
M: Finance
Third Edition

DeMello
Cases in Finance
Second Edition

Grinblatt (editor)
Stephen A. Ross, Mentor: Influence through Generations

Grinblatt and Titman
Financial Markets and Corporate Strategy
Second Edition

Higgins
Analysis for Financial Management
Eleventh Edition

Kellison
Theory of Interest
Third Edition

Ross, Westerfield, Jaffe, and Jordan
Corporate Finance
Eleventh Edition

Ross, Westerfield, Jaffe, and Jordan
Corporate Finance: Core Principles and Applications
Fourth Edition

Ross, Westerfield, and Jordan
Essentials of Corporate Finance
Eighth Edition

Ross, Westerfield, and Jordan
Fundamentals of Corporate Finance
Eleventh Edition

Shefrin
Behavioral Corporate Finance: Decisions that Create Value
First Edition

White
Financial Analysis with an Electronic Calculator
Sixth Edition

INVESTMENTS

Bodie, Kane, and Marcus
Essentials of Investments
Ninth Edition

Bodie, Kane, and Marcus
Investments
Tenth Edition

Hirt and Block
Fundamentals of Investment Management
Tenth Edition

Jordan, Miller, and Dolvin
Fundamentals of Investments: Valuation and Management
Seventh Edition

Stewart, Piros, and Heisler
Running Money: Professional Portfolio Management
First Edition

Sundaram and Das
Derivatives: Principles and Practice
Second Edition

FINANCIAL INSTITUTIONS AND MARKETS

Rose and Hudgins
Bank Management and Financial Services
Ninth Edition

Rose and Marquis
Financial Institutions and Markets
Eleventh Edition

Saunders and Cornett
Financial Institutions Management: A Risk Management Approach
Eighth Edition

Saunders and Cornett
Financial Markets and Institutions
Sixth Edition

INTERNATIONAL FINANCE

Eun and Resnick
International Financial Management
Seventh Edition

REAL ESTATE

Brueggeman and Fisher
Real Estate Finance and Investments
Fourteenth Edition

Ling and Archer
Real Estate Principles: A Value Approach
Fourth Edition

FINANCIAL PLANNING AND INSURANCE

Allen, Melone, Rosenbloom, and Mahoney
Retirement Plans: 401(k)s, IRAs, and Other Deferred Compensation Approaches
Eleventh Edition

Altfest
Personal Financial Planning
First Edition

Harrington and Niehaus
Risk Management and Insurance
Second Edition

Kapoor, Dlabay, Hughes, and Hart
Focus on Personal Finance: An Active Approach to Help You Achieve Financial Literacy
Fifth Edition

Kapoor, Dlabay, and Hughes
Personal Finance
Eleventh Edition

Walker and Walker
Personal Finance: Building Your Future
First Edition

Corporate Finance

ELEVENTH EDITION

Stephen A. Ross
Sloan School of Management
Massachusetts Institute of Technology

Randolph W. Westerfield
Marshall School of Business
University of Southern California

Jeffrey Jaffe
Wharton School of Business
University of Pennsylvania

Bradford D. Jordan
Gatton College of Business and Economics
University of Kentucky

CORPORATE FINANCE, ELEVENTH EDITION

Published by McGraw-Hill Education, 2 Penn Plaza, New York, NY 10121. Copyright © 2016 by McGraw-Hill Education. All rights reserved. Printed in the United States of America. Previous editions © 2013, 2010, 2008, 2005, 2002, 1999, 1996, 1993, 1990, and 1988. No part of this publication may be reproduced or distributed in any form or by any means, or stored in a database or retrieval system, without the prior written consent of McGraw-Hill Education, including, but not limited to, in any network or other electronic storage or transmission, or broadcast for distance learning.

Some ancillaries, including electronic and print components, may not be available to customers outside the United States.

This book is printed on acid-free paper.

5 6 7 8 9 LWI 21 20 19 18

ISBN   978-0-07-786175-9
MHID   0-07-786175-2

Senior Vice President, Products & Markets: *Kurt L. Strand*
Vice President, General Manager, Products & Markets: *Marty Lange*
Vice President, Content Design & Delivery: *Kimberly Meriwether David*
Managing Director: *James Heine*
Brand Manager: *Charles Synovec*
Director, Product Development: *Rose Koos*
Lead Product Developer: *Michele Janicek*
Product Developer: *Jennifer Upton*
Marketing Manager: *Melissa Caughlin*
Director of Digital Content Development: *Douglas Ruby*
Digital Product Developer: *Tobi Philips*
Digital Product Analyst: *Kevin Shanahan*
Director, Content Design & Delivery: *Linda Avenarius*
Program Manager: *Mark Christianson*
Content Project Managers: *Kathryn D. Wright, Bruce Gin, and Karen Jozefowicz*
Buyer: *Jennifer Pickel*
Design: *Matt Diamond*
Content Licensing Specialist: *Beth Thole*
Cover Image: *Getty Images/Jon-Pierre Kelani / EyeEm*
Compositor: *MPS Limited, A Macmillan Company*
Printer: *LSC Communications*

All credits appearing on page or at the end of the book are considered to be an extension of the copyright page.

Library of Congress Cataloging-in-Publication Data
Ross, Stephen A.
    Corporate finance / Stephen A. Ross, Sloan School of Management,
    Massachusetts Institute of Technology, Randolph W. Westerfield, Marshall
    School of Business, University of Southern California, Jeffrey Jaffe,
    Wharton School of Business, University of Pennsylvania, Bradford D. Jordan,
    Gatton College of Business and Economics, University of Kentucky.—Eleventh Edition.
    pages cm.—(Corporate finance)
    Revised edition of Corporate finance, 2013.   ISBN 978-0-07-786175-9 (alk. paper)
    1. Corporations—Finance. I. Westerfield, Randolph. II. Jaffe, Jeffrey F., 1946- III. Title.

HG4026.R675 2016
658.15—dc23   2015028977

www.mhhe.com

To our family and friends
with love and gratitude.

About the Authors

STEPHEN A. ROSS *Sloan School of Management, Massachusetts Institute of Technology*   Stephen A. Ross is the Franco Modigliani Professor of Financial Economics at the Sloan School of Management, Massachusetts Institute of Technology. One of the most widely published authors in finance and economics, Professor Ross is recognized for his work in developing the arbitrage pricing theory, as well as for having made substantial contributions to the discipline through his research in signaling, agency theory, option pricing, and the theory of the term structure of interest rates, among other topics. A past president of the American Finance Association, he currently serves as an associate editor of several academic and practitioner journals and is a trustee of CalTech.

RANDOLPH W. WESTERFIELD *Marshall School of Business, University of Southern California*   Randolph W. Westerfield is Dean Emeritus of the University of Southern California's Marshall School of Business and is the Charles B. Thornton Professor of Finance Emeritus.

Professor Westerfield came to USC from the Wharton School, University of Pennsylvania, where he was the chairman of the finance department and member of the finance faculty for 20 years. He is a member of the Board of Trustees of Oak Tree Capital Mutual Funds. His areas of expertise include corporate financial policy, investment management, and stock market price behavior.

JEFFREY F. JAFFE *Wharton School of Business, University of Pennsylvania*   Jeffrey F. Jaffe has been a frequent contributor to the finance and economics literatures in such journals as the *Quarterly Economic Journal, The Journal of Finance, The Journal of Financial and Quantitative Analysis, The Journal of Financial Economics,* and *The Financial Analysts Journal*. His best-known work concerns insider trading, where he showed both that corporate insiders earn abnormal profits from their trades and that regulation has little effect on these profits. He has also made contributions concerning initial public offerings, regulation of utilities, the behavior of market makers, the fluctuation of gold prices, the theoretical effect of inflation on interest rates, the empirical effect of inflation on capital asset prices, the relationship between small-capitalization stocks and the January effect, and the capital structure decision.

BRADFORD D. JORDAN *Gatton College of Business and Economics, University of Kentucky*   Bradford D. Jordan is professor of finance and holder of the Richard W. and Janis H. Furst Endowed Chair in Finance at the University of Kentucky. He has a long-standing interest in both applied and theoretical issues in corporate finance and has extensive experience teaching all levels of corporate finance and financial management policy. Professor Jordan has published numerous articles on issues such as cost of capital, capital structure, and the behavior of security prices. He is a past president of the Southern Finance Association, and he is coauthor of *Fundamentals of Investments: Valuation and Management,* 7th edition, a leading investments text, also published by McGraw-Hill/Irwin.

Preface

The teaching and the practice of corporate finance are more challenging and exciting than ever before. The last decade has seen fundamental changes in financial markets and financial instruments. In the early years of the 21st century, we still see announcements in the financial press about takeovers, junk bonds, financial restructuring, initial public offerings, bankruptcies, and derivatives. In addition, there are the new recognitions of "real" options, private equity and venture capital, subprime mortgages, bailouts, and credit spreads. As we have learned in the recent global credit crisis and stock market collapse, the world's financial markets are more integrated than ever before. Both the theory and practice of corporate finance have been moving ahead with uncommon speed, and our teaching must keep pace.

These developments have placed new burdens on the teaching of corporate finance. On one hand, the changing world of finance makes it more difficult to keep materials up to date. On the other hand, the teacher must distinguish the permanent from the temporary and avoid the temptation to follow fads. Our solution to this problem is to emphasize the modern fundamentals of the theory of finance and make the theory come to life with contemporary examples. Increasingly, many of these examples are outside the United States.

All too often the beginning student views corporate finance as a collection of unrelated topics that are unified largely because they are bound together between the covers of one book. We want our book to embody and reflect the main principle of finance: Namely, that good financial decisions will add value to the firm and to shareholders and bad financial decisions will destroy value. The key to understanding how value is added or destroyed is cash flows. To add value, firms must generate more cash than they use. We hope this simple principle is manifest in all parts of this book.

The Intended Audience of This Book

This book has been written for the introductory courses in corporate finance at the MBA level and for the intermediate courses in many undergraduate programs. Some instructors will find our text appropriate for the introductory course at the undergraduate level as well.

We assume that most students either will have taken, or will be concurrently enrolled in, courses in accounting, statistics, and economics. This exposure will help students understand some of the more difficult material. However, the book is self-contained, and a prior knowledge of these areas is not essential. The only mathematics prerequisite is basic algebra.

New to Eleventh Edition

Each chapter has been updated and where relevant, "internationalized." We try to capture the excitement of corporate finance with current examples, chapter vignettes, and openers. Spreadsheets applications are spread throughout.

- **CHAPTER 2** has been rewritten to better highlight the notion of cash flow and how it contrasts with accounting income.

- **CHAPTER 6** has been reorganized to better emphasize some special cases of capital budgeting including cost cutting proposals and investments of unequal lives.

- **CHAPTER 9** has updated the many new ways of stock market trading.

- **CHAPTER 10** has updated material on historical risk and return and better motivated the equity risk premium.

- **CHAPTER 13** has sharpened the discussion of how to use the CAPM for the cost of equity and WACC.

- **CHAPTER 14** has updated and added to the discussion of behavioral finance and its challenge to the efficient market hypothesis.

- **CHAPTER 15** expands on its description of equity and debt and has new material on the value of a call provision as well as the differences between book and market values.

- **CHAPTER 19 AND 20** continue to build on the notion of a financial life cycle where capital structure decisions are driven by the varying needs for internal and external finance over a firm's life.

Pedagogy

In this edition of *Corporate Finance*, we have updated and improved our features to present material in a way that makes it coherent and easy to understand. In addition, *Corporate Finance* is rich in valuable learning tools and support, to help students succeed in learning the fundamentals of financial management.

Chapter Opening Vignettes

Each chapter begins with a contemporary vignette that highlights the concepts in the chapter and their relevance to real-world examples.

10 — PART III: RISK

Risk and Return
LESSONS FROM MARKET HISTORY

With the S&P 500 Index returning about 14 percent and the NASDAQ Composite Index up about 13 percent in 2014, stock market performance overall was very good. In particular, investors in outpatient diagnostic imaging services company RadNet, Inc., had to be happy about the 411 percent gain in that stock, and investors in biopharmaceutical company Achillon Pharmaceuticals had to feel pretty good following that company's 269 percent gain. Of course, not all stocks increased in value during the year. Stock in Transocean Ltd. fell 63 percent during the year, and stock in Avon Products dropped 44 percent.

These examples show that there were tremendous potential profits to be made during 2014, but there was also the risk of losing money—and lots of it. So what should you, as a stock market investor, expect when you invest your own money? In this chapter, we study more than eight decades of market history to find out.

10.1 Returns
DOLLAR RETURNS

How did the market do today? Find out at **finance.yahoo.com**.

Suppose the Video Concept Company has several thousand shares of stock outstanding and you are a shareholder. Further suppose that you purchased some of the shares of stock in the company at the beginning of the year; it is now year-end and you want to figure out how well you have done on your investment. The return you get on an investment in stocks, like that in bonds or any other investment, comes in two forms.

As the owner of stock in the Video Concept Company, you are a part owner of the company. If the company is profitable, it generally could distribute some of its profits to the shareholders. Therefore, as the owner of shares of stock, you could receive some cash, called a *dividend*, during the year. This cash is the *income component* of your return. In addition to the dividends, the other part of your return is the *capital gain*—or, if it is negative, the *capital loss* (negative capital gain)—on the investment.

For example, suppose we are considering the cash flows of the investment in Figure 10.1, showing that you purchased 100 shares of stock at the beginning of the year at a price of $37 per share. Your total investment, then, was:

$$C_0 = \$37 \times 100 = \$3,700$$

302

ExcelMaster Icons

Topics covered in the comprehensive ExcelMaster supplement (in Connect Finance) are indicated by an icon in the margin.

EXAMPLE 6.5

Allocated Costs The Voetmann Consulting Corp. devotes one wing of its suite of offices to a library requiring a cash outflow of $100,000 a year in upkeep. A proposed capital budgeting project is expected to generate revenue equal to 5 percent of the overall firm's sales. An executive at the firm, David Pedersen, argues that $5,000 (=5 percent × $100,000) should be viewed as the proposed project's share of the library's costs. Is this appropriate for capital budgeting?

The answer is no. One must ask what the difference is between the cash flows of the entire firm with the project and the cash flows of the entire firm without the project. The firm will spend $100,000 on library upkeep whether or not the proposed project is accepted. Because acceptance of the proposed project does not affect this cash flow, the cash flow should be ignored when calculating the NPV of the project. For example, suppose the project has a positive NPV without the allocated costs but is rejected because of the allocated costs. In this case, the firm is losing positive value that it could have gained otherwise.

6.2 The Baldwin Company: An Example

We next consider the example of a proposed investment in machinery and related items. Our example involves the Baldwin Company and colored bowling balls.

The Baldwin Company, originally established 16 years ago to make footballs, is now a leading producer of tennis balls, baseballs, footballs, and golf balls. Nine years ago, the company introduced "High Flite," its first line of high-performance golf balls. Baldwin management has sought opportunities in whatever businesses seem to have some potential for cash flow. Recently W. C. Meadows, vice president of the Baldwin Company, identified another segment of the sports ball market that looked promising and that he felt was not adequately served by larger manufacturers. That market was for brightly colored bowling balls, and he believed many bowlers valued appearance and style above performance. He also believed that it would be difficult for competitors to take advantage of the opportunity because of both Baldwin's cost advantages and its highly developed marketing skills.

As a result, the Baldwin Company investigated the marketing potential of brightly colored bowling balls. Baldwin sent a questionnaire to consumers in three markets: Philadelphia, Los Angeles, and New Haven. The results of the three questionnaires were much better than expected and supported the conclusion that the brightly colored bowling balls could achieve a 10 to 15 percent share of the market. Of course, some people at Baldwin complained about the cost of the test marketing, which was $250,000. (As we shall see later, this is a sunk cost and should not be included in project evaluation.)

In any case, the Baldwin Company is now considering investing in a machine to produce bowling balls. The bowling balls would be manufactured in a building owned by the firm and located near Los Angeles. This building, which is vacant, and the land can be sold for $150,000 after taxes.

Working with his staff, Meadows is preparing an analysis of the proposed new product. He summarizes his assumptions as follows: The cost of the bowling ball machine is

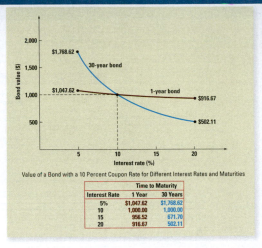

Figure 8.2
Interest Rate Risk and Time to Maturity

Value of a Bond with a 10 Percent Coupon Rate for Different Interest Rates and Maturities

	Time to Maturity	
Interest Rate	1 Year	30 Years
5%	$1,047.62	$1,768.62
10	1,000.00	1,000.00
15	956.52	671.70
20	916.67	502.11

us that a relatively small change in interest rates will lead to a substantial change in the bond's value. In comparison, the one-year bond's price is relatively insensitive to interest rate changes.

Intuitively, shorter-term bonds have less interest rate sensitivity because the $1,000 face amount is received so quickly. For example, the present value of this amount isn't greatly affected by a small change in interest rates if the amount is received in, say, one year. However, even a small change in the interest rate, once compounded for, say, 30 years, can have a significant effect on present value. As a result, the present value of

Figures and Tables

This text makes extensive use of real data and presents them in various figures and tables. Explanations in the narrative, examples, and end-of-chapter problems will refer to many of these exhibits.

Examples

Separate called-out examples are integrated throughout the chapters. Each example illustrates an intuitive or mathematical application in a step-by-step format. There is enough detail in the explanations so students don't have to look elsewhere for additional information.

EXAMPLE 9.5

Calculating the Required Return Pagemaster Enterprises, the company examined in Example 9.4, has 1,000,000 shares of stock outstanding. The stock is selling at $10. What is the required return on the stock?

The payout ratio is the ratio of dividends/earnings. Because Pagemaster's retention ratio is 40 percent, the payout ratio, which is 1 − Retention ratio, is 60 percent. Recall both that Pagemaster just reported earnings of $2,000,000 and that the firm's growth rate is .064.

Earnings a year from now will be $2,128,000 (=$2,000,000 × 1.064), implying that dividends will be $1,276,800 (=.60 × $2,128,000). Dividends per share will be $1.28 (=$1,276,800/1,000,000). Given that $g = .064$, we calculate R from (9.9) as follows:

$$.192 = \frac{\$1.28}{\$10.00} + .064$$

In Their Own Words

ROBERT C. HIGGINS ON SUSTAINABLE GROWTH

Most financial officers know intuitively that it takes money to make money. Rapid sales growth requires increased assets in the form of accounts receivable, inventory, and fixed plant, which, in turn, require money to pay for assets. They also know that if their company does not have the money when needed, it can literally "grow broke." The sustainable growth equation states these intuitive truths explicitly.

Sustainable growth is often used by bankers and other external analysts to assess a company's creditworthiness. They are aided in this exercise by several sophisticated computer software packages that provide detailed analyses of the company's past financial performance, including its annual sustainable growth rate.

Bankers use this information in several ways. Quick comparison of a company's actual growth rate to its sustainable rate tells the banker what issues will be at the top of management's financial agenda. If actual growth consistently exceeds sustainable growth, management's problem will be where to get the cash to finance growth. The banker thus can anticipate interest in loan products. Conversely, if sustainable growth consistently exceeds actual, the banker had best be prepared to talk about

investment products because management's problem will be what to do with all the cash that keeps piling up in the till.

Bankers also find the sustainable growth equation useful for explaining to financially inexperienced small business owners and overly optimistic entrepreneurs that, for the long-run viability of their business, it is necessary to keep growth and profitability in proper balance.

Finally, comparison of actual to sustainable growth rates helps a banker understand why a loan applicant needs money and for how long the need might continue. In one instance, a loan applicant requested $100,000 to pay off several insistent suppliers and promised to repay in a few months when he collected some accounts receivable that were coming due. A sustainable growth analysis revealed that the firm had been growing at four to six times its sustainable growth rate and that this pattern was likely to continue in the foreseeable future. This alerted the banker that impatient suppliers were only a symptom of the much more fundamental disease of overly rapid growth, and that a $100,000 loan would likely prove to be only the down payment on a much larger, multiyear commitment.

SOURCE: Robert C. Higgins is Professor of Finance at the University of Washington. He pioneered the use of sustainable growth as a tool for financial analysis.

"In Their Own Words" Boxes

Located throughout the chapters, this unique series consists of articles written by distinguished scholars or practitioners about key topics in the text. Boxes include essays by Edward I. Altman, Robert S. Hansen, Robert C. Higgins, Michael C. Jensen, Merton Miller, and Jay R. Ritter.

Spreadsheet Applications

Now integrated into select chapters, Spreadsheet Applications boxes reintroduce students to Excel, demonstrating how to set up spreadsheets in order to analyze common financial problems—a vital part of every business student's education. (For even more spreadsheet example problems, check out ExcelMaster in Connect Finance).

This is the stockholders' share in the firm stated in accounting terms. The accounting value of stockholders' equity increases when retained earnings are added. This occurs when the firm retains part of its earnings instead of paying them out as dividends.

VALUE VERSUS COST

The accounting value of a firm's assets is frequently referred to as the *carrying value* or the *book value* of the assets.[2] Under **generally accepted accounting principles (GAAP)**, audited financial statements of firms in the United States carry the assets at cost.[3] Thus the terms *carrying value* and *book value* are unfortunate. They specifically say "value," when in fact the accounting numbers are based on cost. This misleads many readers of financial statements to think that the firm's assets are recorded at true market values. *Market value* is the price at which willing buyers and sellers would trade the assets. It would be only a coincidence if accounting value and market value were the same. In fact, management's job is to create value for the firm that exceeds its cost.

Many people use the balance sheet, but the information each may wish to extract is not the same. A banker may look at a balance sheet for evidence of accounting liquidity and working capital. A supplier may also note the size of accounts payable and therefore the general promptness of payments. Many users of financial statements, including managers and investors, want to know the value of the firm, not its cost. This information is not found on the balance sheet. In fact, many of the true resources of the firm do not appear on the balance sheet: good management, proprietary assets, favorable economic conditions, and so on. Henceforth,

The home page for the Financial Accounting Standards Board (FASB) is **www.fasb.org**.

Explanatory Website Links

These Web links are specifically selected to accompany text material and provide students and instructors with a quick reference to additional information on the Internet.

25.5 Interest Rate Futures Contracts

In this section we consider interest rate futures contracts. Our examples deal with futures contracts on Treasury bonds because of their high popularity. We first price Treasury bonds and Treasury bond forward contracts. Differences between futures and forward contracts are explored. Hedging examples are provided next.

PRICING OF TREASURY BONDS

As mentioned earlier in the text, a Treasury bond pays semiannual interest over its life. In addition, the face value of the bond is paid at maturity. Consider a 20-year, 8 percent coupon bond that was issued on March 1. The first payment is to occur in six months—that is, on September 1. The value of the bond can be determined as follows:

Pricing of Treasury Bond

$$P_{TB} = \frac{\$40}{1 + R_1} + \frac{\$40}{(1 + R_2)^2} + \frac{\$40}{(1 + R_3)^3} + \cdots + \frac{\$40}{(1 + R_{39})^{39}} + \frac{\$1,040}{(1 + R_{40})^{40}} \quad (25.1)$$

Because an 8 percent coupon bond pays interest of $80 a year, the semiannual coupon is $40. Principal and the semiannual coupon are both paid at maturity. As we mentioned in a previous chapter, the price of the Treasury bond, P_{TB}, is determined by discounting each payment on the bond at the appropriate spot rate. Because the payments are semiannual, each spot rate is expressed in semiannual terms. That is, imagine a horizontal term structure where the effective annual yield is 8 percent for all maturities. Because each spot

[3]Ordinarily, an unusual firm name in this textbook is a tip-off that it is fictional. This, however, is a true story.

Numbered Equations

Key equations are numbered and listed on the back endsheets for easy reference.

The end-of-chapter material reflects and builds upon the concepts learned from the chapter and study features.

Summary and Conclusions

1. Firms hedge to reduce risk. This chapter showed a number of hedging strategies.
2. A forward contract is an agreement by two parties to sell an item for cash at a later date. The price is set at the time the agreement is signed. However, cash changes hands on the date of delivery. Forward contracts are generally not traded on organized exchanges.
3. Futures contracts are also agreements for future delivery. They have certain advantages, such as liquidity, that forward contracts do not. An unusual feature of futures contracts is the mark-to-the-market convention. If the price of a futures contract falls on a particular day, every buyer of the contract must pay money to the clearinghouse. Every seller of the contract receives money from the clearinghouse. Everything is reversed if the price rises. The mark-to-the-market convention prevents defaults on futures contracts.
4. We divided hedges into two types: Short hedges and long hedges. An individual or firm that sells a futures contract to reduce risk is instituting a short hedge. Short hedges are generally appropriate for holders of inventory. An individual or firm that buys a futures contract to reduce risk is instituting a long hedge. Long hedges are typically used by firms with contracts to sell finished goods at a fixed price.
5. An interest rate futures contract employs a bond as the deliverable instrument. Because of their popularity, we worked with Treasury bond futures contracts. We showed that Treasury bond futures contracts can be priced using the same type of net present value analysis that is used to price Treasury bonds themselves.
6. Many firms face interest rate risk. They can reduce this risk by hedging with interest rate futures contracts. As with other commodities, a short hedge involves the sale of a futures contract. Firms that are committed to buying mortgages or other bonds are likely to institute short hedges. A long hedge involves the purchase of a futures contract. Firms that have agreed to sell mortgages or other bonds at a fixed price are likely to institute long hedges.
7. Duration measures the average maturity of all the cash flows in a bond. Bonds with high duration have high price variability. Firms frequently try to match the duration of their assets with the duration of their liabilities.
8. Swaps are agreements to exchange cash flows over time. The first major type is an interest rate swap in which one pattern of coupon payments, say, fixed payments, is exchanged for another, say, coupons that float with LIBOR. The second major type is a currency swap, in which an agreement is struck to swap payments denominated in one currency for payments in another currency over time.

Concept Questions

1. **Hedging Strategies** If a firm is selling futures contracts on lumber as a hedging strategy, what must be true about the firm's exposure to lumber prices?
2. **Hedging Strategies** If a firm is buying call options on pork belly futures as a hedging strategy, what must be true about the firm's exposure to pork belly prices?
3. **Forwards and Futures** What is the difference between a forward contract and a futures contract? Why do you think that futures contracts are much more common? Are there any circumstances under which you might prefer to use forwards instead of futures? Explain.

Summary and Conclusions

The summary provides a quick review of key concepts in the chapter.

Questions and Problems

Because solving problems is so critical to a student's learning, new questions and problems have been added, and existing questions and problems have been revised. All problems have also been thoroughly reviewed and checked for accuracy.

Problems have been grouped according to level of difficulty with the levels listed in the margin: Basic, Intermediate, and Challenge.

Additionally, we have tried to make the problems in the critical "concept" chapters, such as those on value, risk, and capital structure, especially challenging and interesting.

We provide answers to selected problems in Appendix B at the end of the book.

Excel Master It! Problems

Included in the end-of-chapter material are problems directly incorporating Excel, and new tips and techniques taught in the chapter's ExcelMaster supplement.

Excel Master It! Problem

Excel is a great tool for solving problems, but with many time value of money problems, you may still need to draw a time line. For example, consider a classic retirement problem. A friend is celebrating her birthday and wants to start saving for her anticipated retirement. She has the following years to retirement and retirement spending goals:

Years until retirement	30
Amount to withdraw each year	$90,000
Years to withdraw in retirement	20

Excel Problems

Indicated by the Excel icon in the margin, these problems can be found at the end of almost all chapters. Located in Connect Finance for Corporate Finance 11e, Excel templates have been created for each of these problems, where students can use the data in the problem to work out the solution using Excel skills.

month in a bond account. The return of the stock account is expected to be 11 percent per year, and the bond account will earn 6 percent per year. When you retire, you will combine your money into an account with an annual return of 8 percent. How much can you withdraw each month from your account assuming a 25-year withdrawal period?

24. **Calculating Rates of Return** Suppose an investment offers to quadruple your money in 12 months (don't believe it). What rate of return per quarter are you being offered?

25. **Calculating Rates of Return** You're trying to choose between two different investments, both of which have up-front costs of $75,000. Investment G returns $125,000 in six years. Investment H returns $185,000 in 10 years. Which of these investments has the higher return?

 26. **Growing Perpetuities** Mark Weinstein has been working on an advanced technology in laser eye surgery. His technology will be available in the near term. He anticipates his first annual cash flow from the technology to be $215,000, received two years from today. Subsequent annual cash flows will grow at 3.8 percent in perpetuity. What is the present value of the technology if the discount rate is 10 percent?

27. **Perpetuities** A prestigious investment bank designed a new security that pays a quarterly dividend of $2.75 in perpetuity. The first dividend occurs one quarter

End-of-Chapter Cases

Located at the end of almost every chapter, these mini cases focus on common company situations that embody important corporate finance topics. Each case presents a new scenario, data, and a dilemma. Several questions at the end of each case require students to analyze and focus on all of the material they learned in that chapter.

Mini Case

THE MBA DECISION

Ben Bates graduated from college six years ago with a finance undergraduate degree. Although he is satisfied with his current job, his goal is to become an investment banker. He feels that an MBA degree would allow him to achieve this goal. After examining schools, he has narrowed his choice to either Wilton University or Mount Perry College. Although internships are encouraged by both schools, to get class credit for the internship, no salary can be paid. Other than internships, neither school will allow its students to work while enrolled in its MBA program.

Ben currently works at the money management firm of Dewey and Louis. His annual salary at the firm is $65,000 per year, and his salary is expected to increase at 3 percent per year until retirement. He is currently 28 years old and expects to work for 40 more years. His current job includes a fully paid health insurance plan, and his current average tax rate is 26 percent. Ben has a savings account with enough money to cover the entire cost of his MBA program.

The Ritter College of Business at Wilton University is one of the top MBA programs in the country. The MBA degree requires two years of full-time enrollment at the university. The annual tuition is $70,000, payable at the beginning of each school year. Books and other supplies are estimated to cost $3,000 per year. Ben expects that after graduation from Wilton, he will receive a job offer for about $110,000 per year, with a $20,000 signing bonus. The salary at this job will increase at 4 percent per year. Because of the higher salary, his average income tax rate will increase to 31 percent.

Comprehensive Teaching and Learning Package

Corporate Finance has many options in terms of the textbook, instructor supplements, student supplements, and multimedia products. Mix and match to create a package that is perfect for your course.

McGraw-Hill Connect Finance

LESS MANAGING. MORE TEACHING. GREATER LEARNING.

McGraw-Hill's Connect Finance is an online assignment and assessment solution that connects students with the tools and resources they will need to achieve success.

Connect helps prepare students for their future by enabling faster learning, more efficient studying, and higher retention of knowledge.

McGraw-Hill Connect Finance Features   Connect Finance offers a number of powerful tools and features to make managing assignments easier, so faculty can spend more time teaching. With Connect Finance, students can engage with their coursework anytime and anywhere, making the learning process more accessible and efficient. Connect Finance offers you the features described below.

Simple assignment management   With Connect Finance, creating assignments is easier than ever, so you can spend more time teaching and less time managing. The assignment management function enables you to:

- Create and deliver assignments easily with selectable end-of-chapter questions and test bank items.
- Streamline lesson planning, student progress reporting, and assignment grading to make classroom management more efficient than ever.
- Go paperless with the eBook and online submission and grading of student assignments.

Smart grading   When it comes to studying, time is precious. Connect Finance helps students learn more efficiently by providing feedback and practice material when they need it, where they need it. When it comes to teaching, your time is also precious. The grading function enables you to:

- Have assignments scored automatically, giving students immediate feedback on their work and side-by-side comparisons with correct answers.
- Access and review each response; manually change grades, or leave comments for students to review.
- Reinforce classroom concepts with practice tests and instant quizzes.

Instructor library   The Connect Finance Instructor Library is your repository for additional resources to improve student engagement in and out of class. You can select and use any asset that enhances your lecture.

Student study center   The Connect Finance Student Study Center is the place for students to access additional resources.

Mc Graw Hill Education | LEARNSMART®

Diagnostic and Adaptive Learning of Concepts: LearnSmart Students want to make the best use of their study time. The LearnSmart adaptive self-study technology within Connect Finance provides students with a seamless combination of practice, assessment, and remediation for every concept in the textbook. LearnSmart's intelligent software adapts to every student response and automatically delivers concepts that will advance the student's understanding while reducing the time devoted to the concepts already mastered. The result for every student is the fastest path to mastery of the chapter. LearnSmart:

- Applies an intelligent concept engine to identify the relationships between ideas and to serve new concepts to each student only when he or she is ready.
- Adapts automatically to each student, so students spend less time on the topics they understand and practice more on those they have yet to master.
- Provides continual reinforcement and remediation, but gives only as much guidance as students need.
- Integrates diagnostics as part of the learning experience.
- Enables you to assess which concepts students have efficiently learned on their own, thus freeing class time for more applications and discussion.

Mc Graw Hill Education | SMARTBOOK®

SmartBook™ uses McGraw-Hill Education's market-leading adaptive technology to provide an ultra-efficient reading and learning experience for students. Students have access to a "smart" eBook, customized to highlight the most important concepts in the chapter and those that the individual student is yet to master. As the student reads, the reading material constantly adapts to ensure the student is focused on the content he or she needs most to close knowledge gaps. Broken into separate modules that have students read, practice the material they just learned, and review material they have covered previously to improve knowledge retention, SmartBook is a next-generation study tool that is proven to improve student learning outcomes and understanding of the material.

Student progress tracking Connect Finance keeps instructors informed about how each student, section, and class is performing, allowing for more productive use of lecture and office hours. The progress-tracking function enables you to:

- View scored work immediately and track individual or group performance with assignment and grade reports.
- Access an instant view of student or class performance relative to learning objectives.

In short, Connect Finance offers you and your students powerful tools and features that optimize your time and energies, enabling you to focus on course content, teaching, and student learning. Connect Finance also offers a wealth of content resources for both instructors and students. This state-of-the-art, thoroughly tested system supports you in preparing students for the world that awaits.

For more information about Connect Finance, go to **connect.mheducation.com**, or contact your local McGraw-Hill sales representative.

Tegrity Campus: Lectures 24/7

Tegrity Campus is a service that makes class time available 24/7 by automatically capturing every lecture in a searchable format for students to review when they study and complete assignments. With a simple one-click start-and-stop process, you capture all computer screens and corresponding audio. Students can replay any part of any class with easy-to-use browser-based viewing on a PC or Mac.

Educators know that the more students can see, hear, and experience class resources, the better they learn. In fact, studies prove it. With Tegrity Campus, students quickly recall key moments by using Tegrity Campus's unique search feature. This search helps students efficiently find what they need, when they need it, across an entire semester of class recordings. Help turn all your students' study time into learning moments immediately supported by your lecture.

To learn more about Tegrity, watch a 2-minute Flash demo at **www.tegrity.com**.

McGraw-Hill Customer Care Contact Information

At McGraw-Hill, we understand that getting the most from new technology can be challenging. That's why our services don't stop after you purchase our products. You can e-mail our product specialists 24 hours a day to get product-training online. Or you can search our knowledge bank of Frequently Asked Questions on our support website. For Customer Support, call **800-331-5094** or visit **mpss.mhhe.com.** One of our Technical Support Analysts will be able to assist you in a timely fashion.

Assurance of Learning Ready

Assurance of Learning is an important element of many accreditation standards. *Corporate Finance*, 11e, is designed specifically to support your assurance of learning initiatives. Every test bank question is labeled with level of difficulty, topic area, Bloom's Taxonomy level, and AACSB skill area. Connect Finance, McGraw-Hill's online homework solution, and *EZ Test*, McGraw-Hill's easy-to-use test bank software, can search the test bank by these and other categories, providing an engine for targeted Assurance of Learning analysis and assessment.

AACSB Statement

The McGraw-Hill Companies is a proud corporate member of AACSB International. Understanding the importance and value of AACSB Accreditation, *Corporate Finance*, 11e, has sought to recognize the curricula guidelines detailed in the AACSB standards for business accreditation by connecting selected questions in the test bank to the general knowledge and skill guidelines found in the AACSB standards.

The statements contained in *Corporate Finance*, 11e, are provided only as a guide for the users of this text. The AACSB leaves content coverage and assessment within the purview of individual schools, the mission of the school, and the faculty. While *Corporate Finance*, 11e, and the teaching package make no claim of any specific AACSB qualification or evaluation, we have, within the test bank, labeled selected questions according to the six general knowledge and skills areas.

Instructor Resources

The Instructor Library in Connect Finance contains all the necessary supplements—Instructor's Manual, Test Bank, Computerized Test Bank, and PowerPoint—all in one place. Go to connect.mheducation.com to find:

- **Instructor's Manual**
  Prepared by Steven D. Dolvin, Butler University

  This is a great place to find new lecture ideas. The IM has three main sections. The first section contains a chapter outline and other lecture materials. The annotated outline for each chapter includes lecture tips, real-world tips, ethics notes, suggested PowerPoint slides, and, when appropriate, a video synopsis.

- **Test Bank**
  Prepared by Kay Johnson

  Here's a great format for a better testing process. The Test Bank has well over 100 questions per chapter that closely link with the text material and provide a variety of question formats (multiple-choice questions/problems and essay questions) and levels of difficulty (basic, intermediate, and challenge) to meet every instructor's testing needs. Problems are detailed enough to make them intuitive for students, and solutions are provided for the instructor.

- **Computerized Test Bank (Windows)**

  These additional questions are found in a computerized test bank utilizing McGraw-Hill's EZ Test software to quickly create customized exams. This user-friendly program allows instructors to sort questions by format, edit existing questions or add new ones, and scramble questions for multiple versions of the same test.

- **PowerPoint Presentation System**
  Prepared by Steven D. Dolvin, Butler University

  Customize our content for your course. This presentation has been thoroughly revised to include more lecture-oriented slides, as well as exhibits and examples both from the book and from outside sources. Applicable slides have Web links that take you directly to specific Internet sites, or a spreadsheet link to show an example in Excel. You can also go to the Notes Page function for more tips on presenting the slides. If you already have PowerPoint installed on your PC, you can edit, print, or rearrange the complete presentation to meet your specific needs.

STUDENT SUPPORT

- **Narrated PowerPoint Examples**

  Each chapter's slides follow the chapter topics and provide steps and explanations showing how to solve key problems. Because each student learns differently, a quick click on each slide will "talk through" its contents with you!

- **Excel Templates**

  Corresponding to most end-of-chapter problems, each template allows the student to work through the problem using Excel. Each end-of-chapter problem with a template is indicated by an Excel icon in the margin beside it.

- **ExcelMaster**

  Developed by the authors for the RWJ franchise, this valuable and comprehensive supplement provides a tutorial for students in using Excel in finance, broken out by chapter sections.

Options Available for Purchase & Packaging

FINGAME ONLINE 5.0   ISBN-10: 0-07-721988-0 / ISBN-13: 978-0-07-721988-8

By LeRoy Brooks, John Carroll University.

Just $15.00 when packaged with this text. In this comprehensive simulation game, students control a hypothetical company over numerous periods of operation. As students make major financial and operating decisions for their company, they will develop and enhance skills in financial management and financial accounting statement analysis.

Acknowledgments

Over the years, many others have contributed their time and expertise to the development and writing of this text. We extend our thanks once again for their assistance and countless insights:

Lucy Ackert
Kennesaw State University

Amanda Adkisson
Texas A&M University

Raj Aggarwal
Federal Reserve Bank of Cleveland

Anne Anderson
Lehigh University

Christopher Anderson
University of Kansas

James J. Angel
Georgetown University

Nasser Arshadi
University of Missouri–St. Louis

Kevin Bahr
University of Wisconsin–Stevens Point

Robert Balik
Western Michigan University

John W. Ballantine
Brandeis University

Thomas Bankston
Angelo State University

Brad Barber
University of California–Davis

Michael Barry
Boston College

Swati Bhatt
Rutgers University

Roger Bolton
Williams College

Gordon Bonner
University of Delaware

Oswald Bowlin
Texas Technical University

Ronald Braswell
Florida State University

William O. Brown
Claremont McKenna College

Kirt Butler
Michigan State University

Bill Callahan
Southern Methodist University

Steven Carvell
Cornell University

Indudeep S. Chhachhi
Western Kentucky University

Kevin Chiang
University of Vermont

Andreas Christofi
Monmouth University

Jonathan Clarke
Georgia Institute of Technology

Jeffrey L. Coles
University of Utah

Mark Copper
Wayne State University

James Cotter
Wake Forest University

Jay Coughenour
University of Delaware

Arnold Cowan
Iowa State University

Raymond Cox
Thompson Rivers University

John Crockett
George Mason University

Mark Cross
Miami University

Ron Crowe
Jacksonville University

William Damon
Vanderbilt University

Sudip Datta
Wayne State University

Ted Day
University of Texas–Dallas

Marcos DeArruda
Drexel University

K. Ozgur Demirtas
Sabanci University

Anand Desai
Wichita State University

Miranda Lam Detzler
University of Massachusetts–Boston

David Distad
University of California–Berkeley

Dennis Draper
Loyola Marymount University

Jean-Francois Dreyfus
New York University

Gene Drzycimski
University of Wisconsin–Oshkosh

Robert Duvic
The University of Texas at Austin

Demissew Ejara
University of New Haven

Robert Eldridge
Southern Connecticut State University

Gary Emery
University of Oklahoma

Theodore Eytan
City University of New York–Baruch College

Don Fehrs
University of Notre Dame

Steven Ferraro
Pepperdine University

Eliezer Fich
Drexel University

Andrew Fields
University of Delaware

Paige Fields
Trinity University

Adlai Fisher
University of British Columbia

Michael Fishman
Northwestern University

Melissa Frye
University of Central Florida–Orlando

Yee-Tien Fu
Stanford University

Partha Gangopadhyay
St. Cloud University

Bruno Gerard
BI Norwegian Business School

Frank Ghannadian
University of Tampa

Stuart Gillan
University of Georgia

Ann Gillette
Kennesaw State University

Michael Goldstein
Babson College

Indra Guertler
Simmons College

Re-Jin Guo
University of Illinois at Chicago

James Haltiner
College of William and Mary

Bill Hamby
Indiana Wesleyan University

Janet Hamilton
Portland State University

Qing Hao
University of Texas-Arlington

Robert Hauswald
American University

Delvin Hawley
University of Mississippi

Hal Heaton
Brigham Young University

John A. Helmuth
University of Michigan–Flint

Michael Hemler
University of Notre Dame

Stephen Heston
University of Maryland

Andrea Heuson
University of Miami

Jim Howard
University of Maryland–University College

Edith Hotchkiss
Boston College

Charles Hu
Claremont McKenna College

Hugh Hunter
Eastern Washington University

James Jackson
Oklahoma State University

Raymond Jackson
University of Massachusetts–Dartmouth

Prem Jain
Georgetown University

Narayanan Jayaraman
Georgia Institute of Technology

Thadavillil Jithendranathan
University of St. Thomas

Jarl Kallberg
New York University

Jonathan Karpoff
University of Washington

Paul Keat
American Graduate School of International Management

Dolly King
University of North Carolina–Charlotte

Brian Kluger
University of Cincinnati

Narayana Kocherlakota
Federal Reserve Bank of Minneapolis

Robert Krell
George Mason University

Ronald Kudla
The University of Akron

Youngsik Kwak
Delaware State University

Nelson Lacey
University of Massachusetts

Gene Lai
Washington State University

Josef Lakonishok
University of Illinois

Dennis Lasser
State University of New York–Binghamton

Paul Laux
University of Delaware

Gregory LaBlanc
University of California–Berkeley

Bong-Su Lee
Florida State University

Youngho Lee
Howard University

Thomas Legg
University of Minnesota

James T. Lindley
University of Southern Mississippi

Dennis Logue
Dartmouth College

Michael Long
Rutgers University

Yulong Ma
California State University–Long Beach

Ileen Malitz
Fairleigh Dickinson University

Terry Maness
Baylor University

Surendra Mansinghka
San Francisco State University

Michael Mazzco
Michigan State University

Robert I. McDonald
Northwestern University

Hugh McLaughlin
Bentley College

Joseph Meredith
Elon University

Larry Merville
University of Texas–Dallas

Joe Messina
San Francisco State University

Roger Mesznik
Columbia University

Rick Meyer
University of South Florida

Timothy Michael
University of Houston–Clear Lake

Vassil Mihov
Texas Christian University

Richard Miller
Wesleyan University

Naval Modani
University of Central Florida

Sheila Moore
California Lutheran University

Angela Morgan
Clemson University

Edward Morris
Lindenwood University

Richard Mull
Fort Lewis College

Jim Musumeci
Bentley University

Robert Nachtmann
University of Texas–El Paso

Edward Nelling
Drexel University

James Nelson
East Carolina University

Gregory Niehaus
University of South Carolina

Peder Nielsen
Aarhus University

Ingmar Nyman
Hunter College

Dennis Officer
University of Kentucky

Joseph Ogden
State University of New York

Darshana Palkar
Nova Southeastern University

Venky Panchapagesan
Washington University–St. Louis

Bulent Parker
University of Wisconsin–Madison

Ajay Patel
Wake Forest University

Dilip Kumar Patro
Rutgers University

Gary Patterson
University of South Florida

Glenn N. Pettengill
Grand Valley State University

Pegaret Pichler
Northeastern University

Christo Pirinsky
Ohio State University

Jeffrey Pontiff
Boston College

Franklin Potts
Baylor University

Annette Poulsen
University of Georgia

N. Prabhala
University of Maryland

Mao Qiu
University of Utah–Salt Lake City

Latha Ramchand
University of Houston

Gabriel Ramirez
Kennesaw State University

Narendar Rao
Northeastern Illinois University

Raghavendra Rau
University of Cambridge

Steven Raymar
Indiana University

Adam Reed
University of North Carolina–Chapel Hill

Bill Reese
Tulane University

Peter Ritchken
Case Western Reserve University

Kimberly Rodgers
American University

Stuart Rosenstein
East Carolina University

Bruce Rubin
Old Dominion University

Patricia Ryan
Colorado State University

Jaime Sabal
Ramon Llull University

Anthony Sanders
George Mason University

Ray Sant
St. Edward's University

Andy Saporoschenko
Lindenwood University

William Sartoris
Indiana University

James Schallheim
University of Utah

Mary Jean Scheuer
California State University–Northridge

Kevin Schieuer
Bellevue University

Faruk Selcuk
University of Bridgeport

Lemma Senbet
University of Maryland

Kuldeep Shastri
University of Pittsburgh

Betty Simkins
Oklahoma State University

Sudhir Singh
Frostburg State University

Scott Smart
Indiana University

Jackie So
Southern Illinois University

Denis Sosyura
University of Michigan

John Stansfield
University of Missouri

Mark Hoven Stohs
California State University–Fullerton

Joeseph Stokes
University of Massachusetts–Amherst

John S. Strong
College of William and Mary

A. Charlene Sullivan
Purdue University

Michael Sullivan
University of Nevada–Las Vegas

Timothy Sullivan
Bentley College

R. Bruce Swensen
Adelphi University

Ernest Swift
Georgia State University

For their help on the eleventh edition, we would like to thank Joe Smolira, Belmont University and Kay Johnson for their work developing the supplements. We also owe a debt of gratitude to Edward I. Altman of New York University; Robert S. Hansen of Tulane; Duke Bristow, Harry DeAngelo, and Suh-Pyng Ku of the University of Southern California; and Jay R. Ritter of the University of Florida, who have provided several thoughtful comments and immeasurable help.

We thank Steve Hailey and Andrew Beeli, University of Kentucky students, for their extensive proofing and problem-checking efforts.

Over the past three years readers have provided assistance by detecting and reporting errors. Our goal is to offer the best textbook available on the subject, so this information was invaluable as we prepared the eleventh edition. We want to ensure that all future editions are error-free—and therefore we offer $10 per arithmetic error to the first individual reporting it. Any arithmetic error resulting in subsequent errors will be counted double. All errors should be reported to Dr. Brad Jordan, c/o Editorial - Finance, McGraw-Hill Education, 1333 Burr Ridge Parkway, Burr Ridge, IL 60527.

Many talented professionals at McGraw-Hill Education have contributed to the development of *Corporate Finance,* Eleventh Edition. We would especially like to thank Chuck Synovec, Jennifer Upton, Melissa Caughlin, Kathryn Wright, Matt Diamond, Michele Janicek, and Bruce Gin.

Finally, we wish to thank our families and friends, Carol, Kate, Jon, Mark, and Lynne, for their forbearance and help.

Stephen A. Ross
Randolph W. Westerfield
Jeffrey F. Jaffe
Bradford D. Jordan

Brief Contents

Contents

CHAPTER 11

Return and Risk: The Capital Asset Pricing Model (CAPM) 331

CHAPTER 12

An Alternative View of Risk and Return: The Arbitrage Pricing Theory 374

CHAPTER 13

Risk, Cost of Capital, and Valuation 396

PART IV Capital Structure and Dividend Policy

CHAPTER 14

Efficient Capital Markets and Behavioral Challenges 431

CHAPTER 15

Long-Term Financing: An Introduction 471

CHAPTER 16

Capital Structure: Basic Concepts 490

CHAPTER 17

Capital Structure: Limits to the Use of Debt 522

PART VII Short-Term Finance

PART VIII Special Topics

1

Introduction to Corporate Finance

George Zimmer, founder of The Men's Wearhouse, for years appeared in televisions ads promising, "You're going to like the way you look. I guarantee it." But, in mid-2013, Zimmer evidently didn't look so good to the company's board of directors, which abruptly fired him. It was reported that Zimmer had a series of disagreements with the board, including a desire to take the company private. Evidently, Zimmer's ideas did not "suit" the board.

Understanding Zimmer's journey from the founder of a clothing store that used a cigar box as a cash register, to corporate executive, and finally to ex-employee takes us into issues involving the corporate form of organization, corporate goals, and corporate control—all of which we discuss in this chapter. You're going to learn a lot if you read it. We guarantee it.

1.1 What Is Corporate Finance?

Suppose you decide to start a firm to make tennis balls. To do this you hire managers to buy raw materials, and you assemble a workforce that will produce and sell finished tennis balls. In the language of finance, you make an investment in assets such as inventory, machinery, land, and labor. The amount of cash you invest in assets must be matched by an equal amount of cash raised by financing. When you begin to sell tennis balls, your firm will generate cash. This is the basis of value creation. The purpose of the firm is to create value for you, the owner. The value is reflected in the framework of the simple balance sheet model of the firm.

THE BALANCE SHEET MODEL OF THE FIRM

Suppose we take a financial snapshot of the firm and its activities at a single point in time. Figure 1.1 shows a graphic conceptualization of the balance sheet, and it will help introduce you to corporate finance.

The assets of the firm are on the left side of the balance sheet. These assets can be thought of as current and fixed. *Fixed assets* are those that will last a long time, such as buildings. Some fixed assets are tangible, such as machinery and equipment. Other fixed assets are intangible, such as patents and trademarks. The other category of assets, *current*

Figure 1.1
The Balance Sheet
Model of the Firm

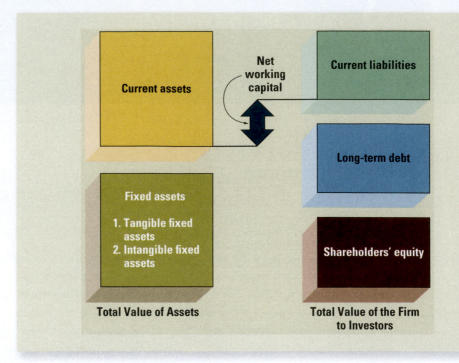

assets, comprises those that have short lives, such as inventory. The tennis balls that your firm has made, but has not yet sold, are part of its inventory. Unless you have overproduced, they will leave the firm shortly.

Before a company can invest in an asset, it must obtain financing, which means that it must raise the money to pay for the investment. The forms of financing are represented on the right side of the balance sheet. A firm will issue (sell) pieces of paper called *debt* (loan agreements) or *equity shares* (stock certificates). Just as assets are classified as long-lived or short-lived, so too are liabilities. A short-term debt is called a *current liability.* Short-term debt represents loans and other obligations that must be repaid within one year. Long-term debt is debt that does not have to be repaid within one year. Shareholders' equity represents the difference between the value of the assets and the debt of the firm. In this sense, it is a residual claim on the firm's assets.

From the balance sheet model of the firm, it is easy to see why finance can be thought of as the study of the following three questions:

1. In what long-lived assets should the firm invest? This question concerns the left side of the balance sheet. Of course the types and proportions of assets the firm needs tend to be set by the nature of the business. We use the term **capital budgeting** to describe the process of making and managing expenditures on long-lived assets.

2. How can the firm raise cash for required capital expenditures? This question concerns the right side of the balance sheet. The answer to this question involves the firm's **capital structure**, which represents the proportions of the firm's financing from current and long-term debt and equity.

3. How should short-term operating cash flows be managed? This question concerns the upper portion of the balance sheet. There is often a mismatch between the timing of cash inflows and cash outflows during operating activities. Furthermore, the amount

and timing of operating cash flows are not known with certainty. Financial managers must attempt to manage the gaps in cash flow. From a balance sheet perspective, short-term management of cash flow is associated with a firm's **net working capital**. Net working capital is defined as current assets minus current liabilities. From a financial perspective, short-term cash flow problems come from the mismatching of cash inflows and outflows. This is the subject of short-term finance.

THE FINANCIAL MANAGER

For current issues facing CFOs, see **www.cfo.com**.

In large firms, the finance activity is usually associated with a top officer of the firm, such as the vice president and chief financial officer, and some lesser officers. Figure 1.2 depicts a general organizational structure emphasizing the finance

Figure 1.2
Hypothetical Organization Chart

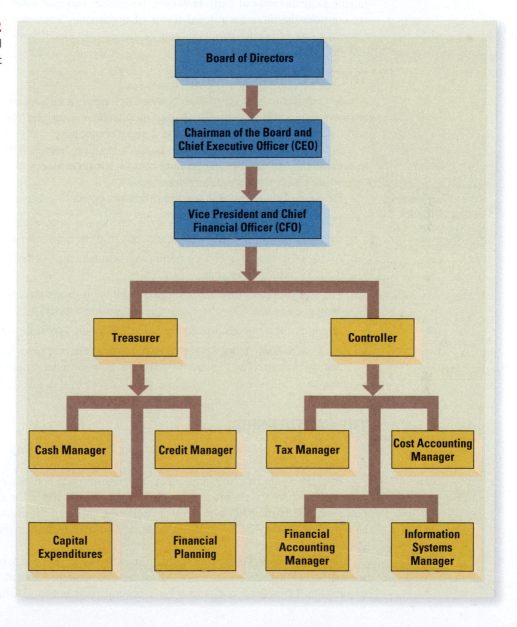

activity within the firm. Reporting to the chief financial officer are the treasurer and the controller. The treasurer is responsible for handling cash flows, managing capital expenditure decisions, and making financial plans. The controller handles the accounting function, which includes taxes, cost and financial accounting, and information systems.

1.2 The Corporate Firm

The firm is a way of organizing the economic activity of many individuals. A basic problem of the firm is how to raise cash. The corporate form of business—that is, organizing the firm as a corporation—is the standard method for solving problems encountered in raising large amounts of cash. However, businesses can take other forms. In this section we consider the three basic legal forms of organizing firms, and we see how firms go about the task of raising large amounts of money under each form.

THE SOLE PROPRIETORSHIP

A **sole proprietorship** is a business owned by one person. Suppose you decide to start a business to produce mousetraps. Going into business is simple: You announce to all who will listen, "Today, I am going to build a better mousetrap."

Most large cities require that you obtain a business license. Afterward, you can begin to hire as many people as you need and borrow whatever money you need. At year-end all the profits and the losses will be yours.

Here are some factors that are important in considering a sole proprietorship:

1. The sole proprietorship is the cheapest business to form. No formal charter is required, and few government regulations must be satisfied for most industries.
2. A sole proprietorship pays no corporate income taxes. All profits of the business are taxed as individual income.
3. The sole proprietorship has unlimited liability for business debts and obligations. No distinction is made between personal and business assets.
4. The life of the sole proprietorship is limited by the life of the sole proprietor.
5. Because the only money invested in the firm is the proprietor's, the equity money that can be raised by the sole proprietor is limited to the proprietor's personal wealth.

For more about business types, see the "Starting a Business" section at **www.sba.gov**.

THE PARTNERSHIP

Any two or more people can get together and form a **partnership**. Partnerships fall into two categories: (1) general partnerships and (2) limited partnerships.

In a *general partnership* all partners agree to provide some fraction of the work and cash and to share the profits and losses. Each partner is liable for all of the debts of the partnership. A partnership agreement specifies the nature of the arrangement. The partnership agreement may be an oral agreement or a formal document setting forth the understanding.

Limited partnerships permit the liability of some of the partners to be limited to the amount of cash each has contributed to the partnership. Limited partnerships usually require that (1) at least one partner be a general partner and (2) the limited partners do not participate in managing the business. Here are some things that are important when considering a partnership:

1. Partnerships are usually inexpensive and easy to form. Written documents are required in complicated arrangements. Business licenses and filing fees may be necessary.

2. General partners have unlimited liability for all debts. The liability of limited partners is usually limited to the contribution each has made to the partnership. If one general partner is unable to meet his or her commitment, the shortfall must be made up by the other general partners.

3. The general partnership is terminated when a general partner dies or withdraws (but this is not so for a limited partner). It is difficult for a partnership to transfer ownership without dissolving. Usually all general partners must agree. However, limited partners may sell their interest in a business.

4. It is difficult for a partnership to raise large amounts of cash. Equity contributions are usually limited to a partner's ability and desire to contribute to the partnership. Many companies, such as Apple Inc., start life as a proprietorship or partnership, but at some point they choose to convert to corporate form.

5. Income from a partnership is taxed as personal income to the partners.

6. Management control resides with the general partners. Usually a majority vote is required on important matters, such as the amount of profit to be retained in the business.

It is difficult for large business organizations to exist as sole proprietorships or partnerships. The main advantage to a sole proprietorship or partnership is the cost of getting started. Afterward, the disadvantages, which may become severe, are (1) unlimited liability, (2) limited life of the enterprise, and (3) difficulty of transferring ownership. These three disadvantages lead to (4) difficulty in raising cash.

THE CORPORATION

Of the forms of business enterprises, the **corporation** is by far the most important. It is a distinct legal entity. As such, a corporation can have a name and enjoy many of the legal powers of natural persons. For example, corporations can acquire and exchange property. Corporations can enter contracts and may sue and be sued. For jurisdictional purposes the corporation is a citizen of its state of incorporation (it cannot vote, however).

Starting a corporation is more complicated than starting a proprietorship or partnership. The incorporators must prepare articles of incorporation and a set of bylaws. The articles of incorporation must include the following:

1. Name of the corporation.

2. Intended life of the corporation (it may be forever).

3. Business purpose.

4. Number of shares of stock that the corporation is authorized to issue, with a statement of limitations and rights of different classes of shares.

5. Nature of the rights granted to shareholders.

6. Number of members of the initial board of directors.

The bylaws are the rules to be used by the corporation to regulate its own existence, and they concern its shareholders, directors, and officers. Bylaws range from the briefest possible statement of rules for the corporation's management to hundreds of pages of text.

In its simplest form, the corporation comprises three sets of distinct interests: the shareholders (the owners), the directors, and the corporation officers (the top management). Traditionally, the shareholders control the corporation's direction, policies, and activities. The shareholders elect a board of directors, who in turn select top management. Members of top management serve as corporate officers and manage the operations of the corporation in the best interest of the shareholders. In closely held corporations with few shareholders, there may be a large overlap among the shareholders, the directors, and the top management. However, in larger corporations, the shareholders, directors, and the top management are likely to be distinct groups.

The potential separation of ownership from management gives the corporation several advantages over proprietorships and partnerships:

1. Because ownership in a corporation is represented by shares of stock, ownership can be readily transferred to new owners. Because the corporation exists independently of those who own its shares, there is no limit to the transferability of shares as there is in partnerships.

2. The corporation has unlimited life. Because the corporation is separate from its owners, the death or withdrawal of an owner does not affect the corporation's legal existence. The corporation can continue on after the original owners have withdrawn.

3. The shareholders' liability is limited to the amount invested in the ownership shares. For example, if a shareholder purchased $1,000 in shares of a corporation, the potential loss would be $1,000. In a partnership, a general partner with a $1,000 contribution could lose the $1,000 plus any other indebtedness of the partnership.

Limited liability, ease of ownership transfer, and perpetual succession are the major advantages of the corporate form of business organization. These give the corporation an enhanced ability to raise cash.

There is, however, one great disadvantage to incorporation. The federal government taxes corporate income (the states do as well). This tax is in addition to the personal income tax that shareholders pay on dividend income they receive. This is double taxation for shareholders when compared to taxation on proprietorships and partnerships. Table 1.1 summarizes our discussion of partnerships and corporations.

Today all 50 states have enacted laws allowing for the creation of a relatively new form of business organization, the limited liability company (LLC). The goal of this entity is to operate and be taxed like a partnership but retain limited liability for owners, so an LLC is essentially a hybrid of partnership and corporation. Although states have differing definitions for LLCs, the more important scorekeeper is the Internal Revenue Service (IRS). The IRS will consider an LLC a corporation, thereby subjecting it to double taxation, unless it meets certain specific criteria. In essence, an LLC cannot be too corporation-like, or it will be treated as one by the IRS. LLCs have become common. For example, Goldman, Sachs and Co., one of Wall Street's last remaining partnerships, decided to convert from a private partnership to an LLC (it later "went public," becoming a publicly held corporation). Large accounting firms and law firms by the score have converted to LLCs.

Table 1.1   A Comparison of Partnerships and Corporations

	Corporation	Partnership
Liquidity and marketability	Shares can be exchanged without termination of the corporation. Common stock can be listed on a stock exchange.	Units are subject to substantial restrictions on transferability. There is usually no established trading market for partnership units.
Voting rights	Usually each share of common stock entitles the holder to one vote per share on matters requiring a vote and on the election of the directors. Directors determine top management.	Some voting rights by limited partners. However, general partners have exclusive control and management of operations.
Taxation	Corporations have double taxation: Corporate income is taxable, and dividends to shareholders are also taxable.	Partnerships are not taxable. Partners pay personal taxes on partnership profits.
Reinvestment and dividend payout	Corporations have broad latitude on dividend payout decisions.	Partnerships are generally prohibited from reinvesting partnership profits. All profits are distributed to partners.
Liability	Shareholders are not personally liable for obligations of the corporation.	Limited partners are not liable for obligations of partnerships. General partners may have unlimited liability.
Continuity of existence	Corporations may have a perpetual life.	Partnerships have limited life.

A CORPORATION BY ANOTHER NAME . . .

The corporate form of organization has many variations around the world. The exact laws and regulations differ from country to country, of course, but the essential features of public ownership and limited liability remain. These firms are often called *joint stock companies*, *public limited companies*, or *limited liability companies*, depending on the specific nature of the firm and the country of origin.

Table 1.2 gives the names of a few well-known international corporations, their countries of origin, and a translation of the abbreviation that follows each company name.

Table 1.2   International Corporations

Company	Country of Origin	Type of Company	
		In Original Language	**Interpretation**
Bayerische Motoren Werke (BMW) AG	Germany	Aktiengesellschaft	Corporation
Red Bull GmbH	Austria	Gesellschaft mit Beschränkter Haftung	Limited liability company
Rolls-Royce PLC	United Kingdom	Public limited company	Public Ltd. Company
Shell UK Ltd.	United Kingdom	Limited	Corporation
Unilever NV	Netherlands	Naamloze Vennootschap	Joint stock company
Fiat SpA	Italy	Società per Azioni	Joint stock company
Volvo AB	Sweden	Aktiebolag	Joint stock company
Peugeot SA	France	Société Anonyme	Joint stock company

Table 1.3   Some Key Skills Needed for the Chief Financial Officers of Large Public Companies

Strategizing	Must be knowledgeable of acquisitions, raising funds, risk management, and joint ventures
Financial reporting	Needs to communicate key financial results to the CEO, board of directors, and senior staff
Accounting	Must prepare important financial and accounting information for auditors, company budgets, and key regulators
Investor relations	Must participate in presentations to current and future shareholders and industry analysts
Information technology	Must lead efforts to incorporate new information technology into administrative information systems

1.3   The Importance of Cash Flows

The most important job of a financial manager is to create value from the firm's capital budgeting, financing, and net working capital activities. How do financial managers create value? The answer is that the firm should:

1. Try to buy assets that generate more cash than they cost.
2. Sell bonds, stocks, and other financial instruments that raise more cash than they cost.

Thus, the firm must create more cash flow than it uses. The cash flows paid to bondholders and stockholders of the firm should be greater than the cash flows put into the firm by the bondholders and stockholders.

The interplay of the firm's activities with the financial markets is illustrated in Figure 1.3. The arrows in Figure 1.3 trace cash flow from the firm to the financial

Figure 1.3

Cash Flows between the Firm and the Financial Markets

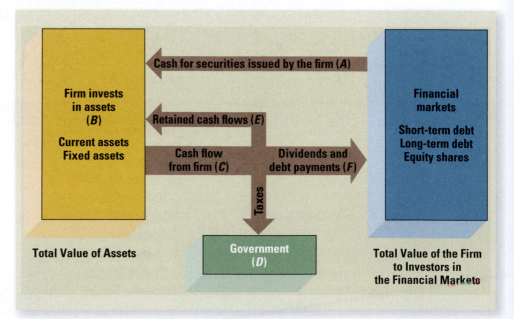

markets and back again. Suppose we begin with the firm's financing activities. To raise money, the firm sells debt and equity shares to investors in the financial markets. This results in cash flows from the financial markets to the firm (*A*). This cash is invested in the investment activities (assets) of the firm (*B*) by the firm's management. The cash generated by the firm (*C*) is paid to shareholders and bondholders (*F*). The shareholders receive cash in the form of dividends; the bondholders who lent funds to the firm receive interest and, when the initial loan is repaid, principal. Not all of the firm's cash is paid out. Some is retained (*E*), and some is paid to the government as taxes (*D*).

Over time, if the cash paid to shareholders and bondholders (*F*) is greater than the cash raised in the financial markets (*A*), value will be created.

Identification of Cash Flows   Unfortunately, it is sometimes not easy to observe cash flows directly. Much of the information we obtain is in the form of accounting statements, and much of the work of financial analysis is to extract cash flow information from these statements. The following example illustrates how this is done.

**EXAMPLE
1.1**

Accounting Profit versus Cash Flows   The Midland Company refines and trades gold. At the end of the year, it sold 2,500 ounces of gold for $1 million. The company had acquired the gold for $900,000 at the beginning of the year. The company paid cash for the gold when it was purchased. Unfortunately it has yet to collect from the customer to whom the gold was sold. The following is a standard accounting of Midland's financial circumstances at year-end:

The Midland Company Accounting View Income Statement Year Ended December 31	
Sales	$1,000,000
−Costs	−900,000
Profit	$ 100,000

By generally accepted accounting principles (GAAP), the sale is recorded even though the customer has yet to pay. It is assumed that the customer will pay soon. From the accounting perspective, Midland seems to be profitable. However, the perspective of corporate finance is different. It focuses on cash flows:

The Midland Company Financial View Income Statement Year Ended December 31	
Cash inflow	$ 0
Cash outflow	−900,000
	−$ 900,000

The perspective of corporate finance is interested in whether cash flows are being created by the gold trading operations of Midland. Value creation depends on cash flows. For Midland, value creation depends on whether and when it actually receives $1 million.

Timing of Cash Flows   The value of an investment made by a firm depends on the timing of cash flows. One of the most important principles of finance is that individuals prefer to receive cash flows earlier rather than later. One dollar received today is worth more than one dollar received next year.

EXAMPLE

Cash Flow Timing   The Midland Company is attempting to choose between two proposals for new products. Both proposals will provide additional cash flows over a four-year period and will initially cost $10,000. The cash flows from the proposals are as follows:

Year	New Product A	New Product B
1	$ 0	$ 4,000
2	0	4,000
3	0	4,000
4	20,000	4,000
Total	$20,000	$16,000

At first it appears that new product A would be best. However, the cash flows from proposal B come earlier than those of A. Without more information, we cannot decide which set of cash flows would create the most value for the bondholders and shareholders. It depends on whether the value of getting cash from B up front outweighs the extra total cash from A.

Risk of Cash Flows   The firm must consider risk. The amount and timing of cash flows are not usually known with certainty. Most investors have an aversion to risk.

EXAMPLE

Risk   The Midland Company is considering expanding operations overseas. It is evaluating Europe and Japan as possible sites. Europe is considered to be relatively safe, whereas operating in Japan is seen as very risky. In both cases the company would close down operations after one year.

After doing a complete financial analysis, Midland has come up with the following cash flows of the alternative plans for expansion under three scenarios—pessimistic, most likely, and optimistic:

	Pessimistic	Most Likely	Optimistic
Europe	$75,000	$100,000	$125,000
Japan	0	150,000	200,000

If we ignore the pessimistic scenario, perhaps Japan is the best alternative. When we take the pessimistic scenario into account, the choice is unclear. Japan appears to be riskier, but it also offers a higher expected level of cash flow. What is risk and how can it be defined? We must try to answer this important question. Corporate finance cannot avoid coping with risky alternatives, and much of our book is devoted to developing methods for evaluating risky opportunities.

1.4 The Goal of Financial Management

Assuming that we restrict our discussion to for-profit businesses, the goal of financial management is to make money or add value for the owners. This goal is a little vague, of course, so we examine some different ways of formulating it to come up with a more precise definition. Such a definition is important because it leads to an objective basis for making and evaluating financial decisions.

POSSIBLE GOALS

If we were to consider possible financial goals, we might come up with some ideas like the following:

- Survive.
- Avoid financial distress and bankruptcy.
- Beat the competition.
- Maximize sales or market share.
- Minimize costs.
- Maximize profits.
- Maintain steady earnings growth.

These are only a few of the goals we could list. Furthermore, each of these possibilities presents problems as a goal for the financial manager.

For example, it's easy to increase market share or unit sales: All we have to do is lower our prices or relax our credit terms. Similarly, we can always cut costs simply by doing away with things such as research and development. We can avoid bankruptcy by never borrowing any money or never taking any risks, and so on. It's not clear that any of these actions are in the stockholders' best interests.

Profit maximization would probably be the most commonly cited goal, but even this is not a precise objective. Do we mean profits this year? If so, then we should note that actions such as deferring maintenance, letting inventories run down, and taking other short-run cost-cutting measures will tend to increase profits now, but these activities aren't necessarily desirable.

The goal of maximizing profits may refer to some sort of "long-run" or "average" profits, but it's still unclear exactly what this means. First, do we mean something like accounting net income or earnings per share? As we will see in more detail in the next chapter, these accounting numbers may have little to do with what is good or bad for the firm. We are actually more interested in cash flows. Second, what do we mean by the long run? As a famous economist once remarked, in the long run, we're all dead! More to the point, this goal doesn't tell us what the appropriate trade-off is between current and future profits.

The goals we've listed here are all different, but they tend to fall into two classes. The first of these relates to profitability. The goals involving sales, market share, and cost control all relate, at least potentially, to different ways of earning or increasing profits. The goals in the second group, involving bankruptcy avoidance, stability, and safety, relate in some way to controlling risk. Unfortunately, these two types of goals are somewhat contradictory. The pursuit of profit normally involves some element of risk, so it isn't really possible to maximize both safety and profit. What we need, therefore, is a goal that encompasses both factors.

THE GOAL OF FINANCIAL MANAGEMENT

The financial manager in a corporation makes decisions for the stockholders of the firm. So, instead of listing possible goals for the financial manager, we really need to answer a more fundamental question: From the stockholders' point of view, what is a good financial management decision?

If we assume that stockholders buy stock because they seek to gain financially, then the answer is obvious: Good decisions increase the value of the stock, and poor decisions decrease the value of the stock.

From our observations, it follows that the financial manager acts in the shareholders' best interests by making decisions that increase the value of the stock. The appropriate goal for the financial manager can thus be stated quite easily:

The goal of financial management is to maximize the current value per share of the existing stock.

The goal of maximizing the value of the stock avoids the problems associated with the different goals we listed earlier. There is no ambiguity in the criterion, and there is no short-run versus long-run issue. We explicitly mean that our goal is to maximize the *current* stock value.

If this goal seems a little strong or one-dimensional to you, keep in mind that the stockholders in a firm are residual owners. By this we mean that they are entitled only to what is left after employees, suppliers, and creditors (and everyone else with legitimate claims) are paid their due. If any of these groups go unpaid, the stockholders get nothing. So if the stockholders are winning in the sense that the leftover, residual portion is growing, it must be true that everyone else is winning also. In other words, managers should make decisions that they believe will achieve the highest firm value because, by doing so, shareholders will benefit the most.

Because the goal of financial management is to maximize the value of the stock, we need to learn how to identify investments and financing arrangements that favorably impact the value of the stock. This is precisely what we will be studying. In the previous section we emphasized the importance of cash flows in value creation. In fact, we could have defined *corporate finance* as the study of the relationship between business decisions, cash flows, and the value of the stock in the business.

A MORE GENERAL GOAL

If our goal is as stated in the preceding section (to maximize the value of the stock), an obvious question comes up: What is the appropriate goal when the firm has no traded stock? Corporations are certainly not the only type of business; and the stock in many corporations rarely changes hands, so it's difficult to say what the value per share is at any particular time.

As long as we are considering for-profit businesses, only a slight modification is needed. The total value of the stock in a corporation is simply equal to the value of the owners' equity. Therefore, a more general way of stating our goal is as follows: Maximize the value of the existing owners' equity.

With this in mind, we don't care whether the business is a proprietorship, a partnership, or a corporation. For each of these, good financial decisions increase the value of the owners' equity, and poor financial decisions decrease it. In fact, although we choose to focus on corporations in the chapters ahead, the principles we develop apply to all forms of business. Many of them even apply to the not-for-profit sector.

Business ethics are considered at **www.business-ethics .com**.

Finally, our goal does not imply that the financial manager should take illegal or unethical actions in the hope of increasing the value of the equity in the firm. What we mean is that the financial manager best serves the owners of the business by identifying goods and services that add value to the firm because they are desired, legal, and valued in the free marketplace.

1.5 The Agency Problem and Control of the Corporation

We've seen that the financial manager acts in the best interests of the stockholders by taking actions that increase the value of the stock. However, in large corporations ownership can be spread over a huge number of stockholders. This dispersion of ownership arguably means that management effectively controls the firm. In this case, will management necessarily act in the best interests of the stockholders? Put another way, might not management pursue its own goals at the stockholders' expense? In the following pages we briefly consider some of the arguments relating to this question.

Corporate governance varies quite a bit around the world. For example, in most countries other than the United States and the United Kingdom, publicly traded companies are usually controlled by one or more large shareholders.[1] Moreover, in countries with limited shareholder protection, when compared to countries with strong shareholder protection like the United States and the United Kingdom, large shareholders may have a greater opportunity to take advantage of minority shareholders. Research shows that a country's investor protection framework is important to understanding a firms' cash holdings and dividend payouts. For example, studies find that shareholders do not highly value cash holdings in firms in countries with low investor protection when compared to firms in the United States where investor protection is high.

In the basic corporate governance setup, the shareholders elect the board of directors who in turn appoint the top corporate managers, such as the CEO. The CEO is usually a member of the board of directors. One aspect of corporate governance that has received attention recently concerns the chair of a firm's board of directors. In a large number of U.S. corporations, the CEO and the board chair are the same person. An argument can be made that combining the CEO and board chair positions can contribute to poor corporate governance. When comparing corporate governance in the United States and the United Kingdom, an edge is often given to the United Kingdom, partly because more than 90 percent of U.K. companies are chaired by outside directors rather than the CEO. This is a contentious issue confronting many United States corporations. For example, in 2012, 20 percent of the S&P 500 companies had named an independent outsider as board chair, up from only 10 percent five years earlier.

AGENCY RELATIONSHIPS

The relationship between stockholders and management is called an *agency relationship*. Such a relationship exists whenever someone (the principal) hires another (the agent) to represent his or her interests. For example, you might hire someone (an agent) to sell a car that you own while you are away at school. In all such relationships there is a possibility of a conflict of interest between the principal and the agent. Such a conflict is called an **agency problem**.

---

[1]For a somewhat contrary view about the concentration of shareholder ownership in the U.S. and around the world, see Clifford G. Holderness "The Myth of Diffuse Ownership in the United States." *The Review of Financial Studies*, volume 22, number 4, April 2009.

Suppose you hire someone to sell your car and you agree to pay that person a flat fee when he or she sells the car. The agent's incentive in this case is to make the sale, not necessarily to get you the best price. If you offer a commission of, say, 10 percent of the sales price instead of a flat fee, then this problem might not exist. This example illustrates that the way in which an agent is compensated is one factor that affects agency problems.

MANAGEMENT GOALS

To see how management and stockholder interests might differ, imagine that a firm is considering a new investment. The new investment is expected to favorably impact the share value, but it is also a relatively risky venture. The owners of the firm will wish to take the investment (because the stock value will rise), but management may not because there is the possibility that things will turn out badly and management jobs will be lost. If management does not take the investment, then the stockholders may lose a valuable opportunity. This is one example of an *agency cost.*

More generally, the term *agency costs* refers to the costs of the conflict of interest between stockholders and management. These costs can be indirect or direct. An indirect agency cost is a lost opportunity, such as the one we have just described.

Direct agency costs come in two forms. The first type is a corporate expenditure that benefits management but costs the stockholders. Perhaps the purchase of a luxurious and unneeded corporate jet would fall under this heading. The second type of direct agency cost is an expense that arises from the need to monitor management actions. Paying outside auditors to assess the accuracy of financial statement information could be one example.

It is sometimes argued that, left to themselves, managers would tend to maximize the amount of resources over which they have control or, more generally, corporate power or wealth. This goal could lead to an overemphasis on corporate size or growth. For example, cases in which management is accused of overpaying to buy up another company just to increase the size of the business or to demonstrate corporate power are not uncommon. Obviously, if overpayment does take place, such a purchase does not benefit the stockholders of the purchasing company.

Our discussion indicates that management may tend to overemphasize organizational survival to protect job security. Also, management may dislike outside interference, so independence and corporate self-sufficiency may be important goals.

DO MANAGERS ACT IN THE STOCKHOLDERS' INTERESTS?

Whether managers will, in fact, act in the best interests of stockholders depends on two factors. First, how closely are management goals aligned with stockholder goals? This question relates, at least in part, to the way managers are compensated. Second, can managers be replaced if they do not pursue stockholder goals? This issue relates to control of the firm. As we will discuss, there are a number of reasons to think that, even in the largest firms, management has a significant incentive to act in the interests of stockholders.

Managerial Compensation Management will frequently have a significant economic incentive to increase share value for two reasons. First, managerial compensation, particularly at the top, is usually tied to financial performance in general and often to share value in particular. For example, managers are frequently given the option to buy stock at a bargain price. The more the stock is worth, the more valuable is this option. In fact, options are often used to motivate employees of all types, not just top management. For example, during 2013, Google expensed about $2.752 billion in stock-related compensation, or about $57,630 per employee. As we mentioned, many firms also give managers an ownership stake in the company by granting stock or stock options. In 2013, the total compensation for Leslie Moonves, CEO of CBS, was reported by *The Wall Street Journal* to be just over $65 million. His base salary was $3.5 million with annual incentives of $32 million, stock option grants of $5.8 million, restricted stock grants of $19.2 million, and performance awards of $4.7 million. Although there are many critics of the high level of CEO compensation, from the stockholders' point of view, sensitivity of compensation to firm performance is usually more important.

The second incentive managers have relates to job prospects. Better performers within the firm will tend to get promoted. More generally, managers who are successful in pursuing stockholder goals will be in greater demand in the labor market and thus command higher salaries.

In fact, managers who are successful in pursuing stockholder goals can reap enormous rewards. During 2013, the median compensation for CEOs at the largest 500 U.S. companies was $10.5 million. The best-paid executive in 2013 was Larry Ellison, the CEO of Oracle; according to *The Wall Street Journal*, he made about $76.9 million. By way of comparison, basketball superstar LeBron James made $72.3 million, and actor Robert Downey Jr. made about $75 million.[2]

Control of the Firm   Control of the firm ultimately rests with stockholders. They elect the board of directors, who, in turn, hire and fire management.

An important mechanism by which unhappy stockholders can replace existing management is called a *proxy fight*. A proxy is the authority to vote someone else's stock. A proxy fight develops when a group solicits proxies in order to replace the existing board and thereby replace existing management. For example, during 2013 and 2014, New York hedge fund Starboard Value was in a protracted battle with Darden Restaurants, operator of chains such as Red Lobster and Olive Garden. Starboard had problems with Olive Garden's restaurant operations, such as the fact that Olive Garden stopped putting salt in its seasoned pasta water in order to extend the warranty on its cooking pots. In October 2014, the proxy battle ended when Starboard convinced enough shareholders to vote to replace all 12 members of Darden's board of directors. Although replacing an entire board of directors does happen, it usually occurs with smaller companies. This episode was unique because Darden is the largest full-service restaurant company in the U.S., with 2013 sales of $8.55 billion.

Another way that management can be replaced is by takeover. Firms that are poorly managed are more attractive as acquisitions than well-managed firms because a greater profit potential exists. Thus, avoiding a takeover by another firm gives management another incentive to act in the stockholders' interests. Unhappy prominent shareholders can suggest different business strategies to a firm's top management. For example, in the chapter opener, we discussed George Zimmer's firing by the board of The Men's Wearhouse. A few months later, rival Jos. A. Bank made a bid to buy the company, despite the fact that Bank was a significantly smaller firm. The offer was rejected. But, in an interesting turn of events, The Men's Wearhouse offered to buy Jos. A. Bank! After months of back and forth, the two companies announced in March 2014 that a deal had

---

[2]This raises the issue of the level of top management pay and its relationship to other employees. According to the *Economic Policy Institute,* the average CEO compensation was greater than 296 times the average employee compensation in 2013 and only 30 times in 1978. However, there is no precise formula that governs the gap between top management compensation and that of employees.

been finalized, with The Men's Wearhouse buying Jos. A. Bank for $65 per share. That price was about 38 percent higher than Bank's stock price when talks began, so The Men's Wearhouse made an excellent "suit-or."

Conclusion   The available theory and evidence are consistent with the view that stockholders control the firm and that stockholder wealth maximization is the relevant goal of the corporation. Even so, there will undoubtedly be times when management goals are pursued at the expense of the stockholders, at least temporarily.

STAKEHOLDERS

Our discussion thus far implies that management and stockholders are the only parties with an interest in the firm's decisions. This is an oversimplification, of course. Employees, customers, suppliers, and even the government all have a financial interest in the firm.

Taken together, these various groups are called **stakeholders** in the firm. In general, a stakeholder is someone other than a stockholder or creditor who potentially has a claim on the cash flows of the firm. Such groups will also attempt to exert control over the firm, perhaps to the detriment of the owners.

1.6 Regulation

Until now, we have talked mostly about the actions that shareholders and boards of directors can take to reduce the conflicts of interest between themselves and management. We have not talked about regulation.[3] Until recently the main thrust of federal regulation has been to require that companies disclose all relevant information to investors and potential investors. Disclosure of relevant information by corporations is intended to put all investors on a level information playing field and, thereby to reduce conflicts of interest. Of course, regulation imposes costs on corporations and any analysis of regulation must include both benefits and costs.

THE SECURITIES ACT OF 1933 AND THE SECURITIES EXCHANGE ACT OF 1934

The Securities Act of 1933 (the 1933 Act) and the Securities Exchange Act of 1934 (the 1934 Act) provide the basic regulatory framework in the United States for the public trading of securities.

The 1933 Act focuses on the issuing of new securities. Basically, the 1933 Act requires a corporation to file a registration statement with the Securities and Exchange Commission (SEC) that must be made available to every buyer of a new security. The intent of the registration statement is to provide potential stockholders with all the necessary information to make a reasonable decision. The 1934 Act extends the disclosure requirements of the 1933 Act to securities trading in markets after they have been issued. The 1934 Act establishes the SEC and covers a large number of issues including corporate reporting, tender offers, and insider trading. The 1934 Act requires corporations to file reports to the SEC on an annual basis (Form 10K), on a quarterly basis (Form 10Q), and on a monthly basis (Form 8K).

---

[3]At this stage in our book, we focus on the regulation of corporate governance. We do not talk about many other regulators in financial markets not to mention non-financial markets such as the Federal Reserve Board. In Chapter 8, we discuss the nationally recognized statistical rating organizations (NRSROs) in the United States. These include Fitch Ratings, Moody's, and Standard & Poor's. Their ratings are used by market participants to help value securities such as corporate bonds. Many critics of the rating agencies blame the 2007–2009 subprime credit crisis on weak regulatory oversight of these agencies.

As mentioned, the 1934 Act deals with the important issue of insider trading. Illegal insider trading occurs when any person who has acquired nonpublic, special information (i.e., inside information) buys or sells securities based upon that information. One section of the 1934 Act deals with insiders such as directors, officers, and large shareholders, while another deals with any person who has acquired inside information. The intent of these sections of the 1934 Act is to prevent insiders or persons with inside information from taking unfair advantage of this information when trading with outsiders.

To illustrate, suppose you learned that ABC firm was about to publicly announce that it had agreed to be acquired by another firm at a price significantly greater than its current price. This is an example of inside information. The 1934 Act prohibits you from buying ABC stock from shareholders who do not have this information. This prohibition would be especially strong if you were the CEO of the ABC firm. Other kinds of inside information could be knowledge of an initial dividend about to be paid, the discovery of a drug to cure cancer, or the default of a debt obligation.

SARBANES-OXLEY

In response to corporate scandals at companies such as Enron, WorldCom, Tyco, and Adelphia, Congress enacted the Sarbanes-Oxley Act in 2002. The act, better known as "Sarbox," is intended to protect investors from corporate abuses. For example, one section of Sarbox prohibits personal loans from a company to its officers, such as the ones that were received by WorldCom CEO Bernie Ebbers.

One of the key sections of Sarbox took effect on November 15, 2004. Section 404 requires, among other things, that each company's annual report must have an assessment of the company's internal control structure and financial reporting. The auditor must then evaluate and attest to management's assessment of these issues. Sarbox also creates the Public Companies Accounting Oversight Board (PCAOB) to establish new audit guidelines and ethical standards. It requires public companies' audit committees of corporate boards to include only independent, outside directors to oversee the annual audits and disclose if the committees have a financial expert (and if not, why not).

Sarbox contains other key requirements. For example, the officers of the corporation must review and sign the annual reports. They must explicitly declare that the annual report does not contain any false statements or material omissions; that the financial statements fairly represent the financial results; and that they are responsible for all internal controls. Finally, the annual report must list any deficiencies in internal controls. In essence, Sarbox makes company management responsible for the accuracy of the company's financial statements.

Of course, as with any law, there are costs. Sarbox has increased the expense of corporate audits, sometimes dramatically. In 2004, the average compliance cost for large firms was $4.51 million, although costs have dropped significantly since then. This added expense has led to several unintended results. For example, in 2003, 198 firms delisted their shares from exchanges, or "went dark," and about the same number delisted in 2004. Both numbers were up from 30 delistings in 1999. Many of the companies that delisted stated the reason was to avoid the cost of compliance with Sarbox.[4]

A company that goes dark does not have to file quarterly or annual reports. Annual audits by independent auditors are not required, and executives do not have to certify the

For an annual survey of Sarbox costs, see **www.protiviti.com /en-US/Documents /Surveys/2014 -SOX-Compliance -Survey-Protiviti .pdf.**

---

[4]But in "Has New York Become Less Competitive in Global Markets? Evaluating Foreign Listing Choices Over Time" *Journal of Financial Economics,* Volume 91, Issue 3, March 2009, pp. 253–77, Craig Doidge, Andrew Karolyi, and René Stulz find that the decline in delistings is not directly related to Sarbanes-Oxley. They conclude that most New York delisting was because of mergers and acquisitions, distress, and restructuring.

accuracy of the financial statements, so the savings can be huge. Of course, there are costs. Stock prices typically fall when a company announces it is going dark. Further, such companies will typically have limited access to capital markets and usually will have a higher interest cost on bank loans.

Sarbox has also probably affected the number of companies choosing to go public in the United States. For example, when Peach Holdings, based in Boynton Beach, Florida, decided to go public in 2006, it shunned the U.S. stock markets, instead choosing the London Stock Exchange's Alternative Investment Market (AIM). To go public in the United States, the firm would have paid a $100,000 fee, plus about $2 million to comply with Sarbox. Instead, the company spent only $500,000 on its AIM stock offering.

Summary and Conclusions

This chapter introduced you to some of the basic ideas in corporate finance:

1. Corporate finance has three main areas of concern:
   a. *Capital budgeting:* What long-term investments should the firm take?
   b. *Capital structure:* Where will the firm get the long-term financing to pay for its investments? Also, what mixture of debt and equity should it use to fund operations?
   c. *Working capital management:* How should the firm manage its everyday financial activities?

2. The goal of financial management in a for-profit business is to make decisions that increase the value of the stock, or, more generally, increase the value of the equity.

3. The corporate form of organization is superior to other forms when it comes to raising money and transferring ownership interests, but it has the significant disadvantage of double taxation.

4. There is the possibility of conflicts between stockholders and management in a large corporation. We called these conflicts *agency problems* and discussed how they might be controlled and reduced.

5. The advantages of the corporate form are enhanced by the existence of financial markets.

Of the topics we've discussed thus far, the most important is the goal of financial management: maximizing the value of the stock. Throughout the text we will be analyzing many different financial decisions, but we will always ask the same question: How does the decision under consideration affect the value of the stock?

Concept Questions

1. **Agency Problems**   Who owns a corporation? Describe the process whereby the owners control the firm's management. What is the main reason that an agency relationship exists in the corporate form of organization? In this context, what kinds of problems can arise?

2. **Not-for-Profit Firm Goals**   Suppose you were the financial manager of a not-for-profit business (a not-for-profit hospital, perhaps). What kinds of goals do you think would be appropriate?

3. **Goal of the Firm**   Evaluate the following statement: Managers should not focus on the current stock value because doing so will lead to an overemphasis on short-term profits at the expense of long-term profits.

4. **Ethics and Firm Goals**   Can the goal of maximizing the value of the stock conflict with other goals, such as avoiding unethical or illegal behavior? In particular, do you think subjects like customer and employee safety, the environment, and the general good of society fit in this framework, or are they essentially ignored? Think of some specific scenarios to illustrate your answer.

5. **International Firm Goal**   Would the goal of maximizing the value of the stock differ for financial management in a foreign country? Why or why not?

6. **Agency Problems**   Suppose you own stock in a company. The current price per share is $25. Another company has just announced that it wants to buy your company and will pay $35 per share to acquire all the outstanding stock. Your company's management immediately begins fighting off this hostile bid. Is management acting in the shareholders' best interests? Why or why not?

7. **Agency Problems and Corporate Ownership**   Corporate ownership varies around the world. Historically, individuals have owned the majority of shares in public corporations in the United States. In Germany and Japan, however, banks, other large financial institutions, and other companies own most of the stock in public corporations. Do you think agency problems are likely to be more or less severe in Germany and Japan than in the United States?

8. **Agency Problems and Corporate Ownership**   In recent years, large financial institutions such as mutual funds and pension funds have become the dominant owners of stock in the United States, and these institutions are becoming more active in corporate affairs. What are the implications of this trend for agency problems and corporate control?

9. **Executive Compensation**   Critics have charged that compensation to top managers in the United States is simply too high and should be cut back. For example, focusing on large corporations, Larry Ellison of Oracle has been one of the best-compensated CEOs in the United States, earning about $76.9 million in 2013. Are such amounts excessive? In answering, it might be helpful to recognize that superstar athletes such as Cristiano Ronaldo, top earners in the entertainment field such as James Cameron and Oprah Winfrey, and many others at the top of their respective fields earn at least as much, if not a great deal more.

10. **Goal of Financial Management**   Why is the goal of financial management to maximize the current value of the company's stock? In other words, why isn't the goal to maximize the future value?

2

Financial Statements and Cash Flow

A write-off by a company frequently means that the value of the company's assets has declined. For example, in July 2014, Ford Motor announced that it was writing off $329 million of the company's investment in Ford Sollers, a joint venture to manufacture Ford cars in Russia. The joint venture had begun in October 2011, but over its less than three-year existence, Ford management came to view the joint venture as problematic. Also in 2014, Maersk Oil announced that it was writing off $1.7 billion related to two Brazilian oil fields, and Royal Dutch Shell wrote off $1.9 billion related to U.S. natural gas assets.

So did stockholders in these companies lose billions of dollars because of the write-offs? The answer is probably not. Understanding why ultimately leads us to the main subject of this chapter: that all-important substance known as *cash flow*.

2.1 The Balance Sheet

The **balance sheet** is an accountant's snapshot of a firm's accounting value on a particular date, as though the firm stood momentarily still. The balance sheet has two sides: On the left are the *assets* and on the right are the *liabilities* and *stockholders' equity*. The balance sheet states what the firm owns and how it is financed. The accounting definition that underlies the balance sheet and describes the balance is:

$$\text{Assets} \equiv \text{Liabilities} + \text{Stockholders' equity}$$

We have put a three-line equality in the balance equation to indicate that it must always hold, by definition. In fact, the stockholders' equity is *defined* to be the difference between the assets and the liabilities of the firm. In principle, equity is what the stockholders would have remaining after the firm discharged its obligations.

Table 2.1 gives the 2015 and 2014 balance sheet for the fictitious U.S. Composite Corporation. The assets in the balance sheet are listed in order by the length of time it normally would take an ongoing firm to convert them into cash. The asset side depends on the nature of the business and how management chooses to conduct it. Management must make decisions about cash versus marketable securities, credit versus cash sales, whether to make or buy commodities, whether to lease or purchase items, the types of business in which to engage, and so on. The liabilities and the stockholders' equity are listed in the order in which they would typically be paid over time.

Two excellent sources for company financial information are **finance.yahoo.com** and **money.cnn.com**.

Table 2.1   The Balance Sheet of the U.S. Composite Corporation

U.S. COMPOSITE CORPORATION Balance Sheet 2015 and 2014 ($ in millions)					
Assets	**2015**	**2014**	**Liabilities (Debt) and Stockholders' Equity**	**2015**	**2014**
Current assets:			Current liabilities:		
Cash and equivalents	$ 198	$ 157	Accounts payable	$ 486	$ 455
Accounts receivable	294	270	Total current liabilities	$ 486	$ 455
Inventory	269	280	Long-term liabilities:		
Total current assets	$ 761	$ 707	Deferred taxes	$ 117	$ 104
Fixed assets:			Long-term debt*	471	458
Property, plant, and equipment	$1,423	$1,274	Total long-term liabilities	$ 588	$ 562
Less accumulated depreciation	550	460	Stockholders' equity:		
Net property, plant, and equipment	873	814	Preferred stock	$ 39	$ 39
			Common stock ($1 par value)	55	32
Intangible assets and others	245	221	Capital surplus	347	327
Total fixed assets	$1,118	$1,035	Accumulated retained earnings	390	347
			Less treasury stock†	26	20
			Total equity	$ 805	$ 725
			Total liabilities and stockholders' equity‡	$1,879	$1,742
Total assets	$1,879	$1,742			

*Long-term debt rose by $471 million − $458 million = $13 million. This is the difference between $86 million new debt and $73 million in retirement of old debt.

†Treasury stock rose by $6 million. This reflects the repurchase of $6 million of U.S. Composite's company stock.

‡U.S. Composite reports $43 million in new equity. The company issued 23 million shares at a price of $1.87. The par value of common stock increased by $23 million, and capital surplus increased by $20 million.

The liabilities and stockholders' equity side reflects the types and proportions of financing, which depend on management's choice of capital structure, as between debt and equity and between current debt and long-term debt.

When analyzing a balance sheet, the financial manager should be aware of three concerns: liquidity, debt versus equity, and value versus cost.

LIQUIDITY

Annual and quarterly financial statements for most public U.S. corporations can be found in the EDGAR database at **www.sec.gov**.

Liquidity refers to the ease and quickness with which assets can be converted to cash (without significant loss in value). *Current assets* are the most liquid and include cash and assets that will be turned into cash within a year from the date of the balance sheet. *Accounts receivable* are amounts not yet collected from customers for goods or services sold to them (after adjustment for potential bad debts). *Inventory* is composed of raw materials to be used in production, work in process, and finished goods. *Fixed assets* are the least liquid kind of assets. Tangible fixed assets include property, plant, and equipment. These assets do not convert to cash from normal business activity, and they are not usually used to pay expenses such as payroll.

Some fixed assets are not tangible. Intangible assets have no physical existence but can be very valuable. Examples of intangible assets are the value of a trademark or the value of a patent. The more liquid a firm's assets, the less likely the firm is to experience problems meeting short-term obligations. Thus, the probability that a firm will avoid financial distress can be linked to the firm's liquidity. Unfortunately, liquid assets frequently have lower rates of return than fixed assets; for example, cash generates no investment income. To the extent a firm invests in liquid assets, it sacrifices an opportunity to invest in potentially more profitable investment vehicles.

DEBT VERSUS EQUITY

Liabilities are obligations of the firm that require a payout of cash within a stipulated period. Many liabilities involve contractual obligations to repay a stated amount and interest over a period. Thus, liabilities are debts and are frequently associated with nominally fixed cash burdens, called *debt service,* that put the firm in default of a contract if they are not paid. *Stockholders' equity* is a claim against the firm's assets that is residual and not fixed. In general terms, when the firm borrows, it gives the bondholders first claim on the firm's cash flow.[1] Bondholders can sue the firm if the firm defaults on its bond contracts. This may lead the firm to declare itself bankrupt. Stockholders' equity is the residual difference between assets and liabilities:

$$\text{Assets} - \text{Liabilities} \equiv \text{Stockholders' equity}$$

This is the stockholders' share in the firm stated in accounting terms. The accounting value of stockholders' equity increases when retained earnings are added. This occurs when the firm retains part of its earnings instead of paying them out as dividends.

VALUE VERSUS COST

The home page for the Financial Accounting Standards Board (FASB) is **www.fasb.org**.

The accounting value of a firm's assets is frequently referred to as the *carrying value* or the *book value* of the assets.[2] Under **generally accepted accounting principles (GAAP)**, audited financial statements of firms in the United States carry the assets at cost.[3] Thus the terms *carrying value* and *book value* are unfortunate. They specifically say "value," when in fact the accounting numbers are based on cost. This misleads many readers of financial statements to think that the firm's assets are recorded at true market values. *Market value* is the price at which willing buyers and sellers would trade the assets. It would be only a coincidence if accounting value and market value were the same. In fact, management's job is to create value for the firm that exceeds its cost.

Many people use the balance sheet, but the information each may wish to extract is not the same. A banker may look at a balance sheet for evidence of accounting liquidity and working capital. A supplier may also note the size of accounts payable and therefore the general promptness of payments. Many users of financial statements, including managers and investors, want to know the value of the firm, not its cost. This information is not found on the balance sheet. In fact, many of the true resources of the firm do not appear on the balance sheet: good management, proprietary assets, favorable economic conditions, and so on. Henceforth,

---

[1]Bondholders are investors in the firm's debt. They are creditors of the firm. In this discussion, the term *bondholder* means the same thing as *creditor.*

[2]Confusion often arises because many financial accounting terms have the same meaning. This presents a problem with jargon for the reader of financial statements. For example, the following terms usually refer to the same thing: *assets minus liabilities, net worth, stockholders' equity, owners' equity, book equity,* and *equity capitalization.*

[3]Generally, GAAP requires assets to be carried at the lower of cost or market value. In most instances, cost is lower than market value. However, in some cases when a fair market value can be readily determined, the assets have their value adjusted to the fair market value.

whenever we speak of the value of an asset or the value of the firm, we will normally mean its market value. So, for example, when we say the goal of the financial manager is to increase the value of the stock, we usually mean the market value of the stock not the book value.

With the increasing globalization of business, there has been a growing need to make accounting standards more comparable across countries. In recent years, U.S. accounting standards have become more closely tied to International Financial Reporting Standards (IFRS). In particular, the Financial Accounting Standards Board, which is in charge of GAAP policies, and the International Accounting Standards Board, in charge of IFRS polices, have been working toward convergence of policies. Although GAAP and IFRS have become similar in several areas, as of late 2014, it appears that a full convergence of accounting policies is off the table, at least for now.

> For more information about IFRS, check out the website **www.ifrs.org**.

EXAMPLE 2.1

Market Value versus Book Value   The Cooney Corporation has fixed assets with a book value of $700 and an appraised market value of about $1,000. Net working capital is $400 on the books, but approximately $600 would be realized if all the current accounts were liquidated. Cooney has $500 in long-term debt, both book value and market value. What is the book value of the equity? What is the market value?

We can construct two simplified balance sheets, one in accounting (book value) terms and one in economic (market value) terms:

COONEY CORPORATION
Balance Sheets
Market Value versus Book Value

Assets			Liabilities and Shareholders' Equity		
	Book	**Market**		**Book**	**Market**
Net working capital	$ 400	$ 600	Long-term debt	$ 500	$ 500
Net fixed assets	700	1,000	Shareholders' equity	600	1,100
	$1,100	$1,600		$1,100	$1,600

In this example, shareholders' equity is actually worth almost twice as much as what is shown on the books. The distinction between book and market values is important precisely because book values can be so different from market values.

2.2 The Income Statement

Excel Master
coverage online

The **income statement** measures performance over a specific period—say a year. The accounting definition of income is:

$$\text{Revenue} - \text{Expenses} \equiv \text{Income}$$

If the balance sheet is like a snapshot, the income statement is like a video recording of what the company did between two snapshots. Table 2.2 gives the income statement for the U.S. Composite Corporation for 2015.

The income statement usually includes several sections. The operations section reports the firm's revenues and expenses from principal operations. One number of

Table 2.2

The Income Statement of the U.S. Composite Corporation

U.S. COMPOSITE CORPORATION Income Statement 2015 ($ in millions)	
Total operating revenues	$2,262
Cost of goods sold	1,655
Selling, general, and administrative expenses	327
Depreciation	90
Operating income	$ 190
Other income	29
Earnings before interest and taxes (EBIT)	$ 219
Interest expense	49
Pretax income	$ 170
Taxes	84
Current: $71	
Deferred: 13	
Net income	$ 86
Addition to retained earnings:	$ 43
Dividends:	43

NOTE: There are 29 million shares outstanding. Earnings per share and dividends per share can be calculated as follows:

$$\text{Earnings per share} = \frac{\text{Net income}}{\text{Total shares outstanding}}$$
$$= \frac{\$86}{29}$$
$$= \$2.97 \text{ per share}$$

$$\text{Dividends per share} = \frac{\text{Dividends}}{\text{Total shares outstanding}}$$
$$= \frac{\$43}{29}$$
$$= \$1.48 \text{ per share}$$

particular importance is earnings before interest and taxes (EBIT), which summarizes earnings before taxes and financing costs. Among other things, the nonoperating section of the income statement includes all financing costs, such as interest expense. Usually a second section reports as a separate item the amount of taxes levied on income. The last item on the income statement is the bottom line, or net income. Net income is frequently expressed per share of common stock—that is, earnings per share.

When analyzing an income statement, the financial manager should keep in mind GAAP, noncash items, time, and costs.

GENERALLY ACCEPTED ACCOUNTING PRINCIPLES

Revenue is recognized on an income statement when the earnings process is virtually completed and an exchange of goods or services has occurred. Therefore, the unrealized appreciation from owning property will not be recognized as income. This provides a device for smoothing income by selling appreciated property at convenient times. For example, if the firm owns a tree farm that has doubled in value, then, in a year when its earnings from other businesses are down, it can raise overall earnings by selling some trees. The matching principle of GAAP dictates that revenues be matched with expenses. Thus, income is reported when it is earned, or accrued, even though no cash flow has necessarily occurred (e.g., when goods are sold for credit, sales and profits are reported).

NONCASH ITEMS

The economic value of assets is intimately connected to their future incremental cash flows. However, cash flow does not appear on an income statement. There are several **noncash items** that are expenses against revenues but do not affect cash flow. The most important of these is *depreciation*. Depreciation reflects the accountant's estimate of the cost of equipment used up in the production process. For example, suppose an asset with a five-year life and no resale value is purchased for $1,000. According to accountants, the $1,000 cost must be expensed over the useful life of the asset. If straight-line depreciation is used, there will be five equal installments, and $200 of depreciation expense will be incurred each year. From a finance perspective, the cost of the asset is the actual negative cash flow incurred when the asset is acquired (i.e., $1,000, *not* the accountant's smoothed $200-per-year depreciation expense).

Another noncash expense is *deferred taxes*. Deferred taxes result from differences between accounting income and true taxable income.[4] Notice that the accounting tax shown on the income statement for the U.S. Composite Corporation is $84 million. It can be broken down as current taxes and deferred taxes. The current tax portion is actually sent to the tax authorities (e.g., the Internal Revenue Service). The deferred tax portion is not. However, the theory is that if taxable income is less than accounting income in the current year, it will be more than accounting income later on. Consequently, the taxes that are not paid today will have to be paid in the future, and they represent a liability of the firm. This shows up on the balance sheet as deferred tax liability. From the cash flow perspective, though, deferred tax is not a cash outflow.

In practice, the difference between cash flows and accounting income can be quite dramatic, so it is important to understand the difference. For example, in the second quarter of 2014, Hecla Mining announced a net loss of $14.5 million. Sounds bad, but the company also reported a positive cash flow of $26.6 million, a difference of $41.1 million.

TIME AND COSTS

It is often useful to visualize all of future time as having two distinct parts, the *short run* and the *long run*. The short run is the period in which certain equipment, resources, and commitments of the firm are fixed; but the time is long enough for the firm to vary its output by using more labor and raw materials. The short run is not a precise period that will be the same for all industries. However, all firms making decisions in the short run have some fixed costs—that is, costs that will not change because of fixed commitments. In real business activity, examples of fixed costs are bond interest, overhead, and property taxes. Costs that are not fixed are variable. Variable costs change as the output of the firm changes; some examples are raw materials and wages for laborers on the production line.

In the long run, all costs are variable. Financial accountants do not distinguish between variable costs and fixed costs. Instead, accounting costs usually fit into a classification that distinguishes product costs from period costs. Product costs are the total production costs incurred during a period—raw materials, direct labor, and manufacturing overhead—and are reported on the income statement as cost of goods sold. Both variable and fixed costs are included in product costs. Period costs are costs that are allocated to a time period; they are called *selling, general,* and *administrative expenses*. One period cost would be the company president's salary.

---

[4]One situation in which taxable income may be lower than accounting income is when the firm uses accelerated depreciation expense procedures for the IRS but uses straight-line procedures allowed by GAAP for reporting purposes.

2.3 Taxes

Excel Master
coverage online

Taxes can be one of the largest cash outflows a firm experiences. In 2013, according to the Department of Commerce, total corporate profits before taxes in the United States were about $2.17 trillion, and taxes on corporate profits were about $474 billion or about 22 percent of pretax profits. The size of the firm's tax bill is determined by the tax code, an often amended set of rules. In this section, we examine corporate tax rates and how taxes are calculated.

If the various rules of taxation seem a little bizarre or convoluted to you, keep in mind that the tax code is the result of political, not economic, forces. As a result, there is no reason why it has to make economic sense. To put the complexity of corporate taxation into perspective, General Electric's 2011 tax return required 57,000 pages, far too much to print.

CORPORATE TAX RATES

Corporate tax rates in effect for 2015 are shown in Table 2.3. A peculiar feature of taxation instituted by the Tax Reform Act of 1986 and expanded in the 1993 Omnibus Budget Reconciliation Act is that corporate tax rates are not strictly increasing. As shown, corporate tax rates rise from 15 percent to 39 percent, but they drop back to 34 percent on income over $335,000. They then rise to 38 percent and subsequently fall to 35 percent.

According to the originators of the current tax rules, there are only four corporate rates: 15 percent, 25 percent, 34 percent, and 35 percent. The 38 and 39 percent brackets arise because of "surcharges" applied on top of the 34 and 35 percent rates. A tax is a tax, however, so there are really six corporate tax brackets, as we have shown.

AVERAGE VERSUS MARGINAL TAX RATES

In making financial decisions, it is frequently important to distinguish between average and marginal tax rates. Your **average tax rate** is your tax bill divided by your taxable income—in other words, the percentage of your income that goes to pay taxes. Your **marginal tax rate** is the tax you would pay (in percent) if you earned one more dollar. The percentage tax rates shown in Table 2.3 are all marginal rates. Put another way, the tax rates apply to the part of income in the indicated range only, not all income.

The difference between average and marginal tax rates can best be illustrated with a simple example. Suppose our corporation has a taxable income of $200,000. What is the tax bill? Using Table 2.3, we can figure our tax bill like this:

Table 2.3
Corporate Tax Rates

Taxable Income	Tax Rate
$ 0– 50,000	15%
50,001– 75,000	25
75,001– 100,000	34
100,001– 335,000	39
335,001–10,000,000	34
10,000,001–15,000,000	35
15,000,001–18,333,333	38
18,333,334+	35

$$.15(\$\ 50,000) \qquad\qquad = \$\ 7,500$$
$$.25(\$\ 75,000 - 50,000) \ = \quad 6,250$$
$$.34(\$100,000 - 75,000) \ = \quad 8,500$$
$$.39(\$200,000 - 100,000) = \underline{\quad 39,000}$$
$$\overline{\$61,250}$$

Our total tax is thus $61,250.

In our example, what is the average tax rate? We had a taxable income of $200,000 and a tax bill of $61,250, so the average tax rate is $61,250/200,000 = 30.625%. What is the marginal tax rate? If we made one more dollar, the tax on that dollar would be 39 cents, so our marginal rate is 39 percent.

The IRS has a great website:
www.irs.gov.

**EXAMPLE
4.2**

Deep in the Heart of Taxes   Algernon, Inc., has a taxable income of $85,000. What is its tax bill? What is its average tax rate? Its marginal tax rate?

From Table 2.3, we see that the tax rate applied to the first $50,000 is 15 percent; the rate applied to the next $25,000 is 25 percent; and the rate applied after that up to $100,000 is 34 percent. So Algernon must pay .15 × $50,000 + .25 × 25,000 + .34 × (85,000 − 75,000) = $17,150. The average tax rate is thus $17,150/85,000 = 20.18%. The marginal rate is 34 percent because Algernon's taxes would rise by 34 cents if it had another dollar in taxable income.

Table 2.4 summarizes some different taxable incomes, marginal tax rates, and average tax rates for corporations. Notice how the average and marginal tax rates come together at 35 percent.

With a *flat-rate* tax, there is only one tax rate, so the rate is the same for all income levels. With such a tax, the marginal tax rate is always the same as the average tax rate. As it stands now, corporate taxation in the United States is based on a modified flat-rate tax, which becomes a true flat rate for the highest incomes.

In looking at Table 2.4, notice that the more a corporation makes, the greater is the percentage of taxable income paid in taxes. Put another way, under current tax law, the average tax rate never goes down, even though the marginal tax rate does. As illustrated, for corporations, average tax rates begin at 15 percent and rise to a maximum of 35 percent.

Normally, the marginal tax rate will be relevant for financial decision making. The reason is that any new cash flows will be taxed at that marginal rate. Because financial

Table 2.4
Corporate Taxes
and Tax Rates

(1) Taxable Income	(2) Marginal Tax Rate	(3) Total Tax	(3)/(1) Average Tax Rate
$ 45,000	15%	$ 6,750	15.00%
70,000	25	12,500	17.86
95,000	34	20,550	21.63
250,000	39	80,750	32.30
1,000,000	34	340,000	34.00
17,500,000	38	6,100,000	34.86
50,000,000	35	17,500,000	35.00
100,000,000	35	35,000,000	35.00

Table 2.5

Average Corporate
Tax Rates

Industry	Number of Companies	Average Tax Rate
Electric utilities (eastern U.S.)	24	33.8%
Trucking	33	32.7
Railroad	15	27.4
Securities brokerage	30	20.5
Banking	481	17.5
Medical supplies	264	11.2
Internet	239	5.9
Pharmaceutical	337	5.6
Biotechnology	121	4.5

decisions usually involve new cash flows or changes in existing ones, this rate will tell us the marginal effect of a decision on our tax bill.

There is one last thing to notice about the tax code as it affects corporations. It's easy to verify that the corporate tax bill is just a flat 35 percent of taxable income if our taxable income is more than $18.33 million. Also, for the many midsize corporations with taxable incomes in the range of $335,000 to $10,000,000, the tax rate is a flat 34 percent. Because we will usually be talking about large corporations, you can assume that the average and marginal tax rates are 35 percent unless we explicitly say otherwise.

We should note that we have simplified the U.S. tax code for presentation purposes. In actuality, the tax code is much more complex, with various tax deductions and loopholes allowed for certain industries, as well as the taxation of multinational companies. In reality, recent evidence shows that the average tax rate can be far from 35 percent for many companies. Table 2.5 shows average tax rates for several industries. As you can see, the average tax rate ranges from 33.8 percent for electric utilities to 4.5 percent for biotechnology firms.

Before moving on, we should note that the tax rates we have discussed in this section relate to federal taxes only. Overall tax rates can be higher if state, local, and any other taxes are considered.

2.4 Net Working Capital

Net working capital is current assets minus current liabilities. Net working capital is positive when current assets are greater than current liabilities. This means the cash that will become available over the next 12 months will be greater than the cash that must be paid out. The net working capital of the U.S. Composite Corporation is $275 million in 2015 and $252 million in 2014.

	Current assets ($ millions)	−	Current liabilities ($ millions)	=	Net working capital ($ millions)
2015	$761	−	$486	=	$275
2014	707	−	455	=	252

In addition to investing in fixed assets (i.e., capital spending), a firm can invest in net working capital. This is called the **change in net working capital**. The change in net working capital in 2015 is the difference between the net working capital in 2015 and 2014—that is,

$275 million − $252 million = $23 million. The change in net working capital is usually positive in a growing firm.[5]

2.5 Cash Flow of the Firm

Excel
Master
coverage online

Perhaps the most important item that can be extracted from financial statements is the actual **cash flow** of the firm. An official accounting statement called the *statement of cash flows* helps to explain the change in accounting cash and equivalents, which for U.S. Composite is $33 million in 2015. (See Section 2.6.) Notice in Table 2.1 that cash and equivalents increase from $107 million in 2014 to $140 million in 2015. However, we will look at cash flow from a different perspective: the perspective of finance. In finance, the value of the firm is its ability to generate financial cash flow. (We will talk more about financial cash flow in a later chapter.)

The first point we should mention is that cash flow is not the same as net working capital. For example, increasing inventory requires using cash. Because both inventories and cash are current assets, this does not affect net working capital. In this case, an increase in inventory is associated with decreasing cash flow.

Just as we established that the value of a firm's assets is always equal to the combined value of the liabilities and the value of the equity, the cash flows received from the firm's assets (i.e., its operating activities), CF(A), must equal the cash flows to the firm's creditors, CF(B), and equity investors, CF(S):

$$CF(A) \equiv CF(B) + CF(S)$$

The first step in determining cash flows of the firm is to figure out the *cash flow from operations*. As can be seen in Table 2.6, operating cash flow is the cash flow generated by business activities, including sales of goods and services. Operating cash flow reflects tax payments, but not financing, capital spending, or changes in net working capital:

	$ in millions
Earnings before interest and taxes	$219
Depreciation	90
Current taxes	−71
Operating cash flow	$238

Another important component of cash flow involves *changes in fixed assets*. For example, when U.S. Composite sold its power systems subsidiary in 2015, it generated $25 million in cash flow. The net change in fixed assets equals the acquisition of

---

[5]A firm's current liabilities sometimes include short-term interest bearing debt usually referred to as *notes payable*. However, financial analysts often distinguish between interest bearing short-term debt and noninterest bearing short-term debt (such as accounts payable). When this distinction is made, only noninterest bearing short-term debt is usually included in the calculation of net working capital. This version of net working capital is called "operating" net working capital. The interest bearing short-term debt is not forgotten but instead is included in cash flow from financing activities, and the interest is considered a return on capital.

Financial analysts also sometimes exclude "excess" cash and short-term investments from the calculation of net working capital because this excess could represent a temporary imbalance to a firm's cash flow and may not be directly related to a firm's normal operating or financing activities.

Table 2.6

Financial Cash Flow of the U.S. Composite Corporation

U.S. COMPOSITE CORPORATION Cash Flow of the Firm 2015 ($ in millions)	
Cash flow of the firm	
Operating cash flow	$238
(Earnings before interest and taxes plus depreciation minus taxes)	
Capital spending	−173
(Acquisitions of fixed assets minus sales of fixed assets)	
Additions to net working capital	−23
Total	$ 42
Cash flow to investors in the firm	
Debt	$ 36
(Interest plus retirement of debt minus long-term debt financing)	
Equity	6
(Dividends plus repurchase of equity minus new equity financing)	
Total	$ 42

fixed assets minus the sales of fixed assets. The result is the cash flow used for capital spending:

Acquisition of fixed assets	$198	
Sales of fixed assets	−25	
Capital spending	$173	($149 + 24 = Increase in property, plant, and equipment + Increase in intangible assets)

We can also calculate capital spending simply as:

$$\text{Capital spending} = \text{Ending net fixed assets} - \text{Beginning net fixed assets}$$
$$+ \text{Depreciation}$$
$$= \$1{,}118 - 1{,}035 + 90$$
$$= \$173$$

Cash flows are also used for making investments in net working capital. In U.S. Composite Corporation in 2015, *additions to net working capital* are:

Additions to net working capital	$23

Note that this $23 million is the change in net working capital we previously calculated. Total cash flows generated by the firm's assets are then equal to:

Operating cash flow	$238
Capital spending	−173
Additions to net working capital	− 23
Total cash flow of the firm	$ 42

The total outgoing cash flow of the firm can be separated into cash flow paid to creditors and cash flow paid to stockholders. The cash flow paid to creditors represents a regrouping of the data in Table 2.6 and an explicit recording of interest expense. Creditors are paid an amount generally referred to as *debt service*. Debt service is interest payments plus repayments of principal (i.e., retirement of debt).

An important source of cash flow is the sale of new debt. U.S. Composite's long-term debt increased by $13 million (the difference between $86 million in new debt and $73 million in retirement of old debt).[6] Thus, an increase in long-term debt is the net effect of new borrowing and repayment of maturing obligations plus interest expense:

Cash Flow Paid to Creditors ($ in millions)	
Interest	$ 49
Retirement of debt	73
Debt service	122
Proceeds from long-term debt sales	−86
Total	$ 36

Cash flow paid to creditors can also be calculated as:

$$\text{Cash flow paid to creditors} = \text{Interest paid} - \text{Net new borrowing}$$
$$= \text{Interest paid} - (\text{Ending long-term debt}$$
$$- \text{Beginning long-term debt})$$
$$= \$49 - (471 - 458)$$
$$= \$36$$

Cash flow of the firm also is paid to the stockholders. It is the net effect of paying dividends plus repurchasing outstanding shares of stock and issuing new shares of stock:

Cash Flow to Stockholders ($ in millions)	
Dividends	$43
Repurchase of stock	6
Cash to stockholders	49
Proceeds from new stock issue	−43
Total	$ 6

In general, cash flow to stockholders can be determined as:

$$\text{Cash flow to stockholders} = \text{Dividends paid} - \text{Net new equity raised}$$
$$= \text{Dividends paid} - (\text{Stock sold}$$
$$- \text{Stock repurchased})$$

To determine stock sold, first notice that the common stock and capital surplus accounts went up by a combined $23 + 20 = $43, which implies that the company sold $43 million worth of stock. Second, treasury stock went up by $6, indicating that the company bought

---

[6]New debt and the retirement of old debt are usually found in the "notes" to the balance sheet.

back $6 million worth of stock. Net new equity is thus $43 − 6 = $37. Dividends paid were $43 million, so the cash flow to stockholders was:

$$\text{Cash flow to stockholders} = \$43 − (43 − 6) = \$6,$$

which is what we previously calculated.

Some important observations can be drawn from our discussion of cash flow:

1. Several types of cash flow are relevant to understanding the financial situation of the firm. **Operating cash flow**, defined as earnings before interest plus depreciation minus taxes, measures the cash generated from operations not counting capital spending or working capital requirements. It is usually positive; a firm is in trouble if operating cash flow is negative for a long time because the firm is not generating enough cash to pay operating costs. **Total cash flow of the firm** includes adjustments for capital spending and additions to net working capital. It will frequently be negative. When a firm is growing at a rapid rate, spending on inventory and fixed assets can be higher than operating cash flow.

2. Net income is not cash flow. The net income of the U.S. Composite Corporation in 2015 was $86 million, whereas cash flow was $42 million. The two numbers are not usually the same. In determining the economic and financial condition of a firm, cash flow is more revealing.

A firm's total cash flow sometimes goes by a different name, **free cash flow**. Of course, there is no such thing as "free" cash (we wish!). Instead, the name refers to cash that the firm is free to distribute to creditors and stockholders because it is not needed for working capital or fixed asset investments. For now, we will stick with "total cash flow of the firm" as our label for this important concept because, in practice, there is some variation in exactly how free cash flow is computed. Nonetheless, whenever you hear the phrase "free cash flow," you should understand that what is being discussed is cash flow from assets that can be distributed to investors.

2.6 The Accounting Statement of Cash Flows

Excel Master coverage online

As previously mentioned, there is an official accounting statement called the *statement of cash flows*. This statement helps explain the change in accounting cash, which for U.S. Composite is $33 million in 2015. It is very useful in understanding financial cash flow.

The first step in determining the change in cash is to figure out cash flow from operating activities. This is the cash flow that results from the firm's normal activities in producing and selling goods and services. The second step is to make an adjustment for cash flow from investing activities. The final step is to make an adjustment for cash flow from financing activities. Financing activities are the net payments to creditors and owners (excluding interest expense) made during the year.

The three components of the statement of cash flows are determined next.

CASH FLOW FROM OPERATING ACTIVITIES

To calculate cash flow from operating activities we start with net income. Net income can be found on the income statement and is equal to $86 million. We now need to add back noncash expenses and adjust for changes in current assets and liabilities (other than cash and notes payable). The result is cash flow from operating activities.

U.S. COMPOSITE CORPORATION
Cash Flow from Operating Activities
2015
($ in millions)

Net income	$ 86
Depreciation	90
Deferred taxes	13
Change in assets and liabilities	
Accounts receivable	−24
Inventories	11
Accounts payable	31
Cash flow from operating activities	**$207**

CASH FLOW FROM INVESTING ACTIVITIES

Cash flow from investing activities involves changes in capital assets: acquisition of fixed assets and sales of fixed assets (i.e., net capital expenditures). The result for U.S. Composite is shown here:

U.S. COMPOSITE CORPORATION
Cash Flow from Investing Activities
2015
($ in millions)

Acquisition of fixed assets	−$198
Sales of fixed assets	25
Cash flow from investing activities	**−$173**

CASH FLOW FROM FINANCING ACTIVITIES

Cash flows to and from creditors and owners include changes in equity and debt:

U.S. COMPOSITE CORPORATION
Cash Flow from Financing Activities
2015
($ in millions)

Retirement of long-term debt	−$73
Proceeds from long-term debt sales	86
Dividends	−43
Repurchase of stock	−6
Proceeds from new stock issue	43
Cash flow from financing activities	**$ 7**

Table 2.7
Statement of
Consolidated
Cash Flows of the
U.S. Composite
Corporation

U.S. COMPOSITE CORPORATION Statement of Cash Flows 2015 ($ in millions)	
Operations	
Net income	$ 86
Depreciation	90
Deferred taxes	13
Changes in assets and liabilities	
Accounts receivable	−24
Inventories	11
Accounts payable	31
Total cash flow from operations	$207
Investing activities	
Acquisition of fixed assets	−$198
Sales of fixed assets	25
Total cash flow from investing activities	−$173
Financing activities	
Retirement of long-term debt	−$ 73
Proceeds from long-term debt sales	86
Dividends	−43
Repurchase of stock	−6
Proceeds from new stock issue	43
Total cash flow from financing activities	$ 7
Change in cash (on the balance sheet)	$ 41

The statement of cash flows is the addition of cash flows from operations, cash flows from investing activities, and cash flows from financing activities, and is produced in Table 2.7. When we add all the cash flows together, we get the change in cash on the balance sheet of $41 million.

There is a close relationship between the official accounting statement called the statement of cash flows and the total cash flow of the firm used in finance. Going back to the previous section, you should note a slight conceptual problem here. Interest paid should really go under financing activities, but unfortunately that is not how the accounting is handled. The reason is that interest is deducted as an expense when net income is computed. As a consequence, a primary difference between the accounting cash flow and the financial cash flow of the firm (see Table 2.6) is interest expense.

2.7 Cash Flow Management

One of the reasons why cash flow analysis is popular is the difficulty in manipulating, or spinning, cash flows. GAAP accounting principles allow for significant subjective decisions to be made regarding many key areas. The use of cash flow as a metric to evaluate a company comes from the idea that there is less subjectivity involved, and, therefore, it is harder to spin the numbers. But several recent examples have shown that companies can still find ways to do it.

Tyco used several ploys to alter cash flows. For example, the company purchased more than $800 million of customer security alarm accounts from dealers. The cash flows from these transactions were reported in the financing activity section of the accounting statement of cash flows. When Tyco received payments from customers, the cash inflows were reported as operating cash flows. Another method used by Tyco was to have acquired companies prepay operating expenses. In other words, the company acquired by Tyco would pay vendors for items not yet received. In one case, the payments totaled more than $50 million. When the acquired company was consolidated with Tyco, the prepayments reduced Tyco's cash outflows, thus increasing the operating cash flows.

Dynegy, the energy giant, was accused of engaging in a number of complex "round-trip trades." The round-trip trades essentially involved the sale of natural resources to a counterparty, with the repurchase of the resources from the same party at the same price. In essence, Dynegy would sell an asset for $100, and immediately repurchase it from the buyer for $100. The problem arose with the treatment of the cash flows from the sale. Dynegy treated the cash from the sale of the asset as an operating cash flow, but classified the repurchase as an investing cash outflow. The total cash flows of the contracts traded by Dynegy in these round-trip trades totaled $300 million.

Adelphia Communications was another company that apparently manipulated cash flows. In Adelphia's case, the company capitalized the labor required to install cable. In other words, the company classified this labor expense as a fixed asset. While this practice is fairly common in the telecommunications industry, Adelphia capitalized a higher percentage of labor than is common. The effect of this classification was that the labor was treated as an investment cash flow, which increased the operating cash flow.

In each of these examples, the companies were trying to boost operating cash flows by shifting cash flows to a different heading. The important thing to notice is that these movements don't affect the total cash flow of the firm, which is why we recommend focusing on this number, not just operating cash flow.

Summary and Conclusions

Besides introducing you to corporate accounting, the purpose of this chapter has been to teach you how to determine cash flow from the accounting statements of a typical company.

1. Cash flow is generated by the firm and paid to creditors and shareholders. It can be classified as:
   a. Cash flow from operations.
   b. Cash flow from changes in fixed assets.
   c. Cash flow from changes in working capital.

2. Calculations of cash flow are not difficult, but they require care and particular attention to detail in properly accounting for noncash expenses such as depreciation and deferred taxes. It is especially important that you do not confuse cash flow with changes in net working capital and net income.

Concept Questions

1. **Liquidity** True or false: All assets are liquid at some price. Explain.

2. **Accounting and Cash Flows** Why might the revenue and cost figures shown on a standard income statement not represent the actual cash inflows and outflows that occurred during a period?

3. **Accounting Statement of Cash Flows** Looking at the accounting statement of cash flows, what does the bottom line number mean? How useful is this number for analyzing a company?

4. **Cash Flows** How do financial cash flows and the accounting statement of cash flows differ? Which is more useful for analyzing a company?

5. **Book Values versus Market Values** Under standard accounting rules, it is possible for a company's liabilities to exceed its assets. When this occurs, the owners' equity is negative. Can this happen with market values? Why or why not?

6. **Cash Flow from Assets** Why is it not necessarily bad for the cash flow from assets to be negative for a particular period?

7. **Operating Cash Flow** Why is it not necessarily bad for the operating cash flow to be negative for a particular period?

8. **Net Working Capital and Capital Spending** Could a company's change in net working capital be negative in a given year? (*Hint:* Yes.) Explain how this might come about. What about net capital spending?

9. **Cash Flow to Stockholders and Creditors** Could a company's cash flow to stockholders be negative in a given year? (*Hint:* Yes.) Explain how this might come about. What about cash flow to creditors?

10. **Firm Values** Referring back to the Ford example at the beginning of the chapter, note that we suggested that Ford's stockholders probably didn't suffer as a result of the reported loss. What do you think was the basis for our conclusion?

Questions and Problems

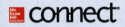

BASIC
(Questions 1–10)

1. **Building a Balance Sheet** Sankey, Inc., has current assets of $4,900, net fixed assets of $25,000, current liabilities of $4,100, and long-term debt of $10,300. What is the value of the shareholders' equity account for this firm? How much is net working capital?

2. **Building an Income Statement** Shelton, Inc., has sales of $435,000, costs of $216,000, depreciation expense of $40,000, interest expense of $21,000, and a tax rate of 35 percent. What is the net income for the firm? Suppose the company paid out $30,000 in cash dividends. What is the addition to retained earnings?

3. **Market Values and Book Values** Klingon Cruisers, Inc., purchased new cloaking machinery three years ago for $9.5 million. The machinery can be sold to the Romulans today for $6.5 million. Klingon's current balance sheet shows net fixed assets of $5.2 million, current liabilities of $2.4 million, and net working capital of $800,000. If all the current assets were liquidated today, the company would receive $2.6 million cash. What is the book value of Klingon's assets today? What is the market value?

4. **Calculating Taxes** The Stefani Co. had $198,000 in taxable income. Using the rates from Table 2.3 in the chapter, calculate the company's income taxes. What is the average tax rate? What is the marginal tax rate?

5. **Calculating OCF** Barrett, Inc., has sales of $19,800, costs of $10,900, depreciation expense of $2,100, and interest expense of $1,250. If the tax rate is 40 percent, what is the operating cash flow, or OCF?

6. **Calculating Net Capital Spending** Gordon Driving School's 2014 balance sheet showed net fixed assets of $1.32 million, and the 2015 balance sheet showed net fixed assets of $1.51 million. The company's 2015 income statement showed a depreciation expense of $137,000. What was the company's net capital spending for 2015?

7. **Building a Balance Sheet** The following table presents the long-term liabilities and stockholders' equity of Information Control Corp. one year ago:

Long-term debt	$ 55,000,000
Preferred stock	3,100,000
Common stock ($1 par value)	12,000,000
Accumulated retained earnings	119,000,000
Capital surplus	56,000,000

During the past year, the company issued 5 million shares of new stock at a total price of $63 million, and issued $30 million in new long-term debt. The company generated $8 million in net income and paid $1.8 million in dividends. Construct the current balance sheet reflecting the changes that occurred at the company during the year.

8. **Cash Flow to Creditors** The 2014 balance sheet of Jordan's Golf Shop, Inc., showed long-term debt of $1.625 million, and the 2015 balance sheet showed long-term debt of $1.73 million. The 2015 income statement showed an interest expense of $185,000. What was the firm's cash flow to creditors during 2015?

9. **Cash Flow to Stockholders** The 2014 balance sheet of Jordan's Golf Shop, Inc., showed $510,000 in the common stock account and $3.6 million in the additional paid-in surplus account. The 2015 balance sheet showed $545,000 and $3.85 million in the same two accounts, respectively. If the company paid out $275,000 in cash dividends during 2015, what was the cash flow to stockholders for the year?

10. **Calculating Cash Flows** Given the information for Jordan's Golf Shop, Inc., in the previous two problems, suppose you also know that the firm's net capital spending for 2015 was $975,000 and that the firm reduced its net working capital investment by $132,000. What was the firm's 2015 operating cash flow, or OCF?

INTERMEDIATE
(Questions 11–23)

11. **Cash Flows** Ritter Corporation's accountants prepared the following financial statements for year-end 2015:
    a. Explain the change in cash during 2015.
    b. Determine the change in net working capital in 2015.
    c. Determine the cash flow generated by the firm's assets during 2015.

RITTER CORPORATION Income Statement 2015	
Revenue	$785
Expenses	575
Depreciation	90
Net income	$120
Dividends	$ 95

RITTER CORPORATION Balance Sheet December 31		
	2015	**2014**
Assets		
Cash	$ 80	$ 60
Other current assets	185	170
Net fixed assets	405	385
Total assets	$670	$615
Liabilities and Equity		
Accounts payable	$140	$125
Long-term debt	160	150
Stockholders' equity	370	340
Total liabilities and equity	$670	$615

12. **Financial Cash Flows**   The Stancil Corporation provided the following current information:

Proceeds from long-term borrowing	$17,800
Proceeds from the sale of common stock	5,000
Purchases of fixed assets	27,000
Purchases of inventories	2,300
Payment of dividends	15,200

Determine the cash flows from the firm and the cash flows to investors of the firm.

13. **Building an Income Statement**   During the year, the Senbet Discount Tire Company had gross sales of $925,000. The firm's cost of goods sold and selling expenses were $490,000 and $220,000, respectively. Senbet also had notes payable of $740,000. These notes carried an interest rate of 4 percent. Depreciation was $120,000. Senbet's tax rate was 35 percent.
    a. What was Senbet's net income?
    b. What was Senbet's operating cash flow?

14. **Calculating Total Cash Flows**   Schwert Corp. shows the following information on its 2015 income statement: sales = $215,000; costs = $117,000; other expenses = $6,700; depreciation expense = $18,400; interest expense = $10,000; taxes = $25,370; dividends = $9,500. In addition, you're told that the firm issued $8,100 in new equity during 2015 and redeemed $7,200 in outstanding long-term debt.
    a. What is the 2015 operating cash flow?
    b. What is the 2015 cash flow to creditors?
    c. What is the 2015 cash flow to stockholders?
    d. If net fixed assets increased by $28,400 during the year, what was the addition to net working capital (NWC)?

15. **Using Income Statements**   Given the following information for O'Hara Marine Co., calculate the depreciation expense: sales = $44,000; costs = $27,500; addition to retained earnings = $5,200; dividends paid = $1,670; interest expense = $1,850; tax rate = 40 percent.

16. **Residual Claims**   Josipovich, Inc., is obligated to pay its creditors $11,300 very soon.
    a. What is the market value of the shareholders' equity if assets have a market value of $12,400?
    b. What if assets equal $9,600?

17. Marginal versus Average Tax Rates (Refer to Table 2.3.) Corporation Growth has $82,500 in taxable income, and Corporation Income has $8,250,000 in taxable income.
 a. What is the tax bill for each firm?
 b. Suppose both firms have identified a new project that will increase taxable income by $10,000. How much in additional taxes will each firm pay? Why is this amount the same?

18. Net Income and OCF During 2015, Rainbow Umbrella Corp. had sales of $590,000. Cost of goods sold, administrative and selling expenses, and depreciation expenses were $455,000, $85,000, and $125,000, respectively. In addition, the company had an interest expense of $65,000 and a tax rate of 35 percent. (Ignore any tax loss carryback or carryforward provisions.)
 a. What is the company's net income for 2015?
 b. What is its operating cash flow?
 c. Explain your results in (a) and (b).

19. Accounting Values versus Cash Flows In Problem 18, suppose Rainbow Umbrella Corp. paid out $34,000 in cash dividends. Is this possible? If spending on net fixed assets and net working capital was zero, and if no new stock was issued during the year, what was the change in the firm's long-term debt account?

20. Calculating Cash Flows Cusic Industries had the following operating results for 2015: sales = $20,300; cost of goods sold = $14,500; depreciation expense = $2,900; interest expense = $690; dividends paid = $660. At the beginning of the year, net fixed assets were $15,470, current assets were $4,630, and current liabilities were $2,520. At the end of the year, net fixed assets were $17,120, current assets were $5,345, and current liabilities were $2,785. The tax rate for 2015 was 40 percent.
 a. What is net income for 2015?
 b. What is the operating cash flow for 2015?
 c. What is the cash flow from assets for 2015? Is this possible? Explain.
 d. If no new debt was issued during the year, what is the cash flow to creditors? What is the cash flow to stockholders? Explain and interpret the positive and negative signs of your answers in (a) through (d).

21. Calculating Cash Flows Consider the following abbreviated financial statements for Weston Enterprises:

WESTON ENTERPRISES 2015 and 2014 Partial Balance Sheets					
Assets			**Liabilities and Owners' Equity**		
	2015	2014		2015	2014
Current assets	$1,176	$ 964	Current liabilities	$ 445	$ 401
Net fixed assets	5,104	4,384	Long-term debt	2,713	2,380

WESTON ENTERPRISES 2015 Income Statement	
Sales	$14,740
Costs	5,932
Depreciation	1,190
Interest paid	328

 a. What is owners' equity for 2014 and 2015?
 b. What is the change in net working capital for 2015?
 c. In 2015, Weston Enterprises purchased $2,350 in new fixed assets. How much in fixed assets did Weston Enterprises sell? What is the cash flow from assets for the year? (The tax rate is 40 percent.)
 d. During 2015, Weston Enterprises raised $455 in new long-term debt. How much long-term debt must Weston Enterprises have paid off during the year? What is the cash flow to creditors?

Use the following information for Ingersoll, Inc., for Problems 22 and 23 (assume the tax rate is 34 percent):

	2014	2015
Sales	$ 9,402	$10,091
Depreciation	1,350	1,351
Cost of goods sold	3,235	3,672
Other expenses	767	641
Interest	630	724
Cash	4,931	6,244
Accounts receivable	6,527	7,352
Short-term notes payable	953	895
Long-term debt	16,152	19,260
Net fixed assets	41,346	42,332
Accounts payable	5,179	5,022
Inventory	11,604	11,926
Dividends	1,147	1,261

22. **Financial Statements**   Draw up an income statement and balance sheet for this company for 2014 and 2015.

23. **Calculating Cash Flow**   For 2015, calculate the cash flow from assets, cash flow to creditors, and cash flow to stockholders.

CHALLENGE
(Questions 24–26)

24. **Cash Flows**   You are researching Time Manufacturing and have found the following accounting statement of cash flows for the most recent year. You also know that the company paid $84 million in current taxes and had an interest expense of $41 million. Use the accounting statement of cash flows to construct the financial statement of cash flows.

TIME MANUFACTURING Statement of Cash Flows ($ in millions)	
Operations	
Net income	$192
Depreciation	76
Deferred taxes	13
Changes in assets and liabilities	
Accounts receivable	−16
Inventories	17
Accounts payable	13
Accrued expenses	−7
Other	2
Total cash flow from operations	$290
Investing activities	
Acquisition of fixed assets	−$198
Sale of fixed assets	21
Total cash flow from investing activities	−$177

Financing activities	
Retirement of long-term debt	−$150
Proceeds from long-term debt sales	115
Change in notes payable	8
Dividends	−81
Repurchase of stock	−11
Proceeds from new stock issue	43
Total cash flow from financing activities	−$ 76
Change in cash (on balance sheet)	$ 37

25. **Net Fixed Assets and Depreciation** On the balance sheet, the net fixed assets (NFA) account is equal to the gross fixed assets (FA) account, which records the acquisition cost of fixed assets, minus the accumulated depreciation (AD) account, which records the total depreciation taken by the firm against its fixed assets. Using the fact that NFA = FA − AD, show that the expression given in the chapter for net capital spending, $NFA_{end} − NFA_{beg} + D$ (where D is the depreciation expense during the year), is equivalent to $FA_{end} − FA_{beg}$.

26. **Tax Rates** Refer to the corporate marginal tax rate information in Table 2.3.
    a. Why do you think the marginal tax rate jumps up from 34 percent to 39 percent at a taxable income of $100,001, and then falls back to a 34 percent marginal rate at a taxable income of $335,001?
    b. Compute the average tax rate for a corporation with exactly $335,001 in taxable income. Does this confirm your explanation in part (a)? What is the average tax rate for a corporation with exactly $18,333,334? Is the same thing happening here?
    c. The 39 percent and 38 percent tax rates both represent what is called a tax "bubble." Suppose the government wanted to lower the upper threshold of the 39 percent marginal tax bracket from $335,000 to $200,000. What would the new 39 percent bubble rate have to be?

Excel Master It! Problem

Using Excel to find the marginal tax rate can be accomplished using the VLOOKUP function. However, calculating the total tax bill is a little more difficult. Below we have shown a copy of the IRS tax table for an individual for 2015 (the income thresholds are indexed to inflation and change through time).

If taxable income is over --	But not over --	The tax is:
$ 0	$ 9,225	10% of the amount over $0
9,226	37,450	$922.50 plus 15% of the amount over $9,225
37,451	90,750	$5,126.25 plus 25% of the amount over $37,450
90,751	189,300	$18,481.25 plus 28% of the amount over $90,750
189,301	411,500	$46,075.25 plus 33% of the amount over $189,300
411,501	413,200	$119,402.25 plus 35% of the amount over $411,500
413,201		$119,996.25 plus 39.6% of the amount over $413,200

In reading this table, the marginal tax rate for taxable income less than $9,225 is 10 percent. If the taxable income is between $9,226 and $37,450, the tax bill is $922.50 plus the marginal taxes. The marginal taxes are calculated as the taxable income minus $9,225 times the marginal tax rate of 15 percent.

a. Create a tax table for corporate taxes similar to the individual tax table shown above.
b. For a given taxable income, what is the marginal tax rate?
c. For a given taxable income, what is the total tax bill?
d. For a given taxable income, what is the average tax rate?

Mini Case

CASH FLOWS AT WARF COMPUTERS, INC.

Warf Computers, Inc., was founded 15 years ago by Nick Warf, a computer programmer. The small initial investment to start the company was made by Nick and his friends. Over the years, this same group has supplied the limited additional investment needed by the company in the form of both equity and short- and long-term debt. Recently the company has developed a virtual keyboard (VK). The VK uses sophisticated artificial intelligence algorithms that allow the user to speak naturally and have the computer input the text, correct spelling and grammatical errors, and format the document according to preset user guidelines. The VK even suggests alternative phrasing and sentence structure, and it provides detailed stylistic diagnostics. Based on a proprietary, very advanced software/hardware hybrid technology, the system is a full generation beyond what is currently on the market. To introduce the VK, the company will require significant outside investment.

Nick has made the decision to seek this outside financing in the form of new equity investments and bank loans. Naturally, new investors and the banks will require a detailed financial analysis. Your employer, Angus Jones & Partners, LLC, has asked you to examine the financial statements provided by Nick. Here are the balance sheets for the two most recent years and the most recent income statement:

WARF COMPUTERS Balance Sheet ($ in thousands)						
	2015	**2014**			**2015**	**2014**
Current assets			Current liabilities			
Cash and equivalents	$ 452	$ 391	Accounts payable		$ 519	$ 485
Accounts receivable	716	668	Accrued expenses		247	401
Inventories	641	663	Total current			
Other	92	78	liabilities		$ 766	$ 886
Total current assets	$1,901	$1,800	Long-term liabilities			
			Deferred taxes		$ 330	$ 159
Fixed assets			Long-term debt		1,179	1,148
Property, plant, and equipment	$4,148	$3,179	Total long-term liabilities		$1,509	$1,307
Less accumulated depreciation	1,340	1,092	Stockholders' equity			
Net property, plant, and equipment	$2,808	$2,087	Preferred stock		$ 21	$ 21
			Common stock		126	126
Intangible assets and others	793	709	Capital surplus		794	779
Total fixed assets	$3,601	$2,796	Accumulated retained earnings		2,478	1,603
			Less treasury stock		192	126
			Total equity		$3,227	$2,403
			Total liabilities and			
Total assets	$5,502	$4,596	shareholders' equity		$5,502	$4,596

Nick has also provided the following information: During the year the company raised $228,000 in new long-term debt and retired $197,000 in long-term debt. The company also sold $15,000 in new stock and repurchased $66,000 in stock. The company purchased $1,482,000 in fixed assets and sold $429,000 in fixed assets.

WARF COMPUTERS Income Statement ($ in thousands)	
Sales	$7,557
Cost of goods sold	4,456
Selling, general, and administrative expense	848
Depreciation	248
Operating income	$2,005
Other income	75
EBIT	$2,080
Interest expense	137
Pretax income	$1,943
Taxes	776
Current: $605	
Deferred: 171	
Net income	$1,167
Dividends	$ 292
Retained earnings	$ 875

Angus has asked you to prepare the financial statement of cash flows and the accounting statement of cash flows. He has also asked you to answer the following questions:

1. How would you describe Warf Computers' cash flows?
2. Which cash flow statement more accurately describes the cash flows at the company?
3. In light of your previous answers, comment on Nick's expansion plans.

3

Financial Statements Analysis and Financial Models

The price of a share of common stock in theme park company SeaWorld closed at about $18 on October 13, 2014. At that price, SeaWorld had a price–earnings (PE) ratio of 17. That is, investors were willing to pay $17 for every dollar in income earned by SeaWorld. At the same time, investors were willing to pay $8, $24, and $28 for each dollar earned by Ford, Coca-Cola, and Google, respectively. At the other extreme were JCPenney and United States Steel. Both had negative earnings for the previous year, but JCPenney was priced at about $7 per share and United States Steel at about $33 per share. Because they had negative earnings,

their PE ratios would have been negative, so they were not reported. At the same time, the typical stock in the S&P 500 Index of large company stocks was trading at a PE of about 17, or about 17 times earnings, as they say on Wall Street.

Price–earnings comparisons are examples of the use of financial ratios. As we will see in this chapter, there are a wide variety of financial ratios, all designed to summarize specific aspects of a firm's financial position. In addition to discussing how to analyze financial statements and compute financial ratios, we will have quite a bit to say about who uses this information and why.

3.1 Financial Statements Analysis

In Chapter 2, we discussed some of the essential concepts of financial statements and cash flows. This chapter continues where our earlier discussion left off. Our goal here is to expand your understanding of the uses (and abuses) of financial statement information.

A good working knowledge of financial statements is desirable simply because such statements, and numbers derived from those statements, are the primary means of communicating financial information both within the firm and outside the firm. In short, much of the language of business finance is rooted in the ideas we discuss in this chapter.

Clearly, one important goal of the accountant is to report financial information to the user in a form useful for decision making. Ironically, the information frequently does not come to the user in such a form. In other words, financial statements don't come with a user's guide. This chapter is a first step in filling this gap.

STANDARDIZING STATEMENTS

One obvious thing we might want to do with a company's financial statements is to compare them to those of other, similar companies. We would immediately have a problem, however. It's almost impossible to directly compare the financial statements for two companies because of differences in size.

For example, Tesla and GM are obviously serious rivals in the auto market, but GM is larger, so it is difficult to compare them directly. For that matter, it's difficult even to compare financial statements from different points in time for the same company if the company's size has changed. The size problem is compounded if we try to compare GM and, say, Toyota. If Toyota's financial statements are denominated in yen, then we have size *and* currency differences.

To start making comparisons, one obvious thing we might try to do is to somehow standardize the financial statements. One common and useful way of doing this is to work with percentages instead of total dollars. The resulting financial statements are called **common-size statements**. We consider these next.

COMMON-SIZE BALANCE SHEETS

For easy reference, Prufrock Corporation's 2014 and 2015 balance sheets are provided in Table 3.1. Using these, we construct common-size balance sheets by expressing each item as a percentage of total assets. Prufrock's 2014 and 2015 common-size balance sheets are shown in Table 3.2.

Notice that some of the totals don't check exactly because of rounding errors. Also notice that the total change has to be zero because the beginning and ending numbers must add up to 100 percent.

Table 3.1

PRUFROCK CORPORATION Balance Sheets as of December 31, 2014 and 2015 ($ in millions)		
Assets	**2014**	**2015**
Current assets		
Cash	$ 84	$ 98
Accounts receivable	165	188
Inventory	393	422
Total	$ 642	$ 708
Fixed assets		
Net plant and equipment	$2,731	$2,880
Total assets	$3,373	$3,588
Liabilities and Owners' Equity		
Current liabilities		
Accounts payable	$ 312	$ 344
Notes payable	231	196
Total	$ 543	$ 540
Long-term debt	$ 531	$ 457
Owners' equity		
Common stock and paid-in surplus	$ 500	$ 550
Retained earnings	1,799	2,041
Total	$2,299	$2,591
Total liabilities and owners' equity	$3,373	$3,588

Table 3.2

PRUFROCK CORPORATION Common-Size Balance Sheets December 31, 2014 and 2015			
Assets	**2014**	**2015**	**Change**
Current assets			
Cash	2.5%	2.7%	+ .2%
Accounts receivable	4.9	5.2	+ .3
Inventory	11.7	11.8	+ .1
Total	19.1	19.7	+ .7
Fixed assets			
Net plant and equipment	80.9	80.3	− .7
Total assets	100.0%	100.0%	.0%
Liabilities and Owners' Equity			
Current liabilities			
Accounts payable	9.2%	9.6%	+ .3%
Notes payable	6.8	5.5	−1.3
Total	16.0	15.1	−1.0
Long-term debt	15.7	12.7	−3.0
Owners' equity			
Common stock and paid-in surplus	14.8	15.3	+ .5
Retained earnings	53.3	56.9	+3.5
Total	68.1	72.2	+4.1
Total liabilities and owners' equity	100.0%	100.0%	.0%

In this form, financial statements are relatively easy to read and compare. For example, just looking at the two balance sheets for Prufrock, we see that current assets were 19.7 percent of total assets in 2015, up from 19.1 percent in 2014. Current liabilities declined from 16.0 percent to 15.1 percent of total liabilities and equity over that same time. Similarly, total equity rose from 68.1 percent of total liabilities and equity to 72.2 percent.

Overall, Prufrock's liquidity, as measured by current assets compared to current liabilities, increased over the year. Simultaneously, Prufrock's indebtedness diminished as a percentage of total assets. We might be tempted to conclude that the balance sheet has grown "stronger."

COMMON-SIZE INCOME STATEMENTS

Table 3.3 describes some commonly used measures of earnings. A useful way of standardizing the income statement shown in Table 3.4 is to express each item as a percentage of total sales, as illustrated for Prufrock in Table 3.5.

This income statement tells us what happens to each dollar in sales. For Prufrock, interest expense eats up $.061 out of every sales dollar, and taxes take another $.081. When all is said and done, $.157 of each dollar flows through to the bottom line (net income), and that amount is split into $.105 retained in the business and $.052 paid out in dividends.

These percentages are useful in comparisons. For example, a relevant figure is the cost percentage. For Prufrock, $.582 of each $1.00 in sales goes to pay for goods sold. It would be interesting to compute the same percentage for Prufrock's main competitors to see how Prufrock stacks up in terms of cost control.

Table 3.3
Measures of Earnings

Investors and analysts look closely at the income statement for clues on how well a company has performed during a particular year. Here are some commonly used measures of earnings (numbers in millions).

Net income   The so-called bottom line, defined as total revenue minus total expenses. Net income for Prufrock in the latest period is $363 million. Net income reflects differences in a firm's capital structure and taxes as well as operating income. Interest expense and taxes are subtracted from operating income in computing net income. Shareholders look closely at net income because dividend payout and retained earnings are closely linked to net income.

EPS   Net income divided by the number of shares outstanding. It expresses net income on a per share basis. For Prufrock, the EPS = (Net income)/(Shares outstanding) = $363/33 = $11.

EBIT   Earnings before interest expense and taxes. EBIT is usually called "income from operations" on the income statement and is income before unusual items, discontinued operations or extraordinary items. To calculate EBIT, operating expenses are subtracted from total operations revenues. Analysts like EBIT because it abstracts from differences in earnings from a firm's capital structure (interest expense) and taxes. For Prufrock, EBIT is $691 million.

EBITDA   Earnings before interest expense, taxes, depreciation, and amortization. EBITDA = EBIT + depreciation and amortization. Here amortization refers to a noncash expense similar to depreciation except it applies to an intangible asset (such as a patent), rather than a tangible asset (such as a machine). The word amortization here does not refer to the payment of debt. There is no amortization in Prufrock's income statement. For Prufrock, EBITDA = $691 + $276 = $967 million. Analysts like to use EBITDA because it adds back two noncash items (depreciation and amortization) to EBIT and thus is a better measure of before-tax operating cash flow.

Sometimes these measures of earnings are preceded by the letters LTM, meaning the last twelve months. For example, LTM EPS is the last twelve months of EPS and LTM EBITDA is the last twelve months of EBITDA. At other times, the letters TTM are used, meaning trailing twelve months. Needless to say, LTM is the same as TTM.

Table 3.4

PRUFROCK CORPORATION 2015 Income Statement ($ in millions)	
Sales	$2,311
Cost of goods sold	1,344
Depreciation	276
Earnings before interest and taxes	$ 691
Interest paid	141
Taxable income	$ 550
Taxes (34%)	187
Net income	$ 363
Dividends	$121
Addition to retained earnings	242

Table 3.5

PRUFROCK CORPORATION	
Common-Size Income Statement 2015	
Sales	100.0%
Cost of goods sold	58.2
Depreciation	11.9
Earnings before interest and taxes	29.9
Interest paid	6.1
Taxable income	23.8
Taxes (34%)	8.1
Net income	15.7%
Dividends	5.2%
Addition to retained earnings	10.5

3.2 Ratio Analysis

Excel Master
coverage online

Another way of avoiding the problems involved in comparing companies of different sizes is to calculate and compare **financial ratios**. Such ratios are ways of comparing and investigating the relationships between different pieces of financial information. We cover some of the more common ratios next (there are many others we don't discuss here).

One problem with ratios is that different people and different sources frequently don't compute them in exactly the same way, and this leads to much confusion. The specific definitions we use here may or may not be the same as ones you have seen or will see elsewhere. If you are using ratios as tools for analysis, you should be careful to document how you calculate each one; and, if you are comparing your numbers to those of another source, be sure you know how their numbers are computed.

We will defer much of our discussion of how ratios are used and some problems that come up with using them until later in the chapter. For now, for each ratio we discuss, several questions come to mind:

Go to
www.reuters.com /finance/stocks
and find the financials link to examine comparative ratios for a huge number of companies.

1. How is it computed?
2. What is it intended to measure, and why might we be interested?
3. What is the unit of measurement?
4. What might a high or low value be telling us? How might such values be misleading?
5. How could this measure be improved?

Financial ratios are traditionally grouped into the following categories:

1. Short-term solvency, or liquidity, ratios.
2. Long-term solvency, or financial leverage, ratios.
3. Asset management, or turnover, ratios.
4. Profitability ratios.
5. Market value ratios.

We will consider each of these in turn. In calculating these numbers for Prufrock, we will use the ending balance sheet (2015) figures unless we explicitly say otherwise.

SHORT-TERM SOLVENCY OR LIQUIDITY MEASURES

As the name suggests, short-term solvency ratios as a group are intended to provide information about a firm's liquidity, and these ratios are sometimes called *liquidity measures*. The primary concern is the firm's ability to pay its bills over the short run without undue stress. Consequently, these ratios focus on current assets and current liabilities.

For obvious reasons, liquidity ratios are particularly interesting to short-term creditors. Because financial managers are constantly working with banks and other short-term lenders, an understanding of these ratios is essential.

One advantage of looking at current assets and liabilities is that their book values and market values are likely to be similar. Often (though not always), these assets and liabilities just don't live long enough for the two to get seriously out of step. On the other hand, like any type of near-cash, current assets and liabilities can and do change fairly rapidly, so today's amounts may not be a reliable guide to the future.

Current Ratio   One of the best-known and most widely used ratios is the *current ratio*. As you might guess, the current ratio is defined as:

$$\text{Current ratio} = \frac{\text{Current assets}}{\text{Current liabilities}} \qquad (3.1)$$

For Prufrock, the 2015 current ratio is:

$$\text{Current ratio} = \frac{\$708}{\$540} = 1.31 \text{ times}$$

Because current assets and liabilities are, in principle, converted to cash over the following 12 months, the current ratio is a measure of short-term liquidity. The unit of measurement is either dollars or times. So, we could say Prufrock has $1.31 in current assets for every $1 in current liabilities, or we could say Prufrock has its current liabilities covered 1.31 times over. Absent some extraordinary circumstances, we would expect to see a current ratio of at least 1; a current ratio of less than 1 would mean that net working capital (current assets less current liabilities) is negative.

The current ratio, like any ratio, is affected by various types of transactions. For example, suppose the firm borrows over the long term to raise money. The short-run effect would be an increase in cash from the issue proceeds and an increase in long-term debt. Current liabilities would not be affected, so the current ratio would rise.

EXAMPLE 3.1

Current Events   Suppose a firm were to pay off some of its suppliers and short-term creditors. What would happen to the current ratio? Suppose a firm buys some inventory. What happens in this case? What happens if a firm sells some merchandise?

The first case is a trick question. What happens is that the current ratio moves away from 1. If it is greater than 1, it will get bigger, but if it is less than 1, it will get smaller. To see this, suppose the firm has $4 in current assets and $2 in current liabilities for a current ratio of 2. If we use $1 in cash to reduce current liabilities, the new current ratio is ($4 − 1)/($2 − 1) = 3. If we reverse the original situation to $2 in current assets and $4 in current liabilities, the change will cause the current ratio to fall to 1/3 from 1/2.

The second case is not quite as tricky. Nothing happens to the current ratio because cash goes down while inventory goes up—total current assets are unaffected.

In the third case, the current ratio would usually rise because inventory is normally shown at cost and the sale would normally be at something greater than cost (the difference is the markup). The increase in either cash or receivables is therefore greater than the decrease in inventory. This increases current assets, and the current ratio rises.

Finally, note that an apparently low current ratio may not be a bad sign for a company with a large reserve of untapped borrowing power.

Quick (or Acid-Test) Ratio Inventory is often the least liquid current asset. It's also the one for which the book values are least reliable as measures of market value because the quality of the inventory isn't considered. Some of the inventory may later turn out to be damaged, obsolete, or lost.

More to the point, relatively large inventories are often a sign of short-term trouble. The firm may have overestimated sales and overbought or overproduced as a result. In this case, the firm may have a substantial portion of its liquidity tied up in slow-moving inventory.

To further evaluate liquidity, the *quick,* or *acid-test, ratio* is computed just like the current ratio, except inventory is omitted:

$$\text{Quick ratio} = \frac{\text{Current assets} - \text{Inventory}}{\text{Current liabilities}} \qquad (3.2)$$

Notice that using cash to buy inventory does not affect the current ratio, but it reduces the quick ratio. Again, the idea is that inventory is relatively illiquid compared to cash.

For Prufrock, this ratio in 2015 was:

$$\text{Quick ratio} = \frac{\$708 - 422}{\$540} = .53 \text{ times}$$

The quick ratio here tells a somewhat different story than the current ratio because inventory accounts for more than half of Prufrock's current assets. To exaggerate the point, if this inventory consisted of, say, unsold nuclear power plants, then this would be a cause for concern.

To give an example of current versus quick ratios, based on recent financial statements, Walmart and ManpowerGroup, had current ratios of .88 and 1.50, respectively. However, ManpowerGroup carries no inventory to speak of, whereas Walmart's current assets are virtually all inventory. As a result, Walmart's quick ratio was only .24, and ManpowerGroup's was 1.50, the same as its current ratio.

Cash Ratio A very short-term creditor might be interested in the *cash ratio:*

$$\text{Cash ratio} = \frac{\text{Cash}}{\text{Current liabilities}} \qquad (3.3)$$

You can verify that this works out to be .18 times for Prufrock.

LONG-TERM SOLVENCY MEASURES

Long-term solvency ratios are intended to address the firm's long-run ability to meet its obligations or, more generally, its financial leverage. These ratios are sometimes called *financial leverage ratios* or just *leverage ratios.* We consider three commonly used measures and some variations.

Total Debt Ratio The *total debt ratio* takes into account all debts of all maturities to all creditors. It can be defined in several ways, the easiest of which is this:

$$\text{Total debt ratio} = \frac{\text{Total assets} - \text{Total equity}}{\text{Total assets}} \qquad (3.4)$$

$$= \frac{\$3,588 - 2,591}{\$3,588} = .28 \text{ times}$$

In this case, an analyst might say that Prufrock uses 28 percent debt.[1] Whether this is high or low or whether it even makes any difference depends on whether capital structure matters, a subject we discuss in a later chapter.

Prufrock has $.28 in debt for every $1 in assets. Therefore, there is $.72 in equity (= $1 − .28) for every $.28 in debt. With this in mind, we can define two useful variations on the total debt ratio, the *debt–equity ratio* and the *equity multiplier:*

The online U.S. Small Business Administration has more information about financial statements, ratios, and small business topics at **www.sba.gov**.

$$\text{Debt–equity ratio} = \text{Total debt/Total equity} \qquad (3.5)$$
$$= \$.28/\$.72 = .39 \text{ times}$$

$$\text{Equity multiplier} = \text{Total assets/Total equity} \qquad (3.6)$$
$$= \$1/\$.72 = 1.39 \text{ times}$$

The fact that the equity multiplier is 1 plus the debt–equity ratio is not a coincidence:

$$\text{Equity multiplier} = \text{Total assets/Total equity} = \$1/\$.72 = 1.39 \text{ times}$$
$$= (\text{Total equity} + \text{Total debt})/\text{Total equity}$$
$$= 1 + \text{Debt–equity ratio} = 1.39 \text{ times}$$

The thing to notice here is that given any one of these three ratios, you can immediately calculate the other two, so they all say exactly the same thing.

Times Interest Earned

Another common measure of long-term solvency is the *times interest earned* (TIE) *ratio*. Once again, there are several possible (and common) definitions, but we'll stick with the most traditional:

$$\text{Times interest earned ratio} = \frac{\text{EBIT}}{\text{Interest}} \qquad (3.7)$$
$$= \frac{\$691}{\$141} = 4.9 \text{ times}$$

As the name suggests, this ratio measures how well a company has its interest obligations covered, and it is often called the *interest coverage ratio.* For Prufrock, the interest bill is covered 4.9 times over.

Cash Coverage

A problem with the TIE ratio is that it is based on EBIT, which is not really a measure of cash available to pay interest. The reason is that depreciation and amortization, noncash expenses, have been deducted out. Because interest is most definitely a cash outflow (to creditors), one way to define the *cash coverage ratio* is:

$$\text{Cash coverage ratio} = \frac{\text{EBIT} + (\text{Depreciation and amortization})}{\text{Interest}} \qquad (3.8)$$
$$= \frac{\$691 + 276}{\$141} = \frac{\$967}{\$141} = 6.9 \text{ times}$$

The numerator here, EBIT plus depreciation and amortization, is often abbreviated EBITDA (earnings before interest, taxes, depreciation, and amortization). It is a basic measure of the firm's ability to generate cash from operations, and it is frequently used as a measure of cash flow available to meet financial obligations.

---

[1]Total equity here includes preferred stock, if there is any. An equivalent numerator in this ratio would be (Current liabilities + Long-term debt).

More recently another long-term solvency measure is increasingly seen in financial statement analysis and in debt covenants. It uses EBITDA and interest bearing debt. Specifically, for Prufrock:

$$\frac{\text{Interest bearing debt}}{\text{EBITDA}} = \frac{\$196 \text{ million} + 457 \text{ million}}{\$967 \text{ million}} = .68 \text{ times}$$

Here we include notes payable (most likely notes payable is bank debt) and long-term debt in the numerator and EBITDA in the denominator. Values below 1 on this ratio are considered very strong and values above 5 are considered weak. However a careful comparison with other comparable firms is necessary to properly interpret the ratio.

ASSET MANAGEMENT OR TURNOVER MEASURES

We next turn our attention to the efficiency with which Prufrock uses its assets. The measures in this section are sometimes called *asset management* or *utilization ratios*. The specific ratios we discuss can all be interpreted as measures of turnover. What they are intended to describe is how efficiently, or intensively, a firm uses its assets to generate sales. We first look at two important current assets: inventory and receivables.

Inventory Turnover and Days' Sales in Inventory   During the year, Prufrock had a cost of goods sold of $1,344. Inventory at the end of the year was $422. With these numbers, *inventory turnover* can be calculated as:

$$\text{Inventory turnover} = \frac{\text{Cost of goods sold}}{\text{Inventory}} \qquad \textbf{(3.9)}$$
$$= \frac{\$1,344}{\$422} = 3.2 \text{ times}$$

In a sense, we sold off, or turned over, the entire inventory 3.2 times during the year. As long as we are not running out of stock and thereby forgoing sales, the higher this ratio is, the more efficiently we are managing inventory.

If we know that we turned our inventory over 3.2 times during the year, we can immediately figure out how long it took us to turn it over on average. The result is the average *days' sales in inventory:*

$$\text{Days' sales in inventory} = \frac{365 \text{ days}}{\text{Inventory turnover}} \qquad \textbf{(3.10)}$$
$$= \frac{365}{3.2} = 114 \text{ days}$$

This tells us that, roughly speaking, inventory sits 114 days on average before it is sold. Alternatively, assuming we used the most recent inventory and cost figures, it will take about 114 days to work off our current inventory.

In practice, inventory levels can vary dramatically from optimal levels. For example, in September 2014, auto industry inventory in the United States stood at 56 days, down from 76 days a month earlier. A 60-day supply is considered normal in the industry. Of course, inventory varied dramatically among manufacturers. Cadillac had a 132-day supply of vehicles. The company had a 141-day supply of the compact ATS and a 167-day supply of the larger CTS. Neither of these was close to the 434-day supply of the slow-moving Dodge Viper. Naturally, the inventory levels are lower for better-selling models. For example, also in September 2014, Subaru had a 17-day supply of cars.

Receivables Turnover and Days' Sales in Receivables   Our inventory measures give some indication of how fast we can sell products. We now look at how fast we collect on those sales. The *receivables turnover* is defined in the same way as inventory turnover:

$$\text{Receivables turnover} = \frac{\text{Sales}}{\text{Accounts receivable}} \tag{3.11}$$

$$= \frac{\$2,311}{\$188} = 12.3 \text{ times}$$

Loosely speaking, we collected our outstanding credit accounts and lent the money again 12.3 times during the year.[2]

This ratio makes more sense if we convert it to days, so the *days' sales in receivables* is:

$$\text{Days' sales in receivables} = \frac{365 \text{ days}}{\text{Receivables turnover}} \tag{3.12}$$

$$= \frac{365}{12.3} = 30 \text{ days}$$

Therefore, on average, we collect on our credit sales in 30 days. For obvious reasons, this ratio is frequently called the *average collection period* (ACP). Also note that if we are using the most recent figures, we can also say that we have 30 days' worth of sales currently uncollected.

<table>
<tr><td>

**EXAMPLE
3.2**

</td><td>

Payables Turnover   Here is a variation on the receivables collection period. How long, on average, does it take for Prufrock Corporation to *pay* its bills? To answer, we need to calculate the accounts payable turnover rate using cost of goods sold. We will assume that Prufrock purchases everything on credit.

The cost of goods sold is $1,344, and accounts payable are $344. The turnover is therefore $1,344/$344 = 3.9 times. So, payables turned over about every 365/3.9 = 94 days. On average, then, Prufrock takes 94 days to pay. As a potential creditor, we might take note of this fact.

</td></tr>
</table>

Total Asset Turnover   Moving away from specific accounts like inventory or receivables, we can consider an important "big picture" ratio, the *total asset turnover* ratio. As the name suggests, total asset turnover is:

$$\text{Total asset turnover} = \frac{\text{Sales}}{\text{Total assets}} \tag{3.13}$$

$$= \frac{\$2,311}{\$3,588} = .64 \text{ times}$$

In other words, for every dollar in assets, we generated $.64 in sales.

<table>
<tr><td>

**EXAMPLE
3.3**

</td><td>

More Turnover   Suppose you find that a particular company generates $.40 in annual sales for every dollar in total assets. How often does this company turn over its total assets?

The total asset turnover here is .40 times per year. It takes 1/.40 = 2.5 years to turn assets over completely.

</td></tr>
</table>

---

[2]Here we have implicitly assumed that all sales are credit sales. If they were not, we would simply use total credit sales in these calculations, not total sales.

PROFITABILITY MEASURES

The three types of measures we discuss in this section are probably the best-known and most widely used of all financial ratios. In one form or another, they are intended to measure how efficiently the firm uses its assets and how efficiently the firm manages its operations.

Profit Margin

Companies pay a great deal of attention to their *profit margins:*

$$\text{Profit margin} = \frac{\text{Net income}}{\text{Sales}} \tag{3.14}$$

$$= \frac{\$363}{\$2,311} = 15.7\%$$

This tells us that Prufrock, in an accounting sense, generates a little less than 16 cents in net income for every dollar in sales.

EBITDA Margin

Another commonly used measure of profitability is the EBITDA margin. As mentioned, EBITDA is a measure of before-tax operating cash flow. It adds back noncash expenses and does not include taxes or interest expense. As a consequence, EBITDA margin looks more directly at operating cash flows than does net income and does not include the effect of capital structure or taxes. For Prufrock, EBITDA margin is:

$$\frac{\text{EBITDA}}{\text{Sales}} = \frac{\$967 \text{ million}}{\$2,311 \text{ million}} = 41.8\%$$

All other things being equal, a relatively high margin is obviously desirable. This situation corresponds to low expense ratios relative to sales. However, we hasten to add that other things are often not equal.

For example, lowering our sales price will usually increase unit volume but will normally cause margins to shrink. Total profit (or, more importantly, operating cash flow) may go up or down, so the fact that margins are smaller isn't necessarily bad. After all, isn't it possible that, as the saying goes, "Our prices are so low that we lose money on everything we sell, but we make it up in volume"?[3]

Margins are very different for different industries. Grocery stores have a notoriously low profit margin, generally around 2 percent. In contrast, the profit margin for the pharmaceutical industry is about 15 percent. So, for example, it is not surprising that recent profit margins for Kroger and Abbott Laboratories were about 1.5 percent and 11.8 percent, respectively.

Return on Assets

Return on assets (ROA) is a measure of profit per dollar of assets. It can be defined several ways,[4] but the most common is:

$$\text{Return on assets} = \frac{\text{Net income}}{\text{Total assets}} \tag{3.15}$$

$$= \frac{\$363}{\$3,588} = 10.1\%$$

---

[3]No, it's not.

[4]For example, we might want a return on assets measure that is neutral with respect to capital structure (interest expense) and taxes. Such a measure for Prufrock would be:

$$\frac{\text{EBIT}}{\text{Total assets}} = \frac{\$691}{\$3,588} = 19.3\%$$

This measure has a very natural interpretation. If 19.3 percent exceeds Prufrock's borrowing rate, Prufrock will earn more money on its investments than it will pay out to its creditors. The surplus will be available to Prufrock's shareholders after adjusting for taxes.

Return on Equity   *Return on equity* (ROE) is a measure of how the stockholders fared during the year. Because benefiting shareholders is our goal, ROE is, in an accounting sense, the true bottom-line measure of performance. ROE is usually measured as:

$$\text{Return on equity} = \frac{\text{Net income}}{\text{Total equity}} \tag{3.16}$$

$$= \frac{\$363}{\$2,591} = 14\%$$

Therefore, for every dollar in equity, Prufrock generated 14 cents in profit; but, again, this is correct only in accounting terms.

Because ROA and ROE are such commonly cited numbers, we stress that it is important to remember they are accounting rates of return. For this reason, these measures should properly be called *return on book assets* and *return on book equity*. In addition, ROE is sometimes called *return on net worth*. Whatever it's called, it would be inappropriate to compare the result to, for example, an interest rate observed in the financial markets.

The fact that ROE exceeds ROA reflects Prufrock's use of financial leverage. We will examine the relationship between these two measures in the next section.

MARKET VALUE MEASURES

Our final group of measures is based, in part, on information not necessarily contained in financial statements—the market price per share of the stock. Obviously, these measures can be calculated directly only for publicly traded companies.

We assume that Prufrock has 33 million shares outstanding and the stock sold for $88 per share at the end of the year. If we recall that Prufrock's net income was $363 million, then we can calculate that its earnings per share were:

$$\text{EPS} = \frac{\text{Net income}}{\text{Shares outstanding}} = \frac{\$363}{33} = \$11 \tag{3.17}$$

Price–Earnings Ratio   The first of our market value measures, the *price–earnings* or *PE ratio* (or multiple), is defined as:

$$\text{PE ratio} = \frac{\text{Price per share}}{\text{Earnings per share}} \tag{3.18}$$

$$= \frac{\$88}{\$11} = 8 \text{ times}$$

In the vernacular, we would say that Prufrock shares sell for eight times earnings, or we might say that Prufrock shares have, or "carry," a PE multiple of 8.

Because the PE ratio measures how much investors are willing to pay per dollar of current earnings, higher PEs are often taken to mean that the firm has significant prospects for future growth. Of course, if a firm had no or almost no earnings, its PE would probably be quite large; so, as always, care is needed in interpreting this ratio.

Market-to-Book Ratio   A second commonly quoted measure is the *market-to-book ratio:*

$$\text{Market-to-book ratio} = \frac{\text{Market value per share}}{\text{Book value per share}} \tag{3.19}$$

$$= \frac{\$88}{\$2,591/33} = \frac{\$88}{\$78.5} = 1.12 \text{ times}$$

Notice that book value per share is total equity (not just common stock) divided by the number of shares outstanding.

Book value per share is an accounting number that reflects historical costs. In a loose sense, the market-to-book ratio therefore compares the market value of the firm's investments to their cost. A value less than 1 could mean that the firm has not been successful overall in creating value for its stockholders.

Market Capitalization

The market capitalization of a public firm is equal to the firm's stock market price per share multiplied by the number of shares outstanding. For Prufrock, this is:

$$\text{Price per share} \times \text{Shares outstanding} = \$88 \times 33 \text{ million} = \$2{,}904 \text{ million}$$

This is a useful number for potential buyers of Prufrock. A prospective buyer of all of the outstanding shares of Prufrock (in a merger or acquisition) would need to come up with at least \$2,904 million plus a premium.

Enterprise Value

Enterprise value is a measure of firm value that is very closely related to market capitalization. Instead of focusing on only the market value of outstanding shares of stock, it measures the market value of outstanding shares of stock plus the market value of outstanding interest bearing debt less cash on hand. We know the market capitalization of Prufrock but we do not know the market value of its outstanding interest bearing debt. In this situation, the common practice is to use the book value of outstanding interest bearing debt less cash on hand as an approximation. For Prufrock, enterprise value is (in millions):

$$\begin{aligned} \text{EV} &= \text{Market capitalization} + \text{Market value of interest bearing debt} - \text{Cash} \quad \textbf{(3.20)} \\ &= \$2{,}904 + (\$196 + 457) - \$98 = \$3{,}459 \text{ million} \end{aligned}$$

The purpose of the EV measure is to better estimate how much it would take to buy all of the outstanding stock of a firm and also to pay off the debt. The adjustment for cash is to recognize that if we were a buyer the cash could be used immediately to buy back debt or pay a dividend.

Enterprise Value Multiples

Financial analysts use valuation multiples based upon a firm's enterprise value when the goal is to estimate the value of the firm's total business rather than just focusing on the value of its equity. To form an appropriate multiple, enterprise value is divided by EBITDA. For Prufrock, the enterprise value multiple is:

$$\frac{\text{EV}}{\text{EBITDA}} = \frac{\$3{,}459 \text{ million}}{\$967 \text{ million}} = 3.6 \text{ times} \quad \textbf{(3.21)}$$

The multiple is especially useful because it allows comparison of one firm with another when there are differences in capital structure (interest expense), taxes, or capital spending. The multiple is not directly affected by these differences.

Similar to PE ratios, we would expect a firm with high growth opportunities to have high EV multiples.

This completes our definition of some common ratios. We could tell you about more of them, but these are enough for now. We'll leave it here and go on to discuss some ways of using these ratios instead of just how to calculate them. Table 3.6 summarizes some of the ratios we've discussed.

Table 3.6   Common Financial Ratios

I. Short-Term Solvency, or Liquidity, Ratios

$$\text{Current ratio} = \frac{\text{Current assets}}{\text{Current liabilities}}$$

$$\text{Quick ratio} = \frac{\text{Current assets} - \text{Inventory}}{\text{Current liabilities}}$$

$$\text{Cash ratio} = \frac{\text{Cash}}{\text{Current liabilities}}$$

$$\text{Days' sales in receivables} = \frac{365 \text{ days}}{\text{Receivables turnover}}$$

$$\text{Total asset turnover} = \frac{\text{Sales}}{\text{Total assets}}$$

$$\text{Capital intensity} = \frac{\text{Total assets}}{\text{Sales}}$$

II. Long-Term Solvency, or Financial Leverage, Ratios

$$\text{Total debt ratio} = \frac{\text{Total assets} - \text{Total equity}}{\text{Total assets}}$$

$$\text{Debt–equity ratio} = \text{Total debt/Total equity}$$

$$\text{Equity multiplier} = \text{Total assets/Total equity}$$

$$\text{Times interest earned ratio} = \frac{\text{EBIT}}{\text{Interest}}$$

$$\text{Cash coverage ratio} = \frac{\text{EBITDA}}{\text{Interest}}$$

IV. Profitability Ratios

$$\text{Profit margin} = \frac{\text{Net income}}{\text{Sales}}$$

$$\text{Return on assets (ROA)} = \frac{\text{Net income}}{\text{Total assets}}$$

$$\text{Return on equity (ROE)} = \frac{\text{Net income}}{\text{Total equity}}$$

$$\text{ROE} = \frac{\text{Net income}}{\text{Sales}} \times \frac{\text{Sales}}{\text{Assets}} \times \frac{\text{Assets}}{\text{Equity}}$$

V. Market Value Ratios

$$\text{Price–earnings ratio} = \frac{\text{Price per share}}{\text{Earnings per share}}$$

$$\text{Market-to-book ratio} = \frac{\text{Market value per share}}{\text{Book value per share}}$$

$$\text{EV multiple} = \frac{\text{Enterprise value}}{\text{EBITDA}}$$

III. Asset Utilization, or Turnover, Ratios

$$\text{Inventory turnover} = \frac{\text{Cost of goods sold}}{\text{Inventory}}$$

$$\text{Days' sales in inventory} = \frac{365 \text{ days}}{\text{Inventory turnover}}$$

$$\text{Receivables turnover} = \frac{\text{Sales}}{\text{Accounts receivable}}$$

EXAMPLE 3.4

Enterprise Value Multiples

Consider the following 2015 data for Atlantic Company, Inc. and The Pacific Depot (billions except for price per share):

	Atlantic Company, Inc.	The Pacific Depot, Inc.
Sales	$53.4	$78.8
EBIT	$ 4.1	$16.6
Net income	$ 2.3	$ 5.4
Cash	$ 0.4	$ 2.0
Depreciation	$ 1.5	$ 1.6
Interest bearing debt	$10.1	$14.7
Total assets	$32.7	$40.5
Price per share	$53	$91
Shares outstanding	1.0	1.4
Shareholder equity	$11.9	$17.9

(continued)

1. Determine the profit margin, ROE, market capitalization, enterprise value, PE multiple, and EV multiple for both Atlantic Company, Inc. and Pacific Depot.

	Atlantic Company, Inc.	Pacific Depot, Inc.
Equity multiplier	32.7/11.9 = 2.7	40.5/17.9 = 2.3
Total asset turnover	53.4/32.7 = 1.6	78.8/40.5 = 1.9
Profit margin	2.3/53.4 = 4.3%	5.4/78.8 = 6.9%
ROE	2.3/11.9 = 19.3%	5.4/17.9 = 30.2%
Market capitalization	1.0 × 53 = $53 billion	1.4 × 91 = $127.4 billion
Enterprise value	(1.0 × 53) + 10.1 −.4 = $62.7 billion	(1.4 × 91) + 14.7 − 2.0 = $140.1 billion
PE multiple	53/2.3 = 23	91/3.86 = 23.6
EBITDA	4.1 + 1.5 = $5.6	16.6 + 1.6 = $18.2
EV multiple	62.7/5.60 = 11.2	140.1/18.2 = 7.7

2. How would you describe these two companies from a financial point of view? Overall, they are similarly situated. In 2014, Pacific Depot had a higher ROE (partially because of a higher total asset turnover and a higher profit margin), but Atlantic had a higher EV multiple. Both companies' PE multiples were somewhat above the general market, indicating possible future growth prospects.

3.3 The DuPont Identity

Excel Master
coverage online

As we mentioned in discussing ROA and ROE, the difference between these two profitability measures reflects the use of debt financing or financial leverage. We illustrate the relationship between these measures in this section by investigating a famous way of decomposing ROE into its component parts.

A CLOSER LOOK AT ROE

To begin, let's recall the definition of ROE:

$$\text{Return on equity} = \frac{\text{Net income}}{\text{Total equity}}$$

If we were so inclined, we could multiply this ratio by Assets/Assets without changing anything:

$$\text{Return on equity} = \frac{\text{Net income}}{\text{Total equity}} = \frac{\text{Net income}}{\text{Total equity}} \times \frac{\text{Assets}}{\text{Assets}}$$
$$= \frac{\text{Net income}}{\text{Assets}} \times \frac{\text{Assets}}{\text{Total equity}}$$

Notice that we have expressed the ROE as the product of two other ratios—ROA and the equity multiplier:

$$\text{ROE} = \text{ROA} \times \text{Equity multiplier} = \text{ROA} \times (1 + \text{Debt–equity ratio})$$

Looking back at Prufrock, for example, we see that the debt–equity ratio was .39 and ROA was 10.12 percent. Our work here implies that Prufrock's ROE, as we previously calculated, is:

$$\text{ROE} = 10.12\% \times 1.39 = 14\%$$

The difference between ROE and ROA can be substantial, particularly for certain businesses. For example, based on recent financial statements, U.S. Bancorp has an ROA of only 1.11 percent, which is actually fairly typical for a bank. However, banks tend to borrow a lot of money, and, as a result, have relatively large equity multipliers. For U.S. Bancorp, ROE is about 11.2 percent, implying an equity multiplier of 10.1.

We can further decompose ROE by multiplying the top and bottom by total sales:

$$\text{ROE} = \frac{\text{Sales}}{\text{Sales}} \times \frac{\text{Net income}}{\text{Assets}} \times \frac{\text{Assets}}{\text{Total equity}}$$

If we rearrange things a bit, ROE is:

$$\text{ROE} = \underbrace{\frac{\text{Net income}}{\text{Sales}} \times \frac{\text{Sales}}{\text{Assets}}}_{\text{Return on assets}} \times \frac{\text{Assets}}{\text{Total equity}} \qquad (3.22)$$

$$= \text{Profit margin} \times \text{Total asset turnover} \times \text{Equity multiplier}$$

What we have now done is to partition ROA into its two component parts, profit margin and total asset turnover. The last expression of the preceding equation is called the **DuPont identity** after the DuPont Corporation, which popularized its use.

We can check this relationship for Prufrock by noting that the profit margin was 15.7 percent and the total asset turnover was .64. ROE should thus be:

$$
\begin{aligned}
\text{ROE} &= \text{Profit margin} \times \text{Total asset turnover} \times \text{Equity multiplier} \\
&= 15.7\% \quad\quad \times \quad\quad .64 \quad\quad \times \quad\quad 1.39 \\
&= 14\%
\end{aligned}
$$

This 14 percent ROE is exactly what we had before.

The DuPont identity tells us that ROE is affected by three things:

1. Operating efficiency (as measured by profit margin).
2. Asset use efficiency (as measured by total asset turnover).
3. Financial leverage (as measured by the equity multiplier).

Weakness in either operating or asset use efficiency (or both) will show up in a diminished return on assets, which will translate into a lower ROE.

Considering the DuPont identity, it appears that the ROE could be leveraged up by increasing the amount of debt in the firm. However, notice that increasing debt also increases interest expense, which reduces profit margins, which acts to reduce ROE. So, ROE could go up or down, depending. More important, the use of debt financing has a number of other effects, and, as we discuss at some length in later chapters, the amount of leverage a firm uses is governed by its capital structure policy.

The decomposition of ROE we've discussed in this section is a convenient way of systematically approaching financial statement analysis. If ROE is unsatisfactory

Table 3.7 The DuPont Breakdown for Yahoo! and Google

Yahoo!								
Twelve Months Ending	**ROE**	**=**	**Profit Margin**	**×**	**Total Asset Turnover**	**×**	**Equity Multiplier**	
12/13	10.5%	=	29.2%	×	.279	×	1.29	
12/12	8.0	=	23.4	×	.292	×	1.17	
12/11	8.4	=	21.0	×	.338	×	1.18	
Google								
Twelve Months Ending	**ROE**	**=**	**Profit Margin**	**×**	**Total Asset Turnover**	**×**	**Equity Multiplier**	
12/13	14.8%	=	21.6%	×	.539	×	1.27	
12/12	15.1	=	21.5	×	.535	×	1.31	
12/11	16.8	=	25.7	×	.522	×	1.25	

by some measure, then the DuPont identity tells you where to start looking for the reasons.[5]

Yahoo! and Google are among the best-known Internet companies. They provide good examples of how DuPont analysis can be useful in helping to ask the right questions about a firm's financial performance. The DuPont breakdowns for Yahoo! and Google are summarized in Table 3.7. As shown, in 2013, Yahoo! had an ROE of 10.4 percent, up from its ROE in 2011 of 8.4 percent. In contrast, in 2013, Google had an ROE of 14.8 percent, down from its ROE in 2011 of 16.7 percent. Given this information, how is it possible that Google's ROE could be so much higher than the ROE of Yahoo! during this period of time, and what accounts for the increase in Yahoo!'s ROE?

Inspecting the DuPont breakdown, we see that Yahoo! and Google have a comparable financial leverage. However, Yahoo!'s profit margin increased from 21.0 percent to 29.2 percent. Meanwhile, Google's profit margin was 21.6 percent in 2013, down from 25.7 percent two years before. What can account for Google's advantage over Yahoo! in ROE? It is clear that the big difference in ROE between the two firms can be attributed to the difference in asset utilization.

PROBLEMS WITH FINANCIAL STATEMENT ANALYSIS

We continue our chapter by discussing some additional problems that can arise in using financial statements. In one way or another, the basic problem with financial statement analysis is that there is no underlying theory to help us identify which quantities to look at and to guide us in establishing benchmarks.

As we discuss in other chapters, there are many cases in which financial theory and economic logic provide guidance in making judgments about value and risk. Little such help exists with financial statements. This is why we can't say which ratios matter the most and what a high or low value might be.

---

[5]Perhaps this is a time to mention Abraham Briloff, a well-known financial commentator who famously remarked that "financial statements are like fine perfume; to be sniffed but not swallowed."

One particularly severe problem is that many firms are conglomerates, owning more or less unrelated lines of business. GE is a well-known example. The consolidated financial statements for such firms don't really fit any neat industry category. More generally, the kind of peer group analysis we have been describing is going to work best when the firms are strictly in the same line of business, the industry is competitive, and there is only one way of operating.

Another problem that is becoming increasingly common is that major competitors and natural peer group members in an industry may be scattered around the globe. The automobile industry is an obvious example. The problem here is that financial statements from outside the United States do not necessarily conform to GAAP. The existence of different standards and procedures makes it difficult to compare financial statements across national borders.

Even companies that are clearly in the same line of business may not be comparable. For example, electric utilities engaged primarily in power generation are all classified in the same group. This group is often thought to be relatively homogeneous. However, most utilities operate as regulated monopolies, so they don't compete much with each other, at least not historically. Many have stockholders, and many are organized as cooperatives with no stockholders. There are several different ways of generating power, ranging from hydroelectric to nuclear, so the operating activities of these utilities can differ quite a bit. Finally, profitability is strongly affected by the regulatory environment, so utilities in different locations can be similar but show different profits.

Several other general problems frequently crop up. First, different firms use different accounting procedures—for inventory, for example. This makes it difficult to compare statements. Second, different firms end their fiscal years at different times. For firms in seasonal businesses (such as a retailer with a large Christmas season), this can lead to difficulties in comparing balance sheets because of fluctuations in accounts during the year. Finally, for any particular firm, unusual or transient events, such as a one-time profit from an asset sale, may affect financial performance. Such events can give misleading signals as we compare firms.

3.4 Financial Models

Financial planning is another important use of financial statements. Most financial planning models use pro forma financial statements, where pro forma means "as a matter of form." In our case, this means that financial statements are the form we use to summarize the projected future financial status of a company.

A SIMPLE FINANCIAL PLANNING MODEL

We can begin our discussion of financial planning models with a relatively simple example. The Computerfield Corporation's financial statements from the most recent year are shown below.

Unless otherwise stated, the financial planners at Computerfield assume that all variables are tied directly to sales and current relationships are optimal. This means that all items will grow at exactly the same rate as sales. This is obviously oversimplified; we use this assumption only to make a point.

COMPUTERFIELD CORPORATION
Financial Statements

Income Statement			Balance Sheet			
Sales	$1,000	Assets	$500	Debt	$250
Costs	800			Equity	250
Net income	$ 200	Total	$500	Total	$500

Suppose sales increase by 20 percent, rising from $1,000 to $1,200. Planners would then also forecast a 20 percent increase in costs, from $800 to $800 × 1.2 = $960. The pro forma income statement would thus look like this:

Pro Forma
Income Statement

Sales	$1,200
Costs	960
Net income	$ 240

The assumption that all variables will grow by 20 percent lets us easily construct the pro forma balance sheet as well:

Pro Forma Balance Sheet

Assets	$600 (+100)	Debt	$300	(+50)
		Equity	300	(+50)
Total	$600 (+100)	Total	$600	(+100)

Notice we have simply increased every item by 20 percent. The numbers in parentheses are the dollar changes for the different items.

Now we have to reconcile these two pro forma statements. How, for example, can net income be equal to $240 and equity increase by only $50? The answer is that Computerfield must have paid out the difference of $240 − 50 = $190, possibly as a cash dividend. In this case dividends are the "plug" variable.

Suppose Computerfield does not pay out the $190. In this case, the addition to retained earnings is the full $240. Computerfield's equity will thus grow to $250 (the starting amount) plus $240 (net income), or $490, and debt must be retired to keep total assets equal to $600.

With $600 in total assets and $490 in equity, debt will have to be $600 − 490 = $110. Because we started with $250 in debt, Computerfield will have to retire $250 − 110 = $140 in debt. The resulting pro forma balance sheet would look like this:

Planware provides insight into cash flow forecasting at **www.planware.org**.

Pro Forma Balance Sheet

Assets	$600 (+100)	Debt	$110	(−140)
		Equity	490	(+240)
Total	$600 (+100)	Total	$600	(+100)

In this case, debt is the plug variable used to balance projected total assets and liabilities.

This example shows the interaction between sales growth and financial policy. As sales increase, so do total assets. This occurs because the firm must invest in net working capital and fixed assets to support higher sales levels. Because assets are growing, total liabilities and equity, the right side of the balance sheet, will grow as well.

The thing to notice from our simple example is that the way the liabilities and owners' equity change depends on the firm's financing policy and its dividend policy. The growth in assets requires that the firm decide on how to finance that growth. This is strictly a managerial decision. Note that in our example the firm needed no outside funds. This won't usually be the case, so we explore a more detailed situation in the next section.

THE PERCENTAGE OF SALES APPROACH

In the previous section, we described a simple planning model in which every item increased at the same rate as sales. This may be a reasonable assumption for some elements. For others, such as long-term borrowing, it probably is not: The amount of long-term borrowing is set by management, and it does not necessarily relate directly to the level of sales.

In this section, we describe an extended version of our simple model. The basic idea is to separate the income statement and balance sheet accounts into two groups, those that vary directly with sales and those that do not. Given a sales forecast, we will then be able to calculate how much financing the firm will need to support the predicted sales level.

The financial planning model we describe next is based on the **percentage of sales approach**. Our goal here is to develop a quick and practical way of generating pro forma statements. We defer discussion of some "bells and whistles" to a later section.

The Income Statement

We start out with the most recent income statement for the Rosengarten Corporation, as shown in Table 3.8. Notice that we have still simplified things by including costs, depreciation, and interest in a single cost figure.

Rosengarten has projected a 25 percent increase in sales for the coming year, so we are anticipating sales of $1,000 × 1.25 = $1,250. To generate a pro forma income statement, we assume that total costs will continue to run at $800/1,000 = 80 percent of sales. With this assumption, Rosengarten's pro forma income statement is as shown in Table 3.9. The effect here of assuming that costs are a constant percentage of sales is to assume that the profit

Table 3.8

ROSENGARTEN CORPORATION Income Statement		
Sales		$1,000
Costs		800
Taxable income		$ 200
Taxes (34%)		68
Net income		$ 132
Dividends	$44	
Addition to retained earnings	88	

Table 3.9

ROSENGARTEN CORPORATION Pro Forma Income Statement	
Sales (projected)	$1,250
Costs (80% of sales)	1,000
Taxable income	$ 250
Taxes (34%)	85
Net income	$ 165

margin is constant. To check this, notice that the profit margin was $132/1,000 = 13.2 percent. In our pro forma statement, the profit margin is $165/1,250 = 13.2 percent; so it is unchanged.

Next, we need to project the dividend payment. This amount is up to Rosengarten's management. We will assume Rosengarten has a policy of paying out a constant fraction of net income in the form of a cash dividend. For the most recent year, the **dividend payout ratio** was:

$$\text{Dividend payout ratio} = \text{Cash dividends/Net income} \qquad (3.23)$$
$$= \$44/132 = 33 \ 1/3\%$$

We can also calculate the ratio of the addition to retained earnings to net income:

$$\text{Addition to retained earnings/Net income} = \$88/132 = 66 \ 2/3\%$$

This ratio is called the **retention ratio** or **plowback ratio**, and it is equal to 1 minus the dividend payout ratio because everything not paid out is retained. Assuming that the payout ratio is constant, the projected dividends and addition to retained earnings will be:

$$\text{Projected dividends paid to shareholders} = \$165 \times 1/3 = \$ 55$$
$$\text{Projected addition to retained earnings} = \$165 \times 2/3 = \underline{\quad 110}$$
$$\underline{\$165}$$

The Balance Sheet   To generate a pro forma balance sheet, we start with the most recent statement, as shown in Table 3.10.

On our balance sheet, we assume that some items vary directly with sales and others do not. For those items that vary with sales, we express each as a percentage of sales for the year just completed. When an item does not vary directly with sales, we write "n/a" for "not applicable."

For example, on the asset side, inventory is equal to 60 percent of sales (=$600/1,000) for the year just ended. We assume this percentage applies to the coming year, so for each $1 increase in sales, inventory will rise by $.60. More generally, the ratio of total assets to sales for the year just ended is $3,000/1,000 = 3, or 300 percent.

This ratio of total assets to sales is sometimes called the **capital intensity ratio**. It tells us the amount of assets needed to generate $1 in sales; the higher the ratio is, the more capital intensive is the firm. Notice also that this ratio is just the reciprocal of the total asset turnover ratio we defined previously.

For Rosengarten, assuming that this ratio is constant, it takes $3 in total assets to generate $1 in sales (apparently Rosengarten is in a relatively capital-intensive business). Therefore, if sales are to increase by $100, Rosengarten will have to increase total assets by three times this amount, or $300.

Table 3.10

ROSENGARTEN CORPORATION Balance Sheet					
Assets			**Liabilities and Owners' Equity**		
	$	**Percentage of Sales**		**$**	**Percentage of Sales**
Current assets			Current liabilities		
Cash	$ 160	16%	Accounts payable	$ 300	30%
Accounts receivable	440	44	Notes payable	100	n/a
Inventory	600	60	Total	$ 400	n/a
Total	$1,200	120	Long-term debt	$ 800	n/a
Fixed assets			Owners' equity		
Net plant and equipment	$1,800	180	Common stock and paid-in surplus	$ 800	n/a
			Retained earnings	1,000	n/a
			Total	$1,800	n/a
Total assets	$3,000	300%	Total liabilities and owners' equity	$3,000	n/a

On the liability side of the balance sheet, we show accounts payable varying with sales. The reason is that we expect to place more orders with our suppliers as sales volume increases, so payables will change "spontaneously" with sales. Notes payable, on the other hand, represents short-term debt such as bank borrowing. This will not vary unless we take specific actions to change the amount, so we mark this item as "n/a."

Similarly, we use "n/a" for long-term debt because it won't automatically change with sales. The same is true for common stock and paid-in surplus. The last item on the right side, retained earnings, will vary with sales, but it won't be a simple percentage of sales. Instead, we will explicitly calculate the change in retained earnings based on our projected net income and dividends.

We can now construct a partial pro forma balance sheet for Rosengarten. We do this by using the percentages we have just calculated wherever possible to calculate the projected amounts. For example, net fixed assets are 180 percent of sales; so, with a new sales level of $1,250, the net fixed asset amount will be 1.80 × $1,250 = $2,250, representing an increase of $2,250 − 1,800 = $450 in plant and equipment. It is important to note that for items that don't vary directly with sales, we initially assume no change and simply write in the original amounts. The result is shown in Table 3.11. Notice that the change in retained earnings is equal to the $110 addition to retained earnings we calculated earlier.

Inspecting our pro forma balance sheet, we notice that assets are projected to increase by $750. However, without additional financing, liabilities and equity will increase by only $185, leaving a shortfall of $750 − 185 = $565. We label this amount *external financing needed* (EFN).

Rather than create pro forma statements, if we were so inclined, we could calculate EFN directly as follows:

$$EFN = \frac{\text{Assets}}{\text{Sales}} \times \Delta \text{Sales} - \frac{\text{Spontaneous liabilities}}{\text{Sales}} \times \Delta \text{Sales} - PM \qquad \textbf{(3.24)}$$
$$\times \text{Projected sales} \times (1 - d)$$

Table 3.11

| | | | ROSENGARTEN CORPORATION
Partial Pro Forma Balance Sheet | | | |

Assets			Liabilities and Owners' Equity			
	Next Year	**Change from Current Year**			**Next Year**	**Change from Current Year**
Current assets			Current liabilities			
Cash	$ 200	$ 40	Accounts payable		$ 375	$ 75
Accounts receivable	550	110	Notes payable		100	0
Inventory	750	150	Total		$ 475	$ 75
Total	$1,500	$300	Long-term debt		$ 800	$ 0
Fixed assets			Owners' equity			
Net plant and equipment	$2,250	$450	Common stock and paid-in surplus		$ 800	$ 0
			Retained earnings		1,110	110
			Total		$1,910	$110
Total assets	$3,750	$750	Total liabilities and owners' equity		$3,185	$185
			External financing needed		$ 565	$565

In this expression, " ΔSales" is the projected change in sales (in dollars). In our example projected sales for next year are $1,250, an increase of $250 over the previous year, so ΔSales = $250. By "Spontaneous liabilities," we mean liabilities that naturally move up and down with sales. For Rosengarten, the spontaneous liabilities are the $300 in accounts payable. Finally, *PM* and *d* are the profit margin and dividend payout ratios, which we previously calculated as 13.2 percent and $33\frac{1}{3}$ percent, respectively. Total assets and sales are $3,000 and $1,000, respectively, so we have:

$$EFN = \frac{\$3,000}{1,000} \times \$250 - \frac{\$300}{1,000} \times \$250 - .132 \times \$1,250 \times \left(1 - \frac{1}{3}\right) = \$565$$

In this calculation, notice that there are three parts. The first part is the projected increase in assets, which is calculated using the capital intensity ratio. The second is the spontaneous increase in liabilities. The third part is the product of profit margin and projected sales, which is projected net income, multiplied by the retention ratio. Thus, the third part is the projected addition to retained earnings.

A Particular Scenario   Our financial planning model now reminds us of one of those good news–bad news jokes. The good news is we're projecting a 25 percent increase in sales. The bad news is this isn't going to happen unless Rosengarten can somehow raise $565 in new financing.

This is a good example of how the planning process can point out problems and potential conflicts. If, for example, Rosengarten has a goal of not borrowing any additional funds and not selling any new equity, then a 25 percent increase in sales is probably not feasible.

Table 3.12

ROSENGARTEN CORPORATION						
Pro Forma Balance Sheet						
Assets				**Liabilities and Owners' Equity**		
	Next Year	Change from Current Year			Next Year	Change from Current Year
Current assets				Current liabilities		
Cash	$ 200	$ 40		Accounts payable	$ 375	$ 75
Accounts receivable	550	110		Notes payable	325	225
Inventory	750	150		Total	$ 700	$300
Total	$1,500	$300		Long-term debt	$1,140	$340
Fixed assets				Owners' equity		
Net plant and equipment	$2,250	$450		Common stock and paid-in surplus	$ 800	$ 0
				Retained earnings	1,110	110
				Total	$1,910	$110
Total assets	$3,750	$750		Total liabilities and owners' equity	$3,750	$750

If we take the need for $565 in new financing as given, we know that Rosengarten has three possible sources: short-term borrowing, long-term borrowing, and new equity. The choice of some combination among these three is up to management; we will illustrate only one of the many possibilities.

Suppose Rosengarten decides to borrow the needed funds. In this case, the firm might choose to borrow some over the short term and some over the long term. For example, current assets increased by $300 whereas current liabilities rose by only $75. Rosengarten could borrow $300 − 75 = $225 in short-term notes payable and leave total net working capital unchanged. With $565 needed, the remaining $565 − 225 = $340 would have to come from long-term debt. Table 3.12 shows the completed pro forma balance sheet for Rosengarten.

We have used a combination of short- and long-term debt as the plug here, but we emphasize that this is just one possible strategy; it is not necessarily the best one by any means. We could (and should) investigate many other scenarios. The various ratios we discussed earlier come in handy here. For example, with the scenario we have just examined, we would surely want to examine the current ratio and the total debt ratio to see if we were comfortable with the new projected debt levels.

3.5 External Financing and Growth

External financing needed and growth are obviously related. All other things staying the same, the higher the rate of growth in sales or assets, the greater will be the need for external financing. In the previous section, we took a growth rate as given, and then we determined the amount of external financing needed to support that growth. In this section, we turn things around a bit. We will take the firm's financial policy as given and then examine the relationship between that financial policy and the firm's ability to finance new investments and thereby grow.

We emphasize that we are focusing on growth not because growth is an appropriate goal; instead, for our purposes, growth is simply a convenient means of examining the interactions between investment and financing decisions. In effect, we assume that the use of growth as a basis for planning is just a reflection of the very high level of aggregation used in the planning process.

EFN AND GROWTH

The first thing we need to do is establish the relationship between EFN and growth. To do this, we introduce the simplified income statement and balance sheet for the Hoffman Company in Table 3.13. Notice that we have simplified the balance sheet by combining short-term and long-term debt into a single total debt figure. Effectively, we are assuming that none of the current liabilities vary spontaneously with sales. This assumption isn't as restrictive as it sounds. If any current liabilities (such as accounts payable) vary with sales, we can assume that any such accounts have been netted out in current assets. Also, we continue to combine depreciation, interest, and costs on the income statement.

Suppose the Hoffman Company is forecasting next year's sales level at $600, a $100 increase. Notice that the percentage increase in sales is $100/500 = 20 percent. Using the percentage of sales approach and the figures in Table 3.13, we can prepare a pro forma income statement and balance sheet as in Table 3.14. As Table 3.14 illustrates, at a 20 percent growth rate, Hoffman needs $100 in new assets. The projected addition to retained earnings is $52.8, so the external financing needed, EFN, is $100 − 52.8 = $47.2.

Table 3.13

HOFFMAN COMPANY
Income Statement and Balance Sheet

Income Statement

Sales		$500
Costs		400
Taxable income		$100
Taxes (34%)		34
Net income		$ 66
Dividends	$22	
Addition to retained earnings	44	

Balance Sheet

Assets			Liabilities and Owners' Equity		
	$	Percentage of Sales		$	Percentage of Sales
Current assets	$200	40%	Total debt	$250	n/a
Net fixed assets	300	60	Owners' equity	250	n/a
Total assets	$500	100%	Total liabilities and owners' equity	$500	n/a

Table 3.14

HOFFMAN COMPANY
Pro Forma Income Statement and Balance Sheet

Income Statement

Sales (projected)	$600.0
Costs (80% of sales)	480.0
Taxable income	$120.0
Taxes (34%)	40.8
Net income	$ 79.2
Dividends	$26.4
Addition to retained earnings	52.8

Balance Sheet

Assets			Liabilities and Owners' Equity		
	$	**Percentage of Sales**		**$**	**Percentage of Sales**
Current assets	$240.0	40%	Total debt	$250.0	n/a
Net fixed assets	360.0	60	Owners' equity	302.8	n/a
Total assets	$600.0	100%	Total liabilities and owners' equity	$552.8	n/a
			External financing needed	$ 47.2	n/a

Notice that the debt–equity ratio for Hoffman was originally (from Table 3.13) equal to $250/250 = 1.0. We will assume that the Hoffman Company does not wish to sell new equity. In this case, the $47.2 in EFN will have to be borrowed. What will the new debt–equity ratio be? From Table 3.14, we know that total owners' equity is projected at $302.8. The new total debt will be the original $250 plus $47.2 in new borrowing, or $297.2 total. The debt–equity ratio thus falls slightly from 1.0 to $297.2/302.8 = .98.

Table 3.15 shows EFN for several different growth rates. The projected addition to retained earnings and the projected debt–equity ratio for each scenario are also given (you should probably calculate a few of these for practice). In determining the debt–equity ratios, we assumed that any needed funds were borrowed, and we also assumed any

Table 3.15

Growth and Projected EFN for the Hoffman Company

Projected Sales Growth	Increase In Assets Required	Addition to Retained Earnings	External Financing Needed, EFN	Projected Debt–Equity Ratio
0%	$ 0	$44.0	−$44.0	.70
5	25	46.2	−21.2	.77
10	50	48.4	1.6	.84
15	75	50.6	24.4	.91
20	100	52.8	47.2	.98
25	125	55.0	70.0	1.05

Figure 3.1

Growth and Related Financing Needed for the Hoffman Company

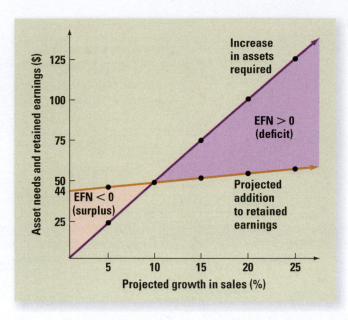

surplus funds were used to pay off debt. Thus, for the zero growth case the debt falls by $44, from $250 to $206. In Table 3.15, notice that the increase in assets required is simply equal to the original assets of $500 multiplied by the growth rate. Similarly, the addition to retained earnings is equal to the original $44 plus $44 times the growth rate.

Table 3.15 shows that for relatively low growth rates, Hoffman will run a surplus, and its debt–equity ratio will decline. Once the growth rate increases to about 10 percent, however, the surplus becomes a deficit. Furthermore, as the growth rate exceeds approximately 20 percent, the debt–equity ratio passes its original value of 1.0.

Figure 3.1 illustrates the connection between growth in sales and external financing needed in more detail by plotting asset needs and additions to retained earnings from Table 3.15 against the growth rates. As shown, the need for new assets grows at a much faster rate than the addition to retained earnings, so the internal financing provided by the addition to retained earnings rapidly disappears.

As this discussion shows, whether a firm runs a cash surplus or deficit depends on growth. Microsoft is a good example. Its revenue growth in the 1990s was amazing, averaging well over 30 percent per year for the decade. Growth slowed down noticeably over the 2000–2010 period, but, nonetheless, Microsoft's combination of growth and substantial profit margins led to enormous cash surpluses. In part because Microsoft paid few dividends, the cash really piled up; in 2014, Microsoft's cash and short-term investment horde exceeded $86 billion.

FINANCIAL POLICY AND GROWTH

Based on our discussion just preceding, we see that there is a direct link between growth and external financing. In this section, we discuss two growth rates that are particularly useful in long-range planning.

The Internal Growth Rate The first growth rate of interest is the maximum growth rate that can be achieved with no external financing of any kind. We will call this the **internal growth rate** because this is the rate the firm can maintain with internal financing only. In Figure 3.1, this internal growth rate is represented by the point where the two lines cross.

At this point, the required increase in assets is exactly equal to the addition to retained earnings, and EFN is therefore zero. We have seen that this happens when the growth rate is slightly less than 10 percent. With a little algebra (see Problem 28 at the end of the chapter), we can define this growth rate more precisely as:

$$\text{Internal growth rate} = \frac{\text{ROA} \times b}{1 - \text{ROA} \times b} \qquad (3.25)$$

where ROA is the return on assets we discussed earlier, and b is the plowback, or retention, ratio also defined earlier in this chapter.

For the Hoffman Company, net income was $66 and total assets were $500. ROA is thus $66/500 = 13.2 percent. Of the $66 net income, $44 was retained, so the plowback ratio, b, is $44/66 = 2/3. With these numbers, we can calculate the internal growth rate as:

$$
\begin{aligned}
\text{Internal growth rate} &= \frac{\text{ROA} \times b}{1 - \text{ROA} \times b} \\
&= \frac{.132 \times (2/3)}{1 - .132 \times (2/3)} \\
&= 9.65\%
\end{aligned}
$$

Thus, the Hoffman Company can expand at a maximum rate of 9.65 percent per year without external financing.

The Sustainable Growth Rate   We have seen that if the Hoffman Company wishes to grow more rapidly than at a rate of 9.65 percent per year, external financing must be arranged. The second growth rate of interest is the maximum growth rate a firm can achieve with no external *equity* financing while it maintains a constant debt–equity ratio. This rate is commonly called the **sustainable growth rate** because it is the maximum rate of growth a firm can maintain without increasing its overall financial leverage.

There are various reasons why a firm might wish to avoid equity sales. For example, new equity sales can be expensive because of the substantial fees that may be involved. Alternatively, the current owners may not wish to bring in new owners or contribute additional equity. Why a firm might view a particular debt–equity ratio as optimal is discussed in later chapters; for now, we will take it as given.

Based on Table 3.15, the sustainable growth rate for Hoffman is approximately 20 percent because the debt–equity ratio is near 1.0 at that growth rate. The precise value can be calculated as follows (see Problem 28 at the end of the chapter):

$$\text{Sustainable growth rate} = \frac{\text{ROE} \times b}{1 - \text{ROE} \times b} \qquad (3.26)$$

This is identical to the internal growth rate except that ROE, return on equity, is used instead of ROA.

For the Hoffman Company, net income was $66 and total equity was $250; ROE is thus $66/250 = 26.4 percent. The plowback ratio, b, is still 2/3, so we can calculate the sustainable growth rate as:

$$
\begin{aligned}
\text{Sustainable growth rate} &= \frac{\text{ROE} \times b}{1 - \text{ROE} \times b} \\
&= \frac{.264 \times (2/3)}{1 - .264 \times (2/3)} \\
&= 21.36\%
\end{aligned}
$$

Thus, the Hoffman Company can expand at a maximum rate of 21.36 percent per year without external equity financing.

EXAMPLE
3.5

Sustainable Growth   Suppose Hoffman grows at exactly the sustainable growth rate of 21.36 percent. What will the pro forma statements look like?

At a 21.36 percent growth rate, sales will rise from $500 to $606.8. The pro forma income statement will look like this:

HOFFMAN COMPANY
Pro Forma Income Statement

Sales (projected)	$606.8
Costs (80% of sales)	485.4
Taxable income	$121.4
Taxes (34%)	41.3
Net income	$ 80.1
Dividends	$26.7
Addition to retained earnings	53.4

We construct the balance sheet just as we did before. Notice, in this case, that owners' equity will rise from $250 to $303.4 because the addition to retained earnings is $53.4.

HOFFMAN COMPANY
Pro Forma Balance Sheet

Assets			Liabilities and Owners' Equity		
	$	Percentage of Sales		$	Percentage of Sales
Current assets	$242.7	40%	Total debt	$250.0	n/a
Net fixed assets	364.1	60	Owners' equity	303.4	n/a
Total assets	$606.8	100%	Total liabilities and owners' equity	$553.4	n/a
			External financing needed	$ 53.4	n/a

As illustrated, EFN is $53.4. If Hoffman borrows this amount, then total debt will rise to $303.4, and the debt–equity ratio will be exactly 1.0, which verifies our earlier calculation. At any other growth rate, something would have to change.

Determinants of Growth   Earlier in this chapter, we saw that the return on equity, ROE, could be decomposed into its various components using the DuPont identity. Because ROE appears so prominently in the determination of the sustainable growth rate, it is obvious that the factors important in determining ROE are also important determinants of growth.

From our previous discussions, we know that ROE can be written as the product of three factors:

$$\text{ROE} = \text{Profit margin} \times \text{Total asset turnover} \times \text{Equity multiplier}$$

If we examine our expression for the sustainable growth rate, we see that anything that increases ROE will increase the sustainable growth rate by making the top bigger and the bottom smaller. Increasing the plowback ratio will have the same effect.

Putting it all together, what we have is that a firm's ability to sustain growth depends explicitly on the following four factors:

1. *Profit margin:* An increase in profit margin will increase the firm's ability to generate funds internally and thereby increase its sustainable growth.

2. *Dividend policy:* A decrease in the percentage of net income paid out as dividends will increase the retention ratio. This increases internally generated equity and thus increases sustainable growth.

3. *Financial policy:* An increase in the debt–equity ratio increases the firm's financial leverage. Because this makes additional debt financing available, it increases the sustainable growth rate.

4. *Total asset turnover:* An increase in the firm's total asset turnover increases the sales generated for each dollar in assets. This decreases the firm's need for new assets as sales grow and thereby increases the sustainable growth rate. Notice that increasing total asset turnover is the same thing as decreasing capital intensity.

The sustainable growth rate is a very useful planning number. What it illustrates is the explicit relationship between the firm's four major areas of concern: its operating efficiency as measured by profit margin, its asset use efficiency as measured by total asset turnover, its dividend policy as measured by the retention ratio, and its financial policy as measured by the debt–equity ratio.

EXAMPLE 3.6

Profit Margins and Sustainable Growth   The Sandar Co. has a debt–equity ratio of .5, a profit margin of 3 percent, a dividend payout ratio of 40 percent, and a capital intensity ratio of 1. What is its sustainable growth rate? If Sandar desired a 10 percent sustainable growth rate and planned to achieve this goal by improving profit margins, what would you think?

ROE is $.03 \times 1 \times 1.5 = 4.5$ percent. The retention ratio is $1 - .40 = .60$. Sustainable growth is thus $.045(.60)/[1 - .045(.60)] = 2.77$ percent.

For the company to achieve a 10 percent growth rate, the profit margin will have to rise. To see this, assume that sustainable growth is equal to 10 percent and then solve for profit margin, PM:

$$.10 = PM(1.5)(.6)/[1 - PM(1.5)(.6)]$$
$$PM = .1/.99 = 10.1\%$$

For the plan to succeed, the necessary increase in profit margin is substantial, from 3 percent to about 10 percent. This may not be feasible.

Given values for all four of these, there is only one growth rate that can be achieved. This is an important point, so it bears restating:

If a firm does not wish to sell new equity and its profit margin, dividend policy, financial policy, and total asset turnover (or capital intensity) are all fixed, then there is only one possible growth rate.

Table 3.16
Summary of Internal
and Sustainable
Growth Rates

I. Internal Growth Rate

$$\text{Internal growth rate} = \frac{\text{ROA} \times b}{1 - \text{ROA} \times b}$$

where

ROA = Return on assets = Net income/Total assets

b = Plowback (retention) ratio
= Addition to retained earnings/Net income

The internal growth rate is the maximum growth rate that can be achieved with no external financing of any kind.

II. Sustainable Growth Rate

$$\text{Sustainable growth rate} = \frac{\text{ROE} \times b}{1 - \text{ROE} \times b}$$

where

ROE = Return on equity = Net income/Total equity

b = Plowback (retention) ratio
= Addition to retained earnings/Net income

The sustainable growth rate is the maximum growth rate that can be achieved with no external equity financing while maintaining a constant debt–equity ratio.

One of the primary benefits of financial planning is that it ensures internal consistency among the firm's various goals. The concept of the sustainable growth rate captures this element nicely. Also, we now see how a financial planning model can be used to test the feasibility of a planned growth rate. If sales are to grow at a rate higher than the sustainable growth rate, the firm must increase profit margins, increase total asset turnover, increase financial leverage, increase earnings retention, or sell new shares.

The two growth rates, internal and sustainable, are summarized in Table 3.16.

A NOTE ABOUT SUSTAINABLE GROWTH RATE CALCULATIONS

Very commonly, the sustainable growth rate is calculated using just the numerator in our expression, ROE $\times$ b. This causes some confusion, which we can clear up here. The issue has to do with how ROE is computed. Recall that ROE is calculated as net income divided by total equity. If total equity is taken from an ending balance sheet (as we have done consistently, and is commonly done in practice), then our formula is the right one. However, if total equity is from the beginning of the period, then the simpler formula is the correct one.

In principle, you'll get exactly the same sustainable growth rate regardless of which way you calculate it (as long as you match up the ROE calculation with the right formula). In reality, you may see some differences because of accounting-related complications. By the way, if you use the average of beginning and ending equity (as some advocate), yet another formula is needed. Also, all of our comments here apply to the internal growth rate as well.

In Their Own Words

ROBERT C. HIGGINS ON SUSTAINABLE GROWTH

Most financial officers know intuitively that it takes money to make money. Rapid sales growth requires increased assets in the form of accounts receivable, inventory, and fixed plant, which, in turn, require money to pay for assets. They also know that if their company does not have the money when needed, it can literally "grow broke." The sustainable growth equation states these intuitive truths explicitly.

Sustainable growth is often used by bankers and other external analysts to assess a company's creditworthiness. They are aided in this exercise by several sophisticated computer software packages that provide detailed analyses of the company's past financial performance, including its annual sustainable growth rate.

Bankers use this information in several ways. Quick comparison of a company's actual growth rate to its sustainable rate tells the banker what issues will be at the top of management's financial agenda. If actual growth consistently exceeds sustainable growth, management's problem will be where to get the cash to finance growth. The banker thus can anticipate interest in loan products. Conversely, if sustainable growth consistently exceeds actual, the banker had best be prepared to talk about investment products because management's problem will be what to do with all the cash that keeps piling up in the till.

Bankers also find the sustainable growth equation useful for explaining to financially inexperienced small business owners and overly optimistic entrepreneurs that, for the long-run viability of their business, it is necessary to keep growth and profitability in proper balance.

Finally, comparison of actual to sustainable growth rates helps a banker understand why a loan applicant needs money and for how long the need might continue. In one instance, a loan applicant requested $100,000 to pay off several insistent suppliers and promised to repay in a few months when he collected some accounts receivable that were coming due. A sustainable growth analysis revealed that the firm had been growing at four to six times its sustainable growth rate and that this pattern was likely to continue in the foreseeable future. This alerted the banker that impatient suppliers were only a symptom of the much more fundamental disease of overly rapid growth, and that a $100,000 loan would likely prove to be only the down payment on a much larger, multiyear commitment.

SOURCE: Robert C. Higgins is Professor of Finance at the University of Washington. He pioneered the use of sustainable growth as a tool for financial analysis.

3.6 Some Caveats Regarding Financial Planning Models

Financial planning models do not always ask the right questions. A primary reason is that they tend to rely on accounting relationships and not financial relationships. In particular, the three basic elements of firm value tend to get left out—namely, cash flow size, risk, and timing.

Because of this, financial planning models sometimes do not produce output that gives the user many meaningful clues about what strategies will lead to increases in value. Instead, they divert the user's attention to questions concerning the association of, say, the debt–equity ratio and firm growth.

The financial model we used for the Hoffman Company was simple—in fact, too simple. Our model, like many in use today, is really an accounting statement generator at heart. Such models are useful for pointing out inconsistencies and reminding us of financial needs, but they offer little guidance concerning what to do about these problems.

In closing our discussion, we should add that financial planning is an iterative process. Plans are created, examined, and modified over and over. The final plan will be a result negotiated between all the different parties to the process. In fact, long-term financial planning in most corporations relies on what might be called the Procrustes approach.[6] Upper-level management has a goal in mind, and it is up to the planning staff to rework and to ultimately deliver a feasible plan that meets that goal.

The final plan will therefore implicitly contain different goals in different areas and also satisfy many constraints. For this reason, such a plan need not be a dispassionate assessment of what we think the future will bring; it may instead be a means of reconciling the planned activities of different groups and a way of setting common goals for the future.

However it is done, the important thing to remember is that financial planning should not become a purely mechanical exercise. If it does, it will probably focus on the wrong things. Nevertheless, the alternative to planning is stumbling into the future. Perhaps the immortal Yogi Berra (the baseball catcher, not the cartoon character), said it best: "Ya gotta watch out if you don't know where you're goin'. You just might not get there."[7]

---

[6]In Greek mythology, Procrustes is a giant who seizes travelers and ties them to an iron bed. He stretches them or cuts off their legs as needed to make them fit the bed.

[7]We're not *exactly* sure what this means, either, but we like the sound of it.

Summary and Conclusions

This chapter focuses on working with information contained in financial statements. Specifically, we studied standardized financial statements, ratio analysis, and long-term financial planning.

1. We explained that differences in firm size make it difficult to compare financial statements, and we discussed how to form common-size statements to make comparisons easier and more meaningful.

2. Evaluating ratios of accounting numbers is another way of comparing financial statement information. We defined a number of the most commonly used ratios, and we discussed the famous DuPont identity.

3. We showed how pro forma financial statements can be generated and used to plan for future financing needs.

After you have studied this chapter, we hope that you have some perspective on the uses and abuses of financial statement information. You should also find that your vocabulary of business and financial terms has grown substantially.

Concept Questions

1. **Financial Ratio Analysis** A financial ratio by itself tells us little about a company because financial ratios vary a great deal across industries. There are two basic methods for analyzing financial ratios for a company: Time trend analysis and peer group analysis. In time trend analysis, you find the ratios for the company over some period, say five years, and examine how each ratio has changed over this period. In peer group analysis, you compare a company's financial ratios to those of its peers. Why might

each of these analysis methods be useful? What does each tell you about the company's financial health?

2. **Industry-Specific Ratios**   So-called "same-store sales" are a very important measure for companies as diverse as McDonald's and Sears. As the name suggests, examining same-store sales means comparing revenues from the same stores or restaurants at two different points in time. Why might companies focus on same-store sales rather than total sales?

3. **Sales Forecast**   Why do you think most long-term financial planning begins with sales forecasts? Put differently, why are future sales the key input?

4. **Sustainable Growth**   In the chapter, we used Rosengarten Corporation to demonstrate how to calculate EFN. The ROE for Rosengarten is about 7.3 percent, and the plowback ratio is about 67 percent. If you calculate the sustainable growth rate for Rosengarten, you will find it is only 5.14 percent. In our calculation for EFN, we used a growth rate of 25 percent. Is this possible? (*Hint:* Yes. How?)

5. **EFN and Growth Rate**   Broslofski Co. maintains a positive retention ratio and keeps its debt–equity ratio constant every year. When sales grow by 20 percent, the firm has a negative projected EFN. What does this tell you about the firm's sustainable growth rate? Do you know, with certainty, if the internal growth rate is greater than or less than 20 percent? Why? What happens to the projected EFN if the retention ratio is increased? What if the retention ratio is decreased? What if the retention ratio is zero?

6. **Common-Size Financials**   One tool of financial analysis is common-size financial statements. Why do you think common-size income statements and balance sheets are used? Note that the accounting statement of cash flows is not converted into a common-size statement. Why do you think this is?

7. **Asset Utilization and EFN**   One of the implicit assumptions we made in calculating the external funds needed was that the company was operating at full capacity. If the company is operating at less than full capacity, how will this affect the external funds needed?

8. **Comparing ROE and ROA**   Both ROA and ROE measure profitability. Which one is more useful for comparing two companies? Why?

9. **Ratio Analysis**   Consider the ratio EBITD/Assets. What does this ratio tell us? Why might it be more useful than ROA in comparing two companies?

10. **Return on Investment**   A ratio that is becoming more widely used is return on investment. Return on investment is calculated as net income divided by long-term liabilities plus equity. What do you think return on investment is intended to measure? What is the relationship between return on investment and return on assets?

Use the following information to answer the next five questions: A small business called The Grandmother Calendar Company began selling personalized photo calendar kits. The kits were a hit, and sales soon sharply exceeded forecasts. The rush of orders created a huge backlog, so the company leased more space and expanded capacity, but it still could not keep up with demand. Equipment failed from overuse and quality suffered. Working capital was drained to expand production, and, at the same time, payments from customers were often delayed until the product was shipped. Unable to deliver on orders, the company became so strapped for cash that employee paychecks began to bounce. Finally, out of cash, the company ceased operations entirely three years later.

11. **Product Sales**   Do you think the company would have suffered the same fate if its product had been less popular? Why or why not?

12. **Cash Flow** The Grandmother Calendar Company clearly had a cash flow problem. In the context of the cash flow analysis we developed in Chapter 2, what was the impact of customers not paying until orders were shipped?

13. **Corporate Borrowing** If the firm was so successful at selling, why wouldn't a bank or some other lender step in and provide it with the cash it needed to continue?

14. **Cash Flow** Which was the biggest culprit here: Too many orders, too little cash, or too little production capacity?

15. **Cash Flow** What are some actions a small company like The Grandmother Calendar Company can take (besides expansion of capacity) if it finds itself in a situation in which growth in sales outstrips production?

Questions and Problems

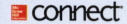

BASIC
(Questions 1–10)

1. **DuPont Identity** If Wilkinson, Inc., has an equity multiplier of 1.35, total asset turnover of 2.10, and a profit margin of 5.2 percent, what is its ROE?

2. **Equity Multiplier and Return on Equity** Synovec Company has a debt–equity ratio of .70. Return on assets is 8.4 percent, and total equity is $840,000. What is the equity multiplier? Return on equity? Net income?

3. **Using the DuPont Identity** Y3K, Inc., has sales of $3,100, total assets of $1,340, and a debt–equity ratio of 1.20. If its return on equity is 15 percent, what is its net income?

4. **EFN** The most recent financial statements for Heine, Inc., are shown here:

Income Statement			Balance Sheet			
Sales	$40,200	Assets	$145,000	Debt	$ 39,000
Costs	27,300			Equity	106,000
Taxable income	$ 12,900	Total	$145,000	Total	$145,000
Taxes (34%)	4,386				
Net income	$ 8,514				

Assets and costs are proportional to sales. Debt and equity are not. A dividend of $3,500 was paid, and the company wishes to maintain a constant payout ratio. Next year's sales are projected to be $45,426. What external financing is needed?

5. **Sales and Growth** The most recent financial statements for Wise Co. are shown here:

Income Statement			Balance Sheet			
Sales	$43,000	Current assets	$ 27,000	Long-term debt	$ 62,000
Costs	21,500	Fixed assets	118,000	Equity	83,000
Taxable income	$21,500	Total	$145,000	Total	$145,000
Taxes (34%)	7,310				
Net income	$14,190				

Assets and costs are proportional to sales. The company maintains a constant 30 percent dividend payout ratio and a constant debt–equity ratio. What is the maximum increase in sales that can be sustained assuming no new equity is issued?

6. **Sustainable Growth**   If the Hunter Corp. has a ROE of 12 percent and a payout ratio of 15 percent, what is its sustainable growth rate?

7. **Sustainable Growth**   Assuming the following ratios are constant, what is the sustainable growth rate?

   Total asset turnover = 2.85
   Profit margin = 5.9%
   Equity multiplier = 1.70
   Payout ratio = 60%

8. **Calculating EFN**   The most recent financial statements for Williamson Inc., are shown here (assuming no income taxes):

Income Statement		Balance Sheet			
Sales	$7,900	Assets	$17,400	Debt	$ 8,400
Costs	6,140			Equity	9,000
Net income	$1,760	Total	$17,400	Total	$17,400

   Assets and costs are proportional to sales. Debt and equity are not. No dividends are paid. Next year's sales are projected to be $9,006. What is the external financing needed?

9. **External Funds Needed**   Dahlia Colby, CFO of Charming Florist Ltd., has created the firm's pro forma balance sheet for the next fiscal year. Sales are projected to grow by 10 percent to $360 million. Current assets, fixed assets, and short-term debt are 20 percent, 75 percent, and 15 percent of sales, respectively. Charming Florist pays out 30 percent of its net income in dividends. The company currently has $105 million of long-term debt and $46 million in common stock par value. The profit margin is 9 percent.

   a. Construct the current balance sheet for the firm using the projected sales figure.
   b. Based on Ms. Colby's sales growth forecast, how much does Charming Florist need in external funds for the upcoming fiscal year?
   c. Construct the firm's pro forma balance sheet for the next fiscal year and confirm the external funds needed that you calculated in part (b).

10. **Sustainable Growth Rate**   The Wintergrass Company has an ROE of 11.4 percent and a payout ratio of 25 percent.
   a. What is the company's sustainable growth rate?
   b. Can the company's actual growth rate be different from its sustainable growth rate? Why or why not?
   c. How can the company increase its sustainable growth rate?

INTERMEDIATE
(Questions 11–23)

11. **Return on Equity**   Firm A and Firm B have debt–total asset ratios of 25 percent and 40 percent and returns on total assets of 8 percent and 7 percent, respectively. Which firm has a greater return on equity?

12. **Ratios and Foreign Companies**   Prince Albert Canning PLC had a net loss of £26,832 on sales of £294,813. What was the company's profit margin? Does the fact that these figures are quoted in a foreign currency make any difference? Why? In dollars, sales were $372,484. What was the net loss in dollars?

**13.	External Funds Needed**　The Optical Scam Company has forecast a sales growth rate of 15 percent for next year. The current financial statements are shown here:

Income Statement	
Sales	$25,380,000
Costs	21,635,000
Taxable income	$ 3,745,000
Taxes	1,498,000
Net income	$ 2,247,000
Dividends	$ 786,450
Addition to retained earnings	1,460,550

Balance Sheet			
Assets		**Liabilities and Owners' Equity**	
Current assets	$ 7,200,000	Short-term debt	$ 5,200,000
		Long-term debt	6,000,000
Fixed assets	17,600,000		
		Common stock	$ 3,200,000
		Accumulated retained earnings	10,400,000
		Total equity	$13,600,000
Total assets	$24,800,000	Total liabilities and equity	$24,800,000

a. Using the equation from the chapter, calculate the external funds needed for next year.
b. Construct the firm's pro forma balance sheet for next year and confirm the external funds needed that you calculated in part (a).
c. Calculate the sustainable growth rate for the company.
d. Can the company eliminate the need for external funds by changing its dividend policy? What other options are available to the company to meet its growth objectives?

**14.	Days' Sales in Receivables**　A company has net income of $314,000 a profit margin of 8.9 percent, and an accounts receivable balance of $152,800. Assuming 80 percent of sales are on credit, what is the company's days' sales in receivables?

**15.	Ratios and Fixed Assets**　The Whisenhunt Company has a ratio of long-term debt to long-term debt and equity of .29 and a current ratio of 1.20. Current liabilities are $1,280, sales are $6,140, profit margin is 8.9 percent, and ROE is 17.6 percent. What is the amount of the firm's net fixed assets?

**16.	Calculating the Cash Coverage Ratio**　Panda Inc.'s net income for the most recent year was $9,620. The tax rate was 34 percent. The firm paid $2,380 in total interest expense and deducted $3,170 in depreciation expense. What was the company's cash coverage ratio for the year?

**17.	DuPont Identity**　The DuPont identity presented in the chapter is commonly referred to as the three-factor DuPont identity. Another common way that the DuPont identity is expressed is the five-factor model, which is:

$$\text{ROE} = \frac{\text{Net income}}{\text{EBT}} \times \frac{\text{EBT}}{\text{EBIT}} \times \frac{\text{EBIT}}{\text{Sales}} \times \frac{\text{Sales}}{\text{Total assets}} \times \frac{\text{Total assets}}{\text{Equity}}$$

Derive the five-factor DuPont identity (EBT is earnings before tax, but after interest). What does each term measure?

18. **Common-Size and Common–Base Year Financial Statements** In addition to common-size financial statements, common–base year financial statements are often used. Common–base year financial statements are constructed by dividing the current year account value by the base year account value. Thus, the result shows the growth rate in the account. Using the following financial statements, construct the common-size balance sheet and common–base year balance sheet for the company. Use 2014 as the base year.

JARROW CORPORATION
2014 and 2015 Balance Sheets

Assets			Liabilities and Owners' Equity		
	2014	2015		2014	2015
Current assets			Current liabilities		
Cash	$ 8,815	$ 11,945	Accounts payable	$ 44,987	$ 55,061
Accounts receivable	22,498	27,524	Notes payable	19,210	20,442
Inventory	40,504	50,156	Total	$ 64,197	$ 75,503
Total	$ 71,817	$ 89,625	Long-term debt	$ 26,500	$ 37,000
Fixed assets			Owners' equity		
Net plant and equipment	$236,907	$292,008	Common stock and paid-in surplus	$ 42,000	$ 43,500
			Retained earnings	176,027	225,630
			Total	$218,027	$269,130
Total assets	$308,724	$381,633	Total liabilities and owners' equity	$308,724	$381,633

Use the following information for Problems 19, 20, and 22:

The discussion of EFN in the chapter implicitly assumed that the company was operating at full capacity. Often, this is not the case. For example, assume that Rosengarten was operating at 90 percent capacity. Full-capacity sales would be $1,000/.90 = $1,111. The balance sheet shows $1,800 in fixed assets. The capital intensity ratio for the company is

$$\text{Capital intensity ratio} = \text{Fixed assets/Full-capacity sales} = \$1,800/\$1,111 = 1.62$$

This means that Rosengarten needs $1.62 in fixed assets for every dollar in sales when it reaches full capacity. At the projected sales level of $1,250, it needs $1,250 × 1.62 = $2,025 in fixed assets, which is $225 lower than our projection of $2,250 in fixed assets. So, EFN is only $565 − 225 = $340.

19. **Full-Capacity Sales** Thorpe Mfg., Inc., is currently operating at only 90 percent of fixed asset capacity. Current sales are $680,000. How much can sales increase before any new fixed assets are needed?

20. **Fixed Assets and Capacity Usage** For the company in the previous problem, suppose fixed assets are $640,000 and sales are projected to grow to $790,000. How much in new fixed assets are required to support this growth in sales?

21. **Calculating EFN** The most recent financial statements for Moose Tours, Inc., appear below. Sales for 2016 are projected to grow by 20 percent. Interest expense will remain

constant; the tax rate and the dividend payout rate will also remain constant. Costs, other expenses, current assets, fixed assets, and accounts payable increase spontaneously with sales. If the firm is operating at full capacity and no new debt or equity is issued, what external financing is needed to support the 20 percent growth rate in sales?

MOOSE TOURS, INC.
2015 Income Statement

Sales	$752,500
Costs	585,600
Other expenses	15,400
Earnings before interest and taxes	$151,500
Interest expense	11,340
Taxable income	$140,160
Taxes	49,056
Net income	$91,104

Dividends	$27,331	
Addition to retained earnings	63,773	

MOOSE TOURS, INC.
Balance Sheet as of December 31, 2015

Assets		Liabilities and Owners' Equity	
Current assets		Current liabilities	
Cash	$ 21,632	Accounts payable	$ 58,140
Accounts receivable	34,799	Notes payable	14,535
Inventory	74,300	Total	$ 72,675
Total	$130,731	Long-term debt	$135,000
		Owners' equity	
Fixed assets		Common stock and paid-in surplus	$115,000
Net plant and equipment	$353,120	Retained earnings	161,176
		Total	$276,176
Total assets	$483,851	Total liabilities and owners' equity	$483,851

22. **Capacity Usage and Growth** In the previous problem, suppose the firm was operating at only 80 percent capacity in 2015. What is EFN now?

23. **Calculating EFN** In Problem 21, suppose the firm wishes to keep its debt–equity ratio constant. What is EFN now?

CHALLENGE (Questions 24–30)

24. **EFN and Internal Growth** Redo Problem 21 using sales growth rates of 15 and 25 percent in addition to 20 percent. Illustrate graphically the relationship between EFN and the growth rate, and use this graph to determine the relationship between them.

25. **EFN and Sustainable Growth** Redo Problem 23 using sales growth rates of 30 and 35 percent in addition to 20 percent. Illustrate graphically the relationship between EFN and the growth rate, and use this graph to determine the relationship between them.

26. **Constraints on Growth** Shinedown, Inc., wishes to maintain a growth rate of 12 percent per year and a debt–equity ratio of .35. Profit margin is 4.9 percent, and the ratio of total

assets to sales is constant at .75. Is this growth rate possible? To answer, determine what the dividend payout ratio must be. How do you interpret the result?

27. **EFN**   Define the following:

S   = Previous year's sales
A   = Total assets
E   = Total equity
g   = Projected growth in sales
PM = Profit margin
b   = Retention (plowback) ratio

Assuming that all debt is constant, show that EFN can be written as:

$$EFN = -PM(S)b + [A - PM(S)b] \times g$$

Hint: Asset needs will equal A × g. The addition to retained earnings will equal PM(S) b × (1 + g).

28. **Sustainable Growth Rate**   Based on the results in Problem 27, show that the internal and sustainable growth rates can be calculated as shown in Equations 3.24 and 3.25. (*Hint:* For the internal growth rate, set EFN equal to zero and solve for g.)

29. **Sustainable Growth Rate**   In the chapter, we discussed one calculation of the sustainable growth rate as:

$$\text{Sustainable growth rate} = \frac{ROE \times b}{1 - ROE \times b}$$

In practice, probably the most commonly used calculation of the sustainable growth rate is ROE × b. This equation is identical to the sustainable growth rate equation presented in the chapter if the ROE is calculated using the beginning of period equity. Derive this equation from the equation presented in the chapter.

30. **Sustainable Growth Rate**   Use the sustainable growth rate equations from the previous problem to answer the following questions. I Am Myself, Inc., had total assets of $410,000 and equity of $230,000 at the beginning of the year. At the end of the year, the company had total assets of $460,000. During the year the company sold no new equity. Net income for the year was $75,000 and dividends were $32,000. What is the sustainable growth rate for the company? What is the sustainable growth rate if you calculate ROE based on the beginning of period equity?

Excel Master It! Problem

Financial planning can be more complex than the percentage of sales approach indicates. Often, the assumptions behind the percentage of sales approach may be too simple. A more sophisticated model allows important items to vary without being a strict percentage of sales.

Consider a new model in which depreciation is calculated as a percentage of beginning fixed assets, and interest expense depends directly on the amount of debt. Debt is still the plug variable. Note that since depreciation and interest now do not necessarily vary directly with sales, the profit margin is no longer constant. Also, for the same reason, taxes and dividends will no longer be a fixed percentage of sales. The parameter estimates used in the new model are:

Cost percentage = Costs / Sales

Depreciation rate = Depreciation / Beginning fixed assets

Interest rate = Interest paid / Total debt

Tax rate = Taxes / Net income

Payout ratio = Dividends / Net income

Capital intensity ratio = Fixed assets / Sales

Fixed assets ratio = Fixed assets / Total assets

The model parameters can be determined by whatever methods the company deems appropriate. For example, they might be based on average values for the last several years, industry standards, subjective estimates, or even company targets. Alternatively, sophisticated statistical techniques can be used to estimate them.

The Loftis Company is preparing its pro forma financial statements for the next year using this model. The abbreviated financial statements are presented below.

Sales growth	20%
Tax rate	34

Income Statement

Sales	$780,000
Costs	415,000
Depreciation	135,000
Interest	68,000
Taxable income	$162,000
Taxes	55,080
Net income	$106,920
Dividends	$ 30,000
Additions to retained earnings	76,920

Balance Sheet

Assets		Liabilities and Equity	
Current assets	$ 240,000	Total debt	$ 880,000
Net fixed assets	1,350,000	Owners' equity	710,000
Total assets	$1,590,000	Total debt and equity	$1,590,000

a. Calculate each of the parameters necessary to construct the pro forma balance sheet.

b. Construct the pro forma balance sheet. What is the total debt necessary to balance the pro forma balance sheet?

c. In this financial planning model, show that it is possible to solve algebraically for the amount of new borrowing.

Mini Case

RATIOS AND FINANCIAL PLANNING AT EAST COAST YACHTS

Dan Ervin was recently hired by East Coast Yachts to assist the company with its short-term financial planning and also to evaluate the company's financial performance. Dan graduated from college five years ago with a finance degree, and he has been employed in the treasury department of a *Fortune* 500 company since then.

East Coast Yachts was founded 10 years ago by Larissa Warren. The company's operations are located near Hilton Head Island, South Carolina, and the company is structured as an LLC.

The company has manufactured custom midsize, high-performance yachts for clients over this period, and its products have received high reviews for safety and reliability. The company's yachts have also recently received the highest award for customer satisfaction. The yachts are primarily purchased by wealthy individuals for pleasure use. Occasionally, a yacht is manufactured for purchase by a company for business purposes.

The custom yacht industry is fragmented, with a number of manufacturers. As with any industry, there are market leaders, but the diverse nature of the industry ensures that no manufacturer dominates the market. The competition in the market, as well as the product cost, ensures that attention to detail is a necessity. For instance, East Coast Yachts will spend 80 to 100 hours on hand-buffing the stainless steel stem-iron, which is the metal cap on the yacht's bow that conceivably could collide with a dock or another boat.

To get Dan started with his analyses, Larissa has provided the following financial statements. Dan has gathered the industry ratios for the yacht manufacturing industry.

EAST COAST YACHTS
2015 Income Statement

Sales	$210,900,000
Cost of goods sold	148,600,000
Other expenses	25,192,000
Depreciation	6,879,000
Earnings before interest and taxes (EBIT)	$ 30,229,000
Interest	3,791,000
Taxable income	$ 26,438,000
Taxes (40%)	10,575,200
Net income	$ 15,862,800
Dividends	$ 4,759,301
Add to RE	$11,103,499

EAST COAST YACHTS
Balance Sheet as of December 31, 2015

Assets		Liabilities & Equity	
Current assets		Current liabilities	
Cash	$ 3,285,600	Accounts payable	$ 6,977,700
Accounts receivable	5,910,800	Notes payable	14,342,600
Inventory	6,627,300	Total	$ 21,320,300
Total	$15,823,700		
Fixed assets		Long-term debt	$ 36,400,000
Net plant and equipment	$101,481,200		
		Shareholders' equity	
		Common stock	$ 5,580,000
		Retained earnings	54,004,600
		Total equity	$ 59,584,600
Total assets	$117,304,900	Total liabilities and equity	$117,304,900

Yacht Industry Ratios			
	Lower Quartile	**Median**	**Upper Quartile**
Current ratio	.50	1.43	1.89
Quick ratio	.21	.38	.62
Total asset turnover	.68	.85	1.38
Inventory turnover	6.85	9.15	16.13
Receivables turnover	6.27	11.81	21.45
Debt ratio	.44	.52	.61
Debt–equity ratio	.79	1.08	1.56
Equity multiplier	1.79	2.08	2.56
Interest coverage	5.18	8.06	9.83
Profit margin	4.05%	6.98%	9.87%
Return on assets	6.05%	10.53%	15.83%
Return on equity	9.93%	16.54%	28.14%

1. Calculate all of the ratios listed in the industry table for East Coast Yachts.

2. Compare the performance of East Coast Yachts to the industry as a whole. For each ratio, comment on why it might be viewed as positive or negative relative to the industry. Suppose you create an inventory ratio calculated as inventory divided by current liabilities. How do you interpret this ratio? How does East Coast Yachts compare to the industry average?

3. Calculate the sustainable growth rate of East Coast Yachts. Calculate external funds needed (EFN) and prepare pro forma income statements and balance sheets assuming growth at precisely this rate. Recalculate the ratios in the previous question. What do you observe?

4. As a practical matter, East Coast Yachts is unlikely to be willing to raise external equity capital, in part because the owners don't want to dilute their existing ownership and control positions. However, East Coast Yachts is planning for a growth rate of 20 percent next year. What are your conclusions and recommendations about the feasibility of East Coast's expansion plans?

5. Most assets can be increased as a percentage of sales. For instance, cash can be increased by any amount. However, fixed assets often must be increased in specific amounts because it is impossible, as a practical matter, to buy part of a new plant or machine. In this case a company has a "staircase" or "lumpy" fixed cost structure. Assume that East Coast Yachts is currently producing at 100 percent of capacity. As a result, to expand production, the company must set up an entirely new line at a cost of $25 million. Calculate the new EFN with this assumption. What does this imply about capacity utilization for East Coast Yachts next year?

Discounted Cash Flow Valuation

The signing of big-name athletes is often accompanied by great fanfare, but the numbers are often misleading. For example, in late 2014, catcher Russell Martin reached a deal with the Toronto Blue Jays, signing a contract with a reported value of $82 million. Not bad, especially for someone who makes a living using the "tools of ignorance" (jock jargon for a catcher's equipment). And also in 2014, football player J.J. Watt signed a $100 million extension with the Houston Texans.

It looks like Brian and J.J. did pretty well, but then there was quarterback Colin Kaepernick, who recently signed a new contract to play for the San Francisco 49ers. Colin's contract had a value of $121 million, but this amount was actually payable over several years. The contract consisted of a $13 million signing bonus, plus $108 million to be paid in the years 2015 through 2019. Brian and J.J.'s payments were similarly spread over time. Because all three contracts called for payments that are made at future dates, we must consider the time value of money, which means none of these players received the quoted amounts. How much did they really get? This chapter gives you the "tools of knowledge" to answer this question.

4.1 Valuation: The One-Period Case

Jim Ellis is trying to sell a piece of raw land in Alaska. Yesterday he was offered $10,000 for the property. He was about ready to accept the offer when another individual offered him $11,424. However, the second offer was to be paid a year from now. Jim has satisfied himself that both buyers are honest and financially solvent, so he has no fear that the offer he selects will fall through. These two offers are pictured as cash flows in Figure 4.1. Which offer should Jim choose?

Mike Tuttle, Jim's financial adviser, points out that if Jim takes the first offer, he could invest the $10,000 in the bank at an insured rate of 12 percent. At the end of one year, he would have:

$$\underset{\substack{\text{Return of}\\\text{principal}}}{\$10,000} + \underset{\substack{\text{Interest}}}{(.12 \times \$10,000)} = \$10,000 \times 1.12 = \$11,200$$

Because this is less than the $11,424 Jim could receive from the second offer, Mike recommends that he take the latter. This analysis uses the concept of **future value (FV)** or **compound value**, which is the value of a sum after investing over one or more periods. The compound or future value of $10,000 at 12 percent is $11,200.

Figure 4.1

Cash Flow for Jim Ellis's Sale

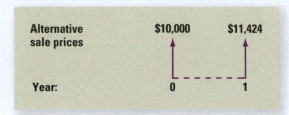

An alternative method employs the concept of **present value (PV)**. One can determine present value by asking the following question: How much money must Jim put in the bank today so that he will have $11,424 next year? We can write this algebraically as:

$$\text{PV} \times 1.12 = \$11,424$$

We want to solve for PV, the amount of money that yields $11,424 if invested at 12 percent today. Solving for PV, we have:

$$\text{PV} = \frac{\$11,424}{1.12} = \$10,200$$

The formula for PV can be written as follows:

Present Value of Investment:

$$\text{PV} = \frac{C_1}{1 + r} \qquad (4.1)$$

where C_1 is cash flow at date 1 and r is the rate of return that Jim Ellis requires on his land sale. It is sometimes referred to as the *discount rate.*

Present value analysis tells us that a payment of $11,424 to be received next year has a present value of $10,200 today. In other words, at a 12 percent interest rate, Jim is indifferent between $10,200 today or $11,424 next year. If you gave him $10,200 today, he could put it in the bank and receive $11,424 next year.

Because the second offer has a present value of $10,200, whereas the first offer is for only $10,000, present value analysis also indicates that Jim should take the second offer. In other words, both future value analysis and present value analysis lead to the same decision. As it turns out, present value analysis and future value analysis must always lead to the same decision.

As simple as this example is, it contains the basic principles that we will be working with over the next few chapters. We now use another example to develop the concept of net present value.

EXAMPLE

4.1

Present Value Diane Badame, a financial analyst at Kaufman & Broad, a leading real estate firm, is thinking about recommending that Kaufman & Broad invest in a piece of land that costs $85,000. She is certain that next year the land will be worth $91,000, a sure $6,000 gain. Given that the interest rate in similar alternative investments is 10 percent, should Kaufman & Broad undertake the investment in land? Diane's choice is described in Figure 4.2 with the cash flow time chart.

A moment's thought should be all it takes to convince her that this is not an attractive business deal. By investing $85,000 in the land, she will have $91,000 available next year. Suppose, instead, that

Figure 4.2   Cash Flows for Land Investment

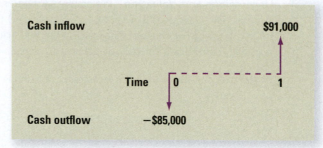

Kaufman & Broad puts the same $85,000 into similar alternative investments. At the interest rate of 10 percent, this $85,000 would grow to:

$$(1 + .10) \times \$85,000 = \$93,500$$

next year.

It would be foolish to buy the land when investing the same $85,000 in similar alternative investments would produce an extra $2,500 (that is, $93,500 from the bank minus $91,000 from the land investment). This is a future value calculation.

Alternatively, she could calculate the present value of the sale price next year as:

$$\text{Present value} = \frac{\$91,000}{1.10} = \$82,727.27$$

Because the present value of next year's sales price is less than this year's purchase price of $85,000, present value analysis also indicates that she should not recommend purchasing the property.

Frequently, financial analysts want to determine the exact *cost* or *benefit* of a decision. In Example 4.1, the decision to buy this year and sell next year can be evaluated as:

$$-\$2,273 = \underset{\substack{\text{Cost of land} \\ \text{today}}}{-\$85,000} + \underset{\substack{\text{Present value of} \\ \text{next year's sales price}}}{\frac{\$91,000}{1.10}}$$

The formula for NPV can be written as follows:

Net Present Value of Investment:
$$\text{NPV} = -\text{Cost} + \text{PV} \tag{4.2}$$

Equation 4.2 says that the value of the investment is −$2,273, after stating all the benefits and all the costs as of date 0. We say that −$2,273 is the **net present value** (NPV) of the investment. That is, NPV is the present value of future cash flows minus the present value of the cost of the investment. Because the net present value is negative, Diane Badame should not recommend purchasing the land.

Both the Ellis and the Badame examples deal with a high degree of certainty. That is, Jim Ellis knows with a high degree of certainty that he could sell his land for $11,424 next year. Similarly, Diane Badame knows with a high degree of certainty that Kaufman & Broad could receive $91,000 for selling its land. Unfortunately, businesspeople frequently do not know future cash flows. This uncertainty is treated in the next example.

**EXAMPLE
4.2**

Uncertainty and Valuation   Professional Artworks, Inc., is a firm that speculates in modern paintings. The manager is thinking of buying an original Picasso for $400,000 with the intention of selling it at the end of one year. The manager expects that the painting will be worth $480,000 in one year. The relevant cash flows are depicted in Figure 4.3.

Figure 4.3   Cash Flows for Investment in Painting

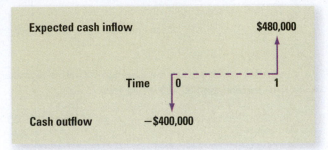

Of course, this is only an expectation—the painting could be worth more or less than $480,000. Suppose the guaranteed interest rate granted by banks is 10 percent. Should the firm purchase the piece of art?

Our first thought might be to discount at the interest rate, yielding:

$$\frac{\$480,000}{1.10} = \$436,364$$

Because $436,364 is greater than $400,000, it looks at first glance as if the painting should be purchased. However, 10 percent is the return one can earn on a low risk investment. Because the painting is quite risky, a higher discount rate is called for. The manager chooses a rate of 25 percent to reflect this risk. In other words, he argues that a 25 percent expected return is fair compensation for an investment as risky as this painting.

The present value of the painting becomes:

$$\frac{\$480,000}{1.25} = \$384,000$$

Thus, the manager believes that the painting is currently overpriced at $400,000 and does not make the purchase.

The preceding analysis is typical of decision making in today's corporations, though real-world examples are, of course, much more complex. Unfortunately, any example with risk poses a problem not faced in a riskless example. Conceptually, the correct discount rate for an expected cash flow is the expected return available in the market on other investments of the same risk. This is the appropriate discount rate to apply because it represents an economic opportunity cost to investors. It is the expected return they will require before committing funding to a project. However, the selection of the discount rate for a risky investment is quite a difficult task. We simply don't know at this point whether the discount rate on the painting in Example 4.2 should be 11 percent, 15 percent, 25 percent, or some other percentage.

Because the choice of a discount rate is so difficult, we merely wanted to broach the subject here. We must wait until the specific material on risk and return is covered in later chapters before a risk-adjusted analysis can be presented.

4.2 The Multiperiod Case

The previous section presented the calculation of future value and present value for one period only. We will now perform the calculations for the multiperiod case.

FUTURE VALUE AND COMPOUNDING

Suppose an individual were to make a loan of $1. At the end of the first year, the borrower would owe the lender the principal amount of $1 plus the interest on the loan at the interest rate of r. For the specific case where the interest rate is, say, 9 percent, the borrower owes the lender:

$$\$1 \times (1 + r) = \$1 \times 1.09 = \$1.09$$

At the end of the year, though, the lender has two choices. She can either take the $1.09—or, more generally, $(1 + r)$—out of the financial market, or she can leave it in and lend it again for a second year. The process of leaving the money in the financial market and lending it for another year is called **compounding**.

Suppose the lender decides to compound her loan for another year. She does this by taking the proceeds from her first one-year loan, $1.09, and lending this amount for the next year. At the end of next year, then, the borrower will owe her:

$$\$1 \times (1 + r) \times (1 + r) = \$1 \times (1 + r)^2 = 1 + 2r + r^2$$
$$\$1 \times (1.09) \times (1.09) = \$1 \times (1.09)^2 = \$1 + \$.18 + \$.0081 = \$1.1881$$

This is the total she will receive two years from now by compounding the loan.

In other words, the capital market enables the investor, by providing a ready opportunity for lending, to transform $1 today into $1.1881 at the end of two years. At the end of three years, the total cash will be $1 \times (1.09)^3 = \$1.2950$.

The most important point to notice is that the total amount the lender receives is not just the $1 that she lent plus two years' worth of interest on $1:

$$2 \times r = 2 \times \$.09 = \$.18$$

The lender also gets back an amount r^2, which is the interest in the second year on the interest that was earned in the first year. The term $2 \times r$ represents **simple interest** over the two years, and the term r^2 is referred to as the *interest on interest*. In our example, this latter amount is exactly:

$$r^2 = (\$.09)^2 = \$.0081$$

When cash is invested at **compound interest**, each interest payment is reinvested. With simple interest, the interest is not reinvested. Benjamin Franklin's statement, "Money makes money and the money that money makes makes more money," is a colorful way of explaining compound interest. The difference between compound interest and simple interest is illustrated in Figure 4.4. In this example, the difference does not amount to much because the loan is for $1. If the loan were for $1 million, the lender would receive $1,188,100 in two years' time. Of this amount, $8,100 is interest on interest. The lesson is that those small numbers beyond the decimal point can add up to big dollar amounts when the transactions are for big amounts. In addition, the longer-lasting the loan, the more important interest on interest becomes.

Figure 4.4
Simple and
Compound Interest

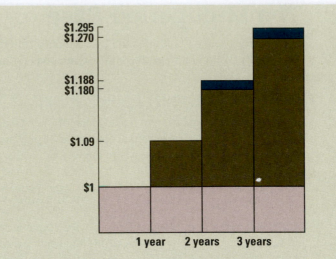

The dark-shaded area indicates the difference between compound and simple interest. The difference is substantial over a period of many years or decades.

The general formula for an investment over many periods can be written as follows:

Future Value of an Investment:

$$FV = C_0 \times (1 + r)^T \tag{4.3}$$

where C_0 is the cash to be invested at Date 0 (i.e., today), r is the interest rate per period, and T is the number of periods over which the cash is invested.

**EXAMPLE
4.3**

Interest on Interest   Suh-Pyng Ku has put $500 in a savings account at the First National Bank of Kent. The account earns 7 percent, compounded annually. How much will Ms. Ku have at the end of three years? The answer is:

$$\$500 \times 1.07 \times 1.07 \times 1.07 = \$500 \times (1.07)^3 = \$612.52$$

Figure 4.5 illustrates the growth of Ms. Ku's account.

Figure 4.5   Suh-Pyng Ku's Savings Account

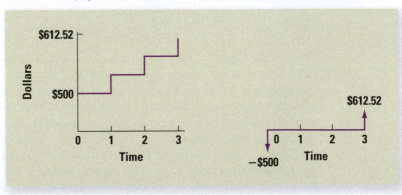

EXAMPLE
4.4

Compound Growth   Jay Ritter invested $1,000 in the stock of the SDH Company. The company pays a current dividend of $2, which is expected to grow by 20 percent per year for the next two years. What will the dividend of the SDH Company be after two years? A simple calculation gives:

$$\$2 \times (1.20)^2 = \$2.88$$

Figure 4.6 illustrates the increasing value of SDH's dividends.

Figure 4.6   The Growth of the SDH Dividends

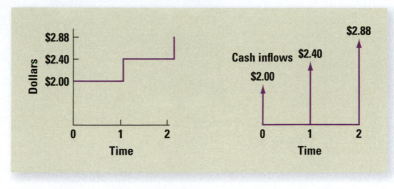

The two previous examples can be calculated in any one of several ways. The computations could be done by hand, by calculator, by spreadsheet, or with the help of a table. We will introduce spreadsheets in a few pages, and we show how to use a calculator in Appendix 4B on the website. The appropriate table is Table A.3, which appears in the back of the text. This table presents *future value of $1 at the end of T periods*. The table is used by locating the appropriate interest rate on the horizontal and the appropriate number of periods on the vertical. For example, Suh-Pyng Ku would look at the following portion of Table A.3:

	Interest Rate		
Period	6%	7%	8%
1	1.0600	1.0700	1.0800
2	1.1236	1.1449	1.1664
3	1.1910	1.2250	1.2597
4	1.2625	1.3108	1.3605

She could calculate the future value of her $500 as:

$$
\underset{\substack{\text{Initial} \\ \text{investment}}}{\$500} \times \underset{\substack{\text{Future value} \\ \text{of }\$1}}{1.2250} = \$612.50
$$

In the example concerning Suh-Pyng Ku, we gave you both the initial investment and the interest rate and then asked you to calculate the future value. Alternatively, the interest rate could have been unknown, as shown in the following example.

**EXAMPLE
4.5**

Finding the Rate Fernando Zapetero, who recently won $10,000 in the lottery, wants to buy a car in five years. Fernando estimates that the car will cost $16,105 at that time. His cash flows are displayed in Figure 4.7.

What interest rate must he earn to be able to afford the car?

Figure 4.7 Cash Flows for Purchase of Fernando Zapetero's Car

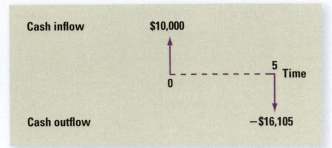

The ratio of purchase price to initial cash is:

$$\frac{\$16{,}105}{\$10{,}000} = 1.6105$$

Thus, he must earn an interest rate that allows $1 to become $1.6105 in five years. Table A.3 tells us that an interest rate of 10 percent will allow him to purchase the car.

We can express the problem algebraically as:

$$\$10{,}000 \times (1 + r)^5 = \$16{,}105$$

where r is the interest rate needed to purchase the car. Because $16,105/$10,000 = 1.6105, we have:

$$(1 + r)^5 = 1.6105$$
$$r = 10\%$$

Either the table, a spreadsheet, or a calculator lets us solve for r.

THE POWER OF COMPOUNDING: A DIGRESSION

Most people who have had any experience with compounding are impressed with its power over long periods. Take the stock market, for example. Ibbotson and Sinquefield have calculated what the stock market returned as a whole from 1926 through 2014.[1] They find that one dollar placed in large U.S. stocks at the beginning of 1926 would have been worth $5316.85 at the end of 2014. This is 10.12 percent compounded annually (rounded to two decimal places) for 89 years—that is, $(1.1012)^{89} = \$5316.85$, ignoring a small rounding error.

The example illustrates the great difference between compound and simple interest. At 10.12 percent, simple interest on $1 is 10.12 cents a year. Simple interest over 89 years is $900.68 (=89 × $10.12). This is quite a bit below the $5316.85 that was obtained by reinvestment of all dividends and capital gains.

The results are more impressive over even longer periods. A person with no experience in compounding might think that the value of $1 at the end of 178 years

---

[1] *Stocks, Bonds, Bills, and Inflation [SBBI]. 2015 Yearbook*. Morningstar, Chicago, 2015.

would be twice the value of $1 at the end of 89 years, if the yearly rate of return stayed the same. Actually the value of $1 at the end of 178 years would be the *square* of the value of $1 at the end of 89 years. That is, if the annual rate of return remained the same, a $1 investment in common stocks would be worth $28,268,893.92 (=$1 × 5316.85 × 5316.85).

A few years ago, an archaeologist unearthed a relic stating that Julius Caesar lent the Roman equivalent of one penny to someone. Because there was no record of the penny ever being repaid, the archaeologist wondered what the interest and principal would be if a descendant of Caesar tried to collect from a descendant of the borrower in the 20th century. The archaeologist felt that a rate of 6 percent might be appropriate. To his surprise, the principal and interest due after more than 2,000 years was vastly greater than the entire wealth on earth.

The power of compounding can explain why the parents of well-to-do families frequently bequeath wealth to their grandchildren rather than to their children. That is, they skip a generation. The parents would rather make the grandchildren very rich than make the children moderately rich. We have found that in these families the grandchildren have a more positive view of the power of compounding than do the children.

EXAMPLE 4.6

How Much for That Island?   Some people have said that it was the best real estate deal in history. Peter Minuit, director general of New Netherlands, the Dutch West India Company's colony in North America, in 1626 allegedly bought Manhattan Island for 60 guilders' worth of trinkets from native Americans. By 1667, the Dutch were forced by the British to exchange it for Suriname (perhaps the worst real estate deal ever). This sounds cheap; but did the Dutch really get the better end of the deal? It is reported that 60 guilders was worth about $24 at the prevailing exchange rate. If the native Americans had sold the trinkets at a fair market value and invested the $24 at 5 percent (tax free), it would now, about 389 years later, be worth about $4.20 billion. Today, Manhattan is undoubtedly worth much more than $4.20 billion, so at a 5 percent rate of return the native Americans got the worst of the deal. However, if invested at 10 percent, the amount of money they received would be worth about:

$$\$24(1 + r)^T = 24 \times 1.1^{389} \cong \$303 \text{ quadrillion}$$

This is a lot of money. In fact, $303 quadrillion is more than all the real estate in the world is worth today. Note that no one in the history of the world has ever been able to find an investment yielding 10 percent every year for 389 years.

PRESENT VALUE AND DISCOUNTING

We now know that an annual interest rate of 9 percent enables the investor to transform $1 today into $1.1881 two years from now. In addition, we would like to know the following:

How much would an investor need to lend today so that she could receive $1 two years from today?

Algebraically, we can write this as:

$$PV \times (1.09)^2 = \$1$$

Figure 4.8
Compounding and Discounting

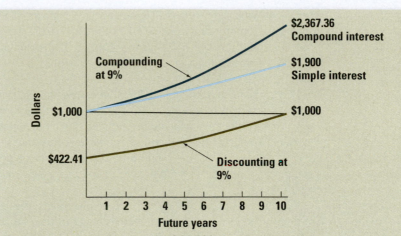

The top line shows the growth of $1,000 at compound interest with the funds invested at 9 percent: $1,000 \times (1.09)^{10} = $2,367.36$. Simple interest is shown on the next line. It is $1,000 + [10 \times ($1,000 \times .09)] = $1,900$. The bottom line shows the discounted value of $1,000 if the interest rate is 9 percent.

In the preceding equation, PV stands for present value, the amount of money we must lend today to receive $1 in two years' time.

Solving for PV in this equation, we have:

$$PV = \frac{\$1}{1.1881} = \$.84$$

This process of calculating the present value of a future cash flow is called **discounting**. It is the opposite of compounding. The difference between compounding and discounting is illustrated in Figure 4.8.

To be certain that $.84 is in fact the present value of $1 to be received in two years, we must check whether or not, if we lent $.84 today and rolled over the loan for two years, we would get exactly $1 back. If this were the case, the capital markets would be saying that $1 received in two years' time is equivalent to having $.84 today. Checking the exact numbers, we get:

$$\$.84168 \times 1.09 \times 1.09 = \$1$$

In other words, when we have capital markets with a sure interest rate of 9 percent, we are indifferent between receiving $.84 today or $1 in two years. We have no reason to treat these two choices differently from each other because if we had $.84 today and lent it out for two years, it would return $1 to us at the end of that time. The value .84 $[=1/(1.09)^2]$ is called the **present value factor**. It is the factor used to calculate the present value of a future cash flow.

In the multiperiod case, the formula for PV can be written as follows:

Present Value of Investment:

$$PV = \frac{C_T}{(1 + r)^T} \tag{4.4}$$

Here, C_T is the cash flow at date T and r is the appropriate discount rate.

**EXAMPLE
4.7**

Multiperiod Discounting   Bernard Dumas will receive $10,000 three years from now. Bernard can earn 8 percent on his investments, so the appropriate discount rate is 8 percent. What is the present value of his future cash flow? The answer is:

$$PV = \$10,000 \times \left(\frac{1}{1.08}\right)^3$$
$$= \$10,000 \times .7938$$
$$= \$7,938$$

Figure 4.9 illustrates the application of the present value factor to Bernard's investment.

Figure 4.9   Discounting Bernard Dumas's Opportunity

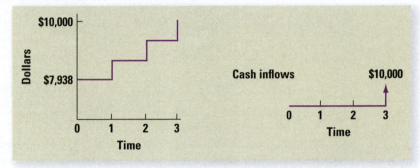

When his investments grow at an 8 percent rate of interest, Bernard Dumas is equally inclined toward receiving $7,938 now and receiving $10,000 in three years' time. After all, he could convert the $7,938 he receives today into $10,000 in three years by lending it at an interest rate of 8 percent.

Bernard Dumas could have reached his present value calculation in one of several ways. The computation could have been done by hand, by calculator, with a spreadsheet, or with the help of Table A.1, which appears in the back of the text. This table presents the *present value of $1 to be received after T periods.* We use the table by locating the appropriate interest rate on the horizontal and the appropriate number of periods on the vertical. For example, Bernard Dumas would look at the following portion of Table A.1:

Period	Interest Rate		
	7%	8%	9%
1	.9346	.9259	.9174
2	.8734	.8573	.8417
3	.8163	.7938	.7722
4	.7629	.7350	.7084

The appropriate present value factor is .7938.

In the preceding example we gave both the interest rate and the future cash flow. Alternatively, the interest rate could have been unknown.

EXAMPLE
4.8

Finding the Rate   A customer of the Chaffkin Corp. wants to buy a tugboat today. Rather than paying immediately, he will pay $50,000 in three years. It will cost the Chaffkin Corp. $38,610 to build the tugboat immediately. The relevant cash flows to Chaffkin Corp. are displayed in Figure 4.10. What interest rate would the Chaffkin Corp. charge to neither gain nor lose on the sale?

Figure 4.10   Cash Flows for Tugboat

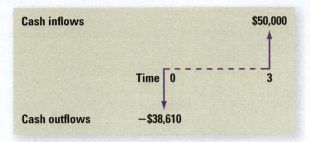

The ratio of construction cost (present value) to sale price (future value) is:

$$\frac{\$38,610}{\$50,000} = .7722$$

We must determine the interest rate that allows $1 to be received in three years to have a present value of $.7722. Table A.1 tells us that 9 percent is that interest rate.

FINDING THE NUMBER OF PERIODS

Suppose we are interested in purchasing an asset that costs $50,000. We currently have $25,000. If we can earn 12 percent on this $25,000, how long until we have the $50,000? Finding the answer involves solving for the last variable in the basic present value equation, the number of periods. There is an easy way to get an approximate answer to this particular problem. Notice that we need to double our money. From the Rule of 72 (see Problem 74 at the end of the chapter), this will take about $72/12 = 6$ years at 12 percent.

To come up with the exact answer, we can again manipulate the basic present value equation. The present value is $25,000, and the future value is $50,000. With a 12 percent discount rate, the basic equation takes one of the following forms:

$$\$25,000 = \$50,000/1.12^t$$
$$\$50,000/25,000 = 1.12^t = 2$$

We thus have a future value factor of 2 for a 12 percent rate. We now need to solve for t. If you look down the column in Table A.3 that corresponds to 12 percent, you will see that a future value factor of 1.9738 occurs at six periods. It will thus take about six years, as we calculated. To get the exact answer, we have to explicitly solve for t (by using a financial calculator or the spreadsheet on the next page). If you do this, you will see that the answer is 6.1163 years, so our approximation was quite close in this case.

SPREADSHEET APPLICATIONS

Using a Spreadsheet for Time Value of Money Calculations

More and more, businesspeople from many different areas (not just finance and accounting) rely on spreadsheets to do all the different types of calculations that come up in the real world. As a result, in this section, we will show you how to use a spreadsheet to handle the various time value of money problems we present in this chapter. We will use Microsoft Excel™, but the commands are similar for other types of software. We assume you are already familiar with basic spreadsheet operations.

As we have seen, you can solve for any one of the following four potential unknowns: future value, present value, the discount rate, or the number of periods. With a spreadsheet, there is a separate formula for each. In Excel, these are shown in a nearby box.

In these formulas, pv and fv are present and future value, nper is the number of periods, and rate is the discount, or interest, rate.

To Find	Enter This Formula
Future value	= FV (rate,nper,pmt,pv)
Present value	= PV (rate,nper,pmt,fv)
Discount rate	= RATE (nper,pmt,pv,fv)
Number of periods	= NPER (rate,pmt,pv,fv)

Two things are a little tricky here. First, unlike a financial calculator, the spreadsheet requires that the rate be entered as a decimal. Second, as with most financial calculators, you have to put a negative sign on either the present value or the future value to solve for the rate or the number of periods. For the same reason, if you solve for a present value, the answer will have a negative sign unless you input a negative future value. The same is true when you compute a future value.

To illustrate how you might use these formulas, we will go back to an example in the chapter. If you invest $25,000 at 12 percent per year, how long until you have $50,000? You might set up a spreadsheet like this:

	A	B	C	D	E	F	G	H
1								
2			Using a spreadsheet for time value of money calculations					
3								
4	If we invest $25,000 at 12 percent, how long until we have $50,000? We need to solve							
5	for the unknown number of periods, so we use the formula NPER(rate, pmt, pv, fv).							
6								
7	Present value (pv):	$25,000						
8	Future value (fv):	$50,000						
9	Rate (rate):	.12						
10								
11	Periods:	6.1162554						
12								
13	The formula entered in cell B11 is =NPER(B9,0,-B7,B8); notice that pmt is zero and that pv							
14	has a negative sign on it. Also notice that rate is entered as a decimal, not a percentage.							

EXAMPLE 4.9

Waiting for Godot   You've been saving up to buy the Godot Company. The total cost will be $10 million. You currently have about $2.3 million. If you can earn 5 percent on your money, how long will you have to wait? At 16 percent, how long must you wait?

At 5 percent, you'll have to wait a long time. From the basic present value equation:

$$\$2.3 \text{ million} = \$10 \text{ million}/1.05^t$$
$$1.05^t = 4.35$$
$$t = 30 \text{ years}$$

At 16 percent, things are a little better. Verify for yourself that it will take about 10 years.

Learn more about using Excel for time value and other calculations at **www.studyfinance.com**.

EXAMPLE 4.10

Cash Flow Valuation   Kyle Mayer has won the Kentucky State Lottery and will receive the following set of cash flows over the next two years:

Year	Cash Flow
1	$20,000
2	50,000

Mr. Mayer can currently earn 6 percent in his money market account, so the appropriate discount rate is 6 percent. The present value of the cash flows is:

Year	Cash Flow × Present Value Factor = Present Value
1	$20,000 \times \dfrac{1}{1.06} = \$20,000 \times \dfrac{1}{1.06} = \$18,867.9$
2	$50,000 \times \left(\dfrac{1}{1.06}\right)^2 = \$50,000 \times \dfrac{1}{(1.06)^2} = \underline{\$44,499.8}$
	Total $63,367.7

In other words, Mr. Mayer is equally inclined toward receiving $63,367.7 today and receiving $20,000 and $50,000 over the next two years.

EXAMPLE 4.11

NPV   Finance.com has an opportunity to invest in a new high-speed computer that costs $50,000. The computer will generate cash flows (from cost savings) of $25,000 one year from now, $20,000 two years from now, and $15,000 three years from now. The computer will be worthless after three years, and no additional cash flows will occur. Finance.com has determined that the appropriate discount rate is 7 percent for this investment. Should Finance.com make this investment in a new high-speed computer? What is the net present value of the investment?

The cash flows and present value factors of the proposed computer are as follows:

	Cash Flows	Present Value Factor
Year 0	−$50,000	$1 = 1$
1	$25,000	$\dfrac{1}{1.07} = .9346$
2	$20,000	$\left(\dfrac{1}{1.07}\right)^2 = .8734$
3	$15,000	$\left(\dfrac{1}{1.07}\right)^3 = .8163$

The present value of the cash flows is:

Cash Flows × Present value factor = Present value

Year 0	−$50,000 × 1	=	−$50,000
1	$25,000 × .9346	=	$23,364.49
2	$20,000 × .8734	=	$17,468.77
3	$15,000 × .8163	=	$12,244.47
		Total:	$ 3,077.73

Finance.com should invest in the new high-speed computer because the present value of its future cash flows is greater than its cost. The NPV is $3,077.73.

THE ALGEBRAIC FORMULA

To derive an algebraic formula for the net present value of a cash flow, recall that the PV of receiving a cash flow one year from now is:

$$PV = C_1/(1 + r)$$

and the PV of receiving a cash flow two years from now is:

$$PV = C_2/(1 + r)^2$$

We can write the NPV of a T-period project as:

$$NPV = -C_0 + \frac{C_1}{1 + r} + \frac{C_2}{(1 + r)^2} + \ldots + \frac{C_T}{(1 + r)^T} = -C_0 + \sum_{i=1}^{T} \frac{C_i}{(1 + r)^i} \quad (4.5)$$

The initial flow, $-C_0$, is assumed to be negative because it represents an investment. The Σ is shorthand for the sum of the series.

We close this section by answering the question we posed at the beginning of the chapter concerning football player Colin Kaepernick's contract. Recall that the contract called for a $13 million signing bonus. The remaining $108 million was to be paid as $12.4 million in 2015, $14.3 million in 2016, $18.5 million in 2017, $19 million in 2018, $20.8 million in 2019, and $23 million in 2020. If 12 percent is the appropriate discount rate, what kind of deal did the 49ers' quarterback get thrown?

To answer, we can calculate the present value by discounting each year's salary back to the present as follows (notice we assume that all the payments are made at year-end):

Year 0 (2014): $13,000,000	= $13,000,000.00
Year 1 (2015): $12,400,000 × 1/1.12^1	= $11,071,428.57
Year 2 (2016): $14,300,000 × 1/1.12^2	= $11,399,872.45
...	
Year 6 (2020): $23,000,000 × 1/1.12^6	= $11,652,515.79

If you fill in the missing rows and then add (do it for practice), you will see that Colin's contract had a present value of about $84.2 million, or about 70 percent of the stated $121 million value (still pretty good!).

4.3 Compounding Periods

So far, we have assumed that compounding and discounting occur yearly. Sometimes, compounding may occur more frequently than just once a year. For example, imagine that a bank pays a 10 percent interest rate "compounded semiannually." This means that a $1,000 deposit in the bank would be worth $1,000 × 1.05 = $1,050 after six months, and $1,050 × 1.05 = $1,102.50 at the end of the year.

The end-of-the-year wealth can be written as:

$$\$1,000 \left(1 + \frac{.10}{2}\right)^2 = \$1,000 \times (1.05)^2 = \$1,102.50$$

Of course, a $1,000 deposit would be worth $1,100 (=$1,000 × 1.10) with yearly compounding. Note that the future value at the end of one year is greater with semiannual compounding than with yearly compounding. With yearly compounding, the original $1,000 remains the investment base for the full year. The original $1,000 is the investment base only for the first six months with semiannual compounding. The base over the second six months is $1,050. Hence one gets *interest on interest* with semiannual compounding.

Because $1,000 × 1.1025 = $1,102.50, 10 percent compounded semiannually is the same as 10.25 percent compounded annually. In other words, a rational investor could not care less whether she is quoted a rate of 10 percent compounded semiannually or a rate of 10.25 percent compounded annually.

Quarterly compounding at 10 percent yields wealth at the end of one year of:

$$\$1,000 \left(1 + \frac{.10}{4}\right)^4 = \$1,103.81$$

More generally, compounding an investment m times a year provides end-of-year wealth of:

$$C_0\left(1 + \frac{r}{m}\right)^m \tag{4.6}$$

where C_0 is the initial investment and r is the **annual percentage rate** (APR). The annual percentage rate is the annual interest rate without consideration of compounding. Banks and other financial institutions may use other names for the annual percentage rate.

EXAMPLE 4.12

EARs   What is the end-of-year wealth if Jane Christine receives an APR of 24 percent compounded monthly on a $1 investment?

Using Equation 4.6, her wealth is:

$$\$1\left(1 + \frac{.24}{12}\right)^{12} = \$1 \times (1.02)^{12}$$
$$= \$1.2682$$

The annual rate of return is 26.82 percent. This annual rate of return is called either the **effective annual rate (EAR)** or the **effective annual yield (EAY)**. Due to compounding, the effective annual interest rate is greater than the APR of 24 percent. Algebraically, we can rewrite the effective annual interest rate as follows:

Effective Annual Rate:
$$\left(1 + \frac{r}{m}\right)^m - 1 \tag{4.7}$$

Students are often bothered by the subtraction of 1 in Equation 4.7. Note that end-of-year wealth is composed of both the interest earned over the year and the original principal. We remove the original principal by subtracting 1 in Equation 4.7.

EXAMPLE
4.13

Compounding Frequencies   If the annual percentage rate, 8 percent, is compounded quarterly, what is the effective annual rate?

Using Equation 4.7, we have:

$$\left(1 + \frac{r}{m}\right)^m - 1 = \left(1 + \frac{.08}{4}\right)^4 - 1 = .0824 = 8.24\%$$

Referring back to our original example where C_0 = $1,000 and r = 10%, we can generate the following table:

C_0	Compounding Frequency (m)	C_1	Effective Annual Rate = $\left(1 + \frac{r}{m}\right)^m - 1$
$1,000	Yearly ($m = 1$)	$1,100.00	.10
1,000	Semiannually ($m = 2$)	1,102.50	.1025
1,000	Quarterly ($m = 4$)	1,103.81	.10381
1,000	Daily ($m = 365$)	1,105.16	.10516

DISTINCTION BETWEEN ANNUAL PERCENTAGE RATE AND EFFECTIVE ANNUAL RATE

The distinction between the annual percentage rate, or APR, and the effective annual rate (EAR) is frequently troubling to students. We can reduce the confusion by noting that the APR becomes meaningful only if the compounding interval is given. For example, for an APR of 10 percent, the future value at the end of one year with semiannual compounding is $[1 + (.10/2)]^2 = 1.1025$. The future value with quarterly compounding is $[1 + (.10/4)]^4 = 1.1038$. If the APR is 10 percent but no compounding interval is given, we cannot calculate future value. In other words, we do not know whether to compound semiannually, quarterly, or over some other interval.

By contrast, the EAR is meaningful *without* a compounding interval. For example, an EAR of 10.25 percent means that a $1 investment will be worth $1.1025 in one year. We can think of this as an APR of 10 percent with semiannual compounding or an APR of 10.25 percent with annual compounding, or some other possibility.

There can be a big difference between an APR and an EAR when interest rates are large. For example, consider "payday loans." Payday loans are short-term loans made to consumers, often for less than two weeks. They are offered by companies such as Check Into Cash and AmeriCash Advance. The loans work like this: You write a check today that is postdated. When the check date arrives, you go to the store and pay the cash for the check, or the company cashes the check. For example, in one particular state, Check Into Cash allows you to write a check for $115 dated 14 days in the future, for which they give you $100 today. So what are the APR and EAR of this arrangement? First, we need to find the interest rate, which we can find by the FV equation as follows:

$$FV = PV \times (1 + r)^1$$
$$\$115 = \$100 \times (1 + r)^1$$
$$1.15 = (1 + r)$$
$$r = .15 \text{ or } 15\%$$

That doesn't seem too bad until you remember this is the interest rate for *14 days!* The APR of the loan is:

$$APR = .15 \times 365/14$$
$$APR = 3.9107 \text{ or } 391.07\%$$

And the EAR for this loan is:

$$EAR = (1 + \text{Quoted rate}/m)^m - 1$$
$$EAR = (1 + .15)^{365/14} - 1$$
$$EAR = 37.2366 \text{ or } 3,723.66\%$$

Now that's an interest rate! Just to see what a difference a small difference in fees can make, AmeriCash Advance will make you write a check for $117.50 for the same amount. Check for yourself that the APR of this arrangement is 456.25 percent and the EAR is 6,598.65 percent. Still not a loan we would like to take out!

By law, lenders are required to report the APR on all loans. In this text, we compute the APR as the interest rate per period multiplied by the number of periods in a year. According to federal law, the APR is a measure of the cost of consumer credit expressed as a yearly rate, and it includes interest and certain noninterest charges and fees. In practice, the APR can be much higher than the interest rate on the loan if the lender charges substantial fees that must be included in the federally mandated APR calculation.

COMPOUNDING OVER MANY YEARS

Equation 4.6 applies for an investment over one year. For an investment over one or more (T) years, the formula becomes this:

Future Value with Compounding:
$$FV = C_0\left(1 + \frac{r}{m}\right)^{mT} \tag{4.8}$$

**EXAMPLE
4.14**

Multiyear Compounding Harry DeAngelo is investing $5,000 at an annual percentage rate of 12 percent per year, compounded quarterly, for five years. What is his wealth at the end of five years?

Using Equation 4.8, his wealth is:

$$\$5,000 \times \left(1 + \frac{.12}{4}\right)^{4\times5} = \$5,000 \times (1.03)^{20} = \$5,000 \times 1.8061 = \$9,030.50$$

CONTINUOUS COMPOUNDING

The previous discussion shows that we can compound much more frequently than once a year. We could compound semiannually, quarterly, monthly, daily, hourly, each minute, or even more often. The limiting case would be to compound every infinitesimal instant, which is commonly called **continuous compounding**. Surprisingly, banks and other financial institutions sometimes quote continuously compounded rates, which is why we study them.

Though the idea of compounding this rapidly may boggle the mind, a simple formula is involved. With continuous compounding, the value at the end of T years is expressed as:

$$C_0 \times e^{rT} \qquad \qquad \textbf{(4.9)}$$

where C_0 is the initial investment, r is the APR, and T is the number of years over which the investment runs. The number e is a constant and is approximately equal to 2.718. It is not an unknown like C_0, r, and T.

EXAMPLE
4.15

Continuous Compounding   Linda DeFond invested $1,000 at a continuously compounded rate of 10 percent for one year. What is the value of her wealth at the end of one year?
From Equation 4.9 we have:

$$\$1,000 \times e^{.10} = \$1,000 \times 1.1052 = \$1,105.20$$

This number can easily be read from Table A.5. We merely set r, the value on the horizontal dimension, to 10 percent and T, the value on the vertical dimension, to 1. For this problem the relevant portion of the table is shown here:

Period (T)	Continuously Compounded Rate (r)		
	9%	10%	11%
1	1.0942	1.1052	1.1163
2	1.1972	1.2214	1.2461
3	1.3100	1.3499	1.3910

Note that a continuously compounded rate of 10 percent is equivalent to an annually compounded rate of 10.52 percent. In other words, Linda DeFond would not care whether her bank quoted a continuously compounded rate of 10 percent or a 10.52 percent rate, compounded annually.

EXAMPLE
4.16

Continuous Compounding, Continued   Linda DeFond's brother, Mark, invested $1,000 at a continuously compounded rate of 10 percent for two years.
The appropriate formula here is:

$$\$1,000 \times e^{.10 \times 2} = \$1,000 \times e^{.20} = \$1,221.40$$

Using the portion of the table of continuously compounded rates shown in the previous example, we find the value to be 1.2214.

Figure 4.11 illustrates the relationship among annual, semiannual, and continuous compounding. Semiannual compounding gives rise to both a smoother curve and a higher ending value than does annual compounding. Continuous compounding has both the smoothest curve and the highest ending value of all.

Figure 4.11
Annual, Semiannual, and Continuous Compounding

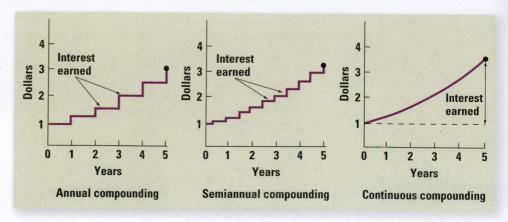

EXAMPLE

Present Value with Continuous Compounding   The Michigan State Lottery is going to pay you $100,000 at the end of four years. If the annual continuously compounded rate of interest is 8 percent, what is the present value of this payment?

$$\$100,000 \times \frac{1}{e^{.08 \times 4}} = \$100,000 \times \frac{1}{1.3771} = \$72,616.37$$

4.4 Simplifications

The first part of this chapter has examined the concepts of future value and present value. Although these concepts allow us to answer a host of problems concerning the time value of money, the human effort involved can be excessive. For example, consider a bank calculating the present value of a 20-year monthly mortgage. This mortgage has 240 ($=20 \times 12$) payments, so a lot of time is needed to perform a conceptually simple task.

Because many basic finance problems are potentially time-consuming, we search for simplifications in this section. We provide simplifying formulas for four classes of cash flow streams:

- Perpetuity.
- Growing perpetuity.
- Annuity.
- Growing annuity.

PERPETUITY

A **perpetuity** is a constant stream of cash flows without end. If you are thinking that perpetuities have no relevance to reality, it will surprise you that there is a well-known case of an unending cash flow stream: The British bonds called *consols*. An investor purchasing a consol is entitled to receive yearly interest from the British government forever.

How can the price of a consol be determined? Consider a consol that pays a coupon of C dollars each year and will do so forever. Simply applying the PV formula gives us:

$$PV = \frac{C}{1+r} + \frac{C}{(1+r)^2} + \frac{C}{(1+r)^3} + \cdots$$

where the dots at the end of the formula stand for the infinite string of terms that continues the formula. Series like the preceding one are called *geometric series*. It is well known that even though they have an infinite number of terms, the whole series has a finite sum because each term is only a fraction of the preceding term. Before turning to our calculus books, though, it is worth going back to our original principles to see if a bit of financial intuition can help us find the PV.

The present value of the consol is the present value of all of its future coupons. In other words, it is an amount of money that, if an investor had it today, would enable him to achieve the same pattern of expenditures that the consol and its coupons would. Suppose an investor wanted to spend exactly C dollars each year. If he had the consol, he could do this. How much money must he have today to spend the same amount? Clearly, he would need exactly enough so that the interest on the money would be C dollars per year. If he had any more, he could spend more than C dollars each year. If he had any less, he would eventually run out of money spending C dollars per year.

The amount that will give the investor C dollars each year, and therefore the present value of the consol, is simply:

$$PV = \frac{C}{r} \tag{4.10}$$

To confirm that this is the right answer, notice that if we lend the amount C/r, the interest it earns each year will be:

$$\text{Interest} = \frac{C}{r} \times r = C$$

which is exactly the consol payment. We have arrived at this formula for a consol:

Formula for Present Value of Perpetuity:

$$PV = \frac{C}{1+r} + \frac{C}{(1+r)^2} + \frac{C}{(1+r)^3} + \cdots \tag{4.11}$$
$$= \frac{C}{r}$$

It is comforting to know how easily we can use a bit of financial intuition to solve this mathematical problem.

EXAMPLE 4.18

Perpetuities   Consider a perpetuity paying $100 a year. If the relevant interest rate is 8 percent, what is the value of the consol?

Using Equation 4.10 we have:

$$PV = \frac{\$100}{.08} = \$1,250$$

Now suppose that interest rates fall to 6 percent. Using Equation 4.10 the value of the perpetuity is:

$$PV = \frac{\$100}{.06} = \$1,666.67$$

Note that the value of the perpetuity rises with a drop in the interest rate. Conversely, the value of the perpetuity falls with a rise in the interest rate.

GROWING PERPETUITY

Imagine an apartment building where cash flows to the landlord after expenses will be $100,000 next year. These cash flows are expected to rise at 5 percent per year. If one assumes that this rise will continue indefinitely, the cash flow stream is termed a **growing perpetuity**. The relevant interest rate is 11 percent. Therefore, the appropriate discount rate is 11 percent, and the present value of the cash flows can be represented as:

$$PV = \frac{\$100,000}{1.11} + \frac{\$100,000(1.05)}{(1.11)^2} + \frac{\$100,000(1.05)^2}{(1.11)^3} + \cdots$$
$$+ \frac{\$100,000(1.05)^{N-1}}{(1.11)^N} + \cdots$$

Algebraically, we can write the formula as:

$$PV = \frac{C}{1+r} + \frac{C \times (1+g)}{(1+r)^2} + \frac{C \times (1+g)^2}{(1+r)^3} + \cdots + \frac{C \times (1+g)^{N-1}}{(1+r)^N} + \cdots$$

where C is the cash flow to be received one period hence, g is the rate of growth per period, expressed as a percentage, and r is the appropriate discount rate.

Fortunately, this formula reduces to the following simplification:

Formula for Present Value of Growing Perpetuity:
$$PV = \frac{C}{r-g}$$

(4.12)

From Equation 4.12 the present value of the cash flows from the apartment building is:

$$\frac{\$100,000}{.11 - .05} = \$1,666,667$$

There are three important points concerning the growing perpetuity formula:

1. *The numerator:* The numerator in Equation 4.12 is the cash flow one period hence, not at date 0. Consider the following example.

EXAMPLE 4.19

Paying Dividends   Popovich Corporation is *just about* to pay a dividend of $3.00 per share. Investors anticipate that the annual dividend will rise by 6 percent a year forever. The applicable discount rate is 11 percent. What is the price of the stock today?

The numerator in Equation 4.12 is the cash flow to be received next period. Since the growth rate is 6 percent, the dividend next year is $3.18 (=$3.00 × 1.06). The price of the stock today is:

$66.60	=	$3.00	+	$\frac{\$3.18}{.11 - .06}$
		Imminent dividend		Present value of all dividends beginning a year from now

The price of $66.60 includes both the dividend to be received immediately and the present value of all dividends beginning a year from now. Equation 4.12 makes it possible to calculate only the present value of all dividends beginning a year from now. Be sure you understand this example; test questions on this subject always seem to trip up a few of our students.

2. *The discount rate and the growth rate:* The discount rate r must be greater than the growth rate g for the growing perpetuity formula to work. Consider the case

in which the growth rate approaches the interest rate in magnitude. Then, the denominator in the growing perpetuity formula gets infinitesimally small and the present value grows infinitely large. The present value is in fact undefined when r is less than g.

3. *The timing assumption:* Cash generally flows into and out of real-world firms both randomly and nearly continuously. However, Equation 4.12 assumes that cash flows are received and disbursed at regular and discrete points in time. In the example of the apartment, we assumed that the net cash flows of $100,000 occurred only once a year. In reality, rent checks are commonly received every month. Payments for maintenance and other expenses may occur anytime within the year.

    We can apply the growing perpetuity formula of Equation 4.12 only by assuming a regular and discrete pattern of cash flow. Although this assumption is sensible because the formula saves so much time, the user should never forget that it is an *assumption*. This point will be mentioned again in the chapters ahead.

A few words should be said about terminology. Authors of financial textbooks generally use one of two conventions to refer to time. A minority of financial writers treat cash flows as being received on exact *dates*—for example Date 0, Date 1, and so forth. Under this convention, Date 0 represents the present time. However, because a year is an interval, not a specific moment in time, the great majority of authors refer to cash flows that occur at the end of a year (or alternatively, the end of a *period*). Under this *end-of-the-year* convention, the end of Year 0 is the present, the end of Year 1 occurs one period hence, and so on. (The beginning of Year 0 has already passed and is not generally referred to.)[2]

The interchangeability of the two conventions can be seen from the following chart:

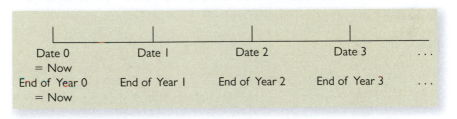

Date 0	Date 1	Date 2	Date 3	. . .
= Now				
End of Year 0	End of Year 1	End of Year 2	End of Year 3	. . .
= Now				

We strongly believe that the *dates convention* reduces ambiguity. However, we use both conventions because you are likely to see the *end-of-year convention* in later courses. In fact, both conventions may appear in the same example for the sake of practice.

ANNUITY

An **annuity** is a level stream of regular payments that lasts for a fixed number of periods. Not surprisingly, annuities are among the most common kinds of financial instruments. The pensions that people receive when they retire are often in the form of an annuity. Leases and mortgages are also often annuities.

To figure out the present value of an annuity we need to evaluate the following equation:

$$\frac{C}{1+r} + \frac{C}{(1+r)^2} + \frac{C}{(1+r)^3} + \cdots + \frac{C}{(1+r)^T}$$

---

[2]Sometimes, financial writers merely speak of a cash flow in Year x. Although this terminology is ambiguous, such writers generally mean the *end of Year x*.

The present value of receiving the coupons for only T periods must be less than the present value of a consol, but how much less? To answer this, we have to look at consols a bit more closely.

Consider the following time chart:

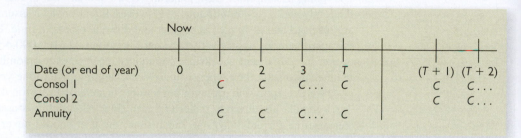

Consol 1 is a normal consol with its first payment at Date 1. The first payment of consol 2 occurs at Date $T + 1$.

The present value of having a cash flow of C at each of T dates is equal to the present value of Consol 1 minus the present value of Consol 2. The present value of Consol 1 is given by:

$$PV = \frac{C}{r} \tag{4.13}$$

Consol 2 is just a consol with its first payment at Date $T + 1$. From the perpetuity formula, this consol will be worth C/r at Date T.[3] However, we do not want the value at Date T. We want the value now, in other words, the present value at Date 0. We must discount C/r back by T periods. Therefore, the present value of Consol 2 is:

$$PV = \frac{C}{r}\left[\frac{1}{(1 + r)^T}\right] \tag{4.14}$$

The present value of having cash flows for T years is the present value of a consol with its first payment at Date 1 minus the present value of a consol with its first payment at Date $T + 1$. Thus the present value of an annuity is Equation 4.13 minus Equation 4.14. This can be written as:

$$\frac{C}{r} - \frac{C}{r}\left[\frac{1}{(1 + r)^T}\right]$$

This simplifies to the following:

Formula for Present Value of Annuity:

$$PV = C\left[\frac{1}{r} - \frac{1}{r(1 + r)^T}\right] \tag{4.15}$$

This can also be written as:

$$PV = C\left[\frac{1 - \frac{1}{(1 + r)^T}}{r}\right]$$

---

[3]Students frequently think that C/r is the present value at Date $T + 1$ because the consol's first payment is at Date $T + 1$. However, the formula values the consol as of one period prior to the first payment.

EXAMPLE 4.20

Lottery Valuation   Mark Young has just won the state lottery, paying $50,000 a year for 20 years. He is to receive his first payment a year from now. The state advertises this as the Million Dollar Lottery because $1,000,000 = $50,000 × 20. If the interest rate is 8 percent, what is the present value of the lottery?

Equation 4.15 yields:

$$\text{Present value of Million Dollar Lottery} = \$50,000 \times \left[\frac{1 - \frac{1}{(1.08)^{20}}}{.08} \right]$$

$$\begin{array}{ccc} \text{Periodic payment} & & \text{Annuity factor} \\ = \$50,000 & \times & 9.8181 \end{array}$$

$$= \$490,905$$

Rather than being overjoyed at winning, Mr. Young sues the state for misrepresentation and fraud. His legal brief states that he was promised $1 million but received only $490,905.

The term we use to compute the present value of the stream of level payments, C, for T years is called a **present value interest factor for annuities**. The present value interest factor for annuities in the current example is 9.8181. Because the present value interest factor for annuities is used so often in PV calculations, we have included it in Table A.2 in the back of this book. The table gives the values of these factors for a range of interest rates, r, and maturity dates, T.

The present value interest factor for annuities as expressed in the brackets of Equation 4.15 is a complex formula. For simplification, we may from time to time refer to the annuity factor as:

$$\text{PVIFA } (r, T)$$

This expression stands for the present value of $1 a year for T years at an interest rate of r.

We can also provide a formula for the future value of an annuity:

$$\text{FV} = C\left[\frac{(1 + r)^T}{r} - \frac{1}{r}\right] = C\left[\frac{(1 + r)^T - 1}{r}\right] \tag{4.16}$$

As with present value factors for annuities, we have compiled future value factors in Table A.4 in the back of this book.

EXAMPLE 4.21

Retirement Investing   Suppose you put $3,000 per year into a Roth IRA. The account pays 6 percent interest per year. How much will you have when you retire in 30 years?

This question asks for the future value of an annuity of $3,000 per year for 30 years at 6 percent, which we can calculate as follows:

$$\text{FV} = C\left[\frac{(1 + r)^T - 1}{r}\right] = \$3,000 \times \left[\frac{1.06^{30} - 1}{.06}\right]$$

$$= \$3,000 \times 79.0582$$

$$= \$237,174.56$$

So, you'll have close to a quarter million dollars in the account.

Our experience is that annuity formulas are not hard, but tricky, for the beginning student. We present four tricks next.

SPREADSHEET APPLICATIONS

Annuity Present Values

Using a spreadsheet to find annuity present values goes like this:

	A	B	C	D	E	F	G
1							
2	Using a spreadsheet to find annuity present values						
3							
4	What is the present value of $500 per year for 3 years if the discount rate is 10 percent?						
5	We need to solve for the unknown present value, so we use the formula PV(rate, nper, pmt, fv).						
6							
7	Payment amount per period:	$500					
8	Number of payments:	3					
9	Discount rate:	0.1					
10							
11	Annuity present value:	$1,243.43					
12							
13	The formula entered in cell B11 is =PV(B9,B8,-B7,0); notice that fv is zero and that						
14	pmt has a negative sign on it. Also notice that rate is entered as a decimal, not a percentage.						
15							
16							
17							

Trick 1: A Delayed Annuity   One of the tricks in working with annuities or perpetuities is getting the timing exactly right. This is particularly true when an annuity or perpetuity begins at a date many periods in the future. We have found that even the brightest beginning student can make errors here. Consider the following example.

EXAMPLE

Delayed Annuities   Danielle Caravello will receive a four-year annuity of $500 per year, beginning at date 6. If the interest rate is 10 percent, what is the present value of her annuity? This situation can be graphed as follows:

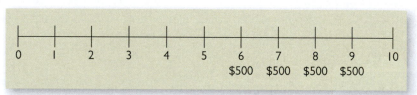

The analysis involves two steps:

1. Calculate the present value of the annuity using Equation 4.15:

Present Value of Annuity at Date 5:

$$\$500 \left[\frac{1 - \frac{1}{(1.10)^4}}{.10} \right] = \$500 \times \text{PVIFA} \,(.10, 4)$$
$$= \$500 \times 3.1699$$
$$= \$1,584.95$$

Note that $1,584.95 represents the present value at *Date 5*.

Students frequently think that $1,584.95 is the present value at Date 6 because the annuity begins at Date 6. However, our formula values the annuity as of one period prior to the first payment. This can be seen in the most typical case where the first payment occurs at Date 1. The formula values the annuity as of Date 0 in that case.

2. Discount the present value of the annuity back to Date 0:

Present Value at Date 0:

$$\frac{\$1,584.95}{(1.10)^5} = \$984.13$$

Again, it is worthwhile mentioning that because the annuity formula brings Danielle's annuity back to Date 5, the second calculation must discount over the remaining five periods. The two-step procedure is graphed in Figure 4.12.

Figure 4.12   Discounting Danielle Caravello's Annuity

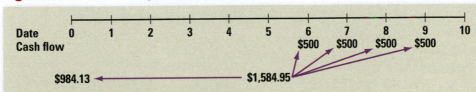

Step one: Discount the four payments back to Date 5 by using the annuity formula.
Step two: Discount the present value at Date 5 ($1,584.95) back to present value at Date 0.

Trick 2: Annuity Due   The annuity formula of Equation 4.15 assumes that the first annuity payment begins a full period hence. This type of annuity is sometimes called an *annuity in arrears* or an *ordinary annuity*. What happens if the annuity begins today—in other words, at Date 0?

EXAMPLE 4.23

Annuity Due   In a previous example, Mark Young received $50,000 a year for 20 years from the state lottery. In that example, he was to receive the first payment a year from the winning date. Let us now assume that the first payment occurs immediately. The total number of payments remains 20.

Under this new assumption, we have a 19-date annuity with the first payment occurring at date 1—plus an extra payment at date 0. The present value is:

$$\underset{\substack{\text{Payment at date 0}}}{\$50,000} \quad + \quad \underset{\substack{\text{19-year annuity}}}{\$50,000 \times \frac{[1 - 1/(1.08)^{19}]}{.08}}$$

$$= \$50,000 + (\$50,000 \times 9.6036)$$
$$= \$530,180$$

$530,180, the present value in this example, is greater than $490,905, the present value in the earlier lottery example. This is to be expected because the annuity of the current example begins earlier. An annuity with an immediate initial payment is called an *annuity in advance* or, more commonly, an *annuity due*. Always remember that Equation 4.15 and Table A.2 in this book refer to an *ordinary annuity*.

Trick 3: The Infrequent Annuity The following example treats an annuity with payments occurring less frequently than once a year.

Infrequent Annuities Ann Chen receives an annuity of $450, payable once every two years. The annuity stretches out over 20 years. The first payment occurs at Date 2—that is, two years from today. The annual interest rate is 6 percent.

The trick is to determine the interest rate over a two-year period. The interest rate over two years is:

$$(1.06 \times 1.06) - 1 = 12.36\%$$

That is, $100 invested over two years will yield $112.36.

What we want is the present value of a $450 annuity over 10 periods, with an interest rate of 12.36 percent per period:

$$\$450 \left[\frac{1 - \frac{1}{(1 + .1236)^{10}}}{.1236} \right] = \$450 \times \text{PVIFA} (.1236, 10) = \$2,505.57$$

Trick 4: Equating Present Value of Two Annuities The following example equates the present value of inflows with the present value of outflows.

Working with Annuities Harold and Helen Nash are saving for the college education of their newborn daughter, Susan. The Nashes estimate that college expenses will run $30,000 per year when their daughter reaches college in 18 years. The annual interest rate over the next few decades will be 14 percent. How much money must they deposit in the bank each year so that their daughter will be completely supported through four years of college?

To simplify the calculations, we assume that Susan is born today. Her parents will make the first of her four annual tuition payments on her 18th birthday. They will make equal bank deposits on each of her first 17 birthdays, but no deposit at Date 0. This is illustrated as follows:

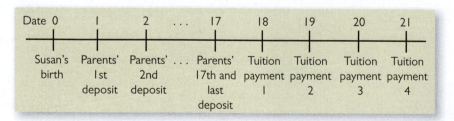

Mr. and Ms. Nash will be making deposits to the bank over the next 17 years. They will be withdrawing $30,000 per year over the following four years. We can be sure they will be able to withdraw fully $30,000 per year if the present value of the deposits is equal to the present value of the four $30,000 withdrawals.

This calculation requires three steps. The first two determine the present value of the withdrawals. The final step determines yearly deposits that will have a present value equal to that of the withdrawals.

1. We calculate the present value of the four years at college using the annuity formula:

$$\$30,000 \times \left[\frac{1 - \frac{1}{(1.14)^4}}{.14} \right] = \$30,000 \times \text{PVIFA } (.14, 4)$$

$$= \$30,000 \times 2.9137 = \$87,411.4$$

We assume that Susan enters college on her 18th birthday. Given our discussion in Trick 1, $87,411 represents the present value at Date 17.

2. We calculate the present value of the college education at Date 0 as:

$$\frac{\$87,411.4}{(1.14)^{17}} = \$9,422.92$$

3. Assuming that Harold and Helen Nash make deposits to the bank at the end of each of the 17 years, we calculate the annual deposit that will yield a present value of all deposits of $9,422.92. This is calculated as:

$$C \times \text{PVIFA } (.14, 17) = \$9,422.92$$

Because PVIFA (.14, 17) = 6.3729,

$$C = \frac{\$9,422.92}{6.3729} = \$1,478.59$$

Thus deposits of $1,478.59 made at the end of each of the first 17 years and invested at 14 percent will provide enough money to make tuition payments of $30,000 over the following four years.

An alternative method in Example 4.25 would be to (1) calculate the present value of the tuition payments at Susan's 18th birthday and (2) calculate annual deposits so that the future value of the deposits at her 18th birthday equals the present value of the tuition payments at that date. Although this technique can also provide the right answer, we have found that it is more likely to lead to errors. Therefore, we equate only present values in our presentation.

GROWING ANNUITY

Cash flows in business are likely to grow over time, due either to real growth or to inflation. The growing perpetuity, which assumes an infinite number of cash flows, provides one formula to handle this growth. We now consider a **growing annuity**, which is a *finite* number of growing cash flows. Because perpetuities of any kind are rare, a formula for a growing annuity would be useful indeed. Here is the formula:

Formula for Present Value of Growing Annuity:

$$\text{PV} = C \left[\frac{1}{r - g} - \frac{1}{r - g} \times \left(\frac{1 + g}{1 + r} \right)^T \right] = C \left[\frac{1 - \left(\frac{1 + g}{1 + r} \right)^T}{r - g} \right] \tag{4.17}$$

As before, C is the payment to occur at the end of the first period, r is the interest rate, g is the rate of growth per period, expressed as a percentage, and T is the number of periods for the annuity.

EXAMPLE
4.26

Growing Annuities   Stuart Gabriel, a second-year MBA student, has just been offered a job at $80,000 a year. He anticipates his salary increasing by 9 percent a year until his retirement in 40 years. Given an interest rate of 20 percent, what is the present value of his lifetime salary?

We simplify by assuming he will be paid his $80,000 salary exactly one year from now, and that his salary will continue to be paid in annual installments. The appropriate discount rate is 20 percent. From Equation 4.17, the calculation is:

$$\text{Present value of Stuart's lifetime salary} = \$80,000 \times \left[\frac{1 - \left(\frac{1.09}{1.20} \right)^{40}}{.20 - .09} \right] = \$711,730.71$$

Though the growing annuity formula is quite useful, it is more tedious than the other simplifying formulas. Whereas most sophisticated calculators have special programs for perpetuity, growing perpetuity, and annuity, there is no special program for a growing annuity. Hence, we must calculate all the terms in Equation 4.17 directly.

EXAMPLE
4.27

More Growing Annuities   In a previous example, Helen and Harold Nash planned to make 17 identical payments to fund the college education of their daughter, Susan. Alternatively, imagine that they planned to increase their payments at 4 percent per year. What would their first payment be?

The first two steps of the previous Nash family example showed that the present value of the college costs was $9,422.92. These two steps would be the same here. However, the third step must be altered. Now we must ask, How much should their first payment be so that, if payments increase by 4 percent per year, the present value of all payments will be $9,422.92?

We set the growing annuity formula equal to $9,422.92 and solve for C:

$$C \left[\frac{1 - \left(\frac{1 + g}{1 + r} \right)^{T}}{r - g} \right] = C \left[\frac{1 - \left(\frac{1.04}{1.14} \right)^{17}}{.14 - .04} \right] = \$9,422.92$$

Here, $C = \$1,192.75$. Thus, the deposit on their daughter's first birthday is $1,192.75, the deposit on the second birthday is $1,240.46 ($= 1.04 \times \$1,192.75$), and so on.

4.5 Loan Amortization

Whenever a lender extends a loan, some provision will be made for repayment of the principal (the original loan amount). A loan might be repaid in equal installments, for example, or it might be repaid in a single lump sum. Because the way that the principal and interest are paid is up to the parties involved, there are actually an unlimited number of possibilities.

In this section, we describe amortized loans. Working with these loans is a very straightforward application of the present value principles that we have already developed.

An *amortized loan* may require the borrower to repay parts of the loan amount over time. The process of providing for a loan to be paid off by making regular principal reductions is called *amortizing* the loan.

A simple way of amortizing a loan is to have the borrower pay the interest each period plus some fixed amount. This approach is common with medium-term business loans. For example, suppose a business takes out a $5,000, five-year loan at 9 percent. The loan agreement calls for the borrower to pay the interest on the loan balance each year and to reduce the loan balance each year by $1,000. Because the loan amount declines by $1,000 each year, it is fully paid in five years.

In the case we are considering, notice that the total payment will decline each year. The reason is that the loan balance goes down, resulting in a lower interest charge each year, whereas the $1,000 principal reduction is constant. For example, the interest in the first year will be $5,000 × .09 = $450. The total payment will be $1,000 + 450 = $1,450. In the second year, the loan balance is $4,000, so the interest is $4,000 × .09 = $360, and the total payment is $1,360. We can calculate the total payment in each of the remaining years by preparing a simple *amortization schedule* as follows:

Year	Beginning Balance	Total Payment	Interest Paid	Principal Paid	Ending Balance
1	$5,000	$1,450	$ 450	$1,000	$4,000
2	4,000	1,360	360	1,000	3,000
3	3,000	1,270	270	1,000	2,000
4	2,000	1,180	180	1,000	1,000
5	1,000	1,090	90	1,000	0
Totals		$6,350	$1,350	$5,000	

Notice that in each year, the interest paid is given by the beginning balance multiplied by the interest rate. Also notice that the beginning balance is given by the ending balance from the previous year.

Probably the most common way of amortizing a loan is to have the borrower make a single, fixed payment every period. Almost all consumer loans (such as car loans) and mortgages work this way. For example, suppose our five-year, 9 percent, $5,000 loan was amortized this way. How would the amortization schedule look?

We first need to determine the payment. From our discussion earlier in the chapter, we know that this loan's cash flows are in the form of an ordinary annuity. In this case, we can solve for the payment as follows:

$$\$5,000 = C \times \{[1 - (1/1.09^5)]/.09\}$$
$$= C \times [(1 - .6499)/.09]$$

This gives us:

$$C = \$5,000/3.8897$$
$$= \$1,285.46$$

The borrower will therefore make five equal payments of $1,285.46. Will this pay off the loan? We will check by filling in an amortization schedule.

In our previous example, we knew the principal reduction each year. We then calculated the interest owed to get the total payment. In this example, we know the total payment. We will thus calculate the interest and then subtract it from the total payment to calculate the principal portion in each payment.

In the first year, the interest is $450, as we calculated before. Because the total payment is $1,285.46, the principal paid in the first year must be:

$$\text{Principal paid} = \$1,285.46 - 450 = \$835.46$$

The ending loan balance is thus:

$$\text{Ending balance} = \$5,000 - 835.46 = \$4,164.54$$

The interest in the second year is $4,164.54 \times .09 = \$374.81$, and the loan balance declines by $1,285.46 - 374.81 = \$910.65$. We can summarize all of the relevant calculations in the following schedule:

Year	Beginning Balance	Total Payment	Interest Paid	Principal Paid	Ending Balance
1	$5,000.00	$1,285.46	$ 450.00	$ 835.46	$4,164.54
2	4,164.54	1,285.46	374.81	910.65	3,253.88
3	3,253.88	1,285.46	292.85	992.61	2,261.27
4	2,261.27	1,285.46	203.51	1,081.95	1,179.32
5	1,179.32	1,285.46	106.14	1,179.32	0.00
Totals		$6,427.30	$1,427.31	$5,000.00	

Because the loan balance declines to zero, the five equal payments do pay off the loan. Notice that the interest paid declines each period. This isn't surprising because the loan balance is going down. Given that the total payment is fixed, the principal paid must be rising each period.

If you compare the two loan amortizations in this section, you will see that the total interest is greater for the equal total payment case: $1,427.31 versus $1,350. The reason for this is that the loan is repaid more slowly early on, so the interest is somewhat higher. This doesn't mean that one loan is better than the other; it simply means that one is effectively paid off faster than the other. For example, the principal reduction in the first year is $835.46 in the equal total payment case as compared to $1,000 in the first case.

EXAMPLE

Partial Amortization, or "Bite the Bullet"   A common arrangement in real estate lending might call for a 5-year loan with, say, a 15-year amortization. What this means is that the borrower makes a payment every month of a fixed amount based on a 15-year amortization. However, after 60 months, the borrower makes a single, much larger payment called a "balloon" or "bullet" to pay off the loan. Because the monthly payments don't fully pay off the loan, the loan is said to be partially amortized.

Suppose we have a $100,000 commercial mortgage with a 12 percent APR and a 20-year (240-month) amortization. Further suppose the mortgage has a five-year balloon. What will the monthly payment be? How big will the balloon payment be?

The monthly payment can be calculated based on an ordinary annuity with a present value of $100,000. There are 240 payments, and the interest rate is 1 percent per month. The payment is:

$$\$100,000 = C \times [1 - (1/1.01^{240})]/.01$$
$$= C \times 90.8194$$
$$C = \$1,101.09$$

Now, there is an easy way and a hard way to determine the balloon payment. The hard way is to actually amortize the loan for 60 months to see what the balance is at that time. The easy way is to recognize that after 60 months, we have a $240 - 60 = 180$-month loan. The payment is still $1,101.09 per month, and the interest rate is still 1 percent per month. The loan balance is thus the present value of the remaining payments:

$$\text{Loan balance} = \$1,101.09 \times [1 - (1/1.01^{180})]/.01$$
$$= \$1,101.09 \times 83.3217$$
$$= \$91,744.69$$

The balloon payment is a substantial $91,744. Why is it so large? To get an idea, consider the first payment on the mortgage. The interest in the first month is $100,000 \times .01 = \$1,000$. Your payment is $1,101.09, so the loan balance declines by only $101.09. Because the loan balance declines so slowly, the cumulative "pay down" over five years is not great.

We will close this section with an example that may be of particular relevance. Federal Stafford loans are an important source of financing for many college students, helping to cover the cost of tuition, books, new cars, condominiums, and many other things. Sometimes students do not seem to fully realize that Stafford loans have a serious drawback: They must be repaid in monthly installments, usually beginning six months after the student leaves school.

Some Stafford loans are subsidized, meaning that the interest does not begin to accrue until repayment begins (this is a good thing). If you are a dependent undergraduate student under this particular option, the total debt you can run up is, at most, $23,000. The interest rate in 2014–2015 is 4.66 percent, or $4.66/12 = .3883$ percent per month. Under the "standard repayment plan," the loans are amortized over 10 years (subject to a minimum payment of $50).

Suppose you max out borrowing under this program. Beginning six months after you graduate (or otherwise depart the ivory tower), what will your monthly payment be? How much will you owe after making payments for four years?

Given our earlier discussions, see if you don't agree that your monthly payment assuming a $23,000 total loan is $240.15 per month. Also, as explained in Example 4.28, after making

SPREADSHEET APPLICATIONS

Loan Amortization Using a Spreadsheet

Loan amortization is a common spreadsheet application. To illustrate, we will set up the problem that we examined earlier: a five-year, $5,000, 9 percent loan with constant payments. Our spreadsheet looks like this:

	A	B	C	D	E	F	G	H
1								
2			Using a spreadsheet to amortize a loan					
3								
4			Loan amount:	$5,000				
5			Interest rate:	0.09				
6			Loan term:	5				
7			Loan payment:	$1,285.46				
8				Note: Payment is calculated using PMT(rate, nper, -pv, fv).				
9			Amortization table:					
10								
11		Year	Beginning	Total	Interest	Principal	Ending	
12			Balance	Payment	Paid	Paid	Balance	
13		1	$5,000.00	$1,285.46	$450.00	$835.46	$4,164.54	
14		2	4,164.54	1,285.46	374.81	910.65	3,253.88	
15		3	3,253.88	1,285.46	292.85	992.61	2,261.27	
16		4	2,261.27	1,285.46	203.51	1,081.95	1,179.32	
17		5	1,179.32	1,285.46	106.14	1,179.32	0.00	
18		Totals		6,427.31	1,427.31	5,000.00		
19								
20			Formulas in the amortization table:					
21								
22		Year	Beginning	Total	Interest	Principal	Ending	
23			Balance	Payment	Paid	Paid	Balance	
24		1	=+D4	=$D$7	=+$D$5*C13	=+D13-E13	=+C13-F13	
25		2	=+G13	=$D$7	=+$D$5*C14	=+D14-E14	=+C14-F14	
26		3	=+G14	=$D$7	=+$D$5*C15	=+D15-E15	=+C15-F15	
27		4	=+G15	=$D$7	=+$D$5*C16	=+D16-E16	=+C16-F16	
28		5	=+G16	=$D$7	=+$D$5*C17	=+D17-E17	=+C17-F17	
29								
30			Note: Totals in the amortization table are calculated using the SUM formula.					
31								

payments for four years, you still owe the present value of the remaining payments. There are 120 payments in all. After you make 48 of them (the first four years), you have 72 to go. By now, it should be easy for you to verify that the present value of $240.15 per month for 72 months at .3883 percent per month is just under $15,058, so you still have a long way to go.

Of course, it is possible to rack up much larger debts. For example, the son of former Federal Reserve Chairman Ben Bernanke was reported to be on track to graduate medical school with over $400,000 in student loans! In fact, according to the Association of American Medical Colleges, medical students who borrowed to attend medical school and graduated in 2013 had an average student loan balance of $169,901. Ouch! How long will it take the average student to pay off her medical school loans?

To answer, let's say she makes a monthly payment of $1,200, and the loan has an interest rate of 7 percent per year, or .5833 percent per month. See if you agree that it will take about 301 months, or about 25 years, to pay off the loan. Maybe MD really stands for "mucho debt"!

4.6 What Is a Firm Worth?

Suppose you are a business appraiser trying to determine the value of small companies. How can you determine what a firm is worth? One way to think about the question of how much a firm is worth is to calculate the present value of its future cash flows.

Let us consider the example of a firm that is expected to generate net cash flows (cash inflows minus cash outflows) of $5,000 at the end of the first year and $2,000 for each of the next five years. The firm can be sold for $10,000 seven years from now. After considering other investments available in the market with similar risks, the owners of the firm would like to be able to make 10 percent on their investment in the firm.

The value of the firm is found by multiplying the net cash flows by the appropriate present value factor. The value of the firm is simply the sum of the present values of the individual net cash flows.

The present value of the net cash flows is given next.

	The Present Value of the Firm		
End of Year	Net Cash Flow of the Firm	Present Value Factor (10%)	Present Value of Net Cash Flows
1	$ 5,000	.90909	$ 4,545.45
2	2,000	.82645	1,652.90
3	2,000	.75131	1,502.62
4	2,000	.68301	1,366.02
5	2,000	.62092	1,241.84
6	2,000	.56447	1,128.94
7	10,000	.51316	5,131.60
		Present value of firm	$16,569.37

Algebraically, we can write:

$$\$5,000/1.1 + 2,000/(1.1)^2 + \cdots + 2,000/(1.1)^6 + 10,000/(1.1)^7$$

We can also use the simplifying formula for an annuity:

$$\frac{\$5,000}{1.1} + \frac{(\$2,000 \times \text{PVIFA}(.10, 5)}{1.1} + \frac{\$10,000}{(1.1)^7} = \$16,569.37$$

where

$$\text{PVIFA}(.10,5) = [1 - 1/(1.1)^5]/.10$$

Suppose you have the opportunity to acquire the firm for $12,000. Should you acquire the firm? The answer is yes because the NPV is positive:

$$NPV = PV - Cost$$
$$\$4,569.37 = \$16,569.37 - \$12,000$$

The incremental value (NPV) of acquiring the firm is $4,569.37.

EXAMPLE
4.29

Firm Valuation   The Trojan Pizza Company is contemplating investing $1 million in four new outlets in Los Angeles. Andrew Lo, the firm's chief financial officer (CFO), has estimated that the investments will pay out cash flows of $200,000 per year for nine years and nothing thereafter. (The cash flows will occur at the end of each year and there will be no cash flow after year 9.) Mr. Lo has determined that the relevant discount rate for this investment is 15 percent. This is the rate of return that the firm can earn on comparable projects. Should the Trojan Pizza Company make the investments in the new outlets?

The decision can be evaluated as follows:

$$
\begin{aligned}
NPV &= -\$1,000,000 + \frac{\$200,000}{1.15} + \frac{\$200,000}{(1.15)^2} + \cdots + \frac{\$200,000}{(1.15)^9} \\
&= -\$1,000,000 + \$200,000 \times PVIFA\,(.15, 9) \\
&= -\$1,000,000 + \$954,316.78 \\
&= -\$45,683.22
\end{aligned}
$$

The present value of the four new outlets is only $954,316.78. The outlets are worth less than they cost. The Trojan Pizza Company should not make the investment because the NPV is −$45,683.22. If the Trojan Pizza Company requires a 15 percent rate of return, the new outlets are not a good investment.

SPREADSHEET APPLICATIONS

How to Calculate Present Values with Multiple Future Cash Flows Using a Spreadsheet

We can set up a basic spreadsheet to calculate the present values of the individual cash flows as follows. Notice that we have simply calculated the present values one at a time and added them up:

	A	B	C	D	E
1					
2			Using a spreadsheet to value multiple future cash flows		
3					
4	What is the present value of $200 in one year, $400 the next year, $600 the next year, and				
5	$800 the last year if the discount rate is 12 percent?				
6					
7	Rate:	0.12			
8					
9	Year	Cash flows	Present values	Formula used	
10	1	$200	$178.57	=PV($B$7,A10,0,−B10)	
11	2	$400	$318.88	=PV($B$7,A11,0,−B11)	
12	3	$600	$427.07	=PV($B$7,A12,0,−B12)	
13	4	$800	$508.41	=PV($B$7,A13,0,−B13)	
14					
15		Total PV:	**$1,432.93**	=SUM(C10:C13)	
16					
17	Notice the negative signs inserted in the PV formulas. These just make the present values have				
18	positive signs. Also, the discount rate in cell B7 is entered as $B$7 (an "absolute" reference)				
19	because it is used over and over. We could have just entered ".12" instead, but our approach is more				
20	flexible.				
21					
22					

Summary and Conclusions

1. Two basic concepts, *future value* and *present value*, were introduced in the beginning of this chapter. With a 10 percent interest rate, an investor with $1 today can generate a future value of $1.10 in a year, $1.21 [=$1 × (1.10)^2] in two years, and so on. Conversely, present value analysis places a current value on a future cash flow. With the same 10 percent interest rate, a dollar to be received in one year has a present value of $.909 (=$1/1.10) in Year 0. A dollar to be received in two years has a present value of $.826 [=$1/(1.10)^2].

2. We commonly express an interest rate as, say, 12 percent per year. However, we can speak of the interest rate as 3 percent per quarter. Although the annual percentage rate remains 12 percent (=3 percent × 4), the effective annual interest rate is 12.55 percent [=(1.03)^4 − 1]. In other words, the compounding process increases the future value of an investment. The limiting case is continuous compounding, where funds are assumed to be reinvested every infinitesimal instant.

3. A basic quantitative technique for financial decision making is net present value analysis. The net present value formula for an investment that generates cash flows (C_i) in future periods is:

$$\text{NPV} = -C_0 + \frac{C_1}{(1 + r)} + \frac{C_2}{(1 + r)^2} + \cdots + \frac{C_T}{(1 + r)^T} = -C_0 + \sum_{i=1}^{T} \frac{C_i}{(1 + r)^i}$$

The formula assumes that the cash flow at date 0 is the initial investment (a cash outflow) and r is the appropriate interest rate reflecting time and risk.

4. Frequently, the actual calculation of present value is long and tedious. The computation of the present value of a long-term mortgage with monthly payments is a good example of this. We presented four simplifying formulas:

$$\text{Perpetuity: } PV = \frac{C}{r}$$

$$\text{Growing perpetuity: } PV = \frac{C}{r - g}$$

$$\text{Annuity: } PV = C\left[\frac{1 - \dfrac{1}{(1 + r)^T}}{r}\right]$$

$$\text{Growing annuity: } PV = C\left[\frac{1 - \left(\dfrac{1 + g}{1 + r}\right)^T}{r - g}\right]$$

5. We stressed a few practical considerations in the application of these formulas:
   a. The numerator in each of the formulas, C, is the cash flow to be received *one full period hence.*
   b. Cash flows are generally irregular in practice. To avoid unwieldy problems, assumptions to create more regular cash flows are made both in this textbook and in the real world.
   c. A number of present value problems involve annuities (or perpetuities) beginning a few periods hence. Students should practice combining the annuity (or perpetuity) formula with the discounting formula to solve these problems.
   d. Annuities and perpetuities may have periods of every two or every n years, rather than once a year. The annuity and perpetuity formulas can easily handle such circumstances.
   e. We frequently encounter problems where the present value of one annuity must be equated with the present value of another annuity.

Concept Questions

1. **Compounding Periods** As you increase the length of time involved, what happens to future values? What happens to present values?

2. **Interest Rates** What happens to the future value of an annuity if you increase the rate r? What happens to the present value?

3. **Present Value** Suppose two athletes sign 10-year contracts for $80 million. In one case, we're told that the $80 million will be paid in 10 equal installments. In the other case, we're told that the $80 million will be paid in 10 installments, but the installments will increase by 5 percent per year. Who got the better deal?

4. **APR and EAR** Should lending laws be changed to require lenders to report EARs instead of APRs? Why or why not?

5. **Time Value** On subsidized Stafford loans, a common source of financial aid for college students, interest does not begin to accrue until repayment begins. Who receives a bigger subsidy, a freshman or a senior? Explain.

Use the following information to answer the next five questions:
Toyota Motor Credit Corporation (TMCC), a subsidiary of Toyota Motor Corporation, offered some securities for sale to the public on March 28, 2008. Under the terms of the deal, TMCC promised to repay the owner of one of these securities $100,000 on March 28, 2038, but investors would receive nothing until then. Investors paid TMCC $24,099 for each of these securities; so they gave up $24,099 on March 28, 2008, for the promise of a $100,000 payment 30 years later.

6. **Time Value of Money** Why would TMCC be willing to accept such a small amount today ($24,099) in exchange for a promise to repay about four times that amount ($100,000) in the future?

7. **Call Provisions** TMCC has the right to buy back the securities on the anniversary date at a price established when the securities were issued (this feature is a term of this particular deal). What impact does this feature have on the desirability of this security as an investment?

8. **Time Value of Money** Would you be willing to pay $24,099 today in exchange for $100,000 in 30 years? What would be the key considerations in answering yes or no? Would your answer depend on who is making the promise to repay?

9. **Investment Comparison** Suppose that when TMCC offered the security for $24,099 the U.S. Treasury had offered an essentially identical security. Do you think it would have had a higher or lower price? Why?

10. **Length of Investment** The TMCC security is bought and sold on the New York Stock Exchange. If you looked at the price today, do you think the price would exceed the $24,099 original price? Why? If you looked in the year 2019, do you think the price would be higher or lower than today's price? Why?

Questions and Problems

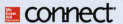

BASIC
(Questions 1–20)

1. **Simple Interest versus Compound Interest** First City Bank pays 7.5 percent simple interest on its savings account balances, whereas Second City Bank pays 7.5 percent interest compounded annually. If you made a $7,000 deposit in each bank, how much more money would you earn from your Second City Bank account at the end of 10 years?

2. **Calculating Future Values** Compute the future value of $1,000 compounded annually for

   a. 10 years at 6 percent.
   b. 10 years at 12 percent.
   c. 20 years at 6 percent.
   d. Why is the interest earned in part (c) not twice the amount earned in part (a)?

3. **Calculating Present Values** For each of the following, compute the present value:

Present Value	Years	Interest Rate	Future Value
	8	7%	$ 13,827
	13	15	43,852
	17	11	725,380
	26	18	590,710

4. **Calculating Interest Rates** Solve for the unknown interest rate in each of the following:

Present Value	Years	Interest Rate	Future Value
$ 242	4		$ 345
410	8		927
51,700	16		152,184
18,750	27		538,600

5. **Calculating the Number of Periods** Solve for the unknown number of years in each of the following:

Present Value	Years	Interest Rate	Future Value
$ 625		7%	$ 1,284
810		12	4,341
16,500		17	402,662
21,500		8	147,350

6. **Calculating the Number of Periods** At 6.5 percent interest, how long does it take to double your money? To quadruple it?

7. **Calculating Present Values** Imprudential, Inc., has an unfunded pension liability of $550 million that must be paid in 20 years. To assess the value of the firm's stock, financial analysts want to discount this liability back to the present. If the relevant discount rate is 6.4 percent, what is the present value of this liability?

8. **Calculating Rates of Return** Although appealing to more refined tastes, art as a collectible has not always performed so profitably. During 2010, Deutscher-Menzies sold *Arkie under the Shower,* a painting by renowned Australian painter Brett Whiteley, at auction for a price of $1,100,000. Unfortunately for the previous owner, he had purchased it three years earlier at a price of $1,680,000. What was his annual rate of return on this painting?

9. **Perpetuities** An investor purchasing a British consol is entitled to receive annual payments from the British government forever. What is the price of a consol that pays

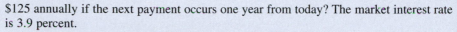

$125 annually if the next payment occurs one year from today? The market interest rate is 3.9 percent.

10. **Continuous Compounding** Compute the future value of $1,900 continuously compounded for

    a. 9 years at an APR of 12 percent.
    b. 5 years at an APR of 8 percent.
    c. 17 years at an APR of 5 percent.
    d. 10 years at an APR of 9 percent.

11. **Present Value and Multiple Cash Flows** Wilkinson Co. has identified an investment project with the following cash flows. If the discount rate is 10 percent, what is the present value of these cash flows? What is the present value at 18 percent? At 24 percent?

Year	Cash Flow
1	$ 675
2	880
3	985
4	1,530

12. **Present Value and Multiple Cash Flows** Investment X offers to pay you $3,900 per year for nine years, whereas Investment Y offers to pay you $6,100 per year for five years. Which of these cash flow streams has the higher present value if the discount rate is 5 percent? If the discount rate is 22 percent?

13. **Calculating Annuity Present Value** An investment offers $5,650 per year for 15 years, with the first payment occurring one year from now. If the required return is 8 percent, what is the value of the investment? What would the value be if the payments occurred for 40 years? For 75 years? Forever?

14 **Calculating Perpetuity Values** The Perpetual Life Insurance Co. is trying to sell you an investment policy that will pay you and your heirs $12,000 per year forever. If the required return on this investment is 4.7 percent, how much will you pay for the policy? Suppose the Perpetual Life Insurance Co. told you the policy costs $275,000. At what interest rate would this be a fair deal?

15. **Calculating EAR** Find the EAR in each of the following cases:

APR	Number of Times Compounded	EAR
6.7%	Quarterly	
12.4	Monthly	
9.8	Daily	
8.4	Infinite	

16. **Calculating APR** Find the APR, in each of the following cases:

APR	Number of Times Compounded	EAR
	Semiannually	8.9%
	Monthly	18.8
	Weekly	10.4
	Infinite	13.6

17. Calculating EAR First National Bank charges 10.3 percent compounded monthly on its business loans. First United Bank charges 10.5 percent compounded semiannually. As a potential borrower, to which bank would you go for a new loan?

18. Interest Rates Well-known financial writer Andrew Tobias argues that he can earn 177 percent per year buying wine by the case. Specifically, he assumes that he will consume one $10 bottle of fine Bordeaux per week for the next 12 weeks. He can either pay $10 per week or buy a case of 12 bottles today. If he buys the case, he receives a 10 percent discount and, by doing so, earns the 177 percent. Assume he buys the wine and consumes the first bottle today. Do you agree with his analysis? Do you see a problem with his numbers?

19. Calculating Number of Periods One of your customers is delinquent on his accounts payable balance. You've mutually agreed to a repayment schedule of $500 per month. You will charge 1.1 percent per month interest on the overdue balance. If the current balance is $18,450, how long will it take for the account to be paid off?

20. Calculating EAR Friendly's Quick Loans, Inc., offers you "three for four or I knock on your door." This means you get $3 today and repay $4 when you get your paycheck in one week (or else). What's the effective annual return Friendly's earns on this lending business? If you were brave enough to ask, what APR would Friendly's say you were paying?

INTERMEDIATE
(Questions 21–50)

21. Future Value What is the future value in six years of $1,000 invested in an account with an APR of 7.5 percent,

   a. Compounded annually?
   b. Compounded semiannually?
   c. Compounded monthly?
   d. Compounded continuously?
   e. Why does the future value increase as the compounding period shortens?

22. Simple Interest versus Compound Interest First Simple Bank pays 4.1 percent simple interest on its investment accounts. If First Complex Bank pays interest on its accounts compounded annually, what rate should the bank set if it wants to match First Simple Bank over an investment horizon of 10 years?

23. Calculating Annuities You are planning to save for retirement over the next 30 years. To do this, you will invest $750 per month in a stock account and $250 per month in a bond account. The return of the stock account is expected to be 11 percent per year, and the bond account will earn 6 percent per year. When you retire, you will combine your money into an account with an annual return of 8 percent. How much can you withdraw each month from your account assuming a 25-year withdrawal period?

24. Calculating Rates of Return Suppose an investment offers to quadruple your money in 12 months (don't believe it). What rate of return per quarter are you being offered?

25. Calculating Rates of Return You're trying to choose between two different investments, both of which have up-front costs of $75,000. Investment G returns $125,000 in six years. Investment H returns $185,000 in 10 years. Which of these investments has the higher return?

26. Growing Perpetuities Mark Weinstein has been working on an advanced technology in laser eye surgery. His technology will be available in the near term. He anticipates his first annual cash flow from the technology to be $215,000, received two years from today. Subsequent annual cash flows will grow at 3.8 percent in perpetuity. What is the present value of the technology if the discount rate is 10 percent?

27. Perpetuities A prestigious investment bank designed a new security that pays a quarterly dividend of $2.75 in perpetuity. The first dividend occurs one quarter from today. What is the price of the security if the APR is 5.3 percent, compounded quarterly?

28. **Annuity Present Values** What is the present value of an annuity of $5,500 per year, with the first cash flow received three years from today and the last one received 25 years from today? Use a discount rate of 8 percent.

29. **Annuity Present Values** What is the value today of a 15-year annuity that pays $900 a year? The annuity's first payment occurs six years from today. The annual interest rate is 11 percent for Years 1 through 5, and 13 percent thereafter.

30. **Balloon Payments** Audrey Sanborn has just arranged to purchase a $650,000 vacation home in the Bahamas with a 20 percent down payment. The mortgage has a 5.2 percent APR, compounded monthly, and calls for equal monthly payments over the next 30 years. Her first payment will be due one month from now. However, the mortgage has an eight-year balloon payment, meaning that the balance of the loan must be paid off at the end of Year 8. There were no other transaction costs or finance charges. How much will Audrey's balloon payment be in eight years?

31. **Calculating Interest Expense** You receive a credit card application from Shady Banks Savings and Loan offering an introductory rate of 2.40 percent per year, compounded monthly for the first six months, increasing thereafter to 18 percent compounded monthly. Assuming you transfer the $10,800 balance from your existing credit card and make no subsequent payments, how much interest will you owe at the end of the first year?

32. **Perpetuities** Young Pharmaceuticals is considering a drug project that costs $3.8 million today and is expected to generate end-of-year annual cash flows of $267,000, forever. At what discount rate would Young be indifferent between accepting or rejecting the project?

33. **Growing Annuity** Southern California Publishing Company is trying to decide whether to revise its popular textbook, *Financial Psychoanalysis Made Simple*. The company has estimated that the revision will cost $135,000. Cash flows from increased sales will be $48,000 the first year. These cash flows will increase by 4 percent per year. The book will go out of print five years from now. Assume that the initial cost is paid now and revenues are received at the end of each year. If the company requires a return of 10 percent for such an investment, should it undertake the revision?

34. **Growing Annuity** Your job pays you only once a year for all the work you did over the previous 12 months. Today, December 31, you just received your salary of $72,500, and you plan to spend all of it. However, you want to start saving for retirement beginning next year. You have decided that one year from today you will begin depositing 5 percent of your annual salary in an account that will earn 9 percent per year. Your salary will increase at 3.7 percent per year throughout your career. How much money will you have on the date of your retirement 40 years from today?

35. **Present Value and Interest Rates** What is the relationship between the value of an annuity and the level of interest rates? Suppose you just bought a 15-year annuity of $4,300 per year at the current interest rate of 10 percent per year. What happens to the value of your investment if interest rates suddenly drop to 5 percent? What if interest rates suddenly rise to 15 percent?

36. **Calculating the Number of Payments** You're prepared to make monthly payments of $240, beginning at the end of this month, into an account that pays 10 percent interest compounded monthly. How many payments will you have made when your account balance reaches $35,000?

37.   Calculating Annuity Present Values   You want to borrow $96,000 from your local bank to buy a new sailboat. You can afford to make monthly payments of $1,950, but no more. Assuming monthly compounding, what is the highest APR you can afford on a 60-month loan?

38.   Calculating Loan Payments   You need a 30-year, fixed-rate mortgage to buy a new home for $250,000. Your mortgage bank will lend you the money at an APR of 4.5 percent for this 360-month loan. However, you can only afford monthly payments of $950, so you offer to pay off any remaining loan balance at the end of the loan in the form of a single balloon payment. How large will this balloon payment have to be for you to keep your monthly payments at $950?

39.   Present and Future Values   The present value of the following cash flow stream is $7,300 when discounted at 7.1 percent annually. What is the value of the missing cash flow?

Year	Cash Flow
1	$1,500
2	?
3	2,700
4	2,900

40.   Calculating Present Values   You just won the TVM Lottery. You will receive $1 million today plus another 10 annual payments that increase by $275,000 per year. Thus, in one year you receive $1.275 million. In two years, you get $1.55 million, and so on. If the appropriate interest rate is 6.2 percent, what is the present value of your winnings?

41.   EAR versus APR   You have just purchased a new warehouse. To finance the purchase, you've arranged for a 30-year mortgage for 80 percent of the $5,200,000 purchase price. The monthly payment on this loan will be $27,500. What is the APR on this loan? The EAR?

42.   Present Value and Break-Even Interest   Consider a firm with a contract to sell an asset for $135,000 three years from now. The asset costs $89,000 to produce today. Given a relevant discount rate on this asset of 13 percent per year, will the firm make a profit on this asset? At what rate does the firm just break even?

43.   Present Value and Multiple Cash Flows   What is the present value of $7,500 per year, at a discount rate of 7.1 percent, if the first payment is received 6 years from now and the last payment is received 25 years from now?

44.   Variable Interest Rates   A 15-year annuity pays $1,750 per month, and payments are made at the end of each month. If the interest rate is 12 percent compounded monthly for the first seven years, and 6 percent compounded monthly thereafter, what is the present value of the annuity?

45.   Comparing Cash Flow Streams   You have your choice of two investment accounts. Investment A is a 15-year annuity that features end-of-month $1,300 payments and has an interest rate of 7.2 percent compounded monthly. Investment B is an 8 percent continuously compounded lump-sum investment, also good for 15 years. How much money would you need to invest in B today for it to be worth as much as Investment A 15 years from now?

46.   Calculating Present Value of a Perpetuity   Given an interest rate of 5.6 percent per year, what is the value at Date $t = 7$ of a perpetual stream of $2,150 annual payments that begins at Date $t = 15$?

47.   Calculating EAR   A local finance company quotes an interest rate of 17 percent on one-year loans. So, if you borrow $23,000, the interest for the year will be $3,910.

Because you must repay a total of $26,910 in one year, the finance company requires you to pay $26,910/12, or $2,242.50, per month over the next 12 months. Is the interest rate on this loan 17 percent? What rate would legally have to be quoted? What is the effective annual rate?

48. **Calculating Present Values**   A 5-year annuity of ten $6,175 semiannual payments will begin 9 years from now, with the first payment coming 9.5 years from now. If the discount rate is 11 percent compounded monthly, what is the value of this annuity five years from now? What is the value three years from now? What is the current value of the annuity?

49. **Calculating Annuities Due**   Suppose you are going to receive $16,250 per year for five years. The appropriate interest rate is 7.5 percent.

    a. What is the present value of the payments if they are in the form of an ordinary annuity? What is the present value if the payments are an annuity due?

    b. Suppose you plan to invest the payments for five years. What is the future value if the payments are an ordinary annuity? What if the payments are an annuity due?

    c. Which has the highest present value, the ordinary annuity or annuity due? Which has the highest future value? Will this always be true?

50. **Calculating Annuities Due**   You want to buy a new sports car from Muscle Motors for $64,000. The contract is in the form of a 60-month annuity due at an APR of 6.15 percent. What will your monthly payment be?

CHALLENGE
(Questions 51–75)

51. **Calculating Annuities Due**   You want to lease a set of golf clubs from Pings Ltd. The lease contract is in the form of 24 equal monthly payments at an APR of 11.2 percent, compounded monthly. Because the clubs cost $2,650 retail, Pings wants the PV of the lease payments to equal $2,650. Suppose that your first payment is due immediately. What will your monthly lease payments be?

52. **Annuities**   You are saving for the college education of your two children. They are two years apart in age; one will begin college 15 years from today and the other will begin 17 years from today. You estimate your children's college expenses to be $65,000 per year per child, payable at the beginning of each school year. The annual interest rate is 8.4 percent. How much money must you deposit in an account each year to fund your children's education? Your deposits begin one year from today. You will make your last deposit when your oldest child enters college. Assume four years of college.

53. **Growing Annuities**   Tom Adams has received a job offer from a large investment bank as a clerk to an associate banker. His base salary will be $63,000. He will receive his first annual salary payment one year from the day he begins to work. In addition, he will get an immediate $10,000 bonus for joining the company. His salary will grow at 3.8 percent each year. Each year he will receive a bonus equal to 10 percent of his salary. Mr. Adams is expected to work for 25 years. What is the present value of the offer if the discount rate is 8.5 percent?

54. **Calculating Annuities**   You have recently won the super jackpot in the Washington State Lottery. On reading the fine print, you discover that you have the following two options:

    a. You will receive 31 annual payments of $250,000, with the first payment being delivered today. The income will be taxed at a rate of 28 percent. Taxes will be withheld when the checks are issued.

    b. You will receive $530,000 now, and you will not have to pay taxes on this amount. In addition, beginning one year from today, you will receive $200,000 each year for 30 years. The cash flows from this annuity will be taxed at 28 percent.

    Using a discount rate of 6.25 percent, which option should you select?

55. Calculating Growing Annuities   You have 30 years left until retirement and want to retire with $2.2 million. Your salary is paid annually, and you will receive $83,000 at the end of the current year. Your salary will increase at 3 percent per year, and you can earn a return of 9 percent on the money you invest. If you save a constant percentage of your salary, what percentage of your salary must you save each year?

56. Balloon Payments   On September 1, 2013, Susan Chao bought a motorcycle for $34,000. She paid $2,000 down and financed the balance with a five-year loan at an annual percentage rate of 7.2 percent, compounded monthly. She started the monthly payments exactly one month after the purchase (i.e., October 1, 2013). Two years later, at the end of October 2015, Susan got a new job and decided to pay off the loan. If the bank charges her a 1 percent prepayment penalty based on the loan balance, how much must she pay the bank on November 1, 2015?

57. Calculating Annuity Values   Bilbo Baggins wants to save money to meet three objectives. First, he would like to be able to retire 30 years from now with a retirement income of $20,000 per month for 20 years, with the first payment received 30 years and 1 month from now. Second, he would like to purchase a cabin in Rivendell in 10 years at an estimated cost of $350,000. Third, after he passes on at the end of the 20 years of withdrawals, he would like to leave an inheritance of $1,500,000 to his nephew Frodo. He can afford to save $2,100 per month for the next 10 years. If he can earn an EAR of 11 percent before he retires and an EAR of 8 percent after he retires, how much will he have to save each month in Years 11 through 30?

58. Calculating Annuity Values   After deciding to buy a new car, you can either lease the car or purchase it with a three-year loan. The car you wish to buy costs $28,000. The dealer has a leasing arrangement where you pay $2,400 today and $380 per month for the next three years. If you purchase the car, you will pay it off in monthly payments over the next three years at an APR of 6 percent. You believe that you will be able to sell the car for $17,000 in three years. Should you buy or lease the car? What break-even resale price in three years would make you indifferent between buying and leasing?

59. Calculating Annuity Values   An All-Pro defensive lineman is in contract negotiations. The team has offered the following salary structure:

Time	Salary
0	$8,500,000
1	3,900,000
2	4,600,000
3	5,300,000
4	5,800,000
5	6,400,000
6	7,300,000

All salaries are to be paid in a lump sum. The player has asked you as his agent to renegotiate the terms. He wants a $10 million signing bonus payable today and a contract value increase of $2,700,000. He also wants an equal salary paid every three months, with the first paycheck three months from now. If the interest rate is 5.7 percent compounded daily, what is the amount of his quarterly check? Assume 365 days in a year.

60. Discount Interest Loans   This question illustrates what is known as *discount interest*. Imagine you are discussing a loan with a somewhat unscrupulous lender. You want to borrow $20,000 for one year. The interest rate is 15.7 percent. You and the lender agree that the interest on the loan will be .157 × $20,000 = $3,140. So, the lender deducts this interest amount from the loan up front and gives you $16,860. In this case, we say that the discount is $3,140. What's wrong here?

61. **Calculating Annuity Values**   You are serving on a jury. A plaintiff is suing the city for injuries sustained after a freak street sweeper accident. In the trial, doctors testified that it will be five years before the plaintiff is able to return to work. The jury has already decided in favor of the plaintiff. You are the foreperson of the jury and propose that the jury give the plaintiff an award to cover the following: (1) The present value of two years' back pay. The plaintiff's annual salary for the last two years would have been $37,000 and $39,000, respectively. (2) The present value of five years' future salary. You assume the salary will be $43,000 per year. (3) $150,000 for pain and suffering. (4) $25,000 for court costs. Assume that the salary payments are equal amounts paid at the end of each month. If the interest rate you choose is an EAR of 7.8 percent, what is the size of the settlement? If you were the plaintiff, would you like to see a higher or lower interest rate?

62. **Calculating EAR with Points**   You are looking at a one-year loan of $10,000. The interest rate is quoted as 8 percent plus three points. A *point* on a loan is simply 1 percent (one percentage point) of the loan amount. Quotes similar to this one are very common with home mortgages. The interest rate quotation in this example requires the borrower to pay three points to the lender up front and repay the loan later with 8 percent interest. What rate would you actually be paying here? What is the EAR for a one-year loan with a quoted interest rate of 11 percent plus two points? Is your answer affected by the loan amount?

63. **EAR versus APR**   Two banks in the area offer 30-year, $225,000 mortgages at 5.6 percent and charge a $2,900 loan application fee. However, the application fee charged by Insecurity Bank and Trust is refundable if the loan application is denied, whereas that charged by I. M. Greedy and Sons Mortgage Bank is not. The current disclosure law requires that any fees that will be refunded if the applicant is rejected be included in calculating the APR, but this is not required with nonrefundable fees (presumably because refundable fees are part of the loan rather than a fee). What are the EARs on these two loans? What are the APRs?

64. **Calculating EAR with Add-On Interest**   This problem illustrates a deceptive way of quoting interest rates called *add-on interest*. Imagine that you see an advertisement for Crazy Judy's Stereo City that reads something like this: "$1,000 Instant Credit! 17.4% Simple Interest! Three Years to Pay! Low, Low Monthly Payments!" You're not exactly sure what all this means and somebody has spilled ink over the APR on the loan contract, so you ask the manager for clarification.

Judy explains that if you borrow $1,000 for three years at 17.4 percent interest, in three years you will owe:

$$\$1,000 \times 1.174^3 = \$1,000 \times 1.61810 = \$1,618.10$$

Judy recognizes that coming up with $1,618.10 all at once might be a strain, so she lets you make "low, low monthly payments" of $1,618.10/36 = $44.95 per month, even though this is extra bookkeeping work for her.

Is the interest rate on this loan 17.4 percent? Why or why not? What is the APR on this loan? What is the EAR? Why do you think this is called add-on interest?

65. **Calculating the Number of Periods**   Your Christmas ski vacation was great, but it unfortunately ran a bit over budget. All is not lost: You just received an offer in the mail to transfer your $10,000 balance from your current credit card, which charges an annual rate of 18.6 percent, to a new credit card charging a rate of 8.2 percent. How much faster could you pay the loan off by making your planned monthly payments of $225 with the new card? What if there was a 2 percent fee charged on any balances transferred?

66. Future Value and Multiple Cash Flows An insurance company is offering a new policy to its customers. Typically the policy is bought by a parent or grandparent for a child at the child's birth. The details of the policy are as follows: The purchaser (say, the parent) makes the following six payments to the insurance company:

First birthday:	$400
Second birthday:	$500
Third birthday:	$600
Fourth birthday:	$700
Fifth birthday:	$800
Sixth birthday:	$900

After the child's sixth birthday, no more payments are made. When the child reaches age 65, he or she receives $250,000. If the relevant interest rate is 11 percent for the first six years and 7 percent for all subsequent years, is the policy worth buying?

67. Annuity Present Values and Effective Rates You have just won the lottery. You will receive $4,500,000 today, and then receive 40 payments of $1,600,000. These payments will start one year from now and will be paid every six months. A representative from Greenleaf Investments has offered to purchase all the payments from you for $30 million. If the appropriate interest rate is an APR of 9 percent compounded daily, should you take the offer? Assume there are 12 months in a year, each with 30 days.

68. Calculating Interest Rates A financial planning service offers a college savings program. The plan calls for you to make six annual payments of $11,000 each, with the first payment occurring today, your child's 12th birthday. Beginning on your child's 18th birthday, the plan will provide $25,000 per year for four years. What return is this investment offering?

69. Break-Even Investment Returns Your financial planner offers you two different investment plans. Plan X is a $20,000 annual perpetuity. Plan Y is a 10-year, $34,000 annual annuity. Both plans will make their first payment one year from today. At what discount rate would you be indifferent between these two plans?

70. Perpetual Cash Flows What is the value of an investment that pays $50,000 every *other* year forever, if the first payment occurs one year from today and the discount rate is 13 percent compounded daily? What is the value today if the first payment occurs four years from today? Assume 365 days in a year.

71. Ordinary Annuities and Annuities Due As discussed in the text, an annuity due is identical to an ordinary annuity except that the periodic payments occur at the beginning of each period and not at the end of the period. Show that the relationship between the value of an ordinary annuity and the value of an otherwise equivalent annuity due is:

$$\text{Annuity due value} = \text{Ordinary annuity value} \times (1 + r)$$

Show this for both present and future values.

72. Calculating EAR A check-cashing store is in the business of making personal loans to walk-up customers. The store makes only one-week loans at 6.5 percent interest per week.

a. What APR must the store report to its customers? What is the EAR that the customers are actually paying?

b. Now suppose the store makes one-week loans at 6.5 percent discount interest per week (see Question 60). What's the APR now? The EAR?

c. The check-cashing store also makes one-month add-on interest loans at 6.5 percent discount interest per week. Thus, if you borrow $100 for one month (four weeks), the interest will be ($100 × 1.065^4) − 100 = $28.65. Because this is discount interest, your net loan proceeds today will be $71.35. You must then repay the store

$100 at the end of the month. To help you out, though, the store lets you pay off this $100 in installments of $25 per week. What is the APR of this loan? What is the EAR?

73. **Present Value of a Growing Perpetuity**   What is the equation for the present value of a growing perpetuity with a payment of C one period from today if the payments grow by C each period?

74. **Rule of 72**   A useful rule of thumb for the time it takes an investment to double with discrete compounding is the "Rule of 72." To use the Rule of 72, you simply divide 72 by the interest rate to determine the number of periods it takes for a value today to double. For example, if the interest rate is 6 percent, the Rule of 72 says it will take $72/6 = 12$ years to double. This is approximately equal to the actual answer of 11.90 years. The Rule of 72 can also be applied to determine what interest rate is needed to double money in a specified period. This is a useful approximation for many interest rates and periods. At what rate is the Rule of 72 exact?

75. **Rule of 69.3**   A corollary to the Rule of 72 is the Rule of 69.3. The Rule of 69.3 is exactly correct except for rounding when interest rates are compounded continuously. Prove the Rule of 69.3 for continuously compounded interest.

Excel Master It! Problem

Excel is a great tool for solving problems, but with many time value of money problems, you may still need to draw a time line. For example, consider a classic retirement problem. A friend is celebrating her birthday and wants to start saving for her anticipated retirement. She has the following years to retirement and retirement spending goals:

Years until retirement	30
Amount to withdraw each year	$90,000
Years to withdraw in retirement	20
Interest rate	8%

Because your friend is planning ahead, the first withdrawal will not take place until one year after she retires. She wants to make equal annual deposits into her account for her retirement fund.

a. If she starts making these deposits in one year and makes her last deposit on the day she retires, what amount must she deposit annually to be able to make the desired withdrawals in retirement?

b. Suppose your friend has just inherited a large sum of money. Rather than making equal annual payments, she has decided to make one lump sum deposit today to cover her retirement needs. What amount does she have to deposit today?

c. Suppose your friend's employer will contribute to the account each year as part of the company's profit sharing plan. In addition, your friend expects a distribution from a family trust several years from now. What amount must she deposit annually now to be able to make the desired withdrawals in retirement? The details are:

Employer's annual contribution	$ 1,500
Years until trust fund distribution	20
Amount of trust fund distribution	$25,000

Mini Case

THE MBA DECISION

Ben Bates graduated from college six years ago with a finance undergraduate degree. Although he is satisfied with his current job, his goal is to become an investment banker. He feels that an MBA degree would allow him to achieve this goal. After examining schools, he has narrowed his choice to either Wilton University or Mount Perry College. Although internships are encouraged by both schools, to get class credit for the internship, no salary can be paid. Other than internships, neither school will allow its students to work while enrolled in its MBA program.

Ben currently works at the money management firm of Dewey and Louis. His annual salary at the firm is $65,000 per year, and his salary is expected to increase at 3 percent per year until retirement. He is currently 28 years old and expects to work for 40 more years. His current job includes a fully paid health insurance plan, and his current average tax rate is 26 percent. Ben has a savings account with enough money to cover the entire cost of his MBA program.

The Ritter College of Business at Wilton University is one of the top MBA programs in the country. The MBA degree requires two years of full-time enrollment at the university. The annual tuition is $70,000, payable at the beginning of each school year. Books and other supplies are estimated to cost $3,000 per year. Ben expects that after graduation from Wilton, he will receive a job offer for about $110,000 per year, with a $20,000 signing bonus. The salary at this job will increase at 4 percent per year. Because of the higher salary, his average income tax rate will increase to 31 percent.

The Bradley School of Business at Mount Perry College began its MBA program 16 years ago. The Bradley School is smaller and less well known than the Ritter College. Bradley offers an accelerated, one-year program, with a tuition cost of $85,000 to be paid upon matriculation. Books and other supplies for the program are expected to cost $4,500. Ben thinks that he will receive an offer of $92,000 per year upon graduation, with an $18,000 signing bonus. The salary at this job will increase at 3.5 percent per year. His average tax rate at this level of income will be 29 percent.

Both schools offer a health insurance plan that will cost $3,000 per year, payable at the beginning of the year. Ben also estimates that room and board expenses will cost $2,000 more per year at both schools than his current expenses, payable at the beginning of each year. The appropriate discount rate is 6.3 percent.

1. How does Ben's age affect his decision to get an MBA?

2. What other, perhaps nonquantifiable factors affect Ben's decision to get an MBA?

3. Assuming all salaries are paid at the end of each year, what is the best option for Ben—from a strictly financial standpoint?

4. Ben believes that the appropriate analysis is to calculate the future value of each option. How would you evaluate this statement?

5. What initial salary would Ben need to receive to make him indifferent between attending Wilton University and staying in his current position?

6. Suppose, instead of being able to pay cash for his MBA, Ben must borrow the money. The current borrowing rate is 5.4 percent. How would this affect his decision?

Appendix 4A   Net Present Value: First Principles of Finance

To access the appendix for this chapter, please logon to Connect for this title.

Appendix 4B   Using Financial Calculators

To access the appendix for this chapter, please logon to Connect for this title.

5

Net Present Value and Other Investment Rules

When a company is deciding whether to invest in a new project, large sums of money can be at stake. For example, in October 2014, Badlands NGL announced plans to build a $4 billion polyethylene plant in North Dakota, which was the largest private-sector investment made in that state's history. Earlier in 2014, Samsung Electronics announced plans to build a $14.7 billion chip facility in South Korea. The chip plant was expected to employ 150,000 workers when it was completed. But neither of these announcements came close to the Artic LNG project, which was being developed by ExxonMobil, ConocoPhillips, BP, pipeline company TransCanada, and the state of Alaska. The Artic LNG project would build a pipeline from Alaska's North Slope to allow natural gas to be sent from the area.

The cost of the pipeline and plant to clean the gas of impurities was expected to be $45 to $65 billion. Decisions such as these, with price tags in the billions, are obviously major undertakings, and the risks and rewards must be carefully weighed. In this chapter, we discuss the basic tools used in making such decisions.

In Chapter 1, we show that increasing the value of a company's stock is the goal of financial management. Thus, what we need to know is how to tell whether a particular investment will achieve that purpose or not. This chapter considers a variety of techniques financial analysts routinely use. More importantly, it shows how many of these techniques can be misleading, and it explains why the net present value approach is the right one.

5.1 Why Use Net Present Value?

Excel Master coverage online

This chapter, as well as the next two, focuses on *capital budgeting,* the decision-making process for accepting or rejecting projects. This chapter develops the basic capital budgeting methods, leaving much of the practical application to subsequent chapters. But we don't have to develop these methods from scratch. In Chapter 4, we pointed out that a dollar received in the future is worth less than a dollar received today. The reason, of course, is that today's dollar can be reinvested, yielding a greater amount in the future. And we showed in Chapter 4 that the exact worth of a dollar to be received in the future is its present value. Furthermore, Section 4.1 suggested calculating the *net present value* of any project. That is, the section suggested calculating the difference between the sum of the present values of the project's future cash flows and the initial cost of the project.

Find out more about capital budgeting for small businesses at **www .missouribusiness .net.**

   The net present value (NPV) method is the first one to be considered in this chapter. We begin by reviewing the approach with a simple example. Then, we ask why the method leads to good decisions.

EXAMPLE

Net Present Value　The Alpha Corporation is considering investing in a riskless project costing $100. The project receives $107 in one year and has no other cash flows. The riskless discount rate on comparable riskless investments is 2 percent.

The NPV of the project can easily be calculated as:

$$\$4.90 = -\$100 + \frac{\$107}{1.02} \tag{5.1}$$

From Chapter 4, we know that the project should be accepted because its NPV is positive. This is true because the project generates $107 of future cash flows from a $100 investment whereas comparable investments only generate $102.

The basic investment rule can be generalized to:

> Accept a project if the NPV is greater than zero.
>
> Reject a project if the NPV is less than zero.

We refer to this as the **NPV rule**.

Why does the NPV rule lead to good decisions? Consider the following two strategies available to the managers of Alpha Corporation:

1. Use $100 of corporate cash to invest in the project. The $107 will be paid as a dividend in one year.

2. Forgo the project and pay the $100 of corporate cash to stockholders as a dividend today.

If Strategy 2 is employed, the stockholder might deposit the cash dividend in a bank for one year. With an interest rate of 2 percent, Strategy 2 would produce cash of $102 (=$100 × 1.02) at the end of the year. The stockholder would prefer Strategy 1 because Strategy 2 produces less than $107 at the end of the year.

Our basic point is:

Accepting positive NPV projects benefits the stockholders.

How do we interpret the exact NPV of $4.90? This is the increase in the value of the firm from the project. For example, imagine that the firm today has productive assets worth $V and has $100 of cash. If the firm forgoes the project, the value of the firm today would simply be:

$$\$V + \$100$$

If the firm accepts the project, the firm will receive $107 in one year but will have no cash today. Thus, the firm's value today would be:

$$\$V + \frac{\$107}{1.02}$$

The difference between these equations is just $4.90, the net present value of Equation 5.1. Thus:

The value of the firm rises by the NPV of the project.

Note that the value of the firm is merely the sum of the values of the different projects, divisions, or other entities within the firm. This property, called **value additivity**, is quite important. It implies that the contribution of any project to a firm's value is simply the

NPV of the project. As we will see later, alternative methods discussed in this chapter do not generally have this nice property.

The NPV rule uses the correct discount rate.

One detail remains. We assumed that the project was riskless, a rather implausible assumption. Future cash flows of real-world projects are invariably risky. In other words, cash flows can only be estimated, rather than known. Imagine that the managers of Alpha *expect* the cash flow of the project to be $107 next year. That is, the cash flow could be higher, say $117, or lower, say $97. With this slight change, the project is risky. Suppose the project is about as risky as the stock market as a whole, where the expected return this year is perhaps 10 percent. Then 10 percent becomes the discount rate, implying that the NPV of the project would be:

$$-\$2.73 = -\$100 + \frac{\$107}{1.10}$$

Because the NPV is negative, the project should be rejected. This makes sense: A stockholder of Alpha receiving a $100 dividend today could invest it in the stock market, expecting a 10 percent return. Why accept a project with the same risk as the market but with an expected return of only 7 percent?

SPREADSHEET APPLICATIONS

Calculating NPVs with a Spreadsheet

Spreadsheets are commonly used to calculate NPVs. Examining the use of spreadsheets in this context also allows us to issue an important warning. Consider the following:

	A	B	C	D	E	F	G	H
1								
2			Using a spreadsheet to calculate net present values					
3								
4	A project's cost is $10,000. The cash flows are $2,000 per year for the first two years,							
5	$4,000 per year for the next two, and $5,000 in the last year. The discount rate is							
6	10 percent; what's the NPV?							
7								
8			Year	Cash flow				
9			0	-$10,000		Discount rate =	10%	
10			1	2,000				
11			2	2,000		NPV =	$2,102.72	(*wrong* answer)
12			3	4,000		NPV =	$2,312.99	(*right* answer)
13			4	4,000				
14			5	5,000				
15								
16	The formula entered in cell F11 is =NPV(F9, C9:C14). However, this gives the wrong answer because the							
17	NPV function actually calculates present values, not *net* present values.							
18								
19	The formula entered in cell F12 is =NPV(F9, C10:C14) + C9. This gives the right answer because the							
20	NPV function is used to calculate the present value of the cash flows and then the initial cost is							
21	subtracted to calculate the answer. Notice that we added cell C9 because it is already negative.							

In our spreadsheet example, notice that we have provided two answers. The first answer is wrong even though we used the spreadsheet's NPV formula. What happened is that the "NPV" function in our spreadsheet is actually a PV function; unfortunately, one of the original spreadsheet programs many years ago got the definition wrong, and subsequent spreadsheets have copied it! Our second answer shows how to use the formula properly.

The example here illustrates the danger of blindly using calculators or computers without understanding what is going on; we shudder to think of how many capital budgeting decisions in the real world are based on incorrect use of this particular function.

Conceptually, the discount rate on a risky project is the return that one can expect to earn on a financial asset of comparable risk. This discount rate is often referred to as an *opportunity cost* because corporate investment in the project takes away the stockholder's option to invest the dividend in other opportunities. Conceptually, we should look for the expected return of investments with similar risks available in the capital markets. The calculation of the discount rate is by no means impossible. We forgo the calculation in this chapter but present it in later chapters of the text.

Having shown that NPV is a sensible approach, how can we tell whether alternative methods are as good as NPV? The key to NPV is its three attributes:

1. *NPV uses cash flows.* Cash flows from a project can be used for other corporate purposes (such as dividend payments, other capital budgeting projects, or payments of corporate interest). By contrast, earnings are an artificial construct. Although earnings are useful to accountants, they should not be used in capital budgeting because they do not represent cash.

2. *NPV uses all the cash flows of the project.* Other approaches ignore cash flows beyond a particular date; beware of these approaches.

3. *NPV discounts the cash flows properly.* Other approaches may ignore the time value of money when handling cash flows. Beware of these approaches as well.

Calculating NPVs by hand can be tedious. A nearby *Spreadsheet Applications* box shows how to do it the easy way and also illustrates an important *caveat calculator*.

5.2 The Payback Period Method

DEFINING THE RULE

One of the most popular alternatives to NPV is **payback**. Here is how payback works: Consider a project with an initial investment of −$50,000. Cash flows are $30,000, $20,000, and $10,000 in the first three years, respectively. These flows are illustrated in Figure 5.1. A useful way of writing down investments like the preceding is with the notation:

$$(-\$50,000, \$30,000, \$20,000, \$10,000)$$

The minus sign in front of the $50,000 reminds us that this is a cash outflow for the investor, and the commas between the different numbers indicate that they are received—or if they are cash outflows, that they are paid out—at different times. In this example we are

Figure 5.1

Cash Flows of an Investment Project

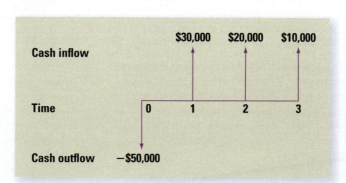

assuming that the cash flows occur one year apart, with the first one occurring the moment we decide to take on the investment.

The firm receives cash flows of $30,000 and $20,000 in the first two years, which add up to the $50,000 original investment. This means that the firm has recovered its investment within two years. In this case, two years is the *payback period* of the investment.

The **payback period rule** for making investment decisions is simple. A particular cutoff date, say two years, is selected. All investment projects that have payback periods of two years or less are accepted, and all of those that pay off in more than two years—if at all—are rejected.

PROBLEMS WITH THE PAYBACK METHOD

There are at least three problems with payback. To illustrate the first two problems, we consider the three projects in Table 5.1. All three projects have the same three-year payback period, so they should all be equally attractive—right?

Actually, they are not equally attractive, as can be seen by a comparison of different *pairs* of projects.

Problem 1: Timing of Cash Flows within the Payback Period   Let

us compare Project A with Project B. In Years 1 through 3, the cash flows of Project A rise from $20 to $50, while the cash flows of Project B fall from $50 to $20. Because the large cash flow of $50 comes earlier with Project B, its net present value must be higher. Nevertheless, we just saw that the payback periods of the two projects are identical. Thus, a problem with the payback method is that it does not consider the timing of the cash flows within the payback period. This example shows that the payback method is inferior to NPV because, as we pointed out earlier, the NPV method *discounts the cash flows properly.*

Problem 2: Payments after the Payback Period   Now consider Projects B

and C, which have identical cash flows within the payback period. However, Project C is clearly preferred because it has a cash flow of $100 in the fourth year. Thus, another problem with the payback method is that it ignores all cash flows occurring after the payback period. Because of the short-term orientation of the payback method, some valuable long-term projects are likely to be rejected. The NPV method does not have this flaw because, as we pointed out earlier, this method *uses all the cash flows of the project.*

Problem 3: Arbitrary Standard for Payback Period   We do not need

to refer to Table 5.1 when considering a third problem with the payback method. Capital markets help us estimate the discount rate used in the NPV method. The riskless rate, perhaps proxied by the yield on a U.S. Treasury instrument, would be the appropriate rate for a riskless investment; a higher rate should be used for risky projects. Later chapters of this

Table 5.1

Expected Cash Flows for Projects A through C ($)

Year	A	B	C
0	−$100	−$100	−$100
1	20	50	50
2	30	30	30
3	50	20	20
4	60	60	$100
Payback period (years)	3	3	3
NPV	21.5	26.3	53.6

textbook show how to use historical returns in the capital markets to estimate the discount rate for a risky project. However, there is no comparable guide for choosing the payback cutoff date, so the choice is somewhat arbitrary.

To illustrate the payback period problems, consider Table 5.1. Suppose the expected return on comparable risky projects is 10 percent. Then we would use a discount rate of 10 percent for these projects. If so, the NPV would be $21.5, $26.3, and $53.6 for A, B, and C respectively. When using the payback period, these projects are equal to one another (i.e. they each have a payback period of 3 years). However, when considering all cash flows, B has a higher NPV than A because of the timing of cash flows within the payback period. And C has the highest NPV because of the $100 cash flow after the payback period.

MANAGERIAL PERSPECTIVE

The payback method is often used by large, sophisticated companies when making relatively small decisions. The decision to build a small warehouse, for example, or to pay for a tune-up for a truck is the sort of decision that is often made by lower-level management. Typically, a manager might reason that a tune-up would cost, say, $200, and if it saved $120 each year in reduced fuel costs, it would pay for itself in less than two years. On such a basis the decision would be made.

Although the treasurer of the company might not have made the decision in the same way, the company endorses such decision making. Why would upper management condone or even encourage such retrograde activity in its employees? One answer would be that it is easy to make decisions using payback. Multiply the tune-up decision into 50 such decisions a month, and the appeal of this simple method becomes clearer.

The payback method also has some desirable features for managerial control. Just as important as the investment decision itself is the company's ability to evaluate the manager's decision-making ability. Under the NPV method, a long time may pass before one decides whether a decision was correct. With the payback method we know in two years whether the manager's assessment of the cash flows was correct.

It has also been suggested that firms with good investment opportunities but no available cash may justifiably use payback. For example, the payback method could be used by small, privately held firms with good growth prospects but limited access to the capital markets. Quick cash recovery increases the reinvestment possibilities for such firms.

Finally, practitioners often argue that standard academic criticisms of the payback method overstate any real-world problems with the method. For example, textbooks typically make fun of payback by positing a project with low cash inflows in the early years but a huge cash inflow right after the payback cutoff date. This project is likely to be rejected under the payback method, though its acceptance would, in truth, benefit the firm. Project C in our Table 5.1 is an example of such a project. Practitioners point out that the pattern of cash flows in these textbook examples is much too stylized to mirror the real world. In fact, a number of executives have told us that for the overwhelming majority of real-world projects, both payback and NPV lead to the same decision. In addition, these executives indicate that if an investment-like Project C were encountered in the real world, decision makers would almost certainly make ad hoc adjustments to the payback rule so that the project would be accepted.

Notwithstanding all of the preceding rationale, it is not surprising to discover that as the decisions grow in importance, which is to say when firms look at bigger projects, NPV becomes the order of the day. When questions of controlling and evaluating the manager become less important than making the right investment decision, payback is used less frequently. For big-ticket decisions, such as whether or not to buy a machine, build a factory, or acquire a company, the payback method is seldom used.

SUMMARY OF PAYBACK

The payback method differs from NPV and is therefore conceptually wrong. With its arbitrary cutoff date and its blindness to cash flows after that date, it can lead to some flagrantly foolish decisions if used too literally. Nevertheless, because of its simplicity, as well as its other mentioned advantages, companies often use it as a screen for making the myriad of minor investment decisions they continually face.

Although this means that you should be wary of trying to change approaches such as the payback method when you encounter them in companies, you should probably be careful not to accept the sloppy financial thinking they represent. After this course, you would do your company a disservice if you used payback instead of NPV when you had a choice.

5.3 The Discounted Payback Period Method

Aware of the pitfalls of payback, some decision makers use a variant called the **discounted payback period method**. Under this approach, we first discount the cash flows. Then we ask how long it takes for the discounted cash flows to equal the initial investment.

For example, suppose that the discount rate is 10 percent and the cash flows on a project are given by:

$$(-\$100, \$50, \$50, \$20)$$

This investment has a payback period of two years because the investment is paid back in that time.

To compute the project's discounted payback period, we first discount each of the cash flows at the 10 percent rate. These discounted cash flows are:

$$[-\$100, \$50/1.1, \$50/(1.1)^2, \$20/(1.1)^3] = (-\$100, \$45.45, \$41.32, \$15.03)$$

The discounted payback period of the original investment is simply the payback period for these discounted cash flows. The payback period for the discounted cash flows is slightly less than three years because the discounted cash flows over the three years are $101.80 (=$45.45 + 41.32 + 15.03). As long as the cash flows and discount rate are positive, the discounted payback period will never be smaller than the payback period because discounting reduces the value of the cash flows.

At first glance discounted payback may seem like an attractive alternative, but on closer inspection we see that it has some of the same major flaws as payback. Like payback, discounted payback first requires us to choose an arbitrary cutoff period, and then it ignores all cash flows after that date.

If we have already gone to the trouble of discounting the cash flows, we might just as well add up all the discounted cash flows and use NPV to make the decision. Although discounted payback looks a bit like NPV, it is just a poor compromise between the payback method and NPV.

5.4 The Internal Rate of Return

Now we come to the most important alternative to the NPV method: The internal rate of return, universally known as the IRR. The IRR is about as close as you can get to the NPV without actually being the NPV. The basic rationale behind the IRR method is that it provides a single number summarizing the merits of a project. That number does not depend on the interest rate prevailing in the capital market. That is why it is called the internal rate

Figure 5.2

Cash Flows for a
Simple Project

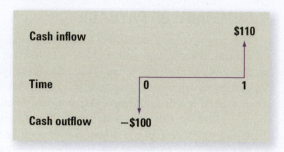

of return; the number is internal or intrinsic to the project and does not depend on anything except the cash flows of the project.

For example, consider the simple project (−$100, $110) in Figure 5.2. For a given rate, the net present value of this project can be described as:

$$NPV = -\$100 + \frac{\$110}{1 + R}$$

where R is the discount rate. What must the discount rate be to make the NPV of the project equal to zero?

We begin by using an arbitrary discount rate of .08, which yields:

$$\$1.85 = -\$100 + \frac{\$110}{1.08}$$

Because the NPV in this equation is positive, we now try a higher discount rate, such as .12. This yields:

$$-\$1.79 = -\$100 + \frac{\$110}{1.12}$$

Because the NPV in this equation is negative, we try lowering the discount rate to .10. This yields:

$$0 = -\$100 + \frac{\$110}{1.10}$$

This trial-and-error procedure tells us that the NPV of the project is zero when R equals 10 percent.[1] Thus, we say that 10 percent is the project's **internal rate of return** (IRR). In general, the IRR is the rate that causes the NPV of the project to be zero. The implication of this exercise is very simple. The firm should be equally willing to accept or reject the project if the discount rate is 10 percent. The firm should accept the project if the discount rate is below 10 percent. The firm should reject the project if the discount rate is above 10 percent.

The general investment rule is clear:

Accept the project if the IRR is greater than the discount rate. Reject the project if the IRR is less than the discount rate.

---

[1]Of course, we could have directly solved for R in this example after setting NPV equal to zero. However, with a long series of cash flows, we cannot generally solve for R directly. Instead, we are forced to use trial and error. Alternatively, we could use a financial calculator or the spreadsheet application on page 144.

Figure 5.3

Cash Flows for a
More Complex
Project

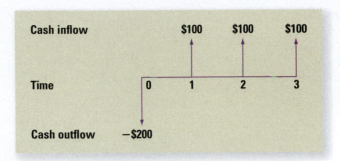

We refer to this as the **basic IRR rule**. Now we can try the more complicated example (−$200, $100, $100, $100) in Figure 5.3.

As we did previously, let's use trial and error to calculate the internal rate of return. We try 20 percent and 30 percent, yielding the following:

Discount Rate	NPV
20%	$10.65
30	−18.39

After much more trial and error, we find that the NPV of the project is zero when the discount rate is 23.38 percent. Thus, the IRR is 23.38 percent. With a 20 percent discount rate, the NPV is positive and we would accept it. However, if the discount rate were 30 percent, we would reject it.

Algebraically, IRR is the unknown in the following equation:[2]

$$0 = -\$200 + \frac{\$100}{1 + IRR} + \frac{\$100}{(1 + IRR)^2} + \frac{\$100}{(1 + IRR)^3}$$

Figure 5.4 illustrates what the IRR of a project means. The figure plots the NPV as a function of the discount rate. The curve crosses the horizontal axis at the IRR of 23.38 percent because this is where the NPV equals zero.

It should also be clear that the NPV is positive for discount rates below the IRR and negative for discount rates above the IRR. If we accept projects like this one when the discount rate is less than the IRR, we will be accepting positive NPV projects. Thus, the IRR rule coincides exactly with the NPV rule.

If this were all there were to it, the IRR rule would always coincide with the NPV rule. But the world of finance is not so kind. Unfortunately, the IRR rule and the NPV rule are consistent with each other only for examples like the one just discussed. Several problems with the IRR approach occur in more complicated situations, a topic to be examined in the next section.

The IRR in the previous example was computed through trial and error. This laborious process can be averted through spreadsheets. A nearby *Spreadsheet Applications* box shows how.

---

[2]As mentioned, we can derive the IRR directly for a problem with an initial cash outflow and up to a couple of inflows. In the case of two subsequent inflows, for example, the quadratic formula is needed. In general, however, only a financial calculator or spreadsheet application will work.

Figure 5.4
Net Present Value
(NPV) and Discount
Rates for a More
Complex Project

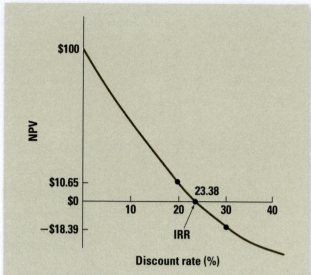

The NPV is positive for discount rates below the IRR and
negative for discount rates above the IRR.

SPREADSHEET APPLICATIONS

Calculating IRRs with a Spreadsheet

Because IRRs are so tedious to calculate by hand, financial calculators and, especially, spreadsheets are generally
used. The procedures used by various financial calculators are too different for us to illustrate here, so we will focus
on using a spreadsheet. As the following example illustrates, using a spreadsheet is very easy.

	A	B	C	D	E	F	G	H
1								
2			**Using a spreadsheet to calculate internal rates of return**					
3								
4	Suppose we have a four-year project that costs $500. The cash flows over the four-year life will be							
5	$100, $200, $300, and $400. What is the IRR?							
6								
7		Year	Cash flow					
8		0	-$500					
9		1	100		IRR =	27.3%		
10		2	200					
11		3	300					
12		4	400					
13								
14								
15	The formula entered in cell F9 is =IRR(C8:C12). Notice that the Year 0 cash flow has a negative							
16	sign representing the initial cost of the project.							
17								

5.5 Problems with the IRR Approach

DEFINITION OF INDEPENDENT AND MUTUALLY EXCLUSIVE PROJECTS

An **independent project** is one whose acceptance or rejection is independent of the acceptance or rejection of other projects. For example, imagine that McDonald's is considering putting a hamburger outlet on a remote island. Acceptance or rejection of this unit is likely to be unrelated to the acceptance or rejection of any other restaurant in its system. The remoteness of the outlet in question ensures that it will not pull sales away from other outlets.

Now consider the other extreme, **mutually exclusive investments**. What does it mean for two projects, A and B, to be mutually exclusive? You can accept A or you can accept B or you can reject both of them, but you cannot accept both of them. For example, A might be a decision to build an apartment house on a corner lot that you own, and B might be a decision to build a movie theater on the same lot.

We now present two general problems with the IRR approach that affect both independent and mutually exclusive projects. Then we deal with two problems affecting mutually exclusive projects only.

TWO GENERAL PROBLEMS AFFECTING BOTH INDEPENDENT AND MUTUALLY EXCLUSIVE PROJECTS

We begin our discussion with Project A, which has the following cash flows:

$$(-\$100, \$130)$$

The IRR for Project A is 30 percent. Table 5.2 provides other relevant information about the project. The relationship between NPV and the discount rate is shown for this project in Figure 5.5. As you can see, the NPV declines as the discount rate rises.

Problem 1: Investing or Financing?   Now consider Project B, with cash flows of:

$$(\$100, -\$130)$$

These cash flows are exactly the reverse of the flows for Project A. In Project B, the firm receives funds first and then pays out funds later. While unusual, projects of this type do exist. For example, consider a corporation conducting a seminar where the participants pay in advance. Because large expenses are frequently incurred at the seminar date, cash inflows precede cash outflows.

Table 5.2 The Internal Rate of Return and Net Present Value

Dates:	Project A			Project B			Project C		
	0	1	2	0	1	2	0	1	2
Cash flows	−$100	$130		$100	−$130		−$100	$230	−$132
IRR	30%			30%			10% and 20%		
NPV @10%	$ 18.2			−$ 18.2			0		
Accept if market rate	<30%			>30%			>10% but <20%		
Financing or investing	Investing			Financing			Mixture		

Figure 5.5   Net Present Value and Discount Rates for Projects A, B, and C

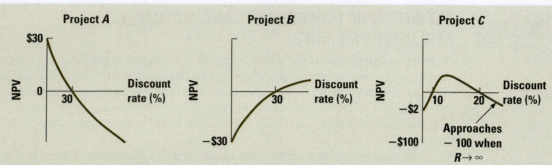

Project A has a cash outflow at Date 0 followed by a cash inflow at Date 1. Its NPV is negatively related to the discount rate.
Project B has a cash inflow at Date 0 followed by a cash outflow at Date 1. Its NPV is positively related to the discount rate.
Project C has two changes of sign in its cash flows. It has an outflow at Date 0, an inflow at Date 1, and an outflow at Date 2.
   Projects with more than one change of sign can have multiple rates of return.

Consider our trial-and-error method to calculate IRR:

$$-\$4 = +\$100 - \frac{\$130}{1.25}$$

$$\$3.70 = +\$100 - \frac{\$130}{1.35}$$

$$\$0 = +\$100 - \frac{\$130}{1.30}$$

As with Project A, the internal rate of return is 30 percent. However, notice that the net present value is *negative* when the discount rate is *below* 30 percent. Conversely, the net present value is positive when the discount rate is above 30 percent. The decision rule is exactly the opposite of our previous result. For this type of project, the following rule applies:

Accept the project when the IRR is less than the discount rate. Reject the project when the IRR is greater than the discount rate.

This unusual decision rule follows from the graph of Project B in Figure 5.5. The curve is upward sloping, implying that NPV is *positively* related to the discount rate.

The graph makes intuitive sense. Suppose the firm wants to obtain $100 immediately. It can either (1) accept Project B or (2) borrow $100 from a bank. Thus, the project is actually a substitute for borrowing. In fact, because the IRR is 30 percent, taking on Project B is equivalent to borrowing at 30 percent. If the firm can borrow from a bank at, say, only 25 percent, it should reject the project. However, if a firm can borrow from a bank only at, say, 35 percent, it should accept the project. Thus Project B will be accepted if and only if the discount rate is *above* the IRR.[3]

This should be contrasted with Project A. If the firm has $100 cash to invest, it can either (1) accept Project A or (2) lend $100 to the bank. The project is actually a substitute for lending. In fact, because the IRR is 30 percent, taking on Project A is tantamount to lending at 30 percent. The firm should accept Project A if the lending rate is below 30 percent. Conversely, the firm should reject Project A if the lending rate is above 30 percent.

---

[3]This paragraph implicitly assumes that the cash flows of the project are risk-free. In this way we can treat the borrowing rate as the discount rate for a firm needing $100. With risky cash flows, another discount rate would be chosen. However, the intuition behind the decision to accept when the IRR is less than the discount rate would still apply.

Because the firm initially pays out money with Project A but initially receives money with Project B, we refer to Project A as an *investing type project* and Project B as a *financing type project*. Investing type projects are the norm. Because the IRR rule is reversed for financing type projects, be careful when using it with this type of project.

Problem 2: Multiple Rates of Return   Suppose the cash flows from a project are:

$$(-\$100, \$230, -\$132)$$

Because this project has a negative cash flow, a positive cash flow, and another negative cash flow, we say that the project's cash flows exhibit two changes of sign, or "flip-flops." Although this pattern of cash flows might look a bit strange at first, many projects require outflows of cash after some inflows. An example would be a strip-mining project. The first stage in such a project is the initial investment in excavating the mine. Profits from operating the mine are received in the second stage. The third stage involves a further investment to reclaim the land and satisfy the requirements of environmental protection legislation. Cash flows are negative at this stage.

Projects financed by lease arrangements may produce a similar pattern of cash flows. Leases often provide substantial tax subsidies, generating cash inflows after an initial investment. However, these subsidies decline over time, frequently leading to negative cash flows in later years. (The details of leasing will be discussed in a later chapter.)

It is easy to verify that this project has not one but two IRRs, 10 percent and 20 percent.[4] In a case like this, the IRR does not make any sense. What IRR are we to use—10 percent or 20 percent? Because there is no good reason to use one over the other, IRR simply cannot be used here.

Why does this project have multiple rates of return? Project C generates multiple internal rates of return because both an inflow and an outflow occur after the initial investment. In general, these flip-flops or changes in sign produce multiple IRRs. In theory, a cash flow stream with K changes in sign can have up to K sensible internal rates of return (IRRs above –100 percent). Therefore, because Project C has two changes in sign, it can have as many as two IRRs. As we pointed out, projects whose cash flows change sign repeatedly can occur in the real world.

NPV Rule   Of course, we should not be too worried about multiple rates of return. After all, we can always fall back on the NPV rule. Figure 5.5 plots the NPV of Project C $(-\$100, \$230, -\$132)$ as a function of the discount rate. As the figure shows, the NPV is zero at both 10 percent and 20 percent and negative outside the range. Thus, the NPV rule tells us to accept the project if the appropriate discount rate is between 10 percent and 20 percent. The project should be rejected if the discount rate lies outside this range.

---

[4]The calculations are:

$$-\$100 + \frac{\$230}{1.1} - \frac{\$132}{(1.1)^2}$$

$$-\$100 + 209.09 - 109.09 = 0$$

and

$$-\$100 + \frac{\$230}{1.2} - \frac{\$132}{(1.2)^2}$$

$$-\$100 + 191.67 - 91.67 = 0$$

Thus, we have multiple rates of return.

Modified IRR As an alternative to NPV, we now introduce the **modified IRR (MIRR)** method, which handles the multiple IRR problem by combining cash flows until only one change in sign remains. To see how it works, consider Project C again. With a discount rate of, say, 14 percent, the value of the last cash flow, $-\$132$, is:

$$-\$132/1.14 = -\$115.79$$

as of Date 1. Because $230 is already received at that time, the "adjusted" cash flow at Date 1 is $114.21 ($=\$230 - 115.79$). Thus, the MIRR approach produces the following two cash flows for the project:

$$(-\$100, \$114.21)$$

Note that by discounting and then combining cash flows, we are left with only one change in sign. The IRR rule can now be applied. The IRR of these two cash flows is 14.21 percent, implying that the project should be accepted given our assumed discount rate of 14 percent.

Of course, Project C is relatively simple to begin with: It has only three cash flows and two changes in sign. However, the same procedure can easily be applied to more complex projects—that is, just keep discounting and combining the later cash flows until only one change of sign remains.

Although this adjustment does correct for multiple IRRs, it appears, at least to us, to violate the "spirit" of the IRR approach. As stated earlier, the basic rationale behind the IRR method is that it provides a single number summarizing the merits of a project. That number does not depend on the discount rate. In fact, that is why it is called the internal rate of return: The number is *internal,* or intrinsic, to the project and does not depend on anything except the project's cash flows. By contrast, MIRR is clearly a function of the discount rate. However, a firm using this adjustment will avoid the multiple IRR problem, just as a firm using the NPV rule will avoid it.[5]

The Guarantee against Multiple IRRs If the first cash flow of a project is negative (because it is the initial investment) and if all of the remaining flows are positive, there can be only a single, unique IRR, no matter how many periods the project lasts. This is easy to understand by using the concept of the time value of money. For example, it is simple to verify that Project A in Table 5.2 has an IRR of 30 percent because using a 30 percent discount rate gives:

$$NPV = -\$100 + \$130/(1.3)$$
$$= \$0$$

---

[5]There is more than one version of modified IRR. In the discussion above, MIRR combines the present values of the later cash flows, leaving a set of cash flows with only one change in sign. Alternatively, investors often combine the future values of the cash flows as of the termination date of the project. In our example, the sum of the future values, as of Date 2, is:

Date of cash flow	1	2	Sum
Future value as of Date 2	$230 (1.14) = $262.20	$-$132	130.20 = 262.20 + (−132)

Under this version, the MIRR of the project becomes:

$$-100 + \frac{130.20}{(1 + MIRR)^2}$$

implying an MIRR of 14.11 percent.

The MIRR here differs from the MIRR of 14.21 percent in the text. However, both MIRRs are above the discount rate of 14 percent, implying acceptance of the project. This consistency should always hold between the two variants of modified IRR. And, as in the version in the text, the multiple IRR problem is avoided.

How do we know that this is the only IRR? Suppose we were to try a discount rate greater than 30 percent. In computing the NPV, changing the discount rate does not change the value of the initial cash flow of −$100 because that cash flow is not discounted. Raising the discount rate can only lower the present value of the future cash flows. In other words, because the NPV is zero at 30 percent, any increase in the rate will push the NPV into the negative range. Similarly, if we try a discount rate of less than 30 percent, the overall NPV of the project will be positive. Though this example has only one positive flow, the above reasoning still implies a single, unique IRR if there are many inflows (but no outflows) after the initial investment.

If the initial cash flow is positive—and if all of the remaining flows are negative— there can only be a single, unique IRR. This result follows from similar reasoning. Both these cases have only one change of sign or flip-flop in the cash flows. Thus, we are safe from multiple IRRs whenever there is only one sign change in the cash flows.

General Rules   The following chart summarizes our rules:

Flows	Number of IRRs	IRR Criterion	NPV Criterion
First cash flow is negative and all remaining cash flows are positive.	1	Accept if IRR > R. Reject if IRR < R.	Accept if NPV > 0. Reject if NPV < 0.
First cash flow is positive and all remaining cash flows are negative.	1	Accept if IRR < R. Reject if IRR > R.	Accept if NPV > 0. Reject if NPV < 0.
Some cash flows after first are positive and some cash flows after first are negative.	May be more than 1.	No valid IRR.	Accept if NPV > 0. Reject if NPV < 0.

Note that the NPV criterion is the same for each of the three cases. In other words, NPV analysis is always appropriate. Conversely, the IRR can be used only in certain cases. When it comes to NPV, the preacher's words, "You just can't lose with the stuff I use," clearly apply.

PROBLEMS SPECIFIC TO MUTUALLY EXCLUSIVE PROJECTS

As mentioned earlier, two or more projects are mutually exclusive if the firm can accept only one of them. We now present two problems dealing with the application of the IRR approach to mutually exclusive projects. These two problems are quite similar, though logically distinct.

The Scale Problem   A professor we know motivates class discussions of this topic with this statement: "Students, I am prepared to let one of you choose between two mutually exclusive 'business' propositions. Opportunity 1—You give me $1 now and I'll give you $1.50 back at the end of the class period. Opportunity 2—You give me $10 and I'll give you $11 back at the end of the class period. You can choose only one of the two opportunities. And you cannot choose either opportunity more than once. I'll pick the first volunteer."

Which would you choose? The correct answer is Opportunity 2.[6] To see this, look at the following chart:

	Cash Flow at Beginning of Class	Cash Flow at End of Class (90 Minutes Later)	NPV[7]	IRR
Opportunity 1	−$ 1	+$ 1.50	$ .50	50%
Opportunity 2	−10	+11.00	1.00	10

As we have stressed earlier in the text, one should choose the opportunity with the highest NPV. This is Opportunity 2 in the example. Or, as one of the professor's students explained it, "I'm bigger than the professor, so I know I'll get my money back. And I have $10 in my pocket right now so I can choose either opportunity. At the end of the class, I'll be able to buy one song on iTunes with Opportunity 2 and still have my original investment, safe and sound. The profit on Opportunity 1 pays for only one half of a song."

This business proposition illustrates a defect with the internal rate of return criterion. The basic IRR rule indicates the selection of Opportunity 1 because the IRR is 50 percent. The IRR is only 10 percent for Opportunity 2.

Where does IRR go wrong? The problem with IRR is that it ignores issues of *scale*. Although Opportunity 1 has a greater IRR, the investment is much smaller. In other words, the high percentage return on Opportunity 1 is more than offset by the ability to earn at least a decent return[8] on a much bigger investment under Opportunity 2.

Because IRR seems to be misguided here, can we adjust or correct it? We illustrate how in the next example.

EXAMPLE 5.2

NPV versus IRR   Stanley Jaffe and Sherry Lansing have just purchased the rights to *Corporate Finance: The Motion Picture*. They will produce this major motion picture on either a small budget or a big budget. Here are the estimated cash flows:

	Cash Flow at Date 0	Cash Flow at Date 1	NPV @25%	IRR
Small budget	−$10 million	$40 million	$22 million	300%
Large budget	−25 million	65 million	27 million	160

Because of high risk, a 25 percent discount rate is considered appropriate. Sherry wants to adopt the large budget because the NPV is higher. Stanley wants to adopt the small budget because the IRR is higher. Who is right?

---

[6]The professor uses real money here. Though many students have done poorly on the professor's exams over the years, no student ever chose Opportunity 1. The professor claims that his students are "money players."

[7]We assume a zero rate of interest because his class lasted only 90 minutes. It just seemed like a lot longer.

[8]A 10 percent return is more than decent over a 90-minute interval!

For the reasons espoused in the classroom example, NPV is correct. Hence Sherry is right. Howwever, Stanley is very stubborn where IRR is concerned. How can Sherry justify the large budget to Stanley using the IRR approach?

This is where *incremental IRR* comes in. Sherry calculates the incremental cash flows from choosing the large budget instead of the small budget as follows:

	Cash Flow at Date 0 (in $ millions)	Cash Flow at Date 1 (in $ millions)
Incremental cash flows from choosing large budget instead of small budget	$-\$25 - (-10) = -\$15$	$\$65 - 40 = \$25$

This chart shows that the incremental cash flows are −$15 million at Date 0 and $25 million at Date 1. Sherry calculates incremental IRR as follows:

Formula for Calculating the Incremental IRR:

$$0 = -\$15 \text{ million} + \frac{\$25 \text{ million}}{1 + IRR}$$

IRR equals 66.67 percent in this equation, implying that the **incremental IRR** is 66.67 percent. Incremental IRR is the IRR on the incremental investment from choosing the large project instead of the small project.

In addition, we can calculate the NPV of the incremental cash flows:

NPV of Incremental Cash Flows:

$$-\$15 \text{ million} + \frac{\$25 \text{ million}}{1.25} = \$5 \text{ million}$$

We know the small-budget picture would be acceptable as an independent project because its NPV is positive. We want to know whether it is beneficial to invest an additional $15 million to make the large-budget picture instead of the small-budget picture. In other words, is it beneficial to invest an additional $15 million to receive an additional $25 million next year? First, our calculations show the NPV on the incremental investment to be positive. Second, the incremental IRR of 66.67 percent is higher than the discount rate of 25 percent. For both reasons, the incremental investment can be justified, so the large-budget movie should be made. The second reason is what Stanley needed to hear to be convinced.

In review, we can handle this example (or any mutually exclusive example) in one of three ways:

1. *Compare the NPVs of the two choices.* The NPV of the large-budget picture is greater than the NPV of the small-budget picture. That is, $27 million is greater than $22 million.

2. *Calculate the incremental NPV from making the large-budget picture instead of the small-budget picture.* Because the incremental NPV equals $5 million, we choose the large-budget picture.

3. *Compare the incremental IRR to the discount rate.* Because the incremental IRR is 66.67 percent and the discount rate is 25 percent, we take the large-budget picture.

All three approaches always give the same decision. However, we must *not* compare the IRRs of the two pictures. If we did, we would make the wrong choice. That is, we would accept the small-budget picture.

Although students frequently think that problems of scale are relatively unimportant, the truth is just the opposite. No real-world project comes in one clear-cut size. Rather, the firm has to *determine* the best size for the project. The movie budget of $25 million is not fixed in stone. Perhaps an extra $1 million to hire a bigger star or to film at a better location will increase the movie's gross. Similarly, an industrial firm must decide whether it wants a warehouse of, say, 500,000 square feet or 600,000 square feet. And, earlier in the chapter, we imagined McDonald's opening an outlet on a remote island. If it does this, it must decide how big the outlet should be. For almost any project, someone in the firm has to decide on its size, implying that problems of scale abound in the real world.

One final note here. Students often ask which project should be subtracted from the other in calculating incremental flows. Notice that we are subtracting the smaller project's cash flows from the bigger project's cash flows. This leaves an *outflow* at Date 0. We then use the basic IRR rule on the incremental flows.[9]

The Timing Problem   Next we illustrate another, somewhat similar problem with the IRR approach to evaluating mutually exclusive projects.

EXAMPLE

Mutually Exclusive Investments   Suppose that the Kaufold Corporation has two alternative uses for a warehouse. It can store toxic waste containers (Investment A) or electronic equipment (Investment B). The cash flows are as follows:

	Cash Flow at Year				NPV			
Year:	0	1	2	3	@ 0%	@10%	@15%	IRR
Investment A	−$10,000	$10,000	$1,000	$ 1,000	$2,000	$669	$109	16.04%
Investment B	−10,000	1,000	1,000	12,000	4,000	751	−484	12.94

We find that the NPV of Investment B is higher with low discount rates, and the NPV of Investment A is higher with high discount rates. This is not surprising if you look closely at the cash flow patterns. The cash flows of A occur early, whereas the cash flows of B occur later. If we assume a high discount rate, we favor Investment A because we are implicitly assuming that the early cash flow (for example, $10,000 in Year 1) can be reinvested at that rate. Because most of Investment B's cash flows occur in Year 3, B's value is relatively high with low discount rates.

The patterns of cash flow for both projects appear in Figure 5.6. Project A has an NPV of $2,000 at a discount rate of zero. This is calculated by simply adding up the cash flows without discounting them. Project B has an NPV of $4,000 at the zero rate. However, the NPV of Project B declines more rapidly as the discount rate increases than does the NPV of Project A. As we mentioned, this occurs because the cash flows of B occur later. Both projects have the same NPV at a discount rate of 10.55 percent. The IRR for a project is

---

[9]Alternatively, we could have subtracted the larger project's cash flows from the smaller project's cash flows. This would have left an *inflow* at Date 0, making it necessary to use the IRR rule for financing situations. This would work, but we find it more confusing.

Figure 5.6

Net Present Value and the Internal Rate of Return for Mutually Exclusive Projects

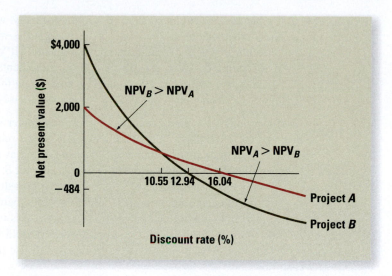

the rate at which the NPV equals zero. Because the NPV of B declines more rapidly, B actually has a lower IRR.

As with the movie example, we can select the better project with one of three different methods:

1. *Compare NPVs of the two projects.* Figure 5.6 aids our decision. If the discount rate is below 10.55 percent, we should choose Project B because B has a higher NPV. If the rate is above 10.55 percent, we should choose Project A because A has a higher NPV.

2. *Compare incremental IRR to discount rate.* Method 1 employed NPV. Another way of determining whether A or B is a better project is to subtract the cash flows of A from the cash flows of B and then to calculate the IRR. This is the incremental IRR approach we spoke of earlier.

   Here are the incremental cash flows:

						NPV of Incremental Cash Flows		
Year:	0	1	2	3	Incremental IRR	@ 0%	@10%	@15%
B − A	0	−$9,000	0	$11,000	10.55%	$2,000	$83	−$593

This chart shows that the incremental IRR is 10.55 percent. In other words, the NPV on the incremental investment is zero when the discount rate is 10.55 percent. Thus, if the relevant discount rate is below 10.55 percent, Project B is preferred to Project A. If the relevant discount rate is above 10.55 percent, Project A is preferred to Project B.

Figure 5.6 shows that the NPVs of the two projects are equal when the discount rate is 10.55 percent. In other words, the *crossover rate* in the figure is 10.55. The incremental cash flows chart shows that the incremental IRR is also 10.55 percent. It is not a coincidence that the crossover rate and the incremental IRR are the same; this equality must *always* hold. The incremental IRR is the rate that causes the incremental cash flows to have zero NPV. The incremental cash flows have zero NPV when the two projects have the same NPV.

3. *Calculate NPV on incremental cash flows.* Finally, we could calculate the NPV on the incremental cash flows. The chart that appears with the previous method displays these NPVs. We find that the incremental NPV is positive when the discount rate is either 0 percent or 10 percent. The incremental NPV is negative if the discount rate is 15 percent. If the NPV is positive on the incremental flows, we should choose *B*. If the NPV is negative, we should choose *A*.

In summary, the same decision is reached whether we (1) compare the NPVs of the two projects, (2) compare the incremental IRR to the relevant discount rate, or (3) examine the NPV of the incremental cash flows. However, as mentioned earlier, we should *not* compare the IRR of Project *A* with the IRR of Project *B*.

We suggested earlier that we should subtract the cash flows of the smaller project from the cash flows of the bigger project. What do we do here when the two projects have the same initial investment? Our suggestion in this case is to perform the subtraction so that the *first* nonzero cash flow is negative. In the Kaufold Corp. example we achieved this by subtracting *A* from *B*. In this way, we can still use the basic IRR rule for evaluating cash flows.

The preceding examples illustrate problems with the IRR approach in evaluating mutually exclusive projects. Both the professor–student example and the motion picture example illustrate the problem that arises when mutually exclusive projects have different initial investments. The Kaufold Corp. example illustrates the problem that arises when mutually exclusive projects have different cash flow timing. When working with mutually exclusive projects, it is not necessary to determine whether it is the scale problem or the timing problem that exists. Very likely both occur in any real-world situation. Instead, the practitioner should simply use either an incremental IRR or an NPV approach.

REDEEMING QUALITIES OF IRR

IRR probably survives because it fills a need that NPV does not. People seem to want a rule that summarizes the information about a project in a single rate of return. This single rate gives people a simple way of discussing projects. For example, one manager in a firm might say to another, "Remodeling the north wing has a 20 percent IRR."

To their credit, however, companies that employ the IRR approach seem to understand its deficiencies. For example, companies frequently restrict managerial projections of cash flows to be negative at the beginning and strictly positive later. Perhaps, then, both the ability of the IRR approach to capture a complex investment project in a single number, and the ease of communicating that number explain the survival of the IRR.

A TEST

To test your knowledge, consider the following two statements:

1. You must know the discount rate to compute the NPV of a project, but you compute the IRR without referring to the discount rate.

2. Hence, the IRR rule is easier to apply than the NPV rule because you don't use the discount rate when applying IRR.

The first statement is true. The discount rate is needed to *compute* NPV. The IRR is *computed* by solving for the rate where the NPV is zero. No mention is made of the discount rate in the mere computation. However, the second statement is false. To *apply* IRR, you must compare the internal rate of return with the discount rate. Thus the discount rate is needed for making a decision under either the NPV or IRR approach.

5.6   The Profitability Index

Another method used to evaluate projects is called the **profitability index**. It is the ratio of the present value of the future expected cash flows *after* initial investment divided by the amount of the initial investment. The profitability index can be represented as:

$$\text{Profitability index (PI)} = \frac{\text{PV of cash flows } \textit{subsequent} \text{ to initial investment}}{\text{Initial investment}}$$

EXAMPLE
5.4

Profitability Index   Hiram Finnegan Inc. (HFI) applies a 12 percent discount rate to two investment opportunities.

Project	Cash Flows ($000,000)			PV @ 12% of Cash Flows Subsequent to Initial Investment ($000,000)	Profitability Index	NPV @12% ($000,000)
	C_0	C_1	C_2			
1	−$20	$70	$10	$70.5	3.53	$50.5
2	−10	15	40	45.3	4.53	35.3

CALCULATION OF PROFITABILITY INDEX

The profitability index is calculated for Project 1 as follows. The present value of the cash flows *after* the initial investment is:

$$\$70.5 = \frac{\$70}{1.12} + \frac{\$10}{(1.12)^2}$$

The profitability index is obtained by dividing this result by the initial investment of $20. This yields:

$$3.53 = \frac{\$70.5}{\$20}$$

Application of the Profitability Index   How do we use the profitability index? We consider three situations:

1. *Independent projects:* Assume that HFI's two projects are independent. According to the NPV rule, both projects should be accepted because NPV is positive in each case. The profitability index (PI) is greater than 1 whenever the NPV is positive. Thus, the PI *decision rule* is:

   • Accept an independent project if PI > 1.
   • Reject it if PI < 1.

2. *Mutually exclusive projects:* Let us now assume that HFI can only accept one of its two projects. NPV analysis says accept Project 1 because this project has the bigger NPV. Because Project 2 has the higher PI, the profitability index leads to the wrong selection.

For mutually exclusive projects, the profitability index suffers from the scale problem that IRR also suffers from. Project 2 is smaller than Project 1. Because the PI is a ratio, it ignores Project 1's larger investment. Thus, like IRR, PI ignores differences of scale for mutually exclusive projects.

However, like IRR, the flaw with the PI approach can be corrected using incremental analysis. We write the incremental cash flows after subtracting Project 2 from Project 1 as follows:

	Cash Flows ($000,000)			PV @ 12% of Cash Flows Subsequent to Initial Investment ($000,000)	Profit-ability Index	NPV @12% ($000,000)
Project	C_0	C_1	C_2			
1–2	−$10	$55	−$30	$25.2	2.52	$15.2

Because the profitability index on the incremental cash flows is greater than 1.0, we should choose the bigger project—that is, Project 1. This is the same decision we get with the NPV approach.

3. *Capital rationing:* The first two cases implicitly assumed that HFI could always attract enough capital to make any profitable investments. Now consider the case when the firm does not have enough capital to fund all positive NPV projects. This is the case of **capital rationing**.

Imagine that the firm has a third project, as well as the first two. Project 3 has the following cash flows:

	Cash Flows ($000,000)			PV @ 12% of Cash Flows Subsequent to Initial Investment ($000,000)	Profit-ability Index	NPV @12% ($000,000)
Project	C_0	C_1	C_2			
3	−$10	−$5	$60	$43.4	4.34	$33.4

Further, imagine that (1) the projects of Hiram Finnegan Inc. are independent, but (2) the firm has only $20 million to invest. Because Project 1 has an initial investment of $20 million, the firm cannot select both this project and another one. Conversely, because Projects 2 and 3 have initial investments of $10 million each, both these projects can be chosen. In other words, the cash constraint forces the firm to choose either Project 1 or Projects 2 and 3.

What should the firm do? Individually, Projects 2 and 3 have lower NPVs than Project 1 has. However, when the NPVs of Projects 2 and 3 are added together, the sum is higher than the NPV of Project 1. Thus, common sense dictates that Projects 2 and 3 should be accepted.

What does our conclusion have to say about the NPV rule or the PI rule? In the case of limited funds, we cannot rank projects according to their NPVs. Instead we should rank them according to the ratio of present value to initial investment. This is the PI rule. Both Project 2 and Project 3 have higher PI ratios than does Project 1. Thus they should be ranked ahead of Project 1 when capital is rationed.

The usefulness of the profitability index under capital rationing can be explained in military terms. The Pentagon speaks highly of a weapon with a lot of "bang for the buck." In capital budgeting, the profitability index measures the bang (the dollar return) for the buck invested. Hence it is useful for capital rationing.

It should be noted that the profitability index does not work if funds are also limited beyond the initial time period. For example, if heavy cash outflows elsewhere in the firm were to occur at Date 1, Project 3, which also has a cash outflow at Date 1, might need to be rejected. In other words, the profitability index cannot handle capital rationing over multiple time periods.

In addition, what economists term *indivisibilities* may reduce the effectiveness of the PI rule. Imagine that HFI has $30 million available for capital investment, not just $20 million. The firm now has enough cash for Projects 1 and 2. Because the sum of the NPVs of these two projects is greater than the sum of the NPVs of Projects 2 and 3, the firm would be better served by accepting Projects 1 and 2. But because Projects 2 and 3 still have the highest profitability indexes, the PI rule now leads to the wrong decision. Why does the PI rule lead us astray here? The key is that Projects 1 and 2 use up all of the $30 million, whereas Projects 2 and 3 have a combined initial investment of only $20 million (= $10 + 10). If Projects 2 and 3 are accepted, the remaining $10 million must be left in the bank.

This situation points out that care should be exercised when using the profitability index in the real world. Nevertheless, while not perfect, the profitability index goes a long way toward handling capital rationing.

5.7 The Practice of Capital Budgeting

So far this chapter has asked "Which capital budgeting methods should companies be using?" An equally important question is this: Which methods *are* companies using? Table 5.3 helps answer this question. As can be seen from the table, approximately three-quarters of U.S. and Canadian companies use the IRR and NPV methods. This is not surprising, given the theoretical advantages of these approaches. Over half of these companies use the payback method, a rather surprising result given the conceptual problems with this approach. And while discounted payback represents a theoretical improvement over regular payback, the usage here is far less. Perhaps companies are attracted to the user-friendly nature of payback. In addition, the flaws of this approach, as mentioned in the current chapter, may be relatively easy to correct. For example, while the payback method ignores

Table 5.3
Percentage of CFOs Who Always or Almost Always Use a Given Technique

	% Always or Almost Always
Internal rate of return (IRR)	75.6%
Net present value (NPV)	74.9
Payback method	56.7
Discounted payback	29.5
Profitability index	11.9

SOURCE: Adapted from Figure 2 from John R. Graham and Campbell R. Harvey, "The Theory and Practice of Corporate Finance: Evidence from the Field," *Journal of Financial Economics* 60 (2001). Based on a survey of 392 CFOs.

all cash flows after the payback period, an alert manager can make ad hoc adjustments for a project with back-loaded cash flows.

Capital expenditures by individual corporations can add up to enormous sums for the economy as a whole. For example, in 2014, ExxonMobil announced that it expected to make about $39.8 billion in capital outlays during the year, down 6 percent from the record $42.5 billion in 2013. The company further indicated that it expected to spend an average of $37 billion per year through 2017. About the same time, Chevron announced that its capital budget for 2014 would be $39.8 billion, down $2 billion from the previous year, and ConocoPhillips announced a capital expenditure budget of $16.7 billion for 2014. Other companies with large capital spending budgets in 2014 were Intel, which projected capital spending of about $11 billion, and Samsung Electronics, which projected capital spending of about $11.5 billion.

Large-scale capital spending is often an industrywide occurrence. For example, in 2014, capital spending in the semiconductor industry was expected to reach $60.9 billion. This tidy sum represented a 5.5 percent increase over industry capital spending in 2013.

According to information released by the U.S. Census Bureau in 2013, capital investment for the economy as a whole was $1.090 trillion in 2009, $1.106 trillion in 2010, and $1.226 trillion in 2011. The totals for the three years therefore equaled approximately $3.422 trillion! Given the sums at stake, it is not too surprising that successful corporations carefully analyze capital expenditures.

One might expect the capital budgeting methods of large firms to be more sophisticated than the methods of small firms. After all, large firms have the financial resources to hire more sophisticated employees. Table 5.4 provides some support for this idea. Here firms indicate frequency of use of the various capital budgeting methods on a scale of 0 (never) to 4 (always). Both the IRR and NPV methods are used more frequently, and payback less frequently, in large firms than in small firms. Conversely, large and small firms employ the last two approaches about equally.

The use of quantitative techniques in capital budgeting varies with the industry. As one would imagine, firms that are better able to estimate cash flows are more likely to use NPV. For example, estimation of cash flow in certain aspects of the oil business is quite feasible. Because of this, energy-related firms were among the first to use NPV analysis. Conversely, the cash flows in the motion picture business are very hard to project. The grosses of great hits like *Spiderman, Harry Potter,* and *Star Wars* were far, far greater than anyone imagined. The big failures like *Alamo* and *Waterworld* were unexpected as well. Because of this, NPV analysis is frowned upon in the movie business.

Table 5.4

Frequency of Use of Various Capital Budgeting Methods

	Large Firms	Small Firms
Internal rate of return (IRR)	3.41	2.87
Net present value (NPV)	3.42	2.83
Payback method	2.25	2.72
Discounted payback	1.55	1.58
Profitability index	.75	.78

Firms indicate frequency of use on a scale from 0 (never) to 4 (always). Numbers in table are averages across respondents.
SOURCE: Adapted from Table 2 from Graham and Harvey (2001), op. cit.

How does Hollywood perform capital budgeting? The information that a studio uses to accept or reject a movie idea comes from the *pitch*. An independent movie producer schedules an extremely brief meeting with a studio to pitch his or her idea for a movie. Consider the following four paragraphs of quotes concerning the pitch from the thoroughly delightful book *Reel Power*:[10]

> "They [studio executives] don't want to know too much," says Ron Simpson. "They want to know concept. . . . They want to know what the three-liner is, because they want it to suggest the ad campaign. They want a title. . . . They don't want to hear any esoterica. And if the meeting lasts more than five minutes, they're probably not going to do the project."
>
> "A guy comes in and says this is my idea: '*Jaws* on a spaceship,'" says writer Clay Frohman (*Under Fire*). "And they say, 'Brilliant, fantastic.' Becomes *Alien*. That is *Jaws* on a spaceship, ultimately. . . . And that's it. That's all they want to hear. Their attitude is 'Don't confuse us with the details of the story.'"
>
> ". . . Some high-concept stories are more appealing to the studios than others. The ideas liked best are sufficiently original that the audience will not feel it has already seen the movie, yet similar enough to past hits to reassure executives wary of anything too far-out. Thus, the frequently used shorthand: It's *Flashdance* in the country (*Footloose*) or *High Noon* in outer space (*Outland*)."
>
> ". . . One gambit not to use during a pitch," says executive Barbara Boyle, "is to talk about big box-office grosses your story is sure to make. Executives know as well as anyone that it's impossible to predict how much money a movie will make, and declarations to the contrary are considered pure malarkey."

---

[10]Mark Litwak, *Reel Power: The Struggle for Influence and Success in the New Hollywood* (New York: William Morrow and Company, Inc., 1986), pp. 73, 74, and 77.

Summary and Conclusions

1. In this chapter, we covered different investment decision rules. We evaluated the most popular alternatives to the NPV: The payback period, the discounted payback period, the internal rate of return, and the profitability index. In doing so we learned more about the NPV.

2. While we found that the alternatives have some redeeming qualities, when all is said and done, they are not the NPV rule; for those of us in finance, that makes them decidedly second-rate.

3. Of the competitors to NPV, IRR must be ranked above payback. In fact, IRR always reaches the same decision as NPV in the normal case where the initial outflows of an independent investment project are followed only by a series of inflows.

4. We classified the flaws of IRR into two types. First, we considered the general case applying to both independent and mutually exclusive projects. There appeared to be two problems here:
   a. Some projects have cash inflows followed by one or more outflows. The IRR rule is inverted here: One should accept when the IRR is *below* the discount rate.
   b. Some projects have a number of changes of sign in their cash flows. Here, there are likely to be multiple internal rates of return. The practitioner must use either NPV or modified internal rate of return here.

5. Next, we considered the specific problems with the IRR for mutually exclusive projects. We showed that, due to differences in either size or timing, the project with the highest IRR need not have the highest NPV. Hence, the IRR rule should not be applied. (Of course, NPV can still be applied.)

    However, we then calculated incremental cash flows. For ease of calculation, we suggested subtracting the cash flows of the smaller project from the cash flows of the larger project. In that way the incremental initial cash flow is negative. One can always reach a correct decision by accepting the larger project if the incremental IRR is greater than the discount rate.

6. We described capital rationing as the case where funds are limited to a fixed dollar amount. With capital rationing the profitability index is a useful method of adjusting the NPV.

Concept Questions

1. **Payback Period and Net Present Value**   If a project with conventional cash flows has a payback period less than the project's life, can you definitively state the algebraic sign of the NPV? Why or why not? If you know that the discounted payback period is less than the project's life, what can you say about the NPV? Explain.

2. **Net Present Value**   Suppose a project has conventional cash flows and a positive NPV. What do you know about its payback? Its discounted payback? Its profitability index? Its IRR? Explain.

3. **Comparing Investment Criteria**   Define each of the following investment rules and discuss any potential shortcomings of each. In your definition, state the criterion for accepting or rejecting independent projects under each rule.

    a. Payback period.
    b. Internal rate of return.
    c. Profitability index.
    d. Net present value.

4. **Payback and Internal Rate of Return**   A project has perpetual cash flows of C per period, a cost of I, and a required return of R. What is the relationship between the project's payback and its IRR? What implications does your answer have for long-lived projects with relatively constant cash flows?

5. **International Investment Projects**   In March 2014, BMW announced plans to spend $1 billion to expand production at its South Carolina plant. The plant produced the second-generation BMW X3 as well as the company's X5 and X6 models. The new investment would allow BMW to build the new, larger X7. BMW apparently felt it would be better able to compete and create value with a U.S.–based facility. In fact, BMW actually expected to export 70 percent of the X3s produced in South Carolina. Also in 2014, Swiss power storage company Alevo Group announced plans to build a $1 billion plant in North Carolina, and gun manufacturer Beretta announced plans to open a plant in Tennessee. What are some of the reasons that foreign manufacturers of products as diverse as automobiles, batteries, and guns might arrive at the same conclusion to build plants in the United States?

6. **Capital Budgeting Problems**   What are some of the difficulties that might come up in actual applications of the various criteria we discussed in this chapter? Which one would be the easiest to implement in actual applications? The most difficult?

7. **Capital Budgeting in Not-for-Profit Entities**   Are the capital budgeting criteria we discussed applicable to not-for-profit corporations? How should such entities make capital budgeting decisions? What about the U.S. government? Should it evaluate spending proposals using these techniques?

8. **Net Present Value**   The investment in Project A is $1 million, and the investment in Project B is $2 million. Both projects have a unique internal rate of return of 20 percent. Is the following statement true or false?

    For any discount rate from 0 percent to 20 percent, Project B has an NPV twice as great as that of Project A.

    Explain your answer.

9. **Net Present Value versus Profitability Index**   Consider the following two mutually exclusive projects available to Global Investments, Inc.:

	C_0	C_1	C_2	Profitability Index	NPV
A	−$1,000	$1,000	$500	1.32	$322
B	−500	500	400	1.57	285

    The appropriate discount rate for the projects is 10 percent. Global Investments chose to undertake Project A. At a luncheon for shareholders, the manager of a pension fund that owns a substantial amount of the firm's stock asks you why the firm chose Project A instead of Project B when Project B has a higher profitability index.

    How would you, the CFO, justify your firm's action? Are there any circumstances under which Global Investments should choose Project B?

10. **Internal Rate of Return**   Projects A and B have the following cash flows:

Year	Project A	Project B
0	−$1,000	−$2,000
1	C1A	C1B
2	C2A	C2B
3	C3A	C3B

    a. If the cash flows from the projects are identical, which of the two projects would have a higher IRR? Why?
    b. If C1B = 2C1A, C2B = 2C2A, and C3B = 2C3A, then is $IRR_A = IRR_B$?

11. **Net Present Value**   You are evaluating Project A and Project B. Project A has a short period of future cash flows, while Project B has relatively long future cash flows. Which project will be more sensitive to changes in the required return? Why?

12. **Modified Internal Rate of Return**   One of the less flattering interpretations of the acronym MIRR is "meaningless internal rate of return." Why do you think this term is applied to MIRR?

13. **Net Present Value**   It is sometimes stated that "the net present value approach assumes reinvestment of the intermediate cash flows at the required return." Is this claim correct? To answer, suppose you calculate the NPV of a project in the usual way. Next, suppose you do the following:

    a. Calculate the future value (as of the end of the project) of all the cash flows other than the initial outlay assuming they are reinvested at the required return, producing a single future value figure for the project.
    b. Calculate the NPV of the project using the single future value calculated in the previous step and the initial outlay. It is easy to verify that you will get the same NPV as in your original calculation only if you use the required return as the reinvestment rate in the previous step.

14. **Internal Rate of Return** It is sometimes stated that "the internal rate of return approach assumes reinvestment of the intermediate cash flows at the internal rate of return." Is this claim correct? To answer, suppose you calculate the IRR of a project in the usual way. Next, suppose you do the following:

   a. Calculate the future value (as of the end of the project) of all the cash flows other than the initial outlay assuming they are reinvested at the IRR, producing a single future value figure for the project.
   b. Calculate the IRR of the project using the single future value calculated in the previous step and the initial outlay. It is easy to verify that you will get the same IRR as in your original calculation only if you use the IRR as the reinvestment rate in the previous step.

Questions and Problems

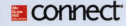

BASIC
(Questions 1–8)

1. **Calculating Payback Period and NPV** Maxwell Software, Inc., has the following mutually exclusive projects.

Year	Project A	Project B
0	−$20,000	−$24,000
1	13,200	14,100
2	8,300	9,800
3	3,200	7,600

   a. Suppose the company's payback period cutoff is two years. Which of these two projects should be chosen?
   b. Suppose the company uses the NPV rule to rank these two projects. Which project should be chosen if the appropriate discount rate is 15 percent?

2. **Calculating Payback** An investment project provides cash inflows of $790 per year for eight years. What is the project payback period if the initial cost is $3,200? What if the initial cost is $4,800? What if it is $7,300?

3. **Calculating Discounted Payback** An investment project has annual cash inflows of $5,000, $5,500, $6,000, and $7,000, and a discount rate of 12 percent. What is the discounted payback period for these cash flows if the initial cost is $8,000? What if the initial cost is $12,000? What if it is $16,000?

4. **Calculating Discounted Payback** An investment project costs $17,500 and has annual cash flows of $4,300 for six years. What is the discounted payback period if the discount rate is 0 percent? What if the discount rate is 10 percent? If it is 17 percent?

5. **Calculating IRR** Vital Silence, Inc., has a project with the following cash flows:

Year	Cash Flows ($)
0	−$24,000
1	9,700
2	13,700
3	6,400

The company evaluates all projects by applying the IRR rule. If the appropriate interest rate is 9 percent, should the company accept the project?

6. **Calculating IRR** Compute the internal rate of return for the cash flows of the following two projects:

	Cash Flows ($)	
Year	Project A	Project B
0	−$5,700	−$3,450
1	2,750	1,380
2	2,800	1,800
3	1,600	1,200

7. **Calculating Profitability Index** Bill plans to open a self-serve grooming center in a storefront. The grooming equipment will cost $265,000, to be paid immediately. Bill expects aftertax cash inflows of $59,000 annually for seven years, after which he plans to scrap the equipment and retire to the beaches of Nevis. The first cash inflow occurs at the end of the first year. Assume the required return is 13 percent. What is the project's PI? Should it be accepted?

8. **Calculating Profitability Index** Suppose the following two independent investment opportunities are available to Relax, Inc. The appropriate discount rate is 8.5 percent.

Year	Project Alpha	Project Beta
0	−$2,100	−$3,700
1	1,200	800
2	1,100	2,300
3	900	2,900

a. Compute the profitability index for each of the two projects.
b. Which project(s) should the company accept based on the profitability index rule?

INTERMEDIATE
(Questions 9–19)

9. **Cash Flow Intuition** A project has an initial cost of I, has a required return of R, and pays C annually for N years.

a. Find C in terms of I and N such that the project has a payback period just equal to its life.
b. Find C in terms of I, N, and R such that this is a profitable project according to the NPV decision rule.
c. Find C in terms of I, N, and R such that the project has a benefit–cost ratio of 2.

10. **Problems with IRR** Suppose you are offered $9,400 today but must make the following payments:

Year	Cash Flows ($)
0	$9,400
1	−4,500
2	−3,100
3	−2,400
4	−1,800

a. What is the IRR of this offer?
b. If the appropriate discount rate is 10 percent, should you accept this offer?
c. If the appropriate discount rate is 20 percent, should you accept this offer?
d. What is the NPV of the offer if the appropriate discount rate is 10 percent? 20 percent?
e. Are the decisions under the NPV rule in part (d) consistent with those of the IRR rule?

11.   NPV versus IRR   Consider the following cash flows on two mutually exclusive projects for the Bahamas Recreation Corporation (BRC). Both projects require an annual return of 14 percent.

Year	Deepwater Fishing	New Submarine Ride
0	−$850,000	−$1,650,000
1	320,000	810,000
2	470,000	750,000
3	410,000	690,000

As a financial analyst for BRC, you are asked the following questions:

a. If your decision rule is to accept the project with the greater IRR, which project should you choose?
b. Because you are fully aware of the IRR rule's scale problem, you calculate the incremental IRR for the cash flows. Based on your computation, which project should you choose?
c. To be prudent, you compute the NPV for both projects. Which project should you choose? Is it consistent with the incremental IRR rule?

12.   Problems with Profitability Index   The Cori's Sausage Corporation is trying to choose between the following two mutually exclusive design projects:

Year	Cash Flow (I)	Cash Flow (II)
0	−$35,000	−$16,000
1	19,800	9,400
2	19,800	9,400
3	19,800	9,400

a. If the required return is 10 percent and the company applies the profitability index decision rule, which project should the firm accept?
b. If the company applies the NPV decision rule, which project should it take?
c. Explain why your answers in (a) and (b) are different.

13.   Problems with IRR   Cutler Petroleum, Inc., is trying to evaluate a generation project with the following cash flows:

Year	Cash Flow
0	−$ 78,000,000
1	110,000,000
2	−13,000,000

a. If the company requires a 10 percent return on its investments, should it accept this project? Why?

b. Compute the IRR for this project. How many IRRs are there? If you apply the IRR decision rule, should you accept the project or not? What's going on here?

14. **Comparing Investment Criteria**   Wii Brothers, a game manufacturer, has a new idea for an adventure game. It can market the game either as a traditional board game or as an interactive DVD, but not both. Consider the following cash flows of the two mutually exclusive projects for the company. Assume the discount rate for both projects is 10 percent.

Year	Board Game	DVD
0	−$950	−$2,100
1	700	1,500
2	550	1,050
3	130	450

a. Based on the payback period rule, which project should be chosen?
b. Based on the NPV, which project should be chosen?
c. Based on the IRR, which project should be chosen?
d. Based on the incremental IRR, which project should be chosen?

15. **Profitability Index versus NPV**   Hanmi Group, a consumer electronics conglomerate, is reviewing its annual budget in wireless technology. It is considering investments in three different technologies to develop wireless communication devices. Consider the following cash flows of the three independent projects available to the company. Assume the discount rate for all projects is 10 percent. Further, the company has only $40 million to invest in new projects this year.

	Cash Flows (in $ millions)		
Year	CDMA	G4	Wi-Fi
0	−$16	−$24	−$40
1	22	20	36
2	15	50	64
3	5	40	40

a. Based on the profitability index decision rule, rank these investments.
b. Based on the NPV, rank these investments.
c. Based on your findings in (a) and (b), what would you recommend to the CEO of the company and why?

16. **Comparing Investment Criteria**   Consider the following cash flows of two mutually exclusive projects for AZ-Motorcars. Assume the discount rate for both projects is 10 percent.

Year	AZM Mini-SUV	AZF Full-SUV
0	−$495,000	−$960,000
1	352,000	385,000
2	198,000	464,000
3	165,000	319,000

a. Based on the payback period, which project should be accepted?

b. Based on the NPV, which project should be accepted?

c. Based on the IRR, which project should be accepted?

d. Based on this analysis, is incremental IRR analysis necessary? If yes, please conduct the analysis.

17. **Comparing Investment Criteria** The treasurer of Amaro Canned Fruits, Inc., has projected the cash flows of Projects A, B, and C as follows:

Year	Project A	Project B	Project C
0	−$225,000	−$450,000	−$225,000
1	165,000	300,000	180,000
2	165,000	300,000	135,000

Suppose the relevant discount rate is 12 percent per year.

a. Compute the profitability index for each of the three projects.

b. Compute the NPV for each of the three projects.

c. Suppose these three projects are independent. Which project(s) should Amaro accept based on the profitability index rule?

d. Suppose these three projects are mutually exclusive. Which project(s) should Amaro accept based on the profitability index rule?

e. Suppose Amaro's budget for these projects is $450,000. The projects are not divisible. Which project(s) should Amaro accept?

18. **Comparing Investment Criteria** Consider the following cash flows of two mutually exclusive projects for Tokyo Rubber Company. Assume the discount rate for both projects is 8 percent.

Year	Dry Prepreg	Solvent Prepreg
0	−$1,700,000	−$750,000
1	1,100,000	375,000
2	900,000	600,000
3	750,000	390,000

a. Based on the payback period, which project should be taken?

b. Based on the NPV, which project should be taken?

c. Based on the IRR, which project should be taken?

d. Based on this analysis, is incremental IRR analysis necessary? If yes, please conduct the analysis.

19. **Comparing Investment Criteria** Consider two mutually exclusive new product launch projects that Nagano Golf is considering. Assume the discount rate for both products is 15 percent.

Project A: Nagano NP-30.

Professional clubs that will take an initial investment of $660,000 at Time 0.

Next five years (Years 1–5) of sales will generate a consistent cash flow of $222,000 per year.

Introduction of new product at Year 6 will terminate further cash flows from this project.

Project *B:*   Nagano NX-20.

High-end amateur clubs that will take an initial investment of $420,000 at Time 0.

Cash flow at Year 1 is $120,000. In each subsequent year cash flow will grow at 10 percent per year.

Introduction of new product at Year 6 will terminate further cash flows from this project.

Year	NP-30	NX-20
0	−$660,000	−$420,000
1	222,000	120,000
2	222,000	132,000
3	222,000	145,200
4	222,000	159,720
5	222,000	175,692

Please fill in the following table:

	NP-30	NX-20	Implications
Payback			
IRR			
PI			
NPV			

CHALLENGE
(Questions 20–28)

20. **NPV and Multiple IRRs**   You are evaluating a project that costs $75,000 today. The project has an inflow of $155,000 in one year and an outflow of $65,000 in two years. What are the IRRs for the project? What discount rate results in the maximum NPV for this project? How can you determine that this is the maximum NPV?

21. **Payback and NPV**   An investment under consideration has a payback of six years and a cost of $573,000. If the required return is 12 percent, what is the worst-case NPV? The best-case NPV? Explain. Assume the cash flows are conventional.

22. **Multiple IRRs**   This problem is useful for testing the ability of financial calculators and computer software. Consider the following cash flows. How many different IRRs are there? (*Hint:* Search between 20 percent and 70 percent.) When should we take this project?

Year	Cash Flow
0	−$ 2,016
1	11,448
2	−24,280
3	22,800
4	−8,000

23. **NPV Valuation**   The Yurdone Corporation wants to set up a private cemetery business. According to the CFO, Barry M. Deep, business is "looking up." As a result, the cemetery project will provide a net cash inflow of $315,000 for the firm during the first

year, and the cash flows are projected to grow at a rate of 4.5 percent per year forever. The project requires an initial investment of $4,100,000.

a. If Yurdone requires a return of 11 percent on such undertakings, should the cemetery business be started?

b. The company is somewhat unsure about the assumption of a growth rate of 4.5 percent in its cash flows. At what constant growth rate would the company just break even if it still required a return of 11 percent on investment?

24. **Calculating IRR** The Utah Mining Corporation is set to open a gold mine near Provo, Utah. According to the treasurer, Monty Goldstein, "This is a golden opportunity." The mine will cost $2,700,000 to open and will have an economic life of 11 years. It will generate a cash inflow of $435,000 at the end of the first year, and the cash inflows are projected to grow at 8 percent per year for the next 10 years. After 11 years, the mine will be abandoned. Abandonment costs will be $400,000 at the end of Year 11.

a. What is the IRR for the gold mine?

b. The Utah Mining Corporation requires a return of 10 percent on such undertakings. Should the mine be opened?

25. **NPV and IRR** Butler International Limited is evaluating a project in Erewhon. The project will create the following cash flows:

Year	Cash Flow
0	−$855,000
1	255,000
2	315,000
3	374,000
4	230,000

All cash flows will occur in Erewhon and are expressed in dollars. In an attempt to improve its economy, the Erewhonian government has declared that all cash flows created by a foreign company are "blocked" and must be reinvested with the government for one year. The reinvestment rate for these funds is 4 percent. If Butler uses a required return of 11 percent on this project, what are the NPV and IRR of the project? Is the IRR you calculated the MIRR of the project? Why or why not?

26. **Calculating IRR** Consider two streams of cash flows, A and B. Stream A's first cash flow is $11,600 and is received three years from today. Future cash flows in Stream A grow by 4 percent in perpetuity. Stream B's first cash flow is −$13,000, is received two years from today, and will continue in perpetuity. Assume that the appropriate discount rate is 12 percent.

a. What is the present value of each stream?

b. Suppose that the two streams are combined into one project, called C. What is the IRR of Project C?

c. What is the correct IRR rule for Project C?

27. **Calculating Incremental Cash Flows** Darin Clay, the CFO of MakeMoney.com, has to decide between the following two projects:

Year	Project Million	Project Billion
0	−$1,200	−$$I_o$
1	I_o + 160	I_o + 400
2	960	1,200
3	1,200	1,600

The expected rate of return for either of the two projects is 12 percent. What is the range of initial investment (I_o) for which Project Billion is more financially attractive than Project Million?

28.   **Problems with IRR**   McKeekin Corp. has a project with the following cash flows:

Year	Cash Flow
0	$20,000
1	−26,000
2	13,000

What is the IRR of the project? What is happening here?

Excel Master It! Problem

As you have already seen, Excel does not have a function to calculate the payback period. We have shown three ways to calculate the payback period, but there are numerous other methods as well. The cash flows for a project are shown below. You need to calculate the payback period using two different methods:

a. Calculate the payback period in a table. The first three columns of the table will be the year, the cash flow for that year, and the cumulative cash flow. The fourth column will show the whole year for the payback. In other words, if the payback period is 3 plus years, this column will have a 3, otherwise it will be a zero. The next column will calculate the fractional part of the payback period, or else it will display zero. The last column will add the previous two columns and display the final payback period calculation. You should also have a cell that displays the final payback period by itself, and a cell that returns the correct accept or reject decision based on the payback criteria.

b. Write a nested IF statement that calculates the payback period using only the project cash flow column. The IF statement should return a value of "Never" if the project has no payback period. In contrast to the example we showed previously, the nested IF function should test for the payback period starting with shorter payback periods and working towards longer payback periods. Another cell should display the correct accept or reject decision based on the payback criteria.

Year	Cash Flow
0	−$250,000
1	41,000
2	48,000
3	63,000
4	79,000
5	88,000
6	64,000
7	41,000
Required payback:	5

BULLOCK GOLD MINING

Seth Bullock, the owner of Bullock Gold Mining, is evaluating a new gold mine in South Dakota. Dan Dority, the company's geologist, has just finished his analysis of the mine site. He has estimated that the mine would be productive for eight years, after which the gold would be completely mined. Dan has taken an estimate of the gold deposits to Alma Garrett, the company's financial officer. Alma has been asked by Seth to perform an analysis of the new mine and present her recommendation on whether the company should open the new mine.

Alma has used the estimates provided by Dan to determine the revenues that could be expected from the mine. She has also projected the expense of opening the mine and the annual operating expenses. If the company opens the mine, it will cost $850 million today, and it will have a cash outflow of $75 million nine years from today in costs associated with closing the mine and reclaiming the area surrounding it. The expected cash flows each year from the mine are shown in the following table. Bullock Mining has a 12 percent required return on all of its gold mines.

Year	Cash Flow
0	−$850,000,000
1	170,000,000
2	190,000,000
3	205,000,000
4	265,000,000
5	235,000,000
6	170,000,000
7	160,000,000
8	105,000,000
9	−75,000,000

1. Construct a spreadsheet to calculate the payback period, internal rate of return, modified internal rate of return, and net present value of the proposed mine.

2. Based on your analysis, should the company open the mine?

3. Bonus question: Most spreadsheets do not have a built-in formula to calculate the payback period. Write a VBA script that calculates the payback period for a project.

6

Making Capital Investment Decisions

Is there green in green? General Electric (GE) thinks so. Through its "Ecomagination" program, the company planned to double research and development spending on green products. In fact, GE originally invested over $5 billion in its Ecomagination program, and it announced plans to invest another $10 billion from 2011 to 2015. With products such as a hybrid railroad locomotive (described as a 200-ton, 6,000-horsepower "Prius on rails"), GE's green initiative seems to be paying off. Revenue from green products has totaled more than $155 billion since its launch in 2005, with $28 billion in 2013 alone. Even further, revenues from Ecomagination products were growing at twice the rate of the rest of the company's revenues. The company's internal commitment to reduced energy consumption through green "Treasure Hunts" saved it more than $100 million, and the

company reduced its water consumption by 30 percent from its 2006 baseline, another considerable cost savings.

As you no doubt recognize from your study of the previous chapter, GE's decision to develop and market green technology represents a capital budgeting decision. In this chapter, we further investigate such decisions—how they are made and how to look at them objectively. We have two main tasks. First, recall that in the last chapter, we saw that cash flow estimates are the critical input into a net present value analysis, but we didn't say much about where these cash flows come from. We will now examine this question in some detail. Our second goal is to learn how to critically examine NPV estimates, and, in particular, how to evaluate the sensitivity of NPV estimates to assumptions made about the uncertain future.

The previous chapter discussed the basic principles behind capital budgeting approaches such as net present value, internal rate of return, and payback. We pointed out there that these three approaches all use cash flows. We did not, however, indicate how cash flows are to be estimated in the real world. Chapter 6 addresses this task. We begin with the idea that one should estimate *incremental* cash flows.

6.1 Incremental Cash Flows: The Key to Capital Budgeting

CASH FLOWS—NOT ACCOUNTING INCOME

You may not have thought about it, but there is a big difference between corporate finance courses and financial accounting courses. Techniques in corporate finance generally use cash flows, whereas financial accounting generally stresses income or earnings numbers.

Certainly our text follows this tradition: Our net present value techniques discount cash flows, not earnings. When considering a single project, we discount the cash flows that the firm receives from the project. When valuing the firm as a whole, we discount dividends—not earnings—because dividends are the cash flows that an investor receives.

**EXAMPLE
6.1**

Relevant Cash Flows   The Weber-Decker Co. just paid $1 million in cash for a building as part of a new capital budgeting project. This entire $1 million is an immediate cash outflow. However, assuming straight-line depreciation over 20 years, only $50,000 (=$1 million/20) is considered an accounting expense in the current year. Current earnings are thereby reduced by only $50,000. The remaining $950,000 is expensed over the following 19 years. For capital budgeting purposes, the relevant cash outflow at Date 0 is the full $1 million, not the reduction in earnings of only $50,000.

Always discount cash flows, not earnings, when performing a capital budgeting calculation. Earnings do not represent real money. You can't spend out of earnings, you can't eat out of earnings, and you can't pay dividends out of earnings. You can do these things only out of cash flows.

In addition, it's not enough to use cash flows. In calculating the NPV of a project, only cash flows that are *incremental* to the project should be used. These cash flows are the changes in the firm's cash flows that occur as a direct consequence of accepting the project. That is, we are interested in the difference between the cash flows of the firm with the project and the cash flows of the firm without the project.

The use of incremental cash flows sounds easy enough, but pitfalls abound in the real world. We describe how to avoid some of the pitfalls of determining incremental cash flows.

SUNK COSTS

A **sunk cost** is a cost that has already occurred. Because sunk costs are in the past, they cannot be changed by the decision to accept or reject the project. Just as we "let bygones be bygones," we should ignore such costs. Sunk costs are not incremental cash outflows.

**EXAMPLE
6.2**

Sunk Costs   The General Milk Company (GMC) is currently evaluating the NPV of establishing a line of chocolate milk. As part of the evaluation, the company paid a consulting firm $100,000 last year for a test marketing analysis. Is this cost relevant for the capital budgeting decision now confronting GMC's management?

The answer is no. The $100,000 is not recoverable, so the $100,000 expenditure is a sunk cost, or spilled milk. In other words, one must ask, "What is the difference between the cash flows of the entire firm with the chocolate milk project and the cash flows of the entire firm without the project?" Since the $100,000 was already spent, acceptance of the project does not affect this cash flow. Therefore, the cash flow should be ignored for capital budgeting purposes.

Of course, the decision to spend $100,000 for a marketing analysis was a capital budgeting decision itself and was perfectly relevant *before* it was sunk. Our point is that once the company incurred the expense, the cost became irrelevant for any future decision.

OPPORTUNITY COSTS

Your firm may have an asset that it is considering selling, leasing, or employing elsewhere in the business. If the asset is used in a new project, potential revenues from alternative uses are lost. These lost revenues can meaningfully be viewed as costs. They are called **opportunity costs** because, by taking the project, the firm forgoes other opportunities for using the assets.

EXAMPLE 6.3

Opportunity Costs   Suppose the Weinstein Trading Company has an empty warehouse in Philadelphia that can be used to store a new line of electronic pinball machines. The company hopes to sell these machines to affluent northeastern consumers. Should the warehouse be considered a cost in the decision to sell the machines?

The answer is yes. The company could sell the warehouse if the firm decides not to market the pinball machines. Thus, the sales price of the warehouse is an opportunity cost in the pinball machine decision.

SIDE EFFECTS

Another difficulty in determining incremental cash flows comes from the side effects of the proposed project on other parts of the firm. A side effect is classified as either **erosion** or **synergy**. Erosion occurs when a new product reduces the sales and, hence, the cash flows of existing products. For example, one of Walt Disney Company's concerns when it built Paris Disneyland was that the new park would drain visitors from the Florida park, a popular vacation destination for Europeans. Synergy occurs when a new project increases the cash flows of existing projects. For example, while a shaving-supplies firm may appear to lose money on its new razor, the increase in sales of its new razor blades may make the razor an overall winner for the firm.

EXAMPLE 6.4

Erosion   Suppose the Innovative Motors Corporation (IMC) is determining the NPV of a new convertible sports car. Some of the would-be purchasers are owners of IMC's compact sedans. Are all sales and profits from the new convertible sports car incremental?

The answer is no because some of the cash flow represents transfers from other elements of IMC's product line. This is erosion, which must be included in the NPV calculation. Without taking erosion into account, IMC might erroneously calculate the NPV of the sports car to be, say, $100 million. If half the customers are transfers from the sedan and lost sedan sales have an NPV of −$150 million, the true NPV is −$50 million (=$100 million − $150 million).

Synergy   IMC is also contemplating the formation of a racing team. The team is forecast to lose money for the foreseeable future, with perhaps the best projection showing an NPV of −$35 million for the operation. However, IMC's managers are aware that the team will likely generate great publicity for all of IMC's products. A consultant estimates that the increase in cash flows elsewhere in the firm has a present value of $65 million. Assuming that the consultant's estimates of synergy are trustworthy, the net present value of the team is $30 million (=$65 million − $35 million). The managers should form the team.

ALLOCATED COSTS

Frequently a particular expenditure benefits a number of projects. Accountants allocate this cost across the different projects when determining income. However, for capital budgeting purposes, this **allocated cost** should be viewed as a cash outflow of a project only if it is an incremental cost of the project.

EXAMPLE 6.5

Allocated Costs   The Voetmann Consulting Corp. devotes one wing of its suite of offices to a library requiring a cash outflow of $100,000 a year in upkeep. A proposed capital budgeting project is expected to generate revenue equal to 5 percent of the overall firm's sales. An executive at the firm, David Pedersen, argues that $5,000 (=5 percent × $100,000) should be viewed as the proposed project's share of the library's costs. Is this appropriate for capital budgeting?

The answer is no. One must ask what the difference is between the cash flows of the entire firm with the project and the cash flows of the entire firm without the project. The firm will spend $100,000 on library upkeep whether or not the proposed project is accepted. Because acceptance of the proposed project does not affect this cash flow, the cash flow should be ignored when calculating the NPV of the project. For example, suppose the project has a positive NPV without the allocated costs but is rejected because of the allocated costs. In this case, the firm is losing potential value that it could have gained otherwise.

6.2 The Baldwin Company: An Example

We next consider the example of a proposed investment in machinery and related items. Our example involves the Baldwin Company and colored bowling balls.

The Baldwin Company, originally established 16 years ago to make footballs, is now a leading producer of tennis balls, baseballs, footballs, and golf balls. Nine years ago, the company introduced "High Flite," its first line of high-performance golf balls. Baldwin management has sought opportunities in whatever businesses seem to have some potential for cash flow. Recently W. C. Meadows, vice president of the Baldwin Company, identified another segment of the sports ball market that looked promising and that he felt was not adequately served by larger manufacturers. That market was for brightly colored bowling balls, and he believed many bowlers valued appearance and style above performance. He also believed that it would be difficult for competitors to take advantage of the opportunity because of both Baldwin's cost advantages and its highly developed marketing skills.

As a result, the Baldwin Company investigated the marketing potential of brightly colored bowling balls. Baldwin sent a questionnaire to consumers in three markets: Philadelphia, Los Angeles, and New Haven. The results of the three questionnaires were much better than expected and supported the conclusion that the brightly colored bowling balls could achieve a 10 to 15 percent share of the market. Of course, some people at Baldwin complained about the cost of the test marketing, which was $250,000. (As we shall see later, this is a sunk cost and should not be included in project evaluation.)

In any case, the Baldwin Company is now considering investing in a machine to produce bowling balls. The bowling balls would be manufactured in a building owned by the firm and located near Los Angeles. This building, which is vacant, and the land can be sold for $150,000 after taxes.

Working with his staff, Meadows is preparing an analysis of the proposed new product. He summarizes his assumptions as follows: The cost of the bowling ball machine is

$100,000 and it is expected to last five years. At the end of five years, the machine will be sold at a price estimated to be $30,000. Production by year during the five-year life of the machine is expected to be as follows: 5,000 units, 8,000 units, 12,000 units, 10,000 units, and 6,000 units. The price of bowling balls in the first year will be $20. The bowling ball market is highly competitive, so Meadows believes that the price of bowling balls will increase at only 2 percent per year, as compared to the anticipated general inflation rate of 5 percent. Conversely, the plastic used to produce bowling balls is rapidly becoming more expensive. Because of this, production cash outflows are expected to grow at 10 percent per year. First-year production costs will be $10 per unit. Meadows has determined, based on Baldwin's taxable income, that the appropriate incremental corporate tax rate in the bowling ball project is 34 percent.

Net working capital is defined as the difference between current assets and current liabilities. Like any other manufacturing firm, Baldwin finds that it must maintain an investment in working capital. It will purchase raw materials before production and sale, giving rise to an investment in inventory. It will maintain cash as a buffer against unforeseen expenditures. And, its credit sales will not generate cash until payment is made at a later date. Management determines that an initial investment (at Year 0) in net working capital of $10,000 is required. Subsequently, net working capital at the end of each year will be equal to 10 percent of sales for that year. In the final year of the project, net working capital will decline to zero as the project is wound down. In other words, the investment in working capital is to be completely recovered by the end of the project's life.

Projections based on these assumptions and Meadows's analysis appear in Tables 6.1 through 6.4. In these tables all cash flows are assumed to occur at the *end* of the year. Because

Table 6.1 Worksheet for Cash Flows of the Baldwin Company ($ in thousands)
(All cash flows occur at the *end* of the year.)

	Year 0	Year 1	Year 2	Year 3	Year 4	Year 5
Investments:						
(1) Bowling ball machine	−$100.00					$ 21.76*
(2) Accumulated depreciation		$ 20.00	$ 52.00	$ 71.20	$ 82.72	94.24
(3) Adjusted basis of machine after depreciation (end of year)		80.00	48.00	28.80	17.28	5.76
(4) Opportunity cost (warehouse)	−150.00					150.00
(5) Net working capital (end of year)	10.00	10.00	16.32	24.97	21.22	
(6) Change in net working capital	−10.00		−6.32	−8.65	3.75	21.22
(7) Total cash flow of investment [(1) + (4) + (6)]	−260.00		−6.32	−8.65	3.75	192.98
Income:						
(8) Sales revenues		$100.00	$163.20	$249.70	$212.24	$129.89
(9) Operating costs		−50.00	−88.00	−145.20	−133.10	−87.85
(10) Depreciation		−20.00	−32.00	−19.20	−11.52	−11.52
(11) Income before taxes [(8) + (9) + (10)]		$ 30.00	$ 43.20	$ 85.30	$ 67.62	$ 30.53
(12) Tax at 34 percent		−10.20	−14.69	−29.00	−22.99	−10.38
(13) Net income		$ 19.80	$ 28.51	$ 56.30	$ 44.63	$ 20.15

*We assume that the sale price of the bowling ball machine at Year 5 will be $30 (in thousands). The machine will have been depreciated to $5.76 at that time. Therefore, the taxable gain from the sale will be $24.24 (=$30 − $5.76). The aftertax salvage value will be $30 − [.34 × ($30 − $5.76)] = $21.76.

of the large amount of information in these tables, it is important to see how the tables are related. Table 6.1 shows the basic data for both investment and income. Supplementary schedules on operations and depreciation, as presented in Tables 6.2 and 6.3, help explain the numbers in Table 6.1. Our goal is to obtain projections of cash flow. The data in Table 6.1 are all that are needed to calculate the relevant cash flows, as shown in Table 6.4.

Table 6.2

Operating Revenues and Costs of the Baldwin Company

(1) Year	(2) Quantity Sold	(3) Price	(4) Sales Revenues	(5) Cost per Unit	(6) Operating Costs
1	5,000	$20.00	$100,000	$10.00	$ 50,000
2	8,000	20.40	163,200	11.00	88,000
3	12,000	20.81	249,696	12.10	145,200
4	10,000	21.22	212,242	13.31	133,100
5	6,000	21.65	129,892	14.64	87,846

Price rises at 2% per year. Unit cost rises at 10% per year. Reported prices and costs (Columns 3 and 5) are rounded to two digits after the decimal. Sales revenues and operating costs (Columns 4 and 6) are calculated using exact, i.e., nonrounded, prices and costs.

Table 6.3

Depreciation under Modified Accelerated Cost Recovery System (MACRS)

| Year | \multicolumn{6}{c}{Recovery Period Class} |

Year	3 Years	5 Years	7 Years	10 Years	15 Years	20 Years
1	.3333	.2000	.1429	.1000	.0500	.03750
2	.4445	.3200	.2449	.1800	.0950	.07219
3	.1481	.1920	.1749	.1440	.0855	.06677
4	.0741	.1152	.1249	.1152	.0770	.06177
5		.1152	.0893	.0922	.0693	.05713
6		.0576	.0892	.0737	.0623	.05285
7			.0893	.0655	.0590	.04888
8			.0446	.0655	.0590	.04522
9				.0656	.0591	.04462
10				.0655	.0590	.04461
11				.0328	.0591	.04462
12					.0590	.04461
13					.0591	.04462
14					.0590	.04461
15					.0591	.04462
16					.0295	.04461
17						.04462
18						.04461
19						.04462
20						.04461
21						.02231

Depreciation is expressed as a percentage of the asset's initial cost. These schedules are based on the IRS Publication 946, entitled *How to Depreciate Property*. Details of depreciation are presented later in the chapter. Five-year depreciation actually carries over six years because the IRS assumes the purchase is made in midyear.

Table 6.4 Incremental Cash Flows for the Baldwin Company ($ in thousands)

	Year 0	Year 1	Year 2	Year 3	Year 4	Year 5
(1) Sales revenue [Line 8, Table 6.1]		$100.00	$163.20	$249.70	$212.24	$129.89
(2) Operating costs [Line 9, Table 6.1]		−50.00	−88.00	−145.20	−133.10	−87.85
(3) Taxes [Line 12, Table 6.1]		−10.20	−14.69	−29.00	−22.99	−10.38
(4) Cash flow from operations [(1) + (2) + (3)]		39.80	60.51	$ 75.50	$ 56.15	$ 31.67
(5) Total cash flow of investment [Line 7, Table 6.1]	−$260.00		−6.32	−8.65	3.75	192.98
(6) Total cash flow of project [(4) + (5)]	−$260.00	$ 39.80	$ 54.19	$ 66.85	$ 59.90	$224.65

NPV @		
	4%	$123.64
	10%	$ 51.59
	15%	$ 5.47
	15.68%	$ 0.00
	20%	($ 31.35)

AN ANALYSIS OF THE PROJECT

For most projects, cash flows follow a common pattern. First, firms invest at the beginning of the project, generating cash outflows. Second, product sales provide cash inflows over the life of the project. Third, plant and equipment are sold off at the end of the project, generating more cash inflow. We now discuss Baldwin's cash flows for each of these three steps.

Investments The investment outlays for the project are summarized in the top segment of Table 6.1. They consist of three parts:

1. *The bowling ball machine:* The purchase requires an immediate (Year 0) cash outflow of $100,000. The firm realizes a cash inflow when the machine is sold in Year 5. These cash flows are shown in Line 1 of Table 6.1. As indicated in the footnote to the table, taxes are incurred when the asset is sold.

2. *The opportunity cost of not selling the warehouse:* If Baldwin accepts the bowling ball project, it will use a warehouse and land that could otherwise be sold. The estimated aftertax sales price of the warehouse and land is therefore included as an *opportunity cost* in Year 0, as presented in Line 4. Opportunity costs are treated as cash outflows for purposes of capital budgeting. However, note that if the project is accepted, management assumes that the warehouse will be sold for $150,000 (after taxes) in Year 5.

   The test marketing cost of $250,000 is not included. As stated earlier, the tests occurred in the past and should be viewed as a *sunk cost.*

3. *The investment in working capital:* Required working capital appears in Line 5. Working capital rises over the early years of the project as expansion occurs. However, all working capital is assumed to be recovered at the end, a common assumption in capital budgeting. In other words, all inventory is sold by the end, the cash balance maintained as a buffer is liquidated, and all accounts receivable are collected.

   Increases in working capital in the early years must be funded by cash generated elsewhere in the firm. Hence, these increases are viewed as cash *outflows.* To reiterate, it is the *increase* in working capital over a year that leads to a cash outflow in that year. Even if working capital is at a high level, there will be no cash outflow over a year if working capital stays constant over that year. Conversely, decreases in working capital in the later years are viewed as cash inflows. All of these cash flows are presented in Line 6 of Table 6.1. A more complete discussion of working capital is provided later in this section.

To recap, there are three investments in this example: the bowling ball machine (Line 1 in Table 6.1), the opportunity cost of the warehouse (Line 4), and the changes in working capital (Line 6). The total cash flow from these three investments is shown in Line 7.

Income and Taxes   Next the determination of income is presented in the bottom segment of Table 6.1. While we are ultimately interested in cash flow—not income—we need the income calculation to determine taxes. Lines 8 and 9 of Table 6.1 show sales revenues and operating costs, respectively. The projections in these lines are based on the sales revenues and operating costs computed in Columns 4 and 6 of Table 6.2. The estimates of revenues and costs follow from assumptions made by the corporate planning staff at Baldwin. In other words, the estimates depend on the forecast that product prices will increase at 2 percent per year and costs per unit will increase at 10 percent per year.

Depreciation of the $100,000 capital investment is shown in Line 10 of Table 6.1. Where do these numbers come from? Depreciation for tax purposes for U.S. companies is based on the Modified Accelerated Cost Recovery System (MACRS). Each asset is assigned a useful life under MACRS, with an accompanying depreciation schedule as shown in Table 6.3. The IRS ruled that Baldwin is to depreciate its capital investment over five years, so the second column of the table applies in this case. Because depreciation in the table is expressed as a percentage of the asset's cost, multiply the percentages in this column by $100,000 to arrive at depreciation in dollars. Notice that the percentages in each column of Table 6.3 sum to 100 percent, implying that the IRS allows the asset to be depreciated to zero.

Income before taxes is calculated in Line 11 of Table 6.1. Taxes are provided in Line 12 of this table, and net income is shown in Line 13.

Salvage Value   When selling an asset, one must pay taxes on the difference between the asset's sales price and its book value. We stated earlier that Baldwin plans to sell the bowling ball machine at the end of Year 5, estimating the sales price at $30,000.

At the end of the fifth year, the book value of the machine would be $5,760, as shown in Line 3 of Table 6.1. If the company sold the machine for $30,000, it would pay taxes on the difference between this sales price and the book value of $5,760. With a 34 percent tax rate, the tax liability would be .34 × ($30,000 − $5,760) = $8,242. The aftertax salvage value of the equipment, a cash inflow to the company, would be $30,000 − $8,242 = $21,758, as indicated in Line 1 of Table 6.1.

Alternatively, if the book value exceeds the market value, the difference is treated as a loss for tax purposes. For example, if Baldwin sold the machine for $4,000, the book value would exceed the market value by $1,760. In this case, taxes of .34 × $1,760 = $598 would be saved.

Cash Flow   Cash flow is finally determined in Table 6.4. We begin by reproducing Lines 8, 9, and 12 in Table 6.1 as Lines 1, 2, and 3 in Table 6.4. Cash flow from operations, which is sales minus both operating costs and taxes, is provided in Line 4 of Table 6.4. Total investment cash flow, taken from Line 7 of Table 6.1, appears as Line 5 of Table 6.4.

Cash flow from operations plus total cash flow of the investment equals total cash flow of the project, which is displayed as Line 6 of Table 6.4.[1]

Net Present Value The NPV of the Baldwin bowling ball project can be calculated from the cash flows in Line 6. As can be seen at the bottom of Table 6.4, the NPV is $51,590 if 10 percent is the appropriate discount rate and −$31,350 if 20 percent is the appropriate discount rate. If the discount rate is 15.68 percent, the project will have a zero NPV. In other words, the project's internal rate of return is 15.68 percent. If the discount rate of the Baldwin bowling ball project is above 15.68 percent, it should not be accepted because its NPV would be negative.

WHICH SET OF BOOKS?

Corporations must provide a computation of profit or loss to both their own stockholders and tax authorities. While you might think that the numbers going to both parties would be the same, this is not the case. In actual fact, U.S. firms keep two sets of books, one for the Internal Revenue Service (IRS), called *tax books,* and another for their annual reports (called *stockholders' books*), with the numbers differing across the two sets.

How can this be? The two sets of books differ because their rules were developed by two separate bodies. The tax books follow the rules of the IRS and the stockholders' books follow the rules of the *Financial Accounting Standards Board* (FASB), the governing body in accounting. For example, interest on municipal bonds is ignored for tax purposes while the FASB treats the interest as income. As another example, companies typically use accelerated depreciation for their taxes and straight-line depreciation for their stockholders' books.

The differences almost always benefit the firm; the rules permit income on the stockholders' books to be higher than income on the tax books. Thus, management can look profitable to its stockholders without having to pay taxes on all of that reported profit. In fact, plenty of large companies consistently report positive earnings to their stockholders while reporting losses to the IRS. A cynical interpretation is that members of Congress, who collectively make tax policy, develop favorable rules to help their constituents. Whether or not this interpretation is true, one thing is clear: Companies are following the law, not breaking the law, by creating two sets of books.

Which set of books is relevant for the present chapter? The numbers in the tax books are the relevant ones, since you can only calculate cash flows after subtracting out taxes. While the stockholders' books are relevant for accounting and financial analysis, they are not used for capital budgeting.

Finally, while U.S. firms are allowed two sets of books, this is not the case in all, or perhaps even a majority, of other countries. Knowledge of local rules is needed before estimating international cash flows.

A NOTE ABOUT NET WORKING CAPITAL

Net working capital is the difference between current assets and current liabilities. Investment in net working capital is an important part of any capital budgeting analysis because it affects cash flows. While we considered net working capital in Lines 5 and 6 of Table 6.1, students may be wondering where the numbers in these lines came from.

---

[1]The total cash flow of the project is frequently referred to as "free cash flow." Free cash flow is the amount of cash that can be distributed to all investors (both debt and equity investors) after all necessary investments have been made.

In capital budgeting, we are most interested in inventory, accounts receivable, accounts payable, and cash. An investment in net working capital arises whenever (1) inventory is purchased, (2) cash is kept in the project as a buffer against unexpected expenditures, and (3) sales are made on credit, generating accounts receivable rather than cash. (The investment in net working capital is reduced by credit purchases, which generate accounts payable.) This investment in net working capital represents a cash *outflow* because cash generated elsewhere in the firm is tied up in the project.

To see how the investment in net working capital is built from its component parts, we focus on Year 1. We see in Table 6.1 that Baldwin's managers predict sales in Year 1 to be $100,000 and operating costs to be $50,000. If both the sales and costs were cash transactions, the firm would receive $50,000 (=$100,000 − $50,000). As stated earlier, this cash flow would occur at the *end* of Year 1.

Now let's give you more information. The managers:

1. Forecast that $9,000 of the sales will be on credit, implying that cash receipts at the end of Year 1 will be only $91,000 (=$100,000 − $9,000). The accounts receivable of $9,000 will be collected at the end of Year 2.

2. Believe that they can defer payment on $3,000 of the $50,000 of costs, implying that cash disbursements at the end of Year 1 will be only $47,000 (=$50,000 − $3,000). Baldwin will pay off the $3,000 of accounts payable at the end of Year 2.

3. Decide that inventory of $2,500 should be left on hand at the end of Year 1 to avoid *stockouts* (i.e., running out of inventory).

4. Decide that cash of $1,500 should be earmarked for the project at the end of Year 1 to avoid running out of cash.

Thus, net working capital at the end of Year 1 is:

$9,000	−	$3,000	+	$2,500	+	$1,500	=	$10,000
Accounts receivable		Accounts payable		Inventory		Cash		Net working capital

Because $10,000 of cash generated elsewhere in the firm must be used to offset this requirement for net working capital, Baldwin's managers correctly view the investment in net working capital as a cash outflow of the project. As the project grows over time, needs for net working capital increase. *Changes* in net working capital from year to year represent further cash flows, as indicated by the negative numbers for the first few years on Line 6 of Table 6.1. However, in the declining years of the project, net working capital is reduced—ultimately to zero. That is, accounts receivable are finally collected, the project's cash buffer is returned to the rest of the corporation, and all remaining inventory is sold off. This frees up cash in the later years, as indicated by positive numbers in Years 4 and 5 on Line 6.

Typically, corporate worksheets (such as Table 6.1) treat net working capital as a whole. The individual components of working capital (receivables, inventory, and the like) do not generally appear in the worksheets. However, the reader should remember that the working capital numbers in the worksheets are not pulled out of thin air. Rather, they result from a meticulous forecast of the components, just as we illustrated for Year 1.

A NOTE ABOUT DEPRECIATION

The Baldwin case made some assumptions about depreciation. Where did these assumptions come from? Depreciation rules are set forth in IRS Publication 946, entitled *How to*

Depreciate Property. This publication sorts different property types into classes, thereby determining their depreciable lives for tax purposes. For example:

- The 3-year class includes certain specialized short-lived property. Tractor units and racehorses over two years old are among the few items fitting into this class.
- The 5-year class includes cars, trucks, computers and peripheral equipment, office machinery, as well as property used in research.
- The 7-year class includes office furniture and fixtures, as well as agricultural machinery and equipment.
- The 10-year class includes vessels, barges, and tugs, as well as some agricultural and horticultural structures.
- The 15-year class includes improvements to land, such as shrubbery, fences, roads, sidewalks, and bridges, as well as certain restaurant property.
- The 20-year class includes farm buildings, as well as land improvements for electric utility plants.
- Real property is separated into two classes: residential and nonresidential. The cost of residential property is recovered over 27½ years and nonresidential property over 39 years.

Items in the 3-, 5-, 7-, 10-, 15-, and 20-year classes are depreciated according to the schedules in Table 6.3. All real estate is depreciated on a straight-line basis.

Calculations of depreciation include a half-year convention, which treats all property as if it were placed in service at midyear. To be consistent, the IRS allows half a year of depreciation for the year in which property is disposed of or retired. The effect of this is to spread the deductions for property over one year more than the name of its class—for example, six tax years for five-year property.

INTEREST EXPENSE

It may have bothered you that interest expense was ignored in the Baldwin example. After all, many projects are at least partially financed with debt, particularly a bowling ball machine that is likely to increase the debt capacity of the firm. As it turns out, our approach of assuming no debt financing is rather standard in the real world. Firms typically calculate a project's cash flows under the assumption that the project is financed only with equity. In this analysis, we want to determine the NPV of the project independent of financing decisions. Any adjustments for debt financing are reflected in the discount rate, not the cash flows. The treatment of debt in capital budgeting will be covered in depth in Chapter 13.

6.3 Alternative Definitions of Operating Cash Flow

As can be seen in the examples of this chapter, proper calculation of cash flow is essential to capital budgeting. A number of different definitions of operating cash flow are in common usage, a fact frequently bedeviling corporate finance students. However, the good news is that these definitions are consistent with each other. That is, if used correctly, they will all lead to the same answer for a given problem. We now consider some of the common definitions, showing in the process that they are identical with each other.[2]

---

[2] For simplicity, working capital is ignored in this discussion.

In the discussion that follows, keep in mind that when we speak of cash flow, we literally mean dollars in less dollars out. This is all we are concerned with.

For a particular project and year under consideration, suppose we have the following estimates:

$$\text{Sales} = \$1,500$$
$$\text{Cash costs}^3 = \$700$$
$$\text{Depreciation} = \$600$$

With these estimates, earnings before taxes (EBT) is:

$$\begin{aligned}
\text{EBT} &= \text{Sales} - \text{Cash costs} - \text{Depreciation} \\
&= \$1,500 - 700 - 600 \\
&= \$200
\end{aligned} \quad\quad (6.1)$$

As is customary in capital budgeting, we assume that no interest is paid, so the tax bill is:

$$\text{Taxes} = (\text{Sales} - \text{Cash costs} - \text{Depreciation}) \times t_c = \text{EBT} \times t_c \quad\quad (6.2)$$
$$(\$1,500 - 700 - 600) \times .34 = \$200 \times .34 = \$68$$

where t_c, the corporate tax rate, is 34 percent.

Now that we have calculated earnings before taxes in Equation 6.1 and taxes in Equation 6.2, how do we determine operating cash flow (OCF)? Below we show three different approaches, all of them consistent with each other. The first is perhaps the most commonsensical because it simply asks, "What cash goes into the owner's pockets and what cash goes out of his pockets?"

THE TOP-DOWN APPROACH

Let's follow the cash. The owner receives sales of $1,500, pays cash costs of $700 and pays taxes of $68. Thus, operating cash flow must equal:

$$\begin{aligned}
\text{OCF} &= \text{Sales} - \text{Cash costs} - \text{Taxes} \\
&= \$1,500 - 700 - 68 \\
&= \$732
\end{aligned} \quad\quad (6.3)$$

We call this the *top-down* approach because we start at the top of the income statement and work our way down to cash flow by subtracting costs, taxes, and other expenses.

Along the way, we left out depreciation. Why? Because depreciation is not a cash outflow. That is, the owner is not writing a $600 check to any Mr. Depreciation! While depreciation is an accounting concept, it is not a cash flow. Nevertheless, does depreciation play a part in the cash flow calculation? Yes, but only indirectly. Under current tax rules, depreciation is a deduction, lowering taxable income. A lower income number leads to lower taxes, which in turn leads to higher cash flow.

THE BOTTOM-UP APPROACH

This is the approach you would have had in an accounting class. First, income is calculated as:

$$\begin{aligned}
\text{Project net income} &= \text{EBT} - \text{Taxes} \\
&= \$200 - 68 \\
&= \$132
\end{aligned}$$

---

[3]Cash costs ignore depreciation.

Next, depreciation is added back, giving us:

$$OCF = \text{Net income} + \text{Depreciation} \qquad (6.4)$$
$$= \$132 + 600$$
$$= \$732$$

Expressing net income in terms of its components, we could write OCF more completely as:

$$OCF = (\text{Sales} - \text{Cash costs} - \text{Depreciation})(1 - t_c) + \text{Depreciation} \qquad (6.4')$$
$$= (\$1,500 - 700 - 600)(1 - .34) + 600 = \$732$$

This is the *bottom-up* approach, whether written as Equation 6.4 or Equation 6.4′. Here we start with the accountant's bottom line (net income) and add back any noncash deductions such as depreciation. It is crucial to remember that this definition of operating cash flow as net income plus depreciation is correct only if there is no interest expense subtracted in the calculation of net income.

A typical man or woman off the street would generally find the top-down approach easier to understand, and that is why we presented it first. The top-down approach simply asks what cash flows come in and what cash flows go out. However, anyone with accounting training may find the bottom-up approach easier because accountants use this latter approach all the time. In fact, a student with an accounting course under her belt knows from force of habit that depreciation is to be added back to get cash flow.

Can we explain intuitively why one should add back depreciation as was done here? Accounting texts devote a lot of space explaining the intuition behind the bottom-up approach, and we don't want to duplicate their efforts in a finance text. However, let's give a two-sentence explanation a try. As mentioned above, while depreciation reduces income, depreciation is *not* a cash outflow. Thus, one must add depreciation back when going from income to cash flow.

THE TAX SHIELD APPROACH

The tax shield approach is just a variant of the top-down approach, as presented in Equation 6.3. One of the terms comprising OCF in Equation 6.3 is taxes, which is defined in Equation 6.2. If we plug the formula for taxes provided in 6.2 into Equation 6.3, we get:

$$OCF = \text{Sales} - \text{Cash costs} - (\text{Sales} - \text{Cash costs} - \text{Depreciation}) \times t_c$$

which simplifies to:

$$OCF = (\text{Sales} - \text{Cash costs}) \times (1 - t_c) + \text{Depreciation} \times t_c \qquad (6.5)$$

where t_c is again the corporate tax rate. Assuming that $t_c = 34$ percent, OCF works out to be:

$$OCF = (\$1,500 - 700) \times .66 + 600 \times .34$$
$$= \$528 + 204$$
$$= \$732$$

This is just what we had before.

This approach views OCF as having two components. The first part is what the project's cash flow would be if there were no depreciation expense. In our example, this would-have-been cash flow is $528.

The second part of OCF in this approach is the depreciation deduction multiplied by the tax rate. This is called the **depreciation tax shield**. We know that depreciation is a non-cash expense. The only cash flow effect of deducting depreciation is to reduce our taxes, a benefit to us. At the current 34 percent corporate tax rate, every dollar in depreciation expense saves us 34 cents in taxes. So, in our example, the $600 depreciation deduction saves us $600 × .34 = $204 in taxes.

Students often think that the tax shield approach contradicts the bottom-up approach because depreciation is added back in Equation 6.4, but only the tax shield on depreciation is added back in Equation 6.5. However, the two formulae are perfectly consistent with each other, an idea most easily seen by comparing Equation 6.4′ to Equation 6.5. Depreciation is subtracted out in the first term on the right-hand side of 6.4′. No comparable subtraction occurs on the right-hand side of 6.5. We add the full amount of depreciation at the end of Equation 6.4′ (and at the end of its equivalent, Equation 6.4) because we subtracted out depreciation earlier in the equation.

CONCLUSION

Now that we've seen that all of these approaches are the same, you're probably wondering why everybody doesn't just agree on one of them. One reason is that different approaches are useful in different circumstances. The best one to use is whichever happens to be the most convenient for the problem at hand.

6.4 Some Special Cases of Discounted Cash Flow Analysis

Excel Master coverage online

Let's now look at three common cases involving discounted cash flow analysis. The first case considers cost-cutting investments. The second case considers competitive bidding. The third case compares equipment with different lives.

There are many other special cases, but these three are particularly common. Also, they illustrate some diverse applications of cash flow analysis and DCF valuation.

EVALUATING COST-CUTTING PROPOSALS

Firms must frequently decide whether to make existing facilities cost-effective. The issue is whether the cost savings are large enough to justify the necessary capital expenditure.

For example, suppose we are considering automating some part of an existing production process. The necessary equipment costs $80,000 to buy and install. The automation will save $22,000 per year (before taxes) by reducing labor and material costs. For simplicity, assume that the equipment has a five-year life and is depreciated to zero on a straight-line basis over that period. It will actually be worth $20,000 in five years. Should we automate? The tax rate is 34 percent, and the discount rate is 10 percent.

Let's begin by identifying the relevant cash flows. Determining the relevant capital spending is easy enough. The initial cost is $80,000. The aftertax salvage value is $20,000 × (1 − .34) = $13,200 because the book value will be zero in five years. There are no working capital consequences here, so we don't need to worry about changes in net working capital.

Operating cash flows must also be considered. Buying the new equipment affects our operating cash flows in three ways. First, we save $22,000 before taxes every year.

In other words, the firm's operating income increases by $22,000, so this is the relevant incremental project operating income.

Second (and it's easy to overlook this), we have an additional depreciation deduction. In this case, the depreciation is $80,000/5 = $16,000 per year.

Because the project has an operating income of $22,000 (the annual pretax cost savings) and a depreciation deduction of $16,000, the project will increase the firm's earnings before interest and taxes (EBIT) by $22,000 − 16,000 = $6,000. In other words, $6,000 is the project's EBIT.

Third, because EBIT is rising for the firm, taxes will increase. This increase in taxes will be $6,000 × .34 = $2,040. With this information, we can compute operating cash flow in the usual way:

EBIT	$ 6,000
+Depreciation	16,000
−Taxes	2,040
Operating cash flow	$19,960

So, our aftertax operating cash flow is $19,960.

We can also calculate operating cash flow using a different approach. What is actually going on here is very simple. First, the cost savings increase our pretax income by $22,000. We have to pay taxes on this amount, so our tax bill increases by .34 × $22,000 = $7,480. In other words, the $22,000 pretax saving amounts to $22,000 × (1 − .34) = $14,520 after taxes.

Second, while the extra $16,000 in depreciation isn't a cash outflow, it does reduce our taxes by $16,000 × .34 = $5,440. The sum of these two components is $14,520 + 5,440 = $19,960, just as we had before. Notice that the $5,440 is the depreciation tax shield we discussed earlier, and we have effectively used the tax shield approach here.

We can now finish our analysis. Based on our discussion, here are the relevant cash flows:

				Year		
	0	1	2	3	4	5
Operating cash flow		$19,960	$19,960	$19,960	$19,960	$19,960
Capital spending	−$80,000					13,200
Total cash flow	−$80,000	$19,960	$19,960	$19,960	$19,960	$33,160

At 10 percent, it's straightforward to verify that the NPV here is $3,860, so we should go ahead and automate.

**EXAMPLE
6.6**

To Buy or Not to Buy We are considering the purchase of a $200,000 computer-based inventory management system. It will be depreciated straight-line to zero over its four-year life. It will be worth $30,000 at the end of that time. The system will save us $60,000 before taxes in inventory-related costs. The relevant tax rate is 39 percent. Because the new setup is more efficient than our existing one, we can carry less total inventory, thereby freeing up $45,000 in net working capital. What is the NPV at 16 percent? What is the IRR on this investment?

(continued)

Let's first calculate the operating cash flow. The aftertax cost savings are $60,000 × (1 − .39) = $36,600 per year. The depreciation is $200,000/4 = $50,000 per year, so the depreciation tax shield is $50,000 × .39 = $19,500. Operating cash flow is thus $36,600 + 19,500 = $56,100 per year.

The system involves a $200,000 up front cost to buy the system. The aftertax salvage is $30,000 × (1 − .39) = $18,300. Finally, and this is somewhat tricky, the initial investment in net working capital (NWC) is a $45,000 *inflow* because the system frees up working capital. Furthermore, we will have to put this back in at the end of the project's life. What this really means is simple: While the system is in operation, we have $45,000 to use elsewhere.

To finish our analysis, we can compute the total cash flows:

	Year				
	0	**1**	**2**	**3**	**4**
Operating cash flow		$56,100	$56,100	$56,100	$56,100
Change in NWC	$ 45,000				−45,000
Capital spending	−200,000				18,300
Total cash flow	−$155,000	$56,100	$56,100	$56,100	$29,400

At 16 percent, the NPV is −$12,768, so the investment is not attractive. After some trial and error, we find that the NPV is zero when the discount rate is 11.48 percent, implying an IRR of about 11.5 percent.

SETTING THE BID PRICE

One generally uses the NPV approach to evaluate a new project. The NPV approach can also be used when submitting a competitive bid to win a job. Under such circumstances, the winner is whoever submits the lowest bid.

There is an old joke concerning this process: The low bidder is whoever makes the biggest mistake. This is called the winner's curse. In other words, if you win, there is a good chance you underbid. In this section, we look at how to go about setting the bid price to avoid the winner's curse. The procedure we describe is useful any time we have to set a price on a product or service.

As with any other capital budgeting project, we must be careful to account for all relevant cash flows. For example, industry analysts estimated that the materials in Microsoft's Xbox 360 cost $470 before assembly. Other items such as the power supply, cables, and controllers increased the materials cost by another $55. At a retail price of $399, Microsoft obviously loses a significant amount on each Xbox 360 it sells. Why would a manufacturer sell at a price well below breakeven? A Microsoft spokesperson stated that the company believed that sales of its game software would make the Xbox 360 a profitable project.

To illustrate how to go about setting a bid price, imagine we are in the business of buying stripped-down truck platforms and then modifying them to customer specifications for resale. A local distributor has requested bids for 5 specially modified trucks each year for the next four years, for a total of 20 trucks in all.

We need to decide what price to bid per truck. The goal of our analysis is to determine the lowest price we can profitably charge. This maximizes our chances of being awarded the contract while guarding against the winner's curse.

Suppose we can buy the truck platforms for $10,000 each. The facilities we need can be leased for $24,000 per year. The labor and material for the modification cost about $4,000 per truck. Total cost per year will thus be $24,000 + 5 × (10,000 + 4,000) = $94,000.

We will need to invest $60,000 in new equipment. This equipment will be depreciated straight-line to a zero salvage value over the four years. It will be worth about $5,000 at the end of that time. We will also need to invest $40,000 in raw materials inventory and other working capital items. The relevant tax rate is 39 percent. What price per truck should we bid if we require a 20 percent return on our investment?

We start by looking at the capital spending and net working capital investment. We have to spend $60,000 today for new equipment. The aftertax salvage value is $5,000 × (1 − .39) = $3,050. Furthermore, we have to invest $40,000 today in working capital. We will get this back in four years.

We can't determine the operating cash flow (OCF) just yet because we don't know the sales price. Thus, if we draw a time line, here is what we have so far:

			Year		
	0	**1**	**2**	**3**	**4**
Operating cash flow		+OCF	+OCF	+OCF	+OCF
Change in NWC	−$ 40,000				$40,000
Capital spending	− 60,000				3,050
Total cash flow	−$100,000	+OCF	+OCF	+OCF	+OCF + $43,050

With this in mind, note that the key observation is the following: The lowest possible price we can profitably charge will result in a zero NPV at 20 percent. At that price, we earn exactly 20 percent on our investment.

Given this observation, we first need to determine what the operating cash flow must be for the NPV to equal zero. To do this, we calculate the present value of the $43,050 nonoperating cash flow from the last year and subtract it from the $100,000 initial investment:

$$\$100,000 - 43,050/1.20^4 = \$100,000 - 20,761 = \$79,239$$

Once we have done this, our time line is:

			Year		
	0	**1**	**2**	**3**	**4**
Total cash flow	−$79,239	+OCF	+OCF	+OCF	+OCF

As the time line suggests, the operating cash flow is now an unknown ordinary annuity amount. The four-year annuity factor for 20 percent, PVIFA (.20, 4), is 2.58873, so we have:

$$NPV = 0 = -\$79,239 + OCF \times 2.58873$$

This implies that:

$$OCF = \$79,239/2.58873 = \$30,609$$

So the operating cash flow needs to be $30,609 each year.

We're not quite finished. The final problem is to find out what sales price results in an operating cash flow of $30,609. The easiest way to do this is to recall that operating cash flow can be written as net income plus depreciation (the bottom-up definition).

The depreciation here is $60,000/4 = $15,000$. Given this, we can determine what net income must be:

$$\text{Operating cash flow} = \text{Net income} + \text{Depreciation}$$
$$\$30,609 = \text{Net income} + \$15,000$$
$$\text{Net income} = \$15,609$$

From here, we work our way backward up the income statement. If net income is $15,609, then our income statement is as follows:

Sales	?
Costs	$94,000
Depreciation	15,000
Taxes (39%)	?
Net income	$15,609

We can solve for sales by noting that:

$$\text{Net income} = (\text{Sales} - \text{Costs} - \text{Depreciation}) \times (1 - T)$$
$$\$15,609 = (\text{Sales} - \$94,000 - \$15,000) \times (1 - .39)$$
$$\text{Sales} = \$15,609/.61 + 94,000 + 15,000$$
$$= \$134,589$$

Sales per year must be $134,589. Because the contract calls for five trucks per year, the sales price has to be $134,589/5 = $26,918$. If we round this up a bit, it looks as though we need to bid about $27,000 per truck. At this price, were we to get the contract, our return would be just over 20 percent.

INVESTMENTS OF UNEQUAL LIVES: THE EQUIVALENT ANNUAL COST METHOD

Suppose a firm must choose between two machines of unequal lives. Both machines can do the same job, but they have different operating costs and will last for different time periods. A simple application of the NPV rule suggests taking the machine whose costs have the lower present value. This choice might be a mistake, however, because the lower-cost machine may need to be replaced before the other one.

Let's consider an example. The Downtown Athletic Club must choose between two mechanical tennis ball throwers. Machine A costs less than Machine B but will not last as long. The cash *outflows* from the two machines are shown here:

Machine	Date				
	0	**1**	**2**	**3**	**4**
A	$500	$120	$120	$120	
B	$600	$100	$100	$100	$100

Machine A costs $500 and lasts three years. There will be maintenance expenses of $120 to be paid at the end of each of the three years. Machine B costs $600 and lasts four years. There will be maintenance expenses of $100 to be paid at the end of each of the four years. We express all costs in real terms, an assumption greatly simplifying the analysis. Revenues per year are assumed to be the same, regardless of machine, so they are not considered in the analysis. Note that all numbers in the chart are *outflows*. For simplicity, we ignore taxes.

To get a handle on the decision, let's take the present value of the costs of each of the two machines. Assuming a discount rate of 10 percent, we have:

$$\text{Machine } A\text{: } \$798.42 = \$500 + \frac{\$120}{1.1} + \frac{\$120}{(1.1)^2} + \frac{\$120}{(1.1)^3}$$

$$\text{Machine } B\text{: } \$916.99 = \$600 + \frac{\$100}{1.1} + \frac{\$100}{(1.1)^2} + \frac{\$100}{(1.1)^3} + \frac{\$100}{(1.1)^4}$$

Machine *B* has a higher present value of outflows. A naive approach would be to select Machine *A* because of its lower present value. However, Machine *B* has a longer life, so perhaps its cost per year is actually lower.

How might one properly adjust for the difference in useful life when comparing the two machines? Perhaps the easiest approach involves calculating something called the *equivalent annual cost* of each machine. This approach puts costs on a per-year basis.

The previous equation for Machine *A* showed that payments of ($500, $120, $120, $120) are equivalent to a single payment of $798.42 at Date 0. We now wish to equate the single payment of $798.42 at Date 0 with a three-year annuity. Using techniques of previous chapters, we have:

$$\$798.42 = C \times \text{PVIFA} (.10, 3)$$

PVIFA (.10, 3) is an annuity of $1 a year for three years, discounted at 10 percent. *C* is the unknown—the annuity payment per year such that the present value of all payments equals $798.42. Because PVIFA (.10, 3) equals 2.4869, *C* equals $321.05 (=$798.42/2.4869). Thus, a payment stream of ($500, $120, $120, $120) is equivalent to annuity payments of $321.05 made at the *end* of each year for three years. We refer to $321.05 as the *equivalent annual cost* of Machine *A*.

This idea is summarized in the following chart:

	Date			
	0	**1**	**2**	**3**
Cash outflows of Machine A	$500	$120	$120	$120
Equivalent annual cost of Machine A		321.05	321.05	321.05

The Downtown Athletic Club should be indifferent between cash outflows of ($500, $120, $120, $120) and cash outflows of ($0, $321.05, $321.05, $321.05). Alternatively, one can say that the purchase of the machine is financially equivalent to a rental agreement calling for annual lease payments of $321.05.

Now let's turn to Machine *B*. We calculate its equivalent annual cost from:

$$\$916.99 = C \times \text{PVIFA} (.10, 4)$$

Because PVIFA (.10, 4) equals 3.1699, *C* equals $916.99/3.1699, or $289.28.

As we did for Machine *A*, we can create the following chart for Machine *B*:

	Date				
	0	**1**	**2**	**3**	**4**
Cash outflows of Machine B	$600	$100	$100	$100	$100
Equivalent annual cost of Machine B		289.28	289.28	289.28	289.28

The decision is easy once the charts of the two machines are compared. Would you rather make annual lease payments of $321.05 or $289.28? Put this way, the problem becomes a no-brainer: A rational person would rather pay the lower amount. Thus, Machine *B* is the preferred choice.

Two final remarks are in order. First, it is no accident that we specified the costs of the tennis ball machines in real terms. Although *B* would still have been the preferred machine had the costs been stated in nominal terms, the actual solution would have been much more difficult. As a general rule, always convert cash flows to real terms when working through problems of this type.

Second, such analysis applies only if one anticipates that both machines can be replaced. The analysis would differ if no replacement were possible. For example, imagine that the only company that manufactured tennis ball throwers just went out of business and no new producers are expected to enter the field. In this case, Machine *B* would generate revenues in the fourth year whereas Machine *A* would not. Here, simple net present value analysis for mutually exclusive projects including both revenues and costs would be appropriate.

6.5 Inflation and Capital Budgeting

To finish our chapter, we look at the effect of inflation on capital budgeting. Inflation (or deflation) can affect both cash flows and discount rates in capital budgeting. We begin our examination of inflation by considering the relationship between interest rates and inflation.

INTEREST RATES AND INFLATION

Suppose a bank offers a one-year interest rate of 10 percent. This means that an individual who deposits $1,000 will receive $1,100 (=$1,000 × 1.10) in one year. Although 10 percent may seem like a handsome return, one can put it in perspective only after examining the rate of inflation.

Imagine that the rate of inflation is 6 percent over the year and it affects all goods equally. For example, a fast-food restaurant charging $1.00 for a hamburger today will charge $1.06 for the same hamburger at the end of the year. You can use your $1,000 to buy 1,000 hamburgers today (Date 0). Alternatively, if you put your money in the bank, you can buy 1,038 (=$1,100/$1.06) hamburgers at Date 1. Thus, lending increases your hamburger consumption by only 3.8 percent.

Because the prices of all goods rise at this 6 percent rate, lending lets you increase your consumption of any single good or any combination of goods by 3.8 percent. Thus, 3.8 percent is what you are *really* earning through your savings account, after adjusting for inflation. Economists refer to the 3.8 percent number as the *real interest rate*. Economists refer to the 10 percent rate as the *nominal interest rate* or simply the *interest rate*. This discussion is illustrated in Figure 6.1.

We have used an example with a specific nominal interest rate and a specific inflation rate. In general, the formula between real and nominal interest rates can be written as follows:

$$1 + \text{Nominal interest rate} = (1 + \text{Real interest rate}) \times (1 + \text{Inflation rate})$$

Rearranging terms, we have:

$$\text{Real interest rate} = \frac{1 + \text{Nominal interest rate}}{1 + \text{Inflation rate}} - 1 \qquad \textbf{(6.6)}$$

Figure 6.1

Calculation of Real Rate of Interest

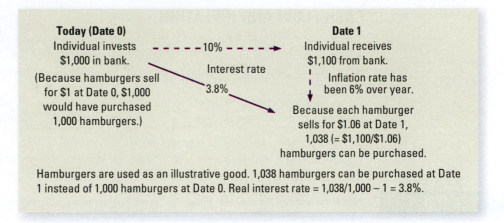

Today (Date 0)
Individual invests $1,000 in bank.

(Because hamburgers sell for $1 at Date 0, $1,000 would have purchased 1,000 hamburgers.)

- - - - 10% - - - - ▶

Interest rate

3.8%

Date 1
Individual receives $1,100 from bank.

Inflation rate has been 6% over year.

Because each hamburger sells for $1.06 at Date 1, 1,038 (= $1,100/$1.06) hamburgers can be purchased.

Hamburgers are used as an illustrative good. 1,038 hamburgers can be purchased at Date 1 instead of 1,000 hamburgers at Date 0. Real interest rate = 1,038/1,000 − 1 = 3.8%.

The formula indicates that the real interest rate in our example is 3.8 percent (=1.10/1.06 − 1).

Equation 6.6 determines the real interest rate precisely. The following formula is an approximation:

$$\text{Real interest rate} \cong \text{Nominal interest rate} - \text{Inflation rate} \tag{6.7}$$

The symbol $\cong$ indicates that the equation is approximately true. This latter formula calculates the real rate in our example as:

$$4\% = 10\% - 6\%$$

You should be aware that, although Equation 6.7 may seem more intuitive than Equation 6.6, 6.7 is only an approximation. This approximation is reasonably accurate for low rates of interest and inflation. In our example the difference between the approximate calculation and the exact one is only .2 percent (= 4 percent − 3.8 percent). Unfortunately, the approximation becomes poor when rates are higher.

EXAMPLE 6.7

Real and Nominal Rates   The little-known monarchy of Gerberovia recently had a nominal interest rate of 300 percent and an inflation rate of 280 percent. According to Equation 6.7, the real interest rate is:

$$300\% - 280\% = 20\% \text{ (Approximate formula)}$$

However, according to Equation 6.6, this rate is:

$$\frac{1 + 300\%}{1 + 280\%} - 1 = 5.26\% \quad \text{(Exact formula)}$$

How do we know that the second formula is indeed the exact one? Let's think in terms of hamburgers again. Had you deposited $1,000 in a Gerberovian bank a year ago, the account would be worth $4,000 [=$1,000 × (1 + 300%)] today. However, while a hamburger cost $1 a year ago, it costs $3.80 (=1 + 280%) today. Therefore, you would now be able to buy 1,052.6 (=$4,000/3.80) hamburgers, implying a real interest rate of 5.26 percent.

CASH FLOW AND INFLATION

The previous analysis defines two types of interest rates, nominal rates and real rates, and relates them through Equation 6.6. Capital budgeting requires data on cash flows as well as on interest rates. Like interest rates, cash flows can be expressed in either nominal or real terms.

A **nominal cash flow** refers to the actual dollars to be received (or paid out). A **real cash flow** refers to the cash flow's purchasing power. These definitions are best explained by examples.

EXAMPLE

Nominal versus Real Cash Flow   Burrows Publishing has just purchased the rights to the next book of famed romantic novelist Barbara Musk. Still unwritten, the book should be available to the public in four years. Currently, romantic novels sell for $10.00 in softcover. The publishers believe that inflation will be 6 percent a year over the next four years. Because romantic novels are so popular, the publishers anticipate that their prices will rise about 2 percent per year more than the inflation rate over the next four years. Burrows Publishing plans to sell the novel at $13.60 [=(1.08)^4 × $10.00] four years from now, anticipating sales of 100,000 copies.

The expected cash flow in the fourth year of $1.36 million (=$13.60 × 100,000) is a *nominal cash flow*. That is, the firm expects to receive $1.36 million at that time. In other words, a nominal cash flow refers to the actual dollars to be received in the future.

The purchasing power of $1.36 million in four years is:

$$\$1.08 \text{ million} = \frac{\$1.36 \text{ million}}{(1.06)^4}$$

The figure of $1.08 million is a *real cash flow* because it is expressed in terms of purchasing power. Extending our hamburger example, the $1.36 million to be received in four years will only buy 1.08 million hamburgers because the price of a hamburger will rise from $1 to $1.26 [=$1 × (1.06)^4] over the period.

EXAMPLE
6.9

Depreciation   EOBII Publishers, a competitor of Burrows, recently bought a printing press for $2,000,000 to be depreciated to zero by the straight-line method over five years. This implies yearly depreciation of $400,000 (=$2,000,000/5). Is this $400,000 figure a real or a nominal quantity?

Depreciation is a *nominal* quantity because $400,000 is the actual tax deduction over each of the next five years. Depreciation becomes a real quantity if it is adjusted for purchasing power. Assuming an annual inflation rate of 6 percent, depreciation in the fourth year expressed as a real quantity is $316,837 [=$400,000/(1.06)^4].

DISCOUNTING: NOMINAL OR REAL?

Our previous discussion showed that interest rates can be expressed in either nominal or real terms. Similarly, cash flows can be expressed in either nominal or real terms. Given these choices, how should one express interest rates and cash flows when performing capital budgeting?

Financial practitioners correctly stress the need to maintain *consistency* between cash flows and discount rates. That is:

> *Nominal* cash flows must be discounted at the *nominal* rate.
>
> *Real* cash flows must be discounted at the *real* rate.

As long as one is consistent, either approach is correct. To minimize computational error, it is generally advisable in practice to choose the approach that is easiest. This idea is illustrated in the following two examples.

EXAMPLE
6.10

Real and Nominal Discounting   Shields Electric forecasts the following nominal cash flows on a particular project:

Cash Flow	0	1	2
	−$1,000	$600	$650

The nominal discount rate is 14 percent, and the inflation rate is forecast to be 5 percent. What is the value of the project?

Using Nominal Quantities   The NPV can be calculated as:

$$\$26.47 = -\$1,000 + \frac{\$600}{1.14} + \frac{\$650}{(1.14)^2}$$

The project should be accepted.

Using Real Quantities   The real cash flows are these:

Cash Flow	0	1	2
	−$1,000	$571.43	$589.57
		$= \left(\frac{\$600}{1.05}\right)$	$= \left(\frac{\$650}{(1.05)^2}\right)$

According to Equation 6.6, the real discount rate is 8.57143 percent ($=1.14/1.05 - 1$). The NPV can be calculated as:

$$\$26.47 = -\$1,000 + \frac{\$571.43}{1.0857143} + \frac{\$589.57}{(1.0857143)^2}$$

The NPV is the same whether cash flows are expressed in nominal or in real quantities. It must always be the case that the NPV is the same under the two different approaches.

Because both approaches always yield the same result, which one should be used? Use the approach that is simpler because the simpler approach generally leads to fewer computational errors. The Shields Electric example begins with nominal cash flows, so nominal quantities produce a simpler calculation here.

EXAMPLE

Real and Nominal NPV Altshuler, Inc., generated the following forecast for a capital budgeting project:

	Year 0	Year 1	Year 2
Capital expenditure	$1,210		
Revenues (in real terms)		$1,900	$2,000
Cash expenses (in real terms)		950	1000
Depreciation (straight-line)		605	605

The CEO, David Altshuler, estimates inflation to be 10 percent per year over the next two years. In addition, he believes that the cash flows of the project should be discounted at the nominal rate of 15.5 percent. His firm's tax rate is 40 percent.

　　Mr. Altshuler forecasts all cash flows in *nominal* terms, leading to the following table and NPV calculation:

	Year 0	Year 1	Year 2
Capital expenditure	−$1,210		
Revenues		$2,090 (=1,900 × 1.10)	$2,420 [=2,000 × (1.10)²]
−Expenses		−1,045 (=950 × 1.10)	−1,210 [=1,000 × (1.10)²]
−Depreciation		−605 (=1210/2)	−605
Taxable income		440	605
−Taxes (40%)		−176	−242
Income after taxes		264	363
+Depreciation		605	605
Cash flow		869	968

$$NPV = -\$1,210 + \frac{\$869}{1.155} + \frac{\$968}{(1.155)^2} = \$268$$

The firm's CFO, Stuart Weiss, prefers working in real terms. He first calculates the real rate to be 5 percent (=1.155/1.10 − 1). Next, he generates the following table in *real* quantities:

	Year 0	Year 1	Year 2
Capital expenditure	−$1,210		
Revenues		$1,900	$2,000
−Expenses		−950	−1,000
−Depreciation		−550 (=605/1.10)	−500 [=605/(1.10)²]
Taxable income		400	500
−Taxes (40%)		−160	−200
Income after taxes		240	300
+Depreciation		550	500
Cash flow		790	800

Mr. Weiss calculates the value of the project as:

$$NPV = -\$1,210 + \frac{\$790}{1.05} + \frac{\$800}{(1.05)^2} = \$268$$

In explaining his calculations to Mr. Altshuler, Mr. Weiss points out these facts:

1. The capital expenditure occurs at Date 0 (today), so its nominal value and its real value are equal.
2. Because yearly depreciation of $605 is a nominal quantity, one converts it to a real quantity by discounting at the inflation rate of 10 percent.

It is no coincidence that both Mr. Altshuler and Mr. Weiss arrive at the same NPV number. Both methods must always generate the same NPV.

Summary and Conclusions

This chapter discussed a number of practical applications of capital budgeting.

1. Capital budgeting must be placed on an incremental basis. This means that sunk costs must be ignored, whereas both opportunity costs and side effects must be considered.

2. In the Baldwin case we computed NPV using the following two steps:
   a. Calculate the net cash flow from all sources for each period.
   b. Calculate the NPV using these cash flows.

3. The discounted cash flow approach can be applied to many areas of capital budgeting. In this chapter we applied the approach to cost-cutting investments, competitive bidding, and choices between equipment of different lives.

4. Operating cash flows (OCF) can be computed in a number of different ways. We presented three different methods for calculating OCF: The top-down approach, the bottom-up approach, and the tax shield approach. The three approaches are consistent with each other.

5. Inflation must be handled consistently. One approach is to express both cash flows and the discount rate in nominal terms. The other approach is to express both cash flows and the discount rate in real terms. Because both approaches yield the same NPV calculation, the simpler method should be used. The simpler method will generally depend on the type of capital budgeting problem.

Concept Questions

1. **Opportunity Cost**   In the context of capital budgeting, what is an opportunity cost?
2. **Incremental Cash Flows**   Which of the following should be treated as an incremental cash flow when computing the NPV of an investment?
   a. A reduction in the sales of a company's other products caused by the investment.
   b. An expenditure on plant and equipment that has not yet been made and will be made only if the project is accepted.
   c. Costs of research and development undertaken in connection with the product during the past three years.
   d. Annual depreciation expense from the investment.

   e. Dividend payments by the firm.

   f. The resale value of plant and equipment at the end of the project's life.

   g. Salary and medical costs for production personnel who will be employed only if the project is accepted.

3. **Incremental Cash Flows** Your company currently produces and sells steel shaft golf clubs. The board of directors wants you to consider the introduction of a new line of titanium bubble woods with graphite shafts. Which of the following costs are *not* relevant?

   a. Land you already own that will be used for the project, but otherwise will be sold for $700,000, its market value.

   b. A $300,000 drop in your sales of steel shaft clubs if the titanium woods with graphite shafts are introduced.

   c. $200,000 spent on research and development last year on graphite shafts.

4. **Depreciation** Given the choice, would a firm prefer to use MACRS depreciation or straight-line depreciation? Why?

5. **Net Working Capital** In our capital budgeting examples, we assumed that a firm would recover all of the working capital it invested in a project. Is this a reasonable assumption? When might it not be valid?

6. **Stand-Alone Principle** Suppose a financial manager is quoted as saying, "Our firm uses the stand-alone principle. Because we treat projects like minifirms in our evaluation process, we include financing costs because they are relevant at the firm level." Critically evaluate this statement.

7. **Equivalent Annual Cost** When is EAC analysis appropriate for comparing two or more projects? Why is this method used? Are there any implicit assumptions required by this method that you find troubling? Explain.

8. **Cash Flow and Depreciation** "When evaluating projects, we're only concerned with the relevant incremental aftertax cash flows. Therefore, because depreciation is a noncash expense, we should ignore its effects when evaluating projects." Critically evaluate this statement.

9. **Capital Budgeting Considerations** A major college textbook publisher has an existing finance textbook. The publisher is debating whether to produce an "essentialized" version, meaning a shorter (and lower-priced) book. What are some of the considerations that should come into play?

   To answer the next three questions, refer to the following example. In 2003, Porsche unveiled its new sports utility vehicle (SUV), the Cayenne. With a price tag of over $40,000, the Cayenne goes from zero to 62 mph in 8.5 seconds. Porsche's decision to enter the SUV market was in response to the runaway success of other high-priced SUVs such as the Mercedes-Benz M class. Vehicles in this class had generated years of very high profits. The Cayenne certainly spiced up the market, and, in 2006, Porsche introduced the Cayenne Turbo S, which goes from zero to 60 mph in 4.8 seconds and has a top speed of 168 mph. The base price for the Cayenne Turbo S in 2014? Almost $115,000!

   Some analysts questioned Porsche's entry into the luxury SUV market. The analysts were concerned because not only was Porsche a late entry into the market, but also the introduction of the Cayenne might damage Porsche's reputation as a maker of high-performance automobiles.

10. **Erosion** In evaluating the Cayenne, would you consider the possible damage to Porsche's reputation as erosion?

11. **Capital Budgeting** Porsche was one of the last manufacturers to enter the sports utility vehicle market. Why would one company decide to proceed with a product when other companies, at least initially, decide not to enter the market?

12. **Capital Budgeting** In evaluating the Cayenne, what do you think Porsche needs to assume regarding the substantial profit margins that exist in this market? Is it likely that they will be maintained as the market becomes more competitive, or will Porsche be able to maintain the profit margin because of its image and the performance of the Cayenne?

Questions and Problems

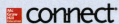

BASIC
(Questions 1–10)

1. **Calculating Project NPV**   Flatte Restaurant is considering the purchase of a $7,500 soufflé maker. The soufflé maker has an economic life of five years and will be fully depreciated by the straight-line method. The machine will produce 1,300 soufflés per year, with each costing $2.15 to make and priced at $5.25. Assume that the discount rate is 14 percent and the tax rate is 34 percent. Should the company make the purchase?

2. **Calculating Project NPV**   The Best Manufacturing Company is considering a new investment. Financial projections for the investment are tabulated here. The corporate tax rate is 34 percent. Assume all sales revenue is received in cash, all operating costs and income taxes are paid in cash, and all cash flows occur at the end of the year. All net working capital is recovered at the end of the project.

	Year 0	Year 1	Year 2	Year 3	Year 4
Investment	$27,400				
Sales revenue		$12,900	$14,000	$15,200	$11,200
Operating costs		2,700	2,800	2,900	2,100
Depreciation		6,850	6,850	6,850	6,850
Net working capital spending	300	200	225	150	?

   a. Compute the incremental net income of the investment for each year.
   b. Compute the incremental cash flows of the investment for each year.
   c. Suppose the appropriate discount rate is 12 percent. What is the NPV of the project?

3. **Calculating Project NPV**   Down Under Boomerang, Inc., is considering a new three-year expansion project that requires an initial fixed asset investment of $1.65 million. The fixed asset will be depreciated straight-line to zero over its three-year tax life, after which it will be worthless. The project is estimated to generate $1.24 million in annual sales, with costs of $485,000. The tax rate is 35 percent and the required return is 12 percent. What is the project's NPV?

4. **Calculating Project Cash Flow from Assets**   In the previous problem, suppose the project requires an initial investment in net working capital of $285,000 and the fixed asset will have a market value of $225,000 at the end of the project. What is the project's Year 0 net cash flow? Year 1? Year 2? Year 3? What is the new NPV?

5. **NPV and Modified ACRS**   In the previous problem, suppose the fixed asset actually falls into the three-year MACRS class. All the other facts are the same. What is the project's Year 1 net cash flow now? Year 2? Year 3? What is the new NPV?

6. **Project Evaluation**   Your firm is contemplating the purchase of a new $530,000 computer-based order entry system. The system will be depreciated straight-line to zero over its five-year life. It will be worth $50,000 at the end of that time. You will save $186,000 before taxes per year in order processing costs, and you will be able to reduce working capital by $85,000 (this is a one-time reduction). If the tax rate is 35 percent, what is the IRR for this project?

7. **Project Evaluation**   Dog Up! Franks is looking at a new sausage system with an installed cost of $345,000. This cost will be depreciated straight-line to zero over the project's five-year life, at the end of which the sausage system can be scrapped for $25,000. The sausage system will save the firm $85,000 per year in pretax operating

costs, and the system requires an initial investment in net working capital of $20,000. If the tax rate is 34 percent and the discount rate is 10 percent, what is the NPV of this project?

8. **Calculating Salvage Value** An asset used in a four-year project falls in the five-year MACRS class for tax purposes. The asset has an acquisition cost of $8,300,000 and will be sold for $1,700,000 at the end of the project. If the tax rate is 35 percent, what is the aftertax salvage value of the asset?

9. **Calculating NPV** Howell Petroleum is considering a new project that complements its existing business. The machine required for the project costs $3.9 million. The marketing department predicts that sales related to the project will be $2.35 million per year for the next four years, after which the market will cease to exist. The machine will be depreciated down to zero over its four-year economic life using the straight-line method. Cost of goods sold and operating expenses related to the project are predicted to be 25 percent of sales. Howell also needs to add net working capital of $150,000 immediately. The additional net working capital will be recovered in full at the end of the project's life. The corporate tax rate is 35 percent. The required rate of return for Howell is 13 percent. Should Howell proceed with the project?

10. **Calculating EAC** You are evaluating two different silicon wafer milling machines. The Techron I costs $245,000, has a three-year life, and has pretax operating costs of $39,000 per year. The Techron II costs $315,000, has a five-year life, and has pretax operating costs of $48,000 per year. For both milling machines, use straight-line depreciation to zero over the project's life and assume a salvage value of $20,000. If your tax rate is 35 percent and your discount rate is 9 percent, compute the EAC for both machines. Which do you prefer? Why?

INTERMEDIATE
(Questions 11–27)

11. **Cost-Cutting Proposals** Massey Machine Shop is considering a four-year project to improve its production efficiency. Buying a new machine press for $730,000 is estimated to result in $270,000 in annual pretax cost savings. The press falls in the MACRS five-year class, and it will have a salvage value at the end of the project of $70,000. The press also requires an initial investment in spare parts inventory of $20,000, along with an additional $3,500 in inventory for each succeeding year of the project. If the shop's tax rate is 35 percent and its discount rate is 8 percent, should Massey buy and install the machine press?

12. **Comparing Mutually Exclusive Projects** Hagar Industrial Systems Company (HISC) is trying to decide between two different conveyor belt systems. System A costs $290,000, has a four-year life, and requires $89,000 in pretax annual operating costs. System B costs $410,000, has a six-year life, and requires $79,000 in pretax annual operating costs. Both systems are to be depreciated straight-line to zero over their lives and will have zero salvage value. Whichever system is chosen, it will *not* be replaced when it wears out. If the tax rate is 34 percent and the discount rate is 7.5 percent, which system should the firm choose?

13. **Comparing Mutually Exclusive Projects** Suppose in the previous problem that HISC always needs a conveyor belt system; when one wears out, it must be replaced. Which system should the firm choose now?

14. **Comparing Mutually Exclusive Projects** Vandalay Industries is considering the purchase of a new machine for the production of latex. Machine A costs $3,100,000 and will last for six years. Variable costs are 35 percent of sales, and fixed costs are $204,000 per year. Machine B costs $6,100,000 and will last for nine years. Variable costs for this machine are 30 percent and fixed costs are $165,000 per year. The sales for each machine will be $13.5 million per year. The required return is 10 percent and the tax rate is 35 percent. Both machines will be depreciated on a straight-line basis. If the company plans to replace the machine when it wears out on a perpetual basis, which machine should you choose?

15. **Capital Budgeting with Inflation**   Consider the following cash flows on two mutually exclusive projects:

Year	Project A	Project B
0	−$30,000	−$45,000
1	18,000	21,000
2	16,000	23,000
3	12,000	25,000

The cash flows of Project A are expressed in real terms, whereas those of Project B are expressed in nominal terms. The appropriate nominal discount rate is 13 percent and the inflation rate is 4 percent. Which project should you choose?

16. **Inflation and Company Value**   Sparkling Water, Inc., expects to sell 2.7 million bottles of drinking water each year in perpetuity. This year each bottle will sell for $1.35 in real terms and will cost $.85 in real terms. Sales income and costs occur at year-end. Revenues will rise at a real rate of 1.3 percent annually, while real costs will rise at a real rate of .8 percent annually. The real discount rate is 6 percent. The corporate tax rate is 34 percent. What is the company worth today?

17. **Calculating Nominal Cash Flow**   Etonic, Inc., is considering an investment of $395,000 in an asset with an economic life of five years. The firm estimates that the nominal annual cash revenues and expenses at the end of the first year will be $255,000 and $82,000, respectively. Both revenues and expenses will grow thereafter at the annual inflation rate of 3 percent. The company will use the straight-line method to depreciate its asset to zero over five years. The salvage value of the asset is estimated to be $45,000 in nominal terms at that time. The one-time net working capital investment of $15,000 is required immediately and will be recovered at the end of the project. The corporate tax rate is 34 percent. What is the project's total nominal cash flow from assets for each year?

18. **Cash Flow Valuation**   Phillips Industries runs a small manufacturing operation. For this fiscal year, it expects real net cash flows of $235,000. The company is an ongoing operation, but it expects competitive pressures to erode its real net cash flows at 3 percent per year in perpetuity. The appropriate real discount rate for the company is 4 percent. All net cash flows are received at year-end. What is the present value of the net cash flows from the company's operations?

19. **Equivalent Annual Cost**   Bridgton Golf Academy is evaluating new golf practice equipment. The "Dimple-Max" equipment costs $64,000, has a three-year life, and costs $7,500 per year to operate. The relevant discount rate is 12 percent. Assume that the straight-line depreciation method is used and that the equipment is fully depreciated to zero. Furthermore, assume the equipment has a salvage value of $7,500 at the end of the project's life. The relevant tax rate is 34 percent. All cash flows occur at the end of the year. What is the equivalent annual cost (EAC) of this equipment?

20. **Calculating Project NPV**   RightPrice Investors, Inc., is considering the purchase of a $415,000 computer with an economic life of five years. The computer will be fully depreciated over five years using the straight-line method. The market value of the computer will be $50,000 in five years. The computer will replace four office employees whose combined annual salaries are $120,000. The machine will also immediately lower the firm's required net working capital by $80,000. This amount of net working capital will need to be replaced once the machine is sold. The corporate tax rate is 34 percent. Is it worthwhile to buy the computer if the appropriate discount rate is 9 percent?

21. **Calculating NPV and IRR for a Replacement**   A firm is considering an investment in a new machine with a price of $15.6 million to replace its existing machine. The current machine has a book value of $5.4 million and a market value of $4.1 million. The new machine is expected to have a four-year life, and the old machine has four years left in

which it can be used. If the firm replaces the old machine with the new machine, it expects to save $6.3 million in operating costs each year over the next four years. Both machines will have no salvage value in four years. If the firm purchases the new machine, it will also need an investment of $250,000 in net working capital. The required return on the investment is 10 percent, and the tax rate is 39 percent. What are the NPV and IRR of the decision to replace the old machine?

22. **Project Analysis and Inflation**   Sanders Enterprises, Inc., has been considering the purchase of a new manufacturing facility for $750,000. The facility is to be fully depreciated on a straight-line basis over seven years. It is expected to have no resale value after the seven years. Operating revenues from the facility are expected to be $635,000, in nominal terms, at the end of the first year. The revenues are expected to increase at the inflation rate of 5 percent. Production costs at the end of the first year will be $395,000, in nominal terms, and they are expected to increase at 4 percent per year. The real discount rate is 7 percent. The corporate tax rate is 34 percent. Should the company accept the project?

23. **Calculating Project NPV**   With the growing popularity of casual surf print clothing, two recent MBA graduates decided to broaden this casual surf concept to encompass a "surf lifestyle for the home." With limited capital, they decided to focus on surf print table and floor lamps to accent people's homes. They projected unit sales of these lamps to be 9,500 in the first year, with growth of 8 percent each year for the next five years. Production of these lamps will require $45,000 in net working capital to start. Total fixed costs are $115,000 per year, variable production costs are $21 per unit, and the units are priced at $53 each. The equipment needed to begin production will cost $190,000. The equipment will be depreciated using the straight-line method over a five-year life and is not expected to have a salvage value. The effective tax rate is 34 percent, and the required rate of return is 18 percent. What is the NPV of this project?

24. **Calculating Project NPV**   You have been hired as a consultant for Pristine Urban-Tech Zither, Inc. (PUTZ), manufacturers of fine zithers. The market for zithers is growing quickly. The company bought some land three years ago for $1 million in anticipation of using it as a toxic waste dump site but has recently hired another company to handle all toxic materials. Based on a recent appraisal, the company believes it could sell the land for $900,000 on an aftertax basis. In four years, the land could be sold for $1,200,000 after taxes. The company also hired a marketing firm to analyze the zither market, at a cost of $125,000. An excerpt of the marketing report is as follows:

> The zither industry will have a rapid expansion in the next four years. With the brand name recognition that PUTZ brings to bear, we feel that the company will be able to sell 6,500, 7,100, 8,900, and 5,800 units each year for the next four years, respectively. Again, capitalizing on the name recognition of PUTZ, we feel that a premium price of $295 can be charged for each zither. Because zithers appear to be a fad, we feel at the end of the four-year period, sales should be discontinued.

PUTZ feels that fixed costs for the project will be $330,000 per year, and variable costs are 15 percent of sales. The equipment necessary for production will cost $3.1 million and will be depreciated according to a three-year MACRS schedule. At the end of the project, the equipment can be scrapped for $280,000. Net working capital of $120,000 will be required immediately. PUTZ has a tax rate of 38 percent, and the required return on the project is 13 percent. What is the NPV of the project? Assume the company has other profitable projects.

25. **Calculating Project NPV**   Pilot Plus Pens is deciding when to replace its old machine. The machine's current salvage value is $2.8 million. Its current book value is $1.6 million. If not sold, the old machine will require maintenance costs of $855,000 at the end of the year for the next five years. Depreciation on the old machine is $320,000 per year. At the end of five years, it will have a salvage value of $140,000 and a book

value of $0. A replacement machine costs $4.5 million now and requires maintenance costs of $350,000 at the end of each year during its economic life of five years. At the end of the five years, the new machine will have a salvage value of $900,000. It will be fully depreciated by the straight-line method. In five years a replacement machine will cost $3,400,000. The company will need to purchase this machine regardless of what choice it makes today. The corporate tax rate is 40 percent and the appropriate discount rate is 8 percent. The company is assumed to earn sufficient revenues to generate tax shields from depreciation. Should the company replace the old machine now or at the end of five years?

26. **EAC and Inflation**   Office Automation, Inc., must choose between two copiers, the XX40 or the RH45. The XX40 costs $1,499 and will last for three years. The copier will require a real aftertax cost of $120 per year after all relevant expenses. The RH45 costs $2,399 and will last five years. The real aftertax cost for the RH45 will be $95 per year. All cash flows occur at the end of the year. The inflation rate is expected to be 3 percent per year, and the nominal discount rate is 9 percent. Which copier should the company choose?

27. **Project Analysis and Inflation**   Dickinson Brothers, Inc., is considering investing in a machine to produce computer keyboards. The price of the machine will be $975,000, and its economic life is five years. The machine will be fully depreciated by the straight-line method. The machine will produce 20,000 keyboards each year. The price of each keyboard will be $43 in the first year and will increase by 3 percent per year. The production cost per keyboard will be $15 in the first year and will increase by 4 percent per year. The project will have an annual fixed cost of $195,000 and require an immediate investment of $25,000 in net working capital. The corporate tax rate for the company is 34 percent. If the appropriate discount rate is 11 percent, what is the NPV of the investment?

CHALLENGE
(Questions 28–38)

28. **Project Evaluation**   Aday Acoustics, Inc., projects unit sales for a new seven-octave voice emulation implant as follows:

Year	Unit Sales
1	81,000
2	89,000
3	97,000
4	92,000
5	77,000

Production of the implants will require $1,500,000 in net working capital to start and additional net working capital investments each year equal to 15 percent of the projected sales increase for the following year. Total fixed costs are $1,850,000 per year, variable production costs are $190 per unit, and the units are priced at $345 each. The equipment needed to begin production has an installed cost of $19,500,000. Because the implants are intended for professional singers, this equipment is considered industrial machinery and thus qualifies as seven-year MACRS property. In five years, this equipment can be sold for about 20 percent of its acquisition cost. The company is in the 35 percent marginal tax bracket and has a required return on all its projects of 18 percent. Based on these preliminary project estimates, what is the NPV of the project? What is the IRR?

29. **Calculating Required Savings**   A proposed cost-saving device has an installed cost of $710,000. The device will be used in a five-year project but is classified as three-year MACRS property for tax purposes. The required initial net working capital investment is $65,000, the marginal tax rate is 35 percent, and the project discount rate is 12 percent. The device has an estimated Year 5 salvage value of $60,000. What level of pretax cost savings do we require for this project to be profitable?

30. **Calculating a Bid Price**   Another utilization of cash flow analysis is setting the bid price on a project. To calculate the bid price, we set the project NPV equal to zero and find the required price. Thus the bid price represents a financial break-even level for the project. Guthrie Enterprises needs someone to supply it with 165,000 cartons of machine screws per year to support its manufacturing needs over the next five years, and you've decided to bid on the contract. It will cost you $2,300,000 to install the equipment necessary to start production; you'll depreciate this cost straight-line to zero over the project's life. You estimate that in five years this equipment can be salvaged for $150,000. Your fixed production costs will be $450,000 per year, and your variable production costs should be $9.25 per carton. You also need an initial investment in net working capital of $130,000. If your tax rate is 35 percent and you require a 14 percent return on your investment, what bid price should you submit?

31. **Financial Break-Even Analysis**   The technique for calculating a bid price can be extended to many other types of problems. Answer the following questions using the same technique as setting a bid price; that is, set the project NPV to zero and solve for the variable in question.

    a. In the previous problem, assume that the price per carton is $18 and find the project NPV. What does your answer tell you about your bid price? What do you know about the number of cartons you can sell and still break even? How about your level of costs?

    b. Solve the previous problem again with the price still at $18—but find the quantity of cartons per year that you can supply and still break even. (*Hint:* It's less than 165,000.)

    c. Repeat (b) with a price of $18 and a quantity of 165,000 cartons per year, and find the highest level of fixed costs you could afford and still break even. (*Hint:* It's more than $450,000.)

32. **Calculating a Bid Price**   Your company has been approached to bid on a contract to sell 15,000 voice recognition (VR) computer keyboards a year for four years. Due to technological improvements, beyond that time they will be outdated and no sales will be possible. The equipment necessary for the production will cost $3.4 million and will be depreciated on a straight-line basis to a zero salvage value. Production will require an investment in net working capital of $75,000 to be returned at the end of the project, and the equipment can be sold for $200,000 at the end of production. Fixed costs are $700,000 per year, and variable costs are $48 per unit. In addition to the contract, you feel your company can sell 4,000, 12,000, 14,000, and 7,000 additional units to companies in other countries over the next four years, respectively, at a price of $145. This price is fixed. The tax rate is 40 percent, and the required return is 13 percent. Additionally, the president of the company will undertake the project only if it has an NPV of $100,000. What bid price should you set for the contract?

33. **Replacement Decisions**   Suppose we are thinking about replacing an old computer with a new one. The old one cost us $450,000; the new one will cost $580,000. The new machine will be depreciated straight-line to zero over its five-year life. It will probably be worth about $130,000 after five years.

    The old computer is being depreciated at a rate of $90,000 per year. It will be completely written off in three years. If we don't replace it now, we will have to replace it in two years. We can sell it now for $230,000; in two years it will probably be worth $60,000. The new machine will save us $85,000 per year in operating costs. The tax rate is 38 percent, and the discount rate is 14 percent.

    a. Suppose we recognize that if we don't replace the computer now, we will be replacing it in two years. Should we replace now or should we wait? (*Hint:* What we effectively have here is a decision either to "invest" in the old computer—by not selling it—or to invest in the new one. Notice that the two investments have unequal lives.)

    b. Suppose we consider only whether we should replace the old computer now without worrying about what's going to happen in two years. What are the relevant cash flows? Should we replace it or not? (*Hint:* Consider the net change in the firm's after-tax cash flows if we do the replacement.)

34. **Project Analysis** Hardwick Enterprises is evaluating alternative uses for a three-story manufacturing and warehousing building that it has purchased for $1,250,000. The company can continue to rent the building to the present occupants for $60,000 per year. The present occupants have indicated an interest in staying in the building for at least another 15 years. Alternatively, the company could modify the existing structure to use for its own manufacturing and warehousing needs. The company's production engineer feels the building could be adapted to handle one of two new product lines. The cost and revenue data for the two product alternatives are as follows:

	Product A	Product B
Initial cash outlay for building modifications	$115,000	$160,000
Initial cash outlay for equipment	220,000	245,000
Annual pretax cash revenues (generated for 15 years)	235,000	265,000
Annual pretax expenditures (generated for 15 years)	85,000	105,000

The building will be used for only 15 years for either Product *A* or Product *B*. After 15 years the building will be too small for efficient production of either product line. At that time, the company plans to rent the building to firms similar to the current occupants. To rent the building again, the company will need to restore the building to its present layout. The estimated cash cost of restoring the building if Product *A* has been undertaken is $75,000. If Product *B* has been manufactured, the cash cost will be $85,000. These cash costs can be deducted for tax purposes in the year the expenditures occur.

The company will depreciate the original building shell (purchased for $1,250,000) over a 30-year life to zero, regardless of which alternative it chooses. The building modifications and equipment purchases for either product are estimated to have a 15-year life. They will be depreciated by the straight-line method. The firm's tax rate is 34 percent, and its required rate of return on such investments is 12 percent.

For simplicity, assume all cash flows occur at the end of the year. The initial outlays for modifications and equipment will occur today (Year 0), and the restoration outlays will occur at the end of Year 15. The company has other profitable ongoing operations that are sufficient to cover any losses. Which use of the building would you recommend to management?

35. **Project Analysis and Inflation** The Biological Insect Control Corporation (BICC) has hired you as a consultant to evaluate the NPV of its proposed toad ranch. The company plans to breed toads and sell them as ecologically desirable insect control mechanisms. They anticipate that the business will continue into perpetuity. Following the negligible start-up costs, the company expects the following nominal cash flows at the end of the year:

Revenues	$325,000
Labor costs	197,000
Other costs	64,000

The company will lease machinery for $150,000 per year. The lease payments start at the end of Year 1 and are expressed in nominal terms. Revenues will increase by 4 percent per year in real terms. Labor costs will increase by 3 percent per year in real terms. Other costs will increase by 1 percent per year in real terms. The rate of inflation is expected to be 6 percent per year. The required rate of return for this project is 10 percent in real terms. The company has a tax rate of 34 percent. All cash flows occur at year-end. What is the NPV of the proposed toad ranch today?

36. Project Analysis and Inflation   O'Bannon Electronics has an investment opportunity to produce a new HDTV. The required investment on January 1 of this year is $145 million. The firm will depreciate the investment to zero using the straight-line method over four years. The investment has no resale value after completion of the project. The firm is in the 34 percent tax bracket. The price of the product will be $435 per unit, in real terms, and will not change over the life of the project. Labor costs for Year 1 will be $16.25 per hour, in real terms, and will increase at 2 percent per year in real terms. Energy costs for Year 1 will be $3.80 per physical unit, in real terms, and will increase at 3 percent per year in real terms. The inflation rate is 5 percent per year. Revenues are received and costs are paid at year-end. Refer to the following table for the production schedule:

	Year 1	Year 2	Year 3	Year 4
Physical production, in units	155,000	175,000	190,000	170,000
Labor input, in hours	1,120,000	1,200,000	1,360,000	1,280,000
Energy input, physical units	210,000	225,000	255,000	240,000

The real discount rate for the project is 4 percent. Calculate the NPV of this project.

37. Project Analysis and Inflation   After extensive medical and marketing research, Pill, Inc., believes it can penetrate the pain reliever market. It is considering two alternative products. The first is a medication for headache pain. The second is a pill for headache and arthritis pain. Both products would be introduced at a price of $7.75 per package in real terms. The headache-only medication is projected to sell 3.2 million packages a year, whereas the headache and arthritis remedy would sell 4.9 million packages a year. Cash costs of production in the first year are expected to be $3.80 per package in real terms for the headache-only brand. Production costs are expected to be $4.35 in real terms for the headache and arthritis pill. All prices and costs are expected to rise at the general inflation rate of 3 percent.

Either product requires further investment. The headache-only pill could be produced using equipment costing $25 million. That equipment would last three years and have no resale value. The machinery required to produce the broader remedy would cost $34 million and last three years. The firm expects that equipment to have a $1 million resale value (in real terms) at the end of Year 3.

Pill, Inc., uses straight-line depreciation. The firm faces a corporate tax rate of 34 percent and believes that the appropriate real discount rate is 7 percent. Which pain reliever should the firm produce?

38. Calculating Project NPV   J. Smythe, Inc., manufactures fine furniture. The company is deciding whether to introduce a new mahogany dining room table set. The set will sell for $6,100, including a set of eight chairs. The company feels that sales will be 1,900, 2,250, 2,700, 2,450, and 2,300 sets per year for the next five years, respectively. Variable costs will amount to 37 percent of sales, and fixed costs are $2.25 million per year. The new tables will require inventory amounting to 10 percent of sales, produced and stockpiled in the year prior to sales. It is believed that the addition of the new table will cause a loss of 250 tables per year of the oak tables the company produces. These tables sell for $4,500 and have variable costs of 40 percent of sales. The inventory for this oak table is also 10 percent of sales. The sales of the oak table will continue indefinitely. J. Smythe currently has excess production capacity. If the company buys the necessary equipment today, it will cost $19 million. However, the excess production capacity means the company can produce the new table without buying the new equipment. The company controller has said that the current excess capacity will end in two years with current production. This means that if the company uses the current excess capacity for the new table, it will be forced to spend the $19 million in two years to accommodate the increased sales of its current products. In five years, the new equipment will have a market value of $3.1 million if purchased today, and $4.7 million if purchased in two years. The equipment is depreciated on a seven-year MACRS schedule. The company has a tax rate of 40 percent, and the required return for the project is 11 percent.

a. Should J. Smythe undertake the new project?

b. Can you perform an IRR analysis on this project? How many IRRs would you expect to find?

c. How would you interpret the profitability index?

Excel Master It! Problems

For this Master It! assignment, refer to the Goodweek Tires, Inc., case at the end of this chapter. For your convenience, we have entered the relevant values such as the price and variable costs in the case on the next page. For this project, answer the following questions:

a. What is the profitability index of the project?

b. What is the IRR of the project?

c. At what OEM price would Goodweek Tires be indifferent to accepting the project? Assume the replacement market price is constant.

d. At what level of variable costs per unit would Goodweek Tires be indifferent to accepting the project?

Mini Cases

BETHESDA MINING COMPANY

Bethesda Mining is a midsized coal mining company with 20 mines located in Ohio, Pennsylvania, West Virginia, and Kentucky. The company operates deep mines as well as strip mines. Most of the coal mined is sold under contract, with excess production sold on the spot market.

The coal mining industry, especially high-sulfur coal operations such as Bethesda, has been hard-hit by environmental regulations. Recently, however, a combination of increased demand for coal and new pollution reduction technologies has led to an improved market demand for high-sulfur coal. Bethesda has just been approached by Mid-Ohio Electric Company with a request to supply coal for its electric generators for the next four years. Bethesda Mining does not have enough excess capacity at its existing mines to guarantee the contract. The company is considering opening a strip mine in Ohio on 5,000 acres of land purchased 10 years ago for $4 million. Based on a recent appraisal, the company feels it could receive $6.5 million on an aftertax basis if it sold the land today.

Strip mining is a process where the layers of topsoil above a coal vein are removed and the exposed coal is removed. Some time ago, the company would simply remove the coal and leave the land in an unusable condition. Changes in mining regulations now force a company to reclaim the land; that is, when the mining is completed, the land must be restored to near its original condition. The land can then be used for other purposes. Because it is currently operating at full capacity, Bethesda will need to purchase additional necessary equipment, which will cost $95 million. The equipment will be depreciated on a seven-year MACRS schedule. The contract runs for only four years. At that time the coal from the site will be entirely mined. The company feels that the equipment can be sold for 60 percent of its initial purchase price in four years. However, Bethesda plans to open another strip mine at that time and will use the equipment at the new mine.

The contract calls for the delivery of 500,000 tons of coal per year at a price of $86 per ton. Bethesda Mining feels that coal production will be 620,000 tons, 680,000 tons, 730,000 tons, and 590,000 tons, respectively, over the next four years. The excess production will be sold in the spot market at an average of $77 per ton. Variable costs amount to $31 per ton, and fixed costs are $4,100,000 per year. The mine will require a net working capital investment of 5 percent of sales. The NWC will be built up in the year prior to the sales.

Bethesda will be responsible for reclaiming the land at termination of the mining. This will occur in Year 5. The company uses an outside company for reclamation of all the company's strip mines. It is estimated the cost of reclamation will be $2.7 million. In order to get the necessary permits for the strip mine, the company agreed to donate the land after reclamation to the state for use as a public park and recreation area. This will occur in Year 6 and result in a charitable expense deduction of $6 million. Bethesda faces a 38 percent tax rate and has a 12 percent required return on new strip mine projects. Assume that a loss in any year will result in a tax credit.

You have been approached by the president of the company with a request to analyze the project. Calculate the payback period, profitability index, net present value, and internal rate of return for the new strip mine. Should Bethesda Mining take the contract and open the mine?

GOODWEEK TIRES, INC.

After extensive research and development, Goodweek Tires, Inc., has recently developed a new tire, the SuperTread, and must decide whether to make the investment necessary to produce and market it. The tire would be ideal for drivers doing a large amount of wet weather and off-road driving in addition to normal freeway usage. The research and development costs so far have totaled about $10 million. The SuperTread would be put on the market beginning this year, and Goodweek expects it to stay on the market for a total of four years. Test marketing costing $5 million has shown that there is a significant market for a SuperTread-type tire.

As a financial analyst at Goodweek Tires, you have been asked by your CFO, Adam Smith, to evaluate the SuperTread project and provide a recommendation on whether to go ahead with the investment. Except for the initial investment that will occur immediately, assume all cash flows will occur at year-end.

Goodweek must initially invest $160 million in production equipment to make the SuperTread. This equipment can be sold for $65 million at the end of four years. Goodweek intends to sell the SuperTread to two distinct markets:

1. *The original equipment manufacturer (OEM) market:* The OEM market consists primarily of the large automobile companies (like General Motors) that buy tires for new cars. In the OEM market, the SuperTread is expected to sell for $41 per tire. The variable cost to produce each tire is $29.

2. *The replacement market:* The replacement market consists of all tires purchased after the automobile has left the factory. This market allows higher margins; Goodweek expects to sell the SuperTread for $62 per tire there. Variable costs are the same as in the OEM market.

Goodweek Tires intends to raise prices at 1 percent above the inflation rate; variable costs will also increase at 1 percent above the inflation rate. In addition, the SuperTread project will incur $43 million in marketing and general administration costs the first year. This cost is expected to increase at the inflation rate in the subsequent years.

Goodweek's corporate tax rate is 40 percent. Annual inflation is expected to remain constant at 3.25 percent. The company uses a 13.4 percent discount rate to evaluate new product decisions. Automotive industry analysts expect automobile manufacturers to produce 6.2 million new cars this year and production to grow at 2.5 percent per year thereafter. Each new car needs four tires (the spare tires are undersized and are in a different category). Goodweek Tires expects the SuperTread to capture 11 percent of the OEM market.

Industry analysts estimate that the replacement tire market size will be 32 million tires this year and that it will grow at 2 percent annually. Goodweek expects the SuperTread to capture an 8 percent market share.

The appropriate depreciation schedule for the equipment is the seven-year MACRS depreciation schedule. The immediate initial working capital requirement is $9 million. Thereafter, the net working capital requirements will be 15 percent of sales. What are the NPV, payback period, discounted payback period, IRR, and PI on this project?

7

Risk Analysis, Real Options, and Capital Budgeting

In mid 2014, the movie *The Legend of Hercules* failed at the task of drawing movie-goers to the theater. And according to critics, just watching the movie amounted to a 13th labor of Hercules. One said, "Somehow more cartoonish than Disney's version, which was a cartoon." Others were even more harsh, saying, "When awfulness reaches a certain point, it achieves unintentional hilarity" and "Even dental extraction is more enjoyable to endure."

Looking at the numbers, Paramount Pictures spent close to $70 million making the movie, plus millions more for marketing and distribution. Unfortunately for Paramount Pictures, *The Legend of Hercules* was not the Golden Hind the

executives believed, pulling in only $18.8 million worldwide. In fact, about 4 of 10 movies lose money in theaters, though DVD sales often help the final tally. Of course, there are movies that do quite well. Also in 2014, the Marvel movie *Guardians of the Galaxy* raked in about $350 million worldwide at a production cost of $170 million.

Obviously, Paramount Pictures didn't *plan* to lose $50 million or so on *The Legend of Hercules,* but it happened. As the box office flop of *The Legend of Hercules,* projects don't always go as companies think they will. This chapter explores how this can happen, and what companies can do to analyze and possibly avoid these situations.

7.1 Sensitivity Analysis, Scenario Analysis, and Break-Even Analysis

One main point of this book is that NPV analysis is a superior capital budgeting technique. In fact, because the NPV approach uses cash flows rather than profits, uses all the cash flows, and discounts the cash flows properly, it is hard to find any theoretical fault with it. However, in our conversations with practical businesspeople, we hear the phrase "a false sense of security" frequently. These people point out that the documentation for capital budgeting proposals is often quite impressive. Cash flows are projected down to the last thousand dollars (or even the last dollar) for each year (or even each month). Opportunity costs and side effects are handled quite properly. Sunk costs are ignored—also quite properly. When a high net present value appears at the bottom, one's temptation is to say yes immediately. Nevertheless, the projected cash flow often goes unmet in practice, and the firm ends up with a money loser.

SENSITIVITY ANALYSIS AND SCENARIO ANALYSIS

How can the firm get the net present value technique to live up to its potential? One approach is **sensitivity analysis**, which examines how sensitive a particular NPV

Table 7.1

Cash Flow Forecasts for Solar Electronics Corporation's Jet Engine: Base Case (millions)*

	Year 1	Years 2–6
Revenues		$6,000
Variable costs		3,000
Fixed costs		1,791
Depreciation		300
Pretax profit		$ 909
Tax ($t_c = .34$)		309
Net profit		$ 600
Cash flow		$ 900
Initial investment costs	$1,500	

*Assumptions: (1) Investment is depreciated in Years 2 through 6 using the straight-line method; (2) tax rate is 34 percent; (3) the company receives no tax benefits for initial development costs.

calculation is to changes in underlying assumptions. Sensitivity analysis is also known as *what-if* analysis and *bop* (best, optimistic, and pessimistic) analysis.

Consider the following example. Solar Electronics Corporation (SEC) has recently developed a solar-powered jet engine and wants to go ahead with full-scale production. The initial (Year 1)[1] investment is $1,500 million, followed by production and sales over the next five years. The preliminary cash flow projection appears in Table 7.1. Should SEC go ahead with investment in and production of the jet engine, the NPV at a discount rate of 15 percent is (in millions):

$$\text{NPV} = -\$1,500 + \sum_{t=1}^{5} \frac{\$900}{(1.15)^t}$$
$$= -\$1,500 + \$900 \times \text{PVIFA}\,(.15, 5)$$
$$= \$1,517$$

Because the NPV is positive, basic financial theory implies that SEC should accept the project. However, is this all there is to say about the venture? Before actual funding, we ought to check out the project's underlying assumptions about revenues and costs.

Revenues   Let's assume that the marketing department has projected annual sales to be:

Number of jet engines sold per year	=	Market share	×	Size of jet engine market per year
3,000	=	.30	×	10,000

Annual sales revenues	=	Number of jet engines sold	×	Price per engine
$6,000 million	=	3,000	×	$2 million

Thus, it turns out that the revenue estimates depend on three assumptions:

1. Market share.
2. Size of jet engine market.
3. Price per engine.

---

[1]Financial custom generally designates Year 0 as "today." However, we use Year 1 as today in this example because later in this chapter we will consider another decision made a year earlier. That decision will have occurred at Year 0.

Costs   Financial analysts frequently divide costs into two types: Variable costs and fixed costs. **Variable costs** change as the output changes, and they are zero when production is zero. Costs of direct labor and raw materials are usually variable. It is common to assume that a variable cost is constant per unit of output, implying that total variable costs are proportional to the level of production. For example, if direct labor is variable and one unit of final output requires $10 of direct labor, then 100 units of final output should require $1,000 of direct labor.

Fixed costs are not dependent on the amount of goods or services produced during the period. Fixed costs are usually measured as costs per unit of time, such as rent per month or salaries per year. Naturally, fixed costs are not fixed forever. They are fixed only over a predetermined time period.

The engineering department has estimated variable costs to be $1 million per engine. Fixed costs are $1,791 million per year. The cost breakdowns are:

$$\begin{array}{ccccc} \text{Variable} \\ \text{cost per year} \end{array} = \begin{array}{c} \text{Variable cost} \\ \text{per unit} \end{array} \times \begin{array}{c} \text{Number of jet engines} \\ \text{sold per year} \end{array}$$

$$\$3{,}000 \text{ million} = \$1 \text{ million} \times 3{,}000$$

$$\begin{array}{c} \text{Total cost before} \\ \text{taxes per year} \end{array} = \begin{array}{c} \text{Variable cost} \\ \text{per year} \end{array} + \text{Fixed cost per year}$$

$$\$4{,}791 \text{ million} = \$3{,}000 \text{ million} + \$1{,}791 \text{ million}$$

These estimates for market size, market share, price, variable cost, and fixed cost, as well as the estimate of initial investment, are presented in the middle column of Table 7.2. These figures represent the firm's expectations or best estimates of the different parameters. For comparison, the firm's analysts also prepared both optimistic and pessimistic forecasts for each of the different variables. These forecasts are provided in the table as well.

Standard sensitivity analysis calls for an NPV calculation for all three possibilities of a single variable, along with the expected forecast for all other variables. This procedure is illustrated in Table 7.3. For example, consider the NPV calculation of $8,154 million provided in the upper right corner of this table. This NPV occurs when the optimistic forecast of 20,000 units per year is used for market size while all other variables are set at their expected forecasts from Table 7.2. Note that each row of the middle column of Table 7.3 shows a value of $1,517 million. This occurs because the expected forecast is used for the variable that was singled out, as well as for all other variables.

Table 7.3 can be used for a number of purposes. First, taken as a whole, the table can indicate whether NPV analysis should be trusted. In other words, it reduces the false sense of security we spoke of earlier. Suppose that NPV is positive when the expected forecast for each variable is used. However, further suppose that every number in the pessimistic column is highly negative and every number in the optimistic column is highly positive. A change in

Table 7.2

Different Estimates for Solar Electronics' Solar Plane Engine

Variable	Pessimistic	Expected or Best	Optimistic
Market size (per year)	5,000	10,000	20,000
Market share	20%	30%	50%
Price	$1.9 million	$2 million	$2.2 million
Variable cost (per plane)	$1.2 million	$1 million	$.8 million
Fixed cost (per year)	$1,891 million	$1,791 million	$1,741 million
Investment	$1,900 million	$1,500 million	$1,000 million

Table 7.3
NPV Calculations
($ in millions) for the
Solar Plane Engine
Using Sensitivity
Analysis

	Pessimistic	Expected or Best	Optimistic
Market size	−$1,802*	$1,517	$8,154
Market share	−696*	1,517	5,942
Price	853	1,517	2,844
Variable cost	189	1,517	2,844
Fixed cost	1,295	1,517	1,628
Investment	1,208	1,517	1,903

Under sensitivity analysis, one input is varied while all other inputs are assumed to meet their expectation. For example, an NPV of −$1,802 occurs when the pessimistic forecast of 5,000 is used for market size, while all other variables are set at their expected forecasts from Table 7.2.

*We assume that the other divisions of the firm are profitable, implying that a loss on this project can offset income elsewhere in the firm, thereby reducing the overall taxes of the firm.

a single forecast greatly alters the NPV estimate, making one leery of the net present value approach. A conservative manager might well scrap the entire NPV analysis in this situation. Fortunately, the solar plane engine does not exhibit this wide dispersion because all but two of the numbers in Table 7.3 are positive. Managers viewing the table will likely consider NPV analysis to be useful for the solar-powered jet engine.

Second, sensitivity analysis shows where more information is needed. For example, an error in the estimate of investment appears to be relatively unimportant because, even under the pessimistic scenario, the NPV of $1,208 million is still highly positive. By contrast, the pessimistic forecast for market share leads to a negative NPV of −$696 million, and a pessimistic forecast for market size leads to a substantially negative NPV of −$1,802 million. Because the effect of incorrect estimates on revenues is so much greater than the effect of incorrect estimates on costs, more information about the factors determining revenues might be needed.

Because of these advantages, sensitivity analysis is widely used in practice. Graham and Harvey[2] report that slightly over 50 percent of the 392 firms in their sample subject their capital budgeting calculations to sensitivity analysis. This number is particularly large when one considers that only about 75 percent of the firms in their sample use NPV analysis.

Unfortunately, sensitivity analysis also suffers from some drawbacks. For example, sensitivity analysis may unwittingly *increase* the false sense of security among managers. Suppose all pessimistic forecasts yield positive NPVs. A manager might feel that there is no way the project can lose money. Of course, the forecasters may simply have an optimistic view of a pessimistic forecast. To combat this, some companies do not treat optimistic and pessimistic forecasts subjectively. Rather, their pessimistic forecasts are always, say, 20 percent less than expected. Unfortunately, the cure in this case may be worse than the disease: A deviation of a fixed percentage ignores the fact that some variables are easier to forecast than others.

In addition, sensitivity analysis treats each variable in isolation when, in reality, the different variables are likely to be related. For example, if ineffective management allows costs to get out of control, it is likely that variable costs, fixed costs, and investment will all rise above expectation at the same time. If the market is not receptive to a solar plane engine, both market share and price should decline together.

---

[2]See Figure 2 of John Graham and Campbell Harvey, "The Theory and Practice of Corporate Finance: Evidence from the Field," *Journal of Financial Economics* (May/June 2001).

Table 7.4

Cash Flow Forecast
($ in millions) under
the Scenario of a
Plane Crash*

	Year 1	Years 2–5
Revenues		$2,800
Variable costs		1,400
Fixed costs		1,791
Depreciation		300
Pretax profit		−691
Tax ($t_c = .34$)†		235
Net profit		$ −456
Cash flow		$ −156
Initial investment cost	−$1,500	

*Assumptions are:

    Market size   7,000 (70 percent of expectation)

    Market share   20% (2/3 of expectation)

Forecasts for all other variables are the expected forecasts as given in Table 7.2.

†Tax loss offsets income elsewhere in firm.

Managers frequently perform **scenario analysis**, a variant of sensitivity analysis, to minimize this problem. Simply put, this approach examines a number of different likely scenarios, where each scenario involves a confluence of factors. As a simple example, consider the effect of a few airline crashes. These crashes are likely to reduce flying in total, thereby limiting the demand for any new engines. Furthermore, even if the crashes do not involve solar-powered aircraft, the public could become more averse to any innovative and controversial technologies. Hence, SEC's market share might fall as well. Perhaps the cash flow calculations would look like those in Table 7.4 under the scenario of a plane crash. Given the calculations in the table, the NPV (in millions) would be:

$$-\$2,023 = -\$1,500 - \$156 \times \text{PVIFA}(.15, 5)$$

A series of scenarios like this might illuminate issues concerning the project better than the standard application of sensitivity analysis would.

BREAK-EVEN ANALYSIS

Our discussion of sensitivity analysis and scenario analysis suggests that there are many ways to examine variability in forecasts. We now present another approach, **break-even analysis**. As its name implies, this approach determines the sales needed to break even. The approach is a useful complement to sensitivity analysis because it also sheds light on the severity of incorrect forecasts. We calculate the break-even point in terms of both accounting profit and present value.

Accounting Profit Annual net profits under four different sales forecasts are as follows:

Annual Unit Sales	Net Profit ($ in millions)
0	−$1,380
1,000	−720
3,000	600
10,000	5,220

Table 7.5   Revenues and Costs of Project under Different Sales Assumptions ($ in millions, except unit sales)

| Year I | | | Years 2–6 | | | | | | |
Initial Invest-ment	Annual Unit Sales	Revenues	Variable Costs	Fixed Costs	Depreci-ation	Taxes* $(t_c = .34)$	Net Profit	Operating Cash Flows	NPV (evaluated Date I)
$1,500	0	$ 0	$ 0	−$1,791	−$300	$ 711	−$1,380	−$1,080	−$ 5,120
1,500	1,000	2,000	−1,000	−1,791	−300	371	−720	−420	−2,908
1,500	3,000	6,000	−3,000	−1,791	−300	−309	600	900	1,517
1,500	10,000	20,000	−10,000	−1,791	−300	−2,689	5,220	5,520	17,004

*Loss is incurred in the first two rows. For tax purposes, this loss offsets income elsewhere in the firm.

Figure 7.1
Break-Even Point
Using Accounting
Numbers

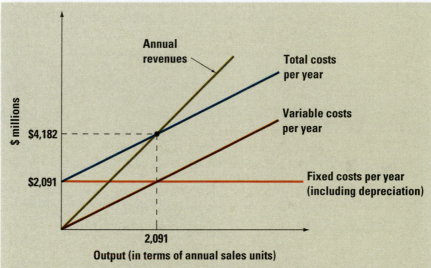

The pretax contribution margin per plane is $1 million. The firm can recover its annual fixed costs of $2,091 million by selling 2,091 planes. Hence, the break-even point occurs with annual sales of 2,091 planes.

A more complete presentation of costs and revenues appears in Table 7.5.

We plot the revenues, costs, and profits under the different assumptions about sales in Figure 7.1. The revenue and cost curves cross at 2,091 jet engines. This is the break-even point—that is, the point where the project generates no profits or losses. As long as annual sales are above 2,091 jet engines, the project will make a profit.

This break-even point can be calculated very easily. Because the sales price is $2 million per engine and the variable cost is $1 million per engine,[3] the difference between sales price and variable cost per engine is:

$$\text{Sales price} - \text{Variable cost} = \$2 \text{ million} - \$1 \text{ million}$$
$$= \$1 \text{ million}$$

---

[3]Though the previous section considered both optimistic and pessimistic forecasts for sales price and variable cost, break-even analysis uses just the expected or best estimates of these variables.

This difference is called the pretax **contribution margin** because each additional engine contributes this amount to pretax profit. (Contribution margin can also be expressed on an aftertax basis.)

Fixed costs are $1,791 million and depreciation is $300 million, implying that the sum of these costs is:

$$\text{Fixed costs} + \text{Depreciation} = \$1{,}791 \text{ million} + \$300 \text{ million}$$
$$= \$2{,}091 \text{ million}$$

That is, the firm incurs costs of $2,091 million per year, regardless of the number of sales. Because each engine contributes $1 million, annual sales must reach the following level to offset the costs:

Accounting Profit Break-Even Point:

$$\frac{\text{Fixed costs} + \text{Depreciation}}{\text{Sales price} - \text{Variable costs}} = \frac{\$2{,}091 \text{ million}}{\$1 \text{ million}} = 2{,}091$$

Thus, 2,091 engines is the break-even point required for an accounting profit.

The astute reader might be wondering why taxes have been ignored in the calculation of break-even accounting profit. The reason is that a firm with a pretax profit of $0 will also have an aftertax profit of $0 because no taxes are paid if no pretax profit is reported. Thus, the number of units needed to break even on a pretax basis must be equal to the number of units needed to break even on an aftertax basis.

Present Value   As we have stated many times, we are more interested in present value than we are in profit. Therefore, we should calculate breakeven in terms of present value. Given a discount rate of 15 percent, the solar plane engine has the following net present values for different levels of annual sales:

Annual Unit Sales	NPV ($ millions)
0	−5,120
1,000	−2,908
3,000	1,517
10,000	17,004

These NPV calculations are reproduced from the last column of Table 7.5.

Figure 7.2 relates the net present value of both the revenues and the costs to output. There are at least two differences between Figure 7.2 and Figure 7.1, one of which is quite important and the other is much less so. First the less important point: The dollar amounts on the vertical dimension of Figure 7.2 are greater than those on the vertical dimension of Figure 7.1 because the net present values are calculated over five years. More important, accounting breakeven occurs when 2,091 units are sold annually, whereas NPV breakeven occurs when 2,315 units are sold annually.

Of course, the NPV break-even point can be calculated directly. The firm originally invested $1,500 million. This initial investment can be expressed as a five-year equivalent annual cost (EAC), determined by dividing the initial investment by the appropriate five-year annuity factor:

$$\text{EAC} = \frac{\text{Initial investment}}{\text{5-year annuity factor at 15\%}} = \frac{\text{Initial investment}}{\text{PVIFA (.15, 5)}}$$
$$= \frac{\$1{,}500 \text{ million}}{3.3522} = \$447.5 \text{ million}$$

Figure 7.2

Break-Even Point
Using Net Present
Value*

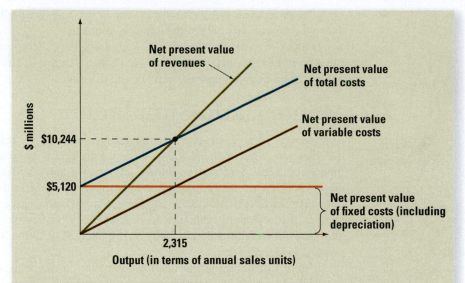

* Net present values of both revenues and costs are calculated on an aftertax basis.

Breakeven in terms of NPV occurs at a higher level of sales than does breakeven for accounting income. Companies that just break even on an accounting basis are not recovering the opportunity cost of the initial investment.

Note that the EAC of $447.5 million is greater than the yearly depreciation of $300 million. This must occur because the calculation of EAC implicitly assumes that the $1,500 million investment could have been invested at 15 percent.

Aftertax costs, regardless of output, can be viewed like this:

$$\begin{array}{ccccccc}
\dfrac{\$1,528}{\text{million}} & = & \dfrac{\$447.5}{\text{million}} & + & \dfrac{\$1,791}{\text{million}} \times & .66 & - & \$300 \text{ million} \times .34 \\[2mm]
& = & \text{EAC} & + & \text{Fixed costs} \times & (1 - t_c) & - & \text{Depreciation} \times t_c
\end{array}$$

That is, in addition to the initial investment's equivalent annual cost of $447.5 million, the firm pays fixed costs each year and receives a depreciation tax shield each year. The depreciation tax shield is written as a negative number because it offsets the costs in the equation. Each plane contributes $.66 million to aftertax profit, so it will take the following sales to offset the costs:

Present Value Break-Even Point:

$$\frac{\text{EAC} + \text{Fixed costs} \times (1 - t_c) - \text{Depreciation} \times t_c}{(\text{Sales price} - \text{Variable costs}) \times (1 - t_c)} = \frac{\$1,528 \text{ million}}{\$.66 \text{ million}} = 2,315$$

Thus, 2,315 planes is the break-even point from the perspective of present value.

Why is the accounting break-even point different from the financial break-even point? When we use accounting profit as the basis for the break-even calculation, we subtract depreciation. Depreciation for the solar jet engines project is $300 million per year. If 2,091 solar jet engines are sold per year, SEC will generate sufficient revenues to cover the $300 million depreciation expense plus other costs. Unfortunately, at this level of sales SEC will not cover the economic opportunity costs of the $1,500 million laid out for the investment. If we take into account that the $1,500 million could have been invested at 15 percent, the true annual cost of the investment is $447.5 million, not $300 million. Depreciation understates the true costs of recovering the initial investment.

Thus companies that break even on an accounting basis are really losing money. They are losing the opportunity cost of the initial investment.

Is break-even analysis important? Very much so: All corporate executives fear losses. Break-even analysis determines how far down sales can fall before the project is losing money, either in an accounting sense or an NPV sense.

7.2 Monte Carlo Simulation

Both sensitivity analysis and scenario analysis attempt to answer the question "What if?" However, while both analyses are frequently used in the real world, each has its own limitations. Sensitivity analysis allows only one variable to change at a time. By contrast, many variables are likely to move at the same time in the real world. Scenario analysis follows specific scenarios, such as changes in inflation, government regulation, or the number of competitors. Although this methodology is often quite helpful, it cannot cover all sources of variability. In fact, projects are likely to exhibit a lot of variability under just one economic scenario.

Monte Carlo simulation is a further attempt to model real-world uncertainty. This approach takes its name from the famous European casino because it analyzes projects the way one might analyze gambling strategies. Imagine a serious blackjack player who wonders if he should take a third card whenever his first two cards total 16. Most likely, a formal mathematical model would be too complex to be practical here. However, he could play thousands of hands in a casino, sometimes drawing a third card when his first two cards add to 16 and sometimes not drawing that third card. He could compare his winnings (or losings) under the two strategies to determine which were better. He would probably lose a lot of money performing this test in a real casino, so simulating the results from the two strategies on a computer might be cheaper. Monte Carlo simulation of capital budgeting projects is in this spirit.

Imagine that Backyard Barbeques, Inc. (BBI), a manufacturer of both charcoal and gas grills, has a blueprint for a new grill that cooks with compressed hydrogen. The CFO, Edward H. Comiskey, dissatisfied with simpler capital budgeting techniques, wants a Monte Carlo simulation for this new grill. A consultant specializing in the Monte Carlo approach, Lester Mauney, takes him through the five basic steps of the method.

STEP 1: SPECIFY THE BASIC MODEL

Les Mauney breaks up cash flow into three components: annual revenue, annual costs, and initial investment. The revenue in any year is viewed as:

$$\begin{array}{l}\text{Number of grills sold} \\ \text{by entire industry}\end{array} \times \begin{array}{l}\text{Market share of BBI's} \\ \text{hydrogen grill (in percent)}\end{array} \times \begin{array}{l}\text{Price per} \\ \text{hydrogen grill}\end{array} \quad (7.1)$$

The cost in any year is viewed as:

Fixed manufacturing costs + Variable manufacturing costs + Marketing costs + Selling costs

Initial investment is viewed as:

Cost of patent + Test marketing costs + Cost of production facility

STEP 2: SPECIFY A DISTRIBUTION FOR EACH VARIABLE IN THE MODEL

Here comes the hard part. Let's start with revenue, which has three components in Equation 7.1. The consultant first models overall market size—that is, the number of

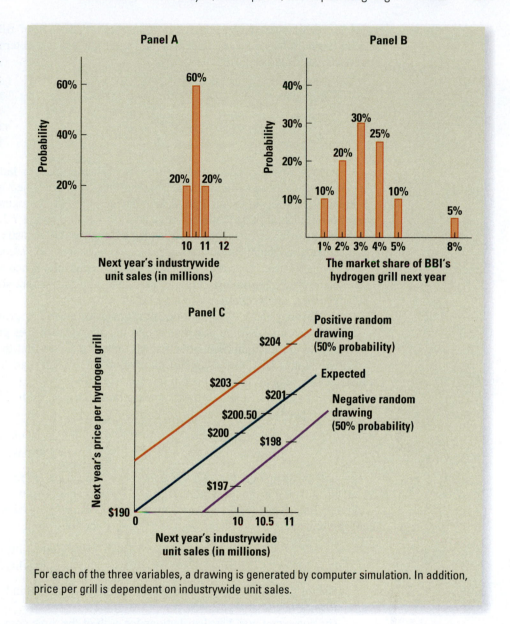

Figure 7.3
Probability Distributions for Industrywide Unit Sales, Market Share of BBI's Hydrogen Grill, and Price of Hydrogen Grill

For each of the three variables, a drawing is generated by computer simulation. In addition, price per grill is dependent on industrywide unit sales.

grills sold by the entire industry. The trade publication *Outdoor Food (OF)* reported that 10 million grills of all types were sold in the continental United States last year, and it forecasts sales of 10.5 million next year. Mr. Mauney, using *OF*'s forecast and his own intuition, creates the following distribution for next year's sales of grills by the entire industry:

Probability	20%	60%	20%
Next Year's Industrywide Unit Sales	10 million	10.5 million	11 million

The tight distribution here reflects the slow but steady historical growth in the grill market. This probability distribution is graphed in Panel A of Figure 7.3.

Lester Mauney realizes that estimating the market share of BBI's hydrogen grill is more difficult. Nevertheless, after a great deal of analysis, he determines the distribution of next year's market share:

Probability	10%	20%	30%	25%	10%	5%
Market Share of BBI's Hydrogen Grill Next Year	1%	2%	3%	4%	5%	8%

Whereas the consultant assumed a symmetrical distribution for industrywide unit sales, he believes a skewed distribution makes more sense for the project's market share. In his mind there is always the small possibility that sales of the hydrogen grill will really take off. This probability distribution is graphed in Panel B of Figure 7.3.

These forecasts assume that unit sales for the overall industry are unrelated to the project's market share. In other words, the two variables are *independent* of each other. Mr. Mauney reasons that although an economic boom might increase industrywide grill sales and a recession might decrease them, the project's market share is unlikely to be related to economic conditions.

Mr. Mauney must determine the distribution of price per grill. Mr. Comiskey, the CFO, informs him that the price will be in the area of $200 per grill, given what other competitors are charging. However, the consultant believes that the price per hydrogen grill will almost certainly depend on the size of the overall market for grills. As in any business, you can usually charge more if demand is high.

After rejecting a number of complex models for price, Mr. Mauney settles on the following specification:

$$\text{Next year's price per hydrogen grill} = \$190 + \$1 \times \frac{\text{Industrywide unit sales}}{\text{(in millions)}} +/- \$3 \qquad (7.2)$$

The grill price in Equation 7.2 depends on the unit sales of the industry. In addition, random variation is modeled via the term "$+/-\$3$," where a drawing of $+\$3$ and a drawing of $-\$3$ each occur 50 percent of the time. For example, if industrywide unit sales are 11 million, the price per share would be either of the following:

$$\$190 + \$11 + \$3 = \$204 \quad (50\% \text{ probability})$$
$$\$190 + \$11 - \$3 = \$198 \quad (50\% \text{ probability})$$

The relationship between the price of a hydrogen grill and industrywide unit sales is graphed in Panel C of Figure 7.3.

The consultant now has distributions for each of the three components of next year's revenue. However, he needs distributions for future years as well. Using forecasts from *Outdoor Food* and other publications, Mr. Mauney forecasts the distribution of growth rates for the entire industry over the second year:

Probability	20%	60%	20%
Growth Rate of Industrywide Unit Sales in Second Year	1%	3%	5%

Given both the distribution of next year's industrywide unit sales and the distribution of growth rates for this variable over the second year, we can generate the distribution of industrywide unit sales for the second year. A similar extension should give Mr. Mauney a distribution for later years as well, though we won't go into the details here. And just as the consultant extended the first component of revenue (industrywide unit sales) to later years, he would want to do the same thing for market share and unit price.

The preceding discussion shows how the three components of revenue can be modeled. Step 2 would be complete once the components of cost and investment are modeled in a similar way. Special attention must be paid to the interactions between variables here because ineffective management will likely allow the different cost components to rise together. However, you are probably getting the idea now, so we will skip the rest of this step.

STEP 3: THE COMPUTER DRAWS ONE OUTCOME

As we said, next year's revenue in our model is the product of three components. Imagine that the computer randomly picks industrywide unit sales of 10 million, a market share for BBI's hydrogen grill of 2 percent, and a +$3 random price variation. Given these drawings, next year's price per hydrogen grill will be:

$$\$190 + \$10 + \$3 = \$203$$

and next year's revenue for BBI's hydrogen grill will be:

$$10 \text{ million} \times .02 \times \$203 = \$40.6 \text{ million}$$

Of course, we are not done with the entire *outcome* yet. We would have to perform drawings for revenue in each future year. In addition, we would perform drawings for costs in each future year. Finally, a drawing for initial investment would have to be made as well. In this way, a single outcome, made up of a drawing for each variable in the model, would generate a cash flow from the project in each future year.

How likely is it that the specific outcome discussed would be drawn? We can answer this because we know the probability of each component. Because industry sales of 10 million units has a 20 percent probability, a market share of 2 percent also has a 20 percent probability, and a random price variation of +$3 has a 50 percent probability, the probability of these three drawings together in the same outcome is:

$$.02 = .20 \times .20 \times .50 \tag{7.3}$$

Of course the probability would get even smaller once drawings for future revenues, future costs, and the initial investment are included in the outcome.

This step generates the cash flow for each year from a single outcome. What we are ultimately interested in is the *distribution* of cash flow each year across many outcomes. We ask the computer to randomly draw over and over again to give us this distribution, which is just what is done in the next step.

STEP 4: REPEAT THE PROCEDURE

The first three steps generate one outcome, but the essence of Monte Carlo simulation is repeated outcomes. Depending on the situation, the computer may be called on to generate thousands or even millions of outcomes. The result of all these drawings is a distribution of cash flow for each future year. This distribution is the basic output of Monte Carlo simulation.

Consider Figure 7.4. Here, repeated drawings have produced the simulated distribution of the third year's cash flow. There would be, of course, a distribution like the one in this figure for each future year. This leaves us with just one more step.

Figure 7.4

Simulated Distribution of the Third Year's Cash Flow for BBI's New Hydrogen Grill

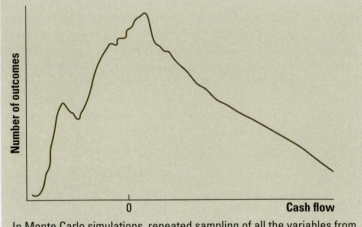

In Monte Carlo simulations, repeated sampling of all the variables from a specific model generates a statistical distribution.

STEP 5: CALCULATE NPV

Given the distribution of cash flow for the third year in Figure 7.4, one can determine the expected cash flow for this year. In a similar manner, one can also determine the expected cash flow for each future year and then calculate the net present value of the project by discounting these expected cash flows at an appropriate rate.

Monte Carlo simulation is often viewed as a step beyond either sensitivity analysis or scenario analysis. Interactions between the variables are explicitly specified in Monte Carlo; so (at least in theory) this methodology provides a more complete analysis. And, as a by-product, having to build a precise model deepens the forecaster's understanding of the project.

Because Monte Carlo simulations have been around for at least 35 years, you might think that most firms would be performing them by now. Surprisingly, this does not seem to be the case. In our experience, executives are frequently skeptical of the complexity. It is difficult to model either the distributions of each variable or the interactions between variables. In addition, the computer output is often devoid of economic intuition. Thus, while Monte Carlo simulations are used in certain real-world situations,[4] the approach is not likely to be "the wave of the future." In fact, Graham and Harvey[5] report that only about 15 percent of the firms in their sample use capital budgeting simulations.

7.3 Real Options

In Chapter 5, we stressed the superiority of net present value (NPV) analysis over other approaches when valuing capital budgeting projects. However, both scholars and practitioners have pointed out problems with NPV. The basic idea here is that NPV analysis, as well as all the other approaches in Chapter 5, ignores the adjustments that a firm can make after a project is accepted. These adjustments are called **real options**. In this respect NPV

---

[4]More than perhaps any other, the pharmaceutical industry has pioneered applications of this methodology. For example, see Nancy A. Nichols, "Scientific Management at Merck: An Interview with CFO Judy Lewent," *Harvard Business Review* (January/February 1994).

[5]See Figure 2 of Graham and Harvey, op. cit.

underestimates the true value of a project. NPV's conservatism is best explained through a series of examples.

THE OPTION TO EXPAND

Conrad Willig, an entrepreneur, recently learned of a chemical treatment causing water to freeze at 100 degrees Fahrenheit rather than 32 degrees. Of all the many practical applications for this treatment, Mr. Willig liked the idea of hotels made of ice more than anything else. Conrad estimated the annual cash flows from a single ice hotel to be $2 million, based on an initial investment of $12 million. He felt that 20 percent was an appropriate discount rate, given the risk of this new venture. Believing that the cash flows would be perpetual, Mr. Willig determined the NPV of the project to be:

$$-\$12{,}000{,}000 + \$2{,}000{,}000/.20 = -\$2 \text{ million}$$

Most entrepreneurs would have rejected this venture, given its negative NPV. But Conrad was not your typical entrepreneur. He reasoned that NPV analysis missed a hidden source of value. While he was pretty sure that the initial investment would cost $12 million, there was some uncertainty concerning annual cash flows. His cash flow estimate of $2 million per year actually reflected his belief that there was a 50 percent probability that annual cash flows will be $3 million and a 50 percent probability that annual cash flows will be $1 million.

The NPV calculations for the two forecasts are given here:

Optimistic forecast: $-\$12$ million $+ \$3$ million$/.20 = \$3$ million

Pessimistic forecast: $-\$12$ million $+ \$1$ million$/.20 = -\$7$ million

On the surface, this new calculation doesn't seem to help Mr. Willig much. An average of the two forecasts yields an NPV for the project of:

$$50\% \times \$3 \text{ million} + 50\% \times (-\$7 \text{ million}) = -\$2 \text{ million}$$

which is just the value he calculated in the first place.

However, if the optimistic forecast turns out to be correct, Mr. Willig would want to *expand*. If he believes that there are, say, 10 locations in the country that can support an ice hotel, the true NPV of the venture would be:

$$50\% \times 10 \times \$3 \text{ million} + 50\% \times (-\$7 \text{ million}) = \$11.5 \text{ million}$$

Figure 7.5, which represents Mr. Willig's decision, is often called a decision tree. The idea expressed in the figure is both basic and universal. The entrepreneur has the option to expand if the pilot location is successful. For example, think of all the people who start restaurants, most of them ultimately failing. These individuals are not necessarily overly

Figure 7.5
Decision Tree for
Ice Hotel

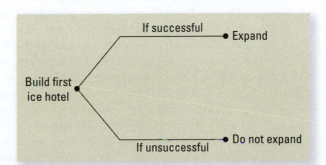

optimistic. They may realize the likelihood of failure but go ahead anyway because of the small chance of starting the next McDonald's or Burger King.

THE OPTION TO ABANDON

Managers also have the option to abandon existing projects. Abandonment may seem cowardly, but it can often save companies a great deal of money. Because of this, the option to abandon increases the value of any potential project.

The example of ice hotels, which illustrated the option to expand, can also illustrate the option to abandon. To see this, imagine that Mr. Willig now believes that there is a 50 percent probability that annual cash flows will be $6 million and a 50 percent probability that annual cash flows will be −$2 million. The NPV calculations under the two forecasts become:

> **Optimistic forecast:** −$12 million + $6 million/.2 = $18 million
> **Pessimistic forecast:** −$12 million − $2 million/.2 = −$22 million

yielding an NPV for the project of:

$$50\% \times \$18 \text{ million} + 50\% \times (-\$22 \text{ million}) = -\$2 \text{ million} \qquad (7.4)$$

Furthermore, now imagine that Mr. Willig wants to own, at most, just one ice hotel, implying that there is no option to expand. Because the NPV in Equation 7.4 is negative, it looks as if he will not build the hotel.

But things change when we consider the abandonment option. As of Date 1, the entrepreneur will know which forecast has come true. If cash flows equal those under the optimistic forecast, Conrad will keep the project alive. If, however, cash flows equal those under the pessimistic forecast, he will abandon the hotel. If Mr. Willig knows these possibilities ahead of time, the NPV of the project becomes:

$$50\% \times \$18 \text{ million} + 50\% \times (-\$12 \text{ million} - \$2 \text{ million}/1.20) = \$2.17 \text{ million}$$

Because Mr. Willig abandons after experiencing the cash flow of −$2 million at Date 1, he does not have to endure this outflow in any of the later years. The NPV is now positive, so Conrad will accept the project.

The example here is clearly a stylized one. Whereas many years may pass before a project is abandoned in the real world, our ice hotel was abandoned after just one year. And, while salvage values generally accompany abandonment, we assumed no salvage value for the ice hotel. Nevertheless, abandonment options are pervasive in the real world.

For example, consider the moviemaking industry. As shown in Figure 7.6, movies begin with either the purchase or development of a script. A completed script might cost a movie studio a few million dollars and potentially lead to actual production. However, the great majority of scripts (perhaps well in excess of 80 percent) are abandoned. Why would studios abandon scripts that they commissioned in the first place? The studios know ahead of time that only a few scripts will be promising, and they don't know which ones. Thus, they cast a wide net, commissioning many scripts to get a few good ones. The studios must be ruthless with the bad scripts because the expenditure here pales in comparison to the huge losses from producing a bad movie.

The few lucky scripts then move into production, where costs might be budgeted in the tens of millions of dollars, if not much more. At this stage, the dreaded phrase is that on-location production gets "bogged down," creating cost overruns. But the studios are

Figure 7.6
The Abandonment
Option in the Movie
Industry

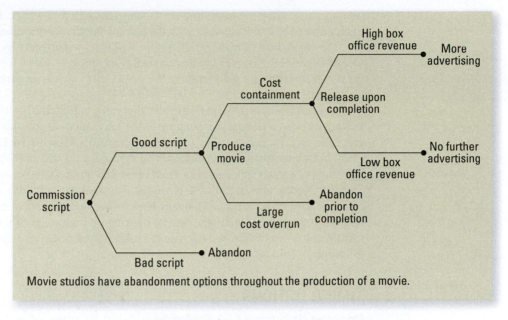

Movie studios have abandonment options throughout the production of a movie.

equally ruthless here. Should these overruns become excessive, production is likely to be abandoned midstream. Interestingly, abandonment almost always occurs due to high costs, not due to the fear that the movie won't be able to find an audience. Little information on that score will be obtained until the movie is actually released.

Release of the movie is accompanied by significant advertising expenditures, perhaps in the range of $10 to $20 million. Advertising will continue following strong ticket sales, but it will likely be abandoned after a few weeks of poor box office performance.

Moviemaking is one of the riskiest businesses around, with studios receiving hundreds of millions of dollars in a matter of weeks from a blockbuster while receiving practically nothing during this period from a flop. The abandonment options contain costs that might otherwise bankrupt the industry.

To illustrate some of these ideas, consider the case of Euro Disney. The deal to open Euro Disney occurred in 1987, and the park opened its doors outside Paris in 1992. Disney's management thought Europeans would go goofy over the new park, but trouble soon began. The number of visitors never met expectations, in part because the company priced tickets too high. Disney also decided not to serve alcohol in a country that was accustomed to wine with meals. French labor inspectors fought Disney's strict dress codes, and so on.

After several years of operations, the park began serving wine in its restaurants, lowered ticket prices, and made other adjustments. In other words, management exercised its option to reformulate the product. The park began to make a small profit. Then the company exercised the option to expand by adding a "second gate," which was another theme park next to Euro Disney named Walt Disney Studios. The second gate was intended to encourage visitors to extend their stays. But the new park flopped. The reasons ranged from high ticket prices, attractions geared toward Hollywood rather than European filmmaking, labor strikes in Paris, and a summer heat wave.

By the summer of 2003, Euro Disney was close to bankruptcy again. Executives discussed a range of options. These options ranged from letting the company go broke (the option to abandon) to pulling the Disney name from the park. In 2005, the company finally agreed to a restructuring with the help of the French government.

The whole idea of managerial options was summed up aptly by Jay Rasulo, the overseer of Disney's theme parks, when he said, "One thing we know for sure is that you never get it 100 percent right the first time. We open every one of our parks with the notion that we're going to add content."

A recent example of the option to abandon came in March 2014 when Panasonic stopped making its plasma televisions. What made the move unusual was that Panasonic made such great plasma TVs. For example, CNET's top four TVs to own were Panasonic plasma TVs. Then, in October 2014, LG announced that it, too, would stop making plasma TVs.

Companies can abandon even quite venerated businesses. For example, in June 2013, Eastman Kodak announced that it would stop making cellulose acetate, an important component of camera film. Although Kodak invented electronic cameras, the company refused to adopt the technology, instead banking on traditional film photography. In a nod to how slow sales of film had become, a spokesperson stated that the company had "years of inventory built up."

TIMING OPTIONS

One often finds urban land that has been vacant for many years. Yet this land is bought and sold from time to time. Why would anyone pay a positive price for land that has no source of revenue? Certainly, one could not arrive at a positive price through NPV analysis. However, the paradox can easily be explained in terms of real options.

Suppose that the land's highest and best use is as an office building. Total construction costs for the building are estimated to be $1 million. Currently, net rents (after all costs) are estimated to be $90,000 per year in perpetuity, and the discount rate is 10 percent. The NPV of this proposed building would be:

$$-\$1 \text{ million} + \$90{,}000/.10 = -\$100{,}000$$

Because this NPV is negative, one would not currently want to build. However, suppose that the federal government is planning various urban revitalization programs for the city. Office rents will likely increase if the programs succeed. In this case, the property's owner might want to erect the office building after all. Conversely, office rents will remain the same, or even fall, if the programs fail. The owner will not build in this case.

We say that the property owner has a *timing option*. Although she does not currently want to build, she will want to build in the future should rents in the area rise substantially. This timing option explains why vacant land often has value. There are costs, such as taxes, from holding raw land, but the value of an office building after a substantial rise in rents may more than offset these holding costs. Of course the exact value of the vacant land depends on both the probability of success in the revitalization program and the extent of the rent increase. Figure 7.7 illustrates this timing option.

Mining operations almost always provide timing options as well. Suppose you own a copper mine where the cost of mining each ton of copper exceeds the sales revenue. It's a no-brainer to say that you would not want to mine the copper currently. And because there are costs of ownership such as property taxes, insurance, and security, you might actually want to pay someone to take the mine off your hands. However, we would caution you not to do so hastily. Copper prices in the future might increase enough so that production is profitable. Given that possibility, you could likely find someone who would pay a positive price for the property today.

Figure 7.7
Decision Tree for
Vacant Land

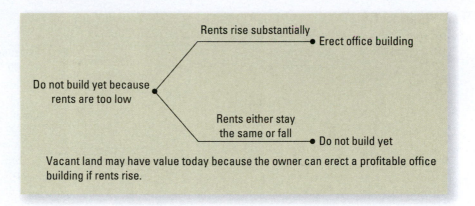

Rents rise substantially
● Erect office building

Do not build yet because
rents are too low

Rents either stay
the same or fall
● Do not build yet

Vacant land may have value today because the owner can erect a profitable office
building if rents rise.

7.4 Decision Trees

Excel
Master
coverage online

As shown in the previous section, managers adjust their decisions on the basis of new
information. For example, a project may be expanded if early experience is promising,
whereas the same project might be abandoned in the wake of bad results. As we said
earlier, the choices available to managers are called *real options* and an individual project
can often be viewed as a series of real options, leading to valuation approaches beyond the
basic present value methodology of earlier chapters.

Earlier in this chapter, we considered Solar Electronics Corporation's (SEC's) solar-
powered jet engine project, with cash flows as shown in Table 7.1. In that example, SEC
planned to invest $1,500 million at Year 1 and expected to receive $900 million per year
in each of the next five years. Our calculations showed an NPV of $1,517 million, so the
firm would presumably want to go ahead with the project.

To illustrate decision trees in more detail, let's move back one year to Year 0, when
SEC's decision was more complicated. At that time, the engineering group had developed
the technology for a solar-powered plane engine, but test marketing had not begun. The
marketing department proposed that SEC develop some prototypes and conduct test marketing of the engine. A corporate planning group, including representatives from production, marketing, and engineering, estimated that this preliminary phase would take a year
and cost $100 million. Furthermore, the group believed there was a 75 percent chance that
the marketing tests would prove successful. After completion of the marketing tests, SEC
would decide whether to engage in full-scale production, necessitating the investment of
$1,500 million.

The marketing tests add a layer of complexity to the analysis. Our previous work on
the example assumed that the marketing tests had already proved successful. How do we
analyze whether we want to go ahead with the marketing tests in the first place? This is
where decision trees come in.

To recap, SEC faces two decisions, both of which are represented in Figure 7.8. First
the firm must decide whether to go ahead with the marketing tests. And if the tests are performed, the firm must decide whether the results of the tests warrant full-scale production.
The important point here, as we will see, is that decision trees answer the two questions in
reverse order. So let's work backward, first considering what to do with the results of the
tests, which can be either successful or unsuccessful.

Figure 7.8
Decision Tree for
SEC ($ millions)

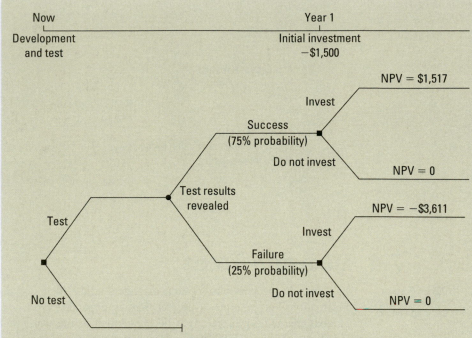

Squares represent decision points. Circle represents receipt of information.
SEC must make two decisions:
  1. Whether to develop and test the engine.
  2. Whether to invest for full-scale production.
With decision trees, decisions are made in reverse order.

Assume tests have been successful (75 percent probability). Table 7.1 tells us that full-scale production will cost $1,500 million and will generate an annual cash flow of $900 million for five years, yielding an NPV of:

$$= -\$1,500 + \sum_{t=1}^{5} \frac{\$900}{(1.15)^t}$$

$$= -\$1,500 + \$900 \times \text{PVIFA}\,(.15, 5)$$

$$= \$1,517$$

Because the NPV is positive, successful marketing tests should lead to full-scale production. (Note that the NPV is calculated as of Year 1, the time at which the investment of $1,500 million is made. Later we will discount this number back to Year 0, when the decision on test marketing is to be made.)

Assume tests have not been successful (25 percent probability). Here, SEC's $1,500 million investment would produce an NPV of −$3,611 million, calculated as of Year 1. (To save space, we will not provide the raw numbers leading to this calculation.) Because the NPV here is negative, SEC will not want full-scale production if the marketing tests are unsuccessful.

Decision on marketing tests. Now we know what to do with the results of the marketing tests. Let's use these results to move back one year. That is, we now want to figure out whether SEC should invest $100 million for the test marketing costs in the first place.

The expected payoff evaluated at Date 1 (in millions) is:

$$
\begin{array}{c}
\text{Expected} \\
\text{payoff}
\end{array}
=
\left(
\begin{array}{c}
\text{Probability} \\
\text{of} \\
\text{success}
\end{array}
\times
\begin{array}{c}
\text{Payoff} \\
\text{if} \\
\text{successful}
\end{array}
\right)
+
\left(
\begin{array}{c}
\text{Probability} \\
\text{of} \\
\text{failure}
\end{array}
\times
\begin{array}{c}
\text{Payoff} \\
\text{if} \\
\text{failure}
\end{array}
\right)
$$

$$
= \quad (.75 \quad \times \quad \$1{,}517) \quad + \quad (.25 \quad \times \quad \$0)
$$

$$
= \$1{,}138
$$

The NPV of testing computed at Date 0 (in millions) is:

$$
\text{NPV} = -\$100 + \frac{\$1{,}138}{1.15}
$$

$$
= \$890
$$

Because the NPV is positive, the firm should test the market for solar-powered jet engines.

Warning   We have used a discount rate of 15 percent for both the testing and the investment decisions. Perhaps a higher discount rate should have been used for the initial test marketing decision, which is likely to be riskier than the investment decision.

Recap   As mentioned above, the analysis is graphed in Figure 7.8. As can be seen from the figure, SEC must make the following two decisions:

1. Whether to develop and test the solar-powered jet engine.
2. Whether to invest for full-scale production following the results of the test.

Using a decision tree, we answered the second question before we answered the first one.

Decision trees represent the best approach to solving SEC's problem, given the information presented so far in the text. However, we will examine a more sophisticated approach to valuing options in a later chapter. Though this approach was first used to value financial options traded on organized option exchanges, it can be used to value real options as well.

Summary and Conclusions

This chapter discussed a number of practical applications of capital budgeting.

1. Though NPV is the best capital budgeting approach conceptually, it has been criticized in practice for giving managers a false sense of security. Sensitivity analysis shows NPV under varying assumptions, giving managers a better feel for the project's risks. Unfortunately, sensitivity analysis modifies only one variable at a time, but many variables are likely to vary together in the real world. Scenario analysis examines a project's performance under different scenarios (such as war breaking out or oil prices skyrocketing). Finally, managers want to know how bad forecasts must be before a project loses money. Break-even analysis calculates the sales figure at which the project breaks even. Though break-even analysis is frequently performed on an accounting profit basis, we suggest that a net present value basis is more appropriate.

2. Monte Carlo simulation begins with a model of the firm's cash flows, based on both the interactions between different variables and the movement of each individual variable over time. Random sampling generates a distribution of these cash flows for each period, leading to a net present value calculation.

3. We analyzed the hidden options in capital budgeting, such as the option to expand, the option to abandon, and timing options.

4. Decision trees represent an approach for valuing projects with these hidden, or real, options.

Concept Questions

1. **Forecasting Risk**   What is forecasting risk? In general, would the degree of forecasting risk be greater for a new product or a cost-cutting proposal? Why?

2. **Sensitivity Analysis and Scenario Analysis**   What is the essential difference between sensitivity analysis and scenario analysis?

3. **Marginal Cash Flows**   A coworker claims that looking at so much marginal this and incremental that is just a bunch of nonsense, and states, "Listen, if our average revenue doesn't exceed our average cost, then we will have a negative cash flow, and we will go broke!" How do you respond?

4. **Break-Even Point**   As a shareholder of a firm that is contemplating a new project, would you be more concerned with the accounting break-even point, the cash break-even point (the point at which operating cash flow is zero), or the financial break-even point? Why?

5. **Break-Even Point**   Assume a firm is considering a new typical project that requires an initial investment with sales, variable costs and fixed costs over its life. Will the project usually reach the accounting, cash, or financial break-even point first? Which will it reach next? Last? Will this order always apply?

6. **Real Options**   Why does traditional NPV analysis tend to underestimate the true value of a capital budgeting project?

7. **Real Options**   The Mango Republic has just liberalized its markets and is now permitting foreign investors. Tesla Manufacturing has analyzed starting a project in the country and has determined that the project has a negative NPV. Why might the company go ahead with the project? What type of option is most likely to add value to this project?

8. **Sensitivity and Break-Even Analysis**   How does sensitivity analysis interact with break-even analysis?

9. **Option to Wait**   An option can often have more than one source of value. Consider a logging company. The company can log the timber today or wait another year (or more) to log the timber. What advantages would waiting one year potentially have?

10. **Project Analysis**   You are discussing a project analysis with a coworker. The project involves real options, such as expanding the project if successful, or abandoning the project if it fails. Your coworker makes the following statement: "This analysis is ridiculous. We looked at expanding or abandoning the project in two years, but there are many other options we should consider. For example, we could expand in one year, and expand further in two years. Or we could expand in one year, and abandon the project in two years. There are too many options for us to examine. Because of this, anything this analysis would give us is worthless." How would you evaluate this statement? Considering that with any capital budgeting project there are an infinite number of real options, when do you stop the option analysis on an individual project?

Questions and Problems

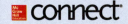

BASIC
(Questions 1–10)

1. **Sensitivity Analysis and Break-Even Point**   We are evaluating a project that costs $588,000, has an eight-year life, and has no salvage value. Assume that depreciation is straight-line to zero over the life of the project. Sales are projected at 70,000 units per year. Price per unit is $36, variable cost per unit is $20, and fixed costs are $695,000 per year. The tax rate is 35 percent, and we require a return of 15 percent on this project.

a. Calculate the accounting break-even point.
   b. Calculate the base-case cash flow and NPV. What is the sensitivity of NPV to changes in the sales figure? Explain what your answer tells you about a 500-unit decrease in projected sales.
   c. What is the sensitivity of OCF to changes in the variable cost figure? Explain what your answer tells you about a $1 decrease in estimated variable costs.

2. **Scenario Analysis**   In the previous problem, suppose the projections given for price, quantity, variable costs, and fixed costs are all accurate to within ±10 percent. Calculate the best-case and worst-case NPV figures.

3. **Calculating Break-Even**   In each of the following cases, find the unknown variable. Ignore taxes.

Accounting Break-Even	Unit Price	Unit Variable Cost	Fixed Costs	Depreciation
86,300	$ 42	$30	$ 820,000	?
143,806	?	81	2,750,000	$1,150,000
7,835	97	?	235,000	105,000

4. **Financial Break-Even**   L.J.'s Toys, Inc., just purchased a $375,000 machine to produce toy cars. The machine will be fully depreciated by the straight-line method over its five-year economic life. Each toy sells for $21. The variable cost per toy is $8, and the firm incurs fixed costs of $280,000 each year. The corporate tax rate for the company is 34 percent. The appropriate discount rate is 12 percent. What is the financial break-even point for the project?

5. **Option to Wait**   Your company is deciding whether to invest in a new machine. The new machine will increase cash flow by $530,000 per year. You believe the technology used in the machine has a 10-year life; in other words, no matter when you purchase the machine, it will be obsolete 10 years from today. The machine is currently priced at $3,400,000. The cost of the machine will decline by $250,000 per year until it reaches $2,650,000, where it will remain. If your required return is 9 percent, should you purchase the machine? If so, when should you purchase it?

6. **Decision Trees**   Ang Electronics, Inc., has developed a new DVDR. If the DVDR is successful, the present value of the payoff (when the product is brought to market) is $27 million. If the DVDR fails, the present value of the payoff is $9 million. If the product goes directly to market, there is a 50 percent chance of success. Alternatively, Ang can delay the launch by one year and spend $1.3 million to test market the DVDR. Test marketing would allow the firm to improve the product and increase the probability of success to 80 percent. The appropriate discount rate is 11 percent. Should the firm conduct test marketing?

7. **Decision Trees**   The manager for a growing firm is considering the launch of a new product. If the product goes directly to market, there is a 50 percent chance of success. For $125,000 the manager can conduct a focus group that will increase the product's chance of success to 65 percent. Alternatively, the manager has the option to pay a consulting firm $285,000 to research the market and refine the product. The consulting firm successfully launches new products 80 percent of the time. If the firm successfully launches the product, the payoff will be $1.8 million. If the product is a failure, the NPV is zero. Which action will result in the highest expected payoff to the firm?

8. **Decision Trees**   B&B has a new baby powder ready to market. If the firm goes directly to the market with the product, there is only a 55 percent chance of success. However, the firm can conduct customer segment research, which will take a year and cost $950,000. By going through research, B&B will be able to better target potential customers and will increase the probability of success to 70 percent.

If successful, the baby powder will bring a present value profit (at time of initial selling) of $18 million. If unsuccessful, the present value payoff is only $5.5 million. Should the firm conduct customer segment research or go directly to market? The appropriate discount rate is 15 percent.

9. **Financial Break-Even Analysis** You are considering investing in a company that cultivates abalone for sale to local restaurants. Use the following information:

Sales price per abalone	= $39
Variable costs per abalone	= $7.15
Fixed costs per year	= $410,000
Depreciation per year	= $120,000
Tax rate	= 35%

The discount rate for the company is 15 percent, the initial investment in equipment is $840,000, and the project's economic life is seven years. Assume the equipment is depreciated on a straight-line basis over the project's life.

  a. What is the accounting break-even level for the project?
  b. What is the financial break-even level for the project?

10. **Financial Break-Even** Niko has purchased a brand new machine to produce its High Flight line of shoes. The machine has an economic life of five years. The depreciation schedule for the machine is straight-line with no salvage value. The machine costs $575,000. The sales price per pair of shoes is $50, while the variable cost is $14. $195,000 of fixed costs per year are attributed to the machine. Assume that the corporate tax rate is 34 percent and the appropriate discount rate is 8 percent. What is the financial break-even point?

INTERMEDIATE
(Questions 11–25)

11. **Break-Even Intuition** Consider a project with a required return of R percent that costs I and will last for N years. The project uses straight-line depreciation to zero over the N-year life; there are neither salvage value nor net working capital requirements.

  a. At the accounting break-even level of output, what is the IRR of this project? The payback period? The NPV?
  b. At the cash break-even level of output, what is the IRR of this project? The payback period? The NPV?
  c. At the financial break-even level of output, what is the IRR of this project? The payback period? The NPV?

12. **Sensitivity Analysis** Consider a four-year project with the following information: Initial fixed asset investment = $410,000; straight-line depreciation to zero over the four-year life; zero salvage value; price = $35; variable costs = $23; fixed costs = $176,000; quantity sold = 90,000 units; tax rate = 34 percent. How sensitive is OCF to changes in quantity sold?

13. **Project Analysis** You are considering a new product launch. The project will cost $760,000, have a four-year life, and have no salvage value; depreciation is straight-line to zero. Sales are projected at 420 units per year; price per unit will be $17,200; variable cost per unit will be $14,300; and fixed costs will be $640,000 per year. The required return on the project is 15 percent, and the relevant tax rate is 35 percent.

  a. Based on your experience, you think the unit sales, variable cost, and fixed cost projections given here are probably accurate to within ±10 percent. What are the upper and lower bounds for these projections? What is the base-case NPV? What are the best-case and worst-case scenarios?
  b. Evaluate the sensitivity of your base-case NPV to changes in fixed costs.
  c. What is the accounting break-even level of output for this project?

14. **Project Analysis**   McGilla Golf has decided to sell a new line of golf clubs. The clubs will sell for $850 per set and have a variable cost of $430 per set. The company has spent $150,000 for a marketing study that determined the company will sell 60,000 sets per year for seven years. The marketing study also determined that the company will lose sales of 12,000 sets of its high-priced clubs. The high-priced clubs sell at $1,100 and have variable costs of $620. The company will also increase sales of its cheap clubs by 15,000 sets. The cheap clubs sell for $400 and have variable costs of $210 per set. The fixed costs each year will be $9,300,000. The company has also spent $1,000,000 on research and development for the new clubs. The plant and equipment required will cost $28,700,000 and will be depreciated on a straight-line basis. The new clubs will also require an increase in net working capital of $1,400,000 that will be returned at the end of the project. The tax rate is 40 percent, and the cost of capital is 14 percent. Calculate the payback period, the NPV, and the IRR.

15. **Scenario Analysis**   In the previous problem, you feel that the values are accurate to within only ±10 percent. What are the best-case and worst-case NPVs? (*Hint:* The price and variable costs for the two existing sets of clubs are known with certainty; only the sales gained or lost are uncertain.)

16. **Sensitivity Analysis**   McGilla Golf would like to know the sensitivity of NPV to changes in the price of the new clubs and the quantity of new clubs sold. What is the sensitivity of the NPV to each of these variables?

17. **Abandonment Value**   We are examining a new project. We expect to sell 7,000 units per year at $38 net cash flow apiece for the next 10 years. In other words, the annual operating cash flow is projected to be $38 × 7,000 = $266,000. The relevant discount rate is 16 percent, and the initial investment required is $1,040,000.

    a. What is the base-case NPV?
    b. After the first year, the project can be dismantled and sold for $820,000. If expected sales are revised based on the first year's performance, when would it make sense to abandon the investment? In other words, at what level of expected sales would it make sense to abandon the project?
    c. Explain how the $820,000 abandonment value can be viewed as the opportunity cost of keeping the project in one year.

18. **Abandonment**   In the previous problem, suppose you think it is likely that expected sales will be revised upward to 9,500 units if the first year is a success and revised downward to 3,800 units if the first year is not a success.

    a. If success and failure are equally likely, what is the NPV of the project? Consider the possibility of abandonment in answering.
    b. What is the value of the option to abandon?

19. **Abandonment and Expansion**   In the previous problem, suppose the scale of the project can be doubled in one year in the sense that twice as many units can be produced and sold. Naturally, expansion would be desirable only if the project were a success. This implies that if the project is a success, projected sales after expansion will be 19,000. Again assuming that success and failure are equally likely, what is the NPV of the project? Note that abandonment is still an option if the project is a failure. What is the value of the option to expand?

20. **Break-Even Analysis**   Your buddy comes to you with a sure-fire way to make some quick money and help pay off your student loans. His idea is to sell T-shirts with the words "I get" on them. "You get it?" He says, "You see all those bumper stickers and T-shirts that say 'got milk' or 'got surf.' So this says, 'I get.' It's funny! All we have to do is buy a used silk screen press for $6,500 and we are in business!" Assume there are no fixed costs, and you depreciate the $6,500 in the first period. Taxes are 30 percent.

a. What is the accounting break-even point if each shirt costs $4.80 to make and you can sell them for $11 apiece?

Now assume one year has passed and you have sold 5,000 shirts! You find out that the Dairy Farmers of America have copyrighted the "got milk" slogan and are requiring you to pay $20,000 to continue operations. You expect this craze will last for another three years and that your discount rate is 12 percent.

b. What is the financial break-even point for your enterprise now?

21. **Decision Trees** Young screenwriter Carl Draper has just finished his first script. It has action, drama, and humor, and he thinks it will be a blockbuster. He takes the script to every motion picture studio in town and tries to sell it but to no avail. Finally, ACME studios offers to buy the script for either (a) $20,000 or (b) 1.5 percent of the movie's profits. There are two decisions the studio will have to make. First is to decide if the script is good or bad, and second if the movie is good or bad. First, there is a 90 percent chance that the script is bad. If it is bad, the studio does nothing more and throws the script out. If the script is good, they will shoot the movie. After the movie is shot, the studio will review it, and there is a 60 percent chance that the movie is bad. If the movie is bad, the movie will not be promoted and will not turn a profit. If the movie is good, the studio will promote heavily; the average profit for this type of movie is $30 million. Carl rejects the $20,000 and says he wants the 1.5 percent of profits. Was this a good decision by Carl?

22. **Option to Wait** Hickock Mining is evaluating when to open a gold mine. The mine has 44,000 ounces of gold left that can be mined, and mining operations will produce 5,500 ounces per year. The required return on the gold mine is 12 percent, and it will cost $29 million to open the mine. When the mine is opened, the company will sign a contract that will guarantee the price of gold for the remaining life of the mine. If the mine is opened today, each ounce of gold will generate an aftertax cash flow of $1,100 per ounce. If the company waits one year, there is a 60 percent probability that the contract price will generate an aftertax cash flow of $1,400 per ounce and a 40 percent probability that the aftertax cash flow will be $900 per ounce. What is the value of the option to wait?

23. **Abandonment Decisions** Allied Products, Inc., is considering a new product launch. The firm expects to have an annual operating cash flow of $13.5 million for the next 10 years. Allied Products uses a discount rate of 13 percent for new product launches. The initial investment is $59 million. Assume that the project has no salvage value at the end of its economic life.

    a. What is the NPV of the new product?
    b. After the first year, the project can be dismantled and sold for $37 million. If the estimates of remaining cash flows are revised based on the first year's experience, at what level of expected cash flows does it make sense to abandon the project?

24. **Expansion Decisions** Applied Nanotech is thinking about introducing a new surface cleaning machine. The marketing department has come up with the estimate that Applied Nanotech can sell 15 units per year at $275,000 net cash flow per unit for the next five years. The engineering department has come up with the estimate that developing the machine will take a $16 million initial investment. The finance department has estimated that a discount rate of 11 percent should be used.

    a. What is the base-case NPV?
    b. If unsuccessful, after the first year the project can be dismantled and will have an aftertax salvage value of $11 million. Also, after the first year, expected cash flows

will be revised up to 20 units per year or to 0 units, with equal probability. What is the revised NPV?

25. **Scenario Analysis**   You are the financial analyst for a tennis racket manufacturer. The company is considering using a graphitelike material in its tennis rackets. The company has estimated the information in the following table about the market for a racket with the new material. The company expects to sell the racket for six years. The equipment required for the project has no salvage value. The required return for projects of this type is 13 percent, and the company has a 40 percent tax rate. Should you recommend the project?

	Pessimistic	**Expected**	**Optimistic**
Market size	120,000	135,000	150,000
Market share	20%	23%	25%
Selling price	$ 147	$ 153	$ 158
Variable costs per unit	$ 104	$ 99	$ 98
Fixed costs per year	$ 965,000	$ 920,000	$ 890,000
Initial investment	$2,100,000	$1,950,000	$1,850,000

CHALLENGE
(Questions 26–30)

26. **Scenario Analysis**   Consider a project to supply Detroit with 25,000 tons of machine screws annually for automobile production. You will need an initial $2,700,000 investment in threading equipment to get the project started; the project will last for five years. The accounting department estimates that annual fixed costs will be $275,000 and that variable costs should be $265 per ton; accounting will depreciate the initial fixed asset investment straight-line to zero over the five-year project life. It also estimates a salvage value of $250,000 after dismantling costs. The marketing department estimates that the automakers will let the contract at a selling price of $345 per ton. The engineering department estimates you will need an initial net working capital investment of $400,000. You require a 13 percent return and face a marginal tax rate of 38 percent on this project.

    a. What is the estimated OCF for this project? The NPV? Should you pursue this project?
    b. Suppose you believe that the accounting department's initial cost and salvage value projections are accurate only to within ±15 percent; the marketing department's price estimate is accurate only to within ±10 percent; and the engineering department's net working capital estimate is accurate only to within ±5 percent. What is your worst-case scenario for this project? Your best-case scenario? Do you still want to pursue the project?

27. **Sensitivity Analysis**   In Problem 26, suppose you're confident about your own projections, but you're a little unsure about Detroit's actual machine screw requirements. What is the sensitivity of the project OCF to changes in the quantity supplied? What about the sensitivity of NPV to changes in quantity supplied? Given the sensitivity number you calculated, is there some minimum level of output below which you wouldn't want to operate? Why?

28. **Abandonment Decisions**   Consider the following project for Hand Clapper, Inc. The company is considering a four-year project to manufacture clap-command garage door openers. This project requires an initial investment of $15 million that will be depreciated straight-line to zero over the project's life. An initial investment in net working capital of $950,000 is required to support spare parts inventory; this cost is fully recoverable

whenever the project ends. The company believes it can generate $10.9 million in pretax revenues with $4.1 million in total pretax operating costs. The tax rate is 38 percent, and the discount rate is 13 percent. The market value of the equipment over the life of the project is as follows:

Year	Market Value ($ millions)
1	$13.0
2	10.0
3	7.5
4	0.0

a. Assuming Hand Clapper operates this project for four years, what is the NPV?
b. Now compute the project NPVs assuming the project is abandoned after only one year, after two years, and after three years. What economic life for this project maximizes its value to the firm? What does this problem tell you about not considering abandonment possibilities when evaluating projects?

29. **Abandonment Decisions**   M.V.P. Games, Inc., has hired you to perform a feasibility study of a new video game that requires an initial investment of $8 million. M.V.P. expects a total annual operating cash flow of $1.5 million for the next 10 years. The relevant discount rate is 10 percent. Cash flows occur at year-end.

a. What is the NPV of the new video game?
b. After one year, the estimate of remaining annual cash flows will be revised either upward to $2.75 million or downward to $345,000. Each revision has an equal probability of occurring. At that time, the video game project can be sold for $3.1 million. What is the revised NPV given that the firm can abandon the project after one year?

30. **Financial Break-Even**   The Cornchopper Company is considering the purchase of a new harvester. Cornchopper has hired you to determine the break-even purchase price in terms of present value of the harvester. This break-even purchase price is the price at which the project's NPV is zero. Base your analysis on the following facts:

- The new harvester is not expected to affect revenues, but pretax operating expenses will be reduced by $13,000 per year for 10 years.
- The old harvester is now 5 years old, with 10 years of its scheduled life remaining. It was originally purchased for $65,000 and has been depreciated by the straight-line method.
- The old harvester can be sold for $21,000 today.
- The new harvester will be depreciated by the straight-line method over its 10-year life.
- The corporate tax rate is 34 percent.
- The firm's required rate of return is 15 percent.
- The initial investment, the proceeds from selling the old harvester, and any resulting tax effects occur immediately.
- All other cash flows occur at year-end.
- The market value of each harvester at the end of its economic life is zero.

Excel Master It! Problem

Dahlia Simmons, CFO of Ulrich Enterprises, is analyzing a new project to sell solar powered batteries for cell phones. Dahlia has estimated the following probability distributions for the variables in the project:

Probability	10%	30%	40%	20%		
Industry demand	80,000,000	95,000,000	108,000,000	124,000,000		
Probability	5%	20%	20%	25%	20%	10%
Ulrich market share	1%	2%	3%	4%	5%	6%
Probability	20%	70%	10%			
Initial cost	$60,000,000	$65,000,000	$72,000,000			
Probability	20%	65%	15%			
VC per unit	$24	$26	$29			
Probability	15%	25%	40%	20%		
Fixed costs	$20,000,000	$24,000,000	$27,000,000	$31,000,000		

The unit price depends on the industry demand since a greater demand will result in a higher price. Dahlia determines that the price per unit will be given by the equation:

$$\text{Price} = \text{Industry demand} / 2{,}000{,}000 +/- \$2$$

The random "+/−$2" term represents an increase or decrease in price according to the following distribution:

Probability	45%	55%
Price randomness	−$2	$2

The length of the project, tax rate, and required return are:

Project length (years)	6
Tax rate	34%
Required return	14%

a. Create a Monte Carlo simulation for the project with at least 500 runs. Calculate the IRR for each run. Note that the IRR function in Excel will return an error if the IRR of the project is too low. For example, what is the IRR if both the initial cash flow and the operating cash flows are negative? The IRR is less than −100 percent. This is not a problem when you are calculating the IRR one time since you can see the IRR is too low, but when you are running 500 or more iterations it can create a problem trying to summarize the results. Because of this issue, you should create an IF statement that tests if the operating cash flow divided by the absolute value of the initial investment is less than .1. If this is the case, the cell will return an IRR of −99.99 percent, or else the cell will calculate the IRR.
b. Create a graph of the distribution of the IRRs from the Monte Carlo simulation for different ranges of IRR.
c. Create a graph for the cumulative probability function for the IRR distribution.

Mini Case

BUNYAN LUMBER, LLC

Bunyan Lumber, LLC, harvests timber and delivers logs to timber mills for sale. The company was founded 70 years ago by Pete Bunyan. The current CEO is Paula Bunyan, the granddaughter of the founder. The company is currently evaluating a 5,000-acre forest it owns in Oregon. Paula has asked Steve Boles, the company's finance officer, to evaluate the project. Paula's concern is when the company should harvest the timber.

Lumber is sold by the company for its "pond value." Pond value is the amount a mill will pay for a log delivered to the mill location. The price paid for logs delivered to a mill is quoted in dollars per thousands of board feet (MBF), and the price depends on the grade of the logs. The forest Bunyan Lumber is evaluating was planted by the company 20 years ago and is made up entirely of Douglas fir trees. The table here shows the current price per MBF for the three grades of timber the company feels will come from the stand:

Timber Grade	Price per MBF
1P	$620
2P	605
3P	595

Steve believes that the pond value of lumber will increase at the inflation rate. The company is planning to thin the forest today, and it expects to realize a positive cash flow of $1,000 per acre from thinning. The thinning is done to increase the growth rate of the remaining trees, and it is always done 20 years following a planting.

The major decision the company faces is when to log the forest. When the company logs the forest, it will immediately replant saplings, which will allow for a future harvest. The longer the forest is allowed to grow, the larger the harvest becomes per acre. Additionally, an older forest has a higher grade of timber. Steve has compiled the following table with the expected harvest per acre in thousands of board feet, along with the breakdown of the timber grades:

Years from Today to Begin Harvest	Harvest (MBF) per Acre	Timber Grade		
		1P	2P	3P
20	14.1	16%	36%	48%
25	16.4	20	40	40
30	17.3	22	43	35
35	18.1	24	45	31

The company expects to lose 5 percent of the timber it cuts due to defects and breakage.

The forest will be clear-cut when the company harvests the timber. This method of harvesting allows for faster growth of replanted trees. All of the harvesting, processing, replanting, and transportation are to be handled by subcontractors hired by Bunyan Lumber. The cost of the logging is expected to be $140 per MBF. A road system has to be constructed and is expected to cost $50 per MBF on average. Sales preparation and administrative costs, excluding office overhead costs, are expected to be $18 per MBF.

As soon as the harvesting is complete, the company will reforest the land. Reforesting costs include the following:

	Cost per Acre
Excavator piling	$150
Broadcast burning	300
Site preparation	145
Planting costs	225

All costs are expected to increase at the inflation rate.

Assume all cash flows occur at the year of harvest. For example, if the company begins harvesting the timber 20 years from today, the cash flow from the harvest will be received 20 years from today. When the company logs the land, it will immediately replant the land with new saplings. The harvest period chosen will be repeated for the foreseeable future. The company's nominal required return is 10 percent, and the inflation rate is expected to be 3.7 percent per year. Bunyan Lumber has a 35 percent tax rate.

Clear-cutting is a controversial method of forest management. To obtain the necessary permits, Bunyan Lumber has agreed to contribute to a conservation fund every time it harvests the lumber. If the company harvested the forest today, the required contribution would be $250,000. The company has agreed that the required contribution will grow by 3.2 percent per year. When should the company harvest the forest?

Interest Rates and Bond Valuation

When states, cities, or other local government entities need to raise money, they can turn to the municipal bond market. With almost $4 trillion in municipal bonds outstanding, it seems that they reach out to this market quite often! There are more than 1 million municipal bond issues outstanding and more than 44,000 issuers. Normally considered a relatively quiet financial market, the municipal bond market became much more exciting because of the potential for municipal bond defaults. The number of defaults that have occurred depends on whom you ask. From 1970 to 2011, Moody's reported that only 71 municipal bonds had defaulted. However, an analysis by the Federal Reserve Bank of New York counted 2,521 defaults. The reason for the difference was that Moody's only included municipal bonds that were

rated, while the New York Fed included all municipal bond defaults. A major cause for concern for municipal bond investors was the bankruptcy filing by Detroit in July 2013, which is the largest municipal bankruptcy in U.S. history. In December 2014, Detroit emerged from bankruptcy, eliminating $7 billion in debt from its balance sheet.

Of course, few municipal bond defaults to date have exceeded the infamous "Whoops" bonds. These were issued by the Washington Public Power Supply System (WPPSS) to fund the construction of five nuclear power plants. WPPSS defaulted on $2.25 billion worth of the bonds in 1983, the largest municipal bond default in U.S. history at that time. Whoops, indeed! In the end, investors received only 10 to 40 percent of their original investment.

This chapter introduces you to bonds. We first use the techniques shown in Chapter 4 to value bonds. We then discuss bond features and how bonds are bought and sold. One important point is that bond values depend, in large part, on interest rates. We therefore cover the behavior of interest rates in the last section of the chapter.

8.1 Bonds and Bond Valuation

Corporations (and governments) frequently borrow money by issuing or selling debt securities called bonds. In this section, we describe the various features of corporate bonds. We then discuss the cash flows associated with a bond and how bonds can be valued using our discounted cash flow procedure.

BOND FEATURES AND PRICES

A bond is normally an interest-only loan, meaning that the borrower will pay the interest every period, but none of the principal will be repaid until the end of the loan.

For example, suppose the Beck Corporation wants to borrow $1,000 for 30 years. The interest rate on similar debt issued by similar corporations is 12 percent. Beck will thus pay .12 × $1,000 = $120 in interest every year for 30 years. At the end of 30 years, Beck will repay the $1,000. As this example suggests, a bond is a fairly simple financing arrangement. There is, however, a rich jargon associated with bonds.

In our example, the $120 regular interest payments are called the bond's **coupons**. Because the coupon is constant and paid every year, this type of bond is sometimes called a *level coupon bond*. The amount repaid at the end of the loan is called the bond's **face value**, or **par value**. As in our example, this par value is usually $1,000 for corporate bonds, and a bond that sells for its par value is called a *par value bond*. Government bonds frequently have much larger face, or par, values. Finally, the annual coupon divided by the face value is called the **coupon rate** on the bond. Since $120/1,000 = 12 percent, the Beck bond has a 12 percent coupon rate.

The number of years until the face value is paid is called the bond's time to **maturity**. A corporate bond will frequently have a maturity of 30 years when it is originally issued, but this varies. Once the bond has been issued, the number of years to maturity declines as time passes.

BOND VALUES AND YIELDS

As time passes, interest rates change in the marketplace. Because the cash flows from a bond stay the same, the value of the bond fluctuates. When interest rates rise, the present value of the bond's remaining cash flows declines, and the bond is worth less. When interest rates fall, the bond is worth more.

To determine the value of a bond at a particular point in time, we need to know the number of periods remaining until maturity, the face value, the coupon, and the market interest rate for bonds with similar features. The interest rate required in the market on a bond is called the bond's **yield to maturity (YTM)**. This rate is sometimes called the bond's *yield* for short. Given all this information, we can calculate the present value of the cash flows as an estimate of the bond's current market value.

For example, suppose the Xanth (pronounced "zanth") Co. were to issue a bond with 10 years to maturity. The Xanth bond has an annual coupon of $80, implying the bond will pay $80 per year for the next 10 years in coupon interest. In addition, Xanth will pay $1,000 to the bondholder in 10 years. The cash flows from the bond are shown in Figure 8.1. As illustrated in the figure, the cash flows have an annuity component (the coupons) and a lump sum (the face value paid at maturity).

Figure 8.1   Cash Flows for Xanth Co. Bond

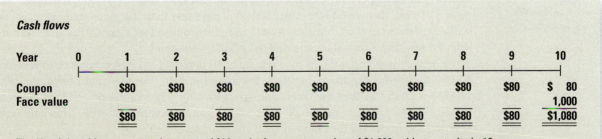

The Xanth bond has an annual coupon of $80 and a face, or par, value of $1,000 paid at maturity in 10 years.

Assuming similar bonds have a yield of 8 percent, what will this bond sell for? We estimate the market value of the bond by calculating the present value of the two components separately and adding the results together. First, at the going rate of 8 percent, the present value of the $1,000 paid in 10 years is:

$$\text{Present value} = \$1,000/1.08^{10} = \$1,000/2.1589 = \$463.19$$

Second, the bond offers $80 per year for 10 years. The present value of this annuity stream is:

$$
\begin{aligned}
\text{Annuity present value} &= \$80 \times (1 - 1/1.08^{10})/.08 \\
&= \$80 \times (1 - 1/2.1589)/.08 \\
&= \$80 \times 6.7101 \\
&= \$536.81
\end{aligned}
$$

We add the values for the two parts together to get the bond's value:

$$\text{Total bond value} = \$463.19 + 536.81 = \$1,000$$

This bond sells for exactly its face value. This is not a coincidence. The going interest rate in the market is 8 percent. Considered as an interest-only loan, what interest rate does this bond have? With an $80 coupon, this bond pays exactly 8 percent interest only when it sells for $1,000.

To illustrate what happens as interest rates change, suppose that a year has gone by. The Xanth bond now has nine years to maturity. If the interest rate in the market has risen to 10 percent, what will the bond be worth? To find out, we repeat the present value calculations with 9 years instead of 10, and a 10 percent yield instead of an 8 percent yield. First, the present value of the $1,000 paid in nine years at 10 percent is:

$$\text{Present value} = \$1,000/1.10^{9} = \$1,000/2.3579 = \$424.10$$

Second, the bond now offers $80 per year for nine years. The present value of this annuity stream at 10 percent is:

$$
\begin{aligned}
\text{Annuity present value} &= \$80 \times (1 - 1/1.10^{9})/.10 \\
&= \$80 \times (1 - 1/2.3579)/.10 \\
&= \$80 \times 5.7590 \\
&= \$460.72
\end{aligned}
$$

We add the values for the two parts together to get the bond's value:

$$\text{Total bond value} = \$424.10 + 460.72 = \$884.82$$

A good bond site to visit is **finance.yahoo.com /bonds**, which has loads of useful information.

Therefore, the bond should sell for about $885. In the vernacular, we say that this bond, with its 8 percent coupon, is priced to yield 10 percent at $885.

The Xanth Co. bond now sells for less than its $1,000 face value. Why? The market interest rate is 10 percent. Considered as an interest-only loan of $1,000, this bond only pays 8 percent, its coupon rate. Since the bond pays less than the going rate, investors are willing to lend only something less than the $1,000 promised repayment. Because the bond sells for less than face value, it is said to be a *discount bond*.

The only way to get the interest rate up to 10 percent is to lower the price to less than $1,000 so that the purchaser, in effect, has a built-in gain. For the Xanth bond, the price of $885 is $115 less than the face value, so an investor who purchased and kept the bond would get $80 per year and would have a $115 gain at maturity as well. This gain compensates the lender for the below-market coupon rate.

Another way to see why the bond is discounted by $115 is to note that the $80 coupon is $20 below the coupon on a newly issued par value bond, based on current market conditions. The bond would be worth $1,000 only if it had a coupon of $100 per year. In a sense, an investor who buys and keeps the bond gives up $20 per year for nine years. At 10 percent, this annuity stream is worth:

$$\text{Annuity present value} = \$20 \times (1 - 1/1.10^9)/.10$$
$$= \$20 \times 5.7590$$
$$= \$115.18$$

Online bond calculators are available at **personal.fidelity.com**; interest rate information is available at **money.cnn.com /data/bonds** and **www.bankrate.com**.

This is just the amount of the discount.

What would the Xanth bond sell for if interest rates had dropped by 2 percent instead of rising by 2 percent? As you might guess, the bond would sell for more than $1,000. Such a bond is said to sell at a *premium* and is called a *premium bond*.

This case is just the opposite of a discount bond. The Xanth bond now has a coupon rate of 8 percent when the market rate is only 6 percent. Investors are willing to pay a premium to get this extra coupon amount. In this case, the relevant discount rate is 6 percent, and there are nine years remaining. The present value of the $1,000 face amount is:

$$\text{Present value} = \$1,000/1.06^9 = \$1,000/1.6895 = \$591.89$$

The present value of the coupon stream is:

$$\text{Annuity present value} = \$80 \times (1 - 1/1.06^9)/.06$$
$$= \$80 \times (1 - 1/1.6895)/.06$$
$$= \$80 \times 6.8017$$
$$= \$544.14$$

We add the values for the two parts together to get the bond's value:

$$\text{Total bond value} = \$591.89 + 544.14 = \$1,136.03$$

Total bond value is therefore about $136 in excess of par value. Once again, we can verify this amount by noting that the coupon is now $20 too high, based on current market conditions. The present value of $20 per year for nine years at 6 percent is:

$$\text{Annuity present value} = \$20 \times (1 - 1/1.06^9)/.06$$
$$= \$20 \times 6.8017$$
$$= \$136.03$$

This is just as we calculated.

Based on our examples, we can now write the general expression for the value of a bond. If a bond has (1) a face value of F paid at maturity, (2) a coupon of C paid per period, (3) T periods to maturity, and (4) a yield of r per period, its value is:

$$\text{Bond value} = C \times [1 - 1/(1 + r)^T]/r + F/(1 + r)^T$$

$$\text{Bond value} = \begin{array}{c} \text{Present value of the} \\ \text{coupons} \end{array} + \begin{array}{c} \text{Present value of} \\ \text{the face amount} \end{array} \qquad \textbf{(8.1)}$$

EXAMPLE 8.1

Semiannual Coupons In practice, bonds issued in the United States usually make coupon payments twice a year. So, if an ordinary bond has a coupon rate of 14 percent, the owner will receive a total of $140 per year, but this $140 will come in two payments of $70 each.

Suppose the yield to maturity on our bond is quoted at 16 percent. Bond yields are quoted like annual percentage rates (APRs); the quoted rate is equal to the actual rate per period multiplied by

(continued)

the number of periods. With a 16 percent quoted yield and semiannual payments, the true yield is 8 percent per six months. If our bond matures in seven years, what is the bond's price? What is the effective annual yield on this bond?

Based on our discussion, we know the bond will sell at a discount because it has a coupon rate of 7 percent every six months when the market requires 8 percent every six months. So, if our answer exceeds $1,000, we know that we have made a mistake.

To get the exact price, we first calculate the present value of the bond's face value of $1,000 paid in seven years. This seven-year period has 14 periods of six months each. At 8 percent per period, the value is:

$$\text{Present value} = \$1,000/1.08^{14} = \$1,000/2.9372 = \$340.46$$

The coupons can be viewed as a 14-period annuity of $70 per period. At an 8 percent discount rate, the present value of such an annuity is:

$$\begin{aligned}
\text{Annuity present value} &= \$70 \times (1 - 1/1.08^{14})/.08 \\
&= \$70 \times (1 - .3405)/.08 \\
&= \$70 \times 8.2442 \\
&= \$577.10
\end{aligned}$$

The total present value is the bond's price:

$$\text{Total present value} = \$340.46 + 577.10 = \$917.56$$

To calculate the effective yield on this bond, note that 8 percent every six months is equivalent to:

$$\text{Effective annual rate} = (1 + .08)^2 - 1 = 16.64\%$$

The effective yield, therefore, is 16.64 percent.

Learn more about bonds at **investorguide.com**.

As we have illustrated in this section, bond prices and interest rates always move in opposite directions. When interest rates rise, a bond's value, like any other present value, declines. Similarly, when interest rates fall, bond values rise. Even if the borrower is certain to make all payments, there is still risk in owning a bond. We discuss this next.

INTEREST RATE RISK

The risk that arises for bond owners from fluctuating interest rates is called *interest rate risk*. How much interest rate risk a bond has depends on how sensitive its price is to interest rate changes. This sensitivity directly depends on two things: the time to maturity and the coupon rate. As we will see momentarily, you should keep the following in mind when looking at a bond:

1. All other things being equal, the longer the time to maturity, the greater the interest rate risk.

2. All other things being equal, the lower the coupon rate, the greater the interest rate risk.

We illustrate the first of these two points in Figure 8.2. As shown, we compute and plot prices under different interest rate scenarios for 10 percent coupon bonds with maturities of 1 year and 30 years. Notice how the slope of the line connecting the prices is much steeper for the 30-year maturity than it is for the 1-year maturity. This steepness tells

Figure 8.2

Interest Rate Risk and
Time to Maturity

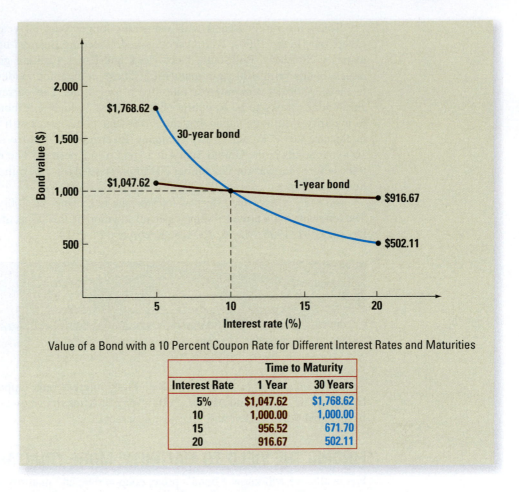

Value of a Bond with a 10 Percent Coupon Rate for Different Interest Rates and Maturities

	Time to Maturity	
Interest Rate	1 Year	30 Years
5%	$1,047.62	$1,768.62
10	1,000.00	1,000.00
15	956.52	671.70
20	916.67	502.11

us that a relatively small change in interest rates will lead to a substantial change in the bond's value. In comparison, the one-year bond's price is relatively insensitive to interest rate changes.

Intuitively, shorter-term bonds have less interest rate sensitivity because the $1,000 face amount is received so quickly. For example, the present value of this amount isn't greatly affected by a small change in interest rates if the amount is received in, say, one year. However, even a small change in the interest rate, once compounded for, say, 30 years, can have a significant effect on present value. As a result, the present value of the face amount will be much more volatile with a longer-term bond.

The other thing to know about interest rate risk is that, like many things in finance and economics, it increases at a decreasing rate. For example, a 10-year bond has much greater interest rate risk than a 1-year bond has. However, a 30-year bond has only slightly greater interest rate risk than a 10-year bond.

The reason that bonds with lower coupons have greater interest rate risk is essentially the same. As we discussed earlier, the value of a bond depends on the present value of both its coupons and its face amount. If two bonds with different coupon rates have the same maturity, the value of the lower-coupon bond is proportionately more dependent on the face amount to be received at maturity. As a result, its value will fluctuate more as interest rates change. Put another way, the bond with the higher coupon has a larger cash flow early in its life, so its value is less sensitive to changes in the discount rate.

Bonds are rarely issued with maturities longer than 30 years, though there are exceptions. In the 1990s, Walt Disney issued "Sleeping Beauty" bonds with a 100-year maturity. Similarly, BellSouth, Coca-Cola, and Dutch banking giant ABN AMRO all issued bonds with 100-year maturities. These companies evidently wanted to lock in the historically low interest rates for a *long* time. The current record holder for corporations looks to be Republic National Bank, which sold bonds with 1,000 years to maturity. Although somewhat rare, 100-year bond issues still occur. For example, in January 2014, French-utility company Électricité de France sold $700 million in 100-year bonds in the United States at a yield of 6.2 percent. The most recent 100-year issue before that was the November 2011 bond issued by U.S. railroad operator Norfolk Southern Corp.

We can illustrate the effect of interest rate risk using the 100-year BellSouth issue. The following table provides some basic information on this issue, along with its prices on December 31, 1995, May 6, 2008, and February 27, 2014.

Maturity	Coupon Rate	Price on 12/31/95	Price on 5/6/08	Percentage Change in Price 1995–2008	Price on 2/27/14	Percentage Change in Price 2008–2014
2095	7.00%	$1,000	$1,008.40	+0.84%	$968.00	−4.0%

Several things emerge from this table. First, interest rates apparently fell between December 31, 1995, and May 6, 2008 (Why?). After that, however, the bond's price first gained 0.84 percent and then lost 4 percent.

FINDING THE YIELD TO MATURITY: MORE TRIAL AND ERROR

Frequently, we will know a bond's price, coupon rate, and maturity date, but not its yield to maturity. For example, suppose we are interested in a six-year, 8 percent coupon bond. A broker quotes a price of $955.14. What is the yield on this bond?

We've seen that the price of a bond can be written as the sum of its annuity and lump-sum components. Knowing that there is an $80 coupon for six years and a $1,000 face value, we can say that the price is:

$$\$955.14 = \$80 \times [1 - 1/(1 + r)^6]/r + 1,000/(1 + r)^6$$

where *r* is the unknown discount rate, or yield to maturity. We have one equation here and one unknown, but we cannot solve for *r* directly without using a financial calculator or a spreadsheet application. Instead, we must use trial and error.

We can speed up the trial-and-error process by using what we know about bond prices and yields. In this case, the bond has an $80 coupon and is selling at a discount. We thus know that the yield is greater than 8 percent. If we compute the price at 10 percent:

$$\text{Bond value} = \$80 \times (1 - 1/1.10^6)/.10 + 1,000/1.10^6$$
$$= \$80 \times 4.3553 + 1,000/1.7716$$
$$= \$912.89$$

Table 8.1
Summary of Bond Valuation

I. Finding the Value of a Bond

Bond value = $C \times [1 - 1/(1 + r)^T]/r + F/(1 + r)^T$
where
C = Coupon paid each period
r = Discount rate per period
T = Number of periods
F = Bond's face value

II. Finding the Yield on a Bond

Given a bond value, coupon, time to maturity, and face value, one can find the implicit discount rate, or yield to maturity, by trial and error. To do this, try different discount rates until the calculated bond value equals the given value (or let a spreadsheet do it for you). Remember that increasing the rate *decreases* the bond value.

Current market rates are available at **www.bankrate.com**.

At 10 percent, the value is lower than the actual price, so 10 percent is too high. The true yield must be somewhere between 8 and 10 percent. At this point, it's "plug and chug" to find the answer. You would probably want to try 9 percent next. If you did, you would see that this is in fact the bond's yield to maturity.

A bond's yield to maturity should not be confused with its **current yield**, which is simply a bond's annual coupon divided by its price. In the present example, the bond's annual coupon is $80, and its price is $955.14. Given these numbers, we see that the current yield is $80/955.14 = 8.38 percent, which is less than the yield to maturity of 9 percent. The reason the current yield is too low is that it only considers the coupon portion of your return; it doesn't consider the built-in gain from the price discount. For a premium bond, the reverse is true, meaning the current yield would be higher because it ignores the built-in loss.

Our discussion of bond valuation is summarized in Table 8.1. A nearby *Spreadsheet Applications* box shows how to find prices and yields the easy way.

EXAMPLE 8.2

Current Events   A bond has a quoted price of $1,080.42. It has a face value of $1,000, a semi-annual coupon of $30, and a maturity of five years. What is its current yield? What is its yield to maturity? Which is bigger? Why?

Notice that this bond makes semiannual payments of $30, so the annual payment is $60. The current yield is thus $60/1,080.42 = 5.55 percent. To calculate the yield to maturity, refer back to Example 8.1. Now, in this case, the bond pays $30 every six months and it has 10 six-month periods until maturity. So, we need to find r as follows:

$$\$1,080.42 = \$30 \times [1 - 1/(1 + r)^{10}]/r + 1,000/(1 + r)^{10}$$

After some trial and error, we find that r is equal to 2.1 percent. But, the tricky part is that this 2.1 percent is the yield *per six months*. We have to double it to get the yield to maturity, so the yield to maturity is 4.2 percent, which is less than the current yield. Why is the yield to maturity less than the current yield? The reason is that the current yield ignores the built-in loss of the premium between now and maturity.

Bond Yields   You're looking at two bonds identical in every way except for their coupons and, of course, their prices. Both have 12 years to maturity. The first bond has a 10 percent coupon rate and sells for $935.08. The second has a 12 percent coupon rate. What do you think it would sell for?

Because the two bonds are very similar, we assume they will be priced to yield about the same rate. We first need to calculate the yield on the 10 percent coupon bond. Proceeding as before, we know that the yield must be greater than 10 percent because the bond is selling at a discount. The bond has a fairly long maturity of 12 years. We've seen that long-term bond prices are relatively sensitive to interest rate changes, so the yield is probably close to 10 percent. A little trial and error reveals that the yield is actually 11 percent:

$$\text{Bond value} = \$100 \times (1 - 1/1.11^{12})/.11 + 1,000/1.11^{12}$$
$$= \$100 \times 6.4924 + 1,000/3.4985$$
$$= \$649.24 + 285.84$$
$$= \$935.08$$

With an 11 percent yield, the second bond will sell at a premium because of its $120 coupon. Its value is:

$$\text{Bond value} = \$120 \times (1 - 1/1.11^{12})/.11 + 1,000/1.11^{12}$$
$$= \$120 \times 6.4924 + 1,000/3.4985$$
$$= \$779.08 + 285.84$$
$$= \$1,064.92$$

ZERO COUPON BONDS

A bond that pays no coupons at all must be offered at a price much lower than its face value. Such bonds are called **zero coupon bonds**, or just zeroes.[1]

**EXAMPLE
8.4**

Yield to Maturity on a Zero under Annual Compounding   Suppose that the Geneva Electronics Co. issues a $1,000 face value, eight-year zero coupon bond. What is the yield to maturity on the bond if the bond is offered at $627? Assume annual compounding.

The yield to maturity, y, can be calculated from the equation:

$$\frac{\$1,000}{(1 + y)^8} = \$627$$

Solving the equation, we find that y equals 6 percent. Thus, the yield to maturity is 6 percent.

The example expresses the yield as an effective annual yield. However, even though no interest payments are made on the bond, zero coupon bond calculations use semiannual periods in practice, to be consistent with the calculations for coupon bonds. We illustrate this practice in the next example.

---

[1]A bond issued with a very low coupon rate (as opposed to a zero coupon rate) is an original-issue discount (OID) bond.

SPREADSHEET APPLICATIONS

How to Calculate Bond Prices and Yields Using a Spreadsheet

Most spreadsheets have fairly elaborate routines available for calculating bond values and yields; many of these routines involve details that we have not discussed. However, setting up a simple spreadsheet to calculate prices or yields is straightforward, as our next two spreadsheets show:

	A	B	C	D	E	F	G	H
1								
2	Using a spreadsheet to calculate bond values							
3								
4	Suppose we have a bond with 22 years to maturity, a coupon rate of 8 percent, and a yield to							
5	maturity of 9 percent. If the bond makes semiannual payments, what is its price today?							
6								
7	Settlement date:	1/1/15						
8	Maturity date:	1/1/37						
9	Annual coupon rate:	.08						
10	Yield to maturity:	.09						
11	Face value (% of par):	100						
12	Coupons per year:	2						
13	Bond price (% of par):	**90.49**						
14								
15	The formula entered in cell B13 is =PRICE(B7,B8,B9,B10,B11,B12); notice that face value and bond							
16	price are given as a percentage of face value.							

	A	B	C	D	E	F	G	H
1								
2	Using a spreadsheet to calculate bond yields							
3								
4	Suppose we have a bond with 22 years to maturity, a coupon rate of 8 percent, and a price of							
5	$960.17. If the bond makes semiannual payments, what is its yield to maturity?							
6								
7	Settlement date:	1/1/15						
8	Maturity date:	1/1/37						
9	Annual coupon rate:	.08						
10	Bond price (% of par):	96.017						
11	Face value (% of par):	100						
12	Coupons per year:	2						
13	Yield to maturity:	**.084**						
14								
15	The formula entered in cell B13 is =YIELD(B7,B8,B9,B10,B11,B12); notice that face value and bond							
16	price are entered as a percentage of face value.							
17								

In our spreadsheets, notice that we had to enter two dates, a settlement date and a maturity date. The settlement date is just the date you actually pay for the bond, and the maturity date is the day the bond actually matures. In most of our problems, we don't explicitly have these dates, so we have to make them up. For example, since our bond has 22 years to maturity, we just picked 1/1/2015 (January 1, 2015) as the settlement date and 1/1/2037 (January 1, 2037) as the maturity date. Any two dates would do as long as they are exactly 22 years apart, but these are particularly easy to work with. Finally, notice that we had to enter the coupon rate and yield to maturity in annual terms and then explicitly provide the number of coupon payments per year.

**EXAMPLE
8.5**

Yield on a Zero under Real-World Convention of Semiannual Compounding   Suppose the Eight-Inch Nails (EIN) Company issues a $1,000 face value, five-year zero coupon bond. The initial price is set at $508.35. What is the yield to maturity using semiannual compounding?

The yield can be expressed as:

$$\frac{\$1,000}{(1 + y)^{10}} = \$508.35$$

The exponent in the denominator is 10, because five years contains 10 semiannual periods. The yield, y, equals 7 percent. Since y is expressed as a return per *six-month* interval, the yield to maturity, expressed as an annual percentage rate, is 14 percent.

8.2 Government and Corporate Bonds

The previous section investigated the basic principles of bond valuation without much discussion of the differences between government and corporate bonds. In this section, we discuss the differences.

GOVERNMENT BONDS

If you're nervous about the level of debt piled up by the U.S. government, *don't* go to **www.publicdebt .treas.gov**, or to **www.brillig.com /debt_clock**! Learn all about government bonds at **www.newyorkfed .org**.

The biggest borrower in the world—by a wide margin—is everybody's favorite family member, Uncle Sam. In 2014, the total debt of the U.S. government was about $18.0 *trillion,* or over $56,000 per citizen (and growing!). When the government wishes to borrow money for more than one year, it sells what are known as Treasury notes and bonds to the public (in fact, it does so every month). Currently, outstanding Treasury notes and bonds have original maturities ranging from 2 to 30 years.

While most U.S. Treasury issues are just ordinary coupon bonds, there are two important things to keep in mind. First, U.S. Treasury issues, unlike essentially all other bonds, have virtually no default risk because (we hope) the Treasury can always come up with the money to make the payments. Second, Treasury issues are exempt from state income taxes (though not federal income taxes). In other words, the coupons you receive on a Treasury note or bond are only taxed at the federal level.

State and local governments also borrow money by selling notes and bonds. Such issues are called *municipal* notes and bonds, or just "munis." Unlike Treasury issues, munis have varying degrees of default risk. The most intriguing thing about munis is that their coupons are exempt from federal income taxes (though not necessarily state income taxes), which makes them very attractive to high-income, high–tax bracket investors. Because of this enormous tax break, the yields on municipal bonds are much lower than the yields on taxable bonds.

**EXAMPLE
8.6**

Another good bond market site is **money.cnn.com**.

Aftertax Yield Comparison   Imagine that a long-term municipal bond selling at par is yielding 4.21 percent while a long-term Treasury bond selling at par yields 6.07 percent.[2] Further suppose an investor is in the 30 percent tax bracket. Ignoring any difference in default risk, would the investor prefer the Treasury bond or the muni?

To answer, we need to compare the *aftertax* yields on the two bonds. Ignoring state and local taxes, the muni pays 4.21 percent on both a pretax and an aftertax basis. The Treasury issue pays 6.07 percent before taxes, but it pays .0607 × (1 − .30) = .0425, or 4.25 percent, once we account for the 30 percent tax bite. Given this, the Treasury bond still has a slightly better yield.

---

[2]Capital gains on municipal bonds are taxed, complicating the analysis somewhat. We avoid capital gains by assuming both bonds are priced at par.

EXAMPLE 8.7

Taxable versus Municipal Bonds   Suppose taxable bonds are currently yielding 8 percent, while at the same time, munis of comparable risk and maturity are yielding 6 percent. Which is more attractive to an investor in a 40 percent tax bracket? What is the break-even tax rate? How do you interpret this rate?

For an investor in a 40 percent tax bracket, a taxable bond yields $8 \times (1 - .40) = 4.8$ percent after taxes, so the muni is much more attractive. The break-even tax rate is the tax rate at which an investor would be indifferent between a taxable and a nontaxable issue. If we let t^* stand for the break-even tax rate, we can solve for this tax rate as follows:

$$.08 \times (1 - t^*) = .06$$
$$1 - t^* = .06/.08 = .75$$
$$t^* = .25$$

Thus, an investor in a 25 percent tax bracket would make 6 percent after taxes from either bond.

CORPORATE BONDS

We pointed out that, while U.S. Treasury issues are default-free, municipal bonds face the possibility of default. Corporate bonds also face the possibility of default. This possibility generates a wedge between the *promised yield* and the *expected return* on a bond.

To understand these two terms, imagine a one-year corporate bond with a par value of $1,000 and an annual coupon of $80. Further assume that fixed-income analysts believe that this bond has a 10 percent chance of default and, in the event of default, each bondholder will receive $800. (Bondholders will likely receive something following default because the proceeds from any liquidation or reorganization go to the bondholders first. The stockholders typically receive a payoff only after the bondholders get paid in full.) Since there is a 90 percent probability that the bond will pay off in full and a 10 percent probability that the bond will default, the expected payoff from the bond at maturity is:

$$.90 \times \$1,080 + .10 \times \$800 = \$1,052$$

Assuming that the discount rate on risky bonds such as this one is 9 percent, the bond's value becomes:

$$\frac{\$1,052}{1.09} = \$965.14$$

What is the expected return on the bond? The expected return is clearly 9 percent, because 9 percent is the discount rate in the previous equation. In other words, an investment of $965.14 today provides an expected payoff at maturity of $1,052, implying a 9 percent expected return.

What is the promised yield? The corporation is promising $1,080 in one year, since the coupon is $80. Because the price of the bond is $965.14, the promised yield can be calculated from the following equation:

$$\$965.14 = \frac{\$1,080}{1 + y} \tag{8.2}$$

In this equation, y, which is the promised yield, is 11.9 percent. Why is the promised yield above the expected return? The promised yield calculation assumes that the bondholder *will* receive the full $1,080. In other words, the promised yield calculation ignores the probability of default. By contrast, the expected return calculation specifically takes the probability of default into account. What about in a risk-free security? The promised yield and the expected return are equal here, since the probability of default is zero, by definition, in a risk-free bond.

Now the promised yield on a corporate bond, as calculated in Equation 8.2, is simply the yield to maturity of the previous section. The promised yield can be calculated for any bond, be it corporate or government. All we need is the coupon rate, par value, and maturity. We do not need to know anything about the probability of default. Calculating the promised yield on a corporate bond is just as easy as calculating the yield to maturity on a government bond. In fact, the two calculations are the *same*. However, the promised yield, or equivalently, the yield to maturity, on a corporate bond is somewhat misleading. Our promised yield of 11.9 percent implies only that the bondholder will receive a return of 11.9 percent if the bond does not default. The promised yield does not tell us what the bondholder *expects* to receive.

For example, the Vanguard Intermediate-Term Treasury Bond Fund (TB Fund), a mutual fund composed of intermediate-term government bonds, had a yield of 1.49 percent in December 2014. The Vanguard High Yield Corporate Bond Fund (HY Fund), a mutual fund composed of intermediate-term corporate bonds with high default probabilities, had a yield of 4.84 percent on the same day. The yield on the HY Fund was 3.25 (=4.84/1.49) times as great as the yield on the TB Fund. Does that mean that an investor in the HY Fund expects a return about 3.25 times the return an investor in the TB Fund expects? Absolutely not. The yields quoted above are promised yields. They do not take into account any chance of default.

A professional analyst might very well find that, because of the high probability of default, the expected return on the HY Fund is actually below that expected on the TB Fund. However, we simply don't know this, one way or the other. Calculation of the expected return on a corporate bond is quite difficult, since one must assess the probability of default. However this number, if it can be calculated, would be very meaningful. As its name implies, it tells us what rate of return the bondholder actually expects to receive.

EXAMPLE 8.8

Yields on Government and Corporate Bonds   Both a default-free two-year government bond and a two-year corporate bond pay a 7 percent coupon. However, the government bond sells at par (or $1,000) and the corporate bond sells at $982.16. What are the yields on these two bonds? Why is there a difference in yields? Are these yields promised yields? Assume annual coupon payments.

Both bonds pay a coupon of $70 per year. The yield on the government bond can be calculated from the following equation:

$$\$1,000 = \frac{\$70}{1 + y} + \frac{\$1,070}{(1 + y)^2}$$

The yield on the government bond, *y*, is 7 percent.

The yield on the corporate bond can be calculated from the following equation:

$$\$982.16 = \frac{\$70}{1 + y} + \frac{\$1,070}{(1 + y)^2}$$

The yield on the corporate bond, *y*, is 8 percent.

The yield on the government bond is below that on the corporate bond because the corporate bond has default risk, while the government bond does not.

For both bonds, the yields we calculated are promised yields, because the coupons are promised coupons. These coupons will not be paid in full if there is a default. The promised yield is equal to the expected return on the government bond, since there is no chance of default. However, the promised yield is greater than the expected return on the corporate bond because default is a possibility.

While our previous discussion on corporate bonds depended heavily on the concept of default probability, estimation of default probabilities is well beyond the scope of this chapter. However, bond ratings provide an easy way to obtain a qualitative appreciation of a bond's default risk.

BOND RATINGS

Firms frequently pay to have their debt rated. The two leading bond-rating firms are Moody's and Standard & Poor's (S&P). The debt ratings are an assessment of the creditworthiness of the corporate issuer. The definitions of creditworthiness used by Moody's and S&P are based on how likely the firm is to default and the protection creditors have in the event of a default.

It is important to recognize that bond ratings are concerned *only* with the possibility of default. Earlier, we discussed interest rate risk, which we defined as the risk of a change in the value of a bond resulting from a change in interest rates. Bond ratings do not address this issue. As a result, the price of a highly rated bond can still be quite volatile.

Bond ratings are constructed from information supplied by the corporation and other sources. The rating classes and some information concerning them are shown in the following table:

	Investment-Quality Bond Ratings				Low-Quality, Speculative, and/or "Junk" Bond Ratings					
	High Grade		Medium Grade		Low Grade		Very Low Grade			
Standard & Poor's	AAA	AA	A	BBB	BB	B	CCC	CC	C	D
Moody's	Aaa	Aa	A	Baa	Ba	B	Caa	Ca	C	

Moody's	S&P	
Aaa	AAA	Debt rated Aaa and AAA has the highest rating. Capacity to pay interest and principal is extremely strong.
Aa	AA	Debt rated Aa and AA has a very strong capacity to pay interest and repay principal. Together with the highest rating, this group comprises the high-grade bond class.
A	A	Debt rated A has a strong capacity to pay interest and repay principal, although it is somewhat more susceptible to the adverse effects of changes in circumstances and economic conditions than debt in higher-rated categories.
Baa	BBB	Debt rated Baa and BBB is regarded as having an adequate capacity to pay interest and repay principal. Whereas it normally exhibits adequate protection parameters, adverse economic conditions or changing circumstances are more likely to lead to a weakened capacity to pay interest and repay principal for debt in this category than in higher-rated categories. These bonds are medium-grade obligations.
Ba; B Caa Ca C	BB; B CCC CC C	Debt rated in these categories is regarded, on balance, as predominantly speculative with respect to capacity to pay interest and repay principal in accordance with the terms of the obligation. BB and Ba indicate the lowest degree of speculation, and Ca, CC, and C the highest degree of speculation. Although such debt is likely to have some quality and protective characteristics, these are outweighed by large uncertainties or major risk exposures to adverse conditions. Issues rated C by Moody's are typically in default.
	D	Debt rated D is in default, and payment of interest and/or repayment of principal is in arrears.

NOTE: At times, both Moody's and S&P use adjustments (called notches) to these ratings. S&P uses plus and minus signs: A+ is the strongest A rating and A− the weakest. Moody's uses a 1, 2, or 3 designation, with 1 being the highest.

Want to know what criteria are commonly used to rate corporate and municipal bonds? Go to **www.standardandpoors.com**, **www.moodys.com**, or **www.fitchratings.com**.

The highest rating a firm's debt can have is AAA or Aaa. Such debt is judged to be the best quality and to have the lowest degree of risk. For example, the 100-year BellSouth issue we discussed earlier was rated AAA. This rating is not awarded very often; AA or Aa ratings indicate very good quality debt and are much more common.

A large part of corporate borrowing takes the form of low-grade, or "junk," bonds. If these low-grade corporate bonds are rated at all, they are rated below investment grade by the major rating agencies. Investment-grade bonds are bonds rated at least BBB by S&P or Baa by Moody's.

Rating agencies don't always agree. Some bonds are known as "crossover" or "5B" bonds. The reason is that they are rated triple-B (or Baa) by one rating agency and double-B (or Ba) by another, implying a "split rating." For example, in September 2014, Arcos Dorados, the largest operator of McDonald's restaurants in Latin America and the Caribbean, issue $375 million of 10-year notes that were rated Ba2 by Moody's and BBB– by S&P.

A bond's credit rating can change as the issuer's financial strength improves or deteriorates. Of course, downgrades can happen to municipal debt as well as corporate debt. For example, in July 2014, Moody's downgraded Atlantic City's debt from Baa2 to Ba1. The major reason given was the significantly weakened tax base. Four of the 12 Atlantic City casinos closed during 2014, with more than one-fourth of casino employees put out of work.

Credit ratings are important because defaults really do occur, and, when they do, investors can lose heavily. For example, in 2000, AmeriServe Food Distribution, Inc., which supplied restaurants such as Burger King with everything from burgers to giveaway toys, defaulted on $200 million in junk bonds. After the default, the bonds traded at just 18 cents on the dollar, leaving investors with a loss of more than $160 million.

Even worse in AmeriServe's case, the bonds had been issued only four months earlier, thereby making AmeriServe an NCAA champion. While that might be a good thing for a college basketball team, NCAA means "No Coupon At All" in the bond market, not a good thing for investors.

8.3 Bond Markets

Bonds are bought and sold in enormous quantities every day. You may be surprised to learn that the trading volume in bonds on a typical day is many, many times larger than the trading volume in stocks (by trading volume, we simply mean the amount of money that changes hands). Here is a finance trivia question: What is the largest securities market in the world? Most people would guess the New York Stock Exchange. In fact, the largest securities market in the world in terms of trading volume is the U.S. Treasury market.

HOW BONDS ARE BOUGHT AND SOLD

Most trading in bonds takes place over the counter, or OTC, which means that there is no particular place where buying and selling occur. Instead, dealers around the country (and around the world) stand ready to buy and sell. The various dealers are connected electronically.

One reason the bond markets are so big is that the number of bond issues far exceeds the number of stock issues. There are two reasons for this. First, a corporation would typically have only one common stock issue outstanding, though there are exceptions. However, a single large corporation could easily have a dozen or more note and bond issues outstanding. Beyond this, federal, state, and local borrowing is simply enormous. For example, even a small city would usually have a wide variety of notes and bonds outstanding, representing money borrowed to pay for items like roads, sewers, and schools. When you think about how many small cities there are in the United States, you begin to get the picture!

Because the bond market is almost entirely OTC, it has historically had little or no *transparency*. A financial market is transparent if its prices and trading volume are easily observed. On the New York Stock Exchange, for example, one can see the price and quantity for every single transaction. In contrast, it is often not possible to observe either in the bond market. Transactions are privately negotiated between parties, and there is little or no centralized reporting of transactions.

Although the total volume of trading in bonds far exceeds that in stocks, only a very small fraction of the total outstanding bond issues actually trades on a given day. This fact, combined with the lack of transparency in the bond market, means that getting up-to-date prices on individual bonds can be difficult or impossible, particularly for smaller corporate or municipal issues. Instead, a variety of sources are commonly used for estimated prices.

BOND PRICE REPORTING

In 2002, transparency in the corporate bond market began to improve dramatically. Under new regulations, corporate bond dealers are now required to report trade information through what is known as the Trade Reporting and Compliance Engine (TRACE).

TRACE bond quotes are available at cxa.marketwatch.com/finra/marketdata. We went to the site and entered "Cisco" to find bonds issued by tech giant Cisco Systems. We found a total of 14 bond issues outstanding.

To learn more about TRACE, visit **www.finra.org**.

Issuer Name	Symbol	Callable	Sub-Product Type	Coupon	Maturity	Moody	S&P	Fitch	Price	Yield
CISCO SYS INC	CSCO.GC	Yes	Corporate Bond	5.500	02/22/2016	A1	AA-		105.830	0.594
CISCO SYS INC	CSCO.GD	Yes	Corporate Bond	5.900	02/15/2039	A1	AA-		123.950	4.297
CISCO SYS INC	CSCO.GE	Yes	Corporate Bond	4.950	02/15/2019	A1	AA-		111.689	2.016
CISCO SYS INC	CSCO.GG	Yes	Corporate Bond	5.500	01/15/2040	A1	AA-		120.358	4.182
CISCO SYS INC	CSCO.GF	Yes	Corporate Bond	4.450	01/15/2020	A1	AA-		110.172	2.320
CISCO SYS INC	CSCO.GI	Yes	Corporate Bond	3.150	03/14/2017	A1	AA-		104.539	1.106
CISCO SYS INC	CSCO4101279		Corporate Bond	0.285	09/03/2015	A1			100.027	
CISCO SYS INC	CSCO4101276		Corporate Bond	0.515	03/03/2017	A1			100.203	
CISCO SYS INC	CSCO4101278		Corporate Bond	0.734	03/01/2019	A1			100.890	
CISCO SYS INC	CSCO4101277	Yes	Corporate Bond	1.100	03/03/2017	A1			100.030	1.086
CISCO SYS INC	CSCO4101280	Yes	Corporate Bond	2.125	03/01/2019	A1			100.341	2.040
CISCO SYS INC	CSCO4100888	Yes	Corporate Bond	2.900	03/04/2021	A1			103.636	2.270
CISCO SYS INC	CSCO4101281	Yes	Corporate Bond	3.625	03/04/2024	A1			106.482	2.822
CISCO SYS INC	CSCO.GH		Corporate Bond	2.900	11/17/2014	WR	NR		100.025	1.592

If you go to the website and click on a particular bond, you will get a lot of information about the bond, including the credit rating, original issue information, and trade information. For example, when we checked, the first bond listed had not traded for two weeks.

As shown in Figure 8.3, the Financial Industry Regulatory Authority (FINRA) provides a daily snapshot of the data from TRACE by reporting the most active issues. The

Figure 8.3

Sample TRACE Bond Quotations

SOURCE: FINRA reported TRACE prices, 12/9/14.

Most Active Investment Grade Bonds

Issuer Name	Symbol	Coupon	Maturity	Moody's/S&P /Fitch	High	Low	Last	Change	Yield%
DEUTSCHE BK AG GLOBAL MEDIUM TERM NTS BO	DB.GKL	3.450%	03/30/2015	A3//A+	100.96000	100.81800	100.81800	-0.050000	0.737301
ROYAL BK SCOTLAND PLC	RBS3681986	4.875%	03/16/2015	Baa1//A	101.10000	101.08000	101.10000	-0.070000	
VERIZON COMMUNICATIONS INC	VZ4050432	3.650%	09/14/2018	Baa1/BBB+/A-	106.85700	105.11500	105.51500	-0.242000	2.115090
BARCLAYS BK PLC	BCS3820939	2.750%	02/23/2015	A2//A	100.46670	100.45600	100.46110	-0.005900	0.500451
MCKESSON CORP NEW	MCK4104769	1.292%	03/10/2017	Baa2//BBB+	100.33300	99.50600	99.58100	-0.026000	1.481994
CREDIT SUISSE FIRST BOSTON USA INC	CS.NP	4.875%	01/15/2015	A1/A/A	100.42900	100.35390	100.42900	0.053000	0.324831
GILEAD SCIENCES INC	GILD4184056	3.500%	02/01/2025	A3/A-/	103.80895	101.73600	101.93100	-0.533000	3.269039
MORGAN STANLEY	MS4175944	3.700%	10/23/2024	Baa2/A-/A	101.21130	100.36900	101.07200	0.316000	3.569753
WELLS FARGO & CO NEW MEDIUM TERM SR NTS	WFC4160708	3.300%	09/09/2024	A2/A+/AA-	100.29100	100.04100	100.15400	0.215000	3.281002
VERIZON COMMUNICATIONS INC	VZ4132476	1.350%	06/09/2017	Baa1/BBB+/A-	99.87300	99.66300	99.67100	0.013000	1.484828

The Federal Reserve Bank of St. Louis maintains dozens of online files containing macroeconomic data as well as rates on U.S. Treasury issues. Go to **research.stlouisfed. org/fred2**.

information in the figure is largely self-explanatory. Notice that the price of the Verizon bond dropped by .242 percentage points on this day. What do you think happened to the yield to maturity for this bond? Figure 8.3 focuses on the most active bonds with investment grade ratings, but the most active high-yield and convertible bonds are also available on the website.

As we mentioned before, the U.S. Treasury market is the largest securities market in the world. As with bond markets in general, it is an OTC market, so there is limited transparency. However, unlike the situation with bond markets in general, trading in Treasury issues, particularly recently issued ones, is very heavy. Each day, representative prices for outstanding Treasury issues are reported.

Figure 8.4 shows a portion of the daily Treasury bond listings from the website wsj .com. Examine the entry that begins "5/15/2023." Reading from left to right, the 05/15/2023 tells us that the bond's maturity is May of 2023. The 1.750 is the bond's coupon rate.

The next two pieces of information are the **bid** and **asked prices**. In general, in any OTC or dealer market, the bid price represents what a dealer is willing to pay for a security, and the asked price (or just "ask" price) is what a dealer is willing to take for it. The difference between the two prices is called the **bid-ask spread** (or just "spread"), and it represents the dealer's profit.

Treasury prices are quoted as a percentage of face value. The bid price, or what a dealer is willing to pay, on the 5/15/2023 bond is 97.1953. With a $1,000 face value, this quote represents a dollar price of $971.953. The asked price, or the price at which the dealer is willing to sell the bond, is 97.2109, or $972.109.

The next number quoted is the change in the asked price from the previous day, measured as a percentage of face value, so this issue's asked price increased by .3438 percent, or $3.438, in value from the previous day. Finally, the last number reported is the yield to maturity, based on the asked price. Notice that this is a discount bond because it sells for less than its face value. Not surprisingly, its yield to maturity (2.113 percent) is greater than its coupon rate (1.75 percent).

Current and historical Treasury yield information is available at **www.treasurydirect .gov**.

The last bond listed, the 11/15/2044, is often called the "bellwether" bond. This bond's yield is the one that is usually reported in the evening news. So, for example, when you hear that long-term interest rates rose, what is really being said is that the yield on

Figure 8.4

Sample *Wall Street Journal* U.S. Treasury Bond Prices

SOURCE: Adapted from www.wsj.com. Copyright © 2014 Dow Jones and Company, Inc., December 9, 2014. All Rights Reserved Worldwide.

Treasury Notes & Bonds

Maturity	Coupon	Bid	Asked	Chg	Asked yield
1/31/2015	2.250	100.2891	100.3047	−0.0313	0.093
2/15/2016	4.500	104.9219	104.9531	−0.0391	0.299
3/15/2017	0.750	99.9688	99.9844	unch.	0.757
3/31/2018	2.875	105.4844	105.5000	0.1250	1.173
5/15/2019	3.125	106.8594	106.8750	0.1719	1.515
8/15/2020	2.625	104.5156	104.5313	0.2422	1.783
6/30/2021	2.125	101.1641	101.1797	0.2578	1.933
11/15/2022	7.625	141.2891	141.3047	0.3594	1.973
5/15/2023	1.750	97.1953	97.2109	0.3438	2.113
11/15/2024	2.250	100.2656	100.2813	0.2969	2.218
2/15/2025	7.625	149.4688	149.4844	0.4453	2.179
8/15/2027	6.375	143.8281	143.8906	0.5000	2.352
11/15/2028	5.250	133.2734	133.3359	0.5313	2.417
2/15/2029	5.250	133.5625	133.6250	0.5313	2.432
8/15/2029	6.125	145.2500	145.3125	0.5781	2.435
5/15/2030	6.250	148.4531	148.5156	0.6016	2.454
2/15/2031	5.375	138.1641	138.2266	0.5625	2.490
2/15/2036	4.500	130.8203	130.8828	0.6719	2.595
2/15/2037	4.750	135.2266	135.2891	0.6641	2.638
5/15/2037	5.000	139.8594	139.9219	0.6875	2.632
2/15/2038	4.375	128.2578	128.3203	0.5625	2.720
8/15/2039	4.500	130.8672	130.8984	0.5313	2.764
11/15/2039	4.375	128.7031	128.7344	0.5391	2.771
2/15/2040	4.625	133.3516	133.3828	0.5313	2.774
5/15/2040	4.375	129.0938	129.1250	0.5234	2.771
8/15/2041	3.750	117.9063	117.9375	0.5391	2.792
11/15/2041	3.125	105.5625	105.5938	0.5469	2.827
2/15/2042	3.125	105.3125	105.3438	0.5703	2.841
11/15/2042	2.750	97.6250	97.6563	0.5156	2.873
2/15/2043	3.125	104.9453	104.9766	0.5703	2.866
2/15/2044	3.625	114.9844	115.0156	0.5859	2.862
11/15/2044	3.000	102.5156	102.5469	0.5781	2.873

this bond went up (and its price went down). Beginning in 2001, the Treasury announced that it would no longer sell 30-year bonds, leaving the 10-year note as the longest maturity issue sold. However, in 2006, the 30-year bond was resurrected and once again assumed bellwether status.

If you examine the yields on the various issues in Figure 8.4, you will clearly see that they vary by maturity. Why this occurs and what it might mean is one of the issues we discuss in our next section. Government (referred to as "sovereign") bond yields also vary by country of origin. Here we show the 10-year bond yields for several countries. The yields vary according to default risks and foreign exchange risks (to be discussed later in the text).

SELECTED INTERNATIONAL GOVERNMENT 10-YEAR BOND YIELDS

	Yield (%)
United States	2.22
United Kingdom	1.89
Japan	.41
Germany	.68
Australia	3.02
Greece	7.98
Spain	1.82
India	7.90
Brazil	4.25

SOURCE: Data pulled from www.bloomberg.com, December 9, 2014.

EXAMPLE 8.9

Treasury Quotes   Locate the Treasury bond in Figure 8.4 maturing in May 2019. What is its coupon rate? What is its bid price? What was the *previous day's* asked price?

The bond's coupon rate is 3.125, or 3.125 percent of face value. The bid price is 106.8594 or 106.8594 percent of face value. The ask price is 106.8750, which is up by .1719 percent from the previous day. This means that the ask price on the previous day was equal to 106.8750 − .1719 = 106.7031.

A NOTE ON BOND PRICE QUOTES

If you buy a bond between coupon payment dates, the price you pay is usually more than the price you are quoted. The reason is that standard convention in the bond market is to quote prices net of "accrued interest," meaning that accrued interest is deducted to arrive at the quoted price. This quoted price is called the **clean price**. The price you actually pay, however, includes the accrued interest. This price is the **dirty price**, also known as the "full" or "invoice" price.

An example is the easiest way to understand these issues. Suppose you buy a bond with a 12 percent annual coupon, payable semiannually. You actually pay $1,080 for this bond, so $1,080 is the dirty, or invoice, price. Further, on the day you buy it, the next coupon is due in four months, so you are between coupon dates. Notice that the next coupon will be $60.

The accrued interest on a bond is calculated by taking the fraction of the coupon period that has passed, in this case two months out of six, and multiplying this fraction by the next coupon, $60. So, the accrued interest in this example is $2/6 \times \$60 = \$20$. The bond's quoted price (i.e., its clean price) would be $1,080 – $20 = $1,060.[3]

---

[3]The calculation of accrued interest differs slightly between Treasury bonds and corporate bonds. The difference involves the calculation of the fractional coupon period. In our example above, we implicitly treated the months as having exactly the same length (i.e., 30 days each, 360 days in a year), which is consistent with the way corporate bonds are quoted. In contrast, actual day counts are used for Treasury bonds. For more on counting the days between coupon payments, check out Excel Master It! Problem for this chapter.

8.4 Inflation and Interest Rates

So far in this chapter, we have not considered the impact of inflation on interest rates. However, we did cover this relationship in Section 6.5. We briefly review our previous discussion before considering additional ideas on the topic.

REAL VERSUS NOMINAL RATES

Suppose the one-year interest rate is 15.5 percent, so that anyone depositing $100 in a bank today will end up with $115.50 next year. Further imagine a pizza costs $5 today, implying that $100 can buy 20 pizzas. Finally, assume that the inflation rate is 5 percent, leading to the price of pizza being $5.25 next year. How many pizzas can you buy next year if you deposit $100 today? Clearly, you can buy $115.50/$5.25 = 22 pizzas. This is up from 20 pizzas, implying a 10 percent increase in purchasing power. Economists say that, while the *nominal* rate of interest is 15.5 percent, the *real* rate of interest is only 10 percent.

The difference between nominal and real rates is important and bears repeating:

The nominal rate on an investment is the percentage change in the number of dollars you have. The real rate on an investment is the percentage change in how much you can buy with your dollars. In other words, the real rate is the percentage change in your buying power.

We can generalize the relation between nominal rates, real rates, and inflation as:

$$1 + R = (1 + r) \times (1 + h)$$

where R is the nominal rate, r is the real rate, and h is the inflation rate.

In the preceding example, the nominal rate was 15.50 percent and the inflation rate was 5 percent. What was the real rate? We can determine it by plugging in these numbers:

$$1 + .1550 = (1 + r) \times (1 + .05)$$
$$1 + r = (1.1550/1.05) = 1.10$$
$$r = 10\%$$

This real rate is the same as we had before.

We can rearrange things a little as follows:

$$1 + R = (1 + r) \times (1 + h)$$
$$R = r + h + r \times h$$

(8.3)

What this tells us is that the nominal rate has three components. First, there is the real rate on the investment, r. Next, there is the compensation for the decrease in the value of the money originally invested because of inflation, h. The third component represents compensation for the fact that the dollars earned on the investment are also worth less because of inflation.

This third component is usually small, so it is often dropped. The nominal rate is then approximately equal to the real rate plus the inflation rate:

$$R \approx r + h$$

(8.4)

Nominal vs. Real Rates   If investors require a 10 percent real rate of return, and the inflation rate is 8 percent, what must be the approximate nominal rate? The exact nominal rate?

First of all, the nominal rate is approximately equal to the sum of the real rate and the inflation rate: 10 percent + 8 percent = 18 percent. From Equation 8.3, we have:

$$1 + R = (1 + r) \times (1 + h)$$
$$= 1.10 \times 1.08$$
$$= 1.1880$$

Therefore, the nominal rate will actually be closer to 19 percent.

It is important to note that financial rates, such as interest rates, discount rates, and rates of return, are almost always quoted in nominal terms. To remind you of this, we will henceforth use the symbol R instead of r in most of our discussions about such rates.

INFLATION RISK AND INFLATION-LINKED BONDS

Consider a 20-year Treasury bond with an 8 percent coupon. If the par value or the principal amount is $1,000, the holder will receive $80 a year for each of the next 20 years and, in addition, receive $1,000 in 20 years. Since the U.S. government has never defaulted, the bondholder is essentially guaranteed to receive these promised payments. Therefore, one can make the case that this is a riskless bond.

But is the bond really riskless after all? That depends on how you define risk. Suppose there is no chance of inflation, meaning that pizzas will always cost $5. We can be sure that the $1,080 ($1,000 of principal and $80 of interest) at maturity will allow us to buy $1,080/$5 = 216 pizzas. Alternatively, suppose that, over the next 20 years, there is a 50 percent probability of no inflation and a 50 percent probability of an annual inflation rate of 10 percent. With a 10 percent inflation rate, a pizza will cost $5 \times (1.10)^{20} = \$33.64$ in 20 years. The $1,080 payment will now allow the holder to buy only $1,080/$33.64 = 32.1 pizzas, not the 216 pizzas we calculated for a world of no inflation. Given the uncertain inflation rate, the investor faces **inflation risk**; while he knows that he will receive $1,080 at maturity, he doesn't know whether he can afford 216 or 32.1 pizzas.

Let's now speak in terms of nominal and real quantities. The *nominal value* of the payment at maturity is simply $1,080, because this is the actual cash the investor will receive. Assuming an inflation rate of 10 percent, the *real value* of this payment is only $1,080/(1.10)^{20} = \$160.54$. The real value measures the purchasing power of the payment. Since bondholders care about the purchasing power of their bond payments, they are ultimately concerned with real values, not nominal values. Inflation can erode the real value of the payments, implying that inflation risk is a serious concern, particularly in a time of high and variable inflation.

Do any bonds avoid inflation risk? As a matter of fact, yes. The U.S. government issues Treasury inflation-protected securities (TIPS), with promised payments specified in real terms, not nominal terms. A number of other countries also issue inflation-linked bonds. Imagine that a particular inflation-linked bond matures in two years, has a par value of $1,000, and pays a 2 percent coupon, where both the par value and the coupon are specified in real terms. Assuming annual payments, the bondholder will receive the following *real* payments:

End of Year 1	End of Year 2
$20	$1,020

Thus, the issuer is promising payments in real terms.

What amounts will the bondholder receive, expressed in nominal terms? Suppose the inflation rate over the first year is 3 percent and the inflation rate over the second year is 5 percent. The bondholder will receive the following *nominal* payments:[4]

End of Year 1	End of Year 2
$20 × 1.03 = $20.60	$1,020 × 1.03 × 1.05 = $1,103.13

While the bondholder knows the size of the payments in real terms when he buys the bond, he doesn't know the size of the payments in nominal terms until the inflation numbers are announced each period. Since TIPS and other inflation-linked bonds guarantee payments in real terms, we say that these bonds eliminate inflation risk.

Index-linked bonds are quoted in real yields. For example, suppose the bond trades at $971.50. The yield, y, would be solved by the following equation:

$$971.50 = \frac{20}{1 + y} + \frac{1,020}{(1 + y)^2}$$

In this example, y turns out to be 3.5 percent. Thus, we say that the real yield of the bond is 3.5 percent.

Are the yields on regular Treasury bonds related to the yields on TIPS? As of September 2014, the real yield on a 20-year TIPS was about 0.8 percent and the (nominal) yield on a 20-year Treasury bond was about 3.0 percent. As a first approximation, one could argue that the differential of 2.2 (= 3.0 − 0.8) percent implies that the market expects an annual rate of inflation of 2.2 percent over the next 20 years.[5]

THE FISHER EFFECT

Imagine a world where, initially, there is no inflation and the nominal interest rate is 2 percent. Suppose that something, an action by the Federal Reserve or a change in the foreign exchange rate, unexpectedly triggers an inflation rate of 5 percent. What do you think will happen to the nominal interest rate? Your first thought might be that the interest rate will rise, because if the rate stays at 2 percent, the real rate would become negative. That is, a bank deposit of $100 today will still turn into $102 at the end of the year. However, if a hamburger priced at $1 today costs $1.05 next year, the $102 will only buy about 97 (=102/1.05) hamburgers next year. Since the initial $100 allows one to buy 100 hamburgers today, there is a reduction in purchasing power.

---

[4] This example is simplified. Actual payment calculations are often complex and differ across countries. For example, TIPS have semiannual payments with a lag in the inflation adjustment.

[5] As mentioned earlier, regular Treasury bonds are subject to inflation risk while TIPS are not subject to this risk.
Since the risks of the two bonds are not equivalent, this approach should be viewed only as a first-pass estimate of anticipated inflation.

How much should the interest rate rise? A well-known economist, Irving Fisher, conjectured many decades ago that the nominal interest rate should rise just enough to keep the real interest rate constant. That is, the real rate should stay at 2 percent in our example. We can use Equation 8.4 to determine that the new nominal rate will be (approximately):

$$2\% + 5\% \cong 7.0\% \text{ (see equation 8.4)}$$

Fisher's thinking is that investors are not foolish. They know that inflation reduces purchasing power and, therefore, they will demand an increase in the nominal rate before lending money. Fisher's hypothesis, typically called the **Fisher effect**, can be stated as:

A rise in the rate of inflation causes the nominal rate to rise just enough so that the real rate of interest is unaffected. In other words, the real rate is invariant to the rate of inflation.

While Fisher's reasoning makes sense, it's important to point out that the claim that the nominal rate will rise to 7.0 percent is only a hypothesis. It may be true and it may be false in any real-world situation; it does not *have* to be true. For example, if investors are foolish after all, the nominal rate could stay at 2 percent, even in the presence of inflation. Alternatively, even if investors understand the impact of inflation, the nominal rate may not rise all the way to 7.0 percent. That is, there may be some unknown force preventing a full rise.

How can one test the Fisher effect empirically? While a precise empirical test is beyond the scope of this chapter, Figure 8.5 gives at least a hint of the evidence. The figure plots two curves, one showing annualized returns on one-month Treasury bills over the last 54 years and the other showing inflation rates over the same period. It is apparent that

Figure 8.5

The Relation between Annualized One-Month Treasury Bill Returns and Inflation

Adapted from *Ibbotson SBBI® Classic Yearbook;* updates made by the authors.

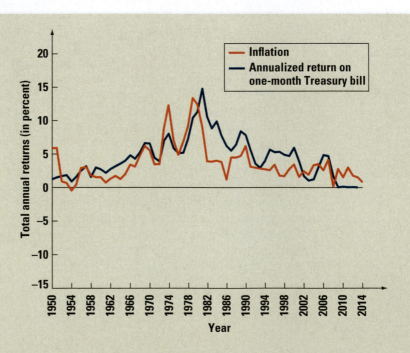

The figure plots both annualized returns on one-month Treasury bills and inflation rates in the United States. The two series appear to move together, implying that the inflation rate is an important determinant of the short-term interest rate.

the two curves move together. Both interest rates and inflation rates rose from the 1950s to the early 1980s while falling in the decades after. Thus, while statistical work is needed to establish a precise relationship, the figure suggests that inflation is an important determinant of the nominal interest rate.

8.5 Determinants of Bond Yields

We are now in a position to discuss the determinants of a bond's yield. As we will see, the yield on any particular bond is a reflection of a variety of factors.

THE TERM STRUCTURE OF INTEREST RATES

At any point in time, short-term and long-term interest rates generally differ. Sometimes short-term rates are higher, sometimes lower. Figure 8.6 provides a long-range perspective on this by showing about two centuries of short- and long-term interest rates. The difference between short- and long-term rates in the figure has ranged from essentially zero to several percentage points, both positive and negative.

The relationship between short- and long-term interest rates is known as the **term structure of interest rates**. To be a little more precise, the term structure of interest rates tells us the *nominal* interest rates on *default-free, pure discount* bonds of all maturities. These rates are, in essence, "pure" interest rates because they contain no risk of default and involve just a single, lump-sum future payment. In other words, the term structure tells us the pure time value of money for different lengths of time.

Figure 8.6   U.S. Interest Rates: 1800–2013

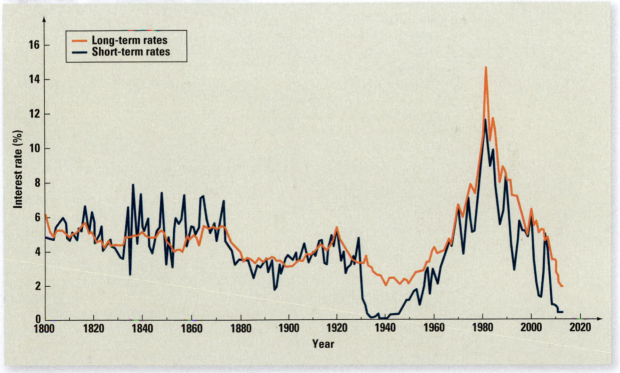

SOURCE: Jeremy J. Siegel, *Stocks for the Long Run*, 4th ed., © McGraw-Hill, 2008, updated by the authors.

When long-term rates are higher than short-term rates, we say that the term structure is upward sloping, and, when short-term rates are higher, we say it is downward sloping. The term structure can also be "humped." When this occurs, it is usually because rates increase at first, but then decline at longer-term maturities. The most common shape of the term structure, particularly in modern times, is upward sloping, but the degree of steepness has varied quite a bit.

What determines the shape of the term structure? There are three basic components. The first two are the ones we discussed in our previous section, the real rate of interest and the rate of inflation. The real rate of interest is the compensation investors demand for forgoing the use of their money. You can think of the real rate as the pure time value of money after adjusting for the effects of inflation.

The real rate of interest is a function of many factors. For example, consider expected economic growth. High expected growth is likely to raise the real rate, and low expected growth is likely to lower it. The real rate of interest may differ across maturities, due to varying growth expectations among other factors. For example, the real rate may be low for short-term bonds and high for long-term ones because the market expects lower economic growth in the short term than in the long term. However, the real rate of interest appears to have only a minor impact on the shape of the term structure.

In contrast, the prospect of future inflation very strongly influences the shape of the term structure. Investors thinking about loaning money for various lengths of time recognize that future inflation erodes the value of the dollars that will be returned. As a result, investors demand compensation for this loss in the form of higher nominal rates. This extra compensation is called the **inflation premium**.

If investors believe that the rate of inflation will be higher in the future, long-term nominal interest rates will tend to be higher than short-term rates. Thus, an upward-sloping term structure may reflect anticipated increases in the rate of inflation. Similarly, a downward-sloping term structure probably reflects the belief that the rate of inflation will be falling in the future.

The third, and last, component of the term structure has to do with interest rate risk. As we discussed earlier in the chapter, longer-term bonds have much greater risk of loss resulting from increases in interest rates than do shorter-term bonds. Investors recognize this risk, and they demand extra compensation in the form of higher rates for bearing it. This extra compensation is called the **interest rate risk premium**. The longer the term to maturity, the greater is the interest rate risk, so the interest rate risk premium increases with maturity. However, as we discussed earlier, interest rate risk increases at a decreasing rate, so the interest rate risk premium does as well.[6]

Putting the pieces together, we see that the term structure reflects the combined effect of the real rate of interest, the inflation premium, and the interest rate risk premium. Figure 8.7 shows how these can interact to produce an upward-sloping term structure (in the top part of Figure 8.7) or a downward-sloping term structure (in the bottom part).

In the top part of Figure 8.7, notice how the rate of inflation is expected to rise gradually. At the same time, the interest rate risk premium increases at a decreasing rate, so the combined effect is to produce a pronounced upward-sloping term structure. In the bottom part of Figure 8.7, the rate of inflation is expected to fall in the future, and the expected decline is enough to offset the interest rate risk premium and produce a downward-sloping term structure. Notice that if the rate of inflation was expected to decline by only a small amount, we could still get an upward-sloping term structure because of the interest rate risk premium.

---

[6]Many years ago, the interest rate risk premium was called a "liquidity" premium. Today, the term *liquidity premium* has an altogether different meaning, which we explore in our next section. Also, the interest rate risk premium is sometimes called a maturity risk premium. Our terminology is consistent with the modern view of the term structure.

Figure 8.7
The Term Structure
of Interest Rates

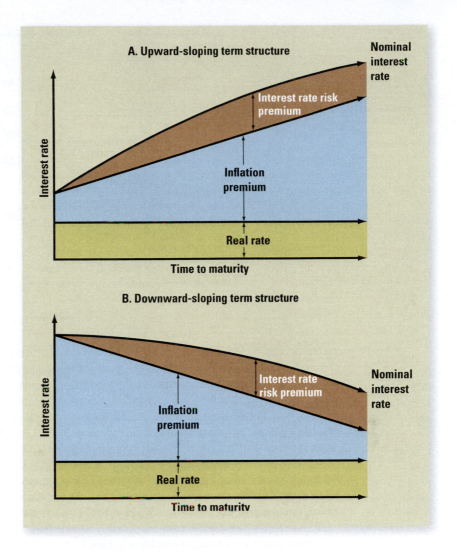

We assumed in drawing Figure 8.7 that the real rate would remain the same. However, as stated earlier, expected future real rates could be larger or smaller than the current real rate. Also, for simplicity, we used straight lines to show expected future inflation rates as rising or declining, but they do not necessarily have to look like this. They could, for example, rise and then fall, leading to a humped yield curve.

BOND YIELDS AND THE YIELD CURVE: PUTTING IT ALL TOGETHER

Going back to Figure 8.4, recall that the yields on Treasury notes and bonds differ across maturities. Each day, in addition to the Treasury prices and yields shown in Figure 8.4, *The Wall Street Journal* provides a plot of Treasury yields relative to maturity. This plot is called the **Treasury yield curve** (or just the yield curve). Figure 8.8 shows the yield curve as of December 2014.

As you probably now suspect, the shape of the yield curve is a reflection of the term structure of interest rates. In fact, the Treasury yield curve and the term structure of interest rates are almost the same thing. The only difference is that the term structure is based on

Online yield curve information is available at **www.bloomberg .com/markets**.

Figure 8.8

The Treasury Yield Curve: December 2014

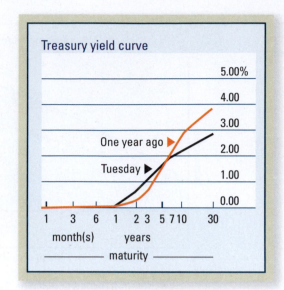

pure discount bonds, whereas the yield curve is based on coupon bond yields. As a result, Treasury yields depend on the three components that underlie the term structure—the real rate, expected future inflation, and the interest rate risk premium.

Treasury notes and bonds have three important features that we need to remind you of: They are default-free, they are taxable, and they are highly liquid. This is not true of bonds in general, so we need to examine what additional factors come into play when we look at bonds issued by corporations or municipalities.

First, consider the possibility of default, commonly called credit risk. Investors recognize that issuers other than the Treasury may or may not make all the promised payments on a bond, so they demand a higher yield as compensation for this risk. This extra compensation is called the **default risk premium**. Earlier in the chapter, we saw how bonds were rated based on their credit risk. What you will find if you start looking at bonds of different ratings is that lower-rated bonds have higher yields.

We stated earlier in this chapter that a bond's yield is calculated assuming that all the promised payments will be made. As a result, it is really a promised yield, and it may or may not be what you will earn. In particular, if the issuer defaults, your actual yield will be lower, probably much lower. This fact is particularly important when it comes to junk bonds. Thanks to a clever bit of marketing, such bonds are now commonly called high-yield bonds, which has a much nicer ring to it; but now you recognize that these are really high *promised* yield bonds.

Next, recall that we discussed earlier how municipal bonds are free from most taxes and, as a result, have much lower yields than taxable bonds. Investors demand the extra yield on a taxable bond as compensation for the unfavorable tax treatment. This extra compensation is the **taxability premium**.

Finally, bonds have varying degrees of liquidity. As we discussed earlier, there are an enormous number of bond issues, most of which do not trade on a regular basis. As a result, if you wanted to sell quickly, you would probably not get as high a price as you could otherwise. Investors prefer liquid assets to illiquid ones, so they demand a **liquidity premium** on top of all the other premiums we have discussed. As a result, all else being the same, less liquid bonds will have higher yields than more liquid bonds.

CONCLUSION

If we combine everything we have discussed, we find that bond yields represent the combined effect of no fewer than six factors. The first is the real rate of interest. On top of the real rate are five premiums representing compensation for (1) expected future inflation, (2) interest rate risk, (3) default risk, (4) taxability, and (5) lack of liquidity. As a result, determining the appropriate yield on a bond requires careful analysis of each of these factors.

Summary and Conclusions

This chapter has explored bonds, bond yields, and interest rates. We saw that:

1. Determining bond prices and yields is an application of basic discounted cash flow principles.
2. Bond values move in the direction opposite that of interest rates, leading to potential gains or losses for bond investors.
3. Bonds are rated based on their default risk. Some bonds, such as Treasury bonds, have no risk of default, whereas so-called junk bonds have substantial default risk.
4. Almost all bond trading is OTC, with little or no market transparency in many cases. As a result, bond price and volume information can be difficult to find for some types of bonds.
5. Bond yields and interest rates reflect six different factors: the real interest rate and five premiums that investors demand as compensation for inflation, interest rate risk, default risk, taxability, and lack of liquidity.

In closing, we note that bonds are a vital source of financing to governments and corporations. Bond prices and yields are a rich subject, and our one chapter, necessarily, touches on only the most important concepts and ideas.

Concept Questions

1. **Treasury Bonds**   Is it true that a U.S. Treasury security is risk-free?
2. **Interest Rate Risk**   Which has greater interest rate risk, a 30-year Treasury bond or a 30-year BB corporate bond?
3. **Treasury Pricing**   With regard to bid and ask prices on a Treasury bond, is it possible for the bid price to be higher? Why or why not?
4. **Yield to Maturity**   Treasury bid and ask quotes are sometimes given in terms of yields, so there would be a bid yield and an ask yield. Which do you think would be larger? Explain.
5. **Coupon Rate**   How does a bond issuer decide on the appropriate coupon rate to set on its bonds? Explain the difference between the coupon rate and the required return on a bond.

6. **Real and Nominal Returns**　Are there any circumstances under which an investor might be more concerned about the nominal return on an investment than the real return?

7. **Bond Ratings**　Companies pay rating agencies such as Moody's and S&P to rate their bonds, and the costs can be substantial. However, companies are not required to have their bonds rated in the first place; doing so is strictly voluntary. Why do you think they do it?

8. **Bond Ratings**　U.S. Treasury bonds are not rated. Why? Often, junk bonds are not rated. Why?

9. **Term Structure**　What is the difference between the term structure of interest rates and the yield curve?

10. **Crossover Bonds**　Looking back at the crossover bonds we discussed in the chapter, why do you think split ratings such as these occur?

11. **Municipal Bonds**　Why is it that municipal bonds are not taxed at the federal level, but are taxable across state lines? Why is it that U.S. Treasury bonds are not taxable at the state level? (You may need to dust off the history books for this one.)

12. **Bond Market**　What are the implications for bond investors of the lack of transparency in the bond market?

13. **Treasury Market**　Take a look back at Figure 8.4. Notice the wide range of coupon rates. Why are they so different?

14. **Rating Agencies**　A controversy erupted regarding bond-rating agencies when some agencies began to provide unsolicited bond ratings. Why do you think this is controversial?

15. **Bonds as Equity**　The 100-year bonds we discussed in the chapter have something in common with junk bonds. Critics charge that, in both cases, the issuers are really selling equity in disguise. What are the issues here? Why would a company want to sell "equity in disguise"?

16. **Bond Prices versus Yields**
    a. What is the relationship between the price of a bond and its YTM?
    b. Explain why some bonds sell at a premium over par value while other bonds sell at a discount. What do you know about the relationship between the coupon rate and the YTM for premium bonds? What about for discount bonds? For bonds selling at par value?
    c. What is the relationship between the current yield and YTM for premium bonds? For discount bonds? For bonds selling at par value?

17. **Interest Rate Risk**　All else being the same, which has more interest rate risk, a long-term bond or a short-term bond? What about a low coupon bond compared to a high coupon bond? What about a long-term, high coupon bond compared to a short-term, low coupon bond?

Questions and Problems

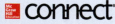

BASIC
(Questions 1–16)

1. **Valuing Bonds**　What is the price of a 15-year, zero coupon bond paying $1,000 at maturity, assuming semiannual compounding, if the YTM is:
    a. 6 percent?
    b. 8 percent?
    c. 10 percent?

2. **Valuing Bonds** Microhard has issued a bond with the following characteristics:

Par: $1,000
Time to maturity: 20 years
Coupon rate: 7 percent
Semiannual payments

Calculate the price of this bond if the YTM is:

a. 7 percent
b. 9 percent
c. 5 percent

3. **Bond Yields** Watters Umbrella Corp. issued 15-year bonds 2 years ago at a coupon rate of 5.9 percent. The bonds make semiannual payments. If these bonds currently sell for 105 percent of par value, what is the YTM?

4. **Coupon Rates** Rhiannon Corporation has bonds on the market with 11.5 years to maturity, a YTM of 7.3 percent, and a current price of $1,080. The bonds make semiannual payments. What must the coupon rate be on these bonds?

5. **Valuing Bonds** Even though most corporate bonds in the United States make coupon payments semiannually, bonds issued elsewhere often have annual coupon payments. Suppose a German company issues a bond with a par value of €1,000, 15 years to maturity, and a coupon rate of 4.5 percent paid annually. If the yield to maturity is 3.9 percent, what is the current price of the bond?

6. **Bond Yields** A Japanese company has a bond outstanding that sells for 106 percent of its ¥100,000 par value. The bond has a coupon rate of 2.8 percent paid annually and matures in 21 years. What is the yield to maturity of this bond?

7. **Zero Coupon Bonds** You find a zero coupon bond with a par value of $10,000 and 17 years to maturity. If the yield to maturity on this bond is 4.9 percent, what is the dollar price of the bond? Assume semiannual compounding periods.

8. **Valuing Bonds** Yan Yan Corp. has a $2,000 par value bond outstanding with a coupon rate of 4.9 percent paid semiannually and 13 years to maturity. The yield to maturity of the bond is 3.8 percent. What is the dollar price of the bond?

9. **Valuing Bonds** Union Local School District has bonds outstanding with a coupon rate of 3.7 percent paid semiannually and 16 years to maturity. The yield to maturity on these bonds is 3.9 percent, and the bonds have a par value of $5,000. What is the dollar price of the bond?

10. **Calculating Real Rates of Return** If Treasury bills are currently paying 3.9 percent and the inflation rate is 2.1 percent, what is the approximate real rate of interest? The exact real rate?

11. **Inflation and Nominal Returns** Suppose the real rate is 2.4 percent and the inflation rate is 3.7 percent. What rate would you expect to see on a Treasury bill?

12. **Nominal and Real Returns** An investment offers a total return of 13 percent over the coming year. Alan Wingspan thinks the total real return on this investment will be only 8 percent. What does Alan believe the inflation rate will be over the next year?

13. **Nominal versus Real Returns** Say you own an asset that had a total return last year of 11.6 percent. If the inflation rate last year was 5.3 percent, what was your real return?

14. **Using Treasury Quotes** Locate the Treasury bond in Figure 8.4 maturing in February 2037. What is its coupon rate? What is its bid price? What was the *previous day's* asked price? Assume a par value of $10,000.

15. **Using Treasury Quotes** Locate the Treasury bond in Figure 8.4 maturing in November 2039. Is this a premium or a discount bond? What is its current yield? What is its yield to maturity? What is the bid-ask spread in dollars? Assume a par value of $1,000.

16. Zero Coupon Bonds You buy a zero coupon bond at the beginning of the year that has a face value of $1,000, a YTM of 6.3 percent, and 25 years to maturity. If you hold the bond for the entire year, how much in interest income will you have to declare on your tax return? Assume semiannual compounding.

INTERMEDIATE
(Questions 17–28)

17. Bond Price Movements Miller Corporation has a premium bond making semiannual payments. The bond pays a coupon of 8.5 percent, has a YTM of 7 percent, and has 13 years to maturity. The Modigliani Company has a discount bond making semiannual payments. This bond pays a coupon of 7 percent, has a YTM of 8.5 percent, and also has 13 years to maturity. If interest rates remain unchanged, what do you expect the price of these bonds to be 1 year from now? In 3 years? In 8 years? In 12 years? In 13 years? What's going on here? Illustrate your answers by graphing bond prices versus time to maturity.

18. Interest Rate Risk Laurel, Inc., and Hardy Corp. both have 6.5 percent coupon bonds outstanding, with semiannual interest payments, and both are priced at par value. The Laurel, Inc., bond has 3 years to maturity, whereas the Hardy Corp. bond has 20 years to maturity. If interest rates suddenly rise by 2 percent, what is the percentage change in the price of these bonds? If interest rates were to suddenly fall by 2 percent instead, what would the percentage change in the price of these bonds be then? Illustrate your answers by graphing bond prices versus YTM. What does this problem tell you about the interest rate risk of longer-term bonds?

19. Interest Rate Risk The Faulk Corp. has a 6 percent coupon bond outstanding. The Gonas Company has a 14 percent bond outstanding. Both bonds have 12 years to maturity, make semiannual payments, and have a YTM of 10 percent. If interest rates suddenly rise by 2 percent, what is the percentage change in the price of these bonds? What if interest rates suddenly fall by 2 percent instead? What does this problem tell you about the interest rate risk of lower coupon bonds?

20. Bond Yields Hacker Software has 6.2 percent coupon bonds on the market with 9 years to maturity. The bonds make semiannual payments and currently sell for 104 percent of par. What is the current yield on the bonds? The YTM? The effective annual yield?

21. Bond Yields RAK Co. wants to issue new 20-year bonds for some much-needed expansion projects. The company currently has 6.4 percent coupon bonds on the market that sell for $1,063, make semiannual payments, and mature in 20 years. What coupon rate should the company set on its new bonds if it wants them to sell at par?

22. Accrued Interest You purchase a bond with an invoice price of $950. The bond has a coupon rate of 5.2 percent, and there are 2 months to the next semiannual coupon date. What is the clean price of the bond?

23. Accrued Interest You purchase a bond with a coupon rate of 5.9 percent and a clean price of $984. If the next semiannual coupon payment is due in four months, what is the invoice price?

24. Finding the Bond Maturity Erna Corp. has 9 percent coupon bonds making annual payments with a YTM of 7.81 percent. The current yield on these bonds is 8.42 percent. How many years do these bonds have left until they mature?

25. Using Bond Quotes Suppose the following bond quote for IOU Corporation appears in the financial page of today's newspaper. Assume the bond has a face value of $1,000, semiannual coupon payments, and the current date is April 15, 2015. What is the yield to maturity of the bond? What is the current yield?

Company (Ticker)	Coupon	Maturity	Last Price	Last Yield	EST Vol (000s)
IOU (IOU)	7.240	Apr 15, 2026	105.312	??	1,827

26. **Finding the Maturity**   You've just found a 10 percent coupon bond on the market that sells for par value. What is the maturity on this bond?

27. **Interest on Zeroes**   Tesla Corporation needs to raise funds to finance a plant expansion, and it has decided to issue 25-year zero coupon bonds to raise the money. The required return on the bonds will be 5.4 percent.

    a. What will these bonds sell for at issuance?
    b. Using the IRS amortization rule, what interest deduction can the company take on these bonds in the first year? In the last year?
    c. Repeat part (b) using the straight-line method for the interest deduction.
    d. Based on your answers in (b) and (c), which interest deduction method would the company prefer? Why?

28. **Zero Coupon Bonds**   Suppose your company needs to raise $50 million and you want to issue 30-year bonds for this purpose. Assume the required return on your bond issue will be 6 percent, and you're evaluating two issue alternatives: A semiannual coupon bond with a 6 percent coupon rate and a zero coupon bond. Your company's tax rate is 35 percent.

    a. How many of the coupon bonds would you need to issue to raise the $50 million? How many of the zeroes would you need to issue?
    b. In 30 years, what will your company's repayment be if you issue the coupon bonds? What if you issue the zeroes?
    c. Based on your answers in (a) and (b), why would you ever want to issue the zeroes? To answer, calculate the firm's aftertax cash outflows for the first year under the two different scenarios. Assume the IRS amortization rules apply for the zero coupon bonds.

CHALLENGE
(Questions 29–35)

29. **Components of Bond Returns**   Bond P is a premium bond with a coupon of 8.5 percent. Bond D has a coupon of 5.5 percent and is selling at a discount. Both bonds make annual payments, have a YTM of 7 percent, and have 10 years to maturity. What is the current yield for Bond P? For Bond D? If interest rates remain unchanged, what is the expected capital gains yield over the next year for Bond P? For Bond D? Explain your answers and the interrelationship among the various types of yields.

30. **Holding Period Yield**   The YTM on a bond is the interest rate you earn on your investment if interest rates don't change. If you actually sell the bond before it matures, your realized return is known as the holding period yield (HPY).

    a. Suppose that today you buy a bond with an annual coupon of 4.9 percent for $930. The bond has 10 years to maturity. What rate of return do you expect to earn on your investment?
    b. Two years from now, the YTM on your bond has declined by 1 percent, and you decide to sell. What price will your bond sell for? What is the HPY on your investment? Compare this yield to the YTM when you first bought the bond. Why are they different?

31. **Valuing Bonds**   The Frush Corporation has two different bonds currently outstanding. Bond M has a face value of $30,000 and matures in 20 years. The bond makes no payments for the first six years, then pays $800 every six months over the subsequent eight years, and finally pays $1,000 every six months over the last six years. Bond N also has a face value of $30,000 and a maturity of 20 years; it makes no coupon payments over the life of the bond. If the required return on both these bonds is 6.4 percent compounded semiannually, what is the current price of Bond M? Of Bond N?

32. **Treasury Bonds**   The following Treasury bond quote appeared in *The Wall Street Journal* on May 11, 2004:

| 9.125 | May 09 | 100:03 | 100:04 | — | –2.15 |

Why would anyone buy this Treasury bond with a negative yield to maturity? How is this possible?

33. **Real Cash Flows** When Marilyn Monroe died, ex-husband Joe DiMaggio vowed to place fresh flowers on her grave every Sunday as long as he lived. The week after she died in 1962, a bunch of fresh flowers that the former baseball player thought appropriate for the star cost about $8. Based on actuarial tables, "Joltin' Joe" could expect to live for 30 years after the actress died. Assume that the EAR is 7.5 percent. Also, assume that the price of the flowers will increase at 3.2 percent per year, when expressed as an EAR. Assuming that each year has exactly 52 weeks, what is the present value of this commitment? Joe began purchasing flowers the week after Marilyn died.

34. **Real Cash Flows** You are planning to save for retirement over the next 30 years. To save for retirement, you will invest $900 per month in a stock account in real dollars and $300 per month in a bond account in real dollars. The effective annual return of the stock account is expected to be 12 percent, and the bond account will earn 7 percent. When you retire, you will combine your money into an account with an effective return of 8 percent. The inflation rate over this period is expected to be 4 percent. How much can you withdraw each month from your account in real terms assuming a withdrawal period of 25 years? What is the nominal dollar amount of your last withdrawal?

35. **Real Cash Flows** Paul Adams owns a health club in downtown Los Angeles. He charges his customers an annual fee of $400 and has an existing customer base of 700. Paul plans to raise the annual fee by 6 percent every year and expects the club membership to grow at a constant rate of 3 percent for the next five years. The overall expenses of running the health club are $125,000 a year and are expected to grow at the inflation rate of 2 percent annually. After five years, Paul plans to buy a luxury boat for $500,000, close the health club, and travel the world in his boat for the rest of his life. What is the annual amount that Paul can spend while on his world tour if he will have no money left in the bank when he dies? Assume Paul has a remaining life of 25 years after he retires and earns 9 percent on his savings.

Excel Master It! Problem

Companies often buy bonds to meet a future liability or cash outlay. Such an investment is called a dedicated portfolio since the proceeds of the portfolio are dedicated to the future liability. In such a case, the portfolio is subject to reinvestment risk. Reinvestment risk occurs because the company will be reinvesting the coupon payments it receives. If the YTM on similar bonds falls, these coupon payments will be reinvested at a lower interest rate, which will result in a portfolio value that is lower than desired at maturity. Of course, if interest rates increase, the portfolio value at maturity will be higher than needed.

Suppose Ice Cubes, Inc., has the following liability due in five years. The company is going to buy five-year bonds today in order to meet the future obligation. The liability and current YTM are below:

Amount of liability	$100,000,000
Current YTM	8%

a. At the current YTM, what is the face value of the bonds the company has to purchase today in order to meet its future obligation? Assume that the bonds in the relevant range will have the same coupon rate as the current YTM and these bonds make semiannual coupon payments.

b. Assume that the interest rates remain constant for the next five years. Thus, when the company reinvests the coupon payments, it will reinvest at the current YTM. What will be the value of the portfolio in five years?

c. Assume that immediately after the company purchases the bonds, interest rates either rise or fall by 1 percent. What will be the value of the portfolio in five years under these circumstances?

One way to eliminate reinvestment risk is called immunization. Rather than buying bonds with the same maturity as the liability, the company instead buys bonds with the same duration as the liability. If you think about the dedicated portfolio, if the interest rate falls, the future value of the reinvested coupon payments decreases. However, as interest rates fall, the price of the bond increases. These effects offset each other in an immunized portfolio.

Another advantage of using duration to immunize a portfolio is that the duration of a portfolio is simply the weighted average of the duration of the assets in the portfolio. In other words, to find the duration of a portfolio, you simply take the weight of each asset multiplied by its duration and then sum the results.

d. What is the duration of the liability for Ice Cubes, Inc.?

e. Suppose the two bonds shown below are the only bonds available to immunize the liability. What face amount of each bond will the company need to purchase to immunize the portfolio?

	Bond A	Bond B
Settlement	1/1/2000	1/1/2000
Maturity	1/1/2003	1/1/2008
Coupon rate	7.00%	8.00%
YTM	7.50%	9.00%
Coupons per year	2	2

Mini Case

FINANCING EAST COAST YACHTS'S EXPANSION PLANS WITH A BOND ISSUE

After Dan's EFN analysis for East Coast Yachts (see the Mini Case in Chapter 3), Larissa has decided to expand the company's operations. She has asked Dan to enlist an underwriter to help sell $50 million in new 20-year bonds to finance new construction. Dan has entered into discussions with Kim McKenzie, an underwriter from the firm of Crowe & Mallard, about which bond features East Coast Yachts should consider and also what coupon rate the issue will likely have. Although Dan is aware of bond features, he is uncertain as to the costs and benefits of some of them, so he isn't clear on how each feature would affect the coupon rate of the bond issue.

1. You are Kim's assistant, and she has asked you to prepare a memo to Dan describing the effect of each of the following bond features on the coupon rate of the bond. She would also like you to list any advantages or disadvantages of each feature.

   a. The security of the bond, that is, whether or not the bond has collateral.

   b. The seniority of the bond.

   c. The presence of a sinking fund.

d. A call provision with specified call dates and call prices.

e. A deferred call accompanying the above call provision.

f. A make-whole call provision.

g. Any positive covenants. Also, discuss several possible positive covenants East Coast Yachts might consider.

h. Any negative covenants. Also, discuss several possible negative covenants East Coast Yachts might consider.

i. A conversion feature (note that East Coast Yachts is not a publicly traded company).

j. A floating rate coupon.

Dan is also considering whether to issue coupon bearing bonds or zero coupon bonds. The YTM on either bond issue will be 7.5 percent. The coupon bond would have a 6.5 percent coupon rate. The company's tax rate is 35 percent.

2. How many of the coupon bonds must East Coast Yachts issue to raise the $50 million? How many of the zeroes must it issue?

3. In 20 years, what will be the principal repayment due if East Coast Yachts issues the coupon bonds? What if it issues the zeroes?

4. What are the company's considerations in issuing a coupon bond compared to a zero coupon bond?

5. Suppose East Coast Yachts issues the coupon bonds with a make-whole call provision. The make-whole call rate is the Treasury rate plus .40 percent. If East Coast calls the bonds in seven years when the Treasury rate is 4.8 percent, what is the call price of the bond? What if it is 8.2 percent?

6. Are investors really made whole with a make-whole call provision?

7. After considering all the relevant factors, would you recommend a zero coupon issue or a regular coupon issue? Why? Would you recommend an ordinary call feature or a make-whole call feature? Why?

9

Stock Valuation

When the stock market closed on December 11, 2014, the common stock of well-known retailer Target was selling for $73.53 per share. On that same day, HSN, Inc., operator of TV retailer The Home Shopping Network, closed at $73.38 per share, while HCA, which operates 165 hospitals, closed at $73.56. Because the stock prices of these three companies were so similar, you might expect they would be offering similar dividends to their stockholders, but be offering similar dividends to their stockholders, but

you would be wrong. In fact, Target's annual dividend was $2.08 per share, HSN's was $1.40 per share, and HCA was paying no dividend at all!

As we will see in this chapter, the current dividend is one of the primary factors in valuing common stocks. However, it is obvious from looking at HCA that current dividends are not the end of the story. This chapter explores dividends, stock values, and the connection between the two.

In our previous chapter, we introduced you to bonds and bond valuation. In this chapter, we turn to the other major source of external financing for corporations, common stock. We first describe the cash flows associated with a share of stock and then develop a well-known result, the dividend growth model. Next, we point out that stocks are frequently priced using comparables as well. We also show that the discounted cash flow approach introduced in Chapters 5 and 6 works for entire firms and shares of stock as well as for projects. We close out the chapter with a discussion of how shares of stock are traded and how stock prices and other important information are reported in the financial press.

9.1 The Present Value of Common Stocks

DIVIDENDS VERSUS CAPITAL GAINS

Our goal in this section is to value common stocks. We learned in previous chapters that an asset's value is determined by the present value of its future cash flows. A stock provides two kinds of cash flows. First, many stocks pay dividends on a regular basis. Second, the stockholder receives the sale price when she sells the stock. Thus, in order to value common stocks, we need to answer an important question: Is the price of a share of stock equal to:

1. The discounted present value of the sum of next period's dividend plus next period's stock price, or
2. The discounted present value of all future dividends?

This is the kind of question that students would love to see on a multiple-choice exam, because both (1) and (2) are correct.

To see that (1) and (2) are the same, let's start with an individual who will buy the stock and hold it for one year. In other words, she has a one-year *holding period*. In addition, she is willing to pay P_0 for the stock today. That is, she calculates:

$$P_0 = \frac{\text{Div}_1}{1 + R} + \frac{P_1}{1 + R}$$ **(9.1)**

Div_1 is the expected dividend paid at year's end and P_1 is the expected price at year's end. P_0 is the present value of the common stock investment. The term in the denominator, R, is the appropriate discount rate for the stock and represents the expected return that investors require in order to commit funds to the stock (or simply, the required return).

That seems easy enough, but where does P_1 come from? P_1 is not pulled out of thin air. Rather, there must be a buyer at the end of Year 1 who is willing to purchase the stock for P_1. This buyer determines the price by:

$$P_1 = \frac{\text{Div}_2}{1 + R} + \frac{P_2}{1 + R}$$ **(9.2)**

Substituting the value of P_1 from Equation 9.2 into Equation 9.1 yields:

$$\begin{aligned} P_0 &= \frac{1}{1 + R}\left[\text{Div}_1 + \left(\frac{\text{Div}_2 + P_2}{1 + R}\right)\right] \\ &= \frac{\text{Div}_1}{1 + R} + \frac{\text{Div}_2}{(1 + R)^2} + \frac{P_2}{(1 + R)^2} \end{aligned}$$ **(9.3)**

We can ask a similar question for Formula 9.3: Where does P_2 come from? An investor at the end of Year 2 is willing to pay P_2 because of the dividend and stock price at Year 3. This process can be repeated *ad nauseam*.[1] At the end, we are left with:

$$P_0 = \frac{\text{Div}_1}{1 + R} + \frac{\text{Div}_2}{(1 + R)^2} + \frac{\text{Div}_3}{(1 + R)^3} + \cdots = \sum_{t=1}^{\infty} \frac{\text{Div}_t}{(1 + R)^t}$$ **(9.4)**

Thus the price of a share of common stock to the investor is equal to the present value of all of the expected future dividends.

This is a very useful result. A common objection to applying present value analysis to stocks is that investors are too shortsighted to care about the long-run stream of dividends. These critics argue that an investor will generally not look past his or her time horizon. Thus, prices in a market dominated by short-term investors will reflect only near-term dividends. However, our discussion shows that a long-run dividend discount model holds even when investors have short-term time horizons. Although an investor may want to cash out early, she must find another investor who is willing to buy. The price this second investor pays is dependent on dividends *after* his date of purchase.

VALUATION OF DIFFERENT TYPES OF STOCKS

The above discussion shows that the price of a share of stock is the present value of its future dividends. How do we apply this idea in practice? Equation 9.4 represents a general model that is applicable whether dividends are expected to grow, decline, or stay the same.

---

[1]This procedure reminds us of the physicist lecturing on the origins of the universe. He was approached by an elderly gentleman in the audience who disagreed with the lecture. The attendee said that the universe rests on the back of a huge turtle. When the physicist asked what the turtle rested on, the gentleman said another turtle. Anticipating the physicist's objections, the attendee said, "Don't tire yourself out, young fellow. It's turtles all the way down."

Figure 9.1
Zero Growth,
Constant Growth,
and Differential
Growth Patterns

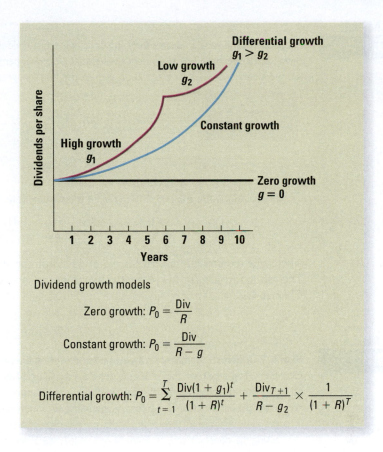

Dividend growth models

$$\text{Zero growth: } P_0 = \frac{\text{Div}}{R}$$

$$\text{Constant growth: } P_0 = \frac{\text{Div}}{R - g}$$

$$\text{Differential growth: } P_0 = \sum_{t=1}^{T} \frac{\text{Div}(1 + g_1)^t}{(1 + R)^t} + \frac{\text{Div}_{T+1}}{R - g_2} \times \frac{1}{(1 + R)^T}$$

The general model can be simplified if dividends are expected to follow some basic patterns: (1) zero growth, (2) constant growth, and (3) differential growth. These cases are illustrated in Figure 9.1.

Case 1 (Zero Growth) The price of a share of stock with a constant dividend is given by:

$$P_0 = \frac{\text{Div}_1}{1 + R} + \frac{\text{Div}_2}{(1 + R)^2} + \cdots = \frac{\text{Div}}{R}$$

Here it is assumed that $\text{Div}_1 = \text{Div}_2 = \cdots = \text{Div}$. This is just an application of the perpetuity formula from Chapter 4 and is useful in valuing preferred stocks where the dividends paid out are constant.

Case 2 (Constant Growth) Dividends are expected to grow at rate g, as follows:

End of Year	1	2	3	4	. . .
Dividend	Div	Div(1 + g)	Div(1 + g)²	Div(1 + g)³	. . .

Note that Div is the dividend at the end of the *first* period.

Projected Dividends Hampshire Products will pay a dividend of $4 per share a year from now. Financial analysts believe that dividends will rise at 6 percent per year for the foreseeable future. What is the dividend per share at the end of each of the first five years?

End of Year	1	2	3	4	5
Dividend	$4.00	$4 × (1.06) = $4.24	$4 × (1.06)² = $4.4944	$4 × (1.06)³ = $4.7641	$4 × (1.06)⁴ = $5.0499

If dividends are expected to grow at a constant rate, the price of a share of stock is:

$$P_0 = \frac{\text{Div}}{1 + R} + \frac{\text{Div}(1 + g)}{(1 + R)^2} + \frac{\text{Div}(1 + g)^2}{(1 + R)^3} + \frac{\text{Div}(1 + g)^3}{(1 + R)^4} + \cdots = \frac{\text{Div}}{R - g}$$

where g is the growth rate. Div is the dividend on the stock at the end of the first period. This is the formula for the present value of a growing perpetuity, which we introduced in Chapter 4.

EXAMPLE

Stock Valuation Suppose an investor is considering the purchase of a share of the Utah Mining Company. The stock will pay a $3 dividend a year from today. This dividend is expected to grow at 10 percent per year ($g = 10\%$) for the foreseeable future. The investor thinks that the required return (R) on this stock is 15 percent, given her assessment of Utah Mining's risk. (We also refer to R as the discount rate of the stock.) What is the price of a share of Utah Mining Company's stock?

Using the constant growth formula of Case 2, we assess the price to be $60:

$$\$60 = \frac{\$3}{.15 - .10}$$

Today's price, P_0 is quite dependent on the value of g. If g had been estimated to be 12½ percent, the value of the share would have been:

$$\$120 = \frac{\$3}{.15 - .125}$$

The stock price doubles (from $60 to $120) when g only increases 25 percent (from 10 percent to 12.5 percent). Because of P_0's dependency on g, one should maintain a healthy sense of skepticism when using this constant growth of dividends model.

Furthermore, note that P_0 is equal to infinity when the growth rate, g, equals the discount rate, R. Because stock prices are never infinite, an estimate of g equal to or greater than R implies an error in estimation. More will be said of this point later.

The assumption of steady dividend growth might strike you as peculiar. Why would the dividend grow at a constant rate? The reason is that, for many companies, steady growth in dividends is an explicit goal. For example, in 2014, Procter & Gamble, the Cincinnati-based maker of personal care and household products, increased its annual dividend by 7 percent to $2.57 per share; this increase was notable because it was the 58th in a row. The subject of dividend growth falls under the general heading of dividend policy, so we will defer further discussion of it to a later chapter.

You might wonder what would happen with the dividend growth model if the growth rate, g, were greater than the discount rate, R. It looks like we would get a negative stock price because $R - g$ would be less than zero. This is not what would happen.

Instead, if the constant growth rate exceeds the discount rate, then the stock price is infinitely large. Why? If the growth rate is bigger than the discount rate, the present value of the dividends keeps getting bigger. Essentially the same is true if the growth rate and the discount rate are equal. In both cases, the simplification that allows us to replace the infinite stream of dividends with the dividend growth model is "illegal," so the answers we get from the dividend growth model are nonsense unless the growth rate is less than the discount rate.

Case 3 (Differential Growth)   In this case, an algebraic formula would be too unwieldy. Instead, we present examples.

**EXAMPLE
9.3**

Differential Growth   Consider Elixir Drug Company, which is expected to enjoy rapid growth from the introduction of its new back-rub ointment. The dividend for a share of Elixir's stock a year from today is expected to be $1.15. During the next four years, the dividend is expected to grow at 15 percent per year ($g_1 = 15\%$). After that, growth (g_2) will be equal to 10 percent per year. Calculate the present value of a share of stock if the required return (R) is 15 percent.

Figure 9.2   Growth in Dividends for Elixir Drug Company

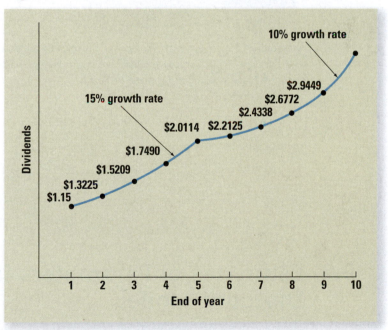

Figure 9.2 displays the growth in Elixir's dividends. We need to apply a two-step process to discount these dividends. We first calculate the present value of the dividends growing at 15 percent per annum. That is, we first calculate the present value of the dividends at the end of each of the first five years. Second, we calculate the present value of the dividends beginning at the end of Year 6.

(continued)

Present Value of First Five Dividends   The present value of dividend payments in Years 1 through 5 is calculated as follows:

Future Year	Growth Rate (g_1)	Expected Dividend	Present Value
1	.15	$1.15	$1
2	.15	1.3225	1
3	.15	1.5209	1
4	.15	1.7490	1
5	.15	2.0114	1
Years 1−5		The present value of dividends = $5	

The growing annuity formula of the previous chapter could normally be used in this step. However, note that dividends grow at 15 percent per year, which is also the discount rate. Since $g = R$, the growing annuity formula cannot be used in this example.

Present Value of Dividends Beginning at End of Year 6   We use the procedure for deferred perpetuities and deferred annuities presented in Chapter 4. The dividends beginning at the end of Year 6 are:

End of Year	6	7	8	9	. . .
Dividend	$Div_5 \times (1 + g_2)$	$Div_5 \times (1 + g_2)^2$	$Div_5 \times (1 + g_2)^3$	$Div_5 \times (1 + g_2)^4$	. . .
	2.0114×1.10	$2.0114 \times (1.10)^2$	$2.0114 \times (1.10)^3$	$2.0114 \times (1.10)^4$	. . .
	= $2.2125	= $2.4338	= $2.6772	= $2.9449	

As stated in Chapter 4, the growing perpetuity formula calculates present value as of one year prior to the first payment. Because the payment begins at the end of Year 6, the present value formula calculates present value as of the end of Year 5.

The price at the end of Year 5 is given by:

$$P_5 = \frac{Div_6}{R - g_2} = \frac{\$2.2125}{.15 - .10} = \$44.25$$

The present value of P_5 as of today is:

$$\frac{P_5}{(1 + R)^5} = \frac{\$44.25}{(1.15)^5} = \$22$$

The present value of *all* dividends as of today is $27 (= $22 + 5).

9.2 Estimates of Parameters in the Dividend Discount Model

The value of the firm is a function of its growth rate, g, and its discount rate, R. How does one estimate these variables?

WHERE DOES *g* COME FROM?

The previous discussion assumed that dividends grow at the rate g. We now want to estimate this rate of growth. Consider a business whose earnings next year are expected to be the same as earnings this year unless a *net investment* is made. This situation is quite plausible because net investment is equal to gross, or total, investment less depreciation. A net investment of zero occurs when *total investment* equals depreciation. If total investment is equal to depreciation, the firm's physical plant is just maintained, consistent with no growth in earnings.

Net investment will be positive only if some earnings are not paid out as dividends, that is, only if some earnings are retained.[2] This leads to the following equation:

$$
\underset{\substack{\text{Earnings} \\ \text{next} \\ \text{year}}}{} = \underset{\substack{\text{Earnings} \\ \text{this} \\ \text{year}}}{} + \underbrace{\underset{\substack{\text{Retained} \\ \text{earnings} \\ \text{this year}}}{} \times \underset{\substack{\text{Return on} \\ \text{retained} \\ \text{earnings}}}{}}_{\text{Increase in earnings}} \qquad (9.5)
$$

The increase in earnings is a function of both the *retained earnings* and the *return on the retained earnings*.

We now divide both sides of Equation 9.5 by earnings this year, yielding

$$
\frac{\text{Earnings next year}}{\text{Earnings this year}} = \frac{\text{Earnings this year}}{\text{Earnings this year}} + \left(\frac{\text{Retained earnings this year}}{\text{Earnings this year}} \right) \qquad (9.6)
$$
$$
\times \text{ Return on retained earnings}
$$

The left-hand side of Equation 9.6 is simply one plus the growth rate in earnings, which we write as $1 + g$. The ratio of retained earnings to earnings is called the **retention ratio**. Thus, we can write

$$
1 + g = 1 + \text{Retention ratio} \times \text{Return on retained earnings} \qquad (9.7)
$$

It is difficult for a financial analyst to determine the return expected on currently retained earnings, because the details on forthcoming projects are not generally public information. However, it is frequently assumed that projects selected in the current year have an anticipated return equal to returns from past projects. Here, we can estimate the anticipated return on current retained earnings by the historical **return on equity** or ROE. After all, ROE is simply the return on the firm's entire equity, which is the return on the cumulation of all the firm's past projects.

From Equation 9.7, we have a simple way to estimate growth in earnings:

Formula for Firm's Growth Rate:
$$
g = \text{Retention ratio} \times \text{Return on retained earnings (ROE)} \qquad (9.8)
$$

The estimate for the growth rate in earnings, g, is also the estimate for the growth rate in dividends under the common assumption that the ratio of dividends to earnings is held constant.[3]

**EXAMPLE
9.4**

Earnings Growth Pagemaster Enterprises just reported earnings of $2 million. The firm plans to retain 40 percent of its earnings in all years going forward. In other words, the retention ratio is 40 percent. We could also say that 60 percent of earnings will be paid out as dividends. The ratio of dividends to earnings is often called the **payout ratio**, so the payout ratio for Pagemaster is

(continued)

---

[2]We ignore the issuance of new shares or the buyback of existing shares of stock. The dividend discount model is valid under both situations. However, these possibilities are considered in later chapters.

[3]In Chapter 3, we also discussed methods for g's calculation.

60 percent. The historical return on equity (ROE) has been .16, a figure expected to continue into the future. How much will earnings grow over the coming year?

We first perform the calculation without reference to Equation 9.8. Then we use (9.8) as a check.

Calculation without Reference to Equation 9.8   The firm will retain $800,000 (= 40% × $2 million). Assuming that historical ROE is an appropriate estimate for future returns, the anticipated increase in earnings is:

$$\$800,000 \times .16 = \$128,000$$

The percentage growth in earnings is:

$$\frac{\text{Change in earnings}}{\text{Total earnings}} = \frac{\$128,000}{\$2 \text{ million}} = .064$$

This implies that earnings in one year will be $2,128,000 (=$2,000,000 × 1.064).

Check Using Equation 9.8   We use g = Retention ratio × ROE. We have:

$$g = .4 \times .16 = .064$$

Since Pagemaster's ratio of dividends to earnings, that is, its payout ratio, is constant going forward, .064 is the growth rate of *both* earnings and dividends.

WHERE DOES *R* COME FROM?

Thus far, we have taken the required return or discount rate, R, as given. Conceptually, the required return is the return on assets with the same risk as the firm's shares. We show how to estimate R in Chapter 13. For now, we want to examine the implications of the dividend growth model for this required return. Earlier, we calculated the price of the stock today, P_0, as:

$$P_0 = \text{Div}/(R - g)$$

Rearranging the equation to solve for R, we get:

$$R - g = \text{Div}/P_0 \qquad \qquad (9.9)$$
$$R = \text{Div}/P_0 + g$$

Equation 9.9 tells us that the required return, R, has two components. The first of these, Div/P_0, is called the **dividend yield**. Because this is calculated as the expected cash dividend divided by the current price, it is conceptually similar to the current yield on a bond.

The second part of the total return is the expected growth rate, g. As we will verify shortly, the dividend growth rate is also the stock price's growth rate. Thus, this growth rate can be interpreted as the **capital gains yield**, that is, the rate at which the value of the investment grows.

To illustrate the components of the required return, suppose we observe a stock selling for $20 per share. The next dividend is expected to be $1 per share. You think that the dividend will grow by 10 percent per year more or less indefinitely. What expected return does this stock offer you?

The dividend growth model calculates total return as:

$$R = \text{Dividend yield} + \text{Capital gains yield}$$
$$R = \quad \text{Div}/P_0 \quad + \quad \quad g$$

In this case, total return works out to be:

$$R = \$1/20 + 10\%$$
$$= 5\% + 10\%$$
$$= 15\%$$

This stock, therefore, has an expected return of 15 percent.

We can verify this answer by calculating the price in one year, P_1, using 15 percent as the required expected return. Since the dividend expected to be received in one year is $1 and the expected growth rate of dividends is 10 percent, the dividend expected to be received in two years, Div_2, is $1.10. Based on the dividend growth model, the stock price in one year will be:

$$P_1 = Div_2/(R - g)$$
$$= \$1.10/(.15 - .10)$$
$$= \$1.10/.05$$
$$= \$22$$

Notice that this $22 is $20 × 1.1, so the stock price has grown by 10 percent as it should. That is, the capital gains yield is 10 percent, which equals the growth rate in dividends.

What is the investor's total expected return? If you pay $20 for the stock today, you will get a $1 dividend at the end of the year, and you will have a $22 − 20 = $2 gain. Your dividend yield is thus $1/20 = 5 percent. Your capital gains yield is $2/20 = 10 percent, so your total expected return would be 5 percent + 10 percent = 15 percent, just as we calculated above.

To get a feel for actual numbers in this context, consider that, according to the 2014 *Value Line Investment Survey,* Procter & Gamble's dividends were expected to grow by 7.0 percent over the next 5 or so years, compared to a historical growth rate of 9.5 percent over the preceding 5 years and 10.5 percent over the preceding 10 years. In 2014, the projected dividend for the coming year was given as $2.60. The stock price at that time was $84.08 per share. What is the expected return investors require on P&G? Here, the dividend yield is 3.1 (=2.60/84.08) percent and the capital gains yield is 7.0 percent, giving a total required return of 10.1 percent on P&G stock.

<table>
<tr><td>**EXAMPLE**
9.5</td><td>**Calculating the Required Return** Pagemaster Enterprises, the company examined in Example 9.4, has 1,000,000 shares of stock outstanding. The stock is selling at $10. What is the required return on the stock?

The payout ratio is the ratio of dividends/earnings. Because Pagemaster's retention ratio is 40 percent, the payout ratio, which is 1 − Retention ratio, is 60 percent. Recall both that Pagemaster just reported earnings of $2,000,000 and that the firm's growth rate is .064.

Earnings a year from now will be $2,128,000 (=$2,000,000 × 1.064), implying that dividends will be $1,276,800 (=.60 × $2,128,000). Dividends per share will be $1.28 (=$1,276,800/1,000,000). Given that $g = .064$, we calculate R from (9.9) as follows:

$$.192 = \frac{\$1.28}{\$10.00} + .064$$</td></tr>
</table>

A HEALTHY SENSE OF SKEPTICISM

It is important to emphasize that our approach merely *estimates* g; our approach does not *determine* g precisely. We mentioned earlier that our estimate of g is based on a number of assumptions. For example, we assume that the return on reinvestment of future retained earnings is equal to the firm's past ROE. We assume that the future retention ratio is equal to the past retention ratio. Our estimate for *g* will be off if these assumptions prove to be wrong.

Unfortunately, the determination of *R* is highly dependent on *g*. For example, if *g* for Pagemaster is estimated to be 0, *R* equals 12.8 percent (= $1.28/$10.00). If *g* is estimated to be 12 percent, *R* equals 24.8 percent (= $1.28/$10.00 + 12%). Thus, one should view estimates of *R* with a healthy sense of skepticism.

Because of the preceding, some financial economists generally argue that the estimation error for *R* for a single security is too large to be practical. Therefore, they suggest calculating the average *R* for an entire industry. This *R* would then be used to discount the dividends of a particular stock in the same industry.

One should be particularly skeptical of two polar cases when estimating *R* for individual securities. First, consider a firm not currently paying a dividend. If the firm initiates a dividend at some point, its dividend growth rate over the interval becomes *infinite*. Thus, Equation 9.9 must be used with extreme caution here, if at all—a point we emphasize later in this chapter.

Second, we mentioned earlier that share price is infinite when *g* is equal to *R*. Because stock prices are never infinite in the real world, an analyst whose estimate of *g* for a particular firm is equal to or above *R* must have made a mistake. Most likely, the analyst's high estimate for *g* is correct for the next few years. However, firms simply cannot maintain an abnormally high growth rate *forever*. The analyst's error was to use a short-run estimate of *g* in a model requiring a perpetual growth rate.

DIVIDENDS OR EARNINGS: WHICH TO DISCOUNT?

As mentioned earlier, this chapter applied the growing perpetuity formula to the valuation of stocks. In our application, we discounted dividends, not earnings. This is sensible since investors select a stock for the cash they can get out of it. They only get two things out of a stock: dividends and the ultimate sales price, which is determined by what future investors expect to receive in dividends.

The calculated stock price would usually be too high were earnings to be discounted instead of dividends. As we saw in our estimation of a firm's growth rate, only a portion of earnings goes to the stockholders as dividends. The remainder is retained to generate future dividends. In our model, retained earnings are equal to the firm's investment. To discount earnings instead of dividends would be to ignore the investment that a firm must make today in order to generate future earnings and dividends.

THE NO-DIVIDEND FIRM

Students frequently ask the following question: If the dividend discount model is correct, why aren't no-dividend stocks selling at zero? This is a good question and gets at the goals of the firm. A firm with many growth opportunities is faced with a dilemma. The firm can pay out dividends now, or it can forgo dividends now so that it can make investments that will generate even greater dividends in the future.[4] This is often a painful choice, because a strategy of dividend deferment may be optimal yet unpopular among certain stockholders.

Many firms choose to pay no dividends—and these firms sell at positive prices. For example, most Internet firms, such as Amazon.com, Google, eBay, and Facebook

---

[4]A third alternative is to issue stock so that the firm has enough cash both to pay dividends and to invest. This possibility is explored in a later chapter.

pay no dividends. Rational shareholders believe that they will either receive dividends at some point or they will receive something just as good. That is, the firm will be acquired in a merger, with the stockholders receiving either cash or shares of stock at that time.

Of course, actual application of the dividend discount model is difficult for no-dividend firms. Clearly, the model for constant growth of dividends does not apply. Though the differential growth model can work in theory, the difficulties of estimating the date of the first dividend, the growth rate of dividends after that date, and the ultimate merger price make application of the model quite difficult in reality.

Empirical evidence suggests that firms with high growth rates are likely to pay lower dividends, a result consistent with the above analysis. For example, consider Microsoft Corporation. The company started in 1975 and grew rapidly for many years. It paid its first dividend in 2003, though it was a multi-billion-dollar company (in both sales and market value of stockholders' equity) prior to that date. Why did it wait so long to pay a dividend? It waited because it had so many positive growth opportunities, such as new software products, to fund.

9.3 Comparables

So far in this chapter, we have valued stocks by discounting dividends. Practitioners often value by comparables as well. The comparables approach is similar to valuation in real estate. If your neighbor's home just sold for $200,000 and it has similar size and amenities to your home, your home is probably worth around $200,000 also. In the stock market, comparable firms are assumed to have similar *multiples*. To see how the comparables approach works, let's look at perhaps the most common multiple, the price-to-earnings (PE) multiple, or PE ratio.

PRICE-TO-EARNINGS RATIO

A stock's price-to-earnings ratio is, as the name suggests, the ratio of the stock's price to its earnings per share. For example, if the stock of Sun Aerodynamic Systems (SAS) is selling at $27.00 per share and its earnings per share over the last year was $4.50, SAS's PE ratio would be 6 (=27/4.50).

It is generally assumed that similar firms have similar PE ratios. For example, imagine the average price-to-earnings (PE) ratio across all publicly traded companies in the specialty retail industry is 12 and a particular company in the industry has earnings of $10 million. If this company is judged to be similar to the rest of the industry, one might estimate the company's value to be $120 million (=12 × $10 million).

Valuation via PE certainly looks easier than valuation via discounted dividends, since the discounted dividend approach calls for estimates of yearly dividends. But is the PE approach better? That depends on the similarity across comparables.

On a particular day in September 2014, *The Wall Street Journal* reported Google's PE ratio to be 30. On that same day, IBM's PE was 12, Hewlett-Packard's was 13, Apple's was 16, and Microsoft's was 17. Why would different stocks in the same industry trade at different PE ratios? Do the differences imply that Google was overpriced and IBM was underpriced? Or are there rational reasons for the differences?

The dividend discount model of Equations 9.1 and 9.4 implies that a firm's PE ratio is related to the value of its future projects. As an example, consider two firms, each having just reported earnings per share of $1. However, one firm has many new projects, each with a positive net present value (NPV), while the other firm has no new projects at all. The firm with the valuable projects should sell at a higher price because an investor is buying both current income of $1 and the new projects.

Suppose that the firm with the projects sells for $16 and the other firm sells for $8. The $1 earnings per share number appears in the denominator of the PE ratio for both firms. Thus, the PE ratio is 16 for the firm with the valuable projects, but only 8 for the firm without the projects.

This explanation seems to hold fairly well in the real world. Electronics and other high-tech stocks generally sell at high PE ratios because they are perceived to have many vaulable projects. In fact, some technology stocks sell at high prices even though the companies have never earned a profit. The PE ratios of these companies are infinite. Conversely, railroads, utilities, and steel companies sell at lower PE ratio because of fewer valuable projects. Table 9.1 contains PE ratios in 2014 for some well-known companies and the S&P 500 Index. Notice the variations across industries.

There are at least two additional factors explaining the PE ratio. The first is the discount rate, R. Since R appears in the denominator of the dividend discount model (in Equation 9.1), the formula implies that the PE ratio is *negatively* related to the firm's discount rate. We have already suggested that the discount rate is positively related to the stock's risk or variability. Thus, the PE ratio is negatively related to the stock's risk. To see that this is a sensible result, consider two firms, A and B, where the stock market *expects* both firms to have annual earnings of $1 per share forever. However, the earnings of Firm A are known with certainty while the earnings of Firm B are quite variable. A rational stockholder is likely to pay more for a share of Firm A because of the absence of risk. If a share of Firm A sells at a higher price and both firms have the same EPS, the PE ratio of Firm A must be higher.

The second additional factor concerns the firm's choice of accounting methods. As an example, consider two identical firms, C and D. Firm C uses LIFO and reports earnings of $2 per share. Firm D uses the less conservative accounting assumptions of FIFO and reports earnings of $3 per share. The market knows that both firms are identical and prices both at $18 per share. The price–earnings ratio is 9 (= $18/$2) for firm C and 6 (= $18/$3) for Firm D. Thus, the firm with the more conservative principles has the higher PE ratio.

Table 9.1
Selected PE Ratios, 2014

Company	Industry	PE Ratio
Chubb	Insurance	11
Coca-Cola	Beverages	21
General Motors	Automotive	13
Goldman Sachs	Financial services	12
Whirlpool	Home appliances	16
Yahoo!	Technology	34
S&P 500 average	n/a	18.79

In conclusion, we have argued that a stock's PE ratio is likely a function of three factors:

1. *Investment opportunities.* Companies with opportunities to invest in projects with large, positive NPVs are likely to have high PE ratios.
2. *Risk.* Low-risk stocks are likely to have high PE ratios.
3. *Accounting practices.* Firms following conservative accounting practices will likely have high PE ratios.

Which of these factors is most important in the real world? The consensus among finance professionals is that investment opportunities typically have the biggest impact on PE ratios. For example, high-tech companies generally have higher PE ratios than, say, utilities, because utilities have fewer valuable investment opportunities, even though utilities typically have lower risk. And, within industries, differences in investment opportunities also generate the biggest differences in PE ratios. In our example at the beginning of this section, Google's high PE is almost certainly due to its investment opportunities, not its low risk or its accounting conservatism. In fact, due to its youth, the risk of Google is likely higher than the risk of many of its competitors. Microsoft's PE is lower than Google's PE because Microsoft's investment opportunities are a small fraction of its existing business lines. However, Microsoft had a much higher PE decades ago, when it had huge investment opportunities but little in the way of existing business.

Thus, while multiples such as the PE ratio can be used to price stocks, care must be taken. Firms in the same industry are likely to have different multiples if they have different investment opportunities, risk levels and accounting treatments. Average multiples should not be calculated across all firms in any industry. Rather, an average multiple should be calculated only across those firms in an industry with similar characteristics.

There are a number of ways to calculate the price-to-earnings ratio, with perhaps the biggest difference involving the denominator. Imagine that a company's stock is selling at $20 today, with the company just reporting earnings per share (EPS) of $2 for the last year. However, the consensus among analysts is that the firm will report earnings next year of $2.50. Some sources calculate the PE ratio as the ratio of current price to the EPS over the last 12 months. The TTM (for "trailing twelve months") earnings would be $2 in this example, and the trailing PE ratio would be 10 (=$20/$2). Other sources use forward earnings—that is, earnings forecasted over the next year—to calculate a PE ratio. The forward PE would be 8 (=$20/$2.50) here.

Which approach makes more sense? There is no right answer. On the one hand, investors should discount future cash flows, not past cash flows, to value stocks, implying that the forward PE is more meaningful. On the other hand, trailing earnings reflect what actually happened, while forward earnings are merely forecasts. So, while we can't say which variant of the PE ratio is more appropriate in a particular situation, you should always be aware of how a particular PE has been calculated.

Often we will be interested in valuing newer companies that both don't pay dividends and are not yet profitable, meaning that earnings are negative. What do we do then? One answer is to use the price–sales ratio. As the name suggests, this ratio is the price per share on the stock divided by sales per share. You use this ratio just like you use the PE ratio, except you use sales per share instead of earnings per share. As with PE ratios, price–sales ratios vary depending on company age and industry. Typical values are in the .8–2.0 range, but they can be much higher for younger, faster-growing companies.

ENTERPRISE VALUE RATIOS

The PE ratio is an equity ratio. That is, the numerator is the price per share of *stock* and the denominator is the earnings per share of *stock*. In addition, practitioners often use ratios involving both equity and debt. Perhaps the most common is the enterprise value (EV) to EBITDA ratio. Enterprise value is equal to the market value of the firm's equity plus the market value of the firm's debt minus cash. Recall, EBITDA stands for earnings before interest, taxes, depreciation, and amortization.

For example, imagine that Illinois Food Products Co. (IFPC) has equity worth $800 million, debt worth $300 million, and cash of $100 million. The enterprise value here is $1 billion (=800 + 300 − 100). Further imagine the firm has the following income statement:

Revenue	$700 million
−Cost of goods sold	−500 million
Earnings before interest, taxes, depreciation, and amortization (EBITDA)	$200 million
−Depreciation and amortization	−100 million
−Interest	−24 million
Pre-tax income	$76 million
−Taxes (@ 30%)	−22.8 million
Profit after taxes	$53.2 million

The EV to EBITDA ratio is 5 (=1 billion/200 million). Note that all the items in the income statement below EBITDA are ignored when calculating this ratio.

As with PE ratios, it is generally assumed that similar firms have similar EV/EBITDA ratios. For example, imagine that the average EV/EBITDA ratio in an industry is 6. If QRT Corporation, a firm in the industry with EBITDA of $50 million, is judged to be similar to the rest of the industry, its enterprise value might be estimated at $300 million (=6 × $50). Now imagine that QRT has $75 million of debt and $25 million of cash. Given our estimate of QRT's enterprise value, QRT's stock would be worth $250 million (=$300 − 75 + 25).

A number of questions arise with value ratios:

1. Is there any advantage to the EV/EBITDA ratio over the PE ratio? Yes. Companies in the same industry may differ by leverage, i.e., the ratio of debt to equity. As you will learn in Chapter 16, leverage increases the risk of equity, impacting the discount rate, R. Thus, while firms in the same industry may be otherwise comparable, they are likely to have different PE ratios if they have different degrees of leverage. Since enterprise value includes debt and equity, the impact of leverage on the EV/EBITDA ratio is less.[5]

2. Why is EBITDA used in the denominator? The numerator and denominator of a ratio should be consistent. Since the numerator of the PE ratio is the price of a share of *stock,* it makes sense that the denominator is the earnings per share (EPS) of *stock.* That is, interest is specifically subtracted before EPS is calculated. By contrast, since EV involves the sum of debt and equity, it is sensible that the denominator is unaffected by interest payments. This is the case with EBITDA since, as its name implies, earnings are calculated before interest is taken out.

---

[5]However, leverage does impact the ratio of EV to EBITDA to some extent. As we discuss in Chapter 16, leverage creates a tax shield, increasing EV. Since leverage should not impact EBITDA, the ratio should increase with leverage.

3. Why does the denominator ignore depreciation and amortization? Many practitioners argue that, since depreciation and amortization are not cash flows, earnings should be calculated before taking out depreciation and amortization. In other words, depreciation and amortization merely reflect the sunk cost of a previous purchase. However, this view is by no means universal. Others point out that depreciable assets will eventually be replaced in an ongoing business. Since depreciation charges reflect the cost of future replacement, it can be argued that these charges should be considered in a calculation of income.

4. What other denominators are used in value ratios? Among others, practitioners may use EBIT (earnings before interest and taxes), EBITA (earnings before interest, taxes, and amortization), and free cash flow.

5. Why is cash subtracted out? Many firms seem to hold amounts of cash well in excess of what is needed. For example, Microsoft held tens of billions of dollars of cash and short-term investments throughout the last decade, far more than many analysts believed was optimal. Since an enterprise value ratio should reflect the ability of *productive* assets to create earnings or cash flow, cash should be subtracted out when calculating the ratio. However, the viewpoint that all cash should be ignored can be criticized. Some cash holdings are necessary to run a business, and this amount of cash should be included in EV.

9.4 Valuing Stocks Using Free Cash Flows

In Chapters 5 and 6, we valued corporate projects by discounting the projects' cash flows. Cash flows were determined by a top-down approach beginning with estimates of revenues and expenses. So far in this chapter, we have discounted dividends to value a single share of stock. As an alternative, one can value entire firms by discounting their free cash flows in a manner analogous to the project valuation of Chapters 5 and 6.

As an example, consider Global Harmonic Control Systems (GHCS). Revenues, which are forecasted to be $500 million in one year, are expected to grow at 10 percent per year for the two years after that, 8 percent per year for the next two years, and 6 percent per year after that. Expenses including depreciation are 60 percent of revenues. Net investment, including net working capital and capital spending less depreciation, is 10 percent of revenues. Because all costs are proportional to revenues, free cash flow grows at the same rate as do revenues. GHCS is an all-equity firm with 12 million shares outstanding. A discount rate of 16 percent is appropriate for a firm of GHCS's risk.

The relevant numbers for the first five years, rounded to two decimals, are:

Year (000,000)	1	2	3	4	5
Revenues	500.0	550.0	605.0	653.4	705.67
−Expenses	300.0	330.0	363.0	392.04	423.40
Earnings before taxes	200.0	220.0	242.0	261.36	282.27
−Taxes (@ 0.40)	80.0	88.0	96.8	104.54	112.91
Earnings after taxes	120.0	132.0	145.2	156.82	169.36
−Net investment	50.0	55.0	60.5	65.34	70.57
Free cash flow	70.0	77.0	84.7	91.48	98.79

Since free cash flow grows at 6 percent per year after Year 5, net cash flow in Year 6 is forecasted to be $104.72 (=98.79 × 1.06). Using the growing perpetuity formula, we can calculate the present value as of Year 5 of all future cash flows to be $1047.22 million (=$104.72/(.16 − .06)).

The present value as of today of that terminal value is:

$$\$1047.22 \times \frac{1}{(1.16)^5} = \$498.59 \text{ million}$$

The present value of the free cash flows during the first five years is:

$$\frac{\$70}{1.16} + \frac{\$77}{(1.16)^2} + \frac{\$84.7}{(1.16)^3} + \frac{\$91.48}{(1.16)^4} + \frac{\$98.79}{(1.16)^5} = \$269.39 \text{ million}$$

Adding in the terminal value, today's value of the firm is $767.98 million (=$269.39 + 498.59). Given the number of shares outstanding, the price per share is $64 (=$767.98/12).

The above calculation assumes a growing perpetuity after Year 5. However, we pointed out in the previous section that stocks are often valued by multiples. An investor might estimate the terminal value of GHCS via a multiple, rather than the growing perpetuity formula. For example, suppose that the price–earnings ratio for comparable firms in GHCS's industry is 7.

Since earnings after tax in Year 5 are $169.36, using the PE multiple of 7, the value of the firm at Year 5 would be estimated as $1,185.52 million (=$169.36 × 7).

The firm's value today is:

$$\frac{\$70}{1.16} + \frac{\$77}{(1.16)^2} + \frac{\$84.7}{(1.16)^3} + \frac{\$91.48}{(1.16)^4} + \frac{\$98.79}{(1.16)^5} + \frac{\$1,185.52}{(1.16)^5} = \$833.83 \text{ million}$$

With 12 million shares outstanding, the price per share of GHCS would be $69.49 (=$833.83/12).

Now we have two estimates of the value of a share of equity in GHCS. The different estimates reflect the different ways of calculating terminal value. Using the constant growth discounted cash flow method for terminal value our estimate of the equity value per share of GHCS is $64, and using the PE comparable method our estimate is $69.49. There is no best method. If the comparable firms were all identical to GHCS, perhaps the PE method would be best. Unfortunately, firms are not identical. On the other hand, if we were very sure of the terminal date and the growth in subsequent cash flows, perhaps the constant growth method would be best. In practice, both methods are used.

Conceptually, the dividend discount model, the comparables method, and the firm cash flow model are mutually consistent and can be used to determine the value of a share of stock. In practice, the dividend discount model is especially useful for firms paying steady dividends and the comparables method is useful for firms with similar investment opportunities. The firm cash flow model is helpful for non-dividend paying firms with external financing needs.

9.5 The Stock Markets

The stock market consists of a **primary market** and a **secondary market**. In the primary, or new-issue market, shares of stock are first brought to the market and sold to investors. In the secondary market, existing shares are traded among investors. In the primary market, companies sell securities to raise money. We will discuss this process in detail in a later chapter.

We therefore focus mainly on secondary-market activity in this section. We conclude with a discussion of how stock prices are quoted in the financial press.

DEALERS AND BROKERS

Because most securities transactions involve dealers and brokers, it is important to understand exactly what is meant by the terms *dealer* and *broker*. A **dealer** maintains an inventory and stands ready to buy and sell at any time. In contrast, **a broker** brings buyers and sellers together but does not maintain an inventory. For example, when we speak of used car dealers and real estate brokers, we recognize that the used car dealer maintains an inventory, whereas the real estate broker does not.

In the securities markets, a dealer stands ready to buy securities from investors wishing to sell them and to sell securities to investors wishing to buy them. The price the dealer is willing to pay is called the *bid price*. The price at which the dealer will sell is called the *ask price* (sometimes called the *asked, offered,* or *offering price*). The difference between the bid and ask prices is called the *spread,* and it is the basic source of dealer profits.

How big is the bid-ask spread on your favorite stock? Check out the latest quotes at **www.bloomberg .com**.

Dealers exist in all areas of the economy, not just the stock markets. For example, your local college bookstore is probably both a primary and a secondary market textbook dealer. If you buy a new book, this is a primary market transaction. If you buy a used book, this is a secondary market transaction, and you pay the store's ask price. If you sell the book back, you receive the store's bid price, often half of the ask price. The bookstore's spread is the difference between the two prices.

In contrast, a securities broker arranges transactions between investors, matching those wishing to buy securities with those wishing to sell securities. The distinctive characteristic of security brokers is that they do not buy or sell securities for their own accounts. Facilitating trades by others is their business.

ORGANIZATION OF THE NYSE

The New York Stock Exchange, or NYSE, popularly known as the Big Board, recently celebrated its bicentennial. It has occupied its current location on Wall Street since the turn of the twentieth century. Measured in terms of dollar volume of activity and the total value of shares listed, it is the largest stock market in the world.

Members   The NYSE has 1,366 exchange **members**. Prior to 2006, the exchange members were said to own "seats" on the exchange, and, collectively, the members of the exchange were also the owners. For this and other reasons, seats were valuable and were bought and sold fairly regularly. Seat prices reached a record $4 million in 2005.

In 2006, all of this changed when the NYSE became a publicly owned corporation. Naturally, its stock is listed on the NYSE. Now, instead of purchasing seats, exchange members must purchase trading licenses, the number of which is still limited to 1,366. In 2014, a license cost $40,000 a year. Having a license entitles you to buy and sell securities on the floor of the exchange. Different members play different roles in this regard.

On April 4, 2007, the NYSE grew even larger when it merged with Euronext to form NYSE Euronext. Euronext was a stock exchange in Amsterdam, with subsidiaries in Belgium, France, Portugal, and the United Kingdom. With the merger, NYSE Euronext became the world's "first global exchange." Further expansion occurred in 2008 when NYSE Euronext merged with the American Stock Exchange. Then, in November 2013, the acquisition of the NYSE by the Intercontinental Exchange (ICE) was completed. ICE, which was founded in May 2000, was originally a commodities exchange, but its rapid growth gave it the necessary $8.2 billion for the acquisition of the NYSE.

With electronic trading, orders to buy and orders to sell are submitted to the exchange. Orders are compared by a computer and whenever there is a match, the orders are executed with no human intervention. Most trades on the NYSE occur this way. For orders that are not handled electronically, the NYSE relies on its license holders. There are three different types of license holders, **designated market makers (DMMs)**, **floor brokers**, and **supplemental liquidity providers (SLPs)**.

The DMMs, formerly known as "specialists," act as dealers in particular stocks. Typically, each stock on the NYSE is assigned to a single DMM. As a dealer, a DMM maintains a two-sided market, meaning that the DMM continually posts and updates bid and ask prices. By doing so, the DMM ensures that there is always a buyer or seller available, thereby promoting market liquidity.

Floor brokers execute trades for customers, trying to get the best price possible. Floor brokers are generally employees of large brokerage firms such as Merrill Lynch, the wealth management division of Bank of America. The interaction between floor brokers and DMMs is the key to non-electronic trading on the NYSE. We discuss this interaction in detail in just a moment.

The SLPs are essentially investment firms that agree to be active participants in stocks assigned to them. Their job is to regularly make a one-sided market (i.e., offering to either buy or sell). They trade purely for their own accounts (using their own money), so they do not represent customers. They are given a small rebate on their buys and sells, thereby encouraging them to be more aggressive. The NYSE's goal is to generate as much liquidity as possible, which makes it easier for ordinary investors to quickly buy and sell at prevailing prices. Unlike DMMs and floor brokers, SLPs do not operate on the floor of the stock exchange.

In recent years, floor brokers have become less important on the exchange floor because of the efficient SuperDOT system (the *DOT* stands for Designated Order Turnaround), which allows orders to be transmitted electronically directly to the DMM. Additionally, the NYSE has introduced NYSE Direct+, an electronic platform for trades. The average time for a trade on the NYSE Direct+ platform is less than 1 second. Electronic trading now accounts for a substantial percentage of all trading on the NYSE, particularly on smaller orders.

Finally, a small number of NYSE members are floor traders who independently trade for their own accounts. Floor traders try to anticipate temporary price fluctuations and profit from them by buying low and selling high. In recent decades, the number of floor traders has declined substantially, suggesting that it has become increasingly difficult to profit from short-term trading on the exchange floor.

Operations Now that we have a basic idea of how the NYSE is organized and who the major players are, we turn to the question of how trading actually takes place. Fundamentally, the business of the NYSE is to attract and process **order flow**. The term *order flow* means the flow of customer orders to buy and sell stocks. The customers of the NYSE are the millions of individual investors and tens of thousands of institutional investors who place their orders to buy and sell shares in NYSE-listed companies. The NYSE has been quite successful in attracting order flow. Currently, it is common for more than one billion shares to change hands in a single day.

Floor Activity It is quite likely that you have seen footage of the NYSE trading floor on television, or you may have visited the NYSE and viewed exchange floor activity from the visitors' gallery. Either way, you would have seen a big room, about the size of a basketball gym. This big room is called, technically, "the Big Room." There are a couple of other, smaller rooms that you normally don't see, one of which is called "the Garage" because that is literally what it was before it was taken over for trading.

On the floor of the exchange are a number of stations, each with a roughly figure-eight shape. These stations have multiple counters with numerous terminal screens above and on the sides. People operate behind and in front of the counters in relatively stationary positions.

Other people move around on the exchange floor, frequently returning to the many telephones positioned along the exchange walls. In all, you may be reminded of worker ants moving around an ant colony. It is natural to wonder, "What are all those people doing down there (and why are so many wearing funny-looking coats)?"

As an overview of exchange floor activity, here is a quick look at what goes on. Each of the counters is a **DMM's post**. DMMs normally operate in front of their posts to monitor and manage trading in the stocks assigned to them. Clerical employees working for the DMMs operate behind the counter. Moving from the many workstations lining the walls of the exchange out to the exchange floor and back again are swarms of floor brokers, receiving customer orders, walking out to DMMs' posts where the orders can be executed, and returning to confirm order executions and receive new customer orders.

To better understand activity on the NYSE trading floor, imagine yourself as a floor broker. Your phone clerk has just handed you an order to sell 20,000 shares of Walmart for a customer of the brokerage company that employs you. The customer wants to sell the stock at the best possible price as soon as possible. You immediately walk (running violates exchange rules) to the DMM's post where Walmart stock is traded.

As you approach the DMM's post where Walmart is traded, you check the terminal screen for information on the current market price. The screen reveals that the last executed trade was at $60.10 per share and that the DMM is bidding $60 per share. You could immediately sell to the DMM at $60 per share, but that would be too easy.

Instead, as the customer's representative, you are obligated to get the best possible price. It is your job to "work" the order, and your job depends on providing satisfactory order execution service. So, you look around for another broker who represents a customer who wants to buy Walmart stock. Luckily, you quickly find another broker at the DMM's post with an order to buy 20,000 shares. Noticing that the DMM is asking $60.10 per share, you both agree to execute your orders with each other at a price of $60.05 per share. This price is exactly halfway between the DMM's bid and ask prices, and it saves each of your customers $.05 × 20,000 = $1,000 as compared to dealing at the posted prices.

For a very actively traded stock, there may be many buyers and sellers around the DMM's post, and most of the trading will be done directly between brokers. This is called trading in the "crowd." In such cases, the DMM's responsibility is to maintain order and to make sure that all buyers and sellers receive a fair price. In other words, the DMM essentially functions as a referee.

More often, however, there will be no crowd at the DMM's post. Going back to our Walmart example, suppose you are unable to quickly find another broker with an order to buy 20,000 shares. Because you have an order to sell immediately, you may have no choice but to sell to the DMM at the bid price of $60 per share. In this case, the need to execute an order quickly takes priority, and the DMM provides the liquidity necessary to allow immediate order execution.

Finally, note that colored coats are worn by many of the people on the floor of the exchange. The color of the coat indicates the person's job or position. Clerks, runners, visitors, exchange officials, and so on wear particular colors to identify themselves. Also, things can get a little hectic on a busy day, with the result that good clothing doesn't last long; the cheap coats offer some protection.

TYPES OF ORDERS

The preceding example involving Walmart stock considers how trades are executed on the NYSE. We now want to discuss a related issue: What sort of trades can an investor make? In the Walmart example, we said that the customer placing the order to sell 20,000 shares of Walmart "wants to sell the stock at the best possible price as soon as possible." An order such as this is called a **market order** because the stock will be sold at or near the current market price. Another investor might want to buy 10,000 shares of, say, Apple Inc. under the same terms. This order is termed a market order to buy.

Are these the only orders that a customer can place? No. Consider an investor who, for whatever reason, wants to own Walmart stock but is not willing to pay as much as $60 per share for it. He might place a **limit order** to buy for, say, $55. This means that the customer is directing his broker only to buy the stock at a price of $55 or less. Because the customer's trade will only get filled at a price of $55 or less, the customer will never get to buy the stock if the price stays above $55. Conversely, imagine another investor would like to sell her Walmart stock, but not for a price as low as $60. She might place a limit order to sell for, say, $65, meaning that her trade will get executed only at a price of $65 or more.

Are there other types of trades? Yes. Imagine an owner of Walmart stock who, while generally optimistic about Walmart's business prospects, is, nevertheless, worried about the possibility of a big price decline. He might place a **stop order** to sell at, say, $50. Here, the order will be executed as a *market order* to sell once the trigger price of $50 is reached. This means that, once another trade occurs at $50 or below, the broker will try to sell the stock at the best possible price as soon as possible. Does this mean that the customer is guaranteed a price of at least $50? Unfortunately, no. In a rapidly falling market, once the price of $50 is reached, the next price might be significantly below $50, implying that the customer might receive a price well below $50. Conversely, another customer might want to execute a stop order to buy at, say $60, implying her stop order will be converted to a market order to buy once the price of $60 is reached.

One more thing is worth mentioning. There is a time dimension to limit and stop orders. That is, one can place, for example, a **day order**, meaning that the limit or stop order will be canceled if it is not executed by the end of the trading day. Conversely, a **good-til-canceled order**, as its name suggests, remains open until the customer specifically cancels it.[6]

NASDAQ OPERATIONS

In terms of total dollar volume of trading, the second largest stock market in the United States is NASDAQ (say "Naz-dak"). The somewhat odd name originally was an acronym for the National Association of Securities Dealers Automated Quotations system, but NASDAQ is now a name in its own right.

Introduced in 1971, the NASDAQ market is a computer network of securities dealers and others that disseminates timely security price quotes to computer screens

---

[6]A more detailed discussion of these and other orders can be found in Bradford Jordan, Thomas Miller, and Steve Dolvin, *Fundamentals of Investments*, 7th ed. (New York: McGraw-Hill, 2015).

worldwide. NASDAQ dealers act as market makers for securities listed on NASDAQ. As market makers, NASDAQ dealers post bid and ask prices at which they accept sell and buy orders, respectively. With each price quote, they also post the number of shares that they obligate themselves to trade at their quoted prices.

Like NYSE DMMs, NASDAQ market makers trade on an inventory basis—that is, using their inventory as a buffer to absorb buy and sell order imbalances. Unlike the NYSE DMM system, NASDAQ features multiple market makers for actively traded stocks. Thus, there are two key differences between the NYSE and NASDAQ:

1. NASDAQ is a computer network and has no physical location where trading takes place.
2. NASDAQ has a multiple market maker system rather than a DMM system.

Traditionally, a securities market largely characterized by dealers who buy and sell securities for their own inventories is called an **over-the-counter (OTC) market**. Consequently, NASDAQ is often referred to as an OTC market. However, in their efforts to promote a distinct image, NASDAQ officials prefer that the term "OTC" not be used when referring to the NASDAQ market. Nevertheless, old habits die hard, and many people still refer to NASDAQ as an OTC market.

The NASDAQ network operates with three levels of information access. Level 1 is designed to provide a timely, accurate source of price quotations. These prices are freely available over the Internet. Level 2 allows users to view price quotes from all NASDAQ market makers. In particular, this level allows access to **inside quotes**. Inside quotes are the highest bid quotes and the lowest asked quotes for a NASDAQ-listed security. Level 2 is now available on the Web, sometimes for a small fee. Level 3 is for the use of market makers only. This access level allows NASDAQ dealers to enter or change their price quote information.

The NASDAQ is actually made up of three separate markets: the NASDAQ Global Select Market, the NASDAQ Global Market, and the NASDAQ Capital Market. As the market for NASDAQ's larger and more actively traded securities, the Global Select Market lists about 1,200 companies (as of 2014), including some of the best-known companies in the world, such as Apple and Google. The Global Market companies are somewhat smaller in size, and NASDAQ lists about 1,450 of these companies. Finally, the smallest companies listed on NASDAQ are in the NASDAQ Capital Market; about 650 are currently listed. Of course, as Capital Market companies become more established, they may move up to the Global Market or the Global Select Market.

ECNs   In a very important development in the late 1990s, the NASDAQ system was opened to so-called **electronic communications networks (ECNs)**. ECNs are basically websites that allow investors to trade directly with one another. Investor buy and sell orders placed on ECNs are transmitted to the NASDAQ and displayed along with market maker bid and ask prices. The ECNs open up the NASDAQ by essentially allowing individual investors, not just market makers, to enter orders. As a result, the ECNs act to increase liquidity and competition.

STOCK MARKET REPORTING

In recent years, stock price quotes and related information have increasingly moved from traditional print media, such as *The Wall Street Journal,* to various websites. Yahoo! Finance (finance.yahoo.com) is a good example. We went there and requested a stock quote on wholesale club Costco, which is listed on the NASDAQ. Here is a portion of what we found:

You can get real-time stock quotes on the Web. See **finance.yahoo.com** for details.

Most of this information is self-explanatory. The price $138.76 is the real-time price of the last trade. Availability of real-time prices for free is a relatively new development. The reported change is from the previous day's closing price. The opening price is the first trade of the day. We see the bid and ask prices of $138.84 and $138.86, respectively, along with the market "depth," which is the number of shares sought at the bid price and offered at the ask price. The "1y Target Est" is the average estimated stock price one year ahead based on estimates from security analysts who follow the stock.

Moving to the second column, we have the range of prices for this day, followed by the range over the previous 52 weeks. Volume is the number of shares traded today, followed by average daily volume over the last three months. Market cap is the number of shares outstanding (from the most recent quarterly financial statements) multiplied by the current price per share. P/E is the PE ratio we discussed earlier in this chapter. The earnings per share (EPS) used in the calculation is "ttm," meaning "trailing twelve months." Finally, we have the dividend on the stock, which is actually the most recent quarterly dividend multiplied by 4, and the dividend yield. Notice that the yield is just the reported dividend divided by the stock price: $1.42/$138.76 = .010, or 1.0%.

Summary and Conclusions

This chapter has covered the basics of stocks and stock valuations. The key points include:

1. A stock can be valued by discounting its dividends. We mention three types of situations:
   a. The case of zero growth of dividends.
   b. The case of constant growth of dividends.
   c. The case of differential growth.

2. An estimate of the growth rate of dividends is needed for the dividend discount model. A useful estimate of the growth rate is:

$$g = \text{Retention ratio} \times \text{Return on retained earnings (ROE)}$$

As long as the firm holds its ratio of dividends to earnings constant, g represents the growth rate of both dividends and earnings.

3. From accounting, we know that earnings are divided into two parts: dividends and retained earnings. Most firms continually retain earnings in order to create future dividends. One should not discount earnings to obtain price per share since part of earnings must be reinvested. Only dividends reach the stockholders and only they should be discounted to obtain share price.

4. Some analysts value stock via multiples, such as the price–earnings ratio. However, we caution that one must apply the same multiple only to similar companies.

5. We suggest that a firm's price–earnings ratio is a function of three factors:
   a. The per-share amount of the firm's valuable investment opportunities.
   b. The risk of the stock.
   c. The type of accounting method used by the firm.

6. As an alternative to discounting dividends or valuing via comparables, one can value an entire firm by discounting its cash flows.

7. The two biggest stock markets in the United States are the NYSE and the NASDAQ. We discussed the organization and operation of these two markets, and we saw how stock price information is reported.

Concept Questions

1. **Stock Valuation**   Why does the value of a share of stock depend on dividends?

2. **Stock Valuation**   A substantial percentage of the companies listed on the NYSE and the NASDAQ don't pay dividends, but investors are nonetheless willing to buy shares in them. How is this possible given your answer to the previous question?

3. **Dividend Policy**   Referring to the previous questions, under what circumstances might a company choose not to pay dividends?

4. **Dividend Growth Model**   Under what two assumptions can we use the dividend growth model presented in the chapter to determine the value of a share of stock? Comment on the reasonableness of these assumptions.

5. **Common versus Preferred Stock**   Suppose a company has a preferred stock issue and a common stock issue. Both have just paid a $2 dividend. Which do you think will have a higher price, a share of the preferred or a share of the common?

6. **Dividend Growth Model**   Based on the dividend growth model, what are the two components of the total return on a share of stock? Which do you think is typically larger?

7. **Growth Rate**   In the context of the dividend growth model, is it true that the growth rate in dividends and the growth rate in the price of the stock are identical?

8. **Price–Earnings Ratio**   What are the three factors that determine a company's price–earnings ratio?

9. **Corporate Ethics**   Is it unfair or unethical for corporations to create classes of stock with unequal voting rights?

10. **Stock Valuation**   Evaluate the following statement: Managers should not focus on the current stock value because doing so will lead to an overemphasis on short-term profits at the expense of long-term profits.

Questions and Problems

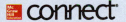

BASIC (Questions 1–10)

1. **Stock Values**   The Starr Co. just paid a dividend of $1.95 per share on its stock. The dividends are expected to grow at a constant rate of 4.5 percent per year, indefinitely. If investors require a return of 11 percent on the stock, what is the current price? What will the price be in three years? In 15 years?

2. **Stock Values** The next dividend payment by ECY, Inc., will be $2.90 per share. The dividends are anticipated to maintain a growth rate of 5.5 percent, forever. If the stock currently sells for $53.10 per share, what is the required return?

3. **Stock Values** For the company in the previous problem, what is the dividend yield? What is the expected capital gains yield?

4. **Stock Values** Shiller Corporation will pay a $2.75 per share dividend next year. The company pledges to increase its dividend by 5 percent per year, indefinitely. If you require a return of 11 percent on your investment, how much will you pay for the company's stock today?

5. **Stock Valuation** Siblings, Inc., is expected to maintain a constant 5.7 percent growth rate in its dividends, indefinitely. If the company has a dividend yield of 4.6 percent, what is the required return on the company's stock?

6. **Stock Valuation** Suppose you know that a company's stock currently sells for $67 per share and the required return on the stock is 10.8 percent. You also know that the total return on the stock is evenly divided between a capital gains yield and a dividend yield. If it's the company's policy to always maintain a constant growth rate in its dividends, what is the current dividend per share?

7. **Stock Valuation** Gruber Corp. pays a constant $9 dividend on its stock. The company will maintain this dividend for the next 13 years and will then cease paying dividends forever. If the required return on this stock is 9.5 percent, what is the current share price?

8. **Valuing Preferred Stock** Ayden, Inc., has an issue of preferred stock outstanding that pays a $4.50 dividend every year, in perpetuity. If this issue currently sells for $87 per share, what is the required return?

9. **Growth Rate** The newspaper reported last week that Bennington Enterprises earned $29 million this year. The report also stated that the firm's return on equity is 17 percent. Bennington retains 80 percent of its earnings. What is the firm's earnings growth rate? What will next year's earnings be?

10. **Stock Valuation and PE** The Spring Flower Co. has earnings of $2.35 per share. The benchmark PE for the company is 18. What stock price would you consider appropriate? What if the benchmark PE were 21?

INTERMEDIATE (Questions 11–28)

11. **Stock Valuation** Universal Laser, Inc., just paid a dividend of $2.90 on its stock. The growth rate in dividends is expected to be a constant 6 percent per year, indefinitely. Investors require a 15 percent return on the stock for the first three years, a 13 percent return for the next three years, and then an 11 percent return thereafter. What is the current share price for the stock?

12. **Nonconstant Growth** Metallica Bearings, Inc., is a young start-up company. No dividends will be paid on the stock over the next nine years, because the firm needs to plow back its earnings to fuel growth. The company will pay a dividend of $17.50 per share in 10 years and will increase the dividend by 5.5 percent per year thereafter. If the required return on this stock is 12 percent, what is the current share price?

13. **Nonconstant Dividends** Bucksnort, Inc., has an odd dividend policy. The company has just paid a dividend of $9 per share and has announced that it will increase the dividend by $4 per share for each of the next five years, and then never pay another dividend. If you require a return of 12 percent on the company's stock, how much will you pay for a share today?

14. **Nonconstant Dividends** Lohn Corporation is expected to pay the following dividends over the next four years: $13, $8, $6.50, and $2.40. Afterwards, the company pledges to maintain a constant 4.5 percent growth rate in dividends forever. If the required return on the stock is 11 percent, what is the current share price?

15. **Differential Growth** Phillips Co. is growing quickly. Dividends are expected to grow at a rate of 25 percent for the next three years, with the growth rate falling off to a constant 5 percent thereafter. If the required return is 12 percent and the company just paid a dividend of $3.10, what is the current share price?

16. **Differential Growth** Synovec Corp. is experiencing rapid growth. Dividends are expected to grow at 30 percent per year during the next three years, 18 percent over the following year, and then 8 percent per year indefinitely. The required return on this stock is 11 percent, and the stock currently sells for $65 per share. What is the projected dividend for the coming year?

17. **Negative Growth** Antiques R Us is a mature manufacturing firm. The company just paid a dividend of $13, but management expects to reduce the payout by 4 percent per year, indefinitely. If you require a return of 10 percent on this stock, what will you pay for a share today?

18. **Finding the Dividend** Mau Corporation stock currently sells for $64.87 per share. The market requires a return of 10.5 percent on the firm's stock. If the company maintains a constant 5 percent growth rate in dividends, what was the most recent dividend per share paid on the stock?

19. **Valuing Preferred Stock** Fifth National Bank just issued some new preferred stock. The issue will pay an annual dividend of $5 in perpetuity, beginning five years from now. If the market requires a return of 4.7 percent on this investment, how much does a share of preferred stock cost today?

20. **Using Stock Quotes** You have found the following stock quote for RJW Enterprises, Inc., in the financial pages of today's newspaper. What is the annual dividend? What was the closing price for this stock that appeared in *yesterday's* paper? If the company currently has 30 million shares of stock outstanding, what was net income for the most recent four quarters?

YTD %Chg	Stock	SYM	YLD	PE	Last	Net Chg
−1.1	RJW Enterp.	RJW	2.1	23	27.82	−.13

21. **Nonconstant Growth and Quarterly Dividends** Pasqually Mineral Water, Inc., will pay a quarterly dividend per share of $.90 at the end of each of the next 12 quarters. Thereafter, the dividend will grow at a quarterly rate of 1 percent, forever. The appropriate rate of return on the stock is 10 percent, compounded quarterly. What is the current stock price?

22. **Finding the Dividend** Briley, Inc., is expected to pay equal dividends at the end of each of the next two years. Thereafter, the dividend will grow at a constant annual rate of 4 percent, forever. The current stock price is $53. What is next year's dividend payment if the required rate of return is 11 percent?

23. **Finding the Required Return** Juggernaut Satellite Corporation earned $23 million for the fiscal year ending yesterday. The firm also paid out 30 percent of its earnings as dividends yesterday. The firm will continue to pay out 30 percent of its earnings as annual, end-of-year dividends. The remaining 70 percent of earnings is retained by the company for use in projects. The company has 2 million shares of common stock outstanding. The current stock price is $97. The historical return on equity (ROE) of 13 percent is expected to continue in the future. What is the required rate of return on the stock?

24. **Dividend Growth** Four years ago, Bling Diamond, Inc., paid a dividend of $1.51 per share. The company paid a dividend of $1.87 per share yesterday. Dividends will grow

over the next five years at the same rate they grew over the last four years. Thereafter, dividends will grow at 5 percent per year. What will the company's cash dividend be in seven years?

25. **Price–Earnings Ratio** Consider Pacific Energy Company and U.S. Bluechips, Inc., both of which reported earnings of $630,000. Without new projects, both firms will continue to generate earnings of $630,000 in perpetuity. Assume that all earnings are paid as dividends and that both firms require a return of 11 percent.

   a. What is the current PE ratio for each company?
   b. Pacific Energy Company has a new project that will generate additional earnings of $100,000 each year in perpetuity. Calculate the new PE ratio of the company.
   c. U.S. Bluechips has a new project that will increase earnings by $200,000 in perpetuity. Calculate the new PE ratio of the firm.

26. **Stock Valuation and PE** Ramsay Corp. currently has an EPS of $3.10, and the benchmark PE for the company is 21. Earnings are expected to grow at 6 percent per year.

   a. What is your estimate of the current stock price?
   b. What is the target stock price in one year?
   c. Assuming the company pays no dividends, what is the implied return on the company's stock over the next year? What does this tell you about the implicit stock return using PE valuation?

27. **Stock Valuation and EV** FFDP Corp. has yearly sales of $42 million and costs of $13 million. The company's balance sheet shows debt of $64 million and cash of $21 million. There are 1,750,000 shares outstanding and the industry EV/EBITDA multiple is 6.8. What is the company's enterprise value? What is the stock price per share?

28. **Stock Valuation and Cash Flows** Fincher Manufacturing has projected sales of $135 million next year. Costs are expected to be $76 million and net investment is expected to be $15 million. Each of these values is expected to grow at 14 percent the following year, with the growth rate declining by 2 percent per year until the growth rate reaches 6 percent, where it is expected to remain indefinitely. There are 5.5 million shares of stock outstanding and investors require a return of 13 percent return on the company's stock. The corporate tax rate is 40 percent.

   a. What is your estimate of the current stock price?
   b. Suppose instead that you estimate the terminal value of the company using a PE multiple. The industry PE multiple is 11. What is your new estimate of the company's stock price?

CHALLENGE
(Questions 29–34)

29. **Capital Gains versus Income** Consider four different stocks, all of which have a required return of 14 percent and a most recent dividend of $3.50 per share. Stocks W, X, and Y are expected to maintain constant growth rates in dividends for the foreseeable future of 7 percent, 0 percent, and −5 percent per year, respectively. Stock Z is a growth stock that will increase its dividend by 30 percent for the next two years and then maintain a constant 8 percent growth rate thereafter. What is the dividend yield for each of these four stocks? What is the expected capital gains yield? Discuss the relationship among the various returns that you find for each of these stocks.

30. **Stock Valuation** Most corporations pay quarterly dividends on their common stock rather than annual dividends. Barring any unusual circumstances during the year, the board raises, lowers, or maintains the current dividend once a year and then pays this dividend out in equal quarterly installments to its shareholders.

   a. Suppose a company currently pays an annual dividend of $3.60 on its common stock in a single annual installment, and management plans on raising this dividend by 4.5 percent per year indefinitely. If the required return on this stock is 11 percent, what is the current share price?

b. Now suppose that the company in (a) actually pays its annual dividend in equal quarterly installments; thus, this company has just paid a dividend of $.90 per share, as it has for the previous three quarters. What is your value for the current share price now? (*Hint:* Find the equivalent annual end-of-year dividend for each year.) Comment on whether or not you think that this model of stock valuation is appropriate.

31. **Nonconstant Growth**   Storico Co. just paid a dividend of $3.40 per share. The company will increase its dividend by 20 percent next year and will then reduce its dividend growth rate by 5 percentage points per year until it reaches the industry average of 5 percent dividend growth, after which the company will keep a constant growth rate forever. If the required return on Storico stock is 13 percent, what will a share of stock sell for today?

32. **Nonconstant Growth**   This one's a little harder. Suppose the current share price for the firm in the previous problem is $62.40 and all the dividend information remains the same. What required return must investors be demanding on Storico stock? (*Hint:* Set up the valuation formula with all the relevant cash flows, and use trial and error to find the unknown rate of return.)

33. **Growth Opportunities**   The Stambaugh Corporation currently has earnings per share of $8.20. The company has no growth and pays out all earnings as dividends. It has a new project that will require an investment of $1.95 per share in one year. The project is only a two-year project, and it will increase earnings in the two years following the investment by $2.75 and $3.05, respectively. Investors require a return of 12 percent on Stambaugh stock.

    a. What is the value per share of the company's stock assuming the firm does not undertake the investment opportunity?
    b. If the company does undertake the investment, what is the value per share now?
    c. Again, assume the company undertakes the investment. What will the price per share be four years from today?

34. **Growth Opportunities**   Burklin, Inc., has earnings of $21 million and is projected to grow at a constant rate of 5 percent forever because of the benefits gained from the learning curve. Currently, all earnings are paid out as dividends. The company plans to launch a new project two years from now that would be completely internally funded and require 30 percent of the earnings that year. The project would start generating revenues one year after the launch of the project and the earnings from the new project in any year are estimated to be constant at $6.7 million. The company has 7.5 million shares of stock outstanding. Estimate the value of the stock. The discount rate is 10 percent.

Excel Master It! Problem

In practice, the use of the dividend discount model is refined from the method we presented in the textbook. Many analysts will estimate the dividend for the next five years and then estimate a perpetual growth rate at some point in the future, typically 10 years. Rather than have the dividend growth fall dramatically from the fast growth period to the perpetual growth period, linear interpolation is applied. That is, the dividend growth is projected to fall by an equal amount each year. For example, if the high-growth period is 15 percent for the next five years and the dividends are expected to fall to a 5 percent perpetual growth rate five years later, the dividend growth rate would decline by 2 percent each year.

The *Value Line Investment Survey* provides information for investors. Below, you will find information for Boeing found in the 2015 edition of *Value Line:*

2014 dividend	$2.92
5-year dividend growth rate	14.5%

a. Assume that a perpetual growth rate of 5 percent begins 11 years from now and use linear interpolation between the high growth rate and perpetual growth rate. Construct a table that shows the dividend growth rate and dividend each year. What is the stock price at Year 10? What is the stock price today?

b. How sensitive is the current stock price to changes in the perpetual growth rate? Graph the current stock price against the perpetual growth rate in 11 years to find out.

Instead of applying the constant dividend growth model to find the stock price in the future, analysts will often combine the dividend discount method with price ratio valuation, often with the PE ratio. Remember that the PE ratio is the price per share divided by the earnings per share. So, if we know what the PE ratio is, we can solve for the stock price. Suppose we also have the following information about Boeing:

Payout ratio	30%
PE ratio at constant growth rate	15

c. Use the PE ratio to calculate the stock price when Boeing reaches a perpetual growth rate in dividends. Now find the value of the stock today by finding the present value of the dividends during the supernormal growth rate and the price you calculated using the PE ratio.

d. How sensitive is the current stock price to changes in PE ratio when the stock reaches the perpetual growth rate? Graph the current stock price against the PE ratio in 11 years to find out.

Mini Case

STOCK VALUATION AT RAGAN ENGINES

Larissa has been talking with the company's directors about the future of East Coast Yachts. To this point, the company has used outside suppliers for various key components of the company's yachts, including engines. Larissa has decided that East Coast Yachts should consider the purchase of an engine manufacturer to allow East Coast Yachts to better integrate its supply chain and get more control over engine features. After investigating several possible companies, Larissa feels that the purchase of Ragan Engines, Inc., is a possibility. She has asked Dan Ervin to analyze Ragan's value.

Ragan Engines, Inc., was founded nine years ago by a brother and sister—Carrington and Genevieve Ragan—and has remained a privately owned company. The company manufactures marine engines for a variety of applications. Ragan has experienced rapid growth because of a proprietary technology that increases the fuel efficiency of its engines with very little sacrifice in performance. The company is equally owned by Carrington and Genevieve. The original agreement between the siblings gave each 150,000 shares of stock.

Larissa has asked Dan to determine a value per share of Ragan stock. To accomplish this, Dan has gathered the following information about some of Ragan's competitors that are publicly traded:

	EPS	DPS	Stock Price	ROE	R
Blue Ribband Motors Corp.	$1.09	$.19	$16.32	10.00%	12.00%
Bon Voyage Marine, Inc.	1.26	.55	13.94	12.00	17.00
Nautilus Marine Engines	(.27)	.57	23.97	N/A	16.00
Industry average	$ .69	$.44	$18.08	11.00%	15.00%

Nautilus Marine Engines's negative earnings per share (EPS) were the result of an accounting write-off last year. Without the write-off, EPS for the company would have been $2.07. Last year, Ragan had an EPS of $5.35 and paid a dividend to Carrington and Genevieve of $320,000 each. The company also had a return on equity of 21 percent. Larissa tells Dan that a required return for Ragan of 18 percent is appropriate.

1. Assuming the company continues its current growth rate, what is the value per share of the company's stock?

2. Dan has examined the company's financial statements, as well as examining those of its competitors. Although Ragan currently has a technological advantage, Dan's research indicates that Ragan's competitors are investigating other methods to improve efficiency. Given this, Dan believes that Ragan's technological advantage will last only for the next five years. After that period, the company's growth will likely slow to the industry average. Additionally, Dan believes that the required return the company uses is too high. He believes the industry average required return is more appropriate. Under Dan's assumptions, what is the estimated stock price?

3. What is the industry average price–earnings ratio? What is Ragan's price–earnings ratio? Comment on any differences and explain why they may exist.

4. Assume the company's growth rate declines to the industry average after five years. What percentage of the stock's value is attributable to growth opportunities?

5. Assume the company's growth rate slows to the industry average in five years. What future return on equity does this imply?

6. Carrington and Genevieve are not sure if they should sell the company. If they do not sell the company outright to East Coast Yachts, they would like to try and increase the value of the company's stock. In this case, they want to retain control of the company and do not want to sell stock to outside investors. They also feel that the company's debt is at a manageable level and do not want to borrow more money. What steps can they take to try and increase the price of the stock? Are there any conditions under which this strategy would *not* increase the stock price?

Risk and Return

LESSONS FROM MARKET HISTORY

With the S&P 500 Index returning about 14 percent and the NASDAQ Composite Index up about 13 percent in 2014, stock market performance overall was very good. In particular, investors in outpatient diagnostic imaging services company RadNet, Inc., had to be happy about the 411 percent gain in that stock, and investors in biopharmaceutical company Achillon Pharmaceuticals had to feel pretty good following that company's 269 percent gain. Of course, not all stocks increased in value during the year. Stock in Transocean Ltd. fell 63 percent during the year, and stock in Avon Products dropped 44 percent.

These examples show that there were tremendous potential profits to be made during 2014, but there was also the risk of losing money—and lots of it. So what should you, as a stock market investor, expect when you invest your own money? In this chapter, we study more than eight decades of market history to find out.

10.1 Returns

DOLLAR RETURNS

Excel Master coverage online

How did the market do today? Find out at **finance.yahoo.com**.

Suppose the Video Concept Company has several thousand shares of stock outstanding and you are a shareholder. Further suppose that you purchased some of the shares of stock in the company at the beginning of the year; it is now year-end and you want to figure out how well you have done on your investment. The return you get on an investment in stocks, like that in bonds or any other investment, comes in two forms.

As the owner of stock in the Video Concept Company, you are a part owner of the company. If the company is profitable, it generally could distribute some of its profits to the shareholders. Therefore, as the owner of shares of stock, you could receive some cash, called a *dividend*, during the year. This cash is the *income component* of your return. In addition to the dividends, the other part of your return is the *capital gain*—or, if it is negative, the *capital loss* (negative capital gain)—on the investment.

For example, suppose we are considering the cash flows of the investment in Figure 10.1, showing that you purchased 100 shares of stock at the beginning of the year at a price of $37 per share. Your total investment, then, was:

$$C_0 = \$37 \times 100 = \$3,700$$

Figure 10.1
Dollar Returns

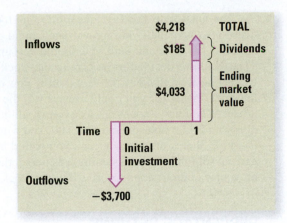

Suppose that over the year the stock paid a dividend of $1.85 per share. During the year, then, you received income of:

$$Div = \$1.85 \times 100 = \$185$$

Suppose, finally, that at the end of the year the market price of the stock is $40.33 per share. Because the stock increased in price, you had a capital gain of:

$$Gain = (\$40.33 - \$37) \times 100 = \$333$$

The capital gain, like the dividend, is part of the return that shareholders require to maintain their investment in the Video Concept Company. Of course, if the price of Video Concept stock had dropped in value to, say, $34.78, you would have recorded this capital loss:

$$Loss = (\$34.78 - \$37) \times 100 = -\$222$$

The *total dollar return* on your investment is the sum of the dividend income and the capital gain or loss on the investment:

$$Total\ dollar\ return = Dividend\ income + Capital\ gain\ (or\ loss)$$

(From now on we will refer to *capital losses* as *negative capital gains* and not distinguish them.) In our first example, the total dollar return is given by:

$$Total\ dollar\ return = \$185 + \$333 = \$518$$

Notice that if you sold the stock at the end of the year, your total amount of cash would be the initial investment plus the total dollar return. In the preceding example you would have:

$$
\begin{aligned}
Total\ cash\ if\ stock\ is\ sold &= Initial\ investment + Total\ dollar\ return \\
&= \$3,700 + \$518 \\
&= \$4,218
\end{aligned}
$$

As a check, notice that this is the same as the proceeds from the sale of stock plus the dividends:

$$
\begin{aligned}
Proceeds\ from\ stock\ sale &+ Dividends \\
&= \$40.33 \times 100 + \$185 \\
&= \$4,033 + \$185 \\
&= \$4,218
\end{aligned}
$$

Suppose, however, that you hold your Video Concept stock and don't sell it at year-end. Should you still consider the capital gain as part of your return? Does this violate our previous present value rule that only cash matters?

The answer to the first question is a strong yes, and the answer to the second question is an equally strong no. The capital gain is every bit as much a part of your return as the dividend, and you should certainly count it as part of your total return. That you have decided to hold onto the stock and not sell, or *realize* the gain or the loss, in no way changes the fact that, if you wanted, you could get the cash value of the stock. After all, you could always sell the stock at year-end and immediately buy it back. The total amount of cash you would have at year-end would be the $518 gain plus your initial investment of $3,700. You would not lose this return when you bought back 100 shares of stock. In fact, you would be in exactly the same position as if you had not sold the stock (assuming, of course, that there are no tax consequences and no brokerage commissions from selling the stock).

PERCENTAGE RETURNS

It is more convenient to summarize the information about returns in percentage terms than in dollars because the percentages apply to any amount invested. The question we want to answer is this: How much return do we get for each dollar invested? To find this out, let t stand for the year we are looking at, let P_t be the price of the stock at the beginning of the year, and let Div_{t+1} be the dividend paid on the stock during the year. Consider the cash flows in Figure 10.2.

In our example, the price at the beginning of the year was $37 per share and the dividend paid during the year on each share was $1.85. Hence, the percentage income return, sometimes called the *dividend yield,* is:

$$
\begin{aligned}
\text{Dividend yield} &= \text{Div}_{t+1}/P_t \\
&= \$1.85/\$37 \\
&= .05 \\
&= 5\%
\end{aligned}
$$

Go to **www.marketwatch .com/markets** for a Java applet that shows today's returns by market sector.

Figure 10.2
Percentage Returns

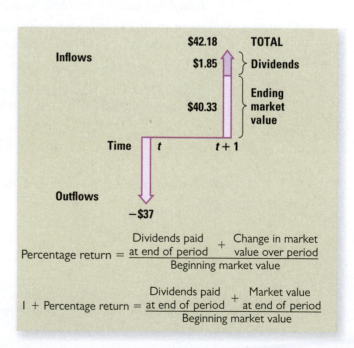

The **capital gain** (or loss) is the change in the price of the stock divided by the initial price. Letting P_{t+1} be the price of the stock at year-end, we can compute the capital gain as follows:

$$
\begin{aligned}
\text{Capital gain} &= (P_{t+1} - P_t)/P_t \\
&= (\$40.33 - \$37)/\$37 \\
&= \$3.33/\$37 \\
&= .09 \\
&= 9\%
\end{aligned}
$$

Combining these two results, we find that the *total return* on the investment in Video Concept stock over the year, which we will label R_{t+1}, was:

$$
\begin{aligned}
R_{t+1} &= \frac{\text{Div}_{t+1}}{P_t} + \frac{(P_{t+1} - P_t)}{P_t} \\
&= 5\% + 9\% \\
&= 14\%
\end{aligned}
$$

From now on, we will refer to returns in percentage terms.

To give a more concrete example, stock in Keurig Green Mountain (GMCR), of coffee making by the cup fame, began 2014 at $75.54 per share. Keurig Green Mountain paid dividends of $1.00 during 2014, and the stock price at the end of the year was $132.40. What was the return on GMCR for the year? For practice, see if you agree that the answer is 76.60 percent. Of course, negative returns occur as well. For example, again in 2014, GameStop's stock price at the end of the year was $33.80 per share, and dividends of $1.32 were paid. The stock began the year at $49.26 per share. Verify that the loss was 28.70 percent for the year.

**EXAMPLE
10.1**

Calculating Returns   Suppose a stock begins the year with a price of $25 per share and ends with a price of $35 per share. During the year, it paid a $2 dividend per share. What are its dividend yield, its capital gains yield, and its total return for the year? We can imagine the cash flows in Figure 10.3.

$$
\begin{aligned}
R_1 &= \frac{\text{Div}_1}{P_0} + \frac{P_1 - P_0}{P_0} \\
&= \frac{\$2}{\$25} + \frac{\$35 - 25}{\$25} = \frac{\$12}{\$25} \\
&= 8\% \ + 40\% \ \ \ \ \ = 48\%
\end{aligned}
$$

Figure 10.3   Cash Flow—An Investment Example

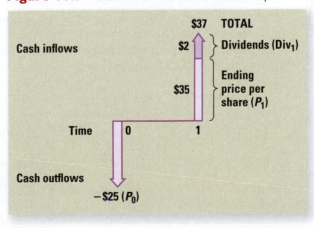

(continued)

Thus, the stock's dividend yield, its capital gains yield, and its total return are 8 percent, 40 percent, and 48 percent, respectively.

Suppose you had $5,000 invested. The total dollar return you would have received on an investment in the stock is $5,000 × .48 = $2,400. If you know the total dollar return on the stock, you do not need to know how many shares you would have had to purchase to figure out how much money you would have made on the $5,000 investment. You just use the total dollar return.

10.2 Holding Period Returns

Excel Master
coverage online

A famous set of studies dealing with rates of return on common stocks, bonds, and Treasury bills is found in *Ibbotson SBBI 2015 Classic U.S. Yearbook.*[1] It presents year-by-year historical rates of return for the following five important types of financial instruments in the United States:

1. *Large-company common stocks:* This common stock portfolio is based on the Standard & Poor's (S&P) Composite Index. At present the S&P Composite includes 500 of the largest (in terms of market value) companies in the United States.

2. *Small-company common stocks:* This is a portfolio corresponding to the bottom fifth of stocks traded on the New York Stock Exchange in which stocks are ranked by market value (i.e., the price of the stock multiplied by the number of shares outstanding).

3. *Long-term corporate bonds:* This is a portfolio of high-quality corporate bonds with 20-year maturities.

4. *Long-term U.S. government bonds:* This is based on U.S. government bonds with maturities of 20 years.

5. *U.S. Treasury bills:* This is based on Treasury bills with a one-month maturity.

None of the returns are adjusted for taxes or transaction costs. In addition to the year-by-year returns on financial instruments, the year-to-year change in the consumer price index is computed. This is a basic measure of inflation. We can calculate year-by-year real returns by subtracting annual inflation.

Before looking closely at the different portfolio returns, we graphically present the returns and risks available from U.S. capital markets in the 89-year period from 1926 to 2014. Figure 10.4 shows the growth of $1 invested at the beginning of 1926. Notice that the vertical axis is logarithmic, so that equal distances measure the same percentage change. The figure shows that if $1 was invested in large-company common stocks and all dividends were reinvested, the dollar would have grown to $5,316.85 by the end of 2014. The biggest growth was in the small stock portfolio. If $1 was invested in small stocks in 1926, the investment would have grown to $27,419.32. However, when you look carefully at Figure 10.4, you can see great variability in the returns on small stocks, especially in the earlier part of the period. A dollar in long-term government bonds was very stable as compared with a dollar in common stocks. Figures 10.5 to 10.8 plot each year-to-year percentage return as a vertical bar drawn from the horizontal axis for large-company common stocks, small-company stocks, long-term bonds and Treasury bills, and inflation, respectively.

---

[1]*Ibbotson SBBI 2015 Classic Yearbook* (Chicago: Morningstar).

Figure 10.4 Wealth Indexes of Investments in the U.S. Capital Markets (Year-End 1925 = $1.00)

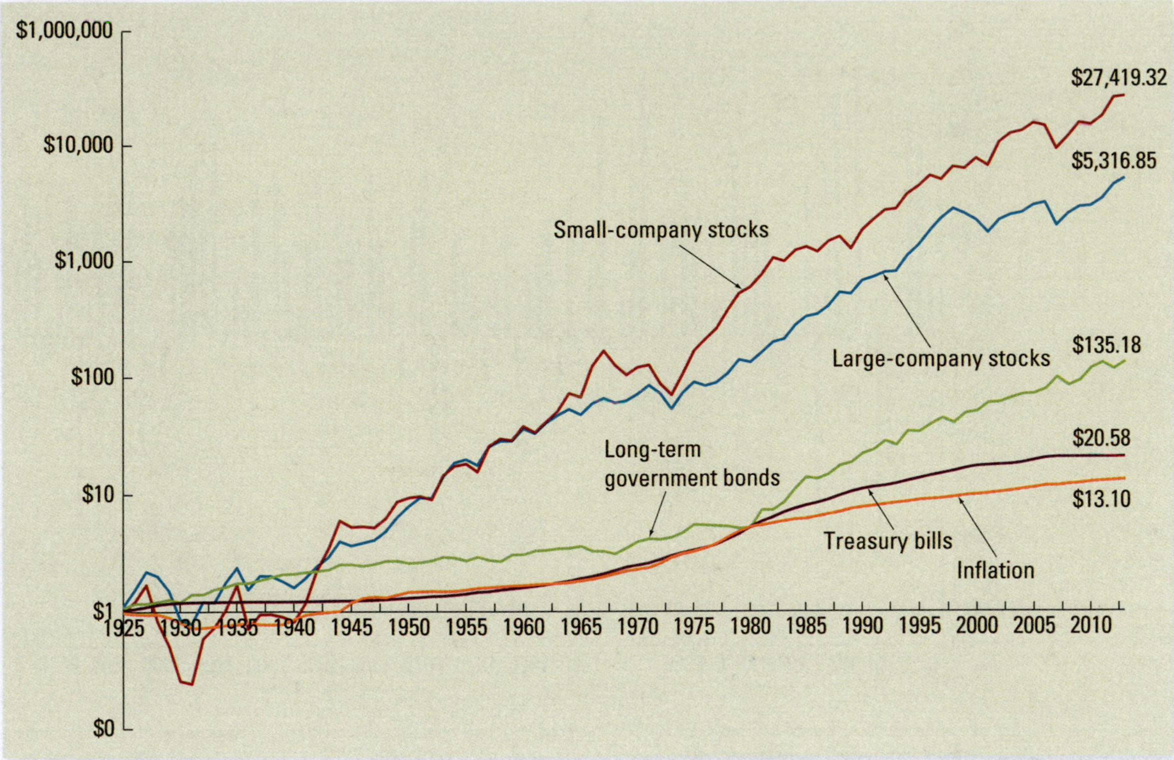

Redrawn from *Stocks, Bonds, Bills and Inflation: 2015 Yearbook,*™ annual updates to the work by Roger G. Ibbotson and Rex A. Sinquefield (Chicago: Morningstar). All rights reserved.

Figure 10.4 gives the growth of a dollar investment in the stock market from 1926 through 2014. In other words, it shows what the value of the investment would have been if the dollar had been left in the stock market and if each year the dividends from the previous year had been reinvested in more stock. If R_t is the return in year t (expressed in decimals), the value you would have at the end of year T is the product of 1 plus the return in each of the years:

$$\text{Value} = (1 + R_1) \times (1 + R_2) \times \cdots \times (1 + R_t) \times \cdots \times (1 + R_T)$$

For example, if the returns were 11 percent, −5 percent, and 9 percent in a three-year period, an investment of $1 at the beginning of the period would be worth:

Go to **bigcharts.marketwatch.com** to see both intraday and long-term charts.

$$\begin{aligned}(1 + R_1) \times (1 + R_2) \times (1 + R_3) &= (\$1 + .11) \times (\$1 - .05) \times (\$1 + .09)\\ &= \$1.11 \times \$.95 \times \$1.09\\ &= \$1.15\end{aligned}$$

at the end of the three years. Notice that .15 or 15 percent is the total return. This includes the return from reinvesting the first-year dividends in the stock market for two more years and reinvesting the second-year dividends for the final year. The 15 percent is called a three-year **holding period return**. Table 10.1 gives the annual returns each year for selected investments from 1926 to 2014. From this table, you can determine holding period returns for any combination of years.

Figure 10.5   Year-by-Year Total Returns on Large-Company Common Stocks

Figure 10.6   Year-by-Year Total Returns on Small-Company Stocks

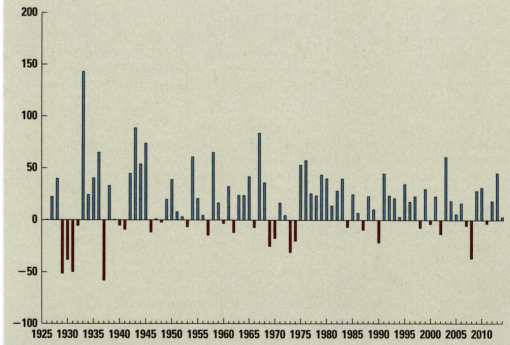

Figure 10.7   Year-by-Year Total Returns on Bonds and U.S. Treasury Bills

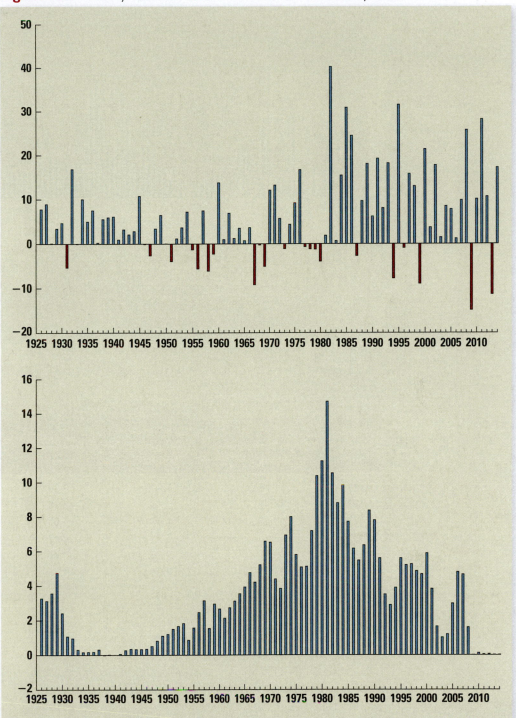

Figure 10.8   Year-by-Year Inflation

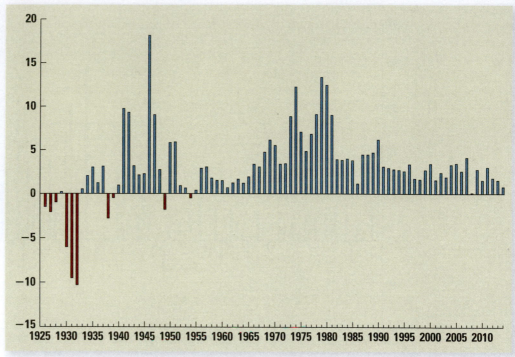

Table 10.1
Year-by-Year Total
Returns, 1926–2014

Year	Large-Company Stocks	Long-Term Government Bonds	U.S. Treasury Bills	Consumer Price Index
1926	11.14%	7.90%	3.30%	−1.12%
1927	37.13	10.36	3.15	−2.26
1928	43.31	−1.37	4.05	−1.16
1929	−8.91	5.23	4.47	.58
1930	−25.26	5.80	2.27	−6.40
1931	−43.86	−8.04	1.15	−9.32
1932	−8.85	14.11	.88	−10.27
1933	52.88	.31	.52	.76
1934	−2.34	12.98	.27	1.52
1935	47.22	5.88	.17	2.99
1936	32.80	8.22	.17	1.45
1937	−35.26	−.13	.27	2.86
1938	33.20	6.26	.06	−2.78
1939	−.91	5.71	.04	.00
1940	−10.08	10.34	.04	.71
1941	−11.77	−8.66	.14	9.93
1942	21.07	2.67	.34	9.03
1943	25.76	2.50	.38	2.96
1944	19.69	2.88	.38	2.30

Table 10.1
Year-by-Year Total
Returns, 1926–2014
(*continued*)

Year	Large-Company Stocks	Long-Term Government Bonds	U.S. Treasury Bills	Consumer Price Index
1945	36.46%	5.17%	.38%	2.25%
1946	−8.18	4.07	.38	18.13
1947	5.24	−1.15	.62	8.84
1948	5.10	2.10	1.06	2.99
1949	18.06	7.02	1.12	−2.07
1950	30.58	−1.44	1.22	5.93
1951	24.55	−3.53	1.56	6.00
1952	18.50	1.82	1.75	.75
1953	−1.10	−.88	1.87	.75
1954	52.40	7.89	.93	−.74
1955	31.43	−1.03	1.80	.37
1956	6.63	−3.14	2.66	2.99
1957	−10.85	5.25	3.28	2.90
1958	43.34	−6.70	1.71	1.76
1959	11.90	−1.35	3.48	1.73
1960	.48	7.74	2.81	1.36
1961	26.81	3.02	2.40	.67
1962	−8.78	4.63	2.82	1.33
1963	22.69	1.37	3.23	1.64
1964	16.36	4.43	3.62	.97
1965	12.36	1.40	4.06	1.92
1966	−10.10	−1.61	4.94	3.46
1967	23.94	−6.38	4.39	3.04
1968	11.00	5.33	5.49	4.72
1969	−8.47	−7.45	6.90	6.20
1970	3.94	12.24	6.50	5.57
1971	14.30	12.67	4.36	3.27
1972	18.99	9.15	4.23	3.41
1973	−14.69	−12.66	7.29	8.71
1974	−26.47	−3.28	7.99	12.34
1975	37.23	4.67	5.87	6.94
1976	23.93	18.34	5.07	4.86
1977	−7.16	2.31	5.45	6.70
1978	6.57	−2.07	7.64	9.02
1979	18.61	−2.76	10.56	13.29
1980	32.50	−5.91	12.10	12.52
1981	−4.92	−.16	14.60	8.92
1982	21.55	49.99	10.94	3.83
1983	22.56	−2.11	8.99	3.79
1984	6.27	16.53	9.90	3.95
1985	31.73	39.03	7.71	3.80
1986	18.67	32.51	6.09	1.10
1987	5.25	−8.09	5.88	4.43
1988	16.61	8.71	6.94	4.42
1989	31.69	22.15	8.44	4.65

Table 10.1

Year-by-Year Total Returns, 1926–2014 *(concluded)*

Year	Large-Company Stocks	Long-Term Government Bonds	U.S. Treasury Bills	Consumer Price Index
1990	−3.10%	5.44%	7.69%	6.11%
1991	30.46	20.04	5.43	3.06
1992	7.62	8.09	3.48	2.90
1993	10.08	22.32	3.03	2.75
1994	1.32	−11.46	4.39	2.67
1995	37.58	37.28	5.61	2.54
1996	22.96	−2.59	5.14	3.32
1997	33.36	17.70	5.19	1.70
1998	28.58	19.22	4.86	1.61
1999	21.04	−12.76	4.80	2.68
2000	−9.10	22.16	5.98	3.39
2001	−11.89	5.30	3.33	1.55
2002	−22.10	14.08	1.61	2.38
2003	28.68	1.62	1.03	1.88
2004	10.88	10.34	1.43	3.26
2005	4.91	10.35	3.30	3.42
2006	15.79	.28	4.97	2.54
2007	5.49	10.85	4.52	4.08
2008	−37.00	19.24	1.24	.09
2009	26.46	−25.61	.15	2.72
2010	15.06	7.73	.14	1.50
2011	2.11	35.75	.06	2.96
2012	16.00	1.80	.08	1.74
2013	32.39	−14.69	.05	1.50
2014	13.7	12.9	.03	.8

SOURCE: Global Financial Data, www.globalfinancialdata.com, copyright 2015. en.m.wikipedia.org, Treasury.gov, bls.gov.

10.3 Return Statistics

Excel Master coverage online

The history of U.S. capital market returns is too complicated to be handled in its undigested form. To use the history, we must first find some manageable ways of describing it, dramatically condensing the detailed data into a few simple statements.

This is where two important numbers summarizing the history come in. The first and most natural number is some single measure that best describes the past annual returns on the stock market. In other words, what is our best estimate of the return that an investor could have realized in a particular year over the 1926 to 2014 period? This is the *average return*.

Figure 10.9 plots the histogram of the yearly stock market returns given in Table 10.1. This plot is the **frequency distribution** of the numbers. The height of the graph gives the number of sample observations in the range on the horizontal axis.

Given a frequency distribution like that in Figure 10.9, we can calculate the **average** or **mean** of the distribution. To compute the average of the distribution, we add up all of the values and divide by the total (T) number (89 in our case because we have 89 years of data). The bar over the R is used to represent the mean, and the formula is the ordinary formula for calculating an average:

$$\text{Mean} = \overline{R} = \frac{(R_1 + \cdots + R_T)}{T}$$

Figure 10.9   Histogram of Returns on U.S. Common Stocks, 1926–2014

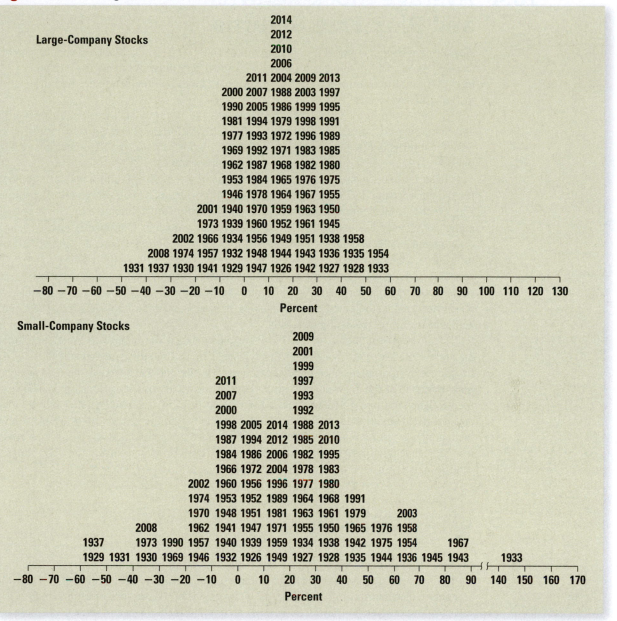

The mean of the 89 annual large-company stock returns from 1926 to 2014 is 12.1 percent.

EXAMPLE 10.2

Calculating Average Returns   Suppose the returns on common stock from 1926 to 1929 are .1370, .3580, .4514, and −.0888, respectively. The average, or mean return over these four years is:

$$\overline{R} = \frac{.1370 + .3580 + .4514 - .0888}{4} = .2144 \text{ or } 21.44\%$$

10.4 Average Stock Returns and Risk-Free Returns

Now that we have computed the average return on the U.S. stock market, it seems sensible to compare it with the returns on other securities. The most obvious comparison is with the low-variability returns in the U.S. government bond market. These are free of most of the volatility we see in the stock market.

An interesting comparison, then, is between the virtually risk-free return on T-bills and the very risky return on common stocks. This difference between risky returns and risk-free returns is often called the *excess return on the risky asset*. Of course, in any particular year the excess return might be positive or negative.

Table 10.2 shows the average stock return, bond return, T-bill return, and inflation rate for the period from 1926 through 2014. From this we can derive average excess returns. The average excess return from large-company common stocks relative to T-bills for the entire period was 8.6 percent (=12.1 percent − 3.5 percent). The average excess return on common stocks is called the historical *equity risk premium* because it is the additional return from bearing risk.

One of the most significant observations of stock market data is this long-term excess of the stock return over the risk-free return. An investor for this period was rewarded for investment in the stock market with an extra, or excess, return over what would have been achieved by simply investing in T-bills.

Why was there such a reward? Does it mean that it never pays to invest in T-bills, and that someone who invested in them instead of in the stock market needs a course in finance? A complete answer to these questions lies at the heart of modern finance. However, part of the answer can be found in the variability of the various types of investments. There are many years when an investment in T-bills achieves higher returns than an investment in large common stocks. Also, we note that the returns from an investment in common stocks are frequently negative, whereas an investment in T-bills has never produced a negative return. So, we now turn our attention to measuring the variability of returns and an introductory discussion of risk.

10.5 Risk Statistics

The second number that we use to characterize the distribution of returns is a measure of the risk in returns. There is no universally agreed-upon definition of risk. One way to think about the risk of returns on common stock is in terms of how spread out the frequency distribution in Figure 10.9 is. The spread, or dispersion, of a distribution is a measure of how much a particular return can deviate from the mean return. If the distribution is very spread out, the returns that will occur are very uncertain. By contrast, a distribution whose returns are all within a few percentage points of each other is tight, and the returns are less uncertain. The measures of risk we will discuss are variance and standard deviation.

VARIANCE

The **variance** and its square root, the **standard deviation**, are the most common measures of variability, or dispersion. We will use Var and σ^2 to denote the variance, and we will use SD and σ to represent the standard deviation. σ is, of course, the Greek letter sigma.

Table 10.2   Total Annual Returns, U.S. Securities Markets, 1926–2014

Series	Arithmetic Mean (%)	Standard Deviation (%)	Distribution (%)
Small-company stocks*	16.7	32.1	
Large-company stocks	12.1	20.1	
Long-term corporate bonds	6.4	8.4	
Long-term government bonds	6.1	10.0	
Intermediate-term government bonds	5.4	5.6	
U.S. Treasury bills	3.5	3.1	
Inflation	3.0	4.1	

−90   0   90

*The 1933 small-company stock total return was 142.9 percent.

SOURCE: Modified from *Stocks, Bonds, Bills and Inflation: 2015 Yearbook,*™ annual updates to the work by Roger G. Ibbotson and Rex A. Sinquefield (Chicago: Morningstar). All rights reserved.

EXAMPLE 10.3

Volatility   Suppose the returns on common stocks are (in decimals) .1370, .3580, .4514, and −.0888, respectively. The variance of this sample is computed as follows:

$$\text{Var} = \frac{1}{T-1}[(R_1 - \bar{R})^2 + (R_2 - \bar{R})^2 + (R_3 - \bar{R})^2 + (R_4 - \bar{R})^2]$$

$$.0582 = \frac{1}{3}[(.1370 - .2144)^2 + (.3580 - .2144)^2$$
$$+ (.4514 - .2144)^2 + (-.0888 - .2144)^2]$$

$$\text{SD} = \sqrt{.0582} = .2412 \text{ or } 24.12\%$$

This formula in Example 10.3 tells us just what to do: Take the T individual returns $(R_1, R_2, \ldots)$ and subtract the average return $\bar{R}$, square the result, and add them up. Finally, this total must be divided by the number of returns less one $(T - 1)$. The standard deviation is always just the square root of the variance.

Using the stock returns for the 89-year period from 1926 through 2014 in this formula, the resulting standard deviation of large-company stock returns is 20.1 percent. The standard deviation is the standard statistical measure of the spread of a sample, and it will be the measure we use most of the time. Its interpretation is facilitated by a discussion of the normal distribution.

Standard deviations are widely reported for mutual funds. For example, the Fidelity Magellan Fund is a large mutual fund. How volatile is it? To find out, we went to www.morningstar.com, entered the ticker symbol FMAGX, and hit the "Ratings & Risk" link. Here is what we found:

MPT Statistics FMAGX

3-Year	5-Year	10-Year	15-Year

3-Year Trailing	Index	R-Squared	Beta	Alpha	Treynor Ratio	Currency
vs. Best-Fit Index						
FMAGX	Russell 1000 Growth TR USD	93.96	1.06	0.34	—	USD
vs. Standard Index						
FMAGX	S&P 500 TR USD	91.54	1.07	0.08	17.50	USD
Category: LG	S&P 500 TR USD	81.44	1.03	-1.38	15.84	USD

01/31/2015

Volatility Measures FMAGX

3-Year	5-Year	10-Year	15-Year

3-Year Trailing	Standard Deviation	Return	Sharpe Ratio	Sortino Ratio	Bear Market Percentile Rank
FMAGX	10.41	18.77	1.71	3.38	—
S&P 500 TR USD	9.31	17.47	1.78	3.31	—
Category: LG	10.72	16.36	1.48	2.74	—

01/31/2015

Over the last three years, the standard deviation of the returns on the Fidelity Magellan Fund was 10.41 percent. When you consider the average stock has a standard deviation of about 50 percent, this seems like a low number. But the Magellan Fund is a relatively well-diversified portfolio, so this is an illustration of the power of diversification, a subject we will discuss in detail later. The return given is the average return; so over the last three years, investors in the Magellan Fund earned an 18.77 percent return per year. Also under the Volatility Measures section, you will see the **Sharpe ratio**. The Sharpe ratio is calculated as the risk premium of the asset divided by the standard deviation. As such, it is a measure of return to the level of risk taken (as measured by standard deviation). The "beta" for the Fidelity Magellan Fund is 1.07. We will have more to say about this number—lots more—in the next chapter.

**EXAMPLE
10.4**

> **Sharpe Ratio**   The Sharpe ratio is the average equity risk premium over a period of time divided by the standard deviation. From 1926 to 2014 the average risk premium (relative to Treasury bills) for large-company stocks was 8.6 percent while the standard deviation was 20.1 percent. The Sharpe ratio of this sample is computed as:
>
> $$\text{Sharpe ratio} = 8.6\%/20.1\% = .428$$
>
> The Sharpe ratio is sometimes referred to as the reward-to-risk ratio where the reward is the average excess return and the risk is the standard deviation.

NORMAL DISTRIBUTION AND ITS IMPLICATIONS FOR STANDARD DEVIATION

A large enough sample drawn from a **normal distribution** looks like the bell-shaped curve drawn in Figure 10.10. As you can see, this distribution is *symmetric* about its mean, not *skewed,* and has a much cleaner shape than the actual distribution of yearly returns drawn in Figure 10.9. Of course, if we had been able to observe stock market returns for 1,000 years, we might have filled in a lot of the jumps and jerks in Figure 10.9 and had a smoother curve.

In classical statistics, the normal distribution plays a central role, and the standard deviation is the usual way to represent the spread of a normal distribution. For the normal distribution, the probability of having a return that is above or below the mean by a certain amount depends only on the standard deviation. For example, the probability of having a

Figure 10.10

The Normal Distribution

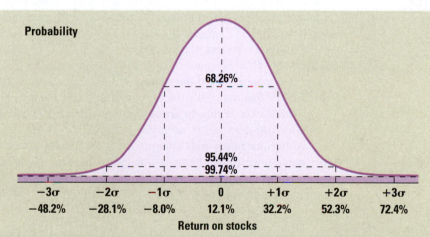

In the case of a normal distribution, there is a 68.26 percent probability that a return will be within one standard deviation of the mean. In this example, there is a 68.26 percent probability that a yearly return will be between −8.0 percent and 32.2 percent.

There is a 95.44 percent probability that a return will be within two standard deviations of the mean. In this example, there is a 95.44 percent probability that a yearly return will be between −28.1 percent and 52.3 percent.

Finally, there is a 99.74 percent probability that a return will be within three standard deviations of the mean. In this example, there is a 99.74 percent probability that a yearly return will be between −48.2 percent and 72.4 percent.

return that is within one standard deviation of the mean of the distribution is approximately .68, or 2/3, and the probability of having a return that is within two standard deviations of the mean is approximately .95.

The 20.1 percent standard deviation we found for stock returns from 1926 through 2014 can now be interpreted in the following way: If stock returns are roughly normally distributed, the probability that a yearly return will fall within 20.1 percent of the mean of 12.1 percent will be approximately 2/3. That is, about 2/3 of the yearly returns will be between −8.0 percent and 32.2 percent. (Note that −8.0 = 12.1 − 20.1 and 32.2 = 12.1 + 20.1.) The probability that the return in any year will fall within two standard deviations is about .95. That is, about 95 percent of yearly returns will be between −28.1 percent and 52.3 percent.

10.6 More on Average Returns

Thus far in this chapter we have looked closely at simple average returns. But there is another way of computing an average return. The fact that average returns are calculated two different ways leads to some confusion, so our goal in this section is to explain the two approaches and also the circumstances under which each is most appropriate.

ARITHMETIC VERSUS GEOMETRIC AVERAGES

Let's start with a simple example. Suppose you buy a particular stock for $100. Unfortunately, the first year you own it, it falls to $50. The second year you own it, it rises back to $100, leaving you where you started (no dividends were paid).

What was your average return on this investment? Common sense seems to say that your average return must be exactly zero because you started with $100 and ended with $100. But if we calculate the returns year-by-year, we see that you lost 50 percent the first year (you lost half of your money). The second year, you made 100 percent (you doubled your money). Your average return over the two years was thus (−50 percent + 100 percent)/2 = 25 percent!

So which is correct, 0 percent or 25 percent? The answer is that both are correct; they just answer different questions. The 0 percent is called the **geometric average return**. The 25 percent is called the **arithmetic average return**. The geometric average return answers the question, *"What was your average compound return per year over a particular period?"* The arithmetic average return answers the question, *"What was your return in an average year over a particular period?"*

Notice that in previous sections, the average returns we calculated were all arithmetic averages, so we already know how to calculate them. What we need to do now is (1) learn how to calculate geometric averages and (2) learn the circumstances under which average is more meaningful than the other.

CALCULATING GEOMETRIC AVERAGE RETURNS

First, to illustrate how we calculate a geometric average return, suppose a particular investment had annual returns of 10 percent, 12 percent, 3 percent, and −9 percent over the last four years. The geometric average return over this four-year period is calculated as $(1.10 \times 1.12 \times 1.03 \times .91)^{1/4} - 1 = 3.66$ percent. In contrast, the average arithmetic return we have been calculating is $(.10 + .12 + .03 - .09)/4 = 4.0$ percent.

In general, if we have T years of returns, the geometric average return over these T years is calculated using this formula:

$$\text{Geometric average return} = [(1 + R_1) \times (1 + R_2) \times \cdots \times (1 + R_T)]^{1/T} - 1 \quad \textbf{(10.1)}$$

This formula tells us that four steps are required:

1. Take each of the T annual returns $R_1, R_2, \ldots, R_T$ and add 1 to each (after converting them to decimals).
2. Multiply all the numbers from step 1 together.
3. Take the result from step 2 and raise it to the power of $1/T$.
4. Finally, subtract 1 from the result of step 3. The result is the geometric average return.

EXAMPLE 10.5

Calculating the Geometric Average Return   Calculate the geometric average return for S&P 500 large-cap stocks for a five-year period using the numbers given here.

First convert percentages to decimal returns, add 1, and then calculate their product:

S&P 500 Returns	Product
13.75%	1.1375
35.70	× 1.3570
45.08	× 1.4508
−8.80	× .9120
−25.13	× .7487
	1.5291

Notice that the number 1.5291 is what our investment is worth after five years if we started with a $1 investment. The geometric average return is then calculated as:

$$\text{Geometric average return} = 1.5291^{1/5} - 1 = .0887, \text{ or } 8.87\%$$

Thus, the geometric average return is about 8.87 percent in this example. Here is a tip: If you are using a financial calculator, you can put $1 in as the present value, $1.5291 as the future value, and 5 as the number of periods. Then solve for the unknown rate. You should get the same answer we did.

You may have noticed in our examples thus far that the geometric average returns seem to be smaller. It turns out that this will always be true (as long as the returns are not all identical, in which case the two "averages" would be the same). To illustrate, Table 10.3 shows the arithmetic averages and standard deviations from Table 10.2, along with the geometric average returns.

As shown in Table 10.3, the geometric averages are all smaller, but the magnitude of the difference varies quite a bit. The reason is that the difference is greater for more volatile investments. In fact, there is a useful approximation. Assuming all the numbers are expressed in decimals (as opposed to percentages), the geometric average return is approximately equal to the arithmetic average return minus half the variance. For example, looking at the large-company stocks, the arithmetic average is 12.1 and the standard deviation is .201, implying that the variance is .040. The approximate geometric average is thus $.121 - \frac{.040}{2} = .100 \, (=10.0\%)$, which is very close to the actual value.

Table 10.3

Geometric versus
Arithmetic Average
Returns: 1926–2014

Series	Geometric Mean	Arithmetic Mean	Standard Deviation
Small-company stocks	12.2%	16.7%	32.1%
Large-company stocks	10.1	12.1	20.1
Long-term corporate bonds	6.1	6.4	8.4
Long-term government bonds	5.7	6.1	10.0
Intermediate-term government bonds	5.3	5.4	5.6
U.S. Treasury bills	3.5	3.5	3.1
Inflation	2.9	3.0	4.1

SOURCE: *Ibbotson SBBI 2015 Classic Yearbook.*

EXAMPLE 10.6

More Geometric Averages   Take a look back at Figure 10.4. There we showed the value of a $1 investment after 89 years. Use the value for the large-company stock investment to check the geometric average in Table 10.3.

In Figure 10.4, the large-company investment grew to $5,316.85 over 89 years. The geometric average return is thus:

$$\text{Geometric average return} = \$5{,}316.85^{1/89} - 1 = .101, \text{ or } 10.1\%$$

This 10.1 percent is the value shown in Table 10.3. For practice, check some of the other numbers in Table 10.3 the same way.

ARITHMETIC AVERAGE RETURN OR GEOMETRIC AVERAGE RETURN?

When we look at historical returns, the difference between the geometric and arithmetic average returns isn't too hard to understand. To put it slightly differently, the geometric average tells you what you actually earned per year on average, compounded annually. The arithmetic average tells you what you earned in a typical year and is an unbiased estimate of the true mean of the distribution. The geometric average is very useful in describing the actual historical investment experience. The arithmetic average is useful in making estimates of the future.[2]

10.7 The U.S. Equity Risk Premium: Historical and International Perspectives

So far, in this chapter, we have studied the United States in the period from 1926 to 2014. As we have discussed, the historical U.S. stock market risk premium has been substantial. Of course, anytime we use the past to predict the future, there is a danger that the past period isn't representative of what the future will hold. Perhaps U.S. investors got lucky over this period

---

[2]Another way of thinking about estimating an investment's return over a particular future horizon is to recall from your statistics class that the arithmetic average is a "sample" mean. As such, it provides an unbiased estimate of the underlying true mean. To use the arithmetic average to estimate the future returns, we must make sure the historical returns are measured using the same interval as the future forecasting period. For example, we could use yearly (annual) returns to estimate next year's return. The arithmetic average would be a good basis for forecasting the next two-year returns if two-year holding period returns were used. We also must be confident that the past distribution of returns is the same as that of the future.

Table 10.4
Estimate of World
Tradable Stock Market
Capitalization, 2015

Country	$ in Trillions	Percent
United States	$19.8	57.7%
Europe (excluding U.K.)	5.8	17.0
Japan	2.9	8.4
United Kingdom	2.7	8.0
Asia (excluding Japan)	1.8	5.3
Canada	1.3	3.7
	$34.3	100%

SOURCE: Uses the website for MSCI World Index, MSCI ASWI, as well as authors' rough estimates as of February 2015. Includes only large and midcap stocks, and accounts for about 85 percent of total world tradable capitalization.

and earned particularly large returns. Data from earlier years for the United States is available, though it is not of the same quality. With that caveat in mind, researchers have tracked returns back to 1802, and the U.S. equity risk premium in the pre-1926 era was smaller. Using the U.S. return data from 1802, the historical equity risk premium was 5.4 percent.[3]

Also, we have not looked at other major countries. Actually, more than half of the value of tradable stock is not in the United States. From Table 10.4, we can see that while the total world stock market capitalization was more than $34 trillion in 2014, only about 58 percent was in the United States. Thanks to Dimson, Marsh, and Staunton, data from earlier periods and other countries are now available to help us take a closer look at equity risk premiums. Table 10.5 and Figure 10.11 show the historical stock market risk premiums for 17 countries around the world in the period from 1900 to 2010. Looking at the numbers, the U.S. historical equity risk premium is the 7th highest at 7.2 percent (which differs from our earlier estimate because of the different time periods examined). The overall world average risk premium is 6.9 percent. It seems clear that U.S. investors did well, but not exceptionally so relative to many other countries. The top-performing countries according to the Sharpe ratio were the United States, Australia, South Africa, and France, while the worst performers were Belgium, Norway, and Denmark. Germany, Japan, and Italy might make an interesting case study because they have the highest stock returns over this period (despite World Wars I and II), but also the highest risk.

So what is a good estimate of the U.S. equity risk premium going forward? Unfortunately, nobody can know for sure what investors expect in the future. If history is a guide, the expected U.S. equity risk premium could be 7.2 percent based upon estimates from 1900–2010. We should also be mindful that the average world equity risk premium was 6.9 percent over this same period. On the other hand, the more recent periods (1926–2014) suggest higher estimates of the U.S. equity risk premium, and earlier periods going back to 1802 suggest lower estimates.

---

[3]Jeremy J. Siegel has estimated the U.S. equity risk premium with data from 1802. As can be seen in the following table, from 1802 to 2011 the historical equity risk premium was 5.4 percent.

	Average Returns 1802–2011 (%)
Common stock	9.6
Treasury bills	4.2
Equity risk premium	5.4

Adopted and updated from J. Siegel, *Stocks for the Long Run,* 4th ed. (New York: McGraw-Hill, 2008).

Table 10.5

Annualized Equity
Risk Premiums and
Sharpe Ratios for
17 Countries,
1900–2010

Country	Historical Equity Risk Premiums (%) (1)	Standard Deviation (%) (2)	The Sharpe Ratio (1)/(2)
Australia	8.3%	17.6%	.47
Belgium	5.5	24.7	.22
Canada	5.6	17.2	.33
Denmark	4.6	20.5	.22
France	8.7	24.5	.36
Germany*	9.8	31.8	.31
Ireland	5.3	21.5	.25
Italy	9.8	32.0	.31
Japan	9.0	27.7	.32
Netherlands	6.5	22.8	.29
Norway	5.9	26.5	.22
South Africa	8.3	22.1	.30
Spain	5.4	21.9	.25
Sweden	6.6	22.1	.30
Switzerland	5.1	18.9	.27
United Kingdom	6.0	19.9	.30
United States	7.2	19.8	.36
Average	**6.9**	**23.0**	**.30**

*Germany omits 1922–1923.

SOURCE: Elroy Dimson, Paul Marsh, and Michael Staunton, Credit Suisse Global Investment Returns Sourcebook, 2011, published by Credit Suisse Research Institute 2011. The Dimson-Marsh-Staunton data set is distributed by Morningstar, Inc.

Figure 10.11

Stock Market Risk
Premiums for
17 Countries:
1900–2010

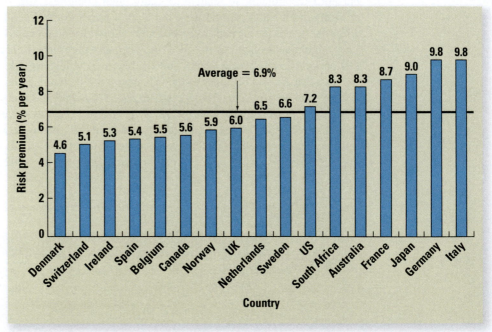

SOURCE: Elroy Dimson, Paul Marsh, and Michael Staunton, "The Worldwide Equity Premium: A Smaller Puzzle," in *Handbook of the Equity Risk Premium*, Rajnish Mehra, ed. (Elsevier, 2007). Updates by the authors.

The standard error (SE) helps with the issue of how much confidence we can have in our historical average of 7.2 percent. The SE is the standard deviation of the historical risk premium and is given by the following formula:

$$\text{SE} = \text{SD}(\overline{R}) = \frac{\text{SD}(R)}{\sqrt{\text{The number of observations}}}$$

If we assume that the distribution of returns is normal and that each year's return is independent of all the others, we know there is a 95.4 percent probability that the true mean return is within two standard errors of the historical average.

More specifically, the 95.4 percent confidence interval for the true equity risk premium is the historical average return $\pm$ (2 $\times$ standard error). As we have seen from 1900 to 2010, the historical equity risk premium of U.S. stocks was 7.2 percent and the standard deviation was 19.8 percent. Therefore 95.4 percent of the time the true equity risk premium should be within 3.43 and 10.97 percent:

$$7.2 \pm 2 \left(\frac{19.8}{\sqrt{111}} \right) = 7.2 \pm 2 \left(\frac{19.8}{10.5} \right) = 7.2 \pm 3.77$$

In other words, we can be 95.4 percent confident that our estimate of the U.S. equity risk premium from historical data is in the range from 3.43 percent to 10.97 percent.

Taking a slightly different approach, Ivo Welch asked the opinions of 226 financial economists regarding the future U.S. equity risk premium, and the median response was 7 percent.[4]

We are comfortable with an estimate based on the historical U.S. equity risk premium of about 7 percent, but estimates of the future U.S. equity risk premium that are somewhat higher or lower could be reasonable if we have good reason to believe the past is not representative of the future.[5] The bottom line is that any estimate of the future equity risk premium will involve assumptions about the future risk environment as well as the amount of risk aversion of future investors.

10.8   2008: A Year of Financial Crisis

2008 entered the record books as one of the worst years for stock market investors in U.S. history. How bad was it? The widely followed S&P 500 Index, which tracks the total market value of 500 of the largest U.S. corporations, decreased 37 percent for the year. Of the 500 stocks in the index, 485 were down for the year.

Over the period 1926–2008, only the year 1931 had a lower return than 2008 (-43 percent versus -37 percent). Making matters worse, the downdraft continued with a further decline of 8.43 percent in January 2009. In all, from November 2007 (when the decline began) through January 2009, the S&P 500 lost 45 percent of its value.

---

[4]For example, see I. Welch, "Views of Financial Economists on the Equity Premium and Other Issues," *Journal of Business,* 73 (2000), pp. 501–537. Shannon P. Pratt and Roger J. Grabowski ("Cost of Capital: Applications and Examples," John Wiley, 2010) conclude, after reviewing a variety of evidence, that the equity risk premium is in the 3.5 to 6 percent range.

[5]In Elroy Dimson, Paul Marsh, and Mike Staunton, "The Worldwide Equity Premium: A Smaller Puzzle," from *Handbook of the Equity Risk Premium,* R. Mehra, ed., the authors argue that a good estimate of the world equity risk premium going forward should be about 5 percent, largely because of nonrecurring factors that positively affected worldwide historical returns. However, it could be argued that the global financial crisis of 2008–2009 was a negative shock to the stock market that has increased the equity risk premium from its historical levels.

Figure 10.12
S&P 500 Monthly
Returns, 2008

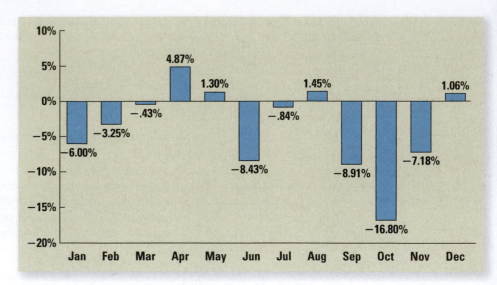

Figure 10.12 shows the month-by-month performance of the S&P 500 decline during 2008. As indicated, returns were negative in eight of the twelve months. Most of the decline occurred in the fall, with investors losing almost 17 percent in October alone. Small stocks fared no better. They also fell 37 percent for the year (with a 21 percent drop in October), their worst performance since losing 58 percent in 1937.

As Figure 10.12 suggests, stock prices were highly volatile at the end the year—more than has been generally true historically. Oddly, the S&P had 126 up days and 126 down days (remember the markets are closed weekends and holidays). Of course, the down days were much worse on average.

The drop in stock prices was a global phenomenon, and many of the world's major markets declined by much more than the S&P. China, India, and Russia, for example, all experienced declines of more than 50 percent. Tiny Iceland saw share prices drop by more than 90 percent for the year. Trading on the Icelandic exchange was temporarily suspended on October 9. In what has to be a modern record for a single day, stocks fell by 76 percent when trading resumed on October 14.

Did any types of securities perform well in 2008? The answer is yes, because, as stock values declined, bond values increased, particularly U.S. Treasury bonds. In fact, long-term Treasury bonds *gained* 20 percent, while shorter-term Treasury bonds were up 13 percent. Higher quality long-term corporate bonds did less well, but still managed to achieve a positive return of about 9 percent. These returns were especially impressive considering that the rate of inflation, as measured by the CPI, was very close to zero.

Of course, stock prices can be volatile in both directions. From March 2009 through February 2011, a period of about 700 days, the S&P 500 doubled in value. This climb was the fastest doubling since 1936 when the S&P did it in just 500 days. So, what lessons should investors take away from this recent, and very turbulent, bit of capital market history? First, and most obviously, stocks have significant risk! But there is a second, equally important lesson. Depending on the mix, a diversified portfolio of stocks and bonds might have suffered in 2008, but the losses would have been much smaller than those experienced by an all-stock portfolio. In other words, diversification matters, a point we will examine in detail in our next chapter.

Summary and Conclusions

1. This chapter presented returns for a number of different asset classes. The general conclusion is that stocks have outperformed bonds over most of the 20th century, though stocks have also exhibited more risk.

2. The statistical measures in this chapter are necessary building blocks for the material of the next three chapters. In particular, standard deviation and variance measure the variability of the returns on an individual security and on portfolios of securities. In the next chapter, we will argue that standard deviation and variance are appropriate measures of the risk of an individual security if an investor's portfolio is composed of that security only.

Concept Questions

1. **Investment Selection**   Given that RadNet was up by about 411 percent for 2014, why didn't all investors hold RadNet?

2. **Investment Selection**   Given that Transocean was down by about 63 percent for 2014, why did some investors hold the stock? Why didn't they sell out before the price declined so sharply?

3. **Risk and Return**   We have seen that over long periods stock investments have tended to substantially outperform bond investments. However, it is not at all uncommon to observe investors with long horizons holding their investments entirely in bonds. Are such investors irrational?

4. **Stocks versus Gambling**   Critically evaluate the following statement: Playing the stock market is like gambling. Such speculative investing has no social value, other than the pleasure people get from this form of gambling.

5. **Effects of Inflation**   Look at Table 10.1 and Figure 10.7 in the text. When were T-bill rates at their highest over the period from 1926 through 2014? Why do you think they were so high during this period? What relationship underlies your answer?

6. **Risk Premiums**   Is it possible for the risk premium to be negative before an investment is undertaken? Can the risk premium be negative after the fact? Explain.

7. **Returns**   Two years ago, General Materials' and Standard Fixtures' stock prices were the same. During the first year, General Materials' stock price increased by 10 percent while Standard Fixtures' stock price decreased by 10 percent. During the second year, General Materials' stock price decreased by 10 percent and Standard Fixtures' stock price increased by 10 percent. Do these two stocks have the same price today? Explain.

8. **Returns**   Two years ago, the Lake Minerals and Small Town Furniture stock prices were the same. The average annual return for both stocks over the past two years was 10 percent. Lake Minerals' stock price increased 10 percent each year. Small Town Furniture's stock price increased 25 percent in the first year and lost 5 percent last year. Do these two stocks have the same price today?

9. **Arithmetic versus Geometric Returns**   What is the difference between arithmetic and geometric returns? Suppose you have invested in a stock for the last 10 years. Which number is more important to you, the arithmetic or geometric return?

10. **Historical Returns**   The historical asset class returns presented in the chapter are not adjusted for inflation. What would happen to the estimated risk premium if we did account for inflation? The returns are also not adjusted for taxes. What would happen to the returns if we accounted for taxes? What would happen to the volatility?

Questions and Problems

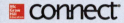

BASIC
(Questions 1–18)

1. **Calculating Returns** Suppose a stock had an initial price of $64 per share, paid a dividend of $1.20 per share during the year, and had an ending share price of $73. Compute the percentage total return.

2. **Calculating Yields** In Problem 1, what was the dividend yield? The capital gains yield?

3. **Calculating Returns** Rework Problems 1 and 2 assuming the ending share price is $57.

4. **Calculating Returns** Suppose you bought a bond with a 5.8 percent coupon rate one year ago for $1,030. The bond sells for $1,059 today.

   a. Assuming a $1,000 face value, what was your total dollar return on this investment over the past year?
   b. What was your total nominal rate of return on this investment over the past year?
   c. If the inflation rate last year was 3 percent, what was your total real rate of return on this investment?

5. **Nominal versus Real Returns** What was the arithmetic average annual return on large-company stocks from 1926 through 2014?

   a. In nominal terms?
   b. In real terms?

6. **Bond Returns** What is the historical real return on long-term government bonds? On long-term corporate bonds?

7. **Calculating Returns and Variability** Using the following returns, calculate the average returns, the variances, and the standard deviations for X and Y:

	Returns	
Year	X	Y
1	9%	12%
2	21	27
3	−27	−32
4	15	14
5	23	36

8. **Risk Premiums** Refer to Table 10.1 in the text and look at the period from 1973 through 1978.

   a. Calculate the arithmetic average returns for large-company stocks and T-bills over this period.
   b. Calculate the standard deviation of the returns for large-company stocks and T-bills over this period.
   c. Calculate the observed risk premium in each year for the large-company stocks versus the T-bills. What was the arithmetic average risk premium over this period? What was the standard deviation of the risk premium over this period?

9. **Calculating Returns and Variability** You've observed the following returns on SkyNet Data Corporation's stock over the past five years: 21 percent, 17 percent, 26 percent, −7 percent, and 4 percent.

   a. What was the arithmetic average return on the company's stock over this five-year period?
   b. What was the variance of the company's returns over this period? The standard deviation?

10. **Calculating Real Returns and Risk Premiums**   In Problem 9, suppose the average inflation rate over this period was 4.2 percent, and the average T-bill rate over the period was 5.1 percent.

   a. What was the average real return on the company's stock?
   b. What was the average nominal risk premium on the company's stock?

11. **Calculating Real Rates**   Given the information in Problem 10, what was the average real risk-free rate over this time period? What was the average real risk premium?

12. **Holding Period Return**   A stock has had returns of 14.38 percent, 8.43 percent, 11.97 percent, 25.83 percent, and −9.17 percent over the past five years, respectively. What was the holding period return for the stock?

13. **Calculating Returns**   You purchased a zero coupon bond one year ago for $160.53. The market interest rate is now 7.5 percent. If the bond had 25 years to maturity when you originally purchased it, what was your total return for the past year?

14. **Calculating Returns**   You bought a share of 3.5 percent preferred stock for $92.07 last year. The market price for your stock is now $96.12. What was your total return for last year?

15. **Calculating Returns**   You bought a stock three months ago for $62.18 per share. The stock paid no dividends. The current share price is $65.37. What is the APR of your investment? The EAR?

16. **Calculating Real Returns**   Refer to Table 10.1. What was the average real return for Treasury bills from 1926 through 1932?

17. **Return Distributions**   Refer back to Table 10.2. What range of returns would you expect to see 68 percent of the time for long-term corporate bonds? What about 95 percent of the time?

18. **Return Distributions**   Refer back to Table 10.2. What range of returns would you expect to see 68 percent of the time for large-company stocks? What about 95 percent of the time?

INTERMEDIATE
(Questions 19–26)

19. **Calculating Returns and Variability**   You find a certain stock that had returns of 12 percent, −15 percent, 13 percent, and 27 percent for four of the last five years. If the average return of the stock over this period was 10.5 percent, what was the stock's return for the missing year? What is the standard deviation of the stock's returns?

20. **Arithmetic and Geometric Returns**   A stock has had returns of 24 percent, 12 percent, 38 percent, −2 percent, 21 percent, and −16 percent over the last six years. What are the arithmetic and geometric returns for the stock?

21. **Arithmetic and Geometric Returns**   A stock has had the following year-end prices and dividends:

Year	Price	Dividend
1	$73.18	—
2	77.98	$ 1.15
3	69.13	1.25
4	84.65	1.36
5	91.37	1.47
6	103.66	1.60

What are the arithmetic and geometric returns for the stock?

22. **Calculating Returns**   Refer to Table 10.1 in the text and look at the period from 1973 through 1980.

   a. Calculate the average return for Treasury bills and the average annual inflation rate (consumer price index) for this period.
   b. Calculate the standard deviation of Treasury bill returns and inflation over this period.
   c. Calculate the real return for each year. What is the average real return for Treasury bills?
   d. Many people consider Treasury bills to be risk-free. What do these calculations tell you about the potential risks of Treasury bills?

23. **Calculating Investment Returns**   You bought one of Bergen Manufacturing Co.'s 6.4 percent coupon bonds one year ago for $1,032.50. These bonds make annual payments and mature six years from now. Suppose you decide to sell your bonds today when the required return on the bonds is 5.5 percent. If the inflation rate was 3.2 percent over the past year, what would be your total real return on the investment?

24. **Using Return Distributions**   Suppose the returns on long-term government bonds are normally distributed. Based on the historical record, what is the approximate probability that your return on these bonds will be less than −3.7 percent in a given year? What range of returns would you expect to see 95 percent of the time? What range would you expect to see 99 percent of the time?

25. **Using Return Distributions**   Assuming that the returns from holding small-company stocks are normally distributed, what is the approximate probability that your money will double in value in a single year? Triple in value?

26. **Distributions**   In the previous problem, what is the probability that the return is less than −100 percent? (Think.) What are the implications for the distribution of returns?

CHALLENGE
(Questions 27–28)

27. **Using Probability Distributions**   Suppose the returns on large-company stocks are normally distributed. Based on the historical record, use the NORMDIST function in Excel® to determine the probability that in any given year you will lose money by investing in common stock.

28. **Using Probability Distributions**   Suppose the returns on long-term corporate bonds and T-bills are normally distributed. Based on the historical record, use the NORMDIST function in Excel® to answer the following questions:

   a. What is the probability that in any given year, the return on long-term corporate bonds will be greater than 10 percent? Less than 0 percent?
   b. What is the probability that in any given year, the return on T-bills will be greater than 10 percent? Less than 0 percent?
   c. In 1979, the return on long-term corporate bonds was −4.18 percent. How likely is it that this low of a return will recur at some point in the future? T-bills had a return of 10.56 percent in this same year. How likely is it that this high of a return on T-bills will recur at some point in the future?

Excel Master It! Problem

As we have seen, over the 1926–2014 period, small company stocks had the highest return and the highest risk, while U.S. Treasury bills had the lowest return and the lowest risk. While we certainly hope you have an 89-year holding period, it is likely your investment horizon will be somewhat shorter. One way risk and return are examined over a shorter investment period is by using rolling returns and standard deviations. Suppose you have a series of annual returns and you want to calculate a 3-year rolling average return. You would calculate the first rolling average at Year 3 using the returns for the first three years. The next rolling average would be calculated using the returns from Years 2, 3, and 4, and so on.

a. Using the annual returns for large company stocks and Treasury bills, calculate both the 5- and 10-year rolling average return and standard deviation.

b. Over how many 5-year periods did Treasury bills outperform large company stocks? How many 10-year periods?

c. Over how many 5-year periods did Treasury bills have a larger standard deviation than large company stocks? Over how many 10-year periods?

d. Graph the rolling 5-year and 10-year average returns for large company stocks and Treasury bills.

e. What conclusions do you draw from the above results?

Mini Case

A JOB AT EAST COAST YACHTS

You recently graduated from college, and your job search led you to East Coast Yachts. Because you felt the company's business was seaworthy, you accepted a job offer. The first day on the job, while you are finishing your employment paperwork, Dan Ervin, who works in Finance, stops by to inform you about the company's 401(k) plan.

A 401(k) plan is a retirement plan offered by many companies. Such plans are tax-deferred savings vehicles, meaning that any deposits you make into the plan are deducted from your current pretax income, so no current taxes are paid on the money. For example, assume your salary will be $50,000 per year. If you contribute $3,000 to the 401(k) plan, you will pay taxes on only $47,000 in income. There are also no taxes paid on any capital gains or income while you are invested in the plan, but you do pay taxes when you withdraw money at retirement. As is fairly common, the company also has a 5 percent match. This means that the company will match your contribution up to 5 percent of your salary, but you must contribute to get the match.

The 401(k) plan has several options for investments, most of which are mutual funds. A mutual fund is a portfolio of assets. When you purchase shares in a mutual fund, you are actually purchasing partial ownership of the fund's assets. The return of the fund is the weighted average of the return of the assets owned by the fund, minus any expenses. The largest expense is typically the management fee, paid to the fund manager. The management fee is compensation for the manager, who makes all of the investment decisions for the fund.

East Coast Yachts uses Bledsoe Financial Services as its 401(k) plan administrator. Here are the investment options offered for employees:

Company Stock   One option in the 401(k) plan is stock in East Coast Yachts. The company is currently privately held. However, when you interviewed with the owner, Larissa Warren, she informed you the company was expected to go public in the next three to four years. Until then, a company stock price is simply set each year by the board of directors.

Bledsoe S&P 500 Index Fund   This mutual fund tracks the S&P 500. Stocks in the fund are weighted exactly the same as the S&P 500. This means the fund return is approximately the return on the S&P 500, minus expenses. Because an index fund purchases assets based on the composition of the index it is following, the fund manager is not required to research stocks and make investment decisions. The result is that the fund expenses are usually low. The Bledsoe S&P 500 Index Fund charges expenses of .15 percent of assets per year.

Bledsoe Small-Cap Fund   This fund primarily invests in small-capitalization stocks. As such, the returns of the fund are more volatile. The fund can also invest 10 percent of its assets in companies based outside the United States. This fund charges 1.70 percent in expenses.

Bledsoe Large-Company Stock Fund   This fund invests primarily in large-capitalization stocks of companies based in the United States. The fund is managed by Evan Bledsoe and has outperformed the market in six of the last eight years. The fund charges 1.50 percent in expenses.

Bledsoe Bond Fund   This fund invests in long-term corporate bonds issued by U.S.–domiciled companies. The fund is restricted to investments in bonds with an investment-grade credit rating. This fund charges 1.40 percent in expenses.

Bledsoe Money Market Fund   This fund invests in short-term, high–credit quality debt instruments, which include Treasury bills. As such, the return on the money market fund is only slightly higher than the return on Treasury bills. Because of the credit quality and short-term nature of the investments, there is only a very slight risk of negative return. The fund charges .60 percent in expenses.

1. What advantages do the mutual funds offer compared to the company stock?

2. Assume that you invest 5 percent of your salary and receive the full 5 percent match from East Coast Yachts. What EAR do you earn from the match? What conclusions do you draw about matching plans?

3. Assume you decide you should invest at least part of your money in large-capitalization stocks of companies based in the United States. What are the advantages and disadvantages of choosing the Bledsoe Large-Company Stock Fund compared to the Bledsoe S&P 500 Index Fund?

4. The returns on the Bledsoe Small-Cap Fund are the most volatile of all the mutual funds offered in the 401(k) plan. Why would you ever want to invest in this fund? When you examine the expenses of the mutual funds, you will notice that this fund also has the highest expenses. Does this affect your decision to invest in this fund?

5. A measure of risk-adjusted performance that is often used is the Sharpe ratio. The Sharpe ratio is calculated as the risk premium of an asset divided by its standard deviation. The standard deviations and returns of the funds over the past 10 years are listed here. Calculate the Sharpe ratio for each of these funds. Assume that the expected return and standard deviation of the company stock will be 16 percent and 65 percent, respectively. Calculate the Sharpe ratio for the company stock. How appropriate is the Sharpe ratio for these assets? When would you use the Sharpe ratio? Assume a 3.2 percent risk-free rate.

	10-Year Annual Return	Standard Deviation
Bledsoe S&P 500 Index Fund	9.18%	20.43%
Bledsoe Small-Cap Fund	14.12	25.13
Bledsoe Large-Company Stock Fund	8.58	23.82
Bledsoe Bond Fund	6.45	9.85

6. What portfolio allocation would you choose? Why? Explain your thinking carefully.

11

Return and Risk

THE CAPITAL ASSET PRICING MODEL (CAPM)

Expected returns on common stocks can vary quite a bit. One important determinant is the industry in which a company operates. For example, according to recent estimates from Morningstar, the median expected return for department stores, which includes companies such as Sears and Kohl's, is 14.47 percent, whereas air transportation companies such as Delta and Southwest have a median expected return of 10.99 percent. Computer software companies such as Microsoft and Oracle have a median expected return of 11.61 percent.

These estimates raise some obvious questions. First, why do these industry expected returns differ so much, and how are these specific numbers calculated? Also, does the higher return offered by department store stocks mean that investors should prefer these to, say, air transportation companies? As we will see in this chapter, the Nobel prize–winning answers to these questions form the basis of our modern understanding of risk and return.

11.1 Individual Securities

In the first part of Chapter 11, we will examine the characteristics of individual securities. In particular, we will discuss:

1. *Expected return:* This is the return that an individual expects a stock to earn over the next period. Of course, because this is only an expectation, the actual return may be either higher or lower. An individual's expectation may simply be the average return per period a security has earned in the past. Alternatively, the expectation may be based on a detailed analysis of a firm's prospects, on some computer-based model, or on special (or inside) information.

2. *Variance and standard deviation:* There are many ways to assess the volatility of a security's return. One of the most common is variance, which is a measure of the squared deviations of a security's return from its expected return. Standard deviation is the square root of the variance.

3. *Covariance and correlation*: Returns on individual securities are related to one another. Covariance is a statistic measuring the interrelationship between two securities. Alternatively, this relationship can be restated in terms of the correlation between the two securities. Covariance and correlation are building blocks to an understanding of the beta coefficient.

11.2 Expected Return, Variance, and Covariance

EXPECTED RETURN AND VARIANCE

Suppose financial analysts believe that there are four equally likely states of the economy: Depression, recession, normal, and boom. The returns on the Supertech Company are expected to follow the economy closely, while the returns on the Slowpoke Company are not. The return predictions are as follows:

	Supertech Returns R_{At}	Slowpoke Returns R_{Bt}
Depression	−20%	5%
Recession	10	20
Normal	30	−12
Boom	50	9

Variance can be calculated in four steps. An additional step is needed to calculate standard deviation. (The calculations are presented in Table 11.1.) The steps are:

1. Calculate the expected return:

Supertech:

$$\frac{-.20 + .10 + .30 + .50}{4} = .175 = 17.5\% = \overline{R}_A$$

Slowpoke:

$$\frac{.05 + .20 - .12 + .09}{4} = .055 = 5.5\% = \overline{R}_B$$

2. For each company, calculate the deviation of each possible return from the company's expected return given previously. This is presented in the third column of Table 11.1.

3. The deviations we have calculated are indications of the dispersion of returns. However, because some are positive and some are negative, it is difficult to work with them in this form. For example, if we were simply to add up all the deviations for a single company, we would get zero as the sum.

    To make the deviations more meaningful, we multiply each one by itself. Now all the numbers are positive, implying that their sum must be positive as well. The squared deviations are presented in the last column of Table 11.1.

4. For each company, calculate the average squared deviation, which is the variance:[1]

Supertech:

$$\frac{.140625 + .005625 + .015625 + .105625}{4} = .066875$$

---

[1] In this example, the four states give rise to four equally likely possible outcomes. The expected return is calculated by taking a probability weighted average of the possible outcomes. For Supertech,

$$.25 \times (-.20) + .25 \times .10 + .25 \times .30 + .25 \times .50 = .175$$

Because the four possible outcomes are equally likely, we can simplify by adding up the possible outcomes and dividing by 4. If outcomes are not equally likely, this simplification does not work.

The same type of calculation is required for variance. We take a probability weighted average of the squared deviations. For Supertech,

$$.25 \times .140625 + .25 \times .005625 + .25 \times .015625 + .25 \times .105625 = .066875$$

This is the same as adding up the possible squared deviations and dividing by 4.

If we use past data (as in Chapter 10), the divisor is always the number of historical observations less 1.

Table 11.1
Calculating Variance and Standard Deviation

(1) State of Economy	(2) Rate of Return	(3) Deviation from Expected Return	(4) Squared Value of Deviation
Supertech		(Expected return = .175)	
	R_{At}	$(R_{At} - \bar{R}_A)$	$(R_{At} - \bar{R}_A)^2$
Depression	−.20	−.375 (= −.20 − .175)	.140625 [= (−.375)²]
Recession	.10	−.075	.005625
Normal	.30	.125	.015625
Boom	.50	.325	.105625
Slowpoke		(Expected return = .055)	
	R_{Bt}	$(R_{Bt} - \bar{R}_B)$	$(R_{Bt} - \bar{R}_B)^2$
Depression	.05	−.005 (= .05 − .055)	.000025 [= (−.005)²]
Recession	.20	.145	.021025
Normal	−.12	−.175	.030625
Boom	.09	.035	.001225

Slowpoke:

$$\frac{.000025 + .021025 + .030625 + .001225}{4} = .013225$$

Thus, the variance of Supertech is .066875, and the variance of Slowpoke is .013225.

5. Calculate standard deviation by taking the square root of the variance:

Supertech:

$$\sqrt{.066875} = .2586 = 25.86\%$$

Slowpoke:

$$\sqrt{.013225} = .1150 = 11.50\%$$

Algebraically, the formula for variance can be expressed as:

$$\text{Var}(R) = \text{Expected value of } (R - \bar{R})^2$$

where $\bar{R}$ is the security's expected return and R is the actual return.

A look at the four-step calculation for variance makes it clear why it is a measure of the spread of the sample of returns. For each observation we square the difference between the actual return and the expected return. We then take an average of these squared differences. Squaring the differences makes them all positive. If we used the differences between each return and the expected return and then averaged these differences, we would get zero because the returns that were above the mean would cancel the ones below.

However, because the variance is still expressed in squared terms, it is difficult to interpret. Standard deviation has a much simpler interpretation, which was provided in Section 10.5. Standard deviation is simply the square root of the variance. The general formula for the standard deviation is:

$$SD(R) = \sqrt{Var(R)}$$

COVARIANCE AND CORRELATION

Variance and standard deviation measure the variability of individual stocks. We now wish to measure the relationship between the return on one stock and the return on another. Enter **covariance** and **correlation**.

Covariance and correlation measure how two random variables are related. We explain these terms by extending the Supertech and Slowpoke example.

Calculating Covariance and Correlation   We have already determined the expected returns and standard deviations for both Supertech and Slowpoke. (The expected returns are .175 and .055 for Supertech and Slowpoke, respectively. The standard deviations are .2586 and .1150, respectively.) In addition, we calculated the deviation of each possible return from the expected return for each firm. Using these data, we can calculate covariance in two steps. An extra step is needed to calculate correlation.

1. For each state of the economy, multiply Supertech's deviation from its expected return by Slowpoke's deviation from its expected return. For example, Supertech's rate of return in a depression is −.20, which is −.375 (=−.20 − .175) from its expected return. Slowpoke's rate of return in a depression is .05, which is −.005 (=.05 − .055) from its expected return. Multiplying the two deviations together yields .001875 [=(−.375) × (−.005)]. The actual calculations are given in the last column of Table 11.2. This procedure can be written algebraically as:

$$(R_{At} - \overline{R}_A) \times (R_{Bt} - \overline{R}_B) \tag{11.1}$$

where R_{At} and R_{Bt} are the returns on Supertech and Slowpoke in state t. $\overline{R}_A$ and $\overline{R}_B$ are the expected returns on the two securities.

2. Calculate the average value of the four states in the last column. This average is the covariance. That is:[2]

$$\sigma_{AB} = Cov(R_A, R_B) = \frac{-.0195}{4} = -.004875$$

Note that we represent the covariance between Supertech and Slowpoke as either $Cov(R_A, R_B)$ or σ_{AB}. Equation 11.1 illustrates the intuition of covariance. Suppose Supertech's return is generally

---

[2]As with variance, we divided by N (4 in this example) because the four states give rise to four equally likely *possible* outcomes.

Table 11.2   Calculating Covariance and Correlation

State of Economy	Rate of Return of Supertech R_{At}	Deviation from Expected Return $(R_{At} - \overline{R}_A)$	Rate of Return of Slowpoke R_{Bt}	Deviation from Expected Return $(R_{Bt} - \overline{R}_B)$	Product of Deviations $(R_{At} - \overline{R}_A) \times (R_{Bt} - \overline{R}_B)$
		(Expected return = .175)		(Expected return = .055)	
Depression	−.20	−.375 (= −.20 − .175)	.05	−.005 (= .05 − .055)	.001875 (= −.375 × −.005)
Recession	.10	−.075	.20	.145	−.010875 (= −.075 × .145)
Normal	.30	.125	−.12	−.175	−.021875 (= .125 × −.175)
Boom	.50	.325	.09	.035	.011375 (= .325 × .035)
					−.0195

above its average when Slowpoke's return is above its average, and Supertech's return is generally below its average when Slowpoke's return is below its average. This shows a positive dependency or a positive relationship between the two returns. Note that the term in Equation 11.1 will be *positive* in any state where both returns are *above* their averages. In addition, Equation 11.1 will still be *positive* in any state where both terms are *below* their averages. Thus a positive relationship between the two returns will give rise to a positive value for covariance.

Conversely, suppose Supertech's return is generally above its average when Slowpoke's return is below its average, and Supertech's return is generally below its average when Slowpoke's return is above its average. This demonstrates a negative dependency or a negative relationship between the two returns. Note that the term in Equation 11.1 will be *negative* in any state where one return is above its average and the other return is below its average. Thus a negative relationship between the two returns will give rise to a negative value for covariance.

Finally, suppose there is no relationship between the two returns. In this case, knowing whether the return on Supertech is above or below its expected return tells us nothing about the return on Slowpoke. In the covariance formula, then, there will be no tendency for the deviations to be positive or negative together. On average, they will tend to offset each other and cancel out, making the covariance zero.

Of course, even if the two returns are unrelated to each other, the covariance formula will not equal zero exactly in any actual history. This is due to sampling error; randomness alone will make the calculation positive or negative. But for a historical sample that is long enough, if the two returns are not related to each other, we should expect the covariance to come close to zero.

The covariance formula seems to capture what we are looking for. If the two returns are positively related to each other, they will have a positive covariance, and if they are negatively related to each other, the covariance will be negative. Last, and very important, if they are unrelated, the covariance should be zero.

(continued)

The formula for covariance can be written algebraically as:

$$\sigma_{AB} = \text{Cov}(R_A, R_B) = \text{Expected value of } [(R_A - \bar{R}_A) \times (R_B - \bar{R}_B)]$$

where $\bar{R}_A$ and $\bar{R}_B$ are the expected returns on the two securities and R_A and R_B are the actual returns. The ordering of the two variables is unimportant. That is, the covariance of A with B is equal to the covariance of B with A. This can be stated more formally as $\text{Cov}(R_A, R_B) = \text{Cov}(R_B, R_A)$ or $\sigma_{AB} = \sigma_{BA}$.

The covariance we calculated is $-.004875$. A negative number like this implies that the return on one stock is likely to be above its average when the return on the other stock is below its average, and vice versa. However, the size of the number is difficult to interpret. Like the variance figure, the covariance is in squared deviation units. Until we can put it in perspective, we don't know what to make of it.

We solve the problem by computing the correlation.

3. To calculate the correlation, divide the covariance by the product of the standard deviations of both of the two securities. For our example, we have:

$$\rho_{AB} = \text{Corr}(R_A, R_B) = \frac{\text{Cov}(R_A, R_B)}{\sigma_A \times \sigma_B} = \frac{-.004875}{.2586 \times .1150} = -.1639 \qquad (11.2)$$

where σ_A and σ_B are the standard deviations of Supertech and Slowpoke, respectively. Note that we represent the correlation between Supertech and Slowpoke either as $\text{Corr}(R_A, R_B)$ or ρ_{AB}. As with covariance, the ordering of the two variables is unimportant. That is, the correlation of A with B is equal to the correlation of B with A. More formally, $\text{Corr}(R_A, R_B) = \text{Corr}(R_B, R_A)$ or $\rho_{AB} = \rho_{BA}$.

Figure 11.1 Examples of Different Correlation Coefficients—Graphs Plotting the Separate Returns on Two Securities through Time

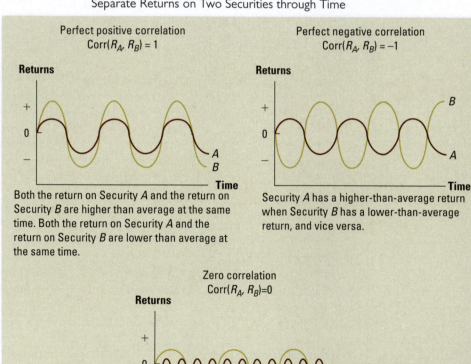

Perfect positive correlation
$\text{Corr}(R_A, R_B) = 1$

Both the return on Security A and the return on Security B are higher than average at the same time. Both the return on Security A and the return on Security B are lower than average at the same time.

Perfect negative correlation
$\text{Corr}(R_A, R_B) = -1$

Security A has a higher-than-average return when Security B has a lower-than-average return, and vice versa.

Zero correlation
$\text{Corr}(R_A, R_B) = 0$

The return on Security A is completely unrelated to the return on Security B.

Because the standard deviation is always positive, the sign of the correlation between two variables must be the same as that of the covariance between the two variables. If the correlation is positive, we say that the variables are *positively correlated;* if it is negative, we say that they are *negatively correlated;* and if it is zero, we say that they are *uncorrelated.* Furthermore, it can be proved that the correlation is always between +1 and −1. This is due to the standardizing procedure of dividing by the product of the two standard deviations.

We can also compare the correlation between different *pairs* of securities. For example, it turns out that the correlation between General Motors and Ford is much higher than the correlation between General Motors and IBM. Hence, we can state that the first pair of securities is more interrelated than the second pair.

Figure 11.1 shows the three benchmark cases for two assets, *A* and *B*. The figure shows two assets with return correlations of +1, −1, and 0. This implies perfect positive correlation, perfect negative correlation, and no correlation, respectively. The graphs in the figure plot the separate returns on the two securities through time.

11.3 The Return and Risk for Portfolios

Suppose an investor has estimates of the expected returns and standard deviations on individual securities and the correlations between securities. How does the investor choose the best combination or **portfolio** of securities to hold? Obviously, the investor would like a portfolio with a high expected return and a low standard deviation of return. It is therefore worthwhile to consider:

1. The relationship between the expected returns on individual securities and the expected return on a portfolio made up of these securities.
2. The relationship between the standard deviations of individual securities, the correlations between these securities, and the standard deviation of a portfolio made up of these securities.

To analyze these two relationships, we will use the same example of Supertech and Slowpoke. The relevant calculations follow.

THE EXPECTED RETURN ON A PORTFOLIO

The formula for expected return on a portfolio is very simple:

The expected return on a portfolio is a weighted average of the expected returns on the individual securities.

Relevant Data from Example of Supertech and Slowpoke		
Item	**Symbol**	**Value**
Expected return on Supertech	$\overline{R}_{Super}$	.175 = 17.5%
Expected return on Slowpoke	$\overline{R}_{Slow}$	.055 = 5.5%
Variance of Supertech	σ^2_{Super}	.066875
Variance of Slowpoke	σ^2_{Slow}	.013225
Standard deviation of Supertech	σ_{Super}	.2586 = 25.86%
Standard deviation of Slowpoke	σ_{Slow}	.1150 = 11.50%
Covariance between Supertech and Slowpoke	$\sigma_{Super,Slow}$	−.004875
Correlation between Supertech and Slowpoke	$\rho_{Super,Slow}$	−.1639

**EXAMPLE
11.2**

Portfolio Expected Returns Consider Supertech and Slowpoke. From our earlier calculations, we find that the expected returns on these two securities are 17.5 percent and 5.5 percent, respectively.

The expected return on a portfolio of these two securities alone can be written as:

$$\text{Expected return on portfolio} = X_{\text{Super}}(17.5\%) + X_{\text{Slow}}(5.5\%) = \bar{R}_P$$

where X_{Super} is the percentage of the portfolio in Supertech and X_{Slow} is the percentage of the portfolio in Slowpoke. If the investor with $100 invests $60 in Supertech and $40 in Slowpoke, the expected return on the portfolio can be written as:

$$\text{Expected return on portfolio} = .6 \times 17.5\% + .4 \times 5.5\% = 12.7\%$$

Algebraically, we can write:

$$\text{Expected return on portfolio} = X_A\bar{R}_A + X_B\bar{R}_B = \bar{R}_P \qquad \text{(11.3)}$$

where X_A and X_B are the proportions of the total portfolio in the assets A and B, respectively. (Because our investor can invest in only two securities, $X_A + X_B$ must equal 1 or 100 percent.) $\bar{R}_A$ and $\bar{R}_B$ are the expected returns on the two securities.

Now consider two stocks, each with an expected return of 10 percent. The expected return on a portfolio composed of these two stocks must be 10 percent, regardless of the proportions of the two stocks held. This result may seem obvious at this point, but it will become important later. The result implies that you do not reduce or *dissipate* your expected return by investing in a number of securities. Rather, the expected return on your portfolio is simply a weighted average of the expected returns on the individual assets in the portfolio.

VARIANCE AND STANDARD DEVIATION OF A PORTFOLIO

The Variance The formula for the variance of a portfolio composed of two securities, A and B, is:

The Variance of the Portfolio:

$$\text{Var(portfolio)} = X_A^2\sigma_A^2 + 2X_AX_B\sigma_{A,B} + X_B^2\sigma_B^2$$

Note that there are three terms on the right side of the equation. The first term involves the variance of Security A (σ_A^2), the second term involves the covariance between the two securities ($\sigma_{A,B}$), and the third term involves the variance of Security B (σ_B^2). (Remember, $\sigma_{A,B} = \sigma_{B,A}$. That is, the ordering of the variables is not relevant when we are expressing the covariance between two securities.)

The formula indicates an important point. The variance of a portfolio depends on both the variances of the individual securities and the covariance between the two securities. The variance of a security measures the variability of an individual security's return. Covariance measures the relationship between the two securities. For given variances of the individual securities, a positive relationship or covariance between the two securities increases the variance of the entire portfolio. A negative relationship or covariance between the two securities decreases the variance of the entire portfolio. This important result seems to square with common sense. If one of your securities tends to go up when the other goes down, or vice versa, your two securities are offsetting each other. You are achieving what we call a *hedge* in finance, and the risk of your entire portfolio will be low. However, if both your securities rise and fall together, you are not hedging at all. Hence, the risk of your entire portfolio will be higher.

The variance formula for our two securities, Super and Slow, is:

$$\text{Var(portfolio)} = X^2_{\text{Super}}\sigma^2_{\text{Super}} + 2X_{\text{Super}}X_{\text{Slow}}\sigma_{\text{Super, Slow}} + X^2_{\text{Slow}}\sigma^2_{\text{Slow}} \qquad \textbf{(11.4)}$$

Given our earlier assumption that an individual with $100 invests $60 in Supertech and $40 in Slowpoke, $X_{\text{Super}} = .6$ and $X_{\text{Slow}} = .4$. Using this assumption and the relevant data from our previous calculations, the variance of the portfolio is:

$$.023851 = .36 \times .066875 + 2 \times [.6 \times .4 \times (-.004875)] + .16 \times .013225 \qquad \textbf{(11.4$'$)}$$

The Matrix Approach

Alternatively, Equation 11.4 can be expressed in the following matrix format:

	Supertech	**Slowpoke**
Supertech	$X^2_{\text{Super}}\sigma^2_{\text{Super}}$ $.024075 = .36 \times .066875$	$X_{\text{Super}}X_{\text{Slow}}\sigma_{\text{Super, Slow}}$ $-.00117 = .6 \times .4 \times (-.004875)$
Slowpoke	$X_{\text{Super}}X_{\text{Slow}}\sigma_{\text{Super, Slow}}$ $-.00117 = .6 \times .4 \times (-.004875)$	$X^2_{\text{Slow}}\sigma^2_{\text{Slow}}$ $.002116 = .16 \times .013225$

There are four boxes in the matrix. We can add the terms in the boxes to obtain Equation 11.4, the variance of a portfolio composed of the two securities. The term in the upper left corner involves the variance of Supertech. The term in the lower right corner involves the variance of Slowpoke. The other two boxes contain the term involving the covariance. These two boxes are identical, indicating why the covariance term is multiplied by two in Equation 11.4.

At this point, students often find the box approach to be more confusing than Equation 11.4. However, the box approach is easily generalized to more than two securities, a task we perform later in this chapter.

Standard Deviation of a Portfolio

Given Equation 11.4$'$, we can now determine the standard deviation of the portfolio's return. This is:

$$\sigma_P = \text{SD(portfolio)} = \sqrt{\text{Var(portfolio)}} = \sqrt{.023851} \qquad \textbf{(11.5)}$$
$$= .1544 = 15.44\%$$

The interpretation of the standard deviation of the portfolio is the same as the interpretation of the standard deviation of an individual security. The expected return on our portfolio is 12.7 percent. A return of -2.74 percent ($=12.7\% - 15.44\%$) is one standard deviation below the mean, and a return of 28.14 percent ($=12.7\% + 15.44\%$) is one standard deviation above the mean. If the return on the portfolio is normally distributed, a return between -2.74 percent and $+28.14$ percent occurs about 68 percent of the time.[3]

---

[3]There are only four equally probable returns for Supertech and Slowpoke, so neither security possesses a normal distribution. Thus, probabilities would be slightly different in our example.

The Diversification Effect It is instructive to compare the standard deviation of the portfolio with the standard deviation of the individual securities. The weighted average of the standard deviations of the individual securities is:

$$\text{Weighted average of standard deviations} = X_{\text{Super}}\sigma_{\text{Super}} + X_{\text{Slow}}\sigma_{\text{Slow}} \tag{11.6}$$
$$.2012 = .6 \times .2586 + .4 \times .115$$

One of the most important results in this chapter concerns the difference between Equations 11.5 and 11.6. In our example, the standard deviation of the portfolio is *less* than a weighted average of the standard deviations of the individual securities.

We pointed out earlier that the expected return on the portfolio is a weighted average of the expected returns on the individual securities. Thus, we get a different type of result for the standard deviation of a portfolio than we do for the expected return on a portfolio.

Our result for the standard deviation of a portfolio is due to diversification. For example, Supertech and Slowpoke are slightly negatively correlated ($\rho = -.1639$). Supertech's return is likely to be a little below average if Slowpoke's return is above average. Similarly, Supertech's return is likely to be a little above average if Slowpoke's return is below average. Thus, the standard deviation of a portfolio composed of the two securities is less than a weighted average of the standard deviations of the two securities.

Our example has negative correlation. Clearly, there will be less benefit from diversification if the two securities exhibit positive correlation. How high must the positive correlation be before all diversification benefits vanish?

To answer this question, let us rewrite Equation 11.4 in terms of correlation rather than covariance. The covariance can be rewritten as:[4]

$$\sigma_{\text{Super,Slow}} = \rho_{\text{Super,Slow}}\sigma_{\text{Super}}\sigma_{\text{Slow}} \tag{11.7}$$

This formula states that the covariance between any two securities is simply the correlation between the two securities multiplied by the standard deviations of each. In other words, covariance incorporates both (1) the correlation between the two assets and (2) the variability of each of the two securities as measured by standard deviation.

From our calculations earlier in this chapter we know that the correlation between the two securities is $-.1639$. Given the variances used in Equation 11.4', the standard deviations are .2586 and .115 for Supertech and Slowpoke, respectively. Thus, the variance of a portfolio can be expressed as follows:

Variance of the Portfolio's Return:

$$= X_{\text{Super}}^2\sigma_{\text{Super}}^2 + 2X_{\text{Super}}X_{\text{Slow}}\rho_{\text{Super, Slow}}\sigma_{\text{Super}}\sigma_{\text{Slow}} + X_{\text{Slow}}^2\sigma_{\text{Slow}}^2 \tag{11.8}$$
$$.023851 = .36 \times .066875 + 2 \times (.6 \times .4 \times (-.1639)$$
$$\times .2586 \times .115) + .16 \times .013225$$

The middle term on the right side is now written in terms of correlation, ρ, not covariance.

Suppose $\rho_{\text{Super,Slow}} = 1$, the highest possible value for correlation. Assume all the other parameters in the example are the same. The variance of the portfolio is:

$$\begin{array}{ll}\text{Variance of the} \\ \text{portfolio's return}\end{array} = .040466 = .36 \times .066875 + 2 \times (.6 \times .4 \times 1 \times .2586 \\ \times .115) + .16 \times .013225$$

---

[4]As with covariance, the ordering of the two securities is not relevant when we express the correlation between the two securities. That is, $\rho_{\text{Super,Slow}} = \rho_{\text{Slow,Super}}$

Table 11.3
Standard Deviations
for Standard & Poor's
500 Index and for
Selected Stocks in the
Index, 2010–2014

Asset	Standard Deviation
S&P 500	13.07%
Johnson & Johnson	13.23
IBM	15.91
Microsoft	20.69
Nordstrom	26.29
Amazon.com	27.43
Boston Scientific	30.20
Bank of America	35.75
Delta Airlines	38.89

As long as the correlations between pairs of securities are less than 1, the standard deviation of an index is less than the weighted average of the standard deviations of the individual securities within the index.

The standard deviation is:

$$\text{Standard deviation of portfolio's return} = \sqrt{.040466} = .2012 = 20.12\% \qquad (11.9)$$

Note that Equations 11.9 and 11.6 are equal. That is, the standard deviation of a portfolio's return is equal to the weighted average of the standard deviations of the individual returns when $\rho = 1$. Inspection of Equation 11.8 indicates that the variance and hence the standard deviation of the portfolio must fall as the correlation drops below 1. This leads to the following result:

As long as $\rho < 1$, the standard deviation of a portfolio of two securities is *less* than the weighted average of the standard deviations of the individual securities.

In other words, the diversification effect applies as long as there is less than perfect correlation (as long as $\rho < 1$). Thus, our Supertech–Slowpoke example is a case of overkill. We illustrated diversification by an example with negative correlation. We could have illustrated diversification by an example with positive correlation—as long as it was not *perfect* positive correlation.

An Extension to Many Assets   The preceding insight can be extended to the case of many assets. That is, as long as correlations between pairs of securities are less than 1, the standard deviation of a portfolio of many assets is less than the weighted average of the standard deviations of the individual securities.

Now consider Table 11.3, which shows the standard deviation of the Standard & Poor's 500 Index and the standard deviations of some of the individual securities listed in the index over a recent 5-year period. Note that all of the individual securities in the table have higher standard deviations than that of the index. In general, the standard deviations of most of the individual securities in an index will be above the standard deviation of the index itself, though a few of the securities could have lower standard deviations than that of the index.

11.4 The Efficient Set for Two Assets

Our results for expected returns and standard deviations are graphed in Figure 11.2. The figure shows a dot labeled Slowpoke and a dot labeled Supertech. Each dot represents both the expected return and the standard deviation for an individual security.

Figure 11.2

Expected Returns and
Standard Deviations
for Supertech,
Slowpoke, and a
Portfolio Composed
of 60 Percent in
Supertech and
40 Percent in
Slowpoke

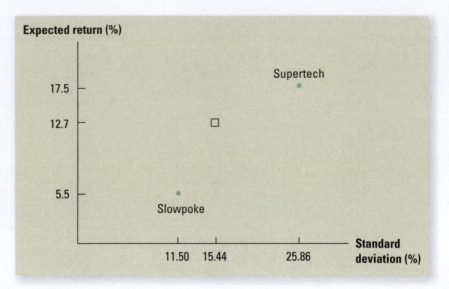

As can be seen, Supertech has both a higher expected return and a higher standard deviation.

The box or "□" in the graph represents a portfolio with 60 percent invested in Supertech and 40 percent invested in Slowpoke. You will recall that we previously calculated both the expected return and the standard deviation for this portfolio.

The choice of 60 percent in Supertech and 40 percent in Slowpoke is just one of an infinite number of portfolios that can be created. The set of portfolios is sketched by the curved line in Figure 11.3.

Consider Portfolio *1*. This is a portfolio composed of 90 percent Slowpoke and 10 percent Supertech. Because the portfolio is weighted so heavily toward Slowpoke, it appears close to the Slowpoke point on the graph. Portfolio *2* is higher on the curve because it is composed of 50 percent Slowpoke and 50 percent Supertech. Portfolio *3* is close to the Supertech point on the graph because it is composed of 90 percent Supertech and 10 percent Slowpoke.

There are a few important points concerning this graph:

1. We previously argued that the diversification effect occurs whenever the correlation between two securities is below 1. The correlation between Supertech and Slowpoke is −.1639. The straight line in the graph represents points that would have been generated had the correlation coefficient between the two securities been 1. Note that the curved line is always to the left of the straight line. Consider Point *1'*. This point represents a portfolio composed of 90 percent in Slowpoke and 10 percent in Supertech *if* the correlation between the two were exactly 1. There is no diversification effect if $\rho = 1$. However, the diversification effect applies to the curved line because Point *1* has the same expected return as Point *1'* but has a lower standard deviation. (Points *2'* and *3'* are omitted to reduce the clutter of Figure 11.3.)

   Though the straight line and the curved line are both represented in Figure 11.3, they do not simultaneously exist in the same world. *Either* $\rho = -.1639$ and the curve exists *or* $\rho = 1$ and the straight line exists. In other words, though an investor can choose between different points on the curve if $\rho = -.1639$, she cannot choose between points on the curve and points on the straight line.

2. Point MV represents the minimum variance portfolio. This is the portfolio with the lowest possible variance. By definition, this portfolio must also have the lowest

Figure 11.3

Set of Portfolios Composed of Holdings in Supertech and Slowpoke (correlation between the two securities is −.1639)

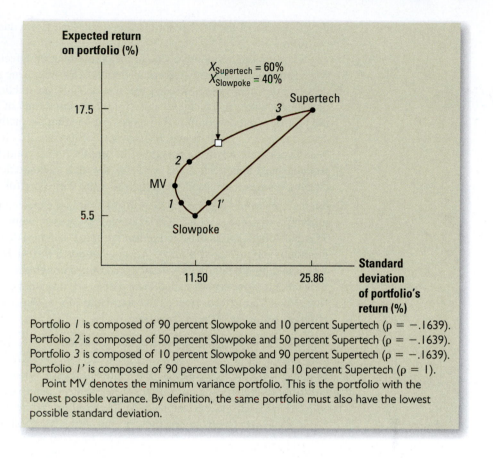

Portfolio *1* is composed of 90 percent Slowpoke and 10 percent Supertech (ρ = −.1639).
Portfolio *2* is composed of 50 percent Slowpoke and 50 percent Supertech (ρ = −.1639).
Portfolio *3* is composed of 10 percent Slowpoke and 90 percent Supertech (ρ = −.1639).
Portfolio *1'* is composed of 90 percent Slowpoke and 10 percent Supertech (ρ = 1).

Point MV denotes the minimum variance portfolio. This is the portfolio with the lowest possible variance. By definition, the same portfolio must also have the lowest possible standard deviation.

possible standard deviation. (The term *minimum variance portfolio* is standard, and we will use that term. Perhaps minimum standard deviation would actually be better because standard deviation, not variance, is measured on the horizontal axis of Figure 11.3.)

3. An individual contemplating an investment in a portfolio of Slowpoke and Supertech faces an **opportunity set** or **feasible set** represented by the curved line in Figure 11.3. That is, he can achieve any point on the curve by selecting the appropriate mix between the two securities. He cannot achieve any point above the curve because he cannot increase the return on the individual securities, decrease the standard deviations of the securities, or decrease the correlation between the two securities. Neither can he achieve points below the curve because he cannot lower the returns on the individual securities, increase the standard deviations of the securities, or increase the correlation. (Of course, he would not want to achieve points below the curve, even if he were able to do so.)

   Were he relatively tolerant of risk, he might choose Portfolio *3*. (In fact, he could even choose the end point by investing all his money in Supertech.) An investor with less tolerance for risk might choose Portfolio *2*. An investor wanting as little risk as possible would choose MV, the portfolio with minimum variance or minimum standard deviation.

4. Note that the curve is backward bending between the Slowpoke point and MV. This indicates that, for a portion of the feasible set, standard deviation actually decreases as we increase expected return. Students frequently ask, "How can an increase in

the proportion of the risky security, Supertech, lead to a reduction in the risk of the portfolio?"

This surprising finding is due to the diversification effect. The returns on the two securities are negatively correlated with each other. One security tends to go up when the other goes down and vice versa. Thus, an addition of a small amount of Supertech acts as a hedge to a portfolio composed only of Slowpoke. The risk of the portfolio is reduced, implying backward bending. Actually, backward bending always occurs if $\rho \leq 0$. It may or may not occur when $\rho > 0$. Of course, the curve bends backward only for a portion of its length. As we continue to increase the percentage of Supertech in the portfolio, the high standard deviation of this security eventually causes the standard deviation of the entire portfolio to rise.

5. No investor would want to hold a portfolio with an expected return below that of the minimum variance portfolio. For example, no investor would choose Portfolio *1*. This portfolio has less expected return but more standard deviation than the minimum variance portfolio has. We say that portfolios such as Portfolio *1* are *dominated* by the minimum variance portfolio. Though the entire curve from Slowpoke to Supertech is called the *feasible set,* investors consider only the curve from MV to Supertech. Hence the curve from MV to Supertech is called the **efficient set** or the **efficient frontier**.

Figure 11.3 represents the opportunity set where $\rho = -.1639$. It is worthwhile to examine Figure 11.4, which shows different curves for different correlations. As can be seen, the lower the correlation, the more the curve bends. This indicates that the diversification effect rises as ρ declines. The greatest bend occurs in the limiting case where $\rho = -1$. This is perfect negative correlation. While this extreme case where $\rho = -1$ seems to fascinate students, it has little practical importance. Most pairs

Figure 11.4

Opportunity Sets Composed of Holdings in Supertech and Slowpoke

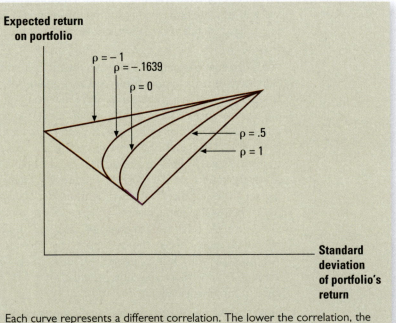

Each curve represents a different correlation. The lower the correlation, the more bend in the curve.

of securities exhibit positive correlation. Very high negative correlations are unusual occurrences.[5]

Note that there is only one correlation between a pair of securities. We stated earlier that the correlation between Slowpoke and Supertech is −.1639. Thus, the curve in Figure 11.4 representing this correlation is the correct one, and the other curves should be viewed as merely hypothetical.

The graphs we examined are not mere intellectual curiosities. Rather, efficient sets can easily be calculated in the real world. As mentioned earlier, data on returns, standard deviations, and correlations are generally taken from past observations, though subjective notions can be used to determine the values of these parameters as well. Once the parameters have been determined, any one of a whole host of software packages can be purchased to generate the efficient set. However, the choice of the preferred portfolio within the efficient set is up to you. As with other important decisions like what job to choose, what house or car to buy, and how much time to allocate to this course, there is no computer program to choose the preferred portfolio.

An efficient set can be generated where the two individual assets are portfolios themselves. For example, the two assets in Figure 11.5 are a diversified portfolio of American stocks and a diversified portfolio of foreign stocks. Expected returns, standard deviations, and the correlation coefficient were calculated over the recent past. No subjectivity entered the analysis. The U.S. stock portfolio with a standard deviation of about .151 is less risky than the foreign stock portfolio, which has a standard deviation of about .166. However, combining a small percentage of the foreign stock portfolio with the U.S. portfolio actually

Figure 11.5

Return/Risk Trade-off for World Stocks: Portfolio of U.S. and Foreign Stocks

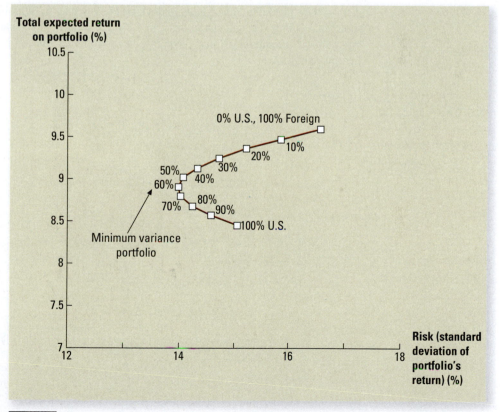

reduces risk, as can be seen by the backward-bending nature of the curve. In other words, the diversification benefits from combining two different portfolios more than offset the introduction of a riskier set of stocks into our holdings. The minimum variance portfolio occurs with about 60 percent of our funds in American stocks and about 40 percent in foreign stocks. Addition of foreign securities beyond this point increases the risk of the entire portfolio. The backward-bending curve in Figure 11.5 is important information that has not bypassed American institutional investors. In recent years, pension funds and other institutions in the United States have sought investment opportunities overseas.

11.5   The Efficient Set for Many Securities

The previous discussion concerned two securities. We found that a simple curve sketched out all the possible portfolios. Because investors generally hold more than two securities, we should look at the same graph when more than two securities are held. The shaded area in Figure 11.6 represents the opportunity set or feasible set when many securities are considered. The shaded area represents all the possible combinations of expected return and standard deviation for a portfolio. For example, in a universe of 100 securities, Point 1 might represent a portfolio of, say, 40 securities. Point 2 might represent a portfolio of 80 securities. Point 3 might represent a different set of 80 securities, or the same 80 securities held in different proportions, or something else. Obviously, the combinations are virtually endless. However, note that all possible combinations fit into a confined region. No security or combination of securities can fall outside the shaded region. That is, no one can choose a portfolio with an expected return above that given by the shaded region. Furthermore, no one can choose a portfolio with a standard deviation below that given in the shaded area. Perhaps more surprisingly, no one can choose an expected return below that given in this area. In other words, the capital markets actually prevent a self-destructive person from taking on a guaranteed loss.[6]

Figure 11.6

The Feasible Set of Portfolios Constructed from Many Securities

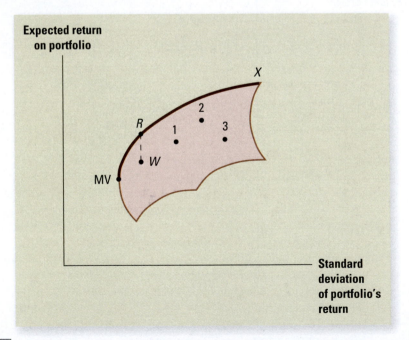

---

[6]Of course, someone dead set on parting with his money can do so. For example, he can trade frequently without purpose, so that commissions more than offset the positive expected returns on the portfolio.

So far, Figure 11.6 is different from the earlier graphs. When only two securities are involved, all the combinations lie on a single curve. Conversely, with many securities the combinations cover an entire area. However, notice that an individual will want to be somewhere on the upper edge between MV and X. The upper edge, which we indicate in Figure 11.6 by a thick curve, is called the *efficient set*. Any point below the efficient set would receive less expected return and the same standard deviation as a point on the efficient set. For example, consider R on the efficient set and W directly below it. If W contains the risk level you desire, you should choose R instead to receive a higher expected return.

In the final analysis, Figure 11.6 is quite similar to Figure 11.3. The efficient set in Figure 11.3 runs from MV to Supertech. It contains various combinations of the securities Supertech and Slowpoke. The efficient set in Figure 11.6 runs from MV to X. It contains various combinations of many securities. The fact that a whole shaded area appears in Figure 11.6 but not in Figure 11.3 is just not an important difference; no informed investor would choose any point below the efficient set in Figure 11.6 anyway.

We mentioned before that an efficient set for two securities can be traced out easily in the real world. The task becomes more difficult when additional securities are included because the number of observations grows. For example, using analysis to estimate expected returns and standard deviations for, say, 100 or 500 securities may very well become overwhelming, and the difficulties with correlations may be greater still. There are almost 5,000 correlations between pairs of securities from a universe of 100 securities.

Though much of the mathematics of efficient set computation had been derived in the 1950s,[7] the high cost of computer time restricted application of the principles. In recent years this cost has been drastically reduced. A number of software packages allow the calculation of an efficient set for portfolios of moderate size. By all accounts these packages sell quite briskly, implying that our discussion is important in practice.

VARIANCE AND STANDARD DEVIATION IN A PORTFOLIO OF MANY ASSETS

We earlier calculated the formulas for variance and standard deviation in the two-asset case. Because we considered a portfolio of many assets in Figure 11.6, it is worthwhile to calculate the formulas for variance and standard deviation in the many-asset case. The formula for the variance of a portfolio of many assets can be viewed as an extension of the formula for the variance of two assets.

To develop the formula, we employ the same type of matrix that we used in the two-asset case. This matrix is displayed in Table 11.4. Assuming that there are N assets, we write the numbers 1 through N on both the horizontal axis and the vertical axis. This creates a matrix of $N \times N = N^2$ boxes. The variance of the portfolio is the sum of the terms in all the boxes.

Consider, for example, the box in the second row and the third column. The term in the box is $X_2 X_3$ $Cov(R_2, R_3)$. X_2 and X_3 are the percentages of the entire portfolio that are invested in the second asset and the third asset, respectively. For example, if an individual with a portfolio of $1,000 invests $100 in the second asset, $X_2 = 10\%$ (=$100/$1,000). $Cov(R_2, R_3)$ is the covariance between the returns on the second asset and the returns on the third asset. Next, note the box in the third row and the second column. The term in this box is $X_3 X_2$ $Cov(R_3, R_2)$. Because $Cov(R_3, R_2) = Cov(R_2, R_3)$, both boxes have the same value. The second security and the third security make up one pair of stocks. In fact, every pair of stocks appears twice in the table: once in the lower left side and once in the upper right side.

---

[7]The classic treatise is Harry Markowitz, *Portfolio Selection* (New York: John Wiley & Sons, 1959). Markowitz won the Nobel Prize in Economics in 1990 for his work on modern portfolio theory.

Table 11.4

Matrix Used to Calculate the Variance of a Portfolio

Stock	1	2	3	. . .	N
1	$X_1^2\sigma_1^2$	$X_1X_2\mathrm{Cov}(R_1,R_2)$	$X_1X_3\mathrm{Cov}(R_1,R_3)$		$X_1X_N\mathrm{Cov}(R_1,R_N)$
2	$X_2X_1\mathrm{Cov}(R_2,R_1)$	$X_2^2\sigma_2^2$	$X_2X_3\mathrm{Cov}(R_2,R_3)$		$X_2X_N\mathrm{Cov}(R_2,R_N)$
3	$X_3X_1\mathrm{Cov}(R_3,R_1)$	$X_3X_2\mathrm{Cov}(R_3,R_2)$	$X_3^2\sigma_3^2$		$X_3X_N\mathrm{Cov}(R_3,R_N)$
.					
.					
.					
N	$X_NX_1\mathrm{Cov}(R_N,R_1)$	$X_NX_2\mathrm{Cov}(R_N,R_2)$	$X_NX_3\mathrm{Cov}(R_N,R_3)$		$X_N^2\sigma_N^2$

The variance of the portfolio is the sum of the terms in all the boxes.

σ_i is the standard deviation of Stock i.

$\mathrm{Cov}(R_i, R_j)$ is the covariance between Stock i and Stock j.

Terms involving the standard deviation of a single security appear on the diagonal. Terms involving covariance between two securities appear off the diagonal.

Table 11.5

Number of Variance and Covariance Terms as a Function of the Number of Stocks in the Portfolio

Number of Stocks in Portfolio	Total Number of Terms	Number of Variance Terms (number of terms on diagonal)	Number of Covariance Terms (number of terms off diagonal)
1	1	1	0
2	4	2	2
3	9	3	6
10	100	10	90
100	10,000	100	9,900
.	.	.	.
.	.	.	.
.	.	.	.
N	N^2	N	$N^2 - N$

In a large portfolio, the number of terms involving covariance between two securities is much greater than the number of terms involving variance of a single security.

Now consider boxes on the diagonal. For example, the term in the first box on the diagonal is $X_1^2\sigma_1^2$. Here, σ_1^2 is the variance of the return on the first security.

Thus, the diagonal terms in the matrix contain the variances of the different stocks. The off-diagonal terms contain the covariances. Table 11.5 relates the numbers of diagonal and off-diagonal elements to the size of the matrix. The number of diagonal terms (number of variance terms) is always the same as the number of stocks in the portfolio. The number of off-diagonal terms (number of covariance terms) rises much faster than the number of diagonal terms. For example, a portfolio of 100 stocks has 9,900 covariance terms. Because the variance of a portfolio's return is the sum of all the boxes, we have the following:

The variance of the return on a portfolio with many securities is more dependent on the covariances between the individual securities than on the variances of the individual securities.

11.6 Diversification

So far, in this chapter we have examined how the risks and returns of individual assets impact the risk and return of the portfolio. We also touched on one aspect of this impact, diversification. To give a recent example, the Dow Jones Industrial Average (DJIA), which contains 30 large, well-known U.S. stocks, rose about 10 percent in 2014, an increase slightly below historical standards. The biggest individual gainers in that year were Intel (up 44.2 percent), Apple (up 40.6 percent), and United Health Group (up 36.5 percent), while the biggest losers were IBM (down 12.2 percent), Chevron (down 7 percent), and ExxonMobil (down 6.1 percent). As can be seen, variation among these individual stocks was reduced through diversification. While this example shows that diversification is good we now want to examine *why* it is good. And just how good is it?

THE ANTICIPATED AND UNANTICIPATED COMPONENTS OF NEWS

We begin the discussion of diversification by focusing on the stock of one company, which we will call Flyers. What will determine this stock's return in, say, the coming month?

The return on any stock consists of two parts. First, the *normal* or *expected return* from the stock is the part of the return that shareholders in the market predict or expect. It depends on all of the information shareholders have that bears on the stock, and it uses all of our understanding of what will influence the stock in the next month.

The second part is the *uncertain* or *risky return* on the stock. This is the portion that comes from information that will be revealed within the month. The list of such information is endless, but here are some examples:

- News about Flyers' research.
- Government figures released for the gross national product (GNP).
- Results of the latest arms control talks.
- Discovery that a rival's product has been tampered with.
- News that Flyers' sales figures are higher than expected.
- A sudden drop in interest rates.
- The unexpected retirement of Flyers' founder and president.

A way to write the return on Flyers' stock in the coming month, then, is:

$$R = \overline{R} + U$$

where R is the actual total return in the month, $\overline{R}$ is the expected part of the return, and U stands for the unexpected part of the return.

RISK: SYSTEMATIC AND UNSYSTEMATIC

The unanticipated part of the return—that portion resulting from surprises—is the true risk of any investment. After all, if we got what we had expected, there would be no risk and no uncertainty.

There are important differences, though, among various sources of risk. Look at our previous list of news stories. Some of these stories are directed specifically at Flyers, and some are more general. Which of the news items are of specific importance to Flyers?

Announcements about interest rates or GNP are clearly important for nearly all companies, whereas the news about Flyers' president, its research, its sales, or the affairs of a rival company are of specific interest to Flyers. We will divide these two types of announcements and the resulting risk, then, into two components: a systematic portion, called *systematic risk,* and the remainder, which we call *specific* or *unsystematic risk.* The following definitions describe the difference:

- A *systematic risk* is any risk that affects a large number of assets, each to a greater or lesser degree.
- An *unsystematic risk* is a risk that specifically affects a single asset or a small group of assets.

Uncertainty about general economic conditions, such as GNP, interest rates, or inflation, are examples of systematic risk. These conditions affect nearly all stocks to some degree. An unanticipated or surprise increase in inflation affects wages and the costs of the supplies that companies buy, the value of the assets that companies own, and the prices at which companies sell their products. These forces to which all companies are susceptible are the essence of systematic risk.

In contrast, the announcement of a small oil strike by a company may affect that company alone or a few other companies. Certainly, it is unlikely to have an effect on the world oil market. To stress that such information is unsystematic and affects only some specific companies, we sometimes call it an *idiosyncratic risk.*

The distinction between a systematic risk and an unsystematic risk is never as exact as we make it out to be. Even the most narrow and peculiar bit of news about a company ripples through the economy. It reminds us of the tale of the war that was lost because one horse lost a shoe; even a minor event may have an impact on the world. But this degree of hairsplitting should not trouble us much. To paraphrase a Supreme Court justice's comment when speaking of pornography, we may not be able to define a systematic risk and an unsystematic risk exactly, but we know them when we see them.

This permits us to break down the risk of Flyers' stock return into its two components: the systematic and the unsystematic. As is traditional, we will use the Greek epsilon, ϵ, to represent the unsystematic risk and write:

$$\begin{aligned} R &= \overline{R} + U \\ &= \overline{R} + m + \epsilon \end{aligned}$$

(11.10)

where we have used the letter m to stand for the systematic risk. Sometimes systematic risk is referred to as *market risk.* This emphasizes the fact that m influences all assets in the market to some extent. $\overline{R}$ is the Flyers' stock expected return.

The important point about the way we have broken the total risk, U, into its two components, m and ϵ, is that ϵ, because it is specific to the company, is unrelated to the specific risk of most other companies. For example, the unsystematic risk on Flyers' stock, ϵ_F, is unrelated to the unsystematic risk of, say, General Electric's stock, ϵ_{GE}. The risk that Flyers' stock will go up or down because of a discovery by its research team—or its failure to discover something—probably is unrelated to any of the specific uncertainties that affect General Electric's stock. This means that the unsystematic risks of Flyers' stock and General Electric's stock are unrelated to each other, or uncorrelated.

THE ESSENCE OF DIVERSIFICATION

Now what happens when we combine Flyers' stock with another stock in a portfolio? Because the unsystematic risks or epsilons of the two stocks are uncorrelated, the epsilon may be positive for one stock when the epsilon of the other is negative. Since the epsilons can offset each other, the unsystematic risk of the portfolio will be lower than the unsystematic risk of either of the two securities. In other words, we see the beginnings of diversification. And, if we add a third security to our portfolio, the unsystematic risk of the portfolio will be lower than the unsystematic risk of the two-security portfolio. The effect continues when we add a fourth, a fifth, or a sixth security. In fact, if we were able, hypothetically, to combine an infinite number of securities, the unsystematic risk of the portfolio would disappear.

Now let's consider what happens to the portfolio's systematic risk when we add a second security. If the return on the second security is also modeled by Equation 11.10, the systematic risk of the portfolio will not be reduced. For example, suppose inflation turns out to be higher than previously anticipated, or GNP turns out to be lower than anticipated. Both stocks will likely decline, implying a decline in the portfolio. And we would get the same result with three securities, four securities, or more. In fact, suppose the portfolio had an infinite number of securities. Bad news for the economy would impact all of these securities negatively, implying a negative impact for the portfolio. Unlike unsystematic risk, systematic risk cannot be diversified away.

This insight can be illustrated in Figure 11.7. The graph, relating the standard deviation of a portfolio to the number of securities in the portfolio, shows a high standard deviation for one security. We often speak of standard deviation as the total risk, or simply the risk, of the portfolio. Addition of a second security reduces standard deviation, or risk, as does the addition of a third security, and so on. The total risk of the portfolio steadily falls with diversification.

But note that diversification does not allow total risk to go to zero. There is a limit to the benefit of diversification, because only unsystematic risk is getting diversified away. Systematic risk is left untouched. Thus, while diversification is good, it is not as good as we might have hoped. Systematic risk just doesn't decrease through diversification.

The previous discussion implicitly assumed that all securities have the same level of systematic risk. While essentially all securities have some systematic risk, certain

Figure 11.7

Relationship between the Standard Deviation of a Portfolio's Return and the Number of Securities in the Portfolio

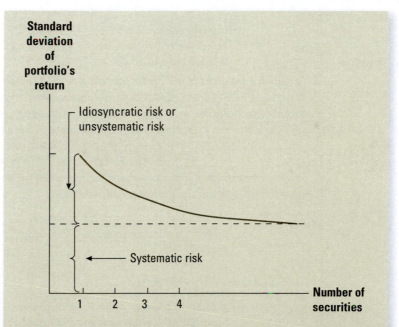

The standard deviation of a portfolio drops as more securities are added to the portfolio. However, it does not drop to zero. Rather, while unsystematic risk can be eliminated through diversification, systematic risk cannot be.

securities have more of this risk than others. The amount of systematic risk is measured by something called *beta,* a concept that will be explained in Section 11.8. But first we must consider the impact of riskless borrowing and lending.

11.7 Riskless Borrowing and Lending

Figure 11.6 assumes that all the securities in the efficient set are risky. Alternatively, an investor could combine a risky investment with an investment in a riskless or *risk-free* security, such as U.S. Treasury bills. This is illustrated in the following example.

EXAMPLE

Riskless Lending and Portfolio Risk   Ms. Bagwell is considering investing in the common stock of Merville Enterprises. In addition, Ms. Bagwell will either borrow or lend at the risk-free rate. The relevant parameters are these:

	Common Stock of Merville	Risk-Free Asset
Expected return	14%	10%
Standard deviation	.20	0

Suppose Ms. Bagwell chooses to invest a total of $1,000, $350 of which is to be invested in Merville Enterprises and $650 placed in the risk-free asset. The expected return on her total investment is simply a weighted average of the two returns:

$$\text{Expected return on portfolio composed of the riskless asset and one risky asset} = .114 = (.35 \times .14) + (.65 \times .10) \qquad \textbf{(11.11)}$$

Because the expected return on the portfolio is a weighted average of the expected return on the risky asset (Merville Enterprises) and the risk-free return, the calculation is analogous to the way we treated two risky assets. In other words, Equation 11.3 applies here.

Using Equation 11.4, the formula for the variance of the portfolio can be written as:

$$X^2_{\text{Merville}} \sigma^2_{\text{Merville}} + 2X_{\text{Merville}} X_{\text{Risk-free}} \sigma_{\text{Merville, Risk-free}} + X^2_{\text{Risk-free}} \sigma^2_{\text{Risk-free}}$$

However, by definition, the risk-free asset has no variability. Thus both $\sigma_{\text{Merville, Risk-free}}$ and $\sigma^2_{\text{Risk-free}}$ are equal to zero, reducing the above expression to:

$$\begin{aligned}\text{Variance of portfolio composed of the riskless asset and one risky asset} &= X^2_{\text{Merville}} \sigma^2_{\text{Merville}} \\ &= (.35)^2 \times (.20)^2 \\ &= .0049\end{aligned} \qquad \textbf{(11.12)}$$

The standard deviation of the portfolio is:

$$\begin{aligned}\text{Standard deviation of portfolio composed of the riskless asset and one risky asset} &= X_{\text{Merville}} \sigma_{\text{Merville}} \\ &= .35 \times .20 \\ &= .07\end{aligned} \qquad \textbf{(11.13)}$$

Figure 11.8 Relationship between Expected Return and Risk for Portfolios Composed of the Riskless Asset and One Risky Asset

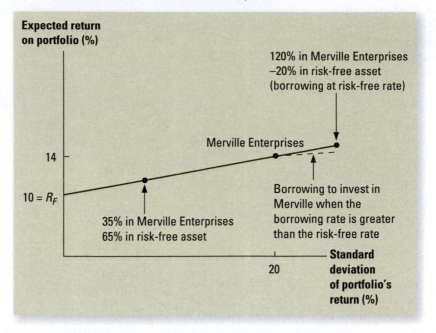

The relationship between risk and expected return for portfolios composed of one risky asset and the riskless asset can be seen in Figure 11.8. Ms. Bagwell's split of 35–65 percent between the two assets is represented on a *straight* line between the risk-free rate and a pure investment in Merville Enterprises. Note that, unlike the case of two risky assets, the opportunity set is straight, not curved.

Suppose that, alternatively, Ms. Bagwell borrows $200 at the risk-free rate. Combining this with her original sum of $1,000, she invests a total of $1,200 in Merville. Her expected return would be:

$$\text{Expected return on portfolio formed by borrowing to invest in risky asset} = 14.8\% = 1.20 \times .14 + (-.2 \times .10)$$

Here, she invests 120 percent of her original investment of $1,000 by borrowing 20 percent of her original investment. Note that the return of 14.8 percent is greater than the 14 percent expected return on Merville Enterprises. This occurs because she is borrowing at 10 percent to invest in a security with an expected return greater than 10 percent.

The standard deviation is:

$$\text{Standard deviation of portfolio formed by borrowing to invest in risky asset} = .24 = 1.20 \times .2$$

The standard deviation of .24 is greater than .20, the standard deviation of the Merville investment, because borrowing increases the variability of the investment. This investment also appears in Figure 11.8.

So far, we have assumed that Ms. Bagwell is able to borrow at the same rate at which she can lend.[8] Now let us consider the case where the borrowing rate is above the lending rate. The dotted line in Figure 11.8 illustrates the opportunity set for borrowing opportunities in this case. The dotted line is below the solid line because a higher borrowing rate lowers the expected return on the investment.

---

[8]Surprisingly, this appears to be a decent approximation because many investors can borrow from a stockbroker (called *going on margin*) when purchasing stocks. The borrowing rate here is very near the riskless rate of interest, particularly for large investors. More will be said about this in a later chapter.

Figure 11.9

Relationship between Expected Return and Standard Deviation for an Investment in a Combination of Risky Securities and the Riskless Asset

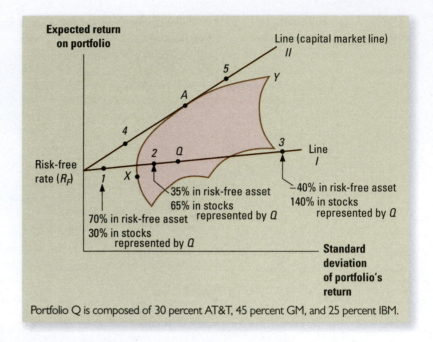

Portfolio Q is composed of 30 percent AT&T, 45 percent GM, and 25 percent IBM.

THE OPTIMAL PORTFOLIO

The previous section concerned a portfolio formed between the riskless asset and one risky asset. In reality, an investor is likely to combine an investment in the riskless asset with a *portfolio* of risky assets. This is illustrated in Figure 11.9.

Consider Point Q, representing a portfolio of securities. Point Q is in the interior of the feasible set of risky securities. Let us assume the point represents a portfolio of 30 percent in AT&T, 45 percent in General Motors (GM), and 25 percent in IBM. Individuals combining investments in Q with investments in the riskless asset would achieve points along the straight line from R_F to Q. We refer to this as Line *I*. For example, Point *1* on the line represents a portfolio of 70 percent in the riskless asset and 30 percent in stocks represented by Q. An investor with $100 choosing Point *1* as his portfolio would put $70 in the risk-free asset and $30 in Q. This can be restated as $70 in the riskless asset, $9 (=.3 × $30) in AT&T, $13.50 (=.45 × $30) in GM, and $7.50 (=.25 × $30) in IBM. Point *2* also represents a portfolio of the risk-free asset and Q, with more (65%) being invested in Q.

Point *3* is obtained by borrowing to invest in Q. For example, an investor with $100 of her own would borrow $40 from the bank or broker to invest $140 in Q. This can be stated as borrowing $40 and contributing $100 of her money to invest $42 (=.3 × $140) in AT&T, $63 (=.45 × $140) in GM, and $35 (=.25 × $140) in IBM.

These investments can be summarized as follows:

	Point Q	Point *I* (Lending $70)	Point *3* (Borrowing $40)
AT&T	$ 30	$ 9.00	$ 42
GM	45	13.50	63
IBM	25	7.50	35
Risk-free	0	70.00	−40
Total investment	$100	$100	$100

Though any investor can obtain any point on Line *I*, no point on the line is optimal. To see this, consider Line *II*, a line running from R_F through *A*. Point *A* represents a portfolio of risky securities. Line *II* represents portfolios formed by combinations of the risk-free asset and the securities in *A*. Points between R_F and *A* are portfolios in which some money is invested in the riskless asset and the rest is placed in *A*. Points past *A* are achieved by borrowing at the riskless rate to buy more of *A* than we could with our original funds alone.

As drawn, Line *II* is tangent to the efficient set of risky securities. Whatever point an individual can obtain on Line *I*, he can obtain a point with the same standard deviation and a higher expected return on Line *II*. In fact, because Line *II* is tangent to the efficient set of risky assets, it provides the investor with the best possible opportunities. In other words, Line *II* can be viewed as the efficient set of *all* assets, both risky and riskless. An investor with a fair degree of risk aversion might choose a point between R_F and *A*, perhaps Point *4*. An individual with less risk aversion might choose a point closer to *A* or even beyond *A*. For example, Point *5* corresponds to an individual borrowing money to increase investment in *A*.

The graph illustrates an important point. With riskless borrowing and lending, the portfolio of *risky* assets held by any investor would always be Point *A*. Regardless of the investor's tolerance for risk, she would never choose any other point on the efficient set of risky assets (represented by Curve *XAY*) nor any point in the interior of the feasible region. Rather, she would combine the securities of *A* with the riskless asset if she had high aversion to risk. She would borrow the riskless asset to invest more funds in *A* if she had low aversion to risk.

This result establishes what financial economists call the **separation principle**. That is, the investor's investment decision consists of two separate steps:

1. After estimating (*a*) the expected returns and variances of individual securities, and (*b*) the covariances between pairs of securities, the investor calculates the efficient set of risky assets, represented by Curve *XAY* in Figure 11.9. He then determines Point *A*, the tangency between the risk-free rate and the efficient set of risky assets (Curve *XAY*). Point *A* represents the portfolio of risky assets that the investor will hold. This point is determined solely from his estimates of returns, variances, and covariances. No personal characteristics, such as degree of risk aversion, are needed in this step.

2. The investor must now determine how he will combine Point *A*, his portfolio of risky assets, with the riskless asset. He might invest some of his funds in the riskless asset and some in Portfolio *A*. He would end up at a point on the line between R_F and *A* in this case. Alternatively, he might borrow at the risk-free rate and contribute some of his own funds as well, investing the sum in Portfolio *A*. He would end up at a point on Line *II* beyond *A*. His position in the riskless asset—that is, his choice of where on the line he wants to be—is determined by his internal characteristics, such as his ability to tolerate risk.

11.8 Market Equilibrium

DEFINITION OF THE MARKET EQUILIBRIUM PORTFOLIO

The preceding analysis concerns one investor. His estimates of the expected returns and variances for individual securities and the covariances between pairs of securities are his and his alone. Other investors would obviously have different estimates of these variables. However, the estimates might not vary much because all investors would be forming expectations from the same data about past price movements and other publicly available information.

Financial economists often imagine a world where all investors possess the *same* estimates of expected returns, variances, and covariances. Though this is never literally true, it is a useful simplifying assumption in a world where investors have access to similar sources of information. This assumption is called **homogeneous expectations**.[9]

If all investors had homogeneous expectations, Figure 11.9 would be the same for all individuals. That is, all investors would sketch out the same efficient set of risky assets because they would be working with the same inputs. This efficient set of risky assets is represented by the Curve *XAY*. Because the same risk-free rate would apply to everyone, all investors would view Point *A* as the portfolio of risky assets to be held.

This Point *A* takes on great importance because all investors would purchase the risky securities that it represents. Investors with a high degree of risk aversion might combine *A* with an investment in the riskless asset, achieving Point *4,* for example. Others with low aversion to risk might borrow to achieve, say, Point *5.* Because this is a very important conclusion, we restate it:

In a world with homogeneous expectations, all investors would hold the portfolio of risky assets represented by Point *A*.

If all investors choose the same portfolio of risky assets, one can determine what that portfolio is. Common sense tells us that it is a market value weighted portfolio of all existing securities. It is the **market portfolio**.

In practice, economists use a broad-based index such as the Standard & Poor's (S&P) 500 as a proxy for the market portfolio. Of course all investors do not hold the same portfolio in practice. However, we know that many investors hold diversified portfolios, particularly when mutual funds or pension funds are included. A broad-based index is a good proxy for the highly diversified portfolios of many investors.

DEFINITION OF RISK WHEN INVESTORS HOLD THE MARKET PORTFOLIO

Earlier in this chapter we pointed out that the risk or standard deviation of a stock could be broken down into systematic and unsystematic risk. Unsystematic risk can be diversified away in a large portfolio but systematic risk cannot. Thus, a diversified investor holding the market portfolio must worry about the systematic risk, but not the unsystematic risk, of every security in a portfolio. Is there a way to measure the systematic risk of a security? Yes, it is best measured by *beta,* which we illustrate in an example. It turns out that beta is the best measure of the risk of an individual security from the point of view of a diversified investor.

EXAMPLE

Beta Consider the following possible returns both on the stock of Jelco, Inc., and on the market:

State	Type of Economy	Return on Market (percent)	Return on Jelco, Inc. (percent)
I	Bull	15	25
II	Bull	15	15
III	Bear	−5	−5
IV	Bear	−5	−15

[9]The assumption of homogeneous expectations states that all investors have the same beliefs concerning returns, variances, and covariances. It does not say that all investors have the same aversion to risk.

Though the return on the market has only two possible outcomes (15% and −5%), the return on Jelco has four possible outcomes. It is helpful to consider the expected return on a security for a given return on the market. Assuming each state is equally likely, we have:

Type of Economy	Return on Market (percent)	Expected Return on Jelco, Inc. (percent)
Bull	15%	$20\% = 25\% \times \frac{1}{2} + 15\% \times \frac{1}{2}$
Bear	−5%	$-10\% = -5\% \times \frac{1}{2} + (-15\%) \times \frac{1}{2}$

Jelco, Inc., responds to market movements because its expected return is greater in bullish states than in bearish states. We now calculate exactly how responsive the security is to market movements. The market's return in a bullish economy is 20 percent [=15% − (−5%)] greater than the market's return in a bearish economy. However, the expected return on Jelco in a bullish economy is 30 percent [=20% − (−10%)] greater than its expected return in a bearish state. Thus Jelco, Inc., has a responsiveness coefficient of 1.5 (=30% / 20%).

Figure 11.10   Performance of Jelco, Inc., and the Market Portfolio

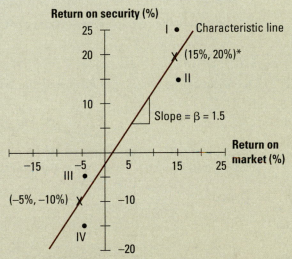

The two points marked X represent the expected return on Jelco for each possible outcome of the market portfolio. The expected return on Jelco is positively related to the return on the market. Because the slope is 1.5, we say that Jelco's beta is 1.5. Beta measures the responsiveness of the security's return to movement in the market.

*(15%, 20%) refers to the point where the return on the market is 15 percent and the return on the security is 20 percent.

This relationship appears in Figure 11.10. The returns for both Jelco and the market in each state are plotted as four points. In addition, we plot the expected return on the security for each of the two possible returns on the market. These two points, each of which we designate by an X, are joined by a line called the **characteristic line** of the security. The slope of the line is 1.5, the number calculated in the previous paragraph. This responsiveness coefficient of 1.5 is the **beta** of Jelco.

The interpretation of beta from Figure 11.10 is intuitive. The graph tells us that the returns of Jelco are magnified 1.5 times over those of the market. When the market does well, Jelco's stock

(continued)

is expected to do even better. When the market does poorly, Jelco's stock is expected to do even worse. Now imagine an individual with a portfolio near that of the market who is considering the addition of Jelco to her portfolio. Because of Jelco's *magnification factor* of 1.5, she will view this stock as contributing much to the risk of the portfolio. (We will show shortly that the beta of the average security in the market is 1.) Jelco contributes more to the risk of a large, diversified portfolio than does an average security because Jelco is more responsive to movements in the market.

Further insight can be gleaned by examining securities with negative betas. One should view these securities as either hedges or insurance policies. The security is expected to do well when the market does poorly and vice versa. Because of this, adding a negative-beta security to a large, diversified portfolio actually reduces the risk of the portfolio.[10]

Table 11.6 presents empirical estimates of betas for individual securities. As can be seen, some securities are more responsive to the market than others. For example, Citigroup has a beta of 1.83. This means that for every 1 percent movement in the market,[11] Citigroup is expected to move 1.83 percent in the same direction. Conversely, Microsoft has a beta of only .69. This means that for every 1 percent movement in the market, Microsoft is expected to move .69 percent in the same direction.

We can summarize our discussion of beta by saying:

Beta measures the responsiveness of a security to movements in the market portfolio.

THE FORMULA FOR BETA

Our discussion so far has stressed the intuition behind beta. The actual definition of beta is:

$$\beta_i = \frac{\text{Cov}(R_i, R_M)}{\sigma^2(R_M)} \tag{11.14}$$

where $\text{Cov}(R_i, R_M)$ is the covariance between the return on Asset i and the return on the market portfolio, and $\sigma^2(R_M)$ is the variance of the market.

Table 11.6
Estimates of Beta for Selected Individual Stocks

Stock	Beta
Dr. Pepper Snapple	.53
Microsoft	.69
Kellogg Company	.95
ExxonMobil	1.10
Google	1.15
3M Company	1.23
Anheuser-Busch InBev	1.36
Cisco Systems	1.40
Citigroup	1.83

The beta is defined as $\text{Cov}(R_i, R_M)/\text{Var}(R_M)$, where $\text{Cov}(R_i, R_M)$ is the covariance of the return on an individual stock, R_i, and the return on the market, R_M. $\text{Var}(R_M)$ is the variance of the return on the market, R_M.

---

[10]Unfortunately, empirical evidence shows that few, if any, stocks have negative betas.

[11]In Table 11.6, we use the Standard & Poor's 500 Index as a proxy for the market portfolio.

One useful property is that the average beta across all securities, when weighted by the proportion of each security's market value to that of the market portfolio, is 1. That is:

$$\sum_{i=1}^{N} X_i \beta_i = 1 \qquad\qquad (11.15)$$

where X_i is the proportion of Security i's market value to that of the entire market and N is the number of securities in the market.

Equation 11.15 is intuitive, once you think about it. If you weight all securities by their market values, the resulting portfolio is the market. By definition, the beta of the market portfolio is 1. That is, for every 1 percent movement in the market, the market must move 1 percent—*by definition*.

A TEST

We have put these questions on past corporate finance examinations:

1. What sort of investor rationally views the variance (or standard deviation) of an individual security's return as the security's proper measure of risk?

2. What sort of investor rationally views the beta of a security as the security's proper measure of risk?

A good response answering both questions might be something like the following:

A rational, risk-averse investor views the variance (or standard deviation) of her portfolio's return as the proper measure of the portfolio's risk. If for some reason the investor can hold only one security, the variance of that security's return becomes the variance of the portfolio's return. Hence, the variance of the security's return is the security's proper measure of risk.

If an individual holds a diversified portfolio, she still views the variance (or standard deviation) of her portfolio's return as the proper measure of the risk of her portfolio. However, she is no longer interested in the variance of each individual security's return. Rather, she is interested in the contribution of an individual security to the variance of the portfolio. The contribution of a security to the variance of a diversified portfolio is best measured by beta. Therefore, beta is the proper measure of the risk of an individual security for a diversified investor.

Beta measures the systematic risk of a security. Thus, diversified investors pay attention to the systematic risk of each security. However, they ignore the unsystematic risks of individual securities, since unsystematic risks are diversified away in a large portfolio.

11.9 Relationship between Risk and Expected Return (CAPM)

It is commonplace to argue that the expected return on an asset should be positively related to its risk. That is, individuals will hold a risky asset only if its expected return compensates for its risk. In this section, we first estimate the expected return on the stock market as a whole. Next, we estimate expected returns on individual securities.

EXPECTED RETURN ON MARKET

Economists frequently argue that the expected return on the market can be represented as:

$$\overline{R}_M = R_F + \text{Risk premium}$$

In words, the expected return on the market is the sum of the risk-free rate plus some compensation for the risk inherent in the market portfolio. Note that the equation refers to the *expected* return on the market, not the actual return in a particular month or year. Because stocks have risk, the actual return on the market over a particular period can, of course, be below R_F or can even be negative.

Because investors want compensation for risk, the risk premium is presumably positive. But exactly how positive is it? It is generally argued that the place to start looking for the risk premium in the future is the average risk premium in the past. As reported in Chapter 10, Dimson, Marsh, and Staunton found the average excess annual return of U.S. common stocks over the risk-free rate (i.e., one-year Treasury bills) was 7.2 percent over 1900–2010. We referred to 7.2 percent as the historical U.S. equity risk premium. The average historical worldwide equity premium was 6.9 percent. Taking into account a number of factors, we find 7 percent to be a reasonable estimate of the future U.S. equity risk premium.

For example, suppose the risk-free rate, estimated by the current yield on a one-year Treasury bill, is 1 percent, the expected return on the market is:

$$8\% = 1\% + 7\%$$

Of course, the future equity risk premium could be higher or lower than the historical equity risk premium. This could be true if future risk is higher or lower than past risk or if individual risk aversions are higher or lower than those of the past.

EXPECTED RETURN ON INDIVIDUAL SECURITY

Now that we have estimated the expected return on the market as a whole, what is the expected return on an individual security? We have argued that the beta of a security is the appropriate measure of its risk in a large, diversified portfolio. Because most investors are diversified, the expected return on a security should be positively related to its beta. This idea is illustrated in Figure 11.11.

Figure 11.11

Relationship between Expected Return on an Individual Security and Beta of the Security

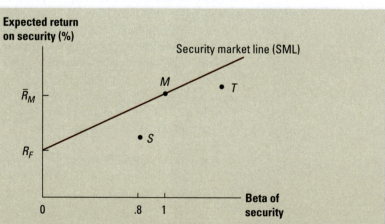

The security market line (SML) is the graphical depiction of the capital asset pricing model (CAPM).

The expected return on a stock with a beta of 0 is equal to the risk-free rate.

The expected return on a stock with a beta of 1 is equal to the expected return on the market.

Actually, economists can be more precise about the relationship between expected return and beta. They posit that under plausible conditions the relationship between expected return and beta can be represented by the following equation:[12]

Capital Asset Pricing Model

$$\overline{R} = R_F + \beta \times (\overline{R}_M - R_F)$$

| Expected return on a security | = | Risk-free rate | + | Beta of the security | × | Difference between expected return on market and risk-free rate | **(11.16)** |

This formula, which is called the **capital asset pricing model** (or CAPM for short), implies that the expected return on a security is linearly related to its beta. Because the average return on the market has been higher than the average risk-free rate over long periods of time, $\overline{R}_M - R_F$ is presumably positive. Thus, the formula implies that the expected return on a security is *positively* related to its beta. The formula can be illustrated by assuming a few special cases:

- *Assume that* $\beta = 0$. Here $\overline{R} = R_F$—that is, the expected return on the security is equal to the risk-free rate. Because a security with zero beta has no relevant risk, its expected return should equal the risk-free rate.

- *Assume that* $\beta = 1$. Equation 11.16 reduces to $\overline{R} = \overline{R}_M$. That is, the expected return on the security is equal to the expected return on the market. This makes sense because the beta of the market portfolio is also 1.

Equation 11.16 can be represented graphically by the upward-sloping line in Figure 11.11. Note that the line begins at R_F and rises to $\overline{R}_M$ when beta is 1. This line is frequently called the **security market line** (SML).

As with any line, the SML has both a slope and an intercept. R_F, the risk-free rate, is the intercept. Because the beta of a security is the horizontal axis, $\overline{R}_M - R_F$ is the slope. The line will be upward-sloping as long as the expected return on the market is greater than the risk-free rate. Because the market portfolio is a risky asset, theory suggests that its expected return is above the risk-free rate, a result consistent with the empirical evidence of the previous chapter.

EXAMPLE
11.5

The stock of Aardvark Enterprises has a beta of 1.5 and that of Zebra Enterprises has a beta of .7. The risk-free rate is assumed to be 3 percent, and the difference between the expected return on the market and the risk-free rate is assumed to be 8.0 percent. The expected returns on the two securities are:

Expected Return for Aardvark

$$15.0\% = 3\% + 1.5 \times 8.0\% \qquad \textbf{(11.17)}$$

Expected Return for Zebra

$$8.6\% = 3\% + .7 \times 8.0\%$$

---

[12]This relationship was first proposed independently by John Lintner and William F. Sharpe.

Three additional points concerning the CAPM should be mentioned:

1. *Linearity:* The intuition behind an upwardly sloping curve is clear. Because beta is the appropriate measure of risk, high-beta securities should have an expected return above that of low-beta securities. However, both Figure 11.11 and Equation 11.16 show something more than an upwardly sloping curve: The relationship between expected return and beta corresponds to a *straight* line.

   It is easy to show that the line of Figure 11.11 is straight. To see this, consider Security *S* with, say, a beta of .8. This security is represented by a point below the security market line in the figure. Any investor could duplicate the beta of Security *S* by buying a portfolio with 20 percent in the risk-free asset and 80 percent in a security with a beta of 1. However, the homemade portfolio would itself lie on the SML. In other words, the portfolio dominates Security *S* because the portfolio has a higher expected return and the same beta.

   Now consider Security *T* with, say, a beta greater than 1. This security is also below the SML in Figure 11.11. Any investor could duplicate the beta of Security *T* by borrowing to invest in a security with a beta of 1. This portfolio must also lie on the SML, thereby dominating Security *T*.

   Because no one would hold either *S* or *T*, their stock prices would drop. This price adjustment would raise the expected returns on the two securities. The price adjustment would continue until the two securities lay on the security market line. The preceding example considered two overpriced stocks and a straight SML. Securities lying above the SML are *underpriced*. Their prices must rise until their expected returns lie on the line. If the SML is itself curved, many stocks would be mispriced. In equilibrium, all securities would be held only when prices changed so that the SML became straight. In other words, linearity would be achieved.

2. *Portfolios as well as securities:* Our discussion of the CAPM considered individual securities. Does the relationship in Figure 11.11 and Equation 11.16 hold for portfolios as well?

   Yes. To see this, consider a portfolio formed by investing equally in our two securities from Example 11.5, Aardvark and Zebra. The expected return on the portfolio is:

   Expected Return on Portfolio:

   $$11.8\% = .5 \times 15.0\% + .5 \times 8.6\% \tag{11.18}$$

The beta of the portfolio is simply a weighted average of the betas of the two securities. Thus, we have:

   Beta of Portfolio:

   $$1.1 = .5 \times 1.5 + .5 \times .7$$

Under the CAPM, the expected return on the portfolio is:

   $$11.8\% = 3\% + 1.1 \times 8.0\% \tag{11.19}$$

Because the expected return in Equation 11.18 is the same as the expected return in Equation 11.19, the example shows that the CAPM holds for portfolios as well as for individual securities.

3. *A potential confusion:* Students often confuse the SML in Figure 11.11 with Line *II* in Figure 11.9. Actually, the lines are quite different. Line *II* traces the efficient set

of portfolios formed from both risky assets and the riskless asset. Each point on the line represents an entire portfolio. Point A is a portfolio composed entirely of risky assets. Every other point on the line represents a portfolio of the securities in A combined with the riskless asset. The axes on Figure 11.9 are the expected return on a *portfolio* and the standard deviation of a *portfolio*. Individual securities do not lie along Line *II*.

The SML in Figure 11.11 relates expected return to beta. Figure 11.11 differs from Figure 11.9 in at least two ways. First, beta appears in the horizontal axis of Figure 11.11, but standard deviation appears in the horizontal axis of Figure 11.9. Second, the SML in Figure 11.11 holds both for all individual securities and for all possible portfolios, whereas Line *II* in Figure 11.9 holds only for efficient portfolios.

We stated earlier that, under homogeneous expectations, Point A in Figure 11.9 becomes the market portfolio. In this situation, Line *II* is referred to as the **capital market line** (CML).

Summary and Conclusions

This chapter set forth the fundamentals of modern portfolio theory. Our basic points are these:

1. This chapter showed us how to calculate the expected return and variance for individual securities, and the covariance and correlation for pairs of securities. Given these statistics, the expected return and variance for a portfolio of two securities A and B can be written as:

$$\text{Expected return on portfolio} = X_A \overline{R}_A + X_B \overline{R}_B$$
$$\text{Var(portfolio)} = X_A^2 \sigma_A^2 + 2X_A X_B \sigma_{AB} + X_B^2 \sigma_B^2$$

2. In our notation, X stands for the proportion of a security in a portfolio. By varying X we can trace out the efficient set of portfolios. We graphed the efficient set for the two-asset case as a curve, pointing out that the degree of curvature or bend in the graph reflects the diversification effect: The lower the correlation between the two securities, the greater the bend. The same general shape of the efficient set holds in a world of many assets.

3. Just as the formula for variance in the two-asset case is computed from a 2×2 matrix, the variance formula is computed from an $N \times N$ matrix in the N-asset case. We showed that with a large number of assets, there are many more covariance terms than variance terms in the matrix. In fact the variance terms are effectively diversified away in a large portfolio, but the covariance terms are not. Thus, a diversified portfolio can eliminate some, but not all, of the risk of the individual securities.

4. The efficient set of risky assets can be combined with riskless borrowing and lending. In this case a rational investor will always choose to hold the portfolio of risky securities represented by Point A in Figure 11.9. Then he can either borrow or lend at the riskless rate to achieve any desired point on Line *II* in the figure.

5. The contribution of a security to the risk of a large, well-diversified portfolio is proportional to the covariance of the security's return with the market's return. This contribution, when standardized, is called the beta. The beta of a security can also be interpreted as the responsiveness of a security's return to that of the market.

6. The CAPM states that:

$$\overline{R} = R_F + \beta(\overline{R}_M - R_F)$$

In other words, the expected return on a security is positively (and linearly) related to the security's beta.

Concept Questions

1. **Diversifiable and Nondiversifiable Risks**   In broad terms, why is some risk diversifiable? Why are some risks nondiversifiable? Does it follow that an investor can control the level of unsystematic risk in a portfolio, but not the level of systematic risk?

2. **Systematic versus Unsystematic Risk**   Classify the following events as mostly systematic or mostly unsystematic. Is the distinction clear in every case?
   a. Short-term interest rates increase unexpectedly.
   b. The interest rate a company pays on its short-term debt borrowing is increased by its bank.
   c. Oil prices unexpectedly decline.
   d. An oil tanker ruptures, creating a large oil spill.
   e. A manufacturer loses a multimillion-dollar product liability suit.
   f. A Supreme Court decision substantially broadens producer liability for injuries suffered by product users.

3. **Expected Portfolio Returns**   If a portfolio has a positive investment in every asset, can the expected return on the portfolio be greater than that on every asset in the portfolio? Can it be less than that on every asset in the portfolio? If you answer yes to one or both of these questions, give an example to support your answer.

4. **Diversification**   True or false: The most important characteristic in determining the expected return of a well-diversified portfolio is the variances of the individual assets in the portfolio. Explain.

5. **Portfolio Risk**   If a portfolio has a positive investment in every asset, can the standard deviation on the portfolio be less than that on every asset in the portfolio? What about the portfolio beta?

6. **Beta and CAPM**   Is it possible that a risky asset could have a beta of zero? Explain. Based on the CAPM, what is the expected return on such an asset? Is it possible that a risky asset could have a negative beta? What does the CAPM predict about the expected return on such an asset? Can you give an explanation for your answer?

7. **Covariance**   Briefly explain why the covariance of a security with the rest of a well-diversified portfolio is a more appropriate measure of the risk of the security than the security's variance.

8. **Beta**   Consider the following quotation from a leading investment manager: "The shares of Southern Co. have traded close to $12 for most of the past three years. Since Southern's stock has demonstrated very little price movement, the stock has a low beta. Texas Instruments, on the other hand, has traded as high as $150 and as low as its current $75. Since TI's stock has demonstrated a large amount of price movement, the stock has a very high beta." Do you agree with this analysis? Explain.

9. **Risk**   A broker has advised you not to invest in oil industry stocks because they have high standard deviations. Is the broker's advice sound for a risk-averse investor like yourself? Why or why not?

10. **Security Selection**   Is the following statement true or false? A risky security cannot have an expected return that is less than the risk-free rate because no risk-averse investor would be willing to hold this asset in equilibrium. Explain.

Questions and Problems

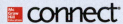

BASIC
(Questions 1–19)

1. **Determining Portfolio Weights**   What are the portfolio weights for a portfolio that has 165 shares of Stock A that sell for $43 per share and 120 shares of Stock B that sell for $74 per share?

2. **Portfolio Expected Return**   You own a portfolio that has $2,700 invested in Stock A and $3,800 invested in Stock B. If the expected returns on these stocks are 9.5 percent and 14 percent, respectively, what is the expected return on the portfolio?

3. **Portfolio Expected Return**   You own a portfolio that is 20 percent invested in Stock X, 45 percent in Stock Y, and 35 percent in Stock Z. The expected returns on these three stocks are 11 percent, 17 percent, and 14 percent, respectively. What is the expected return on the portfolio?

4. **Portfolio Expected Return**   You have $10,000 to invest in a stock portfolio. Your choices are Stock X with an expected return of 13 percent and Stock Y with an expected return of 8.5 percent. If your goal is to create a portfolio with an expected return of 11.9 percent, how much money will you invest in Stock X? In Stock Y?

5. **Calculating Returns and Standard Deviations**   Based on the following information, calculate the expected return and standard deviation for the two stocks:

State of Economy	Probability of State of Economy	Rate of Return if State Occurs	
		Stock A	Stock B
Recession	.30	.06	−.20
Normal	.55	.07	.13
Boom	.15	.11	.33

6. **Calculating Returns and Standard Deviations**   Based on the following information, calculate the expected return and standard deviation:

State of Economy	Probability of State of Economy	Rate of Return if State Occurs
Depression	.15	−.105
Recession	.30	.059
Normal	.45	.130
Boom	.10	.211

7. **Calculating Expected Returns**   A portfolio is invested 20 percent in Stock G, 55 percent in Stock J, and 25 percent in Stock K. The expected returns on these stocks are 9 percent, 11 percent, and 14 percent, respectively. What is the portfolio's expected return? How do you interpret your answer?

8. **Returns and Standard Deviations**   Consider the following information:

State of Economy	Probability of State of Economy	Rate of Return if State Occurs		
		Stock A	Stock B	Stock C
Boom	.65	.06	.16	.33
Bust	.35	.14	.02	−.06

a. What is the expected return on an equally weighted portfolio of these three stocks?

b. What is the variance of a portfolio invested 20 percent each in A and B, and 60 percent in C?

9. **Returns and Standard Deviations** Consider the following information:

State of Economy	Probability of State of Economy	Rate of Return if State Occurs		
		Stock A	Stock B	Stock C
Boom	.25	.24	.45	.33
Good	.40	.09	.10	.15
Poor	.30	.03	−.10	−.05
Bust	.05	−.05	−.25	−.09

a. Your portfolio is invested 30 percent each in A and C, and 40 percent in B. What is the expected return of the portfolio?

b. What is the variance of this portfolio? The standard deviation?

10. **Calculating Portfolio Betas** You own a stock portfolio invested 15 percent in Stock Q, 35 percent in Stock R, 30 percent in Stock S, and 20 percent in Stock T. The betas for these four stocks are .75, 1.90, 1.38, and 1.16, respectively. What is the portfolio beta?

11. **Calculating Portfolio Betas** You own a portfolio equally invested in a risk-free asset and two stocks. If one of the stocks has a beta of 1.73 and the total portfolio is equally as risky as the market, what must the beta be for the other stock in your portfolio?

12. **Using CAPM** A stock has a beta of 1.15, the expected return on the market is 10.6 percent, and the risk-free rate is 4.5 percent. What must the expected return on this stock be?

13. **Using CAPM** A stock has an expected return of 13.4 percent, the risk-free rate is 3.8 percent, and the market risk premium is 7 percent. What must the beta of this stock be?

14. **Using CAPM** A stock has an expected return of 13.4 percent, its beta is 1.20, and the risk-free rate is 4.4 percent. What must the expected return on the market be?

15. **Using CAPM** A stock has an expected return of 11.2 percent, a beta of 1.15, and the expected return on the market is 10.4 percent. What must the risk-free rate be?

16. **Using CAPM** A stock has a beta of 1.13 and an expected return of 12.1 percent. A risk-free asset currently earns 3.6 percent.

a. What is the expected return on a portfolio that is equally invested in the two assets?

b. If a portfolio of the two assets has a beta of .50, what are the portfolio weights?

c. If a portfolio of the two assets has an expected return of 10 percent, what is its beta?

d. If a portfolio of the two assets has a beta of 2.26, what are the portfolio weights? How do you interpret the weights for the two assets in this case? Explain.

17. **Using the SML** Asset W has an expected return of 11.9 percent and a beta of 1.2. If the risk-free rate is 4 percent, complete the following table for portfolios of Asset W and a risk-free asset. Illustrate the relationship between portfolio expected return and portfolio beta by plotting the expected returns against the betas. What is the slope of the line that results?

Percentage of Portfolio in Asset W	Portfolio Expected Return	Portfolio Beta
0%		
25		
50		
75		
100		
125		
150		

18. Reward-to-Risk Ratios Stock Y has a beta of 1.20 and an expected return of 12.7 percent. Stock Z has a beta of .90 and an expected return of 11.1 percent. If the risk-free rate is 4.5 percent and the market risk premium is 7.1 percent, are these stocks correctly priced?

19. Reward-to-Risk Ratios In the previous problem, what would the risk-free rate have to be for the two stocks to be correctly priced?

INTERMEDIATE
(Questions 20–32)

20. Portfolio Returns Using information from the previous chapter about capital market history, determine the return on a portfolio that is equally invested in large-company stocks and long-term government bonds. What is the return on a portfolio that is equally invested in small-company stocks and Treasury bills?

21. CAPM Using the CAPM, show that the ratio of the risk premiums on two assets is equal to the ratio of their betas.

22. Portfolio Returns and Deviations Consider the following information about three stocks:

State of Economy	Probability of State of Economy	Rate of Return if State Occurs Stock A	Stock B	Stock C
Boom	.25	.20	.25	.60
Normal	.55	.15	.11	.05
Bust	.20	.01	−.15	−.50

a. If your portfolio is invested 40 percent each in A and B and 20 percent in C, what is the portfolio expected return? The variance? The standard deviation?

b. If the expected T-bill rate is 3.80 percent, what is the expected risk premium on the portfolio?

c. If the expected inflation rate is 3.50 percent, what are the approximate and exact expected real returns on the portfolio? What are the approximate and exact expected real risk premiums on the portfolio?

23. Analyzing a Portfolio You want to create a portfolio equally as risky as the market, and you have $1,000,000 to invest. Given this information, fill in the rest of the following table:

Asset	Investment	Beta
Stock A	$180,000	.75
Stock B	$290,000	1.25
Stock C		1.45
Risk-free asset		

24. **Analyzing a Portfolio** You have $100,000 to invest in a portfolio containing Stock *X* and Stock *Y*. Your goal is to create a portfolio that has an expected return of 12.9 percent. If Stock *X* has an expected return of 11.2 percent and a beta of 1.30 and Stock *Y* has an expected return of 7.7 percent and a beta of .80, how much money will you invest in Stock *Y*? How do you interpret your answer? What is the beta of your portfolio?

25. **Covariance and Correlation** Based on the following information, calculate the expected return and standard deviation of each of the following stocks. Assume each state of the economy is equally likely to happen. What are the covariance and correlation between the returns of the two stocks?

State of Economy	Return on Stock A	Return on Stock B
Bear	.108	−.067
Normal	.126	.113
Bull	.064	.276

26. **Covariance and Correlation** Based on the following information, calculate the expected return and standard deviation for each of the following stocks. What are the covariance and correlation between the returns of the two stocks?

State of Economy	Probability of State of Economy	Return on Stock J	Return on Stock K
Bear	.30	−.020	.034
Normal	.55	.138	.062
Bull	.15	.218	.092

27. **Portfolio Standard Deviation** Security *F* has an expected return of 10 percent and a standard deviation of 49 percent per year. Security *G* has an expected return of 14 percent and a standard deviation of 73 percent per year.

   a. What is the expected return on a portfolio composed of 30 percent of Security *F* and 70 percent of Security *G*?
   b. If the correlation between the returns of Security *F* and Security *G* is .25, what is the standard deviation of the portfolio described in part (a)?

28. **Portfolio Standard Deviation** Suppose the expected returns and standard deviations of Stocks *A* and *B* are $E(R_A) = .11$, $E(R_B) = .13$, $\sigma_A = .39$, and $\sigma_B = .76$.

   a. Calculate the expected return and standard deviation of a portfolio that is composed of 35 percent *A* and 65 percent *B* when the correlation between the returns on *A* and *B* is .5.
   b. Calculate the standard deviation of a portfolio with the same portfolio weights as in part (a) when the correlation coefficient between the returns on *A* and *B* is −.5.
   c. How does the correlation between the returns on *A* and *B* affect the standard deviation of the portfolio?

29. **Correlation and Beta**   You have been provided the following data about the securities of three firms, the market portfolio, and the risk-free asset:

Security	Expected Return	Standard Deviation	Correlation*	Beta
Firm A	.10	.31	(i)	.85
Firm B	.14	(ii)	.50	1.40
Firm C	.16	.65	.35	(iii)
The market portfolio	.12	.20	(iv)	(v)
The risk-free asset	.05	(vi)	(vii)	(viii)

*With the market portfolio.

   a. Fill in the missing values in the table.
   b. Is the stock of Firm A correctly priced according to the capital asset pricing model (CAPM)? What about the stock of Firm B? Firm C? If these securities are not correctly priced, what is your investment recommendation for someone with a well-diversified portfolio?

30. **CML**   The market portfolio has an expected return of 11 percent and a standard deviation of 19 percent. The risk-free rate is 4.3 percent.

   a. What is the expected return on a well-diversified portfolio with a standard deviation of 9 percent?
   b. What is the standard deviation of a well-diversified portfolio with an expected return of 20 percent?

31. **Beta and CAPM**   A portfolio that combines the risk-free asset and the market portfolio has an expected return of 8 percent and a standard deviation of 17 percent. The risk-free rate is 4.3 percent, and the expected return on the market portfolio is 11 percent. Assume the capital asset pricing model holds. What expected rate of return would a security earn if it had a .45 correlation with the market portfolio and a standard deviation of 60 percent?

32. **Beta and CAPM**   Suppose the risk-free rate is 4.7 percent and the market portfolio has an expected return of 11.2 percent. The market portfolio has a variance of .0382. Portfolio Z has a correlation coefficient with the market of .28 and a variance of .3285. According to the capital asset pricing model, what is the expected return on Portfolio Z?

CHALLENGE
(Questions 33–38)

33. **Systematic versus Unsystematic Risk**   Consider the following information about Stocks I and II:

State of Economy	Probability of State of Economy	Rate of Return if State Occurs	
		Stock I	Stock II
Recession	.15	.11	−.25
Normal	.55	.18	.11
Irrational exuberance	.30	.08	.31

The market risk premium is 7.5 percent, and the risk-free rate is 4 percent. Which stock has the most systematic risk? Which one has the most unsystematic risk? Which stock is "riskier"? Explain.

34. SML   Suppose you observe the following situation:

Security	Beta	Expected Return
Pete Corp.	1.35	12.28%
Repete Co.	.80	8.54

Assume these securities are correctly priced. Based on the CAPM, what is the expected return on the market? What is the risk-free rate?

35. Covariance and Portfolio Standard Deviation   There are three securities in the market. The following chart shows their possible payoffs:

State	Probability of Outcome	Return on Security 1	Return on Security 2	Return on Security 3
1	.15	.20	.20	.05
2	.35	.15	.10	.10
3	.35	.10	.15	.15
4	.15	.05	.05	.20

   a. What are the expected return and standard deviation of each security?
   b. What are the covariances and correlations between the pairs of securities?
   c. What are the expected return and standard deviation of a portfolio with half of its funds invested in Security 1 and half in Security 2?
   d. What are the expected return and standard deviation of a portfolio with half of its funds invested in Security 1 and half in Security 3?
   e. What are the expected return and standard deviation of a portfolio with half of its funds invested in Security 2 and half in Security 3?
   f. What do your answers in parts (a), (c), (d), and (e) imply about diversification?

36. SML   Suppose you observe the following situation:

State of Economy	Probability of State	Return if State Occurs Stock A	Stock B
Bust	.15	−.10	−.08
Normal	.60	.09	.08
Boom	.25	.32	.26

   a. Calculate the expected return on each stock.
   b. Assuming the capital asset pricing model holds and Stock A's beta is greater than Stock B's beta by .25, what is the expected market risk premium?

37. Standard Deviation and Beta   There are two stocks in the market, Stock A and Stock B. The price of Stock A today is $75. The price of Stock A next year will be $64 if the economy is in a recession, $87 if the economy is normal, and $97 if the economy is expanding. The probabilities of recession, normal times, and expansion are .2, .6, and .2, respectively. Stock A pays no dividends and has a correlation of .7 with the market portfolio. Stock B has an expected return of 14 percent, a standard deviation of 34 percent, a correlation with the market portfolio of .24, and a correlation with Stock A of .36. The market portfolio has a standard deviation of 18 percent. Assume the CAPM holds.

   a. If you are a typical, risk-averse investor with a well-diversified portfolio, which stock would you prefer? Why?

b. What are the expected return and standard deviation of a portfolio consisting of 70 percent of Stock A and 30 percent of Stock B?

c. What is the beta of the portfolio in part (b)?

38. **Minimum Variance Portfolio** Assume Stocks A and B have the following characteristics:

Stock	Expected Return (%)	Standard Deviation (%)
A	9	33
B	15	62

The covariance between the returns on the two stocks is .001.

a. Suppose an investor holds a portfolio consisting of only Stock A and Stock B. Find the portfolio weights, X_A and X_B, such that the variance of her portfolio is minimized. (*Hint:* Remember that the sum of the two weights must equal 1.)

b. What is the expected return on the minimum variance portfolio?

c. If the covariance between the returns on the two stocks is $-.05$, what are the minimum variance weights?

d. What is the variance of the portfolio in part (c)?

Excel Master It! Problem

The CAPM is one of the most thoroughly researched models in financial economics. When beta is estimated in practice, a variation of CAPM called the market model is often used. To derive the market model, we start with the CAPM:

$$E(R_i) = R_f + \beta[E(R_M) - R_f]$$

Since CAPM is an equation, we can subtract the risk–free rate from both sides, which gives us:

$$E(R_i) - R_f = \beta[E(R_M) - R_f]$$

This equation is deterministic, that is, exact. In a regression, we realize that there is some indeterminate error. We need to formally recognize this in the equation by adding epsilon, which represents this error:

$$E(R_i) - R_f = \beta[E(R_M) - R_f] + \varepsilon$$

Finally, think of the above equation in a regression. Since there is no intercept in the equation, the intercept is zero. However, when we estimate the regression equation, we can add an intercept term, which we will call alpha:

$$E(R_i) - R_f = \alpha_i + \beta[E(R_M) - R_f] + \varepsilon$$

This equation, known as the market model, is generally the model used for estimating beta. The intercept term is known as Jensen's alpha, and it represents the excess return. If CAPM holds exactly, this intercept should be zero. If you think of alpha in terms of the SML, if the alpha is positive, the stock plots above the SML and if alpha is negative, the stock plots below the SML.

a. You want to estimate the market model for an individual stock and a mutual fund. First, go to finance.yahoo.com and download the adjusted prices for the last 61 months for an individual stock, a mutual fund, and the S&P 500. Next, go to the St. Louis Federal Reserve website at www.stlouisfed.org. You should find the FRED® database there. Look for the 1-Month Treasury Constant Maturity Rate and download this data. This series will be the proxy for the risk-free rate. When using this rate, you should be aware that this interest rate is the annualized interest rate, so while we are using monthly stock returns, you will need to adjust the 1-month T-bill rate. For the stock and mutual fund you select, estimate the beta and alpha using the market model. When you estimate the regression model, find the box that says "Residuals" and check this box when you do each regression. Because you are saving the residuals, you may want to save the regression output in a new worksheet.

1. Are the alpha and beta for each regression statistically different from zero?

2. How do you interpret the alpha and beta for the stock and the mutual fund?

3. Which of the two regression estimates has the highest R-squared? Is this what you would have expected? Why?

b. In part a, you asked Excel to return the residuals of the regression, which is the epsilon in the regression equation. If you remember back to basic statistics, the residuals are the linear distance from each observation to the regression line. In this context, the residuals are the part of the monthly return that is not explained by the market model estimate. The residuals can be used to calculate the appraisal ratio, which is the alpha divided by the standard deviation of the residuals.

1. What do you think the appraisal ratio is intended to measure?

2. Calculate the appraisal ratios for the stock and the mutual fund. Which has a better appraisal ratio?

3. Often, the appraisal ratio is used to evaluate the performance of mutual fund managers. Why do you think the appraisal ratio is used more often for mutual funds, which are portfolios, than for individual stocks?

Mini Case

A JOB AT EAST COAST YACHTS, PART 2

You are discussing your 401(k) with Dan Ervin when he mentions that Sarah Brown, a representative from Bledsoe Financial Services, is visiting East Coast Yachts today. You decide that you should meet with Sarah, so Dan sets up an appointment for you later in the day.

When you sit down with Sarah, she discusses the various investment options available in the company's 401(k) account. You mention to Sarah that you researched East Coast Yachts before you accepted your new job. You are confident in management's ability to lead the company. Analysis of the company has led to your belief that the company is growing and will achieve a greater market share in the future. You also feel you should support your employer. Given these considerations, along with the fact that you are a conservative investor, you are leaning toward investing 100 percent of your 401(k) account in East Coast Yachts stock.

Assume the risk-free rate is 3.2 percent. The correlation between the Bledsoe bond fund and large-cap stock fund is .15. Note that the spreadsheet graphing and "solver" functions may assist you in answering the following questions.

1. Considering the effects of diversification, how should Sarah respond to the suggestion that you invest 100 percent of your 401(k) account in East Coast Yachts stock?

2. Sarah's response to investing your 401(k) account entirely in East Coast Yachts stock has convinced you that this may not be the best alternative. Because you are a conservative investor, you tell Sarah that a 100 percent investment in the bond fund may be the best alternative. Is it?

3. Using the returns for the Bledsoe Large-Cap Stock Fund and the Bledsoe Bond Fund, graph the opportunity set of feasible portfolios.

4. After examining the opportunity set, you notice that you can invest in a portfolio consisting of the bond fund and the large-cap stock fund that will have exactly the same standard deviation as the bond fund. This portfolio will also have a greater expected return. What are the portfolio weights and expected return of this portfolio?

5. Examining the opportunity set, notice there is a portfolio that has the lowest standard deviation. This is the minimum variance portfolio. What are the portfolio weights, expected return, and standard deviation of this portfolio? Why is the minimum variance portfolio important?

6. A measure of risk-adjusted performance that is often used is the Sharpe ratio. The Sharpe ratio is calculated as the risk premium of an asset divided by its standard deviation. The portfolio with the highest possible Sharpe ratio on the opportunity set is called the Sharpe optimal portfolio. What are the portfolio weights, expected return, and standard deviation of the Sharpe optimal portfolio? How does the Sharpe ratio of this portfolio compare to the Sharpe ratios of the bond fund and the large-cap stock fund? Do you see a connection between the Sharpe optimal portfolio and the CAPM? What is the connection?

Appendix 11A Is Beta Dead?

To access Appendix 11A, please logon to Connect Finance.

12

An Alternative View of Risk and Return

THE ARBITRAGE PRICING THEORY

In December 2014, eBay, Alcoa, and Yum! Brands all made major announcements. Following such events, stock prices tend to change, and it was no different in these three cases. For eBay, the market learned that the company would likely lay off 3,000 workers when it spun off its PayPal unit. Aluminum company Alcoa announced that it would purchase titanium and aluminum casting company Tital and that the company's titanium unit would increase sales by 70 percent over the next five years. For Yum! Brands, the company announced that its 2015 earnings growth would be 10 percent or more. You might expect that these three cases represent good news for Alcoa and Yum! Brands and bad news for eBay, and usually you would be right. But here, Alcoa's stock price dropped about 3 percent, Yum! Brands stock dropped by about 6 percent, and eBay's stock price rose about 3 percent.

For these companies, good news seemed to be bad news (and vice versa). So when is good news really good news? The answer is fundamental to understanding risk and return, and—the good news is—this chapter explores it in some detail.

12.1 Introduction

In the previous chapter, we introduced the CAPM. The CAPM shows that if the market portfolio is mean-variance efficient, then the best way to measure the systematic risk of a security is with the beta coefficient. The CAPM implies that the expected return on a security is linearly related to beta. We emphasized the important role of diversification in eliminating unsystematic risks.

In this chapter, we take a closer look at where betas come from and the important role of arbitrage in asset pricing.

12.2 Systematic Risk and Betas

As we have learned, the return of any stock can be written as:

$$R = \overline{R} + U$$

where R is the actual return, $\overline{R}$ is the expected return, and U stands for the unexpected part of the return. The U is the surprise and constitutes the risk.

We also know that the risk of any stock can be further broken down into two components: The systematic and the unsystematic. So, we can write:

$$R = \overline{R} + m + \epsilon$$

where we have used the letter m to represent systematic risk and the Greek letter epsilon, ϵ, to represent unsystematic risk.

The fact that the unsystematic parts of the returns on two companies are unrelated to each other does not mean that the systematic portions are unrelated. On the contrary, because both companies are influenced by the same systematic risks, individual companies' systematic risks, and therefore their total returns, will be related.

For example, a surprise about inflation will influence almost all companies to some extent. How sensitive is a particular stock return to unanticipated changes in inflation? If the stock tends to go up on news that inflation is exceeding expectations, we would say that it is positively related to inflation. If the stock goes down when inflation exceeds expectations and up when inflation falls short of expectations, it is negatively related. In the unusual case where a stock's return is uncorrelated with inflation surprises, inflation has no effect on it.

We capture the influence of a systematic risk like inflation on a stock by using the **beta coefficient**. The beta coefficient, β, tells us the response of the stock's return to a systematic risk. In the previous chapter, beta measured the responsiveness of a security's return to a specific risk factor, the return on the market portfolio. We used this type of responsiveness to develop the capital asset pricing model. Because we now consider many types of systematic risks, our current work can be viewed as a generalization of our work in the previous chapter.

If a company's stock is positively related to the risk of inflation, that stock has a positive inflation beta. If it is negatively related to inflation, its inflation beta is negative; and if it is uncorrelated with inflation, its inflation beta is zero.

It's not hard to imagine some stocks with positive inflation betas and other stocks with negative inflation betas. The stock of a company owning gold mines will probably have a positive inflation beta because an unanticipated rise in inflation is usually associated with an increase in gold prices. On the other hand, an automobile company facing stiff foreign competition might find that an increase in inflation means that the wages it pays are higher, but that it cannot raise its prices to cover the increase. This profit squeeze, as the company's expenses rise faster than its revenues, would give its stock a negative inflation beta.

Some companies that have few assets and that act as brokers—buying items in competitive markets and reselling them in other markets—might be relatively unaffected by inflation because their costs and their revenues would rise and fall together. Their stock would have an inflation beta of zero.

Some structure is useful at this point. Suppose we have identified three systematic risks on which we want to focus. We may believe that these three are sufficient to describe the systematic risks that influence stock returns. Three likely candidates are inflation, GNP, and interest rates. Thus, every stock will have a beta associated with each of these systematic risks: An inflation beta, a GNP beta, and an interest rate beta. We can write the return on the stock, then, in the following form:

$$
\begin{aligned}
R &= \overline{R} + U \\
&= \overline{R} + m + \epsilon \\
&= \overline{R} + \beta_I F_I + \beta_{GNP} F_{GNP} + \beta_r F_r + \epsilon
\end{aligned}
$$

where we have used the symbol β_I to denote the stock's inflation beta, β_{GNP} for its GNP beta, and β_r to stand for its interest rate beta. In the equation, F stands for a surprise, whether it be in inflation, GNP, or interest rates.

Let us go through an example to see how the surprises and the expected return add up to produce the total return, R, on a given stock. To make it more familiar, suppose that the return is over a horizon of a year and not just a month. Suppose that at the beginning of the year, inflation is forecast to be 5 percent for the year, GNP is forecast to increase by 2 percent, and interest rates are expected not to change. Suppose the stock we are looking at has the following betas:

$$\beta_I = 2$$
$$\beta_{GNP} = 1$$
$$\beta_r = -1.8$$

The magnitude of the beta describes how great an impact a systematic risk has on a stock's return. A beta of $+1$ indicates that the stock's return rises and falls one for one with the systematic factor. This means, in our example, that because the stock has a GNP beta of 1, it experiences a 1 percent increase in return for every 1 percent surprise increase in GNP. If its GNP beta were -2, it would fall by 2 percent when there was an unanticipated increase of 1 percent in GNP, and it would rise by 2 percent if GNP experienced a surprise 1 percent decline.

Let us suppose that during the year the following events occur: Inflation rises by 7 percent, GNP rises by only 1 percent, and interest rates fall by 2 percent. Suppose we learn some good news about the company, perhaps that it is succeeding quickly with some new business strategy, and that this unanticipated development contributes 5 percent to its return. In other words:

$$\epsilon = 5\%$$

Let us assemble all of this information to find what return the stock had during the year.

First, we must determine what news or surprises took place in the systematic factors. From our information we know that:

$$\text{Expected inflation} = 5\%$$
$$\text{Expected GNP change} = 2\%$$

and:

$$\text{Expected change in interest rates} = 0\%$$

This means that the market had discounted these changes, and the surprises will be the difference between what actually takes place and these expectations:

$$
\begin{aligned}
F_I &= \text{Surprise in inflation} \\
&= \text{Actual inflation} - \text{Expected inflation} \\
&= 7\% - 5\% \\
&= 2\%
\end{aligned}
$$

Similarly:

$$
\begin{aligned}
F_{GNP} &= \text{Surprise in GNP} \\
&= \text{Actual GNP} - \text{Expected GNP} \\
&= 1\% - 2\% \\
&= -1\%
\end{aligned}
$$

and:

$$
\begin{aligned}
F_r &= \text{Surprise in change in interest rates} \\
&= \text{Actual change} - \text{Expected change} \\
&= -2\% - 0\% \\
&= -2\%
\end{aligned}
$$

The total effect of the systematic risks on the stock return, then, is:

$$m = \text{Systematic risk portion of return}$$
$$= \beta_I F_I + \beta_{GNP} F_{GNP} + \beta_r F_r$$
$$= [2 \times 2\%] + [1 \times (-1\%)] + [(-1.8) \times (-2\%)]$$
$$= 6.6\%$$

Combining this with the unsystematic risk portion, the total risky portion of the return on the stock is:

$$m + \epsilon = 6.6\% + 5\% = 11.6\%$$

Last, if the expected return on the stock for the year was, say, 4 percent, the total return from all three components will be:

$$R = \overline{R} + m + \epsilon$$
$$= 4\% + 6.6\% + 5\%$$
$$= 15.6\%$$

The model we have been looking at is called a **factor model**, and the systematic sources of risk, designated F, are called the *factors*. To be perfectly formal, a *k-factor model* is a model where each stock's return is generated by:

$$R = \overline{R} + \beta_1 F_1 + \beta_2 F_2 + \cdots + \beta_k F_k + \epsilon$$

where ϵ is specific to a particular stock and uncorrelated with the ϵ term for other stocks. In our preceding example we had a three-factor model. We used inflation, GNP, and the change in interest rates as examples of systematic sources of risk, or factors. Researchers have not settled on what is the correct set of factors. Like so many other questions, this might be one of those matters that is never laid to rest.

In practice, researchers frequently use a one-factor model for returns. They do not use all of the sorts of economic factors we used previously as examples; instead they use an index of stock market returns—like the S&P 500, or even a more broadly based index with more stocks in it—as the single factor. Using the single-factor model we can write returns like this:

$$R = \overline{R} + \beta(R_{S\&P500} - \overline{R}_{S\&P500}) + \epsilon$$

When there is only one factor (the returns on the S&P 500 Index), we do not need to put a subscript on the beta. In this form (with minor modifications) the factor model is called a **market model**. This term is employed because the index that is used for the factor is an index of returns on the whole (stock) market. The market model is written as:

$$R = \overline{R} + \beta(R_M - \overline{R}_M) + \epsilon$$

where R_M is the return on the market portfolio.[1] The single β is called the *beta coefficient*.

12.3 Portfolios and Factor Models

Now let us see what happens to portfolios of stocks when each of the stocks follows a one-factor model. For purposes of discussion, we will take the coming one-month period and examine returns. We could have used a day or a year or any other period. If the period

---

[1]Alternatively, the market model could be written as:

$$R = \alpha + \beta R_M + \epsilon$$

Here, alpha (α) is an intercept term equal to $\overline{R} - \beta \overline{R}_M$.

represents the time between decisions, however, we would rather it be short than long, and a month is a reasonable time frame to use.

We will create portfolios from a list of N stocks, and we will use a one-factor model to capture the systematic risk. The ith stock in the list will therefore have returns:

$$R_i = \overline{R}_i + \beta_i F + \epsilon_i \tag{12.1}$$

where we have subscripted the variables to indicate that they relate to the ith stock. Notice that the factor F is not subscripted. The factor that represents systematic risk could be a surprise in GNP, or we could use the market model and let the difference between the S&P 500 return and what we expect that return to be, $R_{\text{S\&P500}} - \overline{R}_{\text{S\&P500}}$, be the factor. In either case, the factor applies to all of the stocks.

The β_i is subscripted because it represents the unique way the factor influences the ith stock. To recapitulate our discussion of factor models, if β_i is zero, the returns on the ith stock are:

$$R_i = \overline{R}_i + \epsilon_i$$

In other words, the ith stock's returns are unaffected by the factor, F, if β_i is zero. If β_i is positive, positive changes in the factor raise the ith stock's returns, and negative changes lower them. Conversely, if β_i is negative, its returns and the factor move in opposite directions.

Figure 12.1 illustrates the relationship between a stock's excess returns, $R_i - \overline{R}_i$, and the factor F for different betas, where $\beta_i > 0$. The lines in Figure 12.1 plot Equation 12.1 on the assumption that there has been no unsystematic risk. That is, $\epsilon_i = 0$. Because we are assuming positive betas, the lines slope upward, indicating that the return on the stock rises with F. Notice that if the factor is zero ($F = 0$), the line passes through zero on the y-axis.

Figure 12.1
The One-Factor Model

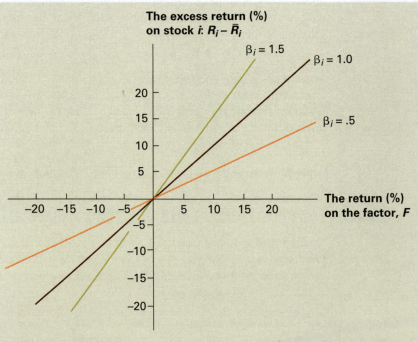

Each line represents a different security, where each security has a different beta.

Now let us see what happens when we create stock portfolios where each stock follows a one-factor model. Let X_i be the proportion of Security i in the portfolio. That is, if an individual with a portfolio of $100 wants $20 in General Motors, we say $X_{GM} = 20\%$. Because the Xs represent the proportions of wealth we are investing in each of the stocks, we know that they must add up to 100 percent, or 1:

$$X_1 + X_2 + X_3 + \cdots + X_N = 1$$

We know that the portfolio return is the weighted average of the returns on the individual assets in the portfolio. Algebraically, this can be written as follows:

$$R_P = X_1 R_1 + X_2 R_2 + X_3 R_3 + \cdots + X_N R_N \tag{12.2}$$

We saw from Equation 12.1 that each asset, in turn, is determined by both the factor F, and the unsystematic risk of ϵ_i. Thus, by substituting Equation 12.1 for each R_i in Equation 12.2, we have:

$$
\begin{aligned}
R_P = \ &X_1(\overline{R}_1 + \beta_1 F + \epsilon_1) &&+ X_2(\overline{R}_2 + \beta_2 F + \epsilon_2) \\
&\text{(Return on Stock 1)} &&\text{(Return on Stock 2)} \\
&+ X_3(\overline{R}_3 + \beta_3 F + \epsilon_3) + \cdots &&+ X_N(\overline{R}_N + \beta_N F + \epsilon_N) \\
&\text{(Return on Stock 3)} &&\text{(Return on Stock } N)
\end{aligned}
\tag{12.3}
$$

Equation 12.3 shows us that the return on a portfolio is determined by three sets of parameters:

1. The expected return on each individual security, $\overline{R}_i$.
2. The beta of each security multiplied by the factor, F.
3. The unsystematic risk of each individual security, ϵ_i.

We express Equation 12.3 in terms of these three sets of parameters like this:

Weighted Average of Expected Returns:

$$R_P = X_1 \overline{R}_1 + X_2 \overline{R}_2 + X_3 \overline{R}_3 + \cdots + X_N \overline{R}_N$$

Weighted Average of Betas $\times$ F:

$$+ (X_1 \beta_1 + X_2 \beta_2 + X_3 \beta_3 + \cdots + X_N \beta_N)F \tag{12.4}$$

Weighted Average of Unsystematic Risks:

$$+ X_1 \epsilon_1 + X_2 \epsilon_2 + X_3 \epsilon_3 + \cdots + X_N \epsilon_N$$

This rather imposing equation is actually straightforward. The first row is the weighted average of each security's expected return. The items in the parentheses of the second row represent the weighted average of each security's beta. This weighted average is, in turn, multiplied by the factor, F. The third row represents a weighted average of the unsystematic risks of the individual securities.

Where does uncertainty appear in Equation 12.4? There is no uncertainty in the first row because only the expected value of each security's return appears there. Uncertainty in the second row is reflected by only one item, F. That is, while we know that the expected value of F is zero, we do not know what its value will be over a particular period. Uncertainty in the third row is reflected by each unsystematic risk, ϵ_i.

PORTFOLIOS AND DIVERSIFICATION

In the previous sections of this chapter, we expressed the return on a single security in terms of our factor model. Portfolios were treated next. Because investors generally hold diversified portfolios, we now want to know what Equation 12.4 looks like in a *large* or diversified portfolio.[2]

As it turns out, something unusual occurs to Equation 12.4: The third row actually *disappears* in a large portfolio. To see this, consider a gambler who divides $1,000 by betting on red over many spins of the roulette wheel. For example, he may participate in 1,000 spins, betting $1 at a time. Though we do not know ahead of time whether a particular spin will yield red or black, we can be confident that red will win about 50 percent of the time. Ignoring the house take, the investor can be expected to end up with just about his original $1,000.

Though we are concerned with stocks, not roulette wheels, the same principle applies. Each security has its own unsystematic risk, where the surprise for one stock is unrelated to the surprise of another stock. By investing a small amount in each security, we bring the weighted average of the unsystematic risks close to zero in a large portfolio.[3]

Although the third row completely vanishes in a large portfolio, nothing unusual occurs in either Row 1 or Row 2. Row 1 remains a weighted average of the expected returns on the individual securities as securities are added to the portfolio. Because there is no uncertainty at all in the first row, there is no way for diversification to cause this row to vanish. The terms inside the parentheses of the second row remain a weighted average of the betas. They do not vanish, either, when securities are added. Because the factor, F, is unaffected when securities are added to the portfolios, the second row does not vanish.

Why does the third row vanish while the second row does not, though both rows reflect uncertainty? The key is that there are many unsystematic risks in Row 3. Because these risks are independent of each other, the effect of diversification becomes stronger as we add more assets to the portfolio. The resulting portfolio becomes less and less risky, and the return becomes more certain. However, the systematic risk, F, affects all securities because it is outside the parentheses in Row 2. Because we cannot avoid this factor by investing in many securities, diversification does not occur in this row.

EXAMPLE

Diversification and Unsystematic Risk   The preceding material can be further explained by the following example. We keep our one-factor model here but make three specific assumptions:

1. All securities have the same expected return of 10 percent. This assumption implies that the first row of Equation 12.4 must also equal 10 percent because this row is a weighted average of the expected returns of the individual securities.

2. All securities have a beta of 1. The sum of the terms inside the parentheses in the second row of Equation 12.4 must equal 1 because these terms are a weighted average of the individual betas. Because the terms inside the parentheses are multiplied by F, the value of the second row is $1 \times F = F$.

---

[2]Technically, we can think of a large portfolio as one where an investor keeps increasing the number of securities without limit. In practice, *effective* diversification would occur if at least a few dozen securities were held.

[3]More precisely, we say that the weighted average of the unsystematic risk approaches zero as the number of equally weighted securities in a portfolio approaches infinity.

3. In this example, we focus on the behavior of one individual, Walter V. Bagehot. Mr. Bagehot decides to hold an equally weighted portfolio. That is, the proportion of each security in his portfolio is $1/N$.

We can express the return on Mr. Bagehot's portfolio as follows:

Return on Walter V. Bagehot's Portfolio

$$R_P = \underset{\substack{\text{From} \\ \text{Row 1 of} \\ \text{Equation 12.4}}}{10\%} + \underset{\substack{\text{From} \\ \text{Row 2 of} \\ \text{Equation 12.4}}}{F} + \underset{\substack{\text{From Row 3 of} \\ \text{Equation 12.4}}}{\left(\frac{1}{N}\epsilon_1 + \frac{1}{N}\epsilon_2 + \frac{1}{N}\epsilon_3 + \cdots + \frac{1}{N}\epsilon_N \right)} \qquad \textbf{(12.4')}$$

We mentioned before that as N increases without limit, Row 3 of Equation 12.4 becomes equal to zero.[4] Thus, the return on Walter Bagehot's portfolio when the number of securities is very large is:

$$R_P = 10\% + F \qquad \textbf{(12.4'')}$$

The key to diversification is exhibited in Equation 12.4''. The unsystematic risk of Row 3 vanishes while the systematic risk of Row 2 remains.

This is illustrated in Figure 12.2. Systematic risk, captured by variation in the factor, F, is not reduced through diversification. Conversely, unsystematic risk diminishes as securities are added, vanishing as the number of securities becomes infinite. Our result is analogous to the diversification example of the previous chapter. In that chapter, we said that undiversifiable or systematic risk arises from positive covariances between securities. In this chapter, we say that systematic risk arises from a common factor, F. Because a common factor causes positive covariances, the arguments of the two chapters are parallel.

Figure 12.2   Diversification and the Portfolio Risk for an Equally Weighted Portfolio

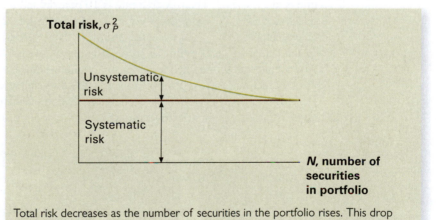

Total risk decreases as the number of securities in the portfolio rises. This drop occurs only in the unsystematic risk component. Systematic risk is unaffected by diversification.

---

[4]Our presentation on this point has not been rigorous. The student interested in more rigor should note that the variance of Row 3 is:

$$\frac{1}{N^2}\sigma_\epsilon^2 + \frac{1}{N^2}\sigma_\epsilon^2 + \frac{1}{N^2}\sigma_\epsilon^2 + \cdots + \frac{1}{N^2}\sigma_\epsilon^2 = \frac{1}{N^2}N\sigma_\epsilon^2$$

where σ_ϵ^2 is the variance of each ϵ. This can be rewritten as σ_ϵ^2/N, which tends to 0 as N goes to infinity.

12.4 Betas, Arbitrage, and Expected Returns

THE LINEAR RELATIONSHIP

We have argued many times that the expected return on a security compensates for its risk. In the previous chapter, we showed that market beta (the standardized covariance of the security's returns with those of the market) was the appropriate measure of risk under the assumptions of homogeneous expectations and riskless borrowing and lending. The capital asset pricing model, which posited these assumptions, implied that the expected return on a security was positively (and linearly) related to its beta. We will find a similar relationship between risk and return in the one-factor model of this chapter.

We begin by noting that the relevant risk in large and well-diversified portfolios is all systematic because unsystematic risk is diversified away. An implication is that when a well-diversified shareholder considers changing her holdings of a particular stock, she can ignore the security's unsystematic risk.

Notice that we are not claiming that stocks, like portfolios, have no unsystematic risk. Nor are we saying that the unsystematic risk of a stock will not affect its returns. Stocks do have unsystematic risk, and their actual returns do depend on the unsystematic risk. Because this risk washes out in a well-diversified portfolio, however, shareholders can ignore this unsystematic risk when they consider whether to add a stock to their portfolio. Therefore, if shareholders are ignoring the unsystematic risk, only the systematic risk of a stock can be related to its *expected* return.

This relationship is illustrated in the security market line of Figure 12.3. Points *P*, *C*, *A*, and *L* all lie on the line emanating from the risk-free rate of 10 percent. The points representing each of these four assets can be created by combinations of the risk-free asset and any of the other three assets. For example, because *A* has a beta of 2.0 and *P* has a beta of 1.0, a portfolio of 50 percent in Asset *A* and 50 percent in the riskless asset has the same beta as Asset *P*. The risk-free rate is 10 percent and the expected return on Security *A* is 35 percent, implying that the combination's return of 22.5 percent [(10% + 35%)/2] is identical to Security *P*'s expected return. Because Security *P* has both the same beta and the same expected return as a combination of the riskless asset and Security *A*, an individual is equally inclined to add a small amount of Security *P* and a small amount of this combination to her portfolio. However, the unsystematic risk of Security *P* need not be equal to the unsystematic risk of the combination of Security *A* and the risk-free asset because unsystematic risk is diversified away in a large portfolio.

Figure 12.3

A Graph of Beta and Expected Return for Individual Stocks Under the One-Factor Model

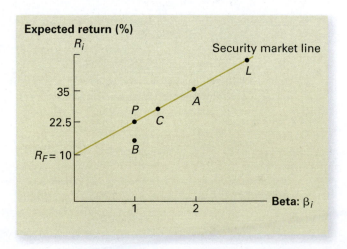

Of course, the potential combinations of points on the security market line are end-less. We can duplicate *P* by combinations of the risk-free asset and either *C* or *L* (or both of them). We can duplicate *C* (or *A* or *L*) by borrowing at the risk-free rate to invest in *P*. The infinite number of points on the security market line that are not labeled can be used as well.

Now consider Security *B*. Because its expected return is below the line, no investor would hold it. Instead, the investor would prefer Security *P*, a combination of Security *A* and the riskless asset, or some other combination. Thus, Security *B*'s price is too high. Its price will fall in a competitive market, forcing its expected return back up to the line in equilibrium. Investors who try to spot situations where securities of the same risk have different expected returns are called arbitrageurs. The arbitrage trade here is to sell short Security *B* and buy Security *P*. The profit would be the difference in the market prices of Security *B* and Security *P*. The idea of arbitrage, and its significance in asset pricing, is referred to as the Arbitrage Pricing Theory.

The preceding discussion allows us to provide an equation for the security market line of Figure 12.3. We know that a line can be described algebraically from two points. It is perhaps easiest to focus on the risk-free asset and security *P* because the risk-free asset has a beta of 0 and *P* has a beta of 1.

Because we know that the return on any zero-beta asset is R_F and the expected return on security *P* is $\overline{R}_P$, it can easily be shown that:

$$\overline{R} = R_F + \beta(\overline{R}_P - R_F) \tag{12.5}$$

In Equation 12.5, $\overline{R}$ can be thought of as the expected return on any security or portfolio lying on the security market line. β is the beta of that security or portfolio.

THE MARKET PORTFOLIO AND THE SINGLE FACTOR

In the CAPM, the beta of a security measures the security's responsiveness to movements in the market portfolio. In the one-factor model of the arbitrage pricing theory (APT), the beta of a security measures its responsiveness to the factor. We now relate the market portfolio to the single factor.

A large, diversified portfolio has no unsystematic risk because the unsystematic risks of the individual securities are diversified away. Assuming enough securities so that the market portfolio is fully diversified and assuming that no security has a disproportionate market share, this portfolio is fully diversified and contains no unsystematic risk.[5] In other words, the market portfolio is perfectly correlated with the single factor, implying that the market portfolio is really a scaled-up or scaled-down version of the factor. After scaling properly, we can treat the market portfolio as the factor itself.

The market portfolio, like every security or portfolio, lies on the security market line. When the market portfolio is the factor, the beta of the market portfolio is 1 by definition. This is shown in Figure 12.4. (We deleted the securities and the specific expected returns from Figure 12.3 for clarity: The two graphs are otherwise identical.) With the market portfolio as the factor, Equation 12.5 becomes:

$$\overline{R} = R_F + \beta(\overline{R}_M - R_F)$$

---

[5]This assumption is plausible in the real world. For example, even the market value of Apple is (at this writing) about 4 percent of the market value of the S&P 500 Index.

Figure 12.4

A Graph of Beta and
Expected Return
for Market Portfolio
under the One-Factor
Model

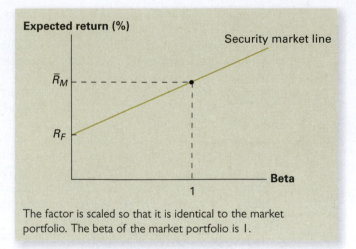

The factor is scaled so that it is identical to the market
portfolio. The beta of the market portfolio is 1.

where $\overline{R}_M$ is the expected return on the market. This equation shows that the expected return on any asset, $\overline{R}$, is linearly related to the security's beta. The equation is identical to that of the CAPM, which we developed in the previous chapter.

12.5 The Capital Asset Pricing Model and the Arbitrage Pricing Theory

The CAPM and the APT are alternative models of risk and return. It is worthwhile to consider the differences between the two models, both in terms of pedagogy and in terms of application.

DIFFERENCES IN PEDAGOGY

We feel that the CAPM has at least one strong advantage from the student's point of view. The derivation of the CAPM necessarily brings the reader through a discussion of efficient sets. This treatment—beginning with the case of two risky assets, moving to the case of many risky assets, and finishing when a riskless asset is added to the many risky ones—is of great intuitive value. This sort of presentation is not as easily accomplished with the APT.

However, the APT has some offsetting advantages. The model adds factors until the unsystematic risk of any security is uncorrelated with the unsystematic risk of every other security. Under this formulation, it is easily shown that (1) unsystematic risk steadily falls (and ultimately vanishes) as the number of securities in the portfolio increases, but (2) the systematic risks do not decrease. This result was also shown in the CAPM, though the intuition was cloudier because the unsystematic risks could be correlated across securities. Also, the APT emphasizes the role of arbitrage in obtaining a linear relationship between expected returns and betas.

DIFFERENCES IN APPLICATION

One advantage of the APT is that it can handle multiple factors while the CAPM ignores them. Although the bulk of our presentation in this chapter focused on the one-factor model, a multifactor model is probably more reflective of reality. That is, we must abstract from many marketwide and industrywide factors before the unsystematic risk of one security becomes uncorrelated with the unsystematic risks of other securities. Under this multifactor version of the APT, the relationship between risk and return can be expressed as:

$$\overline{R} = R_F + (\overline{R}_1 - R_F)\beta_1 + (\overline{R}_2 - R_F)\beta_2 + (\overline{R}_3 - R_F)\beta_3 + \cdots + (\overline{R}_K - R_F)\beta_K \quad \textbf{(12.6)}$$

In this equation, β_1 stands for the security's beta with respect to the first factor, β_2 stands for the security's beta with respect to the second factor, and so on. For example, if the first factor is GNP, β_1 is the security's GNP beta. The term $\overline{R}_1$ is the expected return on a security (or portfolio) whose beta with respect to the first factor is one and whose beta with respect to all other factors is zero. Because the market compensates for risk, $(\overline{R}_1 - R_F)$ will be positive in the normal case.[6] (An analogous interpretation can be given to $\overline{R}_2$, $\overline{R}_3$, and so on.)

The equation states that the security's expected return is related to the security's factor betas. The intuition in Equation 12.6 is straightforward. Each factor represents risk that cannot be diversified away. The higher a security's beta is with regard to a particular factor, the higher the risk that the security bears. In a rational world, the expected return on the security should compensate for this risk. Equation 12.6 states that the expected return is a summation of the risk-free rate plus the compensation for each type of risk that the security bears.

As an example, consider a study where the factors were monthly growth in industrial production (IP), change in expected inflation (ΔEI), unanticipated inflation (UI), unanticipated change in the risk premium between risky bonds and default-free bonds (URP), and unanticipated change in the difference between the return on long-term government bonds and the return on short-term government bonds (UBR).[7] Using the period 1958–1984, the empirical results of the study indicated that the expected monthly return on any stock, $\overline{R}_S$, can be described as:

$$\overline{R}_S = .0041 + .0136\beta_{IP} - .0001\beta_{\Delta EI} - .0006\beta_{UI} + .0072\beta_{URP} - .0052\beta_{UBR}$$

Suppose a particular stock had the following betas: $\beta_{IP} = 1.1$, $\beta_{\Delta EI} = 2$, $\beta_{UI} = 3$, $\beta_{URP} = .1$, $\beta_{UBR} = 1.6$. The expected monthly return on that security would be:

$$\begin{aligned} \overline{R}_S &= .0041 + .0136 \times 1.1 - .0001 \times 2 - .0006 \times 3 + .0072 \times .1 \\ &\quad - .0052 \times 1.6 \\ &= .0095 \end{aligned}$$

Assuming that a firm is unlevered and that one of the firm's projects has risk equivalent to that of the firm, this value of .0095 (i.e., .95%) can be used as the monthly discount rate for the project. (Because annual data are often supplied for capital budgeting purposes, the annual rate of .120 $[=(1.0095)^{12} - 1]$ might be used instead.)

Because many factors appear on the right side of Equation 12.6, the APT formulation has the potential to measure expected returns more accurately than does the CAPM. However, as we mentioned earlier, we cannot easily determine which are the appropriate factors. The factors in the preceding study were included for reasons of both common sense and convenience. They were not derived from theory.

---

[6]Actually, $(\overline{R}_i - R_F)$ could be negative in the case where factor i is perceived as a hedge of some sort.

[7]N. Chen, R. Roll, and S. Ross, "Economic Forces and the Stock Market," *The Journal of Business* (July 1986).

By contrast, the use of the market index in the CAPM formulation is implied by the theory of the previous chapter. We suggested in earlier chapters that the S&P 500 Index reflects overall U.S. stock market movements. Using the Ibbotson-Sinquefield results showing that since 1926 the yearly return on the S&P 500 Index was, on average, about 8.6 percent greater than the risk-free rate, the last chapter showed how to calculate expected returns on different securities using the CAPM.[8]

12.6 Empirical Approaches to Asset Pricing

EMPIRICAL MODELS

The CAPM and the APT by no means exhaust the models and techniques used in practice to measure the expected return on risky assets. Both the CAPM and the APT are *risk-based models*. They each measure the risk of a security by its beta(s) on some systematic factor(s), and they each argue that the expected excess return must be proportional to the beta(s). Although we have seen that this is intuitively appealing and has a strong basis in theory, there are alternative approaches.

Most of these alternatives can be lumped under the broad heading of parametric or **empirical models**. The word *empirical* refers to the fact that these approaches are based less on some theory of how financial markets work and more on simply looking for regularities and relations in the history of market data. In these approaches, the researcher specifies some parameters or attributes associated with the securities in question and then examines the data directly for a relation between these attributes and expected returns. For example, an extensive amount of research has been done on whether the expected return on a firm is related to its size. Is it true that small firms have higher average returns than large firms? Researchers have also examined a variety of accounting measures such as the ratio of the price of a stock to its accounting earnings, its PE ratio, and the closely related ratio of the market value of the stock to the book value of the company, the M/B ratio. Here it might be argued that companies with low PEs or low M/Bs are "undervalued" and can be expected to have higher returns in the future.

To use the empirical approach to determine the expected return, we would estimate the following equation:

$$\overline{R}_i = R_F + k_{P/E} \, (PE)_i + k_{M/B} \, (M/B)_i + k_{size} \, (size)_i$$

where $\overline{R}_i$ is the expected return of Firm i, and where the k's are coefficients that we estimate from stock market data. Notice that this is the same form as Equation 12.6 with the firm's attributes in place of betas and with the k's in place of the excess factor portfolio returns.

When tested with data, these parametric approaches seem to do quite well. In fact, when comparisons are made between using parameters and using betas to predict stock returns, the parameters, such as PE and M/B, seem to work better. There are a variety of possible explanations for these results, and the issues have certainly not been settled.

---

[8]Going back to 1900 the S&P 500 was on average 7.2 percent greater than the risk-free rate. Though many researchers assume that surrogates for the market portfolio are easily found, Richard Roll, "A Critique of the Asset Pricing Theory's Tests," *Journal of Financial Economics* (March 1977), argues that the absence of a universally acceptable proxy for the market portfolio seriously impairs application of the theory. After all, the market must include real estate, racehorses, and other assets that are not in the stock market.

Critics of the empirical approach are skeptical of what they call *data mining*. The particular parameters that researchers work with are often chosen because they have been shown to be related to returns. For instance, suppose that you were asked to explain the change in SAT test scores over the past 40 years in some particular state. Suppose that to do this you searched through all of the data series you could find. After much searching, you might discover, for example, that the change in the scores was directly related to the jackrabbit population in Arizona. We know that any such relation is purely accidental; but if you search long enough and have enough choices, you will find something even if it is not really there. It's a bit like staring at clouds. After a while you will see clouds that look like anything you want—clowns, bears, or whatever—but all you are really doing is data mining.

Needless to say, the researchers on these matters defend their work by arguing that they have not mined the data and have been very careful to avoid such traps by not snooping at the data to see what will work.

Of course, as a matter of pure theory, because anyone in the market can easily look up the PE ratio of a firm, we would certainly not expect to find that firms with low PEs did better than firms with high PEs simply because they were undervalued. In an efficient market, such public measures of undervaluation would be quickly exploited and would not last.

Perhaps a better explanation for the success of empirical approaches lies in a synthesis of the risk-based approaches and the empirical methods. In an efficient market, risk and return are related; so perhaps the parameters or attributes that appear to be related to returns are also better measures of risk. For example, if we were to find that low PE firms outperformed high PE firms and that this was true even for firms that had the same beta(s), then we would have at least two possible explanations. First, we could simply discard the risk-based theories as incorrect. Furthermore, we could argue that markets are inefficient and that buying low PE stocks provides us with an opportunity to make higher-than-predicted returns. Second, we could argue that *both* views of the world are correct and that the PE is really just a better way to measure systematic risk—that is, beta(s)—than directly estimating beta from the data.

STYLE PORTFOLIOS

In addition to their use as a platform for estimating expected returns, stock attributes are also widely used as a way of characterizing money management styles. For example, a portfolio that has a PE ratio much in excess of the market average might be characterized as a high PE portfolio or a **growth stock portfolio**. Similarly, a portfolio made up of stocks with an average PE less than that of a market index might be characterized as a low PE portfolio or a **value portfolio**.

To evaluate how well portfolio managers are doing, their performance is often compared with the performance of some basic indexes. For example, the portfolio returns of managers who purchase large U.S. stocks might be compared to the performance of the S&P 500 Index. In such a case, the S&P 500 is said to be the **benchmark** against which their performance is measured. Similarly, an international manager might be compared against some common index of international stocks. In choosing an appropriate benchmark, care should be taken to identify a benchmark that contains only those types of stocks that the manager targets as representative of his style and that are also available to be purchased. A manager who was told not to purchase any stocks in the S&P 500 Index would not consider it legitimate to be compared against the S&P 500.

In Their Own Words

KENNETH FRENCH ON THE FAMA–FRENCH THREE-FACTOR MODEL

The Fama–French (1993) three-factor model is an empirically motivated implementation of Ross's (1976) arbitrage pricing theory. When we developed the model, researchers had identified two dominant patterns in the cross-section of average stock returns. Small companies, with relatively little market equity, tend to have higher average stock returns than big companies (Banz, 1981). And value companies, which are often defined as those with a high ratio of book equity to market equity, tend to have higher average returns than growth companies (Fama and French, 1992). Our goal was a simple model that captures these patterns in stock returns.

The three-factor model predicts that the expected excess return on portfolio i, $E(R_i) - R_F$, is determined by its loadings on, well, three factors,

$$E(R_i) - R_F = \beta_i[E(R_M) - R_F] + s_i E(SMB) + h_i E(HML)$$

The excess return on the market, $E(R_M) - R_F$, plays much the same role here as it does in the capital asset pricing model. The expected compensation investors receive for bearing market risk equals the quantity of market risk, β_i, times the price per unit, $E(R_M) - R_F$.

The second and third factors are aimed at the size and value effect. The size factor, SMB (small minus big), is the difference between the returns on a portfolio of small stocks and a portfolio of big stocks. The value factor, HML (high minus low), is the difference between the returns on a portfolio of high book-to-market stocks and a portfolio of low book-to-market stocks. Because small stocks tend to outperform big stocks and value stocks

tend to outperform growth stocks, the expected values of SMB and HML are positive. Thus, the three-factor model predicts that the expected return on a portfolio increases linearly with s_i, its loading on SMB, and with h_i, its loading on HML. A portfolio of small value stocks, for example, is likely to have positive loadings on SMB and HML, so the model predicts the portfolio has a high expected return.

You can estimate a portfolio's loadings on $R_M - R_F$, SMB, and HML by regressing its excess return on the three factors,

$$R_{it} - R_{Ft} = \alpha_i + \beta_i(R_{Mt} - R_{Ft}) + s_i SMB_t + h_i HML_t + \epsilon_{it}$$

The model predicts the intercept a_i in this time series regression is zero. I provide daily, monthly, quarterly, and annual returns for the three factors on my website, www.dartmouth.edu/~kfrench. People typically use monthly returns when estimating the model because they offer a good compromise between market microstructure issues that become important as the interval gets shorter and the loss of observations that occurs as the interval gets longer.

The three-factor model is not perfect, but it does a reasonable job explaining the returns on a wide range of stock portfolios. There is controversy, however, about whether the average premiums on SMB and HML are compensation for risk or the result of mispricing. (For what it is worth, I think they are the result of both risk and mispricing.) Fortunately, the answer to this question is irrelevant for many applications of the model. When evaluating a portfolio manager, for example, we can simply interpret SMB and HML as the returns to passive benchmark portfolios.

Increasingly, too, managers are compared not only against an index but also against a peer group of similar managers. The performance of a fund that advertises itself as a growth fund might be measured against the performance of a large sample of similar funds. For instance, the performance over some period is commonly assigned to quartiles. The top 25 percent of the funds are said to be in the first quartile, the next 25 percent in the second quartile, the next 25 percent in the third quartile, and the worst-performing 25 percent of the funds in the last quartile. If the fund we are examining happens to have a performance that falls in the second quartile, then we speak of its manager as a second quartile manager.

Similarly, we call a fund that purchases low M/B stocks a value fund and would measure its performance against a sample of similar value funds. These approaches to measuring performance are relatively new, and they are part of an active and exciting effort to refine our ability to identify and use investment skills.

Summary and Conclusions

The previous chapter developed the capital asset pricing model (CAPM). As an alternative, this chapter developed the arbitrage pricing theory (APT).

1. The APT assumes that stock returns are generated according to factor models. For example, we might describe a stock's return as:

$$R = \bar{R} + \beta_I F_I + \beta_{GNP} F_{GNP} + \beta_r F_r + \epsilon$$

where I, GNP, and r stand for inflation, gross national product, and the interest rate, respectively. The three factors F_I, F_{GNP}, and F_r represent systematic risk because these factors affect many securities. The term ϵ is considered unsystematic risk because it is unique to each individual security.

2. For convenience, we frequently describe a security's return according to a one-factor model:

$$R = \bar{R} + \beta F + \epsilon$$

3. As securities are added to a portfolio, the unsystematic risks of the individual securities offset each other. A fully diversified portfolio has no unsystematic risk but still has systematic risk. This result indicates that diversification can eliminate some, but not all, of the risk of individual securities.

4. Because of this, the expected return on a stock is positively related to its systematic risk. In a one-factor model, the systematic risk of a security is simply the beta of the CAPM. Thus, the implications of the CAPM and the one-factor APT are identical. However, each security has many risks in a multifactor model. The expected return on a security is positively related to its beta with each factor.

5. Empirical or parametric models that capture the relations between returns and stock attributes such as PE or M/B ratios can be estimated directly from the data without any appeal to theory. These ratios are also used to measure the styles of portfolio managers and to construct benchmarks and samples against which they are measured.

Concept Questions

1. **Systematic versus Unsystematic Risk**   Describe the difference between systematic risk and unsystematic risk.

2. **APT**   Consider the following statement: For the APT to be useful, the number of systematic risk factors must be small. Do you agree or disagree with this statement? Why?

3. **APT**   David McClemore, the CFO of Ultra Bread, has decided to use an APT model to estimate the required return on the company's stock. The risk factors he plans to use are the risk premium on the stock market, the inflation rate, and the price of wheat. Because wheat is one of the biggest costs Ultra Bread faces, he feels this is a significant risk factor for Ultra Bread. How would you evaluate his choice of risk factors? Are there other risk factors you might suggest?

4. **Systematic and Usystematic Risk**   You own stock in the Lewis-Striden Drug Company. Suppose you had expected the following events to occur last month:

   a. The government would announce that real GNP had grown 1.2 percent during the previous quarter. The returns of Lewis-Striden are positively related to real GNP.

b. The government would announce that inflation over the previous quarter was 3.7 percent. The returns of Lewis-Striden are negatively related to inflation.

c. Interest rates would rise 2.5 percentage points. The returns of Lewis-Striden are negatively related to interest rates.

d. The president of the firm would announce his retirement. The retirement would be effective six months from the announcement day. The president is well liked: In general, he is considered an asset to the firm.

e. Research data would conclusively prove the efficacy of an experimental drug. Completion of the efficacy testing means the drug will be on the market soon.

Suppose the following events actually occurred:

a. The government announced that real GNP grew 2.3 percent during the previous quarter.

b. The government announced that inflation over the previous quarter was 3.7 percent.

c. Interest rates rose 2.1 percentage points.

d. The president of the firm died suddenly of a heart attack.

e. Research results in the efficacy testing were not as strong as expected. The drug must be tested for another six months, and the efficacy results must be resubmitted to the FDA.

f. Lab researchers had a breakthrough with another drug.

g. A competitor announced that it will begin distribution and sale of a medicine that will compete directly with one of Lewis-Striden's top-selling products.

Discuss how each of the actual occurrences affects the return on your Lewis-Striden stock. Which events represent systematic risk? Which events represent unsystematic risk?

5.   Market Model versus APT   What are the differences between a *k*-factor model and the market model?

6.   APT   In contrast to the CAPM, the APT does not indicate which factors are expected to determine the risk premium of an asset. How can we determine which factors should be included? For example, one risk factor suggested is the company size. Why might this be an important risk factor in an APT model?

7.   CAPM versus APT   What is the relationship between the one-factor model and the CAPM?

8.   Factor Models   How can the return on a portfolio be expressed in terms of a factor model?

9.   Data Mining   What is data mining? Why might it overstate the relation between some stock attribute and returns?

10.   Factor Selection   What is wrong with measuring the performance of a U.S. growth stock manager against a benchmark composed of British stocks?

Questions and Problems

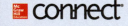

BASIC
(Questions 1–4)

1.   Factor Models   A researcher has determined that a two-factor model is appropriate to determine the return on a stock. The factors are the percentage change in GNP and an interest rate. GNP is expected to grow by 3.6 percent, and the interest rate is expected to be 3.1 percent. A stock has a beta of 1.4 on the percentage change in GNP and a beta of −.53 on the interest rate. If the expected rate of return on the stock is 11.5 percent, what is the revised expected return on the stock if GNP actually grows by 3.2 percent and the interest rate is 3.4 percent?

2. **Factor Models**   Suppose a three-factor model is appropriate to describe the returns of a stock. Information about those three factors is presented in the following chart:

Factor	β	Expected Value	Actual Value
GDP	.0000734	$17,034	$17,863
Inflation	−.90	2.80%	2.6%
Interest rates	−.32	3.70%	3.5%

a. What is the systematic risk of the stock return?
b. Suppose unexpected bad news about the firm was announced that causes the stock price to drop by 1.1 percent. If the expected return on the stock is 11.7 percent, what is the total return on this stock?

3. **Factor Models**   Suppose a factor model is appropriate to describe the returns on a stock. The current expected return on the stock is 10.5 percent. Information about those factors is presented in the following chart:

Factor	β	Expected Value	Actual Value
Growth in GNP	1.67	2.1%	2.6%
Inflation	−1.09	4.3	4.8

a. What is the systematic risk of the stock return?
b. The firm announced that its market share had unexpectedly increased from 11 percent to 15 percent. Investors know from past experience that the stock return will increase by .58 percent for every 1 percent increase in its market share. What is the unsystematic risk of the stock?
c. What is the total return on this stock?

4. **Multifactor Models**   Suppose stock returns can be explained by the following three-factor model:

$$R_i = R_F + \beta_1 F_1 + \beta_2 F_2 - \beta_3 F_3$$

Assume there is no firm-specific risk. The information for each stock is presented here:

	β_1	β_2	β_3
Stock A	1.55	.80	.05
Stock B	.81	1.25	−.20
Stock C	.73	−.14	1.24

The risk premiums for the factors are 4.9 percent, 3.8 percent, and 5.3 percent, respectively. If you create a portfolio with 20 percent invested in Stock A, 20 percent invested in Stock B, and the remainder in Stock C, what is the expression for the return on your portfolio? If the risk-free rate is 3.2 percent, what is the expected return on your portfolio?

INTERMEDIATE
(Questions 5–7)

5. **Multifactor Models** Suppose stock returns can be explained by a two-factor model. The firm-specific risks for all stocks are independent. The following table shows the information for two diversified portfolios:

	β_1	β_2	E(R)
Portfolio A	.85	1.15	16%
Portfolio B	1.45	−.25	12

If the risk-free rate is 4 percent, what are the risk premiums for each factor in this model?

6. **Market Model** The following three stocks are available in the market:

	E(R)	β
Stock A	10.5%	1.20
Stock B	13.0	.98
Stock C	15.7	1.37
Market	14.2	1.00

Assume the market model is valid.

a. Write the market model equation for each stock.
b. What is the return on a portfolio with weights of 30 percent Stock A, 45 percent Stock B, and 25 percent Stock C?
c. Suppose the return on the market is 15 percent and there are no unsystematic surprises in the returns. What is the return on each stock? What is the return on the portfolio?

7. **Portfolio Risk** You are forming an equally weighted portfolio of stocks. Many stocks have the same beta of .84 for Factor 1 and the same beta of 1.69 for Factor 2. All stocks also have the same expected return of 11 percent. Assume a two-factor model describes the return on each of these stocks.

a. Write the equation of the returns on your portfolio if you place only five stocks in it.
b. Write the equation of the returns on your portfolio if you place in it a very large number of stocks that all have the same expected returns and the same betas.

CHALLENGE
(Questions 8–10)

8. **APT** There are two stock markets, each driven by the same common force, F, with an expected value of zero and standard deviation of 10 percent. There are many securities in each market; thus, you can invest in as many stocks as you wish. Due to restrictions, however, you can invest in only one of the two markets. The expected return on every security in both markets is 10 percent.

The returns for each security, i, in the first market are generated by the relationship:

$$R_{1i} = .10 + 1.5F + \epsilon_{1i}$$

where ϵ_{1i} is the term that measures the surprises in the returns of Stock i in Market 1. These surprises are normally distributed; their mean is zero. The returns on Security j in the second market are generated by the relationship:

$$R_{2j} = .10 + .5F + \epsilon_{2j}$$

where ϵ_{2j} is the term that measures the surprises in the returns of Stock j in Market 2. These surprises are normally distributed; their mean is zero. The standard deviation of ϵ_{1i} and ϵ_{2j} for any two stocks, i and j, is 20 percent.

a. If the correlation between the surprises in the returns of any two stocks in the first market is zero, and if the correlation between the surprises in the returns of any two stocks in the second market is zero, in which market would a risk-averse person prefer to invest? (Note: The correlation between ϵ_{1i} and ϵ_{1j} for any i and j is zero, and the correlation between ϵ_{2j} and ϵ_{2j} for any i and j is zero.)

b. If the correlation between ϵ_{1i} and ϵ_{1j} in the first market is .9 and the correlation between ϵ_{2i} and ϵ_{2j} in the second market is zero, in which market would a risk-averse person prefer to invest?

c. If the correlation between ϵ_{1i} and ϵ_{1j} in the first market is zero and the correlation between ϵ_{2i} and ϵ_{2j} in the second market is .5, in which market would a risk-averse person prefer to invest?

d. In general, what is the relationship between the correlations of the disturbances in the two markets that would make a risk-averse person equally willing to invest in either of the two markets?

9. **APT** Assume that the following market model adequately describes the return-generating behavior of risky assets:

$$R_{it} = \alpha_i + \beta_i R_{Mt} + \epsilon_{it}$$

Here:

R_{it} = The return on the ith asset at Time t.

R_{Mt} = The return on a portfolio containing all risky assets in some proportion at Time t.

R_{Mt} and ϵ_{it} are statistically independent.

Short selling (i.e., negative positions) is allowed in the market. You are given the following information:

Asset	β_i	$E(R_i)$	$Var(\epsilon_i)$
A	.7	8.41%	.0100
B	1.2	12.06	.0144
C	1.5	13.95	.0225

The variance of the market is .0121, and there are no transaction costs.

a. Calculate the standard deviation of returns for each asset.

b. Calculate the variance of return of three portfolios containing an infinite number of asset types A, B, or C, respectively.

c. Assume the risk-free rate is 3.3 percent and the expected return on the market is 10.6 percent. Which asset will not be held by rational investors?

d. What equilibrium state will emerge such that no arbitrage opportunities exist? Why?

10. **APT** Assume that the returns on individual securities are generated by the following two-factor model:

$$R_{it} = E(R_{it}) + \beta_{ij}F_{1t} + \beta_{i2}F_{2t}$$

Here:

R_{it} is the return on Security i at Time t.

F_{1t} and F_{2t} are market factors with zero expectation and zero covariance.

In addition, assume that there is a capital market for four securities, and the capital market for these four assets is perfect in the sense that there are no transaction costs and short sales (i.e., negative positions) are permitted. The characteristics of the four securities follow:

Security	β_1	β_2	E(R)
1	1.0	1.5	20%
2	.5	2.0	20
3	1.0	.5	10
4	1.5	.75	10

a. Construct a portfolio containing (long or short) Securities 1 and 2, with a return that does not depend on the market factor, F_{1t}, in any way. (*Hint:* Such a portfolio will have $\beta_1 = 0$.) Compute the expected return and β_2 coefficient for this portfolio.

b. Following the procedure in (a), construct a portfolio containing Securities 3 and 4 with a return that does not depend on the market factor, F_{1t}. Compute the expected return and β_2 coefficient for this portfolio.

c. There is a risk-free asset with an expected return equal to 5 percent, $\beta_1 = 0$, and $\beta_2 = 0$. Describe a possible arbitrage opportunity in such detail that an investor could implement it.

d. What effect would the existence of these kinds of arbitrage opportunities have on the capital markets for these securities in the short run and long run? Graph your analysis.

Excel Master It! Problem

The Fama–French three-factor model has become a popular APT model. However, another model called the Carhart four-factor model has also been proposed (Mark Carhart, 1997, "On Persistence in Mutual Fund Performance," *Journal of Finance* 52, 57–82). In the four-factor model, the first three factors are the same as in the Fama–French three-factor model. The fourth factor is momentum. The momentum factor is constructed by the monthly return difference between the returns on the high and low prior return portfolios.

The factors for the four-factor model are available on Kenneth French's website (http://mba.tuck.dartmouth.edu/pages/faculty/ken.french/index.html). Note that there is a file for the three-factor model as well as a separate file for the momentum factor.

1. The data files are zipped. You will need to open the Zip file, save the text file, and then open the text file in Excel. Make sure you download the monthly factors. The Text Import Wizard in Excel will walk you through the steps necessary to import the text files into columns. When you get the data table set up, estimate the four-factor model and answer the following questions for the stock and mutual fund you selected in the previous chapter.

   a. Would you expect the explanatory power of the four-factor regression to be higher or lower than the market model regression from the previous chapter? Why?

   b. Are the alpha and betas for each regression statistically different from zero?

   c. How do you interpret the betas for each independent variable for the stock and the mutual fund?

   d. Which of the two regression estimates has the highest R squared? Is this what you would have expected? Why?

Mini Case

THE FAMA–FRENCH MULTIFACTOR MODEL AND MUTUAL FUND RETURNS

Dawn Browne, an investment broker, has been approached by client Jack Thomas about the risk of his investments. Dawn has recently read several articles concerning the risk factors that can potentially affect asset returns, and she has decided to examine Jack's mutual fund holdings. Jack is currently invested in the Fidelity Magellan Fund (FMAGX), the Fidelity Low-Priced Stock Fund (FLPSX), and the Baron Small Cap Fund (BSCFX).

Dawn would like to apply the well-known multifactor model proposed by Eugene Fama and Ken French to determine the risk of each mutual fund. Here is the regression equation for the multifactor model she proposes to use:

$$R_{it} - R_{Ft} = \alpha_i + \beta_1(R_{Mt} - R_{Ft}) + \beta_2(SMB_t) + \beta_3(HML_t) + \epsilon_t$$

In the regression equation, R_{it} is the return on Asset i at Time t, R_{Ft} is the risk-free rate at Time t, and R_{Mt} is the return on the market at Time t. Thus, the first risk factor in the Fama–French regression is the market factor often used with the CAPM.

The second risk factor, SMB, or "small minus big," is calculated by taking the difference in the returns on a portfolio of small-cap stocks and a portfolio of big-cap stocks. This factor is intended to pick up the so-called small firm effect. Similarly, the third factor, HML, or "high minus low," is calculated by taking the difference in the returns between a portfolio of "value" stocks and a portfolio of "growth" stocks. Stocks with low market-to-book ratios are classified as value stocks and vice versa for growth stocks. This factor is included because of the historical tendency for value stocks to earn a higher return.

In models such as the one Dawn is considering, the alpha (α) term is of particular interest. It is the regression intercept; but more important, it is also the excess return the asset earned. In other words, if the alpha is positive, the asset earned a return greater than it should have given its level of risk; if the alpha is negative, the asset earned a return lower than it should have given its level of risk. This measure is called "Jensen's alpha," and it is a widely used tool for mutual fund evaluation.

1. For a large-company stock mutual fund, would you expect the betas to be positive or negative for each of the factors in a Fama–French multifactor model?

2. The Fama–French factors and risk-free rates are available at Ken French's website: www.dartmouth.edu/~kfrench. Download the monthly factors and save the most recent 60 months for each factor. The historical prices for each of the mutual funds can be found on various websites, including finance.yahoo.com. Find the prices of each mutual fund for the same time as the Fama–French factors and calculate the returns for each month. Be sure to include dividends. For each mutual fund, estimate the multifactor regression equation using the Fama–French factors. How well do the regression estimates explain the variation in the return of each mutual fund?

3. What do you observe about the beta coefficients for the different mutual funds? Comment on any similarities or differences.

4. If the market is efficient, what value would you expect for alpha? Do your estimates support market efficiency?

5. Which fund has performed best considering its risk? Why?

13

Risk, Cost of Capital, and Valuation

With more than 112,000 employees on five continents, Germany-based BASF is a major international company. It operates in a variety of industries, including agriculture, oil and gas, chemicals, and plastics. In an attempt to increase value, BASF launched Vision 2020, a comprehensive plan that included all functions within the company and challenged and encouraged all employees to act in an entrepreneurial manner. The major financial component of the strategy was that the company expected to earn its weighted average cost of capital, or WACC, plus a premium. So, what exactly is the WACC?

The WACC is the minimum return a company needs to earn to satisfy all of its investors, including stockholders, bondholders, and preferred stockholders. In 2010, for example, BASF pegged its cost of capital at 9 percent and earned a company record premium of €3.9 billion above its cost of capital. From 2011 to 2014, the company pegged its WACC at 11 percent. In this chapter, we learn how to compute a firm's cost of capital and find out what it means to the firm and its investors. We will also learn when to use the firm's cost of capital, and, perhaps more important, when not to use it.

The goal of this chapter is to determine the rate at which cash flows of risky projects and firms are to be discounted. Projects and firms are financed with equity, debt, and other sources of capital, and we must estimate the cost of each of these sources in order to determine the appropriate discount rate. We begin with the cost of equity capital. Since the analysis here builds on beta and the capital asset pricing model (CAPM), we discuss beta in depth, including its calculation, its intuition, and its determinants. We next discuss the cost of debt and the cost of preferred stock. These costs serve as building blocks for the weighted average cost of capital (R_{WACC} or, more simply, WACC), which is used to discount cash flows. We calculate the WACC for a real-world company, Eastman Chemical Co. We show how both firms and projects can be valued using WACC. Finally, we introduce flotation costs.

13.1 The Cost of Capital

Whenever a firm has extra cash, it can take one of two actions. It can pay out the cash directly to its investors. Alternatively, the firm can invest the extra cash in a project, paying out the future cash flows of the project. Which action would the investors prefer? If investors can reinvest the cash in a financial asset (a stock or bond) with the same risk as that

Figure 13.1
Choices of a Firm
with Extra Cash

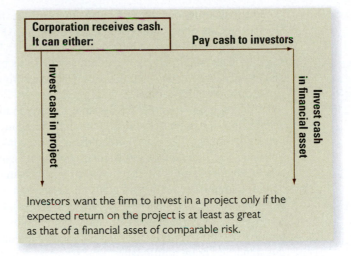

There are various synonyms for the discount rate. For example, the discount rate
is often called the *required return* on the project. This is an appropriate name, since the
project should be accepted only if the project generates a return above what is required.
Alternatively, the discount rate of the project is said to be its *cost of capital*. This name
is also appropriate, since the project must earn enough to pay its suppliers of capital. Our
book will use these three terms, the discount rate, the required return, and the cost of
capital, synonymously.

of the project, the investors would desire the alternative with the higher expected return.
In other words, the project should be undertaken only if its expected return is greater than
that of a financial asset of comparable risk. This idea is illustrated in Figure 13.1. Our
discussion implies a very simple capital budgeting rule:

**The discount rate of a project should be the expected return on a financial asset of
comparable risk.**

   There are various synonyms for the discount rate. For example, the discount rate
is often called the *required return* on the project. This is an appropriate name, since the
project should be accepted only if the project generates a return above what is required.
Alternatively, the discount rate of the project is said to be its *cost of capital*. This name
is also appropriate, since the project must earn enough to pay its suppliers of capital. Our
book will use these three terms, the discount rate, the required return, and the cost of
capital, synonymously.

   Now imagine that all projects of the firm have the same risk. In that case, one could
say that the discount rate is equal to the cost of capital for the firm as a whole. And, if the
firm is all equity, the discount rate is also equal to the firm's cost of equity capital.

13.2 Estimating the Cost of Equity Capital with the CAPM

We start with the cost of equity capital, which is the required return on a stockholders'
investment in the firm. The problem is that stockholders do not tell the firm what their
required returns are. So, what do we do? Luckily, the capital asset pricing model (CAPM)
can be used to estimate the required return.

   Under the CAPM, the expected return on stock can be written as:

$$R_S = R_F + \beta \times (R_M - R_F) \tag{13.1}$$

where R_F is the risk-free rate and $R_M - R_F$ is the difference between the expected return
on the market portfolio and the riskless rate. This difference is often called the expected
excess market return or market risk premium. Note we have dropped the bar denoting

expectations from our expression to simplify the notation, but remember that we are always thinking about *expected* returns with the CAPM.

The expected return on the stock in Equation 13.1 is based on the stock's risk, as measured by beta. Alternatively, we could say that this expected return is the required return on the stock, based on the stock's risk. Similarly, this expected return can be viewed as the firm's cost of equity capital.

It is important to stress the symmetry between the expected return to the shareholder and the cost of capital to the firm. Imagine a company issuing new equity to fund a capital budgeting project. The new shareholder's return comes in the form of dividends and capital gains. These dividends and capital gains represent costs to the firm. It is easier to see this for dividends. Any dividend paid to a new shareholder is cash that cannot be paid to an old shareholder. But capital gains also represent a cost to the firm. Appreciation in the value of a firm's stock is shared by all stockholders. If part of the capital gain goes to new stockholders, only the remainder can be captured by the old stockholders. In other words, the new shareholders dilute the capital gain of the old shareholders. More will be said on this important point a little later.

While academics have long argued for the use of the CAPM in capital budgeting, how prevalent is this approach in practice? One study[1] finds that almost three-fourths of U.S. companies use the CAPM in capital budgeting, indicating that industry has largely adopted this approach. This fraction is likely to increase, since so many of the undergraduates and MBAs who were taught the CAPM in school are now reaching positions of power in corporations.

We now have the tools to estimate a firm's cost of equity capital. To do this, we need to know three things:

- The risk-free rate, R_F.
- The market risk premium, $R_M - R_F$.
- The stock beta, β.

EXAMPLE

Cost of Equity   Suppose the stock of the Quatram Company, a publisher of college textbooks, has a beta (β) of 1.3. The firm is 100 percent equity financed; that is, it has no debt. Quatram is considering a number of capital budgeting projects that will double its size. Because these new projects are similar to the firm's existing ones, the average beta on the new projects is assumed to be equal to Quatram's existing beta. The risk-free rate is 5 percent. What is the appropriate discount rate for these new projects, assuming a market risk premium of 8.4 percent?

We estimate the cost of equity, R_S, for Quatram as:

$$
\begin{aligned}
R_S &= 5\% + (8.4\% \times 1.3) \\
&= 5\% + 10.92\% \\
&= 15.92\%
\end{aligned}
$$

Two key assumptions were made in this example: (1) The beta risk of the new projects is the same as the risk of the firm, and (2) the firm is all equity financed. Given these assumptions, it follows that the cash flows of the new projects should be discounted at the 15.92 percent rate.

---

[1] John R. Graham and Campbell R. Harvey, "The Theory and Practice of Corporate Finance: Evidence from the Field," *Journal of Financial Economics* (2001), report in their Table 3 that 73.49 percent of the companies in their sample use the CAPM for capital budgeting.

**EXAMPLE
13.2**

Project Evaluation and Beta   Suppose Alpha Air Freight is an all-equity firm with a beta of 1.21. Further suppose the market risk premium is 9.5 percent, and the risk-free rate is 5 percent. We can determine the expected return on the common stock of Alpha Air Freight from Equation 13.1. We find that the expected return is:

$$5\% + (1.21 \times 9.5\%) = 16.495\%$$

Because this is the return that shareholders can expect in the financial markets on a stock with a β of 1.21, it is the return they expect on Alpha Air Freight's stock.

Further suppose Alpha is evaluating the following non–mutually exclusive projects:

Project	Project's Beta (β)	Project's Expected Cash Flows Next Year	Project's Internal Rate of Return	Project's NPV When Cash Flows Are Discounted at 16.495%	Accept or Reject
A	1.21	$140	40%	$20.2	Accept
B	1.21	120	20	3.0	Accept
C	1.21	110	10	−5.6	Reject

Each project initially costs $100. All projects are assumed to have the same risk as the firm as a whole. Because the cost of equity capital is 16.495 percent, projects in an all-equity firm are discounted at this rate. Projects A and B have positive NPVs, and C has a negative NPV. Thus, only A and B will be accepted. This result is illustrated in Figure 13.2.

Figure 13.2   Using the Security Market Line to Estimate the Risk-Adjusted Discount Rate for Risky Projects

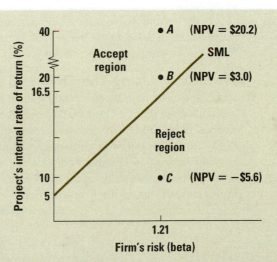

The diagonal line, called the security market line, is a graphical depiction of the CAPM and represents the relationship between the cost of equity capital and the firm's beta. An all-equity firm should accept a project whose internal rate of return is greater than the cost of equity capital, and should reject a project whose internal rate of return is less than the cost of equity capital. (This graph assumes that all projects are as risky as the firm.)

In the above two examples, the values for the risk-free rate, the market risk premium, and the firm's beta were *assumed*. How would we go about estimating these parameters in practice? We will investigate each of these parameters in turn.

THE RISK-FREE RATE

While no bond is completely free of the risk of default, Treasury bills and bonds in the United States are about as close to this ideal as possible. No U.S. Treasury instrument has ever defaulted and, at least at the present time, no instrument is considered to be in the slightest danger of a future default. For this reason, Treasury instruments are generally considered to be risk-free.

However, as we learned from Chapter 8, there is a whole term structure of interest rates, where the yield on any Treasury instrument is a function of that instrument's maturity. Which maturity should have its yield serve as the risk-free rate? The CAPM is a period-by-period model, so a short-term rate would be a good place to start. The one-year Treasury bill rate is used frequently.[2] In a multi-period application, the expected average one-year Treasury could be used.

Another sensible approach is to select a U.S. Treasury security whose "maturity" matches the maturity of a particular project. The match would need to be exact because while U.S. Treasury securities are probably close to default-free, they have interest rate risk. An acceptable rule of thumb for projects with longer term multiple cash flows is to use the yield on a U.S. Treasury security with the average maturity of the cash flows. If you are doing international (non U.S.) valuations, it is common practice to use a government (sovereign) bond in the "local" currency for a risk-free rate. Of course, some foreign government bonds are not actually risk-free.

MARKET RISK PREMIUM

Method 1: Using Historical Data
As mentioned in Chapter 10, the market risk premium is the difference between the expected return on the market portfolio and the risk-free rate. We can use the historical approach of Chapter 10 and settle on an estimate of 7 percent for the market risk premium, though this number should not be interpreted as definitive.

In the current discussion, it is important to remember to use the appropriate risk-free rate measure in defining the market risk premium. In other words, for consistency the risk-free measure should be the same for the risk-free rate and for the market risk premium.

Method 2: Using the Dividend Discount Model (DDM)
Earlier in this chapter, we referenced a study indicating that most corporations use the CAPM for capital budgeting. Does the CAPM imply that risk premiums must be calculated from past returns, as we did above? The answer is no. There is another method, based on the dividend discount model of an earlier chapter, for estimating the risk premium.

In Chapter 9, we pointed out that the price of a share of stock can be thought of as equal to the present value of all of its expected future dividends. Furthermore, we noted in that chapter that, if the firm's dividends are expected to grow at a constant rate, g, the price of a share of stock, P, can be written as:

$$P = \frac{\text{Div}}{R_S - g}$$

---

[2]How can we estimate this expected one-year rate? The anticipated average one-year rate can be estimated from the term structure. Over the period from 1926 to 2014, the average return on 20-year Treasury bonds was 6.1 percent, and the average return on one-year Treasury bills was 3.5 percent. Thus, the term premium, as it is called, was $6.1 - 3.5 = 2.6\%$. This positive term premium is not surprising, since we know that the term structure of interest rates typically slopes upward, reflecting interest rate risk. Suppose the yield on a 20-year Treasury bond is about 3.5 percent. This yield should reflect both the average one-year interest rate over the next 20 years and the term premium. Thus, one can argue that the average one-year interest rate expected over the next 20 years is $3.5 - 2.6 = .9$ percent.

where Div is the dividend per share expected next year, R_s is the discount rate or cost of equity, and g is the constant annual rate of expected growth in dividends. This equation can be rearranged, yielding:

$$R_S = \frac{\text{Div}}{P} + g$$

In words, the annual expected return on a stock is the sum of the dividend yield ($=\text{Div}/P$) over the next year plus the annual expected growth rate in dividends.

Just as this formula can be used to estimate the total expected return on a stock, it can be used to estimate the total expected return on the market as a whole. The first term on the right-hand side is easy to estimate, since a number of print and Internet services calculate the dividend yield for the market. For example, *The Wall Street Journal* recently stated that the average dividend yield across all stocks in the Standard and Poor's (S&P) 500 Index was about 2.1 percent. We will use this number in our estimates.

Next, we need an estimate of the per-share growth rate in dividends across all companies in the market. Security analysts, who are typically employees of investment banking houses, money management firms, and independent research organizations, study individual securities, industries, and the overall stock market. As part of their work, they forecast dividends and earnings, as well as make stock recommendations. For example, suppose the numbers in the *Value Line (VL) Investment Survey* imply a five-year growth rate in dividends for VL's Industrial Composite Index of about 6 percent per year. With a dividend yield of 2.1 percent, the expected return on the market becomes $2.1\% + 6\% = 8.1\%$. Given a one-year yield on Treasury bills of 1.0 percent, the market risk premium would be $8.1\% - 1.0\% = 7.1\%$, almost identical to the 7 percent provided by method 1.

For our firm with a beta of 1.5, the cost of capital becomes:

$$1.0\% + (1.5 \times 7.1\%) = 11.65\%$$

Of course, Value Line is just one source for forecasts. More likely, a firm would either rely on a consensus of many forecasts or use its own subjective growth estimate.

Academics have, nevertheless, long preferred the historical estimated market risk premium for its statistical objectivity. By contrast, estimation of future dividend growth in the DDM seems more error-prone. However, proponents of using the DDM point out that returns in the long run can only come from the current dividend yield and future dividend growth. Anyone who thinks that long-run stock returns will exceed the sum of these two components is fooling himself.[3] The expression, "You can't squeeze blood out of a turnip," applies here.

13.3 Estimation of Beta

In the previous section, we assumed that the beta of the company was known. Of course, beta must be estimated in the real world. We pointed out earlier that the beta of a security is the standardized covariance of a security's return with the return on the market portfolio. As we have seen, the formula for security i is:

$$\text{Beta of security } i = \frac{\text{Cov}(R_i, R_M)}{\text{Var}(R_M)} = \frac{\sigma_{i,M}}{\sigma^2_M} \qquad \textbf{(13.2)}$$

---

[3]For example, see Jay Ritter, "The Biggest Mistakes We Teach," *Journal of Financial Research* (Summer 2002); Eugene Fama and Kenneth French, "The Equity Premium," *Journal of Finance* (2002); and Ravi Jagannathan, E. R. McGrattan, and A. Scherbina, "The Declining U.S. Equity Premium," *Federal Reserve Bank of Minneapolis Quarterly Review* (2000).

Measuring Company Betas

The basic method of measuring company betas is to estimate:

$$\frac{\text{Cov}(R_i, R_M)}{\text{Var}(R_M)}$$

using $t = 1, 2, \ldots, T$ observations.

Problems

1. Betas may vary over time.
2. The sample size may be inadequate.
3. Betas are influenced by changing financial leverage and business risk.

Solutions

1. Problems 1 and 2 can be moderated by more sophisticated statistical techniques.
2. Problem 3 can be lessened by adjusting for changes in business and financial risk.
3. Look at average beta estimates of several comparable firms in the industry.

In words, the beta is the covariance of a security with the market, divided by the variance of the market. Because we calculated both covariance and variance in earlier chapters, calculating beta involves no new material.

REAL-WORLD BETAS

It is instructive to see how betas are determined for actual real-world companies. Figure 13.3 plots monthly returns for four large firms against monthly returns on the S&P 500 Index. Using a standard regression technique, we fit a straight line through the data points. The result is called the "characteristic" line for the security. The slope of the characteristic line is beta. Though we have not shown it in the table, we can also determine the intercept (commonly called alpha) of the characteristic line by regression.

We use five years of monthly data for each plot. Although this choice is arbitrary, it is in line with calculations performed in the real world. Practitioners know that the accuracy of the beta coefficient is suspect when too few observations are used. Conversely, because firms may change their industry over time, observations from the distant past are out of date.

We stated in a previous chapter that the average beta across all stocks in an index is 1. Of course, this need not be true for a subset of the index. For example, of the four securities in our figure, two have betas above 1 and two have betas below 1. Because beta is a measure of the risk of a single security for someone holding a large, diversified portfolio, our results indicate that Procter & Gamble has relatively low risk and Prudential has relatively high risk.

STABILITY OF BETA

We have stated that the beta of a firm is likely to change if the firm changes its industry. It is also interesting to ask the reverse question: Does the beta of a firm stay the same if its industry stays the same?

Figure 13.3

Plots of Five Years of Monthly Returns (2010–2014) on Four Individual Securities against Five Years of Monthly Returns on the Standard & Poor's (S&P) 500 Index

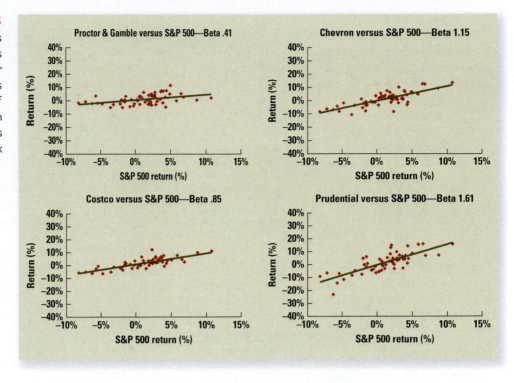

Take the case of Microsoft, which has remained in the same industry for many decades. Figure 13.4 plots the returns on Microsoft and the returns on the S&P 500 for four five-year periods. As can be seen from the figure, Microsoft's beta varies from period to period. However, this movement in beta is probably nothing more than random variation. Thus, for practical purposes, Microsoft's beta has been approximately constant over the two decades covered in the figure. Although Microsoft is just one company, most analysts argue that betas are generally stable for firms remaining in the same industry.

However, this is not to say that, as long as a firm stays in the same industry, its beta will *never* change. Changes in product line, changes in technology, or changes in the market may affect a firm's beta. Furthermore, as we will show in a later section, an increase in the leverage of a firm (i.e., the amount of debt in its capital structure) will increase the firm's beta.

USING AN INDUSTRY BETA

Our approach to estimating the beta of a company from its own past data may seem commonsensical to you. However, it is frequently argued that people can better estimate a firm's beta by involving the whole industry. Consider Table 13.1, which shows the betas of some prominent firms in the software industry. The average beta across all of the firms in the table is 1.08. Imagine a financial executive at Computer Sciences trying to estimate the firm's beta. Because beta estimation is subject to large, random variation in this volatile industry, the

Figure 13.4

Plots of Monthly
Returns on Microsoft
Corporation against
Returns on the
Standard & Poor's
500 Index for
Four Consecutive
Five-Year Periods

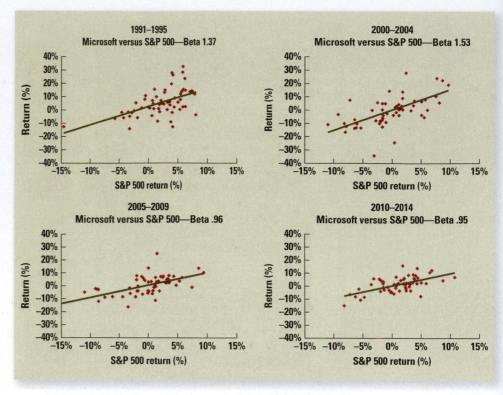

executive may be uncomfortable with the estimate of 1.30. However, the error in beta estimation on a single stock is much higher than the error for a portfolio of securities. Thus, the executive of Computer Sciences may prefer the average industry beta of 1.08 as the estimate of his or her own firm's beta.[4]

Assuming a risk-free rate of 1.0 percent and a risk premium of 7 percent, Computer Sciences might estimate its cost of equity capital as:

$$1.0\% + 1.30 \times 7\% = 10.1\%$$

However, if Computer Sciences believed the industry beta contained less estimation error, it could estimate its cost of equity capital as:

$$1.0\% + 1.08 \times 7\% = 8.56\%$$

The difference is substantial here, presenting a difficult choice for a financial executive at Computer Sciences.

While there is no formula for selecting the right beta, there is a very simple guideline. If you believe that the operations of a firm are similar to the operations of the rest of the

---

[4]Actually, one should adjust for leverage before averaging betas, though not much is gained unless leverage ratios differ significantly. Adjustment for leverage will be discussed in later chapters.

Table 13.1

Betas for Firms in the
Computer Software
Industry

Company	Beta
Microsoft	.98
Apple, Inc.	.94
Automatic Data Processing	.86
Oracle Corp.	1.41
Computer Sciences	1.30
CA, Inc.	1.34
Fiserv, Inc.	1.03
Accenture, Ltd.	1.18
Symantec Corp.	.91
Paychex, Inc.	.89
Equally weighted portfolio	1.08

SOURCE: www.reuters.com December 16, 2014.

industry, you should use the industry beta simply to reduce estimation error. However, if an executive believes that the operations of the firm are fundamentally different from those in the rest of the industry, the firm's beta should be used.

13.4 Determinants of Beta

The regression analysis approach in Section 13.3 doesn't tell us where beta comes from. Of course, the beta of a stock does not come out of thin air. Rather, it is determined by the characteristics of the firm. We consider three factors: The cyclical nature of revenues, operating leverage, and financial leverage.

CYCLICALITY OF REVENUES

The revenues of some firms are quite cyclical. That is, these firms do well in the expansion phase of the business cycle and do poorly in the contraction phase. Empirical evidence suggests high-tech firms, retailers, and automotive firms fluctuate with the business cycle. Firms in industries such as utilities, railroads, food, and airlines are less dependent on the cycle. Because beta measures the responsiveness of a stock's return to the market's return, it is not surprising that highly cyclical stocks have high betas.

It is worthwhile to point out that cyclicality is not the same as variability. For example, a moviemaking firm has highly variable revenues because hits and flops are not easily predicted. However, because the revenues of a studio are more dependent on the quality of its releases than the phase of the business cycle, motion picture companies are not particularly cyclical. In other words, stocks with high standard deviations need not have high betas, a point we have stressed before.

OPERATING LEVERAGE

We distinguished fixed costs from variable costs in Chapter 7. We mentioned that fixed costs do not change as quantity changes. Conversely, variable costs increase as the quantity of output rises. Firms often face a trade-off between fixed and variable costs. For example, a firm can build its own factory, incurring a high level of fixed costs in the process. Alternatively, the firm can outsource production to a supplier, typically generating lower fixed costs but higher variable costs. Fixed costs tend to magnify the impact of sales cyclicality. Fixed costs must be paid, even at a low level of sales, leaving the firm with the possibility of large losses. And with fixed costs replacing variable costs, any additional sales generate low marginal costs, leaving the firm with a substantial increase in profit.

Firms with high fixed costs and low variable costs are generally said to have high **operating leverage**. Conversely, firms with low fixed and high variable costs have low operating leverage. Operating leverage magnifies the effect of the cyclicality of a firm's revenues on beta. That is, a firm with a given sales cyclicality will increase its beta if fixed costs replace variable costs in its production process.

FINANCIAL LEVERAGE AND BETA

As suggested by their names, operating leverage and financial leverage are analogous concepts. Operating leverage refers to the firm's fixed costs of *production*. Financial leverage is the extent to which a firm relies on debt, and a levered firm is a firm with some debt in its capital structure. Because a *levered* firm must make interest payments regardless of the firm's sales, financial leverage refers to the firm's fixed costs of *finance*.

Just as an increase in operating leverage increases beta, an increase in financial leverage (i.e., an increase in debt) increases beta. To see this point, consider a firm with some debt and some equity in its capital structure. Further, imagine an individual who owns all the firm's debt and all its equity. In other words, this individual owns the entire firm. What is the beta of her portfolio of the firm's debt and equity?

As with any portfolio, the beta of this portfolio is a weighted average of the betas of the individual items in the portfolio. Let B stand for the market value of the firm's debt and S stand for the market value of the firm's equity. We have:

$$\beta_{Portfolio} = \beta_{Asset} = \frac{S}{B+S} \times \beta_{Equity} + \frac{B}{B+S} \times \beta_{Debt} \qquad (13.3)$$

where β_{Equity} is the beta of the stock of the *levered* firm. Notice that the beta of debt, β_{Debt}, is multiplied by $B/(B+S)$, the percentage of debt in the capital structure. Similarly, the beta of equity is multiplied by the percentage of equity in the capital structure. Because the portfolio contains both the debt of the firm and the equity of the firm, the beta of the portfolio can be thought of as the beta of the common stock had the firm been all equity. In practice, this beta is called the **asset beta** because its value is dependent only on the assets of the firm.

The beta of debt is very low in practice. If we make the common assumption that the beta of debt is zero (or very close to zero), we have:

$$\beta_{Asset} = \frac{S}{B+S} \times \beta_{Equity} \qquad (13.4)$$

Because $S/(B+S)$ must be below 1 for a levered firm, it follows that $\beta_{Asset} < \beta_{Equity}$. Rearranging this equation, we have:

$$\beta_{Equity} = \beta_{Asset}\left(1 + \frac{B}{S}\right)$$

The equity beta will always be greater than the asset beta with financial leverage (assuming the asset beta is positive).[5] In other words, the equity beta of a levered firm will always be greater than the equity beta of an otherwise identical all-equity firm.

Which beta does regression analysis estimate, the asset beta or the equity beta? Regression, as performed in Section 13.3 and also in the real world, provides us with an equity beta because the technique uses *stock* returns as inputs. We must transform this equity beta using Equation 13.4 to arrive at the asset beta. (Of course, the two betas are the same for an all-equity firm.)

EXAMPLE
13.3

Asset versus Equity Betas   Consider a tree growing company, Rapid Cedars, Inc., which is currently all equity and has a beta of .8. The firm has decided to move to a capital structure of one part debt to two parts equity. Because the firm is staying in the same industry, its asset beta should remain at .8. However, assuming a zero beta for its debt, its equity beta would become:

$$\beta_{Equity} = \beta_{Asset}\left(1 + \frac{B}{S}\right)$$
$$1.2 = .8\left(1 + \frac{1}{2}\right)$$

If the firm had one part debt to one part equity in its capital structure, its equity beta would be:

$$1.6 = .8(1 + 1)$$

However, as long as it stays in the same industry, its asset beta would remain at .8. The effect of leverage, then, is to increase the equity beta.

13.5 The Dividend Discount Model Approach

In Section 13.2, we showed how the CAPM could be used to determine a firm's cost of capital. Among other inputs, we needed an estimate of the market risk premium. One approach used the dividend discount model (DDM) to forecast the expected return on the market as a whole, leading to an estimate of this risk premium. We now use the DDM to estimate the expected return on an individual stock *directly*.

Our discussion in Section 13.2 on the DDM led to the following formula:

$$R_S = \frac{\text{Div}}{P} + g$$

where P is the price per share of a stock, Div is the dividend per share to be received next year, R_S is the discount rate, and g is the expected annual growth rate in dividends per share. The equation tells us that the discount rate on a stock is equal to the sum of the

---

[5]It can be shown that the relationship between a firm's asset beta and its equity beta with corporate taxes is:

$$\beta_{Equity} = \beta_{Asset}\left[1 + (1 - t_C)\frac{B}{S}\right]$$

In this expression, t_C is the corporate tax rate. Tax effects are considered in more detail in later chapters.

stock's dividend yield (=Div/P) and its expected growth rate of dividends. Thus, in order to apply the DDM to a particular stock, we must estimate both the dividend yield and the expected growth rate.

The dividend yield is relatively easy to forecast. Security analysts routinely provide forecasts of next year's dividend for many stocks. Alternatively, we can set next year's dividend as the product of last year's dividend and $1 + g$, using approaches to estimate g that we describe below. The price per share of any publicly traded stock can generally be determined from either financial newspapers or the Internet.

The expected growth rate of dividends can be estimated in one of three ways. First, we can calculate the firm's historical growth rate in dividends from past data. For some firms, this historical growth rate may be a serviceable, though clearly imperfect, estimate of the future growth rate. Second, in Chapter 9, we argued that the growth rate in dividends can be expressed as:

$$g = \text{Retention ratio} \times \text{ROE}$$

where the retention ratio is the ratio of retained earnings to earnings, and ROE stands for return on equity. Return on equity is the ratio of earnings to the accounting book value of the firm's equity. All the variables needed to estimate both the retention ratio and ROE can be found on a firm's income statement and balance sheet. Third, security analysts commonly provide forecasts of future growth. However, analysts' estimates are generally for five-year growth rates in earnings, while the DDM requires long-term growth rates in dividends.

As an example of the third approach, the consensus five-year forecast for annual earnings growth, as recently reported on finance.yahoo.com, was 7.5 percent for Eastman Chemical Co. Assuming a constant payout ratio, this is a 7.5 percent expected growth rate for dividends. The company's dividend yield was 1.04 percent, implying an expected rate of return, and therefore a cost of equity capital, of $1.04\% + 7.5 = 8.54\%$ for Eastman.

The above discussion shows how one can use the DDM to estimate a firm's cost of capital. How accurate is this approach compared to the CAPM? We examine this question in the section below.

COMPARISON OF DDM AND CAPM

Both the dividend discount model and the capital asset pricing model are internally consistent models. Nevertheless, academics have generally favored the CAPM over the DDM. In addition, a recent study[6] reported that slightly fewer than three-fourths of companies use the CAPM to estimate the cost of equity capital, while slightly fewer than one-sixth of companies use the dividend discount model to do so. Why has the pendulum swung over to the CAPM? The CAPM has two primary advantages. First, it explicitly adjusts for risk, and second, it is applicable to companies that pay no dividends or whose dividend growth is difficult to estimate. The primary advantage of the DDM is its simplicity. Unfortunately, the DDM is only applicable to firms that pay steady dividends; it is completely useless if companies do not. Another drawback of the DDM is that it does not explicitly consider risk.

While no one, to our knowledge, has done a systematic comparison of the two approaches, the DDM appears to contain more measurement error than does the

---

[6]John R. Graham and Campbell R. Harvey, "The Theory and Practice of Corporate Finance: Evidence from the Field," *Journal of Financial Economics* (2001), Table 3.

CAPM. The problem is that one is estimating the growth rate of an *individual company* in the DDM, and each of our suggested approaches to estimate *g* is fraught with measurement error for single firms. In contrast, consider the calculation of the beta for the CAPM; Though there is clearly measurement error here as well, it is probably less than for *g*.[7] While we have been critical of the DDM's practical application, DDM provides some important intuition, and can be a useful check on the CAPM estimates.

13.6 Cost of Capital for Divisions and Projects

Previous sections of this chapter all assumed that the risk of a potential project is equal to the risk of the existing firm. How should we estimate the discount rate for a project whose risk differs from that of the firm? The answer is that each project should be discounted at a rate commensurate with its own risk. For example, let's assume that we use the CAPM to determine the discount rate.[8] If a project's beta differs from that of the firm, the project's cash flows should be discounted at a rate commensurate with the project's own beta. This is an important point, since firms frequently speak of a *corporate discount rate*. (As mentioned earlier, *required return* and *cost of capital* are frequently used synonymously.) Unless all projects in the corporation are of the same risk, choosing the same discount rate for all projects is incorrect.

The above paragraph considered the discount rates of individual projects. The same message would apply for whole divisions. If a corporation has a number of divisions, each in a different industry, it would be a mistake to assign the same discount rate to each division.

EXAMPLE 13.4

Project Risk   D. D. Ronnelley Co., a publishing firm, may accept a project in computer software. Noting that computer software companies have high betas, the publishing firm views the software venture as more risky than the rest of its business. It should discount the project at a rate commensurate with the risk of software companies. For example, it might use the average beta of a portfolio of publicly traded software firms. Instead, if all projects in D. D. Ronnelley Co. were discounted at the same rate, a bias would result. The firm would accept too many high-risk projects (software ventures) and reject too many low-risk projects (books and magazines). This point is illustrated in Figure 13.5.

(continued)

---

[7]Of course, there is more to the story since we have to estimate three parameters for the CAPM (risk-free rate, market risk premium, and beta), each one of which contains error. Beta estimation is generally considered the greatest challenge here, because we need a beta for each company. However, as mentioned earlier in the chapter, analysts frequently calculate average betas across the different companies in an industry in order to reduce measurement error. The presumption is that the betas of different firms in an industry are similar. By contrast, we should not calculate average values of *g* across the different firms in an industry. Even though these firms are in the same industry, their growth rates can differ widely.

[8]For simplicity, we consider only the CAPM in this section. However, a similar approach would apply if the cost of capital were determined from the DDM.

Figure 13.5 Relationship between the Firm's Cost of Capital and the Security Market Line (SML)

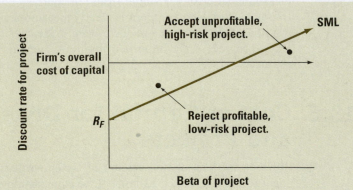

A single cost of capital for all projects in a firm, as indicated by the horizontal line in the figure, may lead to incorrect capital budgeting decisions. Projects with high risk, such as the software venture for D. D. Ronnelley Co., should be discounted at a high rate. By using the firm's cost of capital, the firm is likely to accept too many high-risk projects.

Projects with low risk should be discounted at a low rate. By using the firm's cost of capital, the firm is likely to reject too many low-risk projects.

The D. D. Ronnelley (DDR) example points out that we should discount a project at a rate commensurate with the risk of the project's cash flows. However, practitioners should be concerned with three issues here. First, they must choose the appropriate industry. While this may seem to be an easy task, the problem is that companies often have more than one line of business. For example, suppose that DDR was considering a project in the movie industry, not in computer software. Their first thought might be to look at the betas of the largest and most important companies in the film industry. The six biggest studios are Warner Brothers, Columbia, Fox, Universal, Paramount, and Disney. However, the first five studios are owned by Time-Warner, Sony, News Corporation, Comcast, and Viacom, respectively. These parent corporations are all diversified, with movies making up only a small portion of total revenues. And, while the parent of the sixth studio has the same Walt Disney name, it too is quite diversified, with holdings in television, radio, theme parks, and cruise ships. With all this diversification, it would likely be quite difficult to determine the beta of a pure moviemaking company from the betas of the six parents. Analysts often talk about identifying *pure plays* (i.e., other companies that specialize only in projects similar to the project your firm is considering). Pure plays are easier to find in some situations than in others.

Second, even if all companies in a particular industry are pure plays, the beta of a new project may be greater than the beta of existing firms, because a new project is likely to be particularly responsive to economy-wide movements. For example, a start-up computer venture may fail in a recession while IBM, Microsoft, or Oracle will still be around. Conversely, in an expansion, the venture may grow faster than the older computer firms.

Fortunately, a slight adjustment is all that is needed here. The new venture should be assigned a somewhat higher beta than that of the industry to reflect added risk. The adjustment is necessarily ad hoc, so no formula can be given. Our experience indicates that this approach is in widespread practice today.

Third, a problem arises for the rare project constituting its own industry. For example, consider the firms providing consumer shopping by television. Today, we can obtain a reasonable estimate for the beta of this industry because a few of the firms have publicly traded stock. However, when the ventures began in the 1980s, any beta estimate was suspect. At that time, no one knew whether shopping by TV belonged in the television industry, the retail industry, or in an entirely new industry.

What beta should be used when the project constitutes its own industry? Earlier in this chapter we mentioned three determinants of beta: Cyclicality of revenues, operating leverage, and financial leverage. Comparing the values of these three determinants for the project in question to the values for other firms should provide at least a general feel for the project's beta.

13.7 Cost of Fixed Income Securities

In this section, we examine the cost of both debt and preferred stock. We consider the cost of debt first.

COST OF DEBT

The cost of equity is often difficult to estimate. The task generally involves a fair amount of data gathering and the end result is often measured with error. In general, the cost of debt is easier to determine. For bonds with a small risk of defaulting, the current yield to maturity is a good estimate of investor expected returns and the cost of borrowing. The firm can generally obtain this information either by checking the yield on publicly traded bonds or by talking to commercial and investment bankers.

Imagine that two years ago, the Ritter Manufacturing Corp. (RMC) issued $100 million of debt with a 7 percent coupon. While the bonds were initially issued at par, rising interest rates over the last two years have caused them to sell at a discount. The yield on the bonds is currently 8 percent. In order to finance expansion, RMC is considering another large issue of bonds. What is the cost of the new debt?

The cost of the new debt should be around 8 percent. If the old bonds are selling at 8 percent, the new debt will not sell at a lower yield. The 7 percent is merely a historical number, often called the *embedded cost* of the debt, with no relevance today.

Alternatively, perhaps a firm is issuing debt for the first time. Here, the firm's investment banker can generally indicate to the firm's managers what the yield on the prospective bonds will be. That yield is the cost of debt. Or, perhaps the company will take out a loan with a commercial bank. Again, the borrowing rate on the prospective loan is the cost of debt.

There is only one complication that needs to be discussed. We have ignored taxes so far, obviously an assumption at odds with reality. Under U.S. tax law, interest payments are *tax deductible*. Consider the following example where two firms, Unlevered Corp. and

Levered Corp., differ only in debt. Unlevered Corp. has no debt and Levered Corp. has $100 of debt, with an interest rate of 10 percent.

Unlevered Corp.		Levered Corp.	
Revenue	$180	Revenue	$180
Expenses	−70	Expenses	−70
Pretax earnings	110	Earnings before interest and taxes	110
Taxes (40% rate)	−44	Interest (10% on $100 borrowed)	−10
Aftertax earnings	$ 66	Pretax earnings	100
		Taxes (40% rate)	−40
		Aftertax earnings	$ 60

While the Levered Corp. must pay $10 of interest per year, its aftertax earnings are only $6 (=66 − 60) less than those of the Unlevered Corp. Why? Because the interest payments are tax deductible. That is, while Levered Corp.'s pretax earnings are $10 (=110 − 100) less than those of Unlevered Corp., Levered Corp. pays $4 (=44 − 40) less in taxes than does Unlevered Corp.

The $6 reduction of aftertax earnings is 6 percent of the $100 that Levered Corp. borrowed. Thus, the aftertax cost of debt is 6 percent. In general, the aftertax cost of debt can be written as:

$$\text{Aftertax cost of debt} = (1 - \text{Tax rate}) \times \text{Borrowing rate}$$
$$6\% = (1 - .40) \times 10\%$$

Why have we tax-adjusted the cost of debt while we did not tax-adjust the cost of equity? Because, while firms can deduct their interest payments before paying taxes, dividends are not tax deductible.

COST OF PREFERRED STOCK

The name preferred stock is an unfortunate one, because preferred stock is probably more similar to bonds than to common stock. Preferred stock pays a constant dividend in perpetuity. Interest payments on bonds are quite similar to dividends on preferred stock, though almost all bonds have a finite maturity. By contrast, dividends on common stock are not constant over time.

Suppose a share of the preferred stock of Polytech, Inc., is selling at $17.16 and pays a dividend of $1.50 per year. Since preferred stocks are perpetuities, they should be priced by the perpetuity formula, $PV = C/R_p$, where PV is the present value, or price, C is the cash to be received each year, and R_p is the yield, or rate of return. Rearranging, we have:

$$R_p = C/PV$$

For this preferred issue, the rate of return is 8.7% (=1.50/17.16). The cost of preferred stock is simply this rate of return.

Why don't we tax-adjust the cost of preferred stock the way we did the cost of debt? We don't tax-adjust here, because dividend payments on preferred stock are not tax deductible.

13.8 The Weighted Average Cost of Capital

Sections 13.1 and 13.2 showed how to estimate the discount rate when a project is all equity financed. In this section, we discuss an adjustment when the project is financed with both debt and equity.

Suppose a firm uses both debt and equity to finance its investments. If the firm pays R_B for its debt financing and R_S for its equity, what is the overall or average cost of its capital? The cost of equity is R_S, as discussed in earlier sections. The cost of debt is the firm's borrowing rate, R_B, which we can often observe by looking at the yield to maturity on the firm's debt. If a firm uses both debt and equity, the cost of capital is a weighted average of each. This works out to be:

$$\frac{S}{S + B} \times R_S + \frac{B}{S + B} \times R_B$$

The weights in the formula are, respectively, the proportion of total value represented by equity:

$$\left(\frac{S}{S + B}\right)$$

and the proportion of total value represented by debt:

$$\left(\frac{B}{S + B}\right)$$

This is only natural. If the firm had issued no debt and was therefore an all-equity firm, its average cost of capital would equal its cost of equity, R_S. At the other extreme, if the firm had issued so much debt that its equity was valueless, it would be an all-debt firm, and its average cost of capital would be its cost of debt, R_B.

Interest is tax deductible at the corporate level, as stated in the previous section. The aftertax cost of debt is:

$$\text{Cost of debt (after corporate tax)} = R_B \times (1 - t_C)$$

where t_C is the corporation's tax rate.

Assembling these results, we get the average cost of capital (after tax) for the firm:[9]

$$\text{Average cost of capital} = \left(\frac{S}{S + B}\right) \times R_S + \left(\frac{B}{S + B}\right) \times R_B \times (1 - t_C) \qquad \textbf{(13.5)}$$

Because the average cost of capital weighs the cost of equity and the cost of debt, it is usually referred to as the **weighted average cost of capital, R_{WACC}**, and from now on we will use this term.

**EXAMPLE
13.5**

WACC   Consider a firm whose debt has a market value of $40 million and whose stock has a market value of $60 million (3 million outstanding shares of stock, each selling for $20 per share). The firm pays a 5 percent rate of interest on its new debt and has a beta of 1.41. The corporate tax rate is 34 percent. (Assume that the security market line [SML] holds, that the risk premium on the

(continued)

---

[9]For simplicity, Equation 13.5 ignores preferred stock financing. With the addition of preferred stock, the formula becomes:

$$\text{Average cost of capital} = \frac{S}{S + B + P} \times R_S + \frac{B}{S + B + P} \times R_B \times (1 - t_C) + \frac{P}{S + B + P} \times R_P$$

where P is the amount of preferred stock in the firm's capital structure and R_P is the cost of preferred stock.

market is 9.5 percent [somewhat higher than the historical equity risk premium], and that the current Treasury bill rate is 1 percent.) What is this firm's R_{WACC}?

To compute the R_{WACC} using Equation 13.5, we must know (1) the aftertax cost of debt, $R_B \times (1 - t_c)$, (2) the cost of equity, R_S, and (3) the proportions of debt and equity used by the firm. These three values are determined next:

1. The pretax cost of debt is 5 percent, implying an aftertax cost of 3.3 percent [$=5\% \times (1 - .34)$].

2. We calculate the cost of equity capital by using the SML:

$$R_S = R_F + \beta \times [R_M - R_F]$$
$$= 1\% + 1.41 \times 9.5\%$$
$$= 14.40\%$$

3. We compute the proportions of debt and equity from the market values of debt and equity. Because the market value of the firm is $100 million (=$40 million + $60 million), the proportions of debt and equity are 40 and 60 percent, respectively.

The cost of equity, R_S, is 14.40 percent, and the aftertax cost of debt, $R_B \times (1 - t_c)$, is 3.3 percent. B is $40 million and S is $60 million. Therefore:

$$R_{WACC} = \frac{S}{B + S} \times R_S + \frac{B}{B + S} \times R_B \times (1 - t_c)$$

$$= \left(\frac{60}{100} \times 14.40\%\right) + \left(\frac{40}{100} \times 3.3\%\right) = 9.96\%$$

The above calculations are presented in table form below:

(1) Financing Components	(2) Market Values	(3) Weight	(4) Cost of Capital (after Corporate Tax)	(5) Weighted Cost of Capital
Debt	$ 40,000,000	.40	5% × (1 − .34) = 3.3%	1.32%
Equity	60,000,000	.60	1% + 1.41 × 9.5% = 14.40	8.64
	$100,000,000	1.00		9.96%

The weights used in the previous example are market value weights. Market value weights are more appropriate than book value weights because the market values of the securities are closer to the actual dollars that would be received from their sale. In fact, it is useful to think in terms of "target" market weights. These are the market weights expected to prevail over the life of the firm or project.

13.9 Valuation with R_{WACC}

Now we are in a position to use the weighted average cost of capital, R_{WACC}, to value both projects and entire firms. Our interpretation of R_{WACC} is that it is the overall expected return the firm must earn on its existing assets to maintain its value. The R_{WACC} reflects the risk and the capital structure of the firm's existing assets. As a result the R_{WACC} is an appropriate discount rate for the firm or for a project that is a replica of the firm.

PROJECT EVALUATION AND THE R_{WACC}

When valuing a project we start by determining the correct discount rate and use discounted cash flows to determine NPV.

Suppose a firm has both a current and a target debt–equity ratio of .6, a cost of debt of 5.15 percent, and a cost of equity of 10 percent. The corporate tax rate is 34 percent. What is the firm's weighted average cost of capital?

Our first step calls for transforming the debt–equity (B/S) ratio to a debt–value ratio. A B/S ratio of .6 implies 6 parts debt for 10 parts equity. Because value is equal to the sum of the debt plus the equity, the debt–value ratio is $6/(6 + 10) = .375$. Similarly, the equity–value ratio is $10/(6 + 10) = .625$. The R_{WACC} will then be:

$$R_{WACC} = \left(\frac{S}{S + B}\right) \times R_S + \left(\frac{B}{S + B}\right) \times R_B \times (1 - t_C)$$

$$= .625 \times 10\% + .375 \times 5.15\% \times .66 = 7.52\%$$

Suppose the firm is considering taking on a warehouse renovation costing $60 million that is expected to yield aftertax cost savings of $12 million a year for six years. Using the NPV equation and discounting the six years of expected cash flows from the renovation at the R_{WACC}, we have:

$$NPV = -\$60 + \frac{\$12}{(1 + R_{WACC})} + \cdots + \frac{\$12}{(1 + R_{WACC})^6}$$

$$= -\$60 + \$12 \times \frac{\left[1 - \left(\frac{1}{1.0752}\right)^6\right]}{.0752}$$

$$= -\$60 + (12 \times 4.6910)$$

$$= -\$3.71$$

Should the firm take on the warehouse renovation? The project has a negative NPV using the firm's R_{WACC}. This means that the financial markets offer superior investments in the same risk class (namely, the firm's risk class). The answer is clear: The firm should reject the project.

Of course, we are assuming that the project is in the same risk class as the firm and that the project is an integral part of the overall business.

FIRM VALUATION WITH THE R_{WACC}

When valuing a complete business enterprise our approach is the same as the one used for individual capital projects like the warehouse renovation, except that we use a horizon, and this complicates the calculations. Specifically, we use the firm's weighted average cost of capital as our discount rate, and we set up the usual discounted cash flow model by forecasting the firm's entire net cash flow (sometimes called distributable cash flow, free cash flow, or total cash flow of the firm) up to a horizon along with a terminal value of the firm:

$$PV_0 = \frac{CF_1}{1 + R_{WACC}} + \frac{CF_2}{(1 + R_{WACC})^2} + \frac{CF_3}{(1 + R_{WACC})^3} + \cdots + \frac{CF_T + TV_T}{(1 + R_{WACC})^T}$$

Consistent with the differential growth version of the dividend discount model, the terminal value (TV)[10] is estimated by assuming a constant perpetual growth rate for cash flows beyond the horizon, T, so that:

$$TV_T = \frac{CF_{T+1}}{R_{WACC} - g_{CF}} = \frac{CF_T(1 + g_{CF})}{R_{WACC} - g_{CF}}$$

---

[10]The terminal date is often referred to as the horizon. In general, we choose a horizon whenever we can assume cash flow grows at a constant rate perpetually thereafter. By using the word terminal, we do not rule out the firm continuing to exist. Instead, we are attempting to simplify the cash flow estimation process.

where CF is the net cash flows and is equal to earnings before interest and taxes (EBIT), minus taxes, minus capital spending, minus increases in net working capital plus depreciation.[11] g_{CF} is the growth rate of cash flow beyond T, and R_{WACC} is the weighted average cost of capital.

Consider the Good Food Corporation, a public company headquartered in Barstow, California, that is currently a leading global food service retailer. It operates about 10,000 restaurants in 100 countries. Good Food serves a value-based menu focused on hamburgers and french fries. The company has $4 billion in market valued debt and $2 billion in market valued common stock. Its tax rate is 20 percent. Good Food has estimated its cost of debt as 5 percent and its cost of equity as 10 percent. Its weighted average cost of capital is equal to:

Financial Component	Market Values	Weights	Cost of Capital	Weighted Average
Debt	$4 billion	2/3	5%(1−.2) = 4%	2/3 × 4%
Equity	$2 billion	1/3	10%	1/3 × 10%
	$6 billion			6% = the weighted average cost of capital

Good Food is seeking to grow by acquisition and the investment bankers of Good Food have identified a potential acquisition candidate, Happy Meals, Inc. Happy Meals is currently a private firm with no publicly tradable common stock but has the same product mix as Good Food and is a direct competitor to Good Food in many markets. It operates about 4,000 restaurants mostly in North America and Europe. Happy Meals has $1,318.8 million of debt outstanding with its market value the same as the book value.[12] It has 12.5 million shares outstanding. Since Happy Meals is a private firm, we have no stock market price to rely on for our valuation. Happy Meals expects its EBIT to grow 10 percent a year for the next five years. Increases in net working capital and capital spending are both expected to be 24 percent of EBIT. Depreciation will be 8 percent of EBIT. The perpetual growth rate in cash flow after five years is estimated to be 2 percent.

If Good Food acquires Happy Meals, Good Food analysts estimate the net cash flows from Happy Meals (in $ millions) would be (rounding to one decimal):

Year	1	2	3	4	5
Earnings before interest and taxes (EBIT)	150	165	181.5	199.7	219.6
− Taxes (20%)	30	33	36.3	39.9	43.9
= Earnings after taxes	120	132	145.2	159.8	175.7
+ Depreciation	12	13.2	14.5	16	17.6
− Capital spending	36	39.6	43.6	47.9	52.7
− Increases in net working capital	36	39.6	43.6	47.9	52.7
= Net cash flows (CF)	60	66	72.6	79.9	87.8

---

[11]This definition of cash flow is the same one we used to determine the NPV of capital investments in Chapter 6.

[12]Sometimes analysts refer to a firm's net debt which is the market value of debt minus excess cash. Neither Good Food or Happy Meals has excess cash.

We start our calculations by computing a terminal value of Happy Meals as:

$$TV_5 = \frac{\$87.8 \times 1.02}{.06 - .02} = \$2,238.9$$

Next, we compute the present value of Happy Meals to be:

$$PV_0 = \frac{\$60}{1.06} + \frac{\$66}{(1.06)^2} + \frac{\$72.6}{(1.06)^3} + \frac{\$79.9}{(1.06)^4} + \frac{\$87.8}{(1.06)^5} + \frac{\$2,238.9}{(1.06)^5} = \$1,978.2$$

The present value of net cash flows in Years 1 to 5 is \$305.2, and the present value of the terminal value is:

$$\$2,238.9 \times \left(\frac{1}{1.06}\right)^5 = \$1,673.0$$

so the total value of the company is \$305.2 + \$1,673.0 = \$1,978.2.

To find the value of equity, we subtract the value of debt which gives us \$1,978.2 − \$1,318.8 = \$659.4. To find the equity value per share, we divide the value of equity by the number of shares outstanding: \$659.4/12.5 = \$52.8. Good Food will find Happy Meals an attractive acquisition candidate at a price of less than \$52.8 per share (the less the better).

In doing our valuation of Happy Meals, Inc., it is important to remember that we have assumed that Happy Meals is a pure play for Good Food. Our weighted average cost of capital method only works if Happy Meals has the same business risks as Good Food and the debt-to-equity ratio will remain the same.

The above calculations assume a growing perpetuity after Year 5 (i.e., the horizon). However, we pointed out in Chapter 3 and Chapter 9 that firms as a whole are often valued by multiples. The most common multiple for overall firm valuation is the enterprise value to the EBITDA multiple (i.e., EV/EBITDA). For example, the analysts at Good Food might estimate the terminal value of Happy Meals via an EV/EBITDA multiple, rather than a growing perpetuity. To see how this might work, suppose the EV/EBITDA multiple for comparable firms in the food service industry is 10. The EBITDA for Happy Meals in Year 5 will be equal to EBIT + depreciation or \$237.2 (=\$219.6 + \$17.6). Using the EV/EBITDA multiple of 10, the value of Happy Meals in Year 5 can be estimated as \$2,372.0. The present value of Happy Meals using the EV/EBITDA multiple for terminal value would be:

$$PV_0 = \frac{\$60}{1.06} + \frac{\$66}{(1.06)^2} + \frac{\$72.6}{(1.06)^3} + \frac{\$79.9}{(1.06)^4} + \frac{\$87.8}{(1.06)^5} + \frac{\$2,372}{(1.06)^5} = \$2,077.7$$

The value of the equity of Happy Meals can be estimated as:

$$PV(\text{of entire firm}) \text{ less debt} = \$2,077.7 - \$1,318.8 = \$758.9$$

With 12.5 million shares outstanding, the value of a share of equity would be:

$$\$758.9/12.5 = \$60.7$$

Now we have two estimates of the value of a share of equity in Happy Meals. The different estimates reflect the different ways of calculating terminal value. Using the constant growth discounted cash flow method for terminal value our estimate of the equity value per share of Happy Meals is \$52.8 and using the EV/EBITDA comparable firm method our estimate is $60.7. As mentioned in Chapter 9, there is no perfect method. If the comparable firms were all identical to Happy Meals, perhaps the EV/EBITDA method would be best. Unfortunately firms are not identical. On the other hand, if we were very sure of the terminal date and the growth in subsequent cash flows, perhaps the constant growth method would be best. Both methods are used.

13.10　Estimating Eastman Chemical's Cost of Capital

Excel Master coverage online

In our previous sections, we calculated the cost of capital in examples. We will now calculate the cost of capital for a real company, Eastman Chemical Co., a leading international chemical company and maker of plastics for soft drink containers and other uses. It was created in 1993, when its former parent company, Eastman Kodak, split off the division as a separate company.

Eastman's Cost of Equity　Our first stop for Eastman is www.reuters .com (ticker: EMN). In October 2014, the website reported the market capitalization of EMN's equity, which is share price times number of shares outstanding, as $10.738 billion. To estimate Eastman's cost of equity, we will assume a market risk premium of 7 percent, similar to what we calculated in Chapter 11. Eastman's beta on Reuters is 1.76.

Our estimate of the risk-free rate is the current Treasury bill rate of 1 percent. Of course, we could plausibly use a longer treasury rate.

Using Eastman's beta in the CAPM to estimate the cost of equity,[13] we find:

$$R_S = .01 + (1.76 \times .07) = .1332, \text{ or } 13.32\%$$

Eastman's Cost of Debt　Eastman has eight bond issues that account for essentially all of its debt. To calculate the cost of debt, we will have to combine these eight issues and compute a weighted average. We go to finra-markets.morningstar.com/ BondCenter/ to find quotes on the bonds. We should note here that finding the yield to maturity for all of a company's outstanding bond issues on a single day is unusual. In our previous discussion on bonds, we found that the bond market is not as liquid as the stock market, and on many days, individual bond issues may not trade. To find the book value of the bonds, we can look up the information on each bond at finra-markets. morningstar.com/BondCenter/ or go to www.sec.gov and find the most recent 10K report.

---

[13]Alternatively, one might use an average beta across all companies in the chemical industry, after properly adjusting for leverage. Some argue this averaging approach provides more accuracy, since errors in beta estimation for a single firm are reduced.

The basic information is as follows:

Coupon Rate	Maturity	Book Value (Face Value in $ Millions)	Price (% of Par)	Yield to Maturity
3.00%	2015	$250	102.004%	0.97%
2.40	2017	1,000	101.965	1.58
6.30	2018	160	111.981	3.04
5.50	2019	250	113.176	2.62
2.70	2020	800	100.541	2.58
4.50	2021	250	106.015	3.36
3.60	2022	900	101.411	3.38
7.25	2024	900	127.020	3.72
7.625	2024	54	129.312	3.90
3.80	2025	800	100.626	3.73
7.60	2027	223	129.964	4.39
4.80	2042	500	102.420	4.64
4.65	2044	400	95.440	4.94

To calculate the weighted average cost of debt, we take the percentage of the total debt represented by each issue and multiply by the yield on the issue. We then add to get the overall weighted average debt cost. We use both book values and market values here for comparison. The results of the calculations are as follows:

Coupon Rate	Book Value (Face Value, in $ Millions)	Percentage of Total	Market Value (in $ Millions)	Percentage of Total	Yield to Maturity	Book Value	Market Value
3.00%	$ 250	3.85%	$ 255.01	3.68%	0.97%	0.04%	0.04%
2.40	1,000	15.42	1,019.65	14.73	1.58	0.24	0.23
6.30	160	2.47	178.96	2.59	3.04	0.07	0.08
5.50	250	3.85	282.94	4.09	2.62	0.10	0.11
2.70	800	12.33	804.33	11.62	2.58	0.32	0.30
4.50	250	3.85	265.04	3.83	3.36	0.13	0.13
3.60	900	13.87	912.70	13.19	3.38	0.47	0.45
7.25	900	13.87	1,143.18	16.52	3.72	0.52	0.61
7.63	54	0.83	69.70	1.01	3.90	0.03	0.04
3.80	800	12.33	805.01	11.63	3.73	0.46	0.43
7.60	223	3.44	290.33	4.20	4.39	0.15	0.18
4.80	500	7.71	512.10	7.40	4.64	0.36	0.34
4.65	400	6.17	381.76	5.52	4.94	0.30	0.27
	$6,487	100.00%	$6,920.71	100.00%		3.20%	3.22%

As these calculations show, Eastman's cost of debt is 3.20 percent on a book value basis and 3.22 percent on a market value basis. Thus, for Eastman, whether market values or book values are used makes little difference. The reason is simply that the market values and book values are similar. This will often be the case and explains why companies frequently use book values for debt in WACC calculations. We will, however, use market values in our calculations, because the market reflects current values.

Eastman's WACC   We now have the various pieces necessary to calculate Eastman's WACC. First, we need to calculate the capital structure weights.

The market values of Eastman's debt and equity are $6.921 billion and $10.738 billion, respectively. The total value of the firm is $17.659 billion, implying that the debt and equity percentages are $6.921/17.659 = .392$ and $10.738/17.659 = .608$, respectively. Assuming a tax rate of 35 percent, Eastman's WACC is:

$$R_{WACC} = .392 \times .0322 \times (1 - .35) + .608 \times .1332 = .0892, \text{ or } 8.92\%$$

13.11 Flotation Costs and the Weighted Average Cost of Capital

So far, we have not included issue costs in our discussion of the weighted average cost of capital. When projects are funded by stocks and bonds, the firm will incur these costs, which are commonly called *flotation costs*.

Sometimes it is suggested that the firm's WACC should be adjusted upward to reflect flotation costs. This is really not the best approach because the required return on an investment depends on the risk of the investment, not the source of the funds. This is not to say that flotation costs should be ignored. Since these costs arise as a consequence of the decision to undertake a project, they are relevant cash flows. We therefore briefly discuss how to include them in project analysis.

THE BASIC APPROACH

We start with a simple case. The Spatt Company, an all-equity firm, has a cost of equity of 20 percent. Because this firm is 100 percent equity, its WACC and its cost of equity are the same. Spatt is contemplating a large-scale $100 million expansion of its existing operations. The expansion would be funded by selling new stock.

Based on conversations with its investment banker, Spatt believes its flotation costs will run 10 percent of the amount issued. This means that Spatt's proceeds from the equity sale will be only 90 percent of the amount sold. When flotation costs are considered, what is the cost of the expansion?

Spatt needs to sell enough equity to raise $100 million *after* covering the flotation costs. In other words:

$$\$100 \text{ million} = (1 - .10) \times \text{Amount raised}$$
$$\text{Amount raised} = \$100 \text{ million}/.90 = \$111.11 \text{ million}$$

Spatt's flotation costs are thus $11.11 million, and the true cost of the expansion is $111.11 million including flotation costs.

Things are only slightly more complicated if the firm uses both debt and equity. For example, suppose Spatt's target capital structure is 60 percent equity, 40 percent debt. The flotation costs associated with equity are still 10 percent, but the flotation costs for debt are less—say 5 percent.

Earlier, when we had different capital costs for debt and equity, we calculated a weighted average cost of capital using the target capital structure weights. Here, we will do much the same thing. We can calculate an overall or weighted average flotation cost, f_o, by multiplying the flotation cost for stock, f_S, by the percentage of stock (S/V) and the flotation cost for bonds, f_B, by the percentage of bonds (B/V) and then adding the two together:

$$f_o = (S/V) \times f_S + (B/V) \times f_B \qquad \textbf{(13.6)}$$
$$= 60\% \times .10 + 40\% \times .05$$
$$= 8\%$$

The weighted average flotation cost is thus 8 percent. What this tells us is that for every dollar in outside financing needed for new projects, the firm must actually raise $\$1/(1 - .08) = \$1.087$. In our example, the project cost is $100 million when we ignore flotation costs. If we include them, then the true cost is $100 million$/(1 - f_o) = \$100$ million$/.92 = \$108.7$ million.

In taking issue costs into account, the firm must be careful not to use the wrong weights. The firm should use the target weights, even if it can finance the entire cost of the project with either debt or equity. The fact that a firm can finance a specific project with debt or equity is not directly relevant. If a firm has a target debt–equity ratio of 1, for example, but chooses to finance a particular project with all debt, it will have to raise additional equity later on to maintain its target debt–equity ratio. To take this into account, the firm should always use the target weights in calculating the flotation cost.

EXAMPLE 13.6

Calculating the Weighted Average Flotation Cost   The Weinstein Corporation has a target capital structure of 80 percent equity and 20 percent debt. The flotation costs for equity issues are 20 percent of the amount raised; the flotation costs for debt issues are 6 percent. If Weinstein needs $65 million for a new manufacturing facility, what is the true cost including flotation costs?

We first calculate the weighted average flotation cost, f_o:

$$f_o = S/V \times f_S + B/V \times f_B$$
$$= 80\% \times .20 + 20\% \times .06$$
$$= 17.2\%$$

The weighted average flotation cost is 17.2 percent. The project cost is $65 million without flotation costs. If we include them, then the true cost is $65 million$/(1 - f_o) = \$65$ million$/.828 = \$78.5$ million, again illustrating that flotation costs can be a considerable expense.

FLOTATION COSTS AND NPV

To illustrate how flotation costs can be included in an NPV analysis, suppose the Tripleday Printing Company is currently at its target debt–equity ratio of 100 percent. It is considering building a new $500,000 printing plant in Kansas. This new plant is expected to generate aftertax cash flows of $73,150 per year forever. The tax rate is 34 percent. There are two financing options:

1. A $500,000 new issue of common stock: The issuance costs of the new common stock would be about 10 percent of the amount raised. The required return on the company's new equity is 20 percent.

2. A $500,000 issue of 30-year bonds: The issuance costs of the new debt would be 2 percent of the proceeds. The company can raise new debt at 10 percent.

What is the NPV of the new printing plant?

To begin, since printing is the company's main line of business, we will use the company's weighted average cost of capital, R_{WACC}, to value the new printing plant:

$$R_{WACC} = S/V \times R_S + B/V \times R_B \times (1 - t_C)$$
$$= .50 \times 20\% + .50 \times 10\% \times (1 - .34)$$
$$= 13.3\%$$

Because the cash flows are $73,150 per year forever, the PV of the cash flows at 13.3 percent per year is:

$$PV = \frac{\$73,150}{.133} = \$550,000$$

If we ignore flotation costs, the NPV is:

$$NPV = \$550,000 - 500,000 = \$50,000$$

With no flotation costs, the project generates an NPV that is greater than zero, so it should be accepted.

What about financing arrangements and issue costs? Because new financing must be raised, the flotation costs are relevant. From the information given, we know that the flotation costs are 2 percent for debt and 10 percent for equity. Because Tripleday uses equal amounts of debt and equity, the weighted average flotation cost, f_o, is:

$$f_o = S/V \times f_S + B/V \times f_B$$
$$= .50 \times 10\% + .50 \times 2\%$$
$$= 6\%$$

Remember, the fact that Tripleday can finance the project with all debt or all equity is irrelevant. Since Tripleday needs $500,000 to fund the new plant, the true cost, once we include flotation costs, is $500,000/(1 - f_o) = \$500,000/.94 = \$531,915$. Because the PV of the cash flows is $550,000, the plant has an NPV of $550,000 - 531,915 = $18,085, so it is still a good investment. However, its value is less than we initially might have thought.

INTERNAL EQUITY AND FLOTATION COSTS

Our discussion of flotation costs to this point implicitly assumed that firms always have to raise the capital needed for new investments. In reality, most firms rarely sell equity at all. Instead, their internally generated cash flow is sufficient to cover the equity portion of their capital spending. Only the debt portion must be raised externally.

The use of internal equity doesn't change our approach. However, we now assign a value of zero to the flotation cost of equity because there is no such cost. In our Tripleday example, the weighted average flotation cost would therefore be:

$$f_o = S/V \times f_S + B/V \times f_B$$
$$= .50 \times 0\% + .50 \times 2\%$$
$$= 1\%$$

Notice that whether equity is generated internally or externally makes a big difference because external equity has a relatively high flotation cost.

Summary and Conclusions

Earlier chapters on capital budgeting assumed that projects generate riskless cash flows. The appropriate discount rate in that case is the riskless interest rate. Of course, most cash flows from real-world capital budgeting projects are risky. This chapter discussed the discount rate when cash flows are risky.

1. A firm with excess cash can either pay a dividend or make a capital expenditure. Because stockholders can reinvest the dividend in risky financial assets, the expected return on a capital budgeting project should be at least as great as the expected return on a financial asset of comparable risk.

2. The expected return on any asset is dependent on its beta. Thus, we showed how to estimate the beta of a stock. The appropriate procedure employs regression analysis on historical returns.

3. Both beta and covariance measure the responsiveness of a security to movements in the market. Correlation and beta measure different concepts. Beta is the slope of the regression line and correlation is the tightness of fit around the regression line.

4. We considered the case of a project with beta risk equal to that of the firm. If the firm is unlevered, the discount rate on the project is equal to:

$$R_F + \beta \times (R_M - R_F)$$

where R_M is the expected return on the market portfolio and R_F is the risk-free rate. In words, the discount rate on the project is equal to the CAPM's estimate of the expected return on the security.

5. The beta of a company is a function of a number of factors. Perhaps the three most important are:
   - Cyclicality of revenues.
   - Operating leverage.
   - Financial leverage.

6. If the project's beta differs from that of the firm, the discount rate should be based on the project's beta. We can generally estimate the project's beta by determining the average beta of the project's industry.

7. Sometimes we cannot use the average beta of the project's industry as an estimate of the beta of the project. For example, a new project may not fall neatly into any existing industry. In this case, we can estimate the project's beta by considering the project's cyclicality of revenues and its operating leverage. This approach is qualitative.

8. If a firm uses debt, the discount rate to use is the R_{WACC}. To calculate R_{WACC}, we must estimate the cost of equity and the cost of debt applicable to a project. If the project is similar to the firm, the cost of equity can be estimated using the SML for the firm's equity. Conceptually, a dividend growth model could be used as well, though it is likely to be far less accurate in practice.

9. New projects are often funded by bonds and stock. The costs of issuance, generally called flotation costs, should be included in any NPV analysis.

Concept Questions

1. **Project Risk**   If you can borrow all the money you need for a project at 6 percent, doesn't it follow that 6 percent is your cost of capital for the project?

2. **WACC and Taxes**   Why do we use an aftertax figure for cost of debt but not for cost of equity?

3. **SML Cost of Equity Estimation**   If you use the stock beta and the security market line to compute the discount rate for a project, what assumptions are you implicitly making?

4. **SML Cost of Equity Estimation**   What are the advantages of using the SML approach to finding the cost of equity capital? What are the disadvantages? What are the specific pieces of information needed to use this method? Are all of these variables observable, or do they need to be estimated? What are some of the ways in which you could get these estimates?

5. **Cost of Debt Estimation**   How do you determine the appropriate cost of debt for a company? Does it make a difference if the company's debt is privately placed as opposed to being publicly traded? How would you estimate the cost of debt for a firm whose only debt issues are privately held by institutional investors?

6. **Cost of Capital**   Suppose Tom O'Bedlam, president of Bedlam Products, Inc., has hired you to determine the firm's cost of debt and cost of equity capital.

    a. The stock currently sells for $50 per share, and the dividend per share will probably be about $5. Tom argues, "It will cost us $5 per share to use the stockholders' money this year, so the cost of equity is equal to 10 percent (=$5/$50)." What's wrong with this conclusion?

    b. Based on the most recent financial statements, Bedlam Products' total liabilities are $8 million. Total interest expense for the coming year will be about $1 million. Tom therefore reasons, "We owe $8 million, and we will pay $1 million interest. Therefore, our cost of debt is obviously $1 million/$8 million = 12.5 percent." What's wrong with this conclusion?

    c. Based on his own analysis, Tom is recommending that the company increase its use of equity financing because, "debt costs 12.5 percent, but equity only costs 10 percent; thus equity is cheaper." Ignoring all the other issues, what do you think about the conclusion that the cost of equity is less than the cost of debt?

7. **Company Risk versus Project Risk**   Both Dow Chemical Company, a large natural gas user, and Superior Oil, a major natural gas producer, are thinking of investing in natural gas wells near Houston. Both are all-equity financed companies. Dow and Superior are looking at identical projects. They've analyzed their respective investments, which would involve a negative cash flow now and positive expected cash flows in the future. These cash flows would be the same for both firms. No debt would be used to finance the projects. Both companies estimate that their projects would have a net present value of $1 million at an 18 percent discount rate and a −$1.1 million NPV at a 22 percent discount rate. Dow has a beta of 1.25, whereas Superior has a beta of .75. The expected risk premium on the market is 8 percent, and risk-free bonds are yielding 12 percent. Should either company proceed? Should both? Explain.

8. **Divisional Cost of Capital**   Under what circumstances would it be appropriate for a firm to use different costs of capital for its different operating divisions? If the overall firm WACC was used as the hurdle rate for all divisions, would the riskier divisions or the more conservative divisions tend to get most of the investment projects? Why? If you were to try to estimate the appropriate cost of capital for different divisions, what problems might you encounter? What are two techniques you could use to develop a rough estimate for each division's cost of capital?

9. **Leverage**   Consider a levered firm's projects that have similar risks to the firm as a whole. Is the discount rate for the projects higher or lower than the rate computed using the security market line? Why?

10. **Beta**   What factors determine the beta of a stock? Define and describe each.

Questions and Problems

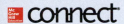

BASIC
(Questions 1–15)

1. **Calculating Cost of Equity** The Dybvig Corporation's common stock has a beta of 1.17. If the risk-free rate is 3.8 percent and the expected return on the market is 11 percent, what is Dybvig's cost of equity capital?

2. **Calculating Cost of Debt** Advance, Inc., is trying to determine its cost of debt. The firm has a debt issue outstanding with 13 years to maturity that is quoted at 95 percent of face value. The issue makes semiannual payments and has a coupon rate of 7 percent. What is the company's pretax cost of debt? If the tax rate is 35 percent, what is the aftertax cost of debt?

3. **Calculating Cost of Debt** Shanken Corp. issued a 30-year, 5.9 percent semiannual bond 6 years ago. The bond currently sells for 108 percent of its face value. The company's tax rate is 35 percent.

   a. What is the pretax cost of debt?
   b. What is the aftertax cost of debt?
   c. Which is more relevant, the pretax or the aftertax cost of debt? Why?

4. **Calculating Cost of Debt** For the firm in the previous problem, suppose the book value of the debt issue is $35 million. In addition, the company has a second debt issue on the market, a zero coupon bond with 12 years left to maturity; the book value of this issue is $80 million and the bonds sell for 61 percent of par. What is the company's total book value of debt? The total market value? What is your best estimate of the aftertax cost of debt now?

5. **Calculating WACC** Mullineaux Corporation has a target capital structure of 70 percent common stock and 30 percent debt. Its cost of equity is 11.5 percent, and the cost of debt is 5.9 percent. The relevant tax rate is 35 percent. What is the company's WACC?

6. **Taxes and WACC** Miller Manufacturing has a target debt–equity ratio of .55. Its cost of equity is 12.5 percent, and its cost of debt is 7 percent. If the tax rate is 35 percent, what is the company's WACC?

7. **Finding the Capital Structure** Fama's Llamas has a weighted average cost of capital of 9.8 percent. The company's cost of equity is 13 percent, and its cost of debt is 6.5 percent. The tax rate is 35 percent. What is Fama's debt–equity ratio?

8. **Book Value versus Market Value** Filer Manufacturing has 8.3 million shares of common stock outstanding. The current share price is $53, and the book value per share is $4. The company also has two bond issues outstanding. The first bond issue has a face value of $70 million and a coupon rate of 7 percent and sells for 108.3 percent of par. The second issue has a face value of $60 million and a coupon rate of 7.5 percent and sells for 108.9 percent of par. The first issue matures in 8 years, the second in 27 years.

   a. What are the company's capital structure weights on a book value basis?
   b. What are the company's capital structure weights on a market value basis?
   c. Which are more relevant, the book or market value weights? Why?

9. **Calculating the WACC** In the previous problem, suppose the company's stock has a beta of 1.15. The risk-free rate is 3.7 percent, and the market risk premium is 7 percent. Assume that the overall cost of debt is the weighted average implied by the two outstanding debt issues. Both bonds make semiannual payments. The tax rate is 35 percent. What is the company's WACC?

10. **WACC** Kose, Inc., has a target debt–equity ratio of .45. Its WACC is 9.8 percent, and the tax rate is 35 percent.

a. If Kose's cost of equity is 13 percent, what is its pretax cost of debt?

b. If instead you know that the aftertax cost of debt is 5.9 percent, what is the cost of equity?

11. Finding the WACC   Given the following information for Huntington Power Co., find the WACC. Assume the company's tax rate is 35 percent.

Debt:	10,000 5.6 percent coupon bonds outstanding, $1,000 par value, 25 years to maturity, selling for 97 percent of par; the bonds make semiannual payments.
Common stock:	425,000 shares outstanding, selling for $61 per share; the beta is .95.
Market:	7 percent market risk premium and 3.8 percent risk-free rate.

12. Finding the WACC   Titan Mining Corporation has 8.7 million shares of common stock outstanding and 230,000 6.4 percent semiannual bonds outstanding, par value $1,000 each. The common stock currently sells for $37 per share and has a beta of 1.20, and the bonds have 20 years to maturity and sell for 104 percent of par. The market risk premium is 7 percent, T-bills are yielding 3.5 percent, and the company's tax rate is 35 percent.

a. What is the firm's market value capital structure?

b. If the company is evaluating a new investment project that has the same risk as the firm's typical project, what rate should the firm use to discount the project's cash flows?

13. SML and WACC   An all-equity firm is considering the following projects:

Project	Beta	IRR
W	.80	9.4%
X	.95	10.9
Y	1.15	13.0
Z	1.45	14.2

The T-bill rate is 3.5 percent, and the expected return on the market is 11 percent.

a. Which projects have a higher expected return than the firm's 11 percent cost of capital?

b. Which projects should be accepted?

c. Which projects would be incorrectly accepted or rejected if the firm's overall cost of capital was used as a hurdle rate?

14. Calculating Flotation Costs   Suppose your company needs $35 million to build a new assembly line. Your target debt–equity ratio is .75. The flotation cost for new equity is 6 percent, but the flotation cost for debt is only 2 percent. Your boss has decided to fund the project by borrowing money because the flotation costs are lower and the needed funds are relatively small.

a. What do you think about the rationale behind borrowing the entire amount?

b. What is your company's weighted average flotation cost, assuming all equity is raised externally?

c. What is the true cost of building the new assembly line after taking flotation costs into account? Does it matter in this case that the entire amount is being raised from debt?

15. Calculating Flotation Costs   Southern Alliance Company needs to raise $55 million to start a new project and will raise the money by selling new bonds. The company will generate no internal equity for the foreseeable future. The company has a target capital structure of 65 percent common stock, 5 percent preferred stock, and 30 percent debt. Flotation costs for issuing new common stock are 7 percent; for new preferred stock,

4 percent; and for new debt, 3 percent. What is the true initial cost figure Southern should use when evaluating its project?

INTERMEDIATE
(Questions 16–21)

16.   WACC and NPV   Och, Inc., is considering a project that will result in initial aftertax cash savings of $2.9 million at the end of the first year, and these savings will grow at a rate of 4 percent per year indefinitely. The company has a target debt–equity ratio of .65, a cost of equity of 13 percent, and an aftertax cost of debt of 5.5 percent. The cost-saving proposal is somewhat riskier than the usual projects the firm undertakes; management uses the subjective approach and applies an adjustment factor of +2 percent to the cost of capital for such risky projects. Under what circumstances should the company take on the project?

17.   Preferred Stock and WACC   The Saunders Investment Bank has the following financing outstanding. What is the WACC for the company?

Debt:	50,000 bonds with a coupon rate of 5.7 percent and a current price quote of 106.5; the bonds have 20 years to maturity. 200,000 zero coupon bonds with a price quote of 17.5 and 30 years until maturity.
Preferred stock:	125,000 shares of 4 percent preferred stock with a current price of $79, and a par value of $100.
Common stock:	2,300,000 shares of common stock; the current price is $65, and the beta of the stock is 1.20.
Market:	The corporate tax rate is 40 percent, the market risk premium is 7 percent, and the risk-free rate is 4 percent.

18.   Flotation Costs   Goodbye, Inc., recently issued new securities to finance a new TV show. The project cost $19 million, and the company paid $1,150,000 in flotation costs. In addition, the equity issued had a flotation cost of 7 percent of the amount raised, whereas the debt issued had a flotation cost of 3 percent of the amount raised. If the company issued new securities in the same proportion as its target capital structure, what is the company's target debt–equity ratio?

19.   Calculating the Cost of Equity   Floyd Industries stock has a beta of 1.15. The company just paid a dividend of $.85, and the dividends are expected to grow at 4.5 percent per year. The expected return on the market is 11 percent, and Treasury bills are yielding 3.9 percent. The most recent stock price for the company is $76.

a. Calculate the cost of equity using the DDM method.
b. Calculate the cost of equity using the SML method.
c. Why do you think your estimates in (a) and (b) are so different?

20.   Firm Valuation   Schultz Industries is considering the purchase of Arras Manufacturing. Arras is currently a supplier for Schultz, and the acquisition would allow Schultz to better control its material supply. The current cash flow from assets for Arras is $6.8 million. The cash flows are expected to grow at 8 percent for the next five years before leveling off to 4 percent for the indefinite future. The cost of capital for Schultz and Arras is 12 percent and 10 percent, respectively. Arras currently has 2.5 million shares of stock outstanding and $30 million in debt outstanding. What is the maximum price per share Schultz should pay for Arras?

21.   Firm Valuation   Happy Times, Inc., wants to expand its party stores into the Southeast. In order to establish an immediate presence in the area, the company is considering the purchase of the privately held Joe's Party Supply. Happy Times currently has debt outstanding with a market value of $140 million and a YTM of 6 percent. The company's market capitalization is $380 million, and the required return on equity is 11 percent. Joe's currently has debt outstanding with a market value of $40 million. The EBIT for Joe's next year is projected to be $16.8 million. EBIT is expected to grow at 10 percent per year for the next five years before slowing to 3 percent in perpetuity. Net working capital, capital spending, and depreciation as a percentage of EBIT are expected to be 9 percent, 15 percent, and 8 percent, respectively. Joe's has 1.95 million shares outstanding and the tax rate for both companies is 38 percent.

a. Based on these estimates, what is the maximum share price that Happy Times should be willing to pay for Joe's?

b. After examining your analysis, the CFO of Happy Times is uncomfortable using the perpetual growth rate in cash flows. Instead, she feels that the terminal value should be estimated using the EV/EBITDA multiple. If the appropriate EV/EBITDA multiple is 8, what is your new estimate of the maximum share price for the purchase?

CHALLENGE
(Questions 22–24)

22. **Flotation Costs and NPV**   Photochronograph Corporation (PC) manufactures time series photographic equipment. It is currently at its target debt–equity ratio of .55. It's considering building a new $50 million manufacturing facility. This new plant is expected to generate aftertax cash flows of $6.7 million a year in perpetuity. The company raises all equity from outside financing. There are three financing options:

    1. *A new issue of common stock:* The flotation costs of the new common stock would be 8 percent of the amount raised. The required return on the company's new equity is 14 percent.
    2. *A new issue of 20-year bonds:* The flotation costs of the new bonds would be 4 percent of the proceeds. If the company issues these new bonds at an annual coupon rate of 8 percent, they will sell at par.
    3. *Increased use of accounts payable financing:* Because this financing is part of the company's ongoing daily business, it has no flotation costs, and the company assigns it a cost that is the same as the overall firm WACC. Management has a target ratio of accounts payable to long-term debt of .20. (Assume there is no difference between the pretax and aftertax accounts payable cost.)

    What is the NPV of the new plant? Assume that PC has a 35 percent tax rate.

23. **Flotation Costs**   Trower Corp. has a debt–equity ratio of .85. The company is considering a new plant that will cost $145 million to build. When the company issues new equity, it incurs a flotation cost of 8 percent. The flotation cost on new debt is 3.5 percent. What is the initial cost of the plant if the company raises all equity externally? What if it typically uses 60 percent retained earnings? What if all equity investments are financed through retained earnings?

24. **Project Evaluation**   This is a comprehensive project evaluation problem bringing together much of what you have learned in this and previous chapters. Suppose you have been hired as a financial consultant to Defense Electronics, Inc. (DEI), a large, publicly traded firm that is the market share leader in radar detection systems (RDSs). The company is looking at setting up a manufacturing plant overseas to produce a new line of RDSs. This will be a five-year project. The company bought some land three years ago for $7.5 million in anticipation of using it as a toxic dump site for waste chemicals, but it built a piping system to safely discard the chemicals instead. The land was appraised last week for $7.1 million. In five years, the aftertax value of the land will be $7.4 million, but the company expects to keep the land for a future project. The company wants to build its new manufacturing plant on this land; the plant and equipment will cost $40 million to build. The following market data on DEI's securities is current:

Debt:	260,000 6.8 percent coupon bonds outstanding, 25 years to maturity, selling for 103 percent of par; the bonds have a $1,000 par value each and make semiannual payments.
Common stock:	9,500,000 shares outstanding, selling for $67 per share; the beta is 1.25.
Preferred stock:	450,000 shares of 5.25 percent preferred stock outstanding, selling for $84 per share and having a par value of $100.
Market:	7 percent expected market risk premium; 3.6 percent risk-free rate.

DEI uses G.M. Wharton as its lead underwriter. Wharton charges DEI spreads of 6.5 percent on new common stock issues, 4.5 percent on new preferred stock issues, and 3 percent on new debt issues. Wharton has included all direct and indirect issuance costs (along with its profit) in setting these spreads. Wharton has recommended to DEI that it raise the funds needed to build the plant by issuing new shares of common stock. DEI's tax rate is 35 percent. The project requires $1,400,000 in initial net working capital investment to get operational. Assume Wharton raises all equity for new projects externally.

a. Calculate the project's initial Time 0 cash flow, taking into account all side effects.

b. The new RDS project is somewhat riskier than a typical project for DEI, primarily because the plant is being located overseas. Management has told you to use an adjustment factor of +2 percent to account for this increased riskiness. Calculate the appropriate discount rate to use when evaluating DEI's project.

c. The manufacturing plant has an eight-year tax life, and DEI uses straight-line depreciation. At the end of the project (i.e., the end of Year 5), the plant and equipment can be scrapped for $8.5 million. What is the aftertax salvage value of this plant and equipment?

d. The company will incur $7,900,000 in annual fixed costs. The plan is to manufacture 18,000 RDSs per year and sell them at $10,900 per machine; the variable production costs are $9,450 per RDS. What is the annual operating cash flow (OCF) from this project?

e. DEI's comptroller is primarily interested in the impact of DEI's investments on the bottom line of reported accounting statements. What will you tell her is the accounting break-even quantity of RDSs sold for this project?

f. Finally, DEI's president wants you to throw all your calculations, assumptions, and everything else into the report for the chief financial officer; all he wants to know is what the RDS project's internal rate of return (IRR) and net present value (NPV) are. What will you report?

Mini Case

COST OF CAPITAL FOR SWAN MOTORS

You have recently been hired by Swan Motors, Inc. (SMI), in its relatively new treasury management department. SMI was founded 8 years ago by Joe Swan. Joe found a method to manufacture a cheaper battery with much greater energy density than was previously possible, giving a car powered by the battery a range of 700 miles before requiring a charge. The cars manufactured by SMI are midsized and carry a price that allows the company to compete with other mainstream auto manufacturers. The company is privately owned by Joe and his family, and it had sales of $97 million last year.

SMI primarily sells to customers who buy the cars online, although it does have a limited number of company-owned dealerships. Most sales are online. The customer selects any customization and makes a deposit of 20 percent of the purchase price. After the order is taken, the car is made to order, typically within 45 days. SMI's growth to date has come from its profits. When the company had sufficient capital, it would expand production. Relatively little formal analysis has been used in its capital budgeting process. Joe has just read about capital budgeting techniques and has come to you for help. For starters, the company has never attempted to determine its cost of capital, and Joe would like you to perform the analysis. Because the company is privately owned, it is difficult to determine the cost of equity for the company. Joe wants you to use the pure play approach to estimate the cost of capital for SMI, and he has chosen Tesla Motors as a representative company. The following questions will lead you through the steps to calculate this estimate.

1. Most publicly traded corporations are required to submit 10Q (quarterly) and 10K (annual) reports to the SEC detailing their financial operations over the previous quarter or year, respectively. These corporate filings are available on the SEC website at www.sec.gov. Go to the SEC website, follow the "Search for Company Filings" link and the "Companies & Other Filers" link, enter "Tesla," and search for SEC filings made by Tesla. Find the most recent 10Q and 10K and download the forms. Look on the balance sheet to find the book value of debt and the book value of equity. If you look further down the report, you should find a section titled either "Long-Term Debt" or "Long-Term Debt and Interest Rate Risk Management" that will list a breakdown of Tesla's long-term debt.

2. To estimate the cost of equity for Tesla, go to finance.yahoo.com and enter the ticker symbol "TSLA." Follow the various links to find answers to the following questions: What is the most recent stock price listed for Tesla? What is the market value of equity, or market capitalization? How many shares of stock does Tesla have outstanding? What is the beta for Tesla? Now go back to finance.yahoo.com and follow the "Bonds" link. What is the yield on 3-month Treasury bills? Using a 7 percent market risk premium, what is the cost of equity for Tesla using the CAPM?

3. Go to www.reuters.com and find the list of competitors in the industry. Find the beta for each of these competitors, and then calculate the industry average beta. Using the industry average beta, what is the cost of equity? Does it matter if you use the beta for Tesla or the beta for the industry in this case?

4. You now need to calculate the cost of debt for Tesla. Go to finra-markets.morningstar .com/BondCenter/Results.jsp, enter Tesla as the company, and find the yield to maturity for each of Tesla's bonds. What is the weighted average cost of debt for Tesla using the book value weights and the market value weights? Does it make a difference in this case if you use book value weights or market value weights?

5. You now have all the necessary information to calculate the weighted average cost of capital for Tesla. Calculate the weighted average cost of capital for SMI using book value weights and market value weights assuming SMI has a 35 percent marginal tax rate. Which cost of capital number is more relevant?

6. You used Tesla as a representative company to estimate the cost of capital for SMI. What are some of the potential problems with this approach in this situation? What improvements might you suggest?

Appendix 13A   Economic Value Added and the Measurement of Financial Performance

To access the appendix for this chapter, please logon to Connect Finance.

Efficient Capital Markets and Behavioral Challenges

The NASDAQ stock market was raging in the late 1990s, gaining about 23 percent, 14 percent, 35 percent, and 87 percent from 1996 to 1999, respectively. Of course, that spectacular run came to a jarring halt, and the NASDAQ lost about 40 percent in 2000, followed by another 30 percent in 2001. The ISDEX, an index of Internet-related stocks, rose from 100 in January 1996 to 1,100 in February 2000, a gain of about 1,000 percent! It then fell like a rock to 600 by May 2000. Of course, a bubble can exist in a single asset as well. For example, many investors saw a tech bubble echo in Tesla Motors, which increased in value more than 590 percent from March 22, 2013, to February 26, 2014. In fact, one analysis of the company's valuation indicated that the stock could be overvalued by about 150 percent.

Nowhere was the tech bubble more evident than in the initial public offering (IPO) market. In the IPO market, companies offer stock for sale for the first time, and large initial gains are not uncommon. However, during 1999 to 2000, stupendous gains became commonplace. For example, stock in VA Linux shot up 698 percent in the first day of trading! Over this period, a total of 194 IPOs doubled, or more than doubled, in value on the first day. In contrast, only 39 companies had done so in the preceding 24 years.

The performance of the NASDAQ over this period, and particularly the rise and fall of Internet stocks, has been described by many as one of the greatest market "bubbles" in history. The argument is that prices were inflated to economically ridiculous levels before investors came to their senses, which then caused the bubble to pop and prices to plunge. Debate over whether the stock market of the late 1990s really was a bubble has generated much controversy. In this chapter, we discuss the competing ideas, present some evidence on both sides, and then examine the implications for financial managers.

14.1 Can Financing Decisions Create Value?

Earlier parts of the book showed how to evaluate projects according to the net present value criterion. The real world is a competitive one where projects with positive net present value are not always easy to come by. However, through hard work or through good fortune, a firm can identify winning projects. For example, to create value from capital budgeting decisions, the firm is likely to:

1. Locate an unsatisfied demand for a particular product or service.
2. Create a barrier to make it more difficult for other firms to compete.
3. Produce products or services at a lower cost than the competition.
4. Be the first to develop a new product.

The next eight chapters concern various aspects of *financing* decisions. Typical financing decisions include how much and what types of debt and equity to sell, and when to sell them. Just as the net present value criterion was used to evaluate capital budgeting projects, we now want to use the same criterion to evaluate financing decisions.

Though the procedure for evaluating financing decisions is identical to the procedure for evaluating projects, the results are different. It turns out that the typical firm has many more capital expenditure opportunities with positive net present values than financing opportunities with positive net present values. In fact, we later show that some plausible financial models imply that no valuable financial opportunities exist at all.

Though this dearth of profitable financing opportunities will be examined in detail later, a few remarks are in order now. We maintain that there are basically three ways to create valuable financing opportunities:

1. *Fool investors.* Assume that a firm can raise capital either by issuing stock or by issuing a more complex security—say, a combination of stock and warrants. Suppose that, in truth, 100 shares of stock are worth the same as 50 units of our complex security. If investors have a misguided, overly optimistic view of the complex security, perhaps the 50 units can be sold for more than the 100 shares of stock. Clearly, this complex security provides a valuable financing opportunity because the firm is getting more than fair value for it.

   Financial managers try to package securities to receive the greatest value. A cynic might view this as attempting to fool investors.

   However, the theory of efficient capital markets implies that investors cannot easily be fooled. It says that securities are appropriately priced at all times, implying that the market as a whole is shrewd indeed. In our example, 50 units of the complex security would sell for the same price as 100 shares of stock. Thus, corporate managers cannot attempt to create value by fooling investors. Instead, managers must create value in other ways.

2. *Reduce costs or increase subsidies.* We show later in the book that certain forms of financing have greater tax advantages than other forms. Clearly, a firm packaging securities to minimize taxes can increase firm value. In addition, any financing technique involves other costs. For example, investment bankers, lawyers, and accountants must be paid. A firm packaging securities to minimize these costs can also increase its value.

EXAMPLE

Valuing Financial Subsidies Suppose Vermont Electronics Company is thinking about relocating its plant to Mexico where labor costs are lower. In the hope that it can stay in Vermont, the company has submitted an application to the state of Vermont to issue $2 million in five-year, tax-exempt industrial bonds. The coupon rate on industrial revenue bonds in Vermont is currently 5 percent. This is an attractive rate because the normal cost of debt capital for Vermont Electronics Company is 10 percent. The firm will pay annual interest of $100,000 (= $2 million × 5%), rather than annual interest of $200,000 (= $2 million × 10%). What is the NPV of this potential financing transaction?

If the application is accepted and the industrial revenue bonds are issued by the Vermont Electronics Company, the NPV (ignoring corporate taxes) is:

$$\text{NPV} = \$2,000,000 - \left[\frac{\$100,000}{1.1} + \frac{\$100,000}{(1.1)^2} + \frac{\$100,000}{(1.1)^3} + \frac{\$100,000}{(1.1)^4} + \frac{\$2,100,000}{(1.1)^5} \right]$$

$$= \$2,000,000 - \$1,620,921$$

$$= \$379,079$$

This transaction has a positive NPV. The Vermont Electronics Company obtains subsidized financing where the value of the subsidy is $379,079.

3. *Create a new security.* There has been a surge in financial innovation in recent decades. For example, in a speech on financial innovation, Nobel laureate Merton Miller asked the rhetorical question, "Can any 20-year period in recorded history have witnessed even a tenth as much new development? Where corporations once issued only straight debt and straight common stock, they now issue zero coupon bonds, adjustable rate notes, floating-rate notes, putable bonds, credit-enhanced debt securities, receivable-backed securities, adjusted-rate preferred stock, convertible adjustable preferred stock, auction rate preferred stock, single-point adjustable rate stock, convertible exchangeable preferred stock, adjustable-rate convertible debt, zero coupon convertible debt, debt with mandatory common stock purchase contracts—to name just a few!"[1] And financial innovation has occurred even more rapidly in the years following Miller's speech.

Though the advantages of each instrument are different, one general theme is that these new securities cannot easily be duplicated by combinations of existing securities. Thus, a previously unsatisfied clientele may pay extra for a specialized security catering to its needs. For example, putable bonds let the purchaser sell the bond at a fixed price back to the firm. This innovation creates a price floor, allowing the investor to reduce her downside risk. Perhaps risk-averse investors or investors with little knowledge of the bond market would find this feature particularly attractive.

Corporations gain by issuing these unique securities at high prices. However, the value captured by the innovator may well be small in the long run because the innovator usually cannot patent or copyright an idea. Soon many firms are issuing securities of the same kind, forcing prices down as a result.

This brief introduction sets the stage for the next several chapters of the book. Most of the rest of this chapter examines how efficient capital markets work. We show that if capital markets are efficient, corporate managers cannot create value by fooling investors. This is quite important because managers must create value in other, perhaps more difficult, ways. We also describe behavioral challenges to the notion of perfectly efficient capital markets.

14.2 A Description of Efficient Capital Markets

An efficient capital market for stocks is one in which stock prices fully reflect available information about the underlying value of the stock. To illustrate how an efficient market works, suppose the F-stop Camera Corporation (FCC) is attempting to develop a camera that will double the speed of the auto-focusing system now available. FCC believes this research has a positive NPV.

Now consider a share of stock in FCC. What determines the willingness of investors to hold shares of FCC at a particular price? One important factor is the probability that FCC will be the first company to develop the new auto-focusing system. In an efficient market, we would expect the price of the shares of FCC to increase if this probability increases.

Suppose FCC hires a well-known engineer to develop the new auto-focusing system. In an efficient market, what will happen to FCC's share price when this is announced? If the engineer is paid a salary that fully reflects his contribution to the firm, the price of the stock will not necessarily change. Suppose instead that hiring the engineer is a positive NPV transaction. In this case, the price of shares in FCC will increase because the firm can pay the engineer a salary below his true value to the company.

---

[1]Merton Miller, "Financial Innovation: The Last Twenty Years and the Next," *Journal of Financial and Quantitative Analysis* (December 1986).

When will the increase in the price of FCC's shares occur? Assume that the hiring announcement is made in a press release on Wednesday morning. In an efficient market, the price of shares in FCC will *immediately* adjust to this new information. Investors should not be able to buy the stock on Wednesday afternoon and make a profit on Thursday. This would imply that it took the stock market a day to realize the implication of the FCC press release. The efficient market hypothesis predicts that the price of shares of FCC stock on Wednesday afternoon will already reflect the information contained in the Wednesday morning press release.

The **efficient market hypothesis** (EMH) has implications for investors and for firms:

- Because information is reflected in prices immediately, investors should only expect to obtain a normal rate of return. Awareness of information when it is released does an investor no good. The price adjusts before the investor has time to trade on it.

- Firms should expect to receive fair value for securities that they sell. *Fair* means that the price they receive from issuing securities is the present value. Thus, valuable financing opportunities that arise from fooling investors are unavailable in efficient capital markets.

Figure 14.1 presents several possible adjustments in stock prices. The solid line represents the stock's price path in an efficient market. In this case, the price adjusts immediately to the new information with no further price changes. The dotted line depicts a slow reaction. Here it takes the market 30 days to fully absorb the information. Finally, the broken line illustrates an overreaction and subsequent correction back to the true price. The broken line and the dotted line show the paths that the stock price might take in an

Figure 14.1

Reaction of Stock Price to New Information in Efficient and Inefficient Markets

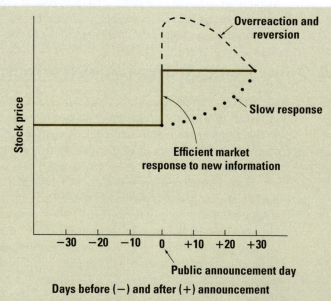

Efficient market response: The price instantaneously adjusts to and fully reflects new information; there is no tendency for subsequent increases and decreases.
Slow response: The price adjusts slowly to the new information; 30 days elapse before the price completely reflects the new information.
Overreaction: The price overadjusts to the new information; there is a bubble in the price sequence.

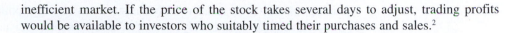

inefficient market. If the price of the stock takes several days to adjust, trading profits would be available to investors who suitably timed their purchases and sales.[2]

FOUNDATIONS OF MARKET EFFICIENCY

Figure 14.1 shows the consequences of market efficiency. But what are the conditions that *cause* market efficiency? Andrei Shleifer argues that there are three conditions, any one of which will lead to efficiency:[3] (1) rationality, (2) independent deviations from rationality, and (3) arbitrage. A discussion of these conditions follows.

Rationality   Imagine that all investors are rational. When new information is released in the marketplace, all investors will adjust their estimates of stock prices in a rational way. In our example, investors will use the information in FCC's press release, in conjunction with existing information about the firm, to determine the NPV of FCC's new venture. If the information in the press release implies that the NPV of the venture is $10 million and there are 2 million shares, investors will calculate that the NPV is $5 per share. While FCC's old price might be, say, $40, no one would now transact at that price. Anyone interested in selling would sell only at a price of at least $45 (= $40 + 5). And anyone interested in buying would now be willing to pay up to $45. In other words, the price would rise by $5. And the price would rise immediately because rational investors would see no reason to wait before trading at the new price.

Of course, we all know times when individuals seem to behave less than perfectly rationally. Thus, perhaps it is too much to ask that *all* investors behave rationally. But the market will still be efficient if the following scenario holds.

Independent Deviations from Rationality   Suppose that FCC's press release is not all that clear. How many new cameras are likely to be sold? At what price? What is the likely cost per camera? Will other camera companies be able to develop competing products? How long will the development of these competing products likely take? If these and other questions cannot be answered easily, it will be difficult to estimate NPV.

With so many unanswered questions, many investors may not be thinking clearly. Some investors might get caught up in the romance of a new product, hoping for and ultimately believing in sales projections well above what is rational. They would overpay for new shares. And if they needed to sell shares (perhaps to finance current consumption), they would do so only at a high price. If these individuals dominate the market, the stock price would likely rise beyond what market efficiency would predict.

However, due to emotional resistance, investors could just as easily react to new information in a pessimistic manner. After all, business historians tell us that investors were initially quite skeptical about the benefits of the telephone, the copier, the automobile, the motion picture, and the computer. Certainly, they could be overly skeptical about this new camera. If investors were primarily of this type, the stock price would likely rise less than market efficiency would predict.

---

[2]Now you should appreciate the following short story. A student was walking down the hall with her finance professor when they both saw a $20 bill on the ground. As the student bent down to pick it up, the professor shook his head slowly and, with a look of disappointment on his face, said patiently to the student, "Don't bother. If it was really there, someone else would have already picked it up."

The moral of the story reflects the logic of the efficient market hypothesis: If you think you have found a pattern in stock prices or a simple device for picking winners, you probably have not. If there was such a simple way to make money, someone else would have found it before. Furthermore, if people tried to exploit the information, their efforts would become self-defeating and the pattern would disappear.

[3]Andrei Shleifer, *Inefficient Markets: An Introduction to Behavioral Finance* (Oxford: Oxford University Press, 2000).

But suppose that about as many individuals were irrationally optimistic as were irrationally pessimistic. Prices would likely rise in a manner consistent with market efficiency, even though most investors would be classified as less than fully rational. Thus, market efficiency does not require rational individuals—only countervailing irrationalities.

However, this assumption of offsetting irrationalities at *all* times may be unrealistic. Perhaps at certain times most investors are swept away by excessive optimism and at other times are caught in the throes of extreme pessimism. But even here there is an assumption that will produce efficiency.

Arbitrage   Imagine a world with two types of individuals: the irrational amateurs and the rational professionals. The amateurs get caught up in their emotions, at times believing irrationally that a stock is undervalued and at other times believing the opposite. If the passions of the different amateurs do not cancel each other out, these amateurs, by themselves, would tend to carry stocks either above or below their efficient prices.

Now let's bring in the professionals. Suppose professionals go about their business methodically and rationally. They study companies thoroughly, they evaluate the evidence objectively, they estimate stock prices coldly and clearly, and they act accordingly. If a stock is underpriced, they would buy it. If it is overpriced, they would sell it. And their confidence would likely be greater than that of the amateurs. Whereas an amateur might risk only a small sum, these professionals might risk large ones, *knowing* as they do that the stock is mispriced. Furthermore, they would be willing to rearrange their entire portfolio in search of a profit. If they find that General Motors is underpriced, they might sell the Ford stock they own to buy GM. *Arbitrage* is the word that comes to mind here because arbitrage generates profit from the simultaneous purchase and sale of different, but substitute, securities. If the arbitrage of professionals dominates the speculation of amateurs, markets would still be efficient.

14.3 The Different Types of Efficiency

In our previous discussion, we assumed that the market responds immediately to all available information. In actuality, certain information may affect stock prices more quickly than other information. To handle differential response rates, researchers separate information into different types. The most common classification system identifies three types: Information about past prices, publicly available information, and all information. The effect of these three information sets on prices is examined next.

THE WEAK FORM

Imagine a trading strategy that recommends buying a stock after it has gone up three days in a row and recommends selling a stock after it has gone down three days in a row. This strategy uses information based only on past prices. It does not use any other information, such as earnings forecasts, merger announcements, or money supply figures. A capital market is said to be *weakly efficient,* or to satisfy **weak form efficiency**, if it fully incorporates the information in past stock prices. Thus, the preceding strategy would not be able to generate profits if weak form efficiency holds.

Often, weak form efficiency is represented mathematically as:

$$P_t = P_{t-1} + \text{Expected return} + \text{Random error}_t \qquad \textbf{(14.1)}$$

Equation 14.1 states that the price today is equal to the sum of the last observed price plus the expected return on the stock (in dollars) plus a random component occurring over the interval. The last observed price could have occurred yesterday, last week, or last month,

Figure 14.2
Investor Behavior
Tends to Eliminate
Cyclical Patterns

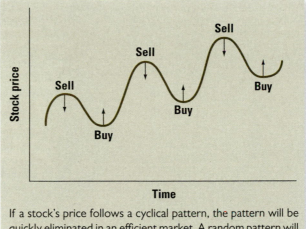

If a stock's price follows a cyclical pattern, the pattern will be quickly eliminated in an efficient market. A random pattern will emerge as investors buy at the trough and sell at the peak of a cycle.

depending on the sampling interval. The expected return is a function of a security's risk and would be based on the models of risk and return in previous chapters. The random component is due to new information about the stock. It could be either positive or negative and has an expectation of zero. The random component in any period is unrelated to the random component in any past period. Hence, this component is not predictable from past prices. If stock prices follow Equation 14.1 they are said to follow a **random walk**.[4]

Weak form efficiency is about the weakest type of efficiency that we would expect a financial market to display because historical price information is the easiest kind of information about a stock to acquire. If it were possible to make extraordinary profits simply by finding patterns in stock price movements, everyone would do it, and any profits would disappear in the scramble.

This effect of competition can be seen in Figure 14.2. Suppose the price of a stock displays a cyclical pattern, as indicated by the wavy curve. Shrewd investors would buy at the low points, forcing those prices up. Conversely, they would sell at the high points, forcing prices down. Via competition, cyclical regularities would be eliminated, leaving only random fluctuations.

THE SEMISTRONG AND STRONG FORMS

If weak form efficiency is controversial, even more contentious are the two stronger types of efficiency, **semistrong form efficiency** and **strong form efficiency**. A market is semistrong form efficient if prices reflect (incorporate) all publicly available information, including information such as published accounting statements for the firm, as well as historical price information. A market is strong form efficient if prices reflect all information, public or private.

The information set of past prices is a subset of the information set of publicly available information, which in turn is a subset of all information. This is shown in Figure 14.3. Thus, strong form efficiency implies semistrong form efficiency, and semistrong form efficiency implies weak form efficiency. The reverse is not true. The distinction between

---

[4]For purposes of this text, the random walk can be considered synonymous with weak form efficiency. Technically, the random walk is a slightly more restrictive hypothesis because it assumes that stock returns are identically distributed through time.

Figure 14.3
Relationship among
Three Different
Information Sets

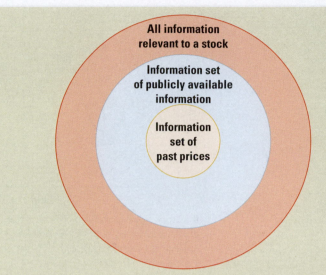

The information set of past prices is a subset of the set of all publicly available information, which in turn is a subset of all information. If today's price reflects only information about past prices, the market is weak form efficient. If today's price reflects all publicly available information, the market is semistrong form efficient. If today's price reflects all information, both public and private, the market is strong form efficient.

Semistrong form efficiency implies weak form efficiency, and strong form efficiency implies semistrong form efficiency.

semistrong form efficiency and weak form efficiency is that semistrong form efficiency requires not only that the market be efficient with respect to historical price information, but that *all* of the information available to the public be reflected in prices.

To illustrate the different forms of efficiency, imagine an investor who always sold a particular stock after its price had risen. A market that was only weak form efficient and not semistrong form efficient would still prevent such a strategy from generating excess or abnormal positive profits. According to weak form efficiency, a recent price rise does not imply that the stock is overvalued.

Now consider a firm reporting increased earnings. An individual might consider investing in the stock after reading the news release providing this information. However, if the market is semistrong form efficient, the price should rise immediately upon the news release. Thus, the investor would end up paying the higher price, eliminating all chance for an abnormal return.

At the furthest end of the spectrum is strong form efficiency. This form says that anything that is pertinent to the value of the stock and that is known to at least one investor is, in fact, fully incorporated into the stock price. A strict believer in strong form efficiency would deny that an insider who knew whether a company mining operation had struck gold could profit from that information. Such a devotee of the strong form efficient market hypothesis might argue that as soon as the insider tried to trade on his information, the market would recognize what was happening, and the price would shoot up before he could buy any of the stock. Alternatively, believers in strong form efficiency argue that there are no secrets, and as soon as the gold is discovered, the secret gets out.

One reason to expect that markets are weak form efficient is that it is so cheap and easy to find patterns in stock prices. Anyone who can program a computer and knows a little bit of statistics can search for such patterns. It stands to reason that if there were such patterns, people would find and exploit them, in the process causing them to disappear.

Semistrong form efficiency, though, implies more sophisticated investors than does weak form efficiency. An investor must be skilled at economics and statistics and steeped in the idiosyncrasies of individual industries and companies. Furthermore, to acquire and use such skills requires talent, ability, and time. In the jargon of the economist, such an effort is costly, and the ability to be successful at it is probably in scarce supply.

As for strong form efficiency, this is just further down the road than semistrong form efficiency. It is difficult to believe that the market is so efficient that someone with valuable inside information cannot prosper from it. And empirical evidence tends to be unfavorable to this form of market efficiency.

SOME COMMON MISCONCEPTIONS ABOUT THE EFFICIENT MARKET HYPOTHESIS

No idea in finance has attracted as much attention as that of efficient markets, and not all of the attention has been flattering. To a certain extent this is because much of the criticism has been based on a misunderstanding of what the hypothesis does and does not say. We illustrate three misconceptions next.

The Efficacy of Dart Throwing
When the notion of market efficiency was first publicized and debated in the popular financial press, it was often characterized by the following quote: ". . . throwing darts at the financial page will produce a portfolio that can be expected to do as well as any managed by professional security analysts."[5,6] This is almost, but not quite, true.

All the efficient market hypothesis really says is that, on average, the manager cannot achieve an abnormal or excess return. The excess return is defined with respect to some benchmark expected return, such as that from the security market line (SML) of Chapter 11. The investor must still decide how risky a portfolio she wants. In addition, a random dart thrower might wind up with all of the darts sticking into one or two high-risk stocks that deal in genetic engineering. Would you really want all of your stock investments in two such stocks?

The failure to understand this has often led to confusion about market efficiency. For example, sometimes it is wrongly argued that market efficiency means that it does not matter what you do because the efficiency of the market will protect the unwary. However, someone once remarked, "The efficient market protects the sheep from the wolves, but nothing can protect the sheep from themselves."

What efficiency does say is that the price investors pay when they buy a share of stock is a fair price in the sense that it reflects the value of that stock given the information that is available about it. Investors need not worry that they are paying too much for a stock with a low dividend or some other characteristic because the market has already incorporated it into the price. However, investors still have to worry about such things as their level of risk exposure and their degree of diversification.

Price Fluctuations
Much of the public is skeptical of efficiency because stock prices fluctuate from day to day. However, daily price movement is in no way inconsistent

---

[5]Burton Malkiel, *A Random Walk Down Wall Street: The Time-Tested Strategy for Successful Investing,* 10th ed. (New York: Norton, 2012).

[6]Older articles often referred to the benchmark of "dart-throwing monkeys." As government involvement in the securities industry grew, the benchmark was often restated as "dart-throwing congressional representatives."

with efficiency; a stock in an efficient market adjusts to new information by changing price. A great deal of new information comes into the stock market each day. In fact, the *absence* of daily price movements in a changing world might suggest an inefficiency.

Stockholder Disinterest Many laypeople are skeptical that the market price can be efficient if only a fraction of the outstanding shares changes hands on any given day. However, the number of traders in a stock on a given day is generally far less than the number of people following the stock. This is true because an individual will trade only when his appraisal of the value of the stock differs enough from the market price to justify incurring brokerage commissions and other transaction costs. Furthermore, even if the number of traders following a stock is small relative to the number of outstanding shareholders, the stock can be expected to be efficiently priced as long as a number of interested traders use the publicly available information. That is, the stock price can reflect the available information even if many stockholders never follow the stock and are not considering trading in the near future.

14.4 The Evidence

The evidence on the efficient market hypothesis is extensive, with studies covering the broad categories of weak form, semistrong form, and strong form efficiency. In the first category we investigate whether stock price changes are random. We review both *event studies* and studies of the performance of mutual funds in the second category. In the third category, we look at the performance of corporate insiders.

THE WEAK FORM

Weak form efficiency implies that a stock's past price movement is unrelated to the stock's future price movement. The work of Chapter 11 allows us to test this implication. In that chapter we discussed the concept of correlation between the returns on two different stocks. For example, the correlation between the return on General Motors and the return on Ford is likely to be relatively high because both stocks are in the same industry. Conversely, the correlation between the return on General Motors and the return on the stock of, say, a European fast-food chain is likely to be low.

Financial economists frequently speak of **serial correlation**, which involves only one security. This is the correlation between the current return on a security and the return on the same security over a later period. A positive coefficient of serial correlation for a particular stock indicates a tendency toward *continuation*. That is, a higher-than-average return today is likely to be followed by higher-than-average returns in the future. Similarly, a lower-than-average return today is likely to be followed by lower-than-average returns in the future.

A negative coefficient of serial correlation for a particular stock indicates a tendency toward *reversal*. A higher-than-average return today is likely to be followed by lower-than-average returns in the future. Similarly, a lower-than-average return today is likely to be followed by higher-than-average returns in the future. Both significantly positive and significantly negative serial correlation coefficients are indications of market inefficiencies; in either case, returns today can be used to predict future returns.

Serial correlation coefficients for stock returns near zero would be consistent with weak form efficiency. Thus, a current stock return that is higher than average is as likely to be followed by lower-than-average returns as by higher-than-average returns. Similarly, a current stock return that is lower than average is as likely to be followed by higher-than-average returns as by lower-than-average returns.

Table 14.1
Serial Correlation
Coefficients for
Selected Companies

Company	Serial Correlation Coefficient in 2013
Duke Energy	.0173
DuPont	.0006
General Electric	.0147
Medtronic	−.0438
Merck	−.0670
Qualcomm	−.0249
United Technologies	−.0349
Average for 100 largest companies in 2013	−.0376
Average for 100 largest companies in 2012	.0167

Duke Energy's coefficient of .0173 is slightly positive, implying that a positive return today makes a positive return tomorrow slightly more likely. Medtronic's coefficient is negative, implying that a positive return today makes a negative return tomorrow slightly more likely. However, the coefficients are so small relative to estimation error and transaction costs that the results are generally considered to be consistent with weak form efficient capital markets.

The first seven rows in Table 14.1 show the serial correlation coefficients for daily price changes for seven large U.S. companies. These coefficients indicate whether there are relationships between yesterday's return and today's return. As can be seen, four of the coefficients are negative, implying that a higher-than-average return today makes a lower-than-average return tomorrow more likely. Conversely, three of the coefficients are positive, implying that a higher-than-average return today makes a higher-than-average return tomorrow more likely.

The next to last line of the table indicates that the average serial correlation coefficient across the 100 largest U.S. stocks in 2013 was −.0376. Because correlation coefficients can, in principle, vary between −1 and +1, this average coefficient is small. Given both estimation errors and transaction costs, a number of this magnitude is generally considered to be consistent with weak form efficiency. In addition, the average coefficient was .0167 in 2012. Since the coefficient changed sign from 2012 to 2013, it is difficult to predict whether the average coefficient will be positive or negative in future years.

The weak form of the efficient market hypothesis has been tested in many other ways as well. Our view of the literature is that the evidence, taken as a whole, is consistent with weak form efficiency.

This finding raises an interesting thought: If price changes are truly random, why do so many believe that prices follow patterns? The work of both psychologists and statisticians suggests that most people simply do not know what randomness looks like. For example, consider Figure 14.4. The top graph was generated by a computer using random numbers and Equation 14.1. Yet we have found that people examining the chart generally see patterns. Different people see different patterns and forecast different future price movements. However, in our experience, viewers are all quite confident of the patterns they see.

Next, consider the bottom graph, which tracks actual movements in The Gap's stock price. This graph may look quite nonrandom to some, suggesting weak form inefficiency. However, it also bears a close visual resemblance to the simulated series, and statistical tests indicate that it indeed behaves like a purely random series. Thus, in our opinion, people claiming to see patterns in stock price data are probably seeing optical illusions.

Figure 14.4
Simulated and
Actual Stock Price
Movements

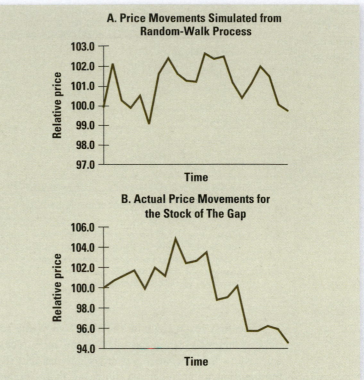

Although stock price movements simulated from a random-walk process are random by definition, people often see patterns. People may also see patterns in The Gap's price movements. However, the price patterns of The Gap are quite similar to those of the randomly simulated series.

THE SEMISTRONG FORM

The semistrong form of the efficient market hypothesis implies that prices should reflect all publicly available information. We present two types of tests of this form.

Event Studies   The *abnormal return* (AR) on a given stock for a particular day can be calculated by subtracting the market's return on the same day (R_m)—as measured by a broad-based index such as the S&P Composite Index—from the actual return (R) on the stock for that day.[7] We write this difference algebraically as:

$$AR = R - R_m$$

The following system will help us understand tests of the semistrong form:

Information released on day $t - 1 \rightarrow AR_{t-1}$
Information released on day $t \qquad \rightarrow AR_t$
Information released on day $t + 1 \rightarrow AR_{t+1}$

The arrows indicate that the abnormal return in any time period is related only to the information released during that period.

---

[7]We can also measure the abnormal return by using the market model. In this case, the abnormal return is:
$$AR = R - (\alpha + \beta R_m)$$

Figure 14.5   Cumulative Abnormal Returns for Companies Announcing Dividend Omissions

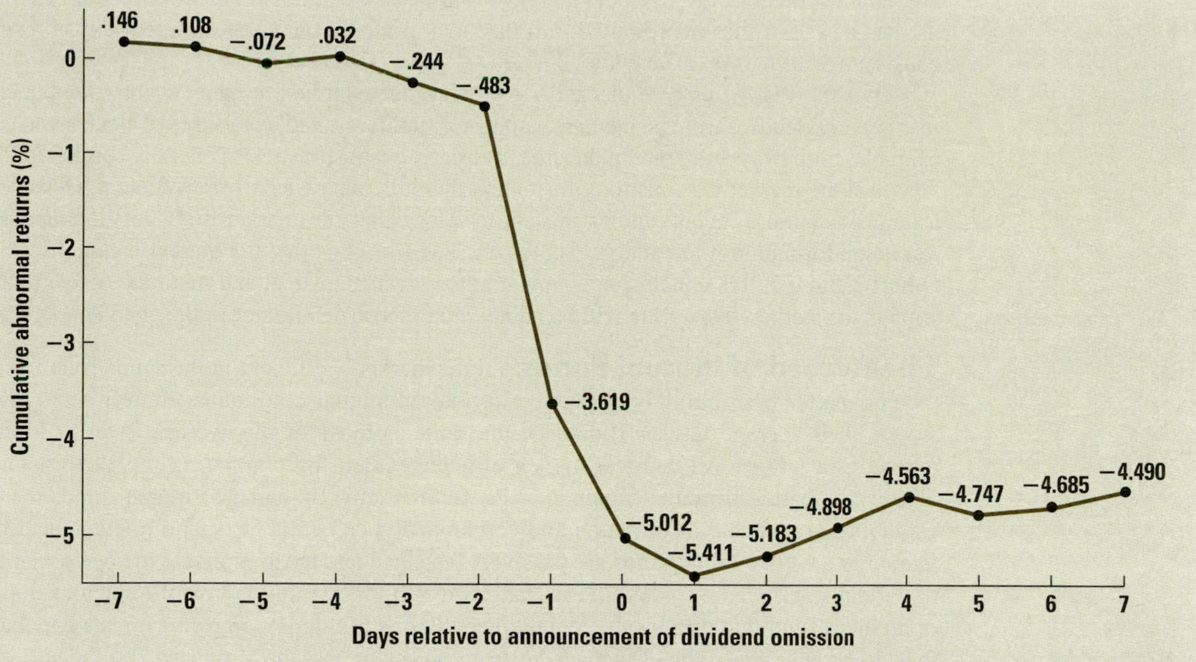

Cumulative abnormal returns (CARs) fall on both the day before the announcement and the day of the announcement of dividend omissions. CARs have little movement after the announcement date. This pattern is consistent with market efficiency.

SOURCE: From Exhibit 2 in Samuel H. Szewczyk, George P. Tsetsekos, and Zaher Z. Zantout, "Do Dividend Omissions Signal Future Earnings or Past Earnings?" *Journal of Investing* (Spring 1997).

According to the efficient market hypothesis, a stock's abnormal return at day t, AR_t, should reflect the release of information at the same day, t. Any information released before then should have no effect on abnormal returns in this period because all of its influence should have been felt before. In other words, an efficient market would already have incorporated previous information into prices. Because a stock's return today cannot depend on what the market does not yet know, information that will be known only in the future cannot influence the stock's return either. Hence, the arrows point in the direction that is shown, with information in any period affecting only that period's abnormal return. *Event studies* are statistical studies that examine whether the arrows are as shown or whether the release of information influences returns on other days.

These studies also speak of *cumulative abnormal returns* (CARs), as well as abnormal returns (ARs). As an example, consider a firm with ARs of 1 percent, −3 percent, and 6 percent for Dates −1, 0, and 1, respectively, relative to a corporate announcement. The CARs for Dates −1, 0, and 1 would be 1 percent, −2 percent [=1 percent + (−3 percent)], and 4 percent [=1 percent + (−3 percent) + 6 percent], respectively.

As an example, consider the study by Szewczyk, Tsetsekos, and Zantout[8] on dividend omissions. Figure 14.5 shows the plot of CARs for a sample of companies announcing dividend omissions. Because dividend omissions are generally considered to be bad events, we would expect abnormal returns to be negative around the time of the announcements. They are, as evidenced by a drop in the CAR on both the day before the announcement

[8]Samuel H. Szewczyk, George P. Tsetsekos, and Zaher Z. Zantout, "Do Dividend Omissions Signal Future Earnings or Past Earnings?" *Journal of Investing* (Spring 1997).

(Day −1) and the day of the announcement (Day 0).[9] However, note that there is virtually no movement in the CARs in the days following the announcement. This implies that the bad news is fully incorporated into the stock price by the announcement day, a result consistent with market efficiency.

Over the years, this type of methodology has been applied to many events. Announcements of dividends, earnings, mergers, capital expenditures, and new issues of stock are a few examples of the vast literature in the area. The early event study tests generally supported the view that the market is semistrong form (and therefore also weak form) efficient. However, a number of more recent studies present evidence that the market does not impound all relevant information immediately. Some conclude from this that the market is not efficient. Others argue that this conclusion is unwarranted given statistical and methodological problems in the studies. This issue will be addressed in more detail later in the chapter.

The Record of Mutual Funds   If the market is efficient in the semistrong form, then no matter what publicly available information mutual fund managers rely on to pick stocks, their average returns should be the same as those of the average investor in the market as a whole. We can test market efficiency, then, by comparing the performance of actively managed mutual funds to index funds. Actively managed mutual funds try to use publicly available information and certain analytical skills to perform better than the market as a whole. Index funds are passively managed and try to replicate the performance of certain stock market indexes. The Vanguard 500 Index Fund is a well-known example of an index fund that mimics the Standard and Poor's 500 Index. Figure 14.6 is a bar chart that shows the percentage of managed equity funds that beat the Vanguard 500 Index Fund in each year from 1986 to 2011. In only 9 of the 26 years did more than half of the professional money managers beat the Vanguard 500 Index Fund.

Perhaps nothing rankles successful stock market investors more than to have some professor tell them that they are not necessarily smart, just lucky. However, while Figure 14.6 represents only one study, there have been many papers on mutual funds. The overwhelming evidence here is that mutual funds, on average, do not beat broad-based indexes.

By and large, mutual fund managers rely on publicly available information. Thus the finding that they do not outperform market indexes is consistent with semistrong form and weak form efficiency.

However, this evidence does not imply that mutual funds are bad investments for individuals. Though these funds fail to achieve better returns than some indexes of the market, they permit the investor to buy a portfolio of many stocks (the phrase "a well-diversified portfolio" is often used). They might also provide a variety of services such as keeping custody and records of all the stocks.

THE STRONG FORM

Even the strongest adherents to the efficient market hypothesis would not be surprised to find that markets are inefficient in the strong form. After all, if an individual has information that no one else has, it is likely that she can profit from it.

---

[9]An astute reader may wonder why the abnormal return is negative on Day −1 as well as on Day 0. To see why, first note that the announcement date is generally taken in academic studies to be the publication date of the story in *The Wall Street Journal* *(WSJ)*. Then consider a company announcing a dividend omission via a press release at noon on Tuesday. The stock should fall on Tuesday. The announcement will be reported in the *WSJ* on Wednesday because the Tuesday edition of the *WSJ* has already been printed. For this firm the stock price falls on the day *before* the announcement in the *WSJ*.

Alternatively, imagine another firm announcing a dividend omission via a press release on Tuesday at 8 p.m. Because the stock market is closed at that late hour, the stock price will fall on Wednesday. Because the *WSJ* will report the announcement on Wednesday, the stock price falls on the day of the announcement in the *WSJ*.

Firms may either make announcements during trading hours or after trading hours, so stocks should fall on both Day −1 and Day 0 relative to publication in the *WSJ*.

Figure 14.6
Percentage of
Managed Equity
Funds Beating
the Vanguard
500 Index Fund, One-
Year Returns

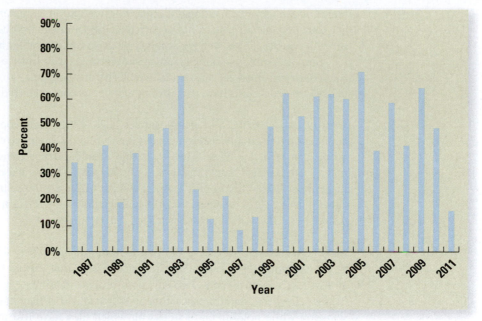

SOURCE: Bradford D. Jordan, Thomas W. Miller, and Steven D. Dolvin, *Fundamentals of Investments,* 7th ed. (New York: McGraw-Hill, 2014).

One group of studies of strong form efficiency investigates insider trading. Insiders in firms have access to information that is not generally available. But if the strong form of the efficient market hypothesis holds, they should not be able to profit by trading on their information. A U.S. government agency, the Securities and Exchange Commission, requires insiders in companies to report trades they make in their own company's stock. By examining records of such trades, we can see whether they made abnormal returns. A number of studies support the view that these trades were abnormally profitable. Thus, strong form efficiency does not seem to be substantiated by the evidence.

14.5 The Behavioral Challenge to Market Efficiency

In Section 14.2 we presented Professor Shleifer's three conditions, any one of which will lead to market efficiency. In that section we made a case that at least one of the conditions is likely to hold in the real world. However, there is definitely disagreement here. Many members of the academic community (including Professor Shleifer) argue that none of the three conditions is likely to hold in reality. This point of view is based on what is called *behavioral finance.* Let us examine the behavioral view of each of these three conditions.

RATIONALITY

Are people really rational? Not always. Just travel to Atlantic City or Las Vegas to see people gambling, sometimes with large sums of money. The casino's take implies a negative expected return for the gambler. Because gambling is risky and has a negative expected return, it can never be a rational thing to do. In addition, gamblers will often bet on black at a roulette table after black has occurred a number of consecutive times, thinking that the run will continue. This strategy is faulty because roulette tables have no memory.

But, of course, gambling is only a sideshow as far as finance is concerned. Do we see irrationality in financial markets as well? The answer seems to be yes, so much so that behavioral economists have names for a number of common irrational investing behaviors.

Overconfidence Academic studies have shown that people are, on average, overconfident. For example, ask someone if he or she is a better driver than average and about 80 percent will say, "Yes." How does this overconfidence translate to investing performance? Researchers argue that overconfidence is likely to cause an investor to overestimate his or her ability to pick the best stocks, leading to more trading. Empirical studies show that the most frequent traders significantly underperform the least frequent ones, primarily because of the costs associated with trading.

Regret/Pride Regret is the bad feeling you get when something goes awry and you are the one responsible. Psychologists tell us that people hate the feeling of regret and will do a lot to avoid it. Does the possibility of feeling regret affect our investments? Studies show that investors are prone to sell stocks that they have made money on (their winners) while holding on to stocks on which they have lost money (their losers). The explanation is that selling your losers causes regret. You look at that round-trip transaction and see a failure. If you still hold on to the stock, you don't have to admit to yourself that you have made a mistake because the stock could still go up. Conversely, selling your winners gives you pride, the opposite of regret. You can see the round-trip transaction as a success.

Selling your winners while holding onto your losers is called the *disposition effect.* Unfortunately, this trading pattern has bad tax consequences. You have to pay taxes on the capital gains from your winners while not being able to take the tax deductions from your losers.

Familiarity Why do most people root for their home-town football team, rather than a football team a thousand miles away? Psychologists tell us that people are often guilty of *familiarity*. That is, we like what we are familiar with. Familiarity is a rather innocuous trait in most areas of life but it can lead to something unfortunate in investing: underdiversification. For example, a number of studies show that individuals overinvest in their own country, reducing their level of international diversification. The investor's attitude appears to be "I live in a particular country, I'm familiar with that country and, doggone it, I'm going to invest in that country." This overinvestment in the stock market of one's home country is often called *home bias*. And there is even domestic home bias. Research shows that individuals often overinvest in stocks headquartered in their home town. Other studies report that employees typically overweight their employer's stock in their 401(k) employer-based savings plan.

Representativeness (also called *Overreaction*) This attribute can be illustrated with the gambling example we used earlier. Gamblers believing a run of black will continue are in error, because the probability of a black spin is still only about 50 percent. These gamblers are guilty of representativeness because they draw conclusions from insufficient data, generally from the recent past. For example, during the great bull market between 1995 and 1999, many investors thought the market would continue its big gains for a long time, forgetting that bear markets also occur.

Conservatism   As *representativeness* is another word for *overreaction, conservatism* is another word for *underreaction*. Human beings often underreact, as was the case with the Telegraph Company, which later became Western Union. The firm was not worried about Alexander Graham Bell's invention of the telephone, as indicated by the following statement the firm released in 1876:[10]

> The "Telephone purports" to transmit the speaking voice over telegraph wires. We found that the voice is very weak and indistinct, and grows even weaker when long wires are used between the sender and receiver. . . . Furthermore, why would any person want to use this ungainly and impractical device when he can send a messenger to the local telegraph office and have a clear written message sent to any large city in the United States?

Does underreaction affect the stock market? Research suggests that investors as a whole often underreact to new information. For example, a number of studies report that prices seem to adjust slowly to the information contained in earnings announcements.[11] These papers suggest that an investor can profit from a strategy of buying a stock after an announcement of a surprisingly high earnings number and selling a stock after an announcement of a surprisingly low earnings number. More will be said of this research in the next section.

Risk-Taking Following Gains or Losses

House Money Effect   How do individuals adjust their risk-taking following gains? A number of studies show that, on average, individuals increase their risk following gains. For example, Las Vegas casinos find that gamblers are more likely to take big risks after winning money from casinos, since they are no longer just playing with their own money but with the *house's money* as well.

Snakebite Effect and Get-Evenitis   How do individuals adjust their risk-taking following losses? Here the evidence is two-sided. Some studies show that individuals reduce their level of risk following losses. In other words, they get *snakebit*. Getting snakebit is quite understandable. Imagine yourself after the stock market fell 22 percent on October 19, 1987. You might never have seen such an extreme drop. In response, you might well reduce your equity holdings, if not get out of the stock market completely: behavior in line with the expression "Once bitten, twice shy."

But that is not the only way to react to losses. A number of studies show that people increase their level of risk in order to get even. In other words, they acquire a case of *get-evenitis*.[12]

INDEPENDENT DEVIATIONS FROM RATIONALITY

The previous list of behavioral traits suggests that investors can be irrational much of the time. Are the deviations from rationality generally random, thereby likely to cancel out in a large population of investors? To the contrary, since psychologists conclude

---

[10]Prof. R. Levine, Electrical Engineering Department, Southern Methodist University, EETS8302 (NTU TC716-N) Digital Telephony, Fall 2001." See Course material from Professor R. Levine, Electrical Engineering Department, Southern Methodist University, course EETS8302 (NTU TC716-N), Digital Telephony, Fall 2001, http://lyle.smu.edu/~levine/ee8320/wulet.pdf.

[11]For example, see Vijay Singal, *Beyond the Random Walk* (New York: Oxford University Press, 2004), Chapter 4.

[12]Joshua Coval and Tyler Shumway, "Do Behavioral Biases Affect Prices," *Journal of Finance* (2005), pp. 1–34.

that the above irrational traits are rather pervasive across individuals, behavioral economists argue that these deviations from rationality cannot be expected to cancel each other out.

Rather than go through all of the traits we discussed, let's work with just two: representativeness and conservatism, where the case can be made that deviations from rationality across individuals do not cancel each other out. We said that individuals have a tendency to overreact to information, particularly if it is recent. Some researchers suggest that this representativeness can cause bubbles. People see a sector of the stock market, for example, some internet stocks having a short history of high revenue growth and extrapolate that the high revenue growth will continue forever, leading to high price–to–earnings and price–to–book–value multiples for these stocks. When the revenue growth inevitably slows, investors reduce these multiples, implying that stock prices will fall.

Other research suggests that the market often underreacts to new information, implying that conservatism dominates the market at times. For example, we mentioned earlier that prices adjust slowly to the information in earnings announcements. This is an example where investors as a whole appear to underreact to information, so that the slowness to respond to new information by some investors is not canceled out by rapid reaction to the same information by other investors.

ARBITRAGE

As discussed above, behavioral economists do not believe that deviations from rationality must be independent across individuals. However, in Section 14.2 we suggested that professional investors, knowing that securities are mispriced, could buy the underpriced ones while selling correctly priced (or even overpriced) substitutes. This might undo any mispricing caused by emotional amateurs.

Trading of this sort is likely to be more risky than it appears at first glance. Suppose professionals generally believed that McDonald's stock was underpriced. They would buy it while selling their holdings in, say, Burger King and Wendy's. However, if amateurs were taking opposite positions, prices would adjust to correct levels only if the positions of amateurs were small relative to those of the professionals. In a world of many amateurs, a few professionals would have to take big positions to bring prices into line, perhaps even engaging heavily in short selling. Buying large amounts of one stock and short selling large amounts of other stocks is quite risky, even if the two stocks are in the same industry. Here, unanticipated bad news about McDonald's and unanticipated good news about the other two stocks would cause the professionals to register large losses.

In addition, if amateurs mispriced McDonald's today, what is to prevent McDonald's from being even *more* mispriced tomorrow? This risk of further mispricing, even in the presence of no new information, may also cause professionals to cut back their arbitrage positions. As an example, imagine a shrewd professional who believed Internet stocks were overpriced in 1998. Had he bet on a decline at that time, he would have lost in the near term since prices rose through March 2000. While his position would have eventually made money because prices later fell, near-term risk may reduce the size of arbitrage strategies.

In conclusion, the arguments presented here suggest that the theoretical underpinnings of the efficient capital markets hypothesis, presented in Section 14.2, might not hold in reality. That is, investors may be irrational, irrationality may be related across investors rather than canceling out across investors, and arbitrage strategies may involve too much risk to eliminate market inefficiencies.

14.6 Empirical Challenges to Market Efficiency

Section 14.4 presented empirical evidence supportive of market efficiency. We now present evidence challenging this hypothesis. (Adherents of market efficiency generally refer to results of this type as *anomalies*.)

1. *Limits to arbitrage:* Royal Dutch Petroleum and Shell Transport agreed to merge their interests in 1907, with all subsequent cash flows being split on a 60 percent–40 percent basis between the two companies. However, both companies continued to be publicly traded. You might imagine that the market value of Royal Dutch would always be 1.5 (=60/40) times that of Shell. That is, if Royal Dutch ever became overpriced, rational investors would buy Shell instead of Royal Dutch. If Royal Dutch were underpriced, investors would buy Royal Dutch. In addition, arbitrageurs would go further by buying the underpriced security and selling the overpriced security short.

    However, Figure 14.7 shows that Royal Dutch and Shell rarely traded at parity (i.e., 60/40) between 1962 and 2005, at which time the two companies merged. Why would these deviations occur? As stated in the previous section, behavioral finance suggests that there are limits to arbitrage. That is, an investor buying the overpriced asset and selling the underpriced asset does not have a sure thing. Deviations from parity could actually *increase* in the short run, implying losses for the arbitrageur. The well-known statement, "Markets can stay irrational longer than you can stay solvent," attributed to John Maynard Keynes, applies here. Thus, risk considerations may force arbitrageurs to take positions that are too small to move prices back to parity.

Figure 14.7

Deviations of the Ratio of the Market Value of Royal Dutch to the Market Value of Shell from Parity

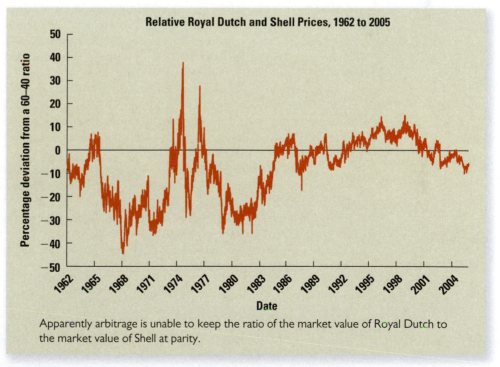

Apparently arbitrage is unable to keep the ratio of the market value of Royal Dutch to the market value of Shell at parity.

SOURCE: Stephen Ross, Randolph Westerfield, and Bradford Jordan, *Fundamentals of Corporate Finance*, 11th ed., Alternate ed., p. 752. (New York: McGraw-Hill, 2016.)

Academics have documented a number of these deviations from parity. Froot and Dabora show similar results for both the twin companies of Unilever N.V. and Unilever PLC and for two classes of SmithKline Beecham stock.[13] Lamont and Thaler present similar findings for 3Com and its subsidiary Palm, Inc. (see Example 14.2 for more about 3Com and Palm).[14] Other researchers find price behavior in closed-end mutual funds suggestive of parity deviations.

2. *Earnings surprises:* Common sense suggests that prices should rise when earnings are reported to be higher than expected and prices should fall when the reverse occurs. However, market efficiency implies that prices will adjust immediately to the announcement, while behavioral finance would predict another pattern. Kolasinski and Li rank companies by the extent of their *earnings surprise*—that is, the difference between current quarterly earnings and an estimate of earnings for that quarter anticipated by the market.[15] The authors form a portfolio of companies with the most

**EXAMPLE
14.2**

Can Stock Market Investors Add and Subtract?   On March 2, 2000, 3Com, a profitable provider of computer networking products and services, sold 5 percent of one of its subsidiaries, Palm, to the public via an initial public offering (IPO). 3Com planned to distribute the remaining Palm shares to 3Com shareholders at a later date. Under the plan, if you owned one share of 3Com, you would receive 1.5 shares of Palm. So after 3Com sold part of Palm via the IPO, investors could buy Palm shares directly or indirectly by purchasing shares of 3Com and waiting.

What makes this case interesting is what happened in the days that followed the Palm IPO. If you owned one 3Com share, you would be entitled, eventually, to 1.5 shares of Palm. Therefore, each 3Com share should be worth *at least* 1.5 times the value of each Palm share. We say *at least* because the other parts of 3Com were profitable. As a result, each 3Com share should have been worth much more than 1.5 times the value of one Palm share. But as you might guess, things did not work out this way.

The day before the Palm IPO, shares in 3Com sold for $104.13. After the first day of trading, Palm closed at $95.06 per share. Multiplying $95.06 by 1.5 results in $142.59, which is the minimum value we would expect to pay for 3Com. But the day Palm closed at $95.06, 3Com shares closed at $81.81, more than $60 lower than the price implied by Palm.

A 3Com price of $81.81 when Palm was selling for $95.06 implies that the market valued the rest of 3Com's businesses (per share) at $81.81 − 142.59 = −$60.78. Given the number of 3Com shares outstanding at the time, this means the market placed a *negative* value of about $22 billion on the rest of 3Com's businesses. Of course, a stock price cannot be negative. This means that the price of Palm relative to 3Com was much too high.

To profit from this mispricing, investors would purchase shares of 3Com and sell shares of Palm. This trade was a no-brainer. In a well-functioning market arbitrage traders would force the prices into alignment quickly. What happened?

As you can see in Figure 14.8, the market valued 3Com and Palm shares in such a way that the non-Palm part of 3Com had a negative value for about two months from March 2, 2000, until May 8, 2000. Thus, the pricing error was corrected by market forces, but not instantly, which is consistent with the existence of limits to arbitrage.

[13]Kenneth A. Froot and Emil M. Dabora, "How Are Stock Prices Affected by the Location of Trade?" *Journal of Financial Economics* 53 (August 1999).

[14]Owen Lamont and Richard Thaler, "Can the Market Add and Subtract? Mispricing in Tech Stock Carve-Outs," *Journal of Political Economy* (April 2003).

[15]Adam Kolasinski and Xu Li, "Can Rational Learning Explain Underreaction Anomalies? Evidence from Insider Trading after Earnings Announcements," (University of Washington unpublished paper, 2011). The authors estimated anticipated earnings by a seasonal random walk model.

Figure 14.8   The Percentage Difference between One Share of 3Com and One and One-Half Shares of Palm, March 2, 2000, to July 27, 2000

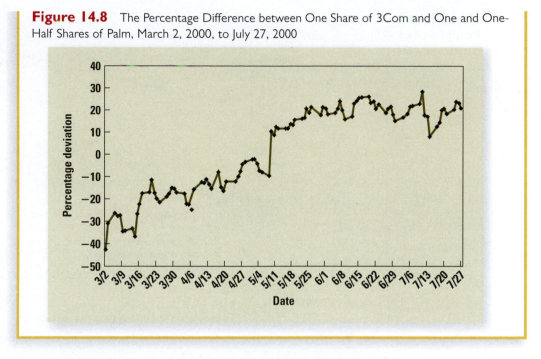

extreme positive surprises and another portfolio of companies with the most extreme negative surprises. Figure 14.9 shows returns from buying the two portfolios, net of the return on the overall market. As can be seen, prices adjust slowly to earnings announcements, with the portfolio with the positive surprises outperforming the portfolio with the negative surprises over the next 275 days. Many other researchers obtain similar results.

Why do prices adjust slowly? Behavioral finance suggests that investors exhibit conservatism because they are slow to adjust to the information contained in the announcements.

3. *Size:* In 1981, two important papers presented evidence that in the United States, the returns on stocks with small market capitalizations were greater than the returns on stocks with large market capitalizations over most of the 20th century.[16] The studies have since been replicated over different periods and in different countries. For example, Figure 14.10 shows average returns over the period from 1926 to 2013 for 10 portfolios of U.S. stocks ranked by size. As can be seen, the average return on small stocks is higher than the average return on large stocks. Although much of the differential performance is merely compensation for the extra risk of small stocks, researchers have generally argued that not all of it can be explained by risk differences. In addition, it appears that most of the difference in performance occurs in the month of January.[17]

4. *Value versus growth:* A number of papers have argued that stocks with high book-value-to-stock-price ratios and/or high earnings-to-price ratios (generally called *value stocks*) outperform stocks with low ratios (*growth stocks*). For example,

---

[16]See Rolt Banz, "The Relationship between Return and Market Value of Common Stocks," *Journal of Financial Economics* (March 1981), and Mark Reinganum, "Misspecification of Capital Asset Pricing: Empirical Anomalies Based on Earnings' Yields and Market Values," *Journal of Financial Economics* (March 1981).

[17]The first paper to document this "January effect," was Donald Keim, "Size-Related Anomalies and Stock Return Seasonality: Further Empirical Evidence," *Journal of Financial Economics* (June 1983).

Figure 14.9

Returns on Two Investment Strategies Based on Earnings Surprise

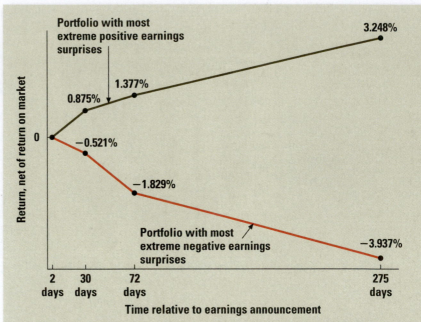

This figure shows returns net of the market return on a strategy of buying stocks with extremely high positive earnings surprises (the difference between current quarterly earnings and an estimate of earnings for that quarter anticipated by the market) and on a strategy of buying stocks with extremely high negative earnings surprises. The strategy begins two days after earnings announcement. The graph shows a slow adjustment to information in earnings announcements.

SOURCE: Adapted from Table 1 of Adam Kolasinski and Xu Li, "Can Rational Learning Explain Underreaction Anomalies? Evidence from Insider Trading after Earnings Announcements," (University of Washington unpublished paper, 2011).

Figure 14.10

Annual Stock Returns on Portfolios Sorted by Size (Market Capitalization) from 1926 to 2013

Historically, the average return on small stocks has been above the average return on large stocks.

SOURCE: Calculated from Index values provided in Table 7.3 of *Ibbotson SBBI® 2014 Classic Yearbook*, Chicago: Morningstar (2014).

Figure 14.11
Monthly Return Difference Between High Book-to-Price Stocks (value stocks) and Low Book-to-Price Stocks (growth stocks) around the World

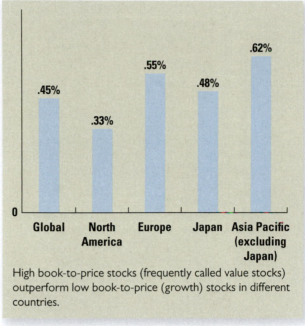

High book-to-price stocks (frequently called value stocks) outperform low book-to-price (growth) stocks in different countries.

SOURCE: Eugene F. Fama, and Kenneth R. French, "Size, Value, and Momentum in International Stock Returns," Journal of Financial Economics 105, no. 3 (2012), Table 1

Fama and French[18] found higher average returns for value stocks than for growth stocks around the world. Figure 14.11 shows the average monthly return differential between value and growth stocks in different geographical regions.

Because the return difference is so large and because these ratios can be obtained so easily for individual stocks, the results may constitute strong evidence against market efficiency. However, a number of papers suggest that the unusual returns are due to differences in risk, not to a true inefficiency.[19] Because the debate revolves around arcane statistical points, we will not pursue the issue further. However, it is safe to say that no conclusion is warranted at this time. As with so many other topics in finance and economics, further research is needed.

5. *Crashes and bubbles*: The stock market crash of October 19, 1987, is extremely puzzling. The market dropped between 20 percent and 25 percent on a Monday following a weekend during which little surprising news was released. A drop of this magnitude for no apparent reason is not consistent with market efficiency. Because the crash of 1929 is still an enigma, it is doubtful that the more recent 1987 debacle will be explained anytime soon—not to mention the crash of 2008, which we discussed in Chapter 10. The recent comments of an eminent historian are apt here: When asked what, in his opinion, the effect of the French Revolution of 1789 was, he replied that it was too early to tell.

Perhaps stock market crashes are evidence consistent with the **bubble theory** of speculative markets. That is, security prices sometimes move wildly above their

---

[18]Taken from Table I of Eugene F. Fama and Kenneth R. French, "Size, Value, and Momentum in International Stock Returns," *Journal of Financial Economics* 105, no. 3 (2012).

[19]For example, see E. F. Fama and K. R. French, "Multifactor Explanations of Asset Pricing Anomalies," *Journal of Finance* 51 (March 1996) and Hengjie Ai and Dana Kiku, "Growth to Value: Option Exercise and the Cross Section of Equity Returns," *Journal of Financial Economics* 107, no. 2 (February 2013).

Figure 14.12
Value of Index of
Internet Stocks

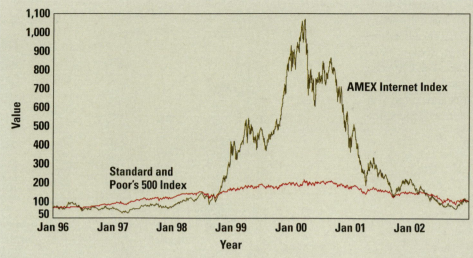

The index of Internet stocks rose over tenfold from the beginning of 1996 to its high in March 2000 before falling to approximately its original level in 2002.

true values. Eventually, prices fall back to their original level, causing great losses for investors. Consider, for example, the behavior of Internet stocks of the late 1990s. Figure 14.12 shows values of an index of Internet stocks from 1996 through 2002. The index rose over tenfold from January 1996 to its high in March 2000 before retreating to approximately its original level in 2002. For comparison, the figure also shows price movement for the Standard & Poor's 500 Index. While this index rose and fell over the same period, the price movement was quite muted relative to that of Internet stocks.

Many commentators describe the rise and fall of Internet stocks as a *bubble*. Is it correct to do so? Unfortunately, there is no precise definition of the term. Some academics argue that the price movement in the figure is consistent with rationality. Prices rose initially, they say, because it appeared that the Internet would soon capture a large chunk of international commerce. Prices fell when later evidence suggested this would not occur quite so quickly. However, others argue that the initial rosy scenario was never supported by the facts. Rather, prices rose due to nothing more than "irrational exuberance."

14.7 Reviewing the Differences

It is fair to say that the controversy over efficient capital markets has not yet been resolved. Rather, academic financial economists have sorted themselves into three camps, with some adhering to market efficiency, some believing in behavioral finance, and others (perhaps the majority) convinced of a combination of the two approaches. This state of affairs is certainly different from, say, 40 years ago, when market efficiency went unchallenged. We think that the evidence suggests security prices in most large capital markets around the world reflect a lot of information. However, it seems it is clear that from time to time behavioral forces can be significant. In any case, the controversy here is one of the most contentious of any area of financial economics.

Adherents of behavioral finance point out, as discussed in Section 14.5, that the three theoretical foundations of market efficiency appear to be violated in the real world. Second, they stress that there are simply too many anomalies, with a number of them having been replicated in out-of-sample tests.[20] Critics of behavioral finance generally make three points in rebuttal:

1. *The file drawer problem:* Scholars generally submit their papers to academic journals, where independent referees judge whether the work is deserving of publication. Papers either get accepted in a journal, leading to potential influence in the field, or they get rejected, leaving the author to, as the phrase goes, bury the paper "in his file drawer." It has been frequently suggested that, holding quality of research constant, referees are more likely to accept a paper with unusual and interesting results. Critics of behavioral finance argue that, since market efficiency has been the received paradigm in finance, any paper challenging efficiency has a higher probability of acceptance than one supporting efficiency. Thus, the publication process may inadvertently favor behavioral finance research.

2. *Risk:* As indicated in Chapter 11, investors try to maximize expected return per unit of risk. However, risk is not always easy to estimate. Efficient market adherents often suggest that some anomalies might disappear if more sophisticated adjustments for risk were made. As an example, we mentioned in the previous section that a number of researchers have argued that the high returns on value stocks can be explained by their higher risk.

3. *Behavioral finance and market prices:* Critics of behavioral finance *often* argue that, even if the data support certain anomalies, it is not clear that these anomalies support behavioral finance. For example, consider representativeness and conservatism, two psychological principles mentioned earlier in this chapter.

Representativeness implies overweighting the results of small samples, as with the gambler who thinks a few consecutive spins of black on the roulette wheel make black a more likely outcome than red on the next spin. Financial economists argue that representativeness can lead to *overreaction* in stock returns. We mentioned earlier that financial bubbles are likely overreactions to news. Internet companies showed great revenue growth for a short time in the late 1990s, causing many to believe that this growth would continue indefinitely. Stock prices rose (too much) at this point. When at last investors realized that this growth could not be sustained, prices plummeted.

Conservatism states that individuals adjust their beliefs too slowly to new information. A market composed of this type of investor would likely lead to stock prices that *underreact* in the presence of new information. The example concerning earnings surprises may illustrate this underreaction. Prices rose slowly following announcements of positive earnings surprises. Announcements of negative surprises had a similar, but opposite, reaction.

Efficient market believers stress that representativeness and conservatism have opposite implications for stock prices. Which principle, they ask, should dominate in any particular situation? In other words, why should investors overreact to news about Internet stocks but underreact to earnings news? Proponents of market efficiency say that unless behaviorists can answer these two questions satisfactorily, we should not reject market efficiency in favor of behavioral finance.[21]

---

[20]Excellent reviews of behavioral finance can be found in Andrei Shleifer, *Inefficient Markets: An Introduction to Behavioral Finance*, op. cit., and in John Nofsinger, *The Psychology of Investing*, 5th ed. (New York: Prentice Hall, 2014).

[21]See, for example, Eugene F. Fama, "Market Efficiency, Long-Term Returns, and Behavioral Finance," *Journal of Financial Economics* 49 (1998).

While we have devoted more space in this section to arguments supporting market efficiency than to arguments supporting behavioral finance, you should not take this difference as evidence against the usefulness of behavioral finance. Rather, the jury, the community of financial economists in this case, is still out here. It does not appear that our textbook, or any textbook, can easily resolve the differing points of view.

14.8 Implications for Corporate Finance

So far this chapter has examined both theoretical arguments and empirical evidence concerning efficient markets. We now ask whether market efficiency has any relevance for corporate financial managers. The answer is that it does. Next, we consider four implications of efficiency for managers.

1. ACCOUNTING CHOICES, FINANCIAL CHOICES, AND MARKET EFFICIENCY

The accounting profession provides firms with a significant amount of leeway in their reporting practices. For example, companies may choose between the last-in, first-out (LIFO) or the first-in, first-out (FIFO) method of valuing inventories. They may choose either the percentage-of-completion or the completed-contract method for construction projects. They may depreciate physical assets by either accelerated or straight-line depreciation.

Managers clearly prefer high stock prices to low stock prices. Should managers use the leeway in accounting choices to report the highest possible income? Not necessarily. That is, accounting choices should not affect stock price if two conditions hold. First, enough information must be provided in the annual report so that financial analysts can construct earnings under the alternative accounting methods. This appears to be the case for many, though not necessarily all, accounting choices. Second, the market must be efficient in the semistrong form. In other words, the market must appropriately use all of this accounting information in determining the market price.

Of course, the issue of whether accounting choices affect stock prices is ultimately an empirical matter. A number of academic papers have addressed this issue. Kaplan and Roll found that the switch from accelerated to straight-line depreciation did not affect stock prices.[22] Kaplan and Roll also looked at changes from the deferral method of accounting for the investment tax credit to the flow-through method.[23] They found that a switch would increase accounting earnings but had no effect on stock prices.

Several other accounting procedures have been studied. Hong, Kaplan, and Mandelker found no evidence that the stock market was affected by the artificially higher earnings reported using the pooling method, compared to the purchase method, for reporting mergers and acquisitions.[24] Biddle and Lindahl found that firms switching to the LIFO method of inventory valuation experienced an increase in stock price.[25] This is to be expected in inflationary environments because LIFO valuation can reduce taxes compared to FIFO. They found that the larger the tax decrease resulting from the use of LIFO, the greater

---

[22]Robert Kaplan and R. Roll, "Investor Evaluation of Accounting Information: Some Empirical Evidence," *Journal of Business* 45 (April 1972).

[23]Before 1987, U.S. tax law allowed a 10 percent tax credit on the purchase of most kinds of capital equipment.

[24]Harrison Hong, R. S. Kaplan, and G. Mandelker, "Pooling vs. Purchase: The Effects of Accounting for Mergers on Stock Prices," *Accounting Review* 53 (1978). The pooling method for mergers is no longer allowed under generally accepted accounting principles.

[25]Gary Biddle and F. W. Lindahl, "Stock Price Reactions to LIFO Adoptions: The Association Between Excess Returns and LIFO Tax Savings," *Journal of Accounting Research* (1982).

was the increase in stock price. In summary, empirical evidence suggests that accounting changes do not fool the market. Therefore, the evidence does not suggest that managers can boost stock prices through accounting practices. In other words, the market appears efficient enough to see through different accounting choices.

One caveat is called for here. Our discussion specifically assumed that "financial analysts can construct earnings under the alternative accounting methods." However, companies like Enron, WorldCom, Global Crossing, and Xerox all simply reported fraudulent numbers in the past. There was no way for financial analysts to construct alternative earnings numbers because these analysts were unaware how the reported numbers were determined. So it was not surprising that the prices of these stocks initially rose well above fair value. Yes, managers can boost prices in this way—as long as they are willing to serve time once they are caught!

Is there anything else that investors can be expected to see through in an efficient market? Consider stock splits and stock dividends. Today, Amarillo Corporation has 1 million shares outstanding and reports $10 million of earnings. In the hopes of boosting the stock price, the firm's chief financial officer (CFO), Ms. Green, recommends to the board of directors that Amarillo have a 2-for-1 stock split. That is, a shareholder with 100 shares prior to the split would have 200 shares after the split. The CFO contends that each investor would feel richer after the split because he would own more shares.

However, this thinking runs counter to market efficiency. A rational investor knows that he would own the same proportion of the firm after the split as before the split. For example, our investor with 100 shares owns 1/10,000 (=100/1 million) of Amarillo's shares prior to the split. His share of the earnings would be $1,000 (=$10 million/10,000). Although he would own 200 shares after the split, there would now be 2 million shares outstanding. Thus, he still would own 1/10,000 of the firm. His share of the earnings would still be $1,000 because the stock split would not affect the earnings of the entire firm.

2. THE TIMING DECISION

Imagine a firm whose managers are contemplating the date to issue equity. This decision is frequently called the *timing* decision. If managers believe that their stock is overpriced, they are likely to issue equity immediately. Here, they are creating value for their current stockholders because they are selling stock for more than it is worth. Conversely, if the managers believe that their stock is underpriced, they are more likely to wait, hoping that the stock price will eventually rise to its true value.

However, if markets are efficient, securities are always correctly priced. Efficiency implies that stock is sold for its true worth, so the timing decision becomes unimportant. Figure 14.13 shows three possible stock price adjustments to the issuance of new stock.

Of course market efficiency is ultimately an empirical issue. Surprisingly, recent research suggests managers have some timing ability. Prof. Jay Ritter's website[26] presents evidence that annual stock returns over the five years following an initial public offering (IPO) are about 1.9 percent less for the issuing company than the returns on a non-issuing company of similar book-to-market ratio. Annual stock returns over this period following a seasoned equity offering (SEO) are about 3.4 percent less for the issuing company than for a comparable nonissuing company. A company's first public offering is called an IPO and all subsequent offerings are termed SEOs. The upper half of Figure 14.14 shows average annual returns of both IPOs and their control group, and the lower half of the figure shows average annual returns of both SEOs and their control group.

---

[26]http://site.warrington.ufl.edu/ritter/

Figure 14.13

Three Stock Price Adjustments after Issuing Equity

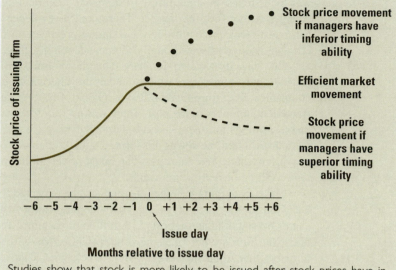

Studies show that stock is more likely to be issued after stock prices have increased. No inferences about market efficiency can be drawn from this result. Rather, market efficiency implies that the stock price of the issuing firm, on average, neither rises nor falls (relative to stock market indexes) after issuance of stock.

The evidence in Ritter's paper suggests that corporate managers issue SEOs when the company's stock is overpriced. In other words, managers appear to time the market successfully. The evidence that managers time their IPOs is less compelling: Returns following IPOs are closer to those of their control group.

Does the ability of a corporate official to issue an SEO when the security is overpriced indicate that the market is inefficient in the semistrong form or the strong form? The answer is actually somewhat more complex than it may first appear. On one hand, managers are likely to have special information that the rest of us do not have, suggesting that the market need only be inefficient in the strong form. On the other hand, if the market were truly semistrong efficient, the price would drop immediately and completely upon the announcement of an upcoming SEO. That is, rational investors would realize that stock is being issued because corporate officials have special information that the stock is overpriced. Indeed, many empirical studies report a price drop on the announcement date. However, Figure 14.14 shows a further price drop in the subsequent years, suggesting that the market is inefficient in the semistrong form.

If firms can time the issuance of common stock, perhaps they can also time the repurchase of stock. Here a firm would like to repurchase when its stock is undervalued. Ikenberry, Lakonishok, and Vermaelen find that stock returns of repurchasing firms are abnormally high in the two years following repurchase, suggesting that timing is effective here.[27]

3. SPECULATION AND EFFICIENT MARKETS

We normally think of individuals and financial institutions as the primary speculators in financial markets. However, industrial corporations speculate as well. For example, many companies make interest rate bets. If the managers of a firm believe that interest rates are

---

[27]David Ikenberry, J. Lakonishok, and T. Vermaelen, "Market Underreaction to Open Market Share Repurchases," *Journal of Financial Economics* (October–November 1995).

Figure 14.14
Returns on Initial
Public Offerings
(IPOs) and Seasoned
Equity Offerings
(SEOs) in Years
Following Issue

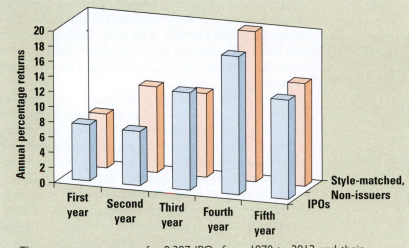

The average raw returns for 8,397 IPOs from 1970 to 2012 and their matching non-issuing firms during the five years after the issue. The first-year return does not include the return on the day of issue.

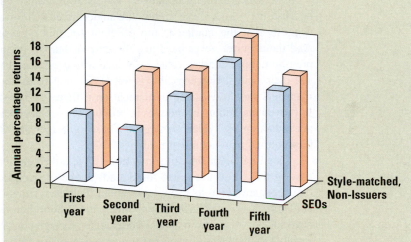

The average raw returns for 10,208 SEOs from 1970 to 2012 and their matching non-issuing firms during the five years after the issue. The first-year return does not include the return on the day of issue.
   On average, IPOs underperform their control groups by about 1.9% per year in the five years following issuance. SEOs underperform by about 3.4% per year.

SOURCE: Jay Ritter, http://site.warrington.ufl.edu/ritter/

likely to rise, they have an incentive to borrow because the present value of the liability will fall with the rate increase. In addition, these managers will have an incentive to borrow long term rather than short term in order to lock in the low rates for a longer period. The thinking can get more sophisticated. Suppose that the long-term rate is already higher than the short-term rate. The manager might argue that this differential reflects the market's view that rates will rise. However, perhaps he anticipates a rate increase even greater than what the market anticipates, as implied by the upward-sloping term structure. Again, the manager will want to borrow long term rather than short term.

Firms also speculate in foreign currencies. Suppose that the CFO of a multinational corporation based in the United States believes that the euro will decline relative to the dollar. She would probably issue euro-denominated debt rather than dollar-denominated debt because she expects the value of the foreign liability to fall. Conversely, she would issue debt domestically if she believes foreign currencies will appreciate relative to the dollar.

We are perhaps getting a little ahead of our story: The subtleties of the term structure and exchange rates are treated in other chapters, not this one. However, the big picture question is this: What does market efficiency have to say about such activity? The answer is clear. If financial markets are efficient, managers should not waste their time trying to forecast the movements of interest rates and foreign currencies. Their forecasts will likely be no better than chance. And they will be using up valuable executive time. This is not to say, however, that firms should flippantly pick the maturity or the denomination of their debt in a random fashion. A firm must *choose* these parameters carefully. However, the choice should be based on other rationales, not on an attempt to beat the market. For example, a firm with a project lasting five years might decide to issue five-year debt. A firm might issue yen-denominated debt because it anticipates expanding into Japan in a big way.

The same thinking applies to acquisitions. Many corporations buy up other firms because they think these targets are underpriced. Unfortunately, the empirical evidence suggests that the market is too efficient for this type of speculation to be profitable. And the acquirer never pays just the current market price. The bidding firm must pay a premium above market value to induce a majority of shareholders of the target firm to sell their shares. However, this is not to say that firms should never be acquired. Rather, managers should consider an acquisition if there are benefits (synergies) from the union. Improved marketing, economies in production, replacement of bad management, and even tax reduction are typical synergies. These synergies are distinct from the perception that the acquired firm is underpriced.

One final point should be mentioned. We talked earlier about empirical evidence suggesting that SEOs are timed to take advantage of overpriced stock. This makes sense—managers are likely to know more about their own firms than the market does. However, while managers may have special information about their own firms, it is unlikely that they have special information about interest rates, foreign currencies, and other firms. There are simply too many participants in these markets, many of whom are devoting all of their time to forecasting. Managers typically spend most of their effort running their own firms, with only a small amount of time devoted to studying financial markets.

INFORMATION IN MARKET PRICES

The previous section argued that it is quite difficult to forecast future market prices. However, the current and past prices of any asset are known—and of great use. Consider, for example, Becher's study of bank mergers.[28] The author finds that stock prices of acquired banks rise about 23 percent on average upon the first announcement of a merger. This is not surprising because companies are generally bought out at a premium above the current stock price. However, the same study shows that prices of acquiring banks fall almost 5 percent on average upon the same announcement. This is pretty strong evidence that bank mergers do not benefit, and may even hurt, acquiring companies. The reason for

---

[28]David A. Becher, "The Valuation Effects of Bank Mergers," *Journal of Corporate Finance* 6 (2000).

Figure 14.15
Stock Performance
Prior to Forced
Departures of
Management

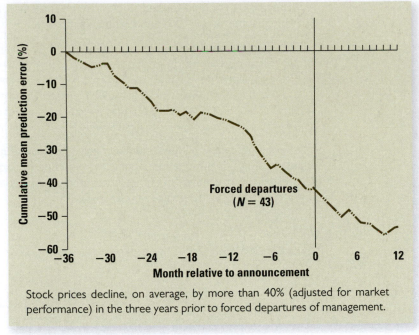

Forced departures
(*N* = 43)

Stock prices decline, on average, by more than 40% (adjusted for market
performance) in the three years prior to forced departures of management.

SOURCE: Adapted from Figure 1 of Warner, Watts, and Wruck, "Stock Prices and Top Management Changes," *Journal of Financial Economics* 20 (1988).

this result is unclear, though perhaps acquirers simply overpay for acquisitions. Regardless of the reason, the *implication* is clear. A bank should think deeply before acquiring another bank.

Furthermore, suppose you are the CFO of a company whose stock price drops significantly upon announcement of an acquisition. The market is telling you that the merger is bad for your firm. Serious consideration should be given to canceling the merger, even if, prior to the announcement, you thought the merger was a good idea.

Of course, mergers are only one type of corporate event. Managers should pay attention to the stock price reaction to any of their announcements, whether it concerns a new venture, a divestiture, a restructuring, or something else.

This is not the only way in which corporations can use the information in market prices. Suppose you are on the board of directors of a company whose stock price has declined precipitously since the current chief executive officer (CEO) was hired. In addition, the stock prices of competitors have risen over the same time. Though there may be extenuating circumstances, this can be viewed as evidence that the CEO is doing a poor job. Perhaps he should be fired. If this seems harsh, consider that Warner, Watts, and Wruck find a strong negative correlation between managerial turnover and prior stock performance.[29] Figure 14.15 shows that stocks fall, on average, about 40 percent in price (relative to market movements) in the three years prior to the forced departure of a top manager.

---

[29] Jerold B. Warner, Ross L. Watts, and Karen H. Wruck, "Stock Prices and Top Management Changes," *Journal of Financial Economics* 20 (1988).

If managers are fired for bad stock price performance, perhaps they are rewarded for stock price appreciation. Hall and Liebman state,

> Our main empirical finding is that CEO wealth often changes by millions of dollars for typical changes in firm value. For example, the median total compensation for CEOs is about $1 million if their firm's stock has a 30th percentile annual return (−7.0 percent) and is $5 million if the firm's stock has a 70th percentile annual return (20.5 percent). Thus, there is a difference of about $4 million in compensation for achieving a moderately above average performance relative to a moderately below average performance.[30]

Market efficiency implies that stock prices reflect all available information. We recommend using this information as much as possible in corporate decisions. And at least with respect to executive firings and executive compensation, it looks as if real-world corporations do pay attention to market prices.

---

[30]Brian J. Hall and Jeffrey B. Liebman, "Are CEOs Really Paid Like Bureaucrats?" *Quarterly Journal of Economics* (August 1998), p. 654.

Summary and Conclusions

1. An efficient securities market processes the information available to investors about the underlying economic value of the securities and incorporates it into the prices of securities. Market efficiency has two general implications. First, in any given time period, a security's abnormal return depends on information or news received by the market in that period. Second, an investor who uses the same information as the market cannot expect to earn abnormal returns. In other words, systems for playing the market are doomed to fail.

2. What information does the market use to determine stock prices?
   a. The weak form of the efficient market hypothesis says that the market uses the history of stock prices and is therefore efficient with respect to these past prices. This implies that stock selection based on patterns of past stock price movements is no better than random stock selection.
   b. The semistrong form states that the market uses all publicly available information in setting prices.
   c. Strong form efficiency states that the market uses all of the information that anybody knows about stocks, even inside information.

3. Behavioral finance states that the market is not always efficient. Adherents argue that:
   a. Investors are not rational.
   b. Deviations from rationality are similar across investors.
   c. Arbitrage, being costly, does not eliminate inefficiencies.

4. Behaviorists point to many studies, including those showing that small stocks outperform large stocks, value stocks outperform growth stocks, and stock prices adjust slowly to earnings surprises, as empirical confirmation of their beliefs.

5. Four implications of market efficiency for corporate finance are:
   a. Managers cannot fool the market through creative accounting.
   b. Firms cannot successfully time issues of debt and equity.
   c. Managers cannot profitably speculate in foreign currencies and other instruments.
   d. Managers can reap many benefits by paying attention to market prices.

The following box summarizes some key issues in the efficient markets debate:

Efficient Market Hypothesis: A Summary

Does Not Say:

- Prices are uncaused.
- Investors are foolish and too stupid to be in the market.
- All shares of stock have the same expected returns.
- Investors should throw darts to select stocks.
- There is no upward trend in stock prices.

Does Say:

- Prices reflect underlying value.
- Financial managers cannot time stock and bond sales.
- Managers cannot profitably speculate in foreign currencies.
- Managers cannot boost stock prices through creative accounting.

Why Doesn't Everybody Believe It?

- There are optical illusions, mirages, and apparent patterns in charts of stock market returns.
- The truth is less interesting.
- There is evidence against efficiency:
  - Two different, but financially identical, classes of stock of the same firm selling at different prices.
  - Earnings surprises.
  - Small versus large stocks.
  - Value versus growth stocks.
  - Crashes and bubbles.

Three Forms:

Weak form: Current prices reflect past prices; chartism (technical analysis) is useless.

Semistrong form: Prices reflect all public information; most financial analysis is useless.

Strong form: Prices reflect all that is knowable; nobody consistently makes superior profits.

Concept Questions

1. **Firm Value**   What rule should a firm follow when making financing decisions? How can firms create valuable financing opportunities?

2. **Efficient Market Hypothesis**   Define the three forms of market efficiency.

3. **Efficient Market Hypothesis**   Which of the following statements are true about the efficient market hypothesis?

    a. It implies perfect forecasting ability.
    b. It implies that prices reflect all available information.

    c. It implies an irrational market.
    d. It implies that prices do not fluctuate.
    e. It results from keen competition among investors.

4.   **Market Efficiency Implications**   Explain why a characteristic of an efficient market is that investments in that market have zero NPVs.

5.   **Efficient Market Hypothesis**   A stock market analyst is able to identify mispriced stocks by comparing the average price for the last 10 days to the average price for the last 60 days. If this is true, what do you know about the market?

6.   **Semistrong Efficiency**   If a market is semistrong form efficient, is it also weak form efficient? Explain.

7.   **Efficient Market Hypothesis**   What are the implications of the efficient market hypothesis for investors who buy and sell stocks in an attempt to "beat the market"?

8.   **Stocks versus Gambling**   Critically evaluate the following statements: Playing the stock market is like gambling. Such speculative investing has no social value other than the pleasure people get from this form of gambling.

9.   **Efficient Market Hypothesis**   Several celebrated investors and stock pickers frequently mentioned in the financial press have recorded huge returns on their investments over the past two decades. Does the success of these particular investors invalidate the EMH? Explain.

10.   **Efficient Market Hypothesis**   For each of the following scenarios, discuss whether profit opportunities exist from trading in the stock of the firm under the conditions that (1) the market is not weak form efficient, (2) the market is weak form but not semistrong form efficient, (3) the market is semistrong form but not strong form efficient, and (4) the market is strong form efficient.

    a. The stock price has risen steadily each day for the past 30 days.
    b. The financial statements for a company were released three days ago, and you believe you've uncovered some anomalies in the company's inventory and cost control reporting techniques that are causing the firm's true liquidity strength to be understated.
    c. You observe that the senior management of a company has been buying a lot of the company's stock on the open market over the past week.

    Use the following information for the next two questions:
    Technical analysis is a controversial investment practice. Technical analysis covers a wide array of techniques, which are all used in an attempt to predict the direction of a particular stock or the market. Technical analysts look at two major types of information: Historical stock prices and investor sentiment. A technical analyst would argue these two information sets provide information about the future direction of a particular stock or the market as a whole.

11.   **Technical Analysis**   What would a technical analyst say about market efficiency?

12.   **Investor Sentiment**   A technical analysis tool that is sometimes used to predict market movements is an investor sentiment index. AAII, the American Association of Individual Investors, publishes an investor sentiment index based on a survey of its members. In the following table you will find the percentage of investors who were bullish, bearish, or neutral during a four-week period:

Week	Bullish	Bearish	Neutral
1	37%	25%	38%
2	52	14	34
3	29	35	36
4	43	26	31

What is the investor sentiment index intended to capture? How might it be useful in technical analysis?

13. **Performance of the Pros** In the middle to late 1990s, the performance of the pros was unusually poor—on the order of 90 percent of all equity mutual funds underperformed a passively managed index fund. How does this bear on the issue of market efficiency?

14. **Efficient Markets** A hundred years ago or so, companies did not compile annual reports. Even if you owned stock in a particular company, you were unlikely to be allowed to see the balance sheet and income statement for the company. Assuming the market is semistrong form efficient, what does this say about market efficiency then compared to now?

15. **Efficient Market Hypothesis** Aerotech, an aerospace technology research firm, announced this morning that it has hired the world's most knowledgeable and prolific space researchers. Before today, Aerotech's stock had been selling for $100. Assume that no other information is received over the next week and the stock market as a whole does not move.

   a. What do you expect will happen to Aerotech's stock?
   b. Consider the following scenarios:
      i. The stock price jumps to $118 on the day of the announcement. In subsequent days it floats up to $123, then falls back to $116.
      ii. The stock price jumps to $116 and remains at that level.
      iii. The stock price gradually climbs to $116 over the next week.

   Which scenario(s) indicate market efficiency? Which do not? Why?

16. **Efficient Market Hypothesis** When the 56-year-old founder of Gulf & Western, Inc., died of a heart attack, the stock price immediately jumped from $18.00 a share to $20.25, a 12.5 percent increase. This is evidence of market inefficiency because an efficient stock market would have anticipated his death and adjusted the price beforehand. Assume that no other information is received and the stock market as a whole does not move. Is this statement about market efficiency true or false? Explain.

17. **Efficient Market Hypothesis** Today, the following announcement was made: "Early today the Justice Department reached a decision in the Universal Product Care (UPC) case. UPC has been found guilty of discriminatory practices in hiring. For the next five years, UPC must pay $2 million each year to a fund representing victims of UPC's policies." Assuming the market is efficient, should investors not buy UPC stock after the announcement because the litigation will cause an abnormally low rate of return? Explain.

18. **Efficient Market Hypothesis** Newtech Corp. is going to adopt a new chip-testing device that can greatly improve its production efficiency. Do you think the lead engineer can profit from purchasing the firm's stock before the news release on the device? After reading the announcement in *The Wall Street Journal,* should you be able to earn an abnormal return from purchasing the stock if the market is efficient?

19. **Efficient Market Hypothesis** TransTrust Corp. has changed how it accounts for inventory. Taxes are unaffected, although the resulting earnings report released this quarter is 20 percent higher than what it would have been under the old accounting system. There is no other surprise in the earnings report, and the change in the accounting treatment was publicly announced. If the market is efficient, will the stock price be higher when the market learns that the reported earnings are higher?

20. **Efficient Market Hypothesis** The Durkin Investing Agency has been the best stock picker in the country for the past two years. Before this rise to fame occurred, the Durkin newsletter had 200 subscribers. Those subscribers beat the market consistently, earning substantially higher returns after adjustment for risk and transaction costs. Subscriptions have skyrocketed to 10,000. Now, when the Durkin Investing Agency recommends a stock, the price instantly rises several points. The subscribers currently earn only a normal return when they buy recommended stock because the price rises before anybody can act on the information. Briefly explain this phenomenon. Is Durkin's ability to pick stocks consistent with market efficiency?

21. **Efficient Market Hypothesis** Your broker commented that well-managed firms are better investments than poorly managed firms. As evidence your broker cited a recent study examining 100 small manufacturing firms that eight years earlier had been listed in an industry magazine as the best-managed small manufacturers in the country. In the ensuing eight years, the 100 firms listed have not earned more than the normal market return. Your broker continued to say that if the firms were well managed, they should have produced better-than-average returns. If the market is efficient, do you agree with your broker?

22. **Efficient Market Hypothesis** A famous economist just announced in *The Wall Street Journal* his findings that the recession is over and the economy is again entering an expansion. Assume market efficiency. Can you profit from investing in the stock market after you read this announcement?

23. **Efficient Market Hypothesis** Suppose the market is semistrong form efficient. Can you expect to earn excess returns if you make trades based on:

   a. Your broker's information about record earnings for a stock?
   b. Rumors about a merger of a firm?
   c. Yesterday's announcement of a successful new product test?

24. **Efficient Market Hypothesis** Imagine that a particular macroeconomic variable that influences your firm's net earnings is positively serially correlated. Assume market efficiency. Would you expect price changes in your stock to be serially correlated? Why or why not?

25. **Efficient Market Hypothesis** The efficient market hypothesis implies that all mutual funds should obtain the same expected risk-adjusted returns. Therefore, we can simply pick mutual funds at random. Is this statement true or false? Explain.

26. **Efficient Market Hypothesis** Assume that markets are efficient. During a trading day American Golf, Inc., announces that it has lost a contract for a large golfing project that, prior to the news, it was widely believed to have secured. If the market is efficient, how should the stock price react to this information if no additional information is released?

27. **Efficient Market Hypothesis** Prospectors, Inc., is a publicly traded gold prospecting company in Alaska. Although the firm's searches for gold usually fail, the prospectors occasionally find a rich vein of ore. What pattern would you expect to observe for Prospectors' cumulative abnormal returns if the market is efficient?

28. **Evidence on Market Efficiency** Some people argue that the efficient market hypothesis cannot explain the 1987 market crash or the high price-to-earnings ratios of Internet stocks during the late 1990s. What alternative hypothesis is currently used for these two phenomena?

Questions and Problems

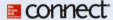

BASIC
(Questions 1–4)

1. **Cumulative Abnormal Returns**   Delta, United, and American Airlines announced purchases of planes on July 18 (7/18), February 12 (2/12), and October 7 (10/7), respectively. Given the following information, calculate the cumulative abnormal return (CAR) for these stocks as a group. Graph the result and provide an explanation. All of the stocks have a beta of 1, and no other announcements are made.

	Delta			United			American	
Date	Market Return	Company Return	Date	Market Return	Company Return	Date	Market Return	Company Return
7/12	−.3	−.5	2/8	−.9	−1.1	10/1	.5	.3
7/13	.0	.2	2/9	−1.0	−1.1	10/2	.4	.6
7/16	.5	.7	2/10	.4	.2	10/3	1.1	1.1
7/17	−.5	−.3	2/11	.6	.8	10/6	.1	−.3
7/18	−2.2	1.1	2/12	−.3	−.1	10/7	−2.2	−.3
7/19	−.9	−.7	2/15	1.1	1.2	10/8	.5	.5
7/20	−1.0	−1.1	2/16	.5	.5	10/9	−.3	−.2
7/23	.7	.5	2/17	−.3	−.2	10/10	.3	.1
7/24	.2	.1	2/18	.3	.2	10/13	.0	−.1

2. **Cumulative Abnormal Returns**   The following diagram shows the cumulative abnormal returns (CAR) for 386 oil exploration companies announcing oil discoveries between 1950 and 1980. Month 0 in the diagram is the announcement month. Assume that no other information is received and the stock market as a whole does not move. Is the diagram consistent with market efficiency? Why or why not?

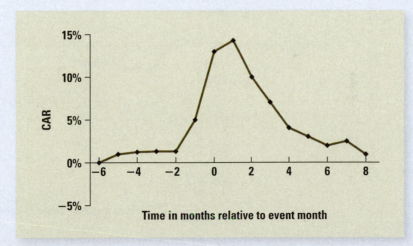

Time in months relative to event month

3. **Cumulative Abnormal Returns**   The following figures present the results of four cumulative abnormal returns (CAR) studies. Indicate whether the results of each study support, reject, or are inconclusive about the semistrong form of the efficient market hypothesis. In each figure, Time 0 is the date of an event.

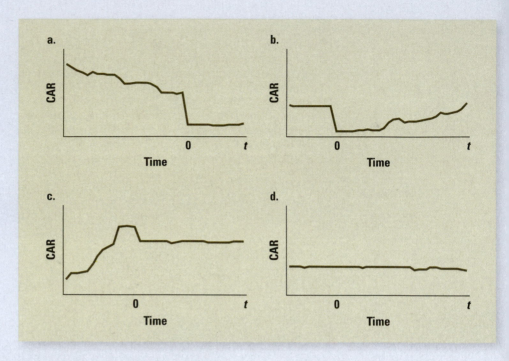

4.   **Cumulative Abnormal Returns**   A study analyzed the behavior of the stock prices of firms that had lost antitrust cases. Included in the diagram are all firms that lost the initial court decision, even if the decision was later overturned on appeal. The event at Time 0 is the initial, pre-appeal court decision. Assume no other information was released, aside from that disclosed in the initial trial. The stock prices all have a beta of 1. Is the diagram consistent with market efficiency? Why or why not?

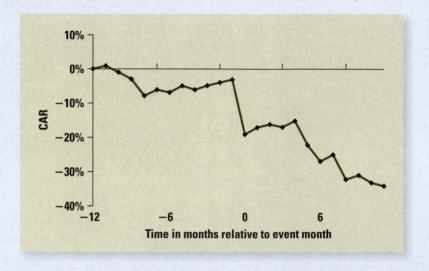

YOUR 401(k) ACCOUNT AT EAST COAST YACHTS

You have been at your job with East Coast Yachts for a week now and have decided you need to sign up for the company's 401(k) plan. Even after your discussion with Sarah Brown, the Bledsoe Financial Services representative, you are still unsure which investment option you should choose. Recall that the options available to you are stock in East Coast Yachts, the Bledsoe S&P 500 Index Fund, the Bledsoe Small-Cap Fund, the Bledsoe Large-Company Stock Fund, the Bledsoe Bond Fund, and the Bledsoe Money Market Fund. You have decided that you should invest in a diversified portfolio, with 70 percent of your investment in equities, 25 percent in bonds, and 5 percent in the money market fund. You have also decided to focus your equity investment on large-cap stocks, but you are debating whether to select the S&P 500 Index Fund or the Large-Company Stock Fund.

In thinking it over, you understand the basic difference in the two funds. One is a purely passive fund that replicates a widely followed large-cap index, the S&P 500, and has low fees. The other is actively managed with the intention that the skill of the portfolio manager will result in improved performance relative to an index. Fees are higher in the latter fund. You're just not certain which way to go, so you ask Dan Ervin, who works in the company's finance area, for advice.

After discussing your concerns, Dan gives you some information comparing the performance of equity mutual funds and the Vanguard 500 Index Fund. The Vanguard 500 is the world's largest equity index mutual fund. It replicates the S&P 500, and its return is only

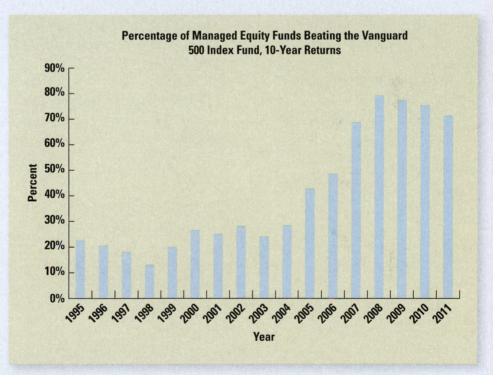

SOURCE: From Bradford Jordan, Thomas Miller, and Steven Dolvin, *Fundamentals of Investments*, 7th ed. McGraw-Hill, New York, 2014.

negligibly different from the S&P 500. Fees are very low. As a result, the Vanguard 500 is essentially identical to the Bledsoe S&P 500 Index Fund offered in the 401(k) plan, but it has been in existence for much longer, so you can study its track record for over two decades. The nearby graph summarizes Dan's comments by showing the percentage of equity mutual funds that outperformed the Vanguard 500 Fund over the previous 10 years.[31] So, for example, from January 1998 to December 2007, about 70 percent of equity mutual funds outperformed the Vanguard 500. Dan suggests that you study the graph and answer the following questions:

1. What implications do you draw from the graph for mutual fund investors?

2. Is the graph consistent or inconsistent with market efficiency? Explain carefully.

3. What investment decision would you make for the equity portion of your 401(k) account? Why?

---

[31]Note that this graph is not hypothetical; it reflects the actual performance of the Vanguard 500 Index Fund relative to a very large population of diversified equity mutual funds. Specialty funds, such as international funds, are excluded. All returns are net of management fees but do not include sales charges (which are known as "loads"), if any. As a result, the performance of actively managed funds is overstated.

15

Long-Term Financing
AN INTRODUCTION

When a corporation with a low credit rating issues bonds, the bonds are referred to as high yield, or "junk," bonds. While junk bonds are more likely to default, they also have higher yields. In 2014, with low interest rates, investors had an appetite for high-yield bonds to improve returns. In April 2014, French telecommunications company Numericable, along with its parent company Altice, met this appetite with a record junk bond issuance. Numericable issued $7.78 billion and €2.25 billion in bonds, and Altice issued $2.9 billion and €2.1 billion in bonds, for a total of $15.8 billion in debt. Previously, the largest junk bond issue was a $6.5 billion sale by Sprint Nextel in 2013. However, neither bond issue came close to the largest bond issue in history. In 2013, Verizon issued $48 billion in BBB bonds to fund its purchase of Vodafone.

15.1 Some Features of Common and Preferred Stocks

In this chapter, we examine specific features of both stocks and bonds. We begin with stock, both common and preferred. In discussing common stock features, we focus on shareholder rights and dividend payments. For preferred stock, we explain what the "preferred" means, and we also debate whether preferred stock is really debt or equity.

COMMON STOCK FEATURES

The term **common stock** means different things to different people, but it is usually applied to stock that has no special preference either in receiving dividends or in bankruptcy.

Shareholder Rights　A corporation's shareholders elect directors who, in turn, hire management to carry out their directives. Shareholders, therefore, control the corporation through the right to elect the directors. Generally, only shareholders have this right.

Directors are elected each year at an annual meeting. Although there are exceptions (discussed next), the general idea is "one share, one vote" (*not* one *shareholder*, one vote). Corporate democracy is thus very different from our political democracy. With corporate democracy, the "golden rule" prevails absolutely.[1]

---

[1] The golden rule: Whosoever has the gold makes the rules.

Directors are elected at an annual shareholders' meeting by a vote of the holders of a majority of shares who are present and entitled to vote. However, the exact mechanism for electing directors differs across companies. The most important difference is whether shares must be voted cumulatively or voted straight.

To illustrate the two different voting procedures, imagine that a corporation has two shareholders: Smith with 20 shares and Jones with 80 shares. Both want to be a director. Jones does not want Smith, however. We assume there are a total of four directors to be elected.

The effect of **cumulative voting** is to allow minority participation.[2] If cumulative voting is permitted, the total number of votes that each shareholder may cast is determined first. This is usually calculated as the number of shares (owned or controlled) multiplied by the number of directors to be elected.

With cumulative voting, the directors are elected all at once. In our example, this means that the top four vote getters will be the new directors. A shareholder can distribute votes however she wishes.

Will Smith get a seat on the board? If we ignore the possibility of a five-way tie, then the answer is yes. Smith will cast $20 \times 4 = 80$ votes, and Jones will cast $80 \times 4 = 320$ votes. If Smith gives all his votes to himself, he is assured of a directorship. The reason is that Jones can't divide 320 votes among four candidates in such a way as to give all of them more than 80 votes, so Smith will finish fourth at worst.

In general, if there are N directors up for election, then $1/(N + 1)$ percent of the stock plus one share will guarantee you a seat. In our current example, this is $1/(4 + 1) = 20$ percent. So the more seats that are up for election at one time, the easier (and cheaper) it is to win one.

With **straight voting**, the directors are elected one at a time. Each time, Smith can cast 20 votes and Jones can cast 80. As a consequence, Jones will elect all of the candidates. The only way to guarantee a seat is to own 50 percent plus one share. This also guarantees that you will win every seat, so it's really all or nothing.

<table>
<tr><td>**EXAMPLE 15.1**</td><td>

Buying the Election   Stock in JRJ Corporation sells for $20 per share and features cumulative voting. There are 10,000 shares outstanding. If three directors are up for election, how much does it cost to ensure yourself a seat on the board?

The question here is how many shares of stock it will take to get a seat. The answer is 2,501, so the cost is $2,501 \times \$20 = \$50,020$. Why 2,501? Because there is no way the remaining 7,499 votes can be divided among three people to give all of them more than 2,501 votes. For example, suppose two people receive 2,502 votes and the first two seats. A third person can receive at most $10,000 - 2,502 - 2,502 - 2,501 = 2,495$, so the third seat is yours.

</td></tr>
</table>

As we've illustrated, straight voting can "freeze out" minority shareholders, which is why many states have mandatory cumulative voting. However, in states where cumulative voting is mandatory, corporations have ways to minimize its impact.

One such way is to stagger the voting for the board of directors. With staggered elections, only a fraction of the directorships are up for election at a particular time. For example, if only two directors are up for election at any one time, it will take $1/(2 + 1) = 33.33$ percent of the stock plus one share to guarantee a seat. Staggered boards are often called *classified* boards because directors are placed into different classes with terms that expire at different times. In recent years, corporations have come under pressure to declassify their boards, meaning that all directors would stand for election every year, and many have done so.

---

[2]By minority participation, we mean participation by shareholders with relatively small amounts of stock.

Overall, staggering has two basic effects:

1. Staggering makes it more difficult for a minority to elect a director under cumulative voting because fewer directors are elected at one time.

2. Staggering deters takeover attempts because of the difficulty of voting in a majority of new directors.

However, staggering can also serve a beneficial purpose. It provides "institutional memory" from continuity on the board of directors. Continuity may be important for corporations with significant long-range plans and projects.

Proxy Voting   At the annual meeting shareholders can vote in person, or they can transfer their right to vote to another party. A **proxy** is the grant of authority by a shareholder to someone else to vote her shares. For convenience, much of the voting in large public corporations is actually done by proxy.

Obviously, management wants to accumulate as many proxies as possible. However, an "outside" group of shareholders can try to obtain proxies in an attempt to replace management by electing enough directors. The resulting battle is called a *proxy fight.*

Classes of Stock   Some firms have more than one class of common stock. Often, the classes are created with unequal voting rights. For example, Ford Motor Company's Class B common stock is held by Ford family interests and trusts and not publicly traded. This class has 40 percent of the voting power, even though it represents less than 10 percent of the total number of shares outstanding.

There are many other cases of corporations with different classes of stock. For example, at one time, General Motors had its "GM Classic" shares (the original) and two additional classes, Class E ("GME") and Class H ("GMH"). These classes were created to help pay for two large acquisitions, Electronic Data Systems and Hughes Aircraft. Another good example is Google, the Web search company, which only recently became publicly owned. Google initially created two classes of common stock, A and B. The Class A shares are held by the public, and each share has one vote. The Class B shares are held by company insiders, and each Class B share has 10 votes. Then, in 2014, the company had a stock split of its Class B shares, creating Class C shares, which have no vote at all. As a result, Google's founders and managers control the company.

Historically, the New York Stock Exchange did not allow companies to create classes of publicly traded common stock with unequal voting rights. However, exceptions (e.g., Ford) appear to have been made. In addition, many non-NYSE companies have dual classes of common stock. Limited-voting stock allows management of a firm to raise equity capital while maintaining control.

The subject of unequal voting rights is controversial in the United States, and the idea of one share, one vote, has a strong following and a long history. Interestingly, however, shares with unequal voting rights are quite common around the world.

Other Rights   The value of a share of common stock in a corporation is directly related to the general rights of shareholders. In addition to the right to vote for directors, shareholders usually have the following rights:

1. The right to share proportionally in dividends.

2. The right to share proportionally in assets remaining after liabilities have been paid in a liquidation.

3. The right to vote on stockholder matters of great importance, such as a merger. Voting usually occurs at the annual meeting or a special meeting.

In addition, corporations sometimes give a *preemptive right* to their stockholders. A preemptive right forces a company to sell stock to its existing stockholders before offering the stock to the general public. The right lets each stockholder protect his proportionate ownership in the corporation.

Dividends Corporations are legally authorized to pay **dividends** to their shareholders. The payment of dividends is at the discretion of the board of directors.

Some important characteristics of dividends include the following:

1. Unless a dividend is declared by the board of directors of a corporation, it is not a liability of the corporation. A corporation cannot default on an undeclared dividend. As a consequence, corporations cannot become bankrupt because of nonpayment of dividends. The amount of the dividend and even whether it is paid are decisions based on the business judgment of the board of directors.

2. Dividends are paid out of the corporation's aftertax cash flow. They are not business expenses and are not deductible for corporate tax purposes.

3. Dividends received by individual shareholders are taxable. However, corporations that own stock in other corporations are permitted to exclude 70 percent of the dividend amounts they receive and are taxed on only the remaining 30 percent.[3]

PREFERRED STOCK FEATURES

Preferred stock pays a cash dividend expressed in terms of dollars per share. Preferred stock has a preference over common stock in the payment of dividends and in the distribution of corporation assets in the event of liquidation. *Preference* means only that holders of preferred shares must receive a dividend (in the case of an ongoing firm) before holders of common shares are entitled to anything. Preferred stock typically has no maturity date.

Preferred stock is a form of equity from a legal and tax standpoint. It is important to note, however, that holders of preferred stock usually have no voting privileges.

Stated Value Preferred shares have a stated liquidating value, usually $100 per share. For example, General Motors' "$5 preferred," paying an annual dividend of $5, translates into a dividend yield of 5 percent of stated value.

Cumulative and Noncumulative Dividends A preferred dividend is *not* like interest on a bond. The decision of the board of directors not to pay the dividends on preferred shares may have nothing to do with the current net income of the corporation.

Dividends payable on preferred stock are either *cumulative* or *noncumulative;* most are cumulative. If preferred dividends are cumulative and are not paid in a particular year, they will be carried forward as an *arrearage.* Usually, both the accumulated (past) preferred dividends and the current preferred dividends must be paid before the common shareholders can receive anything.

Unpaid preferred dividends are *not* debts of the firm. Directors elected by the common shareholders can defer preferred dividends indefinitely. However, in such cases, common

---

[3]More specifically, the 70 percent exclusion applies when the recipient owns less than 20 percent of the outstanding stock in a corporation. If a corporation owns more than 20 percent but less than 80 percent, the exclusion is 80 percent. If more than 80 percent is owned, the corporation can file a single "consolidated" return and the exclusion is effectively 100 percent.

shareholders must also forgo dividends. In addition, holders of preferred shares are sometimes granted voting and other rights if preferred dividends have not been paid for some time. For example, at one point, US Airways had failed to pay dividends on one of its preferred stock issues for six quarters. As a consequence, the holders of the shares were allowed to nominate two people to represent their interests on the airline's board. Because preferred stockholders receive no interest on the accumulated dividends, some have argued that firms have an incentive to delay paying preferred dividends. However, as with USAir, this may mean giving voting rights to preferred stockholders.

Is Preferred Stock Really Debt?   A good case can be made that preferred stock is really debt in disguise. Preferred shareholders receive a stated dividend only, and, if the corporation is liquidated, preferred shareholders get a stated value. Often, preferred stocks carry credit ratings much like those of bonds. Preferred stock is sometimes convertible into common stock. In addition, preferred stocks are often callable, which allows the issuer to repurchase, or "call," part or all of the issue at a stated price. More will be said about the call feature in the next section.

Though preferred stock typically has no maturity date, many issues have obligatory sinking funds. A sinking fund requires a company to retire a portion of its preferred stock each year. A sinking fund effectively creates a final maturity, since the entire issue will ultimately be retired. More will be said on sinking funds in the next section. For these reasons, preferred stock seems to be a lot like debt. However, for tax purposes, preferred dividends are treated like common stock dividends.

In the 1990s, firms began to sell securities that looked a lot like preferred stock but were treated as debt for tax purposes. The new securities were given interesting acronyms like TOPrS (trust-originated preferred securities, or toppers), MIPS (monthly income preferred securities), and QUIPS (quarterly income preferred securities), among others. Because of various specific features, these instruments can be counted as debt for tax purposes, making the interest payments tax deductible. Payments made to investors in these instruments are treated as interest for personal income taxes for individuals. Until 2003, interest payments and dividends were taxed at the same marginal tax rate. When the tax rate on dividend payments was reduced, these instruments were not included, so individuals must still pay their higher income tax rate on dividend payments received from these instruments.

15.2 Corporate Long-Term Debt

In this section, we describe in some detail the basic terms and features of a typical long-term corporate bond. We discuss additional issues associated with long-term debt in subsequent sections.

Securities issued by corporations may be classified roughly as *equity securities* or *debt securities*. A debt represents something that must be repaid; it is the result of borrowing money. When corporations borrow, they generally promise to make regularly scheduled interest payments and to repay the original amount borrowed (i.e., the principal). The person or firm making the loan is called the *creditor,* or *lender.* The corporation borrowing the money is called the *debtor,* or *borrower.*

From a financial point of view, the main differences between debt and equity are:

1. Debt is not an ownership interest in the firm. Creditors generally do not have voting power.

2. The corporation's payment of interest on debt is considered a cost of doing business and is fully tax deductible. Dividends paid to stockholders are *not* tax deductible.

Information for bond investors can be found at **www .investinginbonds .com**.

3. Unpaid debt is a liability of the firm. If it is not paid, the creditors can legally claim the assets of the firm. This action can result in liquidation or reorganization, two of the possible consequences of bankruptcy. Thus, one of the costs of issuing debt is the possibility of financial failure. This possibility does not arise when equity is issued.

IS IT DEBT OR EQUITY?

Sometimes it is not clear if a particular security is debt or equity. For example, suppose a corporation issues a perpetual bond with interest payable solely from corporate income if, and only if, earned. Whether or not this is really a debt is hard to say and is primarily a legal and semantic issue. Courts and taxing authorities would have the final say.

Corporations are adept at creating exotic, hybrid securities that have many features of equity but are treated as debt. Obviously, the distinction between debt and equity is very important for tax purposes. So, one reason that corporations try to create a debt security that is really equity is to obtain the tax benefits of debt and the bankruptcy benefits of equity.

As a general rule, equity represents an ownership interest and is a residual claim. This means that equityholders are paid after debtholders. As a result, the risks and benefits associated with owning debt and equity are different. To give just one example, note that the maximum reward for owning a debt security is ultimately fixed by the amount of the loan, whereas there is no upper limit to the potential reward from owning an equity interest.

Equity versus Debt

Feature	Equity	Debt
Income	Dividends	Interest
Tax status	Dividends are taxed as personal income, although currently capped at 23.8% at the U.S. federal level. Dividends are not a business expense.	Interest is taxed as personal income. Interest is a business expense, and corporations can deduct interest when computing their corporate tax liability.
Control	Common stock usually has voting rights.	Control is exercised with loan agreement.
Default	Firms cannot be forced into bankruptcy for nonpayment of dividends.	Unpaid debt is a liability of the firm. Nonpayment results in default and possible bankruptcy.

Bottom line: Tax status favors debt, but default favors equity. Control features of debt and equity are different, but one is not better than the other.

LONG-TERM DEBT: THE BASICS

Ultimately, all long-term debt securities are promises made by the issuing firm to pay principal when due and to make timely interest payments on the unpaid balance. Beyond this, a number of features distinguish these securities from one another. We discuss some of these features next.

The maturity of a long-term debt instrument is the length of time the debt remains outstanding with some unpaid balance. Debt securities can be short term (with maturities of one year or less) or long term (with maturities of more than one year).[4] Short-term debt is sometimes referred to as *unfunded debt*.[5]

Debt securities are typically called *notes, debentures,* or *bonds.* Strictly speaking, a bond is a secured debt, meaning that certain property is pledged as security for repayment of the debt. However, in common usage, the word *bond* refers to all kinds of secured and unsecured debt. We will therefore continue to use the term generically to refer to long-term debt. Also, usually, the only difference between a note and a bond is the original maturity. Issues with an original maturity of 10 years or less are often called notes. Longer-term issues are called bonds.

Long-term debt can be issued to the public or privately placed. Privately placed debt is issued to a lender and not offered to the public. Because this is a private transaction, the specific terms are up to the parties involved. We concentrate on public-issue bonds. However, most of what we say about them holds true for private-issue, long-term debt as well.

There are many other aspects to long-term debt, including such terms as security, call features, sinking funds, ratings, and protective covenants. The following table illustrates these features for a bond issued by Cisco Systems. If some of these terms are unfamiliar, have no fear. We will discuss them all presently.

> Information on individual bonds can be found at **http://finra -markets .morningstar.com /BondCenter/**.

Features of a Cisco Systems Bond		
Term		**Explanation**
Amount of issue	$1 billion	The company issued $1 billion worth of bonds.
Date of issue	03/03/2014	The bonds were sold on 03/03/2014.
Maturity	03/04/2024	The bonds mature on 3/4/2024.
Face value	$2,000	The denomination of the bonds is $2,000.
Annual coupon	3.625	Each bondholder will receive $72.50 per bond per year (3.625% of face value).
Offer price	99.925	The offer price will be 99.925% of the $2,000 face value, or $1,998.50, per bond.
Coupon payment dates	03/04, 09/04	Coupons of $72.50/2 = $36.25 will be paid on these dates.
Security	None	The bonds are not secured by specific assets.
Sinking fund	None	The bonds have no sinking fund.
Call provision	At any time	The bonds do not have a deferred call.
Call price	Treasury rate plus .15%.	The bonds have a "make whole" call price.
Rating	Moody's A1, S&P AA−	The bonds have a good quality credit rating.

Many of these features will be detailed in the bond indenture, so we discuss this first.

---

[4]There is no universally agreed-upon distinction between short-term and long-term debt. In addition, people often refer to intermediate-term debt, which has a maturity of more than 1 year and less than 3 to 5, or even 10, years.

[5]The word *funding* is part of the jargon of finance. It generally refers to the long term. Thus, a firm planning to "fund" its debt requirements may be replacing short-term debt with long-term debt.

THE INDENTURE

The **indenture** is the written agreement between the corporation (the borrower) and its creditors. It is sometimes referred to as the *deed of trust*.[6] Usually, a trustee (a bank perhaps) is appointed by the corporation to represent the bondholders. The trust company must (1) make sure the terms of the indenture are obeyed, (2) manage the sinking fund (described in the following pages), and (3) represent the bondholders in default, that is, if the company defaults on its payments to them.

The bond indenture is a legal document. It can run several hundred pages and generally makes for very tedious reading. It is an important document, however, because it generally includes the following provisions:

1. The basic terms of the bonds.
2. A description of property used as security.
3. Seniority.
4. The repayment arrangements.
5. The call provisions.
6. Details of the protective covenants.

We discuss these features next.

Terms of a Bond   Corporate bonds usually have a face value (i.e., a denomination) of $1,000. This is called the *principal value* and it is stated on the bond certificate. So, if a corporation wanted to borrow $1 million, 1,000 bonds would have to be sold. The par value (i.e., initial accounting value) of a bond is almost always the same as the face value, and the terms are used interchangeably in practice. Although a par value of $1,000 is most common, essentially any par value is possible. For example, the par value is $2,000 for our Cisco bonds.

Corporate bonds are usually in **registered form**. For example, the indenture might read as follows:

Interest is payable semiannually on July 1 and January 1 of each year to the person in whose name the bond is registered at the close of business on June 15 or December 15, respectively.

This means that the company has a registrar who will record the initial ownership of each bond, as well as any changes in ownership. The company will pay the interest and principal by check mailed directly to the address of the owner of record. A corporate bond may be registered and have attached "coupons." To obtain an interest payment, the owner must separate a coupon from the bond certificate and send it to the company registrar (the paying agent).

Alternatively, the bond could be in **bearer form**. This means that the certificate is the basic evidence of ownership, and the corporation will "pay the bearer." Ownership is not otherwise recorded, and, as with a registered bond with attached coupons, the holder of the bond certificate detaches the coupons and sends them to the company to receive payment.

There are two drawbacks to bearer bonds. First, they are difficult to recover if they are lost or stolen. Second, because the company does not know who owns its bonds, it cannot

---

[6]The phrases *loan agreement,* or *loan contract* are usually used for privately placed debt and term loans.

notify bondholders of important events. Bearer bonds were once the dominant type, but they are now much less common (in the United States) than registered bonds.

Security   Debt securities are classified according to the collateral and mortgages used to protect the bondholder.

Collateral is a general term that frequently means securities (e.g., bonds and stocks) that are pledged as security for payment of debt. For example, collateral trust bonds often involve a pledge of common stock held by the corporation. However, the term *collateral* is commonly used to refer to any asset pledged on a debt.

Mortgage securities are secured by a mortgage on the real property of the borrower. The property involved is usually real estate, such as land or buildings. The legal document that describes the mortgage is called a *mortgage trust indenture* or *trust deed*.

Sometimes mortgages are on specific property, such as a railroad car. More often, blanket mortgages are used. A blanket mortgage pledges all the real property owned by the company.[7]

Bonds frequently represent unsecured obligations of the company. A **debenture** is an unsecured bond for which no specific pledge of property is made. The term **note** is generally used for such instruments if the maturity of the unsecured bond is less than 10 or so years from the date when the bond was originally issued. Debenture holders have a claim only on property not otherwise pledged. In other words, the property that remains after mortgages and collateral trusts are taken into account. The Cisco bonds discussed earlier are an example of such an issue.

The terminology that we use here and elsewhere in this chapter is standard in the United States. Outside the United States, these same terms can have different meanings. For example, bonds issued by the British government ("gilts") are called treasury "stock." Also, in the United Kingdom, a debenture is a *secured* obligation.

At the current time, public bonds issued in the United States by industrial and financial companies are typically debentures. However, most utility and railroad bonds are secured by a pledge of assets.

The Securities Industry and Financial Markets Association (SIFMA) site is **www.sifma.org**.

Seniority   In general terms, *seniority* indicates preference in position over other lenders, and debts are sometimes labeled as *senior* or *junior* to indicate seniority. Some debt is *subordinated,* as in, for example, a subordinated debenture.

In the event of default, holders of subordinated debt must give preference to other specified creditors. Usually, this means that the subordinated lenders will be paid off only after the specified creditors have been compensated. However, debt cannot be subordinated to equity.

Repayment   Bonds can be repaid entirely at maturity, at which time the bondholder receives the stated, or face, value of the bond, or they may be repaid in part or in entirety before maturity. Early repayment in some form is more typical and is often handled through a sinking fund.

A **sinking fund** is an account managed by the bond trustee for the purpose of repaying the bonds. The company makes annual payments to the trustee, who then uses the funds to retire a portion of the debt. The trustee does this by either buying up some of the bonds in the market or calling in a fraction of the outstanding bonds. This second option is discussed in the next section.

---

[7]Real property includes land and things "affixed thereto." It does not include cash or inventories.

There are many different kinds of sinking fund arrangements, and the details are spelled out in the indenture. For example:

1. Some sinking funds start about 10 years after the initial issuance.
2. Some sinking funds establish equal payments over the life of the bond.
3. Some high-quality bond issues establish payments to the sinking fund that are not sufficient to redeem the entire issue. As a consequence, there may be a large "balloon payment" at maturity.

The Call Provision A **call provision** allows the company to repurchase, or "call," part or all of the bond issue at stated prices over a specific period. Corporate bonds are usually callable.

Generally, the call price is above the bond's stated value (i.e., the par value). The difference between the call price and the stated value is the **call premium**. The amount of the call premium may become smaller over time. One arrangement is to initially set the call premium equal to the annual coupon payment and then make it decline to zero as the call date moves closer to the time of maturity.

Call provisions are often not operative during the first part of a bond's life, making the call provision less of a worry for bondholders in the bond's early years. For example, a company might be prohibited from calling its bonds for the first 10 years. This is a **deferred call provision**. During the period of prohibition, the bond is said to be **call protected**.

In recent years, a new type of call provision, a "make-whole" call, has become widespread in the corporate bond market. With such a feature, bondholders receive approximately what the bonds are worth if they are called. Because bondholders don't suffer a loss in the event of a call, they are "made whole."

To determine the make-whole call price, we calculate the present value of the remaining interest and principal payments at a rate specified in the indenture. For example, looking at our Cisco issue, we see that the discount rate is "Treasury rate plus .15%." What this means is that we determine the discount rate by first finding a U.S. Treasury issue with the same maturity. We calculate the yield to maturity on the Treasury issue and then add on an additional .15 percent to get the discount rate we use.

Notice that, with a make-whole call provision, the call price is higher when interest rates are lower and vice versa (why?). Also notice that, as is common with a make-whole call, the Cisco issue does not have a deferred call feature. Why might investors not be too concerned about the absence of this feature?

EXAMPLE
15.2

Callable Bonds

A call provision permits a company to repurchase or call an entire bond issue at some price during a predetermined period. Common sense tells us that call provisions have positive value to the company and negative value to the creditor. If interest rates fall and bond prices go up, the option to buy back the bonds at a call price that is lower than would be true otherwise is valuable. Of course, bond investors know this and take into account the call provision.

Suppose the Venture Capital Corp (VCC) has an outstanding 30-year bond that pays semiannual coupons. It is a 7% bond with a $1,000 par value and is currently selling at par. Further suppose that because of potential changes in interest rates, the price of the VCC bond could be $700 or $1,300 at the end of the year with equal odds.

1. What is the expected value of the VCC bonds after one year?
   Answer: $(.5 \times \$700) + (.5 \times \$1300) = \$1000$

2. What is the expected value of the VCC bonds if they are callable at $1,000?
   Answer: $(.5 \times \$700) + (.5 \times \$1000) = 850$

If the bonds are callable, the expected bond value can be less than if the bonds are not callable. If the actual bond value rises above the call price, the company will call it. Therefore, other things equal, the bond holder will not pay as much for a callable bond.

Want detailed information on the amount and terms of the debt issued by a particular firm? Check out its latest financial statements by searching SEC filings at **www.sec.gov**.

Protective Covenants   A **protective covenant** in the indenture or loan agreement affects certain corporate actions. Protective covenants can be classified into two types: negative covenants and positive (or affirmative) covenants.

A *negative covenant* is a "thou shalt not" type of covenant. It limits or prohibits actions that the company might take. For example, the firm must limit the amount of dividends it pays according to some formula.

A *positive covenant* is a "thou shalt" type of covenant. It specifies an action that the company must take or a condition that the company must abide by. For example, the company must maintain its working capital at or above some specified minimum level.

A particular indenture may feature many different negative and positive covenants.

15.3 Some Different Types of Bonds

Thus far, we have considered only "plain vanilla" corporate bonds. In this section, we look at corporate bonds with unusual features.

FLOATING-RATE BONDS

The conventional bonds we discussed in this chapter have fixed-dollar obligations because the coupon rate is set as a fixed percentage of the par value and the principal is set equal to the par value. With *floating-rate bonds (floaters),* the coupon payments are adjustable. The adjustments are tied to an interest rate index such as the Treasury bill interest rate or the 30-year Treasury bond rate.

The value of a floating-rate bond depends on how the coupon payment adjustments are defined. In most cases, the coupon adjusts with a lag to some base rate. For example, suppose a coupon rate adjustment is made on June 1. The adjustment might be based on the simple average of Treasury bond yields during the previous three months.

In addition, the majority of floaters have the following features:

1. The holder has the right to redeem his note at par on the coupon payment date after some specified amount of time. This is called a *put* provision, and it is discussed in the following section.

2. The coupon rate has a floor and a ceiling, meaning that the coupon is subject to a minimum and a maximum. In this case, the coupon rate is said to be "capped," and the upper and lower rates are sometimes called the *collar*.

OTHER TYPES OF BONDS

Many bonds have unusual or exotic features. One such feature is called a warrant. A warrant gives the buyer of a bond the right to purchase shares of stock in the company at a fixed price. Such a right would be very valuable if the stock price climbed substantially.

(A later chapter discusses this subject in greater depth.) Because of the value of this feature, bonds with warrants are often issued at a very low coupon rate.

Bond features are really only limited by the imaginations of the parties involved. Unfortunately, there are far too many variations for us to cover in detail here. We therefore close out this section by mentioning only a few of the more common types.

Income bonds are similar to conventional bonds, except that coupon payments are dependent on company income. Specifically, coupons are paid to bondholders only if the firm's income is sufficient. This would appear to be an attractive feature, but income bonds are not very common.

A *convertible bond* can be swapped for a fixed number of shares of stock anytime before maturity at the holder's option. Convertibles are relatively common, but the number has been decreasing in recent years.

A *put bond* allows the *holder* to force the issuer to buy the bond back at a stated price. For example, International Paper Co. has bonds outstanding that allow the holder to force International Paper to buy the bonds back at 100 percent of face value if certain "risk" events happen. One such event is a change in credit rating from investment grade to lower than investment grade by Moody's or S&P. The put feature is therefore just the reverse of the call provision.

A given bond may have many unusual features. Two of the most recent exotic bonds are CoCo bonds, which have a coupon payment, and NoNo bonds, which are zero coupon bonds. CoCo and NoNo bonds are contingent convertible, putable, callable, subordinated bonds. The contingent convertible clause is similar to the normal conversion feature, except the contingent feature must be met. For example, a contingent feature may require that the company stock trade at 110 percent of the conversion price for 20 out of the most recent 30 days. Valuing a bond of this sort can be quite complex, and the yield to maturity calculation is often meaningless.

15.4 Bank Loans

In addition to issuing bonds, a firm may simply borrow from a bank. Two important features of bank loans are lines of credit and syndication.

Lines of Credit   Banks often provide a business customer with a line of credit, setting the maximum amount that the bank is willing to lend to the business. The business can then borrow the money according to its need for funds. If the bank is legally obligated, the credit line is generally referred to as a revolving line of credit or a *revolver*. As an example, imagine a revolver for $75 million with a three-year commitment, implying that the business could borrow part or all of the $75 million anytime within the next three years. A commitment fee is generally charged on the unused portion of the revolver. Suppose the commitment fee is .20% and the corporation borrows $25 million in a particular year, leaving $50 million unborrowed. The dollar commitment fee would be $100,000 (= .20% × $50 million) for that year, in addition to the interest on the $25 million actually borrowed.

Syndicated Loans   Very large banks such as Citigroup typically have a larger demand for loans than they can supply, and small regional banks frequently have more funds on hand than they can profitably lend to existing customers. Basically, they cannot generate enough good loans with the funds they have available. As a result, a very large bank may arrange a syndicated loan with a firm or country and then sell portions of it to a syndicate of other banks. With a syndicated loan, each bank has a separate loan agreement with the borrowers.

The syndicate is generally composed of a lead arranger and participant lenders. As the name suggests, the lead arranger takes the lead, creating the relationship with the borrower and negotiating the specifics of the loan. The participant lenders are typically not involved in the negotiation process. The lead arranger works with the participant lenders to determine shares of the loan, and generally lends the most. While all lenders receive interest and principal payments, the lead arranger also receives an up-front fee as compensation for its additional responsibilities.

A syndicated loan may be publicly traded. It may be a line of credit and be "undrawn," or it may be drawn and used by a firm. Syndicated loans are always rated investment grade. However, a *leveraged* syndicated loan is rated speculative grade (i.e., it is "junk").

15.5 International Bonds

A **Eurobond** is a bond issued in multiple countries but denominated in a single currency, usually the issuer's home currency. For example, an American firm may issue a dollar-denominated bond in a number of foreign countries. Such bonds have become an important way to raise capital for many international companies and governments. Eurobonds are issued outside the restrictions that apply to domestic offerings and are syndicated and traded mostly from London. However, trading can and does take place anywhere there are buyers and sellers. Eurobonds had been trading for many years before the euro, the single currency across many European countries, was created in 1999. However, because the two terms are so similar, people mistakenly think Eurobonds must be denominated in euros. To avoid confusion, many refer to Eurobonds as international bonds.

Foreign bonds, unlike Eurobonds, are issued in a single country and are usually denominated in that country's currency. For example, a Canadian firm might issue yen-denominated bonds in Japan. Often, the country in which these bonds are issued will draw distinctions between them and bonds issued by domestic issuers—including different tax laws, restrictions on the amount issued, and tougher disclosure rules.

Foreign bonds often are nicknamed for the country where they are issued: Yankee bonds (United States), Samurai bonds (Japan), Rembrandt bonds (the Netherlands), Bulldog bonds (Britain). Partly because of tougher regulations and disclosure requirements, the foreign bond market hasn't grown in past years with the vigor of the Eurobond market.

15.6 Patterns of Financing

The previous sections of this chapter discussed some institutional details related to long-term financing. We now consider the relationship between long-term financing and investments. As we have seen in earlier chapters, firms want to spend on capital projects with positive NPV. How can these firms get the cash to fund investments in positive NPV projects? First, firms generating positive cash flow internally can use that flow for positive NPV investments. In accounting terms, this cash flow is net income plus depreciation minus dividends. Second, firms can fund positive NPV capital spending through external financing, that is, by issuing debt and equity.

This relationship between investment and financing is described in Figure 15.1. The left-hand side of the figure indicates that cash flow can fund both capital spending and investment in net working capital. The right-hand side of the figure shows the two sources of cash flow, internal and external financing. In the figure, uses of cash flow exceed internal financing. Thus, stocks and bonds must be issued to fill the *financial deficit*.

In practice, what has been the split between internal and external financing? Figure 15.2 breaks down total financing for U.S. businesses into internal financing, financing through new equity, and financing through new debt for each year from 1975 to 2013. Consider 1995, for example. Internal financing in the United States was about 89 percent

Figure 15.1
The Long-Term
Financial Deficit

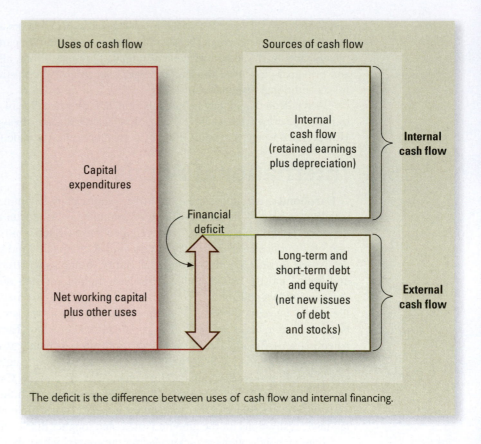

The deficit is the difference between uses of cash flow and internal financing.

Figure 15.2
Financing by U.S.
Nonfinancial
Corporations as a
Percentage of Uses
of Cash Flow

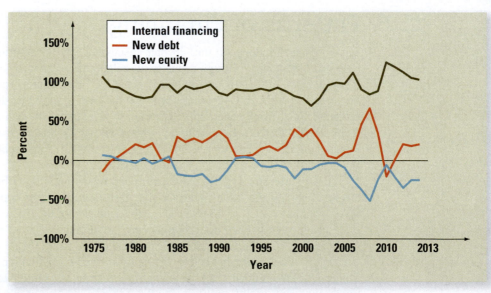

SOURCE: Board of Governors of the Federal Reserve System. "Flow of Funds Accounts of the United States." Federal Reserve Statistical Release. June 5, 2014, http://www.federalreserve.gov/releases/1/20140605/.

of the total, new debt was about 18 percent of the total, and new equity was a negative number. Notice that in this year, as in all the years, the three sources of funds must add to 100 percent. If you are wondering why net equity is a negative number, it is because corporations repurchased more stock than they issued in that year.

The figure illustrates a number of points. First, internally generated cash flow has been the dominant source of financing. Second, this dominance has increased over the sample period, with internal financing actually exceeding 100 percent for most of the years from 2005 to 2013. A number above 100 percent implies that external financing is negative. In other words, corporations are, in dollar terms, redeeming more stocks and bonds than they are issuing. Third, this redemption occurred in equity much more than in debt. New equity was negative in every year since 1994, indicating that the dollar amount of stock buybacks exceeded the dollar amount of stock issues throughout this period. By contrast, new debt financing was positive in every year but 1975, 1983, and 2009. One can view this as share buybacks being financed with new debt.

15.7 Recent Trends in Capital Structure

Figure 15.2 indicates that U.S. firms tended to issue debt while retiring stock. This pattern of financing raises the question: Did the capital structure of firms change over this time period? One might expect the answer to be yes, since debt issuances and stock retirements should raise the ratio of debt to equity. However, look at Figure 15.3, where the ratio of total debt to the book value of equity is shown for each year from 1975 to 2013. The ratio was actually lower in 2013 than it was in 1975. This result is not surprising once retained earnings are considered. As long as net income exceeds dividends, retained earnings will be positive, raising the book value of equity.

Of course, equity can be measured in terms of market value, rather than book value. Figure 15.3 also shows the ratio of total debt to the market value of equity for U.S. firms.

Figure 15.3 Debt to Equity Ratios: Total Debt as a Percentage of Book Value of Equity and Market Value of Equity for U.S. Nonfarm, Nonfinancial Firms from 1975 to 2013

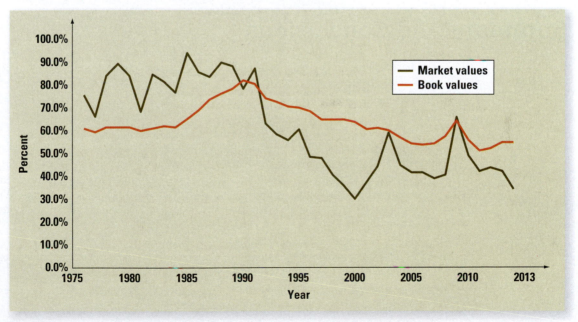

SOURCE: Board of Governors of the Federal Reserve System. "Flow of Funds Accounts of the United States." Federal Reserve Statistical Release. June 4, 2014, http://www.federalreserve.gov/releases/1/20140605/.

While the debt-to-market value ratio is also lower in 2013 than in 1974, the year-by-year pattern is somewhat different than the pattern for debt-to-book value. The debt-to-market value ratio rose significantly from 1999 to 2002 and again in 2008, reflecting the sharp drop in stock prices during those periods. Conversely, the debt-to-market value ratio fell during both the late 1990s and the period from 2008 to 2013, reflecting the sharp rise in stock prices then. Thus, as Figure 15.3 shows, leverage ratios are strongly affected by stock market movements when market values, rather than book values, of equity are used.

WHICH ARE BEST: BOOK OR MARKET VALUES?

Financial economists generally prefer market values when calculating debt ratios, since, as Chapter 14 indicates, market prices reflect current information. However, the use of market values does not mean that book values should be ignored.

Our conversations with corporate treasurers suggest to us that the use of book values is popular because of the volatility of the stock market. It is frequently claimed that the inherent volatility of the stock market makes market-based debt ratios move around too much. In addition, restrictions of debt in bond covenants are usually expressed in book values rather than market values. Moreover, firms such as Standard & Poor's and Moody's use debt ratios expressed in book values to measure credit-worthiness.

A key fact is that whether we use book or market values, debt ratios for U.S. nonfinancial firms generally have been well below 100 percent of total equity in recent years; that is, firms generally use less debt than equity.

Summary and Conclusions

The basic sources of long-term financing are long-term debt, preferred stock, and common stock. This chapter described the essential features of each.

1. We emphasized that common shareholders have:
   a. Residual risk and return in a corporation.
   b. Voting rights.
   c. Dividends are not a business expense and firms cannot be forced into bankruptcy for non payment of a dividend.

2. Long-term debt involves contractual obligations set out in indentures. There are many kinds of debt, but the essential feature is that debt involves a stated amount that must be repaid. Interest payments on debt are considered a business expense and are tax deductible.

3. Preferred stock has some of the features of debt and some of the features of common equity. Holders of preferred stock have preference in liquidation and in dividend payments compared to holders of common equity.

4. Firms need financing for capital expenditures, working capital, and other long-term uses. Most of the financing is provided from internally generated cash flow.

5. For many years, U.S. firms have been retiring large amounts of equity. These share buybacks have been financed with new debt.

Concept Questions

1. **Bond Features**   What are the main features of a corporate bond that would be listed in the indenture?

2. **Preferred Stock and Debt**   What are the differences between preferred stock and debt?

3. **Preferred Stock**   Preferred stock doesn't offer a corporate tax shield on the dividends paid. Why do we still observe some firms issuing preferred stock?

4. **Preferred Stock and Bond Yields**   The yields on nonconvertible preferred stock are lower than the yields on corporate bonds. Why is there a difference? Which investors are the primary holders of preferred stock? Why?

5. **Corporate Financing**   What are the main differences between corporate debt and equity? Why do some firms try to issue equity in the guise of debt?

6. **Call Provisions**   A company is contemplating a long-term bond issue. It is debating whether to include a call provision. What are the benefits to the company from including a call provision? What are the costs? How do these answers change for a put provision?

7. **Proxy**   What is a proxy?

8. **Preferred Stock**   Do you think preferred stock is more like debt or equity? Why?

9. **Long-Term Financing**   As was mentioned in the chapter, new equity issues are generally only a small portion of all new issues. At the same time, companies continue to issue new debt. Why do companies tend to issue little new equity but continue to issue new debt?

10. **Internal versus External Financing**   What is the difference between internal financing and external financing?

11. **Internal versus External Financing**   What factors influence a firm's choice of external versus internal equity financing?

12. **Classes of Stock**   Several publicly traded companies have issued more than one class of stock. Why might a company issue more than one class of stock?

13. **Callable Bonds**   Do you agree or disagree with the following statement: In an efficient market, callable and noncallable bonds will be priced in such a way that there will be no advantage or disadvantage to the call provision. Why?

14. **Bond Prices**   If interest rates fall, will the price of noncallable bonds move up higher than that of callable bonds? Why or why not?

15. **Sinking Funds**   Sinking funds have both positive and negative characteristics for bondholders. Why?

Questions and Problems

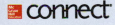

BASIC
(Questions 1–7)

1. **Corporate Voting**   The shareholders of the Stackhouse Company need to elect seven new directors. There are 960,000 shares outstanding currently trading at $48 per share. You would like to serve on the board of directors; unfortunately no one else will be voting for you. How much will it cost you to be certain that you can be elected if the company uses straight voting? How much will it cost you if the company uses cumulative voting?

2. **Cumulative Voting** An election is being held to fill three seats on the board of directors of a firm in which you hold stock. The company has 17,400 shares outstanding. If the election is conducted under cumulative voting and you own 300 shares, how many more shares must you buy to be assured of earning a seat on the board?

3. **Cumulative Voting** The shareholders of Bryant Power Corp. need to elect three new directors to the board. There are 16,500,000 shares of common stock outstanding, and the current share price is $13.75. If the company uses cumulative voting procedures, how much will it cost to guarantee yourself one seat on the board of directors?

4. **Corporate Voting** Beasley, Inc. is going to elect nine board members next month. Betty Brown owns 12.4 percent of the total shares outstanding. How confident can she be of having one of her candidate friends elected under the cumulative voting rule? Will her friend be elected for certain if the voting procedure is changed to the staggering rule, under which shareholders vote on three board members at a time?

5. **Financial Leverage** Kiedis, Corp., has interest-bearing debt with a market value of $65 million. The company also has 2 million shares that sell for $25 per share. What is the debt–equity ratio for this company based on market values?

6. **Financial Leverage** Frusciante, Inc., has 290,000 bonds outstanding. The bonds have a par value of $1,000, a coupon rate of 7 percent paid semiannually, and 8 years to maturity. The current YTM on the bonds is 7.5 percent. The company also has 10 million shares of stock outstanding, with a market price of $23 per share. What is the company's market value debt–equity ratio?

7. **Financial Leverage** Harrison, Inc., has the following book value balance sheet:

Assets		Total Debt and Equity	
Current assets	$200,000,000	Total debt	$220,000,000
		Equity	
		Common stock	$30,000,000
		Capital surplus	80,000,000
		Accumulated retained earnings	170,000,000
Net fixed assets	$300,000,000	Total shareholders' equity	$280,000,000
Total assets	$500,000,000	Total debt and shareholders' equity	$500,000,000

a. What is the debt–equity ratio based on book values?

b. Suppose the market value of the company's debt is $225 million and the market value of equity is $670 million. What is the debt–equity ratio based on market values?

c. Which is more relevant, the debt–equity ratio based on book values or market values? Why?

INTERMEDIATE
(Questions 8–11)

8. **Valuing Callable Bonds** KIC, Inc., plans to issue $5 million of bonds with a coupon rate of 8 percent and 30 years to maturity. The current market interest rates on these bonds are 7 percent. In one year, the interest rate on the bonds will be either 10 percent or 6 percent with equal probability. Assume investors are risk-neutral.

a. If the bonds are noncallable, what is the price of the bonds today?

b. If the bonds are callable one year from today at $1,080, will their price be greater or less than the price you computed in (a)? Why?

9. **Valuing Callable Bonds** New Business Ventures, Inc., has an outstanding perpetual bond with a 10 percent coupon rate that can be called in one year. The bond makes annual coupon payments. The call premium is set at $150 over par value. There is a 60 percent chance that the interest rate in one year will be 12 percent, and a 40 percent chance that the interest rate will be 7 percent. If the current interest rate is 10 percent, what is the current market price of the bond?

10. **Valuing Callable Bonds** Bowdeen Manufacturing intends to issue callable, perpetual bonds with annual coupon payments. The bonds are callable at $1,175. One-year interest rates are 9 percent. There is a 60 percent probability that long-term interest rates one year from today will be 10 percent, and a 40 percent probability that they will be 8 percent. Assume that if interest rates fall the bonds will be called. What coupon rate should the bonds have in order to sell at par value?

11. **Valuing Callable Bonds** Williams Industries has decided to borrow money by issuing perpetual bonds with a coupon rate of 6.5 percent, payable annually. The one-year interest rate is 6.5 percent. Next year, there is a 35 percent probability that interest rates will increase to 8 percent, and there is a 65 percent probability that they will fall to 5 percent.

    a. What will the market value of these bonds be if they are noncallable?
    b. If the company decides instead to make the bonds callable in one year, what coupon will be demanded by the bondholders for the bonds to sell at par? Assume that the bonds will be called if interest rates fall and that the call premium is equal to the annual coupon.
    c. What will be the value of the call provision to the company?

CHALLENGE
(Question 12)

12. **Treasury Bonds** The following Treasury bond quote appeared in *The Wall Street Journal* on May 11, 2004:

9.125	May 09	100.09375	100.12500	. . .	−2.15

    Why would anyone buy this Treasury bond with a negative yield to maturity? How is this possible?

16

Capital Structure

BASIC CONCEPTS

Any way you look at it, 2014 was a banner year for corporate bond issuance. In the United States, corporate bond issuance surpassed $1.5 trillion, and corporate bond issuance worldwide was more than $4 trillion. Online retailer Amazon.com, for example, sold $6 billion in bonds in December 2014, its first issue since a $3 billion offering in 2012.

Amazon's $6 billion deal was a big one, but no match for Apple. In 2013, Apple had a then-record $17 billion bond issue. In April 2014, the company issued another $12 billion in debt, followed by a €2.8 billion ($3.5 billion) bond offering in November 2014.

In issuing all this debt, these companies succeeded in raising capital, but why did they choose to issue bonds instead of stock? A firm's choice of whether to sell debt or equity is known as a capital structure decision. In this chapter, we discuss the basic ideas underlying capital structures and how firms choose them.

16.1 The Capital Structure Question and the Pie Theory

How should a firm choose its debt–equity ratio? We call our approach to the capital structure question the **pie model**. If you are wondering why we chose this name, just take a look at Figure 16.1. The pie in question is the sum of the financial claims of the firm, debt and equity in this case. We *define* the value of the firm to be this sum. Hence the value of the firm, V, is:

$$V \equiv B + S \qquad \textbf{(16.1)}$$

where B is the market value of the debt and S is the market value of the equity. Figure 16.1 presents two possible ways of slicing this pie between stock and debt: 40 percent–60 percent and 60 percent–40 percent. If the goal of the management of the firm is to make the firm as valuable as possible, then the firm should pick the debt–equity ratio that makes the pie—the total value—as big as possible.

This discussion begs two important questions:

1. Why should the stockholders in the firm care about maximizing the value of the entire firm?

2. What ratio of debt to equity maximizes the shareholders' interests?

Let us examine each of the two questions in turn.

Figure 16.1
Two Pie Models of
Capital Structure

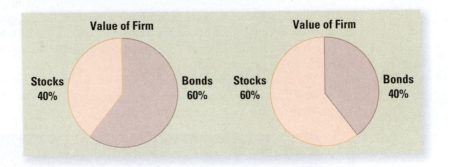

16.2 Maximizing Firm Value versus Maximizing Stockholder Interests

The following example illustrates that the capital structure that maximizes the value of the firm is the one that financial managers should choose for the shareholders.

EXAMPLE
16.1

Debt and Firm Value   Suppose the market value of the J. J. Sprint Company is $1,000. The company currently has no debt, and each of J. J. Sprint's 100 shares of stock sells for $10. A company such as J. J. Sprint with no debt is called an *unlevered* company. Further suppose that J. J. Sprint plans to borrow $500 and pay the $500 proceeds to shareholders as an extra cash dividend of $5 per share. After the issuance of debt, the firm becomes *levered*. The investments of the firm will not change as a result of this transaction. What will the value of the firm be after the proposed restructuring?

Management recognizes that, by definition, only one of three outcomes can occur from restructuring. Firm value after restructuring can be (1) greater than the original firm value of $1,000, (2) equal to $1,000, or (3) less than $1,000. After consulting with investment bankers, management believes that restructuring will not change firm value more than $250 in either direction. Thus it views firm values of $1,250, $1,000, and $750 as the relevant range. The original capital structure and these three possibilities under the new capital structure are presented next:

	No Debt (Original Capital Structure)	Value of Debt plus Equity after Payment of Dividend (Three Possibilities)		
		I	II	III
Debt	$ 0	$ 500	$ 500	$500
Equity	1,000	750	500	250
Firm value	$1,000	$1,250	$1,000	$750

Note that the value of equity is below $1,000 under any of the three possibilities. This can be explained in one of two ways. First, the table shows the value of the equity *after* the extra cash dividend is paid. Because cash is paid out, a dividend represents a partial liquidation of

(*continued*)

the firm. Consequently there is less value in the firm for the equityholders after the dividend payment. Second, in the event of a future liquidation, stockholders will be paid only after bondholders have been paid in full. Thus the debt is an encumbrance of the firm, reducing the value of the equity.

Of course management recognizes that there are infinite possible outcomes. These three are to be viewed as *representative* outcomes only. We can now determine the payoff to stockholders under the three possibilities:

	Payoff to Shareholders after Restructuring		
	I	II	III
Capital gains	−$250	−$500	−$750
Dividends	500	500	500
Net gain or loss to stockholders	$250	$ 0	−$250

No one can be sure ahead of time which of the three outcomes will occur. However, imagine that managers believe that Outcome I is most likely. They should definitely restructure the firm because the stockholders would gain $250. That is, although the price of the stock declines by $250 to $750, they receive $500 in dividends. Their net gain is $250 = −$250 + $500. Also, notice that the value of the firm would rise by $250 = $1,250 − $1,000.

Alternatively, imagine that managers believe that Outcome III is most likely. In this case they should not restructure the firm because the stockholders would expect a $250 loss. That is, the stock falls by $750 to $250 and they receive $500 in dividends. Their net loss is −$250 = −$750 + $500. Also, notice that the value of the firm would change by −$250 = $750 − $1,000.

Finally, imagine that the managers believe that Outcome II is most likely. Restructuring would not affect the stockholders' interest because the net gain to stockholders in this case is zero. Also notice that the value of the firm is unchanged if Outcome II occurs.

This example explains why managers should attempt to maximize the value of the firm. In other words, it answers question (1) in Section 16.1. We find in this example the following wisdom:

Managers should choose the capital structure that they believe will have the highest firm value because this capital structure will be most beneficial to the firm's stockholders.[1]

Clearly, J. J. Sprint should borrow $500 if it expects Outcome I. The crucial question in determining a firm's capital structure is, of course, which outcome is likely to occur. However, this example does not tell us which of the three outcomes is most likely to occur. Thus it does not tell us whether debt should be added to J. J. Sprint's capital structure. In other words, it does not answer question (2) in Section 16.1. This second question is treated in the next section.

---

[1]This result may not hold exactly in a more complex case where debt has a significant possibility of default. Issues of default are treated in the next chapter.

16.3   Financial Leverage and Firm Value: An Example

LEVERAGE AND RETURNS TO SHAREHOLDERS

The previous section shows that the capital structure producing the highest firm value is the one that maximizes shareholder wealth. In this section, we wish to determine that optimal capital structure. We begin by illustrating the effect of capital structure on returns to stockholders. We will use a detailed example that we encourage students to study carefully. Once we have this example under our belts, we will be ready to determine the optimal capital structure.

Trans Am Corporation currently has no debt in its capital structure. The firm is considering issuing debt to buy back some of its equity. Both its current and proposed capital structures are presented in Table 16.1. The firm's assets are $8,000. There are 400 shares of the all-equity firm, implying a market value per share of $20. The proposed debt issue is for $4,000, leaving $4,000 in equity. The interest rate is 10 percent.

The effect of economic conditions on earnings per share is shown in Table 16.2 for the current capital structure (all equity). Consider first the middle column where earnings are expected to be $1,200. Because assets are $8,000, the return on assets (ROA) is 15 percent (=$1,200/$8,000). Assets equal equity for this all-equity firm, so return on equity (ROE) is also 15 percent. Earnings per share (EPS) is $3.00 (=$1,200/400). Similar calculations yield EPS of $1.00 and $5.00 in the cases of recession and expansion, respectively.

The case of leverage is presented in Table 16.3. ROA in the three economic states is identical in Tables 16.2 and 16.3 because this ratio is calculated before interest is considered. Debt is $4,000 here, so interest is $400 (=.10 × $4,000). Thus earnings after interest are $800 (=$1,200 − $400) in the middle (expected) case. Because equity is $4,000, ROE is 20 percent (=$800/$4,000). Earnings per share are $4.00 (=$800/$200). Similar calculations yield earnings of $0 and $8.00 for recession and expansion, respectively.

Tables 16.2 and 16.3 show that the effect of financial leverage depends on the company's earnings before interest. If earnings before interest are equal to $1,200,

Table 16.1

Financial Structure of Trans Am Corporation

	Current	Proposed
Assets	$8,000	$8,000
Debt	$ 0	$4,000
Equity (market and book)	$8,000	$4,000
Interest rate	10%	10%
Market value/share	$ 20	$ 20
Shares outstanding	400	200

The proposed capital structure has leverage, whereas the current structure is all equity.

Table 16.2

Trans Am's Current Capital Structure: No Debt

	Recession	Expected	Expansion
Return on assets (ROA)	5%	15%	25%
Earnings	$400	$1,200	$2,000
Return on equity (ROE) = Earnings/Equity	5%	15%	25%
Earnings per share (EPS)	$1.00	$3.00	$5.00

Table 16.3
Trans Am's Proposed
Capital Structure:
Debt = $4,000

	Recession	Expected	Expansion
Return on assets (ROA)	5%	15%	25%
Earnings before interest (EBI)	$400	$1,200	$2,000
Interest	−400	−400	−400
Earnings after interest	$ 0	$ 800	$1,600
Return on equity (ROE) = Earnings after interest/Equity	0%	20%	40%
Earnings per share (EPS)	$ 0	$ 4.00	$ 8.00

the return on equity (ROE) is higher under the proposed structure. If earnings before interest are equal to $400, the ROE is higher under the current structure.

This idea is represented in Figure 16.2. The solid line represents the case of no leverage. The line begins at the origin, indicating that earnings per share (EPS) would be zero if earnings before interest (EBI) was zero. The EPS rises in tandem with a rise in EBI.

The dotted line represents the case of $4,000 of debt. Here EPS is negative if EBI is zero. This follows because $400 of interest must be paid regardless of the firm's profits.

Now consider the slopes of the two lines. The slope of the dotted line (the line with debt) is higher than the slope of the solid line. This occurs because the levered firm has *fewer* shares of stock outstanding than the unlevered firm. Therefore, any increase in EBI leads to a greater rise in EPS for the levered firm because the earnings increase is distributed over fewer shares of stock.

Because the dotted line has a lower intercept but a higher slope, the two lines must intersect. The *break-even* point occurs at $800 of EBI. Were earnings before interest to

Figure 16.2

Financial Leverage:
EPS and EBI for
the Trans Am
Corporation

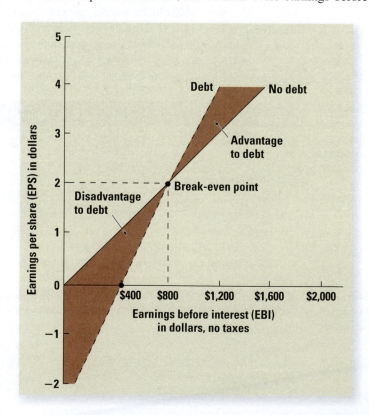

Table 16.4   Payoff and Cost to Shareholders of Trans Am Corporation under the Proposed Structure and under the Current Structure with Homemade Leverage

	Recession	Expected	Expansion
Strategy A: Buy 100 Shares of Levered Equity			
EPS of *levered* equity (taken from last line of Table 16.3)	$0	$ 4	$ 8
Earnings per 100 shares	0	400	800
Initial cost = 100 shares @ $20/share = $2,000			
Strategy B: Homemade Leverage			
Earnings per 200 shares in current	$1 × 200 =	$3 × 200 =	$5 × 200 =
unlevered Trans Am	200	600	1,000
Interest at 10% on $2,000	−200	−200	−200
Net earnings	$ 0	$ 400	$ 800
Initial cost = 200 shares @ $20/share − $2,000 = $2,000			
Cost of stock Amount borrowed			

Investor receives the same payoff whether she (1) buys shares in a levered corporation or (2) buys shares in an unlevered firm and borrows on personal account. Her initial investment is the same in either case. Thus the firm neither helps nor hurts her by adding debt to capital structure.

be $800, both firms would produce $2 of earnings per share (EPS). Because $800 is breakeven, earnings above $800 lead to a greater EPS for the levered firm. Earnings below $800 lead to a greater EPS for the unlevered firm.

THE CHOICE BETWEEN DEBT AND EQUITY

Tables 16.2 and 16.3 and Figure 16.2 are important because they show the effect of leverage on earnings per share. Students should study the tables and figure until they feel comfortable with the calculation of each number in them. However, we have not yet presented the punch line. That is, we have not yet stated which capital structure is better for Trans Am.

At this point many students believe that leverage is beneficial because EPS is expected to be $4.00 with leverage and only $3.00 without leverage. However, leverage also creates *risk*. Note that in a recession, EPS is higher ($1.00 versus $0) for the unlevered firm. Thus a risk-averse investor might prefer the all-equity firm, whereas a risk-neutral (or less risk-averse) investor might prefer leverage. Given this ambiguity, which capital structure *is* better?

Modigliani and Miller (MM or M & M) have a convincing argument that a firm cannot change the total value of its outstanding securities by changing the proportions of its capital structure. In other words, the value of the firm is always the same under different capital structures. In still other words, no capital structure is any better or worse than any other capital structure for the firm's stockholders. This rather pessimistic result is the famous **MM Proposition I**.[2]

Their argument compares a simple strategy, which we call Strategy *A*, with a two-part strategy, which we call Strategy *B*. Both of these strategies for shareholders of Trans Am are illuminated in Table 16.4. Let us now examine the first strategy.

[2]The original paper is Franco Modigliani and Merton Miller, "The Cost of Capital, Corporation Finance and the Theory of Investment," *American Economic Review* (June 1958).

Strategy A: Buy 100 shares of the levered equity

The first line in the top panel of Table 16.4 shows EPS for the proposed levered equity in the three economic states. The second line shows the earnings in the three states for an individual buying 100 shares. The next line shows that the cost of these 100 shares is $2,000.

Let us now consider the second strategy, which has two parts to it.

Strategy B: Homemade leverage

1. Borrow $2,000 from either a bank or, more likely, a brokerage house. (If the brokerage house is the lender, we say that this activity is *going on margin.*)

2. Use the borrowed proceeds plus your own investment of $2,000 (a total of $4,000) to buy 200 shares of the current unlevered equity at $20 per share.

The bottom panel of Table 16.4 shows payoffs under Strategy B, which we call the *homemade leverage* strategy. First observe the middle column, which indicates that 200 shares of the unlevered equity are expected to generate $600 of earnings. Assuming that the $2,000 is borrowed at a 10 percent interest rate, the interest expense is $200 ($=.10 \times \$2,000$). Thus the net earnings are expected to be $400. A similar calculation generates net earnings of either $0 or $800 in recession or expansion, respectively.

Now let us compare these two strategies, both in terms of earnings per year and in terms of initial cost. The top panel of the table shows that Strategy *A* generates earnings of $0, $400, and $800 in the three states. The bottom panel of the table shows that Strategy *B* generates the *same* net earnings in the three states.

The top panel of the table shows that Strategy *A* involves an initial cost of $2,000. Similarly, the bottom panel shows an *identical* net cost of $2,000 for Strategy *B*.

This shows a very important result. Both the cost and the payoff from the two strategies are the same. Thus we must conclude that Trans Am is neither helping nor hurting its stockholders by restructuring. In other words, an investor is not receiving anything from corporate leverage that she could not receive on her own.

Note that, as shown in Table 16.1, the equity of the unlevered firm is valued at $8,000. Because the equity of the levered firm is $4,000 and its debt is $4,000, the value of the levered firm is also $8,000. Now suppose that, for whatever reason, the value of the levered firm were actually greater than the value of the unlevered firm. Here Strategy *A* would cost more than Strategy *B*. In this case an investor would prefer to borrow on his own account and invest in the stock of the unlevered firm. He would get the same net earnings each year as if he had invested in the stock of the levered firm. However, his cost would be less. The strategy would not be unique to our investor. Given the higher value of the levered firm, no rational investor would invest in the stock of the levered firm. Anyone desiring shares in the levered firm would get the same dollar return more cheaply by borrowing to finance a purchase of the unlevered firm's shares. The equilibrium result would be, of course, that the value of the levered firm would fall and the value of the unlevered firm would rise until they became equal. At this point individuals would be indifferent between Strategy *A* and Strategy *B*.

This example illustrates the basic result of Modigliani–Miller (MM) and is, as we have noted, commonly called their Proposition I. We restate this proposition as follows:

MM Proposition I (no taxes): The value of the levered firm is the same as the value of the unlevered firm.

This is one of the most important results in all of corporate finance. In fact, it is generally considered the beginning point of modern managerial finance. Before MM, the effect of leverage on the value of the firm was considered complex and convoluted. Modigliani and Miller showed a blindingly simple result: If levered firms are priced too high, rational investors will simply borrow on their personal accounts to buy shares in unlevered firms. This substitution is often called *homemade leverage.* As long as individuals borrow (and lend) on the same terms as the firms, they can duplicate the effects of corporate leverage on their own.

The example of Trans Am Corporation shows that leverage does not affect the value of the firm. Because we showed earlier that stockholders' welfare is directly related to the firm's value, the example indicates that changes in capital structure cannot affect the stockholders' welfare.

A KEY ASSUMPTION

The MM result hinges on the assumption that individuals can borrow as cheaply as corporations. If, alternatively, individuals can borrow only at a higher rate, we can easily show that corporations can increase firm value by borrowing.

Is this assumption of equal borrowing costs a good one? Individuals who want to buy stock and borrow can do so by establishing a margin account with a broker. Under this arrangement the broker lends the individual a portion of the purchase price. For example, the individual might buy $10,000 of stock by investing $6,000 of her own funds and borrowing $4,000 from the broker. Should the stock be worth $9,000 on the next day, the individual's net worth or equity in the account would be $5,000 = $9,000 − $4,000.[3]

The broker fears that a sudden price drop will cause the equity in the individual's account to be negative, implying that the broker may not get her loan repaid in full. To guard against this possibility, stock exchange rules require that the individual make additional cash contributions (replenish her margin account) as the stock price falls. Because (1) the procedures for replenishing the account have developed over many years and (2) the broker holds the stock as collateral, there is little default risk to the broker.[4] In particular, if margin contributions are not made on time, the broker can sell the stock to satisfy her loan. Therefore, brokers generally charge low interest, with many rates being only slightly above the risk-free rate.

By contrast, corporations frequently borrow using illiquid assets (e.g., plant and equipment) as collateral. The costs to the lender of initial negotiation and ongoing supervision, as well as of working out arrangements in the event of financial distress, can be quite substantial. Thus it is difficult to argue that individuals must borrow at higher rates than corporations.

16.4 Modigliani and Miller: Proposition II (No Taxes)

RISK TO EQUITYHOLDERS RISES WITH LEVERAGE

At a Trans Am corporate meeting, a corporate officer said, "Well, maybe it does not matter whether the corporation or the individual levers—as long as some leverage takes place. Leverage benefits investors. After all, an investor's expected return rises with the amount of the leverage present." He then pointed out that, as shown in Tables 16.2 and 16.3, the expected return on unlevered equity is 15 percent whereas the expected return on levered equity is 20 percent.

---

[3]We are ignoring the one-day interest charge on the loan.

[4]Had this text been published before October 19, 1987, when stock prices declined by more than 20 percent in a single day, we might have used the phrase "virtually no" risk instead of "little" risk.

However, another officer replied, "Not necessarily. Though the expected return rises with leverage, the *risk* rises as well." This point can be seen from an examination of Tables 16.2 and 16.3. With earnings before interest (EBI) varying between $400 and $2,000, earnings per share (EPS) for the stockholders of the unlevered firm vary between $1.00 and $5.00. EPS for the stockholders of the levered firm varies between $0 and $8.00. This greater range for the EPS of the levered firm implies greater risk for the levered firm's stockholders. In other words, levered stockholders have better returns in good times than do unlevered stockholders but have worse returns in bad times. The two tables also show greater range for the ROE of the levered firm's stockholders. The earlier interpretation concerning risk applies here as well.

The same insight can be taken from Figure 16.2. The slope of the line for the levered firm is greater than the slope of the line for the unlevered firm. This means that the levered stockholders have better returns in good times than do unlevered stockholders but have worse returns in bad times, implying greater risk with leverage. In other words, the slope of the line measures the risk to stockholders because the slope indicates the responsiveness of ROE to changes in firm performance (earnings before interest).

PROPOSITION II: REQUIRED RETURN TO EQUITYHOLDERS RISES WITH LEVERAGE

Because levered equity has greater risk, it should have a greater expected return as compensation. In our example, the market *requires* only a 15 percent expected return for the unlevered equity, but it requires a 20 percent expected return for the levered equity.

This type of reasoning allows us to develop **MM Proposition II**. Here MM argue that the expected return on equity is positively related to leverage because the risk to equityholders increases with leverage.

To develop this position recall that the firm's weighted average cost of capital, R_{WACC}, can be written as:[5]

$$R_{WACC} = \frac{S}{B + S} \times R_S + \frac{B}{B + S} \times R_B \qquad (16.2)$$

where:

R_B is the cost of debt.

R_S is the expected return on equity or stock, also called the *cost of equity* or the *required return on equity*.

R_{WACC} is the firm's weighted average cost of capital.

B is the value of the firm's bonds or debt.

S is the value of the firm's stock or equity.

Equation 16.2 is quite intuitive. It simply says that a firm's weighted average cost of capital is a weighted average of its cost of debt and its cost of equity. The weight applied to debt is the proportion of debt in the capital structure, and the weight applied to equity is the proportion of equity in the capital structure. Calculations of R_{WACC} from Equation 16.2 for both the unlevered and the levered firm are presented in Table 16.5.

An implication of MM Proposition I is that R_{WACC} is a constant for a given firm, regardless of the capital structure.[6] For example, Table 16.5 shows that R_{WACC} for Trans Am is 15 percent, with or without leverage.

---

[5]Because we do not have taxes here, the cost of debt is R_B, not $R_B(1 - t_C)$ as it was in Chapter 13.

[6]This statement holds in a world of no taxes. It does not hold in a world with taxes, a point to be brought out later in this chapter (see Figure 16.6).

Table 16.5

Cost of Capital
Calculations for
Trans Am

$$R_{\text{WACC}} = \frac{B}{B+S} \times R_B + \frac{S}{B+S} \times R_S$$

Unlevered firm: $15\% = \dfrac{0}{\$8,000} \times 10\%^* + \dfrac{\$8,000}{\$8,000} \times 15\%^\dagger$

Levered firm: $15\% = \dfrac{\$4,000}{\$8,000} \times 10\%^* + \dfrac{\$4,000}{\$8,000} \times 20\%^\ddagger$

*10% is the cost of debt.

†From the "Expected" column in Table 16.2, we learn that expected earnings for the unlevered firm are $1,200. From Table 16.1 we learn that equity for the unlevered firm is $8,000. Thus R_S for the unlevered firm is:

$$\frac{\text{Expected earnings}}{\text{Equity}} = \frac{\$1,200}{\$8,000} = 15\%$$

‡From the "Expected" column in Table 16.3, we learn that expected earnings after interest for the levered firm are $800. From Table 16.1 we learn that equity for the levered firm is $4,000. Thus R_S for the levered firm is:

$$\frac{\text{Expected earnings after interest}}{\text{Equity}} = \frac{\$800}{\$4,000} = 20\%$$

Let us now define R_0 to be the *cost of capital for an all-equity firm.* For the Trans Am Corp., R_0 is calculated as:

$$R_0 = \frac{\text{Expected earnings to unlevered firm}}{\text{Unlevered equity}} = \frac{\$1,200}{\$8,000} = 15\%$$

As can be seen from Table 16.5, R_{WACC} is equal to R_0 for Trans Am. In fact, R_{WACC} must *always* equal R_0 in a world without corporate taxes.[7]

Proposition II states the expected return on equity, R_S, in terms of leverage. The exact relationship, derived by setting $R_{\text{WACC}} = R_0$ and then rearranging Equation 16.2, is:[8]

MM Proposition II (No Taxes):

$$R_S = R_0 + \frac{B}{S}(R_0 - R_B) \tag{16.3}$$

Equation 16.3 implies that the required return on equity is a linear function of the firm's debt–equity ratio. Examining Equation 16.3, we see that if R_0 exceeds the cost of debt, R_B, then the cost of equity rises with increases in the debt–equity ratio, B/S. Normally R_0 should exceed R_B. That is, because even unlevered equity is risky, it should have an expected return greater than that of less risky debt. Note that Equation 16.3 holds for Trans Am in its levered state:

$$.20 = .15 + \frac{\$4,000}{\$4,000}(.15 - .10)$$

_____

[7]We again emphasize that this statement holds in a world of no taxes. It does not hold in a world with taxes, a point to be brought out later in this chapter (see Figure 16.6).

[8]This can be derived from Equation 16.2 by setting $R_{\text{WACC}} = R_0$, yielding:

$$\frac{B}{B+S}R_B + \frac{S}{B+S}R_S = R_0$$

Multiplying both sides by $(B + S)/S$ yields:

$$\frac{B}{S}R_B + R_S = \frac{B+S}{S}R_0$$

We can rewrite the right side as:

$$\frac{B}{S}R_B + R_S = \frac{B}{S}R_0 + R_0$$

Moving $(B/S)R_B$ to the right side and rearranging yields:

$$R_S = R_0 + \frac{B}{S}(R_0 - R_B)$$

Figure 16.3

The Cost of Equity, the Cost of Debt, and the Weighted Average Cost of Capital: MM Proposition II with No Corporate Taxes

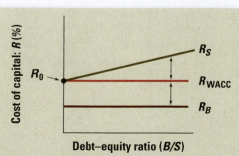

$R_S = R_0 + (R_0 - R_B)B/S$

 R_S is the cost of equity.

 R_B is the cost of debt.

 R_0 is the cost of capital for an all-equity firm.

 R_{WACC} is a firm's weighted average cost of capital. In a world with no taxes, R_{WACC} for a levered firm is equal to R_0.

 R_0 is a single point whereas R_S, R_B, and R_{WACC} are all entire lines.

The cost of equity capital, R_S, is positively related to the firm's debt–equity ratio. The firm's weighted average cost of capital, R_{WACC}, is invariant to the firm's debt–equity ratio.

Figure 16.3 graphs Equation 16.3. As you can see, we have plotted the relation between the cost of equity, R_S, and the debt–equity ratio, B/S, as a straight line. What we witness in Equation 16.3 and illustrate in Figure 16.3 is the effect of leverage on the cost of equity. As the firm raises the debt–equity ratio, each dollar of equity is levered with additional debt. This raises the risk of equity and therefore the required return, R_S, on the equity.

Figure 16.3 also shows that R_{WACC} is unaffected by leverage, a point we have already made. (It is important for students to realize that R_0, the cost of capital for an all-equity firm, is represented by a single dot on the graph. By contrast, R_{WACC} is an entire line.)

EXAMPLE

16.2

MM Propositions I and II   Luteran Motors, an all-equity firm, has expected earnings of $10 million per year in perpetuity. The firm pays all of its earnings out as dividends, so the $10 million may also be viewed as the stockholders' expected cash flow. There are 10 million shares outstanding, implying expected annual cash flow of $1 per share. The cost of capital for this unlevered firm is 10 percent. In addition, the firm will soon build a new plant for $4 million. The plant is expected to generate additional cash flow of $1 million per year. These figures can be described as follows:

Current Company	New Plant
Cash flow: $10 million	Initial outlay: $4 million
Number of outstanding shares: 10 million	Additional annual cash flow: $1 million

The project's net present value is:

$$-\$4 \text{ million} + \frac{\$1 \text{ million}}{.1} = \$6 \text{ million}$$

assuming that the project is discounted at the same rate as the firm as a whole. Before the market knows of the project, the *market value* balance sheet of the firm is this:

LUTERAN MOTORS		
Balance Sheet (All Equity)		
Old assets: $\frac{\$10 \text{ million}}{.1} = \$100$ million	Equity:	$100 million (10 million shares of stock)

The value of the firm is $100 million because the cash flow of $10 million per year is capitalized (discounted) at 10 percent. A share of stock sells for $10 (=$100 million/10 million) because there are 10 million shares outstanding.

The market value balance sheet is a useful tool for financial analysis. Because students are often thrown off guard by it initially, we recommend extra study here. The key is that the market value balance sheet has the same form as the balance sheet that accountants use. That is, assets are placed on the left side whereas liabilities and owners' equity are placed on the right side. In addition, the left and right sides must be equal. The difference between a market value balance sheet and the accountant's balance sheet is in the numbers. Accountants value items in terms of historical cost (original purchase price less depreciation), whereas financial analysts value items in terms of market value.

The firm will issue $4 million of either equity or debt. Let us consider the effect of equity and debt financing in turn.

Stock Financing   Imagine that the firm announces that in the near future it will raise $4 million in equity to build a new plant. The stock price, and therefore the value of the firm, will rise to reflect the positive net present value of the plant. According to efficient markets, the increase occurs immediately. That is, the rise occurs on the day of the announcement, not on the date of either the onset of construction of the plant or the forthcoming stock offering. The market value balance sheet becomes this:

LUTERAN MOTORS			
Balance Sheet			
(upon Announcement of Equity Issue to Construct Plant)			
Old assets	$100 million	Equity	$106 million
			(10 million shares of stock)
NPV of plant:			
-4 million $+ \dfrac{\$1 \text{ million}}{.1} =$	6 million		
Total assets	$106 million		

Note that the NPV of the plant is included in the market value balance sheet. Because the new shares have not yet been issued, the number of outstanding shares remains 10 million. The price per share has now risen to $10.60 (=$106 million/10 million) to reflect news concerning the plant.

Shortly thereafter, $4 million of stock is issued or *floated*. Because the stock is selling at $10.60 per share, 377,358 (=$4 million/$10.60) shares of stock are issued. Imagine that the funds are
(continued)

put in the bank *temporarily* before being used to build the plant. The market value balance sheet becomes this:

LUTERAN MOTORS Balance Sheet (upon Issuance of Stock but Before Construction Begins on Plant)			
Old assets	$100 million	Equity	$110 million
NPV of plant	6 million		(10,377,358 shares of stock)
Proceeds from new issue of stock (currently placed in bank)	4 million		
Total assets	$110 million		

The number of shares outstanding is now 10,377,358 because 377,358 new shares were issued. The price per share is $10.60 (=$110,000,000/10,377,358). Note that the price has not changed. This is consistent with efficient capital markets because the stock price should move due only to new information.

Of course the funds are placed in the bank only temporarily. Shortly after the new issue, the $4 million is given to a contractor who builds the plant. To avoid problems in discounting, we assume that the plant is built immediately. The balance sheet then looks like this:

LUTERAN MOTORS Balance Sheet (upon Completion of the Plant)			
Old assets	$100 million	Equity	$110 million
PV of plant: $\dfrac{\$1 \text{ million}}{.1} =$	10 million		(10,377,358 shares of stock)
Total assets	$110 million		

Though total assets do not change, the composition of the assets does change. The bank account has been emptied to pay the contractor. The present value of cash flows of $1 million a year from the plant is reflected as an asset worth $10 million. Because the building expenditures of $4 million have already been paid, they no longer represent a future cost. Hence they no longer reduce the value of the plant. According to efficient capital markets, the price per share of stock remains $10.60.

Expected yearly cash flow from the firm is $11 million, $10 million of which comes from the old assets and $1 million from the new. The expected return to equityholders is:

$$R_s = \frac{\$11 \text{ million}}{\$110 \text{ million}} = .10$$

Because the firm is all equity, $R_s = R_0 = .10$.

Debt Financing Alternatively, imagine the firm announces that in the near future it will borrow $4 million at 6 percent to build a new plant. This implies yearly interest payments of $240,000

(=$4,000,000 × 6%). Again the stock price rises immediately to reflect the positive net present value of the plant. Thus we have the following:

LUTERAN MOTORS
Balance Sheet
(upon Announcement of Debt Issue to Construct Plant)

Old assets	$100 million	Equity	$106 million
			(10 million shares of stock)
NPV of plant:			
$-\$4 \text{ million} + \dfrac{\$1 \text{ million}}{.1} =$	6 million		
Total assets	$106 million		

The value of the firm is the same as in the equity financing case because (1) the same plant is to be built and (2) MM proved that debt financing is neither better nor worse than equity financing.

At some point $4 million of debt is issued. As before, the funds are placed in the bank temporarily. The market value balance sheet becomes this:

LUTERAN MOTORS
Balance Sheet
(upon Debt Issuance but Before Construction Begins on Plant)

Old assets	$100 million	Debt	$ 4 million
NPV of plant	6 million	Equity	106 million
			(10 million shares of stock)
Proceeds from debt issue (currently invested in bank)	4 million		
Total assets	$110 million	Debt plus equity	$110 million

Note that debt appears on the right side of the balance sheet. The stock price is still $10.60 in accordance with our discussion of efficient capital markets.

Finally, the contractor receives $4 million and builds the plant. The market value balance sheet turns into this:

LUTERAN MOTORS
Balance Sheet
(upon Completion of the Plant)

Old assets	$100 million	Debt	$ 4 million
PV of plant	10 million	Equity	106 million
			(10 million shares of stock)
Total assets	$110 million	Debt plus equity	$110 million

The only change here is that the bank account has been depleted to pay the contractor. The equityholders expect yearly cash flow after interest of:

$10,000,000	+	$1,000,000	−	$240,000	=	$10,760,000
Cash flow on old assets		Cash flow on new assets		Interest: $4 million × 6%		

(continued)

The equityholders expect to earn a return of:

$$\frac{\$10,760,000}{\$106,000,000} = 10.15\%$$

This return of 10.15 percent for levered equityholders is higher than the 10 percent return for the unlevered equityholders. This result is sensible because, as we argued earlier, levered equity is riskier. In fact, the return of 10.15 percent should be exactly what MM Proposition II predicts. This prediction can be verified by plugging the values into:

$$R_S = R_0 + \frac{B}{S} \times (R_0 - R_B)$$

We obtain:

$$10.15\% = 10\% + \frac{\$4,000,000}{\$106,000,000} \times (10\% - 6\%)$$

This example was useful for two reasons. First, we wanted to introduce the concept of market value balance sheets, a tool that will prove useful elsewhere in the text. Among other things, this technique allows us to calculate the price per share of a new issue of stock. Second, the example illustrates three aspects of Modigliani and Miller:

1. The example is consistent with MM Proposition I because the value of the firm is $110 million after either equity or debt financing.

2. Students are often more interested in stock price than in firm value. We show that the stock price is always $10.60, regardless of whether debt or equity financing is used.

3. The example is consistent with MM Proposition II. The expected return to equityholders rises from 10 to 10.15 percent, just as MM Proposition II states. This rise occurs because the equityholders of a levered firm face more risk than do the equityholders of an unlevered firm.

MM: AN INTERPRETATION

The Modigliani–Miller results indicate that managers cannot change the value of a firm by repackaging the firm's securities. Though this idea was considered revolutionary when it was originally proposed in the late 1950s, the MM approach and proof have since met with wide acclaim.[9]

MM argue that the firm's overall cost of capital cannot be reduced as debt is substituted for equity, even though debt appears to be cheaper than equity. The reason for this is that as the firm adds debt, the remaining equity becomes more risky. As this risk rises, the cost of equity capital rises as a result. The increase in the cost of the remaining equity capital offsets the higher proportion of the firm financed by low-cost debt. In fact, MM prove that the two effects exactly offset each other, so that both the value of the firm and the firm's overall cost of capital are invariant to leverage.

MM use an interesting analogy to food. They consider a dairy farmer with two choices. On the one hand, he can sell whole milk. On the other hand, by skimming he can sell a combination of cream and lowfat milk. Though the farmer can get a high price for the cream, he gets a low price for the lowfat milk, implying no net gain. In fact, imagine that the proceeds from the whole-milk strategy were less than those from the cream–lowfat milk strategy. Arbitrageurs would buy the whole milk, perform the skimming operation themselves, and resell the cream and lowfat milk separately. Competition between arbitrageurs would tend

---

[9]Both Merton Miller and Franco Modigliani were awarded separate Nobel Prizes, in part for their work on capital structure.

In Their Own Words

IN PROFESSOR MILLER'S WORDS . . .

The Modigliani–Miller results are not easy to understand fully. This point is related in a story told by Merton Miller.*

"How difficult it is to summarize briefly the contribution of the [Modigliani–Miller] papers was brought home to me very clearly last October after Franco Modigliani was awarded the Nobel Prize in Economics in part—but, of course, only in part—for the work in finance. The television camera crews from our local stations in Chicago immediately descended upon me. 'We understand,' they said, 'that you worked with Modigliani some years back in developing these M and M theorems and we wonder if you could explain them briefly to our television viewers.'

" 'How briefly?' I asked.

" 'Oh, take ten seconds,' was the reply.

"Ten seconds to explain the work of a lifetime! Ten seconds to describe two carefully reasoned articles, each running to more than thirty printed pages and each with sixty or so long footnotes! When they saw the look of dismay on my face, they said, 'You don't have to go into details. Just give us the main points in simple, common-sense terms.'

"The main point of the first or cost-of-capital article was, in principle at least, simple enough to make. It said that in an economist's ideal world of complete and perfect capital markets and with full and symmetric information among all market participants, the total market value of all the securities issued by a firm was governed by the earning power and risk of its underlying real assets and was independent of how the mix of securities issued to finance it was divided between debt instruments and equity capital. . . .

"Such a summary, however, uses too many short-handed terms and concepts, like perfect capital markets, that are rich in connotations to economists but hardly so to the general public. So I thought, instead, of an analogy that we ourselves had invoked in the original paper. . . .

" 'Think of the firm,' I said, 'as a gigantic tub of whole milk. The farmer can sell the whole milk as is. Or he can

*Taken from *GSB Chicago*, University of Chicago (Autumn 1986).

separate out the cream and sell it at a considerably higher price than the whole milk would bring. (That's the analogy of a firm selling low-yield and hence high-priced debt securities.) But, of course, what the farmer would have left would be skim milk with low butterfat content and that would sell for much less than whole milk. That corresponds to the levered equity. The M and M proposition says that if there were no costs of separation (and, of course, no government dairy support programs), the cream plus the skim milk would bring the same price as the whole milk.'

"The television people conferred among themselves and came back to inform me that it was too long, too complicated, and too academic.

" 'Don't you have anything simpler?' they asked. I thought of another way that the M and M proposition is presented these days, which emphasizes the notion of market completeness and stresses the role of securities as devices for 'partitioning' a firm's payoffs in each possible state of the world among the group of its capital suppliers.

" 'Think of the firm,' I said, 'as a gigantic pizza, divided into quarters. If now you cut each quarter in half into eighths, the M and M proposition says that you will have more pieces but not more pizza.'

"Again there was a whispered conference among the camera crew, and the director came back and said:

" 'Professor, we understand from the press releases that there were two M and M propositions. Can we try the other one?' "

[Professor Miller tried valiantly to explain the second proposition, though this was apparently even more difficult to get across. After his attempt:]

"Once again there was a whispered conversation. They shut the lights off. They folded up their equipment. They thanked me for giving them the time. They said that they'd get back to me. But I knew that I had somehow lost my chance to start a new career as a packager of economic wisdom for TV viewers in convenient ten-second bites. Some have the talent for it . . . and some just don't."

to boost the price of whole milk until proceeds from the two strategies became equal. Thus the value of the farmer's milk is invariant to the way in which the milk is packaged.

Food found its way into this chapter earlier when we viewed the firm as a pie. MM argue that the size of the pie does not change no matter how stockholders and bondholders divide it. MM say that a firm's capital structure is irrelevant; it is what it is by some historical accident. The theory implies that firms' debt–equity ratios could be anything.

Summary of Modigliani–Miller Propositions without Taxes

Assumptions

- No taxes.
- No transaction costs.
- Individuals and corporations borrow at same rate.

Results

Proposition I: $V_L = V_U$ (Value of levered firm equals value of unlevered firm)

Proposition II: $R_S = R_0 + \dfrac{B}{S}(R_0 - R_B)$

Intuition

Proposition I: Through homemade leverage individuals can either duplicate or undo the effects of corporate leverage.

Proposition II: The cost of equity rises with leverage because the risk to equity rises with leverage.

They are what they are because of whimsical and random managerial decisions about how much to borrow and how much stock to issue.

Although scholars are always fascinated with far-reaching theories, students are perhaps more concerned with real-world applications. Do real-world managers follow MM by treating capital structure decisions with indifference? Unfortunately for the theory, virtually all companies in certain industries, such as banking, choose high debt–equity ratios. Conversely, companies in other industries, such as pharmaceuticals, choose low debt–equity ratios. In fact, almost any industry has a debt–equity ratio to which companies in that industry tend to adhere. Thus companies do not appear to be selecting their degree of leverage in a frivolous or random manner. Because of this, financial economists (including MM themselves) have argued that real-world factors may have been left out of the theory.

Though many of our students have argued that individuals can borrow only at rates above the corporate borrowing rate, we disagreed with this argument earlier in the chapter. But when we look elsewhere for unrealistic assumptions in the theory, we find two:[10]

1. Taxes were ignored.

2. Bankruptcy costs and other agency costs were not considered.

We turn to taxes in the next section. Bankruptcy costs and other agency costs will be treated in the next chapter. A summary of the main Modigliani–Miller results without taxes is presented in the nearby boxed section.

16.5 Taxes

THE BASIC INSIGHT

The previous part of this chapter showed that firm value is unrelated to debt in a world without taxes. We now show that in the presence of corporate taxes, the firm's value is positively related to its debt. The basic intuition can be seen from a pie chart, such as the

---

[10]MM were aware of both of these issues, as can be seen in their original paper.

Figure 16.4

Two Pie Models of Capital Structure under Corporate Taxes

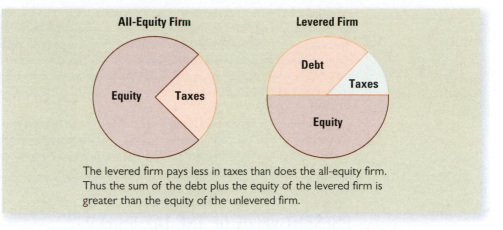

The levered firm pays less in taxes than does the all-equity firm. Thus the sum of the debt plus the equity of the levered firm is greater than the equity of the unlevered firm.

one in Figure 16.4. Consider the all-equity firm on the left. Here both equityholders and the IRS have claims on the firm. The value of the all-equity firm is, of course, that part of the pie owned by the equityholders. The proportion going to taxes is simply a cost.

The pie on the right for the levered firm shows three claims: Equityholders, debtholders, and taxes. The value of the levered firm is the sum of the value of the debt and the value of the equity. In selecting between the two capital structures in the picture, a financial manager should select the one with the higher value. Assuming that the total area is the same for both pies,[11] value is maximized for the capital structure paying the least in taxes. In other words, the manager should choose the capital structure that the IRS hates the most.

We will show that due to a quirk in U.S. tax law, the proportion of the pie allocated to taxes is less for the levered firm than it is for the unlevered firm. Thus, managers should select high leverage.

EXAMPLE
16.3

Taxes and Cash Flow   The Water Products Company has a corporate tax rate, t_C, of 35 percent and expected earnings before interest and taxes (EBIT) of $1 million each year. Its entire earnings after taxes are paid out as dividends.

The firm is considering two alternative capital structures. Under Plan I, Water Products would have no debt in its capital structure. Under Plan II, the company would have $4,000,000 of debt, B. The cost of debt, R_B, is 10 percent.

The chief financial officer for Water Products makes the following calculations:

	Plan I	Plan II
Earnings before interest and corporate taxes (EBIT)	$1,000,000	$1,000,000
Interest ($R_B B$)	0	400,000
Earnings before taxes (EBT) = (EBIT − $R_B B$)	1,000,000	600,000
Taxes ($t_C = .35$)	350,000	210,000
Earnings after corporate taxes	650,000	390,000
(EAT) = [(EBIT − $R_B B$) × (1 − t_C)]		
Total cash flow to both stockholders and bondholders	$ 650,000	$ 790,000
[EBIT × (1 − t_C) + $t_C R_B B$]		

(continued)

[11]Under the MM propositions developed earlier, the two pies should be of the same size.

The most relevant numbers for our purposes are the two on the bottom line. Dividends, which are equal to earnings after taxes in this example, are the cash flow to stockholders, and interest is the cash flow to bondholders.[12] Here we see that more cash flow reaches the owners of the firm (both stockholders and bondholders) under Plan II. The difference is $140,000 = $790,000 − $650,000. It does not take us long to realize the source of this difference. The IRS receives less tax under Plan II ($210,000) than it does under Plan I ($350,000). The difference here is $140,000 = $350,000 − $210,000.

This difference occurs because the way the IRS treats interest is different from the way it treats earnings going to stockholders.[13] Interest totally escapes corporate taxation, whereas earnings after interest but before corporate taxes (EBT) are taxed at the 35 percent rate.

PRESENT VALUE OF THE TAX SHIELD

The previous discussion shows a tax advantage to debt or, equivalently, a tax disadvantage to equity. We now want to value this advantage. The dollar interest is:

$$\text{Interest} = \underbrace{R_B}_{\text{Interest rate}} \times \underbrace{B}_{\text{Amount borrowed}}$$

This interest is $400,000 (=10 percent × $4,000,000) for Water Products. All this interest is tax deductible. That is, whatever the taxable income of Water Products would have been without the debt, the taxable income is now $400,000 *less* with the debt.

Because the corporate tax rate is .35 in our example, the reduction in corporate taxes is $140,000 (=.35 × $400,000). This number is identical to the reduction in corporate taxes calculated previously.

Algebraically, the reduction in corporate taxes is:

$$\underbrace{t_C}_{\text{Corporate tax rate}} \times \underbrace{R_B \times B}_{\text{Dollar amount of interest}} \tag{16.4}$$

That is, whatever the taxes that a firm would pay each year without debt, the firm will pay $t_C R_B B$ less with debt of B. Equation 16.4 is often called the *tax shield from debt*. Note that it is an *annual* amount.

As long as the firm expects to be in a positive tax bracket, we can assume that the cash flow in Equation 16.4 has the same risk as the interest on the debt. Thus its value can be determined by discounting at the cost of debt, R_B. Assuming that the cash flows are perpetual, the present value of the tax shield is:

$$\frac{t_C R_B B}{R_B} = t_C B$$

VALUE OF THE LEVERED FIRM

We have just calculated the present value of the tax shield from debt. Our next step is to calculate the value of the levered firm. The annual aftertax cash flow of an unlevered firm is:

$$\text{EBIT} \times (1 - t_C)$$

---

[12]The reader may wonder why the "total cash flow to both stockholders and bondholders" in this example does not include adjustments for depreciation, capital spending, and working capital that we emphasized in Chapters 2 and 6. It is because we are implicitly assuming that depreciation is equal to capital spending. We are also assuming that the changes in net working capital are zero. These assumptions make sense because the projected cash flows for the Water Products Company are perpetual.

[13]Note that stockholders actually receive more under Plan I ($650,000) than under Plan II ($390,000). Students are often bothered by this because it seems to imply that stockholders are better off without leverage. However, remember that there are more shares outstanding in Plan I than in Plan II. A full-blown model would show that earnings *per share* are higher *with* leverage.

where EBIT is earnings before interest and taxes. The value of an unlevered firm (i.e., a firm with no debt) is the present value of EBIT $\times (1 - t_C)$:

$$V_U = \frac{\text{EBIT} \times (1 - t_C)}{R_0}$$

Here:

$$
\begin{aligned}
V_U &= \text{Present value of an unlevered firm.} \\
\text{EBIT} \times (1 - t_C) &= \text{Firm cash flows after corporate taxes.} \\
t_C &= \text{Corporate tax rate.} \\
R_0 &= \text{The cost of capital to an all-equity firm. As can be seen from} \\
&\quad \text{the formula, } R_0 \text{ now discounts } \textit{aftertax} \text{ cash flows.}
\end{aligned}
$$

As shown previously, leverage increases the value of the firm by the tax shield, which is $t_C B$ for perpetual debt. Thus we merely add this tax shield to the value of the unlevered firm to get the value of the levered firm.

We can write this algebraically as follows:[14]

MM Proposition I (Corporate Taxes):

$$V_L = \frac{\text{EBIT} \times (1 - t_C)}{R_0} + \frac{t_C R_B B}{R_B} = V_U + t_C B \qquad (16.5)$$

Equation 16.5 is MM Proposition I under corporate taxes. The first term in Equation 16.5 is the value of the cash flows of the firm with no debt tax shield. In other words, this term is equal to V_U, the value of the all-equity firm. The value of the levered firm is the value of an all-equity firm plus $t_C B$, the tax rate times the value of the debt. $t_C B$ is the present value of the tax shield in the case of perpetual cash flows.[15] Because the tax shield increases with the amount of debt, the firm can raise its total cash flow and its value by substituting debt for equity.

---

[14]This relationship holds when the debt level is assumed to be constant through time. A different formula would apply if the debt–equity ratio was assumed to be nonconstant over time. For a deeper treatment of this point, see James Miles and John Ezzell, "The Weighted Average Cost of Capital, Perfect Capital Markets, and Project Life: A Clarification," *Journal of Financial and Quantitative Analysis* (September 1980).

[15]The following example calculates the present value if we assume the debt has a finite life. Suppose the Maxwell Company has $1 million in debt with an 8 percent coupon rate. If the debt matures in two years and the cost of debt capital, R_B, is 10 percent, what is the present value of the tax shields if the corporate tax rate is 35 percent? The debt is amortized in equal installments over two years.

Year	Loan Balance	Interest	Tax Shield	Present Value of Tax Shield
0	$1,000,000			
1	500,000	$80,000	.35 × $80,000	$25,454.54
2	0	40,000	.35 × $40,000	11,570.25
				$37,024.79

The present value of the tax saving is:

$$\text{PV} = \frac{.35 \times \$80,000}{1.10} + \frac{.35 \times \$40,000}{(1.10)^2} = \$37,024.79$$

The Maxwell Company's value is higher than that of a comparable unlevered firm by $37,024.79.

MM with Corporate Taxes Divided Airlines is currently an unlevered firm. The company expects to generate $153.85 in earnings before interest and taxes (EBIT) in perpetuity. The corporate tax rate is 35 percent, implying aftertax earnings of $100. All earnings after tax are paid out as dividends.

The firm is considering a capital restructuring to allow $200 of debt. Its cost of debt capital is 10 percent. Unlevered firms in the same industry have a cost of equity capital of 20 percent. What will the new value of Divided Airlines be?

The value of Divided Airlines will be equal to:

$$V_L = \frac{\text{EBIT} \times (1 - t_c)}{R_0} + t_c B$$

$$= \frac{\$100}{.20} + (.35 \times \$200)$$

$$= \$500 + \$70 = \$570$$

The value of the levered firm is $570, which is greater than the unlevered value of $500. Because $V_L = B + S$, the value of levered equity, S, is equal to $570 - $200 = $370. The value of Divided Airlines as a function of leverage is illustrated in Figure 16.5.

Figure 16.5 The Effect of Financial Leverage on Firm Value: MM with Corporate Taxes in the Case of Divided Airlines

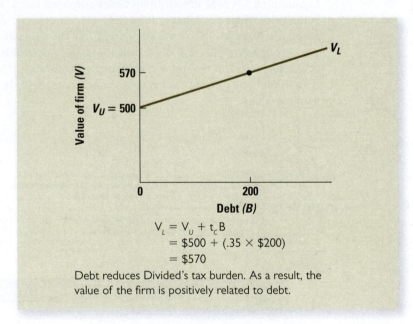

$$V_L = V_U + t_c B$$
$$= \$500 + (.35 \times \$200)$$
$$= \$570$$

Debt reduces Divided's tax burden. As a result, the value of the firm is positively related to debt.

EXPECTED RETURN AND LEVERAGE UNDER CORPORATE TAXES

MM Proposition II under no taxes posits a positive relationship between the expected return on equity and leverage. This result occurs because the risk of equity increases with leverage. The same intuition also holds in a world of corporate taxes. The exact formula in a world of corporate taxes is this:[16]

MM Proposition II (Corporate Taxes):

$$R_S = R_0 + \frac{B}{S} \times (1 - t_C) \times (R_0 - R_B) \qquad (16.6)$$

Applying the formula to Divided Airlines, we get:

$$R_S = .2351 = .20 + \frac{200}{370} \times (1 - .35) \times (.20 - .10)$$

This calculation is illustrated in Figure 16.6.

Whenever $R_0 > R_B$, R_S increases with leverage, a result that we also found in the no-tax case. As stated earlier in this chapter, R_0 should exceed R_B. That is, because equity (even unlevered equity) is risky, it should have an expected return greater than that on the less risky debt.

Let's check our calculations by determining the value of the levered equity in another way. The algebraic formula for the value of levered equity is:

$$S = \frac{(\text{EBIT} - R_B B) \times (1 - t_C)}{R_S}$$

---

[16]This relationship can be shown as follows: Given MM Proposition I under taxes, a levered firm's market value balance sheet can be written as:

$t_C B$ = Tax shield	S = Equity
V_U = Value of unlevered firm	B = Debt

The value of the unlevered firm is simply the value of the assets without benefit of leverage. The balance sheet indicates that the firm's value increases by $t_C B$ when debt of B is added. The expected cash flow *from* the left side of the balance sheet can be written as:

$$V_U R_0 + t_C B R_B \qquad \text{(a)}$$

Because assets are risky, their expected rate of return is R_0. The tax shield has the same risk as the debt, so its expected rate of return is R_B.

The expected cash *to* bondholders and stockholders together is:

$$S R_S + B R_B \qquad \text{(b)}$$

Expression (b) reflects the fact that stock earns an expected return of R_S and debt earns the interest rate R_B.

Because all cash flows are paid out as dividends in our no-growth perpetuity model, the cash flows going into the firm equal those going to stockholders. Hence (a) and (b) are equal:

$$S R_S + B R_B = V_U R_0 + t_C B R_B \qquad \text{(c)}$$

Dividing both sides of (c) by S, subtracting $B R_B$ from both sides, and rearranging yields:

$$R_S = \frac{V_U}{S} \times R_0 - (1 - t_C) \times \frac{B}{S} R_B \qquad \text{(d)}$$

Because the value of the levered firm, V_L, equals $V_U + t_C B = B + S$, it follows that $V_U = S + (1 - t_C) \times B$. Thus (d) can be rewritten as:

$$R_S = \frac{S + (1 - t_C) \times B}{S} \times R_0 - (1 - t_C) \times \frac{B}{S} R_B \qquad \text{(e)}$$

Bringing the terms involving $(1 - t_C) \times (B/S)$ together produces Equation 16.6.

Figure 16.6

The Effect of Financial Leverage on the Cost of Debt and Equity Capital

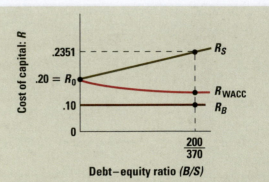

$$R_S = R_0 + (1 - t_C)(R_0 - R_B)B/S = .20 + \left(.65 \times .10 \times \frac{200}{370}\right) = .2351$$

Financial leverage adds risk to the firm's equity. As compensation, the cost of equity rises with the firm's risk. Note that R_0 is a single point whereas R_S, R_B, and R_{WACC} are all entire lines.

The numerator is the expected cash flow to levered equity after interest and taxes. The denominator is the rate at which the cash flow to equity is discounted.

For Divided Airlines we get:

$$\frac{(\$153.85 - .10 \times \$200)(1 - .35)}{.2351} = \$370$$

This is the same result we obtained earlier (ignoring a small rounding error).

THE WEIGHTED AVERAGE COST OF CAPITAL, R_{WACC}, AND CORPORATE TAXES

In Chapter 13, we defined the weighted average cost of capital (with corporate taxes) as follows (note that $V_L = S + B$):

$$R_{WACC} = \frac{S}{V_L}R_S + \frac{B}{V_L}R_B(1 - t_C)$$

Note that the cost of debt capital, R_B, is multiplied by $(1 - t_C)$ because interest is tax deductible at the corporate level. However, the cost of equity, R_S, is not multiplied by this factor because dividends are not deductible. In the no-tax case, R_{WACC} is not affected by leverage. This result is reflected in Figure 16.3, which we discussed earlier. However, because debt is tax-advantaged relative to equity, it can be shown that R_{WACC} declines with leverage in a world with corporate taxes. This result can be seen in Figure 16.6.

For Divided Airlines, R_{WACC} is equal to:

$$R_{WACC} = \left(\frac{370}{570} \times .2351\right) + \left(\frac{200}{570} \times .10 \times .65\right) = .1754$$

Divided Airlines has reduced its R_{WACC} from .20 (with no debt) to .1754 with reliance on debt. This result is intuitively pleasing because it suggests that when a firm lowers its R_{WACC}, the firm's value will increase. Using the R_{WACC} approach, we can confirm that the value of Divided Airlines is $570:

$$V_L = \frac{EBIT \times (1 - t_C)}{R_{WACC}} = \frac{\$100}{.1754} = \$570$$

STOCK PRICE AND LEVERAGE UNDER CORPORATE TAXES

At this point students often believe the numbers—or at least are too intimidated to dispute them. However, they sometimes think we have asked the wrong question. "Why are we choosing to maximize the value of the firm?" they will say. "If managers are looking out for the stockholders' interest, why aren't they trying to maximize stock price?" If this question occurred to you, you have come to the right section.

Our response is twofold: First, we showed in the first section of this chapter that the capital structure that maximizes firm value is also the one that most benefits the interests of the stockholders.

However, that general explanation is not always convincing to students. As a second procedure, we calculate the stock price of Divided Airlines both before and after the exchange of debt for stock. We do this by presenting a set of market value balance sheets. The market value balance sheet for the company in its all-equity form can be represented as follows:

DIVIDED AIRLINES Balance Sheet (All-Equity Firm)	
Physical assets $$\frac{\$153.85}{.20} \times (1 - .35) = \$500$$	Equity $500 (100 shares)

Assuming that there are 100 shares outstanding, each share is worth $5 = $500/100.

Next, imagine the company announces that in the near future it will issue $200 of debt to buy back $200 of stock. We know from our previous discussion that the value of the firm will rise to reflect the tax shield of debt. If we assume that capital markets efficiently price securities, the increase occurs immediately. That is, the rise occurs on the day of the announcement, not on the date of the debt-for-equity exchange. The market value balance sheet now becomes this:

DIVIDED AIRLINES Balance Sheet (upon Announcement of Debt Issue)			
Physical assets	$500	Equity	$570 (100 shares)
Present value of tax shield: $t_c B = 35\% \times \$200 =$	70		
Total assets	$570		

Note that the debt has not yet been issued. Therefore, only equity appears on the right side of the balance sheet. Each share is now worth $570/100 = $5.70, implying that the stockholders have benefited by $70. The equityholders gain because they are the owners of a firm that has improved its financial policy.

The introduction of the tax shield to the balance sheet is perplexing to many students. Although physical assets are tangible, the ethereal nature of the tax shield bothers these students. However, remember that an asset is any item with value. The tax shield has value because it reduces the stream of future taxes. The fact that one cannot touch the shield in the way that one can touch a physical asset is a philosophical, not financial, consideration.

At some point the exchange of debt for equity occurs. Debt of $200 is issued, and the proceeds are used to buy back shares. How many shares of stock are repurchased? Because shares are now selling at $5.70 each, the number of shares that the firm acquires is $200/$5.70 = 35.09. This leaves 64.91 (=100 − 35.09) shares of stock outstanding. The market value balance sheet is now this:

DIVIDED AIRLINES Balance Sheet (after Exchange Has Taken Place)			
Physical assets	$500	Equity	$370
		(100 − 35.09 = 64.91 shares)	
Present value of tax shield	70	Debt	200
Total assets	$570	Debt plus equity	$570

Each share of stock is worth $370/64.91 = $5.70 after the exchange. Notice that the stock price does not change on the exchange date. As we mentioned, the stock price moves on the date of the announcement only. Because the shareholders participating in the exchange receive a price equal to the market price per share after the exchange, they do not care whether they exchange their stock.

This example was provided for two reasons. First, it shows that an increase in the value of the firm from debt financing leads to an increase in the price of the stock. In fact, the stockholders capture the entire $70 tax shield. Second, we wanted to provide more work with market value balance sheets.

A summary of the main results of Modigliani–Miller with corporate taxes is presented in the following boxed section:

Summary of Modigliani–Miller Propositions with Corporate Taxes

Assumptions

- Corporations are taxed at the rate t_C, on earnings after interest.
- No transaction or bankruptcy costs.
- Individuals and corporations borrow at the same rate.

Results

Proposition I: $V_L = V_U + t_C B$ (for a firm with perpetual debt)

Proposition II: $R_S = R_0 + \dfrac{B}{S}(1 - t_C)(R_0 - R_B)$

Intuition

Proposition I: Because corporations can deduct interest payments but not dividend payments, corporate leverage lowers tax payments.

Proposition II: The cost of equity rises with leverage because the risk to equity rises with leverage.

Summary and Conclusions

1. We began our discussion of the capital structure decision by arguing that the particular capital structure that maximizes the value of the firm is also the one that provides the most benefit to the stockholders.

2. In a world of no taxes, the famous Proposition I of Modigliani and Miller proves that the value of the firm is unaffected by the debt–equity ratio. In other words, a firm's capital structure is a matter of indifference in that world. The authors obtain their results by showing that either a high or a low corporate ratio of debt to equity can be offset by homemade leverage. The result hinges on the assumption that individuals can borrow at the same rate as corporations, an assumption we believe to be quite plausible.

3. MM's Proposition II in a world without taxes states that:

$$R_S = R_0 + \frac{B}{S}(R_0 - R_B)$$

This implies that the expected rate of return on equity (also called the *cost of equity* or the *required return on equity*) is positively related to the firm's leverage. This makes intuitive sense because the risk of equity rises with leverage, a point illustrated by Figure 16.3.

4. Although the above work of MM is quite elegant, it does not explain the empirical findings on capital structure very well. MM imply that the capital structure decision is a matter of indifference, whereas the decision appears to be a weighty one in the real world. To achieve real-world applicability, we next considered corporate taxes.

5. In a world with corporate taxes but no bankruptcy costs, firm value is an increasing function of leverage. The formula for the value of the firm is:

$$V_L = V_U + t_C B$$

Expected return on levered equity can be expressed as:

$$R_S = R_0 + (1 - t_C) \times (R_0 - R_B) \times \frac{B}{S}$$

Here, value is positively related to leverage. This result implies that firms should have a capital structure almost entirely composed of debt. Because real-world firms select more moderate levels of debt, the next chapter considers modifications to the results of this chapter.

Concept Questions

1. **MM Assumptions**   List the three assumptions that lie behind the Modigliani–Miller theory in a world without taxes. Are these assumptions reasonable in the real world? Explain.

2. **MM Propositions**   In a world with no taxes, no transaction costs, and no costs of financial distress, is the following statement true, false, or uncertain? If a firm issues equity to repurchase some of its debt, the price per share of the firm's stock will rise because the shares are less risky. Explain.

3. **MM Propositions**   In a world with no taxes, no transaction costs, and no costs of financial distress, is the following statement true, false, or uncertain? Moderate borrowing will not increase the required return on a firm's equity. Explain.

4. **MM Propositions**   What is the quirk in the tax code that makes a levered firm more valuable than an otherwise identical unlevered firm?

5. **Business Risk versus Financial Risk** Explain what is meant by business and financial risk. Suppose Firm *A* has greater business risk than Firm *B*. Is it true that Firm *A* also has a higher cost of equity capital? Explain.

6. **MM Propositions** How would you answer in the following debate?

   Q: Isn't it true that the riskiness of a firm's equity will rise if the firm increases its use of debt financing?

   A: Yes, that's the essence of MM Proposition II.

   Q: And isn't it true that, as a firm increases its use of borrowing, the likelihood of default increases, thereby increasing the risk of the firm's debt?

   A: Yes.

   Q: In other words, increased borrowing increases the risk of the equity *and* the debt?

   A: That's right.

   Q: Well, given that the firm uses only debt and equity financing, and given that the risks of both are increased by increased borrowing, does it not follow that increasing debt increases the overall risk of the firm and therefore decreases the value of the firm?

   A: ?

7. **Optimal Capital Structure** Is there an easily identifiable debt–equity ratio that will maximize the value of a firm? Why or why not?

8. **Financial Leverage** Why is the use of debt financing referred to as financial "leverage"?

9. **Homemade Leverage** What is homemade leverage?

10. **Capital Structure Goal** What is the basic goal of financial management with regard to capital structure?

Questions and Problems

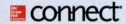

BASIC (Questions 1–16)

1. **EBIT and Leverage** Music City, Inc., has no debt outstanding and a total market value of $295,000. Earnings before interest and taxes, EBIT, are projected to be $23,000 if economic conditions are normal. If there is strong expansion in the economy, then EBIT will be 25 percent higher. If there is a recession, then EBIT will be 40 percent lower. The company is considering an $88,500 debt issue with an interest rate of 8 percent. The proceeds will be used to repurchase shares of stock. There are currently 5,000 shares outstanding. Ignore taxes for this problem.

   a. Calculate earnings per share, EPS, under each of the three economic scenarios before any debt is issued. Also calculate the percentage changes in EPS when the economy expands or enters a recession.

   b. Repeat part (a) assuming that the company goes through with recapitalization. What do you observe?

2. **EBIT, Taxes, and Leverage** Repeat parts (a) and (b) in Problem 1 assuming the company has a tax rate of 35 percent.

3. **ROE and Leverage** Suppose the company in Problem 1 has a market-to-book ratio of 1.0.

   a. Calculate return on equity, ROE, under each of the three economic scenarios before any debt is issued. Also calculate the percentage changes in ROE for economic expansion and recession, assuming no taxes.

b. Repeat part (a) assuming the firm goes through with the proposed recapitalization.

c. Repeat parts (a) and (b) of this problem assuming the firm has a tax rate of 35 percent.

4. **Break-Even EBIT**   Franklin Corporation is comparing two different capital structures, an all-equity plan (Plan I) and a levered plan (Plan II). Under Plan I, the company would have 315,000 shares of stock outstanding. Under Plan II, there would be 225,000 shares of stock outstanding and $4.14 million in debt outstanding. The interest rate on the debt is 10 percent and there are no taxes.

a. If EBIT is $750,000, which plan will result in the higher EPS?

b. If EBIT is $1,750,000, which plan will result in the higher EPS?

c. What is the break-even EBIT?

5. **MM and Stock Value**   In Problem 4, use MM Proposition I to find the price per share of equity under each of the two proposed plans. What is the value of the firm?

6. **Break-Even EBIT and Leverage**   Kolby Corp. is comparing two different capital structures. Plan I would result in 1,300 shares of stock and $80,640 in debt. Plan II would result in 2,900 shares of stock and $19,200 in debt. The interest rate on the debt is 10 percent.

a. Ignoring taxes, compare both of these plans to an all-equity plan assuming that EBIT will be $10,500. The all-equity plan would result in 3,400 shares of stock outstanding. Which of the three plans has the highest EPS? The lowest?

b. In part (a) what are the break-even levels of EBIT for each plan as compared to that for an all-equity plan? Is one higher than the other? Why?

c. Ignoring taxes, when will EPS be identical for Plans I and II?

d. Repeat parts (a), (b), and (c) assuming that the corporate tax rate is 40 percent. Are the break-even levels of EBIT different from before? Why or why not?

7. **Leverage and Stock Value**   Ignoring taxes in Problem 6, what is the price per share of equity under Plan I? Plan II? What principle is illustrated by your answers?

8. **Homemade Leverage**   Star, Inc., a prominent consumer products firm, is debating whether or not to convert its all-equity capital structure to one that is 35 percent debt. Currently there are 6,000 shares outstanding and the price per share is $58. EBIT is expected to remain at $39,600 per year forever. The interest rate on new debt is 7 percent, and there are no taxes.

a. Ms. Brown, a shareholder of the firm, owns 100 shares of stock. What is her cash flow under the current capital structure, assuming the firm has a dividend payout rate of 100 percent?

b. What will Ms. Brown's cash flow be under the proposed capital structure of the firm? Assume that she keeps all 100 of her shares.

c. Suppose the company does convert, but Ms. Brown prefers the current all-equity capital structure. Show how she could unlever her shares of stock to recreate the original capital structure.

d. Using your answer to part (c), explain why the company's choice of capital structure is irrelevant.

9. **Homemade Leverage and WACC**   ABC Co. and XYZ Co. are identical firms in all respects except for their capital structure. ABC is all equity financed with $640,000 in stock. XYZ uses both stock and perpetual debt; its stock is worth $320,000 and the interest rate on its debt is 8 percent. Both firms expect EBIT to be $69,000. Ignore taxes.

a. Richard owns $30,000 worth of XYZ's stock. What rate of return is he expecting?

b. Show how Richard could generate exactly the same cash flows and rate of return by investing in ABC and using homemade leverage.

c. What is the cost of equity for ABC? What is it for XYZ?

d. What is the WACC for ABC? For XYZ? What principle have you illustrated?

10.   MM   Scarlett Corp. uses no debt. The weighted average cost of capital is 8.4 percent. If the current market value of the equity is $43 million and there are no taxes, what is EBIT?

11.   MM and Taxes   In the previous question, suppose the corporate tax rate is 35 percent. What is EBIT in this case? What is the WACC? Explain.

12.   Calculating WACC   Weston Industries has a debt–equity ratio of 1.5. Its WACC is 10.5 percent, and its cost of debt is 6 percent. The corporate tax rate is 35 percent.

   a. What is the company's cost of equity capital?
   b. What is the company's unlevered cost of equity capital?
   c. What would the cost of equity be if the debt–equity ratio were 2? What if it were 1.0? What if it were zero?

13.   Calculating WACC   Shadow Corp. has no debt but can borrow at 6.5 percent. The firm's WACC is currently 9.8 percent, and the tax rate is 35 percent.

   a. What is the company's cost of equity?
   b. If the company converts to 25 percent debt, what will its cost of equity be?
   c. If the company converts to 50 percent debt, what will its cost of equity be?
   d. What is the company's WACC in part (b)? In part (c)?

14.   MM and Taxes   Bruce & Co. expects its EBIT to be $145,000 every year forever. The company can borrow at 8 percent. The company currently has no debt, and its cost of equity is 14 percent. If the tax rate is 35 percent, what is the value of the company? What will the value be if the company borrows $135,000 and uses the proceeds to repurchase shares?

15.   MM and Taxes   In Problem 14, what is the cost of equity after recapitalization? What is the WACC? What are the implications for the firm's capital structure decision?

16.   MM Proposition I   Levered, Inc., and Unlevered, Inc., are identical in every way except their capital structures. Each company expects to earn $23 million before interest per year in perpetuity, with each company distributing all its earnings as dividends. Levered's perpetual debt has a market value of $73 million and costs 8 percent per year. Levered has 2.1 million shares outstanding, currently worth $105 per share. Unlevered has no debt and 4.5 million shares outstanding, currently worth $78 per share. Neither firm pays taxes. Is Levered's stock a better buy than Unlevered's stock?

INTERMEDIATE
(Questions 17–25)

17.   MM   Tool Manufacturing has an expected EBIT of $67,000 in perpetuity and a tax rate of 35 percent. The firm has $130,000 in outstanding debt at an interest rate of 8 percent, and its unlevered cost of capital is 15 percent. What is the value of the company according to MM Proposition I with taxes? Should the company change its debt–equity ratio if the goal is to maximize the value of the company? Explain.

18.   Firm Value   Cavo Corporation expects an EBIT of $26,850 every year forever. The company currently has no debt, and its cost of equity is 14 percent. The tax rate is 35 percent.

   a. What is the current value of the company?
   b. Suppose the company can borrow at 8 percent. What will the value of the company be if it takes on debt equal to 50 percent of its unlevered value? What if it takes on debt equal to 100 percent of its unlevered value?
   c. What will the value of the company be if it takes on debt equal to 50 percent of its levered value? What if the company takes on debt equal to 100 percent of its levered value?

19.   MM Proposition I with Taxes   The Dart Company is financed entirely with equity. The company is considering a loan of $2.6 million. The loan will be repaid in equal installments over the next two years, and it has an interest rate of 8 percent. The company's tax rate is 35 percent. According to MM Proposition I with taxes, what would be the increase in the value of the company after the loan?

20. **MM Proposition I without Taxes**   Alpha Corporation and Beta Corporation are identical in every way except their capital structures. Alpha Corporation, an all-equity firm, has 18,000 shares of stock outstanding, currently worth $35 per share. Beta Corporation uses leverage in its capital structure. The market value of Beta's debt is $85,000, and its cost of debt is 9 percent. Each firm is expected to have earnings before interest of $93,000 in perpetuity. Neither firm pays taxes. Assume that every investor can borrow at 9 percent per year.

   a. What is the value of Alpha Corporation?
   b. What is the value of Beta Corporation?
   c. What is the market value of Beta Corporation's equity?
   d. How much will it cost to purchase 20 percent of each firm's equity?
   e. Assuming each firm meets its earnings estimates, what will be the dollar return to each position in part (d) over the next year?
   f. Construct an investment strategy in which an investor purchases 20 percent of Alpha's equity and replicates both the cost and dollar return of purchasing 20 percent of Beta's equity.
   g. Is Alpha's equity more or less risky than Beta's equity? Explain.

21. **Cost of Capital**   Acetate, Inc., has equity with a market value of $29.5 million and debt with a market value of $8 million. Treasury bills that mature in one year yield 5 percent per year, and the expected return on the market portfolio is 11 percent. The beta of the company's equity is 1.15. The firm pays no taxes.

   a. What is the company's debt–equity ratio?
   b. What is the firm's weighted average cost of capital?
   c. What is the cost of capital for an otherwise identical all-equity firm?

22. **Homemade Leverage**   The Veblen Company and the Knight Company are identical in every respect except that Veblen is not levered. The market value of Knight Company's 6 percent bonds is $1.4 million. Financial information for the two firms appears here. All earnings streams are perpetuities. Neither firm pays taxes. Both firms distribute all earnings available to common stockholders immediately.

	Veblen	Knight
Projected operating income	$ 580,000	$ 580,000
Year-end interest on debt	—	84,000
Market value of stock	4,500,000	3,450,000
Market value of debt	—	1,400,000

   a. An investor who can borrow at 6 percent per year wishes to purchase 5 percent of Knight's equity. Can he increase his dollar return by purchasing 5 percent of Veblen's equity if he borrows so that the initial net costs of the two strategies are the same?
   b. Given the two investment strategies in (a), which will investors choose? When will this process cease?

23. **MM Propositions**   Locomotive Corporation is planning to repurchase part of its common stock by issuing corporate debt. As a result, the firm's debt–equity ratio is expected to rise from 35 percent to 50 percent. The firm currently has $3.1 million worth of debt outstanding. The cost of this debt is 6.7 percent per year. The firm expects to have an EBIT of $1.075 million per year in perpetuity and pays no taxes.

   a. What is the market value of the firm before and after the repurchase announcement?
   b. What is the expected return on the firm's equity before the announcement of the stock repurchase plan?

c. What is the expected return on the equity of an otherwise identical all-equity firm?

d. What is the expected return on the firm's equity after the announcement of the stock repurchase plan?

24. **Stock Value and Leverage** Green Manufacturing, Inc., plans to announce that it will issue $1.8 million of perpetual debt and use the proceeds to repurchase common stock. The bonds will sell at par with a coupon rate of 6 percent. Green is currently an all-equity company worth $5.9 million with 350,000 shares of common stock outstanding. After the sale of the bonds, the company will maintain the new capital structure indefinitely. The company currently generates annual pretax earnings of $1.35 million. This level of earnings is expected to remain constant in perpetuity. The tax rate is 40 percent.

a. What is the expected return on the company's equity before the announcement of the debt issue?

b. Construct the company's market value balance sheet before the announcement of the debt issue. What is the price per share of the firm's equity?

c. Construct the company's market value balance sheet immediately after the announcement of the debt issue.

d. What is the company's stock price per share immediately after the repurchase announcement?

e. How many shares will the company repurchase as a result of the debt issue? How many shares of common stock will remain after the repurchase?

f. Construct the market value balance sheet after the restructuring.

g. What is the required return on the company's equity after the restructuring?

25. **MM with Taxes** Williamson, Inc., has a debt–equity ratio of 2.3. The firm's weighted average cost of capital is 10 percent, and its pretax cost of debt is 6 percent. The tax rate is 35 percent.

a. What is the company's cost of equity capital?

b. What is the company's unlevered cost of equity capital?

c. What would the company's weighted average cost of capital be if the firm's debt–equity ratio were .75? What if it were 1.3?

CHALLENGE
(Questions 26–30)

26. **Weighted Average Cost of Capital** In a world of corporate taxes only, show that the R_{WACC} can be written as $R_{WACC} = R_0 \times [1 - t_C(B/V)]$.

27. **Cost of Equity and Leverage** Assuming a world of corporate taxes only, show that the cost of equity, R_S, is as given in the chapter by MM Proposition II with corporate taxes.

28. **Business and Financial Risk** Assume a firm's debt is risk-free, so that the cost of debt equals the risk-free rate, R_f. Define β_A as the firm's *asset* beta—that is, the systematic risk of the firm's assets. Define β_S to be the beta of the firm's equity. Use the capital asset pricing model, CAPM, along with MM Proposition II to show that $\beta_S = \beta_A \times (1 + B/S)$, where B/S is the debt–equity ratio. Assume the tax rate is zero.

29. **Stockholder Risk** Suppose a firm's business operations mirror movements in the economy as a whole very closely—that is, the firm's asset beta is 1.0. Use the result of the previous problem to find the equity beta for this firm for debt–equity ratios of 0, 1, 5, and 20. What does this tell you about the relationship between capital structure and shareholder risk? How is the shareholders' required return on equity affected? Explain.

30. **Unlevered Cost of Equity** Beginning with the cost of capital equation—that is:

$$R_{WACC} = \frac{S}{B+S}R_S + \frac{B}{B+S}R_B$$

show that the cost of equity capital for a levered firm can be written as follows:

$$R_S = R_0 + \frac{B}{S}(R_0 - R_B)$$

STEPHENSON REAL ESTATE RECAPITALIZATION

Stephenson Real Estate Company was founded 25 years ago by the current CEO, Robert Stephenson. The company purchases real estate, including land and buildings, and rents the property to tenants. The company has shown a profit every year for the past 18 years, and the shareholders are satisfied with the company's management. Prior to founding Stephenson Real Estate, Robert was the founder and CEO of a failed alpaca farming operation. The resulting bankruptcy made him extremely averse to debt financing. As a result, the company is entirely equity financed, with 11 million shares of common stock outstanding. The stock currently trades at $48.50 per share.

Stephenson is evaluating a plan to purchase a huge tract of land in the southeastern United States for $45 million. The land will subsequently be leased to tenant farmers. This purchase is expected to increase Stephenson's annual pretax earnings by $10 million in perpetuity. Kim Weyand, the company's new CFO, has been put in charge of the project. Kim has determined that the company's current cost of capital is 10.5 percent. She feels that the company would be more valuable if it included debt in its capital structure, so she is evaluating whether the company should issue debt to entirely finance the project. Based on some conversations with investment banks, she thinks that the company can issue bonds at par value with a coupon rate of 7 percent. Based on her analysis, she also believes that a capital structure in the range of 70 percent equity/30 percent debt would be optimal. If the company goes beyond 30 percent debt, its bonds would carry a lower rating and a much higher coupon because the possibility of financial distress and the associated costs would rise sharply. Stephenson has a 40 percent corporate tax rate (state and federal).

1. If Stephenson wishes to maximize its total market value, would you recommend that it issue debt or equity to finance the land purchase? Explain.

2. Construct Stephenson's market value balance sheet before it announces the purchase.

3. Suppose Stephenson decides to issue equity to finance the purchase.

    a. What is the net present value of the project?

    b. Construct Stephenson's market value balance sheet after it announces that the firm will finance the purchase using equity. What would be the new price per share of the firm's stock? How many shares will Stephenson need to issue to finance the purchase?

    c. Construct Stephenson's market value balance sheet after the equity issue but before the purchase has been made. How many shares of common stock does Stephenson have outstanding? What is the price per share of the firm's stock?

    d. Construct Stephenson's market value balance sheet after the purchase has been made.

4. Suppose Stephenson decides to issue debt to finance the purchase.

    a. What will the market value of the Stephenson company be if the purchase is financed with debt?

    b. Construct Stephenson's market value balance sheet after both the debt issue and the land purchase. What is the price per share of the firm's stock?

5. Which method of financing maximizes the per-share stock price of Stephenson's equity?

17

Capital Structure

LIMITS TO THE USE OF DEBT

March 2014 was a tough month for fast food. First, on March 10, mall and airport pizza company Sbarro announced it was filing for bankruptcy. The company stated that foot traffic in malls had dropped in recent years. This fact, coupled with the company's debt, meant management was forced to turn to bankruptcy. This filing was Sbarro's second bankruptcy in three years. It had filed for bankruptcy in April 2011, emerging in November 2011. Also in March 2014, sub chain Quiznos announced that it would be toasted without a bankruptcy filing. At one point, the company had more than 5,000 restaurants, but as rival Subway grew, the number of Quiznos stores dropped to 2,100. Women's clothing retailers also faced problems in 2014 as both Coldwater Creek and Dots were forced to file bankruptcy.

As these situations point out, there is a limit to the financial leverage a company can use, and the risk of too much leverage is bankruptcy. In this chapter, we discuss the costs associated with bankruptcies and how companies attempt to avoid this unhappy outcome.

The previous chapter began with the question, "How should a firm choose its debt–equity ratio?" We first presented the Modigliani-Miller (MM) result that, in a world without taxes, the value of the levered firm is the same as the value of the unlevered firm. In other words, the choice of the debt–equity ratio is unimportant here.

We next showed the MM result that, in a world with corporate taxes, the value of the firm increases with leverage, implying that firms should take on as much debt as possible. But this result leaves one with a number of questions. Is this the whole story? Should financial managers really set their firms' debt-to-value ratios near 100 percent? If so, why do real-world companies have, as we show later in this chapter, rather modest levels of debt?

The current chapter bridges the gap between theory and practice. We show that there are good reasons for modest capital structures in practice, even in a world with taxes. We begin with the concept of bankruptcy costs. These costs increase with debt, offsetting the tax advantage of leverage.

17.1 Costs of Financial Distress

BANKRUPTCY RISK OR BANKRUPTCY COST?

As mentioned throughout the previous chapter, debt provides tax benefits to the firm. However, debt puts pressure on the firm because interest and principal payments are obligations. If these obligations are not met, the firm may risk some sort of financial distress. The ultimate distress is *bankruptcy*, where ownership of the firm's assets is legally transferred from the stockholders to the bondholders. These debt obligations are fundamentally different from stock obligations. Although stockholders like and expect dividends, they are not legally entitled to dividends in the way bondholders are legally entitled to interest and principal payments.

We show next that bankruptcy costs, or more generally financial distress costs, tend to offset the advantages to debt. We begin by positing a simple example of bankruptcy. Taxes are ignored to focus only on the costs of debt.

EXAMPLE 17.1

Bankruptcy Costs   The Knight Corporation plans to be in business for one more year. It forecasts a cash flow of either $100 or $50 in the coming year, each occurring with 50 percent probability. The firm has no other assets. Previously issued debt requires payments of $49 of interest and principal. The Day Corporation has identical cash flow prospects but has $60 of interest and principal obligations. The cash flows of these two firms can be represented as follows:

	Knight Corporation		Day Corporation	
	Boom Times (prob. 50%)	**Recession (prob. 50%)**	**Boom Times (prob. 50%)**	**Recession (prob. 50%)**
Cash flow	$100	$50	$100	$50
Payment of interest and principal on debt	49	49	60	50
Distribution to stockholders	$ 51	$ 1	$ 40	$ 0

For Knight Corporation in both boom times and recession and for Day Corporation in boom times, cash flow exceeds interest and principal payments. In these situations the bondholders are paid in full, and the stockholders receive any residual. However, the most interesting of the four columns involves Day Corporation in a recession. Here the bondholders are owed $60, but the firm has only $50 in cash. Because we assume that the firm has no other assets, the bondholders cannot be satisfied in full. Bankruptcy occurs, implying that the bondholders will receive all of the firm's cash, and the stockholders will receive nothing. Importantly, the stockholders do not have to come up with the additional $10 (=$60 − $50). Corporations have limited liability in America and most other countries, implying that bondholders cannot sue the stockholders for the extra $10.[1]

Let's compare the two companies in recession. The bondholders of Knight receive $49 and the stockholders receive $1, for a total of $50. The bondholders of Day receive $50 and the stockholders receive $0, also for a total of $50. There is an important point here. While Day goes bankrupt but Knight does not, the investors of both firms receive $50. In other words, bankruptcy does not reduce the firm's cash flows. One often hears that bankruptcy causes a reduction in value or cash flow. But that is not the case. In our example, it is a recession causing the reduction, not bankruptcy.

(continued)

---

[1]There are situations where the limited liability of corporations can be "pierced." Typically, fraud or misrepresentation must be present.

However, we have left something out. Day's example is not realistic because it ignores an important cash flow. A more realistic set of numbers might be:

Day Corporation		
	Boom Times (prob. 50%)	Recession (prob. 50%)
Earnings	$100	$50
Debt repayment	60	35
Distribution to stockholders	$ 40	$ 0

Why do the bondholders receive only $35 in a recession? If cash flow is only $50, bondholders will be informed that they will not be paid in full. These bondholders are likely to hire lawyers to negotiate or even to sue the company. Similarly, the firm is likely to hire lawyers to defend itself. Further costs will be incurred if the case gets to a bankruptcy court. These fees are always paid before the bondholders get paid. In this example, we are assuming that bankruptcy costs total $15 (=$50 − $35).

Let's compare the example with bankruptcy costs to the example without these costs. Because of its greater leverage, Day Corporation faces the possibility of bankruptcy, while Knight Corporation does not. Nevertheless, as we saw earlier, total cash flow to investors is the same for both firms in a world without bankruptcy costs. However, once we introduce bankruptcy costs, total cash flow to investors becomes lower for the bankrupt company, Day. In a recession, Knight's bondholders receive $49 and the stockholders receive $1, for a total of $50. In a recession, Day's bondholders receive $35 and the stockholders receive $0, for a total of only $35. Thus, we can conclude the following:

Leverage increases the likelihood of bankruptcy. However, bankruptcy does not, by itself, lower the cash flows to investors. Rather, it is the costs associated with bankruptcy that lower cash flows.

Our pie example can provide an explanation. In a world without bankruptcy costs, the bondholders and the stockholders share the entire pie. However, bankruptcy costs eat up some of the pie in the real world, leaving less for the stockholders and bondholders.

17.2 Description of Financial Distress Costs

The preceding example showed that bankruptcy costs can lower the value of the firm. In fact, the same general result holds even if a legal bankruptcy is prevented. Thus *financial distress costs* may be a better phrase than *bankruptcy costs*. It is worthwhile to describe these costs in more detail.

DIRECT COSTS OF FINANCIAL DISTRESS: LEGAL AND ADMINISTRATIVE COSTS OF LIQUIDATION OR REORGANIZATION

As mentioned earlier, lawyers are involved throughout all the stages before and during bankruptcy. With fees often in the hundreds of dollars an hour, these costs can add up quickly. A wag once remarked that bankruptcies are to lawyers what blood is to sharks. In addition, administrative and accounting fees can substantially add to the total bill. And if a trial takes place, we must not forget expert witnesses. Each side may hire a number of these witnesses to testify about the fairness of a proposed settlement. Their fees can easily rival those of lawyers or accountants. (However, we personally look upon these witnesses kindly because they are frequently drawn from the ranks of finance professors.)

One of the most well-publicized bankruptcies in recent years concerned a municipality, Orange County, California, not a corporation. This bankruptcy followed large bond trading losses in the county's financial portfolio. The *Los Angeles Times* stated:

> Orange County taxpayers lost $1.69 billion, and their government, one year ago today, sank into bankruptcy. Now they are spending millions more to get out of it.
>
> Accountants pore over fiscal ledgers at $325 an hour. Lawyers toil into the night—at $385 an hour. Financial advisers from one of the nation's most prominent investment houses labor for the taxpayers at $150,000 a month. Clerks stand by the photocopy machines, running up bills that sometimes exceed $3,000.
>
> Total so far: $29 million. And it's nowhere near over.
>
> The multipronged effort to lift Orange County out of the nation's worst municipal bankruptcy has become a money-eating machine, gobbling up taxpayer funds at a rate of $2.4 million a month. That's $115,000 a day.
>
> County administrators are not alarmed.
>
> They say Orange County's bankruptcy was an epic disaster that will require equally dramatic expenditures of taxpayer cash to help it survive. While they have refused to pay several thousand dollars worth of claimed expenses—lavish dinners, big hotel bills—they have rarely questioned the sky-high hourly fees. They predict the costs could climb much higher.
>
> Indeed, participants in the county's investment pool have agreed to create a separate $50 million fund to pay the costs of doing legal battle with Wall Street.[2]

Of course, Orange County got off cheap when compared with Detroit, which spent $170 million to get out of bankruptcy. Bankruptcy costs in the private sector are often far larger than those in Orange County and Detroit. For example, the direct costs of Enron's and WorldCom's bankruptcies were commonly estimated to exceed $1 billion and $600 million, respectively. The costs of Lehman Brothers' bankruptcy are larger still. The company emerged from bankruptcy in March 2012 as a liquidating trust, with the goal of selling off assets and paying creditors. The direct bankruptcy costs were eye-watering: Lehman spent more than $2.2 billion on lawyers, accountants, consultants, and examiners for its U.S. and European operations. This number is the sum of many large costs. For example, one law firm billed $200,000 for business meals, $439,000 for computerized and other research, $115,000 for local transportation, and $287,000 for copying charges at 10 cents per page. The other costs of the bankruptcy may have been even larger. Some experts estimated that because Lehman rushed into bankruptcy it lost out on $75 billion that it could have earned if the sale of many of its assets had been better planned.

A number of academic studies have measured the direct costs of financial distress. Although large in absolute amount, these costs are actually small as a percentage of firm value. White, Altman, and Weiss estimate the direct costs of financial distress to be about 3 percent of the market value of the firm.[3] In a study of direct financial distress costs of 20 railroad bankruptcies, Warner finds that net financial distress costs were, on average,

---

[2]"The High Cost of Going Bankrupt," *Los Angeles Times Orange County Edition*, December 6, 1995. Taken from Lexis/Nexis.

[3]Michele White, "Bankruptcy Costs and the New Bankruptcy Code," *Journal of Finance* (May 1983); Edward Altman, "A Further Empirical Investigation of the Bankruptcy Cost Question," *Journal of Finance* (September 1984); and Lawrence A. Weiss, "Bankruptcy Resolution: Direct Costs and Violation of Priority of Claims," *Journal of Financial Economics* 27 (1990).

1 percent of the market value of the firm seven years before bankruptcy and were somewhat larger percentages as bankruptcy approached (e.g., 2.5 percent of the market value of the firm three years before bankruptcy).[4] Lubben estimates the average cost of legal fees alone to be about 1.5 percent of total assets for bankrupt firms.[5] Bris, Welch, and Zhu find bankruptcy expenses as measured against asset values to be in the 2 to 10 percent range.[6]

INDIRECT COSTS OF FINANCIAL DISTRESS

Impaired Ability to Conduct Business   Bankruptcy hampers conduct with customers and suppliers. Sales are frequently lost because of both fear of impaired service and loss of trust. For example, in 2008, both General Motors and Chrysler were experiencing significant financial difficulties, and many people felt that one or both companies would eventually file for bankruptcy (both later did). As a result of the bad news surrounding the companies, there was a loss of confidence in their automobiles. A study showed that 75 percent of Americans would not purchase an automobile from a bankrupt company because the company might not honor the warranty, and it might be difficult to obtain replacement parts. This concern resulted in lost potential sales for both companies, which only added to their financial distress. Chrysler actually found itself in a similar situation when it skirted insolvency in the 1970s. Many previously loyal Chrysler customers, fearing the loss of parts and servicing in a bankruptcy, switched to other manufacturers. As another example, gamblers avoided Atlantis casino in Atlantic City after it became technically insolvent. Gamblers are a superstitious bunch. Many wondered, "If the casino itself cannot make money, how can I expect to make money there?" A particularly outrageous story concerned two unrelated stores both named Mitchells in New York City. When one Mitchells declared bankruptcy, customers stayed away from both stores. In time, the second store was forced to declare bankruptcy as well.

Though these costs clearly exist, it is quite difficult to measure them. Altman estimates that both direct and indirect costs of financial distress are frequently greater than 20 percent of firm value.[7] Andrade and Kaplan estimate total distress costs to be between 10 percent and 20 percent of firm value.[8] Bar-Or estimates expected future distress costs for firms that are currently healthy to be 8 to 10 percent of operating value, a number below the estimates of either Altman or Andrade and Kaplan.[9] However, unlike Bar-Or, these authors consider distress costs for firms already in distress, not expected distress costs for currently healthy firms.

Cutler and Summers examine the costs of the well-publicized Texaco bankruptcy.[10] In January 1984, Pennzoil reached what it believed to be a binding agreement to acquire three-sevenths of Getty Oil. However, less than a week later, Texaco acquired all of Getty at a higher per-share price. Pennzoil then sued Getty for breach of contract. Because

---

[4]Jerrod Warner, "Bankruptcy Costs: Some Evidence," *Journal of Finance* (May 1977).

[5]Stephen J. Lubben, "The Direct Costs of Corporate Reorganization: An Empirical Examination of Professional Fees in Large Chapter 11 Cases," *American Bankruptcy Law Journal* (2000).

[6]Arturo Bris, Ivo Welch, and Ning Zhu, "The Costs of Bankruptcy: Chapter 7 Liquidation versus Chapter 11 Reorganization," *Journal of Finance* (June 2006).

[7]Edward Altman, *op. cit.*

[8]Gregor Andrade and Steven N. Kaplan, "How Costly Is Financial (Not Economic) Distress? Evidence from Highly Leveraged Transactions That Became Distressed," *Journal of Finance* (October 1998).

[9]Yuval Bar-Or, "An Investigation of Expected Financial Distress Costs," unpublished paper, Wharton School, University of Pennsylvania (March 2000).

[10]David M. Cutler and Lawrence H. Summers, "The Costs of Conflict Resolution and Financial Distress: Evidence from the Texaco–Pennzoil Litigation," *Rand Journal of Economics* (Summer 1988).

Texaco had previously indemnified Getty against litigation, Texaco became liable for damages.

In November 1985, the Texas State Court awarded damages of $12 billion to Pennzoil, although this amount was later reduced. As a result, Texaco filed for bankruptcy. Cutler and Summers identify nine important events over the course of the litigation. They find that Texaco's market value (stock price times number of shares outstanding) fell a cumulative $4.1 billion over these events, whereas Pennzoil's rose only $682 million. Thus, Pennzoil gained about one-sixth of what Texaco lost, resulting in a net loss to the two firms of almost $3.5 billion.

What could explain this net loss? Cutler and Summers suggest that it is likely due to costs that Texaco and Pennzoil incurred from the litigation and subsequent bankruptcy. The authors argue that direct bankruptcy fees represent only a small part of these costs, estimating Texaco's aftertax legal expenses at about $165 million. Legal costs to Pennzoil were more difficult to assess because Pennzoil's lead lawyer, Joe Jamail, stated publicly that he had no set fee. However, using a clever statistical analysis, the authors estimate his fee was about $200 million. Thus we must search elsewhere for the bulk of the costs.

Indirect costs of financial distress may be the culprit. An affidavit by Texaco stated that, following the lawsuit, some of its suppliers were demanding cash payments. Other suppliers halted or canceled shipments of crude oil. Certain banks restricted Texaco's use of futures contracts on foreign exchange. The affidavit stressed that these constraints were reducing Texaco's ability to run its business, leading to deterioration of its financial condition. Could these sorts of indirect costs explain the $3.5 billion disparity between Texaco's drop and Pennzoil's rise in market value? Unfortunately, although indirect costs likely played a large role here; there is simply no way to obtain a decent quantitative estimate for them.

AGENCY COSTS

When a firm has debt, conflicts of interest arise between stockholders and bondholders. Because of this, stockholders are tempted to pursue selfish strategies. These conflicts of interest, which are magnified when financial distress is incurred, impose **agency costs** on the firm. We describe three kinds of selfish strategies that stockholders use to hurt the bondholders and help themselves. These strategies are costly because they will lower the market value of the whole firm.

Selfish Investment Strategy I: *Incentive to Take Large Risks* Firms near bankruptcy often take great chances because they believe that they are playing with someone else's money. To see this, imagine a levered firm considering two *mutually exclusive* projects, a low-risk one and a high-risk one. There are two equally likely outcomes, recession and boom. The firm is in such dire straits that should a recession hit, it will come near to bankruptcy with one project and actually fall into bankruptcy with the other. The cash flows for the entire firm if the low-risk project is taken can be described as follows:

Value of Entire Firm if Low-Risk Project Is Chosen					
	Probability	Value of Firm	=	Stock	+ Bonds
Recession	.5	$100	=	$ 0	+ $100
Boom	.5	200	=	100	+ 100

If a recession occurs, the value of the firm will be $100; if a boom occurs, the value of the firm will be $200. The expected value of the firm is $150 (=.5 × $100 + .5 × $200).

The firm has promised to pay bondholders $100. Shareholders will obtain the difference between the total payoff and the amount paid to the bondholders. In other words, the bondholders have the prior claim on the payoffs, and the shareholders have the residual claim.

Now suppose that the riskier project can be substituted for the low-risk project. The payoffs and probabilities are as follows:

Value of Entire Firm if High-Risk Project Is Chosen						
	Probability	Value of Firm	=	Stock	+	Bonds
Recession	.5	$ 50	=	$ 0	+	$ 50
Boom	.5	240	=	140	+	100

The expected value of the *firm* is $145 (=.5 × $50 + .5 × $240), which is lower than the expected value of the firm with the low-risk project. Thus the low-risk project would be accepted if the firm were all equity. However, note that the expected value of the *stock* is $70 (=.5 × 0 + .5 × $140) with the high-risk project, but only $50 (=.5 × 0 + .5 × $100) with the low-risk project. Given the firm's present levered state, stockholders will select the high-risk project, even though the high-risk project has a *lower* NPV.

The key is that relative to the low-risk project, the high-risk project increases firm value in a boom and decreases firm value in a recession. The increase in value in a boom is captured by the stockholders because the bondholders are paid in full (they receive $100) regardless of which project is accepted. Conversely, the drop in value in a recession is lost by the bondholders because they are paid in full with the low-risk project but receive only $50 with the high-risk one. The stockholders will receive nothing in a recession anyway, whether the high-risk or low-risk project is selected. Thus, financial economists argue that stockholders expropriate value from the bondholders by selecting high-risk projects.

A story, perhaps apocryphal, illustrates this idea. It seems that Federal Express was near financial collapse within a few years of its inception. The founder, Frederick Smith, took $20,000 of corporate funds to Las Vegas in despair. He won at the gaming tables, providing enough capital to allow the firm to survive. Had he lost, the banks would simply have received $20,000 less when the firm reached bankruptcy.

Selfish Investment Strategy 2: *Incentive toward Underinvestment* Stockholders of a firm with a significant probability of bankruptcy often find that new investment helps the bondholders at the stockholders' expense. The simplest case might be a real estate owner facing imminent bankruptcy. If he takes $100,000 out of his own pocket to refurbish the building, he could increase the building's value by, say, $150,000. Though this investment has a positive net present value, he will turn it down if the increase in value cannot prevent bankruptcy. "Why," he asks, "should I use my own funds to improve the value of a building that the bank will soon repossess?"

This idea is formalized by the following simple example. Consider the firm in Table 17.1, which must decide whether to accept or reject a new project. The project's cost is $1,000. The first two columns in the table show cash flows without the project. The firm receives cash inflows of $5,000 and $2,400 under a boom and a recession, respectively. However, the firm must pay principal and interest of $4,000, implying that the firm will default in a recession.

Table 17.1

Example Illustrating Incentive to Underinvest

	Firm without Project		Firm with Project Costing $1,000	
	Boom	**Recession**	**Boom**	**Recession**
Firm cash flows	$5,000	$2,400	$6,700	$4,100
Bondholders' claim	4,000	2,400	4,000	4,000
Stockholders' claim	$1,000	$ 0	$2,700	$ 100

The project has positive NPV. However, much of its value is captured by bondholders. Rational managers, acting in the stockholders' interest, will reject the project.

Alternatively, as indicated in the next two columns of the table, the firm could raise equity to invest in the new project. Assume that the project generates cash flow of $1,700 in either state, bringing the firm's cash flow to $6,700 (= $5,000 + $1,700) in a boom and $4,100 (= $2,400 + $1,700) in a recession. Since the firm's cash flow of $4,100 in a recession exceeds the bondholders' claim of $4,000, bankruptcy is avoided. Because $1,700 is much greater than the project's cost of $1,000, the project has a positive NPV at any plausible interest rate. Clearly, an all-equity firm would accept the project.

However, the project hurts the stockholders of the levered firm. To see this, imagine the old stockholders contribute the $1,000 *themselves*.[11] Assuming that a boom and a recession are equally likely, the expected value of the stockholders' interest without the project is $500 (=.5 × $1,000 + .5 × 0). The expected value with the project is $1,400 (=.5 × $2,700 + .5 × $100). The stockholders' interest rises by only $900 (= $1,400 − $500) while costing $1,000.

Why does a project with a positive NPV hurt the stockholders? The key is that the stockholders contribute the full $1,000 investment, but the stockholders and bondholders *share* the benefits. The stockholders take the entire gain if a boom occurs. Conversely, the bondholders reap most of the cash flow from the project in a recession.

The discussion of selfish Strategy 1 is quite similar to the discussion of selfish Strategy 2. In both cases, an investment strategy for the levered firm is different from the one for the unlevered firm. Thus, leverage results in distorted investment policy. Whereas the unlevered corporation always chooses projects with positive net present value, the levered firm may deviate from this policy.

Selfish Investment Strategy 3: *Milking the Property* Another strategy is to pay out extra dividends or other distributions in times of financial distress, leaving less in the firm for the bondholders. This is known as *milking the property*, a phrase taken from real estate. Strategies 2 and 3 are very similar. In Strategy 2, the firm chooses not to raise new equity. Strategy 3 goes one step further because equity is actually withdrawn through the dividend.

Summary of Selfish Strategies The distortions just discussed occur only when there is a significant probability of bankruptcy or financial distress. Thus, distortions are unlikely to affect, say, utilities regulated by state commissions, since financial distress is rare among these firms. By contrast, small firms in risky industries, such as the computer field, are more likely to experience financial distress and, in turn, to be affected by such distortions.

Who pays for the cost of selfish investment strategies? We argue that it is ultimately the stockholders. Rational bondholders know that when financial distress is imminent, they

---

[11]The same qualitative results will be obtained if the $1,000 is raised from new stockholders. However, the arithmetic becomes much more difficult because we must determine how many new shares are issued.

cannot expect help from stockholders. Rather, stockholders are likely to choose investment strategies that reduce the value of the bonds. Bondholders protect themselves accordingly by raising the interest rate that they require on the bonds. Because the stockholders must pay these high rates, they ultimately bear the costs of selfish strategies. For firms that face these distortions, debt will be difficult and costly to obtain. These firms will have low leverage ratios.

The relationship between stockholders and bondholders is very similar to the relationship between Errol Flynn and David Niven, good friends and movie stars in the 1930s. Niven reportedly said that the good thing about Flynn was that you knew exactly where you stood with him. When you needed his help, you could always count on him to let you down.

17.3 Can Costs of Debt Be Reduced?

As U.S. senators are prone to say, "A billion here, a billion there. Pretty soon it all adds up." Each of the costs of financial distress we have mentioned is substantial in its own right. The sum of them may well affect debt financing severely. Thus, managers have an incentive to reduce these costs. We now turn to some of their methods. However, it should be mentioned at the outset that the methods here can, at most, reduce the costs of debt. They cannot *eliminate* them entirely.

PROTECTIVE COVENANTS

Because stockholders must pay higher interest rates as insurance against their own selfish strategies, they frequently make agreements with bondholders in hopes of lower rates. These agreements, called **protective covenants**, are incorporated as part of the loan document (or *indenture*) between stockholders and bondholders. The covenants must be taken seriously because a broken covenant can lead to default. Protective covenants can be classified into two types: negative covenants and positive covenants.

A **negative covenant** limits or prohibits actions that the company may take. Here are some typical negative covenants:

1. Limitations are placed on the amount of dividends a company may pay.
2. The firm may not pledge any of its assets to other lenders.
3. The firm may not merge with another firm.
4. The firm may not sell or lease its major assets without approval by the lender.
5. The firm may not issue additional long-term debt.

A **positive covenant** specifies an action that the company agrees to take or a condition the company must abide by. Here are some examples:

1. The company agrees to maintain its working capital at a minimum level.
2. The company must furnish periodic financial statements to the lender.

These lists of covenants are not exhaustive. The authors have seen loan agreements with more than 30 covenants.

Smith and Warner examined public issues of debt and found that 91 percent of the bond indentures included covenants that restricted the issuance of additional debt, 23 percent restricted dividends, 39 percent restricted mergers, and 36 percent limited the sale of assets.[12]

---

[12]Clifford Smith and J. B. Warner, "On Financial Contracting: An Analysis of Bond Covenants," *Journal of Financial Economics* 7 (1979).

Table 17.2   Loan Covenants

Shareholder Action or Firm Circumstances	Covenant Type	Reason for Covenant
As firm approaches financial distress, shareholders may want firm to make high-risk investments.	Financial statement restrictions 1. Minimum working capital 2. Minimum interest coverage 3. Minimum net worth	High-risk investments transfer value from bondholders to stockholders when financial distress is a realistic possibility. Covenants reduce probability of financial distress.
Shareholders may attempt to transfer corporate assets to themselves.	Restrictions on asset disposition 1. Limit on dividends 2. Limit on sale of assets 3. Collateral and mortgages	Covenants limit the ability of shareholders to transfer assets to themselves and to *underinvest*.
Shareholders may attempt to increase risk of firm.	Restrictions on switching assets	Increased firm risk helps shareholders and hurts bondholders.
Shareholders may attempt to issue new debt of equal or greater priority.	Dilution restrictions 1. Limit on leasing 2. Limit on further borrowing	Covenants restrict *dilution of the claim of existing bondholders*.

Protective covenants should reduce the costs of bankruptcy, ultimately increasing the value of the firm. Thus, stockholders are likely to favor all reasonable covenants. To see this, consider three choices by stockholders to reduce bankruptcy costs:

1. *Issue no debt.* Because of the tax advantages to debt, this is a very costly way of avoiding conflicts.

2. *Issue debt with no restrictive and protective covenants.* In this case, bondholders will demand high interest rates to compensate for the unprotected status of their debt.

3. *Write protective and restrictive covenants into the loan contracts.* If the covenants are reasonable and are clearly written, the creditors may receive protection without large costs being imposed on the shareholders. With this protection, the creditors are likely to accept a lower interest rate than they would accept without the covenants.

Thus, bond covenants, even if they reduce flexibility, can increase the value of the firm. They can be the lowest-cost solution to the stockholder–bondholder conflict. A list of typical bond covenants and their uses appears in Table 17.2.

CONSOLIDATION OF DEBT

One reason bankruptcy costs are so high is that different creditors (and their lawyers) contend with each other. This problem can be alleviated by proper coordination between bondholders and stockholders. For example, perhaps one, or at most a few, lenders can shoulder the entire debt. Should financial distress occur, negotiating costs are minimized under this arrangement. In addition, bondholders can purchase stock as well. In this way, stockholders and debtholders are not pitted against each other because they are not separate entities. This appears to be the approach in Japan, where large banks generally take significant stock positions in the firms to which they lend money. Debt–equity ratios in Japan are far higher than those in the United States.

17.4 Integration of Tax Effects and Financial Distress Costs

Modigliani and Miller argue that the firm's value rises with leverage in the presence of corporate taxes. Because this relationship implies that all firms should choose maximum debt, the theory does not predict the behavior of firms in the real world.

Other authors have suggested that bankruptcy and related costs reduce the value of the levered firm. The integration of tax effects and distress costs appears in Figure 17.1. In the top graph of the figure, the diagonal straight line represents the value of the firm in a world without bankruptcy costs. The ∩-shaped curve represents the value of the firm with these costs. This curve rises as the firm moves from all equity to a small amount of debt. Here, the present value of the distress costs is minimal because the probability of distress is so small. However, as more and more debt is added, the present value of these costs rises at an *increasing* rate. At some point, the increase in the present value of these costs from

Figure 17.1

The Optimal Amount of Debt and the Value of the Firm

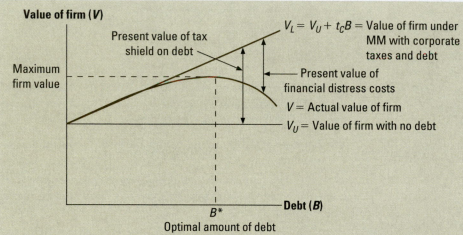

The tax shield increases the value of the levered firm. Financial distress costs lower the value of the levered firm. The two offsetting factors produce an optimal amount of debt at B^*.

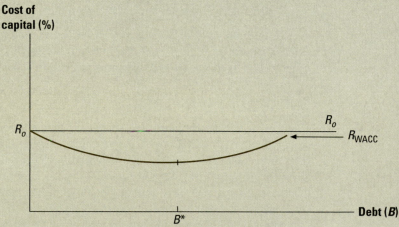

According to the static theory, the R_{WACC} falls initially because of the tax advantage of debt. Beyond point B^*, it begins to rise because of financial distress costs.

an additional dollar of debt equals the increase in the present value of the tax shield. This is the debt level maximizing the value of the firm and is represented by B^* in Figure 17.1. In other words, B^* is the optimal amount of debt. Bankruptcy costs increase faster than the tax shield beyond this point, implying a reduction in firm value from further leverage.

In the bottom graph of Figure 17.1, the weighted average cost of capital (R_{WACC}) falls as debt is added to the capital structure. After reaching B^*, the weighted average cost of capital rises. The optimal amount of debt produces the lowest weighted average cost of capital.

Our discussion implies that a firm's capital structure decision involves a trade-off between the tax benefits of debt and the costs of financial distress. In fact, this approach is frequently called the *trade-off* or the *static trade-off* theory of capital structure. The implication is that there is an optimal amount of debt for any individual firm. This amount of debt becomes the firm's target debt level. Because financial distress costs cannot be expressed in a precise way, no formula has yet been developed to determine a firm's optimal debt level exactly. However, the last section of this chapter offers some rules of thumb for selecting a debt–equity ratio in the real world. Our situation reminds us of a quote from John Maynard Keynes. He reputedly said that although most historians would agree that Queen Elizabeth I was both a better monarch and an unhappier woman than Queen Victoria, no one has yet been able to express the statement in a precise and rigorous formula.

PIE AGAIN

Now that we have considered bankruptcy costs, let's return to the pie approach of the previous chapter. The cash flows (CF) of the firm go to four different claimants: Stockholders, bondholders, the government (in the form of taxes), and, during the bankruptcy process, lawyers (and others). We can express this idea algebraically as:

$$CF = \text{Payments to stockholders}$$
$$+$$
$$\text{Payments to bondholders}$$
$$+$$
$$\text{Payments to the government}$$
$$+$$
$$\text{Payments to lawyers (and others)}$$

It follows that the total value of the firm, V_T, equals the sum of the following four components:

$$V_T = S + B + G + L$$

where S is the value of the equity, B is the value of the bonds, G is the value of the government claims from taxes, and L stands for the value that lawyers and others receive when the firm is under financial distress. This relationship is illustrated in Figure 17.2.

Nor have we begun to exhaust the list of financial claims to the firm's cash flows. To give an unusual example, everyone reading this book has an economic claim to the cash flows of General Motors. After all, if you are injured in an accident, you might sue GM. Win or lose, GM will expend resources dealing with the matter. If you think this is far-fetched and unimportant, ask yourself how much GM might be willing to pay every man, woman, and child in the country to have them promise that they would never sue GM, no matter what happened. The law does not permit such payments, but that does not mean that a value to all of those potential claims does not exist. We guess that it would run into

Figure 17.2

The Pie Model with Real-World Factors

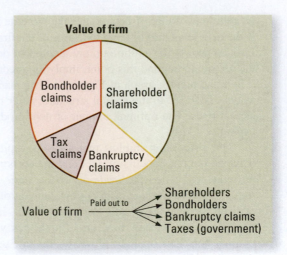

the billions of dollars, and, for GM or any other company, there should be a slice of the pie labeled *LS* for "potential lawsuits."

Figure 17.2 illustrates the essence of MM's intuition. While V_T is determined by the firm's cash flows, the firm's capital structure merely cuts V_T into slices. Capital structure does *not* affect the total value, V_T.

There is, however, a difference between claims such as those of stockholders and bondholders on the one hand and those of government and potential litigants in lawsuits on the other. The first set of claims are **marketable claims**, and the second set are **nonmarketable claims**. Marketable claims can be bought and sold in financial markets, and the nonmarketable claims cannot. This distinction between marketable and nonmarketable claims is important. When stock is issued, stockholders pay cash to the firm for the privilege of later receiving dividends. Similarly, bondholders pay cash to the firm for the privilege of receiving interest in the future. However, the IRS pays nothing to the firm for the privilege of receiving taxes in the future. Similarly, lawyers pay nothing to the firm for the privilege of receiving fees from the firm in the future.

When we speak of the *value of the firm*, we are referring just to the value of the marketable claims, V_M, and not the value of nonmarketable claims, V_N. What we have shown is that capital structure does not affect the total value:

$$V_T = S + B + G + L$$
$$= V_M + V_N$$

But as we saw, the value of the marketable claims, V_M, can change with changes in the capital structure.

By the pie theory, any increase in V_M must imply an identical decrease in V_N. Rational financial managers will choose a capital structure to maximize the value of the marketable claims, V_M. Equivalently, rational managers will work to minimize the value of the nonmarketable claims, V_N. These are taxes and bankruptcy costs in the previous example, but they also include all the other nonmarketable claims such as the *LS* claim.

17.5 Signaling

The previous section pointed out that the corporate leverage decision involves a trade-off between a tax subsidy and financial distress costs. This idea was graphed in Figure 17.1, where the marginal tax subsidy exceeds the distress costs for low levels of debt. The reverse holds for high levels of debt. The firm's capital structure is optimized where the marginal subsidy to debt equals the marginal cost.

Let's explore this idea a little more. What is the relationship between a company's profitability and its debt level? A firm with low anticipated profits will likely take on a low level of debt. A small interest deduction is all that is needed to offset all of this firm's pretax profits. And too much debt would raise the firm's expected distress costs. A more successful firm would probably take on more debt. This firm could use the extra interest to reduce the taxes from its greater earnings. Being more financially secure, this firm would find its extra debt increasing the risk of bankruptcy only slightly. In other words, rational firms raise debt levels (and the concomitant interest payments) when profits are expected to increase.

How do investors react to an increase in debt? Rational investors are likely to infer a higher firm value from a higher debt level. Thus, these investors are likely to bid up a firm's stock price after the firm has, say, issued debt in order to buy back equity. We say that investors view debt as a *signal* of firm value.

Now we get to the incentives of managers to fool the public. Consider a firm whose level of debt is optimal. That is, the marginal tax benefit of debt equals the marginal distress costs of debt. However, imagine that the firm's manager desires to increase the firm's current stock price, perhaps because he knows that many of his stockholders want to sell their stock soon. This manager might want to increase the level of debt just to make investors *think* that the firm is more valuable than it really is. If the strategy works, investors will push up the price of the stock.

This implies that firms can fool investors by taking on *some* additional leverage. Now let's ask the big question. Are there benefits to extra debt but no costs, implying that all firms will take on as much debt as possible? The answer, fortunately, is that there are costs as well. Imagine that a firm has issued extra debt just to fool the public. At some point, the market will learn that the company is not that valuable after all. At this time the stock price should actually fall *below* what it would have been had the debt never been increased. Why? Because the firm's debt level is now above the optimal level. That is, the marginal tax benefit of debt is below the marginal cost of debt. Thus if the current stockholders plan to sell, say, half of their shares now and retain the other half, an increase in debt will help them on immediate sales but likely hurt them on later ones.

Now here is the important point: We said that in a world where managers do not attempt to fool investors, valuable firms issue more debt than less valuable ones. It turns out that even when managers attempt to fool investors, the more valuable firms will still want to issue more debt than the less valuable firms. That is, while all firms will increase debt levels somewhat to fool investors, the costs of extra debt prevent the less valuable firms from issuing more debt than the more valuable firms issue. Thus, investors can still treat debt level as a signal of firm value. In other words, investors can still view an announcement of debt as a positive sign for the firm.

The foregoing is a simplified example of debt signaling, and you might argue that it is too simplified. For example, perhaps the stockholders of some firms want to sell most of their stock immediately, whereas the stockholders of other firms want to sell only a little of theirs now. It is impossible to tell here whether the firms with the most debt are the most valuable or merely the ones with the least skeptical stockholders. Because other objections can be brought up as well, signaling theory is best validated by empirical evidence. And fortunately, the empirical evidence tends to support the theory.

For example, consider the evidence concerning **exchange offers**. Firms often change their debt levels through exchange offers, of which there are two types. The first type of offer allows stockholders to exchange some of their stock for debt, thereby increasing leverage. The second type allows bondholders to exchange some of their debt for stock,

Figure 17.3
Stock Returns at the Time of Announcements of Exchange Offers

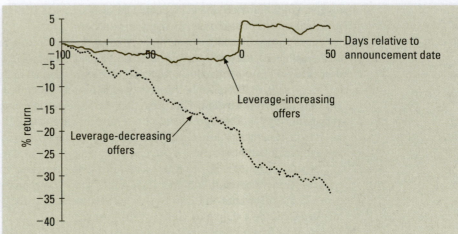

Exchange offers change the debt–equity ratios of firms. The graph shows that stock prices increase for firms whose exchange offers increase leverage. Conversely, stock prices decrease for firms whose offers decrease leverage.

SOURCE: Kshitij Shah, "The Nature of Information Conveyed by Pure Capital Structure Changes," *Journal of Financial Economics* 36 (August 1994).

decreasing leverage. Figure 17.3 shows the stock price behavior of firms that change their proportions of debt and equity via exchange offers. The solid line in the figure indicates that stock prices rise substantially on the date when an exchange offering increasing leverage is announced. (This date is referred to as date 0 in the figure.) Conversely, the dotted line in the figure indicates that stock price falls substantially when an offer decreasing leverage is announced.

The market infers from an increase in debt that the firm is better off, leading to a stock price rise. Conversely, the market infers the reverse from a decrease in debt, implying a stock price fall. Thus, we say that managers signal information when they change leverage.

17.6 Shirking, Perquisites, and Bad Investments: A Note on Agency Cost of Equity

A previous section introduced the static trade-off model, where a rise in debt increases both the tax shield and the costs of distress. We now extend the trade-off model by considering an important agency cost of equity. A discussion of this cost of equity is contained in a well-known quote from Adam Smith:[13]

> The directors of such [joint-stock] companies, however, being the managers of other people's money than of their own, it cannot well be expected that they should watch over it with the same anxious vigilance with which the partners in a private copartnery frequently watch over their own. Like the stewards of a rich man, they are apt to consider attention to small matters as not for their master's honor, and very easily give themselves a dispensation from having it. Negligence and profusion, therefore, must always prevail, more or less, in the management of the affairs of such a company.

---

[13]Adam Smith, *The Wealth of Nations* [1776], Cannon edition (New York: Modern Library, 1937), p. 700, as quoted in Michael Jensen and W. Meckling, "Theory of the Firm: Managerial Behavior, Agency Costs, and Ownership Structure," *Journal of Financial Economics* 3 (1976).

This elegant prose can be restated in modern vocabulary. An individual will work harder for a firm if she is one of its owners than if she is just an employee. In addition, the individual will work harder if she owns a large percentage of the company than if she owns a small percentage. This idea has an important implication for capital structure, which we illustrate with the following example.

EXAMPLE 17.2

Agency Costs   Ms. Pagell is an owner–entrepreneur running a computer services firm worth $1 million. She currently owns 100 percent of the firm. Because of the need to expand, she must raise another $2 million. She can either issue $2 million of debt at 12 percent interest or issue $2 million in stock. The cash flows under the two alternatives are presented here:

	Debt Issue				Stock Issue			
Work Intensity	Cash Flow	Interest	Cash Flow to Equity	Cash Flow to Ms. Pagell (100% of equity)	Cash Flow	Interest	Cash Flow to Equity	Cash Flow to Ms. Pagell ($33\frac{1}{3}$% of equity)
6-hour days	$300,000	$240,000	$ 60,000	$ 60,000	$300,000	0	$300,000	$100,000
10-hour days	400,000	240,000	160,000	160,000	400,000	0	400,000	133,333

Like any entrepreneur, Ms. Pagell can choose the degree of intensity with which she works. In our example, she can work either a 6- or a 10-hour day. With the debt issue, the extra work brings her $100,000 (=$160,000 − $60,000) more income. However, let's assume that with a stock issue she retains only a one-third interest in the equity. Here, the extra work brings her merely $33,333 (=$133,333 − $100,000). Being human, she is likely to work harder if she issues debt. In other words, she has more incentive to *shirk* if she issues equity.

In addition, she is likely to obtain more *perquisites* (a big office, a company car, more expense account meals) if she issues stock. If she is a one-third stockholder, two-thirds of these costs are paid for by the other stockholders. If she is the sole owner, any additional perquisites reduce her equity stake alone.

Finally, she is more likely to take on capital budgeting projects with negative net present values. It might seem surprising that a manager with any equity interest at all would take on negative NPV projects, since the stock price would clearly fall here. However, managerial salaries generally rise with firm size, providing managers with an incentive to accept some unprofitable projects after all the profitable ones have been taken on. That is, when an unprofitable project is accepted, the loss in stock value to a manager with only a small equity interest may be less than the increase in salary. In fact, it is our opinion that losses from accepting bad projects are far greater than losses from either shirking or excessive perquisites. Hugely unprofitable projects have bankrupted whole firms, something that even the largest expense account is unlikely to do.

Thus, as the firm issues more equity, our entrepreneur will likely increase leisure time, work-related perquisites, and unprofitable investments. These three items are called *agency costs* because managers of the firm are agents of the stockholders.[14]

---

[14]As previously discussed, *agency costs* are generally defined as the costs from the conflicts of interest among stockholders, bondholders, and managers.

This example is quite applicable to a small company considering a large stock offering. Because a manager–owner will greatly dilute his or her share of the total equity in this case, a significant drop in work intensity or a significant increase in fringe benefits is possible. However, the example may be less applicable for a large corporation with many stockholders. For example, consider a large company such as General Electric issuing stock for the umpteenth time. The typical manager there already has such a small percentage stake in the firm that any temptation for negligence has probably been experienced before. An additional offering cannot be expected to increase this temptation.

Who bears the burden of these agency costs, the current owner, i.e., Ms. Pagell, or the new stockholders? The new stockholders do not bear these costs as long as they invest with their eyes open. Knowing that Ms. Pagell may work shorter hours, they will pay only a low price for the stock. Thus, it is the owner who is hurt by agency costs. However, Ms. Pagell can protect herself to some extent. Just as stockholders reduce bankruptcy costs through protective covenants, an owner may allow monitoring by new stockholders. However, though proper reporting and surveillance may reduce the agency costs of equity, these techniques are unlikely to eliminate them.

It is commonly suggested that leveraged buyouts (LBOs) significantly reduce these costs of equity. In an LBO, a purchaser (usually a team of existing management) buys out the stockholders at a price above the current market. In other words, the company goes private: The stock is placed in the hands of only a few people. Because the managers now own a substantial chunk of the business, they are likely to work harder than when they were simply hired hands.[15]

EFFECT OF AGENCY COSTS OF EQUITY ON DEBT–EQUITY FINANCING

The preceding discussion of the agency costs of equity should be viewed as an extension of the static trade-off model. That is, we stated in Section 17.4 that the change in the value of the firm when debt is substituted for equity is the difference between (1) the tax shield on debt, and (2) the increase in the costs of financial distress (including the agency costs of debt). Now the change in the value of the firm is (1) the tax shield on debt, plus (2) the reduction in the agency costs of equity, minus (3) the increase in the costs of financial distress (including the agency costs of debt). The optimal debt–equity ratio would be higher in a world with agency costs of equity than in a world without these costs. However, because costs of financial distress are so significant, the costs of equity do not imply 100 percent debt financing.

FREE CASH FLOW

Any reader of murder mysteries knows that a criminal must have both motive and opportunity. The discussion thus far has been about motive. Managers with only a small ownership interest have an incentive for wasteful behavior. For example, they bear only a small portion of the costs of, say, excessive expense accounts, and they reap all of the benefits.

Now let's talk about opportunity. A manager can pad his expense account only if the firm has the cash flow to cover it. Thus, we might expect to see more wasteful activity in a firm with a capacity to generate large cash flows than in one with a capacity to generate only small cash flows. This simple idea, which is formally called the *free cash flow*

---

[15]One professor we know introduces his classes to LBOs by asking the students three questions:

 1. How many of you have ever owned a car?
 2. How many of you have ever rented a car?
 3. How many of you took better care of the car you owned than the car you rented?

Just as it is human nature to take better care of your own car, it is human nature to work harder when you own more of the company.

hypothesis,[16] is backed by a fair amount of empirical research. For example, a frequently cited paper found that firms with high free cash flow are more likely to make bad acquisitions than firms with low free cash flow.[17]

The hypothesis has important implications for capital structure. Since dividends leave the firm, they reduce free cash flow. Thus, according to the free cash flow hypothesis, an increase in dividends should benefit the stockholders by reducing the ability of managers to pursue wasteful activities. Furthermore, since interest and principal also leave the firm, debt reduces free cash flow as well. In fact, firms are legally obligated to pay interest and principal, implying that creditors can push the company into bankruptcy if these payments are withheld. By contrast, firms have no legal obligation to continue paying dividends. Thus, bond payments should have a greater effect than dividends on the free-spending ways of managers. Because of this, the free cash flow hypothesis argues that a shift from equity to debt will boost firm value.

In summary, the free cash flow hypothesis provides still another reason for firms to issue debt. We previously discussed the cost of equity; new equity dilutes the holdings of managers with equity interests, increasing their *motive* to waste corporate resources. We now state that debt reduces free cash flow, because the firm must make interest and principal payments. The free cash flow hypothesis implies that debt reduces the *opportunity* for managers to waste resources.

17.7 The Pecking-Order Theory

Although the trade-off theory has dominated corporate finance circles for a long time, attention is also being paid to the *pecking-order theory*.[18] To understand this view of the world, let's put ourselves in the position of a corporate financial manager whose firm needs new capital. The manager faces a choice between issuing debt and issuing equity. Previously, we evaluated the choice in terms of tax benefits, distress costs, and agency costs. However, there is one consideration that we have so far neglected: timing.

Imagine the manager saying:

> I want to issue stock in one situation only—when it is overvalued. If the stock of my firm is selling at $50 per share, but I think that it is actually worth $60, I will not issue stock. I would actually be giving new stockholders a gift because they would receive stock worth $60 but would only have to pay $50 for it. More important, my current stockholders would be upset because the firm would be receiving $50 in cash but giving away something worth $60. So if I believe that my stock is undervalued, I would issue bonds. Bonds, particularly those with little or no risk of default, are likely to be priced correctly. Their value is determined primarily by the marketwide interest rate, a variable that is publicly known.
>
> But suppose our stock is selling at $70. Now I'd like to issue stock. If I can get some fool to buy our stock for $70 while the stock is really worth only $60, I will be making $10 for our current shareholders.

Although this may strike you as a cynical view, it seems to square well with reality. Before the United States adopted insider trading and disclosure laws, many managers were alleged to have unfairly trumpeted their firm's prospects prior to equity issuance. And even today, managers seem more willing to issue equity after the price of their stock has

---

[16]The seminal theoretical article is Michael C. Jensen, "Agency Costs of Free Cash Flow, Corporate Finance and Takeovers," *American Economic Review* (May 1986), pp. 323–29.

[17]Larry Lang, R. Stulz, and R. Walkling, "Managerial Performance, Tobin's Q and the Gains from Successful Tender Offers," *Journal of Financial Economics* (1989).

[18]The pecking-order theory is generally attributed to Stewart C. Myers, "The Capital Structure Puzzle," *Journal of Finance* 39 (July 1984).

risen than after their stock has fallen in price. Thus, timing might be an important motive in equity issuance, perhaps even more important than the motives in the trade-off model. After all, the firm in the preceding example *immediately* makes $10 by properly timing the issuance of equity. Ten dollars' worth of agency costs and bankruptcy cost reduction might take many years to realize.

The key that makes the example work is asymmetric information: The manager must know more about his firm's prospects than does the typical investor. If the manager's estimate of the true worth of the company is no better than the estimate of a typical investor, any attempts by the manager to time will fail. This assumption of asymmetry is quite plausible. Managers should know more about their company than do outsiders because managers work at the company every day. (One caveat is that some managers are perpetually optimistic about their firm, blurring good judgment.)

But we are not done with this example yet; we must consider the investor. Imagine an investor saying:

> I make investments carefully because they involve my hard-earned money. However, even with all the time I put into studying stocks, I can't possibly know what the managers themselves know. After all, I've got a day job to be concerned with. So I watch what the managers do. If a firm issues stock, the firm was likely overvalued beforehand. If a firm issues debt, the firm was likely undervalued.

When we look at both issuers and investors, we see a kind of poker game, with each side trying to outwit the other. What should the issuing firm do in this poker game? Clearly, the firm should issue debt if the equity is undervalued. But what if the equity is overvalued? Here it gets tricky because a first thought is that the firm should issue equity. However, if a firm issues equity, investors will infer that the stock is overvalued. They will not buy it until the stock has fallen enough to eliminate any advantage from equity issuance. In fact, it can be shown that only the most overvalued firms have any incentive to issue equity. Should even a moderately overpriced firm issue equity, investors will infer that this firm is among the *most* overpriced, causing the stock to fall more than is deserved. Thus, the end result is that virtually no one will issue equity.[19]

This result that essentially all firms should issue debt is clearly an extreme one. It is as extreme as (1) the Modigliani–Miller (MM) result that in a world without taxes, firms are indifferent to capital structure and (2) the MM result that in a world of corporate taxes but no financial distress costs, all firms should be 100 percent debt-financed. Perhaps we in finance have a penchant for extreme models!

But just as we can temper MM's conclusions by combining financial distress costs with corporate taxes, we can temper those of the pure pecking-order theory. This pure version assumes that timing is the financial manager's only consideration. In reality, a manager must consider taxes, financial distress costs, and agency costs as well. Thus, a firm may issue debt only up to a point. If financial distress becomes a real possibility beyond that point, the firm may issue equity instead.

RULES OF THE PECKING ORDER

The previous discussion presented the basic ideas behind the pecking-order theory. What are the practical implications of the theory for financial managers? The theory provides the following two rules for the real world.

---

[19]In the interest of simplicity, we have not presented our results in the form of a rigorous model. To the extent that a reader wants a deeper explanation, we refer him or her to Stewart C. Myers, "The Capital Structure Puzzle," *Journal of Finance* 39 (July 1984).

Rule #1: Use Internal Financing

For expository purposes, we have oversimplified by comparing equity to *riskless* debt. Managers cannot use special knowledge of their firm to determine if this type of debt is mispriced because the rate of interest is the same for all issuers of riskless debt. However, in reality, corporate debt has the possibility of default. Thus, just as managers tend to issue equity when they think it is overvalued, managers also tend to issue debt when they think it is overvalued.

When would managers view their debt as overvalued? Probably in the same situations when they think their equity is overvalued. For example, if the public thinks that the firm's prospects are rosy but the managers see trouble ahead, these managers would view their debt—as well as their equity—as being overvalued. That is, the public might see the debt as nearly risk-free, whereas the managers see a strong possibility of default.

Thus, investors are likely to price a debt issue with the same skepticism that they have when pricing an equity issue. The way managers get out of this box is to finance projects out of retained earnings. You don't have to worry about investor skepticism if you can avoid going to investors in the first place. So the first rule of the pecking order is this:

Use internal financing.

Rule #2: Issue Safe Securities First

Although investors fear mispricing of both debt and equity, the fear is much greater for equity. Corporate debt still has relatively little risk compared to equity because if financial distress is avoided, investors receive a fixed return. Thus, the pecking-order theory implies that if outside financing is required, debt should be issued before equity. Only when the firm's debt capacity is reached should the firm consider equity.

Of course, there are many types of debt. For example, because convertible debt is more risky than straight debt, the pecking-order theory implies that managers should issue straight debt before issuing convertibles. So, the second rule of pecking-order theory is this:

Issue the safest securities first.

IMPLICATIONS

A number of implications associated with the pecking-order theory are at odds with those of the trade-off theory.

1. *There is no target amount of leverage.* According to the trade-off model, each firm balances the benefits of debt, such as the tax shield, with the costs of debt, such as distress costs. The optimal amount of leverage occurs where the marginal benefit of debt equals the marginal cost of debt.

   By contrast, the pecking-order theory does not imply a target amount of leverage. Rather, each firm chooses its leverage ratio based on financing needs. Firms first fund projects out of retained earnings. This should lower the percentage of debt in the capital structure, because profitable, internally funded projects raise both the book value and the market value of equity. Additional projects are funded with debt, clearly raising the debt level. However, at some point the debt capacity of the firm becomes exhausted, giving way to equity issuance. Thus, the amount of leverage is determined by the happenstance of available projects. Firms do not pursue a target debt-to-equity ratio.

2. *Profitable firms use less debt.* Profitable firms generate cash internally, implying less need for outside financing. Because firms desiring outside capital turn to debt first, profitable firms end up relying on less debt. The trade-off model does not have this implication. Here the greater cash flow of more profitable firms creates greater debt

capacity. These firms will use that debt capacity to capture the tax shield and the other benefits of leverage.

3. *Companies like financial slack.* The pecking-order theory is based on the difficulties of obtaining financing at a reasonable cost. A skeptical investing public thinks a stock is overvalued if the managers try to issue more of it, thereby leading to a stock price decline. Because this happens with bonds only to a lesser extent, managers rely first on bond financing. However, firms can only issue so much debt before encountering the potential costs of financial distress.

Wouldn't it be easier to have the cash ahead of time? This is the idea behind *financial slack.* Because firms know that they will have to fund profitable projects at various times in the future, they accumulate cash today. They are then not forced to go to the capital markets when a project comes up. However, there is a limit to the amount of cash a firm will want to accumulate. As mentioned earlier in this chapter, too much free cash may tempt managers to pursue wasteful activities.

17.8 Personal Taxes

So far in this chapter, we have considered corporate taxes only. Because interest on debt is tax deductible whereas dividends on stock are not deductible, we argued that the tax code gives firms an incentive to issue debt. But corporations are not the only ones paying taxes; individuals must pay taxes on both the dividends and the interest that they receive. We cannot fully understand the effect of taxes on capital structure until all taxes, both corporate and personal, are considered.

THE BASICS OF PERSONAL TAXES

Let's begin by examining an all-equity firm that receives $1 of pretax earnings. If the corporate tax rate is t_C, the firm pays taxes of t_C, leaving itself with earnings after taxes of $1 - t_C$. Let's assume that this entire amount is distributed to the stockholders as dividends. If the personal tax rate on stock dividends is t_S, the stockholders pay taxes of $(1 - t_C) \times t_S$, leaving them with $(1 - t_C) \times (1 - t_S)$ after taxes.

Alternatively, imagine that the firm is financed with debt. Here, the entire $1 of earnings will be paid out as interest because interest is deductible at the corporate level. If the personal tax rate on interest is t_B, the bondholders pay taxes of t_B, leaving them with $1 - t_B$ after taxes.

THE EFFECT OF PERSONAL TAXES ON CAPITAL STRUCTURE

To explore the effect of personal taxes on capital structure, let's consider three questions:

1. Ignoring costs of financial distress, what is the firm's optimal capital structure if dividends and interest are taxed at the same personal rate—that is, $t_S = t_B$?

The firm should select the capital structure that gets the most cash into the hands of its investors. This is tantamount to selecting a capital structure that minimizes the total amount of taxes at both the corporate and personal levels.

As we have said, beginning with $1 of pretax corporate earnings, stockholders receive $(1 - t_C) \times (1 - t_S)$, and bondholders receive $1 - t_B$. We can see that if $t_S = t_B$, bondholders receive more than stockholders. Thus, the firm should issue debt, not equity, in this situation. Intuitively, income is taxed twice—once at the corporate level and once at the personal level—if it is paid to stockholders. Conversely, income is taxed only at the personal level if it is paid to bondholders.

Note that the assumption of no personal taxes, which we used in the previous chapter, is a special case of the assumption that both interest and dividends are taxed at the same rate. Without personal taxes, the stockholders receive $1 - t_C$ while the bondholders receive $1. Thus, as we stated in a previous chapter, firms should issue debt in a world without personal taxes.

2. Under what conditions will the firm be indifferent between issuing equity or debt?

The firm will be indifferent if the cash flow to stockholders equals the cash flow to bondholders. That is, the firm is indifferent when:

$$(1 - t_C) \times (1 - t_S) = 1 - t_B \tag{17.1}$$

3. What should companies do in the real world?

Although this is clearly an important question, it is, unfortunately, a hard one—perhaps too hard to answer definitively. Nevertheless, let's begin by working with the highest tax rates. As of 2015, the top corporate tax rate was 35 percent. For investors in the highest marginal tax bracket, interest income was taxed at 39.6 percent. Investors in this highest bracket faced a 20 percent tax rate on dividends.

At these rates, the left side of Equation 17.1 becomes $(1 - .35)(1 - .20)$, which equals .52. The right side of the equation becomes $(1 - .396)$, which equals .604. Starting with $1 of pretax income, any rational firm would rather put $.604 instead of $.52 into its investors' hands. Thus, it appears at first glance that firms should prefer debt over equity, just as we argued in the previous chapter.

Does anything else in the real world alter this conclusion? Perhaps: Our discussion on equity income is not yet complete. Firms can repurchase shares with excess cash instead of paying a dividend. Although capital gains are also taxed at a maximum of 20 percent, the shareholder pays a capital gains tax only on the gain from sale, not on the entire proceeds from the repurchase. Thus, the *effective* tax rate on capital gains is actually lower than 20 percent. Because firms both pay dividends and repurchase shares, the effective personal tax rate on *stock distributions* must be below 20 percent.

This lower effective tax rate makes equity issuance less burdensome, but the lower rate will not induce any firm to choose stocks over bonds. For example, suppose that the effective tax rate on stock distributions is 10 percent. From every dollar of pretax corporate income, stockholders receive $(1 - .35) \times (1 - .10)$, which equals $.59. This amount is less than the $.604 that bondholders receive. In fact, as long as the effective tax rate on stock income is positive, bondholders will still receive more than stockholders from a dollar of pretax corporate income. And we have assumed that all bondholders face a tax rate of .396 on interest income. In reality, plenty of bondholders are in lower tax brackets, further tipping the scales toward bond financing.

Was there ever a time when stocks had a tax advantage over bonds? Very likely, yes. Consider the 1970s, when the marginal tax rate on interest income was as high as 70 percent. While dividends were taxed at the same rate as interest, capital gains were taxed at a much lower rate. Corporate income was taxed at 46 percent. Thus, both the effective tax rate on equity income and the corporate tax rate were well below the maximum rate on interest. Under reasonable assumptions we can make a case that stocks had the tax advantage at that time.[20]

---

[20]Actually, a well-known model of capital structure argues that an equilibrium would have occurred with firms issuing both debt and equity. Investors in low-tax brackets would buy the debt and investors in high-tax brackets would buy the equity. See Merton Miller, "Debt and Taxes," *Journal of Finance* (May 1977).

However, given that bonds appear to have the tax advantage today, is there anything that might cause firms to issue stock rather than bonds? Yes—the same costs of financial distress we discussed earlier in the chapter. We previously said that these costs are an offset to debt's tax advantage, causing firms to employ less than 100 percent leverage. The same point applies in the presence of personal taxes. And as long as the personal tax rate on equity income is below the personal tax rate on interest, the tax advantage to debt is smaller in a world with personal taxes than in a world without personal taxes. Thus, the optimal amount of debt will be lower in a world with personal taxes than in a world without them.

17.9 How Firms Establish Capital Structure

The theories of capital structure are among the most elegant and sophisticated in the field of finance. Financial economists should (and do!) pat themselves on the back for contributions in this area. However, the practical applications of the theories are less than fully satisfying. Consider that our work on net present value produced an *exact* formula for evaluating projects. Prescriptions for capital structure under either the trade-off model or the pecking-order theory are vague by comparison. No exact formula is available for evaluating the optimal debt–equity ratio. Because of this, we turn to evidence from the real world.

The following empirical regularities are worth considering when formulating capital structure policy.

1. *Most nonfinancial corporations have low debt–asset ratios.* How much debt is used in the real world? Figure 17.4 shows the median debt-to-value ratio, defined as book value of debt to market value of the firm, in each of 39 different countries. This ratio ranges from slightly over 50 percent for Korea to slightly under 10 percent for Australia. The ratio for U.S. companies is the fourth lowest.

   Should we view these ratios as being high or low? Because academics generally see corporate tax reduction as a chief motivation for debt, we might wonder if real-world companies issue enough debt to greatly reduce, if not downright eliminate, corporate taxes. The empirical evidence suggests that this is not the case. For example, corporate taxes in the United States for 2014 were more than $300 billion. Thus, it is clear that corporations do not issue debt up to the point where tax shelters are completely used up.[21] There are clearly limits to the amount of debt corporations can issue, perhaps because of the financial distress costs discussed earlier in this chapter.

2. *A number of firms use no debt.* In a fascinating study, Agrawal and Nagarajan examined approximately 100 firms on the New York Stock Exchange without long-term debt.[22] They found that these firms are averse to leverage of any kind, with little short-term debt as well. In addition, they have levels of cash and marketable securities well above their levered counterparts. Typically, the managers of these firms have high equity ownership. Furthermore, there is significantly greater family involvement in all-equity firms than in levered firms.

---

[21]For further insight, see John Graham, "How Big Are the Tax Benefits of Debt?" *Journal of Finance* (2000).

[22]Anup Agrawal and Nandu Nagarajan, "Corporate Capital Structure, Agency Costs, and Ownership Control: The Case of All-Equity Firms," *Journal of Finance* 45 (September 1990).

Figure 17.4 Median Leverage Ratio of Sample Firms in 39 Different Countries (1991–2006)

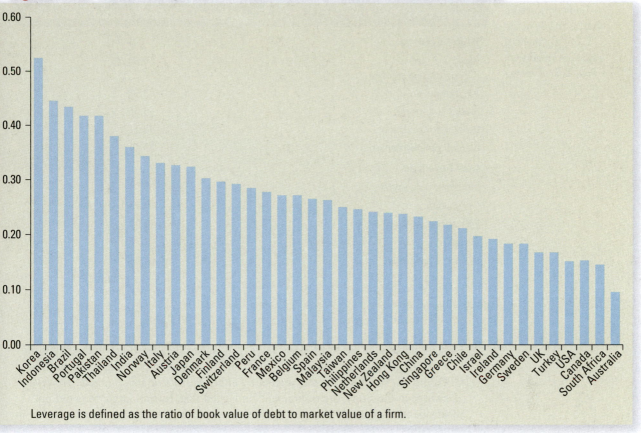

Leverage is defined as the ratio of book value of debt to market value of a firm.

SOURCE: Joseph P. H. Fan, Sheridan Titman, and Garry Twite, "An International Comparison of Capital Structure and Debt Maturity Choices," unpublished paper, University of Texas at Austin (September 2010), Figure 1.

Thus, a story emerges. Managers of all-equity firms are less diversified than the managers of similar, but levered, firms. Because of this, significant leverage represents an added risk that the managers of all-equity firms are loath to accept.

3. *There are differences in the capital structures of different industries.* There are significant interindustry differences in debt ratios that persist over time. As can be seen in Table 17.3, debt ratios tend to be quite low in high-growth industries with ample future investment opportunities, such as the drug and electronics industries. This is true even when the need for external financing is great. Industries with large investments in tangible assets, such as building construction, tend to have high leverage.

4. *Most corporations employ target debt–equity ratios.* Graham and Harvey asked 392 chief financial officers (CFOs) whether their firms use target debt–equity ratios, with the results being presented in Figure 17.5.[23] As can be seen, the great majority of the firms use targets, though the strictness of the targets varies across companies.

---

[23]John Graham and Campbell Harvey, "The Theory and Practice of Corporate Finance," *Journal of Financial Economics* (May/June 2001).

Table 17.3

Capital Structure Ratios for Selected U.S. Nonfinancial Industries (medians), Five-Year Average

	Debt as a Percentage of the Market Value of Equity and Debt (Industry Medians)
High Leverage	
Radio and television broadcasting stations	59.60
Air transport	45.89
Hotels and motels	45.55
Building construction	42.31
Natural gas distribution	33.11
Low Leverage	
Electronic equipment	10.58
Computers	9.53
Educational services	8.93
Drugs	8.79
Biological products	8.05

DEFINITION: Debt is the total of short-term debt and long-term debt.

SOURCE: Ibbotson 2011 *Cost of Capital Yearbook* (Chicago: Morningstar, 2011).

Only 19 percent of the firms avoid target ratios. Results elsewhere in the paper indicate that large firms are more likely than small firms to employ these targets. The CFOs did not specify what they meant by either *flexible* or *strict* targets. However, elsewhere in the study, the respondents indicated that, by and large, they did not rebalance in response to changes in their firm's stock price, suggesting flexibility in target ratios.

Figure 17.5

Survey Results on the Use of Target Debt–Equity Ratios

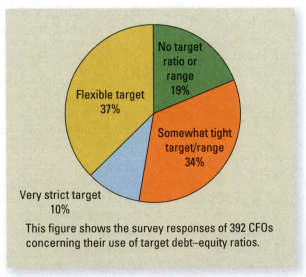

This figure shows the survey responses of 392 CFOs concerning their use of target debt–equity ratios.

SOURCE: Figure 6 of John Graham and Campbell Harvey, "The Theory and Practice of Corporate Finance," *Journal of Financial Economics* (May/June 2001).

How should companies establish target debt–equity ratios? While there is no mathematical formula for establishing a target ratio, we present three important factors affecting the ratio:

- *Taxes:* As we pointed out earlier, firms can deduct interest for tax purposes only to the extent of their profits before interest. Thus, highly profitable firms are more likely to have larger target ratios than less profitable firms.[24]

- *Types of assets:* Financial distress is costly with or without formal bankruptcy proceedings. The costs of financial distress depend on the types of assets that the firm has. For example, if a firm has a large investment in land, buildings, and other tangible assets, it will have smaller costs of financial distress than a firm with a large investment in research and development. Research and development typically has less resale value than land; thus, most of its value disappears in financial distress. Therefore, firms with large investments in tangible assets are likely to have higher target debt–equity ratios than firms with large investments in research and development.

- *Uncertainty of operating income:* Firms with uncertain operating income have a high probability of experiencing financial distress, even without debt. Thus, these firms must finance mostly with equity. For example, pharmaceutical firms have uncertain operating income because no one can predict whether today's research will generate new, profitable drugs. Consequently, these firms issue little debt. By contrast, the operating income of firms in regulated industries, such as utilities, generally has low volatility. Relative to other industries, utilities use a great deal of debt.

5. *Capital structures of individual firms can vary significantly over time.* While Graham and Harvey report that most firms use target leverage ratios, a recent paper nevertheless concludes that capital structures of individual firms often vary widely over time.[25] For example, consider Figure 17.6, which presents leverage ratios for General Motors, IBM, and Eastman Kodak since 1926. Both book leverage (total book value of debt divided by total assets) and market leverage (total book value of debt divided by total book debt plus market value of common stock) are shown. Regardless of the measure, all three companies display significant variations in leverage. Large variations in individual firm leverage over time is evidence that variations in individual firm investment opportunities and the need for financing are important determinants of capital structure and the importance of financial slack (i.e., firms borrow money when they have projects worth spending it on).

One final note is in order. Because no formula supports them, the preceding points may seem too nebulous to assist financial decision making. Instead, many real-world firms simply base their capital structure decisions on industry averages and the need for a certain amount of financial slack. This may strike some as a cowardly approach, but it at least keeps firms from deviating far from accepted practice. After all, the existing firms in any industry are the survivors. Therefore we should pay at least some attention to their decisions.

---

[24]By contrast, the pecking-order theory argues that profitable firms will employ less debt because they can invest out of retained earnings. However, the pecking-order theory argues against the use of target ratios in the first place.

[25]Harry DeAngelo and Richard Roll, "How Stable Are Corporate Capital Structures?" Unpublished paper, Marshall School of Business, University of Southern California (July 2011).

Figure 17.6
Leverage Ratios of
General Motors, IBM,
and Eastman Kodak
over Time

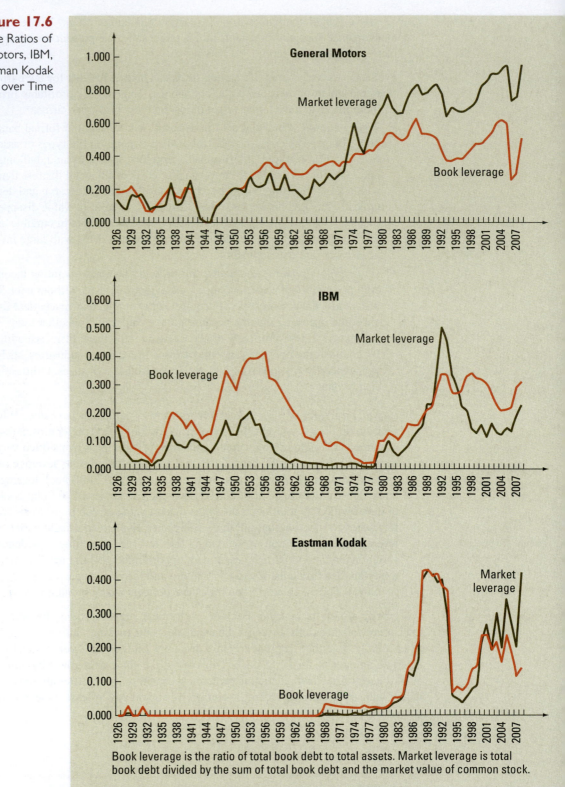

Book leverage is the ratio of total book debt to total assets. Market leverage is total book debt divided by the sum of total book debt and the market value of common stock.

SOURCE: Harry DeAngelo and Richard Roll, "How Stable are Corporate Capital Structures?" Unpublished paper, Marshall School of Business, University of Southern California (July 2011), Figure 1.

Summary and Conclusions

1. We mentioned in the last chapter that according to theory, firms should create all-debt capital structures under corporate taxation. Because firms generally employ moderate amounts of debt in the real world, the theory must have been missing something at that point. We stated in this chapter that costs of financial distress cause firms to restrain their issuance of debt. These costs are of two types: direct and indirect. Lawyers' and accountants' fees during the bankruptcy process are examples of direct costs. We mentioned four examples of indirect costs:

   Impaired ability to conduct business.
   Incentive to take on risky projects.
   Incentive toward underinvestment.
   Distribution of funds to stockholders prior to bankruptcy.

2. Because financial distress costs are substantial and the stockholders ultimately bear them, firms have an incentive to reduce costs. Protective covenants and debt consolidation are two common cost reduction techniques.

3. Because costs of financial distress can be reduced but not eliminated, firms will not finance entirely with debt. Figure 17.1 illustrates the relationship between firm value and debt. In the figure, firms select the debt–equity ratio at which firm value is maximized.

4. Signaling theory argues that profitable firms are likely to increase their leverage because the extra interest payments will offset some of the pretax profits. Rational stockholders will infer higher firm value from a higher debt level. Thus investors view debt as a signal of firm value.

5. Managers owning a small proportion of a firm's equity can be expected to work less, maintain more lavish expense accounts, and accept more pet projects with negative NPVs than managers owning a large proportion of equity. Because new issues of equity dilute a manager's percentage interest in the firm, such agency costs are likely to increase when a firm's growth is financed through new equity rather than through new debt.

6. The pecking-order theory implies that managers prefer internal to external financing. If external financing is required, managers tend to choose the safest securities, such as debt. Firms may accumulate slack to avoid external equity.

7. The results so far have ignored personal taxes. If distributions to equityholders are taxed at a lower effective personal tax rate than are interest payments, the tax advantage to debt at the corporate level is partially offset.

8. Debt–equity ratios vary across industries. We present three factors determining the target debt–equity ratio:
   a. *Taxes:* Firms with high taxable income should rely more on debt than firms with low taxable income.
   b. *Types of assets:* Firms with a high percentage of intangible assets such as research and development should have low debt. Firms with primarily tangible assets should have higher debt.
   c. *Uncertainty of operating income:* Firms with high uncertainty of operating income should rely mostly on equity.

Concept Questions

1. **Bankruptcy Costs**   What are the direct and indirect costs of bankruptcy? Briefly explain each.

2. **Stockholder Incentives**   Do you agree or disagree with the following statement? A firm's stockholders will never want the firm to invest in projects with negative net present values. Why?

3. **Capital Structure Decisions**   Due to large losses incurred in the past several years, a firm has $2 billion in tax loss carryforwards. This means that the next $2 billion of the firm's income will be free from corporate income taxes. Security analysts estimate that it will take many years for the firm to generate $2 billion in earnings. The firm has a moderate amount of debt in its capital structure. The firm's CEO is deciding whether to issue debt or equity to raise the funds needed to finance an upcoming project. Which method of financing would you recommend? Why?

4. **Cost of Debt**   What steps can stockholders take to reduce the costs of debt?

5. **MM and Bankruptcy Costs**   How does the existence of financial distress costs and agency costs affect Modigliani and Miller's theory in a world where corporations pay taxes?

6. **Agency Costs of Equity**   What are the sources of agency costs of equity?

7. **Observed Capital Structures**   Refer to the observed capital structures given in Table 17.3 of the text. What do you notice about the types of industries with respect to their average debt–equity ratios? Are certain types of industries more likely to be highly leveraged than others? What are some possible reasons for this observed segmentation? Do the operating results and tax history of the firms play a role? How about their future earnings prospects? Explain.

8. **Bankruptcy and Corporate Ethics**   As mentioned in the text, some firms have filed for bankruptcy because of actual or likely litigation-related losses. Is this a proper use of the bankruptcy process?

9. **Bankruptcy and Corporate Ethics**   Firms sometimes use the threat of a bankruptcy filing to force creditors to renegotiate terms. Critics argue that in such cases the firm is using bankruptcy laws "as a sword rather than a shield." Is this an ethical tactic?

10. **Bankruptcy and Corporate Ethics**   Continental Airlines once filed for bankruptcy, at least in part, as a means of reducing labor costs. Whether this move was ethical or proper was hotly debated. Give both sides of the argument.

Questions and Problems

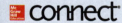

BASIC
(Questions 1–4)

1. **Firm Value**   Janetta Corp. has EBIT of $850,000 per year that is expected to continue in perpetuity. The unlevered cost of equity for the company is 14 percent, and the corporate tax rate is 35 percent. The company also has a perpetual bond issue outstanding with a market value of $1.9 million.

    a. What is the value of the company?
    b. The CFO of the company informs the company president that the value of the company is $4.3 million. Is the CFO correct?

2. **Agency Costs**   Tom Scott is the owner, president, and primary salesperson for Scott Manufacturing. Because of this, the company's profits are driven by the amount of work Tom does. If he works 40 hours each week, the company's EBIT will be $475,000 per year; if he works a 50-hour week, the company's EBIT will be $560,000 per year. The company is currently worth $2.9 million. The company needs a cash infusion of $1.2 million, and it can issue equity or issue debt with an interest rate of 8 percent. Assume there are no corporate taxes.

    a. What are the cash flows to Tom under each scenario?
    b. Under which form of financing is Tom likely to work harder?
    c. What specific new costs will occur with each form of financing?

3. **Nonmarketed Claims**   Dream, Inc., has debt outstanding with a face value of $5 million. The value of the firm if it were entirely financed by equity would be $18.65 million. The company also has 360,000 shares of stock outstanding that sell at a price of $41 per share. The corporate tax rate is 35 percent. What is the decrease in the value of the company due to expected bankruptcy costs?

4. **Capital Structure and Nonmarketed Claims**   Suppose the president of the company in the previous problem stated that the company should increase the amount of debt in its capital structure because of the tax-advantaged status of its interest payments. His argument is that this action would increase the value of the company. How would you respond?

INTERMEDIATE
(Questions 5–8)

5. **Capital Structure and Growth**   Edwards Construction currently has debt outstanding with a market value of $75,000 and a cost of 9 percent. The company has EBIT of $6,750 that is expected to continue in perpetuity. Assume there are no taxes.

   a. What is the value of the company's equity? What is the debt-to-value ratio?
   b. What are the equity value and debt-to-value ratio if the company's growth rate is 3 percent?
   c. What are the equity value and debt-to-value ratio if the company's growth rate is 7 percent?

6. **Costs of Financial Distress**   Steinberg Corporation and Dietrich Corporation are identical firms except that Dietrich is more levered. Both companies will remain in business for one more year. The companies' economists agree that the probability of the continuation of the current expansion is 80 percent for the next year, and the probability of a recession is 20 percent. If the expansion continues, each firm will generate earnings before interest and taxes (EBIT) of $2.7 million. If a recession occurs, each firm will generate earnings before interest and taxes (EBIT) of $1.1 million. Steinberg's debt obligation requires the firm to pay $900,000 at the end of the year. Dietrich's debt obligation requires the firm to pay $1.2 million at the end of the year. Neither firm pays taxes. Assume a discount rate of 13 percent.

   a. What is the value today of Steinberg's debt and equity? What about that for Dietrich's?
   b. Steinberg's CEO recently stated that Steinberg's value should be higher than Dietrich's because the firm has less debt and therefore less bankruptcy risk. Do you agree or disagree with this statement?

7. **Agency Costs**   Fountain Corporation's economists estimate that a good business environment and a bad business environment are equally likely for the coming year. The managers of the company must choose between two mutually exclusive projects. Assume that the project the company chooses will be the firm's only activity and that the firm will close one year from today. The company is obligated to make a $3,500 payment to bondholders at the end of the year. The projects have the same systematic risk but different volatilities. Consider the following information pertaining to the two projects:

Economy	Probability	Low-Volatility Project Payoff	High-Volatility Project Payoff
Bad	.50	$3,500	$2,900
Good	.50	3,700	4,300

   a. What is the expected value of the company if the low-volatility project is undertaken? What if the high-volatility project is undertaken? Which of the two strategies maximizes the expected value of the firm?
   b. What is the expected value of the company's equity if the low-volatility project is undertaken? What is it if the high-volatility project is undertaken?

c. Which project would the company's stockholders prefer? Explain.

d. Suppose bondholders are fully aware that stockholders might choose to maximize equity value rather than total firm value and opt for the high-volatility project. To minimize this agency cost, the firm's bondholders decide to use a bond covenant to stipulate that the bondholders can demand a higher payment if the company chooses to take on the high-volatility project. What payment to bondholders would make stockholders indifferent between the two projects?

8. **Financial Distress**   Good Time Company is a regional chain department store. It will remain in business for one more year. The probability of a boom year is 60 percent and the probability of a recession is 40 percent. It is projected that the company will generate a total cash flow of $148 million in a boom year and $61 million in a recession. The company's required debt payment at the end of the year is $88 million. The market value of the company's outstanding debt is $67 million. The company pays no taxes.

a. What payoff do bondholders expect to receive in the event of a recession?

b. What is the promised return on the company's debt?

c. What is the expected return on the company's debt?

CHALLENGE
(Questions 9–10)

9. **Personal Taxes, Bankruptcy Costs, and Firm Value**   When personal taxes on interest income and bankruptcy costs are considered, the general expression for the value of a levered firm in a world in which the tax rate on equity distributions equals zero is:

$$V_L = V_U + \{1 - [(1 - t_C)/(1 - t_B)]\} \times B - C(B)$$

where:

V_L = The value of a levered firm.
V_U = The value of an unlevered firm.
B = The value of the firm's debt.
t_C = The tax rate on corporate income.
t_B = The personal tax rate on interest income.
$C(B)$ = The present value of the costs of financial distress.

a. In their no-tax model, what do Modigliani and Miller assume about t_C, t_B, and $C(B)$? What do these assumptions imply about a firm's optimal debt–equity ratio?

b. In their model with corporate taxes, what do Modigliani and Miller assume about t_C, t_B, and $C(B)$? What do these assumptions imply about a firm's optimal debt–equity ratio?

c. Consider an all-equity firm that is certain to be able to use interest deductions to reduce its corporate tax bill. If the corporate tax rate is 34 percent, the personal tax rate on interest income is 20 percent, and there are no costs of financial distress, by how much will the value of the firm change if it issues $1 million in debt and uses the proceeds to repurchase equity?

d. Consider another all-equity firm that does not pay taxes due to large tax loss carryforwards from previous years. The personal tax rate on interest income is 20 percent, and there are no costs of financial distress. What would be the change in the value of this firm from adding $1 of perpetual debt rather than $1 of equity?

10. **Personal Taxes, Bankruptcy Costs, and Firm Value**   Overnight Publishing Company (OPC) has $2.5 million in excess cash. The firm plans to use this cash either to retire all of its outstanding debt or to repurchase equity. The firm's debt is held by one institution that is willing to sell it back to OPC for $2.5 million. The institution will not charge OPC any transaction costs. Once OPC becomes an all-equity firm, it will remain unlevered forever. If OPC does not retire the debt, the company will use the $2.5 million

in cash to buy back some of its stock on the open market. Repurchasing stock also has no transaction costs. The company will generate $1,300,000 of annual earnings before interest and taxes in perpetuity regardless of its capital structure. The firm immediately pays out all earnings as dividends at the end of each year. OPC is subject to a corporate tax rate of 35 percent, and the required rate of return on the firm's unlevered equity is 20 percent. The personal tax rate on interest income is 25 percent, and there are no taxes on equity distributions. Assume there are no bankruptcy costs.

a. What is the value of OPC if it chooses to retire all of its debt and become an unlevered firm?

b. What is the value of OPC if is decides to repurchase stock instead of retiring its debt?

(*Hint:* Use the equation for the value of a levered firm with personal tax on interest income from the previous problem.)

c. Assume that expected bankruptcy costs have a present value of $400,000. How does this influence OPC's decision?

Mini Case

McKENZIE CORPORATION'S CAPITAL BUDGETING

Sam McKenzie is the founder and CEO of McKenzie Restaurants, Inc., a regional company. Sam is considering opening several new restaurants. Sally Thornton, the company's CFO, has been put in charge of the capital budgeting analysis. She has examined the potential for the company's expansion and determined that the success of the new restaurants will depend critically on the state of the economy over the next few years.

McKenzie currently has a bond issue outstanding with a face value of $25 million that is due in one year. Covenants associated with this bond issue prohibit the issuance of any additional debt. This restriction means that the expansion will be entirely financed with equity at a cost of $5.7 million. Sally has summarized her analysis in the following table, which shows the value of the company in each state of the economy next year, both with and without expansion:

Economic Growth	Probability	Without Expansion	With Expansion
Low	.30	$20,000,000	$22,000,000
Normal	.50	25,000,000	32,000,000
High	.20	43,000,000	52,000,000

1. What is the expected value of the company in one year, with and without expansion? Would the company's stockholders be better off with or without expansion? Why?

2. What is the expected value of the company's debt in one year, with and without the expansion?

3. One year from now, how much value creation is expected from the expansion? How much value is expected for stockholders? Bondholders?

4. If the company announces that it is not expanding, what do you think will happen to the price of its bonds? What will happen to the price of the bonds if the company does expand?

5. If the company opts not to expand, what are the implications for the company's future borrowing needs? What are the implications if the company does expand?

6. Because of the bond covenant, the expansion would have to be financed with equity. How would it affect your answer if the expansion were financed with cash on hand instead of new equity?

Appendix 17A **Some Useful Formulas of Financial Structure**

Appendix 17B **The Miller Model and the Graduated Income Tax**

To access the appendixes for this chapter, please logon to Connect Finance.

18

Valuation and Capital Budgeting for the Levered Firm

In September 2014, Tesla announced that it would build a $5 billion "gigafactory" in Nevada. So why did Tesla choose Nevada? A major reason was a package granted to the company consisting of $1.25 billion in tax breaks and other perks. For example, Tesla received a 20-year sales tax abatement worth $725 million, a 10-year property tax abatement worth $332 million, and discounted electricity rates for eight years, worth $8 million. The package was the largest ever offered by Nevada and one of the largest ever in the United States.

When a corporation opens a major plant or considers relocation, municipalities often create packages loaded with subsidies such as these. Other common subsidies include subsidized debt, educational training, and road and infrastructure creation.

With subsidized debt, a state or municipality guarantees the debt, which allows the company to borrow at a much lower interest rate. If the interest rate on the debt is lower than the company's normal cost of debt, how does the firm evaluate the financial benefits of this and other such subsidies? In this chapter, we illustrate how to evaluate projects using the adjusted present value and flows to equity approaches to valuation to answer this and related questions.

18.1 Adjusted Present Value Approach

In this chapter, we describe three approaches to valuation for the levered firm. In particular, we describe the adjusted present value (APV) approach, the flow to equity (FTE) approach, and the weighted average cost of capital (WACC) approach. As you may recognize, we have discussed each of these approaches in previous chapters. The analysis of these approaches is relevant for entire firms as well as projects. The specific purpose of this chapter is to tie things together and show that each of the approaches is logically consistent with each other and can give the same answer. However, at times, one approach might be easier to implement than another, and we suggest guidelines for selecting between the approaches. We start with the adjusted present value method.

The **adjusted present value (APV)** method is best described by the following formula:

$$APV = NPV + NPVF$$

In words, the value of a project to a levered firm (APV) is equal to the value of the project to an unlevered firm (NPV) plus the net present value of the financing side effects (NPVF). We can generally think of four side effects:

1. *The tax subsidy to debt*: This was discussed in Chapter 16, where we pointed out that for perpetual debt the value of the tax subsidy is $t_C B$. (t_C is the corporate tax

555

rate, and B is the value of the debt.) The material about valuation under corporate taxes in Chapter 16 is actually an application of the APV approach.

2. *The costs of issuing new securities*: As we will discuss in detail in Chapter 20, investment bankers participate in the public issuance of corporate debt. These bankers must be compensated for their time and effort, a cost that lowers the value of the project.

3. *The costs of financial distress*: The possibility of financial distress, and bankruptcy in particular, arises with debt financing. As stated in the previous chapter, financial distress imposes costs, thereby lowering value.

4. *Subsidies to debt financing*: The interest on debt issued by state and local governments is not taxable to the investor. Because of this, the yield on tax-exempt debt is generally substantially below the yield on taxable debt. Frequently corporations can obtain financing from a municipality at the tax-exempt rate because the municipality can borrow at that rate as well. As with any subsidy, this subsidy adds value.

Although each of the preceding four side effects is important, the tax deduction to debt almost certainly has the highest dollar value in most actual situations. For this reason, the following example considers the tax subsidy but not the other three side effects.[1]

Consider a project of the P. B. Singer Co. with the following characteristics:

Cash inflows: $500,000 per year for the indefinite future.

Cash costs: 72% of sales.

Initial investment: $475,000.

$t_C = 34\%$

$R_0 = 20\%$, where R_0 is the cost of capital for a project of an all-equity firm.

If both the project and the firm are financed with only equity, the project's cash flow is as follows:

Cash inflows	$500,000
Cash costs	−360,000
Operating income	140,000
Corporate tax (34% tax rate)	−47,600
Unlevered cash flow (UCF)	$ 92,400

The distinction between present value and net present value is important for this example. The *present value* of a project is determined before the initial investment at Date 0 is subtracted. The initial investment is subtracted for the calculation of *net* present value.

Given a discount rate of 20 percent, the present value of the project is:

$$\frac{\$92,400}{.20} = \$462,000$$

The net present value (NPV) of the project—that is, the value of the project to an all-equity firm—is:

$$\$462,000 - \$475,000 = -\$13,000$$

Because the NPV is negative, the project would be rejected by an all-equity firm.

Now imagine that the firm finances the project with exactly $126,229.50 in debt, so that the remaining investment of $348,770.50 (= $475,000 − $126,229.50) is financed

---

[1]The Bicksler Enterprises example in Section 18.6 handles both flotation costs and interest subsidies.

with equity. The net present value of the project under leverage, which we call the adjusted present value, or the APV, is:

$$APV = NPV + t_c \times B$$
$$\$29,918 = -\$13,000 + .34 \times \$126,229.50$$

That is, the value of the project when financed with some leverage is equal to the value of the project when financed with all equity plus the tax shield from the debt. Because this number is positive, the project should be accepted.[2]

You may be wondering why we chose such a precise amount of debt. Actually, we chose it so that the ratio of debt to the present value of the project under leverage is .25.[3]

In this example, debt is a fixed proportion of the present value of the project, not a fixed proportion of the initial investment of $475,000. This is consistent with the goal of a target debt-to-*market*-value ratio, which we find in the real world. For example, commercial banks typically lend to real estate developers a fixed percentage of the appraised market value of a project, not a fixed percentage of the initial investment.

18.2 Flow to Equity Approach

The **flow to equity (FTE)** approach is an alternative valuation approach. The formula simply calls for discounting the cash flow from the project to the equityholders of the levered firm at the cost of equity capital, R_S. For a perpetuity this becomes:

$$\frac{\text{Cash flow from project to equityholders of the levered firm}}{R_S}$$

There are three steps to the FTE approach.

STEP 1: CALCULATING LEVERED CASH FLOW (LCF)[4]

Assuming an interest rate of 10 percent, the perpetual cash flow to equityholders in our P. B. Singer Co. example is:

Cash inflows	$500,000.00
Cash costs	−360,000.00
Interest (10% × $126,229.50)	−12,622.95
Income after interest	127,377.05
Corporate tax (34% tax rate)	−43,308.20
Levered cash flow (LCF)	$ 84,068.85

---

[2]This example is meant to dramatize the potential importance of the tax benefits of debt. In practice, the firm will likely find the value of a project to an all-equity firm to have at least an NPV of zero.

[3]That is, the present value of the project after the initial investment has been made is $504,918 (= $29,918 + $475,000). Thus, the debt-to-value ratio of the project is .25 (= $126,229.50/$504,918).

This level of debt can be calculated directly. Note that:

$$\text{Present value of levered project} = \text{Present value of unlevered project} + t_c \times B$$
$$V_{\text{With debt}} = \$462,000 + .34 \times .25 \times V_{\text{With debt}}$$

Rearranging the last line, we have:

$$V_{\text{With debt}} \times (1 - .34 \times .25) = \$462,000$$
$$V_{\text{With debt}} = \$504,918$$

Debt is .25 of value: $126,229.50 = .25 × $504,918.

[4]We use the term *levered cash flow* (LCF) for simplicity. A more complete term would be *distributable cash flow (a.k.a. free cash flow) from the project to the equityholders of a levered firm*. Similarly, a more complete term for *unlevered cash flow* (UCF) would be *distributable cash flow (a.k.a. free cash flow) from the project to the equityholders of an unlevered firm*.

Alternatively, we can calculate levered cash flow (LCF) directly from unlevered cash flow (UCF). The key here is that the difference between the cash flow that equityholders receive in an unlevered firm and the cash flow that equityholders receive in a levered firm is the aftertax interest payment. (Repayment of principal does not appear in this example because the debt is perpetual.) We write this algebraically as:

$$UCF - LCF = (1 - t_C)R_B B$$

The term on the right side of this expression is the aftertax interest payment. Thus, because cash flow to the unlevered equityholders (UCF) is $92,400 and the aftertax interest payment is $8,331.15 ($=.66 \times .10 \times $126,229.50$), cash flow to the levered equityholders (LCF) is:

$$\$92,400 - \$8,331.15 = \$84,068.85$$

which is exactly the number we calculated earlier.

STEP 2: CALCULATING R_S

The next step is to calculate the discount rate, R_S. Note that we assumed that the discount rate on unlevered equity, R_0, is .20. As we saw in an earlier chapter, the formula for R_S is:

$$R_S = R_0 + \frac{B}{S}(1 - t_C)(R_0 - R_B)$$

Note that our target debt-to-value ratio of 1/4 implies a target debt-to-equity ratio of 1/3. Applying the preceding formula to this example, we have:

$$R_S = .222 = .20 + \frac{1}{3}(.66)(.20 - .10)$$

STEP 3: VALUATION

The present value of the project's LCF is:

$$\frac{LCF}{R_S} = \frac{\$84,068.85}{.222} = \$378,688.50$$

Because the initial investment is $475,000 and $126,229.50 is borrowed, the firm must advance the project $348,770.50 ($=$475,000 - $126,229.50$) out of its own cash reserves. The *net* present value of the project is simply the difference between the present value of the project's LCF and the investment not borrowed. Thus, the NPV is:

$$\$378,688.50 - \$348,770.50 = \$29,918$$

which is identical to the result found with the APV approach.

18.3 Weighted Average Cost of Capital Method

Finally, we can value a project or a firm using the **weighted average cost of capital (WACC)** method. Although this method was discussed in earlier chapters, it is worthwhile to review it here. The WACC approach begins with the insight that projects of levered firms are simultaneously financed with both debt and equity. The cost of capital is a weighted average of the cost of debt and the cost of equity. The cost of equity is R_S. Ignoring taxes, the cost of debt is simply the borrowing rate, R_B. However, with corporate taxes, the appropriate cost of debt is $(1 - t_C)R_B$, the aftertax cost of debt.

The formula for determining the weighted average cost of capital, R_{WACC}, is:

$$R_{WACC} = \frac{S}{S + B} R_S + \frac{B}{S + B} R_B (1 - t_C)$$

The weight for equity, $S/(S + B)$, and the weight for debt, $B/(S + B)$, are target ratios. Target ratios are generally expressed in terms of market values, not accounting values. (Recall that another phrase for accounting value is *book value*.)

The formula calls for discounting the *unlevered* cash flow of the project (UCF) at the weighted average cost of capital, R_{WACC}. The net present value of the project can be written algebraically as:

$$\sum_{t=1}^{\infty} \frac{UCF_t}{(1 + R_{WACC})^t} - \text{Initial investment}$$

If the project is a perpetuity, the net present value is:

$$\frac{UCF}{R_{WACC}} - \text{Initial investment}$$

We previously stated that the target debt-to-value ratio of our project is 1/4 and the corporate tax rate is .34, implying that the weighted average cost of capital is:

$$R_{WACC} = \frac{3}{4} \times .222 + \frac{1}{4} \times .10 \times .66 = .183$$

Note that R_{WACC}, .183, is lower than the cost of equity capital for an all-equity firm, .20. This must always be the case because debt financing provides a tax subsidy that lowers the average cost of capital.

We previously determined the UCF of the project to be $92,400, implying that the present value of the project is:

$$\frac{\$92,400}{.183} = \$504,918$$

The initial investment is $475,000, so the NPV of the project is:

$$\$504,918 - \$475,000 = \$29,918$$

Note that all three approaches yield the same value.

18.4 A Comparison of the APV, FTE, and WACC Approaches

In this chapter, we provide three approaches to valuation for projects of a levered firm. The adjusted present value (APV) approach first values the project on an all-equity basis. That is, the project's aftertax cash flows under all-equity financing (called unlevered cash flows, or UCF) are placed in the numerator of the capital budgeting equation. The discount rate, assuming all-equity financing, appears in the denominator. At this point, the calculation is identical to that performed in the early chapters of this book. We then add the net present value of the debt. We point out that the net present value of the debt is likely to be the sum of four parameters: Tax effects, flotation costs, bankruptcy costs, and interest subsidies.

The flow to equity (FTE) approach discounts the aftertax cash flow from a project going to the equityholders of a levered firm (LCF). LCF, which stands for levered cash flow, is the residual to equityholders after interest has been deducted. The discount rate is R_S, the cost of capital to the equityholders of a levered firm. For a firm with leverage,

R_S must be greater than R_0, the cost of capital for an unlevered firm. This follows from our material in Chapter 16 showing that leverage raises the risk to the equityholders.

The last approach is the weighted average cost of capital (WACC) method. This technique calculates the project's aftertax cash flows assuming all-equity financing (UCF). The UCF is placed in the numerator of the capital budgeting equation. The denominator, R_{WACC}, is a weighted average of the cost of equity capital and the cost of debt capital. The tax advantage of debt is reflected in the denominator because the cost of debt capital is determined net of corporate tax. The numerator does not reflect debt at all.

All three approaches perform the same task: Valuation in the presence of debt financing. And as illustrated by the previous example, all three provide the same valuation estimate. However, as we saw before, the approaches are markedly different in technique. Because of this, students often ask questions of the following sort: "How can this be? How can the three approaches look so different and yet give the same answer?" We believe that the best way to handle questions like these is through the following two points:

1. *APV versus WACC:* Of the three approaches, APV and WACC display the greatest similarity. After all, both approaches put the unlevered cash flow (UCF) in the numerator. However, the APV approach discounts these flows at R_0, yielding the value of the unlevered project. Adding the present value of the tax shield gives the value of the project under leverage. The WACC approach discounts UCF at R_{WACC}, which is lower than R_0.

   Thus, both approaches adjust the basic NPV formula for unlevered firms to reflect the tax benefit of leverage. The APV approach makes this adjustment directly. It simply adds in the present value of the tax shield as a separate term. The WACC approach makes the adjustment in a more subtle way. Here, the discount rate is lowered below R_0. Although we do not provide a proof in this book, it can be shown that these two adjustments always have the same quantitative effect.

2. *Entity being valued:* The FTE approach appears at first glance to be far different from the other two. For both the APV and the WACC approaches, the initial investment is subtracted out in the final step ($475,000 in our example). However, for the FTE approach, only the firm's contribution to the initial investment ($348,770.50 = $475,000 − $126,229.50) is subtracted out. This occurs because under the FTE approach only the future cash flows to the levered equityholders (LCF) are valued. By contrast, future cash flows to the unlevered equityholders (UCF) are valued in both the APV and WACC approaches. Thus, because LCFs are net of interest payments, whereas UCFs are not, the initial investment under the FTE approach is correspondingly reduced by debt financing. In this way, the FTE approach produces the same answer that the other two approaches do.

A SUGGESTED GUIDELINE

The net present value of our project is exactly the same under each of the three methods. In theory, this should always be the case.[5] However, one method usually provides an easier computation than another, and, in many cases, one or more of the methods are virtually impossible computationally. We first consider when it is best to use the WACC and FTE approaches.

---

[5]See Ishik Inselbag and H. Kaufold, "Two DCF Approaches for Valuing Companies under Alternative Financial Strategies (and How to Choose between Them)," *Journal of Applied Corporate Finance* (Spring 1997).

If the risk of a project stays constant throughout its life, it is plausible to assume that R_0 remains constant throughout the project's life. This assumption of constant risk appears to be reasonable for most real-world projects. In addition, if the debt-to-value ratio remains constant over the life of the project, both R_S and R_{WACC} will remain constant as well. Under this latter assumption, either the FTE or the WACC approach is easy to apply. However, if the debt-to-value ratio varies from year to year, both R_S and R_{WACC} vary from year to year as well. Using the FTE or the WACC approach when the denominator changes every year is computationally quite complex, and when computations become complex, the error rate rises. Thus, both the FTE and WACC approaches present difficulties when the debt-to-value *ratio* changes over time.

The APV approach is based on the *level* of debt in each future period. Consequently, when the debt level can be specified precisely for future periods, the APV approach is quite easy to use. However, when the debt level is uncertain, the APV approach becomes more problematic. For example, when the debt-to-value ratio is constant, the debt level varies with the value of the project. Because the value of the project in a future year cannot be easily forecast, the level of debt cannot be easily forecast either.

Thus, we suggest the following guideline:

Use WACC or FTE if the firm's target debt-to-value *ratio* applies to the project over its life. Use APV if the project's *level* of debt is known over the life of the project.

There are a number of situations where the APV approach is preferred. For example, in a leveraged buyout (LBO) the firm begins with a large amount of debt but rapidly pays down the debt over a number of years. Because the schedule of debt reduction in the future is known when the LBO is arranged, tax shields in every future year can be easily forecast. Thus, the APV approach is easy to use here. (An illustration of the APV approach applied to LBOs is provided in the appendix to this chapter.) By contrast, the WACC and FTE approaches are virtually impossible to apply here because the debt-to-equity value cannot be expected to be constant over time. In addition, situations involving interest subsidies and flotation costs are much easier to handle with the APV approach. (The Bicksler Enterprises example in Section 18.6 applies the APV approach to subsidies and flotation costs.) Finally, the APV approach handles the lease-versus-buy decision much more easily than does either the FTE or the WACC approach. (A full treatment of the lease-versus-buy decision appears in a later chapter.)

The preceding examples are special cases. Typical capital budgeting situations are more amenable to either the WACC or the FTE approach than to the APV approach. Financial managers generally think in terms of target debt-to-value *ratios*. If a project does better than expected, both its value and its debt capacity will likely rise. The manager will increase debt correspondingly here. Conversely, the manager would be likely to reduce debt if the value of the project were to decline unexpectedly. Of course, because financing is a time-consuming task, the ratio cannot be adjusted daily or monthly. Rather, the adjustment can be expected to occur over the long run. As mentioned before, the WACC and FTE approaches are more appropriate than is the APV approach when a firm focuses on a target debt-to-value ratio.

Because of this, we recommend that the WACC and the FTE approaches, rather than the APV approach, be used in most real-world situations. In addition, frequent discussions with business executives have convinced us that the WACC is by far the most widely used method in the real world. Thus, practitioners seem to agree with us that, outside of the special situations mentioned, the APV approach is a less important method of capital budgeting.

The Three Methods of Valuation with Leverage

1. Adjusted present value (APV) method:

$$\sum_{t=1}^{\infty} \frac{\text{UCF}_t}{(1 + R_0)^t} + \text{Additional effects of debt} - \text{Initial investment}$$

UCF_t = The project's cash flow at date t to the equityholders of an unlevered firm.

R_0 = Cost of capital for project in an unlevered firm.

2. Flow to equity (FTE) method:

$$\sum_{t=1}^{\infty} \frac{\text{LCF}_t}{(1 + R_S)^t} - (\text{Initial investment} - \text{Amount borrowed})$$

LCF_t = The project's cash flow at date t to the equityholders of a levered firm.

R_S = Cost of equity capital with leverage.

3. Weighted average cost of capital (WACC) method:

$$\sum_{t=1}^{\infty} \frac{\text{UCF}_t}{(1 + R_{\text{WACC}})^t} - \text{Initial investment}$$

R_{WACC} = Weighted average cost of capital.

Notes

1. The middle term in the APV formula implies that the value of a project with leverage is greater than the value of the project without leverage. Because $R_{\text{WACC}} < R_0$, the WACC formula implies that the value of a project with leverage is greater than the value of the project without leverage.
2. In the FTE method, cash flow *after interest* (LCF) is used. Initial investment is reduced by *amount borrowed* as well.

Guidelines

1. Use WACC or FTE if the firm's target debt-to-value *ratio* applies to the project over its life.
2. Use APV if the project's *level* of debt is known over the life of the project.

18.5 Valuation When the Discount Rate Must Be Estimated

The previous sections of this chapter introduced APV, FTE, and WACC—the three basic approaches to valuation of a firm with leverage. However, one important detail remains. The example in Sections 18.1 through 18.3 *assumed* a discount rate. We now want to show how this rate is determined for firms with leverage, with an application to the three preceding approaches. The example in this section adds to the work in Chapters 9–13 on the discount rate for levered and unlevered firms along with that in Chapter 16 on the effect of leverage on the cost of capital.

EXAMPLE 18.1

Cost of Capital   World-Wide Enterprises (WWE) is a large conglomerate thinking of entering the widget business, where it plans to finance projects with a debt-to-value ratio of 25 percent (or a debt-to-equity ratio of 1/3). There is currently one firm in the widget industry, American Widgets (AW). This firm is financed with 40 percent debt and 60 percent equity. The beta of AW's equity is 1.5. AW, has a borrowing rate of 12 percent, and WWE expects to borrow for its widget venture at 10 percent. The corporate tax rate for both firms is .40, the market risk premium is 8.5 percent, and the riskless interest rate is 8 percent. What is the appropriate discount rate for WWE to use for its widget venture?

As shown in Sections 18.1–18.3, a corporation may use one of three capital budgeting approaches: APV, FTE, or WACC. The appropriate discount rates for these three approaches are R_0, R_S, and R_{WACC}, respectively. Because AW is WWE's only competitor in widgets, we look at AW's cost of capital to calculate R_0, R_S, and R_{WACC} for WWE's widget venture. The following four-step procedure will allow us to calculate all three discount rates:

1. *Determining AW's cost of equity capital*: First, we determine AW's cost of equity capital using the security market line (SML):

AW's Cost of Equity Capital:

$$R_S = R_F + \beta \times (\overline{R}_M - R_F)$$
$$20.75\% = 8\% + 1.5 \times 8.5\%$$

where $\overline{R}_M$ is the expected return on the market portfolio and R_F is the risk-free rate.

2. *Determining AW's hypothetical all-equity cost of capital*: We must standardize the preceding number in some way because AW's and WWE's widget ventures have different target debt-to-value ratios. The easiest approach is to calculate the hypothetical cost of equity capital for AW, assuming all-equity financing. This can be determined from MM's Proposition II under taxes:

AW's Cost of Capital if All Equity:

$$R_S = R_0 + \frac{B}{S}(1 - t_c)(R_0 - R_B)$$
$$20.75\% = R_0 + \frac{.4}{.6}(.60)(R_0 - 12\%)$$

By solving the equation, we find that $R_0 = .1825$. Of course, R_0 is less than R_S because the cost of equity capital would be less when the firm employs no leverage.

At this point, firms in the real world generally make the assumption that the business risk of their venture is about equal to the business risk of the firms already in the business. Applying this assumption to our problem, we assert that the hypothetical discount rate of WWE's widget venture if all equity financed is also .1825.[6] This discount rate would be employed if WWE uses the APV approach because the APV approach calls for R_0, the project's cost of capital in a firm with no leverage.

3. *Determining R_S for WWE's widget venture*: Alternatively, WWE might use the FTE approach, where the discount rate for levered equity is determined like this:

Cost of Equity Capital for WWE's Widget Venture:

$$R_S = R_0 + \frac{B}{S}(1 - t_c)(R_0 - R_B)$$
$$19.9\% = 18.25\% + \frac{1}{3}(.60)(18.25\% - 10\%)$$

(continued)

---

[6]Alternatively, a firm might assume that its venture would be somewhat riskier because it is a new entrant. Thus, the firm might select a discount rate slightly higher than .1825. Of course, no exact formula exists for adjusting the discount rate upward.

Note that the cost of equity capital for WWE's widget venture, .199, is less than the cost of equity capital for AW, .2075. This occurs because AW has a higher debt-to-equity ratio. (As mentioned, both firms are assumed to have the same business risk.)

4. *Determining R_{WACC} for WWE's widget venture:* Finally, WWE might use the WACC approach. Here is the appropriate calculation:

R_{WACC} for WWE's Widget Venture:

$$R_{WACC} = \frac{B}{S+B}R_B(1-t_c) + \frac{S}{S+B}R_S$$

$$16.425\% = \frac{1}{4}10\%(.60) + \frac{3}{4}19.9\%$$

The preceding example shows how the three discount rates, R_0, R_S, and R_{WACC}, are determined in the real world. These are the appropriate rates for the APV, FTE, and WACC approaches, respectively. Note that R_S for American Widgets is determined first because the cost of equity capital can be determined from the beta of the firm's stock. As discussed in an earlier chapter, beta can easily be estimated for any publicly traded firm such as AW.

18.6 APV Example

As mentioned earlier in this chapter, firms generally set a target debt-to-equity ratio, allowing the use of WACC and FTE for capital budgeting. APV does not work as well here. However, as we also mentioned earlier, APV is the preferred approach when there are side benefits and side costs to debt. Because the analysis here can be tricky, we now devote an entire section to an example where, in addition to the tax subsidy to debt, both flotation costs and interest subsidies come into play.

EXAMPLE

APV Bicksler Enterprises is considering a $10 million project that will last five years, implying straight-line depreciation per year of $2 million. The cash revenues less cash expenses per year are $3,500,000. The corporate tax bracket is 34 percent. The risk-free rate is assumed to be 10 percent, and the cost of unlevered equity is 20 percent.

The cash flow projections each year are these:

	CF_0	CF_1	CF_2	CF_3	CF_4	CF_5
Initial outlay	−$10,000,000					
Depreciation tax shield		.34 × $2,000,000 = $680,000	$ 680,000	$ 680,000	$ 680,000	$ 680,000
Revenue less expenses		(1 − .34) × $3,500,000 = $2,310,000	$2,310,000	$2,310,000	$2,310,000	$2,310,000

We stated before that the APV of a project is the sum of its all-equity value plus the additional effects of debt. We examine each in turn.

All-Equity Value   Assuming the project is financed with all equity, the value of the project is:

$$-\$10,000,000 + \frac{\$680,000}{.10} \times \left[1 - \left(\frac{1}{1.10}\right)^5\right] + \frac{\$2,310,000}{.20} \times \left[1 - \left(\frac{1}{1.20}\right)^5\right] = -\$513,951$$

Initial cost + Depreciation tax shield + Present value of (Cash revenues − Cash expenses)

This calculation uses the techniques presented in the early chapters of this book. Notice that the depreciation tax shield is discounted at the riskless rate of 10 percent (or sometimes at a rate a little higher). The revenues and expenses are discounted at the higher rate of 20 percent.

An all-equity firm would clearly *reject* this project because the NPV is −$513,951. And equity flotation costs (not mentioned yet) would only make the NPV more negative. However, debt financing may add enough value to the project to justify acceptance. We consider the effects of debt next.

Additional Effects of Debt   Bicksler Enterprises can obtain a five-year, nonamortizing loan for $7,500,000 after flotation costs at the risk-free rate of 10 percent. Flotation costs are fees paid when stock or debt is issued. These fees may go to printers, lawyers, and investment bankers, among others. Bicksler Enterprises is informed that flotation costs will be 1 percent of the gross proceeds of its loan. The previous chapter indicates that debt financing alters the NPV of a typical project. We look at the effects of debt next.

Flotation Costs   Given that flotation costs are 1 percent of the gross proceeds, we have:

$$\$7,500,000 = (1 - .01) \times \text{Gross proceeds} = .99 \times \text{Gross proceeds}$$

Thus, the gross proceeds are:

$$\frac{\$7,500,000}{1 - .01} = \frac{\$7,500,000}{.99} = \$7,575,758$$

This implies flotation costs of $75,758 (=1% × $7,575,758). To check the calculation, note that net proceeds are $7,500,000 (=$7,575,758 − $75,758). In other words, Bicksler Enterprises receives only $7,500,000. The flotation costs of $75,758 are received by intermediaries such as investment bankers.

Flotation costs are paid immediately but are deducted from taxes by amortizing on a straight-line basis over the life of the loan. The cash flows from flotation costs are as follows:

	Date 0	Date 1	Date 2	Date 3	Date 4	Date 5
Flotation costs	−**$75,758**					
Deduction		$\frac{\$75,758}{5} = \$15,152$	$15,152	$15,152	$15,152	$15,152
Tax shield from flotation costs		$.34 \times \$15,152$ = **$5,152**	**$5,152**	**$5,152**	**$5,152**	**$5,152**

The relevant cash flows from flotation costs are in boldface. When we discount at 10 percent, the tax shield has a net present value of:

$$\$5,152 \times \text{PVIFA}^5_{.10} = \$19,530$$

This implies a net cost of flotation of:

$$-\$75,758 + \$19,530 = -\$56,228$$

(continued)

The net present value of the project after the flotation costs of debt but before the benefits of debt is:

$$-\$513,951 - \$56,228 = -\$570,179$$

Tax Subsidy Interest must be paid on the gross proceeds of the loan, even though intermediaries receive the flotation costs. Because the gross proceeds of the loan are $7,575,758, annual interest is $757,576 (= $7,575,758 × .10). The interest cost after taxes is $500,000 [= $757,576 × (1 − .34)]. Because the loan is nonamortizing, the entire debt of $7,575,758 is repaid at Date 5. These terms are indicated here:

	Date 0	Date 1	Date 2	Date 3	Date 4	Date 5
Loan (gross proceeds)	**$7,575,758**					
Interest paid		10% × $7,575,758 = $757,576	$ 757,576	$ 757,576	$ 757,576	$ 757,576
Interest cost after taxes		(1 − .34) × $757,576 = **$500,000**	**$500,000**	**$500,000**	**$500,000**	**$ 500,000**
Repayment of debt						**$7,575,758**

The relevant cash flows are listed in boldface in the preceding table. They are (1) loan received, (2) annual interest cost after taxes, and (3) repayment of debt. Note that we include the *gross* proceeds of the loan as an inflow because the flotation costs have previously been subtracted.

In Chapter 16 we mentioned that the financing decision can be evaluated in terms of net present value. The net present value of the loan is simply the sum of the net present values of each of the three cash flows. This can be represented as follows:

$$\text{NPV (loan)} = + \begin{matrix} \text{Amount} \\ \text{borrowed} \end{matrix} - \begin{matrix} \text{Present value} \\ \text{of aftertax} \\ \text{interest payments} \end{matrix} - \begin{matrix} \text{Present value} \\ \text{of loan} \\ \text{repayments} \end{matrix} \qquad \textbf{(18.1)}$$

The calculations for this example are:

$$\$976,415 = +\$7,575,758 - \frac{\$500,000}{.10} \times \left[1 - \left(\frac{1}{1.10}\right)^5\right] - \frac{\$7,575,758}{(1.10)^5} \qquad \textbf{(18.1')}$$

The NPV (loan) is positive, reflecting the interest tax shield.[7]

The adjusted present value of the project with this financing is:

$$\text{APV} = \text{All-equity value} - \text{Flotation costs of debt} + \text{NPV (loan)} \qquad \textbf{(18.2)}$$

$$\$406,236 = -\$513,951 - \$56,228 + \$976,415 \qquad \textbf{(18.2')}$$

Though we previously saw that an all-equity firm would reject the project, a firm would *accept* the project if a $7,500,000 (net) loan could be obtained.

Because the loan just discussed was at the market rate of 10 percent, we have considered only two of the three additional effects of debt (flotation costs and tax subsidy) so far. We now examine another loan where the third effect arises.

---

[7]The NPV (loan) must be zero in a no-tax world because interest provides no tax shield there. To check this intuition, we calculate:

$$\text{No-tax case: } 0 = +\$7,575,758 - \frac{\$757,576}{.10} \times \left[1 - \left(\frac{1}{1.10}\right)^5\right] - \frac{\$7,575,758}{(1.10)^5}$$

Non–Market-Rate Financing   A number of companies are fortunate enough to obtain subsidized financing from a governmental authority. Suppose that the project of Bicksler Enterprises is deemed socially beneficial and the state of New Jersey grants the firm a $7,500,000 loan at 8 percent interest. In addition, all flotation costs are absorbed by the state. Clearly, the company will choose this loan over the one we previously calculated. Here are the cash flows from the loan:

	Date 0	Date 1	Date 2	Date 3	Date 4	Date 5
Loan received	$7,500,000					
Interest paid		8% × $7,500,000 = $600,000	$ 600,000	$ 600,000	$ 600,000	$ 600,000
Aftertax interest		(1 − .34) × $600,000 = **$396,000**	**$396,000**	**$396,000**	**$396,000**	**$ 396,000**
Repayment of debt						**$7,500,000**

The relevant cash flows are listed in boldface in the preceding table. Using Equation 18.1, the NPV (loan) is:

$$\$1,341,939 = +\$7,500,000 - \frac{\$396,000}{.10} \times \left[1 - \left(\frac{1}{1.10}\right)^5\right] - \frac{\$7,500,000}{(1.10)^5} \qquad \textbf{(18.1″)}$$

Why do we discount the cash flows in Equation 18.1″ at 10 percent when the firm is borrowing at 8 percent? We discount at 10 percent because that is the fair or marketwide rate. That is, 10 percent is the rate at which the firm could borrow *without* benefit of subsidization. The net present value of the subsidized loan is larger than the net present value of the earlier loan because the firm is now borrowing at the below-market rate of 8 percent. Note that the NPV (loan) calculation in Equation 18.1″ captures both the tax effect *and* the non–market-rate effect.

The net present value of the project with subsidized debt financing is:

$$APV = \text{All-equity value} - \text{Flotation costs of debt} + \text{NPV (loan)} \qquad \textbf{(18.2)}$$

$$+\$827,988 = -\$513,951 \quad - \quad 0 \quad + \$1,341,939 \qquad \textbf{(18.2″)}$$

The preceding example illustrates the adjusted present value (APV) approach. The approach begins with the present value of a project for the all-equity firm. Next, the effects of debt are added in. The approach has much to recommend it. It is intuitively appealing because individual components are calculated separately and added together in a simple way. And, if the debt from the project can be specified precisely, the present value of the debt can be calculated precisely.

18.7   Beta and Leverage

A previous chapter provides the formula for the relationship between the beta of the common stock and leverage of the firm in a world without taxes. We reproduce this formula here:

The No-Tax Case:

$$\beta_{\text{Equity}} = \beta_{\text{Asset}} \left(1 + \frac{\text{Debt}}{\text{Equity}}\right) \qquad \textbf{(18.3)}$$

As pointed out earlier, this relationship holds under the assumption that the beta of debt is zero.

Because firms must pay corporate taxes in practice, it is worthwhile to provide the relationship in a world with corporate taxes. It can be shown that the relationship between the beta of the unlevered firm and the beta of the levered equity is this:[8]

The Corporate Tax Case:

$$\beta_{\text{Equity}} = \left(1 + \frac{(1 - t_C)\text{Debt}}{\text{Equity}}\right) \beta_{\text{Unlevered firm}} \tag{18.4}$$

when (1) the corporation is taxed at the rate of t_C and (2) the debt has a zero beta.

Because $[1 + (1 - t_C) \text{ Debt/Equity}]$ must be more than 1 for a levered firm, it follows that $\beta_{\text{Unlevered firm}} < \beta_{\text{Equity}}$. The corporate tax case of Equation 18.4 is quite similar to the no-tax case of Equation 18.3 because the beta of levered equity must be greater than the beta of the unlevered firm in either case. The intuition that leverage increases the risk of equity applies in both cases.

However, notice that the two equations are not equal. It can be shown that leverage increases the equity beta less rapidly under corporate taxes. This occurs because, under taxes, leverage creates a *riskless* tax shield, thereby lowering the risk of the entire firm.

---

[8]This result holds only if the beta of debt equals zero. To see this, note that:

$$V_U + t_C B = V_L = B + S \tag{a}$$

where:

V_U = Value of unlevered firm.
V_L = Value of levered firm.
B = Value of debt in a levered firm.
S = Value of equity in a levered firm.

As we stated in the text, the beta of the levered firm is a weighted average of the debt beta and the equity beta:

$$\frac{B}{B + S} \times \beta_B + \frac{S}{B + S} \times \beta_S$$

where β_B and β_S are the betas of the debt and the equity of the levered firm, respectively. Because $V_L = B + S$, we have:

$$\frac{B}{V_L} \times \beta_B + \frac{S}{V_L} \times \beta_S \tag{b}$$

The beta of the levered firm can *also* be expressed as a weighted average of the beta of the unlevered firm and the beta of the tax shield:

$$\frac{V_U}{V_U + t_C B} \times \beta_U + \frac{t_C B}{V_U + t_C B} \times \beta_B$$

where β_U is the beta of the unlevered firm. This follows from Equation (a). Because $V_L = V_U + t_C B$, we have:

$$\frac{V_U}{V_L} \times \beta_U + \frac{t_C B}{V_L} \times \beta_B \tag{c}$$

We can equate (b) and (c) because both represent the beta of a levered firm. Equation (a) tells us that $V_U = S + (1 - t_C) \times B$. Under the assumption that $\beta_B = 0$, equating (b) and (c) and using Equation (a) yields Equation 18.4.

The generalized formula for the levered beta (where β_B is not zero) is:

$$\beta_S = \beta_U + (1 - t_C)(\beta_U - \beta_B)\frac{B}{S}$$

and:

$$\beta_U = \frac{S}{B(1 - t_C) + S}\beta_S + \frac{B(1 - t_C)}{B(1 - t_C) + S}\beta_B$$

EXAMPLE 18.3

Unlevered Betas   C. F. Lee, Incorporated, is considering a scale-enhancing project. The market value of the firm's debt is \$100 million, and the market value of the firm's equity is \$200 million. The debt is considered riskless. The corporate tax rate is 34 percent. Regression analysis indicates that the beta of the firm's equity is 2. The risk-free rate is 10 percent, and the expected market premium is 8.5 percent. What would the project's discount rate be in the hypothetical case that C. F. Lee, Inc., is all equity?

We can answer this question in two steps.

1. *Determining beta of hypothetical all-equity firm:* Rearranging Equation 18.4, we have this:

Unlevered Beta:

$$\frac{\text{Equity}}{\text{Equity} + (1 - t_c) \times \text{Debt}} \times \beta_{\text{Equity}} = \beta_{\text{Unlevered firm}} \qquad (18.5)$$

$$\frac{\$200 \text{ million}}{\$200 \text{ million} + (1 - .34) \times \$100 \text{ million}} \times 2 = 1.50$$

2. *Determining discount rate:* We calculate the discount rate from the security market line (SML) as follows:

Discount Rate:

$$R_S = R_F + \beta \times [\bar{R}_M - R_F]$$
$$22.75\% = 10\% + 1.50 \times 8.5\%$$

THE PROJECT IS NOT SCALE ENHANCING

Because the previous example assumed that the project is scale enhancing, we began with the beta of the firm's equity. If the project is not scale enhancing, we could begin with the equity betas of firms in the industry of the project. For each firm, we could calculate the hypothetical beta of the unlevered equity by Equation 18.5. The SML could then be used to determine the project's discount rate from the average of these betas.

EXAMPLE 18.4

More Unlevered Betas   The J. Lowes Corporation, which currently manufactures staples, is considering a \$1 million investment in a project in the aircraft adhesives industry. The corporation estimates unlevered aftertax cash flows (UCF) of \$300,000 per year into perpetuity from the project. The firm will finance the project with a debt-to-value ratio of .5 (or, equivalently, a debt-to-equity ratio of 1.0).

The three competitors in this new industry are currently unlevered, with betas of 1.2, 1.3, and 1.4. Assuming a risk-free rate of 5 percent, a market risk premium of 9 percent, and a corporate tax rate of 34 percent, what is the net present value of the project?

We can answer this question in five steps.

1. *Calculating the average unlevered beta in the industry:* The average unlevered beta across all three existing competitors in the aircraft adhesives industry is:

$$\frac{1.2 + 1.3 + 1.4}{3} = 1.3$$

(continued)

2. *Calculating the levered beta for J. Lowes's new project:* Assuming the same unlevered beta for this new project as for the existing competitors, we have, from Equation 18.4:

Levered Beta:

$$\beta_{Equity} = \left(1 + \frac{(1 - t_C)\,\text{Debt}}{\text{Equity}}\right)\beta_{Unlevered\ firm}$$

$$2.16 = \left(1 + \frac{.66 \times 1}{1}\right) \times 1.3$$

3. *Calculating the cost of levered equity for the new project:* We calculate the discount rate from the security market line (SML) as follows:

Discount Rate:

$$R_S = R_F + \beta \times [\bar{R}_M - R_F]$$

$$.244 = .05 + 2.16 \times .09$$

4. *Calculating the WACC for the new project:* The formula for determining the weighted average cost of capital, R_{WACC}, is:

$$R_{WACC} = \frac{B}{V}R_B(1 - t_C) + \frac{S}{V}R_S$$

$$.139 = \frac{1}{2} \times .05 \times .66 + \frac{1}{2} \times .244$$

5. *Determining the project's value:* Because the cash flows are perpetual, the NPV of the project is:

$$\frac{\text{Unlevered cash flows (UCF)}}{R_{WACC}} - \text{Initial investment}$$

$$\frac{\$300,000}{.139} - \$1 \text{ million} = \$1.16 \text{ million}$$

Summary and Conclusions

Earlier chapters of this text showed how to value projects and entire firms with and without leverage. In the last three chapters we discuss how to determine the optimal amount of leverage. We pointed out that the introduction of taxes and bankruptcy costs changes a firm's financing decisions. Most rational corporations should employ some debt in a world of this type. The present chapter has discussed three methods for valuation by levered firms: the adjusted present value (APV), flow to equity (FTE), and weighted average cost of capital (WACC) approaches.

Concept Questions

1. **APV**   How is the APV of a project calculated?
2. **WACC and APV**   What is the main difference between the WACC and APV methods?
3. **FTE**   What is the main difference between the FTE approach and the other two approaches?

4. **Capital Budgeting**   You are determining whether your company should undertake a new project and have calculated the NPV of the project using the WACC method when the CFO, a former accountant, notices that you did not use the interest payments in calculating the cash flows of the project. What should you tell him? If he insists that you include the interest payments in calculating the cash flows, what method can you use?

5. **Beta and Leverage**   What are the two types of risk that are measured by a levered beta?

Questions and Problems

BASIC
(Questions 1–9)

1. **NPV and APV**   Zoso is a rental car company that is trying to determine whether to add 25 cars to its fleet. The company fully depreciates all its rental cars over five years using the straight-line method. The new cars are expected to generate $215,000 per year in earnings before taxes and depreciation for five years. The company is entirely financed by equity and has a 35 percent tax rate. The required return on the company's unlevered equity is 13 percent, and the new fleet will not change the risk of the company.

   a. What is the maximum price that the company should be willing to pay for the new fleet of cars if it remains an all-equity company?
   b. Suppose the company can purchase the fleet of cars for $650,000. Additionally, assume the company can issue $430,000 of five-year debt to finance the project at the risk-free rate of 8 percent. All principal will be repaid in one balloon payment at the end of the fifth year. What is the adjusted present value (APV) of the project?

2. **APV**   Gemini, Inc., an all-equity firm, is considering an investment of $1.4 million that will be depreciated according to the straight-line method over its four-year life. The project is expected to generate earnings before taxes and depreciation of $502,000 per year for four years. The investment will not change the risk level of the firm. The company can obtain a four-year, 9.5 percent loan to finance the project from a local bank. All principal will be repaid in one balloon payment at the end of the fourth year. The bank will charge the firm $45,000 in flotation fees, which will be amortized over the four-year life of the loan. If the company financed the project entirely with equity, the firm's cost of capital would be 13 percent. The corporate tax rate is 30 percent. Using the adjusted present value method, determine whether the company should undertake the project.

3. **FTE**   Milano Pizza Club owns three identical restaurants popular for their specialty pizzas. Each restaurant has a debt–equity ratio of 40 percent and makes interest payments of $41,000 at the end of each year. The cost of the firm's levered equity is 19 percent. Each store estimates that annual sales will be $1.45 million; annual cost of goods sold will be $785,000; and annual general and administrative costs will be $435,000. These cash flows are expected to remain the same forever. The corporate tax rate is 40 percent.

   a. Use the flow to equity approach to determine the value of the company's equity.
   b. What is the total value of the company?

4. **WACC**   If Wild Widgets, Inc., were an all-equity company, it would have a beta of .95. The company has a target debt–equity ratio of .40. The expected return on the market portfolio is 11 percent, and Treasury bills currently yield 4 percent. The company has one bond issue outstanding that matures in 20 years and has a coupon rate of 6.5 percent. The bond currently sells for $1,080. The corporate tax rate is 34 percent.

   a. What is the company's cost of debt?
   b. What is the company's cost of equity?
   c. What is the company's weighted average cost of capital?

5.   Beta and Leverage   North Pole Fishing Equipment Corporation and South Pole Fishing Equipment Corporation would have identical equity betas of 1.10 if both were all equity financed. The market value information for each company is shown here:

	North Pole	South Pole
Debt	$2,700,000	$3,900,000
Equity	$3,900,000	$2,700,000

The expected return on the market portfolio is 10.9 percent, and the risk-free rate is 3.2 percent. Both companies are subject to a corporate tax rate of 35 percent. Assume the beta of debt is zero.

a. What is the equity beta of each of the two companies?
b. What is the required rate of return on each of the two companies' equity?

6.   NPV of Loans   Daniel Kaffe, CFO of Kendrick Enterprises, is evaluating a 10-year, 7.5 percent loan with gross proceeds of $4,450,000. The interest payments on the loan will be made annually. Flotation costs are estimated to be 2.5 percent of gross proceeds and will be amortized using a straight-line schedule over the 10-year life of the loan. The company has a tax rate of 40 percent, and the loan will not increase the risk of financial distress for the company.

a. Calculate the net present value of the loan excluding flotation costs.
b. Calculate the net present value of the loan including flotation costs.

7.   NPV for an All-Equity Company   Watson, Inc., is an all-equity firm. The cost of the company's equity is currently 11.9 percent, and the risk-free rate is 3.5 percent. The company is currently considering a project that will cost $10.6 million and last six years. The project will generate revenues minus expenses each year in the amount of $3.1 million. If the company has a tax rate of 40 percent, should it accept the project?

8.   WACC   National Electric Company (NEC) is considering a $68 million project in its power systems division. Tom Edison, the company's chief financial officer, has evaluated the project and determined that the project's unlevered cash flows will be $4.4 million per year in perpetuity. Mr. Edison has devised two possibilities for raising the initial investment: issuing 10-year bonds or issuing common stock. The company's pretax cost of debt is 6.4 percent, and its cost of equity is 10.8 percent. The company's target debt-to-value ratio is 80 percent. The project has the same risk as the company's existing businesses, and it will support the same amount of debt. The tax rate is 34 percent. Should NEC accept the project?

9.   WACC   Bolero, Inc., has compiled the following information on its financing costs:

Type of Financing	Book Value	Market Value	Cost
Short-term debt	$12,000,000	$12,500,000	4.1%
Long-term debt	20,000,000	23,000,000	7.2
Common stock	9,000,000	54,000,000	13.8
Total	$41,000,000	$89,500,000	

The company is in the 35 percent tax bracket and has a target debt–equity ratio of 60 percent. The target short-term debt/long-term debt ratio is 20 percent.

a. What is the company's weighted average cost of capital using book value weights?
b. What is the company's weighted average cost of capital using market value weights?

c. What is the company's weighted average cost of capital using target capital structure weights?

d. What is the difference between WACCs? Which is the correct WACC to use for project evaluation?

INTERMEDIATE
(Questions 10–14)

10. APV   Triad Corporation has established a joint venture with Tobacco Road Construction, Inc., to build a toll road in North Carolina. The initial investment in paving equipment is $93 million. The equipment will be fully depreciated using the straight-line method over its economic life of five years. Earnings before interest, taxes, and depreciation collected from the toll road are projected to be $12.9 million per annum for 20 years starting from the end of the first year. The corporate tax rate is 35 percent. The required rate of return for the project under all-equity financing is 13 percent. The pretax cost of debt for the joint partnership is 8.5 percent. To encourage investment in the country's infrastructure, the U.S. government will subsidize the project with a $30 million, 15-year loan at an interest rate of 5 percent per year. All principal will be repaid in one balloon payment at the end of Year 15. What is the adjusted present value of this project?

11. APV   For the company in the previous problem, what is the value of being able to issue subsidized debt instead of having to issue debt at the terms it would normally receive? Assume the face amount and maturity of the debt issue are the same.

12. APV   MVP, Inc., has produced rodeo supplies for over 20 years. The company currently has a debt–equity ratio of 50 percent and is in the 40 percent tax bracket. The required return on the firm's levered equity is 16 percent. The company is planning to expand its production capacity. The equipment to be purchased is expected to generate the following unlevered cash flows:

Year	Cash Flow
0	−$15,100,000
1	5,400,000
2	8,900,000
3	8,600,000

The company has arranged a debt issue of $8.7 million to partially finance the expansion. Under the loan, the company would pay interest of 9 percent at the end of each year on the outstanding balance at the beginning of the year. The company would also make year-end principal payments of $2,900,000 per year, completely retiring the issue by the end of the third year. Using the adjusted present value method, should the company proceed with the expansion?

13. WACC   Neon Corporation's stock returns have a covariance with the market portfolio of .0415. The standard deviation of the returns on the market portfolio is 20 percent, and the expected market risk premium is 7.5 percent. The company has bonds outstanding with a total market value of $45 million and a yield to maturity of 6.5 percent. The company also has 4.2 million shares of common stock outstanding, each selling for $30. The company's CEO considers the firm's current debt–equity ratio optimal. The corporate tax rate is 35 percent, and Treasury bills currently yield 3.4 percent. The company is considering the purchase of additional equipment that would cost $47 million. The expected unlevered cash flows from the equipment are $13.5 million per year for five years. Purchasing the equipment will not change the risk level of the firm.

a. Use the weighted average cost of capital approach to determine whether Neon should purchase the equipment.

b. Suppose the company decides to fund the purchase of the equipment entirely with debt. What is the cost of capital for the project now? Explain.

14. **Beta and Leverage** Dorman Industries has a new project available that requires an initial investment of $4.3 million. The project will provide unlevered cash flows of $710,000 per year for the next 20 years. The company will finance the project with a debt-to-value ratio of .40. The company's bonds have a YTM of 6.8 percent. The companies with operations comparable to this project have unlevered betas of 1.15, 1.08, 1.30, and 1.25. The risk-free rate is 3.8 percent, and the market risk premium is 7 percent. The company has a tax rate of 34 percent. What is the NPV of this project?

CHALLENGE
(Questions 15–18)

15. **APV, FTE, and WACC** Newkirk, Inc., is an unlevered firm with expected annual earnings before taxes of $21 million in perpetuity. The current required return on the firm's equity is 16 percent, and the firm distributes all of its earnings as dividends at the end of each year. The company has 1.3 million shares of common stock outstanding and is subject to a corporate tax rate of 35 percent. The firm is planning a recapitalization under which it will issue $30 million of perpetual 9 percent debt and use the proceeds to buy back shares.

    a. Calculate the value of the company before the recapitalization plan is announced. What is the value of equity before the announcement? What is the price per share?
    b. Use the APV method to calculate the company value after the recapitalization plan is announced. What is the value of equity after the announcement? What is the price per share?
    c. How many shares will be repurchased? What is the value of equity after the repurchase has been completed? What is the price per share?
    d. Use the flow to equity method to calculate the value of the company's equity after the recapitalization.

16. **APV, FTE, and WACC** Mojito Mint Company has a debt–equity ratio of .35. The required return on the company's unlevered equity is 12.8 percent, and the pretax cost of the firm's debt is 6.5 percent. Sales revenue for the company is expected to remain stable indefinitely at last year's level of $17,500,000. Variable costs amount to 60 percent of sales. The tax rate is 40 percent, and the company distributes all its earnings as dividends at the end of each year.

    a. If the company were financed entirely by equity, how much would it be worth?
    b. What is the required return on the firm's levered equity?
    c. Use the weighted average cost of capital method to calculate the value of the company. What is the value of the company's equity? What is the value of the company's debt?
    d. Use the flow to equity method to calculate the value of the company's equity.

17. **APV, FTE, and WACC** Bruin Industries just issued $265,000 of perpetual 8 percent debt and used the proceeds to repurchase stock. The company expects to generate $123,000 of earnings before interest and taxes in perpetuity. The company distributes all its earnings as dividends at the end of each year. The firm's unlevered cost of capital is 14 percent, and the corporate tax rate is 40 percent.

    a. What is the value of the company as an unlevered firm?
    b. Use the adjusted present value method to calculate the value of the company with leverage.
    c. What is the required return on the firm's levered equity?
    d. Use the flow to equity method to calculate the value of the company's equity.

18. **Projects That Are Not Scale Enhancing** Blue Angel, Inc., a private firm in the holiday gift industry, is considering a new project. The company currently has a target debt–equity ratio of .40, but the industry target debt–equity ratio is .35. The industry average beta is 1.2. The market risk premium is 7 percent, and the risk-free rate is 5 percent. Assume all companies in this industry can issue debt at the risk-free rate. The corporate tax rate is 40 percent. The project requires an initial outlay of $785,000 and is expected to result in a $93,000 cash inflow at the end of the first year. The project will be financed at the company's target debt–equity ratio. Annual cash flows from the project will grow at a constant rate of 5 percent until the end of the fifth year and remain constant forever thereafter. Should Blue Angel invest in the project?

THE LEVERAGED BUYOUT OF CHEEK PRODUCTS, INC.

Cheek Products, Inc. (CPI) was founded 53 years ago by Joe Cheek and originally sold snack foods such as potato chips and pretzels. Through acquisitions, the company has grown into a conglomerate with major divisions in the snack food industry, home security systems, cosmetics, and plastics. Additionally, the company has several smaller divisions. In recent years, the company has been underperforming, but the company's management doesn't seem to be aggressively pursuing opportunities to improve operations (or the stock price).

Meg Whalen is a financial analyst specializing in identifying potential buyout targets. She believes that two major changes are needed at Cheek. First, she thinks that the company would be better off if it sold several divisions and concentrated on its core competencies in snack foods and home security systems. Second, the company is financed entirely with equity. Because the cash flows of the company are relatively steady, Meg thinks the company's debt–equity ratio should be at least .25. She believes these changes would significantly enhance shareholder wealth, but she also believes that the existing board and company management are unlikely to take the necessary actions. As a result, Meg thinks the company is a good candidate for a leveraged buyout.

A leveraged buyout (LBO) is the acquisition by a small group of equity investors of a public or private company. Generally, an LBO is financed primarily with debt. The new shareholders service the heavy interest and principal payments with cash from operations and/or asset sales. Shareholders generally hope to reverse the LBO within three to seven years by way of a public offering or sale of the company to another firm. A buyout is therefore likely to be successful only if the firm generates enough cash to service the debt in the early years and if the company is attractive to other buyers a few years down the road.

Meg has suggested the potential LBO to her partners, Ben Feller and Brenton Flynn. Ben and Brenton have asked Meg to provide projections of the cash flows for the company. Meg has provided the following estimates (in millions):

	2015	2016	2017	2018	2019
Sales	$2,749	$3,083	$3,322	$3,400	$3,539
Costs	731	959	1,009	1,091	1,149
Depreciation	485	516	537	564	575
EBT	$1,533	$1,608	$1,776	$1,745	$1,815
Capital expenditures	$ 279	$ 242	$ 304	$ 308	$ 304
Change in NWC	−$ 122	−$ 186	$ 101	$ 95	$ 108
Asset sales	$1,419	$1,028			

At the end of five years, Meg estimates that the growth rate in cash flows will be 3.5 percent per year. The capital expenditures are for new projects and the replacement of equipment that wears out. Additionally, the company would realize cash flow from the sale of several divisions. Even though the company will sell these divisions, overall sales should increase because of a more concentrated effort on the remaining divisions.

After plowing through the company's financials and various pro forma scenarios, Ben and Brenton feel that in five years they will be able to sell the company to another party or take it public again. They are also aware that they will have to borrow a considerable amount of the purchase price. The interest payments on the debt for each of the next five years if the LBO is undertaken will be these (in millions):

	2015	2016	2017	2018	2019
Interest payments	$1,927	$1,859	$2,592	$2,526	$2,614

The company currently has a required return on assets of 14 percent. Because of the high debt level, the debt will carry a yield to maturity of 12.5 percent for the next five years. When the debt is refinanced in five years, they believe the new yield to maturity will be 8 percent.

CPI currently has 425 million shares of stock outstanding that sell for $29 per share. The corporate tax rate is 40 percent. If Meg, Ben, and Brenton decide to undertake the LBO, what is the most they should offer per share?

Appendix 18A The Adjusted Present Value Approach to Valuing Leveraged Buyouts

To access the appendix for this chapter, please logon to Connect Finance.

19

Dividends and Other Payouts

On December 3, 2014, glass and ceramics company Corning announced a broad plan to reward stockholders for the recent success of the firm's business. Under the plan, Corning would (1) boost its annual dividend by 20 percent, from 10 cents per share to 12 cents per share; and (2) repurchase $1.5 billion of the company's common stock. Investors cheered, bidding up the stock price by about 2.5 percent on the day of the announcement. Why were investors so pleased? To find out, this chapter explores these types of actions and their implications for shareholders.

19.1 Different Types of Payouts

The term *dividend* usually refers to a cash distribution of earnings. If a distribution is made from sources other than current or accumulated retained earnings, the term *distribution* rather than dividend is used. However, it is acceptable to refer to a distribution from earnings as a *dividend* and a distribution from capital as a *liquidating dividend*.

The most common type of dividend is in the form of cash. When public companies pay dividends, they usually pay **regular cash dividends** four times a year. Sometimes firms will pay a regular cash dividend and an *extra cash dividend*. Paying a cash dividend reduces corporate cash and retained earnings—except in the case of a liquidating dividend (where paid-in capital may be reduced).

Another type of dividend is paid out in shares of stock. This dividend is referred to as a **stock dividend**. It is not a true dividend because no cash leaves the firm. Rather, a stock dividend increases the number of shares outstanding, thereby reducing the value of each share. A stock dividend is commonly expressed as a ratio; for example, with a 2 percent stock dividend a shareholder receives 1 new share for every 50 currently owned.

When a firm declares a **stock split**, it increases the number of shares outstanding. Because each share is now entitled to a smaller percentage of the firm's cash flow, the stock price should fall. For example, if the managers of a firm whose stock is selling at $90 declare a three-for-one stock split, the price of a share of stock should fall to about $30. A stock split strongly resembles a stock dividend except that it is usually much larger.

An alternative form of cash payout is a **stock repurchase**. Just as a firm may use cash to pay dividends, it may use cash to buy back shares of its stock. The shares are held by the corporation and accounted for as treasury stock.

19.2 Standard Method of Cash Dividend Payment

The decision to pay a dividend rests in the hands of the board of directors of the corporation. A dividend is distributable to shareholders of record on a specific date. When a dividend has been declared, it becomes a liability of the firm and cannot be easily rescinded by the corporation. The amount of the dividend is expressed as dollars per share (*dividend per share*), as a percentage of the market price (*dividend yield*), or as a percentage of earnings per share (*dividend payout*).

For a list of today's dividends, go to **www.thestreet .com/dividends/.**

The mechanics of a dividend payment can be illustrated by the example in Figure 19.1 and the following chronology:

1. *Declaration date:* On January 15 (the declaration date), the board of directors passes a resolution to pay a dividend of $1 per share on February 16 to all holders of record on January 30.

2. *Date of record:* The corporation prepares a list on January 30 of all individuals believed to be stockholders as of this date. The word *believed* is important here: The dividend will not be paid to individuals whose notification of purchase is received by the company after January 30.

3. *Ex-dividend date:* The procedure for the date of record would be unfair if efficient brokerage houses could notify the corporation by January 30 of a trade occurring on January 29, whereas the same trade might not reach the corporation until February 2 if executed by a less efficient house. To eliminate this problem, all brokerage firms entitle stockholders to receive the dividend if they purchased the stock three business days before the date of record. The second day before the date of record, which is Wednesday, January 28, in our example, is called the *ex-dividend date.* Before this date the stock is said to trade *cum dividend.*

4. *Date of payment:* The dividend checks are mailed to the stockholders on February 16.

Figure 19.1

Example of Procedure for Dividend Payment

Thursday, January 15	Wednesday, January 28	Friday, January 30	Monday, February 16	Days
Declaration date	Ex-dividend date	Record date	Payment date	

1. *Declaration date:* The board of directors declares a payment of dividends.
2. *Record date:* The declared dividends are distributable to shareholders of record on a specific date.
3. *Ex-dividend date:* A share of stock becomes ex dividend on the date the seller is entitled to keep the dividend; under NYSE rules, shares are traded ex dividend on and after the second business day before the record date.
4. *Payment date:* The dividend checks are mailed to shareholders of record.

Figure 19.2

Price Behavior around the Ex-Dividend Date for a $1 Cash Dividend

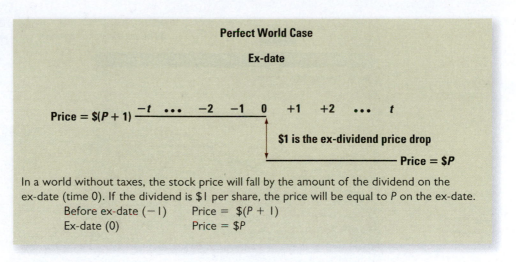

Perfect World Case

Ex-date

$$\text{Price} = \$(P + 1) \quad \frac{-t \quad \cdots \quad -2 \quad -1 \quad 0 \quad +1 \quad +2 \quad \cdots \quad t}{}$$

$1 is the ex-dividend price drop

Price = $P

In a world without taxes, the stock price will fall by the amount of the dividend on the ex-date (time 0). If the dividend is $1 per share, the price will be equal to P on the ex-date.

| Before ex-date (-1) | Price = $(P + 1)$ |
| Ex-date (0) | Price = P |

Obviously, the ex-dividend date is important because an individual purchasing the security before the ex-dividend date will receive the current dividend, whereas another individual purchasing the security on or after this date will not receive the dividend. The stock price will therefore fall on the ex-dividend date (assuming no other events occur). It is worthwhile to note that this drop is an indication of efficiency, not inefficiency, because the market rationally attaches value to a cash dividend. In a world with neither taxes nor transaction costs, the stock price would be expected to fall by the amount of the dividend:

| Before ex-dividend date | Price = $(P + 1)$ |
| On or after ex-dividend date | Price = P |

This is illustrated in Figure 19.2.

The amount of the price drop may depend on tax rates. For example, consider the case with no capital gains taxes. On the day before a stock goes ex dividend, a purchaser must decide either: (1) To buy the stock immediately and pay tax on the forthcoming dividend or (2) To buy the stock tomorrow, thereby missing the dividend. If all investors are in the 20 percent tax bracket and the quarterly dividend is $1, the stock price should fall by $.80 on the ex-dividend date. That is, if the stock price falls by this amount on the ex-dividend date, purchasers will receive the same return from either strategy.

As an example of the price drop on the ex-dividend date, we examine the large dividend paid by Winmark Corp., operator of retail stores such as Plato's Closet and Play It Again Sports, in February 2014. The dividend was $5 per share at a time when the stock price was around $88, so the dividend was about 6 percent of the total stock price.

The stock went ex dividend on February 12, 2014. The stock price chart here shows the change in Winmark stock four days prior to the ex-dividend date and on the ex-dividend date.

The stock closed at \$88.04 on February 11 and opened at \$85.30 on February 12—a drop of \$2.74. With a 20 percent tax rate on dividends, we would have expected a drop of \$4, so the actual price dropped less than we would have expected. We discuss dividends and taxes in more detail in a subsequent section.

19.3 The Benchmark Case: An Illustration of the Irrelevance of Dividend Policy

We have stated in previous chapters that the value of a firm stems from its ability to generate and pay out its distributable (i.e., free) cash flow. Specially, we put forth the idea that the value of a share of stock should be equal to the present value of its future expected dividend payouts (and share repurchases, which we treat in the next section). This still stands. In this section, we discuss dividend policy, which we define as the timing of a firm's dividend payouts given the level of its distributable cash flow.

A powerful argument can be made that the timing of dividends when cash flows do not change does not matter. This will be illustrated with the Bristol Corporation. Bristol is an all-equity firm that started 10 years ago. The current financial managers know at the present time (Date 0) that the firm will dissolve in one year (Date 1). At Date 0 the managers are able to forecast cash flows with perfect certainty. The managers know that the firm will receive a cash flow of \$10,000 immediately and another \$10,000 next year. Bristol has no additional positive NPV projects.

CURRENT POLICY: DIVIDENDS SET EQUAL TO CASH FLOW

At the present time, dividends (Div) at each date are set equal to the available cash flow of \$10,000. The value of the firm can be calculated by discounting these dividends. This value is expressed as:

$$V_0 = \text{Div}_0 + \frac{\text{Div}_1}{1 + R_S}$$

where Div_0 and Div_1 are the cash flows paid out in dividends, and R_S is the discount rate. The first dividend is not discounted because it will be paid immediately.

Assuming $R_S = 10$ percent, the value of the firm is:

$$\$19,090.91 = \$10,000 + \frac{\$10,000}{1.1}$$

If 1,000 shares are outstanding, the value of each share is:

$$\$19.09 = \$10 + \frac{\$10}{1.1} \tag{19.1}$$

To simplify the example, we assume that the ex-dividend date is the same as the date of payment. After the imminent dividend is paid, the stock price will immediately fall to $9.09 (= $19.09 − $10). Several members of Bristol's board have expressed dissatisfaction with the current dividend policy and have asked you to analyze an alternative policy.

ALTERNATIVE POLICY: INITIAL DIVIDEND IS GREATER THAN CASH FLOW

Another policy is for the firm to pay a dividend of $11 per share immediately, which is, of course, a total dividend payout of $11,000. Because the available cash flow is only $10,000, the extra $1,000 must be raised in one of a few ways. Perhaps the simplest would be to issue $1,000 of bonds or stock now (at Date 0). Assume that stock is issued and the new stockholders will desire enough cash flow at Date 1 to let them earn the required 10 percent return on their Date 0 investment. The new stockholders will demand $1,100 of the Date 1 cash flow, leaving only $8,900 to the old stockholders. The dividends to the old stockholders will be these:

	Date 0	Date 1
Aggregate dividends to old stockholders	$11,000	$8,900
Dividends per share	$ 11.00	$ 8.90

The present value of the dividends per share is therefore:

$$\$19.09 = \$11 + \frac{\$8.90}{1.1} \tag{19.2}$$

Students often find it instructive to determine the price at which the new stock is issued. Because the new stockholders are not entitled to the immediate dividend, they would pay $8.09 (= $8.90/1.1) per share. Thus, 123.61 (= $1,000/$8.09) new shares are issued.

THE INDIFFERENCE PROPOSITION

Note that the values in Equations 19.1 and 19.2 are equal. This leads to the initially surprising conclusion that the change in dividend policy did not affect the value of a share of stock as long as all distributable cash flow is paid out. However, on reflection, the result seems sensible. The new stockholders are parting with their money at Date 0 and receiving it back with the appropriate return at Date 1. In other words, they are taking on a zero NPV investment.

HOMEMADE DIVIDENDS

To illustrate the indifference investors have toward dividend policy in our example, we used present value equations. An alternative and perhaps more intuitively appealing explanation avoids the mathematics of discounted cash flows.

Suppose individual investor *X* prefers dividends per share of $10 at both Dates 0 and 1. Would she be disappointed when informed that the firm's management is adopting the alternative dividend policy (dividends of $11 and $8.90 on the two dates, respectively)? Not necessarily: She could easily reinvest the $1 of unneeded funds received on Date 0, yielding an incremental return of $1.10 at Date 1. Thus, she would receive her desired net cash flow of $11 − $1 = $10 at Date 0 and $8.90 + $1.10 = $10 at Date 1.

Conversely, imagine investor *Z* preferring $11 of cash flow at Date 0 and $8.90 of cash flow at Date 1, who finds that management will pay dividends of $10 at both Dates 0 and 1. He can sell off shares of stock at Date 0 to receive the desired amount of cash flow. That is, if he sells off shares (or fractions of shares) at Date 0 totaling $1, his cash flow at Date 0 becomes $10 + $1 = $11. Because a $1 sale of stock at Date 0 will reduce his dividends by $1.10 at Date 1, his net cash flow at Date 1 would be $10 − $1.10 = $8.90.

The example illustrates how investors can make **homemade dividends**. In this instance, corporate dividend policy is being undone by a potentially dissatisfied stockholder. This homemade dividend is illustrated by Figure 19.3. Here the firm's cash flows of $10 per share at both Dates 0 and 1 are represented by Point *A*. This point also represents the initial dividend payout. However, as we just saw, the firm could alternatively pay out $11 per share at Date 0 and $8.90 per share at Date 1, a strategy represented by Point *B*. Similarly, by either issuing new stock or buying back old stock, the firm could achieve a dividend payout represented by any point on the diagonal line.

Figure 19.3

Homemade Dividends: A Trade-off between Dividends per Share at Date 0 and Dividends per Share at Date 1

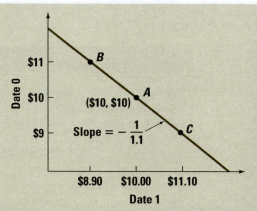

The graph illustrates both (1) how managers can vary dividend policy and (2) how individuals can undo the firm's dividend policy.

Managers varying dividend policy: A firm paying out all cash flows immediately is at Point *A* on the graph. The firm could achieve Point *B* by issuing stock to pay extra dividends or achieve Point *C* by buying back old stock with some of its cash.

Individuals undoing the firm's dividend policy: Suppose the firm adopts the dividend policy represented by Point *B*: dividends per share of $11 at Date 0 and $8.90 at Date 1. An investor can reinvest $1 of the dividends at 10 percent, which will place her at Point *A*. Suppose, alternatively, the firm adopts the dividend policy represented by Point *A*. An investor can sell off $1 of stock at Date 0, placing him at Point *B*. No matter what dividend policy the firm establishes, a shareholder can undo it.

The previous paragraph describes the choices available to the managers of the firm. The same diagonal line also represents the choices available to the shareholder. For example, if the shareholder receives a per-share dividend distribution of ($11, $8.90), he or she can either reinvest some of the dividends to move down and to the right on the graph or sell off shares of stock and move up and to the left.

The implications of the graph can be summarized in two sentences:

1. By varying dividend policy, managers can achieve any payout along the diagonal line in Figure 19.3.
2. Either by reinvesting excess dividends at Date 0 or by selling off shares of stock at this date, an individual investor can achieve any net cash payout along the diagonal line.

Thus, because both the corporation and the individual investor can move only along the diagonal line, dividend policy in this model is irrelevant. The changes the managers make in dividend policy can be undone by an individual who, by either reinvesting dividends or selling off stock, can move to a desired point on the diagonal line.

A TEST

You can test your knowledge of this material by examining these true statements:

1. Dividends are relevant.
2. Dividend policy is irrelevant.

The first statement follows from common sense. Clearly, investors prefer higher dividends to lower dividends at any single date if the dividend level is held constant at every other date. In other words, if the dividend per share at a given date is raised while the dividend per share for each other date is held constant, the stock price will rise. This act can be accomplished by management decisions that improve productivity, increase tax savings, or strengthen product marketing. In fact, you may recall that in Chapter 9 we argued that the value of a firm's equity is equal to the discounted present value of all its future dividends.

The second statement is understandable once we realize that dividend policy cannot raise the dividend per share at one date while holding the dividend level per share constant at all other dates. Rather, dividend policy merely establishes the trade-off between dividends at one date and dividends at another date. As we saw in Figure 19.3, holding cash flows constant, an increase in Date 0 dividends can be accomplished only by a decrease in Date 1 dividends. The extent of the decrease is such that the present value of all dividends is not affected.

DIVIDENDS AND INVESTMENT POLICY

The preceding argument shows that an increase in dividends through issuance of new shares neither helps nor hurts the stockholders. Similarly, a reduction in dividends through share repurchase neither helps nor hurts stockholders. The key to this result is understanding that the overall level of cash flows is assumed to be fixed and that we are not changing the available positive net present value projects.

What about reducing capital expenditures to increase dividends? Earlier chapters show that a firm should accept all positive net present value projects. To do otherwise would reduce the value of the firm. Thus, we have an important point:

Firms should never give up a positive NPV project to increase a dividend (or to pay a dividend for the first time).

This idea was implicitly considered by Miller and Modigliani. One of the assumptions underlying their dividend irrelevance proposition was this: "The investment policy of the firm is set ahead of time and is not altered by changes in dividend policy."

19.4 Repurchase of Stock

Instead of paying dividends, a firm may use cash to repurchase shares of its own stock. Share repurchases have taken on increased importance in recent years. Consider Figure 19.4, which shows the aggregate dollar amounts of dividends, repurchases, and earnings for large U.S. firms in the years from 2004 to 2014. As can be seen, the amount of repurchases was more than the amount of dividends up to 2008. However, the amount of dividends exceeded the amount of repurchases in late 2008 and 2009. This trend reversed after 2009. Notice also from Figure 19.4 that there is "stickiness" to repurchases and dividend payouts. In late 2008 when aggregate corporate earnings turned negative, the level of dividends and share repurchases did not change much. More generally, the volatility of aggregate earnings has been greater than that of dividends and share repurchases.

Share repurchases are typically accomplished in one of three ways. First, companies may simply purchase their own stock, just as anyone would buy shares of a particular stock. In these *open market purchases*, the firm does not reveal itself as the buyer. Thus, the seller does not know whether the shares were sold back to the firm or to just another investor.

Second, the firm could institute a *tender offer*. Here, the firm announces to all of its stockholders that it is willing to buy a fixed number of shares at a specific price. For example, suppose Arts and Crafts (A&C), Inc., has 1 million shares of stock outstanding, with a stock price of $50 per share. The firm makes a tender offer to buy back 300,000 shares

Figure 19.4
Earnings, Dividends, and Net Repurchases for Large U.S. Firms

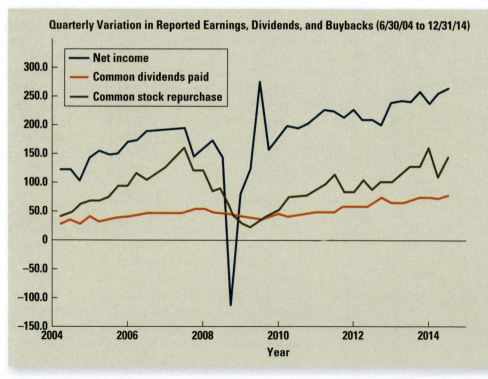

SOURCE: S&P Dow Jones Indices, S&P.

at $60 per share. A&C chooses a price above $50 to induce shareholders to sell—that is, tender—their shares. In fact, if the tender price is set high enough, shareholders may want to sell more than the 300,000 shares. In the extreme case where all outstanding shares are tendered, A&C will buy back 3 out of every 10 shares that a shareholder has. On the other hand, if shareholders do not tender enough shares, the offer can be canceled. A method related to a tender offer is the *Dutch auction.* Here the firm does not set a fixed price for the shares to be sold. Instead, the firm conducts an auction in which it bids for shares. The firm announces the number of shares it is willing to buy back at various prices, and shareholders indicate how many shares they are willing to sell at the various prices. The firm will then pay the lowest price that will achieve its goal.

Finally, firms may repurchase shares from specific individual stockholders, a procedure called a *targeted repurchase.* For example, suppose the International Biotechnology Corporation purchased approximately 10 percent of the outstanding stock of the Prime Robotics Company (P-R Co.) in April at around $38 per share. At that time, International Biotechnology announced to the Securities and Exchange Commission that it might eventually try to take control of P-R Co. In May, P-R Co. repurchased the International Biotechnology holdings at $48 per share, well above the market price at that time. This offer was not extended to other shareholders.

Companies engage in targeted repurchases for a variety of reasons. In some rare cases, a single large stockholder can be bought out at a price lower than that in a tender offer. The legal fees in a targeted repurchase may also be lower than those in a more typical buyback. In addition, the shares of large stockholders are often repurchased to avoid a takeover unfavorable to management.

We now consider an example of a repurchase presented in the theoretical world of a perfect capital market. We next discuss real-world factors involved in the repurchase decision.

DIVIDEND VERSUS REPURCHASE: CONCEPTUAL EXAMPLE

Imagine that Telephonic Industries has excess cash of $300,000 (or $3 per share) and is considering an immediate payment of this amount as an extra dividend. The firm forecasts that, after the dividend, earnings will be $450,000 per year, or $4.50 for each of the 100,000 shares outstanding. Because the price–earnings ratio is 6 for comparable companies, the shares of the firm should sell for $27 (=$4.50 × 6) after the dividend is paid. These figures are presented in the top half of Table 19.1. Because the dividend is $3 per share, the stock would have sold for $30 a share *before* payment of the dividend.

Alternatively, the firm could use the excess cash to repurchase some of its own stock. Imagine that a tender offer of $30 per share is made. Here, 10,000 shares are repurchased

Table 19.1

Dividend versus Repurchase Example for Telephonic Industries

	For Entire Firm	Per Share
Extra Dividend		**(100,000 shares outstanding)**
Proposed dividend	$ 300,000	$ 3.00
Forecasted annual earnings after dividend	450,000	4.50
Market value of stock after dividend	2,700,000	27.00
Repurchase		**(90,000 shares outstanding)**
Forecasted annual earnings after repurchase	$ 450,000	$ 5.00
Market value of stock after repurchase	2,700,000	30.00

so that the total number of shares remaining is 90,000. With fewer shares outstanding, the earnings per share will rise to $5 (=$450,000/90,000). The price–earnings ratio remains at 6 because both the business and financial risks of the firm are the same in the repurchase case as they were in the dividend case. Thus, the price of a share after the repurchase is $30 (=$5 × 6). These results are presented in the bottom half of Table 19.1.

If commissions, taxes, and other imperfections are ignored in our example, the stockholders are indifferent between a dividend and a repurchase. With dividends each stockholder owns a share worth $27 and receives $3 in dividends, so that the total value is $30. This figure is the same as both the amount received by the selling stockholders and the value of the stock for the remaining stockholders in the repurchase case.

This example illustrates the important point that, in a perfect market, the firm is indifferent between a dividend payment and a share repurchase. This result is quite similar to the indifference propositions established by MM for debt versus equity financing and for dividends versus capital gains.

You may often read in the popular financial press that a repurchase agreement is beneficial because earnings per share increase. Earnings per share do rise for Telephonic Industries if a repurchase is substituted for a cash dividend: The EPS is $4.50 after a dividend and $5 after the repurchase. This result holds because the drop in shares after a repurchase implies a reduction in the denominator of the EPS ratio.

However, the financial press frequently places undue emphasis on EPS figures in a repurchase agreement. Given the irrelevance propositions we have discussed, the increase in EPS here is not beneficial. Table 19.1 shows that, in a perfect capital market, the total value to the stockholder is the same under the dividend payment strategy as under the repurchase strategy.

DIVIDENDS VERSUS REPURCHASES: REAL-WORLD CONSIDERATIONS

We previously referred to Figure 19.4, which showed growth in share repurchases relative to dividends. In fact, most firms that pay dividends also repurchase shares of stock. This suggests that repurchasing shares of stock is not always a substitute for paying dividends but rather a complement to it. For example, recently the number of U.S. industrial firms that pay dividends only or repurchase only is about the same as the number of firms paying both dividends and repurchasing shares. Why do some firms choose repurchases over dividends? Here are perhaps five of the most common reasons.

1. Flexibility Firms often view dividends as a commitment to their stockholders and are quite hesitant to reduce an existing dividend. Repurchases do not represent a similar commitment. Thus, a firm with a permanent increase in cash flow is likely to increase its dividend. Conversely, a firm whose cash flow increase is only temporary is likely to repurchase shares of stock.

2. Executive Compensation Executives are frequently given stock options as part of their overall compensation. Let's revisit the Telephonic Industries example of Table 19.1, where the firm's stock was selling at $30 when the firm was considering either a dividend or a repurchase. Further imagine that Telephonic had granted 1,000 stock options to its CEO, Ralph Taylor, two years earlier. At that time, the stock price was, say, only $20. This means that Mr. Taylor can buy 1,000 shares for $20 a share at any time between the grant of the options and their expiration, a procedure called *exercising* the options. His gain from exercising is directly proportional to the rise in the stock price above $20. As we saw in the example, the price of the stock would fall to $27 following a dividend but would remain at $30 following a repurchase. The CEO would clearly prefer a repurchase to a dividend because the difference between the stock price and the exercise price of $20 would be $10 (=$30 − $20) following the repurchase but only $7 (=$27 − $20) following the dividend. Existing stock options will always have greater value when the firm repurchases shares instead of paying a dividend because the stock price will be greater after a repurchase than after a dividend.

3. Offset to Dilution In addition, the exercise of stock options increases the number of shares outstanding. In other words, exercise causes dilution of the stock. Firms frequently buy back shares of stock to offset this dilution. However, it is hard to argue that this is a valid reason for repurchase. As we showed in Table 19.1, repurchase is neither better nor worse for the stockholders than a dividend. Our argument holds whether or not stock options have been exercised previously.

4. Undervaluation Many companies buy back stock because they believe that a repurchase is their best investment. This occurs more frequently when managers believe that the stock price is temporarily depressed.

The fact that some companies repurchase their stock when they believe it is undervalued does not imply that the management of the company must be correct; only empirical studies can make this determination. So far, the evidence is mixed. However, the immediate stock market reaction to the announcement of a stock repurchase is usually quite favorable.

5. Taxes Because taxes for both dividends and share repurchases are treated in depth in the next section, suffice it to say at this point that repurchases provide a tax advantage over dividends.

19.5 Personal Taxes, Dividends, and Stock Repurchases

Section 19.3 asserted that in a world without taxes and other frictions, the timing of dividend payout does not matter if distributable cash flows do not change. Similarly, Section 19.4 concluded that the choice between a share repurchase and a dividend is irrelevant in a world of this type. This section examines the effect of taxes on both dividends and repurchases. Our discussion is facilitated by classifying firms into two types: those without sufficient cash to pay a dividend and those with sufficient cash to do so.

FIRMS WITHOUT SUFFICIENT CASH TO PAY A DIVIDEND

It is simplest to begin with a firm without cash that is owned by a single entrepreneur. If this firm should decide to pay a dividend of $100, it must raise capital. The firm might choose among a number of different stock and bond issues to pay the dividend. However, for simplicity, we assume that the entrepreneur contributes cash to the firm by issuing stock to himself. This transaction, diagrammed in the left side of Figure 19.5, would clearly be a *wash* in a world of no taxes. $100 cash goes into the firm when stock is issued and is immediately paid out as a dividend. Thus, the entrepreneur neither benefits nor loses when the dividend is paid, a result consistent with Miller–Modigliani.

Now assume that dividends are taxed at the owner's personal tax rate of 15 percent. The firm still receives $100 upon issuance of stock. However, the entrepreneur does not

Figure 19.5
Firm Issues Stock to
Pay a Dividend

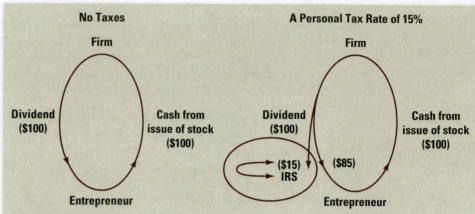

In the no-tax case, the entrepreneur receives the $100 in dividends that he gave to the firm when purchasing stock. The entire operation is called a *wash;* in other words, it has no economic effect. With taxes, the entrepreneur still receives $100 in dividends. However, assume he must pay $15 in taxes to the IRS. The entrepreneur loses and the IRS wins when a firm issues stock to pay a dividend.

get to keep the full $100 dividend. Instead the dividend payment is taxed, implying that the owner receives only $85 net after tax. Thus, the entrepreneur loses $15.

Though the example is clearly contrived and unrealistic, similar results can be reached for more plausible situations. Thus, financial economists generally agree that in a world of personal taxes, firms should not issue stock to pay dividends.

The direct costs of issuance will add to this effect. Investment bankers must be paid when new capital is raised. Thus, the net receipts due to the firm from a new issue are less than 100 percent of total capital raised. Because the size of new issues can be lowered by a reduction in dividends, we have another argument in favor of a low-dividend policy.

Of course, our advice not to finance dividends through new stock issues might need to be modified somewhat in the real world. A company with a large and steady cash flow for many years in the past might be paying a regular dividend. If the cash flow unexpectedly dried up for a single year, should new stock be issued so that dividends could be continued? Although our previous discussion would imply that new stock should not be issued, many managers might issue the stock anyway for practical reasons. In particular, stockholders appear to prefer dividend stability. Thus, managers might be forced to issue stock to achieve this stability, knowing full well the adverse tax consequences.

FIRMS WITH SUFFICIENT CASH TO PAY A DIVIDEND

The previous discussion argued that in a world with personal taxes, a firm should not issue stock to pay a dividend. Does the tax disadvantage of dividends imply the stronger policy, "Never, under any circumstances, pay dividends in a world with personal taxes"?

We argue next that this prescription does not necessarily apply to firms with excess cash. To see this, imagine a firm with $1 million in extra cash after selecting all positive NPV projects and determining the level of prudent cash balances. The firm might consider the following alternatives to a dividend:

1. *Select additional capital budgeting projects.* Because the firm has taken all the available positive NPV projects already, it must invest its excess cash in negative NPV projects. This is clearly a policy at variance with the principles of corporate finance.

In spite of our distaste for this policy, researchers have suggested that many managers purposely take on negative NPV projects in lieu of paying dividends.[1] The idea here is that managers would rather keep the funds in the firm because their prestige, pay, and perquisites are often tied to the firm's size. Although managers may help themselves here, they are hurting stockholders. We broached this subject in the section titled "Free Cash Flow" in Chapter 17, and we will have more to say about it later in this chapter.

2. *Acquire other companies*. To avoid the payment of dividends, a firm might use excess cash to acquire another company. This strategy has the advantage of acquiring profitable assets. However, a firm often incurs heavy costs when it embarks on an acquisition program. In addition, acquisitions are invariably made above the market price. Premiums of 20 to 80 percent are not uncommon. Because of this, a number of researchers have argued that mergers are not generally profitable to the acquiring company, even when firms are merged for a valid business purpose. Therefore, a company making an acquisition merely to avoid a dividend is unlikely to succeed.

3. *Purchase financial assets*. The strategy of purchasing financial assets in lieu of a dividend payment can be illustrated with the following example.

EXAMPLE 19.1

Dividends and Taxes   The Regional Electric Company has $1,000 of extra cash. It can retain the cash and invest it in Treasury bills yielding 10 percent, or it can pay the cash to shareholders as a dividend. Shareholders can also invest in Treasury bills with the same yield. Suppose the corporate tax rate is 34 percent, and the personal tax rate is 28 percent for all individuals. Further suppose, the maximum tax rate on dividends is 15 percent. How much cash will investors have after five years under each policy?

If dividends are paid now, shareholders will receive:

$$\$1,000 \times (1 - .15) = \$850$$

today after taxes. Because their return after personal tax on Treasury bills is 7.2 [$=10 \times (1 - .28)$] percent, shareholders will have:

$$\$850 \times (1.072)^5 = \$1,203.35 \tag{19.3}$$

in five years. Note that interest income is taxed at the personal tax rate (28 percent in this example), but dividends are taxed at the lower rate of 15 percent.

If Regional Electric Company retains the cash to invest in Treasury bills, its aftertax interest rate will be .066 [$=.10 \times (1 - .34)$]. At the end of five years, the firm will have:

$$\$1,000 \times (1.066)^5 = \$1,376.53$$

If these proceeds are then paid as a dividend, the stockholders will receive:

$$\$1,376.53 \times (1 - .15) = \$1,170.05 \tag{19.4}$$

after personal taxes at Date 5. The value in Equation 19.3 is greater than that in Equation 19.4, implying that cash to stockholders will be greater if the firm pays the dividend now.

This example shows that for a firm with extra cash, the dividend payout decision will depend on personal and corporate tax rates. If personal tax rates are higher than corporate tax rates, a firm will have an incentive to reduce dividend payouts. However, if personal tax rates are lower than corporate tax rates, a firm will have an incentive to pay out any excess cash as dividends.

---

[1]See, for example, Michael C. Jensen, "Agency Costs of Free Cash Flow, Corporate Finance, and Takeovers," *American Economic Review* (May 1986).

In the United States, both the highest marginal tax rate for individuals and the corporate tax rate were 39.6 percent in 2014. Because many investors face marginal tax rates well below the maximum, it appears that firms have an incentive not to hoard cash.

However, a quirk in the tax code provides an offsetting incentive. In particular, 70 percent of the dividends that one corporation receives from another corporation are excluded from corporate tax.[2] Individuals are not granted this exclusion. The quirk increases the likelihood that proceeds will be higher if the firm invests cash in other dividend-paying stocks rather than paying out cash as a dividend.

The firm's decision to invest in financial assets or to pay a dividend is a complex one, depending on the tax rate of the firm, the marginal tax rates of its investors, and the application of the dividend exclusion. While there are likely many real-world situations where the numbers favor investment in financial assets, few companies actually seem to hoard cash in this manner without limit. The reason is that Section 532 of the Internal Revenue Code penalizes firms exhibiting "improper accumulation of surplus." Thus, in the final analysis, the purchase of financial assets, like selecting negative NPV projects and acquiring other companies, does not obviate the need for companies with excess cash to pay dividends.

4. *Repurchase shares.* The example we described in the previous section showed that investors are indifferent between share repurchases and dividends in a world without taxes and transaction costs. However, under current tax law, stockholders generally prefer a repurchase to a dividend.

As an example, consider an individual receiving a dividend of $1 on each of 100 shares of a stock. With a 15 percent tax rate, that individual would pay taxes of $15 on the dividend. Selling shareholders would pay lower taxes if the firm repurchased $100 of existing shares. This occurs because taxes are paid only on the *profit* from a sale. The individual's gain on a sale would be only $40 if the shares sold for $100 were originally purchased for, say, $60. The capital gains tax would be $6 ($=.15 \times \$40$), a number below the tax on dividends of $15. Note that the tax from a repurchase is less than the tax on a dividend even though the same 15 percent tax rate applies to both the repurchase and the dividend.

Of all the alternatives to dividends mentioned in this section, the strongest case can be made for repurchases. In fact, academics have long wondered why firms *ever* pay a dividend instead of repurchasing stock. There have been at least two possible reasons for avoiding repurchases. First, Grullon and Michaely point out that in the past the Securities and Exchange Commission (SEC) had accused some firms undergoing share repurchase programs of illegal price manipulation.[3] However, these authors indicate that SEC Rule 10b-18, adopted in 1982, provides guidelines for firms to avoid the charge of price manipulation. These guidelines are relatively easy to follow, so firms should not have to worry about this charge today. In fact, Grullon and Michaely believe that the large increase in buyback programs in recent

---

[2]This exclusion applies if the firm owns less than 20 percent of the stock in the other company. The exclusion rises to 80 percent if the firm owns more than 20 percent of the stock of the other company and is 100 percent if the firm owns more than 80 percent of the stock of the other company. Corporations are not granted an exclusion for interest earned on bonds.

[3]See Gustavo Grullon and Roni Michaely, "Dividends, Share Repurchases, and the Substitution Hypothesis," *Journal of Finance* (August 2002), p. 1677.

years is at least partially the result of 10b-18. Second, the IRS can penalize firms repurchasing their own stocks if the only reason is to avoid the taxes that would be levied on dividends. However, this threat has not materialized with the growth in corporate repurchases. Thus, these two reasons do not seem to justify the avoidance of repurchases.

SUMMARY OF PERSONAL TAXES

This section suggests that because of personal taxes, firms have an incentive to reduce dividends. For example, they might increase capital expenditures, acquire other companies, or purchase financial assets. However, due to financial considerations and legal constraints, rational firms with large cash flows will likely exhaust these activities with plenty of cash left over for dividends.

It is harder to explain why firms pay dividends instead of repurchasing shares. The tax savings from repurchases can be significant, and fear of either the SEC or the IRS seems overblown. Academics are of two minds here. Some argue that corporations were simply slow to grasp the benefits from repurchases. However, since the idea has firmly caught on, the trend toward replacement of dividends with repurchases could continue. Others argue that companies have paid dividends all along for good reasons. We consider potential benefits of dividends in the next section.

19.6 Real-World Factors Favoring a High-Dividend Policy

The previous section pointed out that because individuals pay taxes on dividends, financial managers might seek ways to reduce dividends. While we discussed the problems with taking on more capital budgeting projects, acquiring other firms, and hoarding cash, we stated that a share repurchase has many of the benefits of a dividend with less of a tax disadvantage. This section considers reasons why a firm might pay its shareholders high dividends even in the presence of personal taxes on these dividends.

DESIRE FOR CURRENT INCOME

It has been argued that many individuals desire current income. The classic example is the group of retired people and others living on a fixed income. The argument further states that these individuals would bid up the stock price should dividends rise and bid down the stock price should dividends fall.

This argument does not hold in perfect capital markets because an individual preferring high current cash flow but holding low-dividend securities could easily sell off shares to provide the necessary funds. Thus in a world of no transaction costs, a high current-dividend policy would be of no value to the stockholder.

However, the current income argument is relevant in the real world. Stock sales involve brokerage fees and other transaction costs—direct cash expenses that could be avoided by an investment in high-dividend securities. In addition, stock sales are time-consuming, further leading investors to buy high-dividend securities.

To put this argument in perspective, remember that financial intermediaries such as mutual funds can perform repackaging transactions at low cost. Such intermediaries could buy low-dividend stocks and, by a controlled policy of realizing gains, pay their investors at a higher rate.

BEHAVIORAL FINANCE

Suppose it turned out that the transaction costs in selling no-dividend securities could not account for the preference of investors for dividends. Would there still be a reason for high dividends? We introduced the topic of behavioral finance in Chapter 14, pointing out that the ideas of behaviorists represent a strong challenge to the theory of efficient capital markets. It turns out that behavioral finance also has an argument for high dividends.

The basic idea here concerns *self-control,* a concept that, though quite important in psychology, has received virtually no emphasis in finance. Although we cannot review all that psychology has to say about self-control, let's focus on one example—losing weight. Suppose Al Martin, a college student, just got back from the Christmas break more than a few pounds heavier than he would like. Everyone would probably agree that diet and exercise are the two ways to lose weight. But how should Al put this approach into practice? (We'll focus on exercise, though the same principle would apply to diet as well.) One way—let's call it the economists' way—would involve trying to make rational decisions. Each day Al would balance the costs and the benefits of exercising. Perhaps he would choose to exercise on most days because losing the weight is important to him. However, when he is too busy with exams, he might rationally choose not to exercise because he cannot afford the time. And he wants to be socially active as well. So he may rationally choose to avoid exercise on days when parties and other social commitments become too time-consuming.

This seems sensible—at first glance. The problem is that he must make a choice every day, and there may simply be too many days when his lack of self-control gets the better of him. He may tell himself that he doesn't have the time to exercise on a particular day, simply because he is starting to find exercise boring, not because he really doesn't have the time. Before long, he is avoiding exercise on most days—and overeating in reaction to the guilt from not exercising!

Is there an alternative? One way would be to set rigid rules. Perhaps Al decides to exercise five days a week *no matter what.* This is not necessarily the best approach for everyone, but there is no question that many of us (perhaps most of us) live by a set of rules. For example, Shefrin and Statman[4] suggest some typical rules:

- Jog at least two miles a day.
- Do not consume more than 1,200 calories per day.
- Bank the wife's salary and spend from only the husband's paycheck.
- Save at least 2 percent of every paycheck for children's college education and never withdraw from this fund.
- Never touch a drop of alcohol.

What does this have to do with dividends? Investors must also deal with self-control. Suppose a retiree wants to consume $20,000 a year from savings, in addition to Social Security and her pension. On one hand, she could buy stocks with a dividend yield high enough to generate $20,000 in dividends. On the other hand, she could place her savings in no-dividend stocks, selling off $20,000 each year for consumption. Though these two approaches seem equivalent financially, the second one may allow for too much leeway. If lack of self-control gets the better of her, she might sell off too much, leaving little for her later years. Better, perhaps, to short-circuit this possibility by investing in dividend-paying

---

[4]Hersh M. Shefrin and Meir Statman, "Explaining Investor Preference for Cash Dividends," *Journal of Financial Economics* 13 (1984).

stocks with a firm personal rule of *never* "dipping into principal." Although behaviorists do not claim that this approach is for everyone, they argue that enough people think this way to explain why firms pay dividends—even though, as we said earlier, dividends are tax disadvantaged.

Does behavioral finance argue for increased stock repurchases as well as increased dividends? The answer is no, because investors will sell the stock that firms repurchase. As we have said, selling stock involves too much leeway. Investors might sell too many shares of stock, leaving little for later years. Thus, the behaviorist argument may explain why companies pay dividends in a world with personal taxes.

AGENCY COSTS

Although stockholders, bondholders, and management start firms for mutually beneficial reasons, one party may later gain at the other's expense. For example, take the potential conflict between bondholders and stockholders. Bondholders would like stockholders to leave as much cash as possible in the firm so that this cash would be available to pay the bondholders during times of financial distress. Conversely, stockholders would like to keep this extra cash for themselves. That's where dividends come in. Managers, acting on behalf of the stockholders, may pay dividends simply to keep the cash away from the bondholders. In other words, a dividend can be viewed as a wealth transfer from bond-holders to stockholders. There is empirical evidence for this view of things. For example, DeAngelo and DeAngelo find that firms in financial distress are reluctant to cut dividends.[5] Of course, bondholders know about the propensity of stockholders to transfer money out of the firm. To protect themselves, bondholders frequently create loan agreements stating that dividends can be paid only if the firm has earnings, cash flow, and working capital above specified levels.

Although managers may be looking out for stockholders in any conflict with bond-holders, managers may pursue selfish goals at the expense of stockholders in other situations. For example, as discussed in a previous chapter, managers might pad expense accounts, take on pet projects with negative NPVs, or simply not work hard. Managers find it easier to pursue these selfish goals when the firm has plenty of free cash flow. After all, one cannot squander funds if the funds are not available in the first place. And that is where dividends come in. Several scholars have suggested that the board of directors can use dividends to reduce agency costs.[6] By paying dividends equal to the amount of "surplus" cash flow, a firm can reduce management's ability to squander the firm's resources.

This discussion suggests a reason for increased dividends, but the same argument applies to share repurchases as well. Managers, acting on behalf of stockholders, can just as easily keep cash from bondholders through repurchases as through dividends. And the board of directors, also acting on behalf of stockholders, can reduce the cash available to spendthrift managers just as easily through repurchases as through dividends. Thus, the presence of agency costs is not an argument for dividends over repurchases. Rather, agency costs imply firms may increase either dividends or share repurchases rather than hoard large amounts of cash.

---

[5]Harry DeAngelo and Linda DeAngelo, "Dividend Policy and Financial Distress: An Empirical Investigation of Troubled NYSE Firms," *Journal of Finance* 45 (1990).

[6]Michael Rozeff, "How Companies Set Their Dividend Payout Ratios," in *The Revolution in Corporate Finance,* edited by Joel M. Stern and Donald H. Chew (New York: Basil Blackwell, 1986). See also Robert S. Hansen, Raman Kumar, and Dilip K. Shome, "Dividend Policy and Corporate Monitoring: Evidence from the Regulated Electric Utility Industry," *Financial Management* (Spring 1994).

INFORMATION CONTENT OF DIVIDENDS AND DIVIDEND SIGNALING

Information Content While there are many things researchers do not know about dividends, we know one thing for sure: The stock price of a firm generally rises when the firm announces a dividend increase and generally falls when a dividend reduction is announced. For example, Asquith and Mullins estimate that stock prices rise about 3 percent following announcements of dividend initiations.[7] Michaely, Thaler, and Womack find that stock prices fall about 7 percent following announcements of dividend omissions.[8]

The question is how we should *interpret* this empirical evidence. Consider the following three positions on dividends:

1. From the homemade dividend argument of MM, dividend policy is irrelevant, given that future earnings (and cash flow) are held constant.

2. Because of tax effects, a firm's stock price is negatively related to the current dividend when future earnings (or cash flow) are held constant.

3. Because of stockholders' desire for current income, a firm's stock price is positively related to its current dividend, even when future earnings (or cash flow) are held constant.

At first glance, the empirical evidence that stock prices rise when dividend increases are announced may seem consistent with Position 3 and inconsistent with Positions 1 and 2. In fact, many writers have said this. However, other authors have countered that the observation itself is consistent with all three positions. They point out that companies do not like to cut a dividend. Thus, firms will raise the dividend only when future earnings, cash flow, and so on are expected to rise enough so that the dividend is not likely to be reduced later to its original level. A dividend increase is management's *signal* to the market that the firm is expected to do well.

It is the expectation of good times, and not only the stockholders' affinity for current income, that raises the stock price. The rise in the stock price following the dividend signal is called the **information content effect** of the dividend. To recapitulate, imagine that the stock price is unaffected or even negatively affected by the level of dividends, given that future earnings (or cash flow) are held constant. Nevertheless, the information content effect implies that the stock price may rise when dividends are raised—if dividends simultaneously cause stockholders to *increase* their expectations of future earnings and cash flow.

Dividend Signaling We just argued that the market infers a rise in earnings and cash flows from a dividend increase, leading to a higher stock price. Conversely, the market infers a decrease in cash flows from a dividend reduction, leading to a fall in stock price. This raises an interesting corporate strategy: Could management increase dividends just to make the market *think* that cash flows will be higher, even when management knows that cash flows will not rise?

While this strategy may seem dishonest, academics take the position that managers frequently attempt the strategy. Academics begin with the following accounting identity for an all-equity firm:

$$\text{Cash flow}^9 = \text{Capital expenditures} + \text{Dividends} \qquad \textbf{(19.5)}$$

---

[7]Paul Asquith and Donald Mullins, Jr., "The Impact of Initiating Dividend Payments on Shareholders' Wealth," *Journal of Business* (January 1983).

[8]R. Michaely, R. H. Thaler, and K. Womack, "Price Reactions to Dividend Initiations and Omissions: Overreaction or Drift?" *Journal of Finance* 50 (1995).

[9]The correct representation of Equation 19.5 involves cash flow, not earnings. However, with little loss of understanding, we could discuss dividend signaling in terms of earnings, not cash flow.

Equation 19.5 must hold if a firm is neither issuing nor repurchasing stock. That is, the cash flow from the firm must go somewhere. If it is not paid out in dividends, it must be used in some expenditure. Whether the expenditure involves a capital budgeting project or a purchase of Treasury bills, it is still an expenditure.

Imagine that we are in the middle of the year and investors are trying to make some forecast of cash flow over the entire year. These investors may use Equation 19.5 to estimate cash flow. For example, suppose the firm announces that current dividends will be $50 million and the market believes that capital expenditures are $80 million. The market would then determine cash flow to be $130 million (=$50 + $80).

Now, suppose that the firm had, alternatively, announced a dividend of $70 million. The market might assume that cash flow remains at $130 million, implying capital expenditures of $60 million (=$130 − $70). Here, the increase in dividends would hurt stock price because the market anticipates valuable capital expenditures will be crowded out. Alternatively, the market might assume that capital expenditures remain at $80 million, implying the estimate of cash flow to be $150 million (=$70 + $80). Stock price would likely rise here because stock prices usually increase with cash flow. In general, academics believe that models where investors assume capital expenditures remain the same are more realistic. Thus, an increase in dividends raises stock price.

Now we come to the incentives of managers to fool the public. Suppose you are a manager who wants to boost stock price, perhaps because you are planning to sell some of your personal holdings of the company's stock immediately. You might increase dividends so that the market would raise its estimate of the firm's cash flow, thereby also boosting the current stock price.

If this strategy is appealing, would anything prevent you from raising dividends without limit? The answer is yes because there is also a *cost* to raising dividends. That is, the firm will have to forgo some of its profitable projects. Remember that cash flow in Equation 19.5 is a constant, so an increase in dividends is obtained only by a reduction in capital expenditures. At some point the market will learn that cash flow has not increased, but instead profitable capital expenditures have been cut. Once the market absorbs this information, stock price should fall below what it would have been had dividends never been raised. Thus, if you plan to sell, say, half of your shares and retain the other half, an increase in dividends should help you on the immediate sale but hurt you when you sell your remaining shares years later. So your decision on the level of dividends will be based, among other things, on the timing of your personal stock sales.

This is a simplified example of dividend signaling, where the manager sets dividend policy based on maximum benefit for himself.[10] Alternatively, a given manager may have no desire to sell his shares immediately but knows that, at any one time, plenty of ordinary shareholders will want to do so. Thus, for the benefit of shareholders in general, a manager will always be aware of the trade-off between current and future stock price. And this, then, is the essence of signaling with dividends. It is not enough for a manager to set dividend policy to maximize the true (or intrinsic) value of the firm. He must also consider the effect of dividend policy on the current stock price, even if the current stock price does not reflect true value.

Does a motive to signal imply that managers will increase dividends rather than share repurchases? The answer is likely no: Most academic models imply that dividends and

---

[10]Papers examining fully developed models of signaling include Sudipto Bhattacharya, "Imperfect Information, Dividend Policy, and 'the Bird in the Hand' Fallacy," *Bell Journal of Economics* 10 (1979); Sudipto Bhattacharya, "Nondissipative Signaling Structure and Dividend Policy," *Quarterly Journal of Economics* 95 (1980); S. Ross, "The Determination of Financial Structure: The Incentive-Signalling Approach," *Bell Journal of Economics* 8 (1977); Merton Miller and Kevin Rock, "Dividend Policy under Asymmetric Information," *Journal of Finance* (1985).

share repurchases are perfect substitutes.[11] Rather, these models indicate that managers will consider reducing capital spending (even on projects with positive NPVs) to increase either dividends or share repurchases.

19.7 The Clientele Effect: A Resolution of Real-World Factors?

In the previous two sections, we pointed out that the existence of personal taxes favors a low-dividend policy, whereas other factors favor high dividends. The financial profession had hoped that it would be easy to determine which of these sets of factors dominates. Unfortunately, after years of research, no one has been able to conclude which of the two is more important. This is surprising: we might be skeptical that the two sets of factors would cancel each other out so perfectly.

However, one particular idea, known as the *clientele effect,* implies that the two sets of factors are likely to cancel each other out after all. To understand this idea, let's separate investors in high tax brackets from those in low tax brackets. Individuals in high tax brackets likely prefer either no or low dividends. Low tax bracket investors generally fall into three categories. First, there are individual investors in low brackets. They are likely to prefer some dividends if they desire current income. Second, pension funds pay no taxes on either dividends or capital gains. Because they face no tax consequences, pension funds will also prefer dividends if they have a preference for current income. Finally, corporations can exclude at least 70 percent of their dividend income but cannot exclude any of their capital gains. Thus, corporations are likely to prefer high-dividend stocks, even without a preference for current income.

Suppose that 40 percent of all investors prefer high dividends and 60 percent prefer low dividends, yet only 20 percent of firms pay high dividends while 80 percent pay low dividends. Here, the high-dividend firms will be in short supply, implying that their stock should be bid up while the stock of low-dividend firms should be bid down.

However, the dividend policies of all firms need not be fixed in the long run. In this example, we would expect enough low-dividend firms to increase their payout so that 40 percent of the firms pay high dividends and 60 percent of the firms pay low dividends. After this adjustment, no firm will gain from changing its dividend policy. Once payouts of corporations conform to the desires of stockholders, no single firm can affect its market value by switching from one dividend strategy to another.

Clienteles are likely to form in the following way:

Group	Stocks
Individuals in high tax brackets	Zero- to low-payout stocks
Individuals in low tax brackets	Low- to medium-payout stocks
Tax-free institutions	Medium-payout stocks
Corporations	High-payout stocks

---

[11]Signaling models where dividends and repurchases are not perfect substitutes are contained in Franklin Allen, Antonio Bernardo, and Ivo Welch, "A Theory of Dividends Based on Tax Clienteles," *Journal of Finance* (2000), and Kose John and Joseph Williams, "Dividends, Dilution and Taxes: A Signalling Equilibrium," *Journal of Finance* (1985).

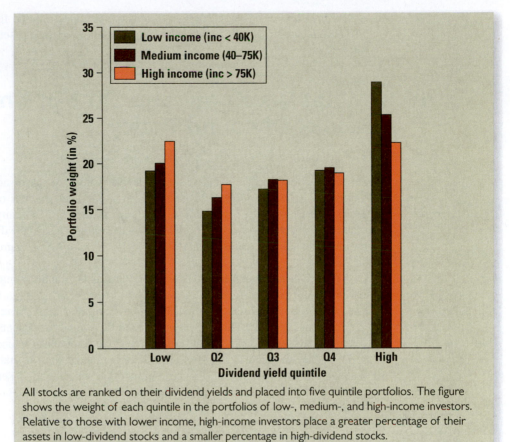

Figure 19.6
Preferences of Investors for Dividend Yield

All stocks are ranked on their dividend yields and placed into five quintile portfolios. The figure shows the weight of each quintile in the portfolios of low-, medium-, and high-income investors. Relative to those with lower income, high-income investors place a greater percentage of their assets in low-dividend stocks and a smaller percentage in high-dividend stocks.

SOURCE: Adapted from Figure 2 of John Graham and Alok Kumar, "Do Dividend Clienteles Exist? Evidence on Dividend Preferences of Retail Investors," *Journal of Finance* 61 (2006), pp. 1305–36.

To see if you understand the clientele effect, consider the following statement: "In a world where many investors like high dividends, a firm can boost its share price by increasing its dividend payout ratio." True or false?

The statement is likely to be false. As long as there are already enough high-dividend firms to satisfy dividend-loving investors, a firm will not be able to boost its share price by paying high dividends. A firm can boost its stock price only if an *unsatisfied* clientele exists.

Our discussion of clienteles followed from the fact that tax brackets vary across investors. If shareholders care about taxes, stocks should attract clienteles based on dividend yield. Is there any evidence that this is the case?

Consider Figure 19.6. Here, John Graham and Alok Kumar[12] rank common stocks by their dividend yields (the ratio of dividend to stock price) and place them into five portfolios, called quintiles. The bottom quintile contains the 20 percent of stocks with the lowest dividend yields; the next quintile contains the 20 percent of stocks with the next lowest dividend yields; and so on. The figure shows the weight of each quintile in the portfolios of low-, medium-, and high-income investors. As can be seen, relative to low-income investors, high-income investors put a greater percentage of their

---

[12]John Graham and Alok Kumar, "Do Dividend Clienteles Exist? Evidence on Dividend Preferences of Retail Investors," *Journal of Finance* (June 2006).

assets into low-dividend securities. Conversely, again relative to low-income investors, high-income investors put a smaller percentage of their assets into high-dividend securities.

19.8 What We Know and Do Not Know about Dividend Policy

CORPORATE DIVIDENDS ARE SUBSTANTIAL

We pointed out earlier in the chapter that dividends are tax disadvantaged relative to capital gains because dividends are taxed upon payment whereas taxes on capital gains are deferred until sale. Nevertheless, dividends in the U.S. economy are substantial. For example, consider Figure 19.7, which shows the ratio of aggregate dividends to aggregate earnings for all U.S. firms from 1980 to 2012. The ratio was approximately 50 percent in 2012.

We might argue that the taxation on dividends is actually minimal, perhaps because dividends are paid primarily to individuals in low tax brackets (currently the tax rate on cash dividends is substantially lower than for ordinary income) or because institutions such as pension funds, which pay no taxes, are the primary recipients. However, Peterson, Peterson, and Ang conducted an in-depth study of dividends for one representative year, 1979.[13] They found that about two-thirds of dividends went to individuals and that the average marginal tax bracket for these individuals was about 40 percent. Thus, we must conclude that large amounts of dividends are paid, even in the presence of substantial taxation.

Figure 19.7

Ratio of Aggregate Dividends to Aggregate Earnings for All U.S. Firms: 1980 to 2012

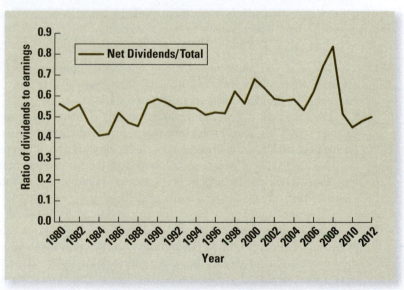

SOURCE: *The Economic Report of the President,* February 2013, Table B-90.

---

[13]P. Peterson, D. Peterson, and J. Ang, "Direct Evidence on the Marginal Rate of Taxation on Dividend Income," *Journal of Financial Economics* 14 (1985).

FEWER COMPANIES PAY DIVIDENDS

Although dividends are substantial, Fama and French (FF) point out that the percentage of companies paying dividends has fallen over the last few decades.[14] FF argue that the decline was caused primarily by an explosion of small, currently unprofitable companies that have recently listed on various stock exchanges. For the most part, firms of this type do not pay dividends. Figure 19.8 shows that the proportion of dividend payers among U.S. industrial firms dropped substantially from 1980 to 2002.

This figure, presented in a paper by DeAngelo, DeAngelo, and Skinner[15] also shows an *increase* in the proportion of dividend payers from 2002 to 2013. One obvious potential explanation is the cut in the maximum tax rate on dividends to 15 percent, signed into law in May 2003.

Figure 19.8 does not imply that dividends across *all* firms declined from 1980 to 2013. DeAngelo, DeAngelo, and Skinner[16] point out that while small firms have shied away from dividends, the largest firms have substantially increased their dividends over recent decades. This increase has created such concentration in dividends that the 25 top dividend-paying firms accounted for more than 50 percent of aggregate dividends in the United States in 2013[17]. DeAngelo and colleagues suggest that "Industrial firms exhibit a two-tier structure in which a small number of firms with

Figure 19.8
Proportion of Dividend Payers among All Publicly Held U.S. Industrial Firms: 1980–2013

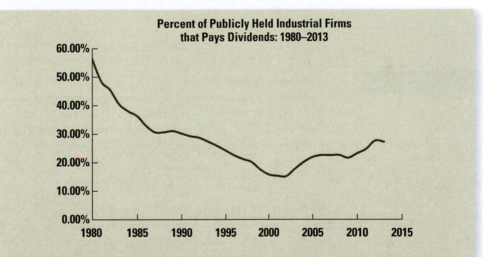

This table reports the proportion of U.S. industrial firms that paid dividends over the years from 1980 to 2013. The proportion dropped significantly from 1980 to 2002, with a rebound over the next several years.

SOURCE: Harry DeAngelo, Linda DeAngelo, and Douglas J. Skinner, "Corporate Payout Policy," in *Foundations and Trends in Finance*, vol. 3 (2008). Data updated by DeAngelo, DeAngelo, and Skinner.

---

[14]Eugene F. Fama and Kenneth R. French, "Disappearing Dividends: Changing Firm Characteristics or Lower Propensity to Pay?" *Journal of Financial Economics* (April 2001).

[15]Harry DeAngelo, Linda DeAngelo, and Douglas J. Skinner, "Corporate Payout Policy," in *Foundations and Trends in Finance*, vol. 3 (2008). Data updated by the authors.

[16]Harry DeAngelo, Linda DeAngelo, and Douglas J. Skinner, "Are Dividends Disappearing? Dividend Concentration and the Consolidation of Earnings," *Journal of Financial Economics* (2004).

[17]In 2013, about 80 percent of the 500 largest U.S. companies (i.e., the S&P 500) paid cash dividends.

very high earnings generates the majority of earnings and dominates the dividend supply, while the majority of firms has at best a modest impact on aggregate earnings and dividends."

CORPORATIONS SMOOTH DIVIDENDS

In 1956, John Lintner made two important observations concerning dividend policy that still ring true.[18] First, real-world companies typically set long-term target ratios of dividends to earnings. A firm is likely to set a low target ratio if it has many positive NPV projects relative to available cash flow and a high ratio if it has few positive NPV projects. Second, managers know that only part of any change in earnings is likely to be permanent. Because managers need time to assess the permanence of any earnings rise, dividend changes appear to lag earnings changes by a number of periods.

Taken together, Lintner's observations suggest that two parameters describe dividend policy: the target payout ratio (t) and the speed of adjustment of current dividends to the target (s). Dividend changes will tend to conform to the following model:

$$\text{Dividend change} \equiv \text{Div}_1 - \text{Div}_0 = s \cdot (t\text{EPS}_1 - \text{Div}_0) \tag{19.6}$$

where Div_1 and Div_0 are dividends in the next year and dividends in the current year, respectively. EPS_1 is earnings per share in the next year.

The limiting cases in Equation 19.6 occur when $s = 1$ and $s = 0$. If $s = 1$, the actual change in dividends will be equal to the target change in dividends. Here, full adjustment

---

**EXAMPLE
19.2**

Dividend Smoothing   Calculator Graphics, Inc. (CGI), has a target payout ratio of .30. Last year's earnings per share were $10, and in accordance with the target, CGI paid dividends of $3 per share last year. However, earnings have jumped to $20 this year. Because the managers do not believe that this increase is permanent, they do *not* plan to raise dividends all the way to $6 (=.30 × $20). Rather, their speed of adjustment coefficient, *s*, is .5, implying that the *increase* in dividends from last year to this year will be:

$$.5 \times (\$6 - \$3) = \$1.50$$

That is, the increase in dividends is the product of the speed of adjustment coefficient, .50, times the difference between what dividends would be with full adjustment [$6 (=.30 × $20)] and last year's dividends. Dividends will increase by $1.50, so dividends this year will be $4.50 (=$3 + $1.50).

Now, suppose that earnings stay at $20 next year. The increase in dividends next year will be:

$$.5 \times (\$6 - \$4.50) = \$.75$$

In words, the increase in dividends from this year to next year will be the speed of adjustment coefficient (.50) times the difference between what dividends would have been next year with full adjustment ($6) and this year's dividends ($4.50). Because dividends will increase by $.75, dividends next year will be $5.25 (=$4.50 + $.75). In this way, dividends will slowly rise every year if earnings in all future years remain at $20. However, dividends will reach $6 only at infinity.

---

[18]John Lintner, "Distribution of Incomes of Corporations Among Dividends, Retained Earnings, and Taxes," *American Economic Review* (May 1956).

occurs immediately. If $s = 0$, $Div_1 = Div_0$. In other words, there is no change in dividends at all. Real-world companies can be expected to set s between 0 and 1.

An implication of Lintner's model is that the dividends-to-earnings ratio rises when a company begins a period of bad times, and the ratio falls when a company starts a period of good times. Thus, dividends display less variability than do earnings. In other words, firms *smooth* dividends.

The Pros and Cons of Paying Dividends

Pros	Cons
1. Dividends may appeal to investors who desire stable cash flow but do not want to incur the transaction costs from periodically selling shares of stock.	1. Dividends have been traditionally taxed as ordinary income.
2. Behavioral finance argues that investors with limited self-control can meet current consumption needs with high-dividend stocks while adhering to the policy of never dipping into principal.	2. Dividends can reduce internal sources of financing. Dividends may force the firm to forgo positive NPV projects or to rely on costly external equity financing.
3. Managers, acting on behalf of stockholders, can pay dividends in order to keep cash from bondholders.	3. Once established, dividend cuts are hard to make without adversely affecting a firm's stock price.
4. The board of directors, acting on behalf of stockholders, can use dividends to reduce the cash available to spendthrift managers.	
5. Managers may increase dividends to signal their optimism concerning future cash flow.	

SOME SURVEY EVIDENCE ABOUT DIVIDENDS

A recent study surveyed a large number of financial executives regarding dividend policy. One of the questions asked was this: "Do these statements describe factors that affect your company's dividend decisions?" Table 19.2 shows some of the results.

As shown in Table 19.2, financial managers are very disinclined to cut dividends. Moreover, they are very conscious of their previous dividends and desire to maintain a relatively steady dividend. In contrast, the cost of external capital and the desire to attract "prudent man" investors (those with fiduciary duties) are less important.

Table 19.3 is drawn from the same survey, but here the responses are to the question, "How important are the following factors to your company's dividend decisions?" Not surprisingly given the responses in Table 19.2 and our earlier discussion, the highest priority is maintaining a consistent dividend policy. The next several items are also consistent with our previous analysis. Financial managers are very concerned about earnings stability and future earnings levels in making dividend decisions, and

Table 19.2

Survey Responses on Dividend Decisions*

Policy Statements	Percentage Who Agree or Strongly Agree
1. We try to avoid reducing dividends per share.	93.8%
2. We try to maintain a smooth dividend from year to year.	89.6
3. We consider the level of dividends per share that we have paid in recent quarters.	88.2
4. We are reluctant to make dividend changes that might have to be reversed in the future.	77.9
5. We consider the change or growth in dividends per share.	66.7
6. We consider the cost of raising external capital to be smaller than the cost of cutting dividends.	42.8
7. We pay dividends to attract investors subject to "prudent man" investment restrictions.	41.7

*Survey respondents were asked the question, "Do these statements describe factors that affect your company's dividend decisions?"

SOURCE: Adapted from Table 4 of Alon Brav, John R. Graham, Campbell R. Harvey, and Roni Michaely, "Payout Policy in the 21st Century," *Journal of Financial Economics* (2005).

they consider the availability of good investment opportunities. Survey respondents also believed that attracting both institutional and individual (retail) investors was relatively important.

In contrast to our discussion in the earlier part of this chapter of taxes and flotation costs, the financial managers in this survey did not think that personal taxes paid on dividends by shareholders are very important. And even fewer think that equity flotation costs are relevant.

Table 19.3

Survey Responses on Dividend Decisions*

Policy Statements	Percentage Who Think This Is Important or Very Important
1. Maintaining consistency with our historic dividend policy.	84.1%
2. Stability of future earnings.	71.9
3. A sustainable change in earnings.	67.1
4. Attracting institutional investors to purchase our stock.	52.5
5. The availability of good investment opportunities for our firm to pursue.	47.6
6. Attracting retail investors to purchase our stock.	44.5
7. Personal taxes our stockholders pay when receiving dividends.	21.1
8. Flotation costs to issuing new equity.	9.3

*Survey respondents were asked the question, "How important are the following factors to your company's dividend decisions?"

SOURCE: Adapted from Table 5 of Alon Brav, John R. Graham, Campbell R. Harvey, and Roni Michaely, "Payout Policy in the 21st Century," *Journal of Financial Economics* (2005).

19.9 Putting It All Together

Much of what we have discussed in this chapter (and much of what we know about dividends from decades of research) can be pulled together and summarized in the following six points:[19]

1. Aggregate dividend and stock repurchases are massive, and they have increased steadily in nominal and real terms over the years.

2. Cash dividends and repurchases are heavily concentrated among a relatively small number of large, mature firms.

3. Managers are very reluctant to cut dividends, normally doing so only due to firm-specific problems.

4. Managers smooth dividends, raising them slowly and incrementally as earnings grow.

5. Stock prices react to unanticipated changes in dividends.

6. The magnitude of stock repurchases tends to vary with transitory earnings.

The challenge now is to fit these six pieces into a reasonably coherent picture. With regard to payouts in general, meaning the combination of stock repurchases and cash dividends, a simple life cycle theory fits Points 1 and 2. The key ideas are straightforward. First, relatively young firms with less available cash generally should not make cash distributions. They need the cash to fund positive NPV projects (and flotation costs discourage the raising of outside cash).

However, as a firm survives and matures, it begins to generate free cash flow (which, you will recall, is internally generated cash flow beyond that needed to fund profitable investment activities). Significant free cash flow can lead to agency problems if it is not distributed. Managers may become tempted to pursue empire building or otherwise spend the excess cash in ways not in the shareholders' best interests. Thus, firms come under shareholder pressure to make distributions rather than hoard cash. And, consistent with what we observe, we expect large firms with a history of profitability to make large distributions.

Thus, the life cycle theory says that firms trade off the agency costs of excess cash retention against the potential future costs of external equity financing. A firm should begin making distributions when it generates sufficient internal cash flow to fund its investment needs now and into the foreseeable future.

The more complex issue concerns the type of distribution, cash dividends versus repurchase. The tax argument in favor of repurchases is a clear and strong one. Repurchases are a much more flexible option (and managers greatly value financial flexibility), so the question is: Why would firms ever choose a cash dividend?

If we are to answer this question, we have to ask a different question. What can a cash dividend accomplish that a share repurchase cannot? One answer is that when a firm makes a commitment to pay a cash dividend now and into the future, it sends a two-part signal to the markets. As we have already discussed, one signal is that the firm anticipates being profitable, with the ability to make the payments on an ongoing basis. Note that a firm cannot benefit by trying to fool the market in this regard because the firm would ultimately be punished when it couldn't make the dividend payment (or couldn't make it

---

[19]This list is distilled in part from a longer list in Harry DeAngelo and Linda DeAngelo, "Payout Policy Pedagogy: What Matters and Why," *European Financial Management* 13 (2007).

without relying on external financing). Thus, a cash dividend may let a firm distinguish itself from less profitable rivals.

A second, and more subtle, signal takes us back to the agency problem of free cash flow. By committing to pay cash dividends now and in the future, the firm signals that it won't be hoarding cash (or at least not as much cash), thereby reducing agency costs and enhancing shareholder wealth.

This two-part signaling story is consistent with Points 3 to 5 on the previous page, but an obvious objection remains. Why don't firms just commit to a policy of setting aside whatever money would be used to pay dividends and use it instead to buy back shares? After all, either way, a firm is committing to pay out cash to shareholders.

A fixed repurchase strategy suffers from two drawbacks. The first is verifiability. A firm could announce an open market repurchase and then simply not do it. By suitably fudging its books, it would be some time before the deception was discovered. Thus, it would be necessary for shareholders to develop a monitoring mechanism, meaning some sort of way for stockholders to know for sure that the repurchase was in fact done. Such a mechanism wouldn't be difficult to build (it could be a simple trustee relationship such as we observe in the bond markets), but it currently does not exist. Of course, a tender offer repurchase needs little or no verification, but such offers have expenses associated with them. The beauty of a cash dividend is that it needs no monitoring. A firm is forced to cut and mail checks four times a year, year in and year out.

Characteristics of a Sensible Payout Policy

- Over time pay out all free cash flows.
- Avoid cutting positive NPV projects to pay dividends or buy back shares.
- Do not initiate dividends until the firm is generating substantial free cash flow.
- Set the current regular dividend consistent with a long-run target payout ratio.
- Set the level of dividends low enough to avoid expensive future external financing.
- Use repurchases to distribute transitory cash flow increases.

A second objection to a fixed repurchase strategy is more controversial. Suppose managers, as insiders, are better able than stockholders to judge whether their stock price is too high or too low. (Note that this idea does not conflict with semistrong market efficiency if inside information is the reason.) In this case, a fixed repurchase commitment forces management to buy back stock even in circumstances when the stock is overvalued. In other words, it forces management into making negative NPV investments.

More research on the cash dividend versus share repurchase question is needed, but the historical trend seems to be favoring continued growth in repurchases relative to dividends. Total corporate payouts seem to be relatively stable over time, but repurchases are becoming a larger portion of that total. Most recently, aggregate repurchases have passed aggregate dividends.

One aspect of aggregate cash dividends that has not received much attention is that there may be a strong legacy effect. Before 1982, the regulatory status of stock repurchases was somewhat murky, creating a significant disincentive. In 1982, the SEC, after years of debate, created a clear set of guidelines for firms to follow, thereby making repurchases much more attractive.

The legacy effect arises because many of the giant firms that pay such a large portion of aggregate dividends were paying dividends before (and perhaps long before) 1982. To the extent that these firms are unwilling to cut their dividends, aggregate cash dividends will be large, but only because of a "lock-in" effect for older firms. If locked-in, legacy payers account for much of the aggregate dividend, what we should observe is (1) a sharply reduced tendency for maturing firms to initiate dividends and (2) a growth in repurchases relative to cash dividends over time. We actually do see evidence of both of these trends; however, as the case of Microsoft clearly shows, legacy effects alone can't account for all cash dividend payers.

19.10   Stock Dividends and Stock Splits

Another type of dividend is paid out in shares of stock. This type of dividend is called a **stock dividend**. A stock dividend is not a true dividend because it is not paid in cash. The effect of a stock dividend is to increase the number of shares that each owner holds. Because there are more shares outstanding, each is simply worth less.

A stock dividend is commonly expressed as a percentage; for example, a 20 percent stock dividend means that a shareholder receives one new share for every five currently owned (a 20 percent increase). Because every shareholder receives 20 percent more stock, the total number of shares outstanding rises by 20 percent. As we will see in a moment, the result is that each share of stock is worth about 20 percent less.

A **stock split** is essentially the same thing as a stock dividend, except that a split is expressed as a ratio instead of a percentage. When a split is declared, each share is split up to create additional shares. For example, in a three-for-one stock split, each old share is split into three new shares.

Information on upcoming stock splits is available on the splits calendar at **www.investmenthouse.com** and **finance.yahoo.com**.

SOME DETAILS ABOUT STOCK SPLITS AND STOCK DIVIDENDS

Stock splits and stock dividends have essentially the same impacts on the corporation and the shareholder. They increase the number of shares outstanding and reduce the value per share. The accounting treatment is not the same, however, and it depends on two things: (1) whether the distribution is a stock split or a stock dividend and (2) the size of the stock dividend if it is called a dividend.

By convention, stock dividends of less than 20 to 25 percent are called *small stock dividends*. The accounting procedure for such a dividend is discussed next. A stock dividend greater than this value of 20 to 25 percent is called a *large stock dividend*. Large stock dividends are not uncommon. For example, in October 2010, water heater manufacturer A.O. Smith announced a three-for-two stock split in the form of a 50 percent stock dividend. The same month, automotive supplier Magna International announced a two-for-one stock split in the form of a 100 percent stock dividend. Except for some relatively minor accounting differences, this has the same effect as a two-for-one stock split.

Example of a Small Stock Dividend   The Peterson Co., a consulting firm specializing in difficult accounting problems, has 10,000 shares of stock outstanding, each selling at $66. The total market value of the equity is $66 × 10,000 = $660,000. With a 10 percent stock dividend, each stockholder receives one additional share for each 10 owned, and the total number of shares outstanding after the dividend is 11,000.

Before the stock dividend, the equity portion of Peterson's balance sheet might look like this:

Common stock ($1 par, 10,000 shares outstanding)	$ 10,000
Capital in excess of par value	200,000
Retained earnings	290,000
Total owners' equity	$500,000

A seemingly arbitrary accounting procedure is used to adjust the balance sheet after a small stock dividend. Because 1,000 new shares are issued, the common stock account is increased by $1,000 (1,000 shares at $1 par value each), for a total of $11,000. The market price of $66 is $65 greater than the par value, so the "excess" of $65 × 1,000 shares = $65,000 is added to the capital surplus account (capital in excess of par value), producing a total of $265,000.

Total owners' equity is unaffected by the stock dividend because no cash has come in or out, so retained earnings are reduced by the entire $66,000, leaving $224,000. The net effect of these machinations is that Peterson's equity accounts now look like this:

Common stock ($1 par, 11,000 shares outstanding)	$ 11,000
Capital in excess of par value	265,000
Retained earnings	224,000
Total owners' equity	$500,000

Example of a Stock Split   A stock split is conceptually similar to a stock dividend, but it is commonly expressed as a ratio. For example, in a three-for-two split, each shareholder receives one additional share of stock for each two held originally, so a three-for-two split amounts to a 50 percent stock dividend. Again, no cash is paid out, and the percentage of the entire firm that each shareholder owns is unaffected.

The accounting treatment of a stock split is a little different from (and simpler than) that of a stock dividend. Suppose Peterson decides to declare a two-for-one stock split. The number of shares outstanding will double to 20,000, and the par value will be halved to $.50 per share. The owners' equity after the split is represented as follows:

For a list of recent stock splits, try **www.stocksplits.net**.

Common stock ($.50 par, 20,000 shares outstanding)	$ 10,000
Capital in excess of par value	200,000
Retained earnings	290,000
Total owners' equity	$500,000

Note that for all three of the categories, the figures on the right are completely unaffected by the split. The only changes are in the par value per share and the number of shares outstanding. Because the number of shares has doubled, the par value of each is cut in half.

Example of a Large Stock Dividend   In our example, if a 100 percent stock dividend were declared, 10,000 new shares would be distributed, so 20,000 shares would be outstanding. At a $1 par value per share, the common stock account would rise by \$10,000, for a total of \$20,000. The retained earnings account would be reduced by \$10,000, leaving \$280,000. The result would be the following:

Common stock (\$1 par, 20,000 shares outstanding)	\$ 20,000
Capital in excess of par value	200,000
Retained earnings	280,000
Total owners' equity	\$500,000

VALUE OF STOCK SPLITS AND STOCK DIVIDENDS

The laws of logic tell us that stock splits and stock dividends can (1) leave the value of the firm unaffected, (2) increase its value, or (3) decrease its value. Unfortunately, the issues are complex enough that we cannot easily determine which of the three relationships holds.

The Benchmark Case   A strong case can be made that stock dividends and splits do not change either the wealth of any shareholder or the wealth of the firm as a whole. In our preceding example, the equity had a total market value of \$660,000. With the small stock dividend, the number of shares increased to 11,000, so it seems that each would be worth \$660,000/11,000 = \$60.

For example, a shareholder who had 100 shares worth \$66 each before the dividend would have 110 shares worth \$60 each afterward. The total value of the stock is \$6,600 either way; so the stock dividend doesn't really have any economic effect.

After the stock split, there are 20,000 shares outstanding, so each should be worth \$660,000/20,000 = \$33. In other words, the number of shares doubles and the price halves. From these calculations, it appears that stock dividends and splits are just paper transactions.

Although these results are relatively obvious, there are reasons that are often given to suggest that there may be some benefits to these actions. The typical financial manager is aware of many real-world complexities, and for that reason the stock split or stock dividend decision is not treated lightly in practice.

Popular Trading Range   Proponents of stock dividends and stock splits frequently argue that a security has a proper **trading range**. When the security is priced above this level, many investors do not have the funds to buy the common trading unit of 100 shares, called a *round lot*. Although securities can be purchased in *odd-lot* form (fewer than 100 shares), the commissions are greater. Thus, firms will split the stock to keep the price in this trading range.

For example, in early 2003, Microsoft announced a two-for-one stock split. This was the ninth split for Microsoft since the company went public in 1986. The stock had split three-for-two on two occasions and two-for-one a total of seven times. So for every share of Microsoft you owned in 1986 when the company first went public, you would own 288 shares as of the most recent stock split in 2003. Similarly, since Walmart went public in 1970, it has split its stock two-for-one 9 times, and Apple has split seven-for-one once and two-for-one three times since going public in 1987. For a really long split history, consider Proctor & Gamble, which has split five-for-one twice, 1.5-to-one once, and two-for-one eight times since 1920. Each share of P&G purchased prior to the company's first stock split would have become 9,600 shares along the way.

Although this argument of a trading range is a popular one, its validity is questionable for a number of reasons. Mutual funds, pension funds, and other institutions have steadily increased their trading activity since World War II and now handle a sizable percentage of total trading volume (e.g., on the order of 80 percent of NYSE trading volume). Because these institutions buy and sell in huge amounts, the individual share price is of little concern.

Furthermore, we sometimes observe share prices that are quite large that do not appear to cause problems. To take an extreme case, consider the Swiss chocolatier Lindt. In January 2015, Lindt shares were selling for around 57,160 Swiss francs each, or about $57,487. A round lot would have cost a cool $5.75 million. This is fairly expensive, but also consider Berkshire-Hathaway, the company run by legendary investor Warren Buffett. In January 2015, each share in the company sold for about $226,000, down from a high of $229,300 in December 2014.

Finally, there is evidence that stock splits may actually decrease the liquidity of the company's shares. Following a two-for-one split, the number of shares traded should more than double if liquidity is increased by the split. This doesn't appear to happen, and the reverse is sometimes observed.

REVERSE SPLITS

A less frequently encountered financial maneuver is the **reverse split**. For example, in January 2014, BioLife Solutions, a medical cold storage company, announced a 1-for-14 reverse stock split, and, in the same month, PeopleString underwent a 1-for-40 reverse split. In a 1-for-40 reverse split, each investor exchanges 40 old shares for 1 new share. The par value is increased by a factor of 40 in the process. In what is one of the biggest reverse splits ever (in terms of market cap), banking giant Citigroup announced in March 2011 that it would do a 1-for-10 reverse split, thereby reducing the number of its shares outstanding from 29 billion to 2.9 billion. As with stock splits and stock dividends, a case can be made that a reverse split has no real effect.

Given real-world imperfections, three related reasons are cited for reverse splits. First, transaction costs to shareholders may be less after the reverse split. Second, the liquidity and marketability of a company's stock might be improved when its price is raised to the popular trading range. Third, stocks selling at prices below a certain level are not considered respectable, meaning that investors underestimate these firms' earnings, cash flow, growth, and stability. Some financial analysts argue that a reverse split can achieve instant respectability. As was the case with stock splits, none of these reasons is particularly compelling, especially not the third one.

There are two other reasons for reverse splits. First, stock exchanges have minimum price per share requirements. A reverse split may bring the stock price up to such a minimum. In 2001–2002, in the wake of a bear market, this motive became an increasingly important one. In 2001, 106 companies asked their shareholders to approve reverse splits. There were 111 reverse splits in 2002 and 75 in 2003, but only 14 by mid-year 2004. The most common reason for these reverse splits is that NASDAQ begins the delisting process for companies whose stock price drops below $1 per share for 30 days. Many companies, particularly Internet-related technology companies, found themselves in danger of being delisted and used reverse splits to boost their stock prices. Second, companies sometimes perform reverse splits and, at the same time, buy out any stockholders who end up with less than a certain number of shares.

For example, in January 2014, Travelzoo completed a reverse/forward split. In this case, the company first did a 1-for-25 reverse stock split and then repurchased all shares held by stockholders with less than one share of stock, thereby eliminating smaller shareholders (and thus reducing the total number of shareholders). The company reduced the number of shareholders from more than 90,000 to fewer than 10,000, saving a considerable amount on administrative expenses. What made the proposal especially imaginative was that immediately after the reverse split, the company did a 25-for-1 ordinary split to restore the stock to its original cost!

Summary and Conclusions

1. The dividend policy of a firm is irrelevant in a perfect capital market because the shareholder can effectively undo the firm's dividend strategy. If a shareholder receives a greater dividend than desired, he or she can reinvest the excess. Conversely, if the shareholder receives a smaller dividend than desired, he or she can sell off extra shares of stock. This argument is due to MM and is similar to their homemade leverage concept, discussed in a previous chapter.

2. Stockholders will be indifferent between dividends and share repurchases in a perfect capital market.

3. Because dividends in the United States are taxed, companies should not issue stock to pay out a dividend.

4. Also because of taxes, firms have an incentive to reduce dividends. For example, they might consider increasing capital expenditures, acquiring other companies, or purchasing financial assets. However, due to financial considerations and legal constraints, rational firms with large cash flows will likely exhaust these activities with plenty of cash left over for dividends.

5. In a world with personal taxes, a strong case can be made for repurchasing shares instead of paying dividends.

6. Nevertheless, there are a number of justifications for dividends even in a world with personal taxes:
   a. Investors in no-dividend stocks incur transaction costs when selling off shares for current consumption.
   b. Behavioral finance argues that investors with limited self-control can meet current consumption needs via high-dividend stocks while adhering to a policy of "never dipping into principal."
   c. Managers, acting on behalf of stockholders, can pay dividends to keep cash from bondholders. The board of directors, also acting on behalf of stockholders, can use dividends to reduce the cash available to spendthrift managers.

7. The stock market reacts positively to increases in dividends (or an initial payment) and negatively to decreases in dividends. This suggests that there is information content in dividend payments.

8. High (low) dividend firms should arise to meet the demands of dividend-preferring (capital gains–preferring) investors. Because of these clienteles, it is not clear that a firm can create value by changing its dividend policy.

Concept Questions

1. **Dividend Policy Irrelevance** How is it possible that dividends are so important, but at the same time dividend policy is irrelevant?

2. **Stock Repurchases** What is the impact of a stock repurchase on a company's debt ratio? Does this suggest another use for excess cash?

3. **Dividend Policy** It is sometimes suggested that firms should follow a "residual" dividend policy. With such a policy, the main idea is that a firm should focus on meeting its investment needs and maintaining its desired debt–equity ratio. Having done so, a firm pays out any leftover, or residual, income as dividends. What do you think would be the chief drawback to a residual dividend policy?

4. **Dividend Chronology**   On Tuesday, December 8, Hometown Power Co.'s board of directors declares a dividend of 75 cents per share payable on Wednesday, January 17, to shareholders of record as of Wednesday, January 3. When is the ex-dividend date? If a shareholder buys stock before that date, who gets the dividends on those shares—the buyer or the seller?

5. **Alternative Dividends**   Some corporations, like one British company that offers its large shareholders free crematorium use, pay dividends in kind (i.e., offer their services to shareholders at below-market cost). Should mutual funds invest in stocks that pay these dividends in kind? (The fundholders do not receive these services.)

6. **Dividends and Stock Price**   If increases in dividends tend to be followed by (immediate) increases in share prices, how can it be said that dividend policy is irrelevant?

7. **Dividends and Stock Price**   Last month, Central Virginia Power Company, which had been having trouble with cost overruns on a nuclear power plant that it had been building, announced that it was "temporarily suspending dividend payments due to the cash flow crunch associated with its investment program." The company's stock price dropped from $28.50 to $25 when this announcement was made. How would you interpret this change in the stock price? (That is, what would you say caused it?)

8. **Dividend Reinvestment Plans**   The DRK Corporation has recently developed a dividend reinvestment plan, or DRIP. The plan allows investors to reinvest cash dividends automatically in DRK in exchange for new shares of stock. Over time, investors in DRK will be able to build their holdings by reinvesting dividends to purchase additional shares of the company.

   More than 1,000 companies offer dividend reinvestment plans. Most companies with DRIPs charge no brokerage or service fees. In fact, the shares of DRK will be purchased at a 10 percent discount from the market price.

   A consultant for DRK estimates that about 75 percent of DRK's shareholders will take part in this plan. This is somewhat higher than the average.

   Evaluate DRK's dividend reinvestment plan. Will it increase shareholder wealth? Discuss the advantages and disadvantages involved here.

9. **Dividend Policy**   For initial public offerings of common stock, 2007 was a relatively slow year, with only about $35.6 billion raised by the process. Relatively few of the 159 firms involved paid cash dividends. Why do you think that most chose not to pay cash dividends?

10. **Investment and Dividends**   The Phew Charitable Trust pays no taxes on its capital gains or on its dividend income or interest income. Would it be irrational for it to have low-dividend, high-growth stocks in its portfolio? Would it be irrational for it to have municipal bonds in its portfolio? Explain.

Use the following information to answer the next two questions:

   Historically, the U.S. tax code treated dividend payments made to shareholders as ordinary income. Thus, dividends were taxed at the investor's marginal tax rate, which was as high as 38.6 percent in 2002. Capital gains were taxed at a capital gains tax rate, which was the same for most investors and fluctuated through the years. In 2002, the capital gains tax rate stood at 20 percent. In an effort to stimulate the economy, President George W. Bush presided over a tax plan overhaul that included changes in dividend and capital gains tax rates. The new tax plan, which was implemented in 2003, called for a 15 percent tax rate on both dividends and capital gains for investors in higher tax brackets. For lower tax bracket investors, the tax rate on dividends and capital gains was set at 5 percent through 2007, dropping to zero in 2008.

11. **Ex-Dividend Stock Prices**   How do you think this tax law change affects ex-dividend stock prices?

12. **Stock Repurchases**   How do you think this tax law change affects the relative attractiveness of stock repurchases compared to dividend payments?

13. **Dividends and Stock Value**   The growing perpetuity model expresses the value of a share of stock as the present value of the expected dividends from that stock. How can you conclude that dividend policy is irrelevant when this model is valid?

14. **Bird-in-the-Hand Argument**   The bird-in-the-hand argument, which states that a dividend today is safer than the uncertain prospect of a capital gain tomorrow, is often used to justify high dividend payout ratios. Explain the fallacy behind this argument.

15. **Dividends and Income Preference**   The desire for current income is not a valid explanation of preference for high current dividend policy because investors can always create homemade dividends by selling a portion of their stocks. Is this statement true or false? Why?

16. **Dividends and Clientele**   Cap Henderson owns Neotech stock because its price has been steadily rising over the past few years and he expects this performance to continue. Cap is trying to convince Sarah Jones to purchase some Neotech stock, but she is reluctant because Neotech has never paid a dividend. She depends on steady dividends to provide her with income.

    a. What preferences are these two investors demonstrating?
    b. What argument should Cap use to convince Sarah that Neotech stock is the stock for her?
    c. Why might Cap's argument not convince Sarah?

17. **Dividends and Taxes**   Your aunt is in a high tax bracket and would like to minimize the tax burden of her investment portfolio. She is willing to buy and sell to maximize her aftertax returns, and she has asked for your advice. What would you suggest she do?

18. **Dividends versus Capital Gains**   If the market places the same value on $1 of dividends as on $1 of capital gains, then firms with different payout ratios will appeal to different clienteles of investors. One clientele is as good as another; therefore, a firm cannot increase its value by changing its dividend policy. Yet empirical investigations reveal a strong correlation between dividend payout ratios and other firm characteristics. For example, small, rapidly growing firms that have recently gone public almost always have payout ratios that are zero; all earnings are reinvested in the business. Explain this phenomenon if dividend policy is irrelevant.

19. **Dividend Irrelevancy**   In spite of the theoretical argument that dividend policy should be irrelevant, the fact remains that many investors like high dividends. If this preference exists, a firm can boost its share price by increasing its dividend payout ratio. Explain the fallacy in this argument.

20. **Dividends and Stock Price**   Empirical research has found that there have been significant increases in stock price on the day an initial dividend (i.e., the first time a firm pays a cash dividend) is announced. What does this finding imply about the information content of initial dividends?

Questions and Problems

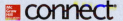

BASIC
(Questions 1–10)

1. **Dividends and Taxes**   Lee Ann, Inc., has declared a $7.50 per-share dividend. Suppose capital gains are not taxed, but dividends are taxed at 15 percent. New IRS regulations require that taxes be withheld when the dividend is paid. The company's stock sells for $93 per share, and is about to go ex-dividend. What do you think the ex-dividend price will be?

2. **Stock Dividends**   The owners' equity accounts for Hexagon International are shown here:

Common stock ($1 par value)	$ 40,000
Capital surplus	155,000
Retained earnings	538,400
Total owners' equity	$733,400

   a. If the company's stock currently sells for $39 per share and a 10 percent stock dividend is declared, how many new shares will be distributed? Show how the equity accounts would change.
   b. If the company declared a 25 percent stock dividend, how would the accounts change?

3. **Stock Splits**   For the company in Problem 2, show how the equity accounts will change if:

   a. The company declares a four-for-one stock split. How many shares are outstanding now? What is the new par value per share?
   b. The company declares a one-for-five reverse stock split. How many shares are outstanding now? What is the new par value per share?

4. **Stock Splits and Stock Dividends**   Roll Corporation (RC) currently has 465,000 shares of stock outstanding that sell for $73 per share. Assuming no market imperfections or tax effects exist, what will the share price be after:

   a. RC has a five-for-three stock split?
   b. RC has a 15 percent stock dividend?
   c. RC has a 42.5 percent stock dividend?
   d. RC has a four-for-seven reverse stock split?

   Determine the new number of shares outstanding in parts (a) through (d).

5. **Regular Dividends**   The balance sheet for Levy Corp. is shown here in market value terms. There are 14,000 shares of stock outstanding.

Market Value Balance Sheet			
Cash	$ 62,000	Equity	$507,000
Fixed assets	445,000		
Total	$507,000	Total	$507,000

   The company has declared a dividend of $1.60 per share. The stock goes ex dividend tomorrow. Ignoring any tax effects, what is the stock selling for today? What will it sell for tomorrow? What will the balance sheet look like after the dividends are paid?

6. **Share Repurchase**   In the previous problem, suppose the company has announced it is going to repurchase $22,400 worth of stock. What effect will this transaction have on the equity of the company? How many shares will be outstanding? What will the price per share be after the repurchase? Ignoring tax effects, show how the share repurchase is effectively the same as a cash dividend.

7. **Stock Dividends**   The market value balance sheet for Outbox Manufacturing is shown here. Outbox has declared a stock dividend of 25 percent. The stock goes ex dividend tomorrow (the chronology for a stock dividend is similar to that for a cash dividend). There are 22,000 shares of stock outstanding. What will the ex-dividend price be?

Market Value Balance Sheet			
Cash	$295,000	Debt	$180,000
Fixed assets	540,000	Equity	655,000
Total	$835,000	Total	$835,000

8.   Stock Dividends   The company with the common equity accounts shown here has declared a stock dividend of 15 percent when the market value of its stock is $57 per share. What effects on the equity accounts will the distribution of the stock dividend have?

Common stock ($1 par value)	$ 435,000
Capital surplus	2,150,000
Retained earnings	5,873,000
Total owners' equity	$8,458,000

9.   Stock Splits   In the previous problem, suppose the company instead decides on a five-for-one stock split. The firm's 45 cent per share cash dividend on the new (postsplit) shares represents an increase of 10 percent over last year's dividend on the presplit stock. What effect does this have on the equity accounts? What was last year's dividend per share?

10.   Dividends and Stock Price   The Mann Company belongs to a risk class for which the appropriate discount rate is 10 percent. Mann currently has 240,000 outstanding shares selling at $105 each. The firm is contemplating the declaration of a $4 dividend at the end of the fiscal year that just began. Assume there are no taxes on dividends. Answer the following questions based on the Miller and Modigliani model, which is discussed in the text.

a. What will be the price of the stock on the ex-dividend date if the dividend is declared?
b. What will be the price of the stock at the end of the year if the dividend is not declared?
c. If Mann makes $4.3 million of new investments at the beginning of the period, earns net income of $1.9 million, and pays the dividend at the end of the year, how many shares of new stock must the firm issue to meet its funding needs?
d. Is it realistic to use the MM model in the real world to value stock? Why or why not?

INTERMEDIATE
(Questions 11–16)

11.   Homemade Dividends   You own 1,000 shares of stock in Avondale Corporation. You will receive a dividend of $2.60 per share in one year. In two years, Avondale will pay a liquidating dividend of $53 per share. The required return on Avondale stock is 14 percent. What is the current share price of your stock (ignoring taxes)? If you would rather have equal dividends in each of the next two years, show how you can accomplish this by creating homemade dividends. (*Hint:* Dividends will be in the form of an annuity.)

12.   Homemade Dividends   In the previous problem, suppose you want only $500 total in dividends the first year. What will your homemade dividend be in two years?

13.   Stock Repurchase   Flychucker Corporation is evaluating an extra dividend versus a share repurchase. In either case $6,300 would be spent. Current earnings are $2.60 per share, and the stock currently sells for $51 per share. There are 1,500 shares outstanding. Ignore taxes and other imperfections in answering parts (a) and (b).

a. Evaluate the two alternatives in terms of the effect on the price per share of the stock and shareholder wealth.

    b. What will be the effect on the company's EPS and PE ratio under the two different scenarios?

    c. In the real world, which of these actions would you recommend? Why?

14. Dividends and Firm Value The net income of Novis Corporation is $85,000. The company has 25,000 outstanding shares and a 100 percent payout policy. The expected value of the firm one year from now is $1,725,000. The appropriate discount rate for the company is 12 percent, and the dividend tax rate is zero.

    a. What is the current value of the firm assuming the current dividend has not yet been paid?

    b. What is the ex-dividend price of the company's stock if the board follows its current policy?

    c. At the dividend declaration meeting, several board members claimed that the dividend is too meager and is probably depressing the company's price. They proposed that the company sell enough new shares to finance a $4.60 dividend.

        i. Comment on the claim that the low dividend is depressing the stock price. Support your argument with calculations.

        ii. If the proposal is adopted, at what price will the new shares sell? How many will be sold?

15. Dividend Policy Gibson Co. has a current period cash flow of $1.3 million and pays no dividends. The present value of the company's future cash flows is $18 million. The company is entirely financed with equity and has 550,000 shares outstanding. Assume the dividend tax rate is zero.

    a. What is the share price of the company's stock?

    b. Suppose the board of directors of the company announces its plan to pay out 50 percent of its current cash flow as cash dividends to its shareholders. How can Jeff Miller, who owns 1,000 shares of the company's stock, achieve a zero payout policy on his own?

16. Dividend Smoothing The Sharpe Co. just paid a dividend of $1.60 per share of stock. Its target payout ratio is 40 percent. The company expects to have earnings per share of $5.10 one year from now.

    a. If the adjustment rate is .3 as defined in the Lintner model, what is the dividend one year from now?

    b. If the adjustment rate is .6 instead, what is the dividend one year from now?

    c. Which adjustment rate is more conservative? Why?

CHALLENGE
(Questions 17–20)

17. Expected Return, Dividends, and Taxes The Gecko Company and the Gordon Company are two firms whose business risk is the same but that have different dividend policies. Gecko pays no dividend, whereas Gordon has an expected dividend yield of 4.7 percent. Suppose the capital gains tax rate is zero, whereas the dividend tax rate is 35 percent. Gecko has an expected earnings growth rate of 13 percent annually, and its stock price is expected to grow at this same rate. If the aftertax expected returns on the two stocks are equal (because they are in the same risk class), what is the pretax required return on Gordon's stock?

18. Dividends and Taxes As discussed in the text, in the absence of market imperfections and tax effects, we would expect the share price to decline by the amount of the dividend payment when the stock goes ex dividend. Once we consider the role of taxes, however, this is not necessarily true. One model has been proposed that incorporates tax effects into determining the ex-dividend price:[20]

$$(P_0 - P_X)/D = (1 - t_P)/(1 - t_G)$$

---

[20]Edwin Elton and Martin Gruber, "Marginal Stockholder Tax Rates and the Clientele Effect," *Review of Economics and Statistics* 52 (February 1970).

Here P_0 is the price just before the stock goes ex, P_X is the ex-dividend share price, D is the amount of the dividend per share, t_p is the relevant marginal personal tax rate on dividends, and t_G is the effective marginal tax rate on capital gains.

a. If $t_p = t_G = 0$, how much will the share price fall when the stock goes ex?

b. If $t_p = 15$ percent and $t_G = 0$, how much will the share price fall?

c. If $t_p = 15$ percent and $t_G = 20$ percent, how much will the share price fall?

d. Suppose the only owners of stock are corporations. Recall that corporations get at least a 70 percent exemption from taxation on the dividend income they receive, but they do not get such an exemption on capital gains. If the corporation's income and capital gains tax rates are both 35 percent, by how much does this model predict the share price will fall?

e. What does this problem tell you about real-world tax considerations and the dividend policy of the firm?

19. **Dividends versus Reinvestment** National Business Machine Co. (NBM) has $4.5 million of extra cash after taxes have been paid. NBM has two choices to make use of this cash. One alternative is to invest the cash in financial assets. The resulting investment income will be paid out as a special dividend at the end of three years. In this case, the firm can invest in either Treasury bills yielding 3 percent or 5 percent preferred stock. IRS regulations allow the company to exclude from taxable income 70 percent of the dividends received from investing in another company's stock. Another alternative is to pay out the cash now as dividends. This would allow the shareholders to invest on their own in Treasury bills with the same yield or in preferred stock. The corporate tax rate is 35 percent. Assume the investor has a 31 percent personal income tax rate, which is applied to interest income and preferred stock dividends. The personal dividend tax rate is 15 percent on common stock dividends. Should the cash be paid today or in three years? Which of the two options generates the highest aftertax income for the shareholders?

20. **Dividends versus Reinvestment** After completing its capital spending for the year, Carlson Manufacturing has $1,000 extra cash. Carlson's managers must choose between investing the cash in Treasury bonds that yield 8 percent or paying the cash out to investors who would invest in the bonds themselves.

a. If the corporate tax rate is 35 percent, what personal tax rate would make the investors equally willing to receive the dividend or to let Carlson invest the money?

b. Is the answer to (a) reasonable? Why or why not?

c. Suppose the only investment choice is a preferred stock that yields 12 percent. The corporate dividend exclusion of 70 percent applies. What personal tax rate will make the stockholders indifferent to the outcome of Carlson's dividend decision?

d. Is this a compelling argument for a low dividend payout ratio? Why or why not?

Mini Case

ELECTRONIC TIMING, INC.

Electronic Timing, Inc. (ETI), is a small company founded 15 years ago by electronics engineers Tom Miller and Jessica Kerr. ETI manufactures integrated circuits to capitalize on the complex mixed-signal design technology and has recently entered the market for frequency timing generators, or silicon timing devices, which provide the timing signals or "clocks" necessary to synchronize electronic systems. Its clock products originally were used in PC video graphics applications, but the market subsequently expanded to include motherboards, PC peripheral devices, and other digital consumer electronics, such as digital television boxes and game consoles. ETI also designs and markets custom application-specific integrated circuits (ASICs) for industrial customers. The ASIC's design combines analog and digital, or mixed-signal, technology. In addition to Tom and Jessica, Nolan Pittman, who provided capital for the company, is the third primary owner. Each owns 25 percent of the $1 million shares outstanding. Several other individuals, including current employees, own the remaining company shares.

Recently, the company designed a new computer motherboard. The company's new design is both more efficient and less expensive to manufacture, and the ETI design is expected to become standard in many personal computers. After investigating the possibility of manufacturing the new motherboard, ETI determined that the costs involved in building a new plant would be prohibitive. The owners also decided that they were unwilling to bring in another large outside owner. Instead, ETI sold the design to an outside firm. The sale of the motherboard design was completed for an aftertax payment of $30 million.

1. Tom believes the company should use the extra cash to pay a special one-time dividend. How will this proposal affect the stock price? How will it affect the value of the company?

2. Jessica believes that the company should use the extra cash to pay off debt and upgrade and expand its existing manufacturing capability. How would Jessica's proposals affect the company?

3. Nolan is in favor of a share repurchase. He argues that a repurchase will increase the company's P/E ratio, return on assets, and return on equity. Are his arguments correct? How will a share repurchase affect the value of the company?

4. Another option discussed by Tom, Jessica, and Nolan would be to begin a regular dividend payment to shareholders. How would you evaluate this proposal?

5. One way to value a share of stock is the dividend growth, or growing perpetuity, model. Consider the following: The dividend payout ratio is 1 minus b, where b is the "retention" or "plowback" ratio. So, the dividend next year will be the earnings next year, E_1, times 1 minus the retention ratio. The most commonly used equation to calculate the sustainable growth rate is the return on equity times the retention ratio. Substituting these relationships into the dividend growth model, we get the following equation to calculate the price of a share of stock today:

$$P_0 = \frac{E_1(1 - b)}{R_S - \text{ROE} \times b}$$

What are the implications of this result in terms of whether the company should pay a dividend or upgrade and expand its manufacturing capability? Explain.

6. Does the question of whether the company should pay a dividend depend on whether the company is organized as a corporation or an LLC?

Raising Capital

On May 18, 2012, in a long-awaited initial public offering (IPO), social network Facebook went public at a price of $38 per share. The stock price opened trading at $42.05 before quickly falling back to $38. To the surprise of many, the stock closed at $38.23, barely unchanged from its IPO price. Over the next few trading days, investors turned antisocial and unfriended the stock, sending it tumbling to $32 per share. In contrast, when Twitter went public on November 7, 2013, at a price of $26, investors went #crazy. The stock quickly jumped to a high of $50.09, before closing the first day at $44.90. Then, on April 17, 2014, Chinese social media platform Weibo went public at a price of $17. The stock price jumped to $20.24 at the end of the day, a 19.1 percent increase.

Businesses large and small have one thing in common: They need long-term capital. This chapter describes how they get it. We pay particular attention to what is probably the most important stage in a company's financial life cycle—the IPO. Such offerings are the process by which companies convert from being privately owned to publicly owned. For many people, starting a company, growing it, and taking it public is the ultimate entrepreneurial dream.

This chapter examines how firms access capital in the real world. The financing method is generally tied to the firm's life cycle. Start-up firms are often financed via venture capital. As firms grow, they may want to "go public." A firm's first public offering is called an IPO, which stands for initial public offering. Later offerings are called SEOs for seasoned equity offerings. This chapter follows the life cycle of the firm, covering venture capital, IPOs, and SEOs. Debt financing is discussed toward the end of the chapter.

20.1 Early-Stage Financing and Venture Capital

One day, you and a friend have a great idea for a new computer software product that will help users communicate using the next-generation meganet. Filled with entrepreneurial zeal, you christen the product Megacomm and set about bringing it to market.

Working nights and weekends, you are able to create a prototype of your product. It doesn't actually work, but at least you can show it around to illustrate your idea. To actually develop the product, you need to hire programmers, buy computers, rent office space, and so on. Unfortunately, because you are both MBA students, your combined assets are not sufficient to fund a pizza party, much less a start-up company. You need what is often referred to as OPM—other people's money.

Your first thought might be to approach a bank for a loan. You would probably discover, however, that banks are generally not interested in making loans to start-up companies with no assets (other than an idea) run by fledgling entrepreneurs with no track record. Instead you search for other sources of capital.

One group of potential investors goes by the name of **angel investors**, or just **angels**. They may just be friends and family, with little knowledge of your product's industry and little experience backing start-up companies. However, some angels are more knowledgeable individuals or groups of individuals who have invested in a number of previous ventures.

VENTURE CAPITAL

Alternatively, you might seek funds in the venture capital (VC) market. While the term *venture capital* does not have a precise definition, it generally refers to financing for new, often high-risk ventures. Venture capitalists share some common characteristics, of which three[1] are particularly important:

1. *VCs are financial intermediaries that raise funds from outside investors.* VC firms are typically organized as limited partnerships. As with any limited partnership, limited partners invest with the general partner, who makes the investment decisions. The limited partners are frequently institutional investors, such as pension plans, endowments, and corporations. Wealthy individuals and families are often limited partners as well.

   This characteristic separates VCs from angels, since angels typically invest just their own money. In addition, corporations sometimes set up internal venture capital divisions to fund fledgling firms. However, Metrick and Yasuda point out that, since these divisions invest the funds of their corporate parent, rather than the funds of others, they are not—in spite of their name—venture capitalists.

2. *VCs play an active role in overseeing, advising, and monitoring the companies in which they invest.* For example, members of venture capital firms frequently join the board of directors. The principals in VC firms are generally quite experienced in business. By contrast, while entrepreneurs at the helm of start-up companies may be bright, creative, and knowledgeable about their products, they often lack much business experience.

3. *VCs generally do not want to own the investment forever.* Rather, VCs look for an exit strategy, such as taking the investment public (a topic we discuss in the next section) or selling it to another company. Corporate venture capital does not share this characteristic, since corporations are frequently content to have the investment stay on the books of the internal VC division indefinitely.

This last characteristic is quite important in determining the nature of typical VC investments. A firm must be a certain size to either go public or be easily sold. Since the investment is generally small initially, it must possess great growth potential; many businesses do not. For example, imagine an individual who wants to open a gourmet restaurant. If the owner is a true "foodie" with no desire to expand beyond one location, it is unlikely the restaurant will ever become large enough to go public. By contrast, firms in high-tech fields often have significant growth potential and many VC firms specialize in this area. Figure 20.1 shows VC investments by industry. As can be seen, a large percentage of these investments are in high-tech fields.

How often do VC investments have successful exits? While data on exits are difficult to come by, Figure 20.2 shows outcomes for more than 11,000 companies funded in the 1990s. As can be seen, nearly 50 percent (=14% + 33%) went public or were acquired. However, the Internet bubble reached its peak in early 2000, so the period covered in the table may have been an unusual one.

---

[1]These characteristics are discussed in depth in Andrew Metrick, and Ayako Yasuda, *Venture Capital and the Finance of Innovation,* 2nd ed. (Hoboken, New Jersey: John Wiley and Sons, 2011).

Figure 20.1   Venture Capital Investments in 2013 by Industry Sector

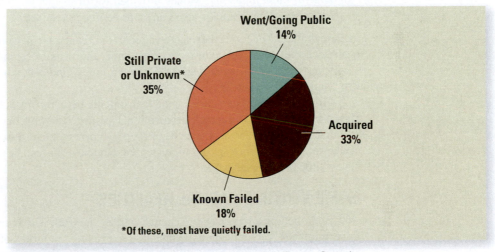

SOURCE: *National Venture Capital Association Yearbook 2014*, (New York: Thomson Reuters), Figure 7.0.

Figure 20.2
The Exit Funnel
Outcomes of the
11,686 Companies
First Funded 1991
to 2000

SOURCE: *National Venture Capital Association Yearbook 2014*, (New York: Thomson Reuters).

STAGES OF FINANCING

Both practitioners and scholars frequently speak of stages in venture capital financing. Well-known classifications for these stages are[2]:

1. *Seed money stage:* A small amount of financing needed to prove a concept or develop a product. Marketing is not included in this stage.

2. *Start-up:* Financing for firms that started within the past year. Funds are likely to pay for marketing and product development expenditures.

---

[2]Albert V. Bruno and Tyzoon T. Tyebjee, "The Entrepreneur's Search for Capital," *Journal of Business Venturing* (Winter 1985); see also Paul Gompers and Josh Lerner, *The Venture Capital Cycle* (Cambridge, MA: MIT Press, 2002).

Figure 20.3
2013 Venture Capital
Investment by
Company Stage

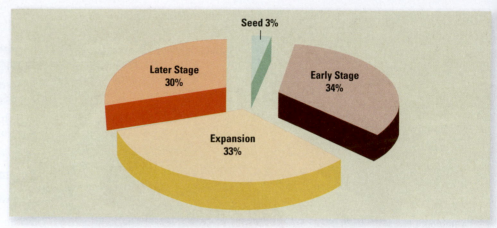

SOURCE: *National Venture Capital Association Yearbook 2014*, (New York: Thomson Reuters), Figure 6.0.

3. *First-round financing:* Additional money to begin sales and manufacturing after a firm has spent its start-up funds.

4. *Second-round financing:* Funds earmarked for working capital for a firm that is currently selling its product but still losing money.

5. *Third-round financing:* Financing for a company that is at least breaking even and is contemplating an expansion. This is also known as *mezzanine financing*.

6. *Fourth-round financing:* Money provided for firms that are likely to go public within half a year. This round is also known as *bridge financing*.

Although these categories may seem vague to the reader, we have found that the terms are well-accepted within the industry. For example, the venture capital firms listed in Pratt's *Guide to Private Equity and Venture Capital Sources*[3] indicate which of these stages they are interested in financing.

Figure 20.3 shows venture capital investments by company stage. The authors of this figure use a slightly different classification scheme. Seed and Early Stage correspond to the first two stages above. Later Stage roughly corresponds to Stages 3 and 4 above and Expansion roughly corresponds to Stages 5 and 6 above. As can be seen, venture capitalists invest little at the Seed stage.

SOME VENTURE CAPITAL REALITIES

Although there is a large venture capital market, the truth is that access to venture capital is very limited. Venture capital companies receive huge numbers of unsolicited proposals, the vast majority of which end up unread in the circular file. Venture capitalists rely heavily on informal networks of lawyers, accountants, bankers, and other venture capitalists to help identify potential investments. As a result, personal contacts are important in gaining access to the venture capital market; it is very much an "introduction" market.

Another simple fact about venture capital is that it is quite expensive. In a typical deal, the venture capitalist will demand (and get) 40 percent or more of the equity in the company. Venture capitalists frequently hold voting preferred stock, giving them various priorities in the event the company is sold or liquidated. The venture capitalist will typically demand (and get) several seats on the company's board of directors and may even appoint one or more members of senior management.

---

[3]Shannon Pratt, *Guide to Private Equity and Venture Capital Sources* (New York: Thompson Reuters, 2014).

Figure 20.4

Capital Commitments
to U.S. Venture Funds
($ in billions) 1985
to 2013

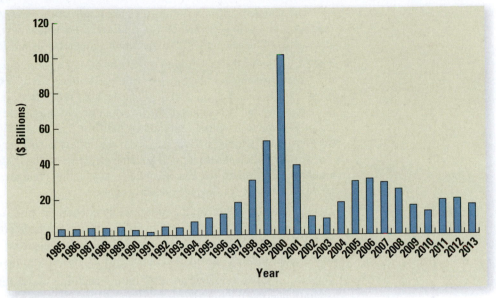

SOURCE: *National Venture Capital Association Yearbook 2014*, (New York: Thomson Reuters), Figure 3.0.

VENTURE CAPITAL INVESTMENTS AND ECONOMIC CONDITIONS

Venture capital investments are strongly influenced by economic conditions. Figure 20.4 shows capital commitments to U.S. venture capital firms over the period from 1985 to 2013. Commitments were essentially flat from 1985 to 1993 but rose rapidly during the rest of the 1990s, reaching their peak in 2000 before falling precipitously. To a large extent, this pattern mirrored the Internet bubble, with prices of high-tech stocks increasing rapidly in the late 1990s, before falling even more rapidly in 2000 and 2001. This relationship between venture capital activity and economic conditions continued in later years. Commitments rose during the bull market years between 2003 and 2006, before dropping from 2007 to 2010 in tandem with the more recent economic crisis.

20.2 The Public Issue

If firms wish to attract a large set of investors, they will issue public securities. There are a lot of regulations for public issues, with perhaps the most important established in the 1930s. The Securities Act of 1933 regulates new interstate securities issues and the Securities Exchange Act of 1934 regulates securities that are already outstanding. The Securities and Exchange Commission (SEC) administers both acts.

The basic steps for issuing securities are:

1. In any issue of securities to the public, management must first obtain approval from the board of directors.

2. The firm must prepare a **registration statement** and file it with the SEC. This statement contains a great deal of financial information, including a financial history, details of the existing business, proposed financing, and plans for the future. It can easily run to 50 or more pages. The document is required for all public issues of securities with two principal exceptions:
   a. Loans that mature within nine months.
   b. Issues that involve less than $5 million.

The second exception is known as the *small-issues exemption*. Issues of less than $5 million are governed by **Regulation A**, for which only a brief offering statement—rather than the full registration statement—is needed.

3. The SEC studies the registration statement during a *waiting period*. During this time, the firm may distribute copies of a preliminary **prospectus**. The preliminary prospectus is called a **red herring** because bold red letters are printed on the cover. A prospectus contains much of the information put into the registration statement, and it is given to potential investors by the firm. The company cannot sell the securities during the waiting period. However, oral offers can be made.

   A registration statement will become effective on the 20th day after its filing unless the SEC sends a *letter of comment* suggesting changes. After the changes are made, the 20-day waiting period starts anew.

4. The registration statement does not initially contain the price of the new issue. On the effective date of the registration statement, a price is determined and a full-fledged selling effort gets under way. A final prospectus must accompany the delivery of securities or confirmation of sale, whichever comes first.

5. **Tombstone** advertisements are used during and after the waiting period. An example is reproduced in Figure 20.5.

The tombstone contains the name of the issuer (the World Wrestling Federation, now known as World Wrestling Entertainment). It provides some information about the issue, and lists the investment banks (the underwriters) involved with selling the issue. The role of the investment banks in selling securities is discussed more fully in the following pages.

The investment banks on the tombstone are divided into groups called *brackets* based on their participation in the issue, and the names of the banks are listed alphabetically within each bracket. The brackets are often viewed as a kind of pecking order. In general, the higher the bracket, the greater is the underwriter's prestige. In recent years, the use of printed tombstones has declined, in part as a cost-saving measure.

Crowdfunding

On April 5, 2012, the JOBS Act was signed into law. A provision of this act allowed companies to raise money through *crowdfunding*, which is the practice of raising small amounts of capital from a large number of people, typically via the Internet. Crowdfunding was first used to underwrite the U.S. tour of British rock band Marillion, but the JOBS Act allows companies to sell equity by crowdfunding. Specifically, the JOBS Act allows a company to issue up to $1 million in securities in a 12-month period, and investors are permitted to invest up to $100,000 in crowdfunding issues per 12 months. Although crowdfunding has been passed into law, the SEC must still set the rules and regulations for these new "exchanges."

20.3 Alternative Issue Methods

When a company decides to issue a new security, it can sell it as a public issue or a private issue. If it is a public issue, the firm is required to register the issue with the SEC. If the issue is sold to fewer than 35 investors, it can be treated as a private issue. A registration statement is not required in this case.[4]

---

[4]However, regulation significantly restricts the resale of unregistered equity securities. For example, the purchaser may be required to hold the securities for at least one year (or more). Many of the restrictions were significantly eased in 1990 for very large institutional investors, however. The private placement of bonds is discussed in a later section.

Figure 20.5
An Example
of a Tombstone
Advertisement

This announcement is neither an offer to sell nor a solicitation of an offer to buy any of these securities.
The offering is made only by the Prospectus.

New Issue

11,500,000 Shares

World Wrestling Federation Entertainment, Inc.

Class A Common Stock

Price $17.00 Per Share

Copies of the Prospectus may be obtained in any State in which this announcement
is circulated from only such of the Underwriters, including the undersigned,
as may lawfully offer these securities in such State.

U.S. Offering

9,200,000 Shares

This portion of the underwriting is being offered in the United States and Canada.

Bear, Stearns & Co., Inc.

Credit Suisse First Boston

Merrill Lynch & Co.

Wit Capital Corporation

Allen & Company Incorporated	Banc of America Securities LLC	Deutsche Banc Alex. Brown	
Donaldson, Lufkin & Jenrette	A.G. Edwards & Sons, Inc.	Hambrecht & Quist	ING Barings
Prudential Securities	SG Cowen	Wassertein Perella Securities, Inc.	Advest, Inc.
Axiom Capital Management, Inc.	Blackford Securities Corp.	J.C. Bradford & Co.	
Joseph Charles & Assoc., Inc.	Chatsworth Securities LLC	Gabelli & Company, Inc.	
Gaines, Berland, Inc.	Jefferies & Company, Inc.	Josephthal & Co., Inc.	Neuberger Berman, LLC
Raymond James & Associates, Inc.		Sanders Morris Mundy	
Tucker Anthony Cleary Gull		Wachovia Securities, Inc.	

International Offering

2,300,000 Shares

This portion of the underwriting is being offered outside of the United States and Canada.

Bear, Stearns International Limited

Credit Suisse First Boston

Merrill Lynch International

Table 20.1   The Methods of Issuing New Securities

Method	Type	Definition
Public		
Traditional negotiated cash offer	Firm commitment cash offer	Company negotiates an agreement with an investment banker to underwrite and distribute the new shares. A specified number of shares are bought by underwriters and sold at a higher price.
	Best-efforts cash offer	Company has investment bankers sell as many of the new shares as possible at the agreed-upon price. There is no guarantee concerning how much cash will be raised.
	Dutch auction cash offer	Company has investment bankers auction shares to determine the highest offer price obtainable for a given number of shares to be sold.
Privileged subscription	Direct rights offer	Company offers the new stock directly to its existing shareholders.
	Standby rights offer	Like the direct rights offer, this contains a privileged subscription arrangement with existing shareholders. The net proceeds are guaranteed by the underwriters.
Nontraditional cash offer	Shelf cash offer	Qualifying companies can authorize all the shares they expect to sell over a two-year period and sell them when needed.
	Competitive firm cash offer	Company can elect to award the underwriting contract through a public auction instead of negotiation.
Private	Direct placement	Securities are sold directly to the purchaser, who, at least until recently, generally could not resell the securities for at least two years.

There are two kinds of public issues: the *general cash offer* and the *rights offer*. Cash offers are sold to all interested investors, and rights offers are sold to existing shareholders. Equity is sold by both the cash offer and the rights offer, though almost all debt is sold by cash offer.

A company's first public equity issue is referred to as an **initial public offering (IPO)** or an **unseasoned equity offering**. All initial public offerings are cash offers because, if the firm's existing shareholders wanted to buy the shares, the firm would not need to sell them publicly. A **seasoned equity offering (SEO)** refers to a new issue where the company's securities have been previously issued. A seasoned equity offering of common stock may be made by either a cash offer or a rights offer.

These methods of issuing new securities are shown in Table 20.1 and discussed in the next few sections.

20.4 The Cash Offer

As just mentioned, stock is sold to interested investors in a **cash offer.** If the cash offer is a public one, **investment banks** are usually involved. Investment banks are financial intermediaries that perform a wide variety of services. In addition to aiding in the sale of securities, they may facilitate mergers and other corporate reorganizations and act as brokers to both individual and institutional clients. You may well have heard of large Wall Street investment banking houses such as Goldman Sachs and Morgan Stanley.

For corporate issuers, investment bankers perform services such as the following:

Formulating the method used to issue the securities.

Pricing the new securities.

Selling the new securities.

There are three basic methods of issuing securities for cash:

1. *Firm commitment:* Under this method, the investment bank (or a group of investment banks) buys the securities for less than the offering price and accepts the risk of not being able to sell them. Because this function involves risk, we say that the investment banker *underwrites* the securities in a firm commitment. In other words, when participating in a firm commitment offering, the investment banker acts as an *underwriter*. (Because firm commitments are so prevalent, we will use *investment banker* and *underwriter* interchangeably in this chapter.)

   To minimize the risks here, a number of investment banks may form an underwriting group (**syndicate**) to share the risk and to help sell the issue. In such a group, one or more managers arrange or comanage the deal. The manager is designated as the lead manager or principal manager, with responsibility for all aspects of the issue. The other investment bankers in the syndicate serve primarily to sell the issue to their clients.

   The difference between the underwriter's buying price and the offering price is called the *gross spread* or *underwriting discount*. It is the basic compensation received by the underwriter. Sometimes the underwriter will get noncash compensation in the form of warrants or stock in addition to the spread.

   Firm commitment underwriting is really just a purchase–sale arrangement, and the syndicate's fee is the spread. The issuer receives the full amount of the proceeds less the spread, and all the risk is transferred to the underwriter. If the underwriter cannot sell all of the issue at the agreed-upon offering price, it may need to lower the price on the unsold shares. However, because the offering price usually is not set until the underwriters have investigated how receptive the market is to the issue, this risk is usually minimal. This is particularly true with seasoned new issues because the price of the new issue can be based on prior trades in the security.

   Since the offering price is usually set just before selling begins, the issuer doesn't know precisely what its net proceeds will be until that time. To determine the offering price, the underwriter will meet with potential buyers, typically large institutional buyers such as mutual funds. Often, the underwriter and company management will do presentations in multiple cities, pitching the stock in what is known as a *road show*. Potential buyers provide information about the price they would be willing to pay and the number of shares they would purchase at a particular price. This process of soliciting information about buyers and the prices and quantities they would demand is known as *bookbuilding*. As we will see, despite the bookbuilding process, underwriters frequently get the price wrong, or so it seems.

2. *Best efforts:* The underwriter bears risk with a firm commitment because it buys the entire issue. Conversely, the syndicate avoids this risk under a best-efforts offering because it does not purchase the shares. Instead, it merely acts as an agent, receiving a commission for each share sold. The syndicate is legally bound to use its best efforts to sell the securities at the agreed-upon offering price. Beyond this, the underwriter does not guarantee any particular amount of money to the issuer. This form of underwriting has become relatively rare.

3. *Dutch auction underwriting:* With **Dutch auction underwriting**, the underwriter does not set a fixed price for the shares to be sold. Instead, the underwriter conducts

an auction in which investors bid for shares. The offer price is determined from the submitted bids. A Dutch auction is also known by the more descriptive name *uniform price auction*. This approach is relatively new in the IPO market and has not been widely used there, but is very common in the bond markets. For example, it is the sole way that the U.S. Treasury sells its notes, bonds, and bills to the public.

To understand a Dutch or uniform price auction, consider a simple example. Suppose the Rial Company wants to sell 400 shares to the public. The company receives five bids as follows:

Bidder	Quantity	Price
A	100 shares	$16
B	100 shares	14
C	100 shares	12
D	200 shares	12
E	200 shares	10

Thus, bidder *A* is willing to buy 100 shares at $16 each, bidder *B* is willing to buy 100 shares at $14, and so on. The Rial Company examines the bids to determine the highest price that will result in all 400 shares being sold. For example, at $14, *A* and *B* would buy only 200 shares, so that price is too high. Working our way down, all 400 shares won't be sold until we hit a price of $12, so $12 will be the offer price in the IPO. Bidders *A* through *D* will receive shares, while bidder *E* will not.

There are two additional important points in our example. First, all the winning bidders will pay $12—even bidders *A* and *B*, who actually bid a higher price. The fact that all successful bidders pay the same price is the reason for the name "uniform price auction." The idea in such an auction is to encourage bidders to bid aggressively by providing some protection against submitting a high bid.

Second, notice that at the $12 offer price, there are actually bids for 500 shares, which exceeds the 400 shares Rial wants to sell. Thus, there has to be some sort of allocation. How this is done varies a bit; but in the IPO market the approach has been to simply compute the ratio of shares offered to shares bid at the offer price or better, which, in our example, is 400/500 = .8, and allocate bidders that percentage of their bids. In other words, bidders *A* through *D* would each receive 80 percent of the shares they bid at a price of $12 per share.

The period after a new issue is initially sold to the public is called the *aftermarket*. During this period, the members of the underwriting syndicate generally do not sell shares of the new issue for less than the offer price.

In most offerings, the principal underwriter is permitted to buy shares if the market price falls below the offering price. The purpose is to *support* the market and *stabilize* the price from temporary downward pressure. If the issue remains unsold after a time (e.g., 30 days), members may leave the group and sell their shares at whatever price the market will allow.

Many underwriting contracts contain a **Green Shoe provision**, which gives the members of the underwriting group the option to purchase additional shares at the offering price.[5] The stated reason for the Green Shoe option is to cover excess demand and over-subscription. Green Shoe options usually last for about 30 days and involve 15 percent of

---

[5]The Green Shoe Corp. was the first firm to allow this provision.

the newly issued shares. The Green Shoe option is a benefit to the underwriting syndicate and a cost to the issuer. If the market price of the new issue goes above the offering price within 30 days, the underwriters can buy shares from the issuer and immediately resell the shares to the public.

Almost all underwriting agreements contain *lockups*. Such arrangements specify how long insiders must wait after an IPO before they can sell some of their stock. Typically, lockup periods are set at 180 days. Thus, insiders must maintain a significant economic interest in the company for six months following the IPO. Lockups are also important because it is not unusual for the number of locked-up insider shares to exceed the number of shares held by the public. Thus, when the lockup period ends, insiders may sell a large number of shares, thereby depressing share price.

Beginning well before an offering and extending for 40 calendar days following an IPO, the SEC requires that a firm and its managing underwriters observe a "quiet period." This means that all communication with the public must be limited to ordinary announcements and other purely factual matters. The SEC's logic is that all relevant information should be contained in the prospectus. An important result of this requirement is that the underwriters' analysts are prohibited from making recommendations to investors. As soon as the quiet period ends, however, the managing underwriters typically publish research reports, usually accompanied by a favorable "buy" recommendation.

Firms that don't stay quiet can have their IPOs delayed. For example, just before Google's IPO, an interview with cofounders Sergey Brin and Larry Page appeared in *Playboy*. The interview almost caused a postponement of the IPO, but Google was able to amend its prospectus in time. However, in May 2004, Salesforce.com's IPO was delayed because an interview with CEO Marc Benioff appeared in *The New York Times*. Salesforce.com finally went public two months later.

INVESTMENT BANKS

Investment banks are at the heart of new security issues. They provide advice, market the securities (after investigating the market's receptiveness to the issue), and underwrite the proceeds. They accept the risk that the market price may fall between the date the offering price is set and the time the issue is sold.

An investment banker's success depends on reputation. A good reputation can help investment bankers retain customers and attract new ones. In other words, financial economists argue that each investment bank has a reservoir of "reputation capital." One measure of this reputation capital is the pecking order among investment banks which, as we mentioned earlier, even extends to the brackets of the tombstone ad in Figure 20.5. MBA students are aware of this order because they know that accepting a job with a top-tier firm is universally regarded as more prestigious than accepting a job with a lower-tier firm.

Investment banks put great importance in their relative rankings and view downward movement in their placement with much distaste. This jockeying for position may seem as unimportant as the currying of royal favor in the court of Louis XVI. However, in any industry where reputation is so important, the firms in the industry must guard theirs with great vigilance.

A firm can offer its securities to the underwriter on either a competitive or a negotiated basis. In a **competitive offer**, the issuing firm sells its securities to the underwriter with the highest bid. In a **negotiated offer**, the issuing firm works with one underwriter. Because the firm generally does not negotiate with many underwriters concurrently, negotiated deals may suffer from lack of competition.

In Their Own Words

Whereas competitive bidding occurs frequently in other areas of commerce, it may surprise you that negotiated deals in investment banking occur with all but the largest issuing firms. Investment bankers point out that they must expend much time and effort learning about the issuer before setting an issue price and a fee schedule. Except in the case of large issues, underwriters could not, it is argued, commit this time without the near certainty of receiving the contract.

Studies generally show that issuing costs are higher in negotiated deals than in competitive ones. However, many financial economists point out that the underwriter gains a great deal of information about the issuing firm through negotiation—information likely to increase the probability of a successful offering.

THE OFFERING PRICE

Determining the correct offering price is the most difficult task the lead investment bank faces in an initial public offering. The issuing firm faces a potential cost if the offering price is set too high or too low. If the issue is priced too high, it may be unsuccessful and have to be withdrawn. If the issue is priced below the true market price, the issuer's existing shareholders will experience an opportunity loss. The process of determining the best offer price is called **bookbuilding**. In bookbuilding, potential investors commit to buying a certain number of shares at various prices.

Table 20.2

Number of Offerings, Average First-Day Return, and Gross Proceeds of Initial Public Offerings: 1960–2014

Year	Number of Offerings*	Average First-Day Return, %†
1960–1969	2,661	21.2%
1970–1979	1,536	7.1
1980–1989	2,044	7.2
1990–1999	4,205	21.0
2000–2009	1,299	29.1
2010–2014	628	16.1
1960–2014	**12,373**	**16.9%**

*The number of offerings excludes IPOs with an offer price of less than $5.00, ADRs, best efforts, units, and Regulation A offers (small issues, raising less than $1.5 million during the 1980s), real estate investment trusts (REITs), partnerships, and closed-end funds. Banks and S&Ls and non-CRSP-listed IPOs are included.

†First-day returns are computed as the percentage return from the offering price to the first closing market price.

‡Gross proceeds data are from Securities Data Co., and they exclude overallotment options but include the international tranche, if any. No adjustments for inflation have been made.

SOURCE: Professor Jay R. Ritter, University of Florida.

Underpricing is fairly common. For example, Ritter examined 12,373 firms that went public between 1960 and 2014 in the United States. He found that the average IPO rose in price 16.9 percent in the first day of trading following issuance (see Table 20.2). These figures are not annualized!

Underpricing obviously helps new shareholders earn a higher return on the shares they buy. However, the existing shareholders of the issuing firm are not helped by underpricing. To them, it is an indirect cost of issuing new securities. For example, consider Chinese online retailer Alibaba's IPO in September 2014. The stock was priced at $68 in the IPO and rose to a first-day high of $99.70, before closing at $93.89, a gain of about 38.1 percent. Based on these numbers, Alibaba was underpriced by about $25.89 per share. Because Alibaba sold 320.1 million shares, the company missed out on an additional $8.3 billion (= $25.89 × 320.1 million), a record amount "left on the table." The previous record of $5.1 billion was held by Visa, set in its 2008 IPO.

UNDERPRICING: A POSSIBLE EXPLANATION

There are several possible explanations for underpricing, but so far there is no agreement among scholars as to which explanation is correct. We now provide two well-known explanations for underpricing. The first explanation begins with the observation that when the price of a new issue is too low, the issue is often *oversubscribed*. This means investors will not be able to buy all of the shares they want, and the underwriters will allocate the shares among investors. The average investor will find it difficult to get shares in an oversubscribed offering because there will not be enough shares to go around. Although initial public offerings have positive initial returns on average, a significant fraction of them have price drops. Thus, an investor submitting an order for all new issues may be allocated more shares in issues that go down in price than in issues that go up in price.

Consider this tale of two investors. Ms. Smarts knows precisely what companies are worth when their shares are offered. Mr. Average knows only that prices usually rise in the first month after the IPO. Armed with this information, Mr. Average decides to buy 1,000 shares of every IPO. Does Mr. Average actually earn an abnormally high average return across all initial offerings?

In Their Own Words

JAY RITTER ON IPO UNDERPRICING AROUND THE WORLD

The United States is not the only country in which initial public offerings (IPOs) of common stock are underpriced. The phenomenon exists in every country with a stock market, although the extent of underpricing varies from country to country.

In general, countries with developed capital markets have more moderate underpricing than in emerging markets. During the Internet bubble of 1999–2000, however, underpricing in the developed capital markets increased dramatically. In the United States, for example, the average first-day return during 1999–2000 was 65 percent. Since the bursting of the Internet bubble in mid-2000, the level of underpricing

in the United States, Germany, and other developed capital markets has returned to more traditional levels.

The underpricing of Chinese IPOs used to be extreme, but in recent years it has moderated. In the 1990s Chinese government regulations required that the offer price could not be more than 15 times earnings, even when comparable stocks had a price–earnings ratio of 45. In 2011–2012, the average first-day return was 21%. But in 2013, there were no IPOs in China at all, due to a moratorium that the government imposed because it thought that an increase in the supply of shares would depress stock prices.

The following table gives a summary of the average first-day returns on IPOs in a number of countries around the world, with the figures collected from a number of studies by various authors.

Country	Sample Size	Time Period	Avg. Initial Return %	Country	Sample Size	Time Period	Avg. Initial Return %
Argentina	26	1991–2013	4.2	Malaysia	474	1980–2013	56.2
Australia	1,562	1976–2011	21.8	Mauritius	40	1989–2005	15.2
Austria	10.3	1971–2013	6.4	Mexico	88	1987–1994	15.9
Belgium	114	1984–2006	13.5	Morocco	19	2004–2007	47.2
Brazil	275	1979–2011	33.1	Netherlands	181	1982–2006	10.2
Bulgaria	9	2004–2007	36.5	New Zealand	214	1979–2006	20.3
Canada	720	1971–2013	6.5	Nigeria	114	1989–2006	12.7
Chile	81	1982–2013	7.4	Norway	153	1984–2006	9.6
China	2,512	1990–2013	118.4	Pakistan	57	2000–2010	32.0
Cyprus	73	1997–2012	20.3	Philippines	123	1987–2006	21.2
Denmark	164	1984–2011	7.4	Poland	309	1991–2012	13.3
Egypt	62	1990–2010	10.4	Portugal	28	1992–2006	11.6
Finland	168	1971–2013	16.9	Russia	40	1999–2006	4.2
France	697	1983–2010	10.5	Saudi Arabia	76	2003–2010	264.5
Germany	736	1978–2011	24.2	Singapore	591	1973–2011	26.1
Greece	373	1976–2013	50.8	South Africa	285	1980–2007	18.0
Hong Kong	1,486	1980–2013	15.8	Spain	128	1986–2006	10.9
India	2,964	1990–2011	88.5	Sri Lanka	105	1987–2008	33.5
Indonesia	441	1990–2013	25.0	Sweden	374	1980–2011	27.2
Iran	279	1991–2004	22.4	Switzerland	159	1983–2008	28.0
Ireland	38	1991–2013	21.6	Taiwan	1,620	1980–2013	38.1
Israel	348	1990–2006	13.8	Thailand	459	1987–2007	36.6
Italy	312	1985–2013	15.2	Turkey	355	1990–2011	10.3
Japan	3,236	1970–2013	41.7	United Kingdom	4,932	1959–2012	16.0
Jordan	53	1999–2008	149.0	United States	12,373	1960–2014	16.9
Korea	1,720	1980–2013	59.3				

Jay R. Ritter is Cordell Professor of Finance at the University of Florida. An outstanding scholar, he is well known for his insightful analyses of new issues and going public.

SOURCE: Jay R. Ritter's website.

The answer is no, and at least one reason is Ms. Smarts. For example, because Ms. Smarts knows that company *XYZ* is underpriced, she invests all her money in its IPO. When the issue is oversubscribed, the underwriters must allocate the shares between Ms. Smarts and Mr. Average. If they do this on a pro rata basis and if Ms. Smarts has bid for, say, twice as many shares as Mr. Average, she will get two shares for each one Mr. Average receives. The net result is that when an issue is underpriced, Mr. Average cannot buy as much of it as he wants.

Ms. Smarts also knows that company *ABC* is overpriced. In this case, she avoids its IPO altogether, and Mr. Average ends up with a full 1,000 shares. To summarize, Mr. Average receives fewer shares when more knowledgeable investors swarm to buy an underpriced issue, but he gets all he wants when the smart money avoids the issue.

This is called the *winner's curse,* and it is one possible reason why IPOs have such a large average return. When the average investor wins and gets his allocation, it is because those who knew better avoided the issue. To counteract the winner's curse and attract the average investor, underwriters underprice issues.[6]

Perhaps a simpler explanation for underpricing is risk. Although IPOs on average have positive initial returns, a significant fraction experience price drops. A price drop would cause the underwriter a loss on his own holdings. In addition, the underwriter risks being sued by angry customers for selling overpriced securities. Underpricing mitigates both problems.

20.5 The Announcement of New Equity and the Value of the Firm

As mentioned, when firms return to the equity markets for additional funds, they arrange for a seasoned equity offering (SEO). The basic processes for an SEO and an IPO are the same. However, something curious happens on the announcement day of an SEO. It seems reasonable that long-term financing is used to fund positive net present value projects. Consequently, when the announcement of external equity financing is made, one might think that the firm's stock price would go up. As we mentioned in an earlier chapter, precisely the opposite actually happens. The firm's stock price tends to decline on the announcement of a new issue of common stock. Plausible reasons for this strange result include:

1. *Managerial information:* If managers have superior information about the market value of the firm, they may know when the firm is overvalued. If they do, they might attempt to issue new shares of stock when the market value exceeds the correct value. This will benefit existing shareholders. However, the potential new shareholders are not stupid. They will infer overvaluation from the new issue, thereby bidding down the stock price on the announcement date of the issue.

2. *Debt capacity:* We argued in an earlier chapter that a firm likely chooses its debt–equity ratio by balancing the tax shield from the debt against the cost of financial distress. When the managers of a firm have special information that the probability of financial distress has risen, the firm is more likely to raise capital through stock than through debt. If the market infers this chain of events, the stock price should fall on the announcement date of an equity issue.

---

[6]This explanation was first suggested in Kevin Rock, "Why New Issues Are Underpriced," *Journal of Financial Economics* 15 (1986).

3. *Issue costs:* As we discuss in the next section, there are substantial costs associated with selling securities.

Whatever the reason, a drop in stock price following the announcement of a new issue is an example of an indirect cost of selling securities. This drop might typically be on the order of 3 percent for an industrial corporation (and somewhat smaller for a public utility); so, for a large company, it can represent a substantial amount of money. We label this drop the *abnormal return* in our discussion of the costs of new issues that follows.

To give a couple of recent examples, in April 2014, 3D printer company Voxeljet announced a secondary offering. Its stock fell about 19.1 percent on the day of the announcement. Also in April 2014, Hi-Crush Partners completed a secondary offering. Its stock dropped 7.4 percent on the day of the announcement.

20.6 The Cost of New Issues

Issuing securities to the public is not free. The costs fall into six categories:

1. Gross spread, or underwriting discount:	The spread is the difference between the price the issuer receives and the price offered to the public.
2. Other direct expenses:	These are costs incurred by the issuer that are not part of the compensation to underwriters. They include filing fees, legal fees, and taxes—all reported in the prospectus.
3. Indirect expenses:	These costs are not reported in the prospectus and include the time management spends on the new issue.
4. Abnormal returns:	In a seasoned issue of stock, the price typically drops by about 3 percent upon the announcement of the issue. The drop protects new shareholders from buying overpriced stock.
5. Underpricing:	For initial public offerings, the stock typically rises substantially after the issue date. This underpricing is a cost to the firm because the stock is sold for less than its efficient price in the aftermarket.
6. Green Shoe option:	The Green Shoe option gives the underwriters the right to buy additional shares at the offer price to cover overallotments. This option is a cost to the firm because the underwriter will buy additional shares only when the offer price is below the price in the aftermarket.

Table 20.3 reports direct costs as a percentage of the gross amount raised for IPOs, SEOs, straight (ordinary) bonds, and convertible bonds sold by U.S. companies over the

Table 20.3 Direct Costs as a Percentage of Gross Proceeds for Equity (IPOs and SEOs) and Straight and Convertible Bonds Offered by Domestic Operating Companies: 1990–2008

Proceeds ($ millions)	IPOs				SEOs			
	Number of Issues	Gross Spread	Other Direct Expense	Total Direct Cost	Number of Issues	Gross Spread	Other Direct Expense	Total Direct Cost
2.00–9.99	1,007	9.40%	15.82%	25.22%	515	8.11%	26.99%	35.11%
10.00–19.99	810	7.39	7.30	14.69	726	6.11	7.76	13.86
20.00–39.99	1,422	6.96	7.06	14.03	1,393	5.44	4.10	9.54
40.00–59.99	880	6.89	2.87	9.77	1,129	5.03	8.93	13.96
60.00–79.99	522	6.79	2.16	8.94	841	4.88	1.98	6.85
80.00–99.99	327	6.71	1.84	8.55	536	4.67	2.05	6.72
100.00–199.99	702	6.39	1.57	7.96	1,372	4.34	.89	5.23
200.00–499.99	440	5.81	1.03	6.84	811	3.72	1.22	4.94
500.00 and up	155	5.01	.49	5.50	264	3.10	.27	3.37
Total/Avg	**6,265**	**7.19**	**3.18**	**10.37**	**7,587**	**5.02**	**2.68**	**7.69**

Proceeds ($ millions)	Straight Bonds				Convertible Bonds			
	Number of Issues	Gross Spread	Other Direct Expense	Total Direct Cost	Number of Issues	Gross Spread	Other Direct Expense	Total Direct Cost
2.00–9.99	3,962	1.64%	2.40%	4.03%	14	6.39%	3.43%	9.82%
10.00–19.99	3,400	1.50	1.71	3.20	23	5.52	3.09	8.61
20.00–39.99	2,690	1.25	.92	2.17	30	4.63	1.67	6.30
40.00–59.99	3,345	.81	.79	1.59	35	3.49	1.04	4.54
60.00–79.99	891	1.65	.80	2.44	60	2.79	.62	3.41
80.00–99.99	465	1.41	.57	1.98	16	2.30	.62	2.92
100.00–199.99	4,949	1.61	.52	2.14	82	2.66	.42	3.08
200.00–499.99	3,305	1.38	.33	1.71	46	2.65	.33	2.99
500.00 and up	1,261	.61	.15	.76	7	2.16	.13	2.29
Total/Avg	**24,268**	**1.38**	**.61**	**2.00**	**313**	**3.07**	**.85**	**3.92**

SOURCE: Inmoo Lee, Scott Lochhead, Jay Ritter, and Quanshiu Zhao, "The Costs of Raising Capital," *Journal of Financial Research* 19 (Spring 1996), updated by the authors.

Table 20.4
Direct and
Indirect Costs,
in Percentages,
of Equity IPOS:
1990–2008

Proceeds ($ millions)	Number of Issues	Gross Spread	Other Direct Expense	Total Direct Cost	Underpricing
2.00–9.99	1,007	9.40%	15.82%	25.22%	20.42%
10.00–19.99	810	7.39	7.30	14.69	10.33
20.00–39.99	1,422	6.96	7.06	14.03	17.03
40.00–59.99	880	6.89	2.87	9.77	28.26
60.00–79.99	522	6.79	2.16	8.94	28.36
80.00–99.99	327	6.71	1.84	8.55	32.92
100.00–199.99	702	6.39	1.57	7.96	21.55
200.00–499.99	440	5.81	1.03	6.84	6.19
500.00 and up	155	5.01	.49	5.50	6.64
Total/Avg	**6,265**	**7.19**	**3.18**	**10.37**	**19.34**

SOURCE: Inmoo Lee, Scott Lochhead, Jay Ritter, and Quanshiu Zhao, "The Costs of Raising Capital," *Journal of Financial Research* 19 (Spring 1996), updated by the authors.

period from 1990 through 2008. Direct costs only include gross spread and other direct expenses (Items 1 and 2 above).

The direct costs alone can be very large, particularly for smaller issues (less than $10 million). On a smaller IPO, for example, the total direct costs amount to 25.22 percent of the amount raised. This means that if a company sells $10 million in stock, it can expect to net only about $7.5 million; the other $2.5 million goes to cover the underwriter spread and other direct expenses.

Overall, four clear patterns emerge from Table 20.3. First, with the possible exception of straight debt offerings (about which we will have more to say later), there are substantial economies of scale. The underwriter spreads are smaller on larger issues, and the other direct costs fall sharply as a percentage of the amount raised—a reflection of the mostly fixed nature of such costs. Second, the costs associated with selling debt are substantially less than the costs of selling equity. Third, IPOs have somewhat higher expenses than SEOs. Finally, straight bonds are cheaper to float than convertible bonds.

As we have discussed, the underpricing of IPOs is an additional cost to the issuer. To give a better idea of the total cost of going public, Table 20.4 combines the information on total direct costs for IPOs in Table 20.3 with data on underpricing. Comparing the total direct costs (in the fifth column) to the underpricing (in the sixth column), we see that, across all size groups, the total direct costs amount to about 10 percent of the proceeds raised, and the underpricing amounts to about 19 percent.

Recall from Chapter 8 that bonds carry different credit ratings. Higher-rated bonds are said to be investment grade, whereas lower-rated bonds are noninvestment grade. Table 20.5 contains a breakdown of direct costs for bond issues after the investment and noninvestment grades have been separated. For the most part, the costs are lower for investment grade. This is not surprising given the risk of noninvestment grade issues. In addition, there are substantial economies of scale for both types of bonds.

THE COSTS OF GOING PUBLIC: A CASE STUDY

On April 10, 2014, Adamas Pharmaceuticals, the Emeryville, California-based pharmaceutical company, went public via an IPO. Adamas issued 3 million shares of stock at a price of $16 each. The lead underwriters on the IPO were Credit Suisse and Piper Jaffray, assisted by a syndicate of other investment banks. Even though the IPO raised a gross sum of $48 million, Adamas got to keep only $41.54 million after expenses. The biggest expense was the 7 percent underwriter spread, which is ordinary for an offering of this size. Adamas sold each of the 3 million shares to the underwriters for $14.88, and the underwriters in turn sold the shares to the public for $16.00 each.

But wait—there's more. Adamas spent $7,999 in SEC registration fees, $9,815 in other filing fees, and $125,000 to be listed on the NASDAQ Global Market. The company also spent $1.5 million in legal fees, $600,000 on accounting to obtain the necessary audits, $5,000 for a transfer agent to physically transfer the shares and maintain a list of shareholders, $260,000 for printing and engraving expenses, and finally, $592,816 in miscellaneous expenses.

As Adamas' outlays show, an IPO can be a costly undertaking! In the end, Adamas' expenses totaled $6.46 million, of which $3.36 million went to the underwriters and $3.1 million went to other parties. All told, the total cost to Adamas was 15.6 percent of the issue proceeds raised by the company.

20.7 Rights

When new shares of common stock are offered to the general public in a seasoned equity offering, the proportionate ownership of existing shareholders is likely to be reduced. However, if a preemptive right is contained in the firm's articles of incorporation, the firm must first offer any new issue of common stock to existing shareholders. This assures that each owner can keep his proportionate share.

An issue of common stock to existing stockholders is called a *rights offering*. Here each shareholder is issued an *option* to buy a specified number of new shares from the firm at a specified price within a specified time, after which the rights expire. For example, a firm whose stock is selling at $30 may let current stockholders buy a fixed number of shares at $10 per share within two months. The terms of the option are evidenced by certificates known as *share warrants* or *rights*. Such rights are often traded on securities exchanges or over the counter. Rights offerings are very common in Europe but not in the United States.

THE MECHANICS OF A RIGHTS OFFERING

We illustrate the mechanics of a rights offering by considering National Power Company. National Power has 1 million shares outstanding and the stock is selling at $20 per share, implying a market capitalization of $20 million. The company plans to raise $5 million of new equity funds by a rights offering.

The process of issuing rights differs from the process of issuing shares of stock for cash. Existing stockholders are notified that they have been given one right for each share of stock they own. Exercise occurs when a shareholder sends payment to the firm's subscription agent (usually a bank) and turns in the required number of rights. Shareholders of National Power will have several choices: (1) subscribe for the full number of entitled shares, (2) sell the rights, or (3) do nothing and let the rights expire.

SUBSCRIPTION PRICE

National Power must first determine the **subscription price**, which is the price that existing shareholders are allowed to pay for a share of stock. A rational shareholder will

Table 20.5 Average Gross Spreads and Total Direct Costs for Domestic Debt Issues: 1990–2008

Convertible Bonds

Proceeds ($ millions)	Investment Grade				Junk or Not Rated			
	Number of Issues	Gross Spread	Other Direct Expense	Total Direct Cost	Number of Issues	Gross Spread	Other Direct Expense	Total Direct Cost
2.00–9.99	—	—	—	—	14	6.39%	3.43%	9.82%
10.00–19.99	1	14.12%	1.87%	15.98%	23	5.52	3.09	8.61
20.00–39.99	—	—	—	—	30	4.63	1.67	6.30
40.00–59.99	3	1.92	.51	2.43	35	3.49	1.04	4.54
60.00–79.99	6	1.65	.44	2.09	60	2.79	.62	3.41
80.00–99.99	4	.89	.27	1.16	16	2.30	.62	2.92
100.00–199.99	27	2.22	.33	2.55	82	2.66	.42	3.08
200.00–499.99	27	2.03	.19	2.22	46	2.65	.33	2.99
500.00 and up	11	1.94	.13	2.06	7	2.16	.13	2.29
Total/Avg	**79**	**2.15**	**.29**	**2.44**	**313**	**3.31**	**.98**	**4.29**

Straight Bonds

Proceeds ($ millions)	Investment Grade				Junk or Not Rated			
	Number of Issues	Gross Spread	Other Direct Expense	Total Direct Cost	Number of Issues	Gross Spread	Other Direct Expense	Total Direct Cost
2.00–9.99	2,709	.62%	1.28%	1.90%	1,253	2.77%	2.50%	5.27%
10.00–19.99	2,564	.59	1.17	1.76	836	3.15	1.97	5.12
20.00–39.99	2,400	.63	.74	1.37	290	3.07	1.13	4.20
40.00–59.99	3,146	.40	.52	.92	199	2.93	1.20	4.14
60.00–79.99	792	.58	.38	.96	99	3.12	1.16	4.28
80.00–99.99	385	.66	.29	.96	80	2.73	.93	3.66
100.00–199.99	4,427	.54	.25	.79	522	2.73	.68	3.41
200.00–499.99	3,031	.52	.25	.76	274	2.59	.39	2.98
500.00 and up	1,207	.31	.08	.39	54	2.38	.25	2.63
Total/Avg	**20,661**	**.52**	**.35**	**.87**	**3,607**	**2.76**	**.81**	**3.57**

SOURCE: Inmoo Lee, Scott Lochhead, Jay Ritter, and Quanshiu Zhao, "The Costs of Raising Capital," *Journal of Financial Research* 19 (Spring 1996), updated by the authors.

subscribe to the rights offering only if the subscription price is below the market price of the stock on the offer's expiration date. For example, if the stock price at expiration is $13 and the subscription price is $15, no rational shareholder will subscribe. Why pay $15 for something worth $13? National Power chooses a price of $10, which is well below the current market price of $20. As long as the market price does not fall by half before expiration, the rights offering will succeed.

NUMBER OF RIGHTS NEEDED TO PURCHASE A SHARE

National Power wants to raise $5 million in new equity. With a subscription price of $10, it will issue 500,000 new shares. This number can be determined by dividing the total amount to be raised by the subscription price:

$$\text{Number of new shares} = \frac{\text{Funds to be raised}}{\text{Subscription price}} = \frac{\$5,000,000}{\$10} = 500,000 \text{ shares}$$

Because stockholders typically get one right for each share of stock they own, National Power will issue 1 million rights. To determine how many rights must be exercised to get one share of stock, we can divide the number of existing (or old) shares of stock by the number of new shares:

$$\frac{\text{Number of rights needed}}{\text{to buy a share of stock}} = \frac{\text{``Old'' shares}}{\text{``New'' shares}} = \frac{1,000,000}{500,000} = 2 \text{ rights}$$

Thus a shareholder must give up two rights plus $10 to receive a share of new stock. If all the stockholders do this, National Power will raise the required $5 million.

Given that National Power wants to raise $5 million, the number of new shares and the number of rights needed to buy one new share follow from the subscription price, as indicated below:

Subscription Price	Number of New Shares	Number of Rights Needed to Buy One Share of Stock
$20	250,000 (= 5,000,000/20)	4 (= 1,000,000/250,000)
10	500,000 (= 5,000,000/10)	2 (= 1,000,000/500,000)
5	1,000,000 (= 5,000,000/5)	1 (= 1,000,000/1,000,000)

As can be seen, a lower subscription price leads the firm both to issue more shares and to reduce the number of rights needed to buy one share.

EFFECT OF RIGHTS OFFERING ON PRICE OF STOCK

Rights clearly have value. In the case of National Power, the right to buy a share of stock worth $20 for $10 is valuable.

Suppose a shareholder of National Power owns two shares of stock just before the rights offering. This situation is depicted in Table 20.6. Initially, the price of National Power is $20 per share, so the shareholder's total holding is worth 2 × $20 = $40. A stockholder with two shares will receive two rights. The National Power rights offer gives shareholders with two rights the opportunity to purchase one additional share for $10. The holding of the shareholder who exercises these rights and buys the new share would increase to three shares. The value of the new holding would be $40 + $10 = $50 (the $40 initial value plus the $10 paid to the company). Because the stockholder now holds

Table 20.6

The Value to the
Individual Shareholder
of National Power's
Rights

Initial Position of Shareholder	
Number of shares	2
Share price	$20
Value of holding	$40
Terms of Offer	
Subscription price	$10
Number of rights issued	2
Number of rights for a share	2
Shareholder Position after Offer	
Number of shares	3
Share price	$16.67
Value of holding	$50
Value of a Right	
Old price − New price	$20 − $16.67 = $3.33
New price − Subscription price	($16.67 − $10)/2 = $3.33
Number of rights for a share	

three shares, the price per share would drop to $50/3 = $16.67 (rounded to two decimal places).

The difference between the old share price of $20 and the new share price of $16.67 reflects the fact that the old shares carried rights to subscribe to the new issue. The difference must be equal to the value of one right—that is, $20 − $16.67 = $3.33. We can also calculate the value of a right in another way. The rights offer lets an individual pay $10 for a share worth $16.67, generating a gain of $6.67. Since the individual needs two rights for this transaction, a rational individual would be willing to pay as much as $3.33 (=$6.67/2) for a single right.

Just as we learned of an ex-dividend date in the previous chapter, there is an **ex-rights date** here. An individual buying the stock prior to the ex-rights date will receive the rights when they are distributed. An individual buying the stock on or after the ex-rights date will not receive the rights. In our example, the price of the stock prior to the ex-rights date is $20. An individual buying on or after the ex-rights date is not entitled to the rights. The price on or after the ex-rights date is $16.67.

Table 20.7 shows what happens to National Power. If all shareholders exercise their rights, the number of shares will increase to 1.5 million (=1 million + .5 million) and the value of the firm will increase to $25 million (=$20 million + $5 million). After the rights offering the value of each share will drop to $16.67 (=$25 million/1.5 million).

An investor holding no shares of National Power stock who wants to subscribe to the new issue can do so by buying rights. An outside investor buying two rights will pay $3.33 × 2 = $6.67 (to account for previous rounding). If the investor exercises the rights at a subscription cost of $10, the total cost would be $10 + $6.67 = $16.67. In return for this expenditure, the investor will receive a share of the new stock, which is worth $16.67.

Of course, outside investors can also buy National Power stock directly at $16.67 per share. In an efficient stock market it will make no difference whether new stock is obtained via rights or via direct purchase.

Table 20.7

National Power
Company Rights
Offering

Initial Position	
Number of shares	1 million
Share price	$20
Value of firm	$20 million
Terms of Offer	
Subscription price	$10
Number of rights issued	1 million
Number of rights for a share	2
After Offer	
Number of shares	1.5 million
Value of firm	$25 million
Share price	$16.67

EFFECTS ON SHAREHOLDERS

Shareholders can either sell their rights or exercise them, though it makes no difference which alternative is chosen. To see this, consider an investor owning two shares. She will be granted two rights. She can sell the two rights for $3.33 each, obtaining $3.33 $\times$ 2 = $6.67 in cash. Because the two shares are each worth $16.67, her holdings are valued at:

$$\begin{aligned}
\text{Shares} &= 2 \times \$16.67 = \$33.33 \\
\text{Sold rights} &= 2 \times \$\ 3.33 = \underline{\$\ 6.67} \\
\text{Total} &\qquad\qquad\ = \$40.00
\end{aligned}$$

Alternatively, if the shareholder exercises her rights, she ends up with three shares worth a total of $16.67 $\times$ 3 = $50. In other words, by spending $10, the value of her holdings are worth $10 more than the $40 value from selling her rights and holding on to her shares. Thus, the individual is indifferent between exercising and selling the rights.

It is obvious that after the rights offering, the new market price of the firm's stock will be lower than the price before the rights offering. As we have seen, however, stockholders have not suffered a loss from the offering. Thus, the stock price decline is very much like that in a stock split, a device described in Chapter 19. The lower the subscription price, the greater is the price decline resulting from a rights offering. Because shareholders receive rights equal in value to the price drop, the rights offering does *not* hurt stockholders.

There is one last issue. How do we set the subscription price in a rights offering? If you think about it, you will see that the subscription price really should not matter. It has to be below the market price of the stock for the rights to have value; but beyond this, the price is arbitrary. In principle, it could be as low as we cared to make it as long as it was not zero.

THE UNDERWRITING ARRANGEMENTS

Undersubscription can occur if investors throw away rights or if bad news causes the market price of the stock to fall below the subscription price. To ensure against these possibilities, rights offerings are typically arranged by **standby underwriting**. Here the underwriter makes a firm commitment to purchase the unsubscribed portion of the issue at the subscription price less a take-up fee. The underwriter usually receives a **standby fee** as compensation for this risk-bearing function.

In practice, the subscription price is usually set well below the current market price, making the probability of a rights failure quite small. Though a small percentage (less than 10 percent) of shareholders fail to exercise valuable rights, shareholders are usually allowed to purchase unsubscribed shares at the subscription price. This **oversubscription privilege** makes it unlikely that the corporate issuer would need to turn to its underwriter for help.

20.8 The Rights Puzzle

Smith calculated the issuance costs from three alternative methods: an equity issue with underwriting, a rights issue with standby underwriting, and a pure rights issue.[7] His results suggest that a pure rights issue is the cheapest of the three alternatives, with total costs as a percentage of proceeds being 6.17 percent, 6.05 percent, and 2.45 percent for the three alternatives, respectively.

If corporate executives are rational, they will raise equity in the cheapest manner. Thus, the preceding evidence suggests that issues of pure rights should dominate. Surprisingly, almost all new equity issues in the United States are sold without rights. Conversely, rights offerings are quite common elsewhere in the world. The avoidance of rights offerings in the United States is generally viewed as an anomaly in the finance profession, though a few explanations have been advanced:

1. Underwriters increase the stock price through their selling effort and enhanced public confidence. However, Smith could find no evidence of this in an examination of 52 rights offerings and 344 underwritten offerings.

2. Because the underwriter buys the shares at the agreed-upon price, it is providing insurance to the firm. That is, the underwriter loses if it is unable to sell all the shares to the public. However, the potential economic loss is probably not large. In most cases the offer price is set within 24 hours of the offering, by which time the underwriter has usually made a careful assessment of the market for the shares.

3. The underwriter certifies that the offering price is consistent with the true value of the issue, providing investors the comfort to purchase the stock.[8] This certification occurs because the underwriting firm obtains special access to the firm and is willing to put its reputation for correct pricing on the line.

4. Other arguments include: (a) The proceeds of underwritten issues are available sooner than are the proceeds from a rights offer; (b) underwriters provide a wider distribution of ownership than would be possible with a rights offering; (c) consulting advice from investment bankers may be beneficial; (d) stockholders find exercising rights a nuisance; and (e) the risk that the market price might fall below the subscription price is significant.

---

[7]Clifford W. Smith, Jr., "Alternative Methods for Raising Capital: Rights versus Underwritten Offerings," *Journal of Financial Economics* 5 (December 1977). Myron Slovin, Marie Sushka, and Kam Wah Lai found a similar difference in the United Kingdom, "Alternative Flotation Methods, Adverse Selection, and Ownership Structure: Evidence from Seasoned Equity Issuance in the U.K.," *Journal of Financial Economics* 57 (2000).

[8]James Booth and R. Smith, "The Certification Role of the Investment Banker in New Issue Pricing," *Midland Corporate Finance Journal* (Spring 1986).

All of the preceding arguments are pieces of the puzzle, but none seems very convincing. Further research on the topic is needed.

20.9 Dilution

A subject that comes up quite a bit in discussions involving the issuance of stock is **dilution**. Dilution refers to a loss in existing shareholders' value. There are several kinds:

1. Dilution of percentage ownership.
2. Dilution of stock price.
3. Dilution of earnings per share.
4. Dilution of book value per share.

Is dilution bad? Though the word "dilution" definitely has a negative connotation, we argue below that only dilution of stock price is unambiguously bad.

DILUTION OF PROPORTIONATE OWNERSHIP

The first type of dilution can arise whenever a firm sells shares to the general public. For example, Joe Smith owns 5,000 shares of Merit Shoe Company. Merit Shoe currently has 50,000 shares of stock outstanding; each share gets one vote. Joe thus controls 10 percent (=5,000/50,000) of the votes and receives 10 percent of the dividends.

If Merit Shoe issues 50,000 new shares of common stock to the public via a general cash offer, Joe's ownership in Merit Shoe may be diluted. If Joe does not participate in the new issue, his ownership will drop to 5 percent (=5,000/100,000). Notice that, if the equity offering is used to fund a positive–NPV project, the value of Joe's shares should rise. However, even in this case, he will now own a smaller percentage of the firm.

Because a rights offering would ensure Joe Smith an opportunity to maintain his proportionate 10 percent share, dilution of the ownership of existing shareholders can be avoided by using a rights offering.

STOCK PRICE DILUTION

To address stock price dilution, let's consider Upper States Manufacturing (USM), an all-equity firm with 1 million shares outstanding and earnings of $1,000,000 (or $1 per share) each year into perpetuity. If the discount rate is .20, the price per share is $5 (=$1/.20). The market value of the equity is $5 million (=$5 × 1 million). For simplicity, we ignore taxes.

Now imagine that USM decides to accept a project costing $2 million and generating earnings in perpetuity of $600,000 per year. The present value of the project is:

$$-\$2,000,000 + \$600,000/.20 = \$1,000,000$$

If the project is accepted, the earnings of the firm will increase to $1,600,000. Once the firm publicly announces the project, the discounted cash flow of the firm rises to:

$$\$1,600,000/.20 - \$2,000,000 = \$6,000,000$$

With a million shares outstanding, the stock price becomes $6.

Of course, new shares must be issued to raise the $2 million. With a stock price of $6, the firm must issue 333,333 (=2,000,000/6) additional shares. We can derive the $6 stock

	Initial	Positive NPV Project	Negative NPV Project	Zero NPV Project
Number of shares in firm	1,000,000	1,333,333	1,500,000	1,400,000
Annual earnings	$1,000,000	$1,600,000	$1,200,000	$1,400,000
Firm market value at announcement	$5,000,000	$6,000,000	$4,000,000	$5,000,000
Firm market value after funding		$8,000,000	$6,000,000	$7,000,000
Price per share	$5	$6	$4	$5
Book value	$10,000,000	$12,000,000	$12,000,000	$12,000,000
Book value per share	$10	$9	$8	$8.57

price in another way. Once the $2 million investment has been spent—that is, the project has been funded—the present value of the firm becomes $1,600,000/.20 = $8,000,000. The price per share can be calculated as $8,000,000/1,333,333 = $6. The basic results of this example are presented in the first two columns of Table 20.8.

Why does the share price rise in this example? Simply because the net present value of the project is positive. Suppose the project still costs $2 million but generates only $200,000 per year. The project has a negative NPV, lowering the stock price. The relevant numbers here are presented in the third column of Table 20.8.

The rule on stock price dilution is quite simple. The stock price rises if the firm issues stock to fund a project with a positive NPV. Conversely, the stock price falls if the project has a negative NPV. These conclusions are consistent with the fifth row of Table 20.8.

BOOK VALUE

We have not mentioned book value yet in this example. Let's now assume that the firm initially has a book value of $10 million, implying book value per share of $10. Why would the firm have a book value above the market value of $5 million? Most likely the firm is not doing well, perhaps because of poor management or bad industry prospects.

As a baseline case here, imagine the firm accepts a project with earnings each year into perpetuity of $400,000. The NPV of this project is:

$$-\$2,000,000 + \$400,000/.20 = 0$$

The price remains at $5 per share, implying the firm must issue 400,000 (= 2,000,000/5) new shares. Since the book value of the project equals its cost of $2,000,000, the book value of the firm rises to $12 million. With 400,000 shares issued, the book value per share falls to $8.57 (=$12 million/1.4 million). These numbers are displayed in the last column of Table 20.8.

Why does the book value per share drop? Simply because the original book value per share of $10 was well above the price or market value per share of $5. Since the project has an NPV of zero, the market value of the cash inflows from the project is equal to the book value or cost of the project, which is $2 million. By combining the book-to-market ratio of 2 for the existing firm with the book to market ratio of 1 for the project, the book-to-market ratio falls when the new project is funded. Since the market value per share stays the same at $5, the book value per share must fall.

Now, a manager might be upset with this decline in book value per share. But, is it really anything to worry about? No, because the price per share has remained at $5, implying that the shareholders have been unaffected. The general rule that managers should accept projects with positive NPVs because they boost stock prices and reject projects with negative NPVs still holds. What happens to book value is largely irrelevant.

Admittedly, we have examined the special case of a project with a zero NPV. If the project had a positive NPV, the resulting book value per share would have been higher than $8.57 because fewer shares would have to be issued. Conversely, if the project had a negative NPV, the resulting book value per share would have been lower. We can see this in Table 20.8 with the book value per share being $9 for the positive NPV project and $8 per share for the negative NPV project. But again, change in book value is irrelevant.

EARNINGS PER SHARE

Does EPS rise and fall in tandem with stock price? Not necessarily, and it is easy to come up with examples that show the difference. Again consider USM with initial EPS of $1. Suppose that the firm accepts a project that costs $2 million, as before. However, now imagine that the project generates just one cash flow, a payment of $5,184,000 three years from today. The net present value of this project is:

$$-\$2,000,000 + \$5,184,000/(1.20)^3 = \$1,000,000$$

The firm's value rises to $6 million (=$5 million + $1 million) and the price per share rises to $6. However, earnings per share in the first year fall below $1. Why? Because new shares must be issued to fund the project but the project does not generate any earnings in the first year. The general rule here is that a project with big growth in earnings over time may reduce EPS initially, even if the NPV is positive. This is an important point, because managerial compensation is frequently based on EPS. Managers compensated on EPS are inadvertently incentivized to avoid a project with low initial earnings, even if the project has a positive net present value. But this is not good for the stockholders. Again, from the shareholders' perspective managers should accept projects with positive NPVs and reject projects with negative NPVs. The immediate impact on EPS, like the impact on book value per share, is just not as important.

CONCLUSION

This example has focused on the impact of new issues of equity on dilution. We examined dilution of proportional ownership, stock price, book value per share, and earnings per share. We concluded that only the impact of new issues on stock price per share is relevant to a firm's stockholders.[9] Dilution of the other variables is irrelevant to the stockholders.

20.10 Shelf Registration

To simplify the procedure for issuing securities, the SEC currently allows **shelf registration**. Shelf registration permits a corporation to register an offering that it reasonably expects to sell within the next two years. A master registration statement is filed at the time of registration.

---

[9]In a rights offering, one should consider the impact on stock price prior to the ex-rights date.

The company is permitted to sell the issue whenever it wants over those two years as long as it distributes a short-form statement. For example, in February 2014, Farmville creator Zynga announced a shelf registration of 28.2 million shares of stock.

Not all companies are allowed shelf registration. The major qualifications are as follows:

1. The company must be rated *investment grade.*
2. The firm cannot have defaulted on its debt in the past three years.
3. The aggregate market value of the firm's outstanding stock must be more than $150 million.
4. The firm must not have violated the Securities Exchange Act of 1934 in the past three years.

Shelf registration allows firms to use the *dribble method* of new equity issuance. With dribbling, a company registers the issue and hires an underwriter to be its selling agent. The company sells shares in small amounts from time to time via a stock exchange. Companies that have used dribble programs include Wells Fargo & Company, Pacific Gas and Electric, and The Southern Company.

The rule has been controversial. Several arguments have been made against shelf registration:

1. The timeliness of disclosure is reduced with shelf registration because the master registration statement may have been prepared up to two years before the actual issue occurs.
2. Some investment bankers have argued that shelf registration will cause a market overhang because registration informs the market of future issues. It has been suggested that this overhang will depress market prices.

20.11 Issuing Long-Term Debt

The general procedures followed in a public issue of bonds are the same as those for stocks. The issue must be registered with the SEC, there must be a prospectus, and so on. The registration statement for a public issue of bonds, however, is different from the one for common stock. For bonds, the registration statement must indicate an indenture.

Another important difference is that more than 50 percent of all debt is issued privately. There are two basic forms of direct private long-term financing: term loans and private placement.

Term loans are direct business loans. These loans have maturities between one and five years. Most term loans are repayable during the life of the loan. The lenders include commercial banks, insurance companies, and other lenders that specialize in corporate finance. **Private placements** are similar to term loans except that the maturity is longer.

The important differences between direct private long-term financing and public issues of debt are:

1. A direct long-term loan avoids the cost of Securities and Exchange Commission registration.
2. Direct placement is likely to have more restrictive covenants.
3. It is easier to renegotiate a term loan or a private placement in the event of a default. It is harder to renegotiate a public issue because hundreds of holders are usually involved.

4. Life insurance companies and pension funds dominate the private placement segment of the bond market. Commercial banks are significant participants in the term loan market.

5. The costs of distributing bonds are lower in the private market.

The interest rates on term loans and private placements are usually higher than those on an equivalent public issue. This difference reflects the trade-off between a higher interest rate and more flexible arrangements in the event of financial distress, as well as the lower costs associated with private placements.

An additional, and very important, consideration is that the flotation costs associated with selling debt are much less than the comparable costs associated with selling equity.

Summary and Conclusions

1. Venture capital is a common source of financing in start-up and privately held firms. Venture capital is particularly important in financing high-tech enterprises. Venture capital financing was at its peak during the Internet bubble around the turn of the century.

2. A company's first public equity issue is called an IPO for initial public offering. IPOs are generally underpriced. That is, the stock price in the aftermarket is normally above the issue price.

3. A seasoned equity offering (SEO) refers to a new issue when the company's securities have already been publicly traded. On average, the stock price of the issuing company falls upon the announcement of an SEO.

4. The underwriter bears risk with a firm commitment because it buys the entire issue. Conversely, the investment banker avoids this risk under a best-efforts offering because it does not purchase the shares. Firm commitment underwriting is far more prevalent for large issues than is best-efforts underwriting.

5. Rights offerings are cheaper than general cash offers and eliminate the problem of underpricing. Yet most new equity issues in the United States are underwritten general cash offers.

6. While dilution in stock price hurts stockholders, dilution of proportionate interest, book value per share, and EPS—by themselves—do not.

7. Shelf registration allows a corporation to register an offering that it reasonably expects to sell within two years.

Concept Questions

1. **Debt versus Equity Offering Size**   In the aggregate, debt offerings are much more common than equity offerings and typically much larger as well. Why?

2. **Debt versus Equity Flotation Costs**   Why are the costs of selling equity so much larger than the costs of selling debt?

3. **Bond Ratings and Flotation Costs**   Why do noninvestment-grade bonds have much higher direct costs than investment-grade issues?

4. **Underpricing in Debt Offerings**   Why is underpricing not a great concern with bond offerings?

Use the following information to answer the next three questions. Zipcar, the car sharing company, went public in April 2011. Assisted by the investment bank Goldman Sachs, Zipcar sold 9.68 million shares at $18 each, thereby raising a total of $174.24 million. By the end of the first day of trading, the stock had zipped to $28 per share, down from a high of $31.50. Based on the end-of-day numbers, Zipcar shares were apparently underpriced by about $10 each, meaning that the company missed out on an additional $96.8 million.

5. **IPO Pricing**   The Zipcar IPO was underpriced by about 56 percent. Should Zipcar be upset at Goldman over the underpricing?

6. **IPO Pricing**   In the previous question, how would it affect your thinking to know that the company was incorporated about 10 years earlier, had only $186 million in revenues in 2010, and had never earned a profit? Additionally, the viability of the company's business model was still unproven.

7. **IPO Pricing**   In the previous two questions, how would it affect your thinking to know that in addition to the 9.68 million shares offered in the IPO, Zipcar had an additional 30 million shares outstanding? Of those 30 million shares, 14.1 million shares were owned by four venture capital firms, and 15.5 million shares were owned by the 12 directors and executive officers.

8. **Cash Offer versus Rights Offer**   Ren-Stimpy International is planning to raise fresh equity capital by selling a large new issue of common stock. Ren-Stimpy is currently a publicly traded corporation, and it is trying to choose between an underwritten cash offer and a rights offering (not underwritten) to current shareholders. Ren-Stimpy management is interested in minimizing the selling costs and has asked you for advice on the choice of issue methods. What is your recommendation and why?

9. **IPO Underpricing**   In 1980, a certain assistant professor of finance bought 12 initial public offerings of common stock. He held each of these for approximately one month and then sold them. The investment rule he followed was to submit a purchase order for every firm commitment initial public offering of oil and gas exploration companies. There were 22 of these offerings, and he submitted a purchase order for approximately $1,000 in stock for each of the companies. With 10 of these, no shares were allocated to this assistant professor. With 5 of the 12 offerings that were purchased, fewer than the requested number of shares were allocated.

The year 1980 was very good for oil and gas exploration company owners: On average, for the 22 companies that went public, the stocks were selling for 80 percent above the offering price a month after the initial offering date. The assistant professor looked at his performance record and found that the $8,400 invested in the 12 companies had grown to $10,000, representing a return of only about 20 percent (commissions were negligible). Did he have bad luck, or should he have expected to do worse than the average initial public offering investor? Explain.

10. **IPO Pricing**   The following material represents the cover page and summary of the prospectus for the initial public offering of the Pest Investigation Control Corporation (PICC), which is going public tomorrow with a firm commitment initial public offering managed by the investment banking firm of Erlanger and Ritter.

Answer the following questions:

a. Assume that you know nothing about PICC other than the information contained in the prospectus. Based on your knowledge of finance, what is your prediction for the price of PICC tomorrow? Provide a short explanation of why you think this will occur.

b. Assume that you have several thousand dollars to invest. When you get home from class tonight, you find that your stockbroker, whom you have not talked to for weeks, has called. She has left a message that PICC is going public tomorrow and that she can get you several hundred shares at the offering price if you call her back first thing in the morning. Discuss the merits of this opportunity.

PROSPECTUS   **PICC**

200,000 shares

PEST INVESTIGATION CONTROL CORPORATION

Of the shares being offered hereby, all 200,000 are being sold by the Pest Investigation Control Corporation, Inc. ("the Company"). Before the offering there has been no public market for the shares of PICC, and no guarantee can be given that any such market will develop.

These securities have not been approved or disapproved by the SEC, nor has the commission passed judgment upon the accuracy or adequacy of this prospectus. Any representation to the contrary is a criminal offense.

	Price to Public	Underwriting Discount	Proceeds to Company*
Per share	$11.00	$1.10	$9.90
Total	$2,200,000	$220,000	$1,980,000

*Before deducting expenses estimated at $27,000 and payable by the company.

This is an initial public offering. The common shares are being offered, subject to prior sale, when, as, and if delivered to and accepted by the Underwriters and subject to approval of certain legal matters by their Counsel and by Counsel for the Company. The Underwriters reserve the right to withdraw, cancel, or modify such offer and to reject offers in whole or in part.

Erlanger and Ritter, Investment Bankers
July 13, 2016

Prospectus Summary

The Company	The Pest Investigation Control Corporation (PICC) breeds and markets toads and tree frogs as ecologically safe insect-control mechanisms.
The Offering	200,000 shares of common stock, no par value.
Listing	The Company will seek listing on NASDAQ and will trade over the counter.
Shares Outstanding	As of June 30, 2016, 400,000 shares of common stock were outstanding. After the offering, 600,000 shares of common stock will be outstanding.
Use of Proceeds	To finance expansion of inventory and receivables and general working capital, and to pay for country club memberships for certain finance professors.

Selected Financial Information (amounts in thousands except per-share data)					
	Fiscal Year Ended June 30			**As of June 30, 2016**	
	2014	**2015**	**2016**	**Actual**	**As Adjusted for This Offering**
Revenues	$60.00	$120.00	$240.00	Working capital $ 8	$1,961
Net earnings	3.80	15.90	36.10	Total assets 511	2,464
Earnings per share	.01	.04	.09	Stockholders' equity 423	2,376

11. **Competitive and Negotiated Offers** What are the comparative advantages of a competitive offer and a negotiated offer, respectively?

12. **Seasoned Equity Offers** What are the possible reasons why the stock price typically drops on the announcement of a seasoned new equity issue?

13. **Raising Capital** Megabucks Industries is planning to raise fresh equity capital by selling a large new issue of common stock. Megabucks, a publicly traded corporation, is trying to choose between an underwritten cash offer and a rights offering (not underwritten) to current shareholders. Megabucks' management is interested in maximizing the wealth of current shareholders and has asked you for advice on the choice of issue methods. What is your recommendation? Why?

14. **Shelf Registration** Explain why shelf registration has been used by many firms instead of syndication.

15. **IPOs** Every IPO is unique, but what are the basic empirical regularities in IPOs?

Questions and Problems

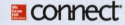

BASIC
(Questions 1–9)

1. **Rights Offerings** Chanelle, Inc., is proposing a rights offering. Presently, there are 625,000 shares outstanding at $87 each. There will be 85,000 new shares offered at $78 each.

   a. What is the new market value of the company?
   b. How many rights are associated with one of the new shares?
   c. What is the ex-rights price?
   d. What is the value of a right?
   e. Why might a company have a rights offering rather than a general cash offer?

2. **Rights Offering** The Clifford Corporation has announced a rights offer to raise $26 million for a new journal, the *Journal of Financial Excess*. This journal will review potential articles after the author pays a nonrefundable reviewing fee of $5,000 per page. The stock currently sells for $28 per share, and there are 2.9 million shares outstanding.

   a. What is the maximum possible subscription price? What is the minimum?
   b. If the subscription price is set at $25 per share, how many shares must be sold? How many rights will it take to buy one share?
   c. What is the ex-rights price? What is the value of a right?
   d. Show how a shareholder with 1,000 shares before the offering and no desire (or money) to buy additional shares is not harmed by the rights offer.

3. **Rights** Stone Shoe Co. has concluded that additional equity financing will be needed to expand operations and that the needed funds will be best obtained through a rights offering. It has correctly determined that as a result of the rights offering, the share price will fall from $64 to $62.05 ($64 is the "rights-on" price; $62.05 is the ex-rights price, also known as the *when-issued* price). The company is seeking $15 million in additional funds with a per-share subscription price equal to $50. How many shares are there currently, before the offering? (Assume that the increment to the market value of the equity equals the gross proceeds from the offering.)

4. **IPO Underpricing** The Woods Co. and the Garcia Co. have both announced IPOs at $40 per share. One of these is undervalued by $11, and the other is overvalued by $3, but you have no way of knowing which is which. You plan on buying 1,000 shares of each issue. If an issue is underpriced, it will be rationed, and only half your order will be filled. If you *could* get 1,000 shares in Woods and 1,000 shares in Garcia, what

would your profit be? What profit do you actually expect? What principle have you illustrated?

5. **Calculating Flotation Costs**   The St. Anger Corporation needs to raise $55 million to finance its expansion into new markets. The company will sell new shares of equity via a general cash offering to raise the needed funds. If the offer price is $32 per share and the company's underwriters charge a spread of 7 percent, how many shares need to be sold?

6. **Calculating Flotation Costs**   In the previous problem, if the SEC filing fee and associated administrative expenses of the offering are $1,900,000, how many shares need to be sold?

7. **Calculating Flotation Costs**   The Green Hills Co. has just gone public. Under a firm commitment agreement, Green Hills received $29.96 for each of the 7.5 million shares sold. The initial offering price was $32 per share, and the stock rose to $34.56 per share in the first few minutes of trading. Green Hills paid $1,950,000 in direct legal and other costs and $425,000 in indirect costs. What was the flotation cost as a percentage of funds raised?

8. **Price Dilution**   Raggio, Inc., has 145,000 shares of stock outstanding. Each share is worth $75, so the company's market value of equity is $10,875,000. Suppose the firm issues 30,000 new shares at the following prices: $75, $70, and $65. What will the effect be of each of these alternative offering prices on the existing price per share?

9. **Stock Offerings**   The Newton Company has 50,000 shares of stock that each sell for $40. Suppose the company issues 9,000 shares of new stock at the following prices: $40, $20, and $10. What is the effect of each of the alternative offering prices on the existing price per share?

INTERMEDIATE
(Questions 10–18)

10. **Dilution**   Teardrop, Inc., wishes to expand its facilities. The company currently has 6.8 million shares outstanding and no debt. The stock sells for $65 per share, but the book value per share is $20. Net income for Teardrop is currently $11.5 million. The new facility will cost $30 million, and it will increase net income by $675,000. The par value of the stock is $1 per share.

    a. Assuming a constant price–earnings ratio, what will the effect be of issuing new equity to finance the investment? To answer, calculate the new book value per share, the new total earnings, the new EPS, the new stock price, and the new market-to-book ratio. What is going on here?

    b. What would the new net income for Teardrop have to be for the stock price to remain unchanged?

11. **Dilution**   The all-equity firm Metallica Heavy Metal Mining (MHMM) Corporation wants to diversify its operations. Some recent financial information for the company is shown here:

Stock price	$75
Number of shares	65,000
Total assets	$9,400,000
Total liabilities	$4,100,000
Net income	$980,000

MHMM is considering an investment that has the same PE ratio as the firm. The cost of the investment is $1,500,000, and it will be financed with a new equity issue. The return on the investment will equal MHMM's current ROE. What will happen to the book value per share, the market value per share, and the EPS? What is the NPV of this investment? Does dilution take place?

12. Dilution   In the previous problem, what would the ROE on the investment have to be if we wanted the price after the offering to be $75 per share? (Assume the PE ratio remains constant.) What is the NPV of this investment? Does any dilution take place?

13. Rights   A company's stock currently sells for $73 per share. Last week the firm issued rights to raise new equity. To purchase a new share, a stockholder must remit $14 and three rights.

    a. What is the ex-rights stock price?
    b. What is the price of one right?
    c. When will the price drop occur? Why will it occur then?

14. Rights   Valley Corp.'s stock is currently selling at $37 per share. There are 1 million shares outstanding. The firm is planning to raise $2.5 million to finance a new project. What are the ex-rights stock price, the value of a right, and the appropriate subscription prices under the following scenarios?

    a. Two shares of outstanding stock are entitled to purchase one additional share of the new issue.
    b. Four shares of outstanding stock are entitled to purchase one additional share of the new issue.
    c. How does the stockholders' wealth change from part (a) to part (b)?

15. Rights   Hoobastink Mfg. is considering a rights offer. The company has determined that the ex-rights price will be $61. The current price is $68 per share, and there are 10 million shares outstanding. The rights offer would raise a total of $67 million. What is the subscription price?

16. Value of a Right   Show that the value of a right can be written as:

$$\text{Value of a right} = P_{RO} - P_X = (P_{RO} - P_S)/(N + 1)$$

where P_{RO}, P_S, and P_X stand for the "rights-on" price, the subscription price, and the ex-rights price, respectively, and N is the number of rights needed to buy one new share at the subscription price.

17. Selling Rights   Wuttke Corp. wants to raise $5,375,000 via a rights offering. The company currently has 950,000 shares of common stock outstanding that sell for $55 per share. Its underwriter has set a subscription price of $30 per share and will charge Wuttke a 6 percent spread. If you currently own 6,000 shares of stock in the company and decide not to participate in the rights offering, how much money can you get by selling your rights?

18. Valuing a Right   Mitsi Inventory Systems, Inc., has announced a rights offer. The company has announced that it will take four rights to buy a new share in the offering at a subscription price of $30. At the close of business the day before the ex-rights day, the company's stock sells for $60 per share. The next morning you notice that the stock sells for $54 per share and the rights sell for $5 each. Are the stock and/or the rights correctly priced on the ex-rights day? Describe a transaction in which you could use these prices to create an immediate profit.

Mini Case

EAST COAST YACHTS GOES PUBLIC

Larissa Warren and Dan Ervin have been discussing the future of East Coast Yachts. The company has been experiencing fast growth, and the future looks like clear sailing. However, the fast growth means that the company's growth can no longer be funded by internal sources, so Larissa and Dan have decided the time is right to take the company public. To this end, they have entered into discussions with the investment bank of Crowe & Mallard. The company has a working relationship with Robin Perry, the underwriter who assisted with the company's previous bond offering. Crowe & Mallard have helped numerous small companies in the IPO process, so Larissa and Dan feel confident with this choice.

Robin begins by telling Larissa and Dan about the process. Although Crowe & Mallard charged an underwriter fee of 4 percent on the bond offering, the underwriter fee is 7 percent on all initial stock offerings of the size of East Coast Yachts' initial offering. Robin tells Larissa and Dan that the company can expect to pay about $1,800,000 in legal fees and expenses, $15,000 in SEC registration fees, and $20,000 in other filing fees. Additionally, to be listed on the NASDAQ, the company must pay $100,000. There are also transfer agent fees of $8,500 and engraving expenses of $525,000. The company should also expect to pay $75,000 for other expenses associated with the IPO.

Finally, Robin tells Larissa and Dan that to file with the SEC, the company must provide three years' worth of audited financial statements. She is unsure of the costs of the audit. Dan tells Robin that the company provides audited financial statements as part of its bond indenture, and the company pays $325,000 per year for the outside auditor.

1. At the end of the discussion Dan asks Robin about the Dutch auction IPO process. What are the differences in the expenses to East Coast Yachts if it uses a Dutch auction IPO versus a traditional IPO? Should the company go public with a Dutch auction or use a traditional underwritten offering?

2. During the discussion of the potential IPO and East Coast Yachts' future, Dan states that he feels the company should raise $75 million. However, Larissa points out that if the company needs more cash soon, a secondary offering close to the IPO would be potentially problematic. Instead, she suggests that the company should raise $100 million in the IPO. How can we calculate the optimal size of the IPO? What are the advantages and disadvantages of increasing the size of the IPO to $100 million?

3. After deliberation, Larissa and Dan have decided that the company should use a firm commitment offering with Crowe & Mallard as the lead underwriter. The IPO will be for $85 million. Ignoring underpricing, how much will the IPO cost the company as a percentage of the funds received?

4. Many of the employees of East Coast Yachts have shares of stock in the company because of an existing employee stock purchase plan. To sell the stock, the employees can tender their shares to be sold in the IPO at the offering price, or the employees can retain their stock and sell it in the secondary market after East Coast Yachts goes public (once the 180-day lockup period expires). Larissa asks you to advise the employees about which option is best. What would you suggest to the employees?

21

Leasing

Have you ever flown on General Electric (GE) Airlines? Probably not; but with more than 1,570 planes, GE Capital Aviation Services (GECAS), part of GE, owns one of the largest aircraft fleets in the world. In fact, this financing arm of GE owns more than $43 billion in assets, generated more than $1 billion in profits during 2014, and has more than 230 customers in 75 countries. Why does GECAS own so many planes? It turns out more than one-third of all commercial jetliners worldwide are leased, which is what GECAS does. But why is GECAS in the business of buying assets, only to lease them out? And why don't the companies that lease from GECAS simply purchase the assets themselves? This chapter answers these and other questions associated with leasing.

21.1 Types of Leases

THE BASICS

A *lease* is a contractual agreement between a lessee and lessor. The agreement establishes that the lessee has the right to use an asset and in return must make periodic payments to the lessor, the owner of the asset. The lessor is either the asset's manufacturer or an independent leasing company. If the lessor is an independent leasing company, it must buy the asset from a manufacturer. Then the lessor delivers the asset to the lessee, and the lease goes into effect.

As far as the lessee is concerned, it is the use of the asset that is most important, not who owns the asset. The use of an asset can be obtained by a lease contract. Because the user can also buy the asset, leasing and buying involve alternative financing arrangements for the use of an asset. This is illustrated in Figure 21.1.

The specific example in Figure 21.1 happens often in the computer industry. Firm *U*, the lessee, might be a hospital, a law firm, or any other firm that uses computers. The lessor is an independent leasing company that purchased the equipment from a manufacturer such as IBM or Apple. Leases of this type are called **direct leases**. In the figure the lessor issued both debt and equity to finance the purchase.

Of course, a manufacturer like IBM could lease its *own* computers, though we do not show this situation in the example. Leases of this type are called **sales-type leasing**. In this case IBM would compete with the independent computer leasing company.

Figure 21.1   Buying versus Leasing

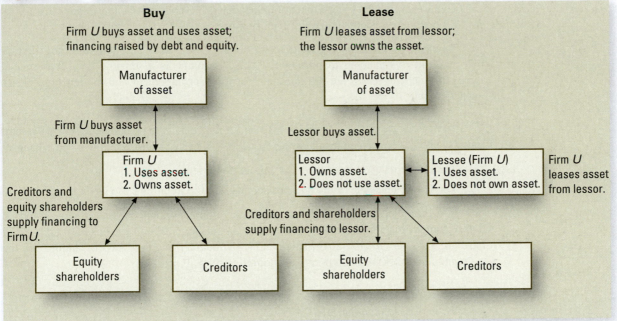

OPERATING LEASES

Years ago, a lease where the lessee received an operator along with the equipment was called an **operating lease**. Though the operating lease defies an exact definition today, this form of leasing has several important characteristics:

1. Operating leases are usually not fully amortized. This means that the payments required under the terms of the lease are not enough to recover the full cost of the asset for the lessor. This occurs because the term, or life, of the operating lease is usually less than the economic life of the asset. Thus, the lessor must expect to recover the costs of the asset by renewing the lease or by selling the asset for its residual value.

2. Operating leases usually require the lessor to maintain and insure the leased assets.

3. Perhaps the most interesting feature of an operating lease is the cancellation option. This option gives the lessee the right to cancel the lease contract before the expiration date. If the option to cancel is exercised, the lessee must return the equipment to the lessor. The value of a cancellation clause depends on whether future technological or economic conditions are likely to make the value of the asset to the lessee less than the value of the future lease payments under the lease.

To leasing practitioners, the preceding characteristics constitute an operating lease. However, accountants use the term in a slightly different way, as we will see shortly.

FINANCIAL LEASES

Financial leases are the exact opposite of operating leases, as is seen from their important characteristics:

1. Financial leases do not provide for maintenance or service by the lessor.
2. Financial leases are fully amortized.

3. The lessee usually has a right to renew the lease on expiration.

4. Generally, financial leases cannot be canceled. In other words, the lessee must make all payments or face the risk of bankruptcy.

Because of these characteristics, particularly (2), this lease provides an alternative method of financing to purchase. Hence, its name is a sensible one. Two special types of financial leases are the sale and leaseback arrangement and the leveraged lease arrangement.

Sale and Leaseback   A **sale and leaseback** occurs when a company sells an asset it owns to another firm and immediately leases it back. In a sale and leaseback two things happen:

1. The lessee receives cash from the sale of the asset.

2. The lessee makes periodic lease payments, thereby retaining use of the asset.

For example, in December 2014, airline Finnair announced that it had signed an agreement with Doric Asset Finance on the €75 million sale and leaseback of six ATR72 aircraft. And, in October 2014, semiconductor industry supplier Axcelis announced the sale and leaseback of its corporate headquarters for $50 million.

Leveraged Leases   A **leveraged lease** is a three-sided arrangement among the lessee, the lessor, and the lenders:

1. As in other leases, the lessee uses the assets and makes periodic lease payments.

2. As in other leases, the lessor purchases the assets, delivers them to the lessee, and collects the lease payments. However, the lessor puts up no more than 40 to 50 percent of the purchase price.

3. The lenders supply the remaining financing and receive interest payments from the lessor. Thus, the arrangement on the right side of Figure 21.1 would be a leveraged lease if the bulk of the financing was supplied by creditors.

The lenders in a leveraged lease typically use a nonrecourse loan. This means that the lessor is not obligated to the lender in case of a default. However, the lender is protected in two ways:

1. The lender has a first lien on the asset.

2. In the event of loan default, the lease payments are made directly to the lender.

The lessor puts up only part of the funds but gets the lease payments and all the tax benefits of ownership. These lease payments are used to pay the debt service of the nonrecourse loan. The lessee benefits because, in a competitive market, the lease payment is lowered when the lessor saves taxes.

21.2 Accounting and Leasing

Before November 1976, a firm could arrange to use an asset through a lease and not disclose the asset or the lease contract on the balance sheet. Lessees needed to report information on leasing activity only in the footnotes of their financial statements. Thus, leasing led to **off–balance sheet financing**.

In November 1976, the Financial Accounting Standards Board (FASB) issued its *Statement of Financial Accounting Standards No. 13* (FAS 13), "Accounting for Leases."

Table 21.1

Examples of Balance Sheets under FAS 13

Balance Sheet			
Truck is purchased with debt (the company owns a $100,000 truck):			
Truck	$100,000	Debt	$100,000
Land	100,000	Equity	100,000
Total assets	$200,000	Total debt plus equity	$200,000
Operating lease (the company has an operating lease for the truck):			
Truck	$ 0	Debt	$ 0
Land	100,000	Equity	100,000
Total assets	$100,000	Total debt plus equity	$100,000
Capital lease (the company has a capital lease for the truck):			
Assets under capital lease	$100,000	Obligations under capital lease	$100,000
Land	100,000	Equity	100,000
Total assets	$200,000	Total debt plus equity	$200,000

Under FAS 13, certain leases are classified as capital leases. For a capital lease, the present value of the lease payments appears on the right side of the balance sheet. The identical value appears on the left side of the balance sheet as an asset.

FASB classifies all other leases as operating leases, though FASB's definition differs from that of nonaccountants. No mention of the lease appears on the balance sheet for operating leases.

The accounting implications of this distinction are illustrated in Table 21.1. Imagine a firm that, years ago, issued $100,000 of equity to purchase land. It now wants to use a $100,000 truck, which it can either purchase or lease. The balance sheet reflecting purchase of the truck is shown at the top of the table. (We assume that the truck is financed entirely with debt.) Alternatively, imagine that the firm leases the truck. If the lease is judged to be an operating one, the middle balance sheet is created. Here, neither the lease liability nor the truck appears on the balance sheet. The bottom balance sheet reflects a capital lease. The truck is shown as an asset and the lease is shown as a liability.

Accountants generally argue that a firm's financial strength is inversely related to the amount of its liabilities. Because the lease liability is hidden with an operating lease, the balance sheet of a firm with an operating lease *looks* stronger than the balance sheet of a firm with an otherwise identical capital lease. Given the choice, firms would probably classify all their leases as operating ones. Because of this tendency, FAS 13 states that a lease must be classified as a capital one if at least one of the following four criteria is met:

1. The present value of the lease payments is at least 90 percent of the fair market value of the asset at the start of the lease.

2. The lease transfers ownership of the property to the lessee by the end of the term of the lease.

3. The lease term is 75 percent or more of the estimated economic life of the asset.

4. The lessee can purchase the asset at a price below fair market value when the lease expires. This is frequently called a *bargain purchase price option*.

These rules capitalize leases that are similar to purchases. For example, the first two rules capitalize leases where the asset is likely to be purchased at the end of the lease period. The last two rules capitalize long-term leases.

Some firms have tried to cook the books by exploiting this classification scheme. Suppose a trucking firm wants to lease a $200,000 truck that it expects to use for 15 years. A clever financial manager could try to negotiate a lease contract for 10 years with lease payments having a present value of $178,000. These terms would get around Criteria (1) and (3). If Criteria (2) and (4) could be circumvented, the arrangement would be an operating lease and would not show up on the balance sheet.

Does this sort of gimmickry pay? The semistrong form of the efficient capital markets hypothesis implies that stock prices reflect all publicly available information. As we discussed earlier in this text, the empirical evidence generally supports this form of the hypothesis. Though operating leases do not appear in the firm's balance sheet, information about these leases must be disclosed elsewhere in the annual report. Because of this, attempts to keep leases off the balance sheet will not affect stock price in an efficient capital market.

21.3 Taxes, the IRS, and Leases

The lessee can deduct lease payments for income tax purposes if the lease is qualified by the Internal Revenue Service. Because tax shields are critical to the economic viability of any lease, all interested parties generally obtain an opinion from the IRS before agreeing to a major lease transaction. The opinion of the IRS will reflect the following guidelines:

1. The term of the lease must be less than 30 years. If the term is greater than 30 years, the transaction will be regarded as a conditional sale.

2. The lease should not have an option to acquire the asset at a price below its fair market value. This type of bargain option would give the lessee the asset's residual scrap value, implying an equity interest.

3. The lease should not have a schedule of payments that is very high at the start of the lease term and thereafter very low. Early *balloon* payments would be evidence that the lease was being used to avoid taxes and not for a legitimate business purpose.

4. The lease payments must provide the lessor with a fair market rate of return. The profit potential of the lease to the lessor should be apart from the deal's tax benefits.

5. The lease should not limit the lessee's right to issue debt or pay dividends while the lease is operative.

6. Renewal options must be reasonable and reflect the fair market value of the asset. This requirement can be met by granting the lessee the first option to meet a competing outside offer.

The reason the IRS is concerned about lease contracts is that many times they appear to be set up solely to avoid taxes. To see how this could happen, suppose a firm plans to purchase a $1 million bus that has a five-year class life. Depreciation expense would be $200,000 per year, assuming straight-line depreciation. Now suppose the firm can lease the bus for $500,000 per year for two years and buy the bus for $1 at the end of the two-year term. The present value of the tax benefits from acquiring the bus would clearly be less than if the bus were leased. The speedup of lease payments would greatly benefit the firm and give it a form of accelerated depreciation. If the tax rates of the lessor and lessee are different, leasing can be a form of tax avoidance.

21.4 The Cash Flows of Leasing

In this section we identify the basic cash flows used in evaluating a lease. Consider the decision confronting the Xomox corporation, which manufactures pipe. Business has been expanding, and Xomox currently has a five-year backlog of pipe orders for the Trans-Honduran Pipeline.

The International Boring Machine Corporation (IBMC) makes a pipe-boring machine that can be purchased for $10,000. Xomox has determined that it needs a new machine, and the IBMC model will save Xomox $6,000 per year in reduced electricity bills for the next five years. These savings are known with certainty because Xomox has a long-term electricity purchase agreement with State Electric Utilities, Inc.

Xomox has a corporate tax rate of 34 percent. We assume that five-year straight-line depreciation is used for the pipe-boring machine, and the machine will be worthless after five years.[1]

However, Friendly Leasing Corporation has offered to lease the same pipe-boring machine to Xomox for $2,500 per year for five years. With the lease, Xomox would remain responsible for maintenance, insurance, and operating expenses.[2]

Simon Smart, a recently hired MBA, has been asked to calculate the incremental cash flows from leasing the IBMC machine in lieu of buying it. He has prepared Table 21.2, which shows the direct cash flow consequences of buying the pipe-boring machine and also signing the lease agreement with Friendly Leasing.

To simplify matters, Simon Smart has prepared Table 21.3, which subtracts the direct cash flows of buying the pipe-boring machine from those of leasing it. Noting that only

Table 21.2

Cash Flows to Xomox from Using the IBMC Pipe-Boring Machine: Buy versus Lease

	Year 0	Year 1	Year 2	Year 3	Year 4	Year 5
Buy						
Cost of machine	−$10,000					
Aftertax operating savings [$3,960 = $6,000 × (1 − .34)]		$3,960	$3,960	$3,960	$3,960	$3,960
Depreciation tax benefit*		680	680	680	680	680
Total	−$10,000	$4,640	$4,640	$4,640	$4,640	$4,640
Lease						
Lease payments		−$2,500	−$2,500	−$2,500	−$2,500	−$2,500
Tax benefits of lease payments ($850 = $2,500 × .34)		850	850	850	850	850
Aftertax operating savings		3,960	3,960	3,960	3,960	3,960
Total		$2,310	$2,310	$2,310	$2,310	$2,310

*Depreciation is straight-line. Because the depreciable base is $10,000, depreciation expense per year is $10,000/5 = $2,000. The depreciation tax benefit per year is equal to:

Tax rate × Depreciation expense per year = Depreciation tax benefit
.34   × $2,000   = $680

---

[1] This is a simplifying assumption because current tax law allows the accelerated method as well. The accelerated method will almost always be the best choice.

[2] For simplicity, we have assumed that lease payments are made at the end of each year. Actually, most leases require lease payments to be made at the beginning of the year.

Table 21.3

Incremental Cash Flow Consequences for Xomox from Leasing instead of Purchasing

Lease Minus Buy	Year 0	Year 1	Year 2	Year 3	Year 4	Year 5
Lease						
Lease payments		−$2,500	−$2,500	−$2,500	−$2,500	−$2,500
Tax benefits of lease payments		850	850	850	850	850
Buy (minus)						
Cost of machine	−(−$10,000)					
Lost depreciation tax benefit		−680	−680	−680	−680	−680
Total	$10,000	−$2,330	−$2,330	−$2,330	−$2,330	−$2,330

The bottom line presents the cash flows from leasing relative to the cash flows from purchase. The cash flows would be exactly the opposite if we considered the purchase relative to the lease.

the net advantage of leasing is relevant to Xomox, he concludes the following from his analysis:

1. Operating costs are not directly affected by leasing. Xomox will save $3,960 (after taxes) from use of the IBMC boring machine regardless of whether the machine is owned or leased. Thus, this cash flow stream does not appear in Table 21.3.

2. If the machine is leased, Xomox will save the $10,000 it would have used to purchase the machine. This saving shows up as an initial cash *inflow* of $10,000 in Year 0.

3. If Xomox leases the pipe-boring machine, it will no longer own this machine and must give up the depreciation tax benefits. These lost tax benefits show up as an *outflow.*

4. If Xomox chooses to lease the machine, it must pay $2,500 per year for five years. The first payment is due at the end of the first year. (This is a break: Often the first payment is due immediately.) The lease payments are tax deductible and, as a consequence, generate tax benefits of $850 (=.34 × $2,500).

The net cash flows have been placed in the bottom line of Table 21.3. These numbers represent the cash flows from *leasing* relative to the cash flows from the purchase. It is arbitrary that we express the cash flows in this way. We could have expressed the cash flows from the *purchase* relative to the cash flows from leasing. These cash flows would look like this:

	Year 0	Year 1	Year 2	Year 3	Year 4	Year 5
Net cash flows from purchase alternative relative to lease alternative	−$10,000	$2,330	$2,330	$2,330	$2,330	$2,330

Of course, the cash flows here are the opposite of those in the bottom line of Table 21.3. Depending on our purpose, we may look at either the purchase relative to the lease or vice versa. Thus, the student should become comfortable with either viewpoint.

Now that we have the cash flows, we can make our decision by discounting the cash flows properly. However, because the discount rate is tricky, we take a detour in the next section before moving back to the Xomox case. In this next section, we show that cash flows in the lease-versus-buy decision should be discounted at the *aftertax* interest rate (i.e., the aftertax cost of debt capital).

21.5 A Detour for Discounting and Debt Capacity with Corporate Taxes

The analysis of leases is difficult, and both financial practitioners and academics have made conceptual errors. These errors revolve around taxes. We hope to avoid their mistakes by beginning with the simplest type of example: a loan for one year. Though this example is unrelated to our lease-versus-buy situation, principles developed here will apply directly to lease–buy analysis.

PRESENT VALUE OF RISKLESS CASH FLOWS

Consider a corporation that lends $100 for a year. If the interest rate is 10 percent, the firm will receive $110 at the end of the year. Of this amount, $10 is interest and the remaining $100 is the original principal. A corporate tax rate of 34 percent implies taxes on the interest of $3.40 (=.34 × $10). Thus, the firm ends up with $106.60 (=$110 − $3.40) after taxes on a $100 investment.

Now consider a company that borrows $100 for a year. With a 10 percent interest rate, the firm must pay $110 to the bank at the end of the year. However, the borrowing firm can take the $10 of interest as a tax deduction. The corporation pays $3.40 (=.34 × $10) less in taxes than it would have paid had it not borrowed the money at all. Thus, considering this reduction in taxes, the firm must pay $106.60 (=$110 − $3.40) on a $100 loan. The cash flows from both lending and borrowing are displayed in Table 21.4.

Table 21.4 Lending and Borrowing in a World with Corporate Taxes (Interest Rate Is 10 Percent and Corporate Tax Rate Is 34 Percent)

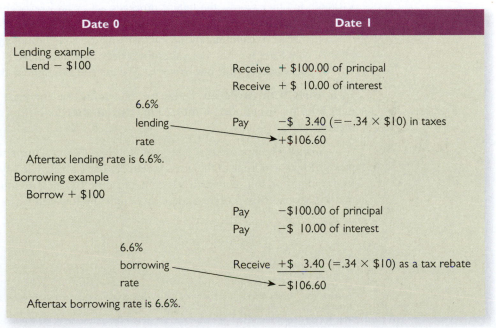

General principle: In a world with corporate taxes, riskless cash flows should be discounted at the aftertax interest rate.

The previous two paragraphs show a very important result: The firm could not care less whether it received $100 today or $106.60 next year.[3] If it received $100 today, it could lend it out, thereby receiving $106.60 after corporate taxes at the end of the year. Conversely, if it knows today that it will receive $106.60 at the end of the year, it could borrow $100 today. The aftertax interest and principal payments on the loan would be paid with the $106.60 that the firm will receive at the end of the year. Because of this interchangeability, we say that a payment of $106.60 next year has a present value of $100. Because $100 = $106.60/1.066, a riskless cash flow should be discounted at the aftertax interest rate of .066 [=.10 × (1 − .34)].

Of course, the preceding discussion is a specific example. The general principle is this:

In a world with corporate taxes, the firm should discount riskless cash flows at the aftertax riskless rate of interest.

OPTIMAL DEBT LEVEL AND RISKLESS CASH FLOWS

In addition, our simple example can illustrate a related point concerning optimal debt level. Consider a firm that has just determined that the current level of debt in its capital structure is optimal. Immediately following that determination, it is surprised to learn that it will receive a guaranteed payment of $106.60 in one year from, say, a tax-exempt government lottery. This future windfall is an asset that, like any asset, should raise the firm's optimal debt level. How much does this payment raise the firm's optimal level?

Our analysis implies that the firm's optimal debt level must be $100 more than it previously was. That is, the firm could borrow $100 today, perhaps paying the entire amount out as a dividend. It would owe the bank $110 at the end of the year. However, because it receives a tax rebate of $3.40 (=.34 × $10), its net repayment will be $106.60. Thus, its borrowing of $100 today is fully offset by next year's government lottery proceeds of $106.60. In other words, the lottery proceeds act as an irrevocable trust that can service the increased debt. Note that we need not know the optimal debt level before the lottery was announced. We are merely saying that whatever this prelottery optimal level was, the optimal debt level is $100 more after the lottery announcement.

Of course, this is just one example. The general principle is this:[4]

In a world with corporate taxes, we determine the increase in the firm's optimal debt level by discounting a future guaranteed aftertax inflow at the aftertax riskless interest rate.

Conversely, suppose that a second, unrelated firm is surprised to learn that it must pay $106.60 next year to the government for back taxes. Clearly, this additional liability impinges on the second firm's debt capacity. By the previous reasoning, it follows that the second firm's optimal debt level must be lowered by exactly $100.

---

[3]For simplicity, assume that the firm received $100 or $106.60 *after* corporate taxes. Because .66 = 1 − .34, the pretax inflows would be $151.52 (=$100/.66) and $161.52 (=$106.60/.66), respectively.

[4]This principle holds for riskless or guaranteed cash flows only. Unfortunately, there is no easy formula for determining the increase in optimal debt level from a *risky* cash flow.

21.6 NPV Analysis of the Lease-versus-Buy Decision

Our detour leads to a simple method for evaluating leases: Discount all cash flows at the aftertax interest rate. From the bottom line of Table 21.3, Xomox's incremental cash flows from leasing versus purchasing are these:

	Year 0	Year 1	Year 2	Year 3	Year 4	Year 5
Net cash flows from lease alternative relative to purchase alternative	$10,000	−$2,330	−$2,330	−$2,330	−$2,330	−$2,330

Let us assume that Xomox can either borrow or lend at the interest rate of 7.57575 percent. If the corporate tax rate is 34 percent, the correct discount rate is the aftertax rate of 5 percent [=7.57575% × (1 − .34)]. When 5 percent is used to compute the NPV of the lease, we have:

$$\text{NPV} = \$10,000 - \$2,330 \times \text{PVIFA}(.05, 5) = -\$87.68 \qquad \textbf{(21.1)}$$

Because the net present value of the incremental cash flows from leasing relative to purchasing is negative, Xomox prefers to purchase.

Equation 21.1 is the correct approach to lease-versus-buy analysis. However, students are often bothered by two things. First, they question whether the cash flows in Table 21.3 are truly riskless. We examine this issue next. Second, they feel that this approach lacks intuition. We address this concern a little later.

THE DISCOUNT RATE

Because we discounted at the aftertax riskless rate of interest, we have implicitly assumed that the cash flows in the Xomox example are riskless. Is this appropriate?

A lease payment is like the debt service on a secured bond issued by the lessee, and the discount rate should be approximately the same as the interest rate on such debt. In general, this rate will be slightly higher than the riskless rate considered in the previous section. The various tax shields could be somewhat riskier than the lease payments for two reasons. First, the value of the depreciation tax benefits depends on the ability of Xomox to generate enough taxable income to use them. Second, the corporate tax rate may change in the future, just as it fell in 1986 and increased in 1993. For these two reasons, a firm might be justified in discounting the depreciation tax benefits at a rate higher than that used for the lease payments. However, our experience is that real-world companies discount both the depreciation shield and lease payments at the same rate. This implies that financial practitioners view these two risks as minor. We adopt the real-world convention of discounting the two flows at the same rate. This rate is the aftertax interest rate on secured debt issued by the lessee.

At this point some students still question why we do not use R_{WACC} as the discount rate in lease-versus-buy analysis. Of course, R_{WACC} should not be used for lease analysis because the cash flows are more like debt service cash flows than operating cash flows and, as such, the risk is much less. The discount rate should reflect the risk of the incremental cash flows.

21.7 Debt Displacement and Lease Valuation

THE BASIC CONCEPT OF DEBT DISPLACEMENT

The previous analysis allows us to calculate the right answer in a simple manner. This clearly must be viewed as an important benefit. However, the analysis has little intuitive appeal. To remedy this, we hope to make lease–buy analysis more intuitive by considering the issue of debt displacement.

A firm that purchases equipment will generally issue debt to finance the purchase. The debt becomes a liability of the firm. A lessee incurs a liability equal to the present value of all future lease payments. Because of this, we argue that leases displace debt. The balance sheets in Table 21.5 illustrate how leasing might affect debt.

Suppose a firm initially has $100,000 of assets and a 150 percent optimal debt–equity ratio. The firm's debt is $60,000, and its equity is $40,000. As in the Xomox case, suppose the firm must use a new $10,000 machine. The firm has two alternatives:

1. *The firm can purchase the machine.* If it does, it will finance the purchase with a secured loan and with equity. The debt capacity of the machine is assumed to be the same as for the firm as a whole.

2. *The firm can lease the asset and get 100 percent financing.* That is, the present value of the future lease payments will be $10,000.

If the firm finances the machine with both secured debt and new equity, its debt will increase by $6,000 and its equity by $4,000. Its optimal debt–equity ratio of 150 percent will be maintained.

Conversely, consider the lease alternative. Because the lessee views the lease payment as a liability, the lessee thinks in terms of a *liability-to-equity* ratio, not just a debt-to-equity ratio. As just mentioned, the present value of the lease liability is $10,000. If the leasing firm is to maintain a liability-to-equity ratio of 150 percent, debt elsewhere in the firm must

Table 21.5

Debt Displacement Elsewhere in the Firm when a Lease is Instituted

Assets		Liabilities	
Initial situation			
Current	$ 50,000	Debt	$ 60,000
Fixed	50,000	Equity	40,000
Total	$100,000	Total	$100,000
Buy with secured loan			
Current	$ 50,000	Debt	$ 66,000
Fixed	50,000	Equity	44,000
Machine	10,000	Total	$110,000
Total	$110,000		
Lease			
Current	$ 50,000	Lease	$ 10,000
Fixed	50,000	Debt	56,000
Machine	10,000	Equity	44,000
Total	$110,000	Total	$110,000

This example shows that leases reduce the level of debt elsewhere in the firm. Though the example illustrates a point, it is not meant to show a precise method for calculating debt displacement.

fall by $4,000 when the lease is instituted. Because debt must be repurchased, net liabilities rise by only $6,000 (=$10,000 − $4,000) when $10,000 of assets are placed under lease.[5]

Debt displacement is a hidden cost of leasing. If a firm leases, it will not use as much regular debt as it would otherwise. The benefits of debt capacity will be lost—particularly the lower taxes associated with interest expense.

OPTIMAL DEBT LEVEL IN THE XOMOX EXAMPLE

The previous section showed that leasing displaces debt. Though the section illustrated a point, it was not meant to show the *precise* method for calculating debt displacement. Here we describe the precise method for calculating the difference in optimal debt levels between purchase and lease in the Xomox example.

From the last line of Table 21.3, we know these cash flows from the *purchase* alternative relative to the cash flows from the lease alternative:[6]

	Year 0	Year 1	Year 2	Year 3	Year 4	Year 5
Net cash flows from purchase alternative relative to lease alternative	−$10,000	$2,330	$2,330	$2,330	$2,330	$2,330

An increase in the optimal debt level at Year 0 occurs because the firm learns at that time of guaranteed cash flows beginning at Year 1. Our detour into discounting and debt capacity told us to calculate this increased debt level by discounting the future riskless cash inflows at the aftertax interest rate.[7] Thus, the additional debt level of the purchase alternative relative to the lease alternative is:

$$\$10,087.68 = \frac{\$2,330}{1.05} + \frac{\$2,330}{(1.05)^2} + \frac{\$2,330}{(1.05)^3} + \frac{\$2,330}{(1.05)^4} + \frac{\$2,330}{(1.05)^5}$$

That is, whatever the optimal amount of debt would be under the lease alternative, the optimal amount of debt would be $10,087.68 more under the purchase alternative.

This result can be stated in another way. Imagine there are two identical firms except that one firm purchases the boring machine and the other leases it. From Table 21.3, we know that the purchasing firm generates $2,330 more cash flow after taxes in each of the five years than does the leasing firm. Further imagine that the same bank lends money to both firms. The bank should lend the purchasing firm more money because it has a greater cash flow each period. How much extra money should the bank lend the purchasing firm so that the incremental loan can be paid off by the extra cash flows of $2,330 per year? The answer is exactly $10,087.68—the increase in the optimal debt level we calculated earlier.

To see this, let us work through the example year by year. Because the purchasing firm borrows $10,087.68 more at Year 0 than does the leasing firm, the purchasing firm

---

[5]Growing firms in the real world will not generally repurchase debt when instituting a lease. Rather, they will issue less debt in the future than they would have without the lease.

[6]The last line of Table 21.3 presents the cash flows from the lease alternative relative to the purchase alternative. As pointed out earlier, our cash flows are now reversed because we are now presenting the cash flows from the purchase alternative relative to the lease alternative.

[7]Though our detour considered only riskless cash flows, the cash flows in a leasing example are not necessarily riskless. As we explained earlier, we therefore adopt the real-world convention of discounting at the aftertax interest rate on secured debt issued by the lessee.

Table 21.6 Calculation of Increase in Optimal Debt Level if Xomox Purchases instead of Leases

	Year 0	Year 1	Year 2	Year 3	Year 4	Year 5
Outstanding balance of loan	$10,087.68	$8,262.07*	$6,345.17	$4,332.42	$2,219.05	$ 0
Interest		764.22	625.91	480.69	328.22	168.11
Tax deduction on interest		259.83	212.81	163.44	111.59	57.16
Aftertax interest expense		$ 504.39	$ 413.10	$ 317.25	$ 216.63	$ 110.95
Extra cash that purchasing firm generates over leasing firm (from Table 21.3)		$2,330.00	$2,330.00	$2,330.00	$2,330.00	$2,330.00
Repayment of loan		$1,825.61†	$1,916.90	$2,012.75	$2,113.37	$2,219.05

Assume that there are two otherwise identical firms: One leases and the other purchases. The purchasing firm can borrow $10,087.68 more than the leasing firm. The extra cash flow each year of $2,330 from purchasing instead of leasing can be used to pay off the loan in five years.

*$8,262.07 = $10,087.68 − $1,825.61.

†$1,825.61 = $2,330 − $504.39.

will pay interest of $764.22 (=$10,087.68 × .0757575) at Year 1 on the additional debt. The interest allows the firm to reduce its taxes by $259.83 (=$764.22 × .34), leaving an aftertax outflow of $504.39 (=$764.22 − $259.83) at Year 1.

We know from Table 21.3 that the purchasing firm generates $2,330 more cash at Year 1 than does the leasing firm. Because the purchasing firm has the extra $2,330 coming in at Year 1 but must pay interest on its loan, how much of the loan can the firm repay at Year 1 and still have the same cash flow as the leasing firm? The purchasing firm can repay $1,825.61 (=$2,330 − $504.39) of the loan at Year 1 and still have the same net cash flow that the leasing firm has. After the repayment, the purchasing firm will have a remaining balance of $8,262.07 (=$10,087.68 − $1,825.61) at Year 1. For each of the five years, this sequence of cash flows is displayed in Table 21.6. The outstanding balance goes to zero over the five years. Thus, the annual cash flow of $2,330, which represents the extra cash from purchasing instead of leasing, fully amortizes the loan of $10,087.68.

Our analysis of debt capacity has two purposes. First, we want to show the additional debt capacity from purchasing. We just completed this task. Second, we want to determine whether the lease is preferred to the purchase. This decision rule follows easily from our discussion. By leasing the equipment and having $10,087.68 less debt than under the purchase alternative, the firm has exactly the same cash flow in Years 1 to 5 that it would have through a levered purchase. Thus, we can ignore cash flows beginning in Year 1 when comparing the lease alternative to the purchase-with-debt alternative. However, the cash flows differ between the alternatives at Year 0:

1. *The purchase cost at Year 0 of $10,000 is avoided by leasing.* This should be viewed as a cash inflow under the leasing alternative.

2. *The firm borrows $10,087.68 less at Year 0 under the lease alternative than it can under the purchase alternative.* This should be viewed as a cash outflow under the leasing alternative.

Because the firm borrows $10,087.68 less by leasing but saves only $10,000 on the equipment, the lease alternative requires an extra cash outflow at Year 0 relative to the purchase alternative of −$87.68 (=$10,000 − $10,087.68). Because cash flows in later years from leasing are identical to those from purchasing with debt, the firm should purchase.

Two Methods for Calculating Net Present Value of Lease Relative to Purchase*

Method 1: Discount all cash flows at the aftertax interest rate:

$$-\$87.68 = \$10,000 - \$2,330 \times \text{PVIFA}(.05, 5)$$

Method 2: Compare purchase price with reduction in optimal debt level under leasing alternative:

$$-\$87.68 = \underset{\substack{\text{Purchase} \\ \text{price}}}{\$10,000} - \underset{\substack{\text{Reduction in} \\ \text{optimal debt} \\ \text{level if leasing}}}{\$10,087.68}$$

*Because we are calculating the NPV of the lease relative to the purchase, a negative value indicates that the purchase alternative is preferred.

This is exactly the same answer we got when, earlier in this chapter, we discounted all cash flows at the aftertax interest rate. Of course, this is no coincidence: The increase in the optimal debt level is also determined by discounting all cash flows at the aftertax interest rate. The accompanying box presents both methods. The numbers in the box are in terms of the NPV of the lease relative to the purchase. Thus, a negative NPV indicates that the purchase alternative should be taken. The NPV of a lease is often called the net advantage of leasing, or NAL.

21.8 Does Leasing Ever Pay? The Base Case

We previously looked at the lease–buy decision from the point of view of the potential lessee, Xomox. Let's now look at the decision from the point of view of the lessor, Friendly Leasing. This firm faces three cash flows, all of which are displayed in Table 21.7. First, Friendly purchases the machine for $10,000 at Year 0. Second, because the asset is depreciated straight-line over five years, the depreciation expense at the end of each of the five years is $2,000 (=$10,000/5). The yearly depreciation tax shield is $680 (=$2,000 × .34). Third, because the yearly lease payment is $2,500, the aftertax lease payment is $1,650 [=$2,500 × (1 − .34)].

Now examine the total cash flows to Friendly Leasing displayed in the bottom line of Table 21.7. Those of you with a healthy memory will notice something interesting. These

Table 21.7   Cash Flows to Friendly Leasing as Lessor of IBMC Pipe-Boring Machine

	Year 0	Year 1	Year 2	Year 3	Year 4	Year 5
Cash for machine	−$10,000					
Depreciation tax benefit ($680 = $2,000 × .34)		$ 680	$ 680	$ 680	$ 680	$ 680
Aftertax lease payment [$1,650 = $2,500 × (1 − .34)]		1,650	1,650	1,650	1,650	1,650
Total	−$10,000	$2,330	$2,330	$2,330	$2,330	$2,330

These cash flows are the opposite of the cash flows to Xomox, the lessee (see the bottom line of Table 21.3).

cash flows are exactly the *opposite* of those of Xomox displayed in the bottom line of Table 21.3. Those of you with a healthy sense of skepticism may be thinking something interesting: "If the cash flows of the lessor are exactly the opposite of those of the lessee, the combined cash flow of the two parties must be zero each year. Thus, there does not seem to be any joint benefit to this lease. Because the net present value to the lessee was −$87.68, the NPV to the lessor must be $87.68. The joint NPV is $0 (=−$87.68 + $87.68). There does not appear to be any way for the NPV of both the lessor and the lessee to be positive at the same time. Because one party would inevitably lose money, the leasing deal could never fly."

This is one of the most important results of leasing. Though Table 21.7 concerns one particular leasing deal, the principle can be generalized. As long as (1) both parties are subject to the same interest and tax rates and (2) transaction costs are ignored, there can be no leasing deal that benefits both parties. However, there is a lease payment for which both parties would calculate an NPV of zero. Given that payment, Xomox would be indifferent to whether it leased or bought, and Friendly Leasing would be indifferent to whether it leased or not.[8]

A student with an even healthier sense of skepticism might be thinking, "This textbook appears to be arguing that leasing is not beneficial. Yet we know that leasing occurs frequently in the real world. Maybe, just maybe, the textbook is wrong." Although we will not admit to being wrong (what authors would?!), we freely admit that our explanation is incomplete at this point. The next section considers factors that give benefits to leasing.

21.9 Reasons for Leasing

Proponents of leasing make many claims about why firms should lease assets rather than buy them. Some of the reasons given to support leasing are good, and some are not. Here we discuss good reasons for leasing and those we think are not.

GOOD REASONS FOR LEASING

Leasing is a good choice if at least one of the following is true:

1. Taxes will be reduced by leasing.
2. The lease contract will reduce certain types of uncertainty.
3. Transaction costs will be higher for buying an asset and financing it with debt or equity than for leasing the asset.

Tax Advantages   The most important reason for long-term leasing is tax reduction. If the corporate income tax were repealed, long-term leasing would probably disappear. The tax advantages of leasing exist because firms are in different tax brackets.

Should a user in a low tax bracket purchase, he will receive little tax benefit from depreciation and interest deductions. Should the user lease, the lessor will receive the depreciation shield and the interest deductions. In a competitive market, the lessor must charge a low lease payment to reflect these tax shields. Thus, the user is likely to lease rather than purchase.

---

[8]The break-even lease payment is $2,469.32 in our example. Both the lessor and lessee can solve for this as follows:

$$\$10,000 = \$680 \times \text{PVIFA}(.05, 5) + L \times (1 - .34) \times \text{PVIFA}(.05, 5)$$

In this case, $L = \$2,469.32$.

In our example with Xomox and Friendly Leasing, the value of the lease to Friendly was $87.68:

$$\$87.68 = -\$10,000 + \$2,330 \times PVIFA(.05, 5)$$

However, the value of the lease to Xomox was exactly the opposite (−$87.68). Because the lessor's gains came at the expense of the lessee, no deal could be arranged.

However, if Xomox pays no taxes and the lease payments are reduced to $2,475 from $2,500, both Friendly and Xomox will find positive NPVs in leasing. Xomox can rework Table 21.3 with $t_C = 0$, finding that its cash flows from leasing are now these:

	Year 0	Year 1	Year 2	Year 3	Year 4	Year 5
Cost of machine	$10,000					
Lease payment		−$2,475	−$2,475	−$2,475	−$2,475	−$2,475

The value of the lease to Xomox is:

$$\begin{aligned} \text{Value of lease} &= \$10,000 - \$2,475 \times PVIFA(.0757575, 5) \\ &= \$6.55 \end{aligned}$$

Notice that the discount rate is the interest rate of 7.57575 percent because tax rates are zero. In addition, the full lease payment of $2,475—and not some lower aftertax number—is used because there are no taxes. Finally, note that depreciation is ignored, also because no taxes apply.

Given a lease payment of $2,475, the cash flows to Friendly Leasing look like this:

	Year 0	Year 1	Year 2	Year 3	Year 4	Year 5
Cost of machine	−$10,000					
Depreciation tax shield ($680 = $2,000 × .34)		$ 680	$ 680	$ 680	$ 680	$ 680
Aftertax lease payment [$1,633.50 = $2,475 × (1 − .34)]		$1,633.50	$1,633.50	$1,633.50	$1,633.50	$1,633.50
Total		$2,313.50	$2,313.50	$2,313.50	$2,313.50	$2,313.50

The value of the lease to Friendly is:

$$\begin{aligned} \text{Value of lease} &= -\$10,000 + \$2,313.50 \times PVIFA(.05, 5) \\ &= -\$10,000 + \$10,016.24 \\ &= \$16.24 \end{aligned}$$

As a consequence of different tax rates, the lessee (Xomox) gains $6.55 and the lessor (Friendly) gains $16.24. Both the lessor and the lessee can gain if their tax rates are different because the lessor uses the depreciation and interest tax shields that cannot be used by the lessee. The IRS loses tax revenue, and some of the tax gains of the lessor are passed on to the lessee in the form of lower lease payments.

Because both parties can gain when tax rates differ, the lease payment is agreed upon through negotiation. Before negotiation begins, each party needs to know the *reservation* payment of both parties. This is the payment that will make one party indifferent to whether it enters the lease deal. In other words, this is the payment that makes the value of the lease zero. These payments are calculated next.

Reservation Payment of Lessee We now solve for L_{MAX}, the payment that makes the value of the lease to the lessee zero. When the lessee is in a zero tax bracket, his cash flows, in terms of L_{MAX}, are as follows:

	Year 0	Year 1	Year 2	Year 3	Year 4	Year 5
Cost of machine	$10,000					
Lease payment		$-L_{MAX}$	$-L_{MAX}$	$-L_{MAX}$	$-L_{MAX}$	$-L_{MAX}$

This table implies that:

$$\text{Value of lease} = \$10,000 - L_{MAX} \times \text{PVIFA}(.0757575, 5)$$

The value of the lease equals zero when:

$$L_{MAX} = \frac{\$10,000}{\text{PVIFA}(.0757575, 5)} = \$2,476.62$$

After performing this calculation, the lessor knows that he will never be able to charge a payment above $2,476.62.

Reservation Payment of Lessor We now solve for L_{MIN}, the payment that makes the value of the lease to the lessor zero. The cash flows to the lessor, in terms of L_{MIN}, are these:

	Year 0	Year 1	Year 2	Year 3	Year 4	Year 5
Cost of machine	$-\$10,000$					
Depreciation tax shield ($680 = $2,000 × .34)		$680	$680	$680	$680	$680
Aftertax lease payment ($t_c = .34$)		$L_{MIN} \times (.66)$	$L_{MIN} \times (.66)$	$L_{MIN} \times (.66)$	$L_{MIN} \times (.66)$	$L_{MIN} \times (.66)$

This table implies that:

$$\text{Value of lease} = -\$10,000 + \$680 \times \text{PVIFA}(.05, 5) + L_{MIN} \times (.66) \times \text{PVIFA}(.05, 5)$$

The value of the lease equals zero when:

$$\begin{aligned} L_{MIN} &= \frac{\$10,000}{.66 \times \text{PVIFA}(.05, 5)} - \frac{\$680}{.66} \\ &= \$3,499.62 - \$1,030.30 \\ &= \$2,469.32 \end{aligned}$$

After performing this calculation, the lessee knows that the lessor will never agree to a lease payment below $2,469.32.

A Reduction of Uncertainty We have noted that the lessee does not own the property when the lease expires. The value of the property at this time is called the *residual value,* and the lessor has a firm claim to it. When the lease contract is signed, there may be substantial uncertainty about what the residual value of the asset will be. Thus, under a lease contract, this residual risk is borne by the lessor. Conversely, the user bears this risk when purchasing.

It is common sense that the party best able to bear a particular risk should do so. If the user has little risk aversion, she will not suffer by purchasing. However, if the user is highly averse to risk, she should find a third-party lessor more capable of assuming this burden.

This latter situation frequently arises when the user is a small or newly formed firm. Because the risk of the entire firm is likely to be quite high and because the principal stockholders are likely to be undiversified, the firm desires to minimize risk wherever possible. A potential lessor, such as a large, publicly held financial institution, is far more capable of bearing the risk. Conversely, this situation is not expected to happen when the user is a blue chip corporation. That potential lessee is more able to bear risk.

Transaction Costs The costs of changing an asset's ownership are generally greater than the costs of writing a lease agreement. Consider the choice that confronts a person who lives in Los Angeles but must do business in New York for two days. It would clearly be cheaper to rent a hotel room for two nights than it would be to buy an apartment condominium for two days and then to sell it.

Unfortunately, leases generate agency costs as well. For example, the lessee might misuse or overuse the asset because she has no interest in the asset's residual value. This cost will be implicitly paid by the lessee through a high lease payment. Although the lessor can reduce these agency costs through monitoring, monitoring itself is costly.

Thus, leasing is most beneficial when the transaction costs of purchase and resale outweigh the agency costs and monitoring costs of a lease. Flath argues that this occurs in short-term leases but not in long-term leases.[9]

BAD REASONS FOR LEASING

Leasing and Accounting Income

In our discussion of accounting and leasing we pointed out that a firm's balance sheet shows fewer liabilities with an operating lease than with either a capitalized lease or a purchase financed with debt. We indicated that a firm desiring to project a strong balance sheet might select an operating lease. In addition, the firm's return on assets (ROA) is generally higher with an operating lease than with either a capitalized lease or a purchase. To see this, we look at the numerator and denominator of the ROA formula in turn.

With an operating lease, lease payments are treated as an expense. If the asset is purchased, both depreciation and interest charges are expenses. At least in the early part of the asset's life, the yearly lease payment is generally less than the sum of yearly depreciation and yearly interest. Thus, accounting income, the numerator of the ROA formula, is higher with an operating lease than with a purchase. Because accounting expenses with a capitalized lease are analogous to depreciation and interest with a purchase, the increase in accounting income does not occur when a lease is capitalized.

In addition, leased assets do not appear on the balance sheet with an operating lease. Thus, the total asset value of a firm, the denominator of the ROA formula, is less with an operating lease than it is with either a purchase or a capitalized lease. The two preceding

---

[9]David Flath, "The Economics of Short-Term Leasing," *Economic Inquiry* 18 (April 1980).

effects imply that the firm's ROA should be higher with an operating lease than with either a purchase or a capitalized lease.

Of course, in an efficient capital market, accounting information cannot be used to fool investors. It is unlikely, then, that leasing's impact on accounting numbers should create value for the firm. Savvy investors should be able to see through attempts by management to improve the firm's financial statements.

One Hundred Percent Financing   It is often claimed that leasing provides 100 percent financing, whereas secured equipment loans require an initial down payment. However, we argued earlier that leases tend to displace debt elsewhere in the firm. Our earlier analysis suggests that leases do not permit a greater level of total liabilities than do purchases with borrowing.

Other Reasons   There are, of course, many special reasons that some companies find advantages in leasing. In one celebrated case, the U.S. Navy leased a fleet of tankers instead of asking Congress for appropriations. Thus, leasing may be used to circumvent capital expenditure control systems set up by bureaucratic firms.

21.10 Some Unanswered Questions

Our analysis suggests that the primary advantage of long-term leasing results from the differential tax rates of the lessor and the lessee. Other valid reasons for leasing are lower contracting costs and risk reduction. There are several questions our analysis has not specifically answered.

ARE THE USES OF LEASES AND DEBT COMPLEMENTARY?

Ang and Peterson find that firms with high debt tend to lease frequently as well.[10] This result should not be puzzling. The corporate attributes that provide high debt capacity may also make leasing advantageous. Thus, even though leasing displaces debt (i.e., leasing and borrowing are substitutes) for an individual firm, high debt and high leasing can be positively associated when we look at a number of firms.

WHY ARE LEASES OFFERED BY BOTH MANUFACTURERS AND THIRD-PARTY LESSORS?

The offsetting effects of taxes can explain why both manufacturers (e.g., computer firms) and third-party lessors offer leases.

1. For manufacturer lessors, the basis for determining depreciation is the manufacturer's cost. For third-party lessors, the basis is the sales price that the lessor paid to the manufacturer. Because the sales price is generally greater than the manufacturer's cost, this is an advantage to third-party lessors.

2. However, the manufacturer must recognize a profit for tax purposes when selling the asset to the third-party lessor. The manufacturer's profit for some equipment can be deferred if the manufacturer becomes the lessor. This provides an incentive for manufacturers to lease.

---

[10]James Ang and Pamela P. Peterson, "The Leasing Puzzle," *Journal of Finance* 39 (September 1984).

WHY ARE SOME ASSETS LEASED MORE THAN OTHERS?

Certain assets appear to be leased more frequently than others. Smith and Wakeman have looked at nontax incentives affecting leasing.[11] Their analysis suggests many asset and firm characteristics that are important in the lease-or-buy decision. The following are among the things they mention:

1. The more sensitive the value of an asset is to use and maintenance decisions, the more likely it is that the asset will be purchased instead of leased. They argue that ownership provides a better incentive to minimize maintenance costs than does leasing.

2. Price discrimination opportunities may be important. Leasing may be a way of circumventing laws against charging too *low* a price.

---

[11]Clifford W. Smith, Jr., and L. M. Wakeman, "Determinants of Corporate Leasing Policy," *Journal of Finance* 40 (July 1985).

Summary and Conclusions

A large fraction of America's equipment is leased rather than purchased. This chapter both described the institutional arrangements surrounding leases and showed how to evaluate leases financially.

1. Leases can be separated into two polar types. Though operating leases allow the lessee to use the equipment, ownership remains with the lessor. Although the lessor in a financial lease legally owns the equipment, the lessee maintains effective ownership because financial leases are fully amortized.

2. When a firm purchases an asset with debt, both the asset and the liability appear on the firm's balance sheet. If a lease meets at least one of a number of criteria, it must be capitalized. This means that the present value of the lease appears as both an asset and a liability. A lease escapes capitalization if it does not meet any of these criteria. Leases not meeting the criteria are called *operating leases,* though the accountant's definition differs somewhat from the practitioner's definition. Operating leases do not appear on the balance sheet. For cosmetic reasons, many firms prefer that a lease be called *operating.*

3. Firms generally lease for tax purposes. To protect its interests, the IRS allows financial arrangements to be classified as leases only if a number of criteria are met.

4. We showed that risk-free cash flows should be discounted at the aftertax risk-free rate. Because both lease payments and depreciation tax shields are nearly riskless, all relevant cash flows in the lease–buy decision should be discounted at a rate near this aftertax rate. We use the real-world convention of discounting at the aftertax interest rate on the lessee's secured debt.

5. Though this method is simple, it lacks certain intuitive appeal. We presented an alternative method in the hopes of increasing the reader's intuition. Relative to a lease, a purchase generates debt capacity. This increase in debt capacity can be calculated by discounting the difference between the cash flows of the purchase and the cash flows of the lease by the aftertax interest rate. The increase in debt capacity from a purchase is compared to the extra outflow at Year 0 from a purchase.

6. If the lessor is in the same tax bracket as the lessee, the cash flows to the lessor are exactly the opposite of the cash flows to the lessee. Thus, the sum of the value of the lease to the lessee plus the value of the lease to the lessor must be zero. Although this suggests that leases can never fly, there are actually at least three good reasons for leasing:

   a. Differences in tax brackets between the lessor and lessee.
   b. Shift of risk bearing to the lessor.
   c. Minimization of transaction costs.

We also documented a number of bad reasons for leasing.

Concept Questions

1. **Leasing vs. Borrowing** What are the key differences between leasing and borrowing? Are they perfect substitutes?

2. **Leasing and Taxes** Taxes are an important consideration in the leasing decision. Which is more likely to lease: A profitable corporation in a high tax bracket or a less profitable one in a low tax bracket? Why?

3. **Leasing and IRR** What are some of the potential problems with looking at IRRs when evaluating a leasing decision?

4. **Leasing** Comment on the following remarks:

   a. Leasing reduces risk and can reduce a firm's cost of capital.
   b. Leasing provides 100 percent financing.
   c. If the tax advantages of leasing were eliminated, leasing would disappear.

5. **Accounting for Leases** Discuss the accounting criteria for determining whether a lease must be reported on the balance sheet. In each case give a rationale for the criterion.

6. **IRS Criteria** Discuss the IRS criteria for determining whether a lease is tax deductible. In each case give a rationale for the criterion.

7. **Off–Balance Sheet Financing** What is meant by the term *off–balance sheet financing?* When do leases provide such financing, and what are the accounting and economic consequences of such activity?

8. **Sale and Leaseback** Why might a firm choose to engage in a sale and leaseback transaction? Give two reasons.

9. **Leasing Cost** Explain why the aftertax borrowing rate is the appropriate discount rate to use in lease evaluation.

   Refer to the following example for Questions 10–12. In April 2014, International Lease Finance Corporation (ILFC) announced a deal to purchase eight Airbus A330-200 and A350-900 passenger aircraft. ILFC then signed a long-term lease contract on the planes with Azul Linhas Aéreas Brasileiras to be used for flights from Brazil to the United States.

10. **Leasing vs. Purchase** Why wouldn't Azul Linhas Aéreas Brasileiras purchase the planes if they were obviously needed for the company's operations?

11. **Reasons to Lease** Why would ILFC be willing to buy planes from Airbus and then lease the planes to Azul Linhas Aéreas Brasileiras? How is this different from just lending money to Azul Linhas Aéreas Brasileiras to buy the planes?

12. **Leasing** What do you suppose happens to the plane at the end of the lease period?

Questions and Problems

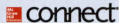

BASIC
(Questions 1–8)

Use the following information to work Problems 1–6. You work for a nuclear research laboratory that is contemplating leasing a diagnostic scanner (leasing is a common practice with expensive, high-tech equipment). The scanner costs $5,800,000, and it would be depreciated straight-line to zero over four years. Because of radiation contamination, it will actually be completely valueless in four years. You can lease it for $1,690,000 per year for four years.

1. **Lease or Buy** Assume that the tax rate is 35 percent. You can borrow at 8 percent before taxes. Should you lease or buy?

2. **Leasing Cash Flows** What are the cash flows from the lease from the lessor's viewpoint? Assume a 35 percent tax bracket.

3. **Finding the Break-Even Payment** What would the lease payment have to be for both the lessor and the lessee to be indifferent about the lease?

4. **Taxes and Leasing Cash Flows** Assume that your company does not contemplate paying taxes for the next several years. What are the cash flows from leasing in this case?

5. **Setting the Lease Payment** In the previous question, over what range of lease payments will the lease be profitable for both parties?

6. **MACRS Depreciation and Leasing** Rework Problem 1 assuming that the scanner will be depreciated as three-year property under MACRS (see Chapter 6 for the depreciation allowances).

7. **Lease or Buy** Super Sonics Entertainment is considering buying a machine that costs $480,000. The machine will be depreciated over five years by the straight-line method and will be worthless at that time. The company can lease the machine with year-end payments of $130,000. The company can issue bonds at an interest rate of 9 percent. If the corporate tax rate is 35 percent, should the company buy or lease?

8. **Setting the Lease Payment** Quartz Corporation is a relatively new firm. Quartz has experienced enough losses during its early years to provide it with at least eight years of tax loss carryforwards. Thus, Quartz's effective tax rate is zero. Quartz plans to lease equipment from New Leasing Company. The term of the lease is five years. The purchase cost of the equipment is $720,000. New Leasing Company is in the 35 percent tax bracket. There are no transaction costs to the lease. Each firm can borrow at 10 percent.

   a. What is Quartz's reservation price?
   b. What is New Leasing Company's reservation price?
   c. Explain why these reservation prices determine the negotiating range of the lease.

INTERMEDIATE
(Questions 9–16)

Use the following information to work Problems 9–11. The Wildcat Oil Company is trying to decide whether to lease or buy a new computer-assisted drilling system for its oil exploration business. Management has decided that it must use the system to stay competitive; it will provide $2.9 million in annual pretax cost savings. The system costs $9.7 million and will be depreciated straight-line to zero over five years. Wildcat's tax rate is 34 percent, and the firm can borrow at 9 percent. Lambert Leasing Company has offered to lease the drilling equipment to Wildcat for payments of $2.15 million per year. Lambert's policy is to require its lessees to make payments at the start of the year.

9. **Lease or Buy** What is the NAL for Wildcat? What is the maximum lease payment that would be acceptable to the company?

10. **Leasing and Salvage Value** Suppose it is estimated that the equipment will have an aftertax residual value of $700,000 at the end of the lease. What is the maximum lease payment acceptable to Wildcat now?

11. **Deposits in Leasing**   Many lessors require a security deposit in the form of a cash payment or other pledged collateral. Suppose Lambert requires Wildcat to pay a $1.5 million security deposit at the inception of the lease. If the lease payment is still $2.15 million, is it advantageous for Wildcat to lease the equipment now?

12. **Debt Capacity**   Monster Magnet Manufacturing is considering leasing some equipment. The annual lease payment would be $295,000 per year for six years. The appropriate interest rate is 7 percent and the company is in the 38 percent tax bracket. How would signing the lease affect the debt capacity for the company?

13. **Setting the Lease Price**   An asset costs $720,000 and will be depreciated in a straight-line manner over its three-year life. It will have no salvage value. The corporate tax rate is 34 percent, and the appropriate interest rate is 10 percent.

    a. What set of lease payments will make the lessee and the lessor equally well off?
    b. Show the general condition that will make the value of a lease to the lessor the negative of the value to the lessee.
    c. Assume that the lessee pays no taxes and the lessor is in the 34 percent tax bracket. For what range of lease payments does the lease have a positive NPV for both parties?

14. **Lease or Buy**   Wolfson Corporation has decided to purchase a new machine that costs $2.8 million. The machine will be depreciated on a straight-line basis and will be worthless after four years. The corporate tax rate is 35 percent. The Sur Bank has offered Wolfson a four-year loan for $2.8 million. The repayment schedule is four yearly principal repayments of $700,000 and an interest charge of 9 percent on the outstanding balance of the loan at the beginning of each year. Both principal repayments and interest are due at the end of each year. Cal Leasing Corporation offers to lease the same machine to Wolfson. Lease payments of $830,000 per year are due at the beginning of each of the four years of the lease.

    a. Should Wolfson lease the machine or buy it with bank financing?
    b. What is the annual lease payment that will make Wolfson indifferent to whether it leases the machine or purchases it?

15. **Setting the Lease Price**   An asset costs $590,000 and will be depreciated in a straight-line manner over its three-year life. It will have no salvage value. The lessor can borrow at 7 percent and the lessee can borrow at 9 percent. The corporate tax rate is 34 percent for both companies.

    a. How does the fact that the lessor and lessee have different borrowing rates affect the calculation of the NAL?
    b. What set of lease payments will make the lessee and the lessor equally well off?
    c. Assume that the lessee pays no taxes and the lessor is in the 34 percent tax bracket. For what range of lease payments does the lease have a positive NPV for both parties?

16. **Automobile Lease Payments**   Automobiles are often leased, and there are several terms unique to auto leases. Suppose you are considering leasing a car. The price you and the dealer agree on for the car is $32,000. This is the base capitalized cost. Other costs that may be added to the capitalized cost price include the acquisition (bank) fee, insurance, or extended warranty. Assume these costs are $450. Capitalized cost reductions include any down payment, credit for a trade-in, or dealer rebate. Assume you make a down payment of $2,000, and there is no trade-in or rebate. If you drive 12,000 miles per year, the lease-end residual value for this car will be $17,000 after three years.

    The lease or "money" factor, which is the interest rate on the loan, is the APR of the loan divided by 2,400. The money factor of 2,400 is the product of three numbers: 2, 12, and 100. The 100 is used to convert the APR, expressed as a percentage, to a decimal number. The 12 converts this rate to a monthly rate. Finally, the monthly rate is applied to the sum of the net capitalization cost plus the residual. If we divide this sum by 2, the result is the average anticipated book value. Thus, the end result of the calculation using the money factor is to multiply a monthly rate by the average book value to get a monthly payment. The lease factor the dealer quotes you is .00215.

The monthly lease payment consists of three parts: Depreciation fee, finance fee, and sales tax. The depreciation fee is the net capitalized cost minus the residual value divided by the term of the lease. The finance fee is the net capitalization cost plus the residual times the money factor, and the monthly sales tax is simply the monthly lease payment times the tax rate. What APR is the dealer quoting you? What is your monthly lease payment for a 36-month lease if the sales tax is 7 percent?

CHALLENGE
(Questions 17–18)

17. **Lease vs. Borrow** Return to the case of the diagnostic scanner discussed in Problems 1 through 6. Suppose the entire $5,800,000 purchase price of the scanner is borrowed. The rate on the loan is 8 percent, and the loan will be repaid in equal installments. Create a lease-versus-buy analysis that explicitly incorporates the loan payments. Show that the NPV of leasing instead of buying is not changed from what it was in Problem 1. Why is this so?

18. **Lease or Buy** High electricity costs have made Farmer Corporation's chicken-plucking machine economically worthless. Only two machines are available to replace it. The International Plucking Machine (IPM) model is available only on a lease basis. The lease payments will be $80,000 for five years, due at the beginning of each year. This machine will save Farmer $29,000 per year through reductions in electricity costs. As an alternative, Farmer can purchase a more energy-efficient machine from Basic Machine Corporation (BMC) for $365,000. This machine will save $32,000 per year in electricity costs. A local bank has offered to finance the machine with a $365,000 loan. The interest rate on the loan will be 10 percent on the remaining balance and will require five annual principal payments of $73,000. Farmer has a target debt-to-asset ratio of 67 percent. Farmer is in the 34 percent tax bracket. After five years, both machines will be worthless. The machines will be depreciated on a straight-line basis.

    a. Should Farmer lease the IPM machine or purchase the more efficient BMC machine?
    b. Does your answer depend on the form of financing for direct purchase?
    c. How much debt is displaced by this lease?

Mini Case

THE DECISION TO LEASE OR BUY AT WARF COMPUTERS

Warf Computers has decided to proceed with the manufacture and distribution of the virtual keyboard (VK) the company has developed. To undertake this venture, the company needs to obtain equipment for the production of the microphone for the keyboard. Because of the required sensitivity of the microphone and its small size, the company needs specialized equipment for production.

Nick Warf, the company president, has found a vendor for the equipment. Clapton Acoustical Equipment has offered to sell Warf Computers the necessary equipment at a price of $3.6 million. Because of the rapid development of new technology, the equipment falls in the three-year MACRS depreciation class. At the end of four years, the market value of the equipment is expected to be $440,000.

Alternatively, the company can lease the equipment from Hendrix Leasing. The lease contract calls for four annual payments of $935,000, due at the beginning of the year. Additionally, Warf Computers must make a security deposit of $210,000 that will be returned when the lease expires. Warf Computers can issue bonds with a yield of 11 percent, and the company has a marginal tax rate of 35 percent.

1. Should Warf buy or lease the equipment?
2. Nick mentions to James Hendrix, the president of Hendrix Leasing, that although the company will need the equipment for four years, he would like a lease contract for two

years instead. At the end of the two years, the lease could be renewed. Nick would also like to eliminate the security deposit, but he would be willing to increase the lease payments to $1,650,000 for each of the two years. When the lease is renewed in two years, Hendrix would consider the increased lease payments in the first two years when calculating the terms of the renewal. The equipment is expected to have a market value of $1.44 million in two years. What is the NAL of the lease contract under these terms? Why might Nick prefer this lease? What are the potential ethical issues concerning the new lease terms?

3. In the leasing discussion, James informs Nick that the contract could include a purchase option for the equipment at the end of the lease. Hendrix Leasing offers three purchase options:

   a. An option to purchase the equipment at the fair market value.
   b. An option to purchase the equipment at a fixed price. The price will be negotiated before the lease is signed.
   c. An option to purchase the equipment at a price of $200,000.

   How would the inclusion of a purchase option affect the value of the lease?

4. James also informs Nick that the lease contract can include a cancellation option. The cancellation option would allow Warf Computers to cancel the lease on any anniversary date of the contract. In order to cancel the lease, Warf Computers would be required to give 30 days' notice prior to the anniversary date. How would the inclusion of a cancellation option affect the value of the lease?

Appendix 21A   APV Approach to Leasing

To access the appendix for this chapter, please logon to Connect Finance.

Options and Corporate Finance

On June 2, 2015, the closing stock prices for women's apparel company The Buckle, hunting and outdoor merchandise retailer Cabela's, and farm products company The Andersons were $52.52, $52.71, and $53.14, respectively. Each company had a call option trading on the Chicago Board Options Exchange with a $50 strike price and an expiration date of August 19—77 days away. You might expect that the prices on these call options would be similar, but they weren't. Buckle's options sold for $2.86, Cabela's options traded at $5.10, and The Anderson's options traded at $6.50. Why would options on these three similarly priced stocks be priced so differently when the strike prices and the time to expiration were exactly the same? A big reason is that the volatility of the underlying stock is an important determinant of an option's underlying value; and, in fact, these three stocks had very different volatilities. In this chapter, we explore this issue—and many others—in much greater depth using the Nobel Prize-winning Black–Scholes option pricing model.

22.1 Options

The Options Industry Council has a web page with lots of educational material at **www.optionseducation.org**.

An **option** is a contract giving its owner the right to buy or sell an asset at a fixed price on or before a given date. For example, an option on a building might give the buyer the right to buy the building for $1 million on or anytime before the Saturday prior to the third Wednesday in January 2019. Options are a unique type of financial contract because they give the buyer the right, but not the *obligation,* to do something. The buyer uses the option only if it is advantageous to do so; otherwise the option can be thrown away.

There is a special vocabulary associated with options. Here are some important definitions:

1. *Exercising the option:* The act of buying or selling the underlying asset via the option contract.

2. *Strike, or exercise, price:* The fixed price in the option contract at which the holder can buy or sell the underlying asset.

3. *Expiration date:* The maturity date of the option; after this date, the option is dead.

4. *American and European options:* An American option may be exercised anytime up to the expiration date. A European option differs from an American option in that it can be exercised only on the expiration date.

22.2 Call Options

The most common type of option is a **call option**. A call option gives the owner the right to buy an asset at a fixed price during a particular period. There is no restriction on the kind of asset, but the most common ones traded on exchanges are options on stocks and bonds.

For example, call options on IBM stock can be purchased on the Chicago Board Options Exchange. IBM does not issue (i.e., sell) call options on its common stock. Instead, individual investors are the original buyers and sellers of call options on IBM common stock. Suppose it is April 1. A representative call option on IBM stock enables an investor to buy 100 shares of IBM on or before September 19 (options expire on the Saturday after the third Friday of the month) at an exercise price of $100. This is a valuable option if there is some probability that the price of IBM common stock will exceed $100 on or before September 19.

THE VALUE OF A CALL OPTION AT EXPIRATION

What is the value of a call option contract on common stock at expiration? The answer depends on the value of the underlying stock at expiration.

Let's continue with the IBM example. Suppose the stock price is $130 at expiration. The buyer[1] of the call option has the right to buy the underlying stock at the exercise price of $100. In other words, he has the right to exercise the call. Having the right to buy something for $100 when it is worth $130 is obviously a good thing. The value of this right is $30 (=$130 − $100) on the expiration day.[2]

The call would be worth even more if the stock price was higher on the expiration day. For example, if IBM were selling for $150 on the date of expiration, the call would be worth $50 (=$150 − $100) at that time. In fact, the call's value increases $1 for every $1 rise in the stock price.

If the stock price is greater than the exercise price, we say that the call is *in the money*. Of course, it is also possible that the value of the common stock will turn out to be less than the exercise price, in which case we say that the call is *out of the money*. The holder will not exercise in this case. For example, if the stock price at the expiration date is $90, no rational investor would exercise. Why pay $100 for stock worth only $90? Because the option holder has no obligation to exercise the call, she can *walk away* from the option. As a consequence, if IBM's stock price is less than $100 on the expiration date, the value of the call option will be $0. In this case the value of the call option is not the difference between IBM's stock price and $100, as it would be if the holder of the call option had the *obligation* to exercise the call.

Here is the payoff of this call option at expiration:

	Payoff on the Expiration Date	
	If Stock Price Is Less Than $100	**If Stock Price Is Greater Than $100**
Call option value	$0	Stock price − $100

---

[1]We use *buyer, owner,* and *holder* interchangeably.

[2]This example assumes that the call lets the holder purchase one share of stock at $100. In reality, one call option contract would let the holder purchase 100 shares. The profit would then equal $3,000 [= ($130 − $100) × 100].

Figure 22.1

The Value of a
Call Option on the
Expiration Date

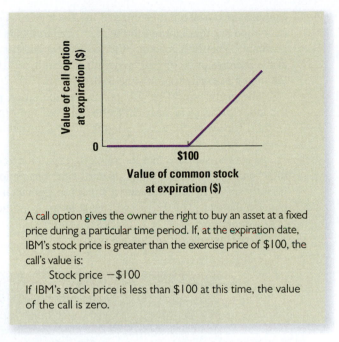

A call option gives the owner the right to buy an asset at a fixed price during a particular time period. If, at the expiration date, IBM's stock price is greater than the exercise price of $100, the call's value is:

Stock price −$100

If IBM's stock price is less than $100 at this time, the value of the call is zero.

Figure 22.1 plots the value of the call option at expiration against the value of IBM's stock. This is referred to as the *hockey stick diagram* of call option values. If the stock price is less than $100, the call is out of the money and worthless. If the stock price is greater than $100, the call is in the money and its value rises one-for-one with increases in the stock price. Notice that the call can never have a negative value. It is a *limited liability instrument,* which means that all the holder can lose is the initial amount she paid for it.

**EXAMPLE
22.1**

Call Option Payoffs   Suppose Mr. Optimist holds a one-year call option on TIX common stock. It is a European call option and can be exercised at $150. Assume that the expiration date has arrived. What is the value of the TIX call option on the expiration date? If TIX is selling for $200 per share, Mr. Optimist can exercise the option—purchase TIX at $150—and then immediately sell the share at $200. Mr. Optimist will have made $50 (=$200 − $150). Thus, the price of this call option must be $50 at expiration.

Instead, assume that TIX is selling for $100 per share on the expiration date. If Mr. Optimist still holds the call option, he will throw it out. The value of the TIX call option on the expiration date will be zero in this case.

22.3 Put Options

A **put option** can be viewed as the opposite of a call option. Just as a call gives the holder the right to buy the stock at a fixed price, a put gives the holder the right to *sell* the stock for a fixed exercise price.

THE VALUE OF A PUT OPTION AT EXPIRATION

The circumstances that determine the value of the put are the opposite of those for a call option because a put option gives the holder the right to sell shares. Let us assume that the exercise price of the put is $50 and the stock price at expiration is $40. The owner of this put option has the right to sell the stock for *more* than it is worth, something that is clearly profitable. That is, he can buy the stock at the market price of $40 and immediately sell it at the exercise price of $50, generating a profit of $10 (=$50 − $40). Thus, the value of the option at expiration must be $10.

The profit would be greater still if the stock price were lower. For example, if the stock price were only $30, the value of the option would be $20 (=$50 − $30). In fact, for every $1 that the stock price declines at expiration, the value of the put rises by $1.

However, suppose that the stock at expiration is trading at $60—or any price above the exercise price of $50. The owner of the put option would not want to exercise here. It is a losing proposition to sell a stock for $50 when it trades in the open market at $60. Instead, the owner of the put will walk away from the option. That is, he will let the put option expire.

Here is the payoff of this put option:

	Payoff on the Expiration Date	
	If Stock Price Is Less Than $50	**If Stock Price Is Greater Than $50**
Put option value	$50 − Stock price	$0

Figure 22.2 plots the values of a put option for all possible values of the underlying stock. It is instructive to compare Figure 22.2 to Figure 22.1 for the call option. The call option is valuable when the stock price is above the exercise price, and the put option is valuable when the stock price is below the exercise price.

Figure 22.2

The Value of a Put Option on the Expiration Date

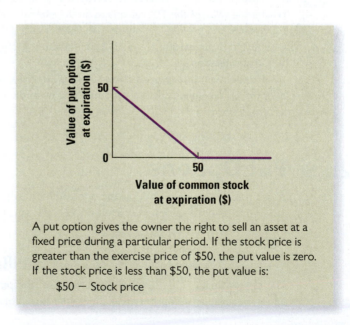

A put option gives the owner the right to sell an asset at a fixed price during a particular period. If the stock price is greater than the exercise price of $50, the put value is zero. If the stock price is less than $50, the put value is:

$50 − Stock price

Put Option Payoffs   Ms. Pessimist believes that BMI will fall from its current $160 per-share price. She buys a put. Her put option contract gives her the right to sell a share of BMI stock at $150 one year from now. If the price of BMI is $200 on the expiration date, she will tear up the put option contract because it is worthless. That is, she will not want to sell stock worth $200 for the exercise price of $150.

On the other hand, if BMI is selling for $100 on the expiration date, she will exercise the option. In this case she can buy a share of BMI in the market for $100 per share and turn around and sell the share at the exercise price of $150. Her profit will be $50 (=$150 − $100). Therefore, the value of the put option on the expiration date will be $50.

22.4 Selling Options

An investor who sells (or *writes*) a call on common stock must deliver shares of the common stock if required to do so by the call option holder. Notice that the seller is *obligated* to do so.

If, at the expiration date, the price of the common stock is greater than the exercise price, the holder will exercise the call and the seller must give the holder shares of stock in exchange for the exercise price. The seller loses the difference between the stock price and the exercise price. For example, assume that the stock price is $60 and the exercise price is $50. Knowing that exercise is imminent, the option seller buys stock in the open market at $60. Because she is obligated to sell at $50, she loses $10 (=$50 − $60). Conversely, if at the expiration date the price of the common stock is below the exercise price, the call option will not be exercised and the seller's liability is zero.

Why would the seller of a call place himself in such a precarious position? After all, the seller loses money if the stock price ends up above the exercise price, and he merely avoids losing money if the stock price ends up below the exercise price. The answer is that the seller is paid to take this risk. On the day that the option transaction takes place, the seller receives the price that the buyer pays.

Now let's look at the seller of puts. An investor who sells a put on common stock agrees to purchase shares of common stock if the put holder should so request. The seller loses on this deal if the stock price falls below the exercise price. For example, assume that the stock price is $40 and the exercise price is $50. The holder of the put will exercise in this case. In other words, she will sell the underlying stock at the exercise price of $50. This means that the seller of the put must buy the underlying stock at the exercise price of $50. Because the stock is worth only $40, the loss here is $10 (=$40 − $50).

The values of the "sell-a-call" and "sell-a-put" positions are depicted in Figure 22.3. The graph on the left side of the figure shows that the seller of a call loses nothing when the stock price at the expiration date is below $50. However, the seller loses a dollar for every dollar that the stock rises above $50. The graph in the center of the figure shows that the seller of a put loses nothing when the stock price at expiration date is above $50. However, the seller loses a dollar for every dollar that the stock falls below $50.

It is worthwhile to spend a few minutes comparing the graphs in Figure 22.3 to those in Figures 22.1 and 22.2. The graph of selling a call (the graph on the left side of

Check out these
option exchanges:
www.cboe.com
www.nasdaq.com
www.cmegroup
.com
www.euronext.com

Figure 22.3   The Payoffs to Sellers of Calls and Puts and to Buyers of Common Stock

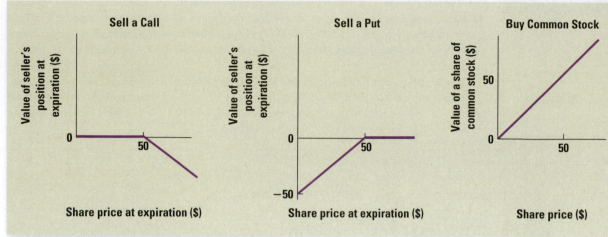

Figure 22.3) is the mirror image of the graph of buying a call (Figure 22.1).[3] This occurs because options are a zero-sum game. The seller of a call loses what the buyer makes. Similarly, the graph of selling a put (the middle graph in Figure 22.3) is the mirror image of the graph of buying a put (Figure 22.2). Again, the seller of a put loses what the buyer makes.

Figure 22.3 also shows the value at expiration of simply buying common stock. Notice that buying the stock is the same as buying a call option on the stock with an exercise price of zero. This is not surprising. If the exercise price is zero, the call holder can buy the stock for nothing, which is really the same as owning it.

22.5   Option Quotes

For more about option ticker symbols, go to the "Symbol Directory" link under "Tools & Resources" at **www.cboe.com**.

Now that we understand the definitions for calls and puts, let's see how these options are quoted. Table 22.1 presents information about Abbott Laboratories options expiring in August 2015, obtained from finance.yahoo.com. At the time of these quotes, Abbott Labs stock was selling for $44.90.

On the left in the table are the available strike prices. On the top are call option quotes; put option quotes are on the bottom. The second column contains the contract name, which uniquely indicates the underlying stock; the type of option; and the strike price. Next, we have the most recent prices on the options ("Last") and the change from the previous day. Bid and ask prices follow. Note that option prices are quoted on a per-option basis, but trading actually occurs in standardized contracts, where each contract calls for the purchase (for calls) or sale (for puts) of 100 shares. Thus, the call option with a strike price of $44 last traded at $3.50 per option, or $350 per contract. The final two columns contain volume, quoted in contracts, and the open interest, which is the number of contracts currently outstanding.

---

[3]Actually, because of differing exercise prices, the two graphs are not quite mirror images of each other. The exercise price in Figure 22.1 is $100, and the exercise price in Figure 22.3 is $50.

Table 22.1 Information about the Options of Abbott Laboratories

CALLS

Strike	Contract Name	Last	Bid	Ask	Change	% Change	Volume	Open Interest	Implied Volatility
40.00	ABT150821C00040000	5.62	5.45	5.80	0.00	0.00%	4	4	19.75%
42.00	ABT150821C00042000	4.80	4.20	4.35	0.00	0.00%	2	7	19.20%
43.00	ABT150821C00043000	4.16	3.55	3.65	0.00	0.00%	10	50	18.53%
44.00	ABT150821C00044000	3.50	2.98	3.10	0.00	0.00%	10	10	18.58%
45.00	ABT150821C00045000	2.65	2.45	2.52	0.00	0.00%	10	14	17.98%
46.00	ABT150821C00046000	1.93	1.98	2.06	0.00	0.00%	23	272	17.80%
47.00	ABT150821C00047000	1.79	1.58	1.65	0.00	0.00%	1	129	17.55%
48.00	ABT150821C00048000	1.51	1.24	1.30	0.00	0.00%	5	69	17.32%
49.00	ABT150821C00049000	1.23	0.96	1.01	0.00	0.00%	1	1	17.12%
50.00	ABT150821C00050000	0.93	0.74	0.78	0.00	0.00%	2	30	16.99%

PUTS

Strike	Contract Name	Last	Bid	Ask	Change	% Change	Volume	Open Interest	Implied Volatility
37.00	ABT150821P00037000	0.62	0.69	0.74	0.00	0.00%	10	71	25.34%
39.00	ABT150821P00039000	0.91	1.01	1.05	0.00	0.00%	12	12	23.78%
40.00	ABT150821P00040000	1.15	1.22	1.26	0.00	0.00%	1	15	23.15%
45.00	ABT150821P00045000	2.73	3.00	3.10	0.00	0.00%	27	49	21.36%

22.6 Combinations of Options

 Excel Master coverage online

Puts and calls can serve as building blocks for more complex option contracts. For example, Figure 22.4 illustrates the payoff from buying a put option on a stock and simultaneously buying the stock.

If the share price is greater than the exercise price, the put option is worthless, and the value of the combined position is equal to the value of the common stock. If, instead, the exercise price is greater than the share price, the decline in the value of the shares will be exactly offset by the rise in the value of the put.

Figure 22.4 Payoff to the Combination of Buying a Put and Buying the Underlying Stock

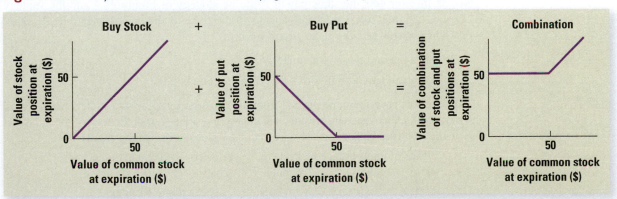

Figure 22.5 Payoff to the Combination of Buying a Call and Buying a Zero Coupon Bond

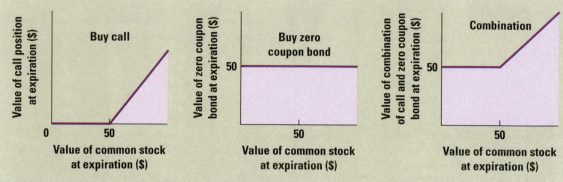

The graph of buying a call and buying a zero coupon bond is the same as the graph of buying a put and buying the stock in Figure 22.4

The strategy of buying a put and buying the underlying stock is called a *protective put*. It is as if we are buying insurance for the stock. The stock can always be sold at the exercise price, regardless of how far the market price of the stock falls.

Note that the combination of buying a put and buying the underlying stock has the same *shape* in Figure 22.4 as the call purchase in Figure 22.1. To pursue this point, let's consider the graph for buying a call, which is shown at the far left of Figure 22.5. This graph is the same as Figure 22.1, except that the exercise price is $50 here. Now let's try the strategy of:

(Leg *A*) Buying a call.

(Leg *B*) Buying a risk-free, zero coupon bond (i.e., a T-bill) with a face value of $50 that matures on the same day that the option expires.

We have drawn the graph of Leg *A* of this strategy at the far left of Figure 22.5, but what does the graph of Leg *B* look like? It looks like the middle graph of the figure. That is, anyone buying this zero coupon bond will be guaranteed to receive $50, regardless of the price of the stock at expiration.

What does the graph of *simultaneously* buying both Leg *A* and Leg *B* of this strategy look like? It looks like the far right graph of Figure 22.5. That is, the investor receives a guaranteed $50 from the bond, regardless of what happens to the stock. In addition, the investor receives a payoff from the call of $1 for every $1 that the price of the stock rises above the exercise price of $50.

The far right graph of Figure 22.5 looks *exactly* like the far right graph of Figure 22.4. Thus, an investor gets the same payoff from the strategy of Figure 22.4 and the strategy of Figure 22.5, regardless of what happens to the price of the underlying stock. In other words, the investor gets the same payoff from:

1. Buying a put and buying the underlying stock.

2. Buying a call and buying a risk-free, zero coupon bond.

If investors have the same payoffs from the two strategies, the two strategies must have the same cost. Otherwise, all investors will choose the strategy with the lower cost and avoid the strategy with the higher cost. This leads to the following interesting result:

$$\underset{\text{stock}}{\text{Price of underlying}} + \underset{\text{put}}{\text{Price of}} = \underset{\text{call}}{\text{Price of}} + \underset{\text{exercise price}}{\text{Present value of}}$$ **(22.1)**

Cost of first strategy = Cost of second strategy

This relationship is known as **put–call parity** and is one of the most fundamental relationships concerning options. It says that there are two ways of buying a protective put. You can buy a put and buy the underlying stock simultaneously. Here, your total cost is the price of the underlying stock plus the price of the put. Or you can buy a call and buy a zero coupon bond. Here, your total cost is the price of the call plus the price of the zero coupon bond. The price of the zero coupon bond is equal to the present value of the exercise price—that is, the present value of $50 in our example.

Equation 22.1 is a very precise relationship. It holds only if the put and the call have both the same exercise price and the same expiration date. In addition, the maturity date of the zero coupon bond must be the same as the expiration date of the options.

To see how fundamental put–call parity is, let's rearrange the formula, yielding:

$$\begin{matrix} \text{Price of underlying} \\ \text{stock} \end{matrix} = \begin{matrix} \text{Price of} \\ \text{call} \end{matrix} - \begin{matrix} \text{Price of} \\ \text{put} \end{matrix} + \begin{matrix} \text{Present value of} \\ \text{exercise price} \end{matrix}$$

This relationship now states that you can replicate the purchase of a share of stock by buying a call, selling a put, and buying a zero coupon bond. (Note that because a minus sign comes before "Price of put," the put is sold, not bought.) Investors in this three-legged strategy are said to have purchased a *synthetic* stock.

Let's do one more transformation:

Covered Call Strategy:

$$\begin{matrix} \text{Price of underlying} \\ \text{stock} \end{matrix} - \begin{matrix} \text{Price} \\ \text{of call} \end{matrix} = - \begin{matrix} \text{Price} \\ \text{of put} \end{matrix} + \begin{matrix} \text{Present value of} \\ \text{exercise price} \end{matrix}$$

Many investors like to buy a stock and write a call on the stock simultaneously. This is a conservative strategy known as *selling a covered call*. The preceding put–call parity relationship tells us that this strategy is equivalent to selling a put and buying a zero coupon bond. Figure 22.6 develops the graph for the covered call. You can verify that the covered call can be replicated by selling a put and simultaneously buying a zero coupon bond.

Figure 22.6   Payoff to the Combination of Buying a Stock and Selling a Call

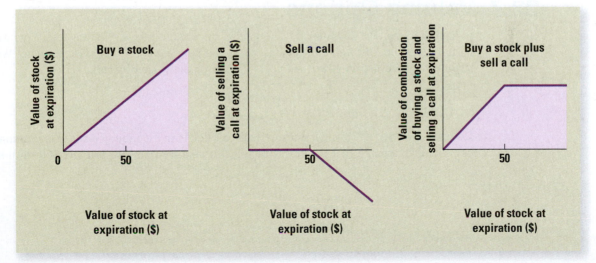

Of course, there are other ways of rearranging the basic put–call relationship. For each rearrangement, the strategy on the left side is equivalent to the strategy on the right side. The beauty of put–call parity is that it shows how any strategy in options can be achieved in two different ways.

To test your understanding of put–call parity, suppose shares of stock in Joseph–Belmont, Inc., are selling for $80. A three-month call option with an $85 strike price goes for $6. The risk-free rate is .5 percent per month. What's the value of a three-month put option with an $85 strike price?

We can rearrange the put–call parity relationship to solve for the price of the put as follows:

$$\begin{array}{llll}
\text{Price of} \\ \text{put} & = - \begin{array}{c}\text{Price of underlying}\\ \text{stock}\end{array} & + \begin{array}{c}\text{Price of}\\ \text{call}\end{array} & + \begin{array}{c}\text{Present value}\\ \text{of strike price}\end{array} \\
& = - \quad\quad \$80 & + \quad \$6 & + \quad \$85/1.005^3 \\
& = \$9.74
\end{array}$$

As shown, the value of the put is $9.74.

**EXAMPLE
22.3**

A Synthetic T-Bill   Suppose shares of stock in Smolira Corp. are selling for $110. A call option on Smolira with one year to maturity and a $110 strike price sells for $15. A put with the same terms sells for $5. What's the risk-free rate?

To answer, we need to use put–call parity to determine the price of a risk-free, zero coupon bond:

Price of underlying stock + Price of put − Price of call = Present value of exercise price

Plugging in the numbers, we get:

$$\$110 + \$5 - \$15 = \$100$$

Because the present value of the $110 strike price is $100, the implied risk-free rate is 10 percent.

22.7 Valuing Options

In the last section we determined what options are worth on the expiration date. Now we wish to determine the value of options when you buy them well before expiration.[4] We begin by considering the lower and upper bounds on the value of a call.

BOUNDING THE VALUE OF A CALL

Lower Bound   Consider an American call that is in the money prior to expiration. For example, assume that the stock price is $60 and the exercise price is $50. In this

---

[4]Our discussion in this section is of American options because they are more commonly traded in the real world. As necessary, we will indicate differences for European options.

case the option cannot sell below $10. To see this, note the following simple strategy if the option sells at, say, $9:

Date		Transaction	
Today	(1)	Buy call.	−$ 9
Today	(2)	Exercise call—that is, buy underlying stock at exercise price.	−$50
Today	(3)	Sell stock at current market price.	+$60
		Arbitrage profit	+$ 1

The type of profit that is described in this transaction is an *arbitrage* profit. Arbitrage profits come from transactions that have no risk or cost and cannot occur regularly in normal, well-functioning financial markets. The excess demand for these options would quickly force the option price up to at least $10 (=$60 − $50).

Of course, the price of the option is likely to be above $10. Investors will rationally pay more than $10 because of the possibility that the stock will rise above $60 before expiration. For example, suppose the call actually sells for $12. In this case we say that the *intrinsic value* of the option is $10, meaning it must always be worth at least this much. The remaining $12 − $10 = $2 is sometimes called the *time premium,* and it represents the extra amount that investors are willing to pay because of the possibility that the stock price will rise before the option expires.

Upper Bound   Is there an upper boundary for the option price as well? It turns out that the upper boundary is the price of the underlying stock. That is, an option to buy common stock cannot have a greater value than the common stock itself. A call option can be used to buy common stock with a payment of the exercise price. It would be foolish to buy stock this way if the stock could be purchased directly at a lower price. The upper and lower bounds are represented in Figure 22.7.

Figure 22.7
The Upper and Lower Boundaries of Call Option Values

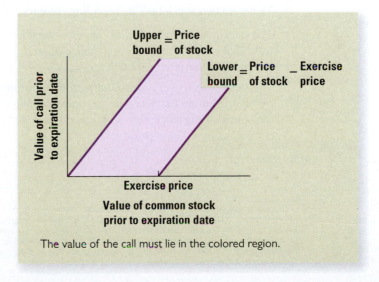

The value of the call must lie in the colored region.

THE FACTORS DETERMINING CALL OPTION VALUES

The previous discussion indicated that the price of a call option must fall somewhere in the shaded region of Figure 22.7. We now will determine more precisely where in the shaded region it should be. The factors that determine a call's value can be broken into two sets. The first set contains the features of the option contract. The two basic contractual features are the exercise price and the expiration date. The second set of factors affecting the call price concerns characteristics of the stock and the market.

Exercise Price
An increase in the exercise price reduces the value of the call. For example, imagine that there are two calls on a stock selling at $60. The first call has an exercise price of $50 and the second one has an exercise price of $40. Which call would you rather have? Clearly, you would rather have the call with an exercise price of $40 because that one is $20 (=$60 − $40) in the money. In other words, the call with an exercise price of $40 should sell for more than an otherwise identical call with an exercise price of $50.

Expiration Date
The value of an American call option must be at least as great as the value of an otherwise identical option with a shorter term to expiration. Consider two American calls: One has a maturity of nine months and the other expires in six months. Obviously, the nine-month call has the same rights as the six-month call, and it also has an additional three months within which these rights can be exercised. It cannot be worth less and will generally be more valuable.[5]

There is a good discussion of options at **www.nasdaqtrader .com**.

Stock Price
Other things being equal, the higher the stock price, the more valuable the call option will be. For example, if a stock is worth $80, a call with an exercise price of $100 isn't worth very much. If the stock soars to $120, the call becomes much more valuable.

Now consider Figure 22.8, which shows the relationship between the call price and the stock price prior to expiration. The curve indicates that the call price increases as the stock price increases. Furthermore, it can be shown that the relationship is represented not by a straight line, but by a *convex* curve. That is, the increase in the call price for a given change in the stock price is greater when the stock price is high than when the stock price is low.

There are two special points regarding the curve in Figure 22.8:

1. *The stock is worthless.* The call must be worthless if the underlying stock is worthless. That is, if the stock has no chance of attaining any value, it is not worthwhile to pay the exercise price to obtain the stock.

2. *The stock price is very high relative to the exercise price.* In this situation the owner of the call knows that she will end up exercising the call. She can view herself as the owner of the stock now with one difference: She must pay the exercise price at expiration.

---

[5]This relationship need not hold for a European call option. Consider a firm with two otherwise identical European call options, one expiring at the end of May and the other expiring a few months later. Further assume that a *huge* dividend is paid in early June. If the first call is exercised at the end of May, its holder will receive the underlying stock. If he does not sell the stock, he will receive the large dividend shortly thereafter. However, the holder of the second call will receive the stock through exercise after the dividend is paid. Because the market knows that the holder of this option will miss the dividend, the value of the second call option could be less than the value of the first.

Figure 22.8

Value of an American
Call as a Function of
Stock Price

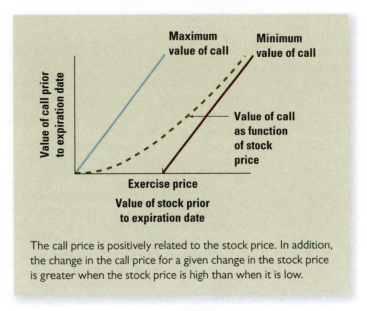

The call price is positively related to the stock price. In addition,
the change in the call price for a given change in the stock price
is greater when the stock price is high than when it is low.

Thus, the value of her position—that is, the value of the call—is:

$$\text{Stock price} - \text{Present value of exercise price}$$

These two points on the curve are summarized in the bottom half of Table 22.2.

The Key Factor: The Variability of the Underlying Asset   The
greater the variability of the underlying asset, the more valuable the call option will be.
Consider the following example. Suppose that just before the call expires, the stock price
will be either $100 with probability .5 or $80 with probability .5. What will be the value of
a call with an exercise price of $110? Clearly, it will be worthless because no matter what
happens to the stock, its price will always be below the exercise price.

Table 22.2

Factors Affecting
American Option
Values

Increase in	Call Option*	Put Option*
Value of underlying asset (stock price)	+	−
Exercise price	−	+
Stock volatility	+	+
Interest rate	+	−
Time to expiration	+	+

In addition to the preceding, we have presented the following four relationships for
American calls:

1. The call price can never be greater than the stock price (*upper bound*).

2. The call price can never be less than either zero or the difference between the stock price
   and the exercise price (*lower bound*).

3. The call is worth zero if the stock is worth zero.

4. When the stock price is much greater than the exercise price, the call price tends toward the
   difference between the stock price and the present value of the exercise price.

*The signs (+, −) indicate the effect of the variables on the value of the option. For example, the two +s for stock volatility indicate
that an increase in volatility will increase both the value of a call and the value of a put.

Figure 22.9

Distribution of Common Stock Price at Expiration for Both Security A and Security B. Options on the Two Securities Have the Same Exercise Price.

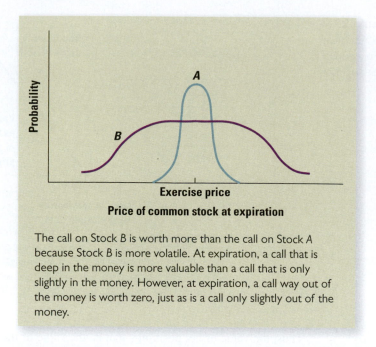

The call on Stock B is worth more than the call on Stock A because Stock B is more volatile. At expiration, a call that is deep in the money is more valuable than a call that is only slightly in the money. However, at expiration, a call way out of the money is worth zero, just as is a call only slightly out of the money.

For an option-oriented site focusing on volatilities, visit **www.ivolatility.com**.

What happens if the stock is more variable? Suppose we add $20 to the best case and take $20 away from the worst case. Now the stock has a one-half chance of being worth $60 and a one-half chance of being worth $120. We have spread the stock returns, but, of course, the expected value of the stock has stayed the same:

$$(1/2 \times \$80) + (1/2 \times \$100) = \$90 = (1/2 \times \$60) + (1/2 \times \$120)$$

Notice that the call option has value now because there is a one-half chance that the stock price will be $120, or $10 above the exercise price of $110. This illustrates an important point. There is a fundamental distinction between holding an option on an underlying asset and holding the underlying asset. If investors in the marketplace are risk-averse, a rise in the variability of the stock will decrease its market value. However, the holder of a call receives payoffs from the positive tail of the probability distribution. As a consequence, a rise in the variability of the underlying stock increases the market value of the call.

This result can also be seen from Figure 22.9. Consider two Stocks, A and B, each of which is normally distributed. For each security, the figure illustrates the probability of different stock prices on the expiration date. As can be seen from the figure, Stock B has more volatility than does Stock A. This means that Stock B has a higher probability of both abnormally high returns and abnormally low returns. Let us assume that options on each of the two securities have the same exercise price. To option holders, a return much below average on Stock B is no worse than a return only moderately below average on Stock A. In either situation the option expires out of the money. However, to option holders, a return much above average on Stock B is better than a return only moderately above average on Stock A. Because a call's price at the expiration date is the difference between the stock price and the exercise price, the value of the call on B at expiration will be higher in this case.

The Interest Rate   Call prices are also a function of the level of interest rates. Buyers of calls do not pay the exercise price until they exercise the option, if they do so at all. The ability to delay payment is more valuable when interest rates are high and less valuable when interest rates are low. Thus, the value of a call is positively related to interest rates.

A QUICK DISCUSSION OF FACTORS DETERMINING PUT OPTION VALUES

Given our extended discussion of the factors influencing a call's value, we can examine the effect of these factors on puts very easily. Table 22.2 summarizes the five factors influencing the prices of both American calls and American puts. The effect of three factors on puts are the opposite of the effect of these three factors on calls:

1. The put's market value *decreases* as the stock price increases because puts are in the money when the stock sells below the exercise price.

2. The value of a put with a high exercise price is *greater* than the value of an otherwise identical put with a low exercise price for the reason given in (1).

3. A high interest rate *adversely* affects the value of a put. The ability to sell a stock at a fixed exercise price sometime in the future is worth less if the present value of the exercise price is reduced by a high interest rate.

The effect of the other two factors on puts is the same as the effect of these factors on calls:

4. The value of an American put with a distant expiration date is greater than an otherwise identical put with an earlier expiration.[6] The longer time to maturity gives the put holder more flexibility, just as it did in the case of a call.

5. Volatility of the underlying stock increases the value of the put. The reasoning is analogous to that for a call. At expiration, a put that is way in the money is more valuable than a put only slightly in the money. However, at expiration, a put way out of the money is worth zero, just as is a put only slightly out of the money.

22.8 An Option Pricing Formula

We have explained *qualitatively* that the value of a call option is a function of five variables:

1. The current price of the underlying asset, which for stock options is the price of a share of common stock.

2. The exercise price.

3. The time to the expiration date.

4. The variance of the underlying asset.

5. The risk-free interest rate.

It is time to replace the qualitative model with a precise option valuation model. The model we choose is the famous Black–Scholes option pricing model. You can put numbers into the Black–Scholes model and get values back.

The Black–Scholes model is represented by a rather imposing formula. A derivation of the formula is simply not possible in this textbook, as many students will be happy to learn. However, some appreciation for the achievement as well as some intuitive understanding are in order.

In the early chapters of this book, we showed how to discount capital budgeting projects using the net present value formula. We also used this approach to value stocks and bonds. Why, students sometimes ask, can't the same NPV formula be used to value

---

[6]Though this result must hold in the case of an American put, it need not hold for a European put.

puts and calls? This is a good question: The earliest attempts at valuing options used NPV. Unfortunately, the attempts were not successful because no one could determine the appropriate discount rate. An option is generally riskier than the underlying stock, but no one knew exactly how much riskier.

Black and Scholes attacked the problem by pointing out that a strategy of borrowing to finance a stock purchase duplicates the risk of a call. Then, knowing the price of a stock already, we can determine the price of a call such that its return is identical to that of the stock-with-borrowing alternative.

We illustrate the intuition behind the Black–Scholes approach by considering a simple example where a combination of a call and a stock eliminates all risk. This example works because we let the future stock price be one of only *two* values. Hence, the example is called a *two-state*, or *binomial option, model.* By eliminating the possibility that the stock price can take on other values, we are able to duplicate the call exactly.

A TWO-STATE OPTION MODEL

Consider the following example. Suppose the current market price of a stock is $50 and the stock will either be $60 or $40 at the end of the year. Further, imagine a call option on this stock with a one-year expiration date and a $50 exercise price. Investors can borrow at 10 percent. Our goal is to determine the value of the call.

To value the call correctly, we need to examine two strategies. The first is to simply buy the call. The second is to:

1. Buy one-half a share of stock.
2. Borrow $18.18, implying a payment of principal and interest at the end of the year of $20 (=$18.18 × 1.10).

As you will see shortly, the cash flows from the second strategy match the cash flows from buying a call. (A little later we will show how we came up with the exact fraction of a share of stock to buy and the exact borrowing amount.) Because the cash flows match, we say that we are *duplicating* the call with the second strategy.

At the end of the year, the future payoffs are set out as follows:

Initial Transactions	Future Payoffs	
	If Stock Price Is $60	If Stock Price Is $40
1. Buy a call	$60 − $50 = $10	$ 0
2. Buy $\frac{1}{2}$ share of stock	$\frac{1}{2}$ × $60 = $30	$\frac{1}{2}$ × $40 = $20
Borrow $18.18 at 10%	−($18.18 × 1.10) = −$20	−$20
Total from stock and borrowing strategy	$10	$ 0

Note that the future payoff structure of the "buy-a-call" strategy is duplicated by the strategy of "buy stock and borrow." That is, under either strategy an investor would end up with $10 if the stock price rose and $0 if the stock price fell. Thus these two strategies are equivalent as far as traders are concerned.

If two strategies always have the same cash flows at the end of the year, how must their initial costs be related? The two strategies must have the *same* initial cost.

Otherwise, there will be an arbitrage possibility. We can easily calculate this cost for our strategy of buying stock and borrowing:

Buy $\frac{1}{2}$ share of stock	$\frac{1}{2} \times \$50 =$	$25.00
Borrow $18.18		$-\$18.18$
		$ 6.82

Because the call option provides the same payoffs at expiration as does the strategy of buying stock and borrowing, the call must be priced at $6.82. This is the value of the call option in a market without arbitrage profits.

We left two issues unexplained in the preceding example.

Determining the Delta   How did we know to buy one-half share of stock in the duplicating strategy? Actually, the answer is easier than it might first appear. The call price at the end of the year will be either $10 or $0, whereas the stock price will be either $60 or $40. Thus, the call price has a potential swing of $10 (=$10 − $0) next period, whereas the stock price has a potential swing of $20 (=$60 − $40). We can write this in terms of the following ratio:

$$\text{Delta} = \frac{\text{Swing of call}}{\text{Swing of stock}} = \frac{\$10 - \$0}{\$60 - \$40} = \frac{1}{2}$$

As indicated, this ratio is called the *delta* of the call. In words, a $1 swing in the price of the stock gives rise to a $.50 swing in the price of the call. Because we are trying to duplicate the call with the stock, it seems sensible to buy one-half share of stock instead of buying one call. In other words, the risk of buying one-half share of stock should be the same as the risk of buying one call.

Determining the Amount of Borrowing   How did we know how much to borrow? Buying one-half share of stock brings us either $30 or $20 at expiration, which is exactly $20 more than the payoffs of $10 and $0, respectively, from the call. To duplicate the call through a purchase of stock, we should also borrow enough money so that we have to pay back exactly $20 of interest and principal. This amount of borrowing is merely the present value of $20, which is $18.18 (=$20/1.10).

Now that we know how to determine both the delta and the borrowing, we can write the value of the call as follows:

$$\text{Value of call} = \text{Stock price} \times \text{Delta} - \text{Amount borrowed} \qquad \textbf{(22.2)}$$

$$\$6.82 = \$50 \times \frac{1}{2} - \$18.18$$

We will find this intuition useful in explaining the Black–Scholes model.

Risk-Neutral Valuation   Before leaving this simple example, we should comment on a remarkable feature. We found the exact value of the option without even knowing the probability that the stock would go up or down! If an optimist thought the probability of an up move was high and a pessimist thought it was low, they would still agree on the option value. How can that be? The answer is that the current $50 stock price already balances the views of the optimists and the pessimists. The option reflects that balance because its value depends on the stock price.

This insight provides us with another approach to valuing the call. If we don't need the probabilities of the two states to value the call, perhaps we can select *any* probabilities we want and still come up with the right answer. Suppose we selected probabilities such that the expected return on the stock is equal to the risk-free rate of 10 percent. We know that the stock return given a rise in the stock's price is 20 percent (=$60/$50 − 1) and the stock return given a fall in the stock's price is −20 percent (=$40/$50 − 1). Thus, we can solve for the probability of a rise necessary to achieve an expected return of 10 percent as follows:

10% = Probability of a rise × 20% + (1 − Probability of rise) × −20%

Solving this formula, we find that the probability of a rise is 3/4 and the probability of a fall is 1/4. If we apply these probabilities to the call, we can value it as:

$$\text{Value of call} = \frac{\frac{3}{4} \times \$10 + \frac{1}{4} \times \$0}{1.10} = \$6.82$$

the same value we got from the duplicating approach.

Why did we select probabilities such that the expected return on the stock is 10 percent? We wanted to work with the special case where investors are *risk-neutral*. This case occurs when the expected return on *any* asset (including both the stock and the call) is equal to the risk-free rate. In other words, this case occurs when investors demand no additional compensation beyond the risk-free rate, regardless of the risk of the asset in question.

What would have happened if we had assumed that the expected return on the stock was greater than the risk-free rate? The value of the call would still be $6.82. However, the calculations would be difficult. For example, if we assumed that the expected return on the stock was 11 percent, we would have had to derive the expected return on the call. Although the expected return on the call would have been higher than 11 percent, it would have taken a lot of work to determine the expected return precisely. Why do any more work than you have to? Because we can't think of any good reason, we (and most other financial economists) choose to assume risk neutrality.

Thus, the preceding material allows us to value a call in the following two ways:

1. Determine the cost of a strategy duplicating the call. This strategy involves an investment in a fractional share of stock financed by partial borrowing.

2. Calculate the probabilities of a rise and a fall in stock prices under the assumption of risk neutrality. Use these probabilities in conjunction with the risk-free rate to discount the payoffs of the call at expiration.

THE BLACK–SCHOLES MODEL

There's a Black–Scholes calculator (and a lot more) at **www.numa.com** **.www.margrabe** **.com/optionpricing** **.html**

The preceding example illustrates the duplicating strategy. Unfortunately, a strategy such as this will not work in the real world over, say, a one-year time frame because there are many more than two possibilities for next year's stock price. However, the number of possibilities is reduced as the period is shortened. Is there a time period over which the stock price can only have two outcomes? Academics argue that the assumption that there are only two possibilities for the stock price over the next infinitesimal instant is quite plausible.[7]

In our opinion, the fundamental insight of Black and Scholes is to shorten the time period. They show that a specific combination of stock and borrowing can indeed duplicate a call over an infinitesimal time horizon. Because the price of the stock will change over the first instant, another combination of stock and borrowing is needed to duplicate the call over the second

---

[7]A full treatment of this assumption can be found in John C. Hull, *Options, Futures and Other Derivatives,* 8th ed. (Upper Saddle River, NJ: Prentice Hall, 2011).

instant and so on. By adjusting the combination from moment to moment, they can continually duplicate the call. It may boggle the mind that a formula can (1) determine the duplicating combination at any moment and (2) value the option based on this duplicating strategy. Suffice it to say that their dynamic strategy allows them to value a call in the real world, just as we showed how to value the call in the two-state model.

This is the basic intuition behind the Black–Scholes (BS) model. Because the actual derivation of their formula is, alas, far beyond the scope of this text, we simply present the formula itself:

Black–Scholes Model:

$$C = SN(d_1) - Ee^{-Rt} N(d_2)$$

where:

$$d_1 = [\ln(S/E) + (R + \sigma^2/2)t]/\sqrt{\sigma^2 t}$$
$$d_2 = d_1 - \sqrt{\sigma^2 t}$$

This formula for the value of a call, C, is one of the most complex in finance. However, it involves only five parameters:

1. S = Current stock price.
2. E = Exercise price of call.
3. R = Annual risk-free rate of return, continuously compounded.
4. σ^2 = Variance (per year) of the continuous return on the stock.
5. t = Time (in years) to expiration date.

In addition, there is this statistical concept:

$$N(d) = \text{Probability that a standardized, normally distributed,}$$
$$\text{random variable will be less than or equal to } d.$$

Rather than discuss the formula in its algebraic state, we illustrate the formula with an example.

EXAMPLE
22.4

Black–Scholes   Consider Private Equipment Company (PEC). On October 4 of Year 0, the PEC April 49 call option had a closing value of $4. The stock itself was selling at $50. On October 4, the option had 199 days to expiration (maturity date = April 21, Year 1). The annual risk-free interest rate, continuously compounded, was 7 percent.

This information determines three variables directly:

1. The stock price, S, is $50.
2. The exercise price, E, is $49.
3. The risk-free rate, R, is .07.

In addition, the time to maturity, t, can be calculated quickly: The formula calls for t to be expressed in *years*.

4. We express the 199-day interval in years as $t = 199/365$.

In the real world, an option trader would know S and E exactly. Traders generally view U.S. Treasury bills as riskless, so a current quote from The *Wall Street Journal* or a similar source would be obtained for the interest rate. The trader would also know (or could count) the number of days to expiration exactly. Thus, the fraction of a year to expiration, t, could be calculated quickly.

(continued)

The problem comes in determining the variance of the stock's return. The formula calls for the variance between the purchase date of October 4 and the expiration date. Unfortunately, this represents the future, so the correct value for variance is not available. Instead, traders frequently estimate variance from past data, just as we calculated variance in an earlier chapter. In addition, some traders may use intuition to adjust their estimate. For example, if anticipation of an upcoming event is likely to increase the volatility of the stock, the trader might adjust her estimate of variance upward to reflect this. (This problem was most severe right after the October 19, 1987, crash. The stock market was quite risky in the aftermath, so estimates using precrash data were too low.)

The preceding discussion was intended merely to mention the difficulties in variance estimation, not to present a solution. For our purposes, we assume that a trader has come up with an estimate of variance:

5. The variance of Private Equipment Co. has been estimated to be .09 per year.

Using these five parameters, we calculate the Black–Scholes value of the PEC call option in three steps:

Step 1: *Calculate d_1 and d_2.* These values can be determined by a straightforward, albeit tedious, insertion of our parameters into the basic formula. We have:

$$d_1 = \left[\ln\left(\frac{S}{E}\right) + (R + \sigma^2/2)t\right]\bigg/\sqrt{\sigma^2 t}$$

$$= \left[\ln\left(\frac{50}{49}\right) + (.07 + .09/2) \times \frac{199}{365}\right]\bigg/\sqrt{.09 \times \frac{199}{365}}$$

$$= [.0202 + .0627]/.2215 = .3742$$

$$d_2 = d_1 - \sqrt{\sigma^2 t}$$

$$= .1527$$

Step 2: *Calculate $N(d_1)$ and $N(d_2)$.* We can best understand the values $N(d_1)$ and $N(d_2)$ by examining Figure 22.10. The figure shows the normal distribution with an expected value of 0 and a standard deviation of 1. This is frequently called the **standardized normal distribution**. We mentioned in an earlier chapter that the probability that a drawing from this distribution will be between −1 and +1 (within one standard deviation of its mean, in other words) is 68.26 percent.

Now let us ask a different question: What is the probability that a drawing from the standardized normal distribution will be *below* a particular value? For example, the probability that a drawing will be below 0 is clearly 50 percent because the normal distribution is symmetric. Using statistical

Figure 22.10   Graph of Cumulative Probability

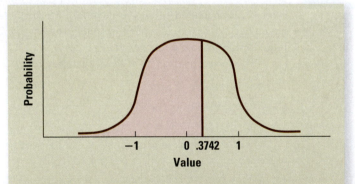

The shaded area represents cumulative probability. Because the probability is .6459 that a drawing from the standard normal distribution will be below .3742, we say that N(.3742) = .6459. That is, the cumulative probability of .3742 is .6459.

terminology, we say that the **cumulative probability** of 0 is 50 percent. Statisticians also say that $N(0) = 50\%$. It turns out that:

$$N(d_1) = N(.3742) = .6459$$
$$N(d_2) = N(.1527) = .5607$$

The first value means that there is a 64.59 percent probability that a drawing from the standardized normal distribution will be below .3742. The second value means that there is a 56.07 percent probability that a drawing from the standardized normal distribution will be below .1527. More generally, $N(d)$ is the probability that a drawing from the standardized normal distribution will be below d. In other words, $N(d)$ is the cumulative probability of d. Note that d_1 and d_2 in our example are slightly above zero, so $N(d_1)$ and $N(d_2)$ are slightly greater than .50.

Perhaps the easiest way to determine $N(d_1)$ and $N(d_2)$ is from the EXCEL function NORMSDIST. In our example, NORMSDIST(.3742) and NORMSDIST(.1527) are .6459 and .5607, respectively.

We can also determine the cumulative probability from Table 22.3. For example, consider $d = .37$. This can be found in the table as .3 on the vertical and .07 on the horizontal. The value in

Table 22.3 Cumulative Probabilities of the Standard Normal Distribution Function

d	.00	.01	.02	.03	.04	.05	.06	.07	.08	.09
.0	.0000	.0040	.0080	.0120	.0160	.0199	.0239	.0279	.0319	.0359
.1	.0398	.0438	.0478	.0517	.0557	.0596	.0636	.0675	.0714	.0753
.2	.0793	.0832	.0871	.0910	.0948	.0987	.1026	.1064	.1103	.1141
.3	.1179	.1217	.1255	.1293	.1331	.1368	.1406	.1443	.1480	.1517
.4	.1554	.1591	.1628	.1664	.1700	.1736	.1772	.1808	.1844	.1879
.5	.1915	.1950	.1985	.2019	.2054	.2088	.2123	.2157	.2190	.2224
.6	.2257	.2291	.2324	.2357	.2389	.2422	.2454	.2486	.2517	.2549
.7	.2580	.2611	.2642	.2673	.2704	.2734	.2764	.2794	.2823	.2852
.8	.2881	.2910	.2939	.2967	.2995	.3023	.3051	.3078	.3106	.3133
.9	.3159	.3186	.3212	.3238	.3264	.3289	.3315	.3340	.3365	.3389
1.0	.3413	.3438	.3461	.3485	.3508	.3531	.3554	.3577	.3599	.3621
1.1	.3643	.3665	.3686	.3708	.3729	.3749	.3770	.3790	.3810	.3830
1.2	.3849	.3869	.3888	.3907	.3925	.3944	.3962	.3980	.3997	.4015
1.3	.4032	.4049	.4066	.4082	.4099	.4115	.4131	.4147	.4162	.4177
1.4	.4192	.4207	.4222	.4236	.4251	.4265	.4279	.4292	.4306	.4319
1.5	.4332	.4345	.4357	.4370	.4382	.4394	.4406	.4418	.4429	.4441
1.6	.4452	.4463	.4474	.4484	.4495	.4505	.4515	.4525	.4535	.4545
1.7	.4554	.4564	.4573	.4582	.4591	.4599	.4608	.4616	.4625	.4633
1.8	.4641	.4649	.4656	.4664	.4671	.4678	.4686	.4693	.4699	.4706
1.9	.4713	.4719	.4726	.4732	.4738	.4744	.4750	.4756	.4761	.4767
2.0	.4773	.4778	.4783	.4788	.4793	.4798	.4803	.4808	.4812	.4817
2.1	.4821	.4826	.4830	.4834	.4838	.4842	.4846	.4850	.4854	.4857
2.2	.4861	.4866	.4868	.4871	.4875	.4878	.4881	.4884	.4887	.4890
2.3	.4893	.4896	.4898	.4901	.4904	.4906	.4909	.4911	.4913	.4916
2.4	.4918	.4920	.4922	.4925	.4927	.4929	.4931	.4932	.4934	.4936
2.5	.4938	.4940	.4941	.4943	.4945	.4946	.4948	.4949	.4951	.4952
2.6	.4953	.4955	.4956	.4957	.4959	.4960	.4961	.4962	.4963	.4964
2.7	.4965	.4966	.4967	.4968	.4969	.4970	.4971	.4972	.4973	.4974
2.8	.4974	.4975	.4976	.4977	.4977	.4978	.4979	.4979	.4980	.4981
2.9	.4981	.4982	.4982	.4982	.4984	.4984	.4985	.4985	.4986	.4986
3.0	.4987	.4987	.4987	.4988	.4988	.4989	.4989	.4989	.4990	.4990

$N(d)$ represents areas under the standard normal distribution function. Suppose that $d_1 = .24$. The table implies a cumulative probability of $.5000 + .0948 = .5948$. If d_1 is equal to .2452, we must estimate the probability by interpolating between $N(.25)$ and $N(.24)$.

(continued)

the table for $d = .37$ is .1443. This value is *not* the cumulative probability of .37. We must first make an adjustment to determine cumulative probability. That is:

$$N(.37) = .50 + .1443 = .6443$$
$$N(-.37) = .50 - .1443 = .3557$$

Unfortunately, our table handles only two significant digits, whereas our value of .3742 has four significant digits. Hence we must interpolate to find N(.3742). Because N(.37) = .6443 and N(.38) = .6480, the difference between the two values is .0037 (=.6480 − .6443). Since .3742 is 42 percent of the way between .37 and .38, we interpolate as:[8]

$$N(.3742) = .6443 + .42 \times .0037 = .6459$$

Step 3: *Calculate C*. We have:

$$
\begin{aligned}
C &= S \times [N(d_1)] - Ee^{-Rt} \times [N(d_2)] \\
&= \$50 \times [N(d_1)] - \$49 \times [e^{-.07 \times (199/365)}] \times N(d_2) \\
&= (\$50 \times .6459) - (\$49 \times .9626 \times .5607) \\
&= \$32.295 - \$26.447 \\
&= \$5.85
\end{aligned}
$$

The estimated price of $5.85 is greater than the $4 actual price, implying that the call option is underpriced. A trader believing in the Black–Scholes model would buy a call. Of course, the Black–Scholes model is fallible. Perhaps the disparity between the model's estimate and the market price reflects error in the trader's estimate of variance.

The previous example stressed the calculations involved in using the Black–Scholes formula. Is there any intuition behind the formula? Yes, and that intuition follows from the stock purchase and borrowing strategy in our binomial example. The first line of the Black–Scholes equation is:

$$C = S \times N(d_1) - Ee^{-Rt} N(d_2)$$

which is exactly analogous to Equation 22.2:

Value of call = Stock price × Delta − Amount borrowed   **(22.2)**

Another good options calculator can be found at **www.margrabe .com/optionpricing .html**.

We presented this equation in the binomial example. It turns out that $N(d_1)$ is the delta in the Black–Scholes model. $N(d_1)$ is .6459 in the previous example. In addition, $Ee^{-Rt} N(d_2)$ is the amount that an investor must borrow to duplicate a call. In the previous example, this value is $26.45 (=$49 × .9626 × .5607). Thus, the model tells us that we can duplicate the call of the preceding example by both:

1. Buying .6459 share of stock.

2. Borrowing $26.45.

It is no exaggeration to say that the Black–Scholes formula is among the most important contributions in finance. It allows anyone to calculate the value of an option given a few parameters. The attraction of the formula is that four of the parameters are observable: The current price of stock, S; the exercise price, E; the interest rate, R; and the time to expiration date, t. Only one of the parameters must be estimated: the variance of return, σ^2.

---

[8]This method is called *linear interpolation*. It is only one of a number of possible methods of interpolation.

To see how truly attractive this formula is, note what parameters are not needed. First, the investor's risk aversion does not affect value. The formula can be used by anyone, regardless of willingness to bear risk. Second, it does not depend on the expected return on the stock! Investors with different assessments of the stock's expected return will nevertheless agree on the call price. As in the two-state example, this is because the call depends on the stock price, and that price already balances investors' divergent views.

22.9   Stocks and Bonds as Options

The previous material in this chapter described, explained, and valued publicly traded options. This is important material to any finance student because much trading occurs in these listed options. The study of options has another purpose for the student of corporate finance.

You may have heard the one-liner about the elderly gentleman who was surprised to learn that he had been speaking prose all of his life. The same can be said about the corporate finance student and options. Although options were formally defined for the first time in this chapter, many corporate policies discussed earlier in the text were actually options in disguise. Though it is beyond the scope of this chapter to recast all of corporate finance in terms of options, the rest of the chapter considers three examples of implicit options:

1. Stocks and bonds as options.
2. Capital structure decisions as options.
3. Capital budgeting decisions as options.

We begin by illustrating the implicit options in stocks and bonds.

EXAMPLE 22.5

Stocks and Bonds as Options   The Popov Company has been awarded the concessions at next year's Olympic Games in Antarctica. Because the firm's principals live in Antarctica and because there is no other concession business on that continent, their enterprise will disband after the games. The firm has issued debt to help finance this venture. Interest and principal due on the debt next year will be $800, at which time the debt will be paid off in full. The firm's cash flows next year are forecast as follows:

	Popov's Cash Flow Schedule			
	Very Successful Games	Moderately Successful Games	Moderately Unsuccessful Games	Outright Failure
Cash flow before interest and principal	$1,000	$ 850	$ 700	$ 550
−interest and principal	−800	−800	−700	−550
Cash flow to stockholders	$ 200	$ 50	$ 0	$ 0

As can be seen, the principals forecast four equally likely scenarios. If either of the first two scenarios occurs, the bondholders will be paid in full. The extra cash flow goes to the stockholders. However, if either of the last two scenarios occurs, the bondholders will not be paid in full. Instead, they will receive the firm's entire cash flow, leaving the stockholders with nothing.

Figure 22.11
Cash Flow to Stockholders of Popov Company as a Function of Cash Flow to Firm

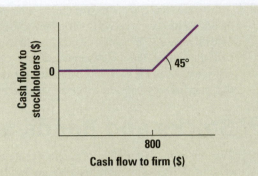

The stockholders can be viewed as having a call option on the firm. If the cash flows of the firm exceed $800, the stockholders pay $800 in order to receive the firm's cash flows. If the cash flows of the firm are less than $800, the stockholders do not exercise their option. They walk away from the firm, receiving nothing.

This example is similar to the bankruptcy examples presented in our chapters about capital structure. Our new insight is that the relationship between the common stock and the firm can be expressed in terms of options. We consider call options first because the intuition is easier. The put option scenario is treated next.

THE FIRM EXPRESSED IN TERMS OF CALL OPTIONS

The Stockholders We now show that stock can be viewed as a call option on the firm. To illustrate this, Figure 22.11 graphs the cash flow to the stockholders as a function of the cash flow to the firm. The stockholders receive nothing if the firm's cash flows are less than $800; here all of the cash flows go to the bondholders. However, the stockholders earn a dollar for every dollar that the firm receives above $800. The graph looks exactly like the call option graphs that we considered earlier in this chapter.

But what is the underlying asset upon which the stock is a call option? The underlying asset is the firm itself. That is, we can view the *bondholders* as owning the firm. However, the stockholders have a call option on the firm with an exercise price of $800.

If the firm's cash flow is above $800, the stockholders would choose to exercise this option. In other words, they would buy the firm from the bondholders for $800. Their net cash flow is the difference between the firm's cash flow and their $800 payment. This would be $200 (=$1,000 − $800) if the games are very successful and $50 (=$850 − $800) if the games are moderately successful.

Should the value of the firm's cash flows be less than $800, the stockholders would not choose to exercise their option. Instead, they would walk away from the firm, as any call option holder would do. The bondholders would then receive the firm's entire cash flow.

This view of the firm is a novel one, and students are frequently bothered by it on first exposure. However, we encourage students to keep looking at the firm in this way until the view becomes second nature to them.

The Bondholders What about the bondholders? Our earlier cash flow schedule showed that they would get the entire cash flow of the firm if the firm generates less cash than $800. Should the firm earn more than $800, the bondholders would receive

Figure 22.12

Cash Flow to Bondholders of Popov Company as a Function of Cash Flow to Firm

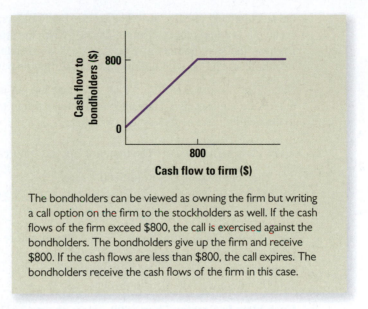

The bondholders can be viewed as owning the firm but writing a call option on the firm to the stockholders as well. If the cash flows of the firm exceed $800, the call is exercised against the bondholders. The bondholders give up the firm and receive $800. If the cash flows are less than $800, the call expires. The bondholders receive the cash flows of the firm in this case.

only $800. That is, they are entitled only to interest and principal. This schedule is graphed in Figure 22.12.

In keeping with our view that the stockholders have a call option on the firm, what does the bondholders' position consist of? The bondholders' position can be described by two claims:

1. They own the firm.
2. They have written a call on the firm with an exercise price of $800.

As we mentioned before, the stockholders walk away from the firm if cash flows are less than $800. Thus, the bondholders retain ownership in this case. However, if the cash flows are greater than $800, the stockholders exercise their option. They call the stock away from the bondholders for $800.

THE FIRM EXPRESSED IN TERMS OF PUT OPTIONS

The preceding analysis expresses the positions of the stockholders and the bondholders in terms of call options. We can now express the situation in terms of put options.

The Stockholders   The stockholders' position can be expressed by three claims:

1. They own the firm.
2. They owe $800 in interest and principal to the bondholders.

If the debt were risk-free, these two claims would fully describe the stockholders' situation. However, because of the possibility of default, we have a third claim as well:

3. The stockholders own a put option on the firm with an exercise price of $800. The group of bondholders is the seller of the put.

Now consider two possibilities.

Cash Flow Is Less Than $800   Because the put has an exercise price of $800, the put is in the money. The stockholders "put"—that is, sell—the firm to the bondholders. Normally, the holder of a put receives the exercise price when the asset is sold. However, the stockholders already owe $800 to the bondholders. Thus, the debt of $800 is simply canceled—and no money changes hands—when the stock is delivered to the bondholders. Because the stockholders give up the stock in exchange for extinguishing the debt, the stockholders end up with nothing if the cash flow is below $800.

Cash Flow Is Greater Than $800   Because the put is out of the money here, the stockholders do not exercise. Thus, the stockholders retain ownership of the firm but pay $800 to the bondholders as interest and principal.

The Bondholders   The bondholders' position can be described by two claims:

1. The bondholders are owed $800.
2. They have sold a put option on the firm to the stockholders with an exercise price of $800.

Cash Flow Is Less Than $800   As mentioned before, the stockholders will exercise the put in this case. This means that the bondholders are obligated to pay $800 for the firm. Because they are owed $800, the two obligations offset each other. Thus, the bondholders simply end up with the firm in this case.

Cash Flow Is Greater Than $800   Here, the stockholders do not exercise the put. Thus, the bondholders merely receive the $800 that is due them.

Expressing the bondholders' position in this way is illuminating. With a riskless default-free bond, the bondholders are owed $800. Thus, we can express the risky bond in terms of a riskless bond and a put:

$$\begin{matrix} \text{Value of risky} \\ \text{bond} \end{matrix} = \begin{matrix} \text{Value of} \\ \text{default-free bond} \end{matrix} - \begin{matrix} \text{Value of} \\ \text{put option} \end{matrix}$$

That is, the value of the risky bond is the value of the default-free bond less the value of the stockholders' option to sell the company for $800.

A RESOLUTION OF THE TWO VIEWS

We have argued that the positions of the stockholders and the bondholders can be viewed either in terms of calls or in terms of puts. These two viewpoints are summarized in Table 22.4.

Table 22.4
Positions of Stockholders and Bondholders in Popov Company in Terms of Calls and Puts

Stockholders	Bondholders
Positions viewed in terms of call options	
1. Stockholders own a call on the firm with an exercise price of $800.	1. Bondholders own the firm.
	2. Bondholders have sold a call on the firm to the stockholders.
Positions viewed in terms of put options	
1. Stockholders own the firm.	1. Bondholders are owed $800 in interest and principal.
2. Stockholders owe $800 in interest and principal to bondholders.	2. Bondholders have sold a put on the firm to the stockholders.
3. Stockholders own a put option on the firm with an exercise price of $800.	

We have found from experience that it is generally harder for students to think of the firm in terms of puts than in terms of calls. Thus, it would be helpful if there were a way to show that the two viewpoints are equivalent. Fortunately, there is *put–call parity.* In an earlier section, we presented the put–call parity relationship as Equation 22.1, which we now repeat:

$$\text{Price of underlying stock} + \text{Price of put} = \text{Price of call} + \text{Present value of exercise price} \qquad \textbf{(22.1)}$$

Using the results of this section, Equation 22.1 can be rewritten like this:

$$\text{Value of call on firm} = \text{Value of firm} + \text{Value of put on firm} - \text{Value of default-free bond} \qquad \textbf{(22.3)}$$

$$\begin{array}{ccc}\text{Stockholders'} & & \text{Stockholders'} \\ \text{position in terms} & = & \text{position in terms} \\ \text{of call options} & & \text{of put options}\end{array}$$

Going from Equation 22.1 to Equation 22.3 involves a few steps. First, we treat the firm, not the stock, as the underlying asset in this section. (In keeping with common convention, we refer to the *value* of the firm and the *price* of the stock.) Second, the exercise price is now $800, the principal and interest on the firm's debt. Taking the present value of this amount at the riskless rate yields the value of a default-free bond. Third, the order of the terms in Equation 22.1 is rearranged in Equation 22.3.

Note that the left side of Equation 22.3 is the stockholders' position in terms of call options, as shown in Table 22.4. The right side of Equation 22.3 is the stockholders' position in terms of put options, as shown in the same table. Thus, put–call parity shows that viewing the stockholders' position in terms of call options is equivalent to viewing the stockholders' position in terms of put options.

Now let's rearrange the terms in Equation 22.3 to yield the following:

$$\text{Value of firm} - \text{Value of call on firm} = \text{Value of default-free bond} - \text{Value of put on firm} \qquad \textbf{(22.4)}$$

$$\begin{array}{ccc}\text{Bondholders' position in} & = & \text{Bondholders' position in} \\ \text{terms of call options} & & \text{terms of put options}\end{array}$$

The left side of Equation 22.4 is the bondholders' position in terms of call options, as shown in Table 22.4. (The minus sign on this side of the equation indicates that the bondholders are *writing* a call.) The right side of the equation is the bondholders' position in terms of put options, as shown in Table 22.4. Thus, put–call parity shows that viewing the bondholders' position in terms of call options is equivalent to viewing the bondholders' position in terms of put options.

A NOTE ABOUT LOAN GUARANTEES

In the Popov example given earlier, the bondholders bore the risk of default. Of course, bondholders generally ask for an interest rate that is high enough to compensate them for bearing risk. When firms experience financial distress, they can no longer attract new debt at moderate interest rates. Thus, firms experiencing distress have frequently sought loan guarantees from the government. Our framework can be used to understand these guarantees.

If the firm defaults on a guaranteed loan, the government must make up the difference. In other words, a government guarantee converts a risky bond into a riskless bond. What is the value of this guarantee?

Recall that with option pricing:

$$\begin{matrix} \text{Value of} \\ \text{default-free bond} \end{matrix} = \begin{matrix} \text{Value of} \\ \text{risky bond} \end{matrix} + \begin{matrix} \text{Value of} \\ \text{put option} \end{matrix}$$

This equation shows that the government is assuming an obligation that has a cost equal to the value of a put option.

This analysis differs from that of both politicians and company spokespeople. They generally say that the guarantee will cost the taxpayers nothing because the guarantee enables the firm to attract debt, thereby staying solvent. However, it should be pointed out that although solvency may be a strong possibility, it is never a certainty. Thus, when the guarantee is made, the government's obligation has a cost in terms of present value. To say that a government guarantee costs the government nothing is like saying a put on the stock of Microsoft has no value because the stock is *likely* to rise in price.

Actually, the U.S. government has had good fortune with loan guarantees. Its two biggest guarantees before the current financial crisis were to the Lockheed Corporation in 1971 and the Chrysler Corporation in 1980. Both firms nearly ran out of cash and defaulted on loans. In both cases the U.S. government came to the rescue by agreeing to guarantee new loans. Under the guarantees, if Lockheed and Chrysler had defaulted on new loans, the lenders could have obtained the full value of their claims from the U.S. government. From the lender's point of view, the loans became as risk-free as Treasury bonds. These guarantees enabled Lockheed and Chrysler to borrow large amounts of cash and to get through a difficult time. As it turned out, neither firm defaulted.

Who benefits from a typical loan guarantee?

1. If existing risky bonds are guaranteed, all gains accrue to the existing bondholders. The stockholders gain nothing because the limited liability of corporations absolves the stockholders of any obligation in bankruptcy.

2. If new debt is issued and guaranteed, the new debtholders do not gain. Rather, in a competitive market, they must accept a low interest rate because of the debt's low risk. The stockholders gain here because they are able to issue debt at a low interest rate. In addition, some of the gains accrue to the old bondholders because the firm's value is greater than would otherwise be true. Therefore, if shareholders want all the gains from loan guarantees, they should renegotiate or retire existing bonds before the guarantee is in place. This happened in the Chrysler case.

22.10 Options and Corporate Decisions: Some Applications

In this section we explore the implications of options analysis in two key areas: Capital budgeting and mergers. We start with mergers and show a very surprising result. We then go on to show that the net present value rule has some important wrinkles in a leveraged firm.

MERGERS AND DIVERSIFICATION

Elsewhere in this book, we discuss mergers and acquisitions. There we mention that diversification is frequently cited as a reason for two firms to merge. Is diversification a good reason to merge? It might seem so. After all, in an earlier chapter, we spent a lot of time explaining why diversification is valuable for investors in their own portfolios because of the elimination of unsystematic risk.

To investigate this issue, let's consider two companies, Sunshine Swimwear (SS) and Polar Winterwear (PW). For obvious reasons, both companies have highly seasonal cash flows; and, in their respective off-seasons, both companies worry about cash flow. If the two companies were to merge, the combined company would have a much more stable cash flow. In other words, a merger would diversify away some of the seasonal variation and, in fact, make bankruptcy much less likely.

Notice that the operations of the two firms are very different, so the proposed merger is a purely "financial" merger. This means that there are no "synergies" or other value-creating possibilities except, possibly, gains from risk reduction. Here is some premerger information:

	Sunshine Swimwear	Polar Winterwear
Market value of assets	$30 million	$10 million
Face value of pure discount debt	$12 million	$ 4 million
Debt maturity	3 years	3 years
Asset return standard deviation	50%	60%

The risk-free rate, continuously compounded, is 5 percent. Given this, we can view the equity in each firm as a call option and calculate the following using Black–Scholes to determine equity values (check these for practice):

	Sunshine Swimwear	Polar Winterwear
Market value of equity	$20.424 million	$7.001 million
Market value of debt	$ 9.576 million	$2.999 million

If you check these, you may get slightly different answers if you use Table 22.3 (we used a spreadsheet). Notice that we calculated the market value of debt using the balance sheet identity.

After the merger, the combined firm's assets will simply be the sum of the premerger values ($30 + $10 = $40 million) because no value was created or destroyed. Similarly, the total face value of the debt is now $16 million. However, we will assume that the combined firm's asset return standard deviation is 40 percent. This is lower than for either of the two individual firms because of the diversification effect.

So, what is the impact of this merger? To find out, we compute the postmerger value of the equity. Based on our discussion, here is the relevant information:

	Combined Firm
Market value of assets	$40 million
Face value of pure discount debt	$16 million
Debt maturity	3 years
Asset return standard deviation	40%

Once again, we can calculate equity and debt values:

	Combined Firm
Market value of equity	$26.646 million
Market value of debt	$13.354 million

What we notice is that this merger is a terrible idea, at least for the stockholders! Before the merger, the stock in the two separate firms was worth a total of $20.424 + 7.001 = $27.425 million compared to only $26.646 million postmerger; so the merger vaporized $27.425 − 26.646 = $.779 million, or almost $1 million, in equity.

Where did the $1 million in equity go? It went to the bondholders. Their bonds were worth $9.576 + 2.999 = $12.575 million before the merger and $13.354 million after, a gain of exactly $.779 million. Thus, this merger neither created nor destroyed value, but it shifted it from the stockholders to the bondholders.

Our example shows that pure financial mergers are a bad idea, and it also shows why. The diversification works in the sense that it reduces the volatility of the firm's return on assets. This risk reduction benefits the bondholders by making default less likely. This is sometimes called the "coinsurance" effect. Essentially, by merging, the firms insure each other's bonds. The bonds are thus less risky, and they rise in value. If the bonds increase in value and there is no net increase in asset values, then the equity must decrease in value. Thus, pure financial mergers are good for creditors but not for stockholders.

Another way to see this is that because the equity is a call option, a reduction in return variance on the underlying asset has to reduce its value. The reduction in value in the case of a purely financial merger has an interesting interpretation. The merger makes default (and thus bankruptcy) *less* likely to happen. That is obviously a good thing from a bondholder's perspective, but why is it a bad thing from a stockholder's perspective? The answer is simple: The right to go bankrupt is a valuable stockholder option. A purely financial merger reduces the value of that option.

OPTIONS AND CAPITAL BUDGETING

We now consider two issues regarding capital budgeting. What we will show is that, for a leveraged firm, the shareholders might prefer a lower NPV project to a higher one. We then show that they might even prefer a *negative* NPV project to a positive NPV project.

As usual, we will illustrate these points first with an example. Here is the basic background information for the firm:

Market value of assets	$20 million
Face value of pure discount debt	$40 million
Debt maturity	5 years
Asset return standard deviation	50%

The risk-free rate is 4 percent. As we have now done several times, we can calculate equity and debt values:

Market value of equity	$ 5.744 million
Market value of debt	$14.256 million

This firm has a fairly high degree of leverage: The debt–equity ratio based on market values is $14.256/5.744 = 2.48, or 248 percent. This is high, but not unheard of. Notice also that the option here is out of the money; as a result, the delta is .547.

The firm has two mutually exclusive investments under consideration. The projects affect both the market value of the firm's assets and the firm's asset return standard deviation as follows:

	Project A	Project B
NPV	$ 4	$ 2
Market value of firm's assets ($20 + NPV)	$24	$22
Firm's asset return standard deviation	40%	60%

Which project is better? It is obvious that Project A has the higher NPV, but by now you are wary of the change in the firm's asset return standard deviation. One project reduces it; the other increases it. To see which project the stockholders like better, we have to go through our now familiar calculations:

	Project A	Project B
Market value of equity	$ 5.965	$ 8.751
Market value of debt	$18.035	$13.249

There is a dramatic difference between the two projects. Project A benefits both the stockholders and the bondholders, but most of the gain goes to the bondholders. Project B has a huge impact on the value of equity, plus it reduces the value of the debt. Clearly the stockholders prefer B.

What are the implications of our analysis? Basically, we have discovered two things. First, when the equity has a delta significantly smaller than 1.0, any value created will go partially to the bondholders. Second, stockholders have a strong incentive to increase the variance of the return on the firm's assets. More specifically, stockholders will have a strong preference for variance-increasing projects as opposed to variance-decreasing ones, even if that means a lower NPV.

Let's do one final example. Here is a different set of numbers:

Market value of assets	$20 million
Face value of pure discount debt	$100 million
Debt maturity	5 years
Asset return standard deviation	50%

The risk-free rate is 4 percent, so the equity and debt values are these:

Market value of equity	$ 2.012 million
Market value of debt	$17.988 million

Notice that the change from our previous example is that the face value of the debt is now $100 million, so the option is far out of the money. The delta is only .24, so most of any value created will go to the bondholders.

The firm has an investment under consideration that must be taken now or never. The project affects both the market value of the firm's assets and the firm's asset return standard deviation as follows:

Project NPV	−$ 1 million
Market value of firm's assets ($20 million + NPV)	$19 million
Firm's asset return standard deviation	70%

Thus, the project has a negative NPV, but it increases the standard deviation of the firm's return on assets. If the firm takes the project, here is the result:

Market value of equity	$ 4.834 million
Market value of debt	$14.166 million

This project more than doubles the value of the equity! Once again, what we are seeing is that stockholders have a strong incentive to increase volatility, particularly when the option is far out of the money. What is happening is that the shareholders have relatively little to lose because bankruptcy is the likely outcome. As a result, there is a strong incentive to go for a long shot, even if that long shot has a negative NPV. It's a bit like using your very last dollar on a lottery ticket. It's a bad investment, but there aren't a lot of other options!

22.11 Investment in Real Projects and Options

Let us quickly review the material about capital budgeting presented earlier in the text. We first considered projects where forecasts for future cash flows were made at Date 0. The expected cash flow in each future period was discounted at an appropriate risky rate, yielding an NPV calculation. For independent projects, a positive NPV meant acceptance and a negative NPV meant rejection. This approach treated risk through the discount rate.

We later considered decision tree analysis, an approach that handles risk in a more sophisticated way. We pointed out that the firm will make investment and operating decisions on a project over its entire life. We value a project today, assuming that future decisions will be optimal. However, we do not yet know what these decisions will be because much information remains to be discovered. The firm's ability to delay its investment and operating decisions until the release of information is an option. We now illustrate this option through an example.

**EXAMPLE
22.6**

Options and Capital Budgeting   Exoff Oil Corporation is considering the purchase of an oil field in a remote part of Alaska. The seller has listed the property for $10,000 and is eager to sell immediately. Initial drilling costs are $500,000. Exoff anticipates that 10,000 barrels of oil can be extracted each year for many decades. Because the termination date is so far in the future and so hard to estimate, the firm views the cash flow stream from the oil as a perpetuity. With oil prices at $50 per barrel and extraction costs at $46 a barrel, the firm anticipates a net margin of $4 per barrel. Because oil prices are expected to rise at the inflation rate, the firm assumes that its cash flow per barrel will always be $4 in real terms. The appropriate real discount rate is 10 percent. The firm has enough tax credits from bad years in the past that it will not need to pay taxes on any profits from the oil field. Should Exoff buy the property?

The NPV of the oil field to Exoff is:

$$-\$110,000 = -\$10,000 - \$500,000 + \frac{\$4 \times 10,000}{.10}$$

According to this analysis, Exoff should not purchase the land.

Though this approach uses the standard capital budgeting techniques of this and other textbooks, it is actually inappropriate for this situation. To see this, consider the analysis of Kirtley Thornton, a consultant to Exoff. He agrees that the price of oil is *expected* to rise at the rate of inflation. However, he points out that the next year will be quite perilous for oil prices. On the one hand, OPEC is considering a long-term agreement that would raise oil prices to $65 per barrel in real terms for many years in the future. On the other hand, National Motors recently indicated that cars using a mixture of sand and water for fuel are currently being tested. Thornton argues that oil will be priced at $35 per barrel in real terms for many years should this development prove successful. Full information about both these developments will be released in exactly one year.

Should oil prices rise to $65 a barrel, the NPV of the project would be:

$$\$1,390,000 = -\$10,000 - \$500,000 + \frac{(\$65 - \$46) \times 10,000}{.10}$$

However, should oil prices fall to $35 a barrel, the NPV of the oil field will be even more negative than it is today.

Mr. Thornton makes two recommendations to Exoff's board. He argues that:

1. The land should be purchased.
2. The drilling decision should be delayed until information about both OPEC's new agreement and National Motors' new automobile is released.

Mr. Thornton explains his recommendations to the board by first assuming that the land has already been purchased. He argues that under this assumption, the drilling decision should be delayed. Second, he investigates his assumption that the land should have been purchased in the first place. This approach of examining the second decision (whether to drill) after assuming that the first decision (to buy the land) has been made was also used in our earlier presentation on decision trees. Let us now work through Mr. Thornton's analysis.

Assume the land has already been purchased. If the land has already been purchased, should drilling begin immediately? If drilling begins immediately, the NPV is −$110,000: If the drilling decision is delayed until new information is released in a year, the optimal choice can be made at that time.

(continued)

If oil prices drop to $35 a barrel, Exoff should not drill. Instead, the firm should walk away from the project, losing nothing beyond its $10,000 purchase price for the land. If oil prices rise to $65, drilling should begin.

Mr. Thornton points out that by delaying, the firm will invest the $500,000 of drilling costs only if oil prices rise. Thus, by delaying, the firm saves $500,000 in the case where oil prices drop. Kirtley concludes that once the land is purchased, the drilling decision should be delayed.[9]

Should the land have been purchased in the first place? We now know that if the land has been purchased, it is optimal to defer the drilling decision until the release of information. Given that we know this optimal decision concerning drilling, should the land be purchased in the first place? Without knowing the exact probability that oil prices will rise, Mr. Thornton is nevertheless confident that the land should be purchased. The NPV of the project at $65 per barrel oil prices is $1,390,000, whereas the cost of the land is only $10,000. Mr. Thornton believes that an oil price rise is possible, though by no means probable. Even so, he argues that the high potential return is clearly worth the risk.

This example presents an approach that is similar to our decision tree analysis of the Solar Equipment Company in a previous chapter. Our purpose in this section is to discuss this type of decision in an option framework. When Exoff purchases the land, it is actually purchasing a call option. That is, once the land has been purchased, the firm has an option to buy an active oil field at an exercise price of $500,000. As it turns out, one should generally not exercise a call option immediately.[10] In this case the firm should delay exercise until relevant information concerning future oil prices is released.

This section points out a serious deficiency in classical capital budgeting: Net present value calculations typically ignore the flexibility that real-world firms have. In our example the standard techniques generated a negative NPV for the land purchase. Yet by allowing the firm the option to change its investment policy according to new information, the land purchase can easily be justified.

We encourage the reader to look for hidden options in projects. Because options are beneficial, managers are shortchanging their firm's projects if capital budgeting calculations ignore flexibility.

---

[9]Actually, there are three separate effects here. First, the firm avoids drilling costs in the case of low oil prices by delaying the decision. This is the effect discussed by Mr. Thornton. Second, the present value of the $500,000 payment is less when the decision is delayed, even if drilling eventually takes place. Third, the firm loses one year of cash inflows through delay.

The first two effects support delaying the decision. The third effect supports immediate drilling. In this example, the first effect greatly outweighs the other two effects. Thus, Mr. Thornton avoided the second and third effects in his presentation.

[10]Actually, it can be shown that a call option on a stock that pays no dividend should *never* be exercised before expiration. However, for a dividend-paying stock, it may be optimal to exercise prior to the ex-dividend date. The analogy applies to our example of an option in real assets.

The firm would receive cash flows from oil earlier if drilling begins immediately. This is equivalent to the benefit from exercising a call on a stock prematurely in order to capture the dividend. However, in our example, this dividend effect is far outweighed by the benefits from waiting.

Summary and Conclusions

This chapter serves as an introduction to options.

1. The most familiar options are puts and calls. These options give the holder the right to sell or buy shares of common stock at a given exercise price. American options can be exercised any time up to and including the expiration date. European options can be exercised only on the expiration date.

2. We showed that a strategy of buying a stock and buying a put is equivalent to a strategy of buying a call and buying a zero coupon bond. From this, the put–call parity relationship was established:

$$\begin{matrix}\text{Value of} \\ \text{stock}\end{matrix} + \begin{matrix}\text{Value of} \\ \text{put}\end{matrix} - \begin{matrix}\text{Value of} \\ \text{call}\end{matrix} = \begin{matrix}\text{Present value of} \\ \text{exercise price}\end{matrix}$$

3. The value of an option depends on five factors:
   a. The price of the underlying asset.
   b. The exercise price.
   c. The expiration date.
   d. The variability of the underlying asset.
   e. The interest rate on risk-free bonds.

   The Black–Scholes model can determine the intrinsic price of an option from these five factors.

4. Much of corporate financial theory can be presented in terms of options. In this chapter, we pointed out that:
   a. Common stock can be represented as a call option on the firm.
   b. Stockholders enhance the value of their call by increasing the risk of their firm.
   c. Real projects have hidden options that enhance value.

Concept Questions

1. **Options** What is a call option? A put option? Under what circumstances might you want to buy each? Which one has greater *potential* profit? Why?

2. **Options** Complete the following sentence for each of these investors:
   a. A buyer of call options.
   b. A buyer of put options.
   c. A seller (writer) of call options.
   d. A seller (writer) of put options.

   "The (buyer/seller) of a (put/call) option (pays/receives) money for the (right/obligation) to (buy/sell) a specified asset at a fixed price for a fixed length of time."

3. **American and European Options** What is the difference between an American option and a European option?

4. **Intrinsic Value** What is the intrinsic value of a call option? Of a put option? How do we interpret these values?

5. **Option Pricing** You notice that shares of stock in the Patel Corporation are going for $50 per share. Call options with an exercise price of $35 per share are selling for $10. What's wrong here? Describe how you can take advantage of this mispricing if the option expires today.

6. **Options and Stock Risk** If the risk of a stock increases, what is likely to happen to the price of call options on the stock? To the price of put options? Why?

7. **Option Risk** True or false: The unsystematic risk of a share of stock is irrelevant for valuing the stock because it can be diversified away; therefore, it is also irrelevant for valuing a call option on the stock. Explain.

8. **Option Pricing** Suppose a certain stock currently sells for $30 per share. If a put option and a call option are available with $30 exercise prices, which do you think will sell for more? Explain.

9. **Option Price and Interest Rates** Suppose the interest rate on T-bills suddenly and unexpectedly rises. All other things being the same, what is the impact on call option values? On put option values?

10. **Contingent Liabilities** When you take out an ordinary student loan, it is usually the case that whoever holds that loan is given a guarantee by the U.S. government, meaning that the government will make up any payments you skip. This is just one example of the many loan guarantees made by the U.S. government. Such guarantees don't show up in calculations of government spending or in official deficit figures. Why not? Should they show up?

11. **Options and Expiration Dates** What is the impact of lengthening the time to expiration on an option's value? Explain.

12. **Options and Stock Price Volatility** What is the impact of an increase in the volatility of the underlying stock's return on an option's value? Explain.

13. **Insurance as an Option** An insurance policy is considered analogous to an option. From the policyholder's point of view, what type of option is an insurance policy? Why?

14. **Equity as a Call Option** It is said that the equityholders of a levered firm can be thought of as holding a call option on the firm's assets. Explain what is meant by this statement.

15. **Option Valuation and NPV** You are the CEO of Titan Industries and have just been awarded a large number of employee stock options. The company has two mutually exclusive projects available. The first project has a large NPV and will reduce the total risk of the company. The second project has a small NPV and will increase the total risk of the company. You have decided to accept the first project when you remember your employee stock options. How might this affect your decision?

16. **Put–Call Parity** You find a put and a call with the same exercise price and maturity. What do you know about the relative prices of the put and call? Prove your answer and provide an intuitive explanation.

17. **Put–Call Parity** A put and a call have the same maturity and strike price. If they have the same price, which one is in the money? Prove your answer and provide an intuitive explanation.

18. **Put–Call Parity** One thing put–call parity tells us is that given any three of a stock, a call, a put, and a T-bill, the fourth can be synthesized or replicated using the other three. For example, how can we replicate a share of stock using a call, a put, and a T-bill?

Questions and Problems

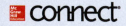

BASIC
(Questions 1–17)

1. **Two-State Option Pricing Model** T-bills currently yield 3.9 percent. Stock in Nina Manufacturing is currently selling for $63 per share. There is no possibility that the stock will be worth less than $61 per share in one year.

   a. What is the value of a call option with a $60 exercise price? What is the intrinsic value?

   b. What is the value of a call option with a $50 exercise price? What is the intrinsic value?

   c. What is the value of a put option with a $60 exercise price? What is the intrinsic value?

2. **Understanding Option Quotes** Use the option quote information shown here to answer the questions that follow. The stock is currently selling for $83.

Option and NY Close	Expiration	Strike Price	Calls Vol.	Calls Last	Puts Vol.	Puts Last
RWJ						
	March	80	230	2.80	160	.80
	April	80	170	6	127	1.40
	July	80	139	8.05	43	3.90
	October	80	60	10.20	11	3.65

   a. Are the call options in the money? What is the intrinsic value of an RWJ Corp. call option?
   b. Are the put options in the money? What is the intrinsic value of an RWJ Corp. put option?
   c. Two of the options are clearly mispriced. Which ones? At a minimum, what should the mispriced options sell for? Explain how you could profit from the mispricing in each case.

3. **Calculating Payoffs** Use the option quote information shown here to answer the questions that follow. The stock is currently selling for $114.

Option and NY Close	Expiration	Strike Price	Calls Vol.	Calls Last	Puts Vol.	Puts Last
Macrosoft						
	February	110	85	7.60	40	.60
	March	110	61	8.80	22	1.55
	May	110	22	10.25	11	2.85
	August	110	3	13.05	3	4.70

   a. Suppose you buy 10 contracts of the February 110 call option. How much will you pay, ignoring commissions?
   b. In part (a), suppose that Macrosoft stock is selling for $140 per share on the expiration date. How much is your options investment worth? What if the terminal stock price is $125? Explain.
   c. Suppose you buy 10 contracts of the August 110 put option. What is your maximum gain? On the expiration date, Macrosoft is selling for $104 per share. How much is your options investment worth? What is your net gain?
   d. In part (c), suppose you *sell* 10 of the August 110 put contracts. What is your net gain or loss if Macrosoft is selling for $103 at expiration? For $132? What is the break-even price—that is, the terminal stock price that results in a zero profit?

4. **Two-State Option Pricing Model** The price of Ervin Corp. stock will be either $53 or $67 at the end of the year. Call options are available with one year to expiration. T-bills currently yield 5 percent.

   a. Suppose the current price of the stock is $58. What is the value of the call option if the exercise price is $50 per share?
   b. Suppose the exercise price is $60 in part (a). What is the value of the call option now?

5. **Two-State Option Pricing Model**   The price of Tara, Inc., stock will be either $50 or $70 at the end of the year. Call options are available with one year to expiration. T-bills currently yield 5 percent.

    a. Suppose the current price of the stock is $62. What is the value of the call option if the exercise price is $35 per share?

    b. Suppose the exercise price is $60 in part (a). What is the value of the call option now?

6. **Put–Call Parity**   A stock is currently selling for $47 per share. A call option with an exercise price of $50 sells for $3.80 and expires in three months. If the risk-free rate of interest is 2.6 percent per year, compounded continuously, what is the price of a put option with the same exercise price?

7. **Put–Call Parity**   A put option that expires in six months with an exercise price of $75 sells for $4.89. The stock is currently priced at $72, and the risk-free rate is 3.6 percent per year, compounded continuously. What is the price of a call option with the same exercise price?

8. **Put–Call Parity**   A put option and a call option with an exercise price of $85 and three months to expiration sell for $6.18 and $5.09, respectively. If the risk-free rate is 4.8 percent per year, compounded continuously, what is the current stock price?

9. **Put–Call Parity**   A put option and a call option with an exercise price of $55 expire in two months and sell for $2.65 and $5.32, respectively. If the stock is currently priced at $57.30, what is the annual continuously compounded rate of interest?

10. **Black–Scholes**   What are the prices of a call option and a put option with the following characteristics?

    Stock price = $57
    Exercise price = $60
    Risk-free rate = 6% per year, compounded continuously
    Maturity = 4 months
    Standard deviation = 54% per year

11. **Black–Scholes**   What are the prices of a call option and a put option with the following characteristics?

    Stock price = $93
    Exercise price = $90
    Risk-free rate = 4% per year, compounded continuously
    Maturity = 5 months
    Standard deviation = 53% per year

12. **Delta**   What are the deltas of a call option and a put option with the following characteristics? What does the delta of the option tell you?

    Stock price = $76
    Exercise price = $70
    Risk-free rate = 5% per year, compounded continuously
    Maturity = 9 months
    Standard deviation = 49% per year

13. **Black–Scholes and Asset Value**   You own a lot in Key West, Florida, that is currently unused. Similar lots have recently sold for $1.3 million. Over the past five years, the price of land in the area has increased 12 percent per year, with an annual standard deviation of 30 percent. A buyer has recently approached you and wants an option to buy the land in the next 12 months for $1.45 million. The risk-free rate of interest is 5 percent per year, compounded continuously. How much should you charge for the option?

14. **Black–Scholes and Asset Value**   In the previous problem, suppose you wanted the option to sell the land to the buyer in one year. Assuming all the facts are the same, describe the transaction that would occur today. What is the price of the transaction today?

15. **Time Value of Options**   You are given the following information concerning options on a particular stock:

> Stock price = $83
> Exercise price = $80
> Risk-free rate = 6% per year, compounded continuously
> Maturity = 6 months
> Standard deviation = 47% per year

   a. What is the intrinsic value of the call option? Of the put option?
   b. What is the time value of the call option? Of the put option?
   c. Does the call or the put have the larger time value component? Would you expect this to be true in general?

16. **Risk-Neutral Valuation**   A stock is currently priced at $84. The stock will either increase or decrease by 17 percent over the next year. There is a call option on the stock with a strike price of $80 and one year until expiration. If the risk-free rate is 8 percent, what is the risk-neutral value of the call option?

17. **Risk-Neutral Valuation**   In the previous problem, assume the risk-free rate is only 5 percent. What is the risk-neutral value of the option now? What happens to the risk-neutral probabilities of a stock price increase and a stock price decrease?

INTERMEDIATE
(Questions 18–29)

18. **Black–Scholes**   A call option matures in six months. The underlying stock price is $75, and the stock's return has a standard deviation of 30 percent per year. The risk-free rate is 4 percent per year, compounded continuously. If the exercise price is $0, what is the price of the call option?

19. **Black–Scholes**   A call option has an exercise price of $80 and matures in six months. The current stock price is $84, and the risk-free rate is 5 percent per year, compounded continuously. What is the price of the call if the standard deviation of the stock is 0 percent per year?

20. **Black–Scholes**   A stock is currently priced at $35. A call option with an expiration of one year has an exercise price of $50. The risk-free rate is 7 percent per year, compounded continuously, and the standard deviation of the stock's return is infinitely large. What is the price of the call option?

21. **Equity as an Option**   Sunburn Sunscreen has a zero coupon bond issue outstanding with a $20,000 face value that matures in one year. The current market value of the firm's assets is $21,700. The standard deviation of the return on the firm's assets is 38 percent per year, and the annual risk-free rate is 5 percent per year, compounded continuously. Based on the Black–Scholes model, what is the market value of the firm's equity and debt?

22. Equity as an Option and NPV Suppose the firm in the previous problem is considering two mutually exclusive investments. Project A has an NPV of $1,200, and Project B has an NPV of $1,600. As a result of taking Project A, the standard deviation of the return on the firm's assets will increase to 55 percent per year. If Project B is taken, the standard deviation will fall to 34 percent per year.

   a. What is the value of the firm's equity and debt if Project A is undertaken? If Project B is undertaken?

   b. Which project would the stockholders prefer? Can you reconcile your answer with the NPV rule?

   c. Suppose the stockholders and bondholders are, in fact, the same group of investors. Would this affect your answer to (b)?

   d. What does this problem suggest to you about stockholder incentives?

23. Equity as an Option Frostbite Thermalwear has a zero coupon bond issue outstanding with a face value of $25,000 that matures in one year. The current market value of the firm's assets is $27,200. The standard deviation of the return on the firm's assets is 53 percent per year, and the annual risk-free rate is 5 percent per year, compounded continuously. Based on the Black–Scholes model, what is the market value of the firm's equity and debt? What is the firm's continuously compounded cost of debt?

24. Mergers and Equity as an Option Suppose Sunburn Sunscreen and Frostbite Thermalwear in the previous problems have decided to merge. Because the two companies have seasonal sales, the combined firm's return on assets will have a standard deviation of 29 percent per year.

   a. What is the combined value of equity in the two existing companies? The value of debt?

   b. What is the value of the new firm's equity? The value of debt?

   c. What was the gain or loss for shareholders? For bondholders?

   d. What happened to shareholder value here?

25. Equity as an Option and NPV A company has a single zero coupon bond outstanding that matures in 10 years with a face value of $10 million. The current value of the company's assets is $9.05 million, and the standard deviation of the return on the firm's assets is 39 percent per year. The risk-free rate is 6 percent per year, compounded continuously.

   a. What is the current market value of the company's equity?

   b. What is the current market value of the company's debt?

   c. What is the company's continuously compounded cost of debt?

   d. The company has a new project available. The project has an NPV of $1,200,000. If the company undertakes the project, what will be the new market value of equity? Assume volatility is unchanged.

   e. Assuming the company undertakes the new project and does not borrow any additional funds, what is the new continuously compounded cost of debt? What is happening here?

26. Two-State Option Pricing Model Ken is interested in buying a European call option written on Southeastern Airlines, Inc., a non-dividend-paying common stock, with a strike price of $65 and one year until expiration. Currently, the company's stock sells for $62 per share. In one year Ken knows that the comapny's stock will be trading at either $76 per share or $54 per share. Ken is able to borrow and lend at the risk-free EAR of 2.5 percent.

   a. What should the call option sell for today?

   b. If no options currently trade on the stock, is there a way to create a synthetic call option with identical payoffs to the call option just described? If there is, how would you do it?

c. How much does the synthetic call option cost? Is this greater than, less than, or equal to what the actual call option costs? Does this make sense?

27. **Two-State Option Pricing Model**   Rob wishes to buy a European put option on BioLabs, Inc., a non-dividend-paying common stock, with a strike price of $50 and six months until expiration. The company's common stock is currently selling for $45 per share, and Rob expects that the stock price will either rise to $68 or fall to $37 in six months. Rob can borrow and lend at the risk-free EAR of 5 percent.

   a. What should the put option sell for today?

   b. If no options currently trade on the stock, is there a way to create a synthetic put option with identical payoffs to the put option just described? If there is, how would you do it?

   c. How much does the synthetic put option cost? Is this greater than, less than, or equal to what the actual put option costs? Does this make sense?

28. **Two-State Option Pricing Model**   Maverick Manufacturing, Inc., must purchase gold in three months for use in its operations. Maverick's management has estimated that if the price of gold were to rise above $1,380 per ounce, the firm would go bankrupt. The current price of gold is $1,270 per ounce. The firm's chief financial officer believes that the price of gold will either rise to $1,465 per ounce or fall to $1,120 per ounce over the next three months. Management wishes to eliminate any risk of the firm going bankrupt. Maverick can borrow and lend at the risk-free EAR of 6.50 percent.

   a. Should the company buy a call option or a put option on gold? To avoid bankruptcy, what strike price and time to expiration would the company like this option to have?

   b. How much should such an option sell for in the open market?

   c. If no options currently trade on gold, is there a way for the company to create a synthetic option with identical payoffs to the option just described? If there is, how would the firm do it?

   d. How much does the synthetic option cost? Is this greater than, less than, or equal to what the actual option costs? Does this make sense?

29. **Black–Scholes and Collar Cost**   An investor is said to take a position in a "collar" if she buys the asset, buys an out-of-the-money put option on the asset, and sells an out-of-the-money call option on the asset. The two options should have the same time to expiration. Suppose Marie wishes to purchase a collar on Hollywood, Inc., a non-dividend–paying common stock, with six months until expiration. She would like the put to have a strike price of $45 and the call to have a strike price of $75. The current price of the stock is $60 per share. Marie can borrow and lend at the continuously compounded risk-free rate of 7 percent per annum, and the annual standard deviation of the stock's return is 50 percent. Use the Black–Scholes model to calculate the total cost of the collar that Marie is interested in buying. What is the effect of the collar?

CHALLENGE
(Questions 30–38)

30. **Debt Valuation and Time to Maturity**   McLemore Industries has a zero coupon bond issue that matures in two years with a face value of $75,000. The current value of the company's assets is $46,000, and the standard deviation of the return on assets is 60 percent per year.

   a. Assume the risk-free rate is 5 percent per year, compounded continuously. What is the value of a risk-free bond with the same face value and maturity as the company's bond?

   b. What price would the bondholders have to pay for a put option on the company's assets with a strike price equal to the face value of the debt?

   c. Using the answers from (a) and (b), what is the value of the company's debt? What is the continuously compounded yield on the company's debt?

d. From an examination of the value of the assets of the company, and the fact that the debt must be repaid in two years, it seems likely that the company will default on its debt. Management has approached bondholders and proposed a plan whereby the company would repay the same face value of debt, but the repayment would not occur for five years. What is the value of the debt under the proposed plan? What is the new continuously compounded yield on the debt? Explain why this occurs.

31. **Debt Valuation and Asset Variance**   Brozik Corp. has a zero coupon bond that matures in five years with a face value of $40,000. The current value of the company's assets is $38,000, and the standard deviation of its return on assets is 50 percent per year. The risk-free rate is 6 percent per year, compounded continuously.

   a. What is the value of a risk-free bond with the same face value and maturity as the current bond?
   b. What is the value of a put option on the company's assets with a strike price equal to the face value of the debt?
   c. Using the answers from (a) and (b), what is the value of the company's debt? What is the continuously compounded yield on the company's debt?
   d. Assume the company can restructure its assets so that the standard deviation of its return on assets increases to 60 percent per year. What happens to the value of the debt? What is the new continuously compounded yield on the debt? Reconcile your answers in (c) and (d).
   e. What happens to bondholders if the company restructures its assets? What happens to shareholders? How does this create an agency problem?

32. **Two-State Option Pricing and Corporate Valuation**   Strudler Real Estate, Inc., a construction firm financed by both debt and equity, is undertaking a new project. If the project is successful, the value of the firm in one year will be $213 million, but if the project is a failure, the firm will be worth only $156 million. The current value of the company is $185 million, a figure that includes the prospects for the new project. Strudler has outstanding zero coupon bonds due in one year with a face value of $175 million. Treasury bills that mature in one year have an EAR of 7 percent. The company pays no dividends.

   a. Use the two-state option pricing model to find the current value of the company's debt and equity.
   b. Suppose the company has 500,000 shares of common stock outstanding. What is the price per share of the company's equity?
   c. Compare the market value of the company's debt to the present value of an equal amount of debt that is riskless with one year until maturity. Is the firm's debt worth more than, less than, or the same as the riskless debt? Does this make sense? What factors might cause these two values to be different?
   d. Suppose that in place of the preceding project, the company's management decides to undertake a project that is even more risky. The value of the company will either increase to $245 million or decrease to $135 million by the end of the year. Surprisingly, management concludes that the value of the company today will remain at exactly $185 million if this risky project is substituted for the less risky one. Use the two-state option pricing model to determine the values of the firm's debt and equity if the company plans on undertaking this new project. Which project do bondholders prefer?

33. **Black–Scholes and Dividends**   In addition to the five factors discussed in the chapter, dividends also affect the price of an option. The Black–Scholes option pricing model with dividends is:

$$C = S \times e^{-dt} \times N(d_1) - E \times e^{-Rt} \times N(d_2)$$
$$d_1 = [\ln(S/E) + (R - d + \sigma^2/2) \times t]/(\sigma \times \sqrt{t})$$
$$d_2 = d_1 - \sigma \times \sqrt{t}$$

All of the variables are the same as the Black–Scholes model without dividends except for the variable d, which is the continuously compounded dividend yield on the stock.

    a. What effect do you think the dividend yield will have on the price of a call option? Explain.

    b. A stock is currently priced at $113 per share, the standard deviation of its return is 50 percent per year, and the risk-free rate is 5 percent per year, compounded continuously. What is the price of a call option with a strike price of $110 and a maturity of six months if the stock has a dividend yield of 2 percent per year?

34. **Put–Call Parity and Dividends** The put–call parity condition is altered when dividends are paid. The dividend-adjusted put–call parity formula is:

$$S \times e^{-dt} - P = E \times e^{-Rt} + C$$

where d is again the continuously compounded dividend yield.

    a. What effect do you think the dividend yield will have on the price of a put option? Explain.

    b. From the previous question, what is the price of a put option with the same strike price and time to expiration as the call option?

35. **Put Delta** In the chapter we noted that the delta for a put option is $N(d_1) - 1$. Is this the same thing as $-N(-d_1)$? (*Hint*: Yes, but why?)

36. **Black–Scholes Put Pricing Model** Use the Black–Scholes model for pricing a call, put–call parity, and the previous question to show that the Black–Scholes model for directly pricing a put can be written as follows:

$$P = E \times e^{-Rt} \times N(-d_2) - S \times N(-d_1)$$

37. **Black–Scholes** A stock is currently priced at $50. The stock will never pay a dividend. The risk-free rate is 12 percent per year, compounded continuously, and the standard deviation of the stock's return is 60 percent. A European call option on the stock has a strike price of $100 and no expiration date, meaning that it has an infinite life. Based on Black–Scholes, what is the value of the call option? Do you see a paradox here? Do you see a way out of the paradox?

38. **Delta** You purchase one call and sell one put with the same strike price and expiration date. What is the delta of your portfolio? Why?

Excel Master It! Problem

In addition to spinners and scroll bars, there are numerous other controls in Excel. For this assignment, you need to build a Black–Scholes Option Pricing Model spreadsheet using several of these controls.

a. Buttons are always used in sets. Using buttons permits you to check an option, and the spreadsheet will use that input. In this case, you need to create two buttons, one for a call option and one for a put option. When using the spreadsheet, if you click the call option, the spreadsheet will calculate a call price, and if you click the put option, it will calculate the price of a put. Notice on the next spreadsheet that cell B20 is empty. This cell should change names. The names should be "Call option price" and "Put option price." In the price cell, only the price for the call option or put option is displayed depending on which button is selected. For the button, use the button under Form Controls.

b. A Combo Box uses a drop-down menu with values entered by the spreadsheet developer. One advantage of a Combo Box is that the user can choose values from the drop-down menu or enter another value if they choose. In this case, you want to create a Combo Box for the stock price and a separate Combo Box for the strike price. On the right-hand side of the spreadsheet, we have values for the drop-down menu. These values should be created in an array before the Combo Box is inserted. To create an ActiveX Combo Box, go to Developer, Insert, and select Combo Box from the ActiveX Controls menu. After you draw the Combo Box, right-click on the box, select Properties, and enter the LinkedCell, which is the cell where you want the output displayed, and the ListFillRange, which is the range that contains the list of values you want displayed in the drop-down menu.

c. In contrast to a Combo Box, a List Box permits the user to scroll through a list of possible values that are predetermined by the spreadsheet developer. No other values can be entered. You need to create a List Box for the interest rate using the interest rate array on the right-hand side of the spreadsheet. To insert a List Box, go to Developer, Insert, and choose the List Box from the ActiveX Controls. To enter the linked cell and array of values, you will need to go to the Properties for the List Box. To do this, right-click on the List Box and select Properties from the menu. We should note here that to edit both the Combo Box and List box you will need to make sure that Design Mode is checked on the Developer tab.

Mini Case

CLISSOLD INDUSTRIES OPTIONS

You are currently working for Clissold Industries. The company, which went public five years ago, engages in the design, production, and distribution of lighting equipment and specialty products worldwide. Because of recent events, Mal Clissold, the company president, is concerned about the company's risk, so he asks for your input.

In your discussion with Mal, you explain that the CAPM proposes that the market risk of the company's stock is the determinant of its expected return. Even though Mal agrees with this, he argues that his portfolio consists entirely of Clissold Industry stock and options, so he is concerned with the total risk, or standard deviation, of the company's stock. Furthermore, even though he has calculated the standard deviation of the company's stock for the past five years, he would like an estimate of the stock's volatility moving forward.

Mal states that you can find the estimated volatility of the stock for future periods by calculating the implied standard deviation of option contracts on the company stock. When you examine the factors that affect the price of an option, all of the factors except the standard deviation of the stock are directly observable in the market. Mal states that because you can observe all of the option factors except the standard deviation, you can simply solve the Black–Scholes model and find the implied standard deviation.

To help you find the implied standard deviation of the company's stock, Mal has provided you with the following option prices on four call options that expire in six months. The risk-free rate is 4 percent, and the current stock price is $53.

Strike Price	Option Price
$50	$12.78
55	10.14
60	7.99
65	5.81

1. How many different volatilities would you expect to see for the stock?
2. Unfortunately, solving for the implied standard deviation is not as easy as Mal suggests. In fact, there is no direct solution for the standard deviation of the stock even if we have all the other variables for the Black–Scholes model. Mal would still like you to estimate the

implied standard deviation of the stock. To do this, set up a spreadsheet using the Solver function in Excel to calculate the implied volatilities for each of the options.

3. Are all of the implied volatilities for the options the same? (*Hint:* No.) What are the possible reasons that can cause different volatilities for these options?

4. After you discuss the importance of volatility on option prices, your boss mentions that he has heard of the VIX. What is the VIX and what does it represent? You might need to visit the Chicago Board Options Exchange (CBOE) at www.cboe.com to help with your answer.

5. When you are on the CBOE website, look for the option quotes for the VIX. What does the implied volatility of a VIX option represent?

23

Options and Corporate Finance

EXTENSIONS AND APPLICATIONS

During most years in the last decade, Larry Ellison, Executive Chairman of Oracle, has been one of the highest paid executives in the United States. Much of Mr. Ellison's pay has been based on employee stock options. From 2006 to 2013, Mr. Ellison was granted 7 million stock options per year. However, in 2014, the board of directors, under pressure from shareholders, reduced Mr. Ellison's stock option grant to 3 million shares, valued at $46 million. At the same time, the stock option grants awarded to co-presidents Mark Hurd and Safra Catz were cut from 5 million to 2.25 million. In this chapter, we discuss employee stock options, as well as the options seen in capital budgeting.

23.1 Executive Stock Options

WHY OPTIONS?

Executive compensation is usually made up of a base salary plus some or all of the following elements:

1. Long-term compensation.
2. Annual bonuses.
3. Retirement contributions.
4. Options.

The final component of compensation, options, is by far the biggest part of total compensation for many top executives. Table 23.1 lists the 5 CEOs who received very large stock option grants during 2014–2015. The rank is in terms of the *face value* of the options granted. This is the number of options times the current stock price.

Knowing the face value of an option does not automatically allow us to determine the market value of the option. We also need to know the exercise price before valuing the option according to either the Black–Scholes model or the binomial model. However, the exercise price is generally set equal to the market price of the stock on the date the executive receives the options. In the next section, we value options under the assumption that the exercise price is equal to the market price.

Table 23.1   2014–2015 Top 5 Option Grants

Company[1]	CEO	Number of Options Granted	Weighted Average Exercise Price	Grant Value of Options[2]
Oracle Corporation	J. Ellison	3,000,000	$40.47	$121,410,000
The Coca Cola Company	M. Kent	2,382,134	37.21	88,627,295
JPMorgan Chase & Co	J. Dimon	2,000,000	39.83	79,660,000
Chevron Corp	J. Watson	662,000	103.71	68,656,020
Honeywell International, Inc.	D. Cote	600,000	93.97	56,382,000

[1]Based on the 200 largest publically-traded, U.S. incorporated companies in the Fortune 500, (market cap) on 2/8/2015

[2]Grant value of options calculated as the number of options times the stock price on the date of grant.

SOURCE: Pearl Meyer & Partners.

Options in the stock of the company are increasingly being granted to executives as an alternative to increases in base pay. Some of the reasons given for using options are these:

1. Options make executives share the same interests as the stockholders. By aligning interests, executives are more likely to make decisions for the benefit of the stockholders.

2. Options allow the company to lower the executive's base pay. This removes pressures on morale caused by disparities between the salaries of executives and those of other employees.

3. Options put an executive's pay at risk, rather than guaranteeing it, regardless of the performance of the firm.

4. Options are a tax-efficient way to pay employees. Under current tax law, if an executive is given options to purchase company stock and the options are "at the money," they are not considered part of taxable income to the employee. The options are taxed only when and if they are eventually exercised.

EXAMPLE 23.1

Options at Starbucks   Stock options are not always restricted to the highest-ranking executives. Starbucks, the coffee chain, has pushed options down to the lowest-level employees. To quote its founder, Howard Schultz, "Even though we were a private company, we would grant stock options to every employee companywide, from the top managers to the baristas, in proportion to their level of base pay. They could then, through their efforts, help make Starbucks more successful every year, and if Starbucks someday went public, their options could eventually be worth a good sum of money."

VALUING EXECUTIVE COMPENSATION

In this section, we value executive stock options. Not surprisingly, the complexity of the total compensation package often makes valuation a difficult task. The economic value of the options depends on factors such as the volatility of the underlying stock and the exact terms of the option grant.

We attempt to estimate the economic value of the options held by the executives listed in Table 23.1. To do so, we employ the Black–Scholes option pricing formula from Chapter 22. Of course, we are missing many features of the particular plans, and the best we can hope for is a rough estimate. Simple matters such as requiring the executive to hold the option for a fixed period, the freeze-out period, before exercising, can significantly diminish the value of a standard option. Equally important, the Black–Scholes formula has to be modified if the stock pays dividends and is no longer applicable if the volatility of the stock is changing randomly over time. Intuitively, a call option on a dividend-paying stock is worth less than a call on a stock that pays no dividends: All other things being equal, the dividends will lower the stock price. Nevertheless, let us see what we can do.

Table 23.2 shows the grant value of the options as well as the actual option values as reported by each of the companies. Most of these companies use the Black–Scholes method to value the options, but they take into account the special features of their plans and their stock, including whether or not it pays dividends. As can be seen, these reported values, while large by ordinary standards, are significantly less than the corresponding grant values.

The values we have computed in Table 23.2 are the economic values of the options if they were to trade in the market. The real question is this: Whose value are we talking about? Are these the costs of the options to the company? Are they the values of the options to the executives?

Suppose a company computes the fair market value of the options as we have done in Table 23.2. For illustration, assume that the options are in the money and that they are worth $25 each. Suppose, too, that the CEO holds 1 million such options for a total value of $25 million. This is the amount that the options would trade at in the financial markets and that traders and investors would be willing to pay for them.[1] If the company were very large, it would not be unreasonable for it to view this as the cost of granting the options to the CEO. Of course, in return, the company would expect

Table 23.2 Value of 2014–2015 Top 5 Option Grants

Company[1]	CEO	Grant Value of Options[2]	Annual Stock Volatility (%)	Black-Scholes Value of Options[3]
Oracle Corporation	J. Ellison	$121,410,000	23.0%	$24,784,947
JPMorgan Chase & Co	J. Dimon	79,660,000	28.0	16,481,929
Chevron Corp	J. Watson	68,656,020	31.3	14,391,664
Honeywell International, Inc.	D. Cote	56,382,000	23.1	9,783,302
The Coca Cola Company	M. Kent	88,627,295	17.0	8,727,893

[1]Based on the 200 largest publically-traded, U.S. incorporated companies in the Fortune 500, (market cap) on 2/8/2015.

[2]Grant value of options calculated as the number of options times the stock price.

[3]Reflects the FASB ASC Topic 718 Black-Scholes value of stock option grants.

[4]Utilized Binomial Model for stock option valuation.

SOURCE: Pearl Meyer & Partners.

---

[1]We ignore warrant dilution in this example. See Chapter 24 for a discussion of warrant dilution.

EXAMPLE
23.2

Options at United Express Corporation According to the proxy statement filed in fiscal year 2015, Rich Pettit, the CEO of United Express Corporation, was granted 1.662 million stock options. The average exercise price of the options was $50.99, and we will assume that all of the options were granted at the money. We'll also assume that the options expire in five years and that the risk-free rate is 5 percent. This information implies that:

1. The stock price (S) equals the exercise price (E), $50.99.
2. The risk-free rate, R, equals .05.
3. The time interval, t, equals 5.

In addition, the stock volatility, σ, is given as 37.46 percent per year, which implies that the variance, σ^2, equals $(.3746)^2 = .1403$.

We now have enough information to estimate the value of Rich Pettit's options using the Black–Scholes model:

$$C = SN(d_1) - Ee^{-Rt}N(d_2)$$
$$d_1 = \frac{(R + \frac{1}{2}\sigma^2)t}{\sqrt{\sigma^2 t}} = .7173$$
$$d_2 = d_1 - \sqrt{\sigma^2 t} = -.1204$$
$$N(d_1) = .7634$$
$$N(d_2) = .4521$$
$$e^{-Rt} = .7788$$
$$C = \$50.99 \times .7634 - \$50.99 \times (.7788 \times .4521) = \$20.97$$

Since Mr. Pettit was granted options on 1.662 million shares, and since each option is worth $20.97, the market value of his options by the above calculations is 1.662 million $\times$ $20.97 = $34.9 million.

the CEO to improve the value of the company to its shareholders by more than this amount. As we have seen, perhaps the main purpose of options is to align the interests of management with those of the shareholders of the firm. Under no circumstances, though, is the $25 million necessarily a fair measure of what the options are worth to the CEO.

As an illustration, suppose that the CEO of ABC has options on 1 million shares with an exercise price of $30 per share, and the current price of ABC stock is $50 per share. If the options were exercised today, they would be worth $20 million (an underestimation of their market value). Suppose, in addition, that the CEO owns $5 million in company stock and has $5 million in other assets. The CEO clearly has a very undiversified personal portfolio. By the standards of modern portfolio theory, having 25/30, or about 83 percent, of your personal wealth in one stock and its options is unnecessarily risky.

Although the CEO is wealthy by most standards, shifts in stock price impact the CEO's economic well-being. If the price drops from $50 per share to $30 per share, the current exercise value of the options on 1 million shares drops from $20 million down to zero. Ignoring the fact that if the options had more time to mature they might not lose all of this value, we nevertheless have a rather startling decline in the CEO's net worth from $30 million to $8 million (=$5 million in other assets plus stock that is now worth

$3 million). But that is the purpose of giving the options and the stock holdings to the CEO—namely, to make the CEO's fortunes rise and fall with those of the company. It is why the company requires the executive to hold the options for at least a freeze-out period rather than letting the executive sell them to realize their value.

The implication is that when options are a large portion of an executive's net worth, the total value of the position to the executive is less than market value. As a purely financial matter, an executive might be happier with $5 million in cash rather than $20 million in options. At least the executive could then diversify his personal portfolio.

23.2 Valuing a Start-Up

Ralph Simmons was not your typical MBA student. Since childhood, he'd had one ambition: To open a restaurant that sold alligator meat. He went to business school because he realized that although he knew 101 ways to cook alligator, he didn't have the business skills necessary to run a restaurant. He was extremely focused, with each course at graduate school being important to him only to the extent that it could further his dream.

While taking his school's course in entrepreneurship, he began to develop a business plan for his restaurant, which he now called Alligator Alley. He thought about marketing; he thought about raising capital; and he thought about dealing with future employees. He even devoted a great deal of time to designing the physical layout of the restaurant. Against the professor's advice in his entrepreneurship class, he designed the restaurant in the shape of an alligator, where the front door went through the animal's mouth. Of course, his business plan would not be complete without financial projections. After much thought, he came up with the projections shown in Table 23.3.

The table starts with sales projections, which rise from $300,000 in the first year to a steady state of $1 million a year. Cash flows from operations are shown in the next line, although we leave out the intermediate calculations needed to move from Line (1) to Line (2). After subtracting working capital, the table shows net cash flows in Line (4). Net cash flows are negative initially, as is quite common in start-ups, but they become positive by Year 3. However, the rest of the table presents the unfortunate truth. The cash flows from the restaurant yield a present value of $582,561, assuming a discount rate of 20 percent. Unfortunately, the cost of the building is greater, at $700,000, implying a negative net present value of –$117,439.

Table 23.3   Financial Projections for Alligator Alley

	Year 1	Year 2	Year 3	Year 4	All Future Years
(1) Sales	$300,000	$600,000	$900,000	$1,000,000	$1,000,000
(2) Cash flows from operations	−100,000	−50,000	+75,000	+250,000	+250,000
(3) Increase in working capital	50,000	20,000	10,000	10,000	0
(4) Net cash flows [(2) − (3)]	−$150,000	−$70,000	$65,000	$240,000	$250,000
Present value of net cash flows in Years 1–4 (discounted at 20%)			−$20,255		
Present value of terminal value	$\left[\dfrac{\$250,000}{.20} \times \dfrac{1}{(1.20)^4}\right] =$		+$602,816		
Present value of restaurant			$582,561		
− Cost of building			−700,000		
Net present value of restaurant			−$117,439		

The projections indicate that Ralph's lifelong dream may not come to pass. He cannot expect to raise the capital needed to open his restaurant; and if he did obtain the funding, the restaurant would likely go under anyway. Ralph checked and rechecked the numbers, hoping in vain to discover either a numerical error or a cost-saving omission that would move his venture from the red to the black. In fact, Ralph saw that, if anything, his forecasts were generous: A 20 percent discount rate and an infinite-lived building are on the optimistic side.

It wasn't until Ralph took a course in corporate strategy that he saw the hidden value in his venture. In that course, his instructor repeatedly stated the importance of positioning a firm to take advantage of new opportunities. Although Ralph didn't see the connection at first, he finally realized the implications for Alligator Alley. His financial projections were based on expectations. There was a 50 percent probability that alligator meat would be more popular than he thought, in which case actual cash flows would exceed projections. And there was a 50 percent probability that the meat would be less popular, in which case the actual flows would fall short of projections.

If the restaurant did poorly, it would probably fold in a few years because he would not want to keep losing money forever. However, if the restaurant did well, he would be in a position to expand. With alligator meat being popular in one locale, it would likely prove popular in other locales as well. Thus, he noticed two options: The option to abandon under bad conditions and the option to expand under good conditions. Although both options can be valued according to the principles of the previous chapter, we focus on the option to expand because it is probably much more valuable.

Ralph reasoned that as much as he personally liked alligator meat, consumer resistance in some regions of the country would doom Alligator Alley. So he developed a strategy of catering only to those regions where alligator meat is somewhat popular already. He forecasts that although he could expand quickly if the first restaurant proved successful, the market would limit him to 30 additional restaurants.

Ralph believes that this expansion will occur about four years from now. He believes that he will need three years of operating the first restaurant to (1) get the initial restaurant running smoothly and (2) have enough information to place an accurate value on the restaurant. If the first restaurant is successful enough, he will need another year to obtain outside capital. Thus, he will be ready to build the 30 additional units around the fourth year.

Ralph will value his enterprise, including the option to expand, according to the Black–Scholes model. From Table 23.3, we see that each unit costs $700,000, implying a total cost over the 30 additional units of $21,000,000 (=30 × $700,000). The present value of the cash inflows from these 30 units is $17,476,830 (=30 × $582,561), according to the table. However, because the expansion will occur around the fourth year, this present value calculation is provided from the point of view of four years in the future. The present value as of today is $8,428,255 [=$17,476,830/(1.20)^4], assuming a discount rate of 20 percent per year. Thus, Ralph views his potential restaurant business as an option, where the exercise price is $21,000,000 and the value of the underlying asset is $8,428,255. The option is currently out of the money, a result that follows from the negative value of a typical restaurant, as calculated in Table 23.3. Of course, Ralph is hoping that the option will move into the money within four years.

Ralph needs three additional parameters to use the Black–Scholes model: R, the continuously compounded interest rate; t, the time to maturity; and σ, the standard deviation of the underlying asset. Ralph uses the yield on a four-year zero coupon bond, which is 3.5 percent, as the estimate of the interest rate. The time to maturity is four years. The estimate of standard deviation is a little trickier because there is no historical data on alligator restaurants. Ralph finds that the average annual standard deviation of the returns on publicly traded restaurants is 35 percent. Because Alligator Alley is a new venture, he reasons that the risk here would be somewhat greater. He finds that the average annual standard deviation for restaurants that have gone public in the last few years is .45. Ralph's restaurant is newer still, so he uses a standard deviation of 50 percent.

There is now enough data to value Ralph's venture. The value according to the Black–Scholes model is $1,454,269. The actual calculations are shown in Table 23.4. Of course, Ralph must start his pilot restaurant before he can take advantage of this option. Thus, the net value of the call option plus the negative net present value of the pilot restaurant is $1,336,830 (=$1,454,269 – $117,439). Because this value is large and positive, Ralph decides to stay with his dream of Alligator Alley. He knows that the probability that the restaurant will fail is greater than 50 percent. Nevertheless, the option to expand is important enough that his restaurant business has value. And if he needs outside capital, he probably can attract the necessary investors.

Table 23.4

Valuing a Start-Up Firm (Alligator Alley) as an Option

Facts

1. The value of a single restaurant is negative, as indicated by the net present value calculation in Table 23.3 of −$117,439. Thus, the restaurant would not be funded if there were no possibility of expansion.

2. If the pilot restaurant is successful, Ralph Simmons plans to create 30 additional restaurants around Year 4. This leads to the following observations:
   a. The total cost of 30 units is $21,000,000 (=30 × $700,000).
   b. The present value of future cash flows as of Year 4 is $17,476,830 (=30 × $582,561).
   c. The present value of these cash flows today is $8,428,255 [=$17,476,830/(1.20)⁴].

Here, we assume that cash flows from the project are discounted at 20% per annum.

Thus, the business is essentially a call option, where the exercise price is $21,000,000 and the underlying asset is worth $8,428,255.

3. Ralph Simmons estimates the standard deviation of the annual return on Alligator Alley's stock to be 50%.

Parameters of the Black–Scholes model:

$$S \text{ (stock price)} = \$8,428,255$$
$$E \text{ (exercise price)} = \$21,000,000$$
$$t \text{ (time to maturity)} = 4 \text{ years}$$
$$\sigma \text{ (standard deviation)} = 50\%$$
$$R \text{ (continuously compounded interest rate)} = 3.5\%$$

Calculation from the Black–Scholes model:

$$C = SN(d_1) - Ee^{-Rt}N(d_2)$$
$$d_1 = [\ln(S/E) + (R + 1/2\sigma^2)t]/\sqrt{\sigma^2 t}$$
$$d_2 = d_1 - \sqrt{\sigma^2 t}$$
$$d_1 = \left[\ln\frac{8,428,255}{21,000,000} + \left(.035 + \frac{1}{2}(.50)^2\right)4\right]\Big/\sqrt{(.50)^2 \cdot 4} = -.27293$$
$$d_2 = -.27293 - \sqrt{(.50)^2 \cdot 4} = -1.27293$$
$$N(d_1) = N(-.27293) = .3925$$
$$N(d_2) = N(-1.27293) = .1015$$
$$C = \$8,428,255 \times .3925 - \$21,000,000 \times e^{-.035 \times 4} \times .1015$$
$$= \$1,454,269$$

Value of business including cost of pilot restaurant = $1,454,269 − $117,439
= $1,336,830

This finding leads to the appearance of a paradox. If Ralph approaches investors to invest in a single restaurant with no possibility of expansion, he will probably not be able to attract capital. After all, Table 23.3 shows a net present value of –$117,439. However, if Ralph thinks bigger, he will likely be able to attract all the capital he needs. But this is really not a paradox at all. By thinking bigger, Ralph is offering investors the option—not the obligation—to expand.

The example we have chosen may seem frivolous, and certainly, we added offbeat characteristics for interest. However, if you think that business situations involving options are unusual or unimportant, let us state emphatically that nothing is further from the truth. The notion of embedded options is at the heart of business. There are two possible outcomes for virtually every business idea. On the one hand, the business may fail, in which case the managers will probably try to shut it down in the most cost-efficient way. On the other hand, the business may prosper, in which case the managers will try to expand. Thus, virtually every business has both the option to abandon and the option to expand. You may have read pundits claiming that the net present value approach to capital budgeting is wrong or incomplete. Although criticism of this type frequently irritates the finance establishment, the pundits definitely have a point. If virtually all projects have embedded options, only an approach such as the one we have outlined can be appropriate. Ignoring the options is likely to lead to serious undervaluation.

23.3 More about the Binomial Model

Earlier in this chapter, we examined two applications of options: Executive compensation and the start-up decision. In both cases we valued an option using the Black–Scholes model. Although this model is justifiably well known, it is not the only approach to option valuation. As mentioned in the previous chapter, the two-state, or binomial, model is an alternative and—in some situations—a superior approach to valuation. The rest of this chapter examines two applications of the binomial model.

HEATING OIL

Two-Date Example Consider Anthony Meyer, a typical heating oil distributor, whose business consists of buying heating oil at the wholesale level and reselling the oil to homeowners at a somewhat higher price. Most of his revenue comes from sales during the winter. Today, September 1, heating oil sells for $2.00 per gallon. Of course, this price is not fixed. Rather, oil prices will vary from September 1 until December 1, the time when his customers will probably make their big winter purchases of heating oil. Let's simplify the situation by assuming that Mr. Meyer believes that oil prices will either be at $2.74 or $1.46 on December 1. Figure 23.1 portrays this possible price movement. This potential price range represents a great deal of uncertainty because Mr. Meyer has no idea which of the two possible prices will actually occur. However, this price variability does not translate into that much risk because he can pass price changes on to his customers. That is, he will charge his customers more if he ends up paying $2.74 per gallon than if he ends up paying $1.46 per gallon.

Of course, Mr. Meyer is avoiding risk by passing on that risk to his customers. His customers accept the risk, perhaps because they are each too small to negotiate a better deal. This is not the case with CECO, a large electric utility in his area. CECO approaches Mr. Meyer with the following proposition. The utility would like to be able to buy *up to* 6 million gallons of oil from him at $2.10 per gallon on December 1.

Figure 23.1

Movement of
Heating Oil Prices
from September 1 to
December 1 in a
Two-Date Example

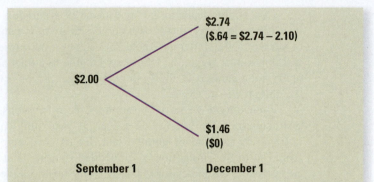

$2.00

$2.74
($.64 = $2.74 − 2.10)

$1.46
($0)

September 1   December 1

The price of heating oil on December 1 will be either $2.74 or $1.46.
Because the price on September 1 is $2.00, we say that $u = 1.37$
($=$2.74/2.00) and $d = .73$ ($=$1.46/2.00). The loss per gallon to
Mr. Meyer (or, equivalently, the gain per gallon to CECO) of $.64 in
the up state or $0 in the down state is shown in parentheses.

Although this arrangement represents a lot of oil, both Mr. Meyer and CECO know
that Mr. Meyer can expect to lose money on it. If prices rise to $2.74 per gallon, the utility
will happily buy all 6 million gallons at only $2.10 per gallon, clearly creating a loss for
the distributor. However, if oil prices decline to $1.46 per gallon, the utility will not buy
any oil. After all, why should CECO pay $2.10 per gallon to Mr. Meyer when the utility
can buy all the oil it wants at $1.46 per gallon in the open market? In other words, CECO
is asking for a *call option* on heating oil. To compensate Mr.Meyer for the risk of loss, the
two parties agree that CECO will pay him $1,000,000 up front for the right to buy up to 6
million gallons of oil at $2.10 per gallon.

Is this a fair deal? Although small distributors may evaluate a deal like this by gut feel,
we can evaluate it more quantitatively by using the binomial model described in the previous chapter. In that chapter, we pointed out that option problems can be handled most easily by assuming *risk-neutral pricing*. In this approach, we first note that oil will either rise
37 percent ($=$2.74/$2.00 − 1$) or fall −27 percent ($=$1.46/$2.00 − 1$) from September
1 to December 1. We can think of these two numbers as the possible returns on heating
oil. In addition, we introduce two new terms, u and d. We define u as $1 + .37 = 1.37$ and
d as $1 − .27 = .73$.[2] Using the methodology of the previous chapter, we value the contract
in the following two steps.

Step 1: Determining the Risk-Neutral Probabilities   We determine the probability of a
price rise such that the expected return on oil exactly equals the risk-free rate. Assuming
an 8 percent annual interest rate, which implies a 2 percent rate over the next three months,
we can solve for the probability of a rise as follows:[3]

$$2\% = \text{Probability of rise} \times .37 + (1 − \text{Probability of rise}) \times (−.27)$$

Solving this equation, we find that the probability of a rise is approximately 45 percent,
implying that the probability of a fall is 55 percent. In other words, if the probability of a
price rise is 45 percent, the expected return on heating oil is 2 percent. In accordance with
what we said in the previous chapter, these are the probabilities that are consistent with a
world of risk neutrality. That is, under risk neutrality, the expected return on any asset would

---

[2]As we will see later, u and d are consistent with a standard deviation of the annual return on heating oil of .63.
[3]For simplicity, we ignore both storage costs and a convenience yield.

equal the riskless rate of interest. No one would demand an expected return above this riskless rate, because risk-neutral individuals do not need to be compensated for bearing risk.

Step 2: Valuing the Contract   If the price of oil rises to $2.74 on December 1, CECO will want to buy oil from Mr. Meyer at $2.10 per gallon. Mr. Meyer will lose $.64 per gallon because he buys oil in the open market at $2.74 per gallon, only to resell it to CECO at $2.10 per gallon. This loss of $.64 is shown in parentheses in Figure 23.1. Conversely, if the market price of heating oil falls to $1.46 per gallon, CECO will not buy any oil from Mr. Meyer. That is, CECO would not want to pay $2.10 per gallon to him when the utility could buy heating oil in the open market at $1.46 per gallon. Thus, we can say that Mr. Meyer neither gains nor loses if the price drops to $1.46. The gain or loss of zero is placed in parentheses under the price of $1.46 in Figure 23.1. In addition, as mentioned earlier, Mr. Meyer receives $1,000,000 up front.

Given these numbers, the value of the contract to Mr. Meyer can be calculated as:

$$\underbrace{[.45 \times (\$2.10 - \$2.74) \times 6 \text{ million} + .55 \times 0]/1.02}_{\text{Value of the call option}} + \$1,000,000 = -\$694,118 \tag{23.1}$$

As in the previous chapter, we are valuing an option using risk-neutral pricing. The cash flows of –$.64 (=$2.10 – $2.74) and $0 per gallon are multiplied by their risk-neutral probabilities. The entire first term in Equation 23.1 is then discounted at 1.02 because the cash flows in that term occur on December 1. The $1,000,000 is not discounted because Mr. Meyer receives it today, September 1. Because the present value of the contract is negative, Mr. Meyer would be wise to reject the contract.

As stated before, the distributor has sold a call option to CECO. The first term in the preceding equation, which equals –$1,694,118, can be viewed as the value of this call option. It is a negative number because the equation looks at the option from Mr. Meyer's point of view. Therefore, the value of the call option would be +$1,694,118 to CECO. On a per-gallon basis, the value of the option to CECO is:

$$[.45 (\$2.74 - \$2.10) + .55 \times 0]/1.02 = \$.282 \tag{23.2}$$

Equation 23.2 shows that CECO will gain $.64 (=$2.74 – $2.10) per gallon in the up state because CECO can buy heating oil worth $2.74 for only $2.10 under the contract. By contrast, the contract is worth nothing to CECO in the down state because the utility will not pay $2.10 for oil selling for only $1.46 in the open market. Using risk-neutral pricing, the formula tells us that the value of the call option on one gallon of heating oil is $.282.

Three-Date Example   Although the preceding example captures a number of aspects of the real world, it has one deficiency. It assumes that the price of heating oil can take on only two values on December 1. This is clearly not plausible: Oil can take on essentially any value, in reality. Although this deficiency seems glaring at first glance, it actually is easily correctable. All we have to do is introduce more intervals over the three-month period of our example.

For example, consider Figure 23.2, which shows the price movement of heating oil over two intervals of 1½ months each.[4] As shown in the figure, the price will be either $2.50 or $1.60 on October 15. We refer to $2.50 as the price in the *up state* and $1.60 as the price in the *down state*. Thus, heating oil has returns of 25 percent (=$2.50/$2.00−1) and −20 percent (=$1.60/$2.00−1) in the two states.

---

[4]Though it is not apparent at first glance, we will see later that the price movement in Figure 23.2 is consistent with the price movement in Figure 23.1.

Figure 23.2

Movement of Heating
Oil Prices in a Three-
Date Model

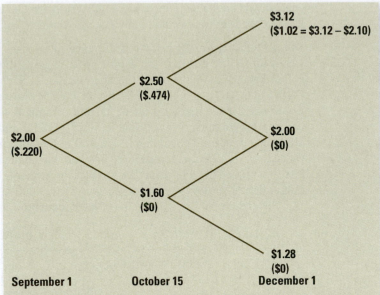

The figure shows the prices of a gallon of heating oil on three dates, given
$u = 1.25$ and $d = .80$. There are three possible prices for heating oil on
December 1. For each one of these three prices, we calculate the price on
December 1 of a call option on a gallon of heating oil with an exercise price
of $2.10. These numbers are in parentheses. Call prices at earlier dates are
determined by the binomial model and are also shown in parentheses.

We assume the same variability as we move forward from October 15 to December 1.
That is, given a price of $2.50 on October 15, the price on December 1 will be either $3.12
(=$2.50 × 1.25) or $2 (=$2.50 × .80). Similarly, given a price of $1.60 on October 15, the
price on December 1 will be either $2 (=$1.60 × 1.25) or $1.28 (=$1.60 × .80). This assumption of constant variability is quite plausible because the rate of new information impacting
heating oil (or most commodities or assets) is likely to be similar from month to month.

Note that there are three possible prices on December 1, but there are two possible prices
on October 15. Also, note that there are two paths to a price of $2 on December 1. The price
could rise to $2.50 on October 15 before falling back down to $2 on December 1. Alternatively,
the price could fall to $1.60 on October 15 before going back up to $2 on December 1. In other
words, the model has symmetry, where an up movement followed by a down movement yields
the same price on December 1 as a down movement followed by an up movement.

How do we value CECO's option in this three-date example? We employ the same
procedure that we used in the two-date example, although we now need an extra step
because of the extra date.

Step 1: Determining the Risk-Neutral Probabilities　As we did in the two-date example,
we determine what the probability of a price rise would be such that the expected return on
heating oil exactly equals the riskless rate. However, in this case we work with an interval
of 1½ months. Assuming an 8 percent annual rate of interest, which implies a 1 percent
rate over a 1½-month interval,[5] we can solve for the probability of a rise like this:

$$1\% = \text{Probability of rise} \times .25 + (1 - \text{Probability of rise}) \times (-.20)$$

---
[5]For simplicity, we ignore interest compounding.

Solving the equation, we find that the probability of a rise here is 47 percent, implying that the probability of a fall is 53 percent. In other words, if the probability of a rise is 47 percent, the expected return on heating oil is 1 percent per each 1½-month interval. Again, these probabilities are determined under the assumption of risk-neutral pricing.

Note that the probabilities of 47 percent and 53 percent hold for both the interval from September 1 to October 15 and the interval from October 15 to December 1. This is the case because the return in the up state is 25 percent and the return in the down state is −20 percent for each of the two intervals. Thus, the preceding equation must apply to each of the intervals separately.

Step 2: Valuing the Option as of October 15 As indicated in Figure 23.2, the option to CECO will be worth $1.02 per gallon on December 1 if the price of heating oil has risen to $3.12 on that date. That is, CECO can buy oil from Mr. Meyer at $2.10 when it would otherwise have to pay $3.12 in the open market. However, the option will be worthless on December 1 if the price of a gallon of heating oil is either $2 or $1.28 on that date. Here, the option is out of the money because the exercise price of $2.10 is above either $2 or $1.28.

Using these option prices on December 1, we can calculate the value of the call option on October 15. If the price of a gallon of heating oil is $2.50 on October 15, Figure 23.2 shows us that the call option will be worth either $1.02 or $0 on December 1. Thus, if the price of heating oil is $2.50 on October 15, the value of the option on one gallon of heating oil at that time is:

$$[.47 \times \$1.02 + .53 \times 0]/1.01 = \$.474$$

Here we are valuing an option using the same risk-neutral pricing approach that we used in the earlier two-date example. This value of $.474 is shown in parentheses in Figure 23.2.

We also want to value the option on October 15 if the price at that time is $1.60. However, the value here is clearly zero, as indicated by this calculation:

$$[.47 \times \$0 + .53 \times \$0]/1.01 = 0$$

This is obvious once we look at Figure 23.2. We see from the figure that the call must end up out of the money on December 1 if the price of heating oil is $1.60 on October15. Thus, the call must have zero value on October 15 if the price of heating oil is $1.60 on that date.

Step 3: Valuing the Option on September 1 In the previous step, we saw that the price of the call on October 15 would be $.474 if the price of a gallon of heating oil was $2.50 on that date. Similarly, the price of the option on October 15 would be $0 if oil was selling at $1.60 on that date. From these values, we can calculate the call option value on September 1:

$$[.47 \times \$.474 + .53 \times \$0]/1.01 = \$.220$$

Notice that this calculation is completely analogous to the calculation of the option value in the previous step, as well as the calculation of the option value in the two-date example that we presented earlier. In other words, the same approach applies regardless of the number of intervals used. As we will see later, we can move to many intervals, which produces greater realism, yet still maintain the same basic methodology.

The previous calculation has given us the value to CECO of its option on one gallon of heating oil. Now we are ready to calculate the value of the contract to Mr. Meyer. Given the calculations from the previous equation, the contract's value can be written as:

$$-\$.220 \times 6,000,000 + \$1,000,000 = -\$320,000$$

That is, Mr. Meyer is giving away an option worth $.220 for each of the 6 million gallons of heating oil. In return, he is receiving only $1,000,000 up front. Overall, he is losing $320,000. Of course, the value of the contract to CECO is the opposite, so the value to the utility is $320,000.

Extension to Many Dates   We have looked at the contract between CECO and Mr. Meyer using both a two-date example and a three-date example. The three-date case is more realistic because more possibilities for price movements are allowed here. However, why stop at just three dates? Moving to 4 dates, 5 dates, 50 dates, 500 dates, and so on should give us even more realism. Note that as we move to more dates, we are merely shortening the interval between dates without increasing the overall time period of three months (September 1 to December 1).

For example, imagine a model with 90 dates over the three months. Here, each interval is approximately one day long because there are about 90 days in a three-month period. The assumption of two possible outcomes in the binomial model is more plausible over a one-day interval than it is over a 1½-month interval, let alone a three-month interval. Of course, we could probably achieve greater realism still by going to an interval of, say, one hour or one minute.

How do we adjust the binomial model to accommodate increases in the number of intervals? It turns out that two simple formulas relate u and d to the standard deviation of the return on the underlying asset:[6]

$$u = e^{\sigma/\sqrt{n}} \quad \text{and} \quad d = 1/u$$

where σ is the standard deviation of the annualized return on the underlying asset (heating oil, in this case) and n is the number of intervals over a year.

When we created the heating oil example, we assumed that the annualized standard deviation of the return on heating oil was .63 (or, equivalently, 63 percent). Because there are four quarters in a year, $u = e^{.63/\sqrt{4}} = 1.37$ and $d = 1/1.37 = .73$, as shown in the two-date example of Figure 23.1. In the three-date example of Figure 23.2, where each interval is 1½ months long, $u = e^{.63/\sqrt{8}} = 1.25$ and $d = 1/1.25 = .80$. Thus, the binomial model can be applied in practice if the standard deviation of the return of the underlying asset can be estimated.

We stated earlier that the value of the call option on a gallon of heating oil was estimated to be $.282 in the two-date model and $.220 in the three-date model. How does the value of the option change as we increase the number of intervals while keeping the time period constant at three months (from September 1 to December 1)? We have calculated the value of the call for various time intervals in Table 23.5.[7] The realism increases with the number of intervals because the restriction of only two possible outcomes is more plausible over a short interval than over a long one. Thus, the value of the call when the number of intervals is 99 or infinity is likely more realistic than this value when the number of intervals is, say, 1 or 2.

However, a very interesting phenomenon can be observed from the table. Although the value of the call changes as the number of intervals increases, convergence occurs quite rapidly. The call's value with 6 intervals is almost identical to the value with 99 intervals. Thus, a small number of intervals appears serviceable for the binomial model. Six intervals

---

[6]See John C. Hull, *Options, Futures, and Other Derivatives,* 8th ed. (Upper Saddle River, NJ: Prentice Hall, 2011), for a derivation of these formulas.

[7]In this discussion, we have used both *intervals* and *dates.* To keep the terminology straight, remember that the number of intervals is always one less than the number of dates. For example, if a model has two dates, it has only one interval.

Table 23.5
Value of a Call
on One Gallon of
Heating Oil

Number of Intervals*	Call Value
1	$.282
2	.220
3	.244
4	.232
6	.228
10	.228
20	.228
30	.228
40	.228
50	.226
99	.226
Black–Scholes Infinity	.226

In this example, the value of the call according to the binomial model varies as the number of intervals increases. However, the value of the call converges rapidly to the Black–Scholes value. Thus, the binomial model, even with only a few intervals, appears to be a good approximation of Black–Scholes.

*The number of intervals is always one less than the number of dates.

in a three-month period implies that each interval is two weeks long. Of course, the assumption that heating oil can take on only one of two prices in two weeks is simply not realistic. The paradox is that this unrealistic assumption still produces a realistic call price.

What happens when the number of intervals goes to infinity, implying that the length of the interval goes to zero? It can be proved mathematically that we end up with the value of the Black–Scholes model. This value is also presented in Table 23.5. Thus, we can argue that the Black–Scholes model is the best approach to value the heating oil option. It is also quite easy to apply. We can use a calculator to value options with Black–Scholes, whereas we must generally use a computer program for the binomial model. However, as shown in Table 23.5, the values from the binomial model, even with relatively few intervals, are quite close to the Black–Scholes value. Thus, although Black–Scholes may save us time, it does not materially affect our estimate of value.

At this point it seems as if the Black–Scholes model is preferable to the binomial model. Who wouldn't want to save time and still get a slightly more accurate value? However, this is not always the case. There are plenty of situations where the binomial model is preferred to the Black–Scholes model. One such situation is presented in the next section.

23.4 Shutdown and Reopening Decisions

Some of the earliest and most important examples of special options have occurred in the natural resources and mining industries.

VALUING A GOLD MINE

The Woe Is Me gold mine was founded in 1882 on one of the richest veins of gold in the West. Thirty years later, by 1912, the mine had been played out; but occasionally, depending on the price of gold, it was reopened. Currently, gold is not actively mined at Woe Is Me, but its stock is still traded on the exchange under the ticker symbol WOE. WOE has no debt and, with about 20 million outstanding shares, its market value (stock price times number of shares outstanding) exceeds $6 billion. WOE owns about 160 acres of land surrounding the mine and has a 100-year government lease to mine gold there. However, land in the desert has a market value of only a few thousand dollars. WOE holds cash securities and other assets worth about $30 million. What could possibly explain why a company with $30 million in assets and a closed gold mine with no cash flow has the market value that WOE has?

The answer lies in the options that WOE implicitly owns in the form of a gold mine. Assume that the current price of gold is about $1,300 per ounce, and the cost of extraction and processing at the mine is about $1,400 per ounce. It is no wonder that the mine is closed. Every ounce of gold extracted costs $1,400 and can be sold for only $1,300, for a loss of $100 per ounce. Presumably, if the price of gold were to rise, the mine could be opened. It costs $20 million to open the mine; when it is opened, production is 50,000 ounces per year. Geologists believe that the amount of gold in the mine is essentially unlimited, and WOE has the right to mine it for the next 100 years. Under the terms of its lease, WOE cannot stockpile gold and each year must sell all the gold it mines that year. Closing the mine, which costs $10 million, requires equipment to be mothballed and some environmental precautions to be put in place. We will refer to the $20 million required to open the mine as the entry fee, or investment, and the $10 million to close it as the closing or abandonment cost. (We cannot avoid the abandonment cost by simply keeping the mine open and not operating.)

From a financial perspective, WOE is really just a package of options on the price of gold disguised as a company and a mine. The basic option is a call on the price of gold where the exercise price is the $1,400 extraction cost. The option is complicated by having an exercise fee of $20 million—the opening cost—whenever it is exercised and a closing fee of $10 million when it is abandoned. It is also complicated by the fact that it is a perpetual option with no final maturity.

THE ABANDONMENT AND OPENING DECISIONS

Before valuing the option implicit in WOE, it is useful to see what we can say by just applying common sense. To begin with, the mine should be opened only when the price of gold is sufficiently above the extraction cost of $1,400 per ounce. Because it costs $20 million to open the mine, the mine should not be opened whenever the price of gold is only slightly above $1,400. At a gold price of, say, $1,401, the mine wouldn't be opened because the one-dollar profit per ounce translates into $50,000 per year (=50,000 ounces × $1/ounce). This would not begin to cover the $20 million opening costs. More significantly, though, the mine probably would not be opened if the price rose to $1,450 per ounce, even though a $50 profit per ounce—$2,500,000 per year—would pay the $20 million opening costs at any reasonable discount rate. The reason is that here, as in all option problems, volatility (in this case the volatility of gold) plays a significant role. Because the gold price is volatile, the price has to rise sufficiently above $1,400 per ounce to make it worth opening the mine. If the price at which the mine is opened is too close to the extraction price of $1,400 per ounce, say at $1,450 per ounce, we would open the mine every time the price jogged above $1,450. Unfortunately, we would then find ourselves operating at a loss or facing a closing decision whenever gold jogged back down $50 per ounce (or only 3 percent) to $1,400.

The estimated volatility of the return on gold is about 25 percent per year. This means that a single annual standard deviation movement in the gold price is 25 percent of $1,300, or $325 per year. Surely with this amount of random movement in the gold price, a threshold of, for example, $1,405 is much too low at which to open the mine. Similar logic applies to the closing decision. If the mine is open, we will clearly keep it open as long as the gold price is above the extraction cost of $1,400 per ounce because we are profiting on every ounce of gold mined. But we also won't close the mine down simply because the gold price drops below $1,400 per ounce. We will tolerate a running loss because gold may later rise back above $1,400. If, alternatively, we closed the mine, we would pay the $10 million abandonment cost, only to pay another $20 million to reopen the mine if the price rose again.

To summarize, if the mine is currently closed, then it will be opened—at a cost of $20 million—whenever the price of gold rises *sufficiently* above the extraction cost of $1,400 per ounce. If the mine is currently operating, then it will be closed down—at a cost of $10 million—whenever the price of gold falls *sufficiently* below the extraction cost of $1,400 per ounce. WOE's problem is to find these two threshold prices at which it opens a closed mine and closes an open mine. We call these prices p*open* and p*close,* respectively, where:

$$p\text{open} > \$1,400/\text{ounce} > p\text{close}$$

In other words, WOE will open the mine if the gold price option is sufficiently in the money and will close it when the option is sufficiently out of the money.

We know that the more volatile the gold price, the further away p*open* and p*close* will be from $1,400 per ounce. We also know that the greater the cost of opening the mine, the higher p*open* will be; and the greater the cost of abandoning the mine, the lower p*close* will be. Interestingly, we should also expect that p*open* will be higher if the abandonment cost is increased. After all, if it costs more to abandon the mine, WOE will need to be more assured that the price will stay above the extraction cost when it decides to open the mine. Otherwise, WOE will face the costly choice between abandonment and operating at a loss if the price falls below $1,400 per ounce. Similarly, raising the cost of opening the mine will make WOE more reluctant to close an open mine. As a result, p*close* will be lower.

The preceding arguments have enabled us to reduce the problem of valuing WOE to two stages. First, we have to determine the threshold prices, p*open* and p*close*. Second, given the best choices for these thresholds, we must determine the value of a gold option that is exercised for a cost of $20 million when the gold price rises above p*open* and is shut down for a cost of $10 million whenever the gold price is below p*close*.

When the mine is open—that is, when the option is exercised—the annual cash flow is equal to the difference between the gold price and the extraction cost of $1,400 per ounce times 50,000 ounces. When the mine is shut down, it generates no cash flow.

The following diagram describes the decisions available at each point in time:

How do we determine the critical values for p*open* and p*close* and then the value of the mine? It is possible to get a good approximation by using the tools we have currently developed.

VALUING THE SIMPLE GOLD MINE

Here is what has to be done both to determine p*open* and p*close* and to value the mine.

Step 1   Find the risk-free interest rate and the volatility. We assume a semiannual interest rate of 3.4 percent and a volatility of 25 percent per year for gold.

Step 2   Construct a binomial tree and fill it in with gold prices. Suppose, for example, that we set the steps of the tree six months apart. If the annual volatility is 25 percent, u is equal to $e^{.25/\sqrt{2}}$, which is approximately equal to 1.19. The other parameter, d, is .84 ($=1/1.19$). Figure 23.3 illustrates the tree. Starting at the current price of $1,300, the first 19 percent increase takes the price to $1,551 in six months. The first 16 percent decrease takes the price to $1,089. Subsequent steps are up 19 percent or down 16 percent from the previous price. The tree extends for the 100-year life of the lease, or 200 six-month steps.

Using our analysis from the previous section, we now compute the risk-adjusted probabilities for each step. Given a semiannual interest rate of 3.4 percent, we have:

$$3.4\% = \text{Probability of a rise} \times .19 + (1 - \text{Probability of a rise}) \times -.16$$

Figure 23.3
A Binomial Tree for Gold Prices

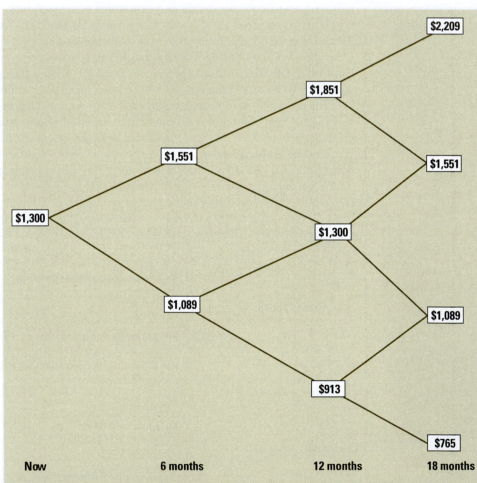

Steps of the binomial tree are six months apart. For each step, u is equal to 1.19 and d is equal to .84. Note that u and d are rounded to two decimal points.

Solving this equation gives us .55 for the probability of a rise, implying that the probability of a fall is .45. These probabilities are the same for each six-month interval. In other words, if the probability of a rise is .55, the expected return on gold is 3.4 percent per each six-month interval. These probabilities are determined under the assumption of risk-neutral pricing. In other words, if investors are risk-neutral, they will be satisfied with an expected return equal to the risk-free rate because the extra risk of gold will not concern them.

Step 3   Now we turn the computer on and let it simulate, say, 5,000 possible paths through the tree. At each node, the computer has a .55 probability of picking an "up" movement in the price and a corresponding .45 probability of picking a "down" movement in the price. A typical path might be represented by whether the price rose or fell each six-month period over the next 100 years; it would be a list like:

up, up, down, up, down, down, . . . , down

where the first "up" means the price rose from $1,300 to $1,551 in the first six months, the next "up" means it again went up in the second half of the year from $1,551 to $1,851, and so on, ending with a down move in the last half of year 100.

With 5,000 such paths, we will have a good sample of all the future possibilities for movement in the gold price.

Step 4   Next, we consider possible choices for the threshold prices, p*open* and p*close*. For p*open,* we let the possibilities be:

p*open* = $1,500 or $1,600 or . . . or $2,900

a total of 15 values. For p*close* we let the possibilities be:

p*close* = $1,300 or $1,200 or . . . or $400

a total of 10 values.

We picked these choices because they seemed reasonable and because increments of $100 for each seemed sensible. To be precise, though, we should let the threshold prices change as we move through the tree and get closer to the end of 100 years. Presumably, for example, if we decided to open the mine with one year left on the lease, the price of gold should be at least high enough to cover the $20 million opening costs in the coming year. Because we mine 50,000 ounces per year, we will open the mine in year 99 only if the gold price is at least $400 above the extraction cost, or $1,800.

Although this will become important at the end of the lease, using a constant threshold shouldn't have too big an impact on the value with 100 years to go. Therefore, we will stick with our approximation of constant threshold prices.

Step 5   We calculate the value of the mine for each pair of choices of p*open* and p*close*. For example, if p*open* = $2,200 and p*close* = $1,100, we use the computer to keep track of the cash flows if we opened the mine whenever it was previously closed and the gold price rose to $2,200, and closed the mine whenever it was previously open and the gold price fell to $1,100. We do this for each of the 5,000 paths we simulated in Step 3.

For example, consider the path illustrated in Figure 23.4:

up, up, down, up, up, down, down, down, down

As can be seen from the figure, the price reaches a peak of $2,209 in 2½ years, only to fall to $1,089 over the following four six-month intervals. If p*open* = $2,200 and p*close* = $1,100, the mine will be opened when the price reaches $2,209, necessitating a cost of $20 million. However, the firm can sell 25,000 ounces of gold at $2,209 per ounce at that time, producing a cash flow of $20.225 million [=25,000 ($2,209 − $1,400)]. When the

Figure 23.4

A Possible Path for
the Price of Gold

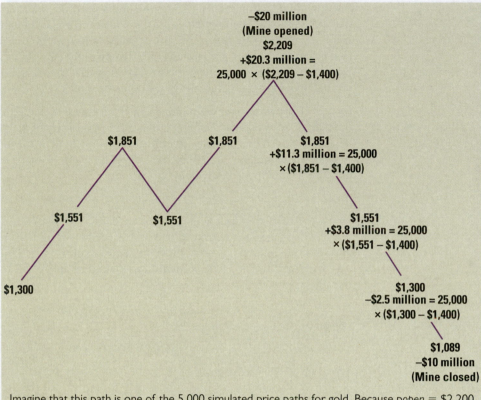

Imagine that this path is one of the 5,000 simulated price paths for gold. Because $p_{open} = \$2,200$ and $p_{close} = \$1,100$, the mine is opened when the price reaches $2,209. The mine is closed when the price reaches $1,089.

price falls to $1,851 six months later, the firm sells another 25,000 ounces, yielding a cash flow of $11.275 million [=25,000 ($1,851 − $1,400)]. The price continues to fall, reaching $1,300 a year later. Here, the firm experiences a cash outflow because production costs are $1,400 per ounce. Next, the price falls to $1,089. Because this price is below p_{close} of $1,100, the mine is closed at a cost of $10 million. Of course, the price of gold will fluctuate in further years, leading to the possibility of future mine openings and closings.

This path is just a possibility. It may or may not occur in any simulation of 5,000 paths. For each of the 5,000 paths that the computer simulated, we have a sequence of semiannual cash flows using a p_{open} of $2,200 and a p_{close} of $1,100. We calculate the present value of each of these cash flows, discounting at the interest rate of 3.4 percent. Summing across all the cash flows, we have the present value of the gold mine for one path.

We then take the average present value of the gold mine across all the 5,000 simulated paths. This number is the expected value of the mine from following a policy of opening the mine whenever the gold price hits $2,200 and closing it at a price of $1,100.

Step 6   The final step is to compare the different expected discounted cash flows from Step 5 for the range of possible choices for p_{open} and p_{close} and to pick the highest one. This is the best estimate of the expected value of the mine. The values for p_{open} and p_{close} corresponding to this estimate are the points at which to open a closed mine and to shut an open one.

As mentioned in Step 4, there are 15 different values for p_{open} and 10 different values for p_{close}, implying 150 (=15 × 10) different pairs. Consider Table 23.6, which shows

Table 23.6

Valuation of Woe Is Me (WOE) Gold Mine for the 20 Best Choices of p*open* and p*close*

p*open*	p*close*	Estimated Value of Gold Mine (in $ millions)
$2,900	$1,200	$6,629
2,200	1,300	6,557
2,000	1,000	6,428
2,000	1,200	6,288
1,800	1,400	6,168
2,900	500	6,140
2,800	500	6,103
2,900	900	6,055
3,000	1,100	6,054
2,600	900	6,050
2,600	600	6,038
3,000	500	6,033
1,900	1,400	5,958
2,100	700	5,939
2,300	500	5,934
2,200	1,400	5,928
1,800	800	5,895
2,300	600	5,892
2,400	1,100	5,862
1,900	500	5,855

For our simulation, WOE opens the mine whenever the gold price rises above p*open* and closes the mine whenever the gold price falls below p*close*.

the present values associated with the 20 best pairs. The table indicates that the best pair is p*open* = $2,900 and p*close* = $1,200, with a present value of $6.629 billion. This number represents the average present value across 5,000 simulations, all assuming the preceding values of p*open* and p*close*. The next best pair is p*open* = $2,200 and p*close* = $1,300, with a present value of $6.557 billion. The third best pair has a somewhat lower present value, and so on.

Of course, our estimate of the value of the mine is $6.629 billion, the present value of the best pair of choices. The market capitalization (Price × Number of shares outstanding) of WOE should reach this value if the market makes the same assumptions that we did. Note that the value of the firm is quite high using an option framework. However, as stated earlier, WOE would appear worthless if a regular discounted cash flow approach were used. This occurs because the initial gold price of $1,300 is below the extraction cost of $1,400.

This example is not easy, neither in concepts nor in implementation. However, the extra work involved in mastering this example is worth it because the example illustrates the type of modeling that actually occurs in corporate finance departments in the real world.

Furthermore, the example illustrates the benefits of the binomial approach. We merely calculate the cash flows associated with each of a number of simulations, discount the cash flows from each simulation, and average present values across the simulations. Because the Black–Scholes model is not amenable to simulations, it cannot be used for this type of problem. In addition, there are a number of other situations where the binomial model is more appropriate than is the Black–Scholes model. For example, it is well known that the Black–Scholes model cannot properly handle options with dividend payments prior to the expiration date. This model also does not adequately handle the valuation of an American put. By contrast, the binomial model can easily handle both of these situations.

Thus, any student of corporate finance should be well versed in both models. The Black–Scholes model should be used whenever appropriate because it is simpler to use than is the binomial model. However, for the more complex situations where the Black–Scholes model breaks down, the binomial model becomes a necessary tool.

Summary and Conclusions

Real options, which are pervasive in business, are not captured by net present value analysis. Chapter 7 valued real options via decision trees. Given the work on options in the previous chapter, we are now able to value real options according to the Black–Scholes model and the binomial model.

In this chapter, we described and valued four different types of options:

1. Executive stock options, which are technically not real options.

2. The embedded option in a start-up company.

3. The option in simple business contracts.

4. The option to shut down and reopen a project.

We tried to keep the presentation simple and straightforward from a mathematical point of view. The binomial approach to option pricing in Chapter 22 was extended to many periods. This adjustment brings us closer to the real world because the assumption of only two prices at the end of an interval is more plausible when the interval is short.

Concept Questions

1. **Employee Stock Options** Why do companies issue options to executives if they cost the company more than they are worth to the executive? Why not just give cash and split the difference? Wouldn't that make both the company and the executive better off?

2. **Real Options** What are the two options that many businesses have?

3. **Project Analysis** Why does a strict NPV calculation typically understate the value of a company or project?

4. **Real Options** Utility companies often face a decision to build new plants that burn coal, oil, or both. If the prices of both coal and gas are highly volatile, how valuable is the decision to build a plant that can burn either coal or oil? What happens to the value of this option as the correlation between coal and oil prices increases?

5. **Real Options** Your company owns a vacant lot in a suburban area. What is the advantage of waiting to develop the lot?

6. **Real Options** Star Mining buys a gold mine, but the cost of extraction is currently too high to make the mine profitable. In option terminology, what type of option(s) does the company have on this mine?

7. **Real Options**   You are discussing real options with a colleague. During the discussion, the colleague states, "Real option analysis makes no sense because it says that a real option on a risky venture is worth more than a real option on a safe venture." How should you respond to this statement?

8. **Real Options and Capital Budgeting**   Your company currently uses traditional capital budgeting techniques, including net present value. After hearing about the use of real option analysis, your boss decides that your company should use real option analysis in place of net present value. How would you evaluate this decision?

9. **Insurance as an Option**   Insurance, whether purchased by a corporation or an individual, is in essence an option. What type of option is an insurance policy?

10. **Real Options**   How would the analysis of real options change if a company has competitors?

Questions and Problems

BASIC
(Questions 1–5)

1. **Employee Stock Options**   Gary Levin is the chief executive officer of Mountainbrook Trading Company. The board of directors has just granted Mr. Levin 25,000 at-the-money European call options on the company's stock, which is currently trading at $55 per share. The stock pays no dividends. The options will expire in five years, and the standard deviation of the returns on the stock is 61 percent. Treasury bills that mature in five years currently yield a continuously compounded interest rate of 6 percent.

   a. Use the Black–Scholes model to calculate the value of the stock options.
   b. You are Mr. Levin's financial adviser. He must choose between the previously mentioned stock option package and an immediate $750,000 bonus. If he is risk-neutral, which would you recommend?
   c. How would your answer to (b) change if Mr. Levin were risk-averse and he could not sell the options prior to expiration?

2. **Employee Stock Options**   Jared Lazarus has just been named the new chief executive officer of BluBell Fitness Centers, Inc. In addition to an annual salary of $475,000, his three-year contract states that his compensation will include 20,000 at-the-money European call options on the company's stock that expire in three years. The current stock price is $41 per share, and the standard deviation of the returns on the firm's stock is 69 percent. The company does not pay a dividend. Treasury bills that mature in three years yield a continuously compounded interest rate of 5 percent. Assume that Mr. Lazarus's annual salary payments occur at the end of the year and that these cash flows should be discounted at a rate of 9 percent. Using the Black–Scholes model to calculate the value of the stock options, determine the total value of the compensation package on the date the contract is signed.

3. **Binomial Model**   Gasworks, Inc., has been approached to sell up to 5 million gallons of gasoline in three months at a price of $2.65 per gallon. Gasoline is currently selling on the wholesale market at $2.34 per gallon and has a standard deviation of 62 percent. If the risk-free rate is 6 percent per year, what is the value of this option?

4. **Real Options**   The Webber Company is an international conglomerate with a real estate division that owns the right to erect an office building on a parcel of land in downtown Sacramento over the next year. This building would cost $55 million to construct. Due to low demand for office space in the downtown area, such a building is worth approximately $53.2 million today. If demand increases, the building would be worth $57.9 million a year from today. If demand decreases, the same office building would be worth only $49.8 million in a year. The company can borrow and lend at the risk-free annual effective rate of

4.8 percent. A local competitor in the real estate business has recently offered $1.8 million for the right to build an office building on the land. Should the company accept this offer? Use a two-state model to value the real option.

5. **Real Options** Jet Black is an international conglomerate with a petroleum division and is currently competing in an auction to win the right to drill for crude oil on a large piece of land in one year. The current market price of crude oil is $103 per barrel, and the land is believed to contain 435,000 barrels of oil. If found, the oil would cost $75 million to extract. Treasury bills that mature in one year yield a continuously compounded interest rate of 4 percent, and the standard deviation of the returns on the price of crude oil is 50 percent. Use the Black–Scholes model to calculate the maximum bid that the company should be willing to make at the auction.

INTERMEDIATE
(Questions 6–8)

6. **Real Options** Sardano and Sons is a large, publicly held company that is considering leasing a warehouse. One of the company's divisions specializes in manufacturing steel, and this particlar warehouse is the only facility in the area that suits the firm's operations. The current price of steel is $690 per ton. If the price of steel falls over the next six months, the company will purchase 500 tons of steel and produce 55,000 steel rods. Each steel rod will cost $18 to manufacture, and the company plans to sell the rods for $29 each. It will take only a matter of days to produce and sell the steel rods. If the price of steel rises or remains the same, it will not be profitable to undertake the project, and the company will allow the lease to expire without producing any steel rods. Treasury bills that mature in six months yield a continuously compounded interest rate of 4.5 percent, and the standard deviation of the returns on steel is 38 percent. Use the Black–Scholes model to determine the maximum amount that the company should be willing to pay for the lease.

7. **Real Options** Wet for the Summer, Inc., manufactures filters for swimming pools. The company is deciding whether to implement a new technology in its pool filters. One year from now the company will know whether the new technology is accepted in the market. If the demand for the new filters is high, the present value of the cash flows in one year will be $14.7 million. Conversely, if the demand is low, the value of the cash flows in one year will be $8.5 million. The value of the project today under these assumptions is $13.1 million, and the risk-free rate is 6 percent. Suppose that in one year, if the demand for the new technology is low, the company can sell the technology for $9.4 million. What is the value of the option to abandon?

8. **Binomial Model** There is a European put option on a stock that expires in two months. The stock price is $82, and the standard deviation of the stock returns is 70 percent. The option has a strike price of $90, and the risk-free interest rate is a 5 percent annual percentage rate. What is the price of the put option today using one-month steps?

CHALLENGE
(Questions 9–10)

9. **Binomial Model** In the previous problem, assume that the exercise style on the option is American rather than European. What is the price of the option now? (*Hint:* How will you find the value of the option if it can be exercised early? When would you exercise the option early?)

10. **Real Options** You are in discussions to purchase an option on an office building with a strike price of $63 million. The building is currently valued at $60 million. The option will allow you to purchase the building either six months from today or one year from today. Six months from today, accrued rent payments from the building in the amount of $900,000 will be made to the owners. If you exercise the option in six months, you will receive the accrued rent payment, otherwise, the payment will be made to the current owners. A second accrued rent payment of $900,000 will be paid one year from today with the same payment terms. The standard deviation of the value of the building is 30 percent, and the risk-free rate is a 6 percent annual percentage rate. What is the price of the option today using six-month steps? (*Hint:* The value of the building in six months will be reduced by the accrued rent payment if you do not exercise the option at that time.)

Mini Case

EXOTIC CUISINES' EMPLOYEE STOCK OPTIONS

As a newly minted MBA, you've taken a management position with Exotic Cuisines, Inc., a restaurant chain that just went public last year. The company's restaurants specialize in exotic main dishes, using ingredients such as alligator, buffalo, and ostrich. A concern you had going in was that the restaurant business is very risky. However, after some due diligence, you discovered a common misperception about the restaurant industry. It is widely thought that 90 percent of new restaurants close within three years; however, recent evidence suggests the failure rate is closer to 60 percent over three years. So it is a risky business, although not as risky as you originally thought.

During your interview process, one of the benefits mentioned was employee stock options. Upon signing your employment contract, you received options with a strike price of $40 for 10,000 shares of company stock. As is fairly common, your stock options have a three-year vesting period and a 10-year expiration, meaning that you cannot exercise the options for three years, and you lose them if you leave before they vest. After the three-year vesting period, you can exercise the options at any time. Thus, the employee stock options are European (and subject to forfeit) for the first three years and American afterward. Of course, you cannot sell the options, nor can you enter into any sort of hedging agreement. If you leave the company after the options vest, you must exercise within 90 days or forfeit.

Exotic Cuisines stock is currently trading at $27.15 per share, a slight increase from the initial offering price last year. There are no market-traded options on the company's stock. Because the company has been traded for only about a year, you are reluctant to use the historical returns to estimate the standard deviation of the stock's return. However, you have estimated that the average annual standard deviation for restaurant company stocks is about 55 percent. Because Exotic Cuisines is a newer restaurant chain, you decide to use a 60 percent standard deviation in your calculations. The company is relatively young, and you expect that all earnings will be reinvested back into the company for the near future. Therefore, you expect no dividends will be paid for at least the next 10 years. A three-year Treasury note currently has a yield of 3.8 percent, and a 10-year Treasury note has a yield of 4.4 percent.

1. You're trying to value your options. What minimum value would you assign? What is the maximum value you would assign?

2. Suppose that in three years the company's stock is trading at $60. At that time, should you keep the options or exercise them immediately? What are some of the important determinants in making such a decision?

3. Your options, like most employee stock options, are not transferable or tradable. Does this have a significant effect on the value of the options? Why?

4. Why do you suppose employee stock options usually have a vesting provision? Why must they be exercised shortly after you depart the company even after they vest?

5. A controversial practice with employee stock options is repricing. What happens is that a company experiences a stock price decrease, which leaves employee stock options far out of the money or "underwater." In such cases, many companies have "repriced" or "restruck" the options, meaning that the company leaves the original terms of the option intact but lowers the strike price. Proponents of repricing argue that because the option is very unlikely to end in the money because of the stock price decline, the motivational force is lost. Opponents argue that repricing is in essence a reward for failure. How do you evaluate this argument? How does the possibility of repricing affect the value of an employee stock option at the time it is granted?

6. As we have seen, much of the volatility in a company's stock price is due to systematic or marketwide risks. Such risks are beyond the control of a company and its employees. What are the implications for employee stock options? In light of your answer, can you recommend an improvement over traditional employee stock options?

24

Warrants and Convertibles

In February 2014, electric car maker Tesla Motors announced the pricing on two new bond issues. The company sold $920 million worth of .25 percent coupon bonds due in 2019 and $1.38 billion of 1.25 percent coupon bonds due in 2021. The bonds were sold at or near par value, so, in both cases, the yield to maturity might seem surprisingly low, particularly given the company's B– credit rating. So how was Tesla able to issue bonds with such a low promised yield?

The answer is these bonds were convertible into shares of the company's common stock at a price of $359.87 per share. Tesla shares were trading at $244.81 when the bonds were issued, so conversion was not immediately profitable, but it could prove to be very lucrative at some point in the future if the stock price were to rise. So, in essence, these convertible bonds are low coupon bonds with an attached call option held by the bondholders.

How do we value a financial instrument that is a combination of bond and call options? This chapter explores this and other issues.

24.1 Warrants

Warrants are securities that give holders the right, but not the obligation, to buy shares of common stock directly from a company at a fixed price for a given period. Each warrant specifies the number of shares of stock that the holder can buy, the exercise price, and the expiration date.

From the preceding description of warrants, it is clear that they are similar to call options. The differences in contractual features between warrants and the call options that trade on the Chicago Board Options Exchange are small. For example, warrants have longer maturity periods.[1] Some warrants are actually perpetual, meaning that they never expire.

Warrants are referred to as *equity kickers* because they are usually issued in combination with privately placed bonds.[2] In most cases, warrants are attached to the bonds when issued. The loan agreement will state whether the warrants are detachable from the bond—that is, whether they can be sold separately. Usually, the warrant can be detached immediately.

For example, AIG International issued warrants on January 19, 2011. Each stockholder received .533933 warrants for every share of stock owned, and each warrant gave

---

[1]Warrants are usually protected against stock splits and dividends in the same way that call options are.

[2]Warrants are also issued with publicly distributed bonds and new issues of common stock.

Figure 24.1
AIG Warrants on
January 14, 2015

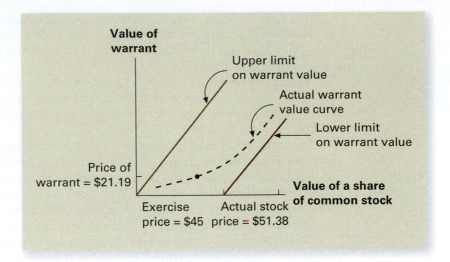

the holder the right to purchase one share of stock at an exercise price of $45. The warrants expired on January 19, 2021. On January 14, 2015, AIG International stock closed at $51.38, and the price of a warrant was $21.19.

The relationship between the value of AIG's warrants and its stock price can be viewed as similar to the relationship between a call option and the stock price, described in a previous chapter. Figure 24.1 depicts the relationship for AIG's warrants. The lower limit on the value of the warrants is zero if AIG's stock price is below $45 per share. If the price of AIG's stock rises above $45 per share, the lower limit is the stock price minus $45. The upper limit is the price of AIG's stock. A warrant to buy one share of stock cannot sell at a price above the price of the underlying stock.

The price of AIG's warrants on January 14, 2015, was higher than the lower limit. The height of the warrant price above the lower limit will depend on the following:

1. The variance of AIG's stock returns.
2. The time to expiration date.
3. The risk-free rate of interest.
4. The stock price of AIG.
5. The exercise price.

These are the same factors that determine the value of a call option.

24.2 The Difference between Warrants and Call Options

From the holder's point of view, warrants are similar to call options on common stock. A warrant, like a call option, gives its holder the right to buy common stock at a specified price. Warrants usually have an expiration date, though in most cases they are issued with longer lives than call options. From the firm's point of view, however, a warrant is very different from a call option on the company's common stock.

The most important difference between call options and warrants is that call options are issued by individuals and warrants are issued by firms. When a warrant is exercised, a firm must issue new shares of stock. Each time a warrant is exercised, then, the number of shares outstanding increases.

To illustrate, suppose the Endrun Company issues a warrant giving holders the right to buy one share of common stock at $25. Furthermore, suppose the warrant is exercised. Endrun must print one new stock certificate. In exchange for the stock certificate, it receives $25 from the holder.

In contrast, when a call option is exercised there is no change in the number of shares outstanding. Suppose Ms. Eager holds a call option on the common stock of the Endrun Company. The call option gives Ms. Eager the right to buy one share of the common stock of the Endrun Company for $25. If Ms. Eager chooses to exercise the call option, a seller, say Mr. Swift, is obligated to give her one share of Endrun's common stock in exchange for $25. If Mr. Swift does not already own a share, he must enter the stock market and buy one. The call option is a side bet between buyers and sellers on the value of the Endrun Company's common stock. When a call option is exercised, one investor gains and the other loses. The total number of shares outstanding of the Endrun Company remains constant, and no new funds are made available to the company.

EXAMPLE
24.1

Warrants and Firm Value   To see how warrants affect the value of the firm, imagine that Mr. Gould and Ms. Rockefeller are two investors who have together purchased six ounces of platinum. At the time they bought the platinum, Mr. Gould and Ms. Rockefeller each contributed half of the cost, which we will assume was $3,000 for six ounces, or $500 an ounce (they each contributed $1,500). They incorporated, printed two stock certificates, and named the firm the GR Company. Each certificate represents a one-half claim to the platinum. Mr. Gould and Ms. Rockefeller each own one certificate. They have formed a company with platinum as its only asset.

A Call Is Issued   Suppose Mr. Gould later decides to sell to Ms. Fiske a call option issued on Mr. Gould's share. The call option gives Ms. Fiske the right to buy Mr. Gould's share for $1,800 within the next year. If the price of platinum rises above $600 per ounce, the firm will be worth more than $3,600, and each share will be worth more than $1,800. If Ms. Fiske decides to exercise her option, Mr. Gould must turn over his stock certificate and receive $1,800.

How would the firm be affected by the exercise? The number of shares will remain the same. There will still be two shares, now owned by Ms. Rockefeller and Ms. Fiske. If the price of platinum rises to $700 an ounce, each share will be worth $2,100 (=$4,200/2). If Ms. Fiske exercises her option at this price, she will gain $300.

A Warrant Is Issued Instead   This story changes if a warrant is issued. Suppose that Mr. Gould does not sell a call option to Ms. Fiske. Instead, Mr. Gould and Ms. Rockefeller have a stockholders' meeting. They vote that GR Company will issue a warrant and sell it to Ms. Fiske. The warrant will give Ms. Fiske the right to receive a share of the company at an exercise price of $1,800.[3]

(continued)

---

[3]The sale of the warrant brings cash into the firm. We assume that the sale proceeds immediately leave the firm through a cash dividend to Mr. Gould and Ms. Rockefeller. This simplifies the analysis because the firm with warrants then has the same total value as the firm without warrants.

If Ms. Fiske decides to exercise the warrant, the firm will issue another stock certificate and give it to Ms. Fiske in exchange for $1,800.

From Ms. Fiske's perspective, the call option and the warrant *seem* to be the same. The exercise prices of the warrant and the call are the same: $1,800. It is still advantageous for Ms. Fiske to exercise the warrant when the price of platinum exceeds $600 per ounce. However, we will show that Ms. Fiske actually makes less in the warrant situation due to dilution.

The GR Company must also consider dilution. Suppose the price of platinum increases to $700 an ounce and Ms. Fiske exercises her warrant. Two things will occur:

1. Ms. Fiske will pay $1,800 to the firm.
2. The firm will print one stock certificate and give it to Ms. Fiske. The stock certificate will represent a one-third claim on the value of the firm.

Because Ms. Fiske contributes $1,800 to the firm, the value of the firm increases. It is now worth:

$$\text{New value of firm} = \text{Value of platinum} + \text{Contribution to the firm by Ms. Fiske}$$
$$= \$4,200 \qquad + \qquad \$1,800$$
$$= \$6,000$$

Because Ms. Fiske has a one-third claim on the firm's value, her share is worth $2,000 (=$6,000/3). By exercising the warrant, Ms. Fiske gains $2,000 − $1,800 = $200. This is illustrated in Table 24.1.

Table 24.1 Effect of Call Option and Warrant on the GR Company*

	Price of Platinum per Share	
Value of Firm If	**$700**	**$600**
No warrant		
Mr. Gould's share	$2,100	$1,800
Ms. Rockefeller's share	2,100	1,800
Firm	$4,200	$3,600
Call option		
Mr. Gould's claim	$ 0	$1,800
Ms. Rockefeller's claim	2,100	1,800
Ms. Fiske's claim	2,100	0
Firm	$4,200	$3,600
Warrant		
Mr. Gould's share	$2,000	$1,800
Ms. Rockefeller's share	2,000	1,800
Ms. Fiske's share	2,000	0
Firm	$6,000	$3,600

*If the price of platinum is $700, the value of the firm is equal to the value of six ounces of platinum plus the excess dollars paid into the firm by Ms. Fiske. This amount is $4,200 + $1,800 = $6,000.

Dilution Why does Ms. Fiske gain only $200 in the warrant case but gain $300 in the call option case? The key is dilution—that is, the creation of another share. In the call option case,

(continued)

she contributes $1,800 and receives one of the two outstanding shares. That is, she receives a share worth $2,100 ($=\frac{1}{2} \times$ $4,200$). Her gain is $300 (=$2,100 − $1,800). We rewrite this gain like this:

Gain on Exercise of Call

$$\frac{\$4,200}{2} - \$1,800 = \$300 \tag{24.1}$$

In the warrant case, she contributes $1,800 and receives a newly created share. She now owns one of the three outstanding shares. Because the $1,800 remains in the firm, her share is worth $2,000 [(=$4,200 + $1,800)/3]. Her gain is $200 (=$2,000 − $1,800). We rewrite this gain as follows:

Gain on Exercise of Warrant

$$\frac{\$4,200 + \$1,800}{2 + 1} - \$1,800 = \$200 \tag{24.2}$$

Warrants also affect accounting numbers. Warrants and (as we shall see) convertible bonds cause the number of shares to increase. This causes the firm's net income to be spread over more shares, thereby decreasing earnings per share. Firms with significant amounts of warrants and convertible issues must report earnings on a *primary* basis and a *fully diluted* basis.

HOW THE FIRM CAN HURT WARRANT HOLDERS

Suppose that the platinum firm owned by Mr. Gould and Ms. Rockefeller has issued a warrant to Ms. Fiske that is *in the money* and about to expire. One way that Mr. Gould and Ms. Rockefeller can hurt Ms. Fiske is to pay themselves a large dividend. This could be funded by selling a substantial amount of platinum. The value of the firm would fall, and the warrant would be worth much less.

24.3 Warrant Pricing and the Black–Scholes Model

We now wish to express the gains from exercising a call and a warrant in more general terms. The gain on a call can be written like this:

Gain from Exercising a Single Call:

$$\frac{\text{Firm's value net of debt}}{\#} - \text{Exercise price} \tag{24.3}$$

$$\text{(Value of a share of stock)}$$

Equation 24.3 generalizes Equation 24.1. We define the *firm's value net of debt* to be the total firm value less the value of the debt. The total firm value is $4,200 in our example, and there is no debt. The # stands for the number of shares outstanding, which is two in our example. The ratio on the left is the value of a share of stock. The gain on a warrant can be written as follows:

Gain from Exercising a Single Warrant:

$$\frac{\text{Firm's value net of debt} + \text{Exercise price} \times \#_w}{\# + \#_w} - \text{Exercise price} \tag{24.4}$$

(Value of a share of stock after warrant is exercised)

Equation 24.4 generalizes Equation 24.2. The numerator of the left term is the firm's value net of debt *after* the warrant is exercised. It is the sum of the firm's value net of debt *prior* to the warrant's exercise plus the proceeds the firm receives from the exercise. The proceeds equal the product of the exercise price multiplied by the number of warrants. The number of warrants appears as $\#_w$. (Our analysis uses the plausible assumption that all warrants in the money will be exercised.) Note that $\#_w = 1$ in our numerical example. The denominator, $\# + \#_w$, is the number of shares outstanding *after* the exercise of the warrants. The ratio on the left is the value of a share of stock after exercise. By rearranging terms, we can rewrite Equation 24.4 as:[4]

Gain from Exercising a Single Warrant:

$$\frac{\#}{\# + \#_w} \times \left(\frac{\text{Firm's value net of debt}}{\#} - \text{Exercise price} \right) \tag{24.5}$$

(Gain from a call on a firm with no warrants)

Formula 24.5 relates the gain on a warrant to the gain on a call. Note that the term within parentheses is Equation 24.3. Thus, the gain from exercising a warrant is a proportion of the gain from exercising a call in a firm without warrants. The proportion $\#/(\# + \#_w)$ is the ratio of the number of shares in the firm without warrants to the number of shares after all the warrants have been exercised. This ratio must always be less than 1. Thus, the gain on a warrant must be less than the gain on an identical call in a firm without warrants. Note that $\#/(\# + \#_w) = \frac{2}{3}$ in our example, which explains why Ms. Fiske gains $300 on her call yet gains only $200 on her warrant.

The preceding implies that the Black–Scholes model must be adjusted for warrants. When a call option is issued to Ms. Fiske, we know that the exercise price is $1,800 and the time to expiration is one year. Though we have not posited the price of the stock, the variance of the stock, or the interest rate, we could easily provide these data for a real-world situation. Thus, we could use the Black–Scholes model to value Ms. Fiske's call.

Suppose that the warrant is to be issued tomorrow to Ms. Fiske. We know the number of warrants to be issued, the warrant's expiration date, and the exercise price. Using our assumption that the warrant proceeds are immediately paid out as a dividend, we could use the Black–Scholes model to value the warrant. We would first calculate the value of an identical call. The warrant price is the call price multiplied by the ratio $\#/(\# + \#_w)$. As mentioned earlier, this ratio is $\frac{2}{3}$ in our example.

---

[4]To derive Formula 24.5, we separate "Exercise price" in Equation 24.4. This yields:

$$\frac{\text{Firm's value net of debt}}{\# + \#_w} - \frac{\#}{\# + \#_w} \times \text{Exercise price}$$

By rearranging terms, we can obtain Formula 24.5.

24.4   Convertible Bonds

A **convertible bond** is similar to a bond with warrants. The most important difference is that a bond with warrants can be separated into distinct securities and a convertible bond cannot. A convertible bond gives the holder the right to exchange it for a given number of shares of stock anytime up to and including the maturity date of the bond.

Preferred stock can frequently be converted into common stock. A convertible preferred stock is the same as a convertible bond except that it has an infinite maturity date.

EXAMPLE

Convertibles   On September 12, 2014, Twitter raised $900 million by issuing convertible subordinated debentures with a 1 percent coupon rate due in 2021. Each bond was convertible into 12.8793 shares of common stock of Twitter any time before maturity. The number of shares received for each bond (12.8793 in this example) is called the **conversion ratio**.

Bond traders also speak of the **conversion price** of the bond. This price is calculated as the ratio of the face value of the bond to the conversion ratio. Because the face value of each Twitter bond was $1,000, the conversion price was $77.64 (=$1,000/12.8793). If a bondholder chose to convert, she would give up a bond with a face value of $1,000 and receive 12.8793 shares of Twitter common stock in return. Thus, the conversion is equivalent to paying $77.64 for each share of Twitter common stock received.

When Twitter issued its convertible bonds, its common stock was trading at $52.11 per share. The conversion price of $77.64 was 49 percent higher than the actual common stock price. This 49 percent is referred to as the **conversion premium**. It reflects the fact that the conversion option in Twitter convertible bonds was *out of the money*, meaning that immediate conversion would be unprofitable. This conversion premium is typical.

Convertibles are almost always protected against stock splits and stock dividends. Thus, if Twitter's common stock were split two-for-one, the conversion ratio would increase from 12.8793 to 25.7586.

Conversion ratio, conversion price, and conversion premium are well-known terms in the real world. For that reason alone, the student should master these concepts. However, conversion price and conversion premium implicitly assume that the bond is selling at par. If the bond is selling at another price, the terms have little meaning. By contrast, conversion ratio can have a meaningful interpretation regardless of the price of the bond.

To give an example of these ideas, consider convertible bonds issued by offshore driller Transocean. The bonds were offered for sale in December 2007 and matured in 2037. The conversion ratio on the bonds was 5.931. This ratio means that the conversion price was $1,000/5.931 = $168.61. In January 2015, Transocean's stock was selling for about $19, so this price implied a conversion premium of 787.4 percent.

24.5   The Value of Convertible Bonds

The value of a convertible bond can be described in terms of three components: straight bond value, conversion value, and option value. We examine these three components next.

STRAIGHT BOND VALUE

The straight bond value is what the convertible bonds would sell for if they could not be converted into common stock. It will depend on the general level of interest rates and on the default risk. Suppose that straight debentures issued by Twitter had been rated BB–, and BB– rated bonds were priced to yield 2.4 percent per six months. Further suppose the semiannual coupons were $5, the principal amount was $1,000, and the maturity was 7 years. The straight bond value of Twitter convertible bonds can be determined by discounting the $5 semiannual coupon payment and principal amount at 2.4 percent:

$$\text{Straight bond value} = \sum_{t=1}^{14} \frac{\$5}{1.024^t} + \frac{\$1,000}{(1.024)^{14}}$$

$$= \$5 \times \text{PVIFA}(.024, 14) + \frac{\$1,000}{(1.024)^{14}}$$

$$= \$58.86 + \$717.46$$

$$= \$776.32$$

The straight bond value of a convertible bond is a minimum value. The price of Twitter's convertible bonds could not have gone lower than the straight bond value.

Figure 24.2 illustrates the relationship between straight bond value and stock price. In Figure 24.2 we have been somewhat dramatic and implicitly assumed that the convertible bond is default free. In this case, the straight bond value does not depend on the stock price, so it is graphed as a straight line.

CONVERSION VALUE

The value of convertible bonds depends on conversion value. **Conversion value** is what the bonds would be worth if they were immediately converted into common stock at current prices. Typically, we compute conversion value by multiplying the number of shares of common stock that will be received when the bond is converted by the current price of the common stock.

Figure 24.2

Minimum Value of a Convertible Bond versus the Value of the Stock for a Given Interest Rate

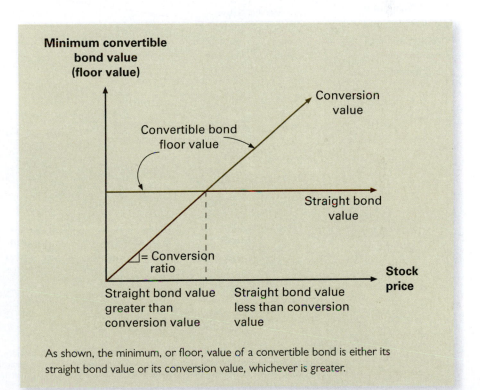

As shown, the minimum, or floor, value of a convertible bond is either its straight bond value or its conversion value, whichever is greater.

On January 15, 2015, each Twitter convertible bond could have been converted into 12.8793 shares of Twitter common stock. Twitter common stock was selling for $36.93. Thus, the conversion value was 12.8793 × $36.93 = $475.63. A convertible cannot sell for less than its conversion value. Arbitrage prevents this from happening. If Twitter's convertible sold for less than $475.63, investors would have bought the bonds and converted them into common stock and sold the stock. The profit would have been the difference between the value of the stock sold and the bond's conversion value.

Thus, convertible bonds have two minimum values: The straight bond value and the conversion value. The conversion value is determined by the value of the firm's underlying common stock. This is illustrated in Figure 24.2. As the value of common stock rises and falls, the conversion value rises and falls with it. When the price of Twitter's common stock increased by $1, the conversion value of its convertible bonds increased by $12.8793.

OPTION VALUE

The value of a convertible bond will generally exceed both the straight bond value and the conversion value.[5] This occurs because holders of convertibles need not convert immediately. Instead, by waiting they can take advantage of whichever is greater in the future: The straight bond value or the conversion value. This option to wait has value, and it raises the value over both the straight bond value and the conversion value.

When the value of the firm is low, the value of convertible bonds is most significantly influenced by their underlying value as straight debt. However, when the value of the firm is very high, the value of convertible bonds is mostly determined by their underlying conversion value. This is illustrated in Figure 24.3.

Figure 24.3

Value of a Convertible Bond versus the Value of the Stock for a Given Interest Rate

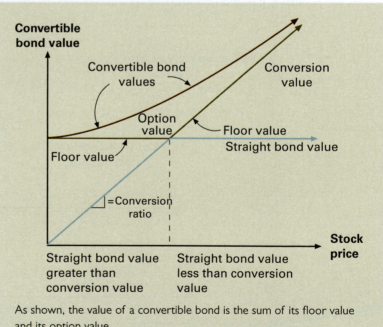

As shown, the value of a convertible bond is the sum of its floor value and its option value.

---

[5]The most plausible exception is when conversion would provide the investor with a dividend much greater than the interest available prior to conversion. The optimal strategy here could very well be to convert immediately, implying that the market value of the bond would exactly equal the conversion value. Other exceptions occur when the firm is in default or the bondholders are forced to convert.

The bottom portion of the figure implies that the value of a convertible bond is the maximum of its straight bond value and its conversion value, plus its option value:

$$\text{Value of convertible bond} = \text{The greater of (Straight bond value, Conversion value)} + \text{Option value}$$

EXAMPLE 24.3

Conversion Suppose the Moulton Company has outstanding 1,000 shares of common stock and 100 bonds. Each bond has a face value of $1,000 at maturity. They are discount bonds and pay no coupons. At maturity each bond can be converted into 10 shares of newly issued common stock.

What circumstances will make it advantageous for the holders of Moulton convertible bonds to convert to common stock at maturity?

If the holders of the convertible bonds convert, they will receive $100 \times 10 = 1,000$ shares of common stock. Because there were already 1,000 shares, the total number of shares outstanding becomes 2,000 upon conversion. Thus, converting bondholders own 50 percent of the value of the firm, V. If they do not convert, they will receive $100,000 or V, whichever is less. The choice for the holders of the Moulton bonds is obvious. They should convert if 50 percent of V is greater than $100,000. This will be true whenever V is greater than $200,000. This is illustrated as follows:

Payoff to Convertible Bondholders and Stockholders of the Moulton Company

	(1) $V \leq 100,000$	(2) $100,000 < V \leq \$200,000$	(3) $V > \$200,000$
Decision:	Bondholders will not convert	Bondholders will not convert	Bondholders will convert
Convertible bondholders	V	$100,000	.5V
Stockholders	0	$V - \$100,000$	.5V

24.6 Reasons for Issuing Warrants and Convertibles

Probably there is no other area of corporate finance where real-world practitioners get as confused as they do on the reasons for issuing convertible debt. To separate fact from fantasy, we present a rather structured argument. We first compare convertible debt to straight debt. Then we compare convertible debt to equity. For each comparison, we ask in what situations is the firm better off with convertible debt and in what situations is it worse off?

CONVERTIBLE DEBT VERSUS STRAIGHT DEBT

Convertible debt pays a lower interest rate than does otherwise identical straight debt. For example, if the interest rate is 10 percent on straight debt, the interest rate on convertible debt might be 9 percent. Investors will accept a lower interest rate on a convertible because of the potential gain from conversion.

Imagine a firm that seriously considers both convertible debt and straight debt, finally deciding to issue convertibles. When would this decision have benefited the firm and when would it have hurt the firm? We consider two situations.

The Stock Price Later Rises So That Conversion Is Indicated The firm clearly likes to see the stock price rise. However, it would have benefited even more had it previously issued straight debt instead of a convertible. Although the firm paid out a lower interest rate than it would have with straight debt, it was obligated to sell the convertible holders a chunk of the equity at a below-market price.

The Stock Price Later Falls or Does Not Rise Enough to Justify Conversion The firm hates to see the stock price fall. However, as long as the stock price does fall, the firm is glad that it had previously issued convertible debt instead of straight debt. This is because the interest rate on convertible debt is lower. Because conversion does not take place, our comparison of interest rates is all that is needed.

Summary Compared to straight debt, the firm is worse off having issued convertible debt if the underlying stock subsequently does well. The firm is better off having issued convertible debt if the underlying stock subsequently does poorly. In an efficient market, we cannot predict future stock price. Thus, we cannot argue that convertibles either dominate or are dominated by straight debt.

CONVERTIBLE DEBT VERSUS COMMON STOCK

Next, imagine a firm that seriously considers both convertible debt and common stock but finally decides to issue convertibles. When would this decision benefit the firm and when would it hurt the firm? We consider our two situations.

The Stock Price Later Rises So That Conversion Is Indicated The firm is better off having previously issued a convertible instead of equity. To see this, consider the Twitter case. The firm could have issued stock for $52.11. Instead, by issuing a convertible, the firm will effectively receive substantially more for a share upon conversion.

The Stock Price Later Falls or Does Not Rise Enough to Justify Conversion No firm wants to see its stock price fall. However, given that the price did fall, the firm would have been better off if it had previously issued stock instead of a convertible. The firm would have benefited by issuing stock above its later market price. That is, the firm would have received more than the subsequent worth of the stock. However, the drop in stock price did not affect the value of the convertible much because the straight bond value serves as a floor.

Summary Compared with equity, the firm is better off having issued convertible debt if the underlying stock subsequently does well. The firm is worse off having issued convertible debt if the underlying stock subsequently does poorly. We cannot predict future stock prices in an efficient market. Thus, we cannot argue that issuing convertibles is better or worse than issuing equity. The preceding analysis is summarized in Table 24.2.

Modigliani–Miller (MM) pointed out that, abstracting from taxes and bankruptcy costs, the firm is indifferent to whether it issues stock or issues debt. The MM relationship is a quite general one. Their pedagogy could be adjusted to show that the firm is indifferent to whether it issues convertibles or issues other instruments. To save space (and the patience of students) we have omitted a full-blown proof of MM in a world with

Table 24.2
The Case for and against Convertible Bonds (CBs)

	If Firm Subsequently Does Poorly	If Firm Subsequently Prospers
Convertible bonds (CBs)	No conversion because of low stock price.	Conversion because of high stock price.
Compared to:		
Straight bonds	CBs provide cheap financing because coupon rate is lower.	CBs provide expensive financing because bonds are converted, which dilutes existing equity.
Common stock	CBs provide expensive financing because firm could have issued common stock at high prices.	CBs provide cheap financing because firm issues stock at high prices when bonds are converted.

convertibles. However, our results are perfectly consistent with MM. Now we turn to the real-world view of convertibles.

THE "FREE LUNCH" STORY

The preceding discussion suggests that issuing a convertible bond is no better and no worse than issuing other instruments. Unfortunately, many corporate executives fall into the trap of arguing that issuing convertible debt is actually better than issuing alternative instruments. This is a free lunch type of explanation, of which we are quite critical.

EXAMPLE 24.4

Are Convertibles Always Better?   The stock price of RW Company is $20. Suppose this company can issue subordinated debentures at 10 percent. It can also issue convertible bonds at 6 percent with a conversion value of $800. The conversion value means that the holders can convert a convertible bond into 40 (=$800/$20) shares of common stock.

A company treasurer who believes in free lunches might argue that convertible bonds should be issued because they represent a cheaper source of financing than both subordinated bonds and common stock. The treasurer will point out that if the company does poorly and the price does not rise above $20, the convertible bondholders will not convert the bonds into common stock. In this case the company will have obtained debt financing at below-market rates by attaching worthless equity kickers. On the other hand, if the firm does well and the price of its common stock rises to $25 or above, convertible holders will convert. The company will issue 40 shares. The company will receive a bond with a face value of $1,000 in exchange for issuing 40 shares of common stock, implying a conversion price of $25. The company will have issued common stock at $25 per share, or 25 percent above the $20 common stock price prevailing when the convertible bonds were issued. This enables it to lower its cost of equity capital. Thus, the treasurer happily points out, regardless of whether the company does well or poorly, convertible bonds are the cheapest form of financing.

Although this argument may sound quite plausible at first, there is a flaw. The treasurer is comparing convertible financing *with straight debt* when the stock subsequently falls. However, the treasurer compares convertible financing *with common stock* when the stock subsequently rises. This is an unfair mixing of comparisons. By contrast, our analysis in Table 24.2 was fair because we examined both stock increases and decreases when comparing a convertible with each alternative instrument. We found that no single alternative dominated convertible bonds in *both* up and down markets.

THE "EXPENSIVE LUNCH" STORY

Suppose we stand the treasurer's argument on its head by comparing (1) convertible financing with straight debt when the stock rises and (2) convertible financing with equity when the stock falls.

From Table 24.2, we see that convertible debt is more expensive than straight debt when the stock subsequently rises. The firm's obligation to sell convertible holders a chunk of equity at a below-market price more than offsets the lower interest rate on a convertible.

Also from Table 24.2, we see that convertible debt is more expensive than equity when the stock subsequently falls. Had the firm issued stock, it would have received a price higher than its subsequent worth. Therefore, the expensive lunch story implies that convertible debt is an inferior form of financing. Of course, we dismiss both the free lunch and the expensive lunch arguments.

A RECONCILIATION

In an efficient financial market there is neither a free lunch nor an expensive lunch. Convertible bonds can be neither cheaper nor more expensive than other instruments. A convertible bond is a package of straight debt and an option to buy common stock. The difference between the market value of a convertible bond and the value of a straight bond is the price investors pay for the call option feature. In an efficient market, this is a fair price.

In general, if a company prospers, issuing convertible bonds will turn out to be worse than issuing straight bonds and better than issuing common stock. In contrast, if a company does poorly, convertible bonds will turn out to be better than issuing straight bonds and worse than issuing common stock.

24.7 Why Are Warrants and Convertibles Issued?

From studies it is known that firms that issue convertible bonds are different from other firms. Here are some of the differences:

1. The bond ratings of firms using convertibles are lower than those of other firms.[6]
2. Convertibles tend to be used by smaller firms with high growth rates and more financial leverage.[7]
3. Convertibles are usually subordinated and unsecured.

The kind of company that uses convertibles provides clues to why they are issued. Here are some explanations that make sense.

MATCHING CASH FLOWS

If financing is costly, it makes sense to issue securities whose cash flows match those of the firm. A young, risky, and (it hopes) growing firm might prefer to issue convertibles or bonds with warrants because these will have lower initial interest costs. When the firm is

[6]Eugene F. Brigham, "An Analysis of Convertible Debentures: Theory and Some Empirical Evidence," *Journal of Finance* 21 (1966).
[7]Wayne H. Mikkelson, "Convertible Calls and Security Returns," *Journal of Financial Economics* 9 (September 1981), p. 3.

Table 24.3
A Hypothetical Case
of the Yields on
Convertible Bonds*

	Firm Risk	
	Low	**High**
Straight bond yield	10%	15%
Convertible bond yield	6	7

*The yields on straight bonds reflect the risk of default. The yields on convertibles are not sensitive to default risk.

successful, the convertibles (or warrants) will be converted. This causes expensive dilution, but it occurs when the firm can most afford it.

RISK SYNERGY

Another argument for convertible bonds and bonds with warrants is that they are useful when it is very costly to assess the risk of the issuing company. Suppose you are evaluating a new product by a start-up company. The new product is a genetically engineered virus that may increase the yields of corn crops in northern climates. It may also cause cancer. This type of product is difficult to value properly. Thus, the risk of the company is very hard to determine: It may be high, or it may be low. If you could be sure the risk of the company was high, you would price the bonds for a high yield, say 15 percent. If it was low, you would price them at a lower yield, say 10 percent.

Convertible bonds and bonds with warrants can protect somewhat against mistakes of risk evaluation. Convertible bonds and bonds with warrants have two components: Straight bonds and call options on the company's underlying stock. If the company turns out to be a low-risk company, the straight bond component will have high value and the call option will have low value. However, if the company turns out to be a high-risk company, the straight bond component will have low value and the call option will have high value. This is illustrated in Table 24.3.

However, although risk has effects on value that cancel each other out in convertibles and bonds with warrants, the market and the buyer nevertheless must make an assessment of the firm's potential to value securities, and it is not clear that the effort involved is that much less than is required for a straight bond.

AGENCY COSTS

Convertible bonds can resolve agency problems associated with raising money. In a previous chapter, we showed that straight bonds are like risk-free bonds minus a put option on the assets of the firm. This creates an incentive for creditors to force the firm into low-risk activities. In contrast, holders of common stock have incentives to adopt high-risk projects. High-risk projects with negative NPV transfer wealth from bondholders to stockholders. If these conflicts cannot be resolved, the firm may be forced to pass up profitable investment opportunities. However, because convertible bonds have an equity component, less expropriation of wealth can occur when convertible debt is issued instead of straight debt.[8] In other words, convertible bonds mitigate agency costs. One implication is that convertible bonds have less restrictive debt covenants than do straight bonds in the real world. Casual empirical evidence seems to bear this out.

[8]Amir Barnea, Robert A. Haugen, and Lemma Senbet, *Agency Problems and Financial Contracting,* Prentice Hall Foundations of Science Series (New York: Prentice Hall, 1985), Chapter VI.

BACKDOOR EQUITY

A popular theory of convertibles views them as backdoor equity.[9] The basic story is that young, small, high-growth firms cannot usually issue debt on reasonable terms due to high financial distress costs. However, the owners may be unwilling to issue equity if current stock prices are too low.

Lewis, Rogalski, and Seward examine the risk shifting and backdoor equity theories of convertible bond debt. They find evidence for both theories.

24.8 Conversion Policy

There is one aspect of convertible bonds that we have omitted so far. Firms are frequently granted a call option on the bond. The typical arrangements for calling a convertible bond are simple. When the bond is called, the holder has about 30 days to choose between the following:

1. Converting the bond to common stock at the conversion ratio.
2. Surrendering the bond and receiving the call price in cash.

What should bondholders do? It should be obvious that if the conversion value of the bond is greater than the call price, conversion is better than surrender; and if the conversion value is less than the call price, surrender is better than conversion. If the conversion value is greater than the call price, the call is said to **force conversion**.

What should financial managers do? Calling the bonds does not change the value of the firm as a whole. However, an optimal call policy can benefit the stockholders at the expense of the bondholders. Because we are speaking about dividing a pie of fixed size, the optimal call policy is simple: Do whatever the bondholders do not want you to do.

Bondholders would love the stockholders to call the bonds when the bonds' market value is below the call price. Shareholders would be giving bondholders extra value. Alternatively, should the value of the bonds rise above the call price, the bondholders would love the stockholders not to call the bonds because bondholders would be allowed to hold onto a valuable asset.

There is only one policy left. This is the policy that maximizes shareholder value and minimizes bondholder value:

Call the bond when its value is equal to the call price.

It is puzzling that firms do not always call convertible bonds when the conversion value reaches the call price. Ingersoll examined the call policies of 124 firms between 1968 and 1975.[10] In most cases he found that the company waited to call the bonds until the conversion value was much higher than the call price. The median company waited until the conversion value of its bonds was 44 percent higher than the call price. This is not even close to our optimal strategy. Why?

---

[9]Jeremy Stein, "Convertible Bonds as Backdoor Equity Financing," *Journal of Financial Economics* 32 (1992). See also Craig M. Lewis, Richard J. Rogalski, and James K. Seward, "Understanding the Design of Convertible Debt," *The Journal of Applied Corporate Finance* (Spring 1998).

[10]J. Ingersoll, "An Examination of Corporate Call Policies on Convertible Securities," *Journal of Finance* (May 1977). See also Milton Harris and A. Raviv, "A Sequential Signalling Model of Convertible Debt Call Policy," *Journal of Finance* (December 1985). Harris and Raviv describe a signal equilibrium that is consistent with Ingersoll's result. They show that managers with favorable information will delay calls to avoid depressing stock prices.

One reason is that if firms attempt to implement the optimal strategy, it may not be truly optimal. Recall that bondholders have 30 days to decide whether to convert bonds to common stock or to surrender bonds for the call price in cash. In 30 days the stock price could drop, forcing the conversion value below the call price. If so, the convertible is "out of the money" and the firm is giving away money. The firm would be giving up cash for common stock worth much less. Because of this possibility, firms in the real world usually wait until the conversion value is substantially above the call price before they trigger the call.[11] This is sensible.

---

[11]See Paul Asquith, "Convertible Bonds Are Not Called Late," *Journal of Finance* (September 1995). On the other hand, the stock market usually reacts negatively to the announcement of a call. For example, see Ajai K. Singh, Arnold R. Cowan, and Nandkumar Nayar, "Underwritten Calls of Convertible Bonds," *Journal of Financial Economics* (March 1991); and Michael A. Mazzeo and William T. Moore, "Liquidity Costs and Stock Price Response to Convertible Security Calls," *Journal of Business* (July 1992).

Ederington, Caton, and Campbell tested various theories about when it is optimal to call convertibles. They found evidence consistent with the preceding 30-day "safety margin" theory. They also found that calls of in-the-money convertibles are highly unlikely if dividends to be received (after conversion) exceed the company's interest payment. See Louis H. Ederington, Gary L. Caton, and Cynthia J. Campbell, "To Call or Not to Call Convertible Debt," *Financial Management* (Spring 1997).

Summary and Conclusions

1. A warrant gives the holder the right to buy shares of common stock at an exercise price for a given period. Typically, warrants are issued in a package with privately placed bonds. Afterwards, they become detached and trade separately.

2. A convertible bond is a combination of a straight bond and a call option. The holder can give up the bond in exchange for shares of stock.

3. Convertible bonds and warrants are like call options. However, there are some important differences:
   a. Warrants and convertible securities are issued by corporations. Call options are traded between individual investors.
      i. Warrants are usually issued privately and are combined with a bond. In most cases, the warrants can be detached immediately after the issue. In some cases, warrants are issued with preferred stock, with common stock, or in executive compensation programs.
      ii. Convertibles are usually bonds that can be converted into common stock.
      iii. Call options are sold separately by individual investors (called *writers* of call options).
   b. Warrants and call options are exercised for cash. The holder of a warrant gives the company cash and receives new shares of the company's stock. The holder of a call option gives another individual cash in exchange for shares of stock. When someone converts a bond, it is exchanged for common stock. As a consequence, bonds with warrants and convertible bonds have different effects on corporate cash flow and capital structure.
   c. Warrants and convertibles cause dilution to the existing shareholders. When warrants are exercised and convertible bonds converted, the company must issue new shares of common stock. The percentage ownership of the existing shareholders will decline. New shares are not issued when call options are exercised.

4. Many arguments, both plausible and implausible, are given for issuing convertible bonds and bonds with warrants. One plausible rationale for such bonds has to do with risk. Convertibles and bonds with warrants are associated with risky companies. Lenders can do several things to protect themselves from high-risk companies:
   a. They can require high yields.
   b. They can lend less or not at all to firms whose risk is difficult to assess.
   c. They can impose severe restrictions on such debt.

   Another useful way to protect against risk is to issue bonds with equity kickers. This gives the lenders the chance to benefit from risks and reduces the conflicts between bondholders and stockholders concerning risk.

5. A certain puzzle particularly vexes financial researchers: Convertible bonds usually have call provisions. Companies appear to delay calling convertibles until the conversion value greatly exceeds the call price. From the shareholders' standpoint, the optimal call policy would be to call the convertibles when the conversion value equals the call price.

Concept Questions

1. **Warrants and Options** What is the primary difference between a warrant and a traded call option?

2. **Warrants** Explain the following limits on the prices of warrants:
   a. If the stock price is below the exercise price of the warrant, the lower bound on the price of a warrant is zero.
   b. If the stock price is above the exercise price of the warrant, the lower bound on the price of a warrant is the difference between the stock price and the exercise price.
   c. An upper bound on the price of any warrant is the current value of the firm's stock.

3. **Convertible Bonds and Stock Volatility** Suppose you are evaluating a callable, convertible bond. If the stock price volatility increases, how will this affect the price of the bond?

4. **Convertible Bond Value** What happens to the price of a convertible bond if interest rates increase?

5. **Dilution** What is dilution, and why does it occur when warrants are exercised?

6. **Warrants and Convertibles** What is wrong with the simple view that it is cheaper to issue a bond with a warrant or a convertible feature because the required coupon is lower?

7. **Warrants and Convertibles** Why do firms issue convertible bonds and bonds with warrants?

8. **Convertible Bonds** Why will convertible bonds not be voluntarily converted to stock before expiration?

9. **Convertible Bonds** When should a firm force conversion of convertibles? Why?

10. **Warrant Valuation** A warrant with six months until expiration entitles its owner to buy 10 shares of the issuing firm's common stock for an exercise price of $31 per share. If the current market price of the stock is $15 per share, will the warrant be worthless?

Questions and Problems

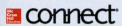

BASIC
(Questions 1–9)

1. **Conversion Price** A convertible bond with a par value of $1,000 has a conversion ratio of 19.2. What is the conversion price?

2. **Conversion Ratio** A convertible bond with a par value of $1,000 has a conversion price of $72.45. What is the conversion ratio of the bond?

3. **Conversion Premium** Eckely, Inc., recently issued bonds with a conversion ratio of 14.5. If the stock price at the time of the bond issue was $53.16, what was the conversion premium?

4. **Convertible Bonds** Hannon Home Products, Inc., recently issued $2 million worth of 3 percent convertible debentures. Each convertible bond has a face value of $1,000. Each convertible bond can be converted into 23.50 shares of common stock anytime before maturity. The stock price is $34.65, and the market value of each bond is $1,070.

   a. What is the conversion ratio?
   b. What is the conversion price?
   c. What is the conversion premium?
   d. What is the conversion value?
   e. If the stock price increases by $2, what is the new conversion value?

5. **Warrant Value** A warrant gives its owner the right to purchase three shares of common stock at an exercise price of $64 per share. The current market price of the stock is $68. What is the minimum value of the warrant?

6. **Convertible Bond Value** An analyst has recently informed you that at the issuance of a company's convertible bonds, one of the two following sets of relationships existed:

	Scenario A	Scenario B
Face value of bond	$1,000	$1,000
Straight value of convertible bond	900	950
Market value of convertible bond	1,000	900

   Assume the bonds are available for immediate conversion. Which of the two scenarios do you believe is more likely? Why?

7. **Convertible Bond Value** Sportime Fitness Center, Inc., issued convertible bonds with a conversion price of $49. The bonds are available for immediate conversion. The current price of the company's common stock is $43 per share. The current market price of the convertible bonds is $990. The convertible bonds' straight value is not known.

   a. What is the minimum price for the convertible bonds?
   b. Explain the difference between the current market price of each convertible bond and the value of the common stock into which it can be immediately converted.

8. **Convertible Bonds** You own a callable, convertible bond with a conversion ratio of 25.18. The stock is currently selling for $47 per share. The issuer of the bond has announced a call at a call price of 110. What are your options here? What should you do?

9. **Warrant Value** General Modems has five-year warrants that currently trade in the open market. Each warrant gives its owner the right to purchase one share of common stock for an exercise price of $55.

   a. Suppose the stock is currently trading for $51 per share. What is the lower limit on the price of the warrant? What is the upper limit?
   b. Suppose the stock is currently trading for $58 per share. What is the lower limit on the price of the warrant? What is the upper limit?

INTERMEDIATE
(Questions 10–13)

10. **Convertible Bonds** Vital Silence Corp. has just issued a 30-year callable, convertible bond with an annual coupon rate of 6 percent. The bond has a conversion price of $93. The company's stock is selling for $28 per share. The owner of the bond will be forced to convert if the bond's conversion value is ever greater than or equal to $1,100. The required return on an otherwise identical nonconvertible bond is 7 percent.

    a. What is the minimum value of the bond?
    b. If the stock price were to grow by 11 percent per year forever, how long would it take for the bond's conversion value to exceed $1,100?

11. **Convertible Bonds** Rob Stevens is the chief executive officer of Isner Construction, Inc., and owns 850,000 shares of stock. The company currently has 5.1 million shares of stock and convertible bonds with a face value of $40 million outstanding. The convertible bonds have a conversion price of $37, and the stock is currently selling for $45.

    a. What percentage of the firm's common stock does Mr. Stevens own?
    b. If the company decides to call the convertible bonds and force conversion, what percentage of the firm's common stock will Mr. Stevens own? He does not own any convertible bonds.

12. **Warrants** Bauble, Inc., an all-equity firm, has eight shares of stock outstanding. Yesterday, the firm's assets consisted of nine ounces of platinum, currently worth $1,650 per ounce. Today, the company issued Ms. Wu a warrant for its fair value of $1,650. The warrant gives Ms. Wu the right to buy a single share of the firm's stock for $2,000 and can be exercised only on its expiration date one year from today. The firm used the proceeds from the issuance to immediately purchase an additional ounce of platinum.

    a. What was the price of a single share of stock *before* the warrant was issued?
    b. What was the price of a single share of stock immediately *after* the warrant was issued?
    c. Suppose platinum is selling for $1,950 per ounce on the warrant's expiration date in one year. What will be the value of a single share of stock on the warrant's expiration date?

13. **Warrants** The capital structure of Ricketti Enterprises, Inc., consists of 25 million shares of common stock and 1.5 million warrants. Each warrant gives its owner the right to purchase one share of common stock for an exercise price of $27. The current stock price is $32, and each warrant is worth $7. What is the new stock price if all warrant holders decide to exercise today?

CHALLENGE
(Questions 14–16)

14. **Convertible Calculations** You have been hired to value a new 20-year callable, convertible bond. The bond has a 5.8 percent coupon rate, payable annually. The conversion price is $150, and the stock currently sells for $32.20. The stock price is expected to grow at 12 percent per year. The bond is callable at $1,150; but based on prior experience, it won't be called unless the conversion value is $1,250. The required return on this bond is 9 percent. What value would you assign to this bond?

15. **Warrant Value** Superior Clamps, Inc., has a capital structure consisting of 7 million shares of common stock and 900,000 warrants. Each warrant gives its owner the right to purchase one share of newly issued common stock for an exercise price of $25.

The warrants are European and will expire one year from today. The market value of the company's assets is $165 million, and the annual variance of the returns on the firm's assets is .20. Treasury bills that mature in one year yield a continuously compounded interest rate of 7 percent. The company does not pay a dividend. Use the Black–Scholes model to determine the value of a single warrant.

16. **Warrant Value**   Omega Airline's capital structure consists of 2.7 million shares of common stock and zero coupon bonds with a face value of $18 million that mature in six months. The firm just announced that it will issue warrants with an exercise price of $95 and six months until expiration to raise the funds to pay off its maturing debt. Each warrant can be exercised only at expiration and gives its owner the right to buy a single newly issued share of common stock. The firm will place the proceeds from the warrant issue immediately into Treasury bills. The market value balance sheet shows that the firm will have assets worth $240 million after the announcement. The company does not pay dividends. The standard deviation of the returns on the firm's assets is 50 percent, and Treasury bills with a six-month maturity yield 6 percent. How many warrants must the company issue today to be able to use the proceeds from the sale to pay off the firm's debt obligation in six months?

Mini Case

S&S AIR'S CONVERTIBLE BOND

Chris Guthrie was recently hired by S&S Air, Inc., to assist the company with its short-term financial planning and to evaluate the company's performance. Chris graduated from college five years ago with a finance degree. He has been employed in the finance department of a Fortune 500 company since then.

S&S Air was founded 10 years ago by two friends, Mark Sexton and Todd Story. The company has manufactured and sold light airplanes over this period, and the company's products have received high reviews for safety and reliability. The company has a niche market in that it sells primarily to individuals who own and fly their own airplanes. The company has two models: The Birdie, which sells for $53,000, and the Eagle, which sells for $78,000.

S&S Air is not publicly traded, but the company needs new funds for investment opportunities. In consultation with Tonisha Jones of underwriter Raines and Warren, Chris decided that a convertible bond issue with a 20-year maturity is the way to go. He met with the owners, Mark and Todd, and presented his analysis of the convertible bond issue. Because the company is not publicly traded, Chris looked at comparable publicly traded companies and determined that the average PE ratio for the industry is 17.5. Earnings per share for the company are $1.75. With this in mind, Chris concluded that the conversion price should be $45 per share.

Several days later Todd, Mark, and Chris met again to discuss the potential bond issue. Both Todd and Mark have researched convertible bonds and have questions for Chris. Todd begins by asking Chris if the convertible bond issue will have a lower coupon rate than a comparable bond without a conversion feature. Chris replies that to sell the bond at par value, the convertible bond issue would require a 5 percent coupon rate with a conversion value of $680.56, while a plain vanilla bond would have an 8 percent coupon rate. Todd nods in agreement, and he explains that the convertible bonds are a win–win form of financing. He states that if the value of the company stock does not rise above the conversion price, the company has issued debt at a cost below the market rate (5 percent instead of 8 percent). If the company's stock does rise to the conversion value, the company has effectively issued stock at above the current value.

Mark immediately disagrees, arguing that convertible bonds are a no-win form of financing. He argues that if the value of the company stock rises to $45, the company is forced to sell stock at the conversion price. This means the new shareholders (those who bought the convertible bonds) benefit from a bargain price. Put another way, if the company prospers, it would have been better to have issued straight debt so that the gains would not be shared.

Chris has gone back to Tonisha for help. As Tonisha's assistant, you've been asked to prepare another memo answering the following questions:

1. Why do you think Chris is suggesting a conversion price of $45? Given that the company is not publicly traded, does it even make sense to talk about a conversion price?

2. What is the floor value of the S&S Air convertible bond?

3. What is the conversion ratio of the bond?

4. What is the conversion premium of the bond?

5. What is the value of the option?

6. Is there anything wrong with Todd's argument that it is cheaper to issue a bond with a convertible feature because the required coupon is lower?

7. Is there anything wrong with Mark's argument that a convertible bond is a bad idea because it allows new shareholders to participate in gains made by the company?

8. How can you reconcile the arguments made by Todd and Mark?

9. During the debate, a question comes up concerning whether the bonds should have an ordinary (not make-whole) call feature. Chris confuses everybody by stating, "The call feature lets S&S Air force conversion, thereby minimizing the problem Mark has identified." What is he talking about? Is he making sense?

25

Derivatives and Hedging Risk

Natural disasters are, of course, a major risk for property and casualty insurance companies. For example, the 2011 tsunami in Japan was estimated to have cost $235 billion, and Hurricane Katrina caused more than $80 billion in damages in 2005. So how do insurance and reinsurance companies handle this risk? One way is to issue catastrophe, or "cat," bonds. With a cat bond, the issuer pays the coupon like any other bond; however, if a "trigger" is hit, the issuer does not have to pay the remaining coupons or repay the principal. In the first quarter of 2014, companies issued $1.2 billion in cat bonds, raising the total to about $21 billion in cat bonds outstanding. Since 1996, there have been $682 million in losses on cat bonds, or about 1.3 percent of the $51 billion issued. As we will see in this chapter, there are a variety of sophisticated financial tools available to deal with risks, including futures, options, and swaps.

25.1 Derivatives, Hedging, and Risk

The name *derivatives* is self-explanatory. A derivative is a financial instrument whose payoffs and values are derived from, or depend on, something else. Often, we speak of the thing that the derivative depends on as the *primitive* or the *underlying*. For example, in Chapter 22 we studied how options work. An option is a derivative. The value of a call option depends on the value of the underlying stock on which it is written. Actually, call options are quite complicated examples of derivatives. The vast majority of derivatives are simpler than call options. Most derivatives are forward or futures agreements or what are called *swaps,* and we will study each of these in some detail.

Why do firms use derivatives? The answer is that derivatives are tools for changing the firm's risk exposure. Someone once said that derivatives are to finance what scalpels are to surgery. By using derivatives, the firm can cut away unwanted portions of risk exposure and even transform the exposures into quite different forms. A central point in finance is that risk is undesirable. In our chapters about risk and return, we pointed out that individuals would choose risky securities only if the expected return compensated for the risk. Similarly, a firm will accept a project with high risk only if the return on the project compensates for this risk. Not surprisingly, then, firms are usually looking for ways to reduce their risk. When the firm reduces its risk exposure with the use of derivatives, it is said to be **hedging**. Hedging offsets the firm's risk, such as the risk in a project, by one or more transactions in the financial markets.

Derivatives can also be used to merely change or even increase the firm's risk exposure. When this occurs, the firm is **speculating** on the movement of some economic variables—those that underlie the derivative. For example, if a derivative is purchased that will rise in value if interest rates rise, and if the firm has no offsetting exposure to interest rate changes, then the firm is speculating that interest rates will rise and give it a profit on its derivatives position. Using derivatives to translate an opinion about whether interest rates or some other economic variable will rise or fall is the opposite of hedging—it is risk enhancing. Speculating on your views on the economy and using derivatives to profit if that view turns out to be correct is not necessarily wrong, but the speculator should always remember that sharp tools cut deep: If the opinions on which the derivatives position is based turn out to be incorrect, then the consequences can prove costly. Efficient market theory teaches how difficult it is to predict what markets will do. Most of the sad experiences with derivatives have occurred not from their use as instruments for hedging and offsetting risk, but rather from speculation.

25.2 Forward Contracts

We can begin our discussion of hedging by considering forward contracts. You have probably been dealing in forward contracts your whole life without knowing it. Suppose you walk into a bookstore on, say, February 1, to buy the best seller *Eating Habits of the Rich and Famous*. The cashier tells you that the book is currently sold out, but he takes your phone number, saying that he will reorder it for you. He says the book will cost $10.00. If you agree on February 1 to pick up and pay $10.00 for the book when called, you and the cashier have engaged in a **forward contract**. That is, you have agreed both to pay for the book and to pick it up when the bookstore notifies you. Because you are agreeing to buy the book at a later date, you are *buying* a forward contract on February 1. In commodity parlance, you will be taking delivery when you pick up the book. The book is called the **deliverable instrument**.

The cashier, acting on behalf of the bookstore, is selling a forward contract. (Alternatively, we say that he is writing a forward contract.) The bookstore has agreed to turn the book over to you at the predetermined price of $10.00 as soon as the book arrives. The act of turning the book over to you is called **making delivery**. Table 25.1 illustrates the book purchase. Note that the agreement takes place on February 1. The price is set and the conditions for sale are set at that time. In this case, the sale will occur when the book arrives. In other cases, an exact date of sale would be given. However, *no* cash changes hands on February 1; cash changes hands only when the book arrives.

Though forward contracts may have seemed exotic to you before you began this chapter, you can see that they are quite commonplace. Dealings in your personal life probably

Table 25.1

Illustration of Book Purchase as a Forward Contract

February 1	Date When Book Arrives
Buyer	
Buyer agrees to:	Buyer:
1. Pay the purchase price of $10.00.	1. Pays purchase price of $10.00.
2. Receive book when book arrives.	2. Receives book.
Seller	
Seller agrees to:	Seller:
1. Give up book when book arrives.	1. Gives up book.
2. Accept payment of $10.00 when book arrives.	2. Accepts payment of $10.00.

have involved forward contracts. Similarly, forward contracts occur all the time in business. Every time a firm orders an item that cannot be delivered immediately, a forward contract takes place. Sometimes, particularly when the order is small, an oral agreement will suffice. Other times, particularly when the order is larger, a written agreement is necessary.

Note that a forward contract is not an option. Both the buyer and the seller are obligated to perform under the terms of the contract. Conversely, the buyer of an option *chooses* whether to exercise the option.

A forward contract should be contrasted with a **cash transaction**—that is, a transaction where exchange is immediate. Had the book been on the bookstore's shelf, your purchase of it would constitute a cash transaction.

25.3 Futures Contracts

A variant of the forward contract takes place on financial exchanges. Contracts on exchanges are usually called **futures contracts**. There are a number of futures exchanges in the United States and elsewhere, and more are being established. The CME Group is among the largest, combining the old Chicago Mercantile Exchange (CME) and the Chicago Board of Trade (CBT). However, the two are still separate trading platforms. Another notable exchange is the London International Financial Futures and Options Exchange (LIFFE). The New York Mercantile Exchange (NYM) is also now owned by the CME.

Table 25.2 gives a partial *Wall Street Journal* listing for selected futures contracts. Taking a look at the corn contracts in the left portion of the table, note that the contracts trade on the CBT, one contract calls for the delivery of 5,000 bushels of corn, and prices are quoted in cents per bushel. The months in which the contracts mature are given in the first column.

For the corn contract with a March maturity, the first number in the row is the opening price (404.75 cents per bushel), the next number is the high price for the day (407.25), and the following number is the low price for the day (395.75). The *settlement price* is the fourth number (396.25), and it essentially is the closing price for the day. For purposes of marking to market, this is the figure used. The change, listed next, is the movement in the settlement price since the previous trading session (−8.75 cents). Finally, the *open interest* (622,973), the number of contracts outstanding at the end of the day, is shown.

To see how large futures trading can be, look at the CBT Treasury bond contracts (under the interest rate heading). One contract is for long-term Treasury bonds with a face, or par, value of $100,000. The total open interest for all months is about 882,093 contracts. The total face value outstanding is therefore $88.21 billion for this one type of contract!

Though we are discussing a futures contract, let us work with a forward contract first. Suppose on a Thursday you wrote a *forward* contract for September wheat at $4.07. From our discussion of forward contracts, this would mean that you would agree to turn over an agreed-upon number of wheat bushels for $4.07 per bushel on some specified date later in the month of September.

A futures contract differs somewhat from a forward contract. First, the seller can choose to deliver the wheat on any day during the delivery month—that is, the month of September. This gives the seller leeway that he would not have with a forward contract. When the seller decides to deliver, he notifies the exchange clearinghouse that he wants to do so. The clearinghouse then notifies an individual who bought a September wheat contract to stand ready to accept delivery within the next few days. Though each exchange

Table 25.2
Data on Futures Contracts, Thursday, January 8, 2015

Published, *The Wall Street Journal.*

Futures Contracts | WSJ.com/commodities

Metal & Petroleum Futures

	Open	Contract High	hi lo	Low	Settle	Chg	Open interest
Copper-High (CMX)-25,000 lbs.; $ per lb.							
Jan	2.7920	2.8090		2.7910	**2.7960**	-0.0080	1,307
March	2.7600	2.7765		2.7480	**2.7585**	-0.0085	120,806
Gold (CMX)-100 troy oz.; $ per troy oz.							
Jan	1219.20	1219.20		1211.80	**1210.60**	-8.70	133
Feb	1219.00	1219.40		1209.10	**1210.70**	-8.70	219,873
April	1220.20	1220.20		1209.80	**1211.50**	-8.70	75,780
June	1219.50	1219.50		1210.40	**1212.00**	-8.70	37,173
Aug	1220.00	1220.00		1214.50	**1212.60**	-8.70	10,648
Dec	1217.00	1218.50		1214.00	**1213.90**	-8.70	22,901
miNY Gold (CMX) - 50 troy oz.; $ per troy oz.							
Feb	1218.50	1219.25		1209.25	**1210.75**	-8.75	502
April	1216.00	1216.75		1211.00	**1211.50**	-8.75	45
June	1218.25	1218.75	▲	1211.00	**1212.00**	-8.75	274
Palladium (NYM) - 50 troy oz.; $ per troy oz.							
Jan	815.10	815.10	▼	812.60	**792.45**	-7.95	10
Feb	818.90	818.90	▼	812.90	**792.45**	-7.95	n.a.
June	802.80	802.80	▼	787.75	**793.20**	-7.85	881
Platinum (NYM)-50 troy oz.; $ per troy oz.							
Jan	1220.20	1222.70		1218.00	**1220.70**	-0.10	314
April	1223.50	1225.10		1214.80	**1220.90**	-0.50	65,367
Silver (CMX)-5,000 troy oz.; $ per troy oz.							
Jan	16.480	16.550	▲	16.480	**16.510**	-0.093	91
March	16.575	16.660		16.300	**16.544**	-0.093	103,248
miNY Silver (CMX) - 2500 troy oz.; $ per troy oz.							
March	16.500	16.575		16.325	**16.544**	-0.093	97
May	...	...		...	**16.575**	-0.094	1
Crude Oil, Light Sweet (NYM)-1,000 bbls.; $ per bbl.							
Feb	48.00	49.31	▼	46.83	**48.65**	0.72	279,774
March	50.44	50.71	▼	50.38	**49.08**	0.62	229,075
April	49.00	50.43	▼	48.04	**49.72**	0.56	79,097
May	49.83	51.15	▼	48.87	**50.48**	0.51	50,290
Sept	53.03	53.86	▼	52.11	**53.25**	0.33	57,655
Dec'16	60.80	61.55	▼	59.82	**60.57**	-0.32	74,198
Heating Oil No. 2 (NYM)-42,000 gal.; $ per gal.							
Feb	1.7020	1.7256	▼	1.6715	**1.6999**	-.0263	100,053
March	1.6784	1.6966	▼	1.6486	**1.6755**	-.0189	71,550
Gasoline-NY RBOB (NYM)-42,000 gal.; $ per gal.							
Feb	1.3750	1.3825	▼	1.3728	**1.3376**	-.0167	90,924
March	1.3782	1.3970	▼	1.3497	**1.3766**	-.0097	54,325
Natural Gas (NYM)-10,000 MMBtu.; $ per MMBtu.							
Feb	2.949	3.012		2.825	**2.871**	-.067	165,201
March	2.937	2.996		2.819	**2.865**	-.059	233,058
April	2.881	2.949		2.796	**2.835**	-.040	107,228
May	2.883	2.958		2.813	**2.849**	-.038	92,948
June	2.950	3.001		2.860	**2.894**	-.038	38,954
Oct	3.003	3.071		2.933	**2.964**	-.042	52,003

Agriculture Futures

	Open	Contract High	hi lo	Low	Settle	Chg	Open interest
Corn (CBT)-5,000 bu.; cents per bu.							
March	404.75	407.25		395.75	**396.25**	-8.75	622,973
Dec	427.75	430.00		419.75	**420.25**	-8.00	189,117
Ethanol (CBT)-29,000 gal.; $ per gal.							
July	1.508	1.508	▼	1.498	**1.506**	-.01	274
Aug	1.505	1.505	▼	1.502	**1.507**	-.01	229
Oats (CBT)-5,000 bu.; cents per bu.							
March	304.00	304.25	▼	300.75	**301.75**	-2.75	5,892
May	305.00	305.00		303.00	**304.00**	-2.00	1,324
Soybeans (CBT)-5,000 bu.; cents per bu.							
Jan	1049.75	1055.25	▲	1044.50	**1052.75**	1.75	7,538
March	1054.25	1061.00	▲	1048.25	**1056.25**	.50	292,948
Soybean Meal (CBT)-100 tons; $ per ton.							
Jan	370.90	372.10	▲	365.30	**368.50**	-2.30	3,942
March	355.00	357.40		351.10	**354.00**	-1.10	179,677
Soybean Oil (CBT)-60,000 lbs.; cents per lb.							
Jan	32.67	33.15	▲	32.67	**32.98**	.29	1,888
March	32.85	33.50	▲	32.69	**33.16**	.29	188,660
Rough Rice (CBT)-2,000 cwt.; $ per cwt.							
Jan	1141.00	1142.00		1139.50	**1141.00**	5.00	469
March	1159.50	1173.00	▲	1158.50	**1165.00**	4.50	7,778
Wheat (CBT)-5,000 bu.; cents per bu.							
March	594.25	594.50		578.50	**579.50**	-12.25	201,155
July	600.00	601.25		586.50	**587.75**	-11.00	65,421
Wheat (KC)-5,000 bu.; cents per bu.							
March	633.50	634.00		619.25	**620.00**	-11.25	73,903
May	635.75	637.75		622.50	**623.50**	-11.75	22,552
Wheat (MPLS)-5,000 bu.; cents per bu.							
March	626.00	628.00	▲	613.50	**615.75**	-9.75	36,416
May	632.00	632.75	▲	620.00	**622.25**	-9.50	15,374
Cattle-Feeder (CME)-50,000 lbs.; cents per lb.							
Jan	225.800	226.275		223.075	**225.650**	.950	7,732
March	222.200	222.225		218.375	**220.325**	-.550	15,427
Cattle-Live (CME)-40,000 lbs.; cents per lb.							
Feb	166.400	166.750		164.975	**165.900**	-.125	111,136
April	165.450	165.450		163.800	**164.725**	-.275	85,028
Hogs-Lean (CME)-40,000 lbs.; cents per lb.							
Feb	78.600	79.875	▼	78.150	**79.325**	.750	85,568
April	81.200	82.575	▼	80.700	**81.875**	.525	60,748
Lumber (CME)-110,000 bd. ft., $ per 1,000 bd. ft.							
Jan	324.50	328.40		319.50	**327.30**	7.60	266
March	317.50	324.90	▼	316.70	**322.70**	5.30	3,512
Milk (CME)-200,000 lbs., cents per lb.							
Jan	15.65	16.11	▲	15.58	**15.80**	.15	5,978
Feb	14.90	15.13		14.70	**14.94**	.24	5,383
Cocoa (ICE-US)-10 metric tons; $ per ton.							
March	2,911	2,923		2,899	**2,912**	10	94,074
May	2,896	2,906		2,883	**2,895**	8	48,577
Coffee (ICE-US)-37,500 lbs.; cents per lb.							
March	175.60	182.85	▲	173.00	**175.05**	.15	87,439
May	178.15	185.40	▲	175.80	**177.75**	.20	28,098
Sugar-World (ICE-US)-112,000 lbs.; cents per lb.							
March	14.94	14.99		14.61	**14.78**	-.09	428,531
May	15.20	15.30		14.97	**15.12**	-.07	152,189
Sugar-Domestic (ICE-US)-112,000 lbs.; cents per lb.							
March	25.00	25.00		25.00	**25.12**	-.02	2,493
May	25.40	25.40	▲	25.40	**25.38**	.06	1,497
Cotton (ICE-US)-50,000 lbs.; cents per lb.							
March	60.10	60.52		59.84	**60.43**	.23	119,551
May	60.76	61.11		60.40	**60.91**	.15	34,748
Orange Juice (ICE-US)-15,000 lbs.; cents per lb.							
Jan	143.10	143.10		143.10	**143.20**	.60	364
March	142.10	143.70		141.20	**142.60**	.35	8,857

Interest Rate Futures

	Open	Contract High	hi lo	Low	Settle	Chg	Open interest
Treasury Bonds (CBT)-$100,000; pts 32nds of 100%							
March	148-160	148-240		147-100	**148-060**	1.0	882,093
June	165-120	165-170		163-290	**165-030**	5.0	1,747
Treasury Notes (CBT)-$100,000; pts 32nds of 100%							
March	128-160	128-220		128-005	**128-150**	3.5	2,667,999
June	127-215	127-300		127-120	**127-255**	4.0	3,229
5 Yr. Treasury Notes (CBT)-$100,000; pts 32nds of 100%							
March	119-240	119-282		119-175	**119-255**	3.2	1,815,691
June	...	119-047		118-302	**119-045**	3.0	290
2 Yr. Treasury Notes (CBT)-$200,000; pts 32nds of 100%							
March	109-130	109-150		109-120	**109-145**	1.5	1,246,072
30 Day Federal Funds (CBT)-$5,000,000; 100 - daily avg.							
Jan	99.890	99.893	▲	99.888	**99.888**	...	54,698
May	99.845	99.855	▲	99.840	**99.845**	.005	98,205
10 Yr. Del. Int. Rate Swaps (CBT)-$100,000; pts 32nds of 100%							
March	108.078	108.203		107.750	**108.125**	-.031	51,865
1 Month Libor (CME)-$3,000,000; pts of 100%							
March	99.8275	99.8275	▲	99.8275	**99.8275**	.0025	256
Eurodollar (CME)-$1,000,000; pts of 100%							
Jan	99.7525	99.7525	▲	99.7475	**99.7475**	-.0025	69,733
March	99.7250	99.7300		99.7200	**99.7250**	.0050	1,106,176
June	99.5750	99.5900		99.5600	**99.5800**	.0150	1,077,137
Dec	99.1400	99.1750		99.1100	**99.1400**	.0150	1,070,443

Currency Futures

	Open	Contract High	hi lo	Low	Settle	Chg	Open interest
Japanese Yen (CME)-¥12,500,000; $ per 100¥							
March	.8439	.8443		.8362	**.8412**	-.0023	226,633
June	.8442	.8443		.8374	**.8420**	-.0023	2,208
Canadian Dollar (CME)-CAD 100,000; $ per CAD							
March	.8434	.8452	▼	.8408	**.8447**	-.0002	93,612
June	.8417	.8432	▼	.8400	**.8429**	-.0002	7,743
British Pound (CME)-£62,500; $ per £							
March	1.5136	1.5148	▼	1.5046	**1.5114**	-.0040	161,207
June	1.5115	1.5143	▼	1.5050	**1.5104**	-.0039	602
Swiss Franc (CME)-CHF 125,000; $ per CHF							
March	.9901	.9918	▼	.9839	**.9879**	-.0051	62,828
June	.9920	.9920	▼	.9865	**.9904**	-.0049	1,317
Australian Dollar (CME)-AUD 100,000; $ per AUD							
March	.8037	.8051	▼	.7993	**.8041**	-.0026	121,806
June	.7988	.7995	▼	.7952	**.7992**	-.0025	341
Mexican Peso (CME)-MXN 500,000; $ per MXN							
March	.06691	.06779	▲	.06676	**.06768**	.00063	130,970
June	.06729	.06729	▲	.06724	**.06728**	.00063	90
Euro (CME)-€125,000; $ per €							
March	1.1884	1.1904	▼	1.1809	**1.1857**	-.0064	403,080
June	1.1880	1.1933	▼	1.1823	**1.1869**	-.0064	3,168
Euro/Japanese Yen (ICE-US)-€125,000; ¥ per €							
March	140.82	141.67	▼	140.74	**140.95**	-.38	524
Euro/British Pound (ICE-US)-€125,000; £ per €							
March	.7852	.7863	▲	.7824	**.7845**	-.0021	1,086
Euro/Swiss Franc (ICE-US)-€125,000; CHF per €							
March	1.2004	1.2005	▼	1.2001	**1.2002**	-.0003	1,031

Index Futures

	Open	Contract High	hi lo	Low	Settle	Chg	Open interest
DJ Industrial Average (CBT)-$10 x index							
March	17332	17332		17505	**17507**	217	6,541
Mini DJ Industrial Average (CBT)-$5 x index							
March	17309	17524	▼	17300	**17507**	217	112,371
June	17239	17444		17239	**17434**	217	223
S&P 500 Index (CME)-$250 x index							
March	1997.10	2024.00	▼	1995.80	**2019.60**	25.20	122,933
June	2003.10	2012.50	▼	1998.20	**2012.40**	25.30	2,776
Mini S&P 500 (CME)-$50 x index							
March	1996.50	2023.75	▼	1995.75	**2019.50**	25.00	2,738,793
June	1989.50	2016.50	▼	1989.50	**2012.50**	25.50	9,661
Mini S&P Midcap 400 (CME)-$100 x index							
March	1407.90	1428.00		1407.90	**1426.10**	19.60	82,531
June	...	...	▲	...	**1424.10**	19.60	3
Nasdaq 100 (CME)-$100 x index							
March	4108.50	4162.50	▼	4108.00	**4151.50**	49.25	6,737
Mini Nasdaq 100 (CME)-$20 x index							
March	4105.5	4163.3	▼	4102.8	**4151.5**	49.3	335,823
June	4094.0	4152.0	▼	4094.0	**4140.8**	49.3	157
Mini Russell 2000 (ICE-US)-$100 x index							
March	1158.80	1172.70		1158.40	**1171.60**	14.70	337,932
June	1160.00	1160.00	▼	1160.00	**1167.80**	14.70	7,096
Mini Russell 1000 (ICE-US)-$100 x index							
March	1117.20	1124.50		1114.70	**1122.80**	13.70	7,897
U.S. Dollar Index (ICE-US)-$1,000 x index							
March	92.00	92.51	▲	91.90	**92.12**	.38	123,258
June	92.33	92.84	▲	92.30	**92.49**	.40	1,930

Source: SIX Financial Information

selects the buyer in a different way, the buyer is generally chosen in a random fashion. Because there are so many buyers at any one time, the buyer selected by the clearinghouse to take delivery almost certainly did not originally buy the contract from the seller now making delivery.

Second, futures contracts are traded on an exchange, whereas forward contracts are generally traded off an exchange. Because of this, there is generally a liquid market in futures contracts. A buyer can net out her futures position with a sale. A seller can net out his futures position with a purchase. If a buyer of a futures contract does not subsequently sell her contract, she must take delivery.

Third, and most important, the prices of futures contracts are **marked to the market** daily. That is, suppose the price falls to $4.05 on Friday's close. Because all buyers lost two cents per bushel on that day, they each must turn over the two cents per bushel to their brokers within 24 hours, who subsequently remit the proceeds to the clearinghouse. All sellers gained two cents per bushel on that day, so they each receive two cents per bushel from their brokers. Their brokers are subsequently compensated by the clearinghouse. Because there is a buyer for every seller, the clearinghouse must break even every day.

Now suppose that the price rises to $4.12 on the close of the following Monday. Each buyer receives seven cents ($4.12 − $4.05) per bushel, and each seller must pay

Illustration of Example Involving Marking to Market in Futures Contracts

Both buyer and seller originally transact at Thursday's closing price. Delivery takes place at Monday's closing price.[*]

	Thursday, September 19	Friday, September 20	Monday, September 23	Delivery (Notification Given by Seller on Monday)
Closing price	$4.07	$4.05	$4.12	
Buyer	Buyer purchases futures contract at closing price of $4.07/bushel.	Buyer must pay two cents/bushel to clearinghouse within one business day.	Buyer receives seven cents/bushel from clearinghouse within one business day.	Buyer pays $4.12 per bushel and receives grain within two business day.

Buyer's net payment of −$4.07 (=−$.02 + $.07 − $4.12) is the same as if buyer purchased a forward contract for $4.07/bushel.

| Seller | Seller sells futures contract at closing price of $4.07/bushel. | Seller receives two cents/bushel from clearinghouse within one business day. | Seller pays seven cents/bushel to clearinghouse within one business day. | Seller receives $4.12 per bushel and delivers grain within two business days. |

Seller's net receipts of $4.07 (=$.02 − $.07 + $4.12) are the same as if seller sold a forward contract for $4.07/bushel.

---

[*]For simplicity, we assume that buyer and seller both (1) initially transact at the same time and (2) meet in the delivery process. This is actually very unlikely to occur in the real world because the clearinghouse assigns the buyer to take delivery in a random manner.

seven cents per bushel. Finally, suppose that on Monday a seller notifies his broker of his intention to deliver.[1] The delivery price will be $4.12, which is Monday's close.

There are clearly many cash flows in futures contracts. However, after all the dust settles, the *net price* to the buyer must be the price at which she bought originally. That is, an individual buying at Thursday's closing price of $4.07 and being called to take delivery on Monday pays two cents per bushel on Friday, receives seven cents per bushel on Monday, and takes delivery at $4.12. Her net outflow per bushel is −$4.07 (=−$.02 + $.07 − $4.12), which is the price at which she contracted on Thursday. (Our analysis ignores the time value of money.) Conversely, an individual selling at Thursday's closing price of $4.07 and notifying his broker concerning delivery the following Monday receives two cents per bushel on Friday, pays seven cents per bushel on Monday, and makes delivery at $4.12. His net inflow per bushel is $4.07 (=$.02 − $.07 + $4.12), which is the price at which he contracted on Thursday.

These details are presented in a nearby box. For simplicity, we assumed that the buyer and seller who initially transact on Thursday's close meet in the delivery process.[2] The point in the example is that the buyer's net payment of $4.07 per bushel is the same as if she purchased a forward contract for $4.07. Similarly, the seller's net receipt of $4.07 per bushel is the same as if he sold a forward contract for $4.07 per bushel. The only difference is the timing of the cash flows. The buyer of a forward contract knows that he will make a single payment of $4.07 on the expiration date. He will not need to worry about any other cash flows in the interim. Conversely, though the cash flows to the buyer of a futures contract will net to exactly $4.07 as well, the pattern of cash flows is not known ahead of time.

The mark-to-the-market provision on futures contracts has two related effects. The first concerns differences in net present value. For example, a large price drop immediately following purchase means an immediate outpayment for the buyer of a futures contract. Though the net outflow of $4.07 is still the same as under a forward contract, the present value of the cash outflows is greater to the buyer of a futures contract. Of course, the present value of the cash outflows is less to the buyer of a futures contract if a price rise follows purchase.[3] Though this effect could be substantial in certain theoretical circumstances, it appears to be of quite limited importance in the real world.[4]

Second, the firm must have extra liquidity to handle a sudden outflow prior to expiration. This added risk may make the futures contract less attractive.

Students frequently ask, "Why in the world would managers of the commodity exchanges ruin perfectly good contracts with these bizarre mark-to-the-market provisions?" Actually, the reason is a very good one. Consider the forward contract in Table 25.1 concerning the bookstore. Suppose the public quickly loses interest in *Eating Habits of the Rich and Famous*. By the time the bookstore calls the buyer, other stores may have dropped the price of the book to $6.00. Because the forward contract was for $10.00, the buyer has an incentive not to take delivery on the forward contract. Conversely, should the book become a hot item selling at $15.00, the bookstore may simply not call the buyer.

As indicated, forward contracts have a big flaw. Whichever way the price of the deliverable instrument moves, one party has an incentive to default. There are many cases

---

[1] He will deliver on Wednesday, two days later.

[2] As pointed out earlier, this is actually very unlikely to occur in the real world.

[3] The direction is reversed for the seller of a futures contract. However, the general point that the net present value of cash flows may differ between forward and futures contracts holds for sellers as well.

[4] See John C. Cox, Jonathan E. Ingersoll, and Stephen A. Ross, "The Relationship between Forward and Future Prices," *Journal of Financial Economics* (1981).

where defaults have occurred in the real world. One famous case concerned Coca-Cola. When the company began in the early 20th century, Coca-Cola made an agreement to supply its bottlers and distributors with cola syrup at a constant price *forever*. Of course, subsequent inflation would have caused Coca-Cola to lose large sums of money had it honored the contract. After much legal effort, Coke and its bottlers put an *inflation escalator clause* in the contract. Another famous case concerned Westinghouse. It seems the firm had promised to deliver uranium to certain utilities at a fixed price. The price of uranium skyrocketed in the 1970s, making Westinghouse lose money on every shipment. Westinghouse defaulted on its agreement. The utilities took Westinghouse to court but did not recover amounts anything near what Westinghouse owed them.

Mark-to-the-market provisions minimize the chance of default on a futures contract. If the price rises, the seller has an incentive to default on a forward contract. However, after paying the clearinghouse, the seller of a futures contract has little reason to default. If the price falls, the same argument can be made for the buyer. Because changes in the value of the underlying asset are recognized daily, there is no accumulation of loss, and the incentive to default is reduced.

Because of this default issue, forward contracts generally involve individuals and institutions who know and can trust each other. But as W. C. Fields said, "Trust everybody, but cut the cards." Lawyers earn a handsome living writing supposedly airtight forward contracts, even among friends. The genius of the mark-to-the-market system is that it can prevent default where it is most likely to occur—among investors who do not know each other. Textbooks on futures contracts from decades ago usually include a statement such as, "No major default has ever occurred on the commodity exchanges." No textbook published after the Hunt Brothers defaulted on silver contracts in the 1970s can make that claim. Nevertheless, the extremely low default rate in futures contracts is truly awe-inspiring.

25.4 Hedging

Now that we have determined how futures contracts work, let us talk about hedging. There are two types of hedges, long and short. We discuss the short hedge first.

EXAMPLE 25.1

Futures Hedging   In June, Bernard Abelman, a Midwestern farmer, anticipates a harvest of 50,000 bushels of wheat at the end of September. He has two alternatives.

1. *Write futures contracts against his anticipated harvest.* The September wheat contract on the Chicago Board of Trade is trading at $3.75 a bushel on June 1. He executes the following transaction:

Date of Transaction	Transaction	Price per Bushel
June 1	Write 10 September futures contracts	$3.75

He notes that transportation costs to the designated delivery point in Chicago are 30 cents/bushel. Thus, his net price per bushel is $3.45 = $3.75 − $.30.

(continued)

2. *Harvest the wheat without writing a futures contract.* Alternatively, Mr. Abelman could harvest the wheat without the benefit of a futures contract. The risk would be quite great here because no one knows what the cash price in September will be. If prices rise, he will profit. Conversely, he will lose if prices fall.

We say that Strategy 2 is an unhedged position because there is no attempt to use the futures markets to reduce risk. Conversely, Strategy 1 involves a hedge. That is, a position in the futures market offsets the risk of a position in the physical—that is, in the actual—commodity.

Though hedging may seem quite sensible to you, it should be mentioned that not everyone hedges. Mr. Abelman might reject hedging for at least two reasons.

First, he may simply be uninformed about hedging. We have found that not everyone in business understands the hedging concept. Many executives have told us that they do not want to use futures markets for hedging their inventories because the risks are too great. However, we disagree. While there are large price fluctuations in these markets, hedging actually reduces the risk that an individual holding inventories bears.

Second, Mr. Abelman may have a special insight or some special information that commodity prices will rise. He would not be wise to lock in a price of $3.75 if he expects the cash price in September to be well above this price.

The hedge of Strategy 1 is called a **short hedge** because Mr. Abelman reduces his risk by *selling* a futures contract. The short hedge is very common in business. It occurs whenever someone either anticipates receiving inventory or is holding inventory. Mr. Abelman is anticipating the harvest of grain. A manufacturer of soybean meal and oil may hold large quantities of raw soybeans that are already paid for. However, the prices to be received for meal and oil are not known because no one knows what the market prices will be when the meal and oil are produced. The manufacturer may write futures contracts in meal and oil to lock in sales prices. An oil company may hold large inventories of petroleum to be processed into heating oil. The firm could sell futures contracts in heating oil to lock in the sales price. A mortgage banker may assemble mortgages slowly before selling them in bulk to a financial institution. Movements of interest rates affect the value of the mortgages while they are in inventory. The mortgage banker could sell Treasury bond futures contracts to offset this interest rate risk. (This last example is treated later in this chapter.)

EXAMPLE

More Hedging   On April 1, Moon Chemical agreed to sell petrochemicals to the U.S. government in the future. The delivery dates and prices have been determined. Because oil is a basic ingredient in the production process, Moon Chemical will need to have large quantities of oil on hand. The firm can get the oil in one of two ways:

1. *Buy the oil as the firm needs it.* This is an unhedged position because, as of April 1, the firm does not know the prices it will later have to pay for the oil. Oil is quite a volatile commodity, so Moon Chemical is bearing a good bit of risk. The key to this risk bearing is that the sales price to the U.S. government has already been fixed. Thus, Moon Chemical cannot pass on increased costs to the consumer.

2. *Buy futures contracts.*[5] The firm can buy futures contracts with expiration months corresponding to the dates the firm needs inventory. The futures contracts lock in the purchase price to Moon

(continued)

---

[5]Alternatively, the firm could buy the oil on April 1 and store it. This would eliminate the risk of price movement because the firm's oil costs would be fixed upon the immediate purchase. However, this strategy would be inferior to Strategy 2 in the common case where the difference between the futures contract quoted on April 1 and the April 1 cash price is less than the storage costs.

Chemical. Because there is a crude oil futures contract for every month, selecting the correct futures contract is not difficult. Many other commodities have only five contracts per year, frequently necessitating buying contracts one month away from the month of production.

As mentioned earlier, Moon Chemical is interested in hedging the risk of fluctuating oil prices because it cannot pass any cost increases on to the consumer. Suppose, alternatively, that Moon Chemical was not selling petrochemicals on a fixed contract to the U.S. government. Instead, imagine that the petrochemicals were to be sold to private industry at currently prevailing prices. The price of petrochemicals should move directly with oil prices because oil is a major component of petrochemicals. Because cost increases are likely to be passed on to the consumer, Moon Chemical would probably not want to hedge in this case. Instead, the firm is likely to choose Strategy 1, buying the oil as it is needed. If oil prices increase between April 1 and, say, September 1, Moon Chemical will, of course, find that its inputs have become quite costly. However, in a competitive market, its revenues are likely to rise as well.

Strategy 2 is called a **long hedge** because one *purchases* a futures contract to reduce risk. In other words, one takes a long position in the futures market. In general, a firm institutes a long hedge when it is committed to a fixed sales price. One class of situations involves actual written contracts with customers, such as the one Moon Chemical had with the U.S. government. Alternatively, a firm may find that it cannot easily pass on costs to consumers or does not want to pass on these costs. For example, a group of students opened a small meat market called *What's Your Beef* near the University of Pennsylvania in the late 1970s.[6] This was a time of volatile consumer prices, especially food prices. Knowing that their fellow students were particularly budget-conscious, the owners vowed to keep food prices constant regardless of price movements in either direction. They accomplished this by purchasing futures contracts in various agricultural commodities.

25.5 Interest Rate Futures Contracts

In this section we consider interest rate futures contracts. Our examples deal with futures contracts on Treasury bonds because of their high popularity. We first price Treasury bonds and Treasury bond forward contracts. Differences between futures and forward contracts are explored. Hedging examples are provided next.

PRICING OF TREASURY BONDS

As mentioned earlier in the text, a Treasury bond pays semiannual interest over its life. In addition, the face value of the bond is paid at maturity. Consider a 20-year, 8 percent coupon bond that was issued on March 1. The first payment is to occur in six months—that is, on September 1. The value of the bond can be determined as follows:

Pricing of Treasury Bond

$$P_{TB} = \frac{\$40}{1 + R_1} + \frac{\$40}{(1 + R_2)^2} + \frac{\$40}{(1 + R_3)^3} + \cdots + \frac{\$40}{(1 + R_{39})^{39}} + \frac{\$1,040}{(1 + R_{40})^{40}} \quad (25.1)$$

Because an 8 percent coupon bond pays interest of $80 a year, the semiannual coupon is $40. Principal and the semiannual coupon are both paid at maturity. As we mentioned in a previous chapter, the price of the Treasury bond, P_{TB}, is determined by discounting each payment on the bond at the appropriate spot rate. Because the payments are semiannual, each spot rate is expressed in semiannual terms. That is, imagine a horizontal term structure where the effective annual yield is 8 percent for all maturities. Because each spot

---

[6]Ordinarily, an unusual firm name in this textbook is a tip-off that it is fictional. This, however, is a true story.

rate, R, is expressed in semiannual terms, each spot rate is $\sqrt{1.08} - 1 = 3.92\%$. Coupon payments occur every six months, so there are 40 spot rates over the 20-year period.

PRICING OF FORWARD CONTRACTS

Now imagine a *forward* contract where, on March 1, you agree to buy a new 20-year, 8 percent coupon Treasury bond in six months (on September 1). As with typical forward contracts, you will pay for the bond on September 1, not March 1. The cash flows from both the Treasury bond issued on March 1 and the forward contract that you purchase on March 1 are presented in Figure 25.1. The cash flows on the Treasury bond begin exactly six months earlier than do the cash flows on the forward contract. The Treasury bond is purchased with cash on March 1 (Date 0). The first coupon payment occurs on September 1 (Date 1). The last coupon payment occurs at Date 40, along with the face value of $1,000. The forward contract compels you to pay $P_{\text{FORW.CONT.}}$, the price of the forward contract, on September 1 (Date 1). You receive a new Treasury bond at that time. The first coupon payment you receive from the bond occurs on March 1 of the following year (Date 2). The last coupon payment occurs at Date 41, along with the face value of $1,000.

Given the 40 spot rates, Equation 25.1 showed how to price a Treasury bond. How do we price the forward contract on a Treasury bond? Just as we saw earlier in the text that net present value analysis can be used to price bonds, we will now show that net present value analysis can be used to price forward contracts. Given the cash flows for the forward contract in Figure 25.1, the price of the forward contract must satisfy the following equation:

$$\frac{P_{\text{FORW.CONT.}}}{1 + R_1} = \frac{\$40}{(1 + R_2)^2} + \frac{\$40}{(1 + R_3)^3} + \frac{\$40}{(1 + R_4)^4} + \cdots + \frac{\$40}{(1 + R_{40})^{40}} + \frac{\$1,040}{(1 + R_{41})^{41}} \quad (25.2)$$

The right side of Equation 25.2 discounts all the cash flows from the delivery instrument (the Treasury bond issued on September 1) back to Date 0 (March 1). Because the first cash flow occurs at Date 2 (March 1 of the subsequent year), it is discounted by $1/(1 + R_2)^2$. The last cash flow of $1,040 occurs at Date 41, so it is discounted by

Figure 25.1

Cash Flows for Both a Treasury Bond and a Forward Contract on a Treasury Bond

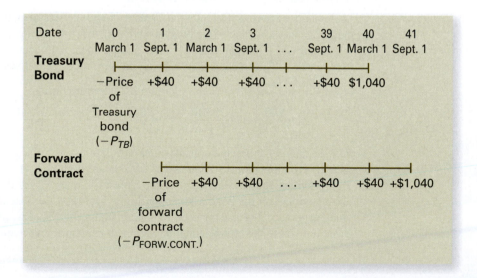

$1/(1 + R_{41})^{41}$. The left side represents the cost of the forward contract as of Date 0. Because the actual outpayment occurs at Date 1, it is discounted by $1/(1 + R_1)$.

Students often ask, "Why are we discounting everything back to Date 0 when we are actually paying for the forward contract on September 1?" The answer is simply that we apply the same techniques to Equation 25.2 that we apply to all capital budgeting problems: We want to put everything in today's (Date 0's) dollars. Given that the spot rates are known in the marketplace, traders should have no more trouble pricing a forward contract by Equation 25.2 than they would have pricing a Treasury bond by Equation 25.1.

Forward contracts are similar to the underlying bonds themselves. If the entire term structure of interest rates unexpectedly shifts upward on March 2, the Treasury bond issued the previous day should fall in value. This can be seen from Equation 25.1. A rise in each of the spot rates lowers the present value of each of the coupon payments. Hence, the value of the bond must fall. Conversely, a fall in the term structure of interest rates increases the value of the bond.

The same relationship holds with forward contracts, as we can see by rewriting Equation 25.2 like this:

$$P_{\text{FORW.CONT.}} = \frac{\$40 \times (1 + R_1)}{(1 + R_2)^2} + \frac{\$40 \times (1 + R_1)}{(1 + R_3)^3} + \frac{\$40 \times (1 + R_1)}{(1 + R_4)^4}$$

$$+ \cdots + \frac{\$40 \times (1 + R_1)}{(1 + R_{40})^{40}} + \frac{\$1{,}040 \times (1 + R_1)}{(1 + R_{41})^{41}} \qquad (25.3)$$

We went from Equation 25.2 to 25.3 by multiplying both the left and the right sides by $(1 + R_1)$. If the entire term structure of interest rates unexpectedly shifts upward on March 2, the *first* term on the right side of Equation 25.3 should fall in value.[7] That is, both R_1 and R_2 will rise an equal amount. However, R_2 enters as a *squared* term, $1/(1 + R_2)^2$, so an increase in R_2 more than offsets the increase in R_1. As we move further to the right, an increase in any spot rate, R_i, more than offsets an increase in R_1. Here, R_i enters as the ith power, $1/(1 + R_i)^i$. Thus, as long as the entire term structure shifts upward an equal amount on March 2, the value of a forward contract must fall on that date. Conversely, as long as the entire term structure shifts downward an equal amount on March 2, the value of a forward contract must rise.

FUTURES CONTRACTS

The previous discussion concerned a forward contract in U.S. Treasury bonds—that is, a forward contract where the deliverable instrument is a U.S. Treasury bond. What about a futures contract on a Treasury bond?[8] We mentioned earlier that futures contracts and forward contracts are quite similar, though there are a few differences between the two. First, futures contracts are generally traded on exchanges, whereas forward contracts are not traded on an exchange. In this case, the Treasury bond futures contract is traded on the Chicago Board of Trade. Second, futures contracts generally allow the seller a period of time in which to deliver, whereas forward contracts generally call for delivery on a particular day. The seller of a Treasury bond futures contract can choose to deliver on any business day during the delivery month.[9] Third, futures contracts are subject to the

---

[7]We are assuming that each spot rate shifts by the same amount. For example, suppose that on March 1 $R_1 = 5\%$, $R_2 = 5.4\%$, and $R_3 = 5.8\%$. Assuming that all rates increase by 1/2 percent on March 2, R_1 becomes 5.5 percent (=5% + 1/2%), R_2 becomes 5.9 percent, and R_3 becomes 6.3 percent.

[8]Futures contracts on bonds are also called *interest rate futures contracts*.

[9]Delivery occurs two days after the seller notifies the clearinghouse of her intention to deliver.

mark-to-the-market convention, whereas forward contracts are not. Traders in Treasury bill futures contracts must adhere to this convention. Fourth, there is generally a liquid market for futures contracts allowing contracts to be quickly netted out. That is, a buyer can sell his futures contract at any time, and a seller can buy back her futures contract at any time. Conversely, because forward markets are generally quite illiquid, traders cannot easily net out their positions. The popularity of the Treasury bond futures contract has produced liquidity even higher than that on other futures contracts. Positions in that contract can be netted out quite easily.

This discussion is not intended to be an exhaustive list of differences between the Treasury bond forward contract and the Treasury bond futures contract. Rather, it is intended to show that both contracts share fundamental characteristics. Though there are differences, the two instruments should be viewed as variations of the same species, not different species. Thus, the pricing of Equation 25.3, which is exact for the forward contract, should be a decent approximation for the futures contract.

HEDGING IN INTEREST RATE FUTURES

Now that we have the basic institutional details under our belts, we are ready for examples of hedging using either futures contracts or forward contracts on Treasury bonds. Because the T-bond futures contract is extremely popular, whereas the forward contract is traded sporadically, our examples use the futures contract.

EXAMPLE 25.3

Interest Rate Hedging   Ron Cooke owns a mortgage banking company. On March 1, he made a commitment to lend a total of $1 million to various homeowners on May 1. The loans are 20-year mortgages carrying a 12 percent coupon, the going interest rate on mortgages at the time. Thus, the mortgages are made at par. Though homeowners would not use the term, we could say that he is buying a *forward contract* on a mortgage. That is, he agrees on March 1 to give $1 million to his borrowers on May 1 in exchange for principal and interest from them every month for the next 20 years.

Like many mortgage bankers, he has no intention of paying the $1 million out of his own pocket. Rather, he intends to sell the mortgages to an insurance company. Thus, the insurance company will actually lend the funds and will receive principal and interest over the next 20 years. Mr. Cooke does not currently have an insurance company in mind. He plans to visit the mortgage departments of insurance companies over the next 60 days to sell the mortgages to one or many of them. He sets April 30 as a deadline for making the sale because the borrowers expect the funds on the following day.

Suppose Mr. Cooke sells the mortgages to the Acme Insurance Co. on April 15. What price will Acme pay for the bonds?

You may think the insurance company will obviously pay $1 million for the loans. However, suppose interest rates have risen above 12 percent by April 15. The insurance company will buy the mortgage at a discount. For example, suppose the insurance company agrees to pay only $940,000 for the mortgages. Because the mortgage banker agreed to lend a full $1 million to the borrowers, the mortgage banker must come up with the additional $60,000 (=$1 million − $940,000) out of his own pocket.

Alternatively, suppose interest rates fall below 12 percent by April 15. The mortgages can be sold at a premium under this scenario. If the insurance company buys the mortgages at $1.05 million, the mortgage banker will have made an unexpected profit of $50,000 (=$1.05 million − $1 million).

Because Ron Cooke is unable to forecast interest rates, this risk is something that he would like to avoid. The risk is summarized in Table 25.3.

(continued)

Table 25.3 Effects of Changing Interest Rates on Ron Cooke, Mortgage Banker

	Mortgage Interest Rate on April 15	
	Above 12%	**Below 12%**
Sale Price to Acme Insurance Company	Below $1 million (we assume $940,000).	Above $1 million (we assume $1.05 million).
Effect on Mortgage Banker	He loses because he must lend the full $1 million to borrowers.	He gains because he lends only $1 million to borrowers.
Dollar Gain or Loss	Loss of $60,000 (=$1 million − $940,000).	Gain of $50,000 (=$1.05 million − $1 million).

The interest rate on March 1, the date when the loan agreement was made with the borrowers, was 12 percent. April 15 is the date the mortgages were sold to Acme Insurance Company.

Seeing the interest rate risk, students at this point may ask, "What does the mortgage banker get out of this loan to offset his risk bearing?" Mr. Cooke wants to sell the mortgages to the insurance company so that he can get two fees. The first is an *origination fee,* which is paid to the mortgage banker by the insurance company on April 15—that is, on the date the loan is sold. An industry standard in certain locales is 1 percent of the value of the loan, which is $10,000 (=1% × $1 million). In addition, Mr. Cooke will act as a collection agent for the insurance company. For this service he will receive a small portion of the outstanding balance of the loan each month. For example, if he is paid .03 percent of the loan each month, he will receive $300 (=.03% × $1 million) in the first month. As the outstanding balance of the loan declines, he will receive less.

Though Mr. Cooke will earn profitable fees on the loan, he bears interest rate risk. He loses money if interest rates rise after March 1, and he profits if interest rates fall after March 1. To hedge this risk, he writes June Treasury bond futures contracts on March 1. As with mortgages, Treasury bond futures contracts fall in value if interest rates rise. Because he *writes* the contract, he makes money on these contracts if they fall in value. Therefore, with an interest rate rise, the loss he endures on the mortgages is offset by the gain he earns in the futures market. Conversely, Treasury bond futures contracts rise in value if interest rates fall. Because he writes the contracts, he suffers losses on them when rates fall. With an interest rate fall, the profit he makes on the mortgages is offset by the loss he suffers in the futures markets.

The details of this hedging transaction are presented in Table 25.4. The column on the left is labeled "Cash Markets" because the deal in the mortgage market is transacted off an exchange. The column on the right shows the offsetting transactions in the futures market. Consider the first row. The mortgage banker enters into a forward contract on March 1. He simultaneously writes Treasury bond futures contracts. Ten contracts are written because the deliverable instrument on each contract is $100,000 of Treasury bonds. The total is $1 million (=10 × $100,000), which is equal to the value of the mortgages. Mr. Cooke would prefer to write May Treasury bond futures contracts. Here, Treasury bonds would be delivered on the futures contract during the same month that the loan is funded. Because there is no May T-bond futures contract, Mr. Cooke achieves the closest match through a June contract.

(continued)

Table 25.4 Illustration of Hedging Strategy for Ron Cooke, Mortgage Banker

	Cash Markets	Futures Markets
March 1	Mortgage banker makes forward contracts to lend $1 million at 12 percent for 20 years. The loans are to be funded on May 1. No cash changes hands on March 1.	Mortgage banker writes 10 June Treasury bond futures contracts.
April 15	Loans are sold to Acme Insurance Company. Mortgage banker will receive sale price from Acme on the May 1 funding date.	Mortgage banker buys back all the futures contracts.
If interest rates rise:	Loans are sold at a price below $1 million. Mortgage banker *loses* because he receives less than the $1 million he must give to borrowers.	Each futures contract is bought back at a price below the sales price, resulting in *profit*. Mortgage banker's profit in futures market offsets loss in cash market.
If interest rates fall:	Loans are sold at a price above $1 million. Mortgage banker *gains* because he receives more than the $1 million he must give to borrowers.	Each futures contract is bought back at a price above the sales price, resulting in *loss*. Mortgage banker's loss in futures market offsets gain in cash market.

If held to maturity, the June contract would obligate the mortgage banker to deliver Treasury bonds in June. Interest rate risk ends in the cash market when the loans are sold. Interest rate risk must be terminated in the futures market at that time. Thus, Mr. Cooke nets out his position in the futures contracts as soon as the loan is sold to Acme Insurance.

As our example shows, risk is clearly reduced via an offsetting transaction in the futures market. However, is risk totally eliminated? Risk would be totally eliminated if losses in the cash markets were *exactly* offset by gains in the futures markets and vice versa. This is unlikely to happen because mortgages and Treasury bonds are not identical instruments. First, mortgages may have different maturities than Treasury bonds. Second, Treasury bonds have a different payment stream than do mortgages. Principal is paid only at maturity on T-bonds, whereas principal is paid every month on mortgages. Because mortgages pay principal continuously, these instruments have a shorter *effective* time to maturity than do Treasury bonds of equal maturity.[10] Third, mortgages have default risk whereas Treasury bonds do not. The term structure applicable to instruments with default risk may change even when the term structure for risk-free assets remains constant. Fourth, mortgages may be paid off early and hence have a shorter *expected maturity* than Treasury bonds of equal maturity.

Because mortgages and Treasury bonds are not identical instruments, they are not identically affected by interest rates. If Treasury bonds are less volatile than mortgages, financial consultants may advise Mr. Cooke to write more than 10 T-bond futures

---

[10]Alternatively, we can say that mortgages have shorter duration than do Treasury bonds of equal maturity. A precise definition of duration is provided later in this chapter.

contracts. Conversely, if these bonds are more volatile, the consultant may state that fewer than 10 futures contracts are needed. An optimal ratio of futures to mortgages will reduce risk as much as possible. However, because the price movements of mortgages and Treasury bonds are not *perfectly correlated,* Mr. Cooke's hedging strategy cannot eliminate all risk.

The preceding strategy is called a *short hedge* because Mr. Cooke sells futures contracts to reduce risk. Though it involves an interest rate futures contract, this short hedge is analogous to short hedges in agricultural and metallurgical futures contracts. We argued at the beginning of this chapter that individuals and firms institute short hedges to offset inventory price fluctuations. Once Mr. Cooke makes a contract to lend money to borrowers, the mortgages effectively become his inventory. He writes a futures contract to offset the price fluctuations of his inventory.

We now consider an example where a mortgage banker institutes a long hedge.

EXAMPLE 25.4

Short versus Long Hedging   Margaret Boswell is another mortgage banker. Her firm faces problems similar to those facing Mr. Cooke's firm. However, she tackles the problems through the use of **advance commitments,** a strategy that is the opposite of Mr. Cooke's. That is, she promises to deliver loans to a financial institution *before* she lines up borrowers. On March 1 her firm agreed to sell mortgages to No-State Insurance Co. The agreement specifies that she must turn over 12 percent coupon mortgages with a face value of $1 million to No-State by May 1. No-State is buying the mortgages at par, implying that they will pay Ms. Boswell $1 million on May 1. As of March 1, Ms. Boswell had not signed up any borrowers. Over the next two months, she will seek out individuals who want mortgages beginning May 1.

As with Mr. Cooke, changing interest rates will affect Ms. Boswell. If interest rates fall before she signs up a borrower, the borrower will demand a premium on a 12 percent coupon loan. That is, the borrower will receive more than par on May 1.[11] Because Ms. Boswell receives par from the insurance company, she must make up the difference.

Conversely, if interest rates rise, a 12 percent coupon loan will be made at a discount. That is, the borrower will receive less than par on May 1. Because Ms. Boswell receives par from the insurance company, the difference is pure profit to her.

The details are provided in Table 25.5. As did Mr. Cooke, Ms. Boswell finds the risk burdensome. Therefore, she offsets her advance commitment with a transaction in the futures markets. Because she *loses* in the cash market when interest rates fall, she *buys* futures contracts to reduce the risk. When interest rates fall, the value of her futures contracts increases. The gain in the futures market offsets the loss in the cash market. Conversely, she gains in the cash markets when interest rates rise. The value of her futures contracts decreases when interest rates rise, offsetting her gain.

We call this a *long hedge* because Ms. Boswell offsets risk in the cash markets by buying a futures contract. Though it involves an interest rate futures contract, this long hedge is analogous to long hedges in agricultural and metallurgical futures contracts. We argued at the beginning of this chapter that individuals and firms institute long hedges when their finished goods are to be sold at a fixed price. Once Ms. Boswell makes the advance commitment with No-State Insurance, she has fixed her sales price. She buys a futures contract to offset the price fluctuation of her raw materials—that is, her mortgages.

(continued)

---

[11] Alternatively, the mortgage would still be at par if a coupon rate below 12 percent were used. However, this is not done because the insurance company wants to buy only 12 percent mortgages.

Table 25.5 Illustration of Advance Commitment for Margaret Boswell, Mortgage Banker

	Cash Markets	Futures Markets
March 1	Mortgage banker makes a forward contract (advance commitment) to deliver $1 million of mortgages to No-State Insurance. The insurance company will pay par to Ms. Boswell for the loans on May 1. The borrowers are to receive their funding from the mortgage banker on May 1. The mortgages are to be 12 percent coupon loans for 20 years.	Mortgage banker buys 10 June Treasury bond futures contracts.
April 15	Mortgage banker signs up borrowers for 12 percent coupon, 20-year mortgages. She promises that the borrowers will receive funds on May 1.	Mortgage banker sells all futures contracts.
If interest rates rise:	Mortgage banker issues mortgages to borrowers at a discount. Mortgage banker *gains* because she receives par from the insurance company.	Futures contracts are sold at a price below purchase price, resulting in *loss*. Mortgage banker's loss in futures market offsets gain in cash market.
If interest rates fall:	Loans to borrowers are issued at a premium. Mortgage banker *loses* because she receives only par from insurance company.	Futures contracts are sold at a price above purchase price, resulting in *gain*. Mortgage banker's gain in futures market offsets loss in cash market.

25.6 Duration Hedging

The last section concerned the risk of interest rate changes. We now want to explore this risk in a more precise manner. In particular we want to show that the concept of duration is a prime determinant of interest rate risk. We begin by considering the effect of interest rate movements on bond prices.

THE CASE OF ZERO COUPON BONDS

Imagine a world where the interest rate is 10 percent across all maturities. A one-year pure discount bond pays $110 at maturity. A five-year pure discount bond pays $161.05 at maturity. Both of these bonds are worth $100, as given by the following:[12]

Value of One-Year Pure Discount Bond:

$$\$100 = \frac{\$110}{1.10}$$

Value of Five-Year Pure Discount Bond:

$$\$100 = \frac{\$161.05}{(1.10)^5}$$

---

[12]Alternatively, we could have chosen bonds that pay $100 at maturity. Their values would be $90.91 (= $100/1.10) and $62.09 [= $100/(1.10)^5]. However, our comparisons to come are made easier if both have the same initial price.

Table 25.6

Value of a Pure Discount Bond as a Function of Interest Rate

Interest Rate	One-Year Pure Discount Bond	Five-Year Pure Discount Bond
8%	$101.85 = \dfrac{\$110}{1.08}$	$109.61 = \dfrac{\$161.05}{(1.08)^5}$
10%	$100.00 = \dfrac{\$110}{1.10}$	$100.00 = \dfrac{\$161.05}{(1.10)^5}$
12%	\$ 98.21 $= \dfrac{\$110}{1.12}$	\$ 91.38 $= \dfrac{\$161.05}{(1.12)^5}$

For a given interest rate change, a five-year pure discount bond fluctuates more in price than does a one-year pure discount bond.

Which bond will change more when interest rates move? To find out, we calculate the value of these bonds when interest rates are either 8 or 12 percent. The results are presented in Table 25.6. As can be seen, the five-year bond has greater price swings than does the one-year bond. That is, both bonds are worth $100 when interest rates are 10 percent. The five-year bond is worth more than the one-year bond when interest rates are 8 percent and worth less than the one-year bond when interest rates are 12 percent. We state that the five-year bond is subject to more price volatility. This point, which was mentioned in passing in an earlier section of the chapter, is not difficult to understand. The interest rate term in the denominator, $1 + R$, is taken to the fifth power for a five-year bond and only to the first power for the one-year bond. Thus, the effect of a changing interest rate is magnified for the five-year bond. The general rule is this:

The percentage price changes of long-term pure discount bonds are greater than the percentage price changes of short-term pure discount bonds.

THE CASE OF TWO BONDS WITH THE SAME MATURITY BUT WITH DIFFERENT COUPONS

The previous example concerned pure discount bonds of different maturities. We now want to see the effect of different coupons on price volatility. To abstract from the effect of differing maturities, we consider two bonds with the same maturity but with different coupons.

Consider a five-year, 10 percent coupon bond and a five-year, 1 percent coupon bond. When interest rates are 10 percent, the bonds are priced like this:

Value of Five-Year, 10 Percent Coupon Bond:

$$\$100 = \frac{\$10}{1.10} + \frac{\$10}{(1.10)^2} + \frac{\$10}{(1.10)^3} + \frac{\$10}{(1.10)^4} + \frac{\$110}{(1.10)^5}$$

Value of Five-Year, 1 Percent Coupon Bond:

$$\$65.88 = \frac{\$1}{1.10} + \frac{\$1}{(1.10)^2} + \frac{\$1}{(1.10)^3} + \frac{\$1}{(1.10)^4} + \frac{\$101}{(1.10)^5}$$

Which bond will change more in *percentage terms* if interest rates change?[13] To find out, we first calculate the value of these bonds when interest rates are either 8 or 12 percent. The results are presented in Table 25.7. As we would expect, the 10 percent coupon bond always sells for more than the 1 percent coupon bond. Also, as we would expect, each bond is worth more when the interest rate is 8 percent than when the interest rate is 12 percent.

---

[13]The bonds are at different prices initially. Thus, we are concerned with percentage price changes, not absolute price changes.

Table 25.7
Value of Coupon Bonds at Different Interest Rates

Interest Rate	Five-Year, 10% Coupon Bond
8%	$107.99 = $\dfrac{\$10}{1.08} + \dfrac{\$10}{(1.08)^2} + \dfrac{\$10}{(1.08)^3} + \dfrac{\$10}{(\$1.08)^4} + \dfrac{\$110}{(1.08)^5}$
10%	$100.00 = $\dfrac{\$10}{1.10} + \dfrac{\$10}{(1.10)^2} + \dfrac{\$10}{(1.10)^3} + \dfrac{\$10}{(1.10)^4} + \dfrac{\$110}{(1.10)^5}$
12%	$\ \ 92.79 = $\dfrac{\$10}{1.12} + \dfrac{\$10}{(1.12)^2} + \dfrac{\$10}{(1.12)^3} + \dfrac{\$10}{(1.12)^4} + \dfrac{\$110}{(1.12)^5}$

Interest Rate	Five-Year, 1% Coupon Bond
8%	$72.05 = $\dfrac{\$1}{1.08} + \dfrac{\$1}{(1.08)^2} + \dfrac{\$1}{(1.08)^3} + \dfrac{\$1}{(1.08)^4} + \dfrac{\$101}{(1.08)^5}$
10%	$65.88 = $\dfrac{\$1}{1.10} + \dfrac{\$1}{(1.10)^2} + \dfrac{\$1}{(1.10)^3} + \dfrac{\$1}{(1.10)^4} + \dfrac{\$101}{(1.10)^5}$
12%	$60.35 = $\dfrac{\$1}{1.12} + \dfrac{\$1}{(1.12)^2} + \dfrac{\$1}{(1.12)^3} + \dfrac{\$1}{(1.12)^4} + \dfrac{\$101}{(1.12)^5}$

We calculate percentage price changes for both bonds as the interest rate changes from 10 to 8 percent and from 10 to 12 percent:

	10% Coupon Bond	1% Coupon Bond
Interest rate changes from 10% to 8%:	$7.99\% = \dfrac{\$107.99}{\$100} - 1$	$9.37\% = \dfrac{\$72.05}{\$65.88} - 1$
Interest rate changes from 10% to 12%:	$-7.21\% = \dfrac{\$92.79}{\$100} - 1$	$-8.39\% = \dfrac{\$60.35}{\$65.88} - 1$

As we can see, the 1 percent coupon bond has a greater percentage price increase than does the 10 percent coupon bond when the interest rate falls. Similarly, the 1 percent coupon bond has a greater percentage price decrease than does the 10 percent coupon bond when the interest rate rises. Thus, we say that the percentage price changes on the 1 percent coupon bond are greater than are the percentage price changes on the 10 percent coupon bond.

DURATION

The question, of course, is "Why?" We can answer this question only after we have explored a concept called **duration**. We begin by noticing that any coupon bond is actually a combination of pure discount bonds. For example, the five-year, 10 percent coupon bond is made up of five pure discount bonds:

1. A pure discount bond paying $10 at the end of year 1.
2. A pure discount bond paying $10 at the end of year 2.
3. A pure discount bond paying $10 at the end of year 3.
4. A pure discount bond paying $10 at the end of year 4.
5. A pure discount bond paying $110 at the end of year 5.

Similarly, the five-year, 1 percent coupon bond is made up of five pure discount bonds. Because the price volatility of a pure discount bond is determined by its maturity, we would like to determine the average maturity of the five pure discount bonds that make up a five-year coupon bond. This leads us to the concept of duration.

We calculate average maturity in three steps. For the 10 percent coupon bond, we have these:

1. *Calculate present value of each payment.* We do this as follows:

Year	Payment	Present Value of Payment by Discounting at 10%
1	$ 10	$ 9.091
2	10	8.264
3	10	7.513
4	10	6.830
5	110	68.302
		$100.00

2. *Express the present value of each payment in relative terms.* We calculate the relative value of a single payment as the ratio of the present value of the payment to the value of the bond. The value of the bond is $100. We obtain these values:

Year	Payment	Present Value of Payment	Relative Value = $\dfrac{\text{Present Value of Payment}}{\text{Value of Bond}}$
1	$ 10	$ 9.091	$9.091/$100 = .09091
2	10	8.264	.08264
3	10	7.513	.07513
4	10	6.830	.06830
5	110	68.302	.68302
		$100.00	1.0

The bulk of the relative value, 68.302 percent, occurs at Year 5 because the principal is paid back at that time.

3. *Weight the maturity of each payment by its relative value:*

$$4.1699 \text{ years} = 1 \text{ year} \times .09091 + 2 \text{ years} \times .08264 + 3 \text{ years} \times .07513$$
$$+ 4 \text{ years} \times .06830 + 5 \text{ years} \times .68302$$

There are many ways to calculate the average maturity of a bond. We have calculated it by weighting the maturity of each payment by the payment's present value. We find that the *effective* maturity of the bond is 4.1699 years. *Duration* is a commonly used word for effective maturity. Thus, the bond's duration is 4.1699 years. Note that duration is expressed in units of time.[14]

---

[14]The mathematical formula for duration is:

$$\text{Duration} = \frac{\text{PV}(C_1)1 + \text{PV}(C_2)2 + \cdots + \text{PV}(C_T)T}{\text{PV}}$$

and

$$\text{PV} = \text{PV}(C_1) + \text{PV}(C_2) + \cdots + \text{PV}(C_T)$$
$$\text{PV}(C_T) = \frac{C_T}{(1 + R)^T}$$

where C_T is the cash to be received in time T, and R is the current discount rate.

Also, note that in our numerical example, we discounted each payment by the interest rate of 10 percent. This was done because we wanted to calculate the duration of the bond before a change in the interest rate occurred. After a change in the rate to, say, 8 or 12 percent, all three of our steps would need to reflect the new interest rate. In other words, the duration of a bond is a function of the current interest rate.

Because the five-year, 10 percent coupon bond has a duration of 4.1699 years, its percentage price fluctuations should be the same as those of a zero coupon bond with a duration of 4.1699 years.[15] It turns out that the five-year, 1 percent coupon bond has a duration of 4.8740 years. Because the 1 percent coupon bond has a higher duration than the 10 percent bond, the 1 percent coupon bond should be subject to greater price fluctuations. This is exactly what we found earlier. In general we say the following:

The percentage price changes of a bond with high duration are greater than the percentage price changes of a bond with low duration.

A final question: Why *does* the 1 percent bond have a greater duration than the 10 percent bond, even though they both have the same five-year maturity? As mentioned earlier, duration is an average of the maturity of the bond's cash flows weighted by the present value of each cash flow. The 1 percent coupon bond receives only $1 in each of the first four years. Thus, the weights applied to Years 1 through 4 in the duration formula will be low. Conversely, the 10 percent coupon bond receives $10 in each of the first four years. The weights applied to Years 1 through 4 in the duration formula will be higher.

MATCHING LIABILITIES WITH ASSETS

Earlier in this chapter, we argued that firms can hedge risk by trading in futures. Because some firms are subject to interest rate risk, we showed how they can hedge with interest rate futures contracts. Firms may also hedge interest rate risk by matching liabilities with assets. This ability to hedge follows from our discussion of duration.

EXAMPLE 25.5

Using Duration The Physical Bank of New York has the following market value balance sheet:

PHYSICAL BANK OF NEW YORK
Market Value Balance Sheet

	Market Value	Duration
Assets		
Overnight money	$ 35 million	0
Accounts receivable–backed loans	500 million	3 months
Inventory loans	275 million	6 months
Industrial loans	40 million	2 years
Mortgages	150 million	14.8 years
	$1,000 million	
Liabilities and Owners' Equity		
Checking and savings accounts	$ 400 million	0
Certificates of deposit	300 million	1 year
Long-term financing	200 million	10 years
Equity	100 million	
	$1,000 million	

(continued)

[15]Actually, this relationship exactly holds only in the case of a one-time shift in a flat yield curve, where the change in the spot rate is identical for all maturities.

The bank has $1,000 million of assets and $900 million of liabilities. Its equity is the difference between the two: $100 million (=$1,000 million − $900 million). Both the market value and the duration of each individual item are provided in the balance sheet. Both overnight money and checking and savings accounts have a duration of zero. This is because the interest paid on these instruments adjusts immediately to changing interest rates in the economy.

The bank's managers think that interest rates are likely to move quickly in the coming months. Because they do not know the direction of the movement, they are worried that their bank is vulnerable to changing rates. They call in a consultant, James Charest, to determine a hedging strategy.

Mr. Charest first calculates the duration of the assets and the duration of the liabilities:[16]

Duration of Assets

$$2.56 \text{ years} = 0 \text{ years} \times \frac{\$35 \text{ million}}{\$1,000 \text{ million}} + \frac{1}{4} \text{ year} \times \frac{\$500 \text{ million}}{\$1,000 \text{ million}} \tag{25.4}$$

$$+ \frac{1}{2} \text{ year} \times \frac{\$275 \text{ million}}{\$1,000 \text{ million}} + 2 \text{ years} \times \frac{\$40 \text{ million}}{\$1,000 \text{ million}}$$

$$+ 14.8 \text{ years} \times \frac{\$150 \text{ million}}{\$1,000 \text{ million}}$$

Duration of Liabilities

$$2.56 = 0 \text{ years} \times \frac{\$400 \text{ million}}{\$900 \text{ million}} + 1 \text{ year} \times \frac{\$300 \text{ million}}{\$900 \text{ million}} + 10 \text{ years} \times \frac{\$200 \text{ million}}{\$900 \text{ million}} \tag{25.5}$$

The duration of the assets, 2.56 years, equals the duration of the liabilities. Because of this, Mr. Charest argues that the firm is immune to interest rate risk.

Just to be on the safe side, the bank calls in a second consultant, Gail Ellert. Ms. Ellert argues that it is incorrect to simply match durations because assets total $1,000 million and liabilities total only $900 million. If both assets and liabilities have the same duration, the price change on a *dollar* of assets should be equal to the price change on a dollar of liabilities. However, the *total* price change will be greater for assets than for liabilities because there are more assets than liabilities in this bank. The firm will be immune to interest rate risk only when the duration of the liabilities is greater than the duration of the assets. Ms. Ellert states that the following relationship must hold if the bank is to be **immunized**—that is, immune to interest rate risk:

$$\begin{matrix} \text{Duration of} \\ \text{assets} \end{matrix} \times \begin{matrix} \text{Market value of} \\ \text{assets} \end{matrix} = \begin{matrix} \text{Duration of} \\ \text{liabilities} \end{matrix} \times \begin{matrix} \text{Market value} \\ \text{of liabilities} \end{matrix} \tag{25.6}$$

She says that the bank should not *equate* the duration of the liabilities with the duration of the assets. Rather, using Equation 25.6, the bank should match the duration of the liabilities to the duration of the assets. She suggests two ways to achieve this match.

1. *Increase the duration of the liabilities without changing the duration of the assets.* Ms. Ellert argues that the duration of the liabilities could be increased to:

$$\text{Duration of assets} \times \frac{\text{Market value of assets}}{\text{Market value of liabilities}} = 2.56 \text{ years} \times \frac{\$1,000 \text{ million}}{\$900 \text{ million}}$$

$$= 2.84 \text{ years}$$

Equation 25.6 then becomes:

$$2.56 \times \$1 \text{ billion} = 2.84 \times \$900 \text{ million}$$

(continued)

---

[16]Note that the duration of a group of items is an average of the duration of the individual items weighted by the market value of each item. This is a simplifying step that greatly increases duration's practicality.

2. *Decrease the duration of the assets without changing the duration of the liabilities.* Alternatively, Ms. Ellert points out that the duration of the assets could be decreased to:

$$\text{Duration of liabilities} \times \frac{\text{Market value of liabilities}}{\text{Market value of assets}} = 2.56 \text{ years} \times \frac{\$900 \text{ million}}{\$1,000 \text{ million}}$$

$$= 2.30 \text{ years}$$

Equation 25.6 then becomes:

$$2.30 \times \$1 \text{ billion} = 2.56 \times \$900 \text{ million}$$

Though we agree with Ms. Ellert's analysis, the bank's current mismatch was small anyway. Huge mismatches have occurred for real-world financial institutions, particularly savings and loans. S&Ls have frequently invested large portions of their assets in mortgages. The durations of these mortgages would clearly be above 10 years. Many of the funds available for mortgage lending were financed by short-term credit, especially savings accounts. As we mentioned, the duration of such instruments is quite small. A thrift institution in this situation faces a large amount of interest rate risk because any increase in interest rates would greatly reduce the value of the mortgages. Because an interest rate rise would reduce the value of the liabilities only slightly, the equity of the firm would fall. As interest rates rose over much of the 1960s and 1970s, many S&Ls found that the market value of their equity approached zero.[17]

Duration and the accompanying immunization strategies are useful in other areas of finance. For example, many firms establish pension funds to meet obligations to retirees. If the assets of a pension fund are invested in bonds and other fixed-income securities, the duration of the assets can be computed. Similarly, the firm views the obligations to retirees as analogous to interest payments on debt. The duration of these liabilities can be calculated as well. The manager of a pension fund would commonly choose pension assets so that the duration of the assets is matched with the duration of the liabilities. In this way, changing interest rates would not affect the net worth of the pension fund.

Life insurance companies receiving premiums today are legally obligated to provide death benefits in the future. Actuaries view these future benefits as analogous to interest and principal payments of fixed-income securities. The duration of these expected benefits can be calculated. Insurance firms frequently invest in bonds where the duration of the bonds is matched to the duration of the future death benefits.

The business of a leasing company is quite simple. The firm issues debt to purchase assets, which are then leased. The lease payments have a duration, as does the debt. Leasing companies frequently structure debt financing so that the duration of the debt matches the duration of the lease. If a firm did not do this, the market value of its equity could be eliminated by a quick change in interest rates.

25.7 Swaps Contracts

Swaps are close cousins to forwards and futures contracts. Swaps are arrangements between two counterparties to exchange cash flows over time. There is enormous flexibility in the forms that swaps can take, but the three basic types are **interest rate swaps**,

---

[17]Actually, the market value of the equity could easily be negative in this example. However, S&Ls in the real world have an asset not shown on our market value balance sheet: The ability to generate new, profitable loans. This should increase the market value of a thrift above the market value of its outstanding loans less its existing debt.

currency swaps, and **credit default swaps**. Often these are combined when interest received in one currency is swapped for interest in another currency.

INTEREST RATE SWAPS

Like other derivatives, swaps are tools that firms can use to easily change their risk exposures and their balance sheets.[18] Consider a firm that has borrowed and carried on its books an obligation to repay a 10-year loan for $100 million of principal with a 9 percent coupon rate paid annually. Ignoring the possibility of calling the loan, the firm expects to have to pay coupons of $9 million every year for 10 years and a balloon payment of $100 million at the end of the 10 years. Suppose, though, that the firm is uncomfortable with having this large fixed obligation on its books. Perhaps the firm is in a cyclical business where its revenues vary and could conceivably fall to a point where it would be difficult to make the debt payment.

Suppose, too, that the firm earns a lot of its revenue from financing the purchase of its products. Typically, for example, a manufacturer might help its customers finance their purchase of its products through a leasing or credit subsidiary. Usually these loans are for relatively short periods and are financed at some premium over the prevailing short-term rate of interest. This puts the firm in the position of having revenues that move up and down with interest rates while its costs are relatively fixed.

What the firm would really prefer is to have a floating-rate loan rather than a fixed-rate loan. That way, when interest rates rise, the firm would have to pay more on the loan, but it would be making more on its product financing. An interest rate swap is ideal in this situation.

Of course, the firm could also just go into the capital markets and borrow $100 million at a variable interest rate and then use the proceeds to retire its outstanding fixed-rate loan. Although this is possible, it is generally quite expensive, requiring underwriting a new loan and the repurchase of the existing loan. The ease of entering a swap is its inherent advantage.

This particular swap would be one that exchanged its fixed obligation for an agreement to pay a floating rate. Every year it would agree to pay a coupon based on whatever the prevailing interest rate was at the time in exchange for an agreement from a counterparty to pay the firm's fixed coupon.

A common reference point for floating-rate commitments is called LIBOR. LIBOR stands for the London Interbank Offered Rate, and it is the rate that most international banks charge one another for dollar-denominated loans in the London market. LIBOR is commonly used as the reference rate for a floating-rate commitment, and, depending on the creditworthiness of the borrower, the rate can vary from LIBOR to LIBOR plus one point (or more) over LIBOR.

If we assume that our firm has a credit rating that requires it to pay LIBOR plus 50 basis points, then in a swap it would be exchanging its fixed 9 percent obligation for the obligation to pay whatever the prevailing LIBOR rate is plus 50 basis points. Table 25.8 displays how the cash flows on this swap would work. In the table, we have assumed that LIBOR starts at 8 percent and rises for three years to 11 percent and then drops to 7 percent. As the table shows, the firm would owe a coupon of 8.5% × $100 million = $8.5 million in Year 1, $9.5 million in Year 2, $10.5 million in Year 3, and $11.5 million in Year 4. The precipitous drop to 7 percent lowers the annual payments to $7.5 million thereafter. In return, the firm receives the fixed payment of $9 million each year. Actually,

---

[18]Under current accounting rules, most derivatives do not usually show up on firms' balance sheets because they do not have a historical cost (i.e., the amount a dealer would pay on the initial transaction day).

Table 25.8 Fixed for Floating Swap: Cash Flows (in $ millions)

Year	Coupons									
	1	2	3	4	5	6	7	8	9	10
A. Swap										
Fixed obligation	9	9	9	9	9	9	9	9	9	9
LIBOR floating	−8.5	−9.5	−10.5	−11.5	−7.5	−7.5	−7.5	−7.5	−7.5	−7.5
B. Original loan										
Fixed obligation	−9	−9	−9	−9	−9	−9	−9	−9	−9	109
Net effect	−8.5	−9.5	10.5	11.5	7.5	7.5	7.5	7.5	7.5	−107.5

rather than swapping the full payments, the cash flows would be netted. Because the firm is paying variable and receiving fixed—which it uses to pay its lender—in the first year, for example, the firm owes $8.5 million and is owed by its counterparty, who is paying fixed, $9 million. Hence, net, the firm would receive a payment of $.5 million. Because the firm has to pay its lender $9 million but gets a net payment from the swap of $.5 million, it really pays out only the difference, or $8.5 million. In each year, then, the firm would effectively pay only LIBOR plus 50 basis points.

Notice, too, that the entire transaction can be carried out without any need to change the terms of the original loan. In effect, by swapping, the firm has found a counterparty that is willing to pay its fixed obligation in return for the firm paying a floating obligation.

CURRENCY SWAPS

FX stands for foreign exchange, and currency swaps are sometimes called FX swaps. Currency swaps are swaps of obligations to pay cash flows in one currency for obligations to pay in another currency.

Currency swaps arise as a natural vehicle for hedging risk in international trade. For example, suppose a U.S. firm sells a broad range of its product line in the German market. Every year the firm can count on receiving revenue from Germany in euros. We will study international finance later in this book, but for now we can just observe that because exchange rates fluctuate, this subjects the firm to considerable risk.

If the firm produces its products in the United States and exports them to Germany, then the firm has to pay its workers and its suppliers in dollars. But it is receiving some of its revenues in euros. The exchange rate between dollars and euros changes over time. As the euro rises in value, the German revenues are worth more dollars, but as it falls they are worth fewer dollars. Suppose the firm can count on selling 100 million euros of goods each year in Germany. If the exchange rate is 2 euros for each dollar, then the firm will receive $50 million. But if the exchange rate were to rise to 3 euros for each dollar, the firm would receive only $33.333 million for its 100 million euros. Naturally the firm would like to protect itself against these currency swings.

To do so the firm can enter a currency swap. We will learn more about exactly what the terms of such a swap might be, but for now we can assume that the swap is for five years at a fixed term of 100 million euros for $50 million each year. Now, no matter what happens to the exchange rate between euros and dollars over the next five years, as long as the firm makes 100 million euros each year from the sale of its products, it will swap this for $50 million each year.

CREDIT DEFAULT SWAPS

A credit default swap (CDS) is like insurance against value loss due to a firm defaulting on a bond. As in other swaps, a person involved in a CDS is called a counterparty. There are always two counterparties in a CDS. In a typical CDS, Counterparty 1 pays Counterparty 2 a periodic payment. In exchange, Counterparty 2 agrees to pay par for a particular bond issue if default occurs. Counterparty 1 is called the protection buyer and Counterparty 2 is called the protection seller. The periodic payment is called the CDS spread.

For example, suppose the Mizuno Company wants to borrow $200 million from United Pacific Bank and is willing to pay a spread of 50 basis points (bps) over LIBOR. United Pacific Bank is interested but cannot justify such a large loan to one company and the attendant credit risks. United Pacific can agree to the loan and buy protection for a 40–basis-point CDS spread. Midland Insurance Company agrees to be the counterparty to United Pacific and, in case the Mizuno Company defaults, will pay the par amount. In exchange, Midland Insurance will receive $800,000 per year (=40 bps × $200 million) for a specified term, say, 5 years.

In this simple example, the terms of the CDS are clear and precise. In practice, there is no organized exchange or template. Each counterparty will attempt to negotiate the best possible agreement.

Swap Pricing   We have not addressed the question of how the market sets prices for swaps—either interest rate swaps, credit default swaps, or currency swaps. In the fixed-for-floating example and in the currency swap, we just quoted some terms. We won't go into great detail on exactly how it is done, but we can stress the most important points.

Swaps, like forwards and futures, are essentially zero-sum transactions, which is to say that in both cases the market sets prices at a fair level, and neither party has any substantial bargain or loss at the moment the deal is struck. For example, in the currency swap, the swap rate is some average of the market expectation of what the exchange rate will be over the life of the swap. In the interest rate swap, the rates are set as the fair floating and fixed rates for the creditor, taking into account the creditworthiness of the counterparties. We can actually price swaps fairly once we know how to price forward contracts. In our interest rate swap example, the firm swapped LIBOR plus 50 basis points for a 9 percent fixed rate, all on a principal amount of $100 million. This is equivalent to a series of forward contracts extending over the life of the swap. In Year 1, for example, having made the swap, the firm is in the same position that it would be if it had sold a forward contract entitling the buyer to receive LIBOR plus 50 basis points on $100 million in return for a fixed payment of $9 million (9 percent of $100 million). Similarly, the currency swap can also be viewed as a series of forward contracts. In a credit default swap, the swap rate is a market expectation of the default rate for a particular bond over a particular time.

EXOTICS

Up to now we have dealt with the meat and potatoes of the derivatives markets: Swaps, options, forwards, and futures. **Exotics** are the complicated blends of these that often produce surprising results for buyers.

One of the more interesting types of exotics is called an *inverse floater.* In our fixed-for-floating swap, the floating payments fluctuated with LIBOR. An inverse floater is one that fluctuates inversely with some rate such as LIBOR. For example, the floater might pay an interest rate of 20 percent minus LIBOR. If LIBOR is 9 percent, then the inverse pays 11 percent, and if LIBOR rises to 12 percent, the payments on the inverse would fall to 8 percent. Clearly, the purchaser of an inverse profits from the inverse if interest rates fall.

Both floaters and inverse floaters have supercharged versions called *superfloaters* and *superinverses* that fluctuate more than one for one with movements in interest rates. As an example of a superinverse floater, consider a floater that pays an interest rate of 30 percent minus *twice* LIBOR. When LIBOR is 10 percent, the inverse pays:

$$30\% - 2 \times 10\% = 30\% - 20\% = 10\%$$

And if LIBOR falls by 3 percent to 7 percent, then the return on the inverse rises by 6 percent from 10 percent to 16 percent:

$$30\% - 2 \times 7\% = 30\% - 14\% = 16\%$$

Sometimes derivatives are combined with options to bound the impact of interest rates. The most important of these instruments are called *caps* and *floors*. A cap is so named because it puts an upper limit or a cap on the impact of a rise in interest rates. A floor, conversely, provides a floor below which the interest rate impact is insulated.

To illustrate the impact of these, consider a firm that is borrowing short term and is concerned that interest rates might rise. For example, using LIBOR as the reference interest rate, the firm might purchase a 7 percent cap. The cap pays the firm the difference between LIBOR and 7 percent on some principal amount, provided that LIBOR is greater than 7 percent. As long as LIBOR is below 7 percent, the holder of the cap receives no payments.

By purchasing the cap, the firm has assured itself that even if interest rates rise above 7 percent, it will not have to pay more than a 7 percent rate. Suppose that interest rates rise to 9 percent. While the firm is borrowing short term and paying 9 percent rates, this is offset by the cap, which is paying the firm the difference between 9 percent and the 7 percent limit. For any LIBOR rate above 7 percent, the firm receives the difference between LIBOR and 7 percent, and, as a consequence, it has capped its cost of borrowing at 7 percent.

On the other side, consider a financial firm that is in the business of lending short term and is concerned that interest rates—and consequently its revenues—might fall. The firm could purchase a floor to protect itself from such declines. If the limit on the floor is 7 percent, then the floor pays the difference between 7 percent and LIBOR whenever LIBOR is below 7 percent, and nothing if LIBOR is above 7 percent. Thus, if interest rates were to fall to, say, 5 percent while the firm is receiving only 5 percent from its lending activities, the floor is paying it the difference between 7 percent and 5 percent, or an additional 2 percent. By purchasing the floor, the firm has assured itself of receiving no less than 7 percent from the combination of the floor and its lending activities.

We have only scratched the surface of what is available in the world of derivatives. Derivatives are designed to meet marketplace needs, and the only binding limitation is the human imagination. Nowhere should the buyer's warning *caveat emptor* be taken more seriously than in the derivatives markets, and this is especially true for the exotics. If swaps are the meat and potatoes of the derivatives markets, then caps and floors are the meat and potatoes of the exotics. As we have seen, they have obvious value as hedging instruments. But much attention has been focused on truly exotic derivatives, some of which appear to have arisen more as the residuals that were left over from more straightforward deals. We won't examine these in any detail, but suffice it to say that some of these are so volatile and unpredictable that market participants have dubbed them "toxic waste."

25.8 Actual Use of Derivatives

Because derivatives do not usually appear in financial statements, it is much more difficult to observe the use of derivatives by firms compared to, say, bank debt. Much of our knowledge of corporate derivative use comes from academic surveys. Most surveys report

Table 25.9
Derivative Usage:
Survey Results

Percent of Companies Using Derivatives	
2010	71%
2009	79

In Which Asset Classes Do You Use Derivatives?

	2010	2009
Interest rates	65%	68%
Currencies	62	58
Credit	13	13
Energy	19	13
Commodities	23	22
Equities	13	9

Do You Expect Your Use of Derivatives to Change?

	2010		2009	
	Increase	Decrease	Increase	Decrease
Interest rates	19%	15%	13%	20%
Currencies	20	8	31	6
Credit	4	4	2	13
Energy	11	7	5	9
Commodities	16	6	12	10
Equities	6	7	7	6

Do You Use an Integrated Risk Management Strategy or Do You Hedge Transactions or Specific Currency Exposures?

	2010	2009
Hedge total risk	31.8%	21.1%
Hedge transactions	34.1	47.4
Hedge specific currency exposures	34.1	31.6

SOURCE: Adapted from *Treasury & Risk* (March 2010 and March 2011).

that the use of derivatives appears to vary widely among large publicly traded firms. Large firms are far more likely to use derivatives than are small firms. Table 25.9 shows that for firms that use derivatives, foreign currency and interest rate derivatives are the most frequently used.

The prevailing view is that derivatives can be very helpful in reducing the variability of firm cash flows, which, in turn, reduces the various costs associated with financial distress. Therefore, it is somewhat puzzling that large firms use derivatives more often than small firms because large firms tend to have less cash flow variability than small firms. Also, some surveys report that firms occasionally use derivatives when they want to speculate about future prices and not just to hedge risks.

However, most of the evidence is consistent with the theory that derivatives are most frequently used by firms where financial distress costs are high and access to the capital markets is constrained.

Summary and Conclusions

1. Firms hedge to reduce risk. This chapter showed a number of hedging strategies.

2. A forward contract is an agreement by two parties to sell an item for cash at a later date. The price is set at the time the agreement is signed. However, cash changes hands on the date of delivery. Forward contracts are generally not traded on organized exchanges.

3. Futures contracts are also agreements for future delivery. They have certain advantages, such as liquidity, that forward contracts do not. An unusual feature of futures contracts is the mark-to-the-market convention. If the price of a futures contract falls on a particular day, every buyer of the contract must pay money to the clearinghouse. Every seller of the contract receives money from the clearinghouse. Everything is reversed if the price rises. The mark-to-the-market convention prevents defaults on futures contracts.

4. We divided hedges into two types: Short hedges and long hedges. An individual or firm that sells a futures contract to reduce risk is instituting a short hedge. Short hedges are generally appropriate for holders of inventory. An individual or firm that buys a futures contract to reduce risk is instituting a long hedge. Long hedges are typically used by firms with contracts to sell finished goods at a fixed price.

5. An interest rate futures contract employs a bond as the deliverable instrument. Because of their popularity, we worked with Treasury bond futures contracts. We showed that Treasury bond futures contracts can be priced using the same type of net present value analysis that is used to price Treasury bonds themselves.

6. Many firms face interest rate risk. They can reduce this risk by hedging with interest rate futures contracts. As with other commodities, a short hedge involves the sale of a futures contract. Firms that are committed to buying mortgages or other bonds are likely to institute short hedges. A long hedge involves the purchase of a futures contract. Firms that have agreed to sell mortgages or other bonds at a fixed price are likely to institute long hedges.

7. Duration measures the average maturity of all the cash flows in a bond. Bonds with high duration have high price variability. Firms frequently try to match the duration of their assets with the duration of their liabilities.

8. Swaps are agreements to exchange cash flows over time. The first major type is an interest rate swap in which one pattern of coupon payments, say, fixed payments, is exchanged for another, say, coupons that float with LIBOR. The second major type is a currency swap, in which an agreement is struck to swap payments denominated in one currency for payments in another currency over time.

Concept Questions

1. **Hedging Strategies** If a firm is selling futures contracts on lumber as a hedging strategy, what must be true about the firm's exposure to lumber prices?

2. **Hedging Strategies** If a firm is buying call options on pork belly futures as a hedging strategy, what must be true about the firm's exposure to pork belly prices?

3. **Forwards and Futures** What is the difference between a forward contract and a futures contract? Why do you think that futures contracts are much more common? Are there any circumstances under which you might prefer to use forwards instead of futures? Explain.

4. **Hedging Commodities** Bubbling Crude Corporation, a large Texas oil producer, would like to hedge against adverse movements in the price of oil because this is the firm's primary source of revenue. What should the firm do? Provide at least two reasons why it probably will not be possible to achieve a completely flat risk profile with respect to oil prices.

5. **Sources of Risk**   A company produces an energy-intensive product and uses natural gas as the energy source. The competition primarily uses oil. Explain why this company is exposed to fluctuations in both oil and natural gas prices.

6. **Hedging Commodities**   If a textile manufacturer wanted to hedge against adverse movements in cotton prices, it could buy cotton futures contracts or buy call options on cotton futures contracts. What would be the pros and cons of the two approaches?

7. **Option**   Explain why a put option on a bond is conceptually the same as a call option on interest rates.

8. **Hedging Interest Rates**   A company has a large bond issue maturing in one year. When it matures, the company will float a new issue. Current interest rates are attractive, and the company is concerned that rates next year will be higher. What are some hedging strategies that the company might use in this case?

9. **Swaps**   Explain why a swap is effectively a series of forward contracts. Suppose a firm enters a swap agreement with a swap dealer. Describe the nature of the default risk faced by both parties.

10. **Swaps**   Suppose a firm enters a fixed for floating interest rate swap with a swap dealer. Describe the cash flows that will occur as a result of the swap.

11. **Transaction versus Economic Exposure**   What is the difference between transactions and economic exposure? Which can be hedged more easily? Why?

12. **Hedging Exchange Rate Risk**   If a U.S. company exports its goods to Japan, how would it use a futures contract on Japanese yen to hedge its exchange rate risk? Would it buy or sell yen futures? Does the way the exchange rate is quoted in the futures contract matter?

13. **Hedging Strategies**   For the following scenarios, describe a hedging strategy using futures contracts that might be considered.

   a. A public utility is concerned about rising costs.
   b. A candy manufacturer is concerned about rising costs.
   c. A corn farmer fears that this year's harvest will be at record high levels across the country.
   d. A manufacturer of photographic film is concerned about rising costs.
   e. A natural gas producer believes there will be excess supply in the market this year.
   f. A bank derives all its income from long-term, fixed-rate residential mortgages.
   g. A stock mutual fund invests in large, blue-chip stocks and is concerned about a decline in the stock market.
   h. A U.S. importer of Swiss army knives will pay for its order in six months in Swiss francs.
   i. A U.S. exporter of construction equipment has agreed to sell some cranes to a German construction firm. The U.S. firm will be paid in euros in three months.

14. **Swaps**   In May 2004, Sysco Corporation, the distributor of food and food-related products (not to be confused with Cisco Systems), announced it had signed an interest rate swap. The interest rate swap effectively converted the company's $100 million, 4.6 percent interest rate bonds for a variable rate payment, which would be the six-month LIBOR minus .52 percent. Why would Sysco use a swap agreement? In other words, why didn't Sysco just go ahead and issue floating-rate bonds because the net effect of issuing fixed-rate bonds and then doing a swap is to create a variable rate bond?

15. **Hedging Strategies**   William Santiago is interested in entering the import/export business. During a recent visit with his financial advisers, he said, "If we play the game right, this is the safest business in the world. By hedging all of our transactions in the foreign exchange futures market, we can eliminate all of our risk." Do you agree with Mr. Santiago's assessment of hedging? Why or why not?

16.   **Hedging Strategies**   Kevin Nomura is a Japanese student who is planning a one-year stay in the United States. He expects to arrive in the United States in eight months. He is worried about depreciation of the yen relative to the dollar over the next eight months and wishes to take a position in foreign exchange futures to hedge this risk. What should Mr. Nomura's hedging position be? Assume the exchange rate between Japanese and U.S. currencies is quoted as yen/dollar.

Questions and Problems

BASIC
(Questions 1–8)

1.   **Futures Quotes**   Refer to Table 25.2 in the text to answer this question. Suppose you purchase a March 2015 cocoa futures contract on January 8, 2015, at the last price of the day. What will your profit or loss be if cocoa prices turn out to be $3,027 per metric ton at expiration?

2.   **Futures Quotes**   Refer to Table 25.2 in the text to answer this question. Suppose you sell five March 2015 silver futures contracts on January 8, 2015, at the last price of the day. What will your profit or loss be if silver prices turn out to be $16.61 per ounce at expiration? What if silver prices are $16.43 per ounce at expiration?

3.   **Put and Call Payoffs**   Suppose a financial manager buys call options on 50,000 barrels of oil with an exercise price of $65 per barrel. She simultaneously sells a put option on 50,000 barrels of oil with the same exercise price of $65 per barrel. Consider her gains and losses if oil prices are $60, $62, $65, $68, and $70. What do you notice about the payoff profile?

4.   **Marking to Market**   You are long 10 gold futures contracts, established at an initial settle price of $1,210 per ounce, where each contract represents 100 ounces. Over the subsequent four trading days, gold settles at $1,217, $1,213, $1,206, and $1,212, respectively. Compute the cash flows at the end of each trading day, and compute your total profit or loss at the end of the trading period.

5.   **Marking to Market**   You are short 25 gasoline futures contracts, established at an initial settle price of $1.36 per gallon, where each contract represents 42,000 gallons. Over the subsequent four trading days, gasoline settles at $1.33, $1.37, $1.39, and $1.44, respectively. Compute the cash flows at the end of each trading day, and compute your total profit or loss at the end of the trading period.

6.   **Duration**   What is the duration of a bond with three years to maturity and a coupon of 6.1 percent paid annually if the bond sells at par?

7.   **Duration**   What is the duration of a bond with four years to maturity and a coupon of 8.6 percent paid annually if the bond sells at par?

8.   **Duration**   Blue Steel Community Bank has the following market value balance sheet:

Asset or Liability	Market Value (in $ millions)	Duration (in years)
Federal funds deposits	$ 31	0
Accounts receivable	540	.20
Short-term loans	320	.65
Long-term loans	98	5.25
Mortgages	435	12.85
Checking and savings deposits	615	0
Certificates of deposit	390	1.60
Long-term financing	285	9.80
Equity	134	N/A

a. What is the duration of the assets?
b. What is the duration of the liabilities?
c. Is the bank immune to interest rate risk?

INTERMEDIATE
(Questions 9–15)

9. **Hedging with Futures** Refer to Table 25.2 in the text to answer this question. Suppose today is January 8, 2015, and your firm produces breakfast cereal and needs 140,000 bushels of corn in March 2015 for an upcoming promotion. You would like to lock in your costs today because you are concerned that corn prices might go up between now and March.

a. How could you use corn futures contracts to hedge your risk exposure? What price would you effectively be locking in based on the closing price of the day?
b. Suppose corn prices are $4.09 per bushel in March. What is the profit or loss on your futures position? Explain how your futures position has eliminated your exposure to price risk in the corn market.

10. **Interest Rate Swaps** ABC Company and XYZ Company need to raise funds to pay for capital improvements at their manufacturing plants. ABC Company is a well-established firm with an excellent credit rating in the debt market; it can borrow funds either at 11 percent fixed rate or at LIBOR + 1 percent floating rate. XYZ Company is a fledgling start-up firm without a strong credit history. It can borrow funds either at 10 percent fixed rate or at LIBOR + 3 percent floating rate.

a. Is there an opportunity here for ABC and XYZ to benefit by means of an interest rate swap?
b. Suppose you've just been hired at a bank that acts as a dealer in the swaps market, and your boss has shown you the borrowing rate information for your clients, ABC and XYZ. Describe how you could bring these two companies together in an interest rate swap that would make both firms better off while netting your bank a 2 percent profit.

11. **Duration** Ted and Alice Hansel have a son who will begin college 10 years from today. School expenses of $30,000 will need to be paid at the beginning of each of the four years that their son plans to attend college. What is the duration of this liability to the couple if they can borrow and lend at the market interest rate of 7.6 percent?

12. **Duration** What is the duration of a bond with two years to maturity if the bond has a coupon rate of 6.4 percent paid semiannually, and the market interest rate is 4.9 percent?

13. **Forward Pricing** The forward price (F) of a contract on an asset with neither carrying costs nor convenience yield is the current spot price of the asset (S_0) multiplied by 1, plus the appropriate interest rate between the initiation of the contract and the delivery date of the asset. Derive this relationship by comparing the cash flows that result from the following two strategies:

Strategy 1: Buy silver on the spot market today and hold it for one year. (*Hint*: Do not use any of your own money to purchase the silver.)
Strategy 2: Take a long position in a silver forward contract for delivery in one year. Assume that silver is an asset with neither carrying costs nor convenience yield.

14. **Forward Pricing** You enter into a forward contract to buy a 10-year, zero coupon bond that will be issued in one year. The face value of the bond is $1,000, and the 1-year and 11-year spot interest rates are 5 percent and 7 percent, respectively.

a. What is the forward price of your contract?
b. Suppose both the 1-year and 11-year spot rates unexpectedly shift downward by 2 percent. What is the new price of the forward contract?

15. **Forward Pricing**   This morning you agreed to buy a one-year Treasury bond in six months. The bond has a face value of $1,000. Use the spot interest rates listed here to answer the following questions:

Time	EAR
6 months	3.61%
12 months	4.05
18 months	4.73
24 months	5.42

   a. What is the forward price of this contract?
   b. Suppose shortly after you purchased the forward contract all rates increased by 30 basis points. For example, the six-month rate increased from 3.61 percent to 3.91 percent. What is the price of a forward contract otherwise identical to yours given these changes?

CHALLENGE
(Question 16)

16. **Financial Engineering**   Suppose there were call options and forward contracts available on coal, but no put options. Show how a financial engineer could synthesize a put option using the available contracts. What does your answer tell you about the general relationship between puts, calls, and forwards?

Mini Case

WILLIAMSON MORTGAGE, INC.

Jennifer Williamson recently received her MBA and has decided to enter the mortgage brokerage business. Rather than work for someone else, she has decided to open her own shop. Her cousin Jerry has approached her about a mortgage for a house he is building. The house will be completed in three months, and he will need the mortgage at that time. Jerry wants a 25-year, fixed-rate mortgage in the amount of $500,000 with monthly payments.

Jennifer has agreed to lend Jerry the money in three months at the current market rate of 5.5 percent. Because Jennifer is just starting out, she does not have $500,000 available for the loan, so she approaches Max Cabell, the president of MC Insurance Corporation, about purchasing the mortgage from her in three months. Max has agreed to purchase the mortgage in three months, but he is unwilling to set a price on the mortgage. Instead, he has agreed in writing to purchase the mortgage at the market rate in three months. There are Treasury bond futures contracts available for delivery in three months. A Treasury bond contract is for $100,000 in face value of Treasury bonds.

1. What is the monthly mortgage payment on Jerry's mortgage?
2. What is the most significant risk Jennifer faces in this deal?
3. How can Jennifer hedge this risk?
4. Suppose that in the next three months the market rate of interest rises to 6.2 percent.
   a. How much will Max be willing to pay for the mortgage?
   b. What will happen to the value of Treasury bond futures contracts? Will the long or short position increase in value?
5. Suppose that in the next three months the market rate of interest falls to 4.6 percent.
   a. How much will Max be willing to pay for the mortgage?
   b. What will happen to the value of Treasury bond futures contracts? Will the long or short position increase in value?
6. Are there any possible risks Jennifer faces in using Treasury bond futures contracts to hedge her interest rate risk?

26

PART VII: SHORT-TERM FINANCE

Short-Term Finance and Planning

With gasoline approaching $2 per gallon in December 2014, sales of the Chevy Volt short-circuited. Because of the sales slump, a Volt sat on a dealer's lot for an average of 40 days. This wait was in sharp contrast to inventory levels seen when gas prices reached $4 a gallon. At that time, there were only 100 Volts in inventory in the entire country. Of course, other automobile models had higher inventory levels. Several months earlier, the Cadillac ELR, GM's Tesla competitor, had a 725-day supply of inventory, or almost two years' worth of sales! As this chapter explores, the length of time goods are carried in inventory until they are sold is an important element of short-term financial management, and companies such as those in the automobile industry pay close attention to it.

To this point, we have described many of the decisions of long-term finance, such as those of capital budgeting, dividend policy, and financial structure. In this chapter, we begin to discuss short-term finance. Short-term finance is primarily concerned with the analysis of decisions that affect current assets and current liabilities.

Frequently, the term *net working capital* is associated with short-term financial decision making. As we have described in previous chapters, net working capital is the difference between current assets and current liabilities. Often, short-term financial management is called *working capital management*. These terms mean the same thing.

There is no universally accepted definition of short-term finance. The most important difference between short-term and long-term finance is in the timing of cash flows. Short-term financial decisions typically involve cash inflows and outflows that occur within a year. For example, short-term financial decisions are involved when a firm orders raw materials, pays in cash, and anticipates selling finished goods in one year for cash. In contrast, long-term financial decisions are involved when a firm purchases a special machine that will reduce operating costs over, say, the next five years.

What types of questions fall under the general heading of short-term finance? To name a few:

1. What is a reasonable level of cash to keep on hand (in a bank) to pay bills?
2. How much should the firm borrow in the short term?
3. How much credit should be extended to customers?

This chapter introduces the basic elements of short-term financial decisions. First, we discuss the short-term operating activities of the firm. We then identify some alternative

Interested in a career in short-term finance? Visit **www.treasury -management.com**

short-term financial policies. Finally, we outline the basic elements in a short-term financial plan and describe short-term financing instruments.

26.1 Tracing Cash and Net Working Capital

In this section, we examine the components of cash and net working capital as they change from one year to the next. We have already discussed various aspects of this subject in Chapters 2 and 3. We briefly review some of that discussion as it relates to short-term financing decisions. Our goal is to describe the short-term operating activities of the firm and their impact on cash and net working capital.

To begin, recall that *current assets* are cash and other assets that are expected to convert to cash within the year. Current assets are presented on the balance sheet in order of their accounting liquidity—the ease with which they can be converted to cash and the time it takes to convert them. Four of the most important items found in the current asset section of a balance sheet are cash and cash equivalents, marketable securities, accounts receivable, and inventories.

Analogous to their investment in current assets, firms use several kinds of short-term debt called *current liabilities*. Current liabilities are obligations that are expected to require cash payment within one year (or within the operating period if it is longer than one year). Three major items found as current liabilities are accounts payable, expenses payable (including accrued wages and taxes), and notes payable.

Because we want to focus on changes in cash, we start off by defining cash in terms of the other elements of the balance sheet. This lets us isolate the cash account and explore the impact on cash from the firm's operating and financing decisions. The basic balance sheet identity can be written as:

$$\text{Net working capital} + \text{Fixed assets} = \text{Long-term debt} + \text{Equity} \qquad \textbf{(26.1)}$$

Net working capital is cash plus other current assets, less current liabilities; that is:

$$\text{Net working capital} = (\text{Cash} + \text{Other current assets}) - \text{Current liabilities} \qquad \textbf{(26.2)}$$

If we substitute this for net working capital in the basic balance sheet identity and rearrange things a bit, we see that cash is:

$$\text{Cash} = \text{Long-term debt} + \text{Equity} + \text{Current liabilities} \\ - \text{Current assets other than cash} - \text{Fixed assets} \qquad \textbf{(26.3)}$$

This tells us in general terms that some activities naturally increase cash and some activities decrease it. We can list these various activities, along with an example of each, as follows:

Activities That Increase Cash

Increasing long-term debt (borrowing over the long term)

Increasing equity (selling some stock)

Increasing current liabilities (getting a 90-day loan)

Decreasing current assets other than cash (selling some inventory for cash)

Decreasing fixed assets (selling some property)

Activities That Decrease Cash

Decreasing long-term debt (paying off a long-term debt)

Decreasing equity (repurchasing some stock)

Decreasing current liabilities (paying off a 90-day loan)

Increasing current assets other than cash (buying some inventory for cash)

Increasing fixed assets (buying some property)

Notice that our two lists are exact opposites. For example, floating a long-term bond issue increases cash (at least until the money is spent). Paying off a long-term bond issue decreases cash.

Activities that increase cash are called *sources of cash*. Those activities that decrease cash are called *uses of cash*. Looking back at our list, we see that sources of cash always involve increasing a liability (or equity) account or decreasing an asset account. This makes sense because increasing a liability means that we have raised money by borrowing it or by selling an ownership interest in the firm. A decrease in an asset means that we have sold or otherwise liquidated an asset. In either case there is a cash inflow.

Uses of cash are just the reverse. A use of cash involves decreasing a liability by paying it off, perhaps, or increasing assets by purchasing something. Both of these activities require that the firm spend some cash.

EXAMPLE 26.1

Sources and Uses   Here is a quick check of your understanding of sources and uses: If accounts payable go up by $100, does this indicate a source or a use? What if accounts receivable go up by $100?

Accounts payable are what we owe our suppliers. This is a short-term debt. If it rises by $100, we have effectively borrowed the money, which is a *source* of cash. Receivables are what our customers owe to us, so an increase of $100 in accounts receivable means that we have loaned the money; this is a *use* of cash.

26.2 The Operating Cycle and the Cash Cycle

The primary concern in short-term finance is the firm's short-run operating and financing activities. For a typical manufacturing firm, these short-run activities might consist of the following sequence of events and decisions:

Event	Decision
1. Buying raw materials	1. How much inventory to order
2. Paying cash	2. Whether to borrow or draw down cash balances
3. Manufacturing the product	3. What choice of production technology to use
4. Selling the product	4. Whether credit should be extended to a particular customer
5. Collecting cash	5. How to collect

These activities create patterns of cash inflows and cash outflows. These cash flows are both unsynchronized and uncertain. They are unsynchronized because, for example, the payment of cash for raw materials does not happen at the same time as the receipt of cash from selling the product. They are uncertain because future sales and costs cannot be precisely predicted.

DEFINING THE OPERATING AND CASH CYCLES

We can start with a simple case. One day, call it Day 0, we purchase $1,000 worth of inventory on credit. We pay the bill 30 days later, and, after 30 more days, someone buys the $1,000 in inventory for $1,400. Our buyer does not actually pay for another 45 days. We can summarize these events chronologically as follows:

Day	Activity	Cash Effect
0	Acquire inventory	None
30	Pay for inventory	−$1,000
60	Sell inventory on credit	None
105	Collect on sale	+$1,400

The Operating Cycle There are several things to notice in our example. First, the entire cycle, from the time we acquire some inventory to the time we collect the cash, takes 105 days. This is called the **operating cycle**.

As we illustrate, the operating cycle is the length of time it takes to acquire inventory, sell it, and collect for it. This cycle has two distinct components. The first part is the time it takes to acquire and sell the inventory. This period, a 60-day span in our example, is called the **inventory period**. The second part is the time it takes to collect on the sale, 45 days in our example. This is called the **accounts receivable period**.

Based on our definitions, the operating cycle is obviously just the sum of the inventory and accounts receivable periods:

$$\text{Operating cycle} = \text{Inventory period} + \text{Accounts receivable period} \quad \textbf{(26.4)}$$
$$105 \text{ days} = 60 \text{ days} + 45 \text{ days}$$

What the operating cycle describes is how a product moves through the current asset accounts. The product begins life as inventory, it is converted to a receivable when it is sold, and it is finally converted to cash when we collect from the sale. Notice that, at each step, the asset is moving closer to cash.

The Cash Cycle The second thing to notice is that the cash flows and other events that occur are not synchronized. For example, we don't actually pay for the inventory until 30 days after we acquire it. The intervening 30-day period is called the **accounts payable period**. Next, we spend cash on Day 30, but we don't collect until Day 105. Somehow, we have to arrange to finance the $1,000 for $105 - 30 = 75$ days. This period is called the **cash cycle**.

The cash cycle, therefore, is the number of days that pass before we collect the cash from a sale, measured from when we actually pay for the inventory. Notice that, based on our definitions, the cash cycle is the difference between the operating cycle and the accounts payable period:

$$\text{Cash cycle} = \text{Operating cycle} - \text{Accounts payable period} \quad \textbf{(26.5)}$$
$$75 \text{ days} = 105 \text{ days} - 30 \text{ days}$$

Figure 26.1

Cash Flow Time Line and the Short-Term Operating Activities of a Typical Manufacturing Firm

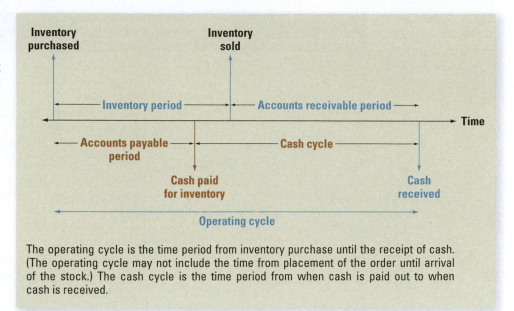

The operating cycle is the time period from inventory purchase until the receipt of cash. (The operating cycle may not include the time from placement of the order until arrival of the stock.) The cash cycle is the time period from when cash is paid out to when cash is received.

Learn more about outsourcing accounts management at **www.businessdebts.com** and **www.opiglobal.com**.

Figure 26.1 depicts the short-term operating activities and cash flows of a typical manufacturing firm by way of a cash flow time line. As shown, the **cash flow time line** presents the operating cycle and the cash cycle in graphical form. In Figure 26.1, the need for short-term financial management is suggested by the gap between the cash inflows and the cash outflows. This is related to the lengths of the operating cycle and the accounts payable period.

The gap between short-term inflows and outflows can be filled either by borrowing or by holding a liquidity reserve in the form of cash or marketable securities. Alternatively, the gap can be shortened by changing the inventory, receivable, and payable periods. These are all managerial options that we discuss in the following sections.

Internet-based bookseller and retailer Amazon.com provides an interesting example of the importance of managing the cash cycle. In January 2015, the market value of Amazon .com was higher than (in fact, more than 100 times as much as) that of Barnes & Noble, king of the brick-and-mortar bookstores.

How could Amazon.com be worth so much more? There are multiple reasons, but short-term management is one factor. During 2014, Amazon turned over its inventory about 7.99 times per year, 2.5 times faster than Barnes & Noble; so, its inventory period was dramatically shorter. Even more striking, Amazon charges a customer's credit card when it ships an order, and it usually gets paid by the credit card firm within a day. This means Amazon has a *negative* cash cycle! In fact, during 2014, Amazon's cash cycle was a negative 73 days. Every sale therefore generates a cash inflow that can be put to work immediately.

Amazon is not the only company with a negative cash cycle. Consider aircraft manufacturer Boeing Company. During 2014, Boeing had an inventory period of 222 days and a receivables period of 28 days, so its operating cycle was a lengthy 250 days Boeing's cash cycle must be fairly long, right? Wrong. Boeing had a payables period of 262 days, so its cash cycle was a negative 11 days (the missing day is due to rounding)!

Title of Manager	Duties Related to Short-Term Financial Management	Assets/Liabilities Influenced
Cash manager	Collection, concentration, disbursement; short-term investments; short-term borrowing; banking relations	Cash, marketable securities, short-term loans
Credit manager	Monitoring and control of accounts receivable; credit policy decisions	Accounts receivable
Marketing manager	Credit policy decisions	Accounts receivable
Purchasing manager	Decisions on purchases, suppliers; may negotiate payment terms	Inventory, accounts payable
Production manager	Setting of production schedules and materials requirements	Inventory, accounts payable
Payables manager	Decisions on payment policies and on whether to take discounts	Accounts payable
Controller	Accounting information on cash flows; reconciliation of accounts payable; application of payments to accounts receivable	Accounts receivable, accounts payable

THE OPERATING CYCLE AND THE FIRM'S ORGANIZATION CHART

Before we examine the operating and cash cycles in greater detail, it is useful for us to take a look at the people involved in managing a firm's current assets and liabilities. As Table 26.1 illustrates, short-term financial management in a large corporation involves a number of different financial and nonfinancial managers. Examining Table 26.1, we see that selling on credit involves at least three different entities: The credit manager, the marketing manager, and the controller. Of these three, only two are responsible to the vice president of finance (the marketing function is usually associated with the vice president of marketing). Thus, there is the potential for conflict, particularly if different managers concentrate on only part of the picture. For example, if marketing is trying to land a new account, it may seek more liberal credit terms as an inducement. However, this may increase the firm's investment in receivables or its exposure to bad-debt risk, and conflict can result.

CALCULATING THE OPERATING AND CASH CYCLES

In our example, the lengths of time that made up the different periods were obvious. If all we have is financial statement information, we will have to do a little more work. We illustrate these calculations next.

To begin, we need to determine various things such as how long it takes, on average, to sell inventory and how long it takes, on average, to collect receivables. We start by gathering some balance sheet information such as the following (in thousands):

Item	Beginning	Ending	Average
Inventory	$2,000	$3,000	$2,500
Accounts receivable	1,600	2,000	1,800
Accounts payable	750	1,000	875

Also, from the most recent income statement, we might have the following figures (in thousands):

Net sales	$11,500
Cost of goods sold	8,200

We now need to calculate some financial ratios. We discussed these in some detail in Chapter 3; here, we just define them and use them as needed.

The Operating Cycle First of all, we need the inventory period. We spent $8.2 million on inventory (our cost of goods sold). Our average inventory was $2.5 million. We thus turned our inventory over $8.2/2.5 times during the year:[1]

$$\text{Inventory turnover} = \frac{\text{Cost of goods sold}}{\text{Average inventory}}$$

$$= \frac{\$8.2 \text{ million}}{\$2.5 \text{ million}} = 3.28 \text{ times}$$

Loosely speaking, this tells us that we bought and sold off our inventory 3.28 times during the year. This means that, on average, we held our inventory for:

$$\text{Inventory period} = \frac{365 \text{ days}}{\text{Inventory turnover}}$$

$$= \frac{365}{3.28} = 111.3 \text{ days}$$

So, the inventory period is about 111 days. On average, in other words, inventory sat for about 111 days before it was sold.[2]

Similarly, receivables averaged $1.8 million, and sales were $11.5 million. Assuming that all sales were credit sales, the receivables turnover is:[3]

$$\text{Receivables turnover} = \frac{\text{Credit sales}}{\text{Average accounts receivable}}$$

$$= \frac{\$11.5 \text{ million}}{\$1.8 \text{ million}} = 6.4 \text{ times}$$

If we turn over our receivables 6.4 times a year, then the receivables period is:

$$\text{Receivables period} = \frac{365 \text{ days}}{\text{Receivables turnover}}$$

$$= \frac{365}{6.4} = 57 \text{ days}$$

The receivables period is also called the *days' sales in receivables,* or the *average collection period.* Whatever it is called, it tells us that our customers took an average of 57 days to pay.

The operating cycle is the sum of the inventory and receivables periods:

$$\text{Operating cycle} = \text{Inventory period} + \text{Accounts receivable period}$$
$$= 111 \text{ days} + 57 \text{ days} = 168 \text{ days}$$

---

[1]Notice that in calculating inventory turnover here, we use the *average* inventory instead of using the ending inventory as we did in Chapter 3. Both approaches are used in the real world. To gain some practice using average figures, we will stick with this approach in calculating various ratios throughout this chapter.

[2]This measure is conceptually identical to the days' sales in inventory figure we discussed in Chapter 3.

[3]If less than 100 percent of our sales were credit sales, then we would just need a little more information, namely, credit sales for the year. See Chapter 3 for more discussion of this measure.

This tells us that, on average, 168 days elapse between the time we acquire inventory and, having sold it, collect for the sale.

The Cash Cycle   We now need the payables period. From the information given earlier, we know that average payables were $875,000 and cost of goods sold was $8.2 million. Our payables turnover is:

$$\text{Payables turnover} = \frac{\text{Cost of goods sold}}{\text{Average payables}}$$

$$= \frac{\$8.2 \text{ million}}{\$.875 \text{ million}} = 9.4 \text{ times}$$

The payables period is:

$$\text{Payables period} = \frac{365 \text{ days}}{\text{Payables turnover}}$$

$$= \frac{365}{9.4} = 39 \text{ days}$$

Thus, we took an average of 39 days to pay our bills.

Finally, the cash cycle is the difference between the operating cycle and the payables period:

$$\text{Cash cycle} = \text{Operating cycle} - \text{Accounts payable period}$$

$$= 168 \text{ days} - 39 \text{ days} = 129 \text{ days}$$

So, on average, there is a 129-day delay between the time we pay for merchandise and the time we collect on the sale.

EXAMPLE 26.2

The Operating and Cash Cycles   You have collected the following information for the Slowpay Company:

Item	Beginning	Ending
Inventory	$5,000	$7,000
Accounts receivable	1,600	2,400
Accounts payable	2,700	4,800

Credit sales for the year just ended were $50,000, and cost of goods sold was $30,000. How long does it take Slowpay to collect on its receivables? How long does merchandise stay around before it is sold? How long does Slowpay take to pay its bills?

We can first calculate the three turnover ratios:

$$\text{Inventory turnover} = \$30,000/6,000 = 5 \text{ times}$$

$$\text{Receivables turnover} = \$50,000/2,000 = 25 \text{ times}$$

$$\text{Payables turnover} = \$30,000/3,750 = 8 \text{ times}$$

We use these to get the various periods:

$$\text{Inventory period} = 365/5 = 73 \text{ days}$$

$$\text{Receivables period} = 365/25 = 14.6 \text{ days}$$

$$\text{Payables period} = 365/8 = 45.6 \text{ days}$$

All told, Slowpay collects on a sale in 14.6 days, inventory sits around for 73 days, and bills get paid after about 46 days. The operating cycle here is the sum of the inventory and receivables periods: $73 + 14.6 = 87.6$ days. The cash cycle is the difference between the operating cycle and the payables period: $87.6 - 45.6 = 42$ days.

INTERPRETING THE CASH CYCLE

Our examples show that the cash cycle depends on the inventory, receivables, and payables periods. The cash cycle increases as the inventory and receivables periods get longer. It decreases if the company is able to defer payment of payables and thereby lengthen the payables period.

Unlike Amazon.com, most firms have a positive cash cycle, and they thus require financing for inventories and receivables. The longer the cash cycle, the more financing is required. Also, changes in the firm's cash cycle are often monitored as an early warning measure. A lengthening cycle can indicate that the firm is having trouble moving inventory or collecting on its receivables. Such problems can be masked, at least partially, by an increased payables cycle, so both cycles should be monitored.

The link between the firm's cash cycle and its profitability can be easily seen by recalling that one of the basic determinants of profitability and growth for a firm is its total asset turnover, which is defined as Sales/Total assets. In Chapter 3, we saw that the higher this ratio is, the greater are the firm's accounting return on assets, ROA, and return on equity, ROE. Thus, all other things being the same, the shorter the cash cycle is, the lower is the firm's investment in inventories and receivables. As a result, the firm's total assets are lower, and total turnover is higher.

A LOOK AT OPERATING AND CASH CYCLES

In 2014, *CFO* magazine published its survey of working capital for various industries. The results of this survey highlight the marked differences in cash and operating cycles across industries. The table below shows four different industries and the median operating and cash cycles for each. Of these, the Food products has the lowest operating cycles. Auto components has the shortest cash cycle.

	Receivables Period (days)	Inventory Period (days)	Operating Cycle (days)	Payables Period (days)	Cash Cycle (days)
Auto components	52	30	82	46	26
Biotechnology	58	27	85	13	72
Food products	24	38	62	24	38
Multiline retail	6	67	73	25	48

Compared to the food products companies, the multiline retailers have slightly longer operating cycles. However, we can see that there is a major difference since the retail industry has a very short receivables period and a much longer inventory period. The inventory period is necessary in this industry so that the shelves are kept stocked, but since customers tend to pay in cash, firms in this industry have little or no receivables.

We've seen that operating and cash cycles can vary quite a bit across industries, but these cycles also can be different for companies within the same industry. Below you will find the operating and cash cycles for selected computer and consumer electronics companies. As you can see, there are differences. Apple and Dell have the best operating and cash cycles in the industry. In fact, Dell has long been known as a leader in current asset management. Both NCR and Diebold have much longer inventory periods.

	Receivables Period (days)	Inventory Period (days)	Operating Cycle (days)	Payables Period (days)	Cash Cycle (days)
Dell	42	9	51	74	−23
Apple	28	4	32	48	−16
Diebold	57	48	105	27	78
NCR	77	47	125	40	85

By examining all parts of the cash and conversion cycles, you can see when a company is performing well, or poorly, as the case may be. Looking at the cash cycles for NCR and Diebold, they appear fairly similar. However, NCR has longer receivables and payables periods to accomplish this.

When you look at the operating and cash cycles, consider that each is really a financial ratio. As with any financial ratio, firm and industry characteristics will have an effect, so take care in your interpretation. For example, in looking at NCR and Diebold, we note both companies' seemingly long inventory period. Is that a bad thing? Maybe not. These companies have a different business model compared to Apple and Dell, and, as a result, aren't really comparable when it comes to inventory levels.

26.3 Some Aspects of Short-Term Financial Policy

The policy that a firm adopts for short-term finance will be composed of at least two elements:

1. *The size of the firm's investment in current assets*: This is usually measured relative to the firm's level of total operating revenues. A flexible or accommodative short-term financial policy would maintain a high ratio of current assets to sales. A restrictive short-term financial policy would entail a low ratio of current assets to sales.

2. *The financing of current assets*: This is measured as the proportion of short-term debt to long-term debt. A restrictive short-term financial policy means a high proportion of short-term debt relative to long-term financing, and a flexible policy means less short-term debt and more long-term debt.

THE SIZE OF THE FIRM'S INVESTMENT IN CURRENT ASSETS

Flexible short-term financial policies include:

1. Keeping large balances of cash and marketable securities.
2. Making large investments in inventory.
3. Granting liberal credit terms, which results in a high level of accounts receivable.

Restrictive short-term financial policies are:

1. Keeping low cash balances and no investment in marketable securities.
2. Making small investments in inventory.
3. Allowing no credit sales and no accounts receivable.

Determining the optimal investment level in short-term assets requires an identification of the different costs of alternative short-term financing policies. The objective is to trade off the costs of restrictive policies against those of the flexible ones to arrive at the best compromise.

Current asset holdings are highest with a flexible short-term financial policy and lowest with a restrictive policy. Thus, flexible short-term financial policies are costly in that they require higher cash outflows to finance cash and marketable securities, inventory, and accounts receivable. However, future cash inflows are highest with a flexible policy. Sales are stimulated by the use of a credit policy that provides liberal financing to customers. A large amount of inventory on hand ("on the shelf") provides a quick delivery service to customers and increases in sales.[4] In addition, the firm can probably charge higher prices for the quick delivery service and the liberal credit terms of flexible policies. A flexible policy also may result in fewer production stoppages because of inventory shortages.[5]

Managing current assets can be thought of as involving a trade-off between costs that rise with the level of investment and costs that fall with the level of investment. Costs that rise with the level of investment in current assets are called **carrying costs**. Costs that fall with increases in the level of investment in current assets are called **shortage costs**.

Carrying costs are generally of two types. First, because the rate of return on current assets is low compared to that of other assets, there is an opportunity cost. Second, there is the cost of maintaining the economic value of the item. For example, the cost of warehousing inventory belongs here.

Shortage costs are incurred when the investment in current assets is low. If a firm runs out of cash, it will be forced to sell marketable securities. If a firm runs out of cash and cannot readily sell marketable securities, it may need to borrow or default on an obligation. (This general situation is called *cash-out*.) If a firm has no inventory (a *stockout*) or if it cannot extend credit to its customers, it will lose customers.

There are two kinds of shortage costs:

1. *Trading, or order, costs*: Order costs are the costs of placing an order for more cash (*brokerage costs*) or more inventory (*production setup costs*).
2. *Costs related to safety reserves*: These are the costs of lost sales, lost customer goodwill, and disruption of production schedules.

Figure 26.2 illustrates the basic nature of carrying costs and shortage costs. The total costs of investing in current assets are determined by adding the carrying costs and the

---

[4]This is true of some types of finished goods.

[5]This is true of inventory of raw materials but not of finished goods.

Determinants of Corporate Liquid Asset Holdings

Firms with High Holdings of Liquid Assets Will Have	Firms with Low Holdings of Liquid Assets Will Have
High-growth opportunities	Low-growth opportunities
High-risk investments	Low-risk investments
Small firms	Large firms
Low-credit firms	High-credit firms

Firms will hold more liquid assets (i.e., cash and marketable securities) to ensure that they can continue investing when cash flow is low relative to positive NPV investment opportunities. Firms that have good access to capital markets will hold less liquid assets.

SOURCE: Tim Opler, Lee Pinkowitz, René Stulz, and Rohan Williamson, "The Determinants and Implications of Corporate Cash Holdings," *Journal of Financial Economics* 52 (1999).

shortage costs. The minimum point on the total cost curve (CA*) reflects the optimal balance of current assets. The curve is generally quite flat at the optimum, and it is difficult, if not impossible, to find the precise optimal balance of shortage and carrying costs. Usually, we are content with a choice near the optimum.

If carrying costs are low or shortage costs are high, the optimal policy calls for substantial current assets. In other words, the optimal policy is a flexible one. This is illustrated in the middle graph of Figure 26.2.

If carrying costs are high or shortage costs are low, the optimal policy is a restrictive one. That is, the optimal policy calls for modest current assets. This is illustrated in the bottom graph of the figure.

Opler, Pinkowitz, Stulz, and Williamson examine the determinants of holdings of cash and marketable securities by publicly traded firms.[6] They find evidence that firms behave according to the static trade-off model described earlier. Their study focuses only on liquid assets (i.e., cash and marketable securities), so that carrying costs are the opportunity costs of holding liquid assets and shortage costs are the risks of not having cash when investment opportunities are good.

ALTERNATIVE FINANCING POLICIES FOR CURRENT ASSETS

In the previous section, we examined the level of investment in current assets. Now we turn to the level of current liabilities, assuming the investment in current assets is optimal.

An Ideal Model   In an ideal economy, short-term assets can always be financed with short-term debt, and long-term assets can be financed with long-term debt and equity. In this economy, net working capital is always zero.

Imagine the simple case of a grain elevator operator. Grain elevator operators buy crops after harvest, store them, and sell them during the year. They have high inventories of grain after the harvest and end with low inventories just before the next harvest.

---

[6]Tim Opler, Lee Pinkowitz, René Stulz, and Rohan Williamson, "The Determinants and Implications of Corporate Cash Holdings," *Journal of Financial Economics* 52 (1999).

Figure 26.2
Carrying Costs and
Shortage Costs

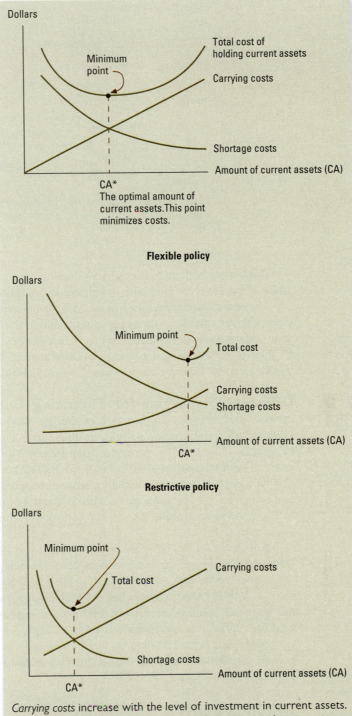

Carrying costs increase with the level of investment in current assets. They include both opportunity costs and the costs of maintaining the asset's economic value. *Shortage costs* decrease with increases in the level of investment in current assets. They include trading costs and the costs of running out of the current asset (e.g., being short on cash).

Figure 26.3
Financing Policy for
an Ideal Economy

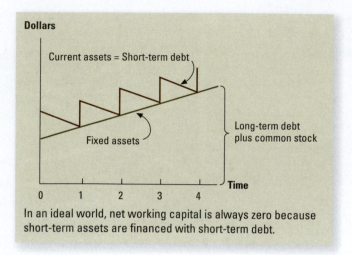

In an ideal world, net working capital is always zero because short-term assets are financed with short-term debt.

Bank loans with maturities of less than one year are used to finance the purchase of grain. These loans are paid with the proceeds from the sale of grain.

The situation is shown in Figure 26.3. Long-term assets are assumed to grow over time, whereas current assets increase at the end of the harvest and then decline during the year. Short-term assets end at zero just before the next harvest. These assets are financed by short-term debt, and long-term assets are financed with long-term debt and equity. Net working capital—current assets minus current liabilities—is always zero.

Different Strategies for Financing Current Assets Current assets cannot be expected to drop to zero in the real world because a long-term rising level of sales will result in some permanent investment in current assets. A growing firm can be thought of as having a permanent requirement for both current assets and long-term assets. This total asset requirement will exhibit balances over time reflecting (1) a secular growth trend, (2) a seasonal variation around the trend, and (3) unpredictable day-to-day and month-to-month fluctuations. This is depicted in Figure 26.4. (We have not tried to show the unpredictable day-to-day and month-to-month variations in the total asset requirement.)

Now let us look at how this asset requirement is financed. First, consider the strategy (Strategy *F* in Figure 26.5) where long-term financing covers more than the total asset requirement, even at seasonal peaks. The firm will have excess cash available for investment in marketable securities when the total asset requirement falls from peaks. Because this approach implies chronic short-term cash surpluses and a large investment in net working capital, it is considered a flexible strategy.

When long-term financing does not cover the total asset requirement, the firm must borrow short term to make up the deficit. This restrictive strategy is labeled Strategy *R* in Figure 26.5.

WHICH IS BEST?

What is the most appropriate amount of short-term borrowing? There is no definitive answer. Several considerations must be included in a proper analysis:

1. *Cash reserves*: The flexible financing strategy implies surplus cash and little short-term borrowing. This strategy reduces the probability that a firm will experience

Figure 26.4
The Total Asset
Requirement
over Time

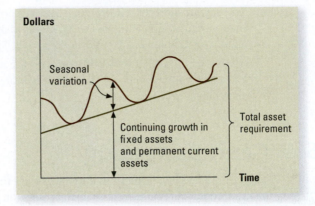

Figure 26.5
Alternative Asset
Financing Policies

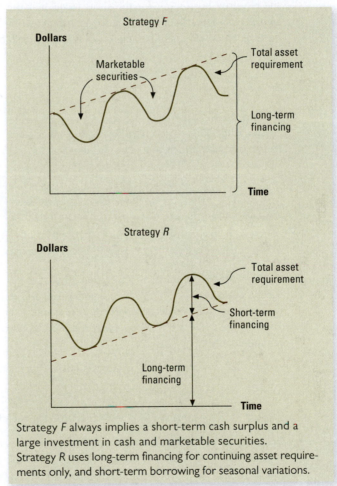

Strategy *F* always implies a short-term cash surplus and a
large investment in cash and marketable securities.
Strategy *R* uses long-term financing for continuing asset requirements only, and short-term borrowing for seasonal variations.

financial distress. Firms may not need to worry as much about meeting recurring
short-term obligations. However, investments in cash and marketable securities are
zero net present value investments at best.

2. *Maturity hedging*: Most firms finance inventories with short-term bank loans and
fixed assets with long-term financing. Firms tend to avoid financing long-lived

assets with short-term borrowing. This type of maturity mismatching would necessitate frequent financing and is inherently risky because short-term interest rates are more volatile than longer rates.

3. *Term structure*: Short-term interest rates are normally lower than long-term interest rates. This implies that, on average, it is more costly to rely on long-term borrowing than on short-term borrowing.

26.4 Cash Budgeting

Excel Master coverage online

The cash budget is a primary tool of short-term financial planning. It allows the financial manager to identify short-term financial needs (and opportunities). It will tell the manager the required borrowing for the short term. It is the way of identifying the cash flow gap on the cash flow time line. The idea of the cash budget is simple: It records estimates of cash receipts and disbursements. We illustrate cash budgeting with the following example of Fun Toys.

EXAMPLE
26.3

Cash Collections   All of Fun Toys' cash inflows come from the sale of toys. Cash budgeting for Fun Toys starts with a sales forecast for the next year by quarter:

	First Quarter	Second Quarter	Third Quarter	Fourth Quarter
Sales ($ in millions)	$100	$200	$150	$100

Fun Toys' fiscal year starts on July 1. Fun Toys' sales are seasonal and are usually very high in the second quarter due to holiday sales. But Fun Toys sells to department stores on credit, and sales do not generate cash immediately. Instead, cash comes later from collections on accounts receivable. Fun Toys has a 90-day collection period, and 100 percent of sales are collected the following quarter. In other words:

$$\text{Collections} = \text{Last quarter's sales}$$

This relationship implies that:

$$\text{Accounts receivable at end of last quarter} = \text{Last quarter's sales} \qquad \textbf{(26.6)}$$

We assume that sales in the fourth quarter of the previous fiscal year were $100 million. From Equation 26.6 we know that accounts receivable at the end of the fourth quarter of the previous fiscal year were $100 million, and collections in the first quarter of the current fiscal year are $100 million.

The first quarter sales of the current fiscal year of $100 million are added to the accounts receivable, but $100 million of collections are subtracted. Therefore, Fun Toys ended the first quarter with accounts receivable of $100 million. The basic relation is:

$$\frac{\text{Ending accounts}}{\text{receivable}} = \frac{\text{Starting accounts}}{\text{receivable}} + \text{Sales} - \text{Collections}$$

Table 26.2 shows cash collections for Fun Toys for the next four quarters. Though collections are the only source of cash here, this need not always be the case. Other sources of cash could include sales of assets, investment income, and long-term financing.

Table 26.2 Sources of Cash ($ in millions)

	First Quarter	Second Quarter	Third Quarter	Fourth Quarter
Sales	$100	$200	$150	$100
Cash collections	100	100	200	150
Starting receivables	100	100	200	150
Ending receivables	100	200	150	100

CASH OUTFLOW

Next, we consider cash disbursements. They can be put into four basic categories, as shown in Table 26.3.

1. *Payments of accounts payable*: These are payments for goods or services, such as raw materials. These payments will generally be made after purchases. Purchases will depend on the sales forecast. In the case of Fun Toys, assume that:

   Payments = Last quarter's purchases

   Purchases = 1/2 next quarter's sales forecast

2. *Wages, taxes, and other expenses*: This category includes all other normal costs of doing business that require actual expenditures. Depreciation, for example, is often thought of as a normal cost of business, but it requires no cash outflow.

3. *Capital expenditures*: These are payments of cash for long-lived assets. Fun Toys plans a major capital expenditure in the fourth quarter.

4. *Long-term financing*: This category includes interest and principal payments on long-term outstanding debt and dividend payments to shareholders.

The total forecast outflow appears in the last line of Table 26.3.

Table 26.3
Disbursement of Cash ($ in millions)

	First Quarter	Second Quarter	Third Quarter	Fourth Quarter
Sales	$100	$200	$150	$100
Purchases	100	75	50	50
Uses of cash				
Payments of accounts payable	50	100	75	50
Wages, taxes, and other expenses	20	40	30	20
Capital expenditures	0	0	0	100
Long-term financing expenses: interest and dividends	10	10	10	10
Total uses of cash	$ 80	$150	$115	$180

Table 26.4
The Cash Balance
($ in millions)

	First Quarter	Second Quarter	Third Quarter	Fourth Quarter
Total cash receipts	$100	$100	$200	$150
Total cash disbursements	80	150	115	180
Net cash flow	20	(50)	85	(30)
Cumulative excess cash balance	20	(30)	55	25
Minimum cash balance	5	5	5	5
Cumulative finance surplus (deficit) requirement	15	(35)	50	20

THE CASH BALANCE

The net cash balance appears in Table 26.4, and a large net cash outflow is forecast in the second quarter. This large outflow is not caused by an inability to earn a profit. Rather, it results from delayed collections on sales. This results in a cumulative cash shortfall of $30 million in the second quarter.

Fun Toys had established a minimum operating cash balance equal to $5 million to facilitate transactions, protect against unexpected contingencies, and maintain compensating balances at its commercial banks. This means that it has a cash shortfall in the second quarter equal to $35 million.

26.5 The Short-Term Financial Plan

Fun Toys has a short-term financing problem. It cannot meet the forecast cash outflows in the second quarter from internal sources. Its financing options include (1) unsecured bank borrowing, (2) secured borrowing, and (3) other sources.

UNSECURED LOANS

The most common way to finance a temporary cash deficit is to arrange a short-term unsecured bank loan. Firms that use short-term bank loans usually ask their bank for either a noncommitted or a committed *line of credit*. A *noncommitted* line of credit is an informal arrangement that allows firms to borrow up to a previously specified limit without going through the normal paperwork. The interest rate on the line of credit is usually set equal to the bank's prime lending rate plus an additional percentage.

Committed lines of credit are formal legal arrangements and usually involve a commitment fee paid by the firm to the bank (usually, the fee is approximately .25 percent of the total committed funds per year). For larger firms, the interest rate is often tied to the London Interbank Offered Rate (LIBOR) or to the bank's cost of funds, rather than the prime rate. Midsized and smaller firms often are required to keep compensating balances in the bank.

Compensating balances are deposits the firm keeps with the bank in low-interest or non-interest-bearing accounts. Compensating balances are commonly on the order of 2 to 5 percent of the amount used. By leaving these funds with the bank without receiving interest, the firm increases the effective interest earned by the bank on the line of credit. For example, if a firm borrowing $100,000 must keep $5,000 as a compensating balance, the firm effectively receives only $95,000. A stated interest rate of 10 percent implies yearly interest payments of $10,000 (=$100,000 × .10). The effective interest rate is 10.53 percent (=$10,000/$95,000).

SECURED LOANS

Banks and other finance companies often require *security* for a loan. Security for short-term loans usually consists of accounts receivable or inventories.

Under **accounts receivable financing**, receivables are either *assigned* or *factored*. Under assignment, the lender not only has a lien on the receivables but also has recourse to the borrower. Factoring involves the sale of accounts receivable. The purchaser, who is called a *factor,* must then collect on the receivables. The factor assumes the full risk of default on bad accounts.

As the name implies, an **inventory loan** uses inventory as collateral. Some common types of inventory loans are:

1. *Blanket inventory lien*: The blanket inventory lien gives the lender a lien against all the borrower's inventories.

2. *Trust receipt*: Under this arrangement, the borrower holds the inventory in trust for the lender. The document acknowledging the loan is called the trust receipt. Proceeds from the sale of inventory are remitted immediately to the lender.

3. *Field warehouse financing*: In field warehouse financing, a public warehouse company supervises the inventory for the lender.

Purchase order financing (or just PO financing) is a popular form of factoring used by small and midsized companies. In a typical scenario, a small business receives a firm order from a customer, but doesn't have sufficient funds to pay the supplier who manufactured the product. With PO financing, the factor pays the supplier. When the sale is completed and the seller is paid, the factor is repaid. A typical interest rate on purchase order factoring is 3.5 percent for the first 30 days, then 1.25 percent every 10 days after, an annual interest rate above 40 percent.

OTHER SOURCES

A variety of other sources of short-term funds are employed by corporations. The most important of these are the issuance of **commercial paper** and financing through **banker's acceptances**. Commercial paper consists of short-term notes issued by large, highly rated firms. Typically, these notes are of short maturity, ranging up to 270 days (beyond that limit the firm must file a registration statement with the SEC). Because the firm issues these directly and because it usually backs the issue with a special bank line of credit, the rate the firm obtains is often significantly below the prime rate the bank would charge it for a direct loan.

A banker's acceptance is an agreement by a bank to pay a sum of money. These agreements typically arise when a seller sends a bill or draft to a customer. The customer's bank *accepts* this bill and notes the acceptance on it, which makes it an obligation of the bank. In this way a firm that is buying something from a supplier can effectively arrange for the bank to pay the outstanding bill. Of course, the bank charges the customer a fee for this service.

Summary and Conclusions

1. This chapter introduced the management of short-term finance. Short-term finance involves short-lived assets and liabilities. We traced and examined the short-term sources and uses of cash as they appear on the firm's financial statements. We saw how current assets and current liabilities arise in the short-term operating activities and the cash cycle of the firm. From an accounting perspective, short-term finance involves net working capital.

2. Managing short-term cash flows involves the minimization of costs. The two major costs are carrying costs (the interest and related costs incurred by overinvesting in short-term assets such as cash) and shortage costs (the cost of running out of short-term assets). The objective of managing short-term finance and short-term financial planning is to find the optimal trade-off between these costs.

3. In an ideal economy, a firm could perfectly predict its short-term uses and sources of cash, and net working capital could be kept at zero. In the real world, net working capital provides a buffer that lets the firm meet its ongoing obligations. The financial manager seeks the optimal level of each of the current assets.

4. The financial manager can use the cash budget to identify short-term financial needs. The cash budget tells the manager what borrowing is required or what lending will be possible in the short term. The firm has a number of possible ways of acquiring funds to meet short-term shortfalls, including unsecured and secured loans.

Concept Questions

1. **Operating Cycle**   What are some of the characteristics of a firm with a long operating cycle?

2. **Cash Cycle**   What are some of the characteristics of a firm with a long cash cycle?

3. **Sources and Uses**   For the year just ended, you have gathered the following information about the Holly Corporation:

   a. A $200 dividend was paid.
   b. Accounts payable increased by $500.
   c. Fixed asset purchases were $900.
   d. Inventories increased by $625.
   e. Long-term debt decreased by $1,200.

   Label each as a source or use of cash and describe its effect on the firm's cash balance.

4. **Cost of Current Assets**   Grohl Manufacturing, Inc., has recently installed a just-in-time (JIT) inventory system. Describe the effect this is likely to have on the company's carrying costs, shortage costs, and operating cycle.

5. **Operating and Cash Cycles**   Is it possible for a firm's cash cycle to be longer than its operating cycle? Explain why or why not.

6. **Shortage Costs**   What are the costs of shortages? Describe them.

7. **Reasons for Net Working Capital**   In an ideal economy, net working capital is always zero. Why might net working capital be positive in a real economy?

Use the following information to answer Questions 8–12: Last month, BlueSky Airline announced that it would stretch out its bill payments to 45 days from 30 days. The reason given was that the company wanted to "control costs and optimize cash flow." The increased payables period will be in effect for all of the company's 4,000 suppliers.

8. **Operating and Cash Cycles**   What impact did this change in payables policy have on BlueSky's operating cycle? Its cash cycle?

9. **Operating and Cash Cycles**   What impact did the announcement have on BlueSky's suppliers?

10. **Corporate Ethics**   Is it ethical for large firms to unilaterally lengthen their payables periods, particularly when dealing with smaller suppliers?

11. **Payables Period**   Why don't all firms simply increase their payables periods to shorten their cash cycles?

12. **Payables Period**   BlueSky lengthened its payables period to "control costs and optimize cash flow." Exactly what is the cash benefit to BlueSky from this change?

Questions and Problems

BASIC
(Questions 1–11)

1. **Changes in the Cash Account**   Indicate the impact of the following corporate actions on cash, using the letter *I* for an increase, *D* for a decrease, or *N* when no change occurs.

   a. A dividend is paid with funds received from a sale of debt.
   b. Real estate is purchased and paid for with short-term debt.
   c. Inventory is bought on credit.
   d. A short-term bank loan is repaid.
   e. Next year's taxes are prepaid.
   f. Preferred stock is redeemed.
   g. Sales are made on credit.
   h. Interest on long-term debt is paid.
   i. Payments for previous sales are collected.
   j. The accounts payable balance is reduced.
   k. A dividend is paid.
   l. Production supplies are purchased and paid with a short-term note.
   m. Utility bills are paid.
   n. Cash is paid for raw materials purchased for inventory.
   o. Marketable securities are sold.

2. **Cash Equation**   Blizzard Corp. has a book value of equity of $14,750. Long-term debt is $8,300. Net working capital, other than cash, is $1,950. Fixed assets are $20,730 and current liabilities are $1,930. How much cash does the company have? What are current assets?

3. **Changes in the Operating Cycle**   Indicate the effect that the following will have on the operating cycle. Use the letter *I* to indicate an increase, the letter *D* for a decrease, and the letter *N* for no change.

   a. Receivables average goes up.
   b. Credit repayment times for customers are increased.
   c. Inventory turnover goes from 3 times to 6 times.

d. Payables turnover goes from 6 times to 11 times.

e. Receivables turnover goes from 7 times to 9 times.

f. Payments to suppliers are accelerated.

4. **Changes in Cycles**   Indicate the impact of the following on the cash and operating cycles, respectively. Use the letter *I* to indicate an increase, the letter *D* for a decrease, and the letter *N* for no change.

   a. The terms of cash discounts offered to customers are made less favorable.

   b. The cash discounts offered by suppliers are increased; thus, payments are made earlier.

   c. An increased number of customers begin to pay in cash instead of with credit.

   d. Fewer raw materials than usual are purchased.

   e. A greater percentage of raw material purchases are paid for with credit.

   f. More finished goods are produced for inventory instead of for order.

5. **Calculating Cash Collections**   The Litzenberger Company has projected the following quarterly sales amounts for the coming year:

	Q1	Q2	Q3	Q4
Sales	$740	$840	$910	$970

   a. Accounts receivable at the beginning of the year are $335. The company has a 45-day collection period. Calculate cash collections in each of the four quarters by completing the following:

	Q1	Q2	Q3	Q4
Beginning receivables				
Sales				
Cash collections				
Ending receivables				

   b. Rework (a) assuming a collection period of 60 days.

   c. Rework (a) assuming a collection period of 30 days.

6. **Calculating Cycles**   Consider the following financial statement information for the Rivers Corporation:

Item	Beginning	Ending
Inventory	$17,385	$19,108
Accounts receivable	13,182	13,973
Accounts payable	15,385	16,676
Net sales		$216,384
Cost of goods sold		165,763

Calculate the operating and cash cycles. How do you interpret your answer?

7. **Calculating Payments** Lewellen Products has projected the following sales for the coming year:

	Q1	Q2	Q3	Q4
Sales	$660	$575	$715	$810

Sales in the year following this one are projected to be 15 percent greater in each quarter.

a. Calculate payments to suppliers assuming that the company places orders during each quarter equal to 30 percent of projected sales for the next quarter. Assume that the company pays immediately. What is the payables period in this case?

	Q1	Q2	Q3	Q4
Payment of accounts	$	$	$	$

b. Rework (a) assuming a 90-day payables period.
c. Rework (a) assuming a 60-day payables period.

8. **Calculating Payments** The Thakor Corporation's purchases from suppliers in a quarter are equal to 75 percent of the next quarter's forecast sales. The payables period is 60 days. Wages, taxes, and other expenses are 20 percent of sales, and interest and dividends are $73 per quarter. No capital expenditures are planned.

Here are the projected quarterly sales:

	Q1	Q2	Q3	Q4
Sales	$1,435	$1,680	$1,520	$1,280

Sales for the first quarter of the following year are projected at $1,645. Calculate the company's cash outlays by completing the following:

	Q1	Q2	Q3	Q4
Payment of accounts				
Wages, taxes, and other expenses				
Long-term financing expenses (interest and dividends)				
Total				

9. **Calculating Cash Collections** The following is the sales budget for Shleifer, Inc., for the first quarter of 2016:

	January	February	March
Sales budget	$258,000	$274,200	$298,000

Credit sales are collected as follows:

65 percent in the month of the sale.
20 percent in the month after the sale.
15 percent in the second month after the sale.

The accounts receivable balance at the end of the previous quarter was $122,800 ($87,750 of which were uncollected December sales).

a. Compute the sales for November.
b. Compute the sales for December.
c. Compute the cash collections from sales for each month from January through March.

10. **Calculating the Cash Budget**   Here are some important figures from the budget of Cornell, Inc., for the second quarter of 2016:

	April	May	June
Credit sales	$601,900	$627,300	$693,790
Credit purchases	232,850	277,900	317,380
Cash disbursements			
Wages, taxes, and expenses	62,964	76,364	79,670
Interest	18,058	18,058	18,058
Equipment purchases	131,400	144,200	0

The company predicts that 5 percent of its credit sales will never be collected, 35 percent of its sales will be collected in the month of the sale, and the remaining 60 percent will be collected in the following month. Credit purchases will be paid in the month following the purchase.

In March 2016, credit sales were $332,640, and credit purchases were $247,100. Using this information, complete the following cash budget:

	April	May	June
Beginning cash balance	$443,500		
Cash receipts			
Cash collections from credit sales			
Total cash available			
Cash disbursements			
Purchases			
Wages, taxes, and expenses			
Interest			
Equipment purchases			
Total cash disbursements			
Ending cash balance			

11. Sources and Uses Here are the most recent balance sheets for Country Kettles, Inc. Excluding accumulated depreciation, determine whether each item is a source or a use of cash, and the amount:

COUNTRY KETTLES, INC. Balance Sheet		
	2015	2016
Assets		
Cash	$ 48,180	$ 45,815
Accounts receivable	100,155	105,413
Inventories	83,600	89,716
Property, plant, and equipment	225,992	249,086
Less: Accumulated depreciation	(77,194)	(85,579)
Total assets	$380,733	$404,451
Liabilities and Equity		
Accounts payable	$ 72,522	$ 50,396
Accrued expenses	10,980	9,840
Long-term debt	49,500	45,000
Common stock	25,000	30,000
Accumulated retained earnings	222,731	269,215
Total liabilities and equity	$380,733	$404,451

INTERMEDIATE
(Questions 12–15)

12. Cash Budgeting The sales budget for your company in the coming year is based on a quarterly growth rate of 10 percent, with the first-quarter sales projection at $185 million. In addition to this basic trend, the seasonal adjustments for the four quarters are 0, −$16, −$8, and $21 million, respectively. Generally, 50 percent of the sales can be collected within the quarter and 45 percent in the following quarter; the rest of the sales are bad debt. The bad debts are written off in the second quarter after the sales are made. The beginning accounts receivable balance is $87 million. Assuming all sales are on credit, compute the cash collections from sales for each quarter.

13. Calculating the Cash Budget Wildcat, Inc., has estimated sales (in millions) for the next four quarters as follows:

	Q1	Q2	Q3	Q4
Sales	$105	$90	$122	$140

Sales for the first quarter of the year after this one are projected at $120 million. Accounts receivable at the beginning of the year were $34 million. Wildcat has a 45-day collection period.

Wildcat's purchases from suppliers in a quarter are equal to 45 percent of the next quarter's forecast sales, and suppliers are normally paid in 36 days. Wages, taxes, and other expenses run about 30 percent of sales. Interest and dividends are $6 million per quarter.

Wildcat plans a major capital outlay in the second quarter of $40 million. Finally, the company started the year with a $32 million cash balance and wishes to maintain a $15 million minimum balance.

a. Complete a cash budget for Wildcat by filling in the following:

WILDCAT, INC. Cash Budget ($ in millions)				
	Q1	Q2	Q3	Q4
Target cash balance	$15			
Net cash inflow				
Ending cash balance				
Minimum cash balance	15			
Cumulative surplus (deficit)				

b. Assume that Wildcat can borrow any needed funds on a short-term basis at a rate of 3 percent per quarter, and can invest any excess funds in short-term marketable securities at a rate of 2 percent per quarter. Prepare a short-term financial plan by filling in the following schedule. What is the net cash cost (total interest paid minus total investment income earned) for the year?

WILDCAT, INC. Short-Term Financial Plan ($ in millions)				
	Q1	Q2	Q3	Q4
Target cash balance	$15			
Net cash inflow				
New short-term investments				
Income from short-term investments				
Short-term investments sold				
New short-term borrowing				
Interest on short-term borrowing				
Short-term borrowing repaid				
Ending cash balance				
Minimum cash balance	15			
Cumulative surplus (deficit)				
Beginning short-term investments				
Ending short-term investments				
Beginning short-term debt				
Ending short-term debt				

14. **Cash Management Policy**   Rework Problem 13 assuming the following:

a. Wildcat maintains a minimum cash balance of $20 million.
b. Wildcat maintains a minimum cash balance of $10 million.

Based on your answers in (a) and (b), do you think the firm can boost its profit by changing its cash management policy? Should other factors be considered as well? Explain.

15. **Short-Term Finance Policy**   Cleveland Compressor and Pnew York Pneumatic are competing manufacturing firms. Their financial statements are printed here.

   a. How are the current assets of each firm financed?
   b. Which firm has the larger investment in current assets? Why?
   c. Which firm is more likely to incur carrying costs, and which is more likely to incur shortage costs? Why?

CLEVELAND COMPRESSOR
Balance Sheet

	2015	2014
Assets		
Current assets:		
Cash	$ 13,862	$ 16,339
Net accounts receivable	23,887	25,778
Inventory	54,867	43,287
Total current assets	$ 92,616	$ 85,404
Fixed assets:		
Plant, property, and equipment	101,543	99,615
Less: Accumulated depreciation	(34,331)	(31,957)
Net fixed assets	$67,212	$67,658
Prepaid expenses	1,914	1,791
Other assets	13,052	13,138
Total assets	$174,794	$167,991
Liabilities and Equity		
Current liabilities:		
Accounts payable	$ 6,494	$ 4,893
Notes payable	10,483	11,617
Accrued expenses	7,422	7,227
Other taxes payable	9,924	8,460
Total current liabilities	34,323	32,197
Long-term debt	22,036	22,036
Total liabilities	$ 56,359	$ 54,233
Equity:		
Common stock	38,000	38,000
Paid-in capital	12,000	12,000
Retained earnings	68,435	63,758
Total equity	118,435	113,758
Total liabilities and equity	$174,794	$167,991

CLEVELAND COMPRESSOR
Income Statement
2015

Income:	
Sales	$162,749
Other income	1,002
Total income	$163,751
Operating expenses:	
Cost of goods sold	103,570
Selling and administrative expenses.	28,495
Depreciation	2,274
Total expenses.	$134,339
Pretax earnings.	29,412
Taxes	14,890
Net earnings.	$ 14,522
Dividends.	$ 9,845
Retained earnings.	$ 4,677

PNEW YORK PNEUMATIC
Balance Sheet

	2015	2014
Assets		
Current assets:		
Cash.	$ 3,307	$ 5,794
Net accounts receivable	22,133	26,177
Inventory	44,661	46,463
Total current assets	$70,101	$78,434
Fixed assets:		
Plant, property, and equipment.	31,116	31,842
Less: Accumulated depreciation.	(18,143)	(19,297)
Net fixed assets.	$12,973	$12,545
Prepaid expenses.	688	763
Other assets.	1,385	1,601
Total assets.	$85,147	$93,343
Liabilities and Equity		
Current liabilities:		
Accounts payable.	$ 5,019	$ 6,008
Bank loans	645	3,722
Accrued expenses	3,295	4,254
Other taxes payable.	4,951	5,688
Total current liabilities	$13,910	$19,672
Equity:		
Common stock	20,576	20,576
Paid-in capital.	5,624	5,624
Retained earnings.	46,164	48,598
Less: Treasury stock	(1,127)	(1,127)
Total equity	$71,237	$73,671
Total liabilities and equity.	$85,147	$93,343

PNEW YORK PNEUMATIC	
Income Statement	
2015	
Income:	
Sales	$91,374
Other income	1,067
Total income	$92,441
Operating expenses:	
Cost of goods sold	59,042
Selling and administrative expenses.	18,068
Depreciation	1,154
Total expenses.	$78,264
Pretax earnings.	14,177
Taxes	6,838
Net earnings.	$ 7,339
Dividends.	$ 4,905
Retained earnings.	$ 2,434

Excel Master It! Problem

Heidi Pedersen, the treasurer for Wood Products, Inc., has just been asked by Justin Wood, the president, to prepare a memo detailing the company's ending cash balance for the next three months. Below, you will see the relevant estimates for this period.

	July	August	September
Credit sales	$1,275,800	$1,483,500	$1,096,300
Credit purchases	765,480	890,160	657,780
Cash disbursements:			
Wages, taxes, and expenses	348,600	395,620	337,150
Interest	29,900	29,900	29,900
Equipment	0	158,900	96,300
Credit sales collections:			
Collected in month of sale	35%		
Collected month after sale	60%		
Never collected	5%		
June credit sales:	$1,135,020		
June credit purchases	$ 681,012		
Beginning cash balance	$ 425,000		

All credit purchases are paid in the month after the purchase.

a. Complete the cash budget for Wood Products for the next three months.

b. Heidi knows that the cash budget will become a standard report completed before each quarter. To help reduce the time preparing the report each quarter, she would like a memo with the appropriate information in Excel linked to the memo. Prepare a memo to Justin that will automatically update when the values are changed in Excel.

KEAFER MANUFACTURING
WORKING CAPITAL MANAGEMENT

You have recently been hired by Keafer Manufacturing to work in its established treasury department. Keafer Manufacturing is a small company that produces highly customized cardboard boxes in a variety of sizes for different purchasers. Adam Keafer, the owner of the company, works primarily in the sales and production areas of the company. Currently, the company basically puts all receivables in one pile and all payables in another, and a part-time bookkeeper periodically comes in and attacks the piles. Because of this disorganized system, the finance area needs work, and that's what you've been brought in to do.

The company currently has a cash balance of $210,000, and it plans to purchase new machinery in the third quarter at a cost of $390,000. The purchase of the machinery will be made with cash because of the discount offered for a cash purchase. Adam wants to maintain a minimum cash balance of $135,000 to guard against unforeseen contingencies. All of Keafer's sales to customers and purchases from suppliers are made with credit, and no discounts are offered or taken.

The company had the following sales each quarter of the year just ended:

	Q1	Q2	Q3	Q4
Gross sales	$1,102,000	$1,141,000	$1,125,000	$1,063,000

After some research and discussions with customers, you're projecting that sales will be 8 percent higher in each quarter next year. Sales for the first quarter of the following year are also expected to grow at 8 percent. You calculate that Keafer currently has an accounts receivable period of 57 days and an accounts receivable balance of $675,000. However, 10 percent of the accounts receivable balance is from a company that has just entered bankruptcy, and it is likely that this portion will never be collected.

You've also calculated that Keafer typically orders supplies each quarter in the amount of 50 percent of the next quarter's projected gross sales, and suppliers are paid in 53 days on average. Wages, taxes, and other costs run about 25 percent of gross sales. The company has a quarterly interest payment of $185,000 on its long-term debt. Finally, the company uses a local bank for its short-term financial needs. It currently pays 1.2 percent per quarter on all short-term borrowing and maintains a money market account that pays .5 percent per quarter on all short-term deposits.

Adam has asked you to prepare a cash budget and short-term financial plan for the company under the current policies. He has also asked you to prepare additional plans based on changes in several inputs.

1. Use the numbers given to complete the cash budget and short-term financial plan.

2. Rework the cash budget and short-term financial plan assuming Keafer changes to a minimum cash balance of $90,000.

3. Rework the sales budget assuming an 11 percent growth rate in sales and a 5 percent growth rate in sales. Assume a $135,000 target cash balance.

4. Assuming the company maintains its target cash balance at $135,000, what sales growth rate would result in a zero need for short-term financing? To answer this question, you may need to set up a spreadsheet and use the "Solver" function.

27

Cash Management

When news breaks about a firm's bank accounts, it's usually because the company is running low on cash. However, that wasn't the case for many companies in early 2015. For example, two of the largest cash balances were held by tech giants Cisco and Microsoft, which held about $52.1 billion and $90.2 billion in cash, respectively. Similarly striking was Google's cash balance of about $61.2 billion, which amounted to about $90 per share! Other companies also had large amounts of cash. General Electric (GE) had a cash balance of about $137.4 billion. But no company came close to investment bank Goldman Sachs, with a cash hoard of $224 billion. Why would firms such as these hold such large quantities of cash? We examine cash management in this chapter to find out.

This chapter is about how firms manage cash. The basic objective of cash management is to keep the investment in cash as low as possible while still keeping the firm operating efficiently and effectively. This goal usually reduces to the dictum, "Collect early and pay late." Accordingly, we discuss ways of accelerating collections and managing disbursements.

In addition, firms must invest temporarily idle cash in short-term marketable securities. As we discuss in various places, these securities can be bought and sold in the financial markets. As a group they have very little default risk, and most are highly marketable. There are different types of these so-called money market securities, and we discuss a few of the most important ones.

27.1 Reasons for Holding Cash

John Maynard Keynes, in his classic work *The General Theory of Employment, Interest, and Money,* identified three motives for liquidity: The speculative motive, the precautionary motive, and the transaction motive. We discuss these next.

THE SPECULATIVE AND PRECAUTIONARY MOTIVES

The **speculative motive** is the need to hold cash in order to be able to take advantage of, for example, bargain purchases that might arise, attractive interest rates, and (in the case of international firms) favorable exchange rate fluctuations.

For most firms, reserve borrowing ability and marketable securities can be used to satisfy speculative motives. Thus, there might be a speculative motive for maintaining liquidity, but not necessarily for holding cash per se. Think of it this way: If you have a credit card with a very large credit limit, then you can probably take advantage of any unusual bargains that come along without carrying any cash.

This is also true, to a lesser extent, for precautionary motives. The **precautionary motive** is the need for a safety supply to act as a financial reserve. Once again, there probably is a precautionary motive for maintaining liquidity. However, given that the value of money market instruments is relatively certain and that instruments such as T-bills are extremely liquid, there is no real need to hold substantial amounts of cash for precautionary purposes.

THE TRANSACTION MOTIVE

Cash is needed to satisfy the **transaction motive**: the need to have cash on hand to pay bills. Transaction-related needs come from the normal disbursement and collection activities of the firm. The disbursement of cash includes the payment of wages and salaries, trade debts, taxes, and dividends.

Cash is collected from product sales, the selling of assets, and new financing. The cash inflows (collections) and outflows (disbursements) are not perfectly synchronized, and some level of cash holdings is necessary to serve as a buffer.

As electronic funds transfers and other high-speed, "paperless" payment mechanisms continue to develop, even the transaction demand for cash may all but disappear. Even if it does, however, there will still be a demand for liquidity and a need to manage it efficiently.

COMPENSATING BALANCES

Compensating balances are another reason to hold cash. As we discussed in the previous chapter, cash balances are kept at commercial banks to compensate for banking services the firm receives. A minimum compensating balance requirement may impose a lower limit on the level of cash a firm holds.

COSTS OF HOLDING CASH

When a firm holds cash in excess of some necessary minimum, it incurs an opportunity cost. The opportunity cost of excess cash (held in currency or bank deposits) is the interest income that could be earned by the next best use, such as investment in marketable securities.

Given the opportunity cost of holding cash, why would a firm hold cash in excess of its compensating balance requirements? The answer is that a cash balance must be maintained to provide the liquidity necessary for transaction needs—paying bills. If the firm maintains too small a cash balance, it may run out of cash. If this happens, the firm may have to raise cash on a short-term basis. This could involve, for example, selling marketable securities or borrowing.

Activities such as selling marketable securities and borrowing involve various costs. As we've discussed, holding cash has an opportunity cost. To determine the appropriate cash balance, the firm must weigh the benefits of holding cash against these costs. We discuss this subject in more detail in the sections that follow.

CASH MANAGEMENT VERSUS LIQUIDITY MANAGEMENT

Before we move on, we should note that it is important to distinguish between true cash management and a more general subject, liquidity management. The distinction is a source of confusion because the word *cash* is used in practice in two different ways. First of all, it has its literal meaning, actual cash on hand. However, financial managers frequently use the word to describe a firm's holdings of cash along with its marketable securities, and marketable securities are sometimes called *cash equivalents,* or *near-cash.* In our discussion of various firms' cash positions at the beginning of the chapter, for example, what was actually being described was their total cash and cash equivalents.

The distinction between liquidity management and cash management is straightforward. Liquidity management concerns the optimal quantity of liquid assets a firm should have on hand, and it is one particular aspect of the current asset management policies we discussed in our previous chapter. Cash management is much more closely related to optimizing mechanisms for collecting and disbursing cash, and it is this subject that we primarily focus on in this chapter.

In general, the firm needs to balance the benefits of holding cash to meet transactions and avoid insolvency against the opportunity costs of lower returns. A sensible cash management policy is to have enough cash on hand to meet the obligations that may arise in the ordinary course of business and to invest some excess cash in marketable securities for precautionary purposes. All other excess cash should be invested in the business or paid out to investors.[1]

27.2　Understanding Float

As you no doubt know, the amount of money you have according to your checkbook can be very different from the amount of money that your bank thinks you have. The reason is that some of the checks you have written haven't yet been presented to the bank for payment. The same thing is true for a business. The cash balance that a firm shows on its books is called the firm's *book*, or *ledger, balance*. The balance shown in its bank account as available to spend is called its *available,* or *collected, balance*. The difference between the available balance and the ledger balance, called the **float**, represents the net effect of checks in the process of *clearing* (moving through the banking system).

DISBURSEMENT FLOAT

Checks written by a firm generate *disbursement float,* causing a decrease in the firm's book balance but no change in its available balance. For example, suppose General Mechanics, Inc. (GMI), currently has $100,000 on deposit with its bank. On June 8, it buys some raw materials and pays with a check for $100,000. The company's book balance is immediately reduced by $100,000 as a result.

GMI's bank, however, will not find out about this check until it is presented to GMI's bank for payment on, say, June 14. Until the check is presented, the firm's available balance is greater than its book balance by $100,000. In other words, before June 8, GMI has a zero float:

$$\text{Float} = \text{Firm's available balance} - \text{Firm's book balance}$$
$$= \$100{,}000 - 100{,}000$$
$$= \$0$$

GMI's position from June 8 to June 14 is:

$$\text{Disbursement float} = \text{Firm's available balance} - \text{Firm's book balance}$$
$$= \$100{,}000 - 0$$
$$= \$100{,}000$$

---

[1]There is some evidence that corporate governance has some role in the cash holdings of U.S. firms. Jarrad Harford, Sattar A. Mansi, and William F. Maxwell, in "Corporate Governance and Firm Cash Holdings in the U.S.," *Journal of Financial Economics* 87, no. 3 (2008), pp. 535–55, find that firms with weaker corporate governance systems have smaller cash reserves. The combination of excess cash and weak governance leads to more capital spending and more acquisitions.

While the check is clearing, GMI has a balance with the bank of $100,000. It can obtain the benefit of this cash during this period. For example, the available balance could be temporarily invested in marketable securities and thus earn some interest. We will return to this subject a little later.

COLLECTION FLOAT AND NET FLOAT

Checks received by the firm create *collection float*. Collection float increases book balances but does not immediately change available balances. For example, suppose GMI receives a check from a customer for $100,000 on October 8. Assume, as before, that the company has $100,000 deposited at its bank and a zero float. It deposits the check and increases its book balance by $100,000 to $200,000. However, the additional cash is not available to GMI until its bank has presented the check to the customer's bank and received $100,000. This will occur on, say, October 14. In the meantime, the cash position at GMI will reflect a collection float of $100,000. We can summarize these events. Before October 8, GMI's position is:

$$\text{Float} = \text{Firm's available balance} - \text{Firm's book balance}$$
$$= \$100,000 - 100,000$$
$$= \$0$$

GMI's position from October 8 to October 14 is:

$$\text{Collection float} = \text{Firm's available balance} - \text{Firm's book balance}$$
$$= \$100,000 - 200,000$$
$$= -\$100,000$$

In general, a firm's payment (disbursement) activities generate disbursement float, and its collection activities generate collection float. The net effect—that is, the sum of the total collection and disbursement floats—is the net float. The net float at a point in time is simply the overall difference between the firm's available balance and its book balance. If the net float is positive, then the firm's disbursement float exceeds its collection float, and its available balance exceeds its book balance. If the available balance is less than the book balance, then the firm has a net collection float.

A firm should be concerned with its net float and available balance more than with its book balance. If a financial manager knows that a check written by the company will not clear for several days, that manager will be able to keep a lower cash balance at the bank than might be possible otherwise. This can generate a great deal of money.

For example, take the case of ExxonMobil. The average daily sales of ExxonMobil are about $1 billion. If ExxonMobil's collections could be sped up by a single day, then ExxonMobil could free up $1 billion for investing. At a relatively modest .01 percent daily rate, the interest earned would be on the order of $100,000 *per day*.

<table>
<tr><td>**EXAMPLE**
27.1</td><td>**Staying Afloat**   Suppose you have $5,000 on deposit. One day, you write a check for $1,000 to pay for books, and you deposit $2,000. What are your disbursement, collection, and net floats?

After you write the $1,000 check, you show a balance of $4,000 on your books, but the bank shows $5,000 while the check is clearing. The difference is a disbursement float of $1,000.

After you deposit the $2,000 check, you show a balance of $6,000. Your available balance doesn't rise until the check clears. This results in a collection float of −$2,000. Your net float is the sum of the collection and disbursement floats, or −$1,000.</td></tr>
</table>

Overall, you show $6,000 on your books. The bank shows a $7,000 balance, but only $5,000 is available because your deposit has not been cleared. The discrepancy between your available balance and your book balance is the net float (−$1,000), and it is bad for you. If you write another check for $5,500, there may not be sufficient available funds to cover it, and it might bounce. This is why financial managers have to be more concerned with available balances than book balances.

FLOAT MANAGEMENT

For a real-world example of float management services, visit **www.carreker** **.fiserv.com**.

Float management involves controlling the collection and disbursement of cash. The objective of cash collection is to speed up collections and reduce the lag between the time customers pay their bills and the time the cash becomes available. The objective of cash disbursement is to control payments and minimize the firm's costs associated with making payments.

Total collection or disbursement times can be broken down into three parts: Mailing time, processing delay, and availability delay:

1. *Mailing time* is the part of the collection and disbursement processes during which checks are trapped in the postal system.

2. *Processing delay* is the time it takes the receiver of a check to process the payment and deposit it in a bank for collection.

3. *Availability delay* refers to the time required to clear a check through the banking system.

Speeding up collections involves reducing one or more of these components. Slowing up disbursements involves increasing one of them. We will describe some procedures for managing collection and disbursement times later. First, we need to discuss how float is measured.

Measuring Float The size of the float depends on both the dollars and the time delay involved. For example, suppose you mail a check for $500 to another state each month. It takes five days in the mail for the check to reach its destination (the mailing time) and one day for the recipient to get over to the bank (the processing delay). The recipient's bank holds out-of-state checks for three days (availability delay). The total delay is 5 + 1 + 3 = 9 days.

In this case, what is your average daily disbursement float? There are two equivalent ways of calculating the answer. First, you have a $500 float for nine days, so we say that the total float is 9 × $500 = $4,500. Assuming 30 days in the month, the average daily float is $4,500/30 = $150.

Alternatively, your disbursement float is $500 for 9 days out of the month and zero the other 21 days (again, assuming 30 days in a month). Your average daily float is thus:

$$\text{Average daily float} = (9 \times \$500 + 21 \times \$0)/30$$
$$= 9/30 \times \$500 + 21/30 \times \$0$$
$$= \$4,500/30$$
$$= \$150$$

This means that, on an average day, your book balance is $150 less than your available balance, representing a $150 average disbursement float.

Things are only a little more complicated when there are multiple disbursements or receipts. To illustrate, suppose Concepts, Inc., receives two items each month as follows:

	Amount	Processing and availability delay	Total float
Item 1:	$5,000,000	× 9	= $45,000,000
Item 2:	$3,000,000	× 5	= $15,000,000
Total:	$8,000,000		$60,000,000

The average daily float is equal to:

$$\text{Average daily float} = \frac{\text{Total float}}{\text{Total days}}$$

$$= \frac{\$60 \text{ million}}{30} = \$2 \text{ million}$$

(27.1)

So, on an average day, there is $2 million that is uncollected and not available.

Another way to see this is to calculate the average daily receipts and multiply by the weighted average delay. Average daily receipts are:

$$\text{Average daily receipts} = \frac{\text{Total receipts}}{\text{Total days}} = \frac{\$8 \text{ million}}{30} = \$266,666.67$$

Of the $8 million total receipts, $5 million, or ⅝ of the total, is delayed for nine days. The other ⅜ is delayed for five days. The weighted average delay is thus:

$$\text{Weighted average delay} = (5/8) \times 9 \text{ days} + (3/8) \times 5 \text{ days}$$

$$= 5.625 + 1.875 = 7.50 \text{ days}$$

The average daily float is thus:

$$\text{Average daily float} = \text{Average daily receipts} \times \text{Weighted average delay}$$

$$= \$266,666.67 \times 7.50 \text{ days} = \$2 \text{ million}$$

(27.2)

Some Details   In measuring float, there is an important difference to note between collection and disbursement float. We defined *float* as the difference between the firm's available cash balance and its book balance. With a disbursement, the firm's book balance goes down when the check is *mailed,* so the mailing time is an important component in disbursement float. However, with a collection, the firm's book balance isn't increased until the check is *received,* so mailing time is not a component of collection float.

This doesn't mean that mailing time is not important. The point is that when collection *float* is calculated, mailing time should not be considered. As we will discuss, when total collection *time* is considered, the mailing time is a crucial component.

Also, when we talk about availability delay, how long it actually takes a check to clear isn't really crucial. What matters is how long we must wait before the bank grants availability—that is, use of the funds. Banks actually use availability schedules to determine how long a check is held based on time of deposit and other factors. Beyond this, availability delay can be a matter of negotiation between the bank and a customer. In a similar vein, for outgoing checks, what matters is the date our account is debited, not when the recipient is granted availability.

Cost of the Float   The basic cost of collection float to the firm is simply the opportunity cost of not being able to use the cash. At a minimum, the firm could earn interest on the cash if it were available for investing.

Figure 27.1

Buildup of the Float

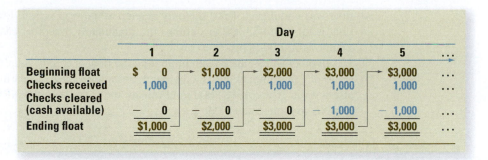

Figure 27.2

Effect of Eliminating the Float

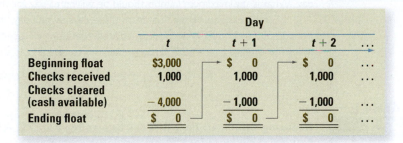

Suppose the Lambo Corporation has average daily receipts of $1,000 and a weighted average delay of three days. The average daily float is thus $3 \times \$1,000 = \$3,000$. This means that, on a typical day, there is $3,000 that is not earning interest. Suppose Lambo could eliminate the float entirely. What would be the benefit? If it costs $2,000 to eliminate the float, what is the NPV of doing so?

Figure 27.1 illustrates the situation for Lambo. Suppose Lambo starts with a zero float. On a given day, Day 1, Lambo receives and deposits a check for $1,000. The cash will become available three days later on Day 4. At the end of the day on Day 1, the book balance is $1,000 more than the available balance, so the float is $1,000. On Day 2, the firm receives and deposits another check. It will collect three days later on Day 5. At the end of Day 2, there are two uncollected checks, and the books show a $2,000 balance. The bank, however, still shows a zero available balance; so the float is $2,000. The same sequence occurs on Day 3, and the float rises to a total of $3,000.

On Day 4, Lambo again receives and deposits a check for $1,000. However, it also collects $1,000 from the Day 1 check. The change in book balance and the change in available balance are identical, +$1,000; so the float stays at $3,000. The same thing happens every day after Day 4; the float therefore stays at $3,000 forever.[2]

Figure 27.2 illustrates what happens if the float is eliminated entirely on some Day *t* in the future. After the float is eliminated, daily receipts are still $1,000. The firm collects the same day because the float is eliminated, so daily collections are also still $1,000. As Figure 27.2 illustrates, the only change occurs the first day. On that day, as usual, Lambo collects $1,000 from the sale made three days before. Because the float is gone, it also collects on the sales made two days before, one day before, and that same day, for an additional $3,000. Total collections on Day *t* are thus $4,000 instead of $1,000.

What we see is that Lambo generates an extra $3,000 on Day *t* by eliminating the float. On every subsequent day, Lambo receives $1,000 in cash just as it did before the

---

[2]This permanent float is sometimes called the *steady-state float.*

float was eliminated. Thus, the only change in the firm's cash flows from eliminating the float is this extra $3,000 that comes in immediately. No other cash flows are affected, so Lambo is $3,000 richer.

In other words, the PV of eliminating the float is simply equal to the total float. Lambo could pay this amount out as a dividend, invest it in interest-bearing assets, or do anything else with it. If it costs $2,000 to eliminate the float, then the NPV is $3,000 − 2,000 = $1,000; so Lambo should do it.

EXAMPLE

Reducing the Float: Part I   Instead of eliminating the float, suppose Lambo can reduce it to one day. What is the maximum Lambo should be willing to pay for this?

If Lambo can reduce the float from three days to one day, then the amount of the float will fall from $3,000 to $1,000. From our immediately preceding discussion, we see right away that the PV of doing this is equal to the $2,000 float reduction. Lambo should thus be willing to pay up to $2,000.

EXAMPLE 27.3

Reducing the Float: Part II   Look back at Example 27.2. A large bank is willing to provide the float reduction service for $175 per year, payable at the end of each year. The relevant discount rate is 8 percent. Should Lambo hire the bank? What is the NPV of the investment? How do you interpret this discount rate? What is the most per year that Lambo should be willing to pay?

The PV to Lambo is still $2,000. The $175 would have to be paid out every year forever to maintain the float reduction; so the cost is perpetual, and its PV is $175/.08 = $2,187.50. The NPV is $2,000 − 2,187.50 = −$187.50; therefore, the service is not a good deal.

Ignoring the possibility of bounced checks, the discount rate here corresponds most closely to the cost of short-term borrowing. The reason is that Lambo could borrow $1,000 from the bank every time a check was deposited and pay it back three days later. The cost would be the interest that Lambo would have to pay.

The most Lambo would be willing to pay is whatever charge results in an NPV of zero. This zero NPV occurs when the $2,000 benefit exactly equals the PV of the costs—that is, when $2,000 = $C/.08$, where C is the annual cost. Solving for C, we find that $C = .08 \times \$2,000 = \$160$ per year.

Ethical and Legal Questions   The cash manager must work with collected bank cash balances and not the firm's book balance (which reflects checks that have been deposited but not collected). If this is not done, a cash manager could be drawing on uncollected cash as a source of funds for short-term investing. Most banks charge a penalty rate for the use of uncollected funds. However, banks may not have good enough accounting and control procedures to be fully aware of the use of uncollected funds. This raises some ethical and legal questions for the firm.

ELECTRONIC DATA INTERCHANGE AND CHECK 21: THE END OF FLOAT?

Electronic data interchange (EDI) is a general term that refers to the growing practice of direct, electronic information exchange between all types of businesses. One important use of EDI, often called *financial EDI,* or *FEDI,* is to electronically transfer financial information and funds between parties, thereby eliminating paper invoices, paper checks, mailing, and handling. For example, it is now possible to arrange to have your checking account directly debited each month to pay many types of bills, and corporations now routinely directly deposit paychecks into employee accounts. More generally, EDI allows a seller to send a bill electronically to a buyer, thereby avoiding the mail. The buyer can then authorize payment, which also occurs electronically. Its bank then transfers the funds to the seller's account at a different bank. The net effect is that the length of time required to initiate and complete a business transaction is shortened considerably, and much of what we normally think of as float is sharply reduced or eliminated. As the use of FEDI increases (which it will), float management will evolve to focus much more on issues surrounding computerized information exchange and funds transfers.

One of the drawbacks of EDI (and FEDI) is that it is expensive and complex to set up. However, with the growth of the Internet, a new form of EDI has emerged: Internet e-commerce. For example, networking giant Cisco Systems books millions in orders each day on its website from resellers around the world. Firms are also linking to critical suppliers and customers via "extranets," which are business networks that extend a company's internal network. Because of security concerns and lack of standardization, don't look for e-commerce and extranets to eliminate the need for EDI anytime soon. In fact, these are complementary systems that will most likely be used in tandem as the future unfolds.

On October 29, 2004, the Check Clearing for the 21st Century Act, also known as Check 21, took effect. Before Check 21, a bank receiving a check was required to send the physical check to the customer's bank before payment could be made. Now a bank can transmit an electronic image of the check to the customer's bank and receive payment immediately. Previously, an out-of-state check might take three days to clear. But with Check 21, the clearing time is typically one day; and often a check can clear the same day it is written. Thus, Check 21 promises to significantly reduce float.

27.3 Cash Collection and Concentration

From our previous discussion, we know that collection delays work against the firm. All other things being the same, a firm will adopt procedures to speed up collections and thereby decrease collection times. In addition, even after cash is collected, firms need procedures to funnel, or concentrate, that cash where it can be best used. We discuss some common collection and concentration procedures next.

COMPONENTS OF COLLECTION TIME

Based on our previous discussion, we can depict the basic parts of the cash collection process as follows. The total time in this process is made up of mailing time, check-processing delay, and the bank's availability delay.

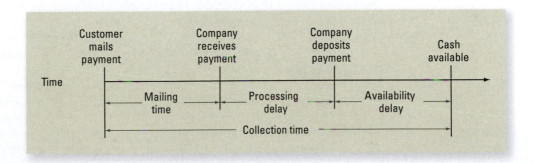

The amount of time that cash spends in each part of the cash collection process depends on where the firm's customers and banks are located and how efficient the firm is in collecting cash.

CASH COLLECTION

How a firm collects from its customers depends in large part on the nature of the business. The simplest case would be a business such as a restaurant chain. Most of its customers will pay with cash, check, or credit card at the point of sale (this is called *over-the-counter collection*), so there is no problem with mailing delay. Normally, the funds will be deposited in a local bank, and the firm will have some means (discussed later) of gaining access to the funds.

When some or all of the payments a company receives are checks that arrive through the mail, all three components of collection time become relevant. The firm may choose to have all the checks mailed to one location; more commonly, the firm might have a number of different mail collection points to reduce mailing times. Also, the firm may run its collection operation itself or might hire an outside firm that specializes in cash collection. We discuss these issues in more detail in the following pages.

Other approaches to cash collection exist. One that is becoming more common is the preauthorized payment arrangement. With this arrangement, the payment amounts and payment dates are fixed in advance. When the agreed-upon date arrives, the amount is automatically transferred from the customer's bank account to the firm's bank account, which sharply reduces or even eliminates collection delays. The same approach is used by firms that have online terminals, meaning that when a sale is rung up, the money is immediately transferred to the firm's accounts.

LOCKBOXES

When a firm receives its payments by mail, it must decide where the checks will be mailed and how the checks will be picked up and deposited. Careful selection of the number and locations of collection points can greatly reduce collection times. Many firms use special post office boxes called **lockboxes** to intercept payments and speed up cash collection.

Figure 27.3 illustrates a lockbox system. The collection process is started by customers mailing their checks to a post office box instead of sending them to the firm. The lockbox is maintained by a local bank. A large corporation may actually maintain more than 20 lockboxes around the country.

In the typical lockbox system, the local bank collects the lockbox checks several times a day. The bank deposits the checks directly to the firm's account. Details of the operation are recorded (in some computer-usable form) and sent to the firm.

A lockbox system reduces mailing time because checks are received at a nearby post office instead of at corporate headquarters. Lockboxes also reduce processing time because the corporation doesn't have to open the envelopes and deposit checks for collection. All in all, a bank lockbox system should enable a firm to get its receipts processed, deposited, and cleared faster than if it were to receive checks at its headquarters and deliver them itself to the bank for deposit and clearing.

Some firms have turned to what are called "electronic lockboxes" as an alternative to traditional lockboxes. In one version of an electronic lockbox, customers use the telephone or the Internet to access their account—say, their credit card account at a bank—review their bill, and authorize payment without paper ever having changed hands on either end of the transaction. Clearly, an electronic lockbox system is far superior to traditional bill

Figure 27.3
Overview of Lockbox
Processing

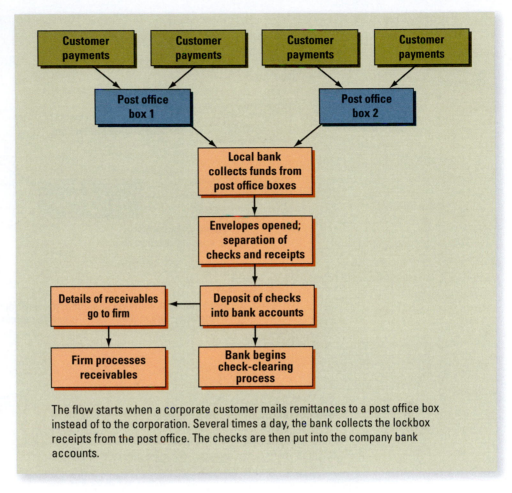

The flow starts when a corporate customer mails remittances to a post office box instead of to the corporation. Several times a day, the bank collects the lockbox receipts from the post office. The checks are then put into the company bank accounts.

payment methods, at least from the biller's perspective. Look for systems like this to continue to grow in popularity.

CASH CONCENTRATION

As we discussed earlier, a firm will typically have a number of cash collection points; as a result, cash collections may end up in many different banks and bank accounts. From here the firm needs procedures to move the cash into its main accounts. This is called **cash concentration**. By routinely pooling its cash, the firm greatly simplifies its cash management by reducing the number of accounts that must be tracked. Also, by having a larger pool of funds available, a firm may be able to negotiate or otherwise obtain a better rate on any short-term investments.

In setting up a concentration system, firms will typically use one or more *concentration banks*. A concentration bank pools the funds obtained from local banks contained within some geographic region. Concentration systems are often used in conjunction with lockbox systems. Figure 27.4 illustrates how an integrated cash collection and cash concentration system might look. As Figure 27.4 illustrates, a key part of the cash collection and concentration process is the transfer of funds to the concentration bank. There are several options available for accomplishing this transfer. The cheapest is a *depository transfer*

Figure 27.4

Lockboxes and Concentration Banks in a Cash Management System

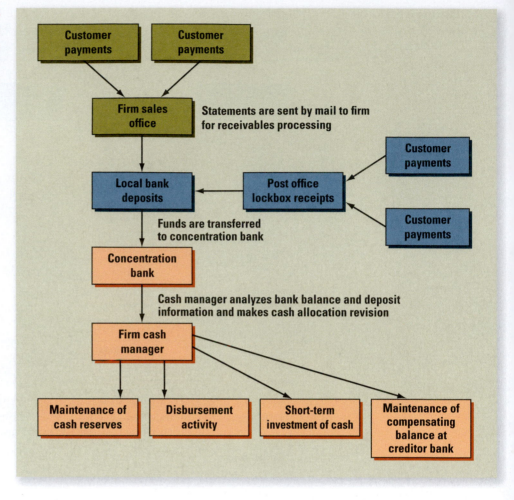

The Association for Financial Professionals has current info about cash management, **www.afponline.org**.

check (DTC), which is a preprinted check that usually needs no signature and is valid only for transferring funds between specific accounts within the *same* firm. The money becomes available one to two days later. *Automated clearinghouse (ACH)* transfers are basically electronic versions of paper checks. These may be more expensive, depending on the circumstances, but the funds are available the next day. The most expensive means of transfer are *wire transfers,* which provide same-day availability. Which approach a firm will choose depends on the number and size of payments. For example, a typical ACH transfer might be $200, whereas a typical wire transfer would be several million dollars. Firms with a large number of collection points and relatively small payments will choose the cheaper route, whereas firms that receive smaller numbers of relatively large payments may choose more expensive procedures.

ACCELERATING COLLECTIONS: AN EXAMPLE

The decision of whether or not to use a bank cash management service incorporating lockboxes and concentration banks depends on where a firm's customers are located and the speed of the U.S. postal system. Suppose Atlantic Corporation, located in Philadelphia, is considering a lockbox system. Its collection delay is currently eight days.

Atlantic does business in the southwestern part of the country (New Mexico, Arizona, and California). The proposed lockbox system would be located in Los Angeles and operated by Pacific Bank. Pacific Bank has analyzed Atlantic's cash-gathering system and has concluded that it can decrease collection time by two days. Specifically, the bank has come up with the following information on the proposed lockbox system:

Reduction in mailing time   = 1.0 day
Reduction in clearing time   = .5 day
Reduction in firm processing time = .5 day
                    Total = 2.0 days

The following is also known:

Daily interest on Treasury bills   = .025%
Average number of daily payments to lockboxes = 2,000
Average size of payment   = $600

The cash flows for the current collection operation are shown in the following cash flow time chart:

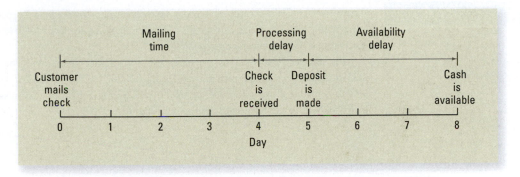

The cash flows for the lockbox collection operation will be as follows:

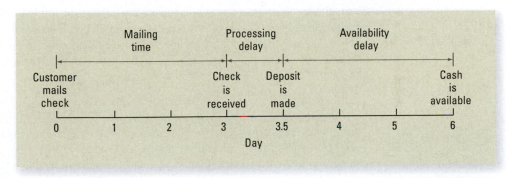

Pacific Bank has agreed to operate this lockbox system for a fee of 25 cents per check processed. Should Atlantic give the go-ahead?

We first need to determine the benefit of the system. The average daily collections from the southwestern region are $1.2 million (=2,000 × $600). The collection time will be decreased by two days, so the lockbox system will increase the collected bank balance by $1.2 million × 2 = $2.4 million. In other words, the lockbox system releases $2.4 million to the firm by reducing processing, mailing, and clearing time by two days. From our earlier discussion, we know that this $2.4 million is the PV of the proposal.

To calculate the NPV, we need to determine the PV of the costs. There are several different ways to proceed. First, at 2,000 checks per day and $.25 per check, the daily cost is $500. This cost will be incurred every day forever. At an interest rate of .025 percent per day, the PV is therefore $500/.00025 = $2 million. The NPV is thus $2.4 million − $2 million = $400,000, and the system appears to be desirable.

Alternatively, Atlantic could invest the $2.4 million at .025 percent per day. The interest earned would be $2.4 million × .00025 = $600 per day. The cost of the system is $500 per day; so running it obviously generates a profit in the amount of $100 per day. The PV of $100 per day forever is $100/.00025 = $400,000, just as we calculated before.

Finally, and most simply, each check is for $600 and is available two days sooner if the system is used. The interest on $600 for two days is 2 × $600 × .00025 = $.30. The cost is 25 cents per check, so Atlantic makes a nickel (=$.30 − .25) on every check. With 2,000 checks per day, the profit is $.05 × 2,000 checks = $100 per day, as we previously calculated.

EXAMPLE
27.4

Accelerating Collections   In our example concerning the Atlantic Corporation's proposed lock-box system, suppose Pacific Bank wants a $20,000 fixed fee (paid annually) in addition to the 25 cents per check. Is the system still a good idea?

To answer, we need to calculate the PV of the fixed fee. The daily interest rate is .025 percent. The annual rate is therefore $1.00025^{365} − 1 = 9.553\%$. The PV of the fixed fee (which is paid each year forever) is $20,000/.09553 = $209,358. Because the NPV without the fee is $400,000, the NPV with the fee is $400,000 − $209,358 = $190,642. It's still a good idea.

27.4 Managing Cash Disbursements

From the firm's point of view, disbursement float is desirable, so the goal in managing disbursement float is to slow down disbursements. To do this, the firm may develop strategies to *increase* mail float, processing float, and availability float on the checks it writes. Beyond this, firms have developed procedures for minimizing cash held for payment purposes. We discuss the most common of these in this section.

INCREASING DISBURSEMENT FLOAT

For a free cash budgeting spreadsheet, go to **www.bizfilings.com /toolkit/tools-forms .aspx**.

As we have seen, slowing down payments comes from the time involved in mail delivery, check processing, and collection of funds. Disbursement float can be increased by writing a check on a geographically distant bank. For example, a New York supplier might be paid with checks drawn on a Los Angeles bank. This will increase the time required for the checks to clear through the banking system. Mailing checks from remote post offices is another way firms slow down disbursement.

Tactics for maximizing disbursement float are debatable on both ethical and economic grounds. First, as we discuss in some detail in the next chapter, payment terms frequently offer a substantial discount for early payment. The discount is usually much larger than any possible savings from "playing the float game." In such cases, increasing mailing time will be of no benefit if the recipient dates payments based on the date received (as is common) as opposed to the postmark date.

Beyond this, suppliers are not likely to be fooled by attempts to slow down disbursements. The negative consequences of poor relations with suppliers can be costly. In broader terms, intentionally delaying payments by taking advantage of mailing times or unsophisticated suppliers may amount to avoiding paying bills when they are due—an unethical business procedure.

CONTROLLING DISBURSEMENTS

We have seen that maximizing disbursement float is probably a poor business practice. However, a firm will still wish to tie up as little cash as possible in disbursements. Firms have therefore developed systems for efficiently managing the disbursement process. The general idea in such systems is to have no more than the minimum amount necessary to pay bills on deposit in the bank. We discuss some approaches to accomplishing this goal next.

Zero-Balance Accounts　With a **zero-balance account** system, the firm, in cooperation with its bank, maintains a master account and a set of subaccounts. When a check written on one of the subaccounts must be paid, the necessary funds are transferred in from the master account. Figure 27.5 illustrates how such a system might work. In this case, the firm maintains two disbursement accounts, one for suppliers and one for payroll. As shown, if the firm does not use zero-balance accounts, then each of these accounts must have a safety stock of cash to meet unanticipated demands. If the firm does use zero-balance accounts, then it can keep one safety stock in a master account and transfer the funds to the two subsidiary accounts as needed. The key is that the total amount of cash held as a buffer is smaller under the zero-balance arrangement, which frees up cash to be used elsewhere.

Controlled Disbursement Accounts　With a **controlled disbursement account** system, almost all payments that must be made in a given day are known in the morning. The bank informs the firm of the total, and the firm transfers (usually by wire) the amount needed.

Figure 27.5　Zero-Balance Accounts

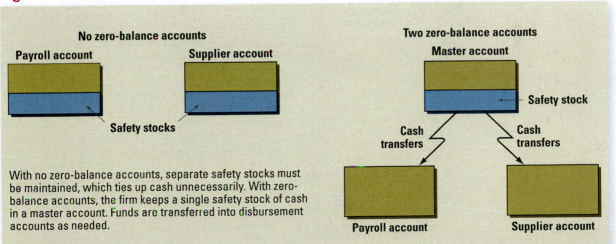

With no zero-balance accounts, separate safety stocks must be maintained, which ties up cash unnecessarily. With zero-balance accounts, the firm keeps a single safety stock of cash in a master account. Funds are transferred into disbursement accounts as needed.

27.5 Investing Idle Cash

If a firm has a temporary cash surplus, it can invest in short-term securities. As we have mentioned at various times, the market for short-term financial assets is called the *money market*. The maturity of short-term financial assets that trade in the money market is one year or less.

Most large firms manage their own short-term financial assets, carrying out transactions through banks and dealers. Some large firms and many small firms use money market mutual funds. These are funds that invest in short-term financial assets for a management fee. The management fee is compensation for the professional expertise and diversification provided by the fund manager.

Among the many money market mutual funds, some specialize in corporate customers. In addition, banks offer arrangements in which the bank takes all excess available funds at the close of each business day and invests them for the firm.

TEMPORARY CASH SURPLUSES

Firms have temporary cash surpluses for various reasons. Two of the most important are the financing of seasonal or cyclical activities of the firm and the financing of planned or possible expenditures.

Seasonal or Cyclical Activities   Some firms have a predictable cash flow pattern. They have surplus cash flows during part of the year and deficit cash flows the rest of the year. For example, Toys "Я" Us, a retail toy firm, has a seasonal cash flow pattern influenced by the holiday season.

A firm such as Toys "Я" Us may buy marketable securities when surplus cash flows occur and sell marketable securities when deficits occur. Of course, bank loans are another short-term financing device. The use of bank loans and marketable securities to meet temporary financing needs is illustrated in Figure 27.6. In this case, the firm is following a compromise working capital policy in the sense we discussed in the previous chapter.

Figure 27.6
Seasonal Cash
Demands

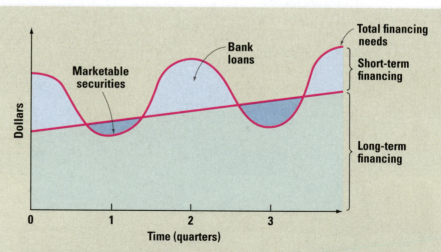

Time 1: A surplus cash flow exists. Seasonal demand for assets is low. The surplus
cash flow is invested in short-term marketable securities.

Time 2: A deficit cash flow exists. Seasonal demand for assets is high. The financial
deficit is financed by selling marketable securities and by bank borrowing.

Planned or Possible Expenditures Firms frequently accumulate temporary investments in marketable securities to provide the cash for a plant construction program, dividend payment, or other large expenditure. Thus, firms may issue bonds and stocks before the cash is needed, investing the proceeds in short-term marketable securities and then selling the securities to finance the expenditures. Also, firms may face the possibility of having to make a large cash outlay. An obvious example would involve the possibility of losing a large lawsuit. Firms may build up cash surpluses against such a contingency.

CHARACTERISTICS OF SHORT-TERM SECURITIES

Given that a firm has some temporarily idle cash, a variety of short-term securities are available for investing. The most important characteristics of these short-term marketable securities are their maturity, default risk, marketability, and taxability.

Maturity From Chapter 8, we know that for a given change in the level of interest rates, the prices of longer-maturity securities will change more than those of shorter-maturity securities. As a consequence, firms that invest in long-term securities are accepting greater risk than firms that invest in securities with short-term maturities.

We called this type of risk *interest rate risk*. Firms often limit their investments in marketable securities to those maturing in less than 90 days to avoid the risk of losses in value from changing interest rates. Of course, the expected return on securities with short-term maturities is usually less than the expected return on securities with longer maturities.

Default Risk *Default risk* refers to the probability that interest and principal will not be paid in the promised amounts on the due dates (or will not be paid at all). In Chapter 8, we observed that various financial reporting agencies, such as Moody's Investors Service and Standard and Poor's, compile and publish ratings of various corporate and other publicly held securities. These ratings are connected to default risk. Of course, some securities have negligible default risk, such as U.S. Treasury bills. Given the purposes of investing idle corporate cash, firms typically avoid investing in marketable securities with significant default risk.

Marketability *Marketability* refers to how easy it is to convert an asset to cash; so marketability and liquidity mean much the same thing. Some money market instruments are much more marketable than others. At the top of the list are U.S. Treasury bills, which can be bought and sold very cheaply and very quickly.

Taxes Interest earned on money market securities that are not some kind of government obligation (either federal or state) is taxable at the local, state, and federal levels. U.S. Treasury obligations such as T-bills are exempt from state taxation, but other government-backed debt is not. Municipal securities are exempt from federal taxes, but they may be taxed at the state level.

SOME DIFFERENT TYPES OF MONEY MARKET SECURITIES

Money market securities are generally highly marketable and short-term. They usually have low risk of default. They are issued by the U.S. government (e.g., U.S. Treasury bills), domestic and foreign banks (e.g., certificates of deposit), and business corporations (e.g., commercial paper). There are many types in all, and we illustrate only a few of the most common here.

U.S. Treasury bills are obligations of the U.S. government that mature in 30, 90, or 180 days. Bills are sold by auction every week.

Short-term tax-exempts are short-term securities issued by states, municipalities, local housing agencies, and urban renewal agencies. Because these are all considered municipal securities, they are exempt from federal taxes. RANs, BANs, and TANs, for example, are revenue, bond, and tax anticipation notes, respectively. In other words, they represent short-term borrowing by municipalities in anticipation of cash receipts.

Short-term tax-exempts have more default risk than U.S. Treasury issues and are less marketable. Because the interest is exempt from federal income tax, the pretax yield on tax-exempts is lower than that on comparable securities such as Treasury bills. Also, corporations face restrictions on holding tax-exempts as investments.

Commercial paper consists of short-term securities issued by finance companies, banks, and corporations. Typically, commercial paper is unsecured. Maturities range from a few weeks to 270 days.

There is no especially active secondary market in commercial paper. As a consequence, the marketability can be low; however, firms that issue commercial paper will often repurchase it directly before maturity. The default risk of commercial paper depends on the financial strength of the issuer. Moody's and S&P publish quality ratings for commercial paper. These ratings are similar to the bond ratings we discussed in Chapter 8.

Certificates of deposit (CDs) are short-term loans to commercial banks. The most common are jumbo CDs—those in excess of $100,000. There are active markets in CDs of 3-month, 6-month, 9-month, and 12-month maturities.

Repurchase agreements (repos) are sales of government securities (e.g., U.S. Treasury bills) by a bank or securities dealer with an agreement to repurchase. Typically, an investor buys some Treasury securities from a bond dealer and simultaneously agrees to sell them back at a later date at a specified higher price. Repurchase agreements usually involve a very short term—overnight to a few days.

Because 70 to 80 percent of the dividends received by one corporation from another are exempt from taxation, the relatively high dividend yields on preferred stock provide a strong incentive for investment. The only problem is that the dividend is fixed with ordinary preferred stock, so the price can fluctuate more than is desirable in a short-term investment. However, money market preferred stock is a fairly recent innovation featuring a floating dividend. The dividend is reset fairly often (usually every 49 days); so this type of preferred has much less price volatility than ordinary preferred, and it has become a popular short-term investment.

> Check out short-term rates online at **www.bloomberg .com**.

Summary and Conclusions

In this chapter, we have examined cash and liquidity management. We saw the following:

1. A firm holds cash to conduct transactions and to compensate banks for the various services they render.

2. The difference between a firm's available balance and its book balance is the firm's net float. The float reflects the fact that some checks have not cleared and are thus uncollected. The financial manager must always work with collected cash balances and not with the company's book balance. To do otherwise is to use the bank's cash without the bank knowing it, which raises ethical and legal questions.

3. The firm can make use of a variety of procedures to manage the collection and disbursement of cash in such a way as to speed up the collection of cash and slow down the payments. Some methods to speed up the collection are the use of lockboxes, concentration banking, and wire transfers.

4. Because of seasonal and cyclical activities, to help finance planned expenditures, or as a contingency reserve, firms temporarily hold a cash surplus. The money market offers a variety of possible vehicles for "parking" this idle cash.

Concept Questions

1. **Cash Management** Is it possible for a firm to have too much cash? Why would shareholders care if a firm accumulates large amounts of cash?

2. **Cash Management** What options are available to a firm if it believes it has too much cash? How about too little?

3. **Agency Issues** Are stockholders and creditors likely to agree on how much cash a firm should keep on hand?

4. **Cash Management versus Liquidity Management** What is the difference between cash management and liquidity management?

5. **Short-Term Investments** Why is a preferred stock with a dividend tied to short-term interest rates an attractive short-term investment for corporations with excess cash?

6. **Collection and Disbursement Floats** Which would a firm prefer: A net collection float or a net disbursement float? Why?

7. **Float** Suppose a firm has a book balance of $2 million. At the automatic teller machine (ATM), the cash manager finds out that the bank balance is $2.5 million. What is the situation here? If this is an ongoing situation, what ethical dilemma arises?

8. **Short-Term Investments** For each of the short-term marketable securities given here, provide an example of the potential disadvantages the investment has for meeting a corporation's cash management goals:
   a. U.S. Treasury bills.
   b. Ordinary preferred stock.
   c. Negotiable certificates of deposit (NCDs).
   d. Commercial paper.
   e. Revenue anticipation notes.
   f. Repurchase agreements.

9. **Agency Issues** It is sometimes argued that excess cash held by a firm can aggravate agency problems (discussed in Chapter 1) and, more generally, reduce incentives for shareholder wealth maximization. How would you describe the issue here?

10. **Use of Excess Cash** One option a firm usually has with any excess cash is to pay its suppliers more quickly. What are the advantages and disadvantages of this use of excess cash?

11. **Use of Excess Cash** Another option usually available is to reduce the firm's outstanding debt. What are the advantages and disadvantages of this use of excess cash?

12. **Float** An unfortunately common practice goes like this (Warning: Don't try this at home): Suppose you are out of money in your checking account; however, your local grocery store will, as a convenience to you as a customer, cash a check for you. So, you cash a check for $200. Of course, this check will bounce unless you do something. To prevent this, you go to the grocery the next day and cash another check

for $200. You take this $200 and deposit it. You repeat this process every day, and, in doing so, you make sure that no checks bounce. Eventually, manna from heaven arrives (perhaps in the form of money from home), and you are able to cover your outstanding checks.

To make it interesting, suppose you are absolutely certain that no checks will bounce along the way. Assuming this is true, and ignoring any question of legality (what we have described is probably illegal check kiting), is there anything unethical about this? If you say yes, then why? In particular, who is harmed?

Questions and Problems

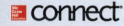

BASIC
(Questions 1–10)

1. **Calculating Float**   In a typical month, the Warren Corporation receives 140 checks totaling $113,500. These are delayed four days on average. What is the average daily float?

2. **Calculating Net Float**   Each business day, on average, a company writes checks totaling $14,400 to pay its suppliers. The usual clearing time for the checks is four days. Meanwhile, the company is receiving payments from its customers each day, in the form of checks, totaling $25,300. The cash from the payments is available to the firm after two days.

   a. Calculate the company's disbursement float, collection float, and net float.
   b. How would your answer to part (a) change if the collected funds were available in one day instead of two?

3. **Costs of Float**   Purple Feet Wine, Inc., receives an average of $13,800 in checks per day. The delay in clearing is typically three days. The current interest rate is .018 percent per day.

   a. What is the company's float?
   b. What is the most the company should be willing to pay today to eliminate its float entirely?
   c. What is the highest daily fee the company should be willing to pay to eliminate its float entirely?

4. **Float and Weighted Average Delay**   Your neighbor goes to the post office once a month and picks up two checks, one for $9,700 and one for $2,600. The larger check takes four days to clear after it is deposited; the smaller one takes five days.

   a. What is the total float for the month?
   b. What is the average daily float?
   c. What are the average daily receipts and weighted average delay?

5. **NPV and Collection Time**   Your firm has an average receipt size of $119. A bank has approached you concerning a lockbox service that will decrease your total collection time by two days. You typically receive 5,650 checks per day. The daily interest rate is .015 percent. If the bank charges a fee of $160 per day, should the lockbox project be accepted? What would the net annual savings be if the service were adopted?

6. **Using Weighted Average Delay**   A mail-order firm processes 5,450 checks per month. Of these, 70 percent are for $55 and 30 percent are for $80. The $55 checks are delayed two days on average; the $80 checks are delayed three days on average.

   a. What is the average daily collection float? How do you interpret your answer?
   b. What is the weighted average delay? Use the result to calculate the average daily float.
   c. How much should the firm be willing to pay to eliminate the float?

d. If the interest rate is 7 percent per year, calculate the daily cost of the float.

e. How much should the firm be willing to pay to reduce the weighted average float by 1.5 days?

7. **Value of Lockboxes** Paper Submarine Manufacturing is investigating a lockbox system to reduce its collection time. It has determined the following:

Average number of payments per day	410
Average value of payment	$865
Variable lockbox fee (per transaction)	$.50
Daily interest rate on money market securities	.02%

The total collection time will be reduced by three days if the lockbox system is adopted.

a. What is the PV of adopting the system?

b. What is the NPV of adopting the system?

c. What is the net cash flow per day from adopting? Per check?

8. **Lockboxes and Collections** It takes Cookie Cutter Modular Homes, Inc., about five days to receive and deposit checks from customers. Cookie Cutter's management is considering a lockbox system to reduce the firm's collection times. It is expected that the lockbox system will reduce receipt and deposit times to three days total. Average daily collections are $126,500, and the required rate of return is 9 percent per year.

a. What is the reduction in outstanding cash balance as a result of implementing the lockbox system?

b. What is the dollar return that could be earned on these savings?

c. What is the maximum monthly charge Cookie Cutter should pay for this lockbox system if the payment is due at the end of the month? What if the payment is due at the beginning of the month?

9. **Value of Delay** No More Pencils, Inc., disburses checks every two weeks that average $61,700 and take seven days to clear. How much interest can the company earn annually if it delays transfer of funds from an interest-bearing account that pays .015 percent per day for these seven days? Ignore the effects of compounding interest.

10. **NPV and Reducing Float** No More Books Corporation has an agreement with Floyd Bank, whereby the bank handles $2.9 million in collections a day and requires a $350,000 compensating balance. No More Books is contemplating canceling the agreement and dividing its eastern region so that two other banks will handle its business. Banks A and B will each handle $1.45 million of collections a day, and each requires a compensating balance of $190,000. No More Books' financial management expects that collections will be accelerated by one day if the eastern region is divided. Should the company proceed with the new system? What will be the annual net savings? Assume that the T-bill rate is 5 percent annually.

INTERMEDIATE
(Questions 11–12)

11. **Lockboxes and Collection Time** Bird's Eye Treehouses, Inc., a Kentucky company, has determined that a majority of its customers are located in the Pennsylvania area. It therefore is considering using a lockbox system offered by a bank located in Pittsburgh. The bank has estimated that use of the system will reduce collection time by two days. Based on the following information, should the lockbox system be adopted?

Average number of payments per day	850
Average value of payment	$630
Variable lockbox fee (per transaction)	$.22
Annual interest rate on money market securities	7%

How would your answer change if there were a fixed charge of $5,000 per year in addition to the variable charge?

12. **Calculating Transactions Required** Cow Chips, Inc., a large fertilizer distributor based in California, is planning to use a lockbox system to speed up collections from its customers located on the East Coast. A Philadelphia-area bank will provide this service for an annual fee of $12,000 plus 10 cents per transaction. The estimated reduction in collection and processing time is one day. If the average customer payment in this region is $4,800, how many customers are needed, on average, each day to make the system profitable for Cow Chips? Treasury bills are currently yielding 5 percent per year.

Mini Case

CASH MANAGEMENT AT RICHMOND CORPORATION

Richmond Corporation was founded 20 years ago by its president, Daniel Richmond. The company originally began as a mail-order company but has grown rapidly in recent years, in large part due to its website. Because of the wide geographical dispersion of the company's customers, it currently employs a lockbox system with collection centers in San Francisco, St. Louis, Atlanta, and Boston.

Steve Dennis, the company's treasurer, has been examining the current cash collection policies. On average, each lockbox center handles $185,000 in payments each day. The company's current policy is to invest these payments in short-term marketable securities daily at the collection center banks. Every two weeks the investment accounts are swept, and the proceeds are wire-transferred to Richmond's headquarters in Dallas to meet the company's payroll. The investment accounts each pay .068 percent per day, and the wire transfers cost .20 percent of the amount transferred.

Steve has been approached by Third National Bank, located just outside Dallas, about the possibility of setting up a concentration banking system for Richmond Corp. Third National will accept the lockbox centers' daily payments via automated clearinghouse (ACH) transfers in lieu of wire transfers. The ACH-transferred funds will not be available for use for one day. Once cleared, the funds will be deposited in a short-term account, which will yield .075 percent per day. Each ACH transfer will cost $200. Daniel has asked Steve to determine which cash management system will be the best for the company. Steve has asked you, his assistant, to answer the following questions:

1. What is Richmond Corporation's total net cash flow from the current lockbox system available to meet payroll?
2. Under the terms outlined by Third National Bank, should the company proceed with the concentration banking system?
3. What cost of ACH transfers would make the company indifferent between the two systems?

Appendix 27A Determining the Target Cash Balance

Appendix 27B Adjustable Rate Preferred Stock, Auction Rate Preferred Stock, and Floating-Rate Certificates of Deposit

To access the appendixes for this chapter, please logon to Connect Finance.

28

Credit and Inventory Management

Bitterly cold winter weather during the first quarter of 2014 was blamed for a slowdown in many areas, including auto sales. But when temperatures warmed up, so did sales. In fact, demand for rail transportation of new cars from manufacturing plants to dealers was up by more than 11 percent in the second quarter of 2014. While this might normally be considered good news, rail companies were caught off guard, causing a backup in delivery from a few days to a few weeks.

In fact, Chrysler had to park about 4,000 cars at the Michigan State Fairgrounds, and Ford was forced to park autos ready for transportation at a closed plant and at a parking lot. As these examples show, inventory disruptions can cause major problems for businesses. Further, companies such as these dislike carrying excessive inventory levels for a variety of reasons. In this chapter, we discuss, among other things, how companies arrive at an optimal inventory level.

28.1 Credit and Receivables

When a firm sells goods and services, it can demand cash on or before the delivery date, or it can extend credit to customers and allow some delay in payment. The next few sections provide an idea of what is involved in the firm's decision to grant credit to its customers. Granting credit is making an investment in a customer—an investment tied to the sale of a product or service.

Why do firms grant credit? Not all do, but the practice is extremely common. The obvious reason is that offering credit is a way of stimulating sales. The costs associated with granting credit are not trivial. First, there is the chance that the customer will not pay. Second, the firm has to bear the costs of carrying the receivables. The credit policy decision thus involves a trade-off between the benefits of increased sales and the costs of granting credit.

From an accounting perspective, when credit is granted, an account receivable is created. Such receivables include credit to other firms, called *trade credit,* and credit granted to consumers, called *consumer credit.* About one-sixth of all the assets of U.S. industrial firms are in the form of accounts receivable, so receivables obviously represent a major investment of financial resources by U.S. businesses.

COMPONENTS OF CREDIT POLICY

If a firm decides to grant credit to its customers, then it must establish procedures for extending credit and collecting. In particular, the firm will have to deal with the following components of credit policy:

1. **Terms of sale:** The terms of sale establish how the firm proposes to sell its goods and services. A basic decision is whether the firm will require cash or will extend credit. If the firm does grant credit to a customer, the terms of sale will specify (perhaps implicitly) the credit period, the cash discount and discount period, and the type of credit instrument.

2. **Credit analysis:** In granting credit, a firm determines how much effort to expend trying to distinguish between customers who will pay and customers who will not pay. Firms use a number of devices and procedures to determine the probability that customers will not pay; put together, these are called credit analysis.

3. **Collection policy:** After credit has been granted, the firm has the potential problem of collecting the cash, for which it must establish a collection policy.

In the next several sections, we will discuss these components of credit policy that collectively make up the decision to grant credit.

THE CASH FLOWS FROM GRANTING CREDIT

In a previous chapter, we described the accounts receivable period as the time it takes to collect on a sale. There are several events that occur during this period. These events are the cash flows associated with granting credit, and they can be illustrated with a cash flow diagram:

These companies assist businesses with working capital management: **www.pnc.com** and **www.treasurystrat .com.**

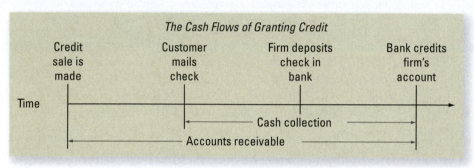

The Cash Flows of Granting Credit

As our time line indicates, the typical sequence of events when a firm grants credit is as follows: (1) The credit sale is made, (2) the customer sends a check to the firm, (3) the firm deposits the check, and (4) the firm's account is credited for the amount of the check.

Based on our discussion in the previous chapter, it is apparent that one of the factors influencing the receivables period is float. Thus, one way to reduce the receivables period is to speed up the check mailing, processing, and clearing. Because we cover this subject elsewhere, we will ignore float in the subsequent discussion and focus on what is likely to be the major determinant of the receivables period: Credit policy.

THE INVESTMENT IN RECEIVABLES

For more on accounts receivable management, visit **www.insidearm .com.**

The investment in accounts receivable for any firm depends on the amount of credit sales and the average collection period. For example, if a firm's average collection period, ACP, is 30 days, then, at any given time, there will be 30 days' worth of sales outstanding. If credit sales run $1,000 per day, the firm's accounts receivable will then be equal to 30 days × $1,000 per day = $30,000, on average.

As our example illustrates, a firm's receivables generally will be equal to its average daily sales multiplied by its average collection period:

$$\text{Accounts receivable} = \text{Average daily sales} \times \text{ACP} \qquad \textbf{(28.1)}$$

Thus, a firm's investment in accounts receivable depends on factors that influence credit sales and collections.

We have seen the average collection period in various places, including Chapters 3 and 26. Recall that we use the terms *days' sales in receivables, receivables period,* and *average collection period* interchangeably to refer to the length of time it takes for the firm to collect on a sale.

28.2   Terms of the Sale

As we described previously, the terms of a sale are made up of three distinct elements:

1. The period for which credit is granted (the credit period).
2. The cash discount and the discount period.
3. The type of credit instrument.

Within a given industry, the terms of sale are usually fairly standard, but these terms vary quite a bit across industries. In many cases, the terms of sale are remarkably archaic and literally date to previous centuries. Organized systems of trade credit that resemble current practice can be easily traced to the great fairs of medieval Europe, and they almost surely existed long before then.

THE BASIC FORM

The easiest way to understand the terms of sale is to consider an example. Terms such as 2/10, net 60 are common. This means that customers have 60 days from the invoice date (discussed a bit later) to pay the full amount; however, if payment is made within 10 days, a 2 percent cash discount can be taken.

Consider a buyer who places an order for $1,000, and assume that the terms of the sale are 2/10, net 60. The buyer has the option of paying $1,000 × (1 − .02) = $980 in 10 days, or paying the full $1,000 in 60 days. If the terms are stated as just net 30, then the customer has 30 days from the invoice date to pay the entire $1,000, and no discount is offered for early payment.

In general, credit terms are interpreted in the following way:

<take this discount off the invoice price>/<if you pay in this many days>,

<or pay the full invoice amount in this many days>

Thus, 5/10, net 45 means take a 5 percent discount from the full price if you pay within 10 days, or else pay the full amount in 45 days.

For more about the credit process for small businesses, visit the National Association of Credit Management at **www.nacm.org**.

THE CREDIT PERIOD

The **credit period** is the basic length of time for which credit is granted. The credit period varies widely from industry to industry, but it is almost always between 30 and 120 days. If a cash discount is offered, then the credit period has two components: The net credit period and the cash discount period.

The net credit period is the length of time the customer has to pay. The cash discount period is the time during which the discount is available. With 2/10, net 30, for example, the net credit period is 30 days and the cash discount period is 10 days.

The Invoice Date   The invoice date is the beginning of the credit period. An **invoice** is a written account of merchandise shipped to the buyer. For individual items, by convention, the invoice date is usually the shipping date or the billing date, *not* the date on which the buyer receives the goods or the bill.

Many other arrangements exist. For example, the terms of sale might be ROG, for *receipt of goods*. In this case, the credit period starts when the customer receives the order. This might be used when the customer is in a remote location.

With EOM dating, all sales made during a particular month are assumed to be made at the end of that month. This is useful when a buyer makes purchases throughout the month, but the seller bills only once a month.

For example, terms of 2/10, EOM tell the buyer to take a 2 percent discount if payment is made by the 10th of the month; otherwise the full amount is due. Confusingly, the end of the month is sometimes taken to be the 25th day of the month. MOM, for middle of month, is another variation.

Seasonal dating is sometimes used to encourage sales of seasonal products during the off-season. A product sold primarily in the summer (e.g., suntan oil) can be shipped in January with credit terms of 2/10, net 30. However, the invoice might be dated May 1 so that the credit period actually begins at that time. This practice encourages buyers to order early.

Length of the Credit Period   Several factors influence the length of the credit period. Two important ones are the *buyer's* inventory period and operating cycle. All else equal, the shorter these are, the shorter the credit period will be.

From Chapter 26, the operating cycle has two components: The inventory period and the receivables period. The buyer's inventory period is the time it takes the buyer to acquire inventory (from us), process it, and sell it. The buyer's receivables period is the time it then takes the buyer to collect on the sale. Note that the credit period we offer is effectively the buyer's payables period.

By extending credit, we finance a portion of our buyer's operating cycle and thereby shorten that buyer's cash cycle (see Figure 26.1). If our credit period exceeds the buyer's inventory period, then we are financing not only the buyer's inventory purchases, but part of the buyer's receivables as well.

Furthermore, if our credit period exceeds our buyer's operating cycle, then we are effectively providing financing for aspects of our customer's business beyond the immediate purchase and sale of our merchandise. The reason is that the buyer effectively has a loan from us even after the merchandise is resold, and the buyer can use that credit for other purposes. For this reason, the length of the buyer's operating cycle is often cited as an appropriate upper limit to the credit period.

There are a number of other factors that influence the credit period. Many of these also influence our customer's operating cycles; so, once again, these are related subjects. Among the most important are these:

1. *Perishability and collateral value:* Perishable items have relatively rapid turnover and relatively low collateral value. Credit periods are thus shorter for such goods. For example, a food wholesaler selling fresh fruit and produce might use net seven days. Alternatively, jewelry might be sold for 5/30, net four months.

2. *Consumer demand:* Products that are well established generally have more rapid turnover. Newer or slow-moving products will often have longer credit periods associated with them to entice buyers. Also, as we have seen, sellers may

choose to extend much longer credit periods for off-season sales (when customer demand is low).

3. *Cost, profitability, and standardization:* Relatively inexpensive goods tend to have shorter credit periods. The same is true for relatively standardized goods and raw materials. These all tend to have lower markups and higher turnover rates, both of which lead to shorter credit periods. However, there are exceptions. Auto dealers, for example, generally pay for cars as they are received.

4. *Credit risk:* The greater the credit risk of the buyer, the shorter the credit period is likely to be (if credit is granted at all).

5. *Size of the account:* If an account is small, the credit period may be shorter because small accounts cost more to manage, and the customers are less important.

6. *Competition:* When the seller is in a highly competitive market, longer credit periods may be offered as a way of attracting customers.

7. *Customer type:* A single seller might offer different credit terms to different buyers. A food wholesaler, for example, might supply groceries, bakeries, and restaurants. Each group would probably have different credit terms. More generally, sellers often have both wholesale and retail customers, and they frequently quote different terms to the two types.

CASH DISCOUNTS

As we have seen, **cash discounts** are often part of the terms of sale. The practice of granting discounts for cash purchases in the United States dates to the Civil War and is widespread today. One reason discounts are offered is to speed up the collection of receivables. This will have the effect of reducing the amount of credit being offered, and the firm must trade this off against the cost of the discount.

Notice that when a cash discount is offered, the credit is essentially free during the discount period. The buyer pays for the credit only after the discount expires. With 2/10, net 30, a rational buyer either pays in 10 days to make the greatest possible use of the free credit or pays in 30 days to get the longest possible use of the money in exchange for giving up the discount. By giving up the discount, the buyer effectively gets $30 - 10 = 20$ days' credit.

Another reason for cash discounts is that they are a way of charging higher prices to customers that have had credit extended to them. In this sense, cash discounts are a convenient way of charging for the credit granted to customers.

Visit the National Association of Credit Management at **www.nacm.org**.

Cost of the Credit   In our examples, it might seem that the discounts are rather small. With 2/10, net 30, for example, early payment gets the buyer only a 2 percent discount. Does this provide a significant incentive for early payment? The answer is yes because the implicit interest rate is extremely high.

To see why the discount is important, we will calculate the cost to the buyer of not paying early. To do this, we will find the interest rate that the buyer is effectively paying for the trade credit. Suppose the order is for $1,000. The buyer can pay $980 in 10 days or wait another 20 days and pay $1,000. It's obvious that the buyer is effectively borrowing $980 for 20 days and that the buyer pays $20 in interest on the "loan." What's the interest rate?

This interest is ordinary discount interest, which we discussed in Chapter 4. With $20 in interest on $980 borrowed, the rate is $20/$980 = 2.0408%. This is relatively low, but remember that this is the rate per 20-day period. There are 365/20 = 18.25 such periods in a year; so, by not taking the discount, the buyer is paying an effective annual rate (EAR) of:

$$EAR = 1.020408^{18.25} - 1 = .4459, \text{ or } 44.59\%$$

From the buyer's point of view, this is an expensive source of financing!

Given that the interest rate is so high here, it is unlikely that the seller benefits from early payment. Ignoring the possibility of default by the buyer, the decision of a customer to forgo the discount almost surely works to the seller's advantage.

Trade Discounts   In some circumstances, the discount is not really an incentive for early payment but is instead a *trade discount,* a discount routinely given to some type of buyer. For example, with our 2/10, EOM terms, the buyer takes a 2 percent discount if the invoice is paid by the 10th, but the bill is considered due on the 10th, and overdue after that. Thus, the credit period and the discount period are effectively the same, and there is no reward for paying before the due date.

The Cash Discount and the ACP   To the extent that a cash discount encourages customers to pay early, it will shorten the receivables period and, all other things being equal, reduce the firm's investment in receivables.

For example, suppose a firm currently has terms of net 30 and an average collection period (ACP) of 30 days. If it offers terms of 2/10, net 30, then perhaps 50 percent of its customers (in terms of volume of purchases) will pay in 10 days. The remaining customers will still take an average of 30 days to pay. What will the new ACP be? If the firm's annual sales are $15 million (before discounts), what will happen to the investment in receivables?

If half of the customers take 10 days to pay and half take 30, then the new average collection period will be:

$$\text{New ACP} = .50 \times 10 \text{ days} + .50 \times 30 \text{ days} = 20 \text{ days}$$

The ACP thus falls from 30 days to 20 days. Average daily sales are $15 million/365 = $41,096 per day. Receivables will thus fall by $41,096 \times 10 = $410,960.

CREDIT INSTRUMENTS

The **credit instrument** is the basic evidence of indebtedness. Most trade credit is offered on *open account.* This means that the only formal instrument of credit is the invoice, which is sent with the shipment of goods and which the customer signs as evidence that the goods have been received. Afterward, the firm and its customers record the exchange on their books of account.

At times the firm may require that the customer sign a *promissory note.* This is a basic IOU and might be used when the order is large, when there is no cash discount involved, or when the firm anticipates a problem in collections. Promissory notes are not common, but they can eliminate possible controversies later about the existence of debt.

One problem with promissory notes is that they are signed after delivery of the goods. One way to obtain a credit commitment from a customer before the goods are delivered is to arrange a *commercial draft.* Typically, the firm draws up a commercial draft calling for the customer to pay a specific amount by a specified date. The draft is then sent to the customer's bank with the shipping invoices.

If immediate payment is required on the draft, it is called a *sight draft.* If immediate payment is not required, then the draft is a *time draft.* When the draft is presented and the buyer "accepts" it, meaning that the buyer promises to pay it in the future, then it is called a *trade acceptance* and is sent back to the selling firm. The seller can then keep the acceptance or sell it to someone else. If a bank accepts the draft, meaning that the bank is guaranteeing payment, then the draft becomes a *banker's acceptance.* This arrangement is common in international trade, and banker's acceptances are actively traded in the money market.

A firm can also use a conditional sales contract as a credit instrument. With such an arrangement, the firm retains legal ownership of the goods until the customer has completed payment. Conditional sales contracts usually are paid in installments and have an interest cost built into them.

28.3 Analyzing Credit Policy

In this section, we take a closer look at the factors that influence the decision to grant credit. Granting credit makes sense only if the NPV from doing so is positive. We thus need to look at the NPV of the decision to grant credit.

CREDIT POLICY EFFECTS

In evaluating credit policy, there are five basic factors to consider:

1. *Revenue effects:* If the firm grants credit, then there will be a delay in revenue collections as some customers take advantage of the credit offered and pay later. However, the firm may be able to charge a higher price if it grants credit and it may be able to increase the quantity sold. Total revenues may thus increase.

2. *Cost effects:* Although the firm may experience delayed revenues if it grants credit, it will still incur the costs of sales immediately. Whether the firm sells for cash or credit, it will still have to acquire or produce the merchandise (and pay for it).

3. *The cost of debt:* When the firm grants credit, it must arrange to finance the resulting receivables. As a result, the firm's cost of short-term borrowing is a factor in the decision to grant credit.[1]

4. *The probability of nonpayment:* If the firm grants credit, some percentage of the credit buyers will not pay. This can't happen, of course, if the firm sells for cash.

5. *The cash discount:* When the firm offers a cash discount as part of its credit terms, some customers will choose to pay early to take advantage of the discount.

EVALUATING A PROPOSED CREDIT POLICY

To illustrate how credit policy can be analyzed, we will start with a relatively simple case. Locust Software has been in existence for two years, and it is one of several successful firms that develop computer programs. Currently, Locust sells for cash only.

Locust is evaluating a request from some major customers to change its current policy to net one month (30 days). To analyze this proposal, we define the following:

P = Price per unit

v = Variable cost per unit

Q = Current quantity sold per month

Q' = Quantity sold under new policy

R = Monthly required return

---

[1]The cost of short-term debt is not necessarily the required return on receivables, although it is commonly assumed to be. As always, the required return on an investment depends on the risk of the investment, not the source of the financing. The *buyer's* cost of short-term debt is closer in spirit to the correct rate. We will maintain the implicit assumption that the seller and the buyer have the same short-term debt cost. In any case, the time periods in credit decisions are relatively short, so a relatively small error in the discount rate will not have a large effect on our estimated NPV.

For now, we ignore discounts and the possibility of default. Also, we ignore taxes because they don't affect our conclusions.

NPV of Switching Policies   To illustrate the NPV of switching credit policies, suppose we have the following for Locust:

$$P = \$49$$
$$v = \$20$$
$$Q = 100$$
$$Q' = 110$$

If the required return, R, is 2 percent per month, should Locust make the switch?

Currently, Locust has monthly sales of $P \times Q = \$4,900$. Variable costs each month are $v \times Q = \$2,000$, so the monthly cash flow from this activity is:

$$\text{Cash flow with old policy} = (P - v)Q \qquad \textbf{(28.2)}$$
$$= (\$49 - 20) \times 100$$
$$= \$2,900$$

This is not the total cash flow for Locust, of course, but it is all that we need to look at because fixed costs and other components of cash flow are the same whether or not the switch is made.

If Locust does switch to net 30 days on sales, then the quantity sold will rise to $Q' = 110$. Monthly revenues will increase to $P \times Q'$, and costs will be $v \times Q'$. The monthly cash flow under the new policy will thus be:

$$\text{Cash flow with new policy} = (P - v)Q' \qquad \textbf{(28.3)}$$
$$= (\$49 - 20) \times 110$$
$$= \$3,190$$

Going back to Chapter 6, we know that the relevant incremental cash flow is the difference between the new and old cash flows:

$$\text{Incremental cash inflow} = (P - v)(Q' - Q)$$
$$= (\$49 - 20) \times (110 - 100)$$
$$= \$290$$

This says that the benefit each month of changing policies is equal to the gross profit per unit sold, $P - v = \$29$, multiplied by the increase in sales, $Q' - Q = 10$. The present value of the future incremental cash flows is thus:

$$\text{PV} = [(P - v)(Q' - Q)]/R \qquad \textbf{(28.4)}$$

For Locust, this present value works out to be:

$$\text{PV} = (\$29 \times 10)/.02 = \$14,500$$

Notice that we have treated the monthly cash flow as a perpetuity because the same benefit will be realized each month forever.

Now that we know the benefit of switching, what's the cost? There are two components to consider. First, because the quantity sold will rise from Q to Q', Locust will have to produce $Q' - Q$ more units at a cost of $v(Q' - Q) = \$20 \times (110 - 100) = \$200$. Second, the sales that would have been collected this month under the current policy ($P \times Q = \$4,900$) will not be collected. Under the new policy, the sales made this month won't be collected until 30 days later. The cost of the switch is the sum of these two components:

$$\text{Cost of switching} = PQ + v(Q' - Q) \qquad (28.5)$$

For Locust, this cost would be $4,900 + $200 = $5,100.

Putting it all together, we see that the NPV of the switch is:

$$\text{NPV of switching} = -[PQ + v(Q' - Q)] + [(P - v)(Q' - Q)]/R \qquad (28.6)$$

For Locust, the cost of switching is $5,100. As we saw earlier, the benefit is $290 per month, forever. At 2 percent per month, the NPV is:

$$\begin{aligned}
\text{NPV} &= -\$5,100 + \$290/.02 \\
&= -\$5,100 + 14,500 \\
&= \$9,400
\end{aligned}$$

Therefore, the switch is very profitable.

EXAMPLE 28.1

We'd Rather Fight Than Switch   Suppose a company is considering a switch from all cash to net 30, but the quantity sold is not expected to change. What is the NPV of the switch? Explain.

In this case, $Q' - Q$ is zero, so the NPV is just $-PQ$. What this says is that the effect of the switch is simply to postpone one month's collections forever, with no benefit from doing so.

A Break-Even Application   Based on our discussion thus far, the key variable for Locust is $Q' - Q$, the increase in unit sales. The projected increase of 10 units is only an estimate, so there is some forecasting risk. Under the circumstances, it's natural to wonder what increase in unit sales is necessary to break even.

Earlier, the NPV of the switch was defined as:

$$\text{NPV} = -[PQ + v(Q' - Q)] + [(P - v)(Q' - Q)]/R$$

We can calculate the break-even point explicitly by setting the NPV equal to zero and solving for $(Q' - Q)$:

$$\begin{aligned}
\text{NPV} = 0 &= -[PQ + v(Q' - Q)] + [(P - v)(Q' - Q)]/R \qquad (28.7) \\
Q' - Q &= PQ/[(P - v)/R - v]
\end{aligned}$$

For Locust, the break-even sales increase is thus:

$$\begin{aligned}
Q' - Q &= \$4,900/(\$29/.02 - \$20) \\
&= 3.43 \text{ units}
\end{aligned}$$

This tells us that the switch is a good idea as long as Locust is confident that it can sell at least 3.43 more units per month.

28.4 Optimal Credit Policy

For business reports on credit, visit **www.creditworthy .com**.

So far, we've discussed how to compute net present values for a switch in credit policy. We have not discussed the optimal amount of credit or the optimal credit policy. In principle, the optimal amount of credit is determined by the point at which the incremental cash flows from increased sales are exactly equal to the incremental costs of carrying the increase in investment in accounts receivable.

THE TOTAL CREDIT COST CURVE

The trade-off between granting credit and not granting credit isn't hard to identify, but it is difficult to quantify precisely. As a result, we can only describe an optimal credit policy.

To begin, the carrying costs associated with granting credit come in three forms:

1. The required return on receivables.
2. The losses from bad debts.
3. The costs of managing credit and credit collections.

We have already discussed the first and second of these. The third cost, the cost of managing credit, consists of the expenses associated with running the credit department. Firms that don't grant credit have no such department and no such expense. These three costs will all increase as credit policy is relaxed.

If a firm has a very restrictive credit policy, then all of the associated costs will be low. In this case, the firm will have a "shortage" of credit, so there will be an opportunity cost. This opportunity cost is the extra potential profit from credit sales that are lost because credit is refused. This forgone benefit comes from two sources: The increase in quantity sold, Q' minus Q, and (potentially) a higher price. The opportunity costs go down as credit policy is relaxed.

The sum of the carrying costs and the opportunity costs of a particular credit policy is called the total **credit cost curve**. We have drawn such a curve in Figure 28.1. As Figure 28.1 illustrates, there is a point where the total credit cost is minimized. This point corresponds to the optimal amount of credit or, equivalently, the optimal investment in receivables.

Figure 28.1
The Costs of Granting Credit

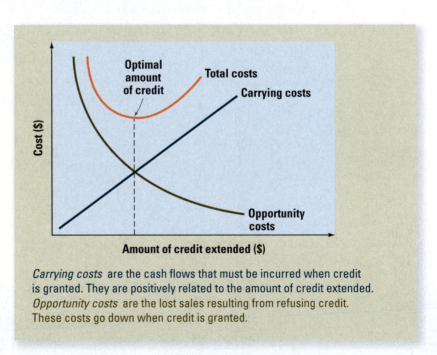

Carrying costs are the cash flows that must be incurred when credit is granted. They are positively related to the amount of credit extended.
Opportunity costs are the lost sales resulting from refusing credit. These costs go down when credit is granted.

If the firm extends more credit than this minimum, the additional net cash flow from new customers will not cover the carrying costs of the investment in receivables. If the level of receivables is below this amount, then the firm is forgoing valuable profit opportunities.

In general, the costs and benefits from extending credit will depend on characteristics of particular firms and industries. All other things being equal, for example, it is likely that firms with (1) excess capacity, (2) low variable operating costs, and (3) repeat customers will extend credit more liberally than other firms. See if you can explain why each of these characteristics contributes to a more liberal credit policy.

ORGANIZING THE CREDIT FUNCTION

Firms that grant credit have the expense of running a credit department. In practice, firms often choose to contract out all or part of the credit function to a factor, an insurance company, or a captive finance company. Chapter 26 discusses factoring, an arrangement in which the firm sells its receivables. Depending on the specific arrangement, the factor may have full responsibility for credit checking, authorization, and collection. Smaller firms may find such an arrangement cheaper than running a credit department.

Firms that manage internal credit operations are self-insured against default. An alternative is to buy credit insurance through an insurance company. The insurance company offers coverage up to a preset dollar limit for accounts. As you would expect, accounts with a higher credit rating merit higher insurance limits. This type of insurance is particularly important for exporters, and government insurance is available for certain types of exports.

Large firms often extend credit through a **captive finance company**, which is simply a wholly owned subsidiary that handles the credit function for the parent company. Ford Motor Credit (FMC) is a well-known example. Ford sells to car dealers, who in turn sell to customers. FMC finances the dealers' inventory of cars and also finances customers who buy the cars.

Why would a firm choose to set up a separate company to handle the credit function? There are a number of reasons, but a primary one is to separate the production and financing of the firm's products for management, financing, and reporting. For example, the finance subsidiary can borrow in its own name, using its receivables as collateral, and the subsidiary often carries a better credit rating than the parent. This may allow the firm to achieve a lower overall cost of debt than could be obtained if production and financing were commingled.

28.5 Credit Analysis

Thus far, we have focused on establishing credit terms. Once a firm decides to grant credit to its customers, it must then establish guidelines for determining who will and who will not be allowed to buy on credit. *Credit analysis* refers to the process of deciding whether or not to extend credit to a particular customer. It usually involves two steps: Gathering relevant information and determining creditworthiness.

Credit analysis is important simply because potential losses on receivables can be substantial. On their balance sheets, companies report the amount of receivables they expect not to collect. In 2014, IBM reported that $316 million of accounts receivable were doubtful, and GE reported a staggering $5.2 billion as an allowance for losses.

WHEN SHOULD CREDIT BE GRANTED?

Imagine that a firm is trying to decide whether or not to grant credit to a customer. This decision can get complicated. For example, note that the answer depends on what will happen if credit is refused. Will the customer simply pay cash? Or will the customer not make the purchase at all? To avoid being bogged down by this and other difficulties, we will use some special cases to illustrate the key points.

A One-Time Sale We start by considering the simplest case. A new customer wishes to buy one unit on credit at a price of P per unit. If credit is refused, the customer will not make the purchase.

Furthermore, we assume that, if credit is granted, then, in one month, the customer will either pay up or default. The probability of the second of these events is π. In this case, the probability (π) can be interpreted as the percentage of *new* customers who will not pay. Our business does not have repeat customers, so this is strictly a one-time sale. Finally, the required return on receivables is R per month, and the variable cost is v per unit.

The analysis here is straightforward. If the firm refuses credit, then the incremental cash flow is zero. If it grants credit, then it spends v (the variable cost) this month and expects to collect $(1 - \pi)P$ next month. The NPV of granting credit is:

$$\text{NPV} = -v + (1 - \pi)P/(1 + R) \tag{28.8}$$

For example, for Locust Software, this NPV is:

$$\text{NPV} = -\$20 + (1 - \pi) \times \$49/1.02$$

With, say, a 20 percent rate of default, this works out to be:

$$\text{NPV} = -\$20 + .80 \times \$49/1.02 = \$18.43$$

Therefore, credit should be granted. Notice that we have divided by $(1 + R)$ here instead of by R because we now assume that this is a one-time transaction.

Our example illustrates an important point. In granting credit to a new customer, a firm risks its variable cost (v). It stands to gain the full price (P). For a new customer, then, credit may be granted even if the default probability is high. For example, the break-even probability in this case can be determined by setting the NPV equal to zero and solving for π:

$$\text{NPV} = 0 = -\$20 + (1 - \pi) \times \$49/1.02$$
$$1 - \pi = \$20/\$49 \times 1.02$$
$$\pi = 58.4\%$$

Locust should extend credit as long as there is a $1 - .584 = 41.6\%$ chance or better of collecting. This explains why firms with higher markups tend to have looser credit terms.

This percentage (58.4 percent) is the maximum acceptable default probability for a *new* customer. If a returning, cash-paying customer wanted to switch to a credit basis, the analysis would be different, and the maximum acceptable default probability would be much lower.

The important difference is that, if we extend credit to a returning customer, we risk the total sales price (P), because this is what we collect if we don't extend credit. If we extend credit to a new customer, we risk only our variable cost.

Repeat Business A second, very important factor to keep in mind is the possibility of repeat business. We can illustrate this by extending our one-time sale example. We make one important assumption: A new customer who does not default the first time around will remain a customer forever and never default.

If the firm grants credit, it spends v this month. Next month, it gets nothing if the customer defaults, or it gets P if the customer pays. If the customer pays, then the customer will buy another unit on credit and the firm will spend v again. The net cash inflow for the month is thus $P - v$. In every subsequent month, this same $P - v$ will occur as the customer pays for the previous month's order and places a new one.

It follows from our discussion that, in one month, the firm will receive $0 with probability π. With probability $(1 - \pi)$, however, the firm will have a permanent new customer. The value of a new customer is equal to the present value of $(P - v)$ every month forever:

$$PV = (P - v)/R$$

The NPV of extending credit is therefore:

$$NPV = -v + (1 - \pi)(P - v)/R \tag{28.9}$$

For Locust, this is:

$$NPV = -\$20 + (1 - \pi) \times (\$49 - 20)/.02$$
$$= -\$20 + (1 - \pi) \times \$1{,}450$$

Even if the probability of default is 90 percent, the NPV is:

$$NPV = -\$20 + .10 \times \$1{,}450 = \$125$$

Locust should extend credit unless default is a virtual certainty. The reason is that it costs only $20 to find out who is a good customer and who is not. A good customer is worth $1,450, however, so Locust can afford quite a few defaults.

Our repeat business example probably exaggerates the acceptable default probability, but it does illustrate that it will often turn out that the best way to do credit analysis is simply to extend credit to almost anyone. It also points out that the possibility of repeat business is a crucial consideration. In such cases, the important thing is to control the amount of credit initially offered to any one customer so that the possible loss is limited. The amount can be increased with time. Most often, the best predictor of whether or not someone will pay in the future is whether or not they have paid in the past.

CREDIT INFORMATION

Web-surfing students should peruse the Dun & Bradstreet home page. This major supplier of credit information can be found at **www.dnb.com**.

If a firm wants credit information about customers, there are a number of sources. Information sources commonly used to assess creditworthiness include the following:

1. *Financial statements:* A firm can ask a customer to supply financial statements such as balance sheets and income statements. Minimum standards and rules of thumb based on financial ratios like the ones we discussed in Chapter 3 can then be used as a basis for extending or refusing credit.

2. *Credit reports about the customer's payment history with other firms:* Quite a few organizations sell information about the credit strength and credit history of business firms. The best-known and largest firm of this type is Dun & Bradstreet, which provides subscribers with credit reports on individual firms. Experian is another well-known credit-reporting firm. Ratings and information are available for a huge number of firms, including very small ones. Equifax, Transunion, and Experian are the major suppliers of consumer credit information.

3. *Banks:* Banks will generally provide some assistance to their business customers in acquiring information about the creditworthiness of other firms.

4. *The customer's payment history with the firm:* The most obvious way to obtain information about the likelihood of customers not paying is to examine whether they have settled past obligations (and how quickly).

CREDIT EVALUATION AND SCORING

There are no magical formulas for assessing the probability that a customer will not pay. In very general terms, the classic **five Cs of credit** are the basic factors to be evaluated:

1. *Character:* The customer's willingness to meet credit obligations.
2. *Capacity:* The customer's ability to meet credit obligations out of operating cash flows.
3. *Capital:* The customer's financial reserves.
4. *Collateral:* An asset pledged in the case of default.
5. *Conditions:* General economic conditions in the customer's line of business.

Credit scoring is the process of calculating a numerical rating for a customer based on information collected; credit is then granted or refused based on the result. For example, a firm might rate a customer on a scale of 1 (very poor) to 10 (very good) on each of the five Cs of credit using all the information available about the customer. A credit score could then be calculated by totaling these ratings. Based on experience, a firm might choose to grant credit only to customers with a score above, say, 30.

Firms such as credit card issuers have developed statistical models for credit scoring. Usually, all of the legally relevant and observable characteristics of a large pool of customers are studied to find their historic relation to defaults. Based on the results, it is possible to determine the variables that best predict whether a customer will pay and then calculate a credit score based on those variables.

Because credit-scoring models and procedures determine who is and who is not creditworthy, it is not surprising that they have been the subject of government regulation. In particular, the kinds of background and demographic information that can be used in the credit decision are limited.

28.6 Collection Policy

Collection policy is the final element in credit policy. Collection policy involves monitoring receivables to spot trouble and obtaining payment on past-due accounts.

MONITORING RECEIVABLES

To keep track of payments by customers, most firms will monitor outstanding accounts. First of all, a firm will normally keep track of its average collection period (ACP) through time. If a firm is in a seasonal business, the ACP will fluctuate during the year; but unexpected increases in the ACP are a cause for concern. Either customers in general are taking longer to pay, or some percentage of accounts receivable are seriously overdue.

The **aging schedule** is a second basic tool for monitoring receivables. To prepare one, the credit department classifies accounts by age.[2] Suppose a firm has $100,000 in

---

[2]Aging schedules are also used elsewhere in business such as inventory tracking.

receivables. Some of these accounts are only a few days old, but others have been outstanding for quite some time. The following is an example of an aging schedule:

Aging Schedule		
Age of Account	Amount	Percentage of Total Value of Accounts Receivable
0–10 days	$ 50,000	50%
11–60 days	25,000	25
61–80 days	20,000	20
Over 80 days	5,000	5
	$100,000	100%

If this firm has a credit period of 60 days, then 25 percent of its accounts are late. Whether or not this is serious depends on the nature of the firm's collections and customers. It is often the case that accounts beyond a certain age are almost never collected. Monitoring the age of accounts is very important in such cases.

Firms with seasonal sales will find the percentages on the aging schedule changing during the year. For example, if sales in the current month are very high, then total receivables will also increase sharply. This means that the older accounts, as a percentage of total receivables, become smaller and might appear less important. Some firms have refined the aging schedule so that they have an idea of how it should change with peaks and valleys in their sales.

COLLECTION EFFORT

A firm usually goes through the following sequence of procedures for customers whose payments are overdue:

1. It sends out a delinquency letter informing the customer of the past-due status of the account.
2. It makes a telephone call to the customer.
3. It employs a collection agency.
4. It takes legal action against the customer.

At times, a firm may refuse to grant additional credit to customers until arrearages are cleared up. This may antagonize a normally good customer, which points to a potential conflict between the collections department and the sales department.

In probably the worst case, the customer files for bankruptcy. When this happens, the credit-granting firm is just another unsecured creditor. The firm can simply wait, or it can sell its receivable. For example, when bookseller Borders filed for bankruptcy in 2011, it owed $178.8 million to its vendors and $18.6 million to its landlords. One of the largest vendors was publisher Penguin Putnam, which was owed $41.1 million. Of course, the firm could simply give up on its claim. Book publisher Wiley had already written off $9 million in debt for books sold to Borders.

28.7 Inventory Management

Like receivables, inventories represent a significant investment for many firms. For a typical manufacturing operation, inventories will often exceed 15 percent of assets. For a retailer, inventories could represent more than 25 percent of assets. From our discussion in Chapter 26, we know that a firm's operating cycle is made up of its inventory period and its receivables period. This is one reason for considering credit and inventory policy in the same chapter. Beyond this, both credit policy and inventory policy are used to drive sales, and the two must be coordinated to ensure that the process of acquiring inventory, selling it, and collecting on the sale is a smooth one. For example, changes in credit policy designed to stimulate sales must be accompanied by planning for adequate inventory.

THE FINANCIAL MANAGER AND INVENTORY POLICY

Despite the size of a typical firm's investment in inventories, the financial manager of a firm will not normally have primary control over inventory management. Instead, other functional areas such as purchasing, production, and marketing will usually share decision-making authority regarding inventory. Inventory management has become an increasingly important specialty in its own right, and financial management will often only have input into the decision. For this reason, we will just survey some basics of inventory and inventory policy.

Visit the Society for Inventory Management Benchmarking Analysis at **www.simba.org**.

INVENTORY TYPES

For a manufacturer, inventory is normally classified into one of three categories. The first category is *raw materials*. This is whatever the firm uses as a starting point in its production process. Raw materials might be something as basic as iron ore for a steel manufacturer or something as sophisticated as disk drives for a computer manufacturer.

The second type of inventory is *work-in-progress,* which is just what the name suggests—unfinished product. How big this portion of inventory is depends in large part on the length of the production process. For an airframe manufacturer, for example, work-in-progress can be substantial. The third and final type of inventory is *finished goods*—that is, products ready to ship or sell.

Keep in mind three things concerning inventory types. First, the names for the different types can be a little misleading because one company's raw materials can be another's finished goods. For example, going back to our steel manufacturer, iron ore would be a raw material, and steel would be the final product. An auto body panel stamping operation will have steel as its raw material and auto body panels as its finished goods, and an automobile assembler will have body panels as raw materials and automobiles as finished products.

The second thing to keep in mind is that the various types of inventory can be quite different in terms of their liquidity. Raw materials that are commodity-like or relatively standardized can be easy to convert to cash. Work-in-progress, on the other hand, can be quite illiquid and have little more than scrap value. As always, the liquidity of finished goods depends on the nature of the product.

Finally, a very important distinction between finished goods and other types of inventories is that the demand for an inventory item that becomes a part of another item is usually termed *derived* or *dependent demand* because the firm's need for these inventory types depends on its need for finished items. In contrast, the firm's demand for finished goods is not derived from demand for other inventory items, so it is sometimes said to be *independent.*

INVENTORY COSTS

As we discussed in Chapter 26, two basic types of costs are associated with current assets in general and with inventory in particular. The first of these is *carrying costs*. Here, carrying costs represent all of the direct and opportunity costs of keeping inventory on hand. These include:

1. Storage and tracking costs.
2. Insurance and taxes.
3. Losses due to obsolescence, deterioration, or theft.
4. The opportunity cost of capital on the invested amount.

The sum of these costs can be substantial, ranging roughly from 20 to 40 percent of inventory value per year.

The other type of costs associated with inventory is *shortage costs.* Shortage costs are costs associated with having inadequate inventory on hand. The two components of shortage costs are restocking costs and costs related to safety reserves. Depending on the firm's business, restocking or order costs are either the costs of placing an order with suppliers or the costs of setting up a production run. The costs related to safety reserves are opportunity losses such as lost sales and loss of customer goodwill that result from having inadequate inventory.

A basic trade-off exists in inventory management because carrying costs increase with inventory levels, whereas shortage or restocking costs decline with inventory levels. The basic goal of inventory management is thus to minimize the sum of these two costs. We consider ways to reach this goal in the next section.

Just to give you an idea of how important it is to balance carrying costs with shortage costs, consider the delay in auto deliveries we discussed at the beginning of the chapter. The major reason for the delay was that rail companies had reduced the number of rail cars they owned because of the recent recession. Therefore, rail companies were unable to increase the number of shipments as fast as they once could have and lost the potential revenue they could have gained.

28.8　Inventory Management Techniques

As we described earlier, the goal of inventory management is usually framed as cost minimization. Three techniques are discussed in this section, ranging from the relatively simple to the very complex.

THE ABC APPROACH

The ABC approach is a simple approach to inventory management in which the basic idea is to divide inventory into three (or more) groups. The underlying rationale is that a small portion of inventory in terms of quantity might represent a large portion in terms of inventory value. For example, this situation would exist for a manufacturer that uses some relatively expensive, high-tech components and some relatively inexpensive basic materials in producing its products.

Figure 28.2 illustrates an ABC comparison of items in terms of the percentage of inventory value represented by each group versus the percentage of items represented. As Figure 28.2 shows, the A Group constitutes only 10 percent of inventory by item count, but it represents more than half of the value of inventory. The A Group items are thus monitored closely, and inventory levels are kept relatively low. At the other end, basic inventory items, such as nuts and bolts, also exist; but, because these are crucial and inexpensive, large quantities are ordered and kept on hand. These would be C Group items. The B Group is made up of in-between items.

Figure 28.2
ABC Inventory
Analysis

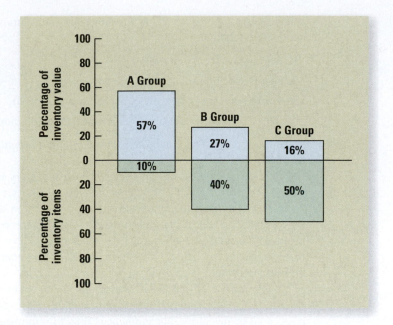

THE ECONOMIC ORDER QUANTITY MODEL

The economic order quantity (EOQ) model is the best-known approach for explicitly establishing an optimal inventory level. The basic idea is illustrated in Figure 28.3, which plots the various costs associated with holding inventory (on the vertical axis) against inventory levels (on the horizontal axis). As shown, inventory carrying costs

Figure 28.3
Costs of Holding
Inventory

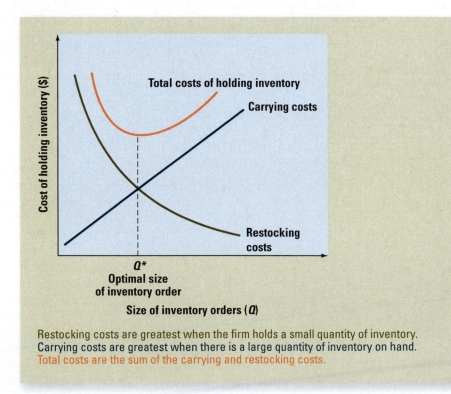

Restocking costs are greatest when the firm holds a small quantity of inventory.
Carrying costs are greatest when there is a large quantity of inventory on hand.
Total costs are the sum of the carrying and restocking costs.

rise and restocking costs decrease as inventory levels increase. From our general discussion in Chapter 26 and our discussion of the total credit cost curve in this chapter, the general shape of the total inventory cost curve is familiar. With the EOQ model, we will attempt to specifically locate the minimum total cost point, Q^*.

In our discussion that follows, an important point to keep in mind is that the actual cost of the inventory itself is not included. The reason is that the *total* amount of inventory the firm needs in a given year is dictated by sales. What we are analyzing here is how much the firm should have on hand at any particular time. More precisely, we are trying to determine what order size the firm should use when it restocks its inventory.

Inventory Depletion   To develop the EOQ, we will assume that the firm's inventory is sold off at a steady rate until it hits zero. At that point, the firm restocks its inventory back to some optimal level. For example, suppose the Eyssell Corporation starts out today with 3,600 units of a particular item in inventory. Annual sales of this item are 46,800 units, which is 900 per week. If Eyssell sells 900 units of inventory each week, all the available inventory will be sold after four weeks, and Eyssell will restock by ordering (or manufacturing) another 3,600 and start over. This selling and restocking process produces a sawtooth pattern for inventory holdings; this pattern is illustrated in Figure 28.4. As the figure shows, Eyssell always starts with 3,600 units in inventory and ends up at zero. On average, then, inventory is half of 3,600, or 1,800 units.

The Carrying Costs   As Figure 28.3 illustrates, carrying costs are normally assumed to be directly proportional to inventory levels. Suppose we let Q be the quantity

Figure 28.4
Inventory Holdings for the Eyssell Corporation

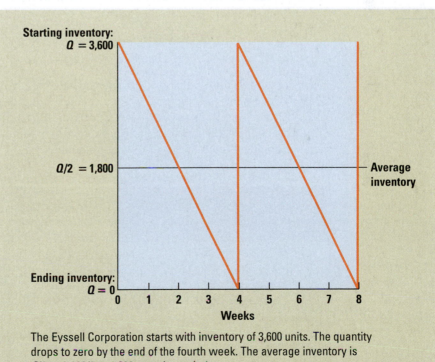

The Eyssell Corporation starts with inventory of 3,600 units. The quantity drops to zero by the end of the fourth week. The average inventory is $Q/2 = 3,600/2 = 1,800$ over the period.

of inventory that Eyssell orders each time (3,600 units); we will call this the *restocking quantity*. Average inventory would then just be $Q/2$, or 1,800 units. If we let CC be the carrying cost per unit per year, Eyssell's total carrying costs will be:

$$\text{Total carrying costs} = \text{Average inventory} \times \text{Carrying costs per unit} \quad \textbf{(28.10)}$$
$$= (Q/2) \times \text{CC}$$

In Eyssell's case, if carrying costs were $.75 per unit per year, total carrying costs would be the average inventory of 1,800 multiplied by $.75, or $1,350 per year.

The Shortage Costs   For now, we will focus only on the restocking costs. In essence, we will assume that the firm never actually runs short on inventory, so that costs relating to safety reserves are not important. We will return to this issue later.

Restocking costs are normally assumed to be fixed. In other words, every time we place an order, fixed costs are associated with that order (remember that the cost of the inventory itself is not considered here). Suppose we let T be the firm's total unit sales per year. If the firm orders Q units each time, then it will need to place a total of T/Q orders. For Eyssell, annual sales are 46,800, and the order size is 3,600. Eyssell thus places a total of $46,800/3,600 = 13$ orders per year. If the fixed cost per order is F, the total restocking cost for the year would be:

$$\text{Total restocking cost} = \text{Fixed cost per order} \times \text{Number of orders} \quad \textbf{(28.11)}$$
$$= F \times (T/Q)$$

For Eyssell, order costs might be $50 per order, so the total restocking cost for 13 orders would be $50 \times 13 = $650 per year.

The Total Costs   The total costs associated with holding inventory are the sum of the carrying costs and the restocking costs:

$$\text{Total costs} = \text{Carrying costs} + \text{Restocking costs} \quad \textbf{(28.12)}$$

$$= (Q/2) \times \text{CC} + F \times (T/Q)$$

Our goal is to find the value of Q, the restocking quantity, that minimizes this cost. To see how we might go about this, we can calculate total costs for some different values of Q. For the Eyssell Corporation, we had carrying costs (CC) of $.75 per unit per year, fixed costs (F) of $50 per order, and total sales (T) of 46,800 units. With these numbers, here are some possible total costs (check some of these for practice):

Restocking Quantity (Q)	Carrying Costs (Q/2 × CC)	+	Restocking Costs (F × T/Q)	=	Total Costs
500	$ 187.5		$4,680.0		$ 4,867.50
1,000	375.0		2,340.0		2,715.00
1,500	562.5		1,560.0		2,122.50
2,000	750.0		1,170.0		1,920.00
2,500	**937.5**		**936.0**		**1,873.50**
3,000	1,125.0		780.0		1,905.00
3,500	1,312.5		668.6		1,981.10

Inspecting the numbers, we see that total costs start out at almost $5,000 and decline to just under $1,900. The cost-minimizing quantity is about 2,500.

To find the cost-minimizing quantity, we can look back at Figure 28.3. What we notice is that the minimum point occurs right where the two lines cross. At this point, carrying costs and restocking costs are the same. For the particular types of costs we have assumed here, this will always be true; so we can find the minimum point just by setting these costs equal to each other and solving for Q^*:

$$\text{Carrying costs} = \text{Restocking costs} \tag{28.13}$$
$$(Q^*/2) \times CC = F \times (T/Q^*)$$

With a little algebra, we get:

$$Q^{*2} = \frac{2T \times F}{CC} \tag{28.14}$$

To solve for Q^*, we take the square root of both sides to find:

$$Q^* = \sqrt{\frac{2T \times F}{CC}} \tag{28.15}$$

This reorder quantity, which minimizes the total inventory cost, is called the **economic order quantity (EOQ)**. For the Eyssell Corporation, the EOQ is:

$$
\begin{aligned}
Q^* &= \sqrt{\frac{2T \times F}{CC}} \\
&= \sqrt{\frac{(2 \times 46{,}800) \times \$50}{.75}} \\
&= \sqrt{6{,}240{,}000} \\
&= 2{,}498 \text{ units}
\end{aligned}
$$

Thus, for Eyssell, the economic order quantity is 2,498 units. At this level, verify that the restocking costs and carrying costs are both $936.75.

EXAMPLE 28.2

Carrying Costs   Thiewes Shoes begins each period with 100 pairs of hiking boots in stock. This stock is depleted each period and reordered. If the carrying cost per pair of boots per year is $3, what are the total carrying costs for the hiking boots?

Inventories always start at 100 items and end up at zero, so average inventory is 50 items. At an annual cost of $3 per item, total carrying costs are $150.

EXAMPLE 28.3

Restocking Costs   In Example 28.2, suppose Thiewes sells a total of 600 pairs of boots in a year. How many times per year does Thiewes restock? Suppose the restocking cost is $20 per order. What are total restocking costs?

Thiewes orders 100 items each time. Total sales are 600 items per year, so Thiewes restocks six times per year, or about every two months. The restocking costs would be 6 orders × $20 per order = $120.

The EOQ   Based on our previous two examples, what size orders should Thiewes place to minimize costs? How often will Thiewes restock? What are the total carrying and restocking costs? The total costs?

We know that the total number of pairs of boots ordered for the year (T) is 600. The restocking cost (F) is \$20 per order, and the carrying cost (CC) is \$3 per unit per year. We can calculate the EOQ for Thiewes as follows:

$$
\begin{aligned}
\text{EOQ} &= \sqrt{\frac{2T \times F}{\text{CC}}} \\
&= \sqrt{\frac{(2 \times 600) \times \$20}{3}} \\
&= \sqrt{8,000} \\
&= 89.44 \text{ units}
\end{aligned}
$$

Because Thiewes sells 600 pairs per year, it will restock $600/89.44 = 6.71$ times. The total restocking costs will be $\$20 \times 6.71 = \$134.16$. Average inventory will be $89.44/2 = 44.72$. The carrying costs will be $\$3 \times 44.72 = \$134.16$, the same as the restocking costs. The total costs are thus \$268.32.

EXTENSIONS TO THE EOQ MODEL

Thus far, we have assumed that a company will let its inventory run down to zero and then reorder. In reality, a company will wish to reorder before its inventory goes to zero for two reasons. First, by always having at least some inventory on hand, the firm minimizes the risk of a stockout and the resulting losses of sales and customers. Second, when a firm does reorder, there will be some time lag before the inventory arrives. Thus, to finish our discussion of the EOQ, we consider two extensions: Safety stocks and reordering points.

Safety Stocks   A *safety stock* is the minimum level of inventory that a firm keeps on hand. Inventories are reordered whenever the level of inventory falls to the safety stock level. The top of Figure 28.5 illustrates how a safety stock can be incorporated into an EOQ model. Notice that adding a safety stock simply means that the firm does not run its inventory all the way down to zero. Other than this, the situation here is identical to that described in our earlier discussion of the EOQ.

Reorder Points   To allow for delivery time, a firm will place orders before inventories reach a critical level. The *reorder points* are the times at which the firm will actually place its inventory orders. These points are illustrated in the middle of Figure 28.5. As shown, the reorder points simply occur some fixed number of days (or weeks or months) before inventories are projected to reach zero.

One of the reasons that a firm will keep a safety stock is to allow for uncertain delivery times. We can therefore combine our reorder point and safety stock discussions in the bottom part of Figure 28.5. The result is a generalized EOQ model in which the firm orders in advance of anticipated needs and also keeps a safety stock of inventory.

MANAGING DERIVED-DEMAND INVENTORIES

The third type of inventory management technique is used to manage derived-demand inventories. As we described earlier, demand for some inventory types is derived from, or dependent on, other inventory needs. A good example is given by the auto manufacturing industry, in which the demand for finished products depends on consumer demand, marketing programs, and other factors related to projected unit sales. The demand for inventory

Figure 28.5
Safety Stocks and
Reorder Points

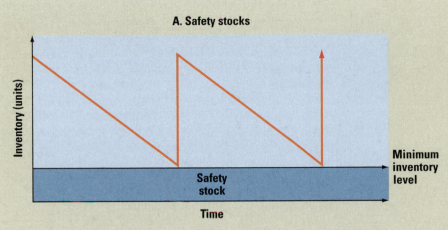

A. Safety stocks

With a safety stock, the firm reorders when inventory reaches a minimum level.

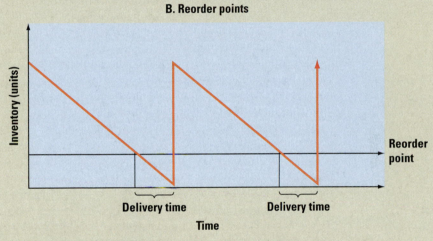

B. Reorder points

When there are lags in delivery or production times, the firm reorders when inventory reaches the reorder point.

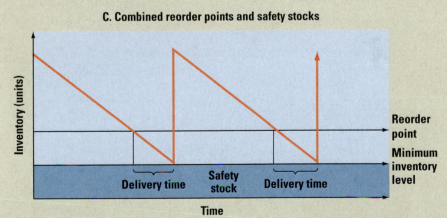

C. Combined reorder points and safety stocks

By combining safety stocks and reorder points, the firm maintains a buffer against unforeseen events.

items such as tires, batteries, headlights, and other components is then completely determined by the number of autos planned. Materials requirements planning and just-in-time inventory management are two methods for managing demand-dependent inventories.

Materials Requirements Planning   Production and inventory specialists have developed computer-based systems for ordering and/or scheduling production of demand-dependent types of inventories. These systems fall under the general heading of **materials requirements planning (MRP)**. The basic idea behind MRP is that, once finished goods inventory levels are set, it is possible to determine what levels of work-in-progress inventories must exist to meet the need for finished goods. From there, it is possible to calculate the quantity of raw materials that must be on hand. This ability to schedule backward from finished goods inventories stems from the dependent nature of work-in-progress and raw materials inventories. MRP is particularly important for complicated products for which a variety of components are needed to create the finished product.

Just-in-Time Inventory   **Just-in-time (JIT) inventory** is a modern approach to managing dependent inventories. The goal of JIT is to minimize such inventories, thereby maximizing turnover. The approach began in Japan, and it is a fundamental part of Japanese manufacturing philosophy. As the name suggests, the basic goal of JIT is to have only enough inventory on hand to meet immediate production needs.

The result of the JIT system is that inventories are reordered and restocked frequently. Making such a system work and avoiding shortages requires a high degree of cooperation among suppliers. Japanese manufacturers often have a relatively small, tightly integrated group of suppliers with whom they work closely to achieve the needed coordination. These suppliers are a part of a large manufacturer's (such as Toyota's) industrial group, or *keiretsu*. Each large manufacturer tends to have its own *keiretsu*. It also helps to have suppliers located nearby, a situation that is common in Japan.

The *kanban* is an integral part of a JIT inventory system, and JIT systems are sometimes called *kanban systems*. The literal meaning of *kanban* is "card" or "sign"; but, broadly speaking, a kanban is a signal to a supplier to send more inventory. For example, a kanban can literally be a card attached to a bin of parts. When a worker pulls that bin, the card is detached and routed back to the supplier, who then supplies a replacement bin.

A JIT inventory system is an important part of a larger production planning process. A full discussion of it would necessarily shift our focus away from finance to production and operations management, so we will leave it here.

Summary and Conclusions

This chapter has covered the basics of credit and inventory policy. The major topics we discussed include these:

1. *The components of credit policy:* We discussed the terms of sale, credit analysis, and collection policy. Under the general subject of terms of sale, the credit period, the cash discount and discount period, and the credit instrument were described.

2. *Credit policy analysis:* We developed the cash flows from the decision to grant credit and showed how the credit decision can be analyzed in an NPV setting. The NPV of granting credit depends on five factors: Revenue effects, cost effects, the cost of debt, the probability of nonpayment, and the cash discount.

3. *Optimal credit policy:* The optimal amount of credit the firm should offer depends on the competitive conditions under which the firm operates. These conditions will determine the carrying costs associated with granting credit and the opportunity costs of the lost sales resulting from refusing to offer credit. The optimal credit policy minimizes the sum of these two costs.

4. *Credit analysis:* We looked at the decision to grant credit to a particular customer. We saw that two considerations are very important: The cost relative to the selling price and the possibility of repeat business.

5. *Collection policy:* Collection policy determines the method of monitoring the age of accounts receivable and dealing with past-due accounts. We described how an aging schedule can be prepared and the procedures a firm might use to collect on past-due accounts.

6. *Inventory types:* We described the different inventory types and how they differ in terms of liquidity and demand.

7. *Inventory costs:* The two basic inventory costs are carrying and restocking costs; we discussed how inventory management involves a trade-off between these two costs.

8. *Inventory management techniques:* We described the ABC approach and the EOQ model approach to inventory management. We also briefly touched on materials requirements planning (MRP) and just-in-time (JIT) inventory management.

Concept Questions

1. **Credit Instruments**   Describe each of the following:
   a. Sight draft.
   b. Time draft.
   c. Banker's acceptance.
   d. Promissory note.
   e. Trade acceptance.

2. **Trade Credit Forms**   In what form is trade credit most commonly offered? What is the credit instrument in this case?

3. **Receivables Costs**   What costs are associated with carrying receivables? What costs are associated with not granting credit? What do we call the sum of the costs for different levels of receivables?

4. **Five Cs of Credit**   What are the five Cs of credit? Explain why each is important.

5. **Credit Period Length**   What are some of the factors that determine the length of the credit period? Why is the length of the buyer's operating cycle often considered an upper bound on the length of the credit period?

6. **Credit Period Length**   In each of the following pairings, indicate which firm would probably have a longer credit period and explain your reasoning.
   a. Firm *A* sells a miracle cure for baldness; Firm *B* sells toupees.
   b. Firm *A* specializes in products for landlords; Firm *B* specializes in products for renters.
   c. Firm *A* sells to customers with an inventory turnover of 10 times; Firm *B* sells to customers with an inventory turnover of 20 times.
   d. Firm *A* sells fresh fruit; Firm *B* sells canned fruit.
   e. Firm *A* sells and installs carpeting; Firm *B* sells rugs.

7. **Inventory Types**   What are the different inventory types? How do the types differ? Why are some types said to have dependent demand, whereas other types are said to have independent demand?

8. **Just-in-Time Inventory**   If a company moves to a JIT inventory management system, what will happen to inventory turnover? What will happen to total asset turnover? What will happen to return on equity (ROE)? (*Hint:* Remember the DuPont equation from Chapter 3.)

9. **Inventory Costs**   If a company's inventory carrying costs are $5 million per year and its fixed order costs are $8 million per year, do you think the firm keeps too much inventory on hand or too little? Why?

10. **Inventory Period**   At least part of Dell's corporate profits can be traced to its inventory management. Using just-in-time inventory, Dell typically maintains an inventory of three to four days' sales. Competitors such as Hewlett-Packard and IBM have attempted to match Dell's inventory policies, but lag far behind. In an industry where the price of PC components continues to decline, Dell clearly has a competitive advantage. Why would you say that it is to Dell's advantage to have such a short inventory period? If doing this is valuable, why don't all other PC manufacturers switch to Dell's approach?

Questions and Problems

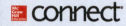

BASIC
(Questions 1–12)

1. **Cash Discounts**   You place an order for 400 units of inventory at a unit price of $115. The supplier offers terms of 1/10, net 30.

   a. How long do you have to pay before the account is overdue? If you take the full period, how much should you remit?

   b. What is the discount being offered? How quickly must you pay to get the discount? If you do take the discount, how much should you remit?

   c. If you don't take the discount, how much interest are you paying implicitly? How many days' credit are you receiving?

2. **Size of Accounts Receivable**   The Paden Corporation has annual sales of $29.5 million. The average collection period is 27 days. What is the average investment in accounts receivable as shown on the balance sheet?

3. **ACP and Accounts Receivable**   Kyoto Joe, Inc., sells earnings forecasts for Japanese securities. Its credit terms are 1/15, net 30. Based on experience, 70 percent of all customers will take the discount.

   a. What is the average collection period for the company?

   b. If the company sells 1,300 forecasts every month at a price of $1,550 each, what is its average balance sheet amount in accounts receivable?

4. **Size of Accounts Receivable**   Tidwell, Inc., has weekly credit sales of $31,400, and the average collection period is 29 days. The cost of production is 75 percent of the selling price. What is the average accounts receivable figure?

5. **Terms of Sale**   A firm offers terms of 1/10, net 30. What effective annual interest rate does the firm earn when a customer does not take the discount? Without doing any calculations, explain what will happen to this effective rate if:

   a. The discount is changed to 2 percent.

   b. The credit period is increased to 60 days.

   c. The discount period is increased to 15 days.

6. **ACP and Receivables Turnover**   Chen, Inc., has an average collection period of 34 days. Its average daily investment in receivables is $61,300. What are annual credit sales? What is the receivables turnover?

7. **Size of Accounts Receivable**   Essence of Skunk Fragrances, Ltd., sells 5,450 units of its perfume collection each year at a price per unit of $480. All sales are on credit with terms of 1/10, net 40. The discount is taken by 35 percent of the customers. What is the total amount of the company's accounts receivable? In reaction to sales by its main competitor, Sewage Spray, Essence of Skunk is considering a change in its credit policy to terms of 2/10, net 30 to preserve its market share. How will this change in policy affect accounts receivable?

8. **Size of Accounts Receivable**   The Arizona Bay Corporation sells on credit terms of net 30. Its accounts are, on average, 5 days past due. If annual credit sales are $8.95 million, what is the company's balance sheet amount in accounts receivable?

9. **Evaluating Credit Policy**   Air Spares is a wholesaler that stocks engine components and test equipment for the commercial aircraft industry. A new customer has placed an order for eight high-bypass turbine engines, which increase fuel economy. The variable cost is $2.6 million per unit, and the credit price is $2.815 million each. Credit is extended for one period, and based on historical experience, payment for about 1 out of every 200 such orders is never collected. The required return is 2.9 percent per period.

   a. Assuming that this is a one-time order, should it be filled? The customer will not buy if credit is not extended.
   b. What is the break-even probability of default in part (a)?
   c. Suppose that customers who don't default become repeat customers and place the same order every period forever. Further assume that repeat customers never default. Should the order be filled? What is the break-even probability of default?
   d. Describe in general terms why credit terms will be more liberal when repeat orders are a possibility.

10. **Credit Policy Evaluation**   Leeloo, Inc., is considering a change in its cash-only sales policy. The new terms of sale would be net one month. Based on the following information, determine if the company should proceed or not. Describe the buildup of receivables in this case. The required return is .95 percent per month.

	Current Policy	New Policy
Price per unit	$720	$720
Cost per unit	$495	$495
Unit sales per month	1,130	1,190

11. **EOQ**   Fhloston Manufacturing uses 1,860 switch assemblies per week and then reorders another 1,860. If the relevant carrying cost per switch assembly is $6.25, and the fixed order cost is $730, is the company's inventory policy optimal? Why or why not?

12. **EOQ**   The Trektronics store begins each week with 675 phasers in stock. This stock is depleted each week and reordered. If the carrying cost per phaser is $73 per year and the fixed order cost is $340, what is the total carrying cost? What is the restocking cost? Should the company increase or decrease its order size? Describe an optimal inventory policy for the company in terms of order size and order frequency.

INTERMEDIATE
(Questions 13–16)

13. **EOQ Derivation**   Prove that when carrying costs and restocking costs are as described in the chapter, the EOQ must occur at the point where the carrying costs and restocking costs are equal.

14. **Credit Policy Evaluation**   The Harrington Corporation is considering a change in its cash-only policy. The new terms would be net one period. Based on the following information, determine if Harrington should proceed or not. The required return is 2.5 percent per period.

	Current Policy	New Policy
Price per unit	$104	$108
Cost per unit	$ 47	$ 47
Unit sales per month	2,870	2,915

15. **Credit Policy Evaluation** Happy Times currently has an all-cash credit policy. It is considering making a change in the credit policy by going to terms of net 30 days. Based on the following information, what do you recommend? The required return is .95 percent per month.

	Current Policy	New Policy
Price per unit	$289	$296
Cost per unit	$226	$229
Unit sales per month	1,105	1,125

16. **Credit Policy** The Silver Spokes Bicycle Shop has decided to offer credit to its customers during the spring selling season. Sales are expected to be 700 bicycles. The average cost to the shop of a bicycle is $650. The owner knows that only 96 percent of the customers will be able to make their payments. To identify the remaining 4 percent, the company is considering subscribing to a credit agency. The initial charge for this service is $950, with an additional charge of $15 per individual report. Should she subscribe to the agency?

CHALLENGE
(Questions 17–22)

17. **Break-Even Quantity** In Problem 14, what is the break-even quantity for the new credit policy?

18. **Credit Markup** In Problem 14, what is the break-even price per unit that should be charged under the new credit policy? Assume that the sales figure under the new policy is 3,150 units and all other values remain the same.

19. **Credit Markup** In Problem 15, what is the break-even price per unit under the new credit policy? Assume all other values remain the same.

20. **Safety Stocks and Order Points** Saché, Inc., expects to sell 700 of its designer suits every week. The store is open seven days a week and expects to sell the same number of suits every day. The company has an EOQ of 500 suits and a safety stock of 100 suits. Once an order is placed, it takes three days for Saché to get the suits in. How many orders does the company place per year? Assume that it is Monday morning before the store opens, and a shipment of suits has just arrived. When will Saché place its next order?

21. **Evaluating Credit Policy** Solar Engines manufactures solar engines for tractor-trailers. Given the fuel savings available, new orders for 125 units have been made by customers requesting credit. The variable cost is $11,400 per unit, and the credit price is $13,000 each. Credit is extended for one period. The required return is 1.9 percent per period. If Solar Engines extends credit, it expects that 30 percent of the customers will be repeat customers and place the same order every period forever, and the remaining customers will place one-time orders. Should credit be extended?

22. **Evaluating Credit Policy** In the previous problem, assume that the probability of default is 15 percent. Should the orders be filled now? Assume the number of repeat customers is affected by the defaults. In other words, 30 percent of the customers who do not default are expected to be repeat customers.

Mini Case

CREDIT POLICY AT BRAAM INDUSTRIES

Tricia Haltiwinger, the president of Braam Industries, has been exploring ways of improving the company's financial performance. Braam Industries manufactures and sells office equipment to retailers. The company's growth has been relatively slow in recent years, but with an expansion in the economy, it appears that sales may increase more quickly in the future. Tricia has asked Andrew Preston, the company's treasurer, to examine Braam's credit policy to see if a different credit policy can help increase profitability.

The company currently has a policy of net 30. As with any credit sales, default rates are always of concern. Because of Braam's screening and collection process, the default rate on credit is currently only 2.1 percent. Andrew has examined the company's credit policy in relation to other vendors, and has determined that three options are available.

The first option is to relax the company's decision on when to grant credit. The second option is to increase the credit period to net 45, and the third option is a combination of the relaxed credit policy and the extension of the credit period to net 45. On the positive side, each of the three policies under consideration would increase sales. The three policies have the drawbacks that default rates would increase, the administrative costs of managing the firm's receivables would increase, and the receivables period would increase. The credit policy change would impact all four of these variables in different degrees. Andrew has prepared the following table outlining the effect on each of these variables:

	Annual Sales (millions)	Default Rate (% of sales)	Administrative Costs (% of sales)	Receivables Period
Current policy	$116	1.90%	1.60%	38 days
Option 1	130	2.60	2.40	41
Option 2	129	2.20	1.90	51
Option 3	132	2.50	2.10	49

Braam's variable costs of production are 45 percent of sales, and the relevant interest rate is a 6 percent effective annual rate. Which credit policy should the company use? Also, notice that in Option 2 the default rate and administrative costs are below those in Option 3. Is this plausible? Why or why not?

Appendix 28A ## More about Credit Policy Analysis

To access the appendix for this chapter, please logon to Connect Finance.

29

Mergers, Acquisitions, and Divestitures

The year 2014 was a banner one for mergers and acquisitions (M&A). Worldwide, M&A activity hit $3.5 trillion, with the United States reporting $1.53 trillion in M&A activity, both record totals. In one of the larger deals during the year, pharmaceutical company Actavis agreed to acquire Allergan for $219 per share, for a total of $66 billion. Actavis believed that the acquisition would result in annual savings of $1.8 billion per year. Of course, not all announced mergers are finalized. In July, AbbVie announced that it was acquiring Dublin-based Shire for about $55 billion. The

acquisition was designed as a "tax inversion." While AbbVie was the larger company, the new combined company would be headquartered in Ireland, where the corporate tax rate is much lower. However, before the deal was finalized, the U.S. Treasury Department announced new rules for tax inversion deals, and the acquisition was canceled.

How do companies like Actavis determine whether an acquisition is a good idea? This chapter explores reasons that mergers should take place—and just as important, reasons why they should not.

29.1 The Basic Forms of Acquisitions

Acquisitions follow one of three basic forms: (1) merger or consolidation, (2) acquisition of stock, and (3) acquisition of assets.

MERGER OR CONSOLIDATION

A **merger** refers to the absorption of one firm by another. The acquiring firm retains its name and identity, and it acquires all of the assets and liabilities of the acquired firm. After a merger, the acquired firm ceases to exist as a separate business entity.

A **consolidation** is the same as a merger except that an entirely new firm is created. In a consolidation, both the acquiring firm and the acquired firm terminate their previous legal existence and become part of the new firm.

EXAMPLE 29.1

Merger Basics   Suppose Firm A acquires Firm B in a merger. Further, suppose Firm B's shareholders are given one share of Firm A's stock in exchange for two shares of Firm B's stock. From a legal standpoint, Firm A's shareholders are not directly affected by the merger. However, Firm B's shares cease to exist. In a consolidation, the shareholders of Firm A and Firm B exchange their shares for shares of a new firm (e.g., Firm C).

Because of the similarities between mergers and consolidations, we shall refer to both types of reorganization as mergers. Here are two important points about mergers and consolidations:

1. A merger is legally straightforward and does not cost as much as other forms of acquisition. It avoids the necessity of transferring title of each individual asset of the acquired firm to the acquiring firm.

2. The stockholders of each firm must approve a merger.[1] Typically, two-thirds of share owners must vote in favor for it to be approved. In addition, shareholders of the acquired firm have *appraisal rights*. This means that they can demand that the acquiring firm purchase their shares at a fair value. Often, the acquiring firm and the dissenting shareholders of the acquired firm cannot agree on a fair value, which results in expensive legal proceedings.

ACQUISITION OF STOCK

A second way to acquire another firm is to purchase the firm's voting stock in exchange for cash, shares of stock, or other securities. This process may start as a private offer from the management of one firm to another. At some point the offer is taken directly to the selling firm's stockholders, often by a tender offer. A **tender offer** is a public offer to buy shares of a target firm. It is made by one firm directly to the shareholders of another firm. The offer is communicated to the target firm's shareholders by public announcements such as newspaper advertisements. Sometimes a general mailing is used in a tender offer. However, a general mailing is difficult because the names and addresses of the stockholders of record are not usually available.

The following factors are involved in choosing between an acquisition of stock and a merger:

1. In an acquisition of stock, shareholder meetings need not be held and a vote is not required. If the shareholders of the target firm do not like the offer, they are not required to accept it and need not tender their shares.

2. In an acquisition of stock, the bidding firm can deal directly with the shareholders of a target firm via a tender offer. The target firm's management and board of directors are bypassed.

3. Target managers often resist acquisition. In such cases, acquisition of stock circumvents the target firm's management. Resistance by the target firm's management often makes the cost of acquisition of stock higher than the cost by merger.

4. Frequently a minority of shareholders will hold out in a tender offer, and thus, the target firm cannot be completely absorbed.

5. Complete absorption of one firm by another requires a merger. Many acquisitions of stock end with a formal merger.

ACQUISITION OF ASSETS

One firm can acquire another by buying all of its assets. The selling firm does not necessarily vanish because its "shell" can be retained. A formal vote of the target stockholders is required in an acquisition of assets. An advantage here is that although the acquirer is often

---

[1]Mergers between corporations require compliance with state laws. In virtually all states, the shareholders of each corporation must give their assent.

Figure 29.1
Varieties of
Takeovers

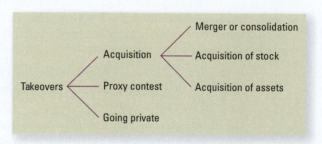

left with minority shareholders in an acquisition of stock, this does not happen in an acquisition of assets. Minority shareholders often present problems, such as holdouts. However, asset acquisition involves transferring title to individual assets, which can be costly.

A CLASSIFICATION SCHEME

Financial analysts have typically classified acquisitions into three types:

1. *Horizontal acquisition:* Here, both the acquirer and acquired are in the same industry. Actavis' acquisition of Allergan, which we mentioned at the beginning of the chapter, would be a horizontal acquisition.

2. *Vertical acquisition:* A vertical acquisition involves firms at different steps of the production process. The solar panel industry has seen a large number vertical acquisitions. For example, in June 2014, SolarCity, the largest U.S. rooftop solar installer, announced that it was acquiring Silevo, a high-efficiency photovoltaic module manufacturer. Another vertical acquisition was Microsoft's 2014 acquisition of Nokia's Devices and Services division. This acquisition guaranteed Microsoft that Nokia would continue to offer telephones with Microsoft's mobile operating system.

3. *Conglomerate acquisition:* The acquiring firm and the acquired firm are not related to each other. Conglomerate acquisitions are popular in the technology arena. For example, by 2015, Google had acquired more than 170 companies since 2003. And while you may be familiar with Google's Android OS for cell phones, what you may not be aware of is that Google acquired Android in 2005.

A NOTE ABOUT TAKEOVERS

Takeover is a general and imprecise term referring to the transfer of control of a firm from one group of shareholders to another.[2] A firm that has decided to take over another firm is usually referred to as the **bidder**. The bidder offers to pay cash or securities to obtain the stock or assets of another company. If the offer is accepted, the **target** firm will give up control over its stock or assets to the bidder in exchange for *consideration* (i.e., its stock, its debt, or cash).[3]

Takeovers can occur by acquisitions, proxy contests, and going-private transactions. Thus, takeovers encompass a broader set of activities than acquisitions, as depicted in Figure 29.1.

If a takeover is achieved by acquisition, it will be by merger, tender offer for shares of stock, or purchase of assets. In mergers and tender offers, the acquiring firm buys the voting common stock of the acquired firm.

---

[2]*Control* can usually be defined as having a majority vote on the board of directors.

[3]Audra L. Boone and J. Harold Mulherin in "How Are Firms Sold?" *Journal of Finance* (April 2007), look closely at the takeover process and the chain of negotiations and competitive bidding.

Proxy contests can result in takeovers as well. Proxy contests occur when a group of shareholders attempts to gain seats on the board of directors. A *proxy* is written authorization for one shareholder to vote the stock of another shareholder. In a proxy contest, an insurgent group of shareholders solicits proxies from other shareholders.

In *going-private transactions,* a small group of investors purchases all the equity shares of a public firm. The group usually includes members of incumbent management and some outside investors. The shares of the firm are delisted from stock exchanges and can no longer be purchased in the open market.

29.2 Synergy

The previous section discussed the basic forms of acquisition. We now examine why firms are acquired. (Although the previous section pointed out that acquisitions and mergers have different definitions, these differences will be unimportant in this, and many of the following, sections. Thus, unless otherwise stated, we will refer to acquisitions and mergers synonymously.)

Much of our thinking here can be organized around the following four questions:

1. Is there a rational reason for mergers? Yes—in a word, *synergy.*

   Suppose firm A is contemplating acquiring firm B. The value of firm A is V_A and the value of firm B is V_B. (It is reasonable to assume that for public companies, V_A and V_B can be determined by observing the market prices of the outstanding securities.) The difference between the value of the combined firm (V_{AB}) and the sum of the values of the firms as separate entities is the synergy from the acquisition:

   $$\text{Synergy} = V_{AB} - (V_A + V_B)$$

   In words, synergy occurs if the value of the combined firm after the merger is greater than the sum of the value of the acquiring firm and the value of the acquired firm before the merger.

2. Where does this magic force, synergy, come from?

   Increases in cash flow create value. We define ΔCF_t as the difference between the cash flows at date t of the combined firm and the sum of the cash flows of the two separate firms. From the chapters about capital budgeting, we know that the cash flow in any period t can be written as:

   $$\Delta CF_t = \Delta Rev_t - \Delta Costs_t - \Delta Taxes_t - \Delta Capital\ Requirements_t$$

   where ΔRev_t is the incremental revenue of the acquisition; $\Delta Costs_t$ is the incremental costs of the acquisition; $\Delta Taxes_t$ is the incremental acquisition taxes; and $\Delta Capital\ Requirements_t$ is the incremental new investment required in working capital and fixed assets.

   It follows from our classification of incremental cash flows that the possible sources of synergy fall into four basic categories: Revenue enhancement, cost reduction, lower taxes, and lower capital requirements.[4] Improvements in at least one of

---

[4]Many reasons are given by firms to justify mergers and acquisitions. When two firms merge, the boards of directors of the two firms adopt an *agreement of merger.* The agreement of merger of U.S. Steel and Marathon Oil is typical. It lists the economic benefits that shareholders can expect from the merger (key words have been italicized):

> U.S. Steel believes that the acquisition of Marathon provides U.S. Steel with an attractive opportunity to *diversify* into the energy business. Reasons for the merger include, but are not limited to, the facts that consummation of the merger will allow U.S. Steel to consolidate Marathon into U.S. Steel's federal *income tax return,* will also contribute to *greater efficiency,* and will enhance the ability to manage capital by permitting the movement of cash between U.S. Steel and Marathon. Additionally, the merger will eliminate the possibility of conflicts of interests between the interests of minority and majority shareholders and will enhance management flexibility. The acquisition will provide Marathon shareholders with a substantial premium over historical market prices for their shares. However, shareholders will no longer continue to share in the future prospects of the company.

these four categories create synergy. Each of these categories will be discussed in detail in the next section.

In addition, reasons are often provided for mergers where improvements are not expected in any of these four categories. These "bad" reasons for mergers will be discussed in Section 29.4.

3. How are these synergistic gains shared? In general, the acquiring firm pays a premium for the acquired, or target, firm. For example, if the stock of the target is selling for $50, the acquirer might need to pay $60 a share, implying a premium of $10, or 20 percent. The gain to the target in this example is $10. Suppose that the synergy from the merger is $30. The gain to the acquiring firm, or bidder, would be $20 (=$30 − $10). The bidder would actually lose if the synergy were less than the premium of $10. A more detailed treatment of these gains or losses will be provided in Section 29.6.

4. Are there other motives for a merger besides synergy? Yes.

As we have said, synergy is the source of benefit to stockholders. However, the *managers* are likely to view a potential merger differently. Even if the synergy from the merger is less than the premium paid to the target, the managers of the acquiring firm may still benefit. For example, the revenues of the combined firm after the merger will almost certainly be greater than the revenues of the bidder before the merger. The managers may receive higher compensation once they are managing a larger firm. Even beyond the increase in compensation, managers generally experience greater prestige and power when managing a larger firm. Conversely, the managers of the target could lose their jobs after the acquisition. They might very well oppose the takeover even if their stockholders would benefit from the premium. These issues will be discussed in more detail in Section 29.9.

29.3 Sources of Synergy

In this section, we discuss sources of synergy.[5]

REVENUE ENHANCEMENT

A combined firm may generate greater revenues than two separate firms. Increased revenues can come from marketing gains, strategic benefits, and market power.

Marketing Gains It is frequently claimed that, due to improved marketing, mergers and acquisitions can increase operating revenues. Improvements can be made in the following areas:

1. Ineffective media programming and advertising efforts.
2. A weak distribution network.
3. An unbalanced product mix.

Strategic Benefits Some acquisitions promise a *strategic* benefit, which is more like an option than a standard investment opportunity. For example, imagine

---

[5]Matthew Rhodes-Kropf and David Robinson, in "The Market for Mergers and the Boundaries of the Firm," *Journal of Finance* (June 2008), address a related question of who buys whom. Contrary to conventional wisdom, they argue that it does not appear that firms with relatively high market value tend to buy firms with relatively low values. Instead, they show firms tend to pair with other firms having similar ratios.

Figure 29.2
Economies of Scale and the Optimal Size of the Firm

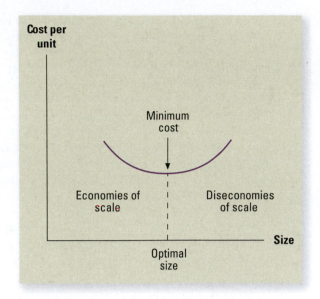

that a sewing machine company acquires a computer company. The firm will be well positioned if technological advances allow computer-driven sewing machines in the future.

Michael Porter has used the word *beachhead* to denote the strategic benefits from entering a new industry.[6] He uses the example of Procter & Gamble's acquisition of the Charmin Paper Company as a beachhead that allowed Procter & Gamble to develop a highly interrelated cluster of paper products—disposable diapers, paper towels, feminine hygiene products, and bathroom tissue.

Market or Monopoly Power One firm may acquire another to reduce competition. If so, prices can be increased, generating monopoly profits. However, mergers that reduce competition do not benefit society, and the U.S. Department of Justice or the Federal Trade Commission may challenge them.

COST REDUCTION

A combined firm may operate more efficiently than two separate firms. When Bank of America agreed to acquire Security Pacific, lower costs were cited as the primary reason. A merger can increase operating efficiency in the following ways:

Economy of Scale Economy of scale means that the average cost of production falls as the level of production increases. Figure 29.2 illustrates the relation between cost per unit and size for a typical firm. As can be seen, average cost first falls and then rises. In other words, the firm experiences economies of scale until optimal firm size is reached. Diseconomies of scale arise after that.

Though the precise nature of economies of scale is not known, it is one obvious benefit of horizontal mergers. The phrase *spreading overhead* is frequently used in connection

---

[6]Michael Porter, *Competitive Advantage* (New York: Free Press, 1998).

with economies of scale. This refers to sharing central facilities such as corporate headquarters, top management, and computer systems.

Economies of Vertical Integration

Operating economies can be gained from vertical combinations as well as from horizontal combinations. The main purpose of vertical acquisitions is to make coordination of closely related operating activities easier. This is probably why most forest product firms that cut timber also own sawmills and hauling equipment. Because petroleum is used to make plastics and other chemical products, the DuPont–Conoco merger was motivated by DuPont's need for a steady supply of oil. Economies of vertical integration probably explain why most airline companies own airplanes. They also may explain why some airline companies have purchased hotels and car rental companies.

Technology Transfer

Technology transfer is another reason for a merger. An automobile manufacturer might well acquire an aircraft company if aerospace technology can improve automotive quality. This technology transfer was the motivation behind the merger of Google and Android.

Complementary Resources

Some firms acquire others to improve usage of existing resources. A ski equipment store merging with a tennis equipment store will smooth sales over both the winter and summer seasons, thereby making better use of store capacity.

Elimination of Inefficient Management

A change in management can often increase firm value. Some managers overspend on perquisites and pet projects, making them ripe for takeover. For example, the leveraged buyout of RJR Nabisco was instituted primarily to halt the profligate behavior of CEO Ross Johnson. Alternatively, incumbent managers may not understand changing market conditions or new technology, making it difficult for them to abandon old strategies. Although the board of directors should replace these managers, the board is often unable to act independently. Thus, a merger may be needed to make the necessary replacements.

Michael C. Jensen cites the oil industry as an example of managerial inefficiency.[7] In the late 1970s, changes in the oil industry included expectations of lower oil prices, increased exploration and development costs, and higher real interest rates. As a result of these changes, substantial reductions in exploration and development were called for. However, many oil company managers were unable to downsize their firms. Acquiring companies sought out oil firms in order to reduce their investment levels. For example, T. Boone Pickens of Mesa Petroleum attempted to buy three oil companies—Unocal, Phillips, and Getty—to install more frugal management. Although he was unable to make the acquisitions, his attempts spurred existing management to reduce expenditures on exploration and development, generating huge gains to the shareholders of these firms, including himself.

Mergers and acquisitions can be viewed as part of the labor market for top management. Michael Jensen and Richard Ruback have used the phrase "market for corporate control," in which alternative management teams compete for the right to manage corporate activities.[8]

---

[7]Michael C. Jensen, "Agency Costs of Free Cash Flow, Corporate Finance, and Takeovers," *American Economic Review* (1986).

[8]Michael C. Jensen and R. S. Ruback, "The Market for Corporate Control: The Scientific Evidence," *Journal of Financial Economics* 11 (1983).

Table 29.1
Tax Effect of Merger
of Firms **A** and **B**

| | Before Merger | | | | After Merger | |
| | Firm *A* | | Firm *B* | | Firm *AB* | |
	If State 1	If State 2	If State 1	If State 2	If State 1	If State 2
Taxable income	$200	−$100	−$100	$200	$100	$100
Taxes	68	0	0	68	34	34
Net income	$132	−$100	−$100	$132	$ 66	$ 66

Neither firm will be able to deduct its losses prior to the merger. The merger allows the losses from *A* to offset the taxable profits from *B*—and vice versa.

TAX GAINS

Tax reduction may be a powerful incentive for some acquisitions. This reduction can come from:

1. The use of tax losses.

2. The use of unused debt capacity.

3. The use of surplus funds.

Net Operating Losses   A firm with a profitable division and an unprofitable one will have a low tax bill because the loss in one division offsets the income in the other. However, if the two divisions are actually separate companies, the profitable firm will not be able to use the losses of the unprofitable one to offset its income. Thus, in the right circumstances, a merger can lower taxes.

Consider Table 29.1, which shows pretax income, taxes, and aftertax income for Firms *A* and *B*. Firm *A* earns $200 in State 1 but loses money in State 2. The firm pays taxes in State 1 but is not entitled to a tax rebate in State 2. Conversely, Firm *B* turns a profit in State 2 but not in State 1. This firm pays taxes only in State 2. The table shows that the combined tax bill of the two separate firms is always $68, regardless of which situation occurs.

However, the last two columns of the table show that after a merger, the combined firm will pay taxes of only $34. Taxes drop after the merger, because a loss in one division offsets the gain in the other.

The message of this example is that firms need taxable profits to take advantage of potential losses. These losses are often referred to as *net operating losses,* or *NOL* for short. Mergers can sometimes bring losses and profits together. However, there are two qualifications to the previous example:

1. Federal tax laws permit firms that experience alternating periods of profits and losses to equalize their taxes by carryback and carryforward provisions. The accounting rules are complicated but generally a firm that has been profitable but has a loss in the current year can get refunds of income taxes paid in the *two previous years* and can carry the loss *forward for 20 years*. Thus, a merger to exploit unused tax shields must offer tax savings over and above what can be accomplished by firms via carryovers.[9]

---

[9]Under the 1986 Tax Reform Act, a corporation's ability to carry forward net operating losses (and other tax credits) is limited when more than 50 percent of the stock changes hands over a three-year period.

2. The IRS may disallow an acquisition if the principal purpose of the acquisition is to avoid federal tax. This is one of the catch-22s of the Internal Revenue Code.

Debt Capacity   There are at least two cases where mergers allow for increased debt and a larger tax shield. In the first case, the target has too little debt, and the acquirer can infuse the target with the missing debt. In the second case, both the target and acquirer have optimal debt levels. A merger leads to risk reduction, generating greater debt capacity and a larger tax shield. We treat each case in turn.

Case 1: Unused Debt Capacity   In Chapter 17, we pointed out that every firm has a certain amount of debt capacity. This debt capacity is beneficial because greater debt leads to a greater tax shield. More formally, every firm can borrow a certain amount before the marginal costs of financial distress equal the marginal tax shield. This debt capacity is a function of many factors, perhaps the most important being the risk of the firm. Firms with high risk generally cannot borrow as much as firms with low risk. For example, a utility or a supermarket, both firms with low risk, can have a higher debt-to-value ratio than a technology firm.

Some firms, for whatever reason, have less debt than is optimal. Perhaps the managers are risk-averse, or perhaps the managers simply don't know how to assess debt capacity properly. Is it bad for a firm to have too little debt? The answer is yes. As we have said, the optimal level of debt occurs when the marginal cost of financial distress equals the marginal tax shield. Too little debt reduces firm value.

This is where mergers come in. A firm with little or no debt is an inviting target. An acquirer could raise the target's debt level after the merger to create a bigger tax shield.

Case 2: Increased Debt Capacity   Let's move back to the principles of modern portfolio theory, as presented in Chapter 11. Consider two stocks in different industries, where both stocks have the same risk or standard deviation. A portfolio of these two stocks has lower risk than that of either stock separately. In other words, the two-stock portfolio is somewhat diversified, whereas each stock by itself is completely undiversified.[10]

Now, rather than considering an individual buying both stocks, consider a merger between the two underlying firms. Because the risk of the combined firm is less than that of either one separately, banks should be willing to lend more money to the combined firm than the total of what they would lend to the two firms separately. In other words, the risk reduction that the merger generates leads to greater debt capacity.

For example, imagine that each firm can borrow $100 on its own before the merger. Perhaps the combined firm after the merger will be able to borrow $250. Debt capacity has increased by $50 (=$250 − $200).

Remember that debt generates a tax shield. If debt rises after the merger, taxes will fall. That is, simply because of the greater interest payments after the merger, the tax bill of the combined firm should be less than the sum of the tax bills of the two separate firms before the merger. In other words, the increased debt capacity from a merger can reduce taxes.

To summarize, we first considered the case where the target had too little leverage. The acquirer could infuse the target with more debt, generating a greater tax shield. Next, we considered the case where both the target and acquirer began with optimal debt levels. A merger leads to more debt even here. That is, the risk reduction from the merger creates greater debt capacity and thus a greater tax shield.

MICHAEL C. JENSEN ON MERGERS AND ACQUISITIONS

Economic analysis and evidence indicate that takeovers, LBOs, and corporate restructurings are playing an important role in helping the economy adjust to major competitive changes in the last two decades. The competition among alternative management teams and organizational structures for control of corporate assets has enabled vast economic resources to move more quickly to their highest-valued use. In the process, substantial benefits for the economy as a whole as well as for shareholders have been created. Overall gains to selling-firm shareholders from mergers, acquisitions, leveraged buyouts, and other corporate restructurings in the 12-year period 1977–1988 totaled over $500 billion in 1988 dollars. I estimate gains to buying-firm shareholders to be at least $50 billion for the same period. These gains equaled 53 percent of the total cash dividends (valued in 1988 dollars) paid to investors by the entire corporate sector in the same period.

Mergers and acquisitions are a response to new technologies or market conditions that require a strategic change in a company's direction or use of resources. Compared to current management, a new owner is often better able to accomplish major change in the existing organizational structure. Alternatively, leveraged buyouts bring about organizational change by creating entrepreneurial incentives for management and by eliminating the centralized bureaucratic obstacles to maneuverability that are inherent in large public corporations.

When managers have a substantial ownership interest in the organization, the conflicts of interest between shareholders and managers over the payout of the company's free cash flow are reduced. Management's incentives are focused on maximizing the value of the enterprise, rather than building empires—often through poorly conceived diversification acquisitions—without regard to shareholder value. Finally, the required repayment of debt replaces management's discretion in paying dividends and the tendency to overretain cash. Substantial increases in efficiency are thereby created.

Michael C. Jensen is Jesse Isidor Straus Professor of Business Administration, Emeritus at Harvard University. An outstanding scholar and researcher, he is famous for his pathbreaking analysis of the modern corporation and its relations with its stockholders.

Surplus Funds   Another quirk in the tax law involves surplus funds. Consider a firm that has *free cash flow*. That is, it has cash flow available after payment of all taxes and after all positive net present value projects have been funded. In this situation, aside from purchasing securities, the firm can either pay dividends or buy back shares.

We have already seen in our previous discussion of dividend policy that an extra dividend will increase the income tax paid by some investors. Investors pay lower taxes in a share repurchase.[11] However, a share repurchase is not a legal option if the sole purpose is to avoid taxes on dividends.

Instead, the firm might make acquisitions with its excess funds. Here, the shareholders of the acquiring firm avoid the taxes they would have paid on a dividend.[12] And no taxes are paid on dividends remitted from the acquired firm.

REDUCED CAPITAL REQUIREMENTS

Earlier in this chapter, we stated that due to economies of scale, mergers can reduce operating costs. It follows that mergers can reduce capital requirements as well. Accountants typically divide capital into two components: Fixed capital and working capital.

When two firms merge, the managers will likely find duplicate facilities. For example, if both firms had their own headquarters, all executives in the merged firm could be moved to one headquarters building, allowing the other headquarters to be sold. Some plants might be

---

[11]A dividend is taxable to all tax-paying recipients. A repurchase creates a tax liability only for those who choose to sell (and do so at a profit).

[12]The situation is actually a little more complex: The target's shareholders must pay taxes on their capital gains. These stockholders will likely demand a premium from the acquirer to offset this tax.

redundant as well. Or two merging firms in the same industry might consolidate their research and development, permitting some R&D facilities to be sold.

The same goes for working capital. The inventory-to-sales ratio and the cash-to-sales ratio often decrease as firm size increases. A merger permits these economies of scale to be realized, allowing a reduction in working capital.

29.4 Two Financial Side Effects of Acquisitions

EARNINGS GROWTH

An acquisition can create the appearance of earnings growth, perhaps fooling investors into thinking that the firm is worth more than it really is. Let's consider two companies, Global Resources, Ltd., and Regional Enterprises, as depicted in the first two columns of Table 29.2. As can be seen, earnings per share are $1 for both companies. However, Global sells for $25 per share, implying a price–earnings (P/E) ratio of 25 (=$25/$1). By contrast, Regional sells for $10, implying a P/E ratio of 10. This means that an investor in Global pays $25 to get $1 in earnings, whereas an investor in Regional receives the same $1 in earnings on only a $10 investment. Are investors getting a better deal with Regional? Not necessarily. Perhaps Global's earnings are expected to grow faster than are Regional's earnings. If this is the case, an investor in Global will expect to receive high earnings in later years, making up for low earnings in the short term. In fact, Chapter 9 argues that the primary determinant of a firm's P/E ratio is the market's expectation of the firm's growth rate in earnings.

Now let's imagine that Global acquires Regional, with the merger creating no value. If the market is smart, it will realize that the combined firm is worth the sum of the values of the separate firms. In this case, the market value of the combined firm will be $3,500, which is equal to the sum of the values of the separate firms before the merger.

At these values, Global will acquire Regional by exchanging 40 of its shares for 100 shares of Regional, so that Global will have 140 shares outstanding after the merger.[13] Global's stock price remains at $25 (=$3,500/140). With 140 shares outstanding and $200 of earnings after the merger, Global earns $1.43 (=$200/140) per share after the merger. Its P/E ratio becomes 17.5 (=$25/$1.43), a drop from 25 before the merger. This scenario is represented by the third column of Table 29.2. Why has the P/E dropped? The combined

Table 29.2

Financial Positions of Global Resources, Ltd., and Regional Enterprises

	Global Resources before Merger	Regional Enterprises before Merger	Global Resources after Merger	
			The Market Is "Smart"	The Market Is "Fooled"
Earnings per share	$ 1.00	$ 1.00	$ 1.43	$ 1.43
Price per share	$ 25.00	$ 10.00	$ 25.00	$ 35.71
Price–earnings ratio	25	10	17.5	25
Number of shares	100	100	140	140
Total earnings	$ 100	$ 100	$ 200	$ 200
Total value	$2,500	$1,000	$3,500	$5,000

Exchange ratio: 1 share in Global for 2.5 shares in Regional.

___

[13]This ratio implies a fair exchange because a share of Regional is selling for 40 percent (=$10/$25) of the price of a share of Global.

firm's P/E will be an average of Global's high P/E and Regional's low P/E before the merger. This is common sense once you think about it. Global's P/E should drop when it takes on a new division with low growth.

Let us now consider the possibility that the market is fooled. As we just said, the acquisition enables Global to increase its earnings per share from $1 to $1.43. If the market is fooled, it might mistake the 43 percent increase in earnings per share for true growth. In this case, the price–earnings ratio of Global may not fall after the merger. Suppose the price–earnings ratio of Global remains at 25. The total value of the combined firm will increase to $5,000 ($=$25 \times$ $200), and the stock price per share of Global will increase to $35.71 ($=$5,000/140). This is reflected in the last column of the table.

This is earnings growth magic. Can we expect this magic to work in the real world? Managers of a previous generation certainly thought so, with firms such as LTV Industries, ITT, and Litton Industries all trying to play the P/E-multiple game in the 1960s. However, in hindsight, it looks as if they played the game without much success. These operators have all dropped out with few, if any, replacements. It appears that the market is too smart to be fooled this easily.

DIVERSIFICATION

Diversification is often mentioned as a benefit of one firm acquiring another. Earlier in this chapter, we noted that U.S. Steel included diversification as a benefit in its acquisition of Marathon Oil. At the time of the merger, U.S. Steel was a cash-rich company, with more than 20 percent of its assets in cash and marketable securities. It is not uncommon to see firms with surplus cash articulating a need for diversification.

However, we argue that diversification, by itself, may not produce increases in value. To see this, recall that part of a business's variability of return can be attributed to what is specific to the business and called *unsystematic* risk.

As you recall from Chapter 11 in our discussion of the CAPM, conceptually unsystematic risk can be diversified away through mergers. However, the investor does not need widely diversified companies such as General Electric to eliminate unsystematic risk. Shareholders can diversify more easily than corporations by simply purchasing common stock in different corporations. For example, the shareholders of U.S. Steel could have purchased shares in Marathon if they believed there would be diversification gains in doing so. Thus, diversification through conglomerate merger may not benefit shareholders.[14]

Diversification can produce gains to the acquiring firm if one of three things is true:

1. Diversification decreases the unsystematic variability at lower costs than by investors' adjustments to personal portfolios. This seems very unlikely.

2. Diversification reduces risk and thereby increases debt capacity. This possibility was mentioned earlier in the chapter.

3. Internal capital or labor allocations are better for diversified firms than would be true otherwise.

Otherwise, one should be cautious in accepting diversification as a benefit in a merger or acquisition.

---

[14] In fact, a number of scholars have argued that diversification can *reduce* firm value by weakening corporate focus, a point to be developed in a later section of this chapter.

29.5 A Cost to Stockholders from Reduction in Risk

We considered two financial side effects of mergers in the previous section. Merging for either of these two reasons will not necessarily destroy value. Rather, it is just unlikely that merging for these two reasons will increase value. In this section, we examine a by-product of acquisitions that could actually destroy value, at least from the stockholders' point of view. As we will see, mergers increase the safety of bonds, raising the value of these bonds and hurting the stockholders.

In Chapter 11, we considered an individual adding one security after another, all of equal risk, to a portfolio. We saw that as long as the securities were less than perfectly positively correlated with each other, the risk of this portfolio fell as the number of securities rose. In a word, this risk reduction reflected *diversification*. Diversification also happens in a merger. When two firms merge, the volatility of their combined value is usually less than their volatilities as separate entities.

However, there is a surprising result here. Whereas an individual benefits from portfolio diversification, diversification from a merger may actually hurt the stockholders. The reason is that the bondholders are likely to gain from the merger because their debt is now "insured" by two firms, not just one. It turns out that this gain to the bondholders is at the stockholders' expense.

THE BASE CASE

Consider an example where Firm A acquires Firm B. Panel I of Table 29.3 shows the net present values of Firm A and Firm B prior to the merger in the two possible states of the economy. Because the probability of each state is .50, the market value of each firm is the average of its values in the two states. For example, the market value of Firm A is:

$$.5 \times \$80 + .5 \times \$20 = \$50$$

Now imagine that the merger of the two firms generates no synergy. The combined Firm AB will have a market value of $75 (=$50 + $25), the sum of the values of Firm A and Firm B. Further imagine that the stockholders of Firm B receive stock in AB equal to Firm B's stand-alone market value of $25. In other words, Firm B receives no premium. Because the value of AB is $75, the stockholders of Firm A have a value of $50 (=$75 − $25) after the merger—just what they had before the merger. Thus, the stockholders of both Firms A and B are indifferent to the merger.

BOTH FIRMS HAVE DEBT

Alternatively, imagine that Firm A has debt with a face value of $30 in its capital structure, as shown in panel II of Table 29.3. Without a merger, Firm A will default on its debt in State 2 because the value of Firm A in this state is $20, less than the face value of the debt of $30. As a consequence, Firm A cannot pay the full value of the debt claim; the bondholders receive only $20 in this state. The creditors take the possibility of default into account, valuing the debt at $25 (=.5 × $30 + .5 × $20).

Firm B's debt has a face value of $15. Firm B will default in State 1 because the value of the firm in this state is $10, less than the face value of the debt of $15. The value of Firm B's debt is $12.50 (=.5 × $10 + .5 × $15). It follows that the sum of the value of Firm A's debt and the value of Firm B's debt is $37.50 (=$25 + $12.50).

Now let's see what happens after the merger. Firm AB is worth $90 in State 1 and $60 in State 2, implying a market value of $75 (=.5 × $90 + .5 × $60). The face value of the debt

Table 29.3
Stock-Swap Mergers

	NPV		
	State 1	State 2	Market Value
Probability	.5	.5	
I. Base case (no debt in either firm's capital structure)			
Values before merger:			
Firm A	$80	$20	$50
Firm B	10	40	25
Values after merger:*			
Firm AB	$90	$60	$75
II. Debt with face value of $30 in Firm A's capital structure Debt with face value of $15 in Firm B's capital structure			
Values before merger:			
Firm A	$80	$20	$50
Debt	30	20	25
Equity	50	0	25
Firm B	$10	$40	$25
Debt	10	15	12.50
Equity	0	25	12.50
Values after merger:†			
Firm AB	$90	$60	$75
Debt	45	45	45
Equity	45	15	30

Values of both Firm A's debt and Firm B's debt rise after the merger. Values of both Firm A's stock and Firm B's stock fall after the merger.

*Stockholders in Firm A receive $50 of stock in Firm AB. Stockholders in Firm B receive $25 of stock in Firm AB. Thus, stockholders in both firms are indifferent to the merger.

†Stockholders in Firm A receive stock in Firm AB worth $20. Stockholders in Firm B receive stock in Firm AB worth $10. Gains and losses from the merger are:

Loss to stockholders in Firm A: $20 − $25 = −$5
Loss to stockholders in Firm B: $10 − $12.50 = −$2.50
Combined gain to bondholders in both firms: $45.00 − $37.50 = $7.50

in the combined firm is $45 (=$30 + $15). Because the value of the firm is greater than $45 in either state, the bondholders always get paid in full. Thus, the value of the debt is its face value of $45. This value is $7.50 greater than the sum of the values of the two debts before the merger, which we just found to be $37.50. Therefore, the merger benefits the bondholders.

What about the stockholders? Because the equity of Firm A was worth $25 and the equity of Firm B was worth $12.50 before the merger, let's assume that Firm AB issues two shares to Firm A's stockholders for every share issued to Firm B's stockholders. Firm AB's equity is $30, so Firm A's shareholders get shares worth $20 and Firm B's shareholders get shares worth $10. Firm A's stockholders lose $5 (=$20 − $25) from the merger. Similarly, Firm B's stockholders lose $2.50 (=$10 − $12.50). The total loss to the stockholders of both firms is $7.50, exactly the gain to the bondholders from the merger.

There are a lot of numbers in this example. The point is that the bondholders gain $7.50 and the stockholders lose $7.50 from the merger. Why does this transfer of value occur? To see what is going on, notice that when the two firms are separate, Firm B does not guarantee Firm A's debt. That is, if Firm A defaults on its debt, Firm B does not help the bondholders of

Firm *A*. However, after the merger the bondholders can draw on the cash flows from both *A* and *B*. When one of the divisions of the combined firm fails, creditors can be paid from the profits of the other division. This mutual guarantee, which is called the *coinsurance effect,* makes the debt less risky and more valuable than before.

There is no net benefit to the firm as a whole. The bondholders gain the coinsurance effect, and the stockholders lose the coinsurance effect. Some general conclusions emerge from the preceding analysis:

1. Mergers can help bondholders. The size of the gain to bondholders depends on the reduction in the probability of bankruptcy after the combination. That is, the less risky the combined firm is, the greater are the gains to bondholders.

2. Stockholders are hurt by the amount that bondholders gain.

3. Conclusion 2 applies to mergers without synergy. In practice, much depends on the size of the synergy.

HOW CAN SHAREHOLDERS REDUCE THEIR LOSSES FROM THE COINSURANCE EFFECT?

The coinsurance effect raises bondholder values and lowers shareholder values. However, there are at least two ways in which shareholders can reduce or eliminate the coinsurance effect. First, the shareholders of Firm *A* could retire its debt *before* the merger announcement date and reissue an equal amount of debt after the merger. Because debt is retired at the low premerger price, this type of refinancing transaction can neutralize the coinsurance effect to the bondholders.

Also, note that the debt capacity of the combined firm is likely to increase because the acquisition reduces the probability of financial distress. Thus, the shareholders' second alternative is simply to issue more debt after the merger. An increase in debt following the merger will have two effects, even without the prior action of debt retirement. The interest tax shield from new corporate debt raises firm value, as discussed in an earlier section of this chapter. In addition, an increase in debt after the merger raises the probability of financial distress, thereby reducing or eliminating the bondholders' gain from the coinsurance effect.

29.6 The NPV of a Merger

Firms typically use NPV analysis when making acquisitions. The analysis is relatively straightforward when the consideration is cash. The analysis becomes more complex when the consideration is stock.

CASH

Suppose Firm *A* and Firm *B* have values as separate entities of $500 and $100, respectively. They are both all-equity firms. If Firm *A* acquires Firm *B*, the merged Firm *AB* will have a combined value of $700 due to synergies of $100. The board of Firm *B* has indicated that it will sell Firm *B* if it is offered $150 in cash.

Should Firm *A* acquire Firm *B*? Assuming that Firm *A* finances the acquisition out of its own retained earnings, its value after the acquisition is:[15]

$$\text{Value of Firm } A \text{ after the acquisition} = \text{Value of combined firm} - \text{Cash paid}$$
$$= \$700 - \$150$$
$$= \$550$$

---

[15]The analysis will be essentially the same if new stock is issued. However, the analysis will differ if new debt is issued to fund the acquisition because of the tax shield to debt. An adjusted present value (APV) approach would be necessary here.

Table 29.4   Cost of Acquisition: Cash versus Common Stock

| | Before Acquisition | | After Acquisition: Firm A | | |
	(1)	(2)	(3)	(4) Common Stock† Exchange Ratio (.75:1)	(5) Common Stock† Exchange Ratio (.6819:1)
	Firm A	Firm B	Cash*		
Market value (V_A, V_B)	$500	$100	$550	$700	$700
Number of shares	25	10	25	32.5	31.819
Price per share	$ 20	$ 10	$ 22	$ 21.54	$ 22

*Value of Firm A after acquisition: Cash

$$V_A = V_{AB} - \text{Cash}$$
$$\$550 = \$700 - \$150$$

†Value of Firm A after acquisition: Common stock

$$V_A = V_{AB}$$
$$\$700 = \$700$$

Because Firm *A* was worth $500 prior to the acquisition, the NPV to Firm *A*'s stockholders is:

$$\$50 = \$550 - \$500 \tag{29.1}$$

Assuming that there are 25 shares in Firm *A*, each share of the firm is worth $20 (=$500/25) prior to the merger and $22 (=$550/25) after the merger. These calculations are displayed in the first and third columns of Table 29.4. Looking at the rise in stock price, we conclude that Firm *A* should make the acquisition.

We spoke earlier of both the synergy and the premium of a merger. We can also value the NPV of a merger to the acquirer:

$$\text{NPV of a merger to acquirer} = \text{Synergy} - \text{Premium}$$

Because the value of the combined firm is $700 and the premerger values of *A* and *B* were $500 and $100, respectively, the synergy is $100 [=$700 − ($500 + $100)]. The premium is $50 (=$150 − $100). Thus, the NPV of the merger to the acquirer is:

$$\text{NPV of merger to firm } A = \$100 - \$50 = \$50$$

One caveat is in order. This textbook has consistently argued that the market value of a firm is the best estimate of its true value. However, we must adjust our analysis when discussing mergers. If the true price of Firm *A* *without the merger* is $500, the market value of Firm *A* may actually be above $500 when merger negotiations take place. This happens because the market price reflects the possibility that the merger will occur. For example, if the probability is 60 percent that the merger will take place, the market price of Firm *A* will be:

	Market value of Firm *A* with merger	×	Probability of merger	+	Market value of Firm *A* without merger	×	Probability of no merger
$530 =	$550	×	.60	+	$500	×	.40

The managers would underestimate the NPV from the merger in Equation 29.1 if the market price of Firm *A* were used. Thus, managers face the difficult task of valuing their own firm without the acquisition.

COMMON STOCK

Of course, Firm *A* could purchase Firm *B* with common stock instead of cash. Unfortunately, the analysis is not as straightforward here. To handle this scenario, we need to know how many shares are outstanding in Firm *B*. We assume that there are 10 shares outstanding, as indicated in Column 2 of Table 29.4.

Suppose Firm *A* exchanges 7.5 of its shares for the entire 10 shares of Firm *B*. We call this an exchange ratio of .75:1. The value of each share of Firm *A*'s stock before the acquisition is $20. Because $7.5 \times \$20 = \$150$, this exchange *appears* to be the equivalent of purchasing Firm *B* in cash for $150.

This is incorrect: The true cost to Firm *A* is greater than $150. To see this, note that Firm *A* has 32.5 (=25 + 7.5) shares outstanding after the merger. Firm *B* shareholders own 23 percent (=7.5/32.5) of the combined firm. Their holdings are valued at $161 (=23% × $700). Because these stockholders receive stock in Firm *A* worth $161, the cost of the merger to Firm *A*'s stockholders must be $161, not $150.

This result is shown in Column 4 of Table 29.4. The value of each share of Firm *A*'s stock after a stock-for-stock transaction is only $21.54 (=$700/32.5). We found out earlier that the value of each share is $22 after a cash-for-stock transaction. The difference is that the cost of the stock-for-stock transaction to Firm *A* is higher.

This nonintuitive result occurs because the exchange ratio of 7.5 shares of Firm *A* for 10 shares of Firm *B* was based on the *premerger* prices of the two firms. However, because the stock of Firm *A* rises after the merger, Firm *B* stockholders receive more than $150 in Firm *A* stock.

What should the exchange ratio be so that Firm *B* stockholders receive only $150 of Firm *A*'s stock? We begin by defining α, the proportion of the shares in the combined firm that Firm *B*'s stockholders own. Because the combined firm's value is $700, the value of Firm *B* stockholders after the merger is:

Value of Firm *B* Stockholders after Merger:

$$\alpha \times \$700$$

Setting $\alpha \times \$700 = \$150$, we find that $\alpha = 21.43\%$. In other words, Firm *B*'s stockholders will receive stock worth $150 if they receive 21.43 percent of the firm after the merger.

Now we determine the number of shares issued to Firm *B*'s shareholders. The proportion, α, that Firm *B*'s shareholders have in the combined firm can be expressed as follows:

$$\alpha = \frac{\text{New shares issued}}{\text{Old shares + New shares issued}} = \frac{\text{New shares issued}}{25 + \text{New shares issued}}$$

Plugging our value of α into the equation yields:

$$.2143 = \frac{\text{New shares issued}}{25 + \text{New shares issued}}$$

Solving for the unknown, we have:

$$\text{New shares} = 6.819 \text{ shares}$$

Total shares outstanding after the merger are 31.819 (=25 + 6.819). Because 6.819 shares of Firm *A* are exchanged for 10 shares of Firm *B*, the exchange ratio is .6819:1.

Results at the exchange ratio of .6819:1 are displayed in Column 5 of Table 29.4. Because there are now 31.819 shares, each share of common stock is worth $22 (=$700/31.819), exactly what it is worth in the cash-for-stock transaction. Thus, given that the board of

Firm *B* will sell its firm for $150, this is the fair exchange ratio, not the ratio of .75:1 mentioned earlier.

CASH VERSUS COMMON STOCK

In this section, we have examined both cash deals and stock-for-stock deals. Our analysis leads to the following question: When do bidders want to pay with cash and when do they want to pay with stock? There is no easy formula: The decision hinges on a few variables, with perhaps the most important being the price of the bidder's stock.

In the example of Table 29.4, Firm *A*'s market price per share prior to the merger was $20. Let's now assume that at the time Firm *A*'s managers believed the "true" price was $15. In other words, the managers believed that their stock was overvalued. Is it likely for managers to have a different view than that of the market? Yes—managers often have more information than does the market. After all, managers deal with customers, suppliers, and employees daily and are likely to obtain private information.

Now imagine that Firm *A*'s managers are considering acquiring Firm *B* with either cash or stock. The overvaluation would have no impact on the merger terms in a cash deal; Firm *B* would still receive $150 in cash. However, the overvaluation would have a big impact on a stock-for-stock deal. Although Firm *B* receives $150 worth of *A*'s stock as calculated at market prices, Firm *A*'s managers know that the true value of the stock is less than $150.

How should Firm *A* pay for the acquisition? Clearly, Firm *A* has an incentive to pay with stock because it would end up giving away less than $150 of value. This conclusion might seem rather cynical because Firm *A* is, in some sense, trying to cheat Firm *B*'s stockholders. However, both theory and empirical evidence suggest that firms are more likely to acquire with stock when their own stocks are overvalued.[16]

The story is not quite this simple. Just as the managers of Firm *A* think strategically, Firm *B*'s managers will likely think this way as well. Suppose that in the merger negotiations, Firm *A*'s managers push for a stock-for-stock deal. This might tip off Firm *B*'s managers that Firm *A* is overpriced. Perhaps Firm *B*'s managers will ask for better terms than Firm *A* is currently offering. Alternatively, Firm *B* may resolve to accept cash or not to sell at all.

And just as Firm *B* learns from the negotiations, the market learns also. Empirical evidence shows that the acquirer's stock price generally falls upon the announcement of a stock-for-stock deal.[17]

However, this discussion does not imply that mistakes are never made. For example, consider the stock-for-stock merger in January 2001 between AOL, an Internet service provider, and Time Warner (TW), a media firm. Although the deal was presented as a merger of equals and the combined company is now called Time Warner, AOL appears, in retrospect, to have been the acquirer. The merger was one of the biggest of all time, with a combined market capitalization between the two firms of about $350 billion at the time of the announcement in January 2000. (The delay of about a year between merger announcement and merger completion was due to regulatory review.) It is also considered one of the worst deals of all time, with Time Warner having a market value of about $68 billion in early 2015. Interestingly, AOL was purchased by Verizon in 2015.

---

[16]The basic theoretical ideas are presented in Stewart Myers and Nicholas Majluf, "Corporate Financing and Investment Decisions When Firms Have Information That Investors Do Not Have," *Journal of Financial Economics* (1984).

[17]For example, see Gregor Andrade, Mark Mitchell, and Erik Stafford, "New Evidence and Perspectives on Mergers," *Journal of Economic Perspectives* (Spring 2001); and Randall Heron and Erik Lie, "Operating Performance and the Method of Payment in Takeovers," *Journal of Financial and Quantitative Analysis* (2002).

AOL was in a precarious position at the time of the merger, providing narrow-band Internet service when consumers were hungering for broadband. Also, at least in retrospect, Internet stocks were greatly overpriced. The deal allowed AOL to offer its inflated stock as currency for a company not in the technology industry and, therefore, not nearly as overpriced, if overpriced at all. Had TW looked at the deal in this way, it might have simply called it off. (Alternatively, it could have demanded cash, though it is unlikely that AOL had the financial resources to pay in this way.)

Just as TW's managers did not understand all the implications of the merger right away, it appears that the market did not either. TW's stock price rose more than 25 percent relative to the market in the week following the merger announcement.

29.7 Friendly versus Hostile Takeovers

Mergers are generally initiated by the acquiring, not the acquired, firm. Thus, the acquirer must decide to purchase another firm, select the tactics to effectuate the merger, determine the highest price it is willing to pay, set an initial bid price, and make contact with the target firm. Often the CEO of the acquiring firm simply calls the CEO of the target and proposes a merger. Should the target be receptive, a merger eventually occurs. Of course there may be many meetings, with negotiations over price, terms of payment, and other parameters. The target's board of directors generally has to approve the acquisition. Sometimes the bidder's board must also give its approval. Finally, an affirmative vote by the stockholders is needed. But when all is said and done, an acquisition that proceeds in this way is viewed as *friendly*.

Of course, not all acquisitions are friendly. The target's management may resist the merger, in which case the acquirer must decide whether to pursue the merger and, if so, what tactics to use. Facing resistance, the acquirer may begin by purchasing some of the target's stock in secret. This position is often called a *toehold*. The Williams Act, passed in 1968 and one of the landmark pieces of legislation of the era, requires that the acquirer file a Schedule 13D with the Securities and Exchange Commission (SEC) within 10 days of obtaining a 5 percent holding in the target's stock. The acquirer must provide detailed information, including its intentions and its position in the target, on this schedule. Secrecy ends at this point because the acquirer must state that it plans to acquire the target. The price of the target's shares will probably rise after the filing, with the new stock price reflecting the possibility that the target will be bought out at a premium. Acquirers will, however, often make the most of this 10-day delay, buying as much stock as possible at the low prefiling price during this period.

Although the acquirer may continue to purchase shares in the open market, an acquisition is unlikely to be effectuated in this manner. Rather, the acquirer is more likely at some point to make a *tender offer* (an offer made directly to the stockholders to buy shares at a premium above the current market price). The tender offer may specify that the acquirer will purchase all shares that are tendered—that is, turned in to the acquirer. Alternatively, the offer may state that the acquirer will purchase all shares up to, say, 50 percent of the number of shares outstanding. If more shares are tendered, prorating will occur. For example, if, in the extreme case, all of the shares are tendered, each stockholder will be allowed to sell one share for every two shares tendered. The acquirer may also say that it will accept the tendered shares only if a minimum number of shares have been tendered.

Under the Williams Act, a tender offer must be held open for at least 20 days. This delay gives the target time to respond. For example, the target may want to notify its stockholders not to tender their shares. It may release statements to the press criticizing the offer. The target may also encourage other firms to enter the bidding process.

At some point, the tender offer ends, at which time the acquirer finds out how many shares have been tendered. The acquirer does not necessarily need 100 percent of the shares to obtain control of the target. In some companies, a holding of 20 percent or so may be enough for control. In others the percentage needed for control is much higher. *Control* is a vague term, but you might think of it operationally as control over the board of directors. Stockholders elect members of the board, who, in turn, appoint managers. If the acquirer receives enough stock to elect a majority of the board members, these members can appoint the managers whom the acquirer wants, and effective control can often be achieved with less than a majority. As long as some of the original board members vote with the acquirer, a few new board members can gain the acquirer a working majority.

Sometimes, once the acquirer gets working control, it proposes a merger to obtain the few remaining shares that it does not already own. The transaction is now friendly because the board of directors will approve it. Mergers of this type are often called *cleanup* mergers.

A tender offer is not the only way to gain control of a *hostile* target. Alternatively, the acquirer may continue to buy more shares in the open market until control is achieved. This strategy, often called a *street sweep,* is infrequently used, perhaps because of the difficulty of buying enough shares to obtain control. Also, as mentioned, tender offers often allow the acquirer to return the tendered shares if fewer shares than the desired number are tendered. By contrast, shares purchased in the open market cannot be returned.

Another means to obtain control is a *proxy fight*—a procedure involving corporate voting. Elections for seats on the board of directors are generally held at the annual stockholders' meeting, perhaps four to five months after the end of the firm's fiscal year. After purchasing shares in the target company, the acquirer nominates a slate of candidates to run against the current directors. The acquirer generally hires a proxy solicitor, who contacts shareholders prior to the stockholders' meeting, making a pitch for the insurgent slate. Should the acquirer's candidates win a majority of seats on the board, the acquirer will control the firm. And as with tender offers, effective control can often be achieved with less than a majority. The acquirer may just want to change a few specific policies of the firm, such as the firm's capital budgeting program or its diversification plan. Or it may simply want to replace management. If some of the original board members are sympathetic to the acquirer's plans, a few new board members can give the acquirer a working majority.

For example, in early 2015, DuPont Co. was in the middle of a proxy fight with investment company Trian Fund Management, headed by Nelson Peltz. Trian argued that the conglomerate structure of DuPont made it especially difficult for the company to give reliable earnings estimates to investors. DuPont argued back that the company was exceeding long-term goals set out in 2010 and had outperformed the stock market over the past five years. DuPont also rebuffed Trian's attempt to name four directors to its board.

Whereas mergers end up with the acquirer owning all of the target's stock, the victor in a proxy fight does not gain additional shares. The reward to the proxy victor is simply share price appreciation if the victor's policies prove effective. In fact, just the threat of a proxy fight may raise share prices because management may improve operations to head off the fight. For example, in November 2013, offshore driller Transocean avoided a proxy fight with activist investor Carl Icahn by agreeing to support one of

Icahn's nominees for its board. Additionally, Transocean agreed to pay a $3 dividend to shareholders, reduce the number of board members from 14 to 11, and make several other changes suggested by Icahn. Transocean's stock price increased 3.6 percent after the announcement.

29.8 Defensive Tactics

Target firm managers frequently resist takeover attempts. Actions to defeat a takeover may benefit the target shareholders if the bidding firm raises its offer price or another firm makes a bid. Alternatively, resistance may simply reflect self-interest at the shareholders' expense. That is, the target managers might fight a takeover to preserve their jobs. Sometimes management resists while simultaneously improving corporate policies. Stockholders can benefit in this case, even if the takeover fails.

In this section, we describe various ways in which target managers resist takeovers. A company is said to be "in play" if one or more suitors are currently interested in acquiring it. It is useful to separate defensive tactics before a company is in play from tactics after the company is in play.

DETERRING TAKEOVERS BEFORE BEING IN PLAY

Corporate Charters The corporate charter refers to the articles of incorporation and corporate bylaws governing a firm.[18] Among other provisions, the charter establishes conditions allowing a takeover. Firms frequently amend charters to make acquisitions more difficult. As examples, consider the following two amendments:

1. *Classified board:* In an unclassified board of directors, stockholders elect all of the directors each year. In a classified, or staggered, board, only a fraction of the board is elected each year, with terms running for multiple years. For example, one-third of the board might stand for election each year, with terms running for three years. Classified boards increase the time an acquirer needs to obtain a majority of seats on the board. In the previous example, the acquirer can gain control of only one-third of the seats in the first year after acquisition. Another year must pass before the acquirer is able to control two-thirds of the seats. Therefore, the acquirer may not be able to change management as quickly as it would like. However, some argue that classified boards are not necessarily effective because the old directors often choose to vote with the acquirer. The use of classified boards has been declining in recent years. In 2005, about 53 percent of the companies in the S&P 500 had classified boards. That percentage declined to less than 15 percent by 2015.

2. *Supermajority provisions:* Corporate charters determine the percentage of voting shares needed to approve important transactions such as mergers. A supermajority provision in the charter means that this percentage is above 50 percent. Two-thirds majorities are common, though the number can be much higher. A supermajority

---

[18]Ronald Masulis, Cong Wang, and Fei Xie in "Corporate Governance and Acquirer Returns," *Journal of Finance* (August 2007), find that acquirer firms with more antitakeover provisions receive lower stock market returns than otherwise.

provision clearly increases the difficulty of acquisition in the face of hostile management. Many charters with supermajority provisions have what is known as a *board out* clause as well. Here supermajority does not apply if the board of directors approves the merger. This clause makes sure that the provision hinders only hostile takeovers.

Golden Parachutes This colorful term refers to generous severance packages provided to management in the event of a takeover. The argument is that golden parachutes will deter takeovers by raising the cost of acquisition. However, some authorities point out that the deterrence effect is likely to be unimportant because a severance package, even a generous one, is probably a small part of the cost of acquiring a firm. In addition, some argue that golden parachutes actually *increase* the probability of a takeover. The reasoning here is that management has a natural tendency to resist any takeover because of the possibility of job loss. A large severance package softens the blow of a takeover, reducing management's inclination to resist.

Poison Pills The poison pill is a sophisticated defensive tactic that Martin Lipton, a well-known New York attorney, developed in the early 1980s. Since then a number of variants have surfaced, so there is no single definition of a poison pill. For example, in October 2013, famed auction house Sotheby's enacted a poison pill to ward off hedge fund Third Point, which was run by activist investor Dan Loeb. Sotheby's poison pill was somewhat unique in that it kicked in if an activist investor acquired more than 10 percent of the company's stock or a passive investor acquired more than 20 percent of the company's stock. If either of these events happened, every shareholder except the shareholder causing the poison pill to become active would be given the right to buy new stock at half price. At the time, Sotheby's had about 69 million shares outstanding. If Third Point acquired more than 10% of the stock, (6.9 million shares), every shareholder *except Third Point* could have bought a new share for every one previously held. If all shareholders exercised this option, Sotheby's would have had to issue 62.1 million ($= .90 \times 69$ million) new shares, bringing its total to 131.1 million. The stock price would drop sharply because the company would be selling shares at half price. The bidder's percentage of the firm would drop from 10 percent to 5.3 percent ($= 6.9$ million/131.1 million). Dilution of this magnitude causes some critics to argue that poison pills are insurmountable.

DETERRING A TAKEOVER AFTER THE COMPANY IS IN PLAY

Greenmail and Standstill Agreements Managers may arrange a *targeted repurchase* to forestall a takeover attempt. In a targeted repurchase, a firm buys back its own stock from a potential bidder, usually at a substantial premium, with the proviso that the seller promises not to acquire the company for a specified period. Critics of such payments label them *greenmail*.

A *standstill agreement* occurs when the acquirer, for a fee, agrees to limit its holdings in the target. As part of the agreement, the acquirer often promises to offer the target a right of first refusal in the event that the acquirer sells its shares. This promise prevents the block of shares from falling into the hands of another would-be acquirer.

**EXAMPLE
29.2**

Takeover Defenses Suppose on April 2, 2012, Torrance Oil, Inc., a large independent oil refinery, had 28 million shares outstanding, and the company's stock price closed the day before at $49.25 per share on the New York Stock Exchange. Further suppose that on April 2, Torrance's board of directors made two decisions:

1. The board approved management's agreement with the Strauss family of Canada to buy, for $51 a share, the Strauss' 2.6 million shares in Torrance. This was part of a greenmail agreement ending the Strauss family's attempt to control Torrance.

2. The board authorized the company to repurchase 7.5 million shares (27 percent of the outstanding shares) of its stock. The board simultaneously established an employee stock ownership plan to be funded with 4.9 million shares of Torrance stock.

These two actions made Torrance invulnerable to unfriendly takeover attempts. In effect, the company was selling about 20 percent of its stock to the employee stock ownership plan. Earlier, Torrance had put in place a provision that said 80 percent of the stockholders have to approve a takeover. Torrance's stock price fell by $.25 over the next two days. Because this move can probably be explained by random error, there is no evidence that Torrance's actions reduced shareholder value.

Greenmail has been a colorful part of the financial lexicon since its first application in the late 1970s. Since then, pundits have commented numerous times on either its ethical or unethical nature. Greenmail has declined in recent years, perhaps for two reasons. First, Congress has imposed a tax on the profits from greenmail. Second, the law on greenmail is currently unsettled, causing recipients to worry about potential lawsuits.

White Knight and White Squire
A firm facing an unfriendly merger offer might arrange to be acquired by a friendly suitor, commonly referred to as a *white knight*. The white knight might be favored simply because it is willing to pay a higher purchase price. Alternatively, it might promise not to lay off employees, fire managers, or sell off divisions.

Management instead may wish to avoid any acquisition at all. A third party, termed a *white squire*, might be invited to make a significant investment in the firm, under the condition that it vote with management and not purchase additional shares. White knights can often increase the amount paid to the target firm. For example, in 2013, Aurizon Mines received a bid of C$4.65 from Alamos Gold, Inc., which was already Aurizon's largest shareholder. In response, Aurizon found a white knight in Hecla Mining, which purchased Aurizon for C$4.75 per share.

Recapitalizations and Repurchases
Target management will often issue debt to pay out a dividend—a transaction called a *leveraged recapitalization*. A *share repurchase*, where debt is issued to buy back shares, is a similar transaction. The two transactions fend off takeovers in a number of ways. First, the stock price may rise, perhaps because of the increased tax shield from greater debt. A rise in stock price makes the acquisition less attractive to the bidder. However, the price will rise only if the firm's debt level before the recapitalization was below the optimum, so a levered recapitalization is not recommended for every target. Consultants point out that firms with low debt but with stable cash flows are ideal candidates for "recaps." Second, as part of the recapitalization, management may issue new securities that give management greater voting control than

it had before the recap. The increase in control makes a hostile takeover more difficult. Third, firms with a lot of cash on their balance sheets are often seen as attractive targets. As part of the recap, the target may use this cash to pay a dividend or buy back stock, reducing the firm's appeal as a takeover candidate.

Exclusionary Self-Tenders   An *exclusionary self-tender* is the opposite of a targeted repurchase. Here, the firm makes a tender offer for a given amount of its own stock while excluding targeted stockholders.

In a particularly celebrated case, Unocal, a large integrated oil firm, made a tender offer for 29 percent of its shares while excluding its largest shareholder, Mesa Partners II (led by T. Boone Pickens). Unocal's self-tender was for $72 per share, which was $16 over the prevailing market price. It was designed to defeat Mesa's attempted takeover of Unocal by transferring wealth, in effect, from Mesa to Unocal's other stockholders.

Asset Restructurings   In addition to altering capital structure, firms may sell off existing assets or buy new ones to avoid takeover. Targets generally sell, or divest, assets for two reasons. First, a target firm may have assembled a hodgepodge of assets in different lines of business, with the various segments fitting together poorly. Value might be increased by placing these divisions into separate firms. Academics often emphasize the concept of *corporate focus*. The idea here is that firms function best by focusing on those few businesses that they really know. A rise in stock price following a divestiture will reduce the target's appeal to a bidder.

The second reason is that a bidder might be interested in a specific division of the target. The target can reduce the bidder's interest by selling off this division. Although the strategy may fend off a merger, it can hurt the target's stockholders if the division is worth more to the target than to the division's buyer. Authorities frequently talk of selling off the *crown jewels* or pursuing a *scorched earth policy*.

While some targets divest existing assets, others buy new ones. Two reasons are generally given here. First, the bidder may like the target as is. The addition of an unrelated business makes the target less appealing to the acquirer. However, a bidder can always sell off the new business, so the purchase is likely not a strong defense. Second, antitrust legislation is designed to prohibit mergers that reduce competition. Antitrust law is enforced by both the Department of Justice (DOJ) and the Federal Trade Commission (FTC). A target may purchase a company, knowing that this new division will pose antitrust problems for the bidder. However, this strategy might not be effective because, in its filings with the DOJ and the FTC, the bidder can state its intention to sell off the unrelated business.

29.9 Have Mergers Added Value?

In Section 29.2, we stated that synergy occurs if the value of the combined firm after the merger is greater than the sum of the value of the acquiring firm and the value of the acquired firm before the merger. Section 29.3 provided a number of sources of synergy in mergers, implying that mergers *can* create value. We now want to know whether mergers actually create value in practice. This is an empirical question and must be answered by empirical evidence.

There are a number of ways to measure value creation, but many academics favor *event studies*. These studies estimate abnormal stock returns on, and around, the merger announcement date. An *abnormal return* is usually defined as the difference between an

Table 29.5   Percentage and Dollar Returns for Mergers

Time Period	Gain or Loss to Merger (Both Acquired and Acquiring Firms)		Gain or Loss to Acquiring Firms	
	Abnormal Percentage Return	Aggregate Dollar Gain or Loss	Abnormal Percentage Return	Aggregate Dollar Gain or Loss
1980–2001	1.35%	−$ 79 billion	1.10%	−$220 billion
1980–1990	2.41	$ 12 billion	.64	−$ 4 billion
1991–2001	1.04	−$ 90 billion	1.20	−$216 billion
1998–2001	.29	−$134 billion	.69	−$240 billion

SOURCE: Adapted from Sara Moeller, Frederik Schlingemann, and René Stulz, "Wealth Destruction on a Massive Scale? A Study of Acquiring-Firm Returns in the Recent Merger Wave," *Journal of Finance* (April 2005), Table 1.

actual stock return and the return on a market index or control group of stocks. This control group is used to net out the effect of marketwide or industrywide influences.

Consider Table 29.5, where returns around the announcement days of mergers are reported. The average abnormal percentage return across all mergers from 1980 to 2001 is 1.35 percent. This number combines the returns on both the acquiring company and the acquired company. Because 1.35 percent is positive, the market believes that mergers on average create value. The other three returns in the first column are positive as well, implying value creation in the different subperiods. Many other academic studies have provided similar results. Thus, it appears from this column that the synergies we mentioned in Section 29.3 show up in the real world.

However, the next column tells us something different. Across all mergers from 1980 to 2001, the aggregate dollar change around the day of merger announcement is −$79 billion. This means that the market is, on average, *reducing* the combined stock value of the acquiring and acquired companies around the merger announcement date. Though the difference between the two columns may seem confusing, there is an explanation. Although most mergers have created value, mergers involving the very largest firms have lost value. The abnormal percentage return is an unweighted average in which the returns on all mergers are treated equally. A positive return here reflects all those small mergers that created value. However, losses in a few large mergers cause the aggregate dollar change to be negative.

But there is more. The rest of the second column indicates that the aggregate dollar losses occurred only in the 1998 to 2001 period. While there were losses of −$134 billion in this period, there were gains of $12 billion from 1980 to 1990. And interpolation of the table indicates that there were gains of $44 billion (=$134 − $90) from 1991 through 1997. Thus, it appears that some large mergers lost a great deal of value from 1998 to 2001.

The results in a table such as Table 29.5 should have important implications for public policy because Congress is always wondering whether mergers are to be encouraged or discouraged. However, the results in that table are, unfortunately, ambiguous. On the one hand, you could focus on the first column, saying that mergers create value on average. Proponents of this view might argue that the great losses in the few large mergers were flukes, not likely to occur again. On the other hand, we cannot easily ignore the fact that over the entire period, mergers destroyed more value than they created. A proponent of this position might quote the old adage, "Except for World War I and World War II, the 20th century was quite peaceful."

Before we move on, some final thoughts are in order. Readers may be bothered that abnormal returns are taken only around the time of the acquisition, well before all of the acquisition's impact is revealed. Academics look at long-term returns but they have a special fondness for short-term returns. If markets are efficient, the short-term return provides an unbiased estimate of the total effect of the merger. Long-term returns, while capturing more information about a merger, also reflect the impact of many unrelated events.

RETURNS TO BIDDERS

The preceding results combined returns on both bidders and targets. Investors want to separate the bidders from the targets. Columns 3 and 4 of Table 29.5 provide returns for acquiring companies alone. The third column shows that abnormal percentage returns for bidders have been positive for the entire sample period and for each of the individual subperiods—a result similar to that for bidders and targets combined. The fourth column indicates aggregate dollar losses, suggesting that large mergers did worse than small ones. The time pattern for these aggregate dollar losses to bidders is presented in Figure 29.3. Again, the large losses occurred from 1998 to 2001, with the greatest loss in 2000.

Let's fast-forward a few decades and imagine that you are the CEO of a company. In that position you will certainly be faced with potential acquisitions. Does the evidence in Table 29.5 and Figure 29.3 encourage you to make acquisitions or not? Again, the evidence is ambiguous. On the one hand, you could focus on the averages in Column 3 of the table, likely increasing your appetite for acquisitions. On the other hand, Column 4 of the table, as well as the figure, might give you pause.

Figure 29.3
Yearly Aggregate Dollar Gain or Loss for the Shareholders of Acquiring Firms

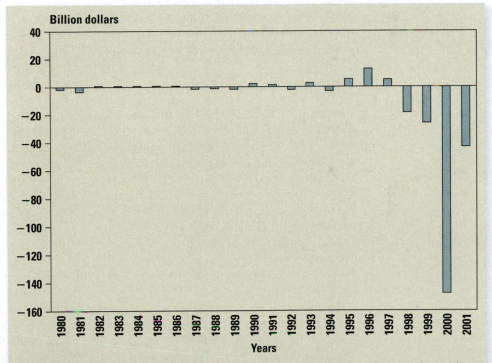

The graph shows the aggregate dollar gain or loss across all acquiring firms each year from 1980 to 2001.

SOURCE: Sara Moeller, Frederik Schlingemann, and René Stulz, "Wealth Destruction on a Massive Scale? A Study of Acquiring-Firm Returns in the Recent Merger Wave," *Journal of Finance* (April 2005), Figure 1.

TARGET COMPANIES

Although the evidence just presented for both the combined entity and the bidder alone is ambiguous, the evidence for targets is crystal clear. Acquisitions benefit the target's stockholders. Consider the following chart, which shows the median merger *premium* over different periods in the United States:[19]

Time Period	1973–1998	1973–1979	1980–1989	1990–1998
Premium	37.9%	47.2%	37.7%	34.5%

The premium is the difference between the acquisition price per share and the target's pre-acquisition share price, divided by the target's pre-acquisition share price. The average premium is quite high for the entire sample period and for the various subsamples. For example, a target stock selling at $100 per share before the acquisition that is later acquired for $137.9 per share generates a premium of 37.9 percent. Clearly, stockholders of any firm trading at $100 would love to be able to sell their holdings for $137.9 per share.

Though other studies may provide different estimates of the average premium, all studies show positive premiums. Thus, we can conclude that mergers benefit the target stockholders. This conclusion leads to at least two implications. First, we should be somewhat skeptical of target managers who resist takeovers. These managers may claim that the target's stock price does not reflect the true value of the company. Or they may say that resistance will induce the bidder to raise its offer. These arguments could be true in certain situations, but they may also provide cover for managers who are simply scared of losing their jobs after acquisition. Second, the premium creates a hurdle for the acquiring company. Even in a merger with true synergies, the acquiring stockholders will lose if the premium exceeds the dollar value of these synergies.

THE MANAGERS VERSUS THE STOCKHOLDERS

Managers of Bidding Firms The preceding discussion was presented from the stockholders' point of view. Because, in theory, stockholders pay the salaries of managers, we might think that managers would look at things from the stockholders' point of view. However, it is important to realize that individual stockholders have little clout with managers. For example, the typical stockholder is simply not in a position to pick up the phone and give the managers a piece of her mind. It is true that the stockholders elect the board of directors, which monitors the managers. However, an elected director has little contact with individual stockholders.

Thus, it is fair to ask whether managers are held fully accountable for their actions. This question is at the heart of what economists call *agency theory*. Researchers in this area often argue that managers work less hard, get paid more, and make worse business decisions than they would if stockholders had more control over them. And there is a special place in agency theory for mergers. Managers frequently receive bonuses for acquiring other companies. In addition, their pay is often positively related to the size of their firm. Finally, managers' prestige is also tied to firm size. Because firm size increases with acquisitions, managers are disposed to look favorably on acquisitions, perhaps even ones with a negative NPV.

---

[19]Gregor Andrade, Mark Mitchell, and Erik Stafford, "New Evidence and Perspectives on Mergers," *Journal of Economic Perspectives* (Spring 2001), Table 1.

A fascinating study[20] compared companies where managers received a lot of options on their own company's stock as part of their compensation package with companies where the managers did not. Because option values rise and fall in tandem with the firm's stock price, managers receiving options have an incentive to forgo mergers with negative NPVs. The paper reported that the acquisitions by firms where managers receive lots of options (termed *equity-based compensation* in the paper) create more value than the acquisitions by firms where managers receive few or no options.

Agency theory may also explain why the biggest merger failures have involved large firms. Managers owning a small fraction of their firm's stock have less incentive to behave responsibly because the great majority of any losses are borne by other stockholders. Managers of large firms likely have a smaller percentage interest in their firm's stock than do managers of small firms (a large percentage of a large firm is too costly to acquire). Thus, the merger failures of large acquirers may be due to the small percentage ownership of the managers.

An earlier chapter of this text discussed the free cash flow hypothesis. The idea here is that managers can spend only what they have. Managers of firms with low cash flow are likely to run out of cash before they run out of good (positive NPV) investments. Conversely, managers of firms with high cash flow are likely to have cash on hand even after all the good investments are taken. Managers are rewarded for growth, so managers with cash flow above that needed for good projects have an incentive to spend the remainder on bad (negative NPV) projects. A paper tested this conjecture, finding that "cash-rich firms are more likely than other firms to attempt acquisitions. . . . cash-rich bidders destroy seven cents in value for every dollar of cash reserves held. . . . consistent with the stock return evidence, mergers in which the bidder is cash-rich are followed by abnormal declines in operating performance."[21]

The previous discussion has considered the possibility that some managers are knaves—more interested in their own welfare than in the welfare of their stockholders. However, one paper entertained the idea that other managers were more fools than knaves. Malmendier and Tate[22] classified certain CEOs as overconfident, either because they refused to exercise stock options on their own company's stock when it was rational to do so or because the press portrayed them as confident or optimistic. The authors find that these overconfident managers are more likely to make acquisitions than are other managers. In addition, the stock market reacts more negatively to announcements of acquisitions when the acquiring CEO is overconfident.

Managers of Target Firms   Our discussion has just focused on the managers of acquiring firms, finding that these managers sometimes make more acquisitions than they should. However, that is only half of the story. Stockholders of target firms may have just as hard a time controlling their managers. While there are many ways that managers of target firms can put themselves ahead of their stockholders, two seem to stand out. First, we said earlier that because premiums are positive, takeovers are beneficial to the target's stockholders. However, if managers may be fired after their firms are acquired, they may resist these takeovers.[23] Tactics employed to resist takeover, generally called defensive

---

[20] Sudip Datta, Mai Iskandar-Datta, and Kartik Raman, "Executive Compensation and Corporate Acquisition Decisions," *Journal of Finance* (December 2001).

[21] From Jarrad Harford, "Corporate Cash Reserves and Acquisitions," *Journal of Finance* (December 1999), p. 1969.

[22] Ulrike Malmendier and Geoffrey Tate, "Who Makes Acquisitions? CEO Overconfidence and the Market's Reaction," published in *Journal of Financial Economics* in 2008.

[23] However, as stated earlier, managers may resist takeovers to raise the offer price, not to prevent the merger.

tactics, were discussed in an earlier section of this chapter. Second, managers who cannot avoid takeover may bargain with the bidder, getting a good deal for themselves at the expense of their shareholders.

Consider Wulf's fascinating work on *mergers of equals* (MOEs).[24] Some deals are announced as MOEs, primarily because both firms have equal ownership in and equal representation on the board of directors of the merged entity. AOL and Time Warner, Daimler-Benz and Chrysler, Morgan Stanley and Dean Witter, and Fleet Financial Group and BankBoston are generally held out as examples of MOEs. Nevertheless, authorities point out that in any deal one firm is typically "more equal" than the other. That is, the target and the bidder can usually be distinguished in practice. For example, Daimler-Benz is commonly classified as the bidder and Chrysler as the target in their merger.

Wulf finds that targets get a lower percentage of the merger gains, as measured by abnormal returns around the announcement date, in MOEs than in other mergers. And the percentage of the gains going to the target is negatively related to the representation of the target's officers and directors on the postmerger board. These and other findings lead Wulf to conclude, "They [the findings of the paper] suggest that CEOs trade power for premium in merger of equals transactions."

29.10 The Tax Forms of Acquisitions

If one firm buys another, the transaction may be taxable or tax-free. In a *taxable acquisition,* the shareholders of the acquired firm are considered to have sold their shares, and their realized capital gains or losses will be taxed. In a taxable transaction, the *appraised value* of the assets of the selling firm may be revalued, as we explain next.

In a *tax-free acquisition,* the selling shareholders are considered to have exchanged their old shares for new ones of equal value, and they have experienced no capital gains or losses. In a tax-free acquisition, the assets are not revalued.

EXAMPLE

Taxes   Suppose that 15 years ago Bill Evans started the Samurai Machinery (SM) Corp., which purchased plant and equipment costing $80,000. These have been the only assets of SM, and the company has no debts. Bill is the sole proprietor of SM and owns all the shares. For tax purposes the assets of SM have been depreciated using the straight-line method over 10 years and have no salvage value. The annual depreciation expense has been $8,000 (=$80,000/10). The machinery has no accounting value today (i.e., it has been written off the books). However, because of inflation, the fair market value of the machinery is $200,000. As a consequence, the S. A. Steel Company has bid $200,000 for all of the outstanding stock of Samurai.

Tax-Free Transaction   If Bill Evans receives *shares* of S. A. Steel worth $200,000, the IRS will treat the sale as a tax-free transaction. Thus, Bill will not have to pay taxes on any gain received from the stock. In addition, S. A. Steel will be allowed the same depreciation deduction that Samurai Machinery was allowed. Because the asset has already been fully depreciated, S. A. Steel will receive no depreciation deduction.

---

[24]Julie Wulf, "Do CEOs in Mergers Trade Power for Premium? Evidence From 'Mergers of Equals,'" *Journal of Law, Economics, and Organization* (Spring 2004).

Taxable Transaction If S. A. Steel pays $200,000 in *cash* for Samurai Machinery, the transaction will be taxable with the following consequences:

1. In the year of the merger, Bill Evans must pay taxes on the difference between the merger price of $200,000 and his initial contribution to the firm of $80,000. Thus, his taxable income is $120,000 (=$200,000 − $80,000).

2. S. A. Steel may *elect to write up* the value of the machinery. In this case, S. A. Steel will be able to depreciate the machinery from an initial tax basis of $200,000. If S. A. Steel depreciates straight-line over 10 years, depreciation will be $20,000 (=$200,000/10) per year.

    If S. A. Steel elects to write up the machinery, S. A. Steel must treat the $200,000 write-up as taxable income immediately.[25]

3. Should S. A. Steel *not* elect the write-up, there is no increase in depreciation. Thus, depreciation remains zero in this example. In addition, because there is no write-up, S. A. Steel does not need to recognize any additional taxable income.

    Because the tax benefits from depreciation occur slowly over time and the taxable income is recognized immediately, the acquirer generally elects *not* to write up the value of the machinery in a taxable transaction.

Because the write-up is not allowed for tax-free transactions and is generally not chosen for taxable ones, the only real tax difference between the two types of transactions concerns the taxation of the selling shareholders. These individuals can defer taxes under a tax-free situation but must pay taxes immediately under a taxable situation, so the tax-free transaction has better tax consequences. The tax implications for both types of transactions are displayed in Table 29.6.

Table 29.6 The Tax Consequences of S. A. Steel Company's Acquisition of Samurai Machinery

	Type of Acquisition	
Buyer or Seller	**Taxable Acquisition**	**Tax-Free Acquisition**
Bill Evans (Seller)	Immediate tax on $120,000 ($200,000 − $80,000)	Capital gains tax not paid until Evans sells shares of S. A. Steel
S. A. Steel (Buyer)	S. A. Steel may elect to write up assets: 1. Assets of Samurai are written up to $200,000 (with useful life of 10 years). Annual depreciation expense is $20,000. 2. Immediate tax on $200,000 write-up of assets. Alternatively, S. A. Steel may elect not to write up assets. Here there is neither additional depreciation nor immediate tax. Typically acquirers elect *not* to write up assets.	No additional depreciation

S. A. Steel acquires Samurai Machinery for $200,000, which is the market value of Samurai's equipment. The book value of the equipment is $0. Bill Evans started Samurai Steel 15 years ago with a contribution of $80,000.

The tax consequences of a tax-free acquisition are better than the tax consequences of a taxable acquisition because the seller pays no immediate tax on a tax-free acquisition.

---

[25]Technically, Samurai Machinery pays this tax. However, because Samurai is now a subsidiary of S. A. Steel, S. A. Steel is the effective taxpayer.

29.11 Accounting for Acquisitions

Earlier in this text we mentioned that firms keep two distinct sets of books: The stockholders' books and the tax books. The previous section concerned the effects of acquisitions on the tax books. We now consider the stockholders' books. When one firm acquires another, the buyer uses the purchase method to account for the acquisition.

The **purchase** method requires that the assets of the acquired firm be reported at their fair market value on the books of the acquiring firm. This allows the acquiring firm to establish a new cost basis for the acquired assets.

In a purchase, an accounting term called *goodwill* is created. **Goodwill** is the excess of the purchase price over the sum of the fair market values of the individual assets acquired.

EXAMPLE
29.4

Acquisitions and Accounting   Suppose firm *A* acquires Firm *B*, creating a new firm, *AB*. Firm *A*'s and Firm *B*'s financial positions at the date of the acquisition are shown in Table 29.7. The book value of Firm *B* on the date of the acquisition is $10 million. This is the sum of $8 million in buildings and $2 million in cash. However, an appraiser states that the sum of the fair market values of the individual buildings is $14 million. With $2 million in cash, the sum of the market values of the individual assets in Firm *B* is $16 million. This represents the value to be received if the firm is liquidated by selling off the individual assets separately. However, the whole is often worth more than the sum of the parts in business. Firm *A* pays $19 million in cash for Firm *B*. This difference of $3 million (=$19 million − $16 million) is goodwill. It represents the increase in value from keeping the firm as an ongoing business. Firm *A* issued $19 million in new debt to finance the acquisition.

The total assets of Firm *AB* increase to $39 million. The buildings of Firm *B* appear in the new balance sheet at their current market value. That is, the market value of the assets of the acquired firm becomes part of the book value of the new firm. However, the assets of the acquiring firm (Firm *A*) remain at their old book value. They are not revalued upward when the new firm is created.

The excess of the purchase price over the sum of the fair market values of the individual assets acquired is $3 million. This amount is reported as goodwill. Financial analysts generally ignore goodwill because it has no cash flow consequences. Each year the firm must assess the value of its goodwill. If the value goes down (this is called *impairment* in accounting speak), the amount of goodwill on the balance sheet must be decreased accordingly. Otherwise no amortization is required.

Table 29.7   Accounting for Acquisitions: Purchase ($ in millions)

Firm A				Firm B				Firm AB			
Cash	$ 4	Equity	$20	Cash	$ 2	Equity	$10	Cash	$ 6	Debt	$19
Land	16			Land	0			Land	16	Equity	20
Buildings	0			Buildings	8			Buildings	14		
								Goodwill	3		
Total	$20		$20	Total	$10		$10	Total	$39		$39

When the purchase method is used, the assets of the acquired firm (Firm *B*) appear in the combined firm's books at their fair market value.

29.12 Going Private and Leveraged Buyouts

Going-private transactions and leveraged buyouts have much in common with mergers, and it is worthwhile to discuss them in this chapter. A publicly traded firm *goes private* when a private group, usually composed of existing management, purchases its stock. As a consequence, the firm's stock is taken off the market (if it is an exchange-traded stock, it is delisted) and is no longer traded. Thus, in going-private transactions, shareholders of publicly held firms are forced to accept cash for their shares.

Going-private transactions are frequently *leveraged buyouts* (LBOs). In a leveraged buyout the cash offer price is financed with large amounts of debt. Part of the appeal of LBOs is that the arrangement calls for little equity capital. This equity capital is generally supplied by a small group of investors, some of whom are likely to be managers of the firm being purchased.

The selling stockholders are invariably paid a premium above market price in an LBO, just as in a merger. As with a merger, the acquirer profits only if the synergy created is greater than the premium. Synergy is quite plausible in a merger of *two* firms, and we delineated a number of types of synergy earlier in the chapter. However, it is more difficult to explain synergy in an LBO because only *one* firm is involved.

Two reasons are generally given for value creation in an LBO. First, the extra debt provides a tax deduction, which, as earlier chapters suggested, leads to an increase in firm value. Most LBOs center around firms with stable earnings and with low to moderate debt. The LBO may simply increase the firm's debt to its optimum level.

The second source of value comes from increased efficiency and is often explained in terms of "the carrot and the stick." Managers become owners under an LBO, giving them an incentive to work hard. This incentive is commonly referred to as the carrot, and the carrots in some LBOs have been huge. For example, consider the LBO of Nashville-based hospital company HCA. In 2007, an investment consortium led by KKR, Bain Capital LLC, and Dr. Thomas Frist, who founded HCA in 1968, purchased HCA for $33 billion. Because of the leveraged nature of the transaction, the investment group only put up about $5.3 billion and borrowed the rest. In 2010, HCA paid a dividend of $4.3 billion to the LBO investors. Then, in 2011, the company went public again, raising about $3.79 billion. In the IPO, the LBO investment group received about $1 billion, which meant that all of the capital the group had invested in HCA had been returned. Of course, this was not all the investors received. After the LBO, they still held about $11 billion in HCA stock! And this was not the first LBO for HCA. In 1989, a group including Dr. Frist's son took HCA private in an LBO valued at $5.1 billion. When they took the company public in 1992, they earned an 800 percent gain.

Interest payments from the high level of debt constitute the stick. Large interest payments can easily turn a profitable firm before an LBO into an unprofitable one after the LBO. Management must make changes, either through revenue increases or cost reductions, to keep the firm in the black. Agency theory, a topic mentioned earlier in this chapter, suggests that managers can be wasteful with a large free cash flow. Interest payments reduce this cash flow, forcing managers to curb the waste.

Though it is easy to measure the additional tax shields from an LBO, it is difficult to measure the gains from increased efficiency. Nevertheless, this increased efficiency is considered at least as important as the tax shield in explaining the LBO phenomenon.

Academic research suggests that LBOs have, on average, created value. First, premiums are positive, as they are with mergers, implying that selling stockholders benefit. Second, studies indicate that LBOs that eventually go public generate high returns for the management group. Finally, other studies show that operating performance increases after the LBO. However, we cannot be completely confident of value creation because researchers have difficulty obtaining data about LBOs that do not go public. If these LBOs generally destroy value, the sample of firms going public would be a biased one. Regardless of the average performance of firms undertaking an LBO, we can be sure of one thing: Because of the great leverage involved, the risk is huge.

29.13 Divestitures

This chapter has primarily been concerned with acquisitions, but it is also worthwhile to consider their opposite—divestitures. Divestitures come in a number of different varieties, the most important of which we discuss next.

SALE

The most basic type of divestiture is the *sale* of a division, business unit, segment, or set of assets to another company. The buyer generally, but not always, pays in cash. A number of reasons are provided for sales. First, in an earlier section of this chapter we considered asset sales as a defense against hostile takeovers. It was pointed out in that section that sales often improve corporate focus, leading to greater overall value for the seller. This same rationale applies when the selling company is not in play. Second, asset sales provide needed cash to liquidity-poor firms. Third, it is often argued that the paucity of data about individual business segments makes large, diversified firms hard to value. Investors may discount the firm's overall value because of this lack of transparency. Sell-offs streamline a firm, making it easier to value. However, this argument is inconsistent with market efficiency because it implies that large, diversified firms sell below their true value. Fourth, firms may simply want to sell unprofitable divisions. However, unprofitable divisions are likely to have low values to anyone. A division should be sold only if its value is greater to the buyer than to the seller.

There has been a fair amount of research on sell-offs, with academics reaching two conclusions. First, event studies show that returns on the seller's stock are positive around the time of the announcement of sale, suggesting that sell-offs create value to the seller. Second, acquisitions are often sold off down the road. For example, Kaplan and Weisbach[26] found that more than 40 percent of acquisitions were later divested, a result that does not reflect well on mergers. The average time between acquisition and divestiture was about seven years.

SPIN-OFF

In a spin-off, a parent firm turns a division into a separate entity and distributes shares in this entity to the parent's stockholders. Spin-offs differ from sales in at least two ways. First, the parent firm receives no cash from a spin-off: Shares are sent for free to the stockholders. Second, the initial stockholders of the spun-off division are the same as the parent's stockholders. By contrast, the buyer in a sell-off is most likely another firm. However, because the shares of the division are publicly traded after the spin-off, the identities of the stockholders will change over time.

At least four reasons are generally given for a spin-off. First, as with a sell-off, the spin-off may increase corporate focus. Second, because the spun-off division is now publicly traded, the Securities and Exchange Commission requires additional information to be disseminated—so investors may find it easier to value the parent and subsidiary after the spin-off. Third, corporations often compensate executives with shares of stock

---

[26]Steven Kaplan and Michael Weisbach, "The Success of Acquisitions: Evidence from Divestitures," *Journal of Finance* (March 1992).

in addition to cash. The stock acts as an incentive: Good performance from managers leads to stock price increases. However, prior to the spin-off, executives can receive stock only in the parent company. If the division is small relative to the entire firm, price movement in the parent's stock will be less related to the performance of the manager's division than to the performance of the rest of the firm. Thus, divisional managers may see little relation between their effort and stock appreciation. However, after the spin-off, the manager can be given stock in the subsidiary. The manager's effort should directly impact price movement in the subsidiary's stock. Fourth, the tax consequences from a spin-off are generally better than from a sale because the parent receives no cash from a spin-off.

CARVE-OUT

In a carve-out, the firm turns a division into a separate entity and then sells shares in the division to the public. Generally the parent retains a large interest in the division. This transaction is similar to a spin-off, and the first three benefits listed for a spin-off apply to a carve-out as well. However, the big difference is that the firm receives cash from a carve-out, but not from a spin-off. The receipt of cash can be both good and bad. On the one hand, many firms need cash. Michaely and Shaw[27] find that large, profitable firms are more likely to use carve-outs, whereas small, unprofitable firms are more likely to use spin-offs. One interpretation is that firms generally prefer the cash that comes with a carve-out. However, small and unprofitable firms have trouble issuing stock. They must resort to a spin-off, where stock in the subsidiary is merely given to their own stockholders.

Unfortunately, there is also a dark side to cash, as developed in the free cash flow hypothesis. That is, firms with cash exceeding that needed for profitable capital budgeting projects may spend it on unprofitable ones. Allen and McConnell[28] find that the stock market reacts positively to announcements of carve-outs if the cash is used to reduce debt. The market reacts neutrally if the cash is used for investment projects.

TRACKING STOCKS

A parent corporation issues tracking stock to "track" the performance of a specific division of the corporation. For example, if the tracking stock pays dividends, the size of the dividend depends on the division's performance. However, although "trackers" trade separately from the parent's stock, the division stays with the parent. By contrast, the subsidiary separates from the parent in a spin-off.

The first tracking stock was tied to the performance of EDS, a subsidiary of General Motors. Later, large firms such as Walt Disney and Sony issued trackers. However, few companies have issued tracking stocks in recent years, and parents have pulled most of those issued in earlier times.

Perhaps the biggest problem with tracking stocks is their lack of clearly defined property rights. An optimistic accountant can increase the earnings of a particular division, leading to a larger dividend. A pessimistic accountant will have the reverse effect. Although accountants affect the earnings of regular companies, a change in earnings will not directly impact dividends.

---

[27]Roni Michaely and Wayne Shaw, "The Choice of Going Public: Spin-offs vs. Carve-outs," *Financial Management* (Autumn 1995).

[28]Jeffrey Allen and John McConnell, "Equity Carve-outs and Managerial Discretion," *Journal of Finance* (February 1998).

Summary and Conclusions

1. One firm can acquire another in several different ways. The three legal forms of acquisition are merger and consolidation, acquisition of stock, and acquisition of assets. Mergers and consolidations are the least costly from a legal standpoint, but they require a vote of approval by the shareholders. Acquisition of stock does not require a shareholder vote and is usually done via a tender offer. However, it is difficult to obtain 100 percent control with a tender offer. Acquisition of assets is comparatively costly because it requires more difficult transfer of asset ownership.

2. The synergy from an acquisition is defined as the value of the combined firm (V_{AB}) less the value of the two firms as separate entities (V_A and V_B):

$$\text{Synergy} = V_{AB} - (V_A + V_B)$$

The shareholders of the acquiring firm will gain if the synergy from the merger is greater than the premium.

3. The possible benefits of an acquisition come from the following:
   a. Revenue enhancement.
   b. Cost reduction.
   c. Lower taxes.
   d. Reduced capital requirements.

4. Stockholders may not benefit from a merger that is done only to achieve diversification or earnings growth. And the reduction in risk from a merger may actually help bondholders and hurt stockholders.

5. A merger is said to be friendly when the managers of the target support it. A merger is said to be hostile when the target managers do not support it. Some of the most colorful language of finance stems from defensive tactics in hostile takeover battles. *Poison pills, golden parachutes, crown jewels,* and *greenmail* are terms that describe various antitakeover tactics.

6. The empirical research on mergers and acquisitions is extensive. On average, the shareholders of acquired firms fare very well. The effect of mergers on acquiring stockholders is less clear.

7. Mergers and acquisitions involve complicated tax and accounting rules. Mergers and acquisitions can be taxable or tax-free transactions. In a taxable transaction each selling shareholder must pay taxes on the stock's capital appreciation. Should the acquiring firm elect to write up the assets, additional tax implications arise. However, acquiring firms do not generally elect to write up the assets for tax purposes. The selling stockholders do not pay taxes at the time of a tax-free acquisition. The purchase method is used to account for mergers and acquisitions.

8. In a *going-private* transaction, a buyout group, usually including the firm's management, buys all the shares of the other stockholders. The stock is no longer publicly traded. A *leveraged buyout* is a going-private transaction financed by extensive leverage.

Concept Questions

1. **Merger Accounting** Explain the purchase accounting method for mergers. What is the effect on cash flows? On EPS?

2. **Merger Concepts** Indicate whether you think the following claims regarding takeovers are true or false. In each case, provide a brief explanation for your answer.
   a. By merging competitors, takeovers have created monopolies that will raise product prices, reduce production, and harm consumers.

    b. Managers act in their own interests at times and in reality may not be answerable to shareholders. Takeovers may reflect runaway management.

    c. In an efficient market, takeovers would not occur because market prices would reflect the true value of corporations. Thus, bidding firms would not be justified in paying premiums above market prices for target firms.

    d. Traders and institutional investors, having extremely short time horizons, are influenced by their perceptions of what other market traders will be thinking of stock prospects and do not value takeovers based on fundamental factors. Thus, they will sell shares in target firms despite the true value of the firms.

    e. Mergers are a way of avoiding taxes because they allow the acquiring firm to write up the value of the assets of the acquired firm.

    f. Acquisitions analysis frequently focuses on the total value of the firms involved. An acquisition, however, will usually affect relative values of stocks and bonds, as well as their total value.

3. Merger Rationale Explain why diversification *per se* is probably not a good reason for merger.

4. Corporate Split No matter how you look at it, Dow Chemical had busy years in 2014 and 2015. In 2014, Dow announced that it was planning to sell its subsidiaries Angus Chemical Company, Sodium Borohydride, and AgroFresh. Dow had also recently has completed the sale of a portion of its North America rail car fleet. Additionally, the company was in the process of a planned carveout of its U.S. Gulf Coast chlor-alkali/chlor-vinyl, global chlorinated organics, and epoxy businesses that would be completed in 2015. Why might a company split off a division? Is there a possibility of reverse synergy?

5. Poison Pills Are poison pills good or bad for stockholders? How do you think acquiring firms are able to get around poison pills?

6. Merger and Taxes Describe the advantages and disadvantages of a taxable merger as opposed to a tax-free exchange. What is the basic determinant of tax status in a merger? Would an LBO be taxable or nontaxable? Explain.

7. Economies of Scale What does it mean to say that a proposed merger will take advantage of available economies of scale? Suppose Eastern Power Co. and Western Power Co. are located in different time zones. Both operate at 60 percent of capacity except for peak periods, when they operate at 100 percent of capacity. The peak periods begin at 9:00 a.m. and 5:00 p.m. local time and last about 45 minutes. Explain why a merger between Eastern and Western might make sense.

8. Hostile Takeovers What types of actions might the management of a firm take to fight a hostile acquisition bid from an unwanted suitor? How do the target firm shareholders benefit from the defensive tactics of their management team? How are the target firm shareholders harmed by such actions? Explain.

9. Merger Offers Suppose a company in which you own stock has attracted two take over offers. Would it ever make sense for your company's management to favor the lower offer? Does the form of payment affect your answer at all?

10. Merger Profit Acquiring firm stockholders seem to benefit little from takeovers. Why is this finding a puzzle? What are some of the reasons offered for it?

Questions and Problems

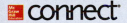

BASIC
(Questions 1–8)

1. Calculating Synergy Holmes, Inc., has offered $295 million cash for all of the common stock in Watson Corporation. Based on recent market information, Watson is worth $278 million as an independent operation. If the merger makes economic sense for Holmes, what is the minimum estimated value of the synergistic benefits from the merger?

2. **Balance Sheets for Mergers**   Consider the following premerger information about firm *X* and firm *Y*:

	Firm X	Firm Y
Total earnings	$105,000	$48,300
Shares outstanding	43,900	33,000
Per-share values:		
Market	$ 53	$ 19
Book	$ 21	$ 9

Assume that Firm *X* acquires Firm *Y* by paying cash for all the shares outstanding at a merger premium of $5 per share. Assuming that neither firm has any debt before or after the merger, construct the postmerger balance sheet for Firm *X* assuming the use of the purchase accounting method.

3. **Balance Sheets for Mergers**   Assume that the following balance sheets are stated at book value. Suppose that Jurion Co. purchases James, Inc. Then suppose the fair market value of James's fixed assets is $23,000 versus the $13,300 book value shown. Jurion pays $30,400 for James and raises the needed funds through an issue of long-term debt. Construct the postmerger balance sheet under the purchase method of accounting.

Jurion Co.			
Current assets	$27,000	Current liabilities	$ 7,700
Net fixed assets	49,000	Long-term debt	13,800
		Equity	54,500
Total	$76,000	Total	$76,000

James, Inc.			
Current assets	$5,200	Current liabilities	$3,300
Net fixed assets	13,300	Long-term debt	2,100
		Equity	13,100
Total	$18,500	Total	$18,500

4. **Balance Sheets for Mergers**   Silver Enterprises has acquired All Gold Mining in a merger transaction. Construct the balance sheet for the new corporation if the merger is treated as a purchase for accounting purposes. The market value of All Gold Mining's fixed assets is $6,300; the market values for current and other assets are the same as the book values. Assume that Silver Enterprises issues $12,500 in new long-term debt to finance the acquisition. The following balance sheets represent the premerger book values for both firms:

Silver Enterprises			
Current assets	$ 8,600	Current liabilities	$ 5,200
Other assets	1,800	Long-term debt	3,700
Net fixed assets	15,800	Equity	17,300
Total	$26,200	Total	$26,200

All Gold Mining			
Current assets	$2,300	Current liabilities	$ 2,300
Other assets	750	Long-term debt	0
Net fixed assets	5,400	Equity	6,150
Total	$8,450	Total	$ 8,450

5. **Cash versus Stock Payment**   Penn Corp. is analyzing the possible acquisition of Teller Company. Both firms have no debt. Penn believes the acquisition will increase its total aftertax annual cash flow by $1.3 million indefinitely. The current market value of Teller is $27 million, and that of Penn is $62 million. The appropriate discount rate for the incremental cash flows is 11 percent. Penn is trying to decide whether it should offer 35 percent of its stock or $37 million in cash to Teller's shareholders.

  a. What is the cost of each alternative?
  b. What is the NPV of each alternative?
  c. Which alternative should Penn choose?

6. **EPS, PE, and Mergers**   The shareholders of Flannery Company have voted in favor of a buyout offer from Stultz Corporation. Information about each firm is given here:

	Flannery	Stultz
Price–earnings ratio	6.35	12.70
Shares outstanding	73,000	146,000
Earnings	$230,000	$690,000

Flannery's shareholders will receive one share of Stultz stock for every three shares they hold in Flannery.

  a. What will the EPS of Stultz be after the merger? What will the PE ratio be if the NPV of the acquisition is zero?
  b. What must Stultz feel is the value of the synergy between these two firms? Explain how your answer can be reconciled with the decision to go ahead with the takeover.

7. **Merger Rationale**   Cholern Electric Company (CEC) is a public utility that provides electricity to the central Colorado area. Recent events at its Mile-High Nuclear Station have been discouraging. Several shareholders have expressed concern over last year's financial statements.

Income Statement Last Year ($ in millions)		Balance Sheet End of Year ($ in millions)	
Revenue	$110	Assets	$400
Fuel	50	Debt	300
Other expenses	30	Equity	100
Interest	30		
Net income	$ 0		

Recently, a wealthy group of individuals has offered to purchase half of CEC's assets at fair market price. Management recommends that this offer be accepted because "We believe our expertise in the energy industry can be better exploited by CEC if we sell our electricity generating and transmission assets and enter the telecommunications business. Although telecommunications is a riskier business than providing electricity as a public utility, it is also potentially very profitable."

Should the management approve this transaction? Why or why not?

8. **Cash versus Stock as Payment**   Consider the following premerger information about a bidding firm (Firm *B*) and a target firm (Firm *T*). Assume that both firms have no debt outstanding.

	Firm B	Firm T
Shares outstanding	8,300	3,400
Price per share	$46	$21

Firm *B* has estimated that the value of the synergistic benefits from acquiring Firm *T* is $12,600.

a. If Firm *T* is willing to be acquired for $24 per share in cash, what is the NPV of the merger?

b. What will the price per share of the merged firm be assuming the conditions in (a)?

c. In part (a), what is the merger premium?

d. Suppose Firm *T* is agreeable to a merger by an exchange of stock. If *B* offers one of its shares for every two of *T*'s shares, what will the price per share of the merged firm be?

e. What is the NPV of the merger assuming the conditions in (d)?

INTERMEDIATE (Questions 9–14)

9. **Cash versus Stock as Payment**   In the previous problem, are the shareholders of Firm *T* better off with the cash offer or the stock offer? At what exchange ratio of *B* shares to *T* shares would the shareholders in *T* be indifferent between the two offers?

10. **Effects of a Stock Exchange**   Consider the following premerger information about Firm *A* and Firm *B*:

	Firm A	Firm B
Total earnings	$2,100	$750
Shares outstanding	900	300
Price per share	$ 60	$ 12

Assume that Firm *A* acquires Firm *B* via an exchange of stock at a price of $13 for each share of *B*'s stock. Both *A* and *B* have no debt outstanding.

a. What will the earnings per share, EPS, of Firm *A* be after the merger?

b. What will Firm *A*'s price per share be after the merger if the market incorrectly analyzes this reported earnings growth (i.e., the price–earnings ratio does not change)?

c. What will the price–earnings ratio of the postmerger firm be if the market correctly analyzes the transaction?

d. If there are no synergy gains, what will the share price of *A* be after the merger? What will the price–earnings ratio be? What does your answer for the share price tell you about the amount *A* bid for *B*? Was it too high? Too low? Explain.

11. **Merger NPV**   Show that the NPV of a merger can be expressed as the value of the synergistic benefits, ΔV, less the merger premium.

12. **Merger NPV**   Fly-By-Night Couriers is analyzing the possible acquisition of Flash-in-the-Pan Restaurants. Neither firm has debt. The forecasts of Fly-By-Night show that the purchase would increase its annual aftertax cash flow by $425,000 indefinitely. The current market value of Flash-in-the-Pan is $7.3 million. The current market value of Fly-By-Night is $24 million. The appropriate discount rate for the incremental cash flows is 8 percent. Fly-By-Night is trying to decide whether it would offer 30 percent of its stock or $11.4 million in cash to Flash-in-the-Pan.

a. What is the synergy from the merger?

b. What is the value of Flash-in-the-Pan to Fly-By-Night?

c. What is the cost to Fly-By-Night of each alternative?

d. What is the NPV to Fly-By-Night of each alternative?

e. What alternative should Fly-By-Night use?

13. **Merger NPV**   Harrods PLC has a market value of £360 million and 30 million shares outstanding. Selfridge Department Store has a market value of £144 million and 18 million shares outstanding. Harrods is contemplating acquiring Selfridge. Harrods's CFO concludes that the combined firm with synergy will be worth £540 million, and Selfridge can be acquired at a premium of £15 million.

a. If Harrods offers 11 million shares of its stock in exchange for the 18 million shares of Selfridge, what will the stock price of Harrods be after the acquisition?

b. What exchange ratio between the two stocks would make the value of the stock offer equivalent to a cash offer of £159 million?

14. **Mergers and Shareholder Value**   Bentley Corp. and Rolls Manufacturing are considering a merger. The possible states of the economy and each company's value in that state are shown here:

State	Probability	Bentley	Rolls
Boom	.65	$290,000	$260,000
Recession	.35	110,000	80,000

Bentley currently has a bond issue outstanding with a face value of $125,000. Rolls is an all-equity company.

a. What is the value of each company before the merger?

b. What are the values of each company's debt and equity before the merger?

c. If the companies continue to operate separately, what are the total value of the companies, the total value of the equity, and the total value of the debt?

d. What would be the value of the merged company? What would be the value of the merged company's debt and equity?

e. Is there a transfer of wealth in this case? Why?

f. Suppose that the face value of Bentley's debt was $90,000. Would this affect the transfer of wealth?

CHALLENGE
(Questions 15–16)

15. Calculating NPV Plant, Inc., is considering making an offer to purchase Palmer Corp. Plant's vice president of finance has collected the following information:

	Plant	Palmer
Price–earnings ratio	14.5	10
Shares outstanding	1,500,000	750,000
Earnings	$4,200,000	$960,000
Dividends	1,050,000	470,000

Plant also knows that securities analysts expect the earnings and dividends of Palmer to grow at a constant rate of 4 percent each year. Plant management believes that the acquisition of Palmer will provide the firm with some economies of scale that will increase this growth rate to 6 percent per year.

a. What is the value of Palmer to Plant?

b. What would Plant's gain be from this acquisition?

c. If Plant were to offer $20 in cash for each share of Palmer, what would the NPV of the acquisition be?

d. What is the most Plant should be willing to pay in cash per share for the stock of Palmer?

e. If Plant were to offer 225,000 of its shares in exchange for the outstanding stock of Palmer, what would the NPV be?

f. Should the acquisition be attempted? If so, should it be as in (c) or as in (e)?

g. Plant's outside financial consultants think that the 6 percent growth rate is too optimistic and a 5 percent rate is more realistic. How does this change your previous answers?

16. Mergers and Shareholder Value The Chocolate Ice Cream Company and the Vanilla Ice Cream Company have agreed to merge and form Fudge Swirl Consolidated. Both companies are exactly alike except that they are located in different towns. The end-of-period value of each firm is determined by the weather, as shown below. There will be no synergy to the merger.

State	Probability	Value
Rainy	.1	$230,000
Warm	.4	450,000
Hot	.5	905,000

The weather conditions in each town are independent of those in the other. Furthermore, each company has an outstanding debt claim of $450,000. Assume that no premiums are paid in the merger.

a. What are the possible values of the combined company?

b. What are the possible values of end-of-period debt and stock after the merger?

c. Show that the bondholders are better off and the stockholders are worse off in the combined firm than they would have been if the firms had remained separate.

Mini Case

THE BIRDIE GOLF—HYBRID GOLF MERGER

Birdie Golf, Inc., has been in merger talks with Hybrid Golf Company for the past six months. After several rounds of negotiations, the offer under discussion is a cash offer of $352 million for Hybrid Golf. Both companies have niche markets in the golf club industry, and the companies believe a merger will result in significant synergies due to economies of scale in manufacturing and marketing, as well as significant savings in general and administrative expenses.

Bryce Bichon, the financial officer for Birdie, has been instrumental in the merger negotiations. Bryce has prepared the following pro forma financial statements for Hybrid Golf assuming the merger takes place. The financial statements include all synergistic benefits from the merger:

	2015	2016	2017	2018	2019
Sales	$512,000,000	$576,000,000	$640,000,000	$720,000,000	$800,000,000
Production costs	359,200,000	403,200,000	448,000,000	505,600,000	564,000,000
Depreciation	48,000,000	51,200,000	52,800,000	53,120,000	53,600,000
Other expenses	51,200,000	57,600,000	64,000,000	72,320,000	77,600,000
EBIT	$ 53,600,000	$ 64,000,000	$ 75,200,000	$ 88,960,000	$104,800,000
Interest	12,160,000	14,080,000	15,360,000	16,000,000	17,280,000
Taxable income	$ 41,440,000	$ 49,920,000	$ 59,840,000	$ 72,960,000	$ 87,520,000
Taxes (40%)	16,576,000	19,968,000	23,936,000	29,184,000	35,008,000
Net income	$ 24,864,000	$ 29,952,000	$ 35,904,000	$ 43,776,000	$ 52,512,000

Bryce is also aware that the Hybrid Golf division will require investments each year for continuing operations, along with sources of financing. The following table outlines the required investments and sources of financing:

	2015	2016	2017	2018	2019
Investments:					
Net working capital	$12,800,000	$16,000,000	$16,000,000	$19,200,000	$19,200,000
Fixed assets	9,600,000	16,000,000	11,520,000	76,800,000	4,480,000
Total	$22,400,000	$32,000,000	$27,520,000	$96,000,000	$23,680,000
Sources of financing:					
New debt	$22,400,000	$10,240,000	$10,240,000	$ 9,600,000	$ 7,680,000
Profit retention	0	21,760,000	17,280,000	17,280,000	16,000,000
Total	$22,400,000	$32,000,000	$27,520,000	$26,880,000	$23,680,000

The management of Birdie Golf feels that the capital structure at Hybrid Golf is not optimal. If the merger takes place, Hybrid Golf will immediately increase its leverage with a $71 million debt issue, which would be followed by a $96 million dividend payment to Birdie Golf. This will increase Hybrid's debt-to-equity ratio from .50 to 1.00. Birdie Golf will also be able to use a $16 million tax loss carryforward in 2016 and 2017 from Hybrid Golf's previous operations. The total value of Hybrid Golf is expected to be $576 million in five years, and the company will have $192 million in debt at that time.

Stock in Birdie Golf currently sells for $94 per share, and the company has 11.6 million shares of stock outstanding. Hybrid Golf has 5.2 million shares of stock outstanding. Both companies can borrow at an 8 percent interest rate. The risk-free rate is 6 percent, and the expected return on the market is 13 percent. Bryce believes the current cost of capital for Birdie Golf is 11 percent. The beta for Hybrid Golf stock at its current capital structure is 1.30.

Bryce has asked you to analyze the financial aspects of the potential merger. Specifically, he has asked you to answer the following questions:

1. Suppose Hybrid shareholders will agree to a merger price of $68.75 per share. Should Birdie proceed with the merger?

2. What is the highest price per share that Birdie should be willing to pay for Hybrid?

3. Suppose Birdie is unwilling to pay cash for the merger but will consider a stock exchange. What exchange ratio would make the merger terms equivalent to the original merger price of $68.75 per share?

4. What is the highest exchange ratio Birdie would be willing to pay and still undertake the merger?

30

Financial Distress

Building casinos in Atlantic City turned out to be a bad bet for many. During 2014, four of the city's 12 casinos folded, including the Revel. The Revel was unique in that it cost $2.4 billion to build, opened on April 2, 2012, filed for bankruptcy in February 2013, and then filed bankruptcy again in September 2014. So, the Revel filed two bankruptcies within two and a half years of first opening! A fifth casino in Atlantic City, the Trump Taj Mahal, barely escaped the same fate after billionaire Carl Icahn put up $20 million to keep its roulette wheels spinning. Then, in January 2015, Caesars Entertainment filed bankruptcy. The Caesars bankruptcy included Caesars Palace Las Vegas, two casinos in Atlantic City, and a dozen Harrah's or Horseshoe casinos in smaller U.S. markets such as Tunica, Mississippi, and Reno, Nevada.

These bankruptcies are examples of companies experiencing significant financial distress, the subject of this chapter. A firm with insufficient cash flow to make contractually required financial obligations, such as interest payments, is in financial distress. A firm that defaults on a required payment may be forced to liquidate its assets, but, more often, a defaulting firm will reorganize its financial structure. Financial restructuring involves replacing old financial claims with new ones and takes place with private workouts or legal bankruptcy. Private workouts are voluntary arrangements to restructure a company's debt, such as postponing a payment or reducing the size of the payment. If a private workout is not possible, formal bankruptcy is usually required.

30.1 What Is Financial Distress?

Financial distress is surprisingly hard to define precisely. This is true partly because of the variety of events befalling firms under financial distress. The list of events is almost endless, but here are some examples:

Dividend reductions

Plant closings

Losses

Layoffs

CEO resignations

Plummeting stock prices

Financial distress is a situation where a firm's operating cash flows are not sufficient to satisfy current obligations (such as trade credits or interest expenses) and the firm is

Figure 30.1

Insolvency

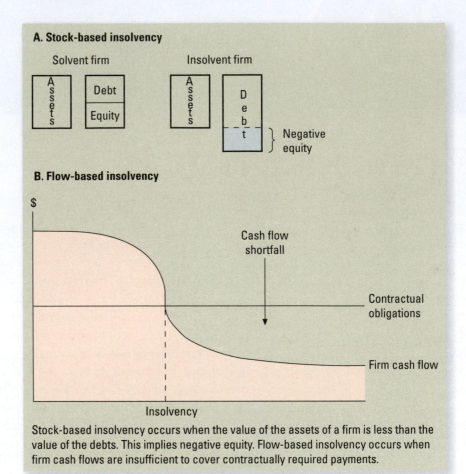

Stock-based insolvency occurs when the value of the assets of a firm is less than the value of the debts. This implies negative equity. Flow-based insolvency occurs when firm cash flows are insufficient to cover contractually required payments.

forced to take corrective action.[1] Financial distress may lead a firm to default on a contract, and it may involve financial restructuring between the firm, its creditors, and its equity investors. Usually the firm is forced to take actions that it would not have taken if it had sufficient cash flow.

Our definition of financial distress can be expanded somewhat by linking it to insolvency. Insolvency is defined in *Black's Law Dictionary* as:[2]

> Inability to pay one's debts; lack of means of paying one's debts. Such a condition of a woman's (or man's) assets and liabilities that the former made immediately available would be insufficient to discharge the latter.

This definition has two general themes: stocks and flows.[3] These two ways of thinking about insolvency are depicted in Figure 30.1. Stock-based insolvency occurs when a firm has negative net worth, so the value of assets is less than the value of its debts. Flow-based insolvency occurs when operating cash flow is insufficient to meet current obligations. Flow-based insolvency refers to the inability to pay one's debts. Insolvency may lead to bankruptcy. Some of the largest U.S. bankruptcies are in Table 30.1.

---

[1]This definition is close to the one used by Karen Wruck, "Financial Distress, Reorganization, and Organizational Efficiency," *Journal of Financial Economics* 27 (1990), p. 425.

[2]Taken from *Black's Law Dictionary,* 5th ed. (St. Paul, MN: West Publishing Company), p. 716.

[3]Edward Altman was one of the first to distinguish between stock-based insolvency and flow-based insolvency. See Edward Altman, *Corporate Financial Distress: A Complete Guide to Predicting, Avoiding, and Dealing with Bankruptcy,* 2nd ed. (New York: John Wiley & Sons, 1993).

Table 30.1

Large U.S. Bankruptcies

Firm	Liabilities ($ in millions)	Bankruptcy Date
1 Lehman Brothers Holdings, Inc.	$613,000.00	15-Sep-08
2 General Motors Corp.	172,810.00	01-Jun-09
3 CIT Group, Inc.	64,901.20	01-Nov-09
4 Conseco, Inc.	56,639.30	02-Dec-02
5 Chrysler, LLC	55,200.00	30-Apr-09
6 WorldCom, Inc.	45,984.00	21-Jul-02
7 MF Global Holdings Ltd.	39,683.92	31-Oct-11
8 Refco, Inc.	33,300.00	05-Oct-05
9 Enron Corp.	31,237.00	02-Dec-01
10 Delta Air Lines, Inc.	28,546.00	05-Sep-05

SOURCE: Supplied by Edward I. Altman, NYU Salomon Center, Stern School of Business.

30.2 What Happens in Financial Distress?

In June 2008, General Motors (GM) reported second quarter net income of negative $15 million. It also lost money in 2005 and 2007 and steadily lost its market share to rivals such as Toyota, BMW, and Honda. Its accounting shareholder equity turned negative in 2006 and its stock price decreased from $50 in late 2003 to about $1 in 2009. Automobile customers had good reason to worry about buying cars from GM. GM struggled to increase sales, cut costs, attempted to sell assets (e.g., the Hummer line), drew down bank debt, and arranged for more long-term financing. GM was clearly a firm experiencing financial distress. GM filed for bankruptcy on June 1, 2009. GM emerged from bankruptcy six weeks later and shares of GM were sold in the world's largest IPO (at the time) in November 2010. Most of the shares were owned by the U.S. Treasury in what had been one of the biggest "bail outs" of a private firm by the U.S. Treasury. GM began paying cash dividends in 2014 and has five consecutive years of positive cash flow. Of course, many firms experiencing financial distress and bankruptcy do not fare as well as GM.

Firms deal with financial distress in several ways, such as these:

1. Selling major assets.
2. Merging with another firm.
3. Reducing capital spending and research and development.
4. Issuing new securities.
5. Negotiating with banks and other creditors.
6. Exchanging debt for equity.
7. Filing for bankruptcy.

Items (1), (2), and (3) concern the firm's assets. Items (4), (5), (6), and (7) involve the right side of the firm's balance sheet and are examples of financial restructuring. Financial

Figure 30.2

What Happens in
Financial Distress with
Large Public Firms

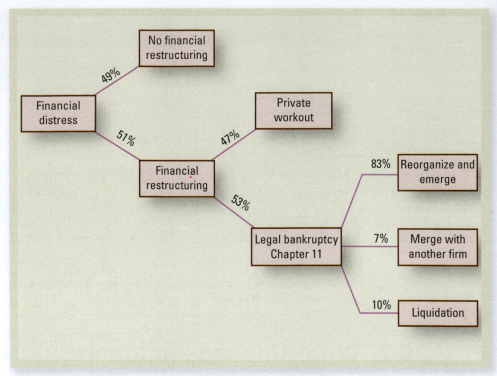

SOURCE: Karen H. Wruck, "Financial Distress, Reorganization, and Organizational Efficiency," *Journal of Financial Economics* 27 (1990), Figure 2. See also Stuart C. Gilson, Kose John, and Larry H. P. Lang, "Troubled Debt Restructurings: An Empirical Study of Private Reorganization of Firms in Default," *Journal of Financial Economics* 27 (1990); and Lawrence A. Weiss, "Bankruptcy Resolution: Direct Costs and Violation of Priority of Claims," *Journal of Financial Economics* 27 (1990).

distress may involve both asset restructuring and financial restructuring (i.e., changes on both sides of the balance sheet).

Some firms may actually benefit from financial distress by restructuring their assets. For example, a levered recapitalization can change a firm's behavior and force a firm to dispose of unrelated businesses. A firm going through a levered recapitalization will add a great deal of debt and, as a consequence, its cash flow may not be sufficient to cover required payments, and it may be forced to sell its noncore businesses. For some firms, financial distress may bring about new organizational forms and new operating strategies. However, in this chapter we focus on financial restructuring.

Financial restructuring may occur in a private workout or a bankruptcy reorganization under Chapter 11 of the U.S. bankruptcy code. Figure 30.2 shows how large public firms move through financial distress. Approximately half of the financial restructurings have been done via private workouts. Most large public firms (approximately 83 percent) that file for Chapter 11 bankruptcy are able to reorganize and continue to do business.[4]

Financial distress can serve as a firm's "early warning" system for trouble. Firms with more debt will experience financial distress earlier than firms with less debt. However, firms that experience financial distress earlier will have more time for private workouts and reorganization. Firms with low leverage will experience financial distress later and, in many instances, be forced to liquidate.

---

[4]However, less than 20 percent of all firms (public or private) going through a Chapter 11 bankruptcy are successfully reorganized.

30.3 Bankruptcy Liquidation and Reorganization

Firms that cannot or choose not to make contractually required payments to creditors have two basic options: Liquidation or reorganization. This section discusses bankruptcy liquidation and reorganization.[5]

Liquidation means termination of the firm as a going concern; it involves selling the assets of the firm for salvage value. The proceeds, net of transactions costs, are distributed to creditors in order of established priority.

Reorganization is the option of keeping the firm a going concern; it sometimes involves issuing new securities to replace old securities.

Liquidation and formal reorganization may be done by bankruptcy. *Bankruptcy* is a legal proceeding and can be done voluntarily with the corporation filing the petition or involuntarily with the creditors filing the petition.

BANKRUPTCY LIQUIDATION

Chapter 7 of the Bankruptcy Reform Act of 1978 deals with "straight" liquidation. The following sequence of events is typical:

1. A petition is filed in a federal court. A corporation may file a voluntary petition, or involuntary petitions may be filed against the corporation.

2. A bankruptcy trustee is elected by the creditors to take over the assets of the debtor corporation. The trustee will attempt to liquidate the assets.

3. When the assets are liquidated, after payment of the costs of administration, proceeds are distributed among the creditors.

4. If any assets remain after expenses and payments to creditors, they are distributed to the shareholders.

Conditions Leading to Involuntary Bankruptcy   An involuntary bankruptcy petition may be filed by creditors if both the following conditions are met:

1. The corporation is not paying debts as they become due.

2. If there are more than 12 creditors, at least three with claims totaling $13,475 or more must join in the filing. If there are fewer than 12 creditors, then only one with a claim of $13,475 is required to file.

Priority of Claims   Once a corporation is determined to be bankrupt, liquidation takes place. The distribution of the proceeds of the liquidation occurs according to the following priority:

1. Administration expenses associated with liquidating the bankrupt company's assets.

2. Unsecured claims arising after the filing of an involuntary bankruptcy petition.

3. Wages, salaries, and commissions.

4. Contributions to employee benefit plans arising within 180 days before the filing date.

---

[5]One of the most important choices a bankrupt firm must make is whether to liquidate or reorganize. Arturo Bris, Ivo Welch, and Ning Zhu have looked closely at this choice in "The Costs of Bankruptcy: Chapter 7 Liquidation versus Chapter 11 Reorganization," *Journal of Finance* (June 2006). They find:

- Very small firms (i.e., with assets less than $100,000), are more likely to liquidate than reorganize compared to large firms.
- Firms with a large number of secured creditors are more likely to try to reorganize.
- Firms with an unsecured creditor, especially a bank, are more likely to choose liquidation.
- Firms that have large negative equity are more likely to try to reorganize.

5. Consumer claims.

6. Tax claims.

7. Secured and unsecured creditors' claims.

8. Preferred stockholders' claims.

9. Common stockholders' claims.

The priority rule in liquidation is the **absolute priority rule (APR)**.

One qualification to this list concerns secured creditors. Liens on property are outside APR ordering. However, if the secured property is liquidated and provides cash insufficient to cover the amount owed them, the secured creditors join with unsecured creditors in dividing the remaining liquidating value. In contrast, if the secured property is liquidated for proceeds greater than the secured claim, the net proceeds are used to pay unsecured creditors and others.

EXAMPLE 30.1

APR   The B. O. Drug Company is to be liquidated. Its liquidating value is $2.7 million. Bonds worth $1.5 million are secured by a mortgage on the B.O. Drug Company corporate headquarters building, which is sold for $1 million; $200,000 is used to cover administrative costs and other claims (including unpaid wages, pension benefits, consumer claims, and taxes). After paying $200,000 to the administrative priority claims, the amount available to pay secured and unsecured creditors is $2.5 million. This is less than the amount of unpaid debt of $4 million.

Under APR, all creditors must be paid before shareholders, and the mortgage bondholders have first claim on the $1 million obtained from the sale of the headquarters building.

The trustee has proposed the following distribution:

Type of Claim	Prior Claim	Cash Received under Liquidation
Bonds (secured by mortgage)	$ 1,500,000	$1,500,000
Subordinated debentures	2,500,000	1,000,000
Common stockholders	10,000,000	0
Total	$14,000,000	$2,500,000

Calculation of the Distribution

Cash received from sale of assets available for distribution	$2,500,000
Cash paid to secured bondholders on sale of mortgaged property	1,000,000
Available to bond and debenture holders	$1,500,000
Total claims remaining ($4,000,000 less payment of $1,000,000 on secured bonds)	$3,000,000
Distribution of remaining $1,500,000 to cover total remaining claims of $3,000,000	

Type of Claim Remaining	Claim on Liquidation Proceeds	Cash Received
Bonds	$ 500,000	$ 500,000
Debentures	2,500,000	1,000,000
Total	$3,000,000	$1,500,000

BANKRUPTCY REORGANIZATION

Corporate reorganization takes place under Chapter 11 of the Federal Bankruptcy Reform Act of 1978, as amended by the Bankruptcy Abuse Prevention and Consumer Protection Act of 2005.[6] The general objective of a proceeding under Chapter 11 is to plan to restructure the corporation with some provision for repayment of creditors. A typical sequence of events follows:

1. A voluntary petition can be filed by the corporation, or an involuntary petition can be filed by three or more creditors (or one creditor if the total creditors are fewer than 12—see the previous section). The involuntary petition must allege that the corporation is not paying its debts.

2. Usually, a federal judge approves the petition, and a time for filing proofs of claims of creditors and of shareholders is set.

3. In most cases, the corporation (the "debtor in possession") continues to run the business.[7]

4. For 120 days only the corporation can file a reorganization plan. If it does, the corporation is given 180 days from the filing date to gain acceptance of the plan.

5. Creditors and shareholders are divided into classes. A class of creditors accepts the plan if two-thirds of the class (in dollar amount) and one-half of the class (in number) have indicated approval.[8]

6. After acceptance by creditors, the plan is confirmed by the court.

7. Payments in cash, property, and securities are made to creditors and shareholders. The plan may provide for the issuance of new securities.

Recently, Section 363 of the bankruptcy code has been in the news. In a traditional Chapter 11 filing, the bankruptcy plan is described to creditors and shareholders in a prospectus-like disclosure. The plan must then be approved in a vote by the interested parties. A Section 363 bankruptcy is more like an auction. An initial bidder, known as a "stalking horse," bids on all or part of the bankrupt company's assets. Other bidders are then invited into the process in an attempt to produce the highest possible bid. The main advantage of a Section 363 bankruptcy is speed. Since a traditional bankruptcy requires the approval of interested parties, it is not uncommon for the process to take several years, while a Section 363 bankruptcy is generally much quicker. For example, in the middle of 2009, both General Motors and Chrysler sped through the bankruptcy process in less than 45 days because of Section 363 auctions.

---

[6]Do bankruptcy codes matter? The answer is yes for Sergei A. Davydenko and Julian R. Franks in "Do Bankruptcy Codes Matter? A Study of Defaults in France, Germany, and the U.K.," *Journal of Finance* (April 2008). They find that the different bankruptcy codes of France, Germany, and the U.K. produce different outcomes of financial distress situations even though banks make significant adjustments in response to creditors' friendly or unfriendly codes, respectively.

[7]In Chapter 11 bankruptcies, the firm (now called "debtor in possession") continues to operate. In many cases, the firm will seek to borrow new money and use the proceeds to pay off secured creditors and to continue to operate until a reorganization plan is approved.

[8]We are describing the standard events in a bankruptcy reorganization. Petitions are almost always accepted, and the general rule is that a reorganization plan will be accepted by the court if all of the creditor classes accept it and it will be rejected if all of the creditor classes reject it. However, if one or more (but not all) of the classes accept it, the plan may be eligible for a "cram down" procedure. A cram down takes place if the bankruptcy court finds a plan fair and equitable and accepts the plan for all creditors.

In Their Own Words

EDWARD I. ALTMAN* ON CORPORATE FINANCIAL DISTRESS AND BANKRUPTCY

Financial distress of private and public entities throughout the world is a frequent occurrence with important implications for their many stakeholders. While the role of corporate bankruptcy laws is clear—either to provide a legal procedure that permits firms which have temporary liquidity problems to restructure and successfully emerge as continuing entities or to provide an orderly process to liquidate assets for the benefit of creditors before asset values are dissipated—bankruptcy laws differ markedly from country to country. It is generally agreed upon that the U.S. Chapter 11 provisions under the Bankruptcy Reform Act of 1978 provide the most protection for bankrupt firms' assets and result in a greater likelihood of successful reorganization than is found in other countries where liquidation and sale of the assets for the benefit of creditors is more likely the result. But the U.S. code's process is usually lengthy (averaging close to two years, except where a sufficient number of creditors agree in advance via a prepackaged Chapter 11) and expensive, and the reorganized entity is not always successful in avoiding subsequent distress. If the reorganization is not successful, then liquidation under Chapter 7 will usually ensue.

Bankruptcy processes in the industrialized world outside the United States strongly favor senior creditors who obtain control of the firm and seek to enforce greater adherence to debt contracts. The U.K. process, for example, is speedy and less costly, but the reduced costs can result in undesirable liquidations, unemployment, and underinvestment. The new bankruptcy code in Germany attempts to reduce the considerable power of secured creditors but it is still closer to the U.K. system. In the United States, creditors and owners can negotiate "violations" to the "absolute priority rule"—this "rule" holds that more senior creditors must be paid in full, prior to any payments to more junior creditors or to owners. (However, the so-called "violations" to absolute priority have empirically been shown to be relatively small—such as under 10 percent of firm value.) Finally, the U.S. system gives the court the right to sanction postpetition debt financing, usually with superpriority status over existing claims, thereby facilitating the continuing operation of the firm. Recently, France had a similar successful experience.

A measure of performance of the U.S. bankruptcy system is the proportion of firms that emerge successfully. The results in the United States of late are somewhat mixed, with close to 83 percent of large firms emerging but probably less than 20 percent of smaller entities. And a not insignificant number of firms suffer subsequent distress and may file again.

Regardless of the location, one of the objectives of bankruptcy and other distressed workout arrangements is

---

EXAMPLE 30.2

Chapter 11   Suppose B.O. Drug Co. decides to reorganize under Chapter 11. Generally senior claims are honored in full before various other claims receive anything. Assume that the "going concern" value of B.O. Drug Co. is $3 million and that its balance sheet is as shown:

Assets	$3,000,000
Liabilities	
Mortgage bonds	1,500,000
Subordinated debentures	2,500,000
Stockholders' equity	−1,000,000

The firm has proposed the following reorganization plan:

Old Security	Old Claim	New Claim with Reorganization Plan
Mortgage bonds	$1,500,000	$1,500,000
Subordinated debentures	2,500,000	1,500,000

that creditors and other suppliers of capital clearly know their rights and expected recoveries in the event of a distressed situation. When these are not transparent and/or are based on outdated processes with arbitrary and possibly corrupt outcomes, then the entire economic system suffers and growth is inhibited. Such is the case in several emerging market countries. Revision of these outdated systems should be a priority.

In addition to the comparative benefits of different national restructuring systems, a number of intriguing theoretical and empirical issues are related to the distressed firm. Among these are corporate debt capacity, manager–creditor–owner incentives, ability to predict distress, data and computations for default rate estimation, investment in securities of distressed firms, and post-reorganization performance assessment.

Corporate distress has a major impact on creditor–debtor relationships and, combined with business risk and tax considerations, affects the capital structure of companies. One key question is how costly are the *expected* distress costs compared to the *expected* tax benefits of using leverage—the so-called trade-off theory. Most analysts agree that the sum of direct (e.g., legal fees) and indirect costs is in the range of 10–20 percent of firm value.

Whether the taking of excess risk and overinvestment are examples of agency conflicts between managers and creditors rests upon one's view as to who are the true residual owners of a distressed firm—the existing equityholders or creditors who will more than likely be the new owners of a reorganized entity. Existing management has the exclusive right to file the first plan of reorganization within 120 days of filing, with exclusivity extensions possible. Their incentives and influence can be biased, however, and not always in accord with other stakeholders, primarily creditors. Limiting this exclusivity would appear to be desirable to speed up the process and restrict managerial abuse.

Distress prediction models have intrigued researchers and practitioners for more than 50 years. Models have evolved from univariate financial statement ratios to multivariate statistical classification models, to contingent claim and market value–based approaches, and finally to using artificial intelligence techniques. Most large financial institutions have one or more of these types of models in place as more sophisticated credit risk management frameworks are being introduced, sometimes combined with aggressive credit asset portfolio strategies. Increasingly, private credit assets are being treated as securities with estimates of default and recovery given default the critical inputs to their valuation.

Perhaps the most intriguing by-product of corporate distress is the development of a relatively new class of investors known as *vultures*. These money managers specialize in securities of distressed and defaulted companies.

*Edward I. Altman is Max L. Heine Professor of Finance, NYU Stern School of Business. He is widely recognized as one of the world's experts on bankruptcy and credit analysis, as well as the distressed debt and high-yield bond markets.

The firm has also proposed a distribution of new securities under a new claim with this reorganization plan:

Old Security	Received under Proposed Reorganization Plan
Mortgage bonds	$1,000,000 in 9% senior debentures
	$500,000 in 11% subordinated debentures
Debentures	$1,000,000 in 8% preferred stock
	$500,000 in common stock

However, it will be difficult for the firm to convince secured creditors (mortgage bonds) to accept unsecured debentures of equal face value. In addition, the corporation may wish to allow the old stockholders to retain some participation in the firm. Needless to say, this would be a violation of the absolute priority rule, and the holders of the debentures would not be happy.

30.4 Private Workout or Bankruptcy: Which Is Best?

A firm that defaults on its debt payments will need to restructure its financial claims. The firm will have two choices: Formal bankruptcy or **private workout**. The previous section described two types of formal bankruptcies: Bankruptcy liquidation and bankruptcy reorganization. This section compares private workouts with bankruptcy reorganizations. Both types of financial restructuring involve exchanging new financial claims for old financial claims. Usually, senior debt is replaced with junior debt and junior debt is replaced with equity. Much recent academic research has described what happens in private workouts and formal bankruptcies.[9]

- Historically, half of financial restructurings have been private, but recently, formal bankruptcies have dominated.
- Firms that emerge from private workouts experience stock price increases that are much greater than those for firms emerging from formal bankruptcies.
- The direct costs of private workouts are much less than the costs of formal bankruptcies.
- Top management usually loses pay and sometimes jobs in both private workouts and formal bankruptcies.

These facts, when taken together, seem to suggest that a private workout is much better than a formal bankruptcy. We then ask: Why do firms ever use formal bankruptcies to restructure?

Absolute Priority Rule (APR)

The absolute priority rule states that senior claims are fully satisfied before junior claims receive anything.

Deviation from Rule

Equityholders	Expectation: No payout
	Reality: Payout in 81 percent of cases
Unsecured creditors	Expectation: Full payout after secured creditors
	Reality: Violation in 78 percent of cases
Secured creditors	Expectation: Full payout
	Reality: Full payout in 92 percent of cases

Reasons for Violations

Creditors want to avoid the expense of litigation. Debtors are given a 120-day opportunity to cause delay and harm value.

Managers often own equity and demand to be compensated.

Bankruptcy judges like consensual plans and pressure parties to compromise.

SOURCE: Lawrence A. Weiss, "Bankruptcy Resolution: Direct Costs and Violation of Priority of Claims," *Journal of Financial Economics* 27 (1990).

THE MARGINAL FIRM

For the average firm, a formal bankruptcy is more costly than a private workout, but for other firms formal bankruptcy is better. Formal bankruptcy allows firms to issue debt that

---

[9]For example, see Stuart Gilson, "Managing Default: Some Evidence on How Firms Choose between Workouts and Chapter 11," *Journal of Applied Corporate Finance* (Summer 1991); and Stuart C. Gilson, Kose John, and Larry H. P. Lang, "Troubled Debt Restructurings: An Empirical Study of Private Reorganization of Firms in Default," *Journal of Financial Economics* 27 (1990).

is senior to all previously incurred debt. This new debt is "debtor in possession" (DIP) debt. For firms that need a temporary injection of cash, DIP debt makes bankruptcy reorganization an attractive alternative to a private workout. There are some tax advantages to bankruptcy. Firms do not lose tax carryforwards in bankruptcy, and the tax treatment of the cancellation of indebtedness is better in bankruptcy. Also, interest on prebankruptcy unsecured debt stops accruing in formal bankruptcy.

HOLDOUTS

Bankruptcy is usually better for the equity investors than it is for the creditors. Using DIP debt and stopping prebankruptcy interest from accruing on unsecured debt helps the stockholders and hurts the creditors. As a consequence, equity investors can usually hold out for a better deal in bankruptcy. The absolute priority rule, which favors creditors over equity investors, is usually violated in formal bankruptcies. One recent study found that in 81 percent of recent bankruptcies the equity investor obtained some compensation.[10] Under Chapter 11, the creditors are often forced to give up some of their seniority rights to get management and the equity investors to agree to a deal.

COMPLEXITY

A firm with a complicated capital structure will have more trouble putting together a private workout. Firms with secured creditors and trade creditors such as Macy's and Carter Hawley Hale will usually use formal bankruptcy because it is too hard to reach an agreement with many different types of creditors.

LACK OF INFORMATION

There is an inherent conflict of interest between equity investors and creditors, and the conflict is accentuated when both have incomplete information about the circumstances of financial distress. When a firm initially experiences a cash flow shortfall, it may not know whether the shortfall is permanent or temporary. If the shortfall is permanent, creditors will push for a formal reorganization or liquidation. However, if the cash flow shortfall is temporary, formal reorganization or liquidation may not be necessary. Equity investors will push for this viewpoint. This conflict of interest cannot easily be resolved.

These last two points are especially important. They suggest that financial distress will be more expensive (cheaper) if complexity is high (low) and information is incomplete (complete). Complexity and lack of information make cheap workouts less likely.

30.5 Prepackaged Bankruptcy[11]

On March 14, 2014, sub shop Quiznos filed for Chapter 11 reorganization under the U.S. bankruptcy code. At the time, the company listed less than $1 million in assets and more than $500 million in liabilities. A firm in this situation could reasonably expect to spend

[10]Lawrence A. Weiss, "Bankruptcy Resolution: Direct Costs and Violation of Priority of Claims," *Journal of Financial Economics* 27 (1990). However, William Beranek, Robert Boehmer, and Brooke Smith, in "Much Ado about Nothing: Absolute Priority Deviations in Chapter 11," *Financial Management* (Autumn 1996), find that 33.8 percent of bankruptcy reorganizations leave the stockholders with nothing. They also point out that deviations from the absolute priority rule are to be expected because the bankruptcy code allows creditors to waive their rights if they perceive a waiver to be in their best interests. A rejoinder can be found in Allan C. Eberhart and Lawrence A. Weiss, "The Importance of Deviations from the Absolute Priority Rule in Chapter 11 Bankruptcy Proceedings," *Financial Management* 27 (1998).

[11]John McConnell and Henri Servaes, "The Economics of Prepackaged Bankruptcy," *Journal of Applied Corporate Finance* (Summer 1991), describe prepackaged bankruptcy.

a year or more in bankruptcy. Not so with Quiznos group. Its reorganization plan was confirmed by the U.S. Bankruptcy Court on July 1, 2014, less than four months after the date of the filing!

Firms typically file bankruptcy to seek protection from their creditors, essentially admitting that they cannot meet their financial obligations as they are presently structured. Once in bankruptcy, the firm attempts to reorganize its financial picture so that it can survive. A key to this process is that the creditors must ultimately give their approval to the restructuring plan. The time a firm spends in Chapter 11 depends on many things, but it usually depends most on the time it takes to get creditors to agree to a plan of reorganization.

Prepackaged bankruptcy is a combination of a private workout and legal bankruptcy. Prior to filing bankruptcy, the firm approaches its creditors with a plan for reorganization. The two sides negotiate a settlement and agree on the details of how the firm's finances will be restructured in bankruptcy. Then, the firm puts together the necessary paperwork for the bankruptcy court before filing for bankruptcy. A filing is a prepack if the firm walks into court and, at the same time, files a reorganization plan complete with the documentation of the approval of its creditors, which is exactly what Quiznos did.

The key to the prepackaged reorganization process is that both sides have something to gain and something to lose. If bankruptcy is imminent, it may make sense for the creditors to expedite the process even though they are likely to take a financial loss in the restructuring. Quiznos' bankruptcy was painful for both stockholders and bondholders. Under the terms of the agreement, stockholders were wiped out entirely and three senior lenders exchanged $445 million in debt for 70 percent of the equity in the company and $200 million in new debt.

In another example of a prepack, let's go back to the Atlantic City casino Revel we mentioned in our opener. Recall that it closed its doors in September 2014. On February 19, 2013, Revel Atlantic City filed for a prepack bankruptcy. Debt holders who put up $1.155 billion in February 2011 would own 82 percent of the company's equity when it emerged from bankruptcy. On May 21, 2013, the company formally emerged from Chapter 11 bankruptcy. As an aside, in 2010, investment bank Morgan Stanley walked away from its entire $932 million investment in the company, so all-in-all, the Revel proved to be an expensive bet.

Prepackaged bankruptcy arrangements require that most creditors reach agreement privately. Prepackaged bankruptcy doesn't seem to work when there are thousands of reluctant trade creditors, such as in the case of a retail firm like Macy's or Revco D. S.[12]

The main benefit of prepackaged bankruptcy is that it forces holdouts to accept a bankruptcy reorganization. If a large fraction of a firm's creditors can agree privately to a reorganization plan, the holdout problem may be avoided. It makes a reorganization plan in formal bankruptcy easier to put together.[13]

A study by McConnell, Lease, and Tashjian reports that prepackaged bankruptcies offer many of the advantages of a formal bankruptcy, but they are also more efficient. Their

---

[12]Sris Chatterjee, Upinder S. Dhillon, and Gabriel G. Ramirez, in "Resolution of Financial Distress: Debt Restructurings via Chapter 11, Prepackaged Bankruptcies and Workouts," *Financial Management* (Spring 1996), find that firms using prepackaged bankruptcy arrangements are smaller and in better financial shape and have greater short-term liquidity problems than firms using private workouts or Chapter 11.

[13]During bankruptcy, a proposed plan can be "crammed down" on a class of creditors. A bankruptcy court can force creditors to participate in a reorganization if it can be shown that the plan is "fair and equitable."

results suggest that the time spent and the direct costs of resolving financial distress are less in a prepackaged bankruptcy than in a formal bankruptcy.[14]

30.6 Predicting Corporate Bankruptcy: The Z-Score Model

Many potential lenders use credit scoring models to assess the creditworthiness of prospective borrowers. The general idea is to find factors that enable the lenders to discriminate between good and bad credit risks. To put it more precisely, lenders want to identify attributes of the borrower that can be used to predict default or bankruptcy.

Edward Altman, a professor at New York University, has developed a model using financial statement ratios and multiple discriminant analyses to predict bankruptcy for publicly traded manufacturing firms. The resultant model is of the form:

$$Z = 3.3 \frac{\text{EBIT}}{\text{Total assets}} + 1.2 \frac{\text{Net working capital}}{\text{Total assets}}$$

$$+ 1.0 \frac{\text{Sales}}{\text{Total assets}} + .6 \frac{\text{Market value of equity}}{\text{Book value of debt}}$$

$$+ 1.4 \frac{\text{Accumulated retained earnings}}{\text{Total assets}}$$

where Z is an index of bankruptcy.

A score of Z less than 2.675 indicates that a firm has a 95 percent chance of becoming bankrupt within one year. However, Altman's results show that in practice scores between 1.81 and 2.99 should be thought of as a gray area. In actual use, bankruptcy would be predicted if $Z \leq 1.81$ and nonbankruptcy if $Z \geq 2.99$. Altman shows that bankrupt firms and nonbankrupt firms have very different financial profiles one year before bankruptcy.[15] These different financial ratios are the key intuition behind the Z-score model and are depicted in Table 30.2.

Table 30.2

Financial Statement Ratios One Year before Bankruptcy: Manufacturing Firms

	Average Ratios One Year before Bankruptcy of:	
	Bankrupt Firms	**Nonbankrupt Firms**
$\dfrac{\text{Net working capital}}{\text{Total assets}}$	−6.1%	41.4%
$\dfrac{\text{Accumulated retained earnings}}{\text{Total assets}}$	−62.6%	35.5%
$\dfrac{\text{EBIT}}{\text{Total assets}}$	−31.8%	15.4%
$\dfrac{\text{Market value of equity}}{\text{Total liabilities}}$	40.1%	247.7%
$\dfrac{\text{Sales}}{\text{Assets}}$	150%	190%

SOURCE: Edward I. Altman, *Corporate Financial Distress and Bankruptcy* (New York: John Wiley & Sons, 1993), Table 3.1, p. 109.

---

[14] John J. McConnell, Ronald Lease, and Elizabeth Tashjian, "Prepacks as a Mechanism for Resolving Financial Distress: The Evidence," *Journal of Applied Corporate Finance* 8 (1996).

[15] Although these are the original values proposed by Altman, in a more recent interview, he stated that a negative Z-score was now an indicator of potential bankruptcy. http://americasmarkets.usatoday.com/2014/09/18/z-score-predicts-doom-of-6-companies/.

Altman's original Z-score model requires a firm to have publicly traded equity and be a manufacturer. He uses a revised model to make it applicable for private firms and nonmanufacturers. The resulting model is this:

$$Z = 6.56 \frac{\text{Net working capital}}{\text{Total assets}} + 3.26 \frac{\text{Accumulated retained earnings}}{\text{Total assets}}$$

$$+ 1.05 \frac{\text{EBIT}}{\text{Total assets}} + 6.72 \frac{\text{Book value of equity}}{\text{Total liabilities}}$$

where $Z < 1.23$ indicates a bankruptcy prediction,
$1.23 \leq Z \leq 2.90$ indicates a gray area,
and $Z > 2.90$ indicates no bankruptcy.

EXAMPLE
30.3

U.S. Composite Corporation is attempting to increase its line of credit with First National State Bank. The director of credit management of First National State Bank uses the Z-score model to determine creditworthiness. U.S. Composite Corporation is not an actively traded firm and market prices are not always very reliable, so the revised Z-score model can be used.

The balance sheet and income statement of U.S. Composite Corporation are in Tables 2.1 and 2.2 (Chapter 2).

The first step is to determine the value of each of the financial statement variables and apply them in the revised Z-score model:

($ in millions)

$$\frac{\text{Net working capital}}{\text{Total assets}} = \frac{275}{1,879} = .146$$

$$\frac{\text{Accumulated retained earnings}}{\text{Total assets}} = \frac{390}{1,879} = .208$$

$$\frac{\text{EBIT}}{\text{Total assets}} = \frac{219}{1,879} = .117$$

$$\frac{\text{Book value of equity}}{\text{Total liabilities}} = \frac{805}{588} = 1.369$$

The next step is to calculate the revised Z-score:

$$Z = 6.56 \times .146 + 3.26 \times .208 + 1.05 \times .117 + 6.72 \times 1.369$$

$$= 10.96$$

Finally, we determine that the Z-score is above 2.9, and we conclude that U.S. Composite is a good credit risk.

Summary and Conclusions

This chapter examined what happens when firms experience financial distress.

1. Financial distress is a situation where a firm's operating cash flow is not sufficient to cover contractual obligations. Financially distressed firms are often forced to take corrective action and undergo financial restructuring. Financial restructuring involves exchanging new financial claims for old ones.

2. Financial restructuring can be accomplished with a private workout or formal bankruptcy. Financial restructuring can involve liquidation or reorganization. However, liquidation is not as common.

3. Corporate bankruptcy involves Chapter 7 liquidation or Chapter 11 reorganization. An essential feature of the U.S. bankruptcy code is the absolute priority rule. The absolute priority rule states that senior creditors are paid in full before junior creditors receive anything. However, in practice the absolute priority rule is often violated.

4. A newer form of financial restructuring is prepackaged bankruptcy. It is a hybrid of a private workout and formal bankruptcy.

5. Firms experiencing financial distress can be identified by different-looking financial statements. The Z-score model captures some of these differences.

Concept Questions

1. **Financial Distress**   Define *financial distress* using the stock-based and flow-based approaches.

2. **Financial Distress**   What are some benefits of financial distress?

3. **Prepackaged Bankruptcy**   What is prepackaged bankruptcy? What is the main benefit of prepackaged bankruptcy?

4. **Financial Distress**   Why doesn't financial distress always cause firms to die?

5. **Liquidation versus Reorganization**   What is the difference between liquidation and reorganization?

6. **APR**   What is the absolute priority rule?

7. **DIP Loans**   What are DIP loans? Where do DIP loans fall in the APR?

8. **Bankruptcy Ethics**   Firms sometimes use the threat of a bankruptcy filing to force creditors to renegotiate terms. Critics argue that in such cases the firm is using bankruptcy laws "as a sword rather than a shield." Is this an ethical tactic?

9. **Bankruptcy Ethics**   Several firms have entered bankruptcy, or threatened to enter bankruptcy, at least in part as a means of reducing labor costs. Whether this move is ethical, or proper, is hotly debated. Is this an ethical use of bankruptcy?

10. **Bankruptcy versus Private Workouts**   Why do so many firms file for legal bankruptcy when private workouts are so much less expensive?

Questions and Problems

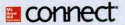

BASIC
(Questions 1–2)

1. **Chapter 7**   When the Beacon Computer Company filed for bankruptcy under Chapter 7 of the U.S. bankruptcy code, it had the following balance sheet information:

Liquidating Value		Claims	
		Trade credit	$ 4,700
		Secured mortgage notes	7,400
		Senior debentures	12,000
		Junior debentures	19,000
Total assets	$31,400	Equity	−11,700

Assuming there are no legal fees associated with the bankruptcy, as a trustee, what distribution of liquidating value do you propose?

2. **Chapter 11**   When the Master Printing Company filed for bankruptcy, it filed under Chapter 11 of the U.S. bankruptcy code. Key information is shown here:

Assets		Claims	
		Mortgage bonds	$20,000
		Senior debentures	10,500
		Junior debentures	7,500
Going concern value	$29,000	Book equity	−9,000

As a trustee, what reorganization plan would you accept?

INTERMEDIATE
(Questions 3–4)

3. **Z-Score**   Fair-to-Midland Manufacturing, Inc. (FMM), has applied for a loan at True Credit Bank. Jon Fulkerson, the credit analyst at the bank, has gathered the following information from the company's financial statements:

Total assets	$95,000
EBIT	7,300
Net working capital	3,800
Book value of equity	21,000
Accumulated retained earnings	19,600
Sales	104,000

The stock price of FMM is $27 per share and there are 7,500 shares outstanding. What is the Z-score for this company?

4. **Z-Score**   Jon Fulkerson has also received a credit application from Seether, LLC, a private company. An abbreviated portion of the financial information provided by the company is shown below:

Total assets	$73,000
EBIT	7,900
Net working capital	4,200
Book value of equity	18,000
Accumulated retained earnings	16,000
Total liabilities	64,000

What is the Z-score for this company?

31

International Corporate Finance

Worldwide, 2014 was a year with low or negative economic growth for most developed countries. To combat slow growth, many central banks lowered domestic interest rates. In fact, in early 2015, savers in Denmark were charged interest to keep deposits in a bank! Even though overall economic growth in the United States was weak, it was strong relative to most other developed countries. As a result, the U.S. dollar strengthened. For example, the dollar gained about 10 percent against the euro, 13 percent against the Japanese yen, and 31 percent against the Argentine peso. The stronger dollar hurt U.S. exporters and multinational companies, but also meant that imports were cheaper. In this chapter, we explore the important role played by currencies and exchange rates in international finance, along with a number of other key topics.

Corporations with significant foreign operations are often called *international corporations* or *multinationals*. Such corporations must consider many financial factors that do not directly affect purely domestic firms. These include foreign exchange rates, differing interest rates from country to country, complex accounting methods for foreign operations, foreign tax rates, and foreign government intervention.

The basic principles of corporate finance still apply to international corporations; like domestic companies, these firms seek to invest in projects that create more value for the shareholders than they cost and to arrange financing that raises cash at the lowest possible cost. In other words, the net present value principle holds for both foreign and domestic operations, although it is usually more complicated to apply the NPV rule to foreign investments.

One of the most significant complications of international finance is foreign exchange. The foreign exchange markets provide important information and opportunities for an international corporation when it undertakes capital budgeting and financing decisions. As we will discuss, international exchange rates, interest rates, and inflation rates are closely related. We will spend much of this chapter exploring the connection between these financial variables.

We won't have much to say here about the role of cultural and social differences in international business. Neither will we be discussing the implications of differing political and economic systems. These factors are of great importance to international businesses, but it would take another book to do them justice. Consequently, we will focus only on some purely financial considerations in international finance and some key aspects of foreign exchange markets.

31.1 Terminology

A common buzzword for the student of business finance is *globalization*. The first step in learning about the globalization of financial markets is to conquer the new vocabulary. As with any specialty, international finance is rich in jargon. Accordingly, we get started on the subject with a highly eclectic vocabulary exercise.

The terms that follow are presented alphabetically, and they are not all of equal importance. We choose these in particular because they appear frequently in the financial press or because they illustrate the colorful nature of the language of international finance.

See **www.adr.com** for more.

1. An **American depositary receipt (ADR)** is a security issued in the United States that represents shares of a foreign stock, allowing that stock to be traded in the United States. Foreign companies use ADRs, which are issued in U.S. dollars, to expand the pool of potential U.S. investors. ADRs are available in two forms for a large and growing number of foreign companies: Company sponsored, which are listed on an exchange, and unsponsored, which usually are held by the investment bank that makes a market in the ADR. Both forms are available to individual investors, but only company-sponsored issues are quoted daily in newspapers.

2. The **cross-rate** is the implicit exchange rate between two currencies (usually non-U.S.) when both are quoted in some third currency, usually the U.S. dollar.

3. **Eurocurrency** is money deposited in a financial center outside of the country whose currency is involved. For instance, Eurodollars—the most widely used Eurocurrency—are U.S. dollars deposited in banks outside the U.S. banking system.

4. **Gilts,** technically, are British and Irish government securities, although the term also includes issues of local British authorities and some overseas public-sector offerings.

For current LIBOR rates, see **www.bloomberg.com**.

5. The **London Interbank Offered Rate (LIBOR)** is the rate that most international banks charge one another for overnight loans of Eurodollars in the London market. LIBOR is a cornerstone in the pricing of money market issues and other short-term debt issues by both government and corporate borrowers. Interest rates are frequently quoted as some spread over LIBOR, and they then float with the LIBOR rate.

31.2 Foreign Exchange Markets and Exchange Rates

The **foreign exchange market** is undoubtedly the world's largest financial market. It is the market where one country's currency is traded for another's. Most of the trading takes place in a few currencies: The U.S. dollar ($), the British pound sterling (£), the Japanese yen (¥), and the euro (€). Table 31.1 lists some of the more common currencies and their symbols.

The foreign exchange market is an over-the-counter market, so there is no single location where traders get together. Instead, market participants are located in the major commercial and investment banks around the world. They communicate using computers, telephones, and other telecommunication devices. For example, one communication network for foreign transactions is maintained by the Society for Worldwide Interbank Financial Telecommunication (SWIFT), a Belgian not-for-profit cooperative. Using data transmission lines, a bank in New York can send messages to a bank in London via SWIFT regional processing centers.

Table 31.1

International Currency Symbols

Country	Currency	Symbol
Australia	Dollar	A$
Canada	Dollar	Can$
Denmark	Krone	DKr
EMU	Euro	€
India	Rupee	Rs
Iran	Rial	Rl
Japan	Yen	¥
Kuwait	Dinar	KD
Mexico	Peso	Ps
Norway	Krone	NKr
Saudi Arabia	Riyal	SR
Singapore	Dollar	S$
South Africa	Rand	R
Sweden	Krona	SKr
Switzerland	Franc	SF
United Kingdom	Pound	£
United States	Dollar	$

The many different types of participants in the foreign exchange market include the following:

1. Importers who pay for goods using foreign currencies.
2. Exporters who receive foreign currency and may want to convert to the domestic currency.
3. Portfolio managers who buy or sell foreign stocks and bonds.
4. Foreign exchange brokers who match buy and sell orders.
5. Traders who "make a market" in foreign currencies.
6. Speculators who try to profit from changes in exchange rates.

Visit SWIFT at **www.swift.com**.

EXCHANGE RATES

An **exchange rate** is simply the price of one country's currency expressed in terms of another country's currency. In practice, almost all trading of currencies takes place in terms of the U.S. dollar. For example, both the Swiss franc and the Japanese yen are traded with their prices quoted in U.S. dollars. Exchange rates are constantly changing.

Exchange Rate Quotations Figure 31.1 reproduces exchange rate quotations as they appeared on www.wsj.com in 2014. The first column (labeled "USD equiv") gives the number of dollars it takes to buy one unit of foreign currency. Because this is the price in dollars of a foreign currency, it is called a *direct* or *American quote* (remember that

Figure 31.1 Exchange Rate Quotations

Exchange Rates: New York Closing Snapshot for Friday, November 28, 2014

Country/currency	USD equiv	Currency per USD	US$ vs. YTD % chg	Country/currency	USD equiv	Currency per USD	US$ vs. YTD % chg
Americas				**Europe**			
Argentina peso	0.1173	8.5280	30.8	Czech Rep. koruna	0.04507	22.188	11.6
Brazil real	0.3897	2.5658	8.6	Denmark krone	0.1673	5.9757	10.1
Canada dollar	0.8759	1.1417	7.5	Euro area euro	1.2452	0.8031	10.4
Chile peso	0.001642	609.1000	15.8	Hungary forint	0.00406209	246.1800	13.9
Colombia peso	0.0004511	2217	14.9	Norway krone	0.1422	7.0305	15.8
Ecuador US dollar	1	1	unch	Poland zloty	0.2976	3.3598	11.1
Mexico peso	0.0718	13.9334	6.8	Romania leu	0.2808	3.5617	9.5
Peru new sol	0.3424	2.9210	4.2	Russia ruble	0.01989	50.274	52.7
Uruguay peso	0.04247	23.545	11.1	Sweden krona	0.1342	7.4518	15.8
Venezuela b. fuerte	0.15748031	6.3500	unch	Switzerland franc	1.0357	0.9655	8.1
				1-mos forward	1.0362	0.9651	7.5
Asia-Pacific				3-mos forward	1.0369	0.9644	7.5
Australian dollar	0.8507	1.1755	4.8	6-mos forward	1.0382	0.9632	7.4
1-mos forward	0.8489	1.1780	4.6	Turkey lira	0.4505	2.2200	3.3
3-mos forward	0.8452	1.1831	4.6	UK pound	1.5649	0.6390	5.8
6-mos forward	0.8397	1.1909	4.7	1-mos forward	1.5646	0.6391	5.5
China yuan	0.1628	6.1431	1.4	3-mos forward	1.5639	0.6394	5.5
Hong Kong dollar	0.129	7.7546	unch	6-mos forward	1.5626	0.6400	5.5
India rupee	0.01606	62.25095	0.6				
Indonesia rupiah	0.0000817	12246	0.7	**Middle East/Africa**			
Japan yen	0.00843	118.62	12.6	Bahrain dinar	2.6516	0.3771	unch
1-mos forward	0.00844	118.54	11.2	Egypt pound	0.1399	7.1471	2.8
3-mos forward	0.00844	118.49	11.2	Israel shekel	0.2567	3.8950	12.3
6-mos forward	0.00845	118.37	11.1	Jordan dinar	1.4187	0.7049	-0.4
Malaysia ringgit	0.2951	3.3887	3.2	Kenya shilling	0.01109	90.149	4.3
New Zealand dollar	0.7843	1.2750	4.8	Kuwait dinar	3.429	0.2916	3.3
Pakistan rupee	0.00982	101.805	-3.4	Lebanon pound	0.0006612	1512.45	0.5
Philippines peso	0.0223	44.905	1.2	Saudi Arabia riyal	0.2665	3.7529	0.1
Singapore dollar	0.7667	1.3043	3.3	South Africa rand	0.0903	11.0695	5.5
South Korea won	0.0008983	1113.2	5.4	UAE dirham	0.2723	3.6731	unch
Taiwan dollar	0.03226	30.999	3.6				
Thailand baht	0.03045	32.843	0.4				
Vietnam dong	0.00005	21355	1.1				

SOURCE: *The Wall Street Journal*, © 2015 Dow Jones and Company, Inc., November 28, 2014.

"Americans are direct"). For example, the Australian dollar is quoted at 0.8507, which means that you can buy one Australian dollar with U.S. $0.8507.

The second column shows the *indirect,* or *European, exchange rate* (even though the currency may not be European). This is the amount of foreign currency per U.S. dollar. The Australian dollar is quoted here at 1.1755, so you can get 1.1755 Australian dollars for one U.S. dollar. Naturally this second exchange rate is just the reciprocal of the first one (possibly with a little rounding error): 1/0.8507 = 1.1755. The third column shows the year-to-date (YTD) percentage change in the dollar's value versus another currency.

You can also find exchange rates on a number of websites. Suppose you have just returned from your dream vacation to Jamaica and feel rich because you have 10,000 Jamaican dollars left over. You now need to convert these to U.S. dollars. How much will you have? We went to www.xe.com and used the currency converter on the site to find out. This is what we found:

Get up-to-the-minute exchange rates at **www.xe.com** and **www.exchangerate.com**.

10,000.00 JMD = 86.7528 USD

Jamaican Dollar ↔ US Dollar

1 JMD = 0.00867528 USD   1 USD = 115.270 JMD

Mid-market rates: 2015-02-14 22:53 UTC

Looks like you left Jamaica just before you ran out of money.

EXAMPLE
31.1

A Yen for Euros   Suppose you have $1,000. Based on the rates in Figure 31.1, how many Japanese yen can you get? Alternatively, if a Porsche costs €100,000 (recall that € is the symbol for the euro), how many dollars will you need to buy it?

The exchange rate in terms of yen per dollar (second column) is 118.62. Your $1,000 will thus get you:

$$\$1,000 \times 118.62 \text{ yen per } \$1 = 118,620 \text{ yen}$$

Because the exchange rate in terms of dollars per euro (first column) is 1.2452, you will need:

$$€100,000 \times \$1.2452 \text{ per } € = \$124,520$$

Cross-Rates and Triangle Arbitrage   Using the U.S. dollar as the common denominator in quoting exchange rates greatly reduces the number of possible cross-currency quotes. For example, with five major currencies, there would potentially be 10 exchange rates instead of just 4.[1] Also, the fact that the dollar is used throughout cuts down on inconsistencies in the exchange rate quotations.

Earlier, we defined the cross-rate as the exchange rate for a non-U.S. currency expressed in terms of another non-U.S. currency. For example, suppose we observe the following for the euro (€) and the Swiss franc (SF):

$$€ \text{ per } \$1 = 1.00$$
$$SF \text{ per } \$1 = 2.00$$

Suppose the cross-rate is quoted as:

$$€ \text{ per } SF = .40$$

What do you think?

The cross-rate here is inconsistent with the exchange rates. To see this, suppose you have $100. If you convert this to Swiss francs, you will receive:

$$\$100 \times SF \ 2 \text{ per } \$1 = SF \ 200$$

---

[1]There are four exchange rates instead of five because one exchange rate would involve the exchange of a currency for itself. More generally, it might seem that there should be 25 exchange rates with five currencies. There are 25 different combinations, but, of these, 5 involve the exchange of a currency for itself. Of the remaining 20, half are redundant because they are just the reciprocals of another exchange rate. Of the remaining 10, 6 can be eliminated by using a common denominator.

If you convert this to euros at the cross-rate, you will have:

$$\text{SF } 200 \times \text{€.4 per SF } 1 = \text{€80}$$

However, if you just convert your dollars to euros without going through Swiss francs, you will have:

$$\$100 \times \text{€1 per } \$1 = \text{€100}$$

What we see is that the euro has two prices, €1 per $1 and €.80 per $1, with the price we pay depending on how we get the euros.

To make money, we want to buy low and sell high. The important thing to note is that euros are cheaper if you buy them with dollars because you get 1 euro instead of just .8. You should proceed as follows:

1. Buy 100 euros for $100.

2. Use the 100 euros to buy Swiss francs at the cross-rate. Because it takes .4 euros to buy a Swiss franc, you will receive €100/.4 = SF 250.

3. Use the SF 250 to buy dollars. Because the exchange rate is SF 2 per dollar, you receive SF 250/2 = $125, for a round-trip profit of $25.

4. Repeat steps 1 through 3.

This particular activity is called *triangle arbitrage* because the arbitrage involves moving through three different exchange rates:

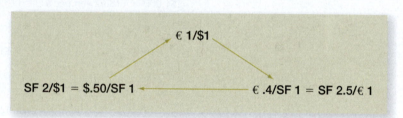

To prevent such opportunities, it is not difficult to see that because a dollar will buy you either one euro or two Swiss francs, the cross-rate must be:

$$(\text{€1}/\$1)/(\text{SF } 2/\$1) = \text{€1}/\text{SF } 2$$

That is, the cross-rate must be one euro per two Swiss francs. If it were anything else, there would be a triangle arbitrage opportunity.

Shedding Some Pounds　Suppose the exchange rates for the British pound and Swiss franc are:

$$\text{Pounds per } \$1 = .60$$

$$\text{SF per } \$1 = 2.00$$

The cross-rate is three francs per pound. Is this consistent? Explain how to go about making some money.

The cross-rate should be SF 2.00/£.60 = SF 3.33 per pound. You can buy a pound for SF 3 in one market, and you can sell a pound for SF 3.33 in another. So we want to first get some francs, then use the francs to buy some pounds, and then sell the pounds. Assuming you have $100, you could:

1. Exchange dollars for francs: $100 × 2 = SF 200.
2. Exchange francs for pounds: SF 200/3 = £66.67.
3. Exchange pounds for dollars: £66.67/.60 = $111.12.

This would result in an $11.12 round-trip profit.

Types of Transactions

There are two basic types of trades in the foreign exchange market: Spot trades and forward trades. A **spot trade** is an agreement to exchange currency "on the spot," which actually means that the transaction will be completed or settled within two business days. The exchange rate on a spot trade is called the **spot exchange rate**. Implicitly, all of the exchange rates and transactions we have discussed so far have referred to the spot market.

A **forward trade** is an agreement to exchange currency at some time in the future. The exchange rate that will be used is agreed upon today and is called the **forward exchange rate**. A forward trade will normally be settled sometime in the next 12 months.

If you look back at Figure 31.1, you will see forward exchange rates quoted for some of the major currencies. For example, the spot exchange rate for the Swiss franc is SF 1 = $1.0357. The 180-day (6-month) forward exchange rate is SF 1 = $1.0382. This means that you can buy a Swiss franc today for $1.0357, or you can agree to take delivery of a Swiss franc in 180 days and pay $1.0382 at that time.

Notice that the Swiss franc is more expensive in the forward market ($1.0382 versus $1.0357). Because the Swiss franc is more expensive in the future than it is today, it is said to be selling at a *premium* relative to the dollar. For the same reason, the dollar is said to be selling at a *discount* relative to the Swiss franc.

Why does the forward market exist? One answer is that it allows businesses and individuals to lock in a future exchange rate today, thereby eliminating any risk from unfavorable shifts in the exchange rate.

EXAMPLE 31.3

Looking Forward   Suppose you are expecting to receive a million British pounds in six months, and you agree to a forward trade to exchange your pounds for dollars. Based on Figure 31.1, how many dollars will you get in six months? Is the pound selling at a discount or a premium relative to the dollar?

In Figure 31.1, the spot exchange rate and the 180-day forward rate in terms of dollars per pound are $1.5649 = £1 and $1.5626 = £1, respectively. If you expect £1 million in 180 days, then you will get £1 million × $1.5626 per pound = $1.5626 million. Because it is less expensive to buy a pound in the forward market than in the spot market ($1.5626 versus $1.5649), the pound is said to be selling at a discount relative to the dollar.

As we mentioned earlier, it is standard practice around the world (with a few exceptions) to quote exchange rates in terms of the U.S. dollar. This means that rates are quoted as the amount of currency per U.S. dollar. For the remainder of this chapter, we will stick with this form. Things can get extremely confusing if you forget this. Thus, when we say things like "the exchange rate is expected to rise," it is important to remember that we are talking about the exchange rate quoted as units of foreign currency per dollar.

31.3 Purchasing Power Parity

Now that we have discussed what exchange rate quotations mean, we can address an obvious question: What determines the level of the spot exchange rate? In addition, because we know that exchange rates change through time, we can ask the related question: what determines the rate of change in exchange rates? At least part of the answer in both cases goes by the name of **purchasing power parity** (**PPP**), the idea that the exchange rate adjusts to keep purchasing power constant among currencies. As we discuss next, there are two forms of PPP, *absolute* and *relative*.

ABSOLUTE PURCHASING POWER PARITY

The basic idea behind *absolute purchasing power parity* is that a commodity costs the same regardless of what currency is used to purchase it or where it is selling. This is a very straightforward concept. If a beer costs £2 in London, and the exchange rate is £.60 per dollar, then a beer costs £2/.60 = $3.33 in New York. In other words, absolute PPP says that $1 will buy you the same number of, say, cheeseburgers anywhere in the world. (This concept is sometimes referred to as the "law of one price.")

More formally, let S_0 be the spot exchange rate between the British pound and the U.S. dollar today (time 0), and remember that we are quoting exchange rates as the amount of foreign currency per dollar. Let P_{US} and P_{UK} be the current U.S. and British prices, respectively, on a particular commodity, say, apples. Absolute PPP simply says that:

$$P_{UK} = S_0 \times P_{US}$$

This tells us that the British price for something is equal to the U.S. price for that same something multiplied by the exchange rate.

The rationale behind absolute PPP is similar to that behind triangle arbitrage. If PPP did not hold, arbitrage would be possible (in principle) if apples were moved from one country to another. For example, suppose apples are selling in New York for $4 per bushel, whereas in London the price is £2.40 per bushel. Absolute PPP implies that:

$$
\begin{aligned}
P_{UK} &= S_0 \times P_{US} \\
£2.40 &= S_0 \times \$4 \\
S_0 &= £2.40/\$4 = £.60
\end{aligned}
$$

That is, the implied spot exchange rate is £.60 per dollar. Equivalently, a pound is worth $1/£.60 = $1.67.

Suppose instead that the actual exchange rate is £.50. Starting with $4, a trader could buy a bushel of apples in New York, ship it to London, and sell it there for £2.40. Our trader could then convert the £2.40 into dollars at the prevailing exchange rate, S_0 = £.50, yielding a total of £2.40/.50 = $4.80. The round-trip gain would be 80 cents.

Because of this profit potential, forces are set in motion to change the exchange rate and/or the price of apples. In our example, apples would begin moving from New York to London. The reduced supply of apples in New York would raise the price of apples there, and the increased supply in Britain would lower the price of apples in London.

In addition to moving apples around, apple traders would be busily converting pounds back into dollars to buy more apples. This activity would increase the supply of pounds and simultaneously increase the demand for dollars. We would expect the value of a pound to fall. This means that the dollar would be getting more valuable, so it would take more pounds to buy one dollar. Because the exchange rate is quoted as pounds per dollar, we would expect the exchange rate to rise from £.50.

For absolute PPP to hold absolutely, several things must be true:

1. The transaction costs of trading apples—shipping, insurance, spoilage, and so on—must be zero.

2. There must be no barriers to trading apples—no tariffs, taxes, or other political barriers.

3. Finally, an apple in New York must be identical to an apple in London. It won't do any good for you to send red apples to London if the English eat only green apples.

Given the fact that the transaction costs are not zero and that the other conditions are rarely met exactly, it is not surprising that absolute PPP is really applicable only to traded goods, and then only to very uniform ones.

For this reason, absolute PPP does not imply that a Mercedes costs the same as a Ford or that a nuclear power plant in France costs the same as one in New York. In the case of the cars, they are not identical. In the case of the power plants, even if they were identical, they are expensive and would be very difficult to ship. On the other hand, we would be very surprised to see a significant violation of absolute PPP for gold.

For example, *The Economist* publishes the Big Mac Index, which shows whether a currency is overvalued or undervalued relative to the U.S. dollar based on the price of a McDonald's Big Mac. In the January 2015 index, 3 of the 43 currencies in the index were overvalued by more than 10 percent, and 32 currencies were undervalued by more than 10 percent. To illustrate, the average price of a Big Mac in the United States in January 2015 was $4.79 and in Japan it was $3.14. At market exchange rates, this could indicate the yen was undervalued by 34 percent and should rise in the future to close the gap. Similarly, at market exchange rates, the price of a Big Mac in China was $2.77, implying the yuan was undervalued by 42 percent.

> To see the current Big Mac Index, check out **http://www.economist.com/content/big-mac-index**

RELATIVE PURCHASING POWER PARITY

As a practical matter, a relative version of purchasing power parity has evolved. *Relative purchasing power parity* does not tell us what determines the absolute level of the exchange rate. Instead, it tells us what determines the *change* in the exchange rate over time.

The Basic Idea Suppose the British pound–U.S. dollar exchange rate is currently $S_0 = £.50$. Further suppose that the inflation rate in Britain is predicted to be 10 percent over the coming year, and (for the moment) the inflation rate in the United States is predicted to be zero. What do you think the exchange rate will be in a year?

If you think about it, you see that a dollar currently costs .50 pounds in Britain. With 10 percent inflation, we expect prices in Britain to generally rise by 10 percent. So we expect that the price of a dollar will go up by 10 percent, and the exchange rate should rise to £.50 × 1.1 = £.55.

If the inflation rate in the United States is not zero, then we need to worry about the *relative* inflation rates in the two countries. For example, suppose the U.S. inflation rate is predicted to be 4 percent. Relative to prices in the United States, prices in Britain are rising at a rate of 10 percent − 4 percent = 6 percent per year. So we expect the price of the dollar to rise by 6 percent, and the predicted exchange rate is £.50 × 1.06 = £.53.

The Result In general, relative PPP says that the change in the exchange rate is determined by the difference in the inflation rates of the two countries. To be more specific, we will use the following notation:

S_0 = Current (Time 0) spot exchange rate (foreign currency per dollar).

$E(S_t)$ = Expected exchange rate in t periods.

h_{US} = Inflation rate in the United States.

h_{FC} = Foreign country inflation rate.

Based on our preceding discussion, relative PPP says that the expected percentage change in the exchange rate over the next year, $[E(S_1) - S_0]/S_0$, is:

$$[E(S_1) - S_0]/S_0 \cong h_{FC} - h_{US} \tag{31.1}$$

In words, relative PPP simply says that the expected percentage change in the exchange rate is equal to the difference in inflation rates.[2] If we rearrange this slightly, we get:

$$E(S_1) \cong S_0 \times [1 + (h_{FC} - h_{US})] \tag{31.2}$$

This result makes a certain amount of sense, but care must be used in quoting the exchange rate.

In our example involving Britain and the United States, relative PPP tells us that the exchange rate will rise by $h_{FC} - h_{US}$ = 10 percent − 4 percent = 6 percent per year. Assuming the difference in inflation rates doesn't change, the expected exchange rate in two years, $E(S_2)$, will therefore be:

$$
\begin{aligned}
E(S_2) &= E(S_1) \times (1 + .06) \\
&= .53 \times 1.06 \\
&= .562
\end{aligned}
$$

Notice that we could have written this as:

$$
\begin{aligned}
E(S_2) &= .53 \times 1.06 \\
&= .50 \times (1.06 \times 1.06) \\
&= .50 \times 1.06^2
\end{aligned}
$$

In general, relative PPP says that the expected exchange rate at some time in the future, $E(S_t)$, is:

$$E(S_t) \cong S_0 \times [1 + (h_{FC} - h_{US})]^t \tag{31.3}$$

As we will see, this is a very useful relationship.

EXAMPLE 31.4

It's All Relative   Suppose the Japanese exchange rate is currently 105 yen per dollar. The inflation rate in Japan over the next three years will run, say, 2 percent per year, whereas the U.S. inflation rate will be 6 percent. Based on relative PPP, what will the exchange rate be in three years?

Because the U.S. inflation rate is higher, we expect that a dollar will become less valuable. The exchange rate change will be 2 percent − 6 percent = −4 percent per year. Over three years the exchange rate will fall to:

$$
\begin{aligned}
E(S_3) &\cong S_0 \times [1 + (h_{FC} - h_{US})]^3 \\
&\cong 105 \times [1 + (-.04)]^3 \\
&\cong 92.90
\end{aligned}
$$

[2]Equation 31.1 is actually an approximation; the relative PPP predicts that:

$$\frac{E(S_1)}{S_0} = \frac{1 + h_{FC}}{1 + h_{FC}} \text{ and } \frac{E(S_1) - S_0}{S_0} = \frac{E(S_1)}{S_0} - 1$$

will hold precisely. So, in our example, the change in the value of a UK pound per dollar would be:

$$1.058 = \frac{1 + .10}{1 + .04}$$

or 5.8 percent instead of 6 percent. This is a widely used approximation, and we use it from time to time for ease of exposition.

Because we don't really expect absolute PPP to hold for most goods, we will focus on relative PPP in our following discussion. Henceforth, when we refer to PPP without further qualification, we mean relative PPP.

Currency Appreciation and Depreciation   We frequently hear things like "the dollar strengthened (or weakened) in financial markets today" or "the dollar is expected to appreciate (or depreciate) relative to the pound." When we say that the dollar strengthens or appreciates, we mean that the value of a dollar rises, so it takes more foreign currency to buy a dollar.

What happens to the exchange rates as currencies fluctuate in value depends on how exchange rates are quoted. Because we are quoting them as units of foreign currency per dollar, the exchange rate moves in the same direction as the value of the dollar: It rises as the dollar strengthens, and it falls as the dollar weakens.

Relative PPP tells us that the exchange rate will rise if the U.S. inflation rate is lower than the foreign country's. This happens because the foreign currency depreciates in value and therefore weakens relative to the dollar.

31.4 Interest Rate Parity, Unbiased Forward Rates, and the International Fisher Effect

The next issue we need to address is the relationship between spot exchange rates, forward exchange rates, and interest rates. To get started, we need some additional notation:

F_t = Forward exchange rate for settlement at time t.

R_{US} = U.S. nominal risk-free interest rate.

R_{FC} = Foreign country nominal risk-free interest rate.

As before, we will use S_0 to stand for the spot exchange rate. You can take the U.S. nominal risk-free rate, R_{US}, to be the T-bill rate.

COVERED INTEREST ARBITRAGE

Suppose we observe the following information about U.S. and Swiss currencies in the market:

S_0 = SF 2.00

F_1 = SF 1.90

R_{US} = 10%

R_S = 5%

where R_S is the nominal risk-free rate in Switzerland. The period is one year, so F_1 is the 360-day forward rate.

Do you see an arbitrage opportunity here? There is one. Suppose you have $1 to invest, and you want a riskless investment. One option you have is to invest the $1 in a riskless U.S. investment such as a 360-day T-bill. If you do this, then in one period your $1 will be worth:

$$\$ \text{ value in 1 period} = \$1 \times (1 + R_{US})$$
$$= \$1.10$$

Alternatively, you can invest in the Swiss risk-free investment. To do this, you need to convert your $1 to Swiss francs and simultaneously execute a forward trade to convert francs back to dollars in one year. The necessary steps would be as follows:

1. Convert your $1 to $1 $\times S_0$ = SF 2.00.

2. At the same time, enter into a forward agreement to convert Swiss francs back to dollars in one year. Because the forward rate is SF 1.90, you will get $1 for every SF 1.90 that you have in one year.

3. Invest your SF 2.00 in Switzerland at R_S. In one year you will have:

$$\text{SF value in 1 year} = \text{SF } 2.00 \times (1 + R_S)$$
$$= \text{SF } 2.00 \times 1.05$$
$$= \text{SF } 2.10$$

4. Convert your SF 2.10 back to dollars at the agreed-upon rate of SF 1.90 = $1. You end up with:

$$\$ \text{ value in 1 year} = \text{SF } 2.10/1.90$$
$$= \$1.1053$$

Notice that the value in one year resulting from this strategy can be written as:

$$\$ \text{ value in 1 year} = \$1 \times S_0 \times (1 + R_S)/F_1$$
$$= \$1 \times 2 \times 1.05/1.90$$
$$= \$1.1053$$

The return on this investment is apparently 10.53 percent. This is higher than the 10 percent we get from investing in the United States. Because both investments are risk-free, there is an arbitrage opportunity.

To exploit the difference in interest rates, you need to borrow, say, $5 million at the lower U.S. rate and invest it at the higher Swiss rate. What is the round-trip profit from doing this? To find out, we can work through the steps outlined previously:

1. Convert the $5 million at SF 2 = $1 to get SF 10 million.

2. Agree to exchange Swiss francs for dollars in one year at SF 1.90 to the dollar.

3. Invest the SF 10 million for one year at R_S = 5 percent. You end up with SF 10.5 million.

4. Convert the SF 10.5 million back to dollars to fulfill the forward contract. You receive SF 10.5 million/1.90 = $5,526,316.

5. Repay the loan with interest. You owe $5 million plus 10 percent interest for a total of $5.5 million. You have $5,526,316, so your round-trip profit is a risk-free $26,316.

The activity that we have illustrated here goes by the name of *covered interest arbitrage*. The term *covered* refers to the fact that we are covered in the event of a change in the exchange rate because we lock in the forward exchange rate today.

INTEREST RATE PARITY

If we assume that significant covered interest arbitrage opportunities do not exist, then there must be some relationship between spot exchange rates, forward exchange rates, and relative interest rates. To see what this relationship is, note that in general Strategy 1 from the preceding discussion, investing in a riskless U.S. investment, gives us $1 + R_{US}$ for every dollar we invest. Strategy 2, investing in a foreign risk-free investment, gives us $S_0 \times (1 + R_{FC})/F_1$ for every dollar we invest. Because these have to be equal to prevent arbitrage, it must be the case that:

$$1 + R_{US} = S_0 \times (1 + R_{FC})/F_1$$

Rearranging this a bit gets us the famous **interest rate parity (IRP)** condition:

$$F_1/S_0 = (1 + R_{FC})/(1 + R_{US}) \qquad \textbf{(31.4)}$$

There is a very useful approximation for IRP that illustrates clearly what is going on and is not difficult to remember.[3] If we define the percentage forward premium or discount as $(F_1 - S_0)/S_0$, then IRP says that this percentage premium or discount is *approximately* equal to the difference in interest rates:

$$(F_1 - S_0)/S_0 \cong R_{FC} - R_{US} \qquad \textbf{(31.5)}$$

Loosely, IRP says that any difference in interest rates between two countries for some period is just offset by the change in the relative value of the currencies, thereby eliminating any arbitrage possibilities. Notice that we could also write:

$$F_1 \cong S_0 \times [1 + (R_{FC} - R_{US})] \qquad \textbf{(31.6)}$$

In general, if we have t periods instead of just one, the IRP approximation is written like this:

$$F_t \cong S_0 \times [1 + (R_{FC} - R_{US})]^t \qquad \textbf{(31.7)}$$

EXAMPLE 31.5

Parity check   Suppose the exchange rate for Japanese yen, S_0, is currently ¥120 = \$1. If the interest rate in the United States is R_{US} = 10 percent and the interest rate in Japan is R_J = 5 percent, then what must the forward rate be to prevent covered interest arbitrage?

From IRP, we have:

$$F_1 \cong S_0 \times [1 + (R_J - R_{US})]$$
$$\cong ¥120 \times [1 + (.05 - .10)]$$
$$\cong ¥120 \times .95$$
$$\cong ¥114$$

Notice that the yen will sell at a premium relative to the dollar. (Why?)

FORWARD RATES AND FUTURE SPOT RATES

In addition to PPP and IRP, there is one more basic relationship we need to discuss. What is the connection between the forward rate and the expected future spot rate? The **unbiased forward rates (UFR)** condition says that the forward rate, F_1, is equal to the *expected* future spot rate, $E(S_1)$:

$$F_1 = E(S_1)$$

With t periods, UFR would be written as:

$$F_t = E(S_t)$$

---

[3]Here we note that $F_1/S_0 - 1 = (F_1 - S_0)/S_0$ and $(1 + R_{FC})/(1 + R_{US})$ is approximately equal to $R_{FC} - R_{US}$.

Loosely, the UFR condition says that, on average, the forward exchange rate is equal to the future spot exchange rate.

If we ignore risk, then the UFR condition should hold. Suppose the forward rate for the Japanese yen is consistently lower than the future spot rate by, say, 10 yen. This means that anyone who wanted to convert dollars to yen in the future would consistently get more yen by not agreeing to a forward exchange. The forward rate would have to rise to get anyone interested in a forward exchange.

Similarly, if the forward rate were consistently higher than the future spot rate, then anyone who wanted to convert yen to dollars would get more dollars per yen by not agreeing to a forward trade. The forward exchange rate would have to fall to attract such traders.

For these reasons, the forward and actual future spot rates should be equal to each other on average. What the future spot rate will actually be is uncertain, of course. The UFR condition may not hold if traders are willing to pay a premium to avoid this uncertainty. If the condition does hold, then the 180-day forward rate that we see today should be an unbiased predictor of what the exchange rate will actually be in 180 days.

PUTTING IT ALL TOGETHER

We have developed three relationships—PPP, IRP, and UFR—that describe the interactions between key financial variables such as interest rates, exchange rates, and inflation rates. We now explore the implications of these relationships as a group.

Uncovered Interest Parity To start, it is useful to collect our international financial market relationships in one place:

$$\text{PPP:} \quad E(S_1) \cong S_0 \times [1 + (h_{FC} - h_{US})]$$
$$\text{IRP:} \quad F_1 \cong S_0 \times [1 + (R_{FC} - R_{US})]$$
$$\text{UFR:} \quad F_1 = E(S_1)$$

We begin by combining UFR and IRP. Because we know that $F_1 = E(S_1)$ from the UFR condition, we can substitute $E(S_1)$ for F_1 in IRP.[4] The result is:

$$\text{UIP: } E(S_1) \cong S_0 \times [1 + (R_{FC} - R_{US})] \tag{31.8}$$

This important relationship is called **uncovered interest parity (UIP)**, and it will play a key role in our international capital budgeting discussion that follows. With t periods, UIP becomes:

$$E(S_t) \cong S_0 \times [1 + (R_{FC} - R_{US})]^t \tag{31.9}$$

The International Fisher Effect Next we compare PPP and UIP. Both of them have $E(S_1)$ on the left side, so their right sides must be equal. We thus have:

$$S_0 \times [1 + (h_{FC} - h_{US})] = S_0 \times [1 + (R_{FC} - R_{US})]$$
$$h_{FC} - h_{US} = R_{FC} - R_{US}$$

---

[4]Here again, we are dealing in an approximation for ease of exposition. The exact equations are:

$$\text{PPP: } E(S_1) = S_0 \times \left[\frac{(1 + h_{FC})}{(1 + h_{US})}\right]$$

$$\text{IRP: } F_1 = S_0 \times \left[\frac{(1 + R_{FC})}{(1 + R_{US})}\right]$$

This tells us that the difference in returns between the United States and a foreign country is just equal to the difference in inflation rates. Rearranging this slightly gives us the **international Fisher effect (IFE)**:

$$\text{IFE: } R_{US} - h_{US} = R_{FC} - h_{FC} \tag{31.10}$$

The IFE says that *real* rates are equal across countries.[5]

The conclusion that real returns are equal across countries is really basic economics. If real returns were higher in, say, Brazil than in the United States, money would flow out of U.S. financial markets and into Brazilian markets. Asset prices in Brazil would rise and their returns would fall. At the same time, asset prices in the United States would fall and their returns would rise. This process acts to equalize real returns.

Having said all this, we need to note a couple of things. First, we really haven't explicitly dealt with risk in our discussion. We might reach a different conclusion about real returns once we do, particularly if people in different countries have different tastes and attitudes toward risk. Second, there are many barriers to the movement of money and capital around the world. Real returns might be different in two different countries for long periods if money can't move freely between them.

Despite these problems, we expect that capital markets will become increasingly internationalized. As this occurs, any differences in real rates will probably diminish. The laws of economics have little respect for national boundaries.

31.5 International Capital Budgeting

Kihlstrom Equipment, a U.S.-based international company, is evaluating an overseas investment. Kihlstrom's exports of drill bits have increased to such a degree that it is considering building a distribution center in France. The project will cost €2 million to launch. The cash flows are expected to be €.9 million a year for the next three years.

The current spot exchange rate for euros is €.5. Recall that this is euros per dollar, so a euro is worth $1/.5 = $2. The risk-free rate in the United States is 5 percent, and the risk-free rate in France is 7 percent. Note that the exchange rate and the two interest rates are observed in financial markets, not estimated.[6] Kihlstrom's WACC on dollar investments of this sort is 10 percent.[7]

Should Kihlstrom take this investment? As always, the answer depends on the NPV; but how do we calculate the net present value of this project in U.S. dollars? There are two basic methods:

1. *The home currency approach:* Convert all the euro cash flows into dollars, and then discount at 10 percent to find the NPV in dollars. Notice that for this approach we

---

[5]Notice that our result here is in terms of the approximate real rate, $R - h$ (see Chapter 8) because we used approximations for PPP and IRP. For the exact result, see Problem 18 at the end of the chapter.

[6]For example, the interest rates might be the short-term Eurodollar and euro deposit rates offered by large banks.

[7]Kihlstrom's WACC is determined in the usual way. Suppose that the market values of debt and equity and associated capital costs are:

Debt	$500	5%
Equity	$500	16%
	$1,000	

with the corporate tax rate equal to 20 percent. It follows that:

$$
\begin{aligned}
\text{WACC} &= \frac{S}{B + S} + \frac{B}{B + S} R_B (1 - T_c) \\
&= \left(\tfrac{1}{2}\right)16\% + \left(\tfrac{1}{2}\right)(5\%)(1 - .20) \\
&= 10\%
\end{aligned}
$$

have to come up with the future exchange rates to convert the future projected euro cash flows into dollars.

2. *The foreign currency approach:* Determine the required return on euro investments, and then discount the euro cash flows to find the NPV in euros. Then convert this euro NPV to a dollar NPV. This approach requires us to somehow convert the 10 percent dollar required return to the equivalent euro required return.

The difference between these two approaches is primarily a matter of when we convert from euros to dollars. In the first case, we convert before estimating the NPV. In the second case, we convert after estimating NPV.

It might appear that the second approach is superior because for it we have to come up with only one number, the euro discount rate. Furthermore, because the first approach requires us to forecast future exchange rates, it probably seems that there is greater room for error with this approach. As we illustrate next, however, based on our previous results, the two approaches are really the same.

METHOD 1: THE HOME CURRENCY APPROACH

To convert the project's future cash flows into dollars, we will invoke the uncovered interest parity, or UIP, relation to come up with the projected exchange rates. Based on our earlier discussion, the expected exchange rate at time t, $E(S_t)$, is:

$$E(S_t) = S_0 \times [1 + (R_{\text{€}} - R_{US})]^t$$

where $R_{\text{€}}$ stands for the nominal risk-free rate in France. Because $R_{\text{€}}$ is 7 percent, R_{US} is 5 percent, and the current exchange rate (S_0) is €.5:

$$E(S_t) = .5 \times [1 + (.07 - .05)]^t$$
$$= .5 \times 1.02^t$$

The projected exchange rates for the drill bit project are shown here:

Year	Expected Exchange Rate
1	€.5 × 1.02^1 = €.5100
2	€.5 × 1.02^2 = €.5202
3	€.5 × 1.02^3 = €.5306

Using these exchange rates, along with the current exchange rate, we can convert all of the euro cash flows to dollars (note that all of the cash flows in this example are in millions):

Year	(1) Cash Flow in €mil	(2) Expected Exchange Rate	(3) Cash Flow in $mil (1)/(2)
0	−€2.0	€.5000	−$4.00
1	.9	.5100	1.76
2	.9	.5202	1.73
3	.9	.5306	1.70

To finish off, we calculate the NPV in the ordinary way:

$$NPV_\$ = -\$4 + \$1.76/1.10 + \$1.73/1.10^2 + \$1.70/1.10^3$$
$$= \$.3 \text{ million}$$

So, the project appears to be profitable.

METHOD 2: THE FOREIGN CURRENCY APPROACH

Kihlstrom requires a nominal return of 10 percent on the dollar-denominated cash flows. We need to convert this to a rate suitable for euro-denominated cash flows. Based on the international Fisher effect, we know that the difference in the nominal rates is:

$$R_\text{€} - R_{US} = h_\text{€} - h_{US}$$
$$= 7\% - 5\% = 2\%$$

The appropriate discount rate for estimating the euro cash flows from the drill bit project is approximately equal to 10 percent plus an extra 2 percent to compensate for the greater euro inflation rate.

If we calculate the NPV of the euro cash flows at this rate, we get:

$$NPV_\text{€} = -\text{€}2 + \text{€}.9/1.12 + \text{€}.9/1.12^2 + \text{€}.9/1.12^3$$
$$= \text{€}.16 \text{ million}$$

The NPV of this project is €.16 million. Taking this project makes us €.16 million richer today. What is this in dollars? Because the exchange rate today is €.5, the dollar NPV of the project is:

$$NPV_\$ = NPV_\text{€}/S_0 = \text{€}.16/.5 = \$.3 \text{ million}$$

This is the same dollar NPV that we previously calculated.

The important thing to recognize from our example is that the two capital budgeting procedures are actually the same and will always give the same answer.[8] In this second approach, the fact that we are implicitly forecasting exchange rates is simply hidden. Even so, the foreign currency approach is computationally a little easier.

UNREMITTED CASH FLOWS

The previous example assumed that all aftertax cash flows from the foreign investment could be remitted to (paid out to) the parent firm. Actually, substantial differences can exist between the cash flows generated by a foreign project and the amount that can be remitted, or "repatriated," to the parent firm.

A foreign subsidiary can remit funds to a parent in many forms, including the following:

1. Dividends.
2. Management fees for central services.
3. Royalties on the use of trade names and patents.

However cash flows are repatriated, international firms must pay special attention to remittances because there may be current and future controls on remittances. Many governments are sensitive to the charge of being exploited by foreign national firms.

---

[8]Actually, there will be a slight difference because we are using the approximate relationships. If we calculate the required return as $1.10 \times (1 + .02) - 1 = .122$ (12.2%), then we get exactly the same NPV. See Problem 18 for more detail.

In such cases, governments are tempted to limit the ability of international firms to remit cash flows. Funds that cannot currently be remitted are sometimes said to be *blocked*.

THE COST OF CAPITAL FOR INTERNATIONAL FIRMS

In the previous chapter, we expressed some skepticism concerning the benefits of firm diversification. We can make a stronger case for diversification in international firms than for purely domestic firms. Suppose barriers prevented shareholders in the United States from holding foreign securities; the financial markets of different countries would be segmented. Further suppose that firms in the United States were not subject to the same barriers. In such a case, a firm engaging in international investing could provide indirect diversification for U.S. shareholders that they could not achieve by investing within the United States. This could lead to the lowering of the risk premium on international projects. In general, if the costs of investing abroad are lower for a firm than for its shareholders, there is an advantage to international diversification by firms, and this advantage will be reflected in a lower risk-adjusted discount rate.

Alternatively, if there were no barriers to international investing for shareholders, shareholders could obtain the benefit of international diversification for themselves by buying foreign securities. In this case, the project cost of capital for a firm in the United States would not depend on whether the project was in the United States or in a foreign country. In practice, holding foreign securities involves substantial expenses. These expenses include taxes, the costs of obtaining information, and trading costs. This implies that although U.S. investors are free to hold foreign securities, they will not be perfectly internationally diversified.

Firms may determine that international investments inherently involve more political risk than domestic investments. This extra risk may offset the gains from international diversification. Firms may increase the discount rate to allow for the risk of expropriation and foreign exchange remittance controls.

31.6 Exchange Rate Risk

Exchange rate risk is the natural consequence of international operations in a world where relative currency values move up and down. Managing exchange rate risk is an important part of international finance. As we discuss next, there are three different types of exchange rate risk or exposure: Short-term exposure, long-term exposure, and translation exposure.

SHORT-TERM EXPOSURE

The day-to-day fluctuations in exchange rates create short-term risks for international firms. Most such firms have contractual agreements to buy and sell goods in the near future at set prices. When different currencies are involved, such transactions have an extra element of risk.

For example, imagine that you are importing imitation pasta from Italy and reselling it in the United States under the Impasta brand name. Your largest customer has ordered 10,000 cases of Impasta. You place the order with your supplier today, but you won't pay until the goods arrive in 60 days. Your selling price is $6 per case. Your cost is 8.4 euros per case, and the exchange rate is currently €1.50, so it takes 1.50 euros to buy $1.

At the current exchange rate, your cost in dollars of filling the order is €8.4/1.5 = $5.60 per case, so your pretax profit on the order is 10,000 × ($6 − 5.60) = $4,000. However, the exchange rate in 60 days will probably be different, so your profit will depend on what the future exchange rate turns out to be.

For example, if the rate goes to €1.6, your cost is €8.4/1.6 = $5.25 per case. Your profit goes to $7,500. If the exchange rate goes to, say, €1.4, then your cost is €8.4/1.4 = $6, and your profit is zero.

The short-term exposure in our example can be reduced or eliminated in several ways. The most obvious way is by entering into a forward exchange agreement to lock in an exchange rate. For example, suppose the 60-day forward rate is €1.58. What will be your profit if you hedge? What profit should you expect if you don't?

If you hedge, you lock in an exchange rate of €1.58. Your cost in dollars will thus be €8.4/1.58 = $5.32 per case, so your profit will be 10,000 × ($6 − 5.32) = $6,800. If you don't hedge, then, assuming that the forward rate is an unbiased predictor (in other words, assuming the UFR condition holds), you should expect that the exchange rate will actually be €1.58 in 60 days. You should expect to make $6,800.

Alternatively, if this strategy is not feasible, you could simply borrow the dollars today, convert them into euros, and invest the euros for 60 days to earn some interest. Based on IRP, this amounts to entering into a forward contract.

LONG-TERM EXPOSURE

In the long term, the value of a foreign operation can fluctuate because of unanticipated changes in relative economic conditions. For example, imagine that we own a labor-intensive assembly operation located in another country to take advantage of lower wages. Through time, unexpected changes in economic conditions can raise the foreign wage levels to the point where the cost advantage is eliminated or even becomes negative.

The impact of changes in exchange rate levels can be substantial. For example, during the fourth quarter of 2014, Coca-Cola estimated that it lost $393 million because of the devaluation of the Venezuelan bolivar alone. Previously, in the first quarter of 2014, Coca-Cola was forced to write off $247 million because of the bolivar's devaluation in that quarter. The dramatic effect of exchange rate movements on profitability is also shown by the analysis done by Iluka Resources, Ltd., an Australian mining company, which stated that a one-cent movement in the Australian dollar–U.S. dollar exchange rate would change its net income by $5 million.

Hedging long-term exposure is more difficult than hedging short-term risks. For one thing, organized forward markets don't exist for such long-term needs. Instead, the primary option that firms have is to try to match up foreign currency inflows and outflows. The same thing goes for matching foreign currency–denominated assets and liabilities. For example, a firm that sells in a foreign country might try to concentrate its raw material purchases and labor expenses in that country. That way, the dollar values of its revenues and costs will move up and down together. Probably the best examples of this type of hedging are the so-called transplant auto manufacturers such as BMW, Honda, Mercedes, and Toyota, which now build a substantial portion of the cars they sell in the United States at plants located in the United States, thereby obtaining some degree of immunization against exchange rate movements.

For example, BMW produces 350,000 cars in South Carolina and exports about 250,000 of them. The costs of manufacturing the cars are paid mostly in dollars, and, when BMW exports the cars to Europe, it receives euros. When the dollar weakens, these vehicles become more profitable for BMW. At the same time, BMW exports many hundreds of thousands of cars to the United States each year. The costs of manufacturing these imported cars are mostly in euros, so they become less profitable when the dollar weakens. Taken together, these gains and losses tend to offset each other and give BMW a natural hedge.

Similarly, a firm can reduce its long-term exchange rate risk by borrowing in the foreign country. Fluctuations in the value of the foreign subsidiary's assets will then be at least partially offset by changes in the value of the liabilities.

TRANSLATION EXPOSURE

When a U.S. company calculates its accounting net income and EPS for some period, it must translate everything into dollars. This can create some problems for the accountants when there are significant foreign operations. In particular, two issues arise:

1. What is the appropriate exchange rate to use for translating each balance sheet account?

2. How should balance sheet accounting gains and losses from foreign currency translation be handled?

To illustrate the accounting problem, suppose we started a small foreign subsidiary in Lilliputia a year ago. The local currency is the gulliver, abbreviated GL. At the beginning of the year, the exchange rate was GL 2 = $1, and the balance sheet in gullivers looked like this:

Assets	GL 1,000	Liabilities	GL 500
		Equity	500

At two gullivers to the dollar, the beginning balance sheet in dollars was as follows:

Assets	$500	Liabilities	$250
		Equity	250

Lilliputia is a quiet place, and nothing at all actually happened during the year. As a result, net income was zero (before consideration of exchange rate changes). However, the exchange rate did change to 4 gullivers = $1 purely because the Lilliputian inflation rate is much higher than the U.S. inflation rate.

Because nothing happened, the accounting ending balance sheet in gullivers is the same as the beginning one. However, if we convert it to dollars at the new exchange rate, we get these figures:

Assets	$250	Liabilities	$125
		Equity	125

Notice that the value of the equity has gone down by $125, even though net income was exactly zero. Despite the fact that absolutely nothing happened, there is a $125 accounting loss. How to handle this $125 loss has been a controversial accounting question.

One obvious and consistent way to handle this loss is simply to report the loss on the parent's income statement. During periods of volatile exchange rates, this kind of treatment can dramatically impact an international company's reported EPS. This is purely an accounting phenomenon, but even so, such fluctuations are disliked by some financial managers.

The current approach to handling translation gains and losses is based on rules set out in the Financial Accounting Standards Board (FASB) *Statement of Financial Accounting*

Standards No. 52 (*FASB 52*), issued in December 1981. For the most part, *FASB 52* requires that all assets and liabilities be translated from the subsidiary's currency into the parent's currency using the exchange rate that currently prevails.

Any translation gains and losses that occur are accumulated in a special account within the shareholders' equity section of the balance sheet. This account might be labeled something like "unrealized foreign exchange gains (losses)." The amounts involved can be substantial, at least from an accounting standpoint. These gains and losses are not reported on the income statement. As a result, the impact of translation gains and losses will not be recognized explicitly in net income until the underlying assets and liabilities are sold or otherwise liquidated.

MANAGING EXCHANGE RATE RISK

For a large multinational firm, the management of exchange rate risk is complicated by the fact that there can be many different currencies involved in many different subsidiaries. It is likely that a change in some exchange rate will benefit some subsidiaries and hurt others. The net effect on the overall firm depends on its net exposure.

For example, suppose a firm has two divisions. Division *A* buys goods in the United States for dollars and sells them in Britain for pounds. Division *B* buys goods in Britain for pounds and sells them in the United States for dollars. If these two divisions are of roughly equal size in terms of their inflows and outflows, then the overall firm obviously has little exchange rate risk.

In our example, if the firm's net position in pounds (the amount coming in less the amount going out) is small, the exchange rate risk is small. However, if one division, acting on its own, were to start hedging its exchange rate risk, then the overall firm's exchange rate risk would go up. The moral of the story is that multinational firms have to be conscious of the overall position that the firm has in a foreign currency. For this reason, management of exchange rate risk is probably best handled on a centralized basis.

31.7 Political Risk

One final element of risk in international investing is **political risk**: Changes in value that arise as a consequence of political actions. This is not a problem faced exclusively by international firms. For example, changes in U.S. tax laws and regulations may benefit some U.S. firms and hurt others, so political risk exists nationally as well as internationally.

Some countries have more political risk than others, however. When firms have operations in these riskier countries, the extra political risk may lead the firms to require higher returns on overseas investments to compensate for the possibility that funds may be blocked, critical operations interrupted, and contracts abrogated. In the most extreme case, the possibility of outright confiscation may be a concern in countries with relatively unstable political environments.

Political risk also depends on the nature of the business: Some businesses are less likely to be confiscated because they are not particularly valuable in the hands of a different owner. An assembly operation supplying subcomponents that only the parent company uses would not be an attractive takeover target, for example. Similarly, a manufacturing operation that requires the use of specialized components from the parent is of little value without the parent company's cooperation.

Natural resource developments, such as copper mining and oil drilling, are just the opposite. Once the operation is in place, much of the value is in the commodity.

The political risk for such investments is much higher for this reason. Also, the issue of exploitation is more pronounced with such investments, again increasing the political risk.

Political risk can be hedged in several ways, particularly when confiscation or nationalization is a concern. The use of local financing, perhaps from the government of the foreign country in question, reduces the possible loss because the company can refuse to pay the debt in the event of unfavorable political activities. Based on our discussion in this section, structuring the operation in such a way that it requires significant parent company involvement to function is another way to reduce political risk.

Summary and Conclusions

The international firm has a more complicated life than the purely domestic firm. Management must understand the connection between interest rates, foreign currency exchange rates, and inflation, and it must become aware of many different financial market regulations and tax systems. This chapter is intended to be a concise introduction to some of the financial issues that come up in international finance.

Our coverage has been necessarily brief. The main topics we discussed are the following:

1. **Some basic vocabulary:** We briefly defined some exotic terms such as *LIBOR* and *Eurocurrency.*

2. **The basic mechanics of exchange rate quotations:** We discussed the spot and forward markets and how exchange rates are interpreted.

3. **The fundamental relationships between international financial variables:**
   a. Absolute and relative purchasing power parity, PPP.
   b. Interest rate parity, IRP.
   c. Unbiased forward rates, UFR.

   Absolute purchasing power parity states that $1 should have the same purchasing power in each country. This means that an orange costs the same whether you buy it in New York or in Tokyo.

   Relative purchasing power parity means that the expected percentage change in exchange rates between the currencies of two countries is equal to the difference in their inflation rates.

   Interest rate parity implies that the percentage difference between the forward exchange rate and the spot exchange rate is equal to the interest rate differential. We showed how covered interest arbitrage forces this relationship to hold.

   The unbiased forward rates condition indicates that the current forward rate is a good predictor of the future spot exchange rate.

4. **International capital budgeting:** We showed that the basic foreign exchange relationships imply two other conditions:
   a. Uncovered interest parity.
   b. The international Fisher effect.

   By invoking these two conditions, we learned how to estimate NPVs in foreign currencies and how to convert foreign currencies into dollars to estimate NPV in the usual way.

5. **Exchange rate and political risk:** We described the various types of exchange rate risk and discussed some common approaches to managing the effect of fluctuating exchange rates on the cash flows and value of the international firm. We also discussed political risk and some ways of managing exposure to it.

Concept Questions

1. **Spot and Forward Rates**   Suppose the exchange rate for the Swiss franc is quoted as SF 1.09 in the spot market and SF 1.11 in the 90-day forward market.

   a. Is the dollar selling at a premium or a discount relative to the franc?
   b. Does the financial market expect the franc to strengthen relative to the dollar? Explain.
   c. What do you suspect is true about relative economic conditions in the United States and Switzerland?

2. **Purchasing Power Parity**   Suppose the rate of inflation in Mexico will run about 3 percent higher than the U.S. inflation rate over the next several years. All other things being the same, what will happen to the Mexican peso versus dollar exchange rate? What relationship are you relying on in answering?

3. **Exchange Rates**   The exchange rate for the Australian dollar is currently A$1.40. This exchange rate is expected to rise by 10 percent over the next year.

   a. Is the Australian dollar expected to get stronger or weaker?
   b. What do you think about the relative inflation rates in the United States and Australia?
   c. What do you think about the relative nominal interest rates in the United States and Australia? Relative real rates?

4. **Exchange Rates**   Are exchange rate changes necessarily good or bad for a particular company?

5. **International Risks**   At one point, Duracell International confirmed that it was planning to open battery manufacturing plants in China and India. Manufacturing in these countries allows Duracell to avoid import duties of between 30 and 35 percent that have made alkaline batteries prohibitively expensive for some consumers. What additional advantages might Duracell see in this proposal? What are some of the risks to Duracell?

6. **Multinational Corporations**   Given that many multinationals based in many countries have much greater sales outside their domestic markets than within them, what is the particular relevance of their domestic currency?

7. **Exchange Rate Movements**   Are the following statements true or false? Explain why.

   a. If the general price index in Great Britain rises faster than that in the United States, we would expect the pound to appreciate relative to the dollar.
   b. Suppose you are a German machine tool exporter, and you invoice all of your sales in foreign currency. Further suppose that the euro monetary authorities begin to undertake an expansionary monetary policy. If it is certain that the easy money policy will result in higher inflation rates in Germany relative to those in other countries, then you should use the forward markets to protect yourself against future losses resulting from the deterioration in the value of the euro.
   c. If you could accurately estimate differences in the relative inflation rates of two countries over a long period while other market participants were unable to do so, you could successfully speculate in spot currency markets.

8. **Exchange Rate Movements**   Some countries encourage movements in their exchange rate relative to those of some other country as a short-term means of addressing foreign trade imbalances. For each of the following scenarios, evaluate the impact the announcement would have on an American importer and an American exporter doing business with the foreign country:

   a. Officials in the administration of the U.S. government announce that they are comfortable with a rising euro relative to the dollar.
   b. British monetary authorities announce that they feel the pound has been driven too low by currency speculators relative to the dollar.

c. The Brazilian government announces that it will print billions of new reais and inject them into the economy in an effort to reduce the country's unemployment rate.

9. **International Capital Market Relationships** We discussed five international capital market relationships: Relative PPP, IRP, UFR, UIP, and the international Fisher effect. Which of these would you expect to hold most closely? Which do you think would be most likely to be violated?

10. **Exchange Rate Risk** If you are an exporter who must make payments in foreign currency three months after receiving each shipment and you predict that the domestic currency will appreciate in value over this period, is there any value in hedging your currency exposure?

11. **International Capital Budgeting** Suppose it is your task to evaluate two different investments in new subsidiaries for your company, one in your own country and the other in a foreign country. You calculate the cash flows of both projects to be identical after exchange rate differences. Under what circumstances might you choose to invest in the foreign subsidiary? Give an example of a country where certain factors might influence you to alter this decision and invest at home.

12. **International Capital Budgeting** An investment in a foreign subsidiary is estimated to have a positive NPV after the discount rate used in the calculations is adjusted for political risk and any advantages from diversification. Does this mean the project is acceptable? Why or why not?

13. **International Borrowing** If a U.S. firm raises funds for a foreign subsidiary, what are the disadvantages to borrowing in the United States? How would you overcome them?

14. **International Investment** If financial markets are perfectly competitive and the Eurodollar rate is above that offered in the U.S. loan market, you would immediately want to borrow money in the United States and invest it in Eurodollars. True or false? Explain.

Questions and Problems

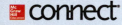

BASIC
(Questions 1–13)

1. **Using Exchange Rates** Take a look back at Figure 31.1 to answer the following questions:

   a. If you have $100, how many euros can you get?
   b. How much is one euro worth in dollars?
   c. If you have 5 million euros, how many dollars do you have?
   d. Which is worth more, a New Zealand dollar or a Singapore dollar?
   e. Which is worth more, a Mexican peso or a Chilean peso?
   f. How many Mexican pesos can you get for a euro? What do you call this rate?
   g. Per unit, what is the most valuable currency of those listed? The least valuable?

2. **Using the Cross-Rate** Use the information in Figure 31.1 to answer the following questions:

   a. Which would you rather have, $100 or £100? Why?
   b. Which would you rather have, 100 Swiss francs (SF) or £100? Why?
   c. What is the cross-rate for Swiss francs in terms of British pounds? For British pounds in terms of Swiss francs?

3. **Forward Exchange Rates** Use the information in Figure 31.1 to answer the following questions:

   a. What is the six-month forward rate for the Japanese yen in yen per U.S. dollar? Is the yen selling at a premium or a discount? Explain.

b. What is the three-month forward rate for British pounds in U.S. dollars per pound? Is the dollar selling at a premium or a discount? Explain.

c. What do you think will happen to the value of the dollar relative to the yen and the pound, based on the information in the figure? Explain.

4. **Using Spot and Forward Exchange Rates**   Suppose the spot exchange rate for the Canadian dollar is Can\$1.13 and the six-month forward rate is Can\$1.16.

   a. Which is worth more, a U.S. dollar or a Canadian dollar?

   b. Assuming absolute PPP holds, what is the cost in the United States of an Elkhead beer if the price in Canada is Can\$2.50? Why might the beer actually sell at a different price in the United States?

   c. Is the U.S. dollar selling at a premium or a discount relative to the Canadian dollar?

   d. Which currency is expected to appreciate in value?

   e. Which country do you think has higher interest rates—the United States or Canada? Explain.

5. **Cross-Rates and Arbitrage**   Suppose the Japanese yen exchange rate is ¥126 = \$1, and the British pound exchange rate is £1 = \$1.53.

   a. What is the cross-rate in terms of yen per pound?

   b. Suppose the cross-rate is ¥195.8 = £1. Is there an arbitrage opportunity here? If there is, explain how to take advantage of the mispricing.

6. **Interest Rate Parity**   Use Figure 31.1 to answer the following questions. Suppose interest rate parity holds, and the current six-month risk-free rate in the United States is 1.9 percent. What must the six-month risk-free rate be in Great Britain? In Japan? In Switzerland?

7. **Interest Rates and Arbitrage**   The treasurer of a major U.S. firm has \$30 million to invest for three months. The annual interest rate in the United States is .17 percent per month. The interest rate in Great Britain is .61 percent per month. The spot exchange rate is £.64, and the three-month forward rate is £.65. Ignoring transaction costs, in which country would the treasurer want to invest the company's funds? Why?

8. **Inflation and Exchange Rates**   Suppose the current exchange rate for the Polish zloty is Z 3.29. The expected exchange rate in three years is Z 3.41. What is the difference in the annual inflation rates for the United States and Poland over this period? Assume that the anticipated rate is constant for both countries. What relationship are you relying on in answering?

 9. **Exchange Rate Risk**   Suppose your company imports computer motherboards from Singapore. The exchange rate is given in Figure 31.1. You have just placed an order for 30,000 motherboards at a cost to you of 141.30 Singapore dollars each. You will pay for the shipment when it arrives in 90 days. You can sell the motherboards for \$115 each. Calculate your profit if the exchange rate goes up or down by 10 percent over the next 90 days. What is the break-even exchange rate? What percentage rise or fall does this represent in terms of the Singapore dollar versus the U.S. dollar?

10. **Exchange Rates and Arbitrage**   Suppose the spot and six-month forward rates on the Norwegian krone are Kr 6.97 and Kr 7.06, respectively. The annual risk-free rate in the United States is 3 percent, and the annual risk-free rate in Norway is 5 percent.

   a. Is there an arbitrage opportunity here? If so, how would you exploit it?

   b. What must the six-month forward rate be to prevent arbitrage?

11. **The International Fisher Effect**   You observe that the inflation rate in the United States is 1.8 percent per year and that T-bills currently yield 1.95 percent annually. What do you estimate the inflation rate to be in:

   a. Australia if short-term Australian government securities yield 4 percent per year?

   b. Canada if short-term Canadian government securities yield 6 percent per year?

   c. Taiwan if short-term Taiwanese government securities yield 9 percent per year?

12. **Spot versus Forward Rates** Suppose the spot and three-month forward rates for the yen are ¥115.13 and ¥114.35, respectively.

   a. Is the yen expected to get stronger or weaker?
   b. What would you estimate is the difference between the inflation rates of the United States and Japan?

13. **Expected Spot Rates** Suppose the spot exchange rate for the Hungarian forint is HUF 251. The inflation rate in the United States is 2.8 percent per year and is 3.7 percent in Hungary. What do you predict the exchange rate will be in one year? In two years? In five years? What relationship are you using?

INTERMEDIATE
(Questions 14–16)

14. **Capital Budgeting** Lakonishok Equipment has an investment opportunity in Europe. The project costs €19 million and is expected to produce cash flows of €3.6 million in Year 1, €4.1 million in Year 2, and €5.1 million in Year 3. The current spot exchange rate is $1.04/€ and the current risk-free rate in the United States is 3.1 percent, compared to that in Europe of 2.9 percent. The appropriate discount rate for the project is estimated to be 10.5 percent, the U.S. cost of capital for the company. In addition, the subsidiary can be sold at the end of three years for an estimated €12.7 million. What is the NPV of the project?

15. **Capital Budgeting** You are evaluating a proposed expansion of an existing subsidiary located in Switzerland. The cost of the expansion would be SF 25 million. The cash flows from the project would be SF 6.9 million per year for the next five years. The dollar required return is 12 percent per year, and the current exchange rate is SF 1.17. The going rate on Eurodollars is 6 percent per year. It is 5 percent per year on Swiss francs.

   a. What do you project will happen to exchange rates over the next four years?
   b. Based on your answer in (a), convert the projected franc flows into dollar flows and calculate the NPV.
   c. What is the required return on franc flows? Based on your answer, calculate the NPV in francs and then convert to dollars.

16. **Translation Exposure** Atreides International has operations in Arrakis. The balance sheet for this division in Arrakeen solaris shows assets of 43,000 solaris, debt in the amount of 14,000 solaris, and equity of 29,000 solaris.

   a. If the current exchange ratio is 1.20 solaris per dollar, what does the balance sheet look like in dollars?
   b. Assume that one year from now the balance sheet in solaris is exactly the same as at the beginning of the year. If the exchange rate is 1.40 solaris per dollar, what does the balance sheet look like in dollars now?
   c. Rework part (b) assuming the exchange rate is 1.12 solaris per dollar.

CHALLENGE
(Questions 17–18)

17. **Translation Exposure** In the previous problem, assume the equity increases by 1,750 solaris due to retained earnings. If the exchange rate at the end of the year is 1.24 solaris per dollar, what does the balance sheet look like?

18. **Using the Exact International Fisher Effect** From our discussion of the Fisher effect in Chapter 8, we know that the actual relationship between a nominal rate, R, a real rate, r, and an inflation rate, h, can be written as follows:

$$1 + r = (1 + R)/(1 + h)$$

This is the *domestic* Fisher effect.

   a. What is the nonapproximate form of the international Fisher effect?
   b. Based on your answer in (a), what is the exact form for UIP? (*Hint:* Recall the exact form of IRP and use UFR.)
   c. What is the exact form for relative PPP? (*Hint:* Combine your previous two answers.)
   d. Recalculate the NPV for the Kihlstrom drill bit project (discussed in Section 31.5) using the exact forms for the UIP and the international Fisher effect. Verify that you get precisely the same answer either way.

Excel Master It! Problem

The St. Louis Federal Reserve has historical exchange rates on its website, www.stlouisfed .org. On the website, look for the FRED data. Download the exchange rate with U.S. dollars over the past five years for the following currencies: Brazilian reals, Canadian dollars, Hong Kong dollars, Japanese yen, Mexican new pesos, South Korean won, Indian rupees, Swiss francs, Australian dollars, and euros. Graph the exchange rate for each of these currencies in a dashboard that can be printed on one page.

Mini Case

EAST COAST YACHTS GOES INTERNATIONAL

Larissa Warren, the owner of East Coast Yachts, has been in discussions with a yacht dealer in Monaco about selling the company's yachts in Europe. Jarek Jachowicz, the dealer, wants to add East Coast Yachts to his current retail line. Jarek has told Larissa that he feels the retail sales will be approximately €8 million per month. All sales will be made in euros, and Jarek will retain 5 percent of the retail sales as commission, which will be paid in euros. Because the yachts will be customized to order, the first sales will take place in one month. Jarek will pay East Coast Yachts for the order 90 days after it is filled. This payment schedule will continue for the length of the contract between the two companies.

Larissa is confident the company can handle the extra volume with its existing facilities, but she is unsure about any potential financial risks of selling yachts in Europe. In her discussion with Jarek she found that the current exchange rate is $1.34/€. At this exchange rate the company would spend 80 percent of the sales income on production costs. This number does not reflect the sales commission to be paid to Jarek.

Larissa has decided to ask Dan Ervin, the company's financial analyst, to prepare an analysis of the proposed international sales. Specifically, she asks Dan to answer the following questions:

1. What are the pros and cons of the international sales plan? What additional risks will the company face?

2. What will happen to the company's profits if the dollar strengthens? What if the dollar weakens?

3. Ignoring taxes, what are East Coast Yachts' projected gains or losses from this proposed arrangement at the current exchange rate of $1.34/€? What will happen to profits if the exchange rate changes to $1.25/€? At what exchange rate will the company break even?

4. How can the company hedge its exchange rate risk? What are the implications for this approach?

5. Taking all factors into account, should the company pursue international sales further? Why or why not?

Appendix A

Mathematical Tables

Table A.1
Present Value of \$1 to Be Received after T Periods $= 1/(1 + r)^T$

Table A.2
Present Value of an Annuity of \$1 per Period for T Periods $= [1 - 1/(1 + r)^T]/r$

Table A.3
Future Value of \$1 at the End of T Periods $= (1 + r)^T$

Table A.4
Future Value of an Annuity of \$1 per Period for T Periods $= [(1 + r)^T - 1]/r$

Table A.5
Future Value of \$1 with a Continuously Compounded Rate r for T Periods:
Values of e^{rT}

Table A.6
Present Value of \$1 with a Continuous Discount Rate r for T Periods: Values of e^{-rT}

Table A.1 Present Value of $1 to Be Received after T Periods = $1/(1 + r)^T$

Period	1%	2%	3%	4%	5%	6%	7%	8%	9%
1	.9901	.9804	.9709	.9615	.9524	.9434	.9346	.9259	.9174
2	.9803	.9612	.9426	.9246	.9070	.8900	.8734	.8573	.8417
3	.9706	.9423	.9151	.8890	.8638	.8396	.8163	.7938	.7722
4	.9610	.9238	.8885	.8548	.8227	.7921	.7629	.7350	.7084
5	.9515	.9057	.8626	.8219	.7835	.7473	.7130	.6806	.6499
6	.9420	.8880	.8375	.7903	.7462	.7050	.6663	.6302	.5963
7	.9327	.8706	.8131	.7599	.7107	.6651	.6227	.5835	.5470
8	.9235	.8535	.7894	.7307	.6768	.6274	.5820	.5403	.5019
9	.9143	.8368	.7664	.7026	.6446	.5919	.5439	.5002	.4604
10	.9053	.8203	.7441	.6756	.6139	.5584	.5083	.4632	.4224
11	.8963	.8043	.7224	.6496	.5847	.5268	.4751	.4289	.3875
12	.8874	.7885	.7014	.6246	.5568	.4970	.4440	.3971	.3555
13	.8787	.7730	.6810	.6006	.5303	.4688	.4150	.3677	.3262
14	.8700	.7579	.6611	.5775	.5051	.4423	.3878	.3405	.2992
15	.8613	.7430	.6419	.5553	.4810	.4173	.3624	.3152	.2745
16	.8528	.7284	.6232	.5339	.4581	.3936	.3387	.2919	.2519
17	.8444	.7142	.6050	.5134	.4363	.3714	.3166	.2703	.2311
18	.8360	.7002	.5874	.4936	.4155	.3503	.2959	.2502	.2120
19	.8277	.6864	.5703	.4746	.3957	.3305	.2765	.2317	.1945
20	.8195	.6730	.5537	.4564	.3769	.3118	.2584	.2145	.1784
21	.8114	.6598	.5375	.4388	.3589	.2942	.2415	.1987	.1637
22	.8034	.6468	.5219	.4220	.3418	.2775	.2257	.1839	.1502
23	.7954	.6342	.5067	.4057	.3256	.2618	.2109	.1703	.1378
24	.7876	.6217	.4919	.3901	.3101	.2470	.1971	.1577	.1264
25	.7798	.6095	.4776	.3751	.2953	.2330	.1842	.1460	.1160
30	.7419	.5521	.4120	.3083	.2314	.1741	.1314	.0994	.0754
40	.6717	.4529	.3066	.2083	.1420	.0972	.0668	.0460	.0318
50	.6080	.3715	.2281	.1407	.0872	.0543	.0339	.0213	.0134

Period	10%	12%	14%	15%	16%	18%	20%	24%	28%	32%	36%
1	.9091	.8929	.8772	.8696	.8621	.8475	.8333	.8065	.7813	.7576	.7353
2	.8264	.7972	.7695	.7561	.7432	.7182	.6944	.6504	.6104	.5739	.5407
3	.7513	.7118	.6750	.6575	.6407	.6086	.5787	.5245	.4768	.4348	.3975
4	.6830	.6355	.5921	.5718	.5523	.5158	.4823	.4230	.3725	.3294	.2923
5	.6209	.5674	.5194	.4972	.4761	.4371	.4019	.3411	.2910	.2495	.2149
6	.5645	.5066	.4556	.4323	.4104	.3704	.3349	.2751	.2274	.1890	.1580
7	.5132	.4523	.3996	.3759	.3538	.3139	.2791	.2218	.1776	.1432	.1162
8	.4665	.4039	.3506	.3269	.3050	.2660	.2326	.1789	.1388	.1085	.0854
9	.4241	.3606	.3075	.2843	.2630	.2255	.1938	.1443	.1084	.0822	.0628
10	.3855	.3220	.2697	.2472	.2267	.1911	.1615	.1164	.0847	.0623	.0462
11	.3505	.2875	.2366	.2149	.1954	.1619	.1346	.0938	.0662	.0472	.0340
12	.3186	.2567	.2076	.1869	.1685	.1372	.1122	.0757	.0517	.0357	.0250
13	.2897	.2292	.1821	.1625	.1452	.1163	.0935	.0610	.0404	.0271	.0184
14	.2633	.2046	.1597	.1413	.1252	.0985	.0779	.0492	.0316	.0205	.0135
15	.2394	.1827	.1401	.1229	.1079	.0835	.0649	.0397	.0247	.0155	.0099
16	.2176	.1631	.1229	.1069	.0930	.0708	.0541	.0320	.0193	.0118	.0073
17	.1978	.1456	.1078	.0929	.0802	.0600	.0451	.0258	.0150	.0089	.0054
18	.1799	.1300	.0946	.0808	.0691	.0508	.0376	.0208	.0118	.0068	.0039
19	.1635	.1161	.0829	.0703	.0596	.0431	.0313	.0168	.0092	.0051	.0029
20	.1486	.1037	.0728	.0611	.0514	.0365	.0261	.0135	.0072	.0039	.0021
21	.1351	.0926	.0638	.0531	.0443	.0309	.0217	.0109	.0056	.0029	.0016
22	.1228	.0826	.0560	.0462	.0382	.0262	.0181	.0088	.0044	.0022	.0012
23	.1117	.0738	.0491	.0402	.0329	.0222	.0151	.0071	.0034	.0017	.0008
24	.1015	.0659	.0431	.0349	.0284	.0188	.0126	.0057	.0027	.0013	.0006
25	.0923	.0588	.0378	.0304	.0245	.0160	.0105	.0046	.0021	.0010	.0005
30	.0573	.0334	.0196	.0151	.0116	.0070	.0042	.0016	.0006	.0002	.0001
40	.0221	.0107	.0053	.0037	.0026	.0013	.0007	.0002	.0001	*	*
50	.0085	.0035	.0014	.0009	.0006	.0003	.0001	*	*	*	*

*The factor is zero to four decimal places.

Table A.2 Present Value of an Annuity of $1 per Period for T Periods = $[1 - 1/(1 + r)^T]/r$

					Interest Rate				
Number of Periods	1%	2%	3%	4%	5%	6%	7%	8%	9%
1	.9901	.9804	.9709	.9615	.9524	.9434	.9346	.9259	.9174
2	1.9704	1.9416	1.9135	1.8861	1.8594	1.8334	1.8080	1.7833	1.7591
3	2.9410	2.8839	2.8286	2.7751	2.7232	2.6730	2.6243	2.5771	2.5313
4	3.9020	3.8077	3.7171	3.6299	3.5460	3.4651	3.3872	3.3121	3.2397
5	4.8534	4.7135	4.5797	4.4518	4.3295	4.2124	4.1002	3.9927	3.8897
6	5.7955	5.6014	5.4172	5.2421	5.0757	4.9173	4.7665	4.6229	4.4859
7	6.7282	6.4720	6.2303	6.0021	5.7864	5.5824	5.3893	5.2064	5.0330
8	7.6517	7.3255	7.0197	6.7327	6.4632	6.2098	5.9713	5.7466	5.5348
9	8.5660	8.1622	7.7861	7.4353	7.1078	6.8017	6.5152	6.2469	5.9952
10	9.4713	8.9826	8.5302	8.1109	7.7217	7.3601	7.0236	6.7101	6.4177
11	10.3676	9.7868	9.2526	8.7605	8.3064	7.8869	7.4987	7.1390	6.8052
12	11.2551	10.5753	9.9540	9.3851	8.8633	8.3838	7.9427	7.5361	7.1607
13	12.1337	11.3484	10.6350	9.9856	9.3936	8.8527	8.3577	7.9038	7.4869
14	13.0037	12.1062	11.2961	10.5631	9.8986	9.2950	8.7455	8.2442	7.7862
15	13.8651	12.8493	11.9379	11.1184	10.3797	9.7122	9.1079	8.5595	8.0607
16	14.7179	13.5777	12.5611	11.6523	10.8378	10.1059	9.4466	8.8514	8.3126
17	15.5623	14.2919	13.1661	12.1657	11.2741	10.4773	9.7632	9.1216	8.5436
18	16.3983	14.9920	13.7535	12.6593	11.6896	10.8276	10.0591	9.3719	8.7556
19	17.2260	15.6785	14.3238	13.1339	12.0853	11.1581	10.3356	9.6036	8.9501
20	18.0456	16.3514	14.8775	13.5903	12.4622	11.4699	10.5940	9.8181	9.1285
21	18.8570	17.0112	15.4150	14.0292	12.8212	11.7641	10.8355	10.0168	9.2922
22	19.6604	17.6580	15.9369	14.4511	13.1630	12.0416	11.0612	10.2007	9.4424
23	20.4558	18.2922	16.4436	14.8568	13.4886	12.3034	11.2722	10.3741	9.5802
24	21.2434	18.9139	16.9355	15.2470	13.7986	12.5504	11.4693	10.5288	9.7066
25	22.0232	19.5235	17.4131	15.6221	14.0939	12.7834	11.6536	10.6748	9.8226
30	25.8077	22.3965	19.6004	17.2920	15.3725	13.7648	12.4090	11.2578	10.2737
40	32.8347	27.3555	23.1148	19.7928	17.1591	15.0463	13.3317	11.9246	10.7574
50	39.1961	31.4236	25.7298	21.4822	18.2559	15.7619	13.8007	12.2335	10.9617

Number of Periods	10%	12%	14%	15%	16%	18%	20%	24%	28%	32%
1	.9091	.8929	.8772	.8696	.8621	.8475	.8333	.8065	.7813	.7576
2	1.7355	1.6901	1.6467	1.6257	1.6052	1.5656	1.5278	1.4568	1.3916	1.3315
3	2.4869	2.4018	2.3216	2.2832	2.2459	2.1743	2.1065	1.9813	1.8684	1.7663
4	3.1699	3.0373	2.9137	2.8550	2.7982	2.6901	2.5887	2.4043	2.2410	2.0957
5	3.7908	3.6048	3.4331	3.3522	3.2743	3.1272	2.9906	2.7454	2.5320	2.3452
6	4.3553	4.1114	3.8887	3.7845	3.6847	3.4976	3.3255	3.0205	2.7594	2.5342
7	4.8684	4.5638	4.2883	4.1604	4.0386	3.8115	3.6046	3.2423	2.9370	2.6775
8	5.3349	4.9676	4.6389	4.4873	4.3436	4.0776	3.8372	3.4212	3.0758	2.7860
9	5.7590	5.3282	4.9464	4.7716	4.6065	4.3030	4.0310	3.5655	3.1842	2.8681
10	6.1446	5.6502	5.2161	5.0188	4.8332	4.4941	4.1925	3.6819	3.2689	2.9304
11	6.4951	5.9377	5.4527	5.2337	5.0286	4.6560	4.3271	3.7757	3.3351	2.9776
12	6.8137	6.1944	5.6603	5.4206	5.1971	4.7932	4.4392	3.8514	3.3868	3.0133
13	7.1034	6.4235	5.8424	5.5831	5.3423	4.9095	4.5327	3.9124	3.4272	3.0404
14	7.3667	6.6282	6.0021	5.7245	5.4675	5.0081	4.6106	3.9616	3.4587	3.0609
15	7.6061	6.8109	6.1422	5.8474	5.5755	5.0916	4.6755	4.0013	3.4834	3.0764
16	7.8237	6.9740	6.2651	5.9542	5.6685	5.1624	4.7296	4.0333	3.5026	3.0882
17	8.0216	7.1196	6.3729	6.0472	5.7487	5.2223	4.7746	4.0591	3.5177	3.0971
18	8.2014	7.2497	6.4674	6.1280	5.8178	5.2732	4.8122	4.0799	3.5294	3.1039
19	8.3649	7.3658	6.5504	6.1982	5.8775	5.3162	4.8435	4.0967	3.5386	3.1090
20	8.5136	7.4694	6.6231	6.2593	5.9288	5.3527	4.8696	4.1103	3.5458	3.1129
21	8.6487	7.5620	6.6870	6.3125	5.9731	5.3837	4.8913	4.1212	3.5514	3.1158
22	8.7715	7.6446	6.7429	6.3587	6.0113	5.4099	4.9094	4.1300	3.5558	3.1180
23	8.8832	7.7184	6.7921	6.3988	6.0442	5.4321	4.9245	4.1371	3.5592	3.1197
24	8.9847	7.7843	6.8351	6.4338	6.0726	5.4509	4.9371	4.1428	3.5619	3.1210
25	9.0770	7.8431	6.8729	6.4641	6.0971	5.4669	4.9476	4.1474	3.5640	3.1220
30	9.4269	8.0552	7.0027	6.5660	6.1772	5.5168	4.9789	4.1601	3.5693	3.1242
40	9.7791	8.2438	7.1050	6.6418	6.2335	5.5482	4.9966	4.1659	3.5712	3.1250
50	9.9148	8.3045	7.1327	6.6605	6.2463	5.5541	4.9995	4.1666	3.5714	3.1250

Table A.3   Future Value of $1 at the End of T Periods $= (1 + r)^T$

					Interest Rate				
Period	**1%**	**2%**	**3%**	**4%**	**5%**	**6%**	**7%**	**8%**	**9%**
1	1.0100	1.0200	1.0300	1.0400	1.0500	1.0600	1.0700	1.0800	1.0900
2	1.0201	1.0404	1.0609	1.0816	1.1025	1.1236	1.1449	1.1664	1.1881
3	1.0303	1.0612	1.0927	1.1249	1.1576	1.1910	1.2250	1.2597	1.2950
4	1.0406	1.0824	1.1255	1.1699	1.2155	1.2625	1.3108	1.3605	1.4116
5	1.0510	1.1041	1.1593	1.2167	1.2763	1.3382	1.4026	1.4693	1.5386
6	1.0615	1.1262	1.1941	1.2653	1.3401	1.4185	1.5007	1.5869	1.6771
7	1.0721	1.1487	1.2299	1.3159	1.4071	1.5036	1.6058	1.7138	1.8280
8	1.0829	1.1717	1.2668	1.3686	1.4775	1.5938	1.7182	1.8509	1.9926
9	1.0937	1.1951	1.3048	1.4233	1.5513	1.6895	1.8385	1.9990	2.1719
10	1.1046	1.2190	1.3439	1.4802	1.6289	1.7908	1.9672	2.1589	2.3674
11	1.1157	1.2434	1.3842	1.5395	1.7103	1.8983	2.1049	2.3316	2.5804
12	1.1268	1.2682	1.4258	1.6010	1.7959	2.0122	2.2522	2.5182	2.8127
13	1.1381	1.2936	1.4685	1.6651	1.8856	2.1329	2.4098	2.7196	3.0658
14	1.1495	1.3195	1.5126	1.7317	1.9799	2.2609	2.5785	2.9372	3.3417
15	1.1610	1.3459	1.5580	1.8009	2.0789	2.3966	2.7590	3.1722	3.6425
16	1.1726	1.3728	1.6047	1.8730	2.1829	2.5404	2.9522	3.4259	3.9703
17	1.1843	1.4002	1.6528	1.9479	2.2920	2.6928	3.1588	3.7000	4.3276
18	1.1961	1.4282	1.7024	2.0258	2.4066	2.8543	3.3799	3.9960	4.7171
19	1.2081	1.4568	1.7535	2.1068	2.5270	3.0256	3.6165	4.3157	5.1417
20	1.2202	1.4859	1.8061	2.1911	2.6533	3.2071	3.8697	4.6610	5.6044
21	1.2324	1.5157	1.8603	2.2788	2.7860	3.3996	4.1406	5.0338	6.1088
22	1.2447	1.5460	1.9161	2.3699	2.9253	3.6035	4.4304	5.4365	6.6586
23	1.2572	1.5769	1.9736	2.4647	3.0715	3.8197	4.7405	5.8715	7.2579
24	1.2697	1.6084	2.0328	2.5633	3.2251	4.0489	5.0724	6.3412	7.9111
25	1.2824	1.6406	2.0938	2.6658	3.3864	4.2919	5.4274	6.8485	8.6231
30	1.3478	1.8114	2.4273	3.2434	4.3219	5.7435	7.6123	10.063	13.268
40	1.4889	2.2080	3.2620	4.8010	7.0400	10.286	14.974	21.725	31.409
50	1.6446	2.6916	4.3839	7.1067	11.467	18.420	29.457	46.902	74.358
60	1.8167	3.2810	5.8916	10.520	18.679	32.988	57.946	101.26	176.03

Period	**10%**	**12%**	**14%**	**15%**	**16%**	**18%**	**20%**	**24%**	**28%**	**32%**	**36%**
1	1.1000	1.1200	1.1400	1.1500	1.1600	1.1800	1.2000	1.2400	1.2800	1.3200	1.3600
2	1.2100	1.2544	1.2996	1.3225	1.3456	1.3924	1.4400	1.5376	1.6384	1.7424	1.8496
3	1.3310	1.4049	1.4815	1.5209	1.5609	1.6430	1.7280	1.9066	2.0972	2.3000	2.5155
4	1.4641	1.5735	1.6890	1.7490	1.8106	1.9388	2.0736	2.3642	2.6844	3.0360	3.4210
5	1.6105	1.7623	1.9254	2.0114	2.1003	2.2878	2.4883	2.9316	3.4360	4.0075	4.6526
6	1.7716	1.9738	2.1950	2.3131	2.4364	2.6996	2.9860	3.6352	4.3980	5.2899	6.3275
7	1.9487	2.2107	2.5023	2.6600	2.8262	3.1855	3.5832	4.5077	5.6295	6.9826	8.6054
8	2.1436	2.4760	2.8526	3.0590	3.2784	3.7589	4.2998	5.5895	7.2058	9.2170	11.703
9	2.3579	2.7731	3.2519	3.5179	3.8030	4.4355	5.1598	6.9310	9.2234	12.166	15.917
10	2.5937	3.1058	3.7072	4.0456	4.4114	5.2338	6.1917	8.5944	11.806	16.060	21.647
11	2.8531	3.4785	4.2262	4.6524	5.1173	6.1759	7.4301	10.657	15.112	21.199	29.439
12	3.1384	3.8960	4.8179	5.3503	5.9360	7.2876	8.9161	13.215	19.343	27.983	40.037
13	3.4523	4.3635	5.4924	6.1528	6.8858	8.5994	10.699	16.386	24.759	36.937	54.451
14	3.7975	4.8871	6.2613	7.0757	7.9875	10.147	12.839	20.319	31.691	48.757	74.053
15	4.1772	5.4736	7.1379	8.1371	9.2655	11.974	15.407	25.196	40.565	64.359	100.71
16	4.5950	6.1304	8.1372	9.3576	10.748	14.129	18.488	31.243	51.923	84.954	136.97
17	5.0545	6.8660	9.2765	10.761	12.468	16.672	22.186	38.741	66.461	112.14	186.28
18	5.5599	7.6900	10.575	12.375	14.463	19.673	26.623	48.039	86.071	148.02	253.34
19	6.1159	8.6128	12.056	14.232	16.777	23.214	31.948	59.568	108.89	195.39	344.54
20	6.7275	9.6463	13.743	16.367	19.461	27.393	38.338	73.864	139.38	257.92	468.57
21	7.4002	10.804	15.668	18.822	22.574	32.324	46.005	91.592	178.41	340.45	637.26
22	8.1403	12.100	17.861	21.645	26.186	38.142	55.206	113.57	228.36	449.39	866.67
23	8.9543	13.552	20.362	24.891	30.376	45.008	66.247	140.83	292.30	593.20	1178.7
24	9.8497	15.179	23.212	28.625	35.236	53.109	79.497	174.63	374.14	783.02	1603.0
25	10.835	17.000	26.462	32.919	40.874	62.669	95.396	216.54	478.90	1033.6	2180.1
30	17.449	29.960	50.950	66.212	85.850	143.37	237.38	634.82	1645.5	4142.1	10143.
40	45.259	93.051	188.88	267.86	378.72	750.38	1469.8	5455.9	19427.	66521.	*
50	117.39	289.00	700.23	1083.7	1670.7	3927.4	9100.4	46890.	*	*	*
60	304.48	897.60	2595.9	4384.0	7370.2	20555.	56348.	*	*	*	*

*FVIV > 99,999.

Table A.4 Future Value of an Annuity of $1 per Period for T Periods $= [(1 + r)^T - 1]/r$

				Interest Rate				

Number of Periods	1%	2%	3%	4%	5%	6%	7%	8%	9%
1	1.0000	1.0000	1.0000	1.0000	1.0000	1.0000	1.0000	1.0000	1.0000
2	2.0100	2.0200	2.0300	2.0400	2.0500	2.0600	2.0700	2.0800	2.0900
3	3.0301	3.0604	3.0909	3.1216	3.1525	3.1836	3.2149	3.2464	3.2781
4	4.0604	4.1216	4.1836	4.2465	4.3101	4.3746	4.4399	4.5061	4.5731
5	5.1010	5.2040	5.3091	5.4163	5.5256	5.6371	5.7507	5.8666	5.9847
6	6.1520	6.3081	6.4684	6.6330	6.8019	6.9753	7.1533	7.3359	7.5233
7	7.2135	7.4343	7.6625	7.8983	8.1420	8.3938	8.6540	8.9228	9.2004
8	8.2857	8.5830	8.8932	9.2142	9.5491	9.8975	10.260	10.637	11.028
9	9.3685	9.7546	10.159	10.583	11.027	11.491	11.978	12.488	13.021
10	10.462	10.950	11.464	12.006	12.578	13.181	13.816	14.487	15.193
11	11.567	12.169	12.808	13.486	14.207	14.972	15.784	16.645	17.560
12	12.683	13.412	14.192	15.026	15.917	16.870	17.888	18.977	20.141
13	13.809	14.680	15.618	16.627	17.713	18.882	20.141	21.495	22.953
14	14.947	15.974	17.086	18.292	19.599	21.015	22.550	24.215	26.019
15	16.097	17.293	18.599	20.024	21.579	23.276	25.129	27.152	29.361
16	17.258	18.639	20.157	21.825	23.657	25.673	27.888	30.324	33.003
17	18.430	20.012	21.762	23.698	25.840	28.213	30.840	33.750	36.974
18	19.615	21.412	23.414	25.645	28.132	30.906	33.999	37.450	41.301
19	20.811	22.841	25.117	27.671	30.539	33.760	37.379	41.446	46.018
20	22.019	24.297	26.870	29.778	33.066	36.786	40.995	45.762	51.160
21	23.239	25.783	28.676	31.969	35.719	39.993	44.865	50.423	56.765
22	24.472	27.299	30.537	34.248	38.505	43.392	49.006	55.457	62.873
23	25.716	28.845	32.453	36.618	41.430	46.996	53.436	60.893	69.532
24	26.973	30.422	34.426	39.083	44.502	50.816	58.177	66.765	76.790
25	28.243	32.030	36.459	41.646	47.727	54.865	63.249	73.106	84.701
30	34.785	40.568	47.575	56.085	66.439	79.058	94.461	113.28	136.31
40	48.886	60.402	75.401	95.026	120.80	154.76	199.64	259.06	337.88
50	64.463	84.579	112.80	152.67	209.35	290.34	406.53	573.77	815.08
60	81.670	114.05	163.05	237.99	353.58	533.13	813.52	1253.2	1944.8

Number of Periods	10%	12%	14%	15%	16%	18%	20%	24%	28%	32%	36%
1	1.0000	1.0000	1.0000	1.0000	1.0000	1.0000	1.0000	1.0000	1.0000	1.0000	1.0000
2	2.1000	2.1200	2.1400	2.1500	2.1600	2.1800	2.2000	2.2400	2.2800	2.3200	2.3600
3	3.3100	3.3744	3.4396	3.4725	3.5056	3.5724	3.6400	3.7776	3.9184	4.0624	4.2096
4	4.6410	4.7793	4.9211	4.9934	5.0665	5.2154	5.3680	5.6842	6.0156	6.3624	6.7251
5	6.1051	6.3528	6.6101	6.7424	6.8771	7.1542	7.4416	8.0484	8.6999	9.3983	10.146
6	7.7156	8.1152	8.5355	8.7537	8.9775	9.4420	9.9299	10.980	12.136	13.406	14.799
7	9.4872	10.089	10.730	11.067	11.414	12.142	12.916	14.615	16.534	18.696	21.126
8	11.436	12.300	13.233	13.727	14.240	15.327	16.499	19.123	22.163	25.678	29.732
9	13.579	14.776	16.085	16.786	17.519	19.086	20.799	24.712	29.369	34.895	41.435
10	15.937	17.549	19.337	20.304	21.321	23.521	25.959	31.643	38.593	47.062	57.352
11	18.531	20.655	23.045	24.349	25.733	28.755	32.150	40.238	50.398	63.122	78.998
12	21.384	24.133	27.271	29.002	30.850	34.931	39.581	50.895	65.510	84.320	108.44
13	24.523	28.029	32.089	34.352	36.786	42.219	48.497	64.110	84.853	112.30	148.47
14	27.975	32.393	37.581	40.505	43.672	50.818	59.196	80.496	109.61	149.24	202.93
15	31.772	37.280	43.842	47.580	51.660	60.965	72.035	100.82	141.30	198.00	276.98
16	35.950	42.753	50.980	55.717	60.925	72.939	87.442	126.01	181.87	262.36	377.69
17	40.545	48.884	59.118	65.075	71.673	87.068	105.93	157.25	233.79	347.31	514.66
18	45.599	55.750	68.394	75.836	84.141	103.74	128.12	195.99	300.25	459.45	700.94
19	51.159	64.440	78.969	88.212	98.603	123.41	154.74	244.03	385.32	607.47	954.28
20	57.275	72.052	91.025	102.44	115.38	146.63	186.69	303.60	494.21	802.86	1298.8
21	64.002	81.699	104.77	118.81	134.84	174.02	225.03	377.46	633.59	1060.8	1767.4
22	71.403	92.503	120.44	137.63	157.41	206.34	271.03	469.06	812.00	1401.2	2404.7
23	79.543	104.60	138.30	159.28	183.60	244.49	326.24	582.63	1040.4	1850.6	3271.3
24	88.497	118.16	158.66	184.17	213.98	289.49	392.48	723.46	1332.7	2443.8	4450.0
25	98.347	133.33	181.87	212.79	249.21	342.60	471.98	898.09	1706.8	3226.8	6053.0
30	164.49	241.33	356.79	434.75	530.31	790.95	1181.9	2640.9	5873.2	12941.	28172.3
40	442.59	767.09	1342.0	1779.1	2360.8	4163.2	7343.9	22729.	69377.	*	*
50	1163.9	2400.0	4994.5	7217.7	10436.	21813.	45497.	*	*	*	*
60	3034.8	7471.6	18535.	29220.	46058.	*	*	*	*	*	*

*FVIFA > 99,999.

Table A.5 Future Value of $1 with a Continuously Compounded Rate r for T Periods: Values of e^{rT}

Period (T)	1%	2%	3%	4%	5%	6%	7%	8%	9%	10%	11%	12%	13%	14%
						Continuously Compounded Rate (r)								
1	1.0101	1.0202	1.0305	1.0408	1.0513	1.0618	1.0725	1.0833	1.0942	1.1052	1.1163	1.1275	1.1388	1.1503
2	1.0202	1.0408	1.0618	1.0833	1.1052	1.1275	1.1503	1.1735	1.1972	1.2214	1.2461	1.2712	1.2969	1.3231
3	1.0305	1.0618	1.0942	1.1275	1.1618	1.1972	1.2337	1.2712	1.3100	1.3499	1.3910	1.4333	1.4770	1.5220
4	1.0408	1.0833	1.1275	1.1735	1.2214	1.2712	1.3231	1.3771	1.4333	1.4918	1.5527	1.6161	1.6820	1.7507
5	1.0513	1.1052	1.1618	1.2214	1.2840	1.3499	1.4191	1.4918	1.5683	1.6487	1.7333	1.8221	1.9155	2.0138
6	1.0618	1.1275	1.1972	1.2712	1.3499	1.4333	1.5220	1.6161	1.7160	1.8221	1.9348	2.0544	2.1815	2.3164
7	1.0725	1.1503	1.2337	1.3231	1.4191	1.5220	1.6323	1.7507	1.8776	2.0138	2.1598	2.3164	2.4843	2.6645
8	1.0833	1.1735	1.2712	1.3771	1.4918	1.6161	1.7507	1.8965	2.0544	2.2255	2.4109	2.6117	2.8292	3.0649
9	1.0942	1.1972	1.3100	1.4333	1.5683	1.7160	1.8776	2.0544	2.2479	2.4596	2.6912	2.9447	3.2220	3.5254
10	1.1052	1.2214	1.3499	1.4918	1.6487	1.8221	2.0138	2.2255	2.4596	2.7183	3.0042	3.3201	3.6693	4.0552
11	1.1163	1.2461	1.3910	1.5527	1.7333	1.9348	2.1598	2.4109	2.6912	3.0042	3.3535	3.7434	4.1787	4.6646
12	1.1275	1.2712	1.4333	1.6161	1.8221	2.0544	2.3164	2.6117	2.9447	3.3201	3.7434	4.2207	4.7588	5.3656
13	1.1388	1.2969	1.4770	1.6820	1.9155	2.1815	2.4843	2.8292	3.2220	3.6693	4.1787	4.7588	5.4195	6.1719
14	1.1503	1.3231	1.5220	1.7507	2.0138	2.3164	2.6645	3.0649	3.5254	4.0552	4.6646	5.3656	6.1719	7.0993
15	1.1618	1.3499	1.5683	1.8221	2.1170	2.4596	2.8577	3.3201	3.8574	4.4817	5.2070	6.0496	7.0287	8.1662
16	1.1735	1.3771	1.6161	1.8965	2.2255	2.6117	3.0649	3.5966	4.2207	4.9530	5.8124	6.8210	8.0045	9.3933
17	1.1853	1.4049	1.6653	1.9739	2.3396	2.7732	3.2871	3.8962	4.6182	5.4739	6.4883	7.6906	9.1157	10.8049
18	1.1972	1.4333	1.7160	2.0544	2.4596	2.9447	3.5254	4.2207	5.0531	6.0496	7.2427	8.6711	10.3812	12.4286
19	1.2092	1.4623	1.7683	2.1383	2.5857	3.1268	3.7810	4.5722	5.5290	6.6859	8.0849	9.7767	11.8224	14.2963
20	1.2214	1.4918	1.8221	2.2255	2.7183	3.3201	4.0552	4.9530	6.0496	7.3891	9.0250	11.0232	13.4637	16.4446
21	1.2337	1.5220	1.8776	2.3164	2.8577	3.5254	4.3492	5.3656	6.6194	8.1662	10.0744	12.4286	15.3329	18.9158
22	1.2461	1.5527	1.9348	2.4109	3.0042	3.7434	4.6646	5.8124	7.2427	9.0250	11.2459	14.0132	17.4615	21.7584
23	1.2586	1.5841	1.9937	2.5093	3.1582	3.9749	5.0028	6.2965	7.9248	9.9742	12.5535	15.7998	19.8857	25.0281
24	1.2712	1.6161	2.0544	2.6117	3.3201	4.2207	5.3656	6.8210	8.6711	11.0232	14.0132	17.8143	22.6464	28.7892
25	1.2840	1.6487	2.1170	2.7183	3.4903	4.4817	5.7546	7.3891	9.4877	12.1825	15.6426	20.0855	25.7903	33.1155
30	1.3499	1.8221	2.4596	3.3204	4.4817	6.0496	8.1662	11.0232	14.8797	20.0855	27.1126	36.5982	49.4024	66.6863
35	1.4191	2.0138	2.8577	4.0552	5.7546	8.1662	11.5883	16.4446	23.3361	33.1155	46.9931	66.6863	94.6324	134.2898
40	1.4918	2.2255	3.3201	4.9530	7.3891	11.0232	16.4446	24.5235	36.5982	54.5982	81.4509	121.5104	181.2722	270.4264
45	1.5683	2.4596	3.8574	6.0496	9.4877	14.8797	23.3361	36.5982	57.3975	90.0171	141.1750	221.4064	347.2344	544.5719
50	1.6487	2.7183	4.4817	7.3891	12.1825	20.0855	33.1155	54.5982	90.0171	148.4132	244.6919	403.4288	665.1416	1096.633
55	1.7333	3.0042	5.2070	9.0250	15.6426	27.1126	46.9931	81.4509	141.1750	244.6919	424.1130	735.0952	1274.106	2208.348
60	1.8221	3.3201	6.0496	11.0232	20.0855	36.5982	66.6863	121.5104	221.4064	403.4288	735.0952	1339.431	2440.602	4447.067

Continuously Compounded Rate (r)

Period (T)	15%	16%	17%	18%	19%	20%	21%	22%	23%	24%	25%	26%	27%	28%
1	1.1618	1.1735	1.1853	1.1972	1.2092	1.2214	1.2337	1.2461	1.2586	1.2712	1.2840	1.2969	1.3100	1.3231
2	1.3499	1.3771	1.4049	1.4333	1.4623	1.4918	1.5220	1.5527	1.5841	1.6161	1.6487	1.6820	1.7160	1.7507
3	1.5683	1.6161	1.6653	1.7160	1.7683	1.8221	1.8776	1.9348	1.9937	2.0544	2.1170	2.1815	2.2479	2.3164
4	1.8221	1.8965	1.9739	2.0544	2.1383	2.2255	2.3164	2.4109	2.5093	2.6117	2.7183	2.8292	2.9447	3.0649
5	2.1170	2.2255	2.3396	2.4596	2.5857	2.7183	2.8577	3.0042	3.1582	3.3201	3.4903	3.6693	3.8574	4.0552
6	2.4596	2.6117	2.7732	2.9447	3.1268	3.3201	3.5254	3.7434	3.9749	4.2207	4.4817	4.7588	5.0351	5.3656
7	2.8577	3.0649	3.2871	3.5254	3.7810	4.0552	4.3492	4.6646	5.0028	5.3656	5.7546	6.1719	6.6194	7.0993
8	3.3201	3.5966	3.8962	4.2207	4.5722	4.9530	5.3656	5.8124	6.2965	6.8210	7.3891	8.0045	8.6711	9.3933
9	3.8574	4.2207	4.6182	5.0531	5.5290	6.0496	6.6194	7.2427	7.9248	8.6711	9.4877	10.3812	11.3589	12.4286
10	4.4817	4.9530	5.4739	6.0496	6.6859	7.3891	8.1662	9.0250	9.9742	11.0232	12.1825	13.4637	14.8797	16.4446
11	5.2070	5.8124	6.4883	7.2427	8.0849	9.0250	10.0744	11.2459	12.5535	14.0132	15.6426	17.4615	19.4919	21.7584
12	6.0496	6.8210	7.6906	8.6711	9.7767	11.0232	12.4286	14.0132	15.7998	17.8143	20.0855	22.6464	25.5337	28.7892
13	7.0287	8.0045	9.1157	10.3812	11.8224	13.4637	15.3329	17.4615	19.8857	22.6464	25.7903	29.3708	33.4483	38.0918
14	8.1662	9.3933	10.8049	12.4286	14.2963	16.4446	18.9158	21.7584	25.0281	28.7892	33.1155	38.0918	43.8160	50.4004
15	9.4877	11.0232	12.0871	14.8797	17.2878	20.0855	23.3361	27.1126	31.5004	36.5982	42.5211	49.4024	57.3975	66.6863
16	11.0232	12.9358	15.1803	17.8143	20.9052	24.5325	28.7892	33.7844	39.6464	46.5255	54.5982	64.0715	75.1886	88.2347
17	12.8071	15.1803	17.9933	21.3276	25.2797	29.9641	35.5166	42.0980	49.8990	59.1455	70.1054	83.0963	98.4944	116.7459
18	14.8797	17.8143	21.3276	25.5337	30.5694	36.5982	43.8160	52.4573	62.8028	75.1886	90.0171	107.7701	129.0242	154.4700
19	17.2878	20.9052	25.2797	30.5694	36.9661	44.7012	54.0549	65.3659	79.0436	95.5835	115.5843	139.7702	169.0171	204.3839
20	20.0855	24.5325	29.9641	36.5982	44.7012	54.5982	66.6863	81.4509	99.4843	121.5104	148.4132	181.2722	221.4064	270.4264
21	23.3361	28.7892	35.5166	43.8160	54.0549	66.6863	82.2695	101.4940	125.2110	154.4700	190.5663	235.0974	290.0345	357.8092
22	27.1126	33.7844	42.0980	52.4573	65.3659	81.4509	101.4940	126.4694	157.5905	196.3699	244.6919	304.9049	379.9349	473.4281
23	31.5004	39.6464	49.8990	62.8028	79.0436	99.4843	125.2110	157.5905	198.3434	249.6350	314.1907	395.4404	497.7013	626.4068
24	36.5982	46.5255	59.1455	75.1886	95.5835	121.5104	154.4700	196.3699	249.6350	317.3483	403.4288	512.8585	651.9709	828.8175
25	42.5211	54.5982	70.1054	90.0171	115.5843	148.4132	190.5663	244.6919	314.1907	403.4288	518.0128	665.1416	854.0588	1096.633
30	90.0171	121.5104	164.0219	221.4064	298.8674	403.4288	544.5719	735.0952	992.2747	1339.431	1808.042	2440.602	3294.468	4447.067
35	190.5663	270.4264	383.7533	544.5719	772.7843	1096.633	1556.197	2208.348	3133.795	4447.067	6310.688	8955.293	12708.17	18033.74
40	403.4288	601.8450	897.8473	1339.431	1998.196	2980.958	4447.067	6634.244	9897.129	14764.78	22026.47	32859.63	49020.80	73130.44
45	854.0588	1339.431	2100.646	3294.468	5166.754	8103.084	12708.17	19930.37	31257.04	49020.80	76879.92	120571.7	189094.1	296558.6
50	1808.042	2980.958	4914.769	8103.084	13359.73	22026.47	36315.50	59874.14	98715.77	162754.8	268337.3	442413.4	729416.4	1202604.
55	3827.626	6634.244	11498.82	19930.37	34544.37	59874.14	103777.0	179871.9	311763.4	540364.9	936589.2	1623346.	2813669.	4876801.
60	8103.084	14764.78	26903.19	49020.80	89321.72	162754.8	296558.6	540364.9	984609.1	1794075.	3269017.	5956538.	10853520.	19776403.

Table A.6 Present Value of $1 with a Continuous Discount Rate r for T Periods: Values of e^{-rT}

	Continuous Discount Rate (r)																
Period (T)	**1%**	**2%**	**3%**	**4%**	**5%**	**6%**	**7%**	**8%**	**9%**	**10%**	**11%**	**12%**	**13%**	**14%**	**15%**	**16%**	**17%**
1	.9900	.9802	.9704	.9608	.9512	.9418	.9324	.9231	.9139	.9048	.8958	.8869	.8781	.8694	.8607	.8521	.8437
2	.9802	.9608	.9418	.9231	.9048	.8869	.8694	.8521	.8353	.8187	.8025	.7866	.7711	.7558	.7408	.7261	.7118
3	.9704	.9418	.9139	.8869	.8607	.8353	.8106	.7866	.7634	.7408	.7189	.6977	.6771	.6570	.6376	.6188	.6005
4	.9608	.9231	.8869	.8521	.8187	.7866	.7558	.7261	.6977	.6703	.6440	.6188	.5945	.5712	.5488	.5273	.5066
5	.9512	.9048	.8607	.8187	.7788	.7408	.7047	.6703	.6376	.6065	.5769	.5488	.5220	.4966	.4724	.4493	.4274
6	.9418	.8869	.8353	.7866	.7408	.6977	.6570	.6188	.5827	.5488	.5169	.4868	.4584	.4317	.4066	.3829	.3606
7	.9324	.8694	.8106	.7558	.7047	.6570	.6126	.5712	.5326	.4966	.4630	.4317	.4025	.3753	.3499	.3263	.3042
8	.9231	.8521	.7866	.7261	.6703	.6188	.5712	.5273	.4868	.4493	.4148	.3829	.3535	.3263	.3012	.2780	.2576
9	.9139	.8353	.7634	.6977	.6376	.5827	.5326	.4868	.4449	.4066	.3716	.3396	.3104	.2837	.2592	.2369	.2165
10	.9048	.8187	.7408	.6703	.6065	.5488	.4966	.4493	.4066	.3679	.3329	.3012	.2725	.2466	.2231	.2019	.1827
11	.8958	.8025	.7189	.6440	.5769	.5169	.4630	.4148	.3716	.3329	.2982	.2671	.2393	.2144	.1920	.1720	.1541
12	.8869	.7866	.6977	.6188	.5488	.4868	.4317	.3829	.3396	.3012	.2671	.2369	.2101	.1864	.1653	.1466	.1300
13	.8781	.7711	.6771	.5945	.5220	.4584	.4025	.3535	.3104	.2725	.2393	.2101	.1845	.1620	.1423	.1249	.1097
14	.8694	.7558	.6570	.5712	.4966	.4317	.3753	.3263	.2837	.2466	.2144	.1864	.1620	.1409	.1225	.1065	.0926
15	.8607	.7408	.6376	.5488	.4724	.4066	.3499	.3012	.2592	.2231	.1920	.1653	.1423	.1225	.1054	.0907	.0781
16	.8521	.7261	.6188	.5273	.4493	.3829	.3263	.2780	.2369	.2019	.1720	.1466	.1249	.1065	.0907	.0773	.0659
17	.8437	.7118	.6005	.5066	.4274	.3606	.3042	.2567	.2165	.1827	.1541	.1300	.1097	.0926	.0781	.0659	.0556
18	.8353	.6977	.5827	.4868	.4066	.3396	.2837	.2369	.1979	.1653	.1381	.1153	.0963	.0805	.0672	.0561	.0469
19	.8270	.6839	.5655	.4677	.3867	.3198	.2645	.2187	.1809	.1496	.1237	.1023	.0846	.0699	.0578	.0478	.0396
20	.8187	.6703	.5488	.4493	.3679	.3012	.2466	.2019	.1653	.1353	.1108	.0907	.0743	.0608	.0498	.0408	.0334
21	.8106	.6570	.5326	.4317	.3499	.2837	.2299	.1864	.1511	.1225	.0993	.0805	.0652	.0529	.0429	.0347	.0282
22	.8025	.6440	.5169	.4148	.3329	.2671	.2144	.1720	.1381	.1108	.0889	.0714	.0573	.0460	.0369	.0296	.0238
23	.7945	.6313	.5016	.3985	.3166	.2516	.1999	.1588	.1262	.1003	.0797	.0633	.0503	.0400	.0317	.0252	.0200
24	.7866	.6188	.4868	.3829	.3012	.2369	.1864	.1466	.1153	.0907	.0714	.0561	.0442	.0347	.0273	.0215	.0169
25	.7788	.6065	.4724	.3679	.2865	.2231	.1738	.1353	.1054	.0821	.0639	.0498	.0388	.0302	.0235	.0183	.0143
30	.7408	.5488	.4066	.3012	.2231	.1653	.1225	.0907	.0672	.0498	.0369	.0273	.0202	.0150	.0111	.0082	.0061
35	.7047	.4966	.3499	.2466	.1738	.1225	.0863	.0608	.0429	.0302	.0213	.0150	.0106	.0074	.0052	.0037	.0026
40	.6703	.4493	.3012	.2019	.1353	.0907	.0608	.0408	.0273	.0183	.0123	.0082	.0055	.0037	.0025	.0017	.0011
45	.6376	.4066	.2592	.1653	.1054	.0672	.0429	.0273	.0174	.0111	.0071	.0045	.0029	.0018	.0012	.0007	.0005
50	.6065	.3679	.2231	.1353	.0821	.0498	.0302	.0183	.0111	.0067	.0041	.0025	.0015	.0009	.0006	.0003	.0002
55	.5769	.3329	.1920	.1108	.0639	.0369	.0213	.0123	.0071	.0041	.0024	.0014	.0008	.0005	.0003	.0002	.0001
60	.5488	.3012	.1653	.0907	.0498	.0273	.0150	.0082	.0045	.0025	.0014	.0007	.0004	.0002	.0001	.0001	.0000

Continuous Discount Rate (r)

Period (T)	18%	19%	20%	21%	22%	23%	24%	25%	26%	27%	28%	29%	30%	31%	32%	33%	34%	35%
1	.8353	.8270	.8187	.8106	.8025	.7945	.7866	.7788	.7711	.7634	.7558	.7483	.7408	.7334	.7261	.7189	.7118	.7047
2	.6977	.6839	.6703	.6570	.6440	.6313	.6188	.6065	.5945	.5827	.5712	.5599	.5488	.5379	.5273	.5169	.5066	.4966
3	.5827	.5655	.5488	.5326	.5169	.5016	.4868	.4724	.4584	.4449	.4317	.4190	.4066	.3946	.3829	.3716	.3606	.3499
4	.4868	.4677	.4493	.4317	.4148	.3985	.3829	.3679	.3535	.3396	.3263	.3135	.3012	.2894	.2780	.2671	.2567	.2466
5	.4066	.3867	.3679	.3499	.3329	.3166	.3012	.2865	.2725	.2592	.2466	.2346	.2231	.2122	.2019	.1920	.1827	.1738
6	.3396	.3198	.3012	.2837	.2671	.2516	.2369	.2231	.2101	.1979	.1864	.1755	.1653	.1557	.1466	.1381	.1300	.1225
7	.2837	.2645	.2466	.2299	.2144	.1999	.1864	.1738	.1620	.1511	.1409	.1313	.1225	.1142	.1065	.0993	.0926	.0863
8	.2369	.2187	.2019	.1864	.1720	.1588	.1466	.1353	.1249	.1153	.1065	.0983	.0907	.0837	.0773	.0714	.0659	.0608
9	.1979	.1809	.1653	.1511	.1381	.1262	.1153	.1054	.0963	.0880	.0805	.0735	.0672	.0614	.0561	.0513	.0469	.0429
10	.1653	.1496	.1353	.1225	.1108	.1003	.0907	.0821	.0743	.0672	.0608	.0550	.0498	.0450	.0408	.0369	.0334	.0302
11	.1381	.1237	.1108	.0993	.0889	.0797	.0714	.0639	.0573	.0513	.0460	.0412	.0369	.0330	.0296	.0265	.0238	.0213
12	.1154	.1023	.0907	.0805	.0714	.0633	.0561	.0498	.0442	.0392	.0347	.0308	.0273	.0242	.0215	.0191	.0169	.0150
13	.0963	.0846	.0743	.0652	.0573	.0503	.0442	.0388	.0340	.0299	.0263	.0231	.0202	.0178	.0156	.0137	.0120	.0106
14	.0805	.0699	.0608	.0529	.0460	.0400	.0347	.0302	.0263	.0228	.0198	.0172	.0150	.0130	.0113	.0099	.0086	.0074
15	.0672	.0578	.0498	.0429	.0369	.0317	.0273	.0235	.0202	.0174	.0150	.0129	.0111	.0096	.0082	.0071	.0061	.0052
16	.0561	.0478	.0408	.0347	.0296	.0252	.0215	.0183	.0156	.0133	.0113	.0097	.0082	.0070	.0060	.0051	.0043	.0037
17	.0469	.0396	.0334	.0282	.0238	.0200	.0169	.0143	.0120	.0102	.0086	.0072	.0061	.0051	.0043	.0037	.0031	.0026
18	.0392	.0327	.0273	.0228	.0191	.0159	.0133	.0111	.0093	.0078	.0065	.0054	.0045	.0038	.0032	.0026	.0022	.0018
19	.0327	.0271	.0224	.0185	.0153	.0127	.0105	.0087	.0072	.0059	.0049	.0040	.0033	.0028	.0023	.0019	.0016	.0013
20	.0273	.0224	.0183	.0150	.0123	.0101	.0082	.0067	.0055	.0045	.0037	.0030	.0025	.0020	.0017	.0014	.0011	.0009
21	.0228	.0185	.0150	.0122	.0099	.0080	.0065	.0052	.0043	.0034	.0028	.0023	.0018	.0015	.0012	.0010	.0008	.0006
22	.0191	.0153	.0123	.0099	.0079	.0063	.0051	.0041	.0033	.0026	.0021	.0017	.0014	.0011	.0009	.0007	.0006	.0005
23	.0159	.0127	.0101	.0080	.0063	.0050	.0040	.0032	.0025	.0020	.0016	.0013	.0010	.0008	.0006	.0005	.0004	.0003
24	.0133	.0105	.0082	.0065	.0051	.0040	.0032	.0025	.0019	.0015	.0012	.0009	.0007	.0006	.0005	.0004	.0003	.0002
25	.0111	.0087	.0067	.0052	.0041	.0032	.0025	.0019	.0015	.0012	.0009	.0007	.0006	.0004	.0003	.0003	.0002	.0002
30	.0045	.0033	.0025	.0018	.0014	.0010	.0007	.0006	.0004	.0003	.0002	.0002	.0001	.0001	.0001	.0001	.0000	.0000
35	.0018	.0013	.0009	.0006	.0005	.0003	.0002	.0002	.0001	.0001	.0001	.0000	.0000	.0000	.0000	.0000	.0000	.0000
40	.0007	.0005	.0003	.0002	.0002	.0001	.0001	.0000	.0000	.0000	.0000	.0000	.0000	.0000	.0000	.0000	.0000	.0000
45	.0003	.0002	.0001	.0001	.0001	.0000	.0000	.0000	.0000	.0000	.0000	.0000	.0000	.0000	.0000	.0000	.0000	.0000
50	.0001	.0001	.0000	.0000	.0000	.0000	.0000	.0000	.0000	.0000	.0000	.0000	.0000	.0000	.0000	.0000	.0000	.0000
55	.0001	.0000	.0000	.0000	.0000	.0000	.0000	.0000	.0000	.0000	.0000	.0000	.0000	.0000	.0000	.0000	.0000	.0000
60	.0000	.0000	.0000	.0000	.0000	.0000	.0000	.0000	.0000	.0000	.0000	.0000	.0000	.0000	.0000	.0000	.0000	.0000

Appendix B

Solutions to Selected End-of-Chapter Problems

CHAPTER 2

2.2 $102,700; $72,700
2.6 $327,000
2.10 $878,000
2.14 a. $65,930
  b. $17,200
  c. $1,400
  d. $530
2.16 $1,100; $0

CHAPTER 3

3.2 1.80 times; 17.46; $128,331
3.6 11.61%
3.10 8.53%
3.14 23.27 days
3.16 8.91 times

CHAPTER 4

4.2 a. $1,628.89
  b. $2,593.74
  c. $2,653.30
4.4 6.13%; 10.27%; 7.41%; 12.79%
4.10 a. $4,401.10
  b. $3,132.57
  c. $3,462.003
  d. $3,826.13
4.14 $88,461.54; 4.69%
4.18 EAR = 176.68%
4.22 4.14%
4.26 $2,477,552
4.30 $386,994.11
4.34 $2,279,147
4.38 $385,664.73
4.42 $3,700.77; 14.81%
4.44 $134,455.36
4.52 $11,571.48
4.56 $18,451.74
4.60 EAR = 17.65%
4.64 APR = 35.71%; EAR = 42.18%

CHAPTER 5

5.2 3.81 years; 5.71 years; Never
5.6 10.38%; 19.16%

5.10 a. 12.40%
  d. −$293.70; $803.24
5.14 a. 1.33 years; 1.59 years
  b. $257.51; $347.26
  c. 33.79%; 23.31%
  d. 15.86%
5.18 a. 1.67 years; 1.63 years
  b. $607,287.75; $397,789.63
  c. 30.90%; 36.51%
  d. 25.52%
5.22 25.00%; 33.33%; 42.86%; 66.67%

CHAPTER 6

6.2 $1,553.87
6.6 20.06%
6.10 −$83,329.16; −$82,554.30
6.16 $24,486,000
6.18 $1,266,667
6.22 $30,170.71
6.28 $6,106,959; 27.54%
6.32 $182.60

CHAPTER 7

7.2 NPV_{Best} = $2,475,317
  NPV_{Worst} = −$969,375.68
7.6 Go to market NPV = $23,000,000
  Test market NPV = $25,666,667
7.10 7,043 units
7.14 Payback = 2.97 years
  NPV = $14,246,367
  IRR = 27.89%
7.20 a. 1,018
  b. 1,622

CHAPTER 8

8.2 a. $1,000
  b. $837.11
  c. $1,209.30
8.6 3.34%
8.10 6.84%
8.12 Current yield = 4.27%
  YTM = 4.23%
8.18 6.44%

CHAPTER 9
9.2 10.91%
9.6 $3.91
9.8 6.78%
9.13 $73.26
9.18 $3.61
9.22 $48.26
9.29 a. $53.81
     b. $60.09

CHAPTER 10
10.2 1.61%; 14.67%
10.6 2.91%; 3.20%
10.10 a. 6.14%
      b. 5.50%
10.14 5.51%
10.20 Arithmetic average = 7.83%
      Geometric average = 5.22%

CHAPTER 11
11.2 12.81%
11.6 E(R) = 10.50%
     σ_A = 8.64%
11.10 1.42
11.14 10.44%
11.18 Market risk premium = 7.30%

CHAPTER 12
12.2 a. −1.73%
     b. 9.97%
12.5 F_1 = 6.49%
     F_2 = 5.64%

CHAPTER 13
13.2 8.67%; 5.57%
13.6 10.65%
13.10 a. 4.24%
      b. 13.36%
13.14 b. 5.29%
      c. $21,116,139
13.18 .4775
13.22 $6,251,949

CHAPTER 15
15.2 1,601
15.6 $927.27
15.9 8.45%
15.11 $119.73

CHAPTER 16
16.2 a. $1.64; $2.473; $3.41
     b. $.95; $2.66; $3.72

16.6 a. $2.14; $2.94; $3.15
     b. $9,855
     c. $9,855
     d. $1.29; $1.76; $1.89
       Breakeven = $9,855
16.10 $3,330,000
16.14 V_U = $751,562.50
      V = $798,812.50

CHAPTER 17
17.3 $650,000
17.8 a. $76,000,000
     b. 32.53%
     c. 16.14%

CHAPTER 18
18.2 $68,510.88
18.6 a. $1,256,127
     b. $1,149,131
18.10 $5,845,477
18.13 $4,020,681

CHAPTER 19
19.2 a. New shares issued = 3,000
     b. New shares issued = 7,500
19.6 11,412; $38.75
19.10 a. $106
      b. $110
      c. 40,909
19.14 a. $1,625,179
      b. $61.61
      c. $1,625,179
      d. 496.63

CHAPTER 20
20.2 a. $27
     b. 1,120,000; 2.59
     c. $26.44; $.56
     d. 27,000; 27,000
20.6 1,626,778
20.12 20.10%
20.15 $28.15

CHAPTER 21
21.2 −$95,405.20
21.6 $52,107.92
21.10 $1,852,606
21.14 a. −$46,247.78
      b. $930,668

CHAPTER 22
22.4 a. $13.33
     b. $2.60
22.6 $5.54

22.10 Call = $5.24; Put = $7.34
22.14 $163,712.78
22.18 $75.00
22.22 Project A: Equity = $7,603.04; Debt = $19,896.96
Project B: Equity = $5,921.30; Debt = $21,978.70
22.26 a. $9.38
b. .64; Borrow $40.77
c. $9.38
22.34 $10.58

CHAPTER 23
23.2 $1,298,460
23.6 $258,609.04
23.10 $6,961,860

CHAPTER 24
24.2 16.26
24.5 $15
24.10 a. $875.28
b. 12.42 years
24.14 $803.05

CHAPTER 25
25.2 −$5,075; $8,175
25.6 2.808 years
25.9 $11,200
25.14 a. $498.85
b. $602.22

CHAPTER 26
26.2 Cash = $820
Current assets = $4,655
26.6 Operating cycle = 75.23 days
Cash cycle = 33.55 days
26.10 Ending cash balance = $358,344; $457,690; $679,018

CHAPTER 27
27.2 a. Disbursement float = $68,000
Collection float = −$57,000
Net float = $11,000
b. Disbursement float = $68,000
Collection float = −$28,500
Net float = $39,500

27.6 a. $30,780
b. 2.49 days
c. $30,780
d. $5.71
e. $18,525
27.10 $3,710,000; $158,500

CHAPTER 28
28.2 $3,073,973
28.6 10.1389 times; $591,097.22
28.10 $135,568.42
28.14 $313,055
28.18 $103.85

CHAPTER 29
29.2 Assets = $1,846,800
29.6 Goodwill = $1,350
29.10 a. $2,300
b. $36.48
c. $7,200
d. $36.55
e. $3,116.67
29.14 a. $4,875,000
b. $11,875,000
c. $9,000,000; $10,162,500
d. NPV_{Cash} = $2,875,000
NPV_{Stock} = $1,712,500

CHAPTER 30
30.4 3.519

CHAPTER 31
31.2 £ = $158.260
SF/£ = 1.3957
£/SF = .7165
31.6 Great Britian = 2.04%
Japan = 1.58%
Switzerland = 1.26%
31.10 Kr/$ = 5.6658
31.14 $986,351.89

Appendix C

Using the HP 10B and TI BA II Plus Financial Calculators

This appendix is intended to help you use your Hewlett-Packard HP 10B or Texas Instruments TI BA II Plus financial calculator to solve problems encountered in an introductory finance course. It describes the various calculator settings and provides keystroke solutions for nine selected problems from this book. Please see your owner's manual for more complete instructions. For more examples and problem-solving techniques, please see *Financial Analysis with an Electronic Calculator,* 7th edition, by Mark A. White (New York: McGraw-Hill, 2007).

Calculator Settings

Most calculator errors in introductory finance courses are the result of inappropriate settings. Before beginning a calculation, you should ask yourself the following questions:

1. Did I clear the financial registers?
2. Is the compounding frequency set to once per period?
3. Is the calculator in END mode?
4. Did I enter negative numbers using the +/− key?

CLEARING THE REGISTERS

All calculators have areas of memory, called registers, where variables and intermediate results are stored. There are two sets of financial registers, the time value of money (TVM) registers and the cash flow (CF) registers. These must be cleared before beginning a new calculation. On the Hewlett-Packard HP 10B, pressing {CLEAR ALL} clears both the TVM and the CF registers.[1] To clear the TVM registers on the TI BA II Plus, press **2nd** {CLR TVM}. Press **2nd** {CLR Work} from within the cash flow worksheet to clear the CF registers.

COMPOUNDING FREQUENCY

Both the HP 10B and the TI BA II Plus are hardwired to assume monthly compounding, that is, compounding 12 times per period. Because very few problems in introductory finance courses make this assumption, you should change this default setting to once per period. On the HP 10B, press 1 {P/YR}. To verify that the default has been changed, press the key, then press and briefly hold the **INPUT** key.[2] The display should read "1P_Yr".

On the TI BA II Plus, you can specify both payment frequency and compounding frequency, although they should normally be set to the same number. To set both to once per period, press the key sequence **2nd** {P/Y} 1 **ENTER**,

then press ↓ 1 **ENTER**. Pressing **2nd** {QUIT} returns you to standard calculator mode.

END MODE AND ANNUITIES DUE

In most problems, payment is made at the end of a period, and this is the default setting (end mode) for both the HP 10B and the TI BA II Plus. *Annuities due* assume payments are made at the *beginning* of each period (begin mode). On the HP 10B, pressing {BEG/END} toggles between begin and end mode. Press the key sequence **2nd** {BGN} **2nd** [SET] **2nd** {QUIT} to accomplish the same task on the TI BA II Plus. Both calculators will indicate on the display that your calculator is set for begin mode.

SIGN CHANGES

Sign changes are used to identify the direction of cash inflows and outflows. Generally, cash inflows are entered as positive numbers and cash outflows are entered as negative numbers. To enter a negative number on either the HP 10B or the TI BA II Plus, first press the appropriate digit keys and then press the change sign key, +/−. Do *not* use the minus sign key, −, as its effects are quite unpredictable.

Sample Problems

This section provides keystroke solutions for selected problems from the text illustrating the nine basic financial calculator skills.

1. FUTURE VALUE OR PRESENT VALUE OF A SINGLE SUM

Compute the future value of $2,250 at a 17 percent annual rate for 30 years.

HP 10B		TI BA II Plus	
−2,250.00 **PV**		−2,250.00 **PV**	
30.00 **N**		30.00 **N**	
17.00 **I/YR**		17.00 **I/Y**	
FV	249,895.46	**CPT** **FV**	249,895.46

The future value is $249,895.46.

2. PRESENT VALUE OR FUTURE VALUE OF AN ORDINARY ANNUITY

Betty's Bank offers you a $20,000, seven-year term loan at 11 percent annual interest. What will your annual loan payment be?

HP 10B		TI BA II Plus		
−20,000.00 **PV**		−20,000.00 **PV**		
7.00 **N**		7.00 **N**		
11.00 **I/YR**		11.00 **I/Y**		
PMT 4,244.31		**CPT** **PMT** 4,244.31		

Your annual loan payment will be $4,244.31.

3. FINDING AN UNKNOWN INTEREST RATE

Assume that the total cost of a college education will be $75,000 when your child enters college in 18 years. You presently have $7,000 to invest. What rate of interest must you earn on your investment to cover the cost of your child's college education?

HP 10B		TI BA II Plus	
−7,000.00 **PV**		−7,000.00 **PV**	
18.00 **N**		18.00 **N**	
75,000.00 **FV**		75,000.00 **FV**	
I/YR 14.08		**CPT** **I/Y** 14.08	

You must earn an annual interest rate of at least 14.08 percent to cover the expected future cost of your child's education.

4. FINDING AN UNKNOWN NUMBER OF PERIODS

One of your customers is delinquent on his accounts payable balance. You've mutually agreed to a repayment schedule of $374 per month. You will charge 1.4 percent per month interest on the overdue balance. If the current balance is $12,000, how long will it take for the account to be paid off?

HP 10B		TI BA II Plus	
−12,000.00 **PV**		−12,000.00 **PV**	
1.40 **I/YR**		1.40 **I/Y**	
374.00 **PMT**		374.00 **PMT**	
N 42.90		**CPT** **N** 42.90	

The loan will be paid off in 42.90 months.

5. SIMPLE BOND PRICING

Mullineaux Co. issued 11-year bonds one year ago at a coupon rate of 8.25 percent. The bonds make semiannual payments. If the YTM on these bonds is 7.10 percent, what is the current bond price?

HP 10B		TI BA II Plus	
41.25 **PMT**		41.25 **PMT**	
1,000.00 **FV**		1,000.00 **FV**	
20.00 **N**		20.00 **N**	
3.55 **I/YR**		3.55 **I/Y**	
PV −1,081.35		**CPT** **PV** −1,081.35	

Because the bonds make semiannual payments, we must halve the coupon payment (8.25 ÷ 2 = 4.125 ==> $41.25), halve the YTM (7.10 ÷ 2 ==> 3.55), and double the number of periods (10 years remaining × 2 = 20 periods). Then, the current bond price is $1,081.35.

6. SIMPLE BOND YIELDS TO MATURITY

Vasicek Co. has 12.5 percent coupon bonds on the market with eight years left to maturity. The bonds make annual payments. If one of these bonds currently sells for $1,145.68, what is its YTM?

HP 10B		TI BA II Plus	
−1,145.68 **PV**		−1,145.68 **PV**	
125.00 **PMT**		125.00 **PMT**	
1,000.00 **FV**		1,000.00 **FV**	
8.00 **N**		8.00 **N**	
I/YR 9.79		**CPT** **I/Y** 9.79	

The bond has a yield to maturity of 9.79 percent.

7. CASH FLOW ANALYSIS

What are the IRR and NPV of the following set of cash flows? Assume a discount rate of 10 percent.

Year	Cash Flow
0	−$1,300
1	400
2	300
3	1,200

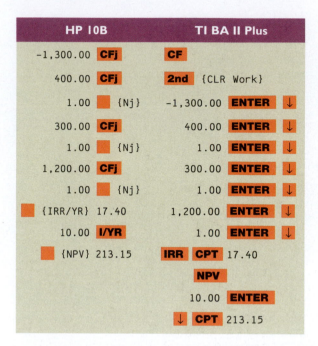

The project has an IRR of 17.40 percent and an NPV of $213.15.

8. LOAN AMORTIZATION

Prepare an amortization schedule for a three-year loan of $24,000. The interest rate is 16 percent per year, and the loan calls for equal annual payments. How much interest is paid in the third year? How much total interest is paid over the life of the loan?

To prepare a complete amortization schedule, you must amortize each payment one at a time:

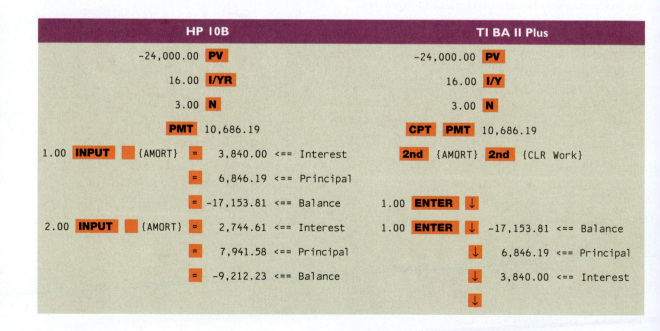

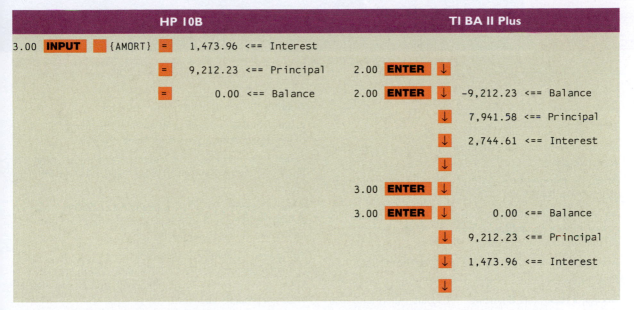

Interest of $1,473.96 is paid in the third year.

Enter both a beginning and an ending period to compute the total amount of interest or principal paid over a particular period of time.

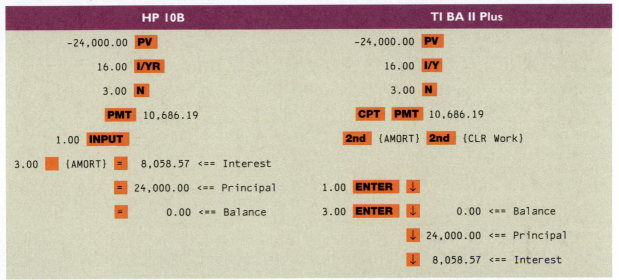

Total interest of $8,058.57 is paid over the life of the loan.

9. INTEREST RATE CONVERSIONS

Find the effective annual rate, EAR, corresponding to a 7 percent annual percentage rate, APR, compounded quarterly.

The effective annual rate equals 7.19 percent.

Glossary

ACP   Average collections period.

ADR   American depository receipt.

APR   Annual percentage rate.

APT   Arbitrage pricing theory.

Abnormal return   The difference between the actual and expected return.

Absolute priority rule (APR)   Establishes priority of claims under liquidation.

Absolute purchasing power parity   Idea that a commodity costs the same regardless of what currency is used to purchase it or where it is selling.

Accounts payable   Money the firm owes to suppliers.

Accounts receivable   Money owed to the firm by customers.

Accounts receivable financing   A secured short-term loan that involves either the assigning of receivables or the factoring of receivables.

Additions to net working capital   Component of cash flow of firm. Another term from change in net working capital.

Adjusted present value   Net present value adjusted for taxes, financial distress costs, and other financial side effects.

Advance commitment   A promise to sell an asset before the seller has lined up purchase of the asset.

Agency costs   Costs of conflicts of interest among stockholders, bondholders, and managers.

Agency problem   A conflict of interest between a principal and an agent.

Aging schedule   A compilation of accounts receivable by the age of account.

Allocated cost   A cost arising from use of a resource that is used in multiple projects.

American depository receipt (ADR)   A security issued in the United States to represent shares of a foreign stock. Enables the stock to be traded in the United States.

American option   An option contract that may be exercised anytime up to the expiration date. In contrast, a European option may be exercised only on the expiration date.

Amortized loan   Requires the borrower to repay parts of the loan amount over time.

Angel investors   Individuals providing initial capital to start-ups.

Annual percentage rate (APR)   The annual interest rate without consideration of compounding. Also called the stated annual interest rate.

Annuity   A level stream of equal dollar payments that lasts for a fixed time.

Annuity due   An annuity with an immediate initial payment.

Annuity factor   A term used to calculate the present value of the stream of level payments for a fixed period.

Annuity in arrears   An annuity with a first payment on date 1 rather than on date 0. Also called an ordinary annuity.

Appraisal rights   Right of shareholders of an acquired firm that allows them to demand that their shares be purchased at a fair value by the acquiring firm.

Arbitrage   Buying an asset in one market at a lower price and simultaneously selling an identical asset in another market at a higher price. This is done with no risk and after all costs are properly accounted for.

Arbitrage pricing theory (APT)   An equilibrium asset pricing theory that is derived from a factor model by using diversification and arbitrage. It shows that the expected return on any risky asset is a linear combination of various factors.

Arithmetic average   The sum of the values observed divided by the total number of observations—sometimes referred to as the mean.

Ask price   The price at which a dealer is willing to sell a security.

Asset beta   The sensitivity of the value of the firm's assets to changes in the market. Also called unlevered beta.

Assets   Anything that the firm owns that generates future benefits.

Availability float   Refers to the time required to clear a check through the banking system.

Average   Usually refers to the arithmetic mean.

Average collection period (ACP)   Average amount of time required to collect an account receivable. Also referred to as days' sales in receivables.

Average cost of capital   The weighted average cost of a firm's common equity, preferred stock, and debt. Typically called the weighted average cost of capital.

Average tax rate   Tax bill divided by taxable income.

Balance sheet   A statement showing a firm's accounting value on a particular date. It reflects the fact that assets must be equal to the sum of liabilities and equity.

Balloon payment   A large final payment on a loan.

Banker's acceptance   Agreement by a bank to pay a given sum of money at a future date.

Bankruptcy   State of being unable to pay debts. The owner-ship of the firm's assets is transferred from the stockholders to the bondholders.

Bankruptcy costs   An old term for financial distress costs.

Bargain purchase price option   Gives a lessee the option to purchase the asset at a price below fair market value when the lease expires.

Bearer form   A form of bond without record of the owner's name. Whoever holds the bond (the bearer) is the owner.

Benchmark   An index or average whose movement is considered a general indicator of the direction of the over-all market. Used as a comparison for other portfolio's performance.

Best-efforts underwriting   An offering in which an under-writer agrees to distribute as much of the offering as possible and to return any unsold shares to the issuer.

Beta   A measure of the sensitivity of a security's return to a systematic risk.

Bid price   What a dealer is willing to pay for a security.

Bid-ask spread   The difference between the bid and ask prices.

Bidder   A firm or person that has made an offer to take over a firm.

Binomial model   Method for valuing options that rests on the assumption that each period the price of an asset can take only one of two values.

Black-Scholes pricing equation   An exact formula for the price of an option. The formula requires five variables: the risk-free interest rate, the variance of the underlying stock, the exercise price, the price of the underlying stock, and the time to expiration.

Blanket inventory lien   A secured loan that gives the lender a lien against all the borrower's inventories.

Bond   A long-term debt of a firm. In common usage, the term bond often refers to both secured and unsecured debt.

Bookbuilding   The process of soliciting information about price and quantity for a new security offering.

Book value   The value as stated on the balance sheet.

Book value per share   Total accounting equity divided by the number of outstanding shares.

Brackets   The pecking order of banks involved in a secu-rity's issue.

Break-even analysis   Analysis of the level of sales at which a project would earn zero profit.

Broker   An entity that brings security buyers and sellers to-gether but does not maintain an inventory.

Bubble theory (of speculative markets)   Security prices sometimes move wildly above their fundamental values.

CAPM   Capital asset pricing model.

CAR   Cumulative abnormal return.

CD   Certificate of deposit.

CDS   Credit default swap.

Call option   The right—but not the obligation—to buy the underlying asset at a stated price within a specified time.

Call premium   The difference between the call price of a bond and its stated value.

Call price of a bond   Price at which a firm has the right to re-purchase its bonds or debentures before the stated maturity date. The call price is always set equal to or more than the par value.

Call protected   Describes a bond that is not allowed to be called at the current date.

Call provision   A written agreement between an issuing corporation and its bondholders that gives the corporation the option to redeem the bond at a specified price before the maturity date.

Callable bond   Refers to a bond that can be repurchased at a stated call price before maturity.

Capital asset pricing model (CAPM)   An equilibrium asset pricing theory that shows that the equilibrium expected return on all risky assets is a function of their covariance with the market portfolio.

Capital budgeting   The decision-making process for ac-cepting or rejecting projects.

Capital gains   The positive change in the value of an asset. A negative capital gain is a capital loss.

Capital gains yield   The rate at which the value of an invest-ment grows.

Capital intensity ratio   The ratio total assets to sales. Measures the amount of assets needed to generate one dollar of sales.

Capital market line   The efficient set of all assets, both risky and riskless, which provides the investor with the best possible opportunities.

Capital rationing   The case where funds are limited to a fixed dollar amount and must be allocated among competing projects.

Capital structure   The mix of the various debt and equity capital maintained by a firm.

Captive finance company   A wholly owned subsidiary that handles the credit function for the parent company.

Carrying costs   Costs that increase with increases in the level of investment in assets (usually refers to current assets).

Carrying value   Book value.

Cash budget   A forecast of cash receipts and disbursements expected by a firm in the upcoming periods. It is a short-term financial planning tool.

Cash concentration   Process a firm follows to move cash into its main accounts after collection.

Cash cow   A company that pays out a substantial proportion of earnings to stockholders as dividends.

Cash cycle   In general, the time between cash disbursement and cash collection. In net working capital management, it can be thought of as the operating cycle less the average accounts payable period.

Cash discount   A discount given for a cash purchase. Often offered to speed up the collection of receivables.

Cash equivalents   Marketable securities held by a firm. Also called near-cash.

Cash flow   Cash generated by the firm and paid to creditors and shareholders. It can be classified as (1) cash flow from operations, (2) cash flow from changes in fixed assets, and (3) cash flow from changes in net working capital.

Cash flow from operations   Cash flow generated from business activities such as sales of goods and services.

Cash offer   A public equity issue that is sold to all interested investors.

Cash ratio   Cash divided by current liabilities. Used to measure the short term solvency of the firm.

Cash transaction   A transaction where exchange is immediate. Contrasted with a forward contract which calls for future delivery of an asset at an agreed-upon price.

Cashout   Refers to a situation where a firm runs out of cash.

Certificates of deposit (CD)   Short-term loans to commercial banks.

Change in fixed assets   Cost of new fixed assets less proceeds from sales of fixed assets.

Change in net working capital   Change in difference between current assets and current liabilities from one period to the next.

Characteristic line   The line relating the expected return on a security to different returns on the market.

Classified board   A method of voting for a firm's board of directors that places only a portion of the board up for election each year.

Clean price   The quoted price on a bond.

Clientele effect   Argument that stocks attract clienteles based on dividend yield or taxes.

Coinsurance effect   Refers to the fact that the merger of two firms decreases the probability of default on either's debt.

Collateral   Assets that are pledged as security for payment of debt.

Collection float   An increase in book cash with no immediate change in bank cash. Generated by checks deposited by the firm that have not cleared.

Collection policy   Procedures followed by a firm in attempting to collect accounts receivable.

Commercial draft   A demand for payment sent to a customer's bank along with a shipping invoice.

Commercial paper   Short-term, unsecured promissory notes issued by corporations, usually with investment-grade credit. Their maturity ranges up to 270 days.

Common stock   Equity claims held by the "residual owners" of the firm who are the last to receive any distribution of earnings or assets.

Common-size statements   Financial statements expressed in percentages instead of total dollars to allow for comparison.

Compensating balance   Deposit that the firm keeps with the bank in a low-interest or non-interest-bearing account to compensate banks for bank loans or services.

Competitive offer   Method of selecting an investment bank for a new issue by offering the securities to the underwriter with the highest bid.

Compound interest   Interest that is earned both on the initial principal and on interest earned on the initial principal in previous periods.

Compound value   Value of a sum after investing it over one or more periods. Also called future value (FV).

Compounding   Process of reinvesting each interest payment to earn more interest. Compounding is based on the idea that interest itself becomes principal and therefore also earns interest in subsequent periods.

Concentration bank   A bank that pools funds obtained from local banks contained within some geographic region.

Conditional sales contract   An arrangement whereby the firm retains legal ownership of the goods until the customer has completed payment.

Conglomerate acquisition   Acquisition in which the acquired firm and the acquiring firm are not related, unlike a horizontal or a vertical acquisition.

Conservatism   A deviation from rationality in which a person is too slow to update their beliefs to new information.

Consol   A bond that never matures and carries a promise to pay a coupon forever.

Consolidation   A merger in which an entirely new firm is created.

Continuous compounding   Interest compounded continuously rather than at fixed intervals.

Contribution margin   Amount that each additional sale contributes to the profit of the whole project.

Controlled disbursement account   Allows a bank to determine total payments on an account in a given day and request that amount from a firm.

Conversion premium   Difference between the conversion price and the current stock price divided by the current stock price.

Conversion price   The ratio of the face value of a bond to the conversion ratio.

Conversion ratio   The number of shares per bond that a bondholder would receive if the bond were converted.

Conversion value   What a convertible bond would be worth if it were immediately converted into the common stock at the current price.

Convertible bond   A bond that may be converted into another form of security, typically common stock, at the option of the holder at a specified price for a specified period of time.

Corporate bond   A bond issued by a corporation.

Corporation   Form of business organization that is created as a distinct "legal person" composed of one or more actual individuals or legal entities.

Correlation   A standardized statistical measure of the dependence of two random variables. Defined as the covariance divided by the standard deviations of the two variables.

Cost of capital   The minimum rate of return required to undertake a project. Also called the required return.

Cost of debt   The cost of borrowing.

Cost of equity   The required return on the company's common stock in capital markets. It is a cost from the firm's perspective.

Coupon   The stated interest payment on a debt instrument.

Coupon rate   The annual coupon a bond pays divided by its face value.

Covariance   A statistical measure of the degree to which random variables move together.

Covered call   Buying an asset and selling a call on the same asset. Equivalent to selling a put on the same asset and investing at the risk-free rate.

Covered interest arbitrage   Borrowing in one country and investing in another to create an arbitrage profit made available by differentials in spot rates, future rates, and interest rates.

Credit analysis   The process of determining whether a credit applicant meets the firm's standards and what amount of credit the applicant should receive.

Credit default swap   A derivative investment that provides insurance against loss due to a bond default.

Credit instrument   Device by which a firm offers credit, such as an invoice or a promissory note.

Credit period   Time allowed for a credit purchaser to remit the full payment for credit purchases.

Credit scoring   Determining the probability of default when granting customers credit.

Creditor   Person or institution that holds the debt issued by a firm or individual.

Cross-rate   The exchange rate between two foreign currencies that are both quoted in some third currency.

Crown jewels   An antitakeover tactic in which major assets—the crown jewels—are sold by a firm when faced with a takeover threat.

Cum dividend   With dividend.

Cumulative abnormal return (CAR)   Sum of differences between the expected return on a stock and the actual return.

Cumulative dividend   Type of dividend on preferred stock that takes priority over dividend payments on common stock. Dividends may not be paid on the common stock until all past dividends on the preferred stock have been paid.

Cumulative probability   The probability that a draw from a distribution will be below a particular value.

Cumulative voting   A procedure whereby a shareholder may cast all of his or her votes for one member of the board of directors.

Currency swap   Agreement to pay cash flows in one currency and receive them in another.

Current asset   Asset that is in the form of cash or that is expected to be converted into cash in the next 12 months, such as inventory.

Current liability   Obligation that is expected to require cash payment within one year or the operating period.

Current ratio   Total current assets divided by total current liabilities. Used to measure short-term solvency of a firm.

Current yield   A bond's annual coupon divided by its current market.

DDM   Dividend discount model.

DMM   Designated market marker.

Data mining   Searching without the use of theory for relationships in data.

Date of payment   Date that dividend checks are mailed. Also called payment date.

Date of record   Date on which holders of record in a firm's stock ledger are designated as the recipients of either dividends or stock rights. Also called record date.

Dates convention   Treating cash flows as being received on exact dates—date 0, date 1, and so forth—as opposed to the end-of-year convention.

Days' sales in receivables   Average amount of time required to collect an account receivable. Also called the average collection period (ACP).

Dealer   An entity that maintains an inventory and stands ready to buy and sell at any time.

Debenture An unsecured bond, usually with maturity of 10 years or more. A debt obligation backed by the general credit of the issuing corporation.

Debt Loan agreement that is a liability of the firm. An obligation to repay a specified amount at a particular time.

Debt capacity Ability to borrow. The amount a firm can borrow up to the point where the firm value no longer increases.

Debt displacement The amount of borrowing that leasing displaces. Firms that do a lot of leasing will be forced to cut back on borrowing.

Debt service Interest payments plus repayments of principal to creditors, that is, retirement of debt.

Decision trees A graphical representation of alternative sequential decisions and the possible outcomes of those decisions.

Declaration date Date on which the board of directors passes a resolution to pay a dividend of a specified amount to all qualified holders of record on a specified date.

Deed of trust Written agreement between the corporate debt issuer and the lender. Sets forth maturity date, interest rate, and other terms. Also called indenture.

Default risk The chance that interest or principal will not be paid on the due date and/or in the promised amount.

Default risk premium Extra compensation required by bond holders because of the risk of a bond issuer defaulting.

Deferred call A provision that prohibits the company from calling the bond before a certain date. During this period the bond is said to be call protected.

Deferred taxes A noncash liability resulting from differences between accounting and true taxable income.

Deficit The amount by which a sum of money is less than the required amount; an excess of liabilities over assets, of losses over profits, or of expenditure over income.

Deliverable instrument The asset in a forward contract that will be delivered in the future at an agreed-upon price.

Depreciation A noncash expense, such as the cost of plant or equipment, charged against earnings to write off the cost of an asset during its estimated useful life.

Depreciation tax shield Portion of an investment that can be deducted from taxable income.

Designated market marker (DMM) A person assigned by a security exchange to maintain a fair and orderly market for a group of securities.

Dilution Loss in existing shareholders' value. There are several kinds of dilution: (1) dilution of ownership, (2) dilution of market value, and (3) dilution of book value and earnings.

Direct lease A lease under which a lessor buys equipment from a manufacturer and leases it to a lessee.

Direct placement Selling new securities directly to a purchaser rather than to the public.

Direct quote Price of a unit of foreign currency expressed in the buyer's home currency. Also called an American quote.

Dirty price The price of a bond including accrued interest.

Disbursement float A decrease in book cash but no immediate change in bank cash. Generated by checks written by the firm.

Discount bond If a bond is selling below its face value, it is said to sell at a discount.

Discount period Time allowed for a credit purchaser to remit the full payment for credit purchases less a discount.

Discount rate Rate used to calculate the present value of future cash flows.

Discounted payback period The length of time it takes for a project's discounted cash flows to equal its initial investment.

Discounting Calculating the present value of a future amount. The process is the opposite of compounding.

Distribution A type of dividend paid by a firm to its owners from sources other than current or accumulated retained earnings.

Diversifiable risk Any risk that specifically affects a single asset or a small group of assets. Also called unique, idiosyncratic, or unsystematic risk.

Dividend Payment made by a firm to its owners, either in cash or in stock. Also called the income component of the return on an investment in stock.

Dividend discount model (DDM) A model wherein a firm is valued by discounting its expected future stream of dividends.

Dividend payout ratio Amount of cash paid to shareholders expressed as a percentage of earnings.

Dividend yield Dividends per share of common stock divided by market price per share.

Dividends per share Amount of cash paid to shareholders expressed in dollars per share.

DuPont identity States that return on equity (ROE) can be expressed as the product of profit margin, total asset turnover, and the equity multiplier (one plus the debt to equity ratio).

Duration The weighted average time of an asset's cash flows. Often called effective maturity.

Dutch Auction A security offering in which the underwriter sets the offer price through an auction. Also called a uniform price auction.

EAC Equivalent annual cost.

EAR Effective annual rate.

EBIT Earnings before interest and taxes.

ECN   Electronic communications network.

EDI   Electronic data interchange.

EFN   External financing needed.

EMH   Efficient market hypothesis.

EOQ   Economic order quantity.

Earnings per share (EPS)   Net income divided by shares outstanding. Measures the profit generated per share.

Economic order quantity (EOQ)   Approach for explicitly establishing an optimal inventory level.

Effective annual rate (EAR)   The interest rate if it were compounded once per time period rather than several times per period.

Efficient market hypothesis (EMH)   States that prices of securities fully reflect available information. Investors buying bonds and stocks should expect to obtain an equilibrium rate of return. Firms should expect to receive the fair value for the securities they sell.

Efficient set   Graph representing a set of portfolios that maximize expected return at each level of portfolio risk. Also called the efficient frontier.

Electronic communications network (ECN)   A type of website that allows investors to trade directly with one another.

Electronic data Interchange (EDI)   General term referring to the practice of direct, electronic information exchange between all types of business.

Empirical models   Models based less on theory and more on regularities and relationships in market history.

End-of-the-year convention   Treating cash flows as if they occur at the end of a year (or, alternatively, at the end of a period).

Enterprise value   The cost to purchase all shares outstanding of a firm and pay off all debt less the firm's cash holdings.

Equity   Ownership interest in a firm.

Equity beta   The asset beta adjusted for leverage. The beta of the publically traded stock of the firm.

Equity kicker   Used to refer to warrants because warrants usually are issued in combination with privately placed bonds.

Equity share   Ownership interest.

Equivalent annual cost (EAC)   The net present value of cost divided by an annuity factor that has the same life as the investment.

Erosion   Cash-flow amount transferred to a new project from customers and sales of other products of the firm.

Eurobond   An international bond sold primarily in countries other than the country in whose currency the issue is denominated.

Eurocurrency   Money deposited in a financial center outside of the country whose currency is involved.

Eurodollar   A dollar deposited in a bank outside the United States.

European option   An option contract that may be exercised only on the expiration date. In contrast, an American option may be exercised any time up to the expiration date.

Event study   A statistical study that examines the effect of different events on outcomes, such as merger announcements on prices.

Exchange offers   Occur when a firm offers to exchange stock for debt, or vice versa.

Exchange rate   Price of one country's currency for another's.

Exchange rate risk   Risk that arises from holding currencies other than an entity's home currency when future exchange rates are uncertain.

Exclusionary self-tender   The firm makes a tender offer for a given amount of its own stock while excluding targeted stockholders.

Ex-dividend date   An individual purchasing a stock on or after its ex-dividend date will not receive the current dividend.

Exercise price   Price at which the put option or call option can be exercised. Also called the strike price.

Exercising the option   The act of buying or selling the underlying asset via the option contract.

Exotics   Complicated blends of derivative instruments.

Expected return   Average of possible returns weighted by their probability.

Expiration date   Maturity date of an option.

Ex-rights date   An individual purchasing a stock on or after its ex-rights date will not receive the rights.

External financing needed (EFN)   The plug variable used to balance pro forma statements.

Extra cash dividend   A dividend paid in addition to the regular cash dividend.

FASB   Financial Accounting Standards Board.

FIFO   First in-first out.

FTE   Flow to equity.

FV   Future value.

Face value   The value of a bond that appears on its face. Also referred to as par value or principal.

Factor   A financial institution that buys a firm's accounts receivables and collects the debt.

Factor model   A model in which each stock's return is generated by common factors derived from systematic sources of risk.

Factoring Sale of a firm's accounts receivable to a financial institution known as a factor.

Fair market value Amount an asset would sell for between a willing buyer and a willing seller both having knowledge of the relevant facts.

Feasible set The best possible expected return—standard deviation pairs that can be constructed from a set of assets. Also called an opportunity set.

Field warehouse financing A form of inventory loan in which a public warehouse company supervises the inventory for the lender.

File drawer problem The publication of research favors unusual and interesting results which skews the distribution of publications on certain topics.

Financial Accounting Standards Board (FASB) The governing body for U.S. accounting.

Financial distress Events preceding and including bankruptcy such as violation of loan contracts.

Financial distress costs Legal and administrative costs of liquidation or reorganization (direct costs); an impaired ability to do business and an incentive toward selfish strategies such as taking large risks, underinvesting, and milking the property (indirect costs).

Financial lease A long-term, noncancelable lease that generally requires the lessee to pay all maintenance fees.

Financial leverage Extent to which a firm relies on debt.

Financial ratio Ratio of two measures of firm status or performance.

Finished goods A form of inventory. Composed of products that are ready to ship or sell.

Firm commitment underwriting A type of underwriting in which an investment banking firm commits to buy the entire issue and assumes all financial responsibility for any unsold shares.

First in-first out (FIFO) An inventory accounting method that expenses inventory in the order it was acquired.

Fisher Effect The real rate of interest is invariant to the rate of inflation.

Fixed asset Long-lived property owned by a firm that is used by a firm in the production of its income. Tangible fixed assets include real estate, plant, and equipment. Intangible fixed assets include patents, trademarks, and customer recognition.

Fixed cost A cost that is not dependent on the amount of goods or services produced during the period.

Float The difference between bank cash and book cash. Represents the net effect of checks in the process of collection or clearing.

Floatation costs Costs firms incur when issuing new securities.

Floating-rate bond A debt obligation with an adjustable coupon payment. Also called a floater.

Flow to equity (FTE) A valuation approach that emphasizes cash flows to equity.

Forced conversion If the conversion value of a convertible is greater than the call price, the call can be used to force conversion.

Foreign bond An international bond issued by foreign borrowers in another nation's capital market and traditionally denominated in that nation's currency.

Foreign exchange market Market in which arrangements are made to exchange foreign currencies.

Forward contract An arrangement calling for future delivery of an asset at an agreed-upon price.

Forward trade An agreement to buy or sell based on exchange rates established today for settlement in the future.

Forward-exchange rate A future day's exchange rate between two major currencies.

Free cash flow Cash flow that is free to distribute to creditors and stockholders because it is not needed for working capital or fixed asset investments.

Frequency distribution The organization of data to show how often certain values or ranges of values occur.

Friendly takeover A takeover that occurs with the support of stockholders in the acquired firm.

Future value (FV) Value of a sum after investing it over one or more periods. Also called compound value.

Futures contract Obliges traders to purchase or sell an asset at an agreed-upon price on a specified future date. Futures differ from forward contracts in their standardization, exchange trading, margin requirements, and daily settling (mark to market).

GAAP Generally accepted accounting principles.

General cash offer A public issue of a security that is sold to all interested investors rather than only to existing shareholders.

General partnership Form of business organization in which all partners agree to provide some portion of the work and cash and to share profits and losses. Each partner is liable for the debts of the partnership.

Generally accepted accounting principles (GAAP) A common set of accounting concepts, standards, and procedures by which financial statements are prepared.

Geometric average Average compound return per period.

Gilts British and Irish government securities.

Going-private transaction Publicly owned stock in a firm is replaced with complete equity ownership by a private group. The shares are delisted from stock exchanges and can no longer be purchased in the open market.

Golden parachute   Compensation paid to top-level management when they are asked to leave the firm, such as if a takeover occurs.

Goodwill   The excess of the purchase price over the sum of the fair market values of the individual assets acquired.

Government bonds   Bonds issued by a government.

Green Shoe provision   A contract provision that gives the underwriter the option to purchase additional shares at the offering price to cover overallotments.

Greenmail   Payments to potential bidders to cease unfriendly takeover attempts.

Gross spread   Difference between the underwriter's buying price and the offering price. The spread is a fee for the service of the underwriting syndicate.

Growing annuity   A finite number of growing cash flows.

Growing perpetuity   A constant stream of cash flows without end that is expected to rise indefinitely.

Growth opportunity   Opportunity to invest in a positive NPV project.

Growth stock portfolio   A portfolio that has an average P/E ratio much in excess of the market average P/E.

Hedging   Taking a position in two or more securities that are negatively correlated (taking opposite trading positions) to reduce risk.

High-yield bond   Junk bond.

Holding period   Length of time that an individual holds a security.

Holding period return   The rate of return over a given period.

Homemade dividends   An individual investor can undo corporate dividend policy by reinvesting excess dividends or selling off shares of stock to receive a desired cash flow.

Homemade leverage   Idea that as long as individuals borrow (and lend) on the same terms as the firm, they can duplicate the effects of corporate leverage on their own.

Homogeneous expectations   Idea that all individuals have the same beliefs concerning future expected returns, variances, and covariances.

Horizontal acquisition   Merger between two companies producing similar goods or services.

Hostile takeover   A takeover that occurs against the wishes of stockholders in the acquired firm.

IFE   International Fisher effect.

IPO   Initial public offering.

IRP   Interest rate parity.

IRR   Internal rate of return.

Idiosyncratic risk   An unsystematic risk.

Immunized   Immune to interest-rate risk.

In the money   Describes an option whose exercise would produce profits. Out of the money describes an option whose exercise would not be profitable.

Income bond   A bond on which the payment of interest is contingent on sufficient earnings.

Income statement   Financial report that summarizes a firm's performance over a specified time period.

Incremental cash flows   Difference between the firm's cash flows with and without a project.

Incremental IRR   IRR on the incremental investment from choosing a large project instead of a smaller project.

Indenture   Written agreement between the corporate debt issuer and the lender. Sets forth maturity date, interest rate, and other terms. Also called deed of trust.

Independent project   A project whose acceptance or rejection is independent of the acceptance or rejection of other projects.

Indirect Quote   Price of a foreign currency expressed per unit of the buyer's home currency. Also called a European quote.

Inflation   A fall in the buying power of a unit of currency.

Inflation premium   The extra compensation required by bondholders because of inflation.

Inflation risk   Risk faced by Investors due to uncertainty about future inflation.

Information content effect   The rise in the stock price following the dividend signal.

Initial public offering (IPO)   The original sale of a company's securities to the public. Also called an unseasoned new issue.

Inside information   Nonpublic knowledge about a corporation.

Instruments   Financial securities.

Interest rate   The price paid for borrowing money.

Interest rate parity (IRP)   The interest rate differential between two countries is driven by the difference between the forward-exchange rate and the spot-exchange rate of the two countries' currencies.

Interest rate risk   The chance that a change in the interest rate will result in a change in the value of a security.

Interest rate risk premium   Extra compensation required by bond holders because of uncertainty about future interest rates.

Interest rate swap   Agreement to exchange one series of interest payments for another.

Internal growth rate   The maximum growth rate that can be achieved with no external financing of any kind.

Internal rate of return (IRR)   The discount rate at which the net present value of an investment is zero. A method of evaluating capital expenditure proposals.

International Fisher effect (IFE) States that real interest rates are equal from country to country.

Inventory A current asset composed of raw materials to be used in production, work in process, and finished goods.

Inventory loan A secured short-term loan using inventory as collateral. The three basic forms are a blanket inventory lien, a trust receipt, and field warehouse financing.

Inventory turnover ratio Ratio of annual sales to inventory. Measures how quickly inventory is produced and sold.

Investment banks Financial intermediaries who perform a variety of services including aiding in the sale of securities, facilitating mergers and other corporate reorganizations, acting as brokers to both individual and institutional clients, and trading for their own accounts.

Investment grade bond Debt that is rated BBB and above by Standard & Poor's or Baa and above by Moody's.

Invoice Bill written by a seller of goods or services and submitted to the purchaser.

Just-in-time inventory (JIT) An inventory management approach that emphasizes minimizing inventory and maximizing turnover.

Junk bond A speculative grade bond. Sometimes marketed as a high-yield bond.

LBO Leveraged buyout.

LIBOR London Interbank Offered Rate.

Last in-first out (LIFO) An inventory accounting method that expenses inventory in the reverse order of how it was acquired.

Law of one price (LOP) A commodity will cost the same regardless of what currency is used to purchase it.

Lease A contractual arrangement to grant the use of specific fixed assets for a specified time in exchange for payment, usually in the form of rent.

Lend To provide money temporarily on the condition that it or its equivalent will be returned, typically with an interest fee.

Lessee One that receives the use of assets under a lease.

Lessor One that conveys the use of assets under a lease.

Letter of comment A communication to the firm from the Securities and Exchange Commission (SEC) that suggests changes to a registration statement.

Level-coupon bond Bond with a stream of coupon payments that are the same throughout the life of the bond.

Leveraged buyout (LBO) Takeover of a company by using borrowed funds, usually by a group including some member of existing management.

Leveraged equity Stock in a firm that relies on financial leverage. Holders of leveraged equity face the benefits and costs of using debt.

Leveraged lease Tax-oriented leasing arrangement that involves one or more third-party lenders.

Leveraged recapitalization Using debt to repurchase shares or issue a dividend. Used to fend off takeover attempts.

Levered cash flow Unlevered cash flow less aftertax interest payments.

Liabilities Debts of the firm in the form of financial claims on a firm's assets.

Liability-to-equity ratio Similar to debt-to-equity ratio but takes into account off-balance sheet financing such as leases.

Limited partnership Form of business organization that permits the liability of some partners to be limited by the amount of cash contributed to the partnership.

Limited-liability instrument A security, such as a call option, or common stock, in which all the holder can lose is the initial amount put into it.

Line of credit An agreement that allows firms to borrow up to a previously specified limit. Can be committed (formal arrangement with commitment fee) or noncommitted (informal with little paperwork).

Liquidating dividend Payment by a firm to its owners from capital rather than from earnings.

Liquidation Termination of the firm as a going concern. Involves selling the assets of the firm and distributing cash to creditors and equity holders in order of established priority.

Liquidity Refers to the ease and quickness of converting assets to cash. Also called marketability.

Liquidity premium Extra compensation required by bondholders because of an asset's illiquidity.

Lockbox Post office box set up to intercept payments. The most widely used device to speed up the collection of cash.

Lockup Part of an underwriting agreement that specifies how long insiders must wait to sell their stock after an IPO. Typically 180 days.

London Interbank Offered Rate (LIBOR) Rate the most creditworthy banks charge one another for large loans of Eurodollars overnight in the London market.

Long hedge Protecting the future cost of a purchase by purchasing a futures contract to protect against changes in the price of an asset.

Long run A period of time in which all costs are variable.

Long-term debt An obligation having a maturity of more than one year from the date it was issued.

MIRR Modified IRR.

MRP Materials requirements planning.

Mail float Refers to the part of the collection and disbursement process wherein checks are trapped in the postal system.

Make a market To stand ready to buy or sell an asset.

Making delivery   Refers to the seller of a forward contract actually turning over to the buyer the asset agreed upon in the contract.

Marginal tax rate   Tax rate on the next dollar of income.

Marked to the market   Describes the daily settlement of obligations on futures positions.

Market capitalization   Price per share of stock multiplied by the number of shares outstanding.

Market model   A one-factor model for returns where the the factor is an index of the returns on the whole market.

Market portfolio   In concept, a value-weighted index of all securities. In practice, it is an index, such as the S&P 500.

Market price   The current price a security is trading at in the market.

Market risk   Systematic risk. This term emphasizes the fact that systematic risk influences to some extent all assets in the market.

Marketability   Refers to the ease and quickness of converting an asset to cash. Also called liquidity.

Marketable claims   Claims that can be bought and sold in financial markets, such as those of stockholders and bondholders.

Market-to-book ratio   Market price per share of common stock divided by book value per share.

Materials requirements planning (MRP)   A system for planning the levels of work-in-progress and raw materials a firm needs based on projected finished goods needs.

Maturity   The number of years until the face value of a bond is paid.

Mean   The sum of the values observed divided by the total number of observations—sometimes referred to as the average.

Merger   The absorption of one firm by another.

Minimum variance portfolio   The portfolio of risky assets with the lowest possible variance. By definition, this portfolio must also have the lowest possible standard deviation.

Modified IRR (MIRR)   An IRR calculation method that changes cash flows such that only one IRR exists. Cash flows are adjusted so that the sign on the cash flows only changes once.

Money market   Financial markets for debt securities that pay off in the short term (usually less than one year).

Monte Carlo simulation   An exercise that generates possible outcomes for a project based on a model of the underlying factors that drive project performance.

Mortgage securities   A debt obligation secured by a mortgage on the real property of the borrower.

Multiples   Another name for price ratios.

Municipal bonds   Bonds issued by a municipality such as a city or state.

Mutually exclusive investments   Investments where the acceptance of one project precludes the acceptance of one or more alternative projects.

NASDAQ   A computer network of securities dealers and others that disseminate security price quotes. Uses a multiple market maker system.

NOL   Net operating losses.

NPV   Net present value.

NPVGO model   A model for valuing the firm in which the net present value of new investment opportunities is explicitly examined. NPVGO stands for net present value of growth opportunities.

NYSE   New York Stock Exchange.

Negative covenant   Part of the indenture or loan agreement that limits or prohibits actions that the company may take.

Negative float   The firm's disbursement float is less than its collections float. Book balance is greater than available balance.

Negotiated offer   The issuing firm negotiates a deal with one underwriter to offer a new issue rather than taking competitive bids.

Net float   Sum of disbursement float and collection float.

Net operating losses (NOL)   Losses that a firm can take advantage of to reduce taxes.

Net present value (NPV)   The present value of future cash returns discounted at the appropriate market interest rate minus the present value of the cost of the investment.

Net working capital   Current assets minus current liabilities.

New York Stock Exchange (NYSE)   The largest stock market in the world in terms of dollar volume and total value of shares listed.

Nominal cash flow   A cash flow expressed in actual currency.

Nominal interest rate   Interest rate unadjusted for inflation.

Noncash item   Expense against revenue that does not directly affect cash flow such as depreciation and deferred taxes.

Nonmarketable claims   Claims that cannot be easily bought and sold in the financial markets, such as those of the government and litigants in lawsuits.

Normal distribution   Symmetric bell-shaped frequency distribution that can be completely defined by its mean and standard deviation.

Note   Unsecured debt, usually with maturity of less than 10 years.

OTC   Over the counter.

Odd-lot   Stock trading unit of less than 100 shares.

Off-balance sheet financing   Financing that is not shown as a liability on a company's balance sheet.

Offer price   The price at which a new security offering is made available to the public.

Open account   A credit account for which the only formal instrument of credit is the invoice.

Open market repurchase   Firm uses the market to buy back its own shares without revealing itself as the buyer.

Operating activities   Activities such as buying and paying for raw materials, manufacturing and selling a product, and collecting cash.

Operating cash flow   Earnings before interest plus depreciation minus taxes. Cash generated from operations less capital spending and working capital requirements.

Operating cycle   The time interval between the arrival of inventory stock and the date when cash is collected from receivables.

Operating lease   Type of lease where the period of contract is less than the life of the equipment and the lessor pays all maintenance and servicing costs.

Operating leverage   The degree to which a company's costs of operation are fixed as opposed to variable. The larger the fixed costs compared to variable costs, the larger the operating leverage.

Opportunity cost   Most valuable alternative that is given up. The discount rate used in NPV computation is an opportunity interest rate.

Opportunity set   The possible expected return—standard deviation pairs that can be constructed from a set of assets. Also called a feasible set.

Option   A right—but not an obligation—to do something.

Option writer   The seller of the option.

Order flow   The flow of customer orders to buy and sell stocks.

Ordinary annuity   An annuity with a first payment on Date 1 rather than on Date 0. Also called an annuity in arrears.

Out of the money   Describes an option whose exercise would not be profitable. In the money describes an option whose exercise would produce profits.

Over the counter (OTC) market   An informal network of brokers and dealers who negotiate sales of securities (not a formal exchange).

Oversubscribed issue   Investors are not able to buy all the shares they want, so underwriters must allocate the shares among investors. This occurs when a new issue is underpriced.

Oversubscription privilege   Allows shareholders to purchase unsubscribed shares in a rights offering at the subscription price.

PPP   Purchasing power parity.

PV   Present value.

Par value   The nominal or face value of stocks or bonds. For stock, it is a relatively unimportant value except for bookkeeping purposes.

Partnership   Form of business organization in which two or more co-owners form a business.

Payables turnover   Cost of goods sold divided by average payables. Used to measure how effectively a firm is managing its accounts payable.

Payback period   The length of time it takes for a project to return its initial investment.

Payment date   Date that dividend checks are mailed. Also called date of payment.

Payout ratio   Proportion of net income paid out in cash dividends.

Pecking order theory   Hierarchy of financing strategies in which using internally generated cash is at the top, issuing new equity is at the bottom, and issuing new debt is in the middle.

Percentage of sales approach   A financial planning protocol that specifies balance sheet and income statement items as a proportion of sales.

Perpetuity   A constant stream of cash flows without end.

Perquisites   Management amenities such as a big office, a company car, or expense-account meals.

Pie model of capital structure   A visual depiction of the firm that shows its full value as a circle with different claims dividing it into portions. Claims may be either marketable (stockholders) or nonmarketable (government).

Plug   A variable used to balance a financial plan.

Poison pill   Strategy by a takeover target to make their stock less appealing to a company that wishes to acquire it.

Political risk   Changes in value that arise as a consequence of political actions.

Portfolio   Combined holding of more than one stock, bond, real estate asset, or other asset by an investor.

Portfolio variance   Weighted sum of the covariances and variances of the assets in a portfolio.

Positive covenant   Part of the indenture or loan agreement that specifies an action that the company must undertake.

Positive float   The firm's disbursement float exceeds its collection float. Available balance exceeds book balance.

Post   Particular place on the floor of an exchange where transactions in stocks listed on the exchange occur.

Precautionary motive   The need for a safety supply of cash to act as a financial reserve.

Preemptive right   The right to share proportionally in any new stock sold.

Preferred stock A type of stock whose holders are given certain priority over common stockholders in the payment of dividends. Usually the dividend rate is fixed at the time of issue and no voting rights are given.

Premium bond If a bond is selling above its face value, it is said to sell at a premium.

Prepackaged bankruptcy Bankruptcy arrangements are worked out before the formal filing.

Present value (PV) The value of a future cash stream discounted to present day.

Present value factor Factor used to calculate the present value of an amount to be received in a future period.

Price-earnings (PE) ratio Current market price of common stock divided by current annual earnings per share.

Primary market Where new issues of securities are offered to the public.

Principal The value of a bond that must be repaid at maturity. Also called the face value or par value.

Private placement The direct sale of a bond or other security to a limited number of investors.

Private workout Financial restructuring that takes place in lieu of formal bankruptcy.

Pro forma statements Projected financial statements for future periods.

Processing float Refers to the time it takes the receiver of a check to process the payment and deposit it in a bank for collection.

Profit margin Net income divided by sales. Measures how much profit is generated per dollar of sales.

Profitability index A method used to evaluate projects. It is the ratio of the present value of the future expected cash flows after initial investment divided by the initial investment.

Promissory note Written promise to pay.

Prospectus The legal document that must be given to every investor who contemplates purchasing registered securities in an offering. It describes the details of the company and the particular offering.

Protective covenant A part of the indenture or loan agreement that limits or requires certain actions by a company during the term of the loan to protect the lender's interest.

Protective put Buying a put and the underlying asset.

Proxy A grant of authority by the shareholder to transfer his or her voting rights to someone else.

Proxy contest An attempt to gain control of a firm by soliciting a sufficient number of stockholder votes to replace the existing management.

Public issue Sales of securities to the public.

Purchase accounting Method of reporting acquisitions that requires that the assets of the acquired firm be reported at their fair market value on the books of the acquiring firm.

Purchasing power parity (PPP) The idea that the exchange rate adjusts to keep purchasing power constant among currencies.

Pure discount bond Bonds that pay no coupons and only pay back face value at maturity. Also referred to as "bullets" and "zeros."

Put bond A bond that allows the holder to force the issuer to buy the bond back at a stated price.

Put option The right—but not the obligation—to sell the underlying asset at a stated price within a specified time.

Put provision Gives the holder of a bond the right to sell back the bond to the issuer at a predetermined price.

Put-call parity The value of a European call equals the value of the underlying stock and a put minus the cost of investing in a risk-free asset such that the asset is worth the option strike price at expiration.

Quick ratio Quick assets (current assets minus inventories) divided by total current liabilities. Used to measure short-term solvency of a firm.

ROA Return on assets.

ROE Return on equity.

Random walk A statistical model where stock price changes from day to day are random; the changes are independent of each other and have the same probability distribution.

Raw materials A form of inventory. Composed of whatever materials exist at the starting point of a firm's production process.

Real cash flow A cash flow is expressed in terms of purchasing power, not actual dollars.

Real interest rate Interest rate expressed in terms of real goods. The nominal interest rate adjusted for the expected inflation rate.

Real option The option to perform an action in managing a business or as part of a project.

Receivables turnover ratio Total operating revenues divided by receivables. Used to measure how effectively a firm is managing its accounts receivable.

Record date The date on which holders of record in a firm's stock ledger are designated as the recipients of either dividends or stock rights. Also called date of record.

Red herring The first document released by an underwriter of a new issue to prospective investors.

Registered form A form of bond issuance wherein a registrar records who initially owns the bonds and updates records for changes in ownership.

Registration statement   Discloses all the pertinent information concerning a corporation that wants to make a public offering. The statement is filed with the Securities and Exchange Commission.

Regular cash dividend   Cash payment by firm to its shareholders, usually four times a year.

Regulation A   The securities regulation that exempts small public offerings (those valued at less than $5 million) from most registration requirements.

Relative purchasing power parity (RPPP)   Idea that the rate of change in the price levels in one country relative to the price level in another determines the change in exchange rate between the two countries' currencies.

Reorganization   Financial restructuring of a failed firm. Both the firm's asset structure and its financial structure are changed to reflect their true value, and claims are settled.

Replacement value   Current cost of replacing the firm's assets.

Representativeness   A deviation from rationality in which a person believes that small samples are accurate representations of true distributions.

Repurchase agreement (repos)   Short-term, often overnight, sales of government securities with an agreement to repurchase the securities at a slightly higher price.

Required return   The minimum rate of return required to undertake a project. Also called the cost of capital.

Residual value   Usually refers to the value of a lessor's property at the time the lease expires.

Retained earnings   Earnings not paid out as dividends.

Retention ratio   Retained earnings divided by net income. Also called the plowback ratio.

Return   Profit on capital investment or securities.

Return on assets (ROA)   Net income divided by total assets. Measures the profit per dollar of assets.

Return on equity (ROE)   Net income divided by total equity. Measures the profit per dollar of book equity.

Reverse split   A procedure whereby the number of outstanding stock shares is reduced; for example, two outstanding shares are combined to create only one.

Rights offer   An offer that gives a current shareholder the opportunity to maintain a proportionate interest in the company before the shares are offered to the public.

Risk aversion   The level of reward required to accept a unit of risk.

Risk premium   The excess return on the risky asset that is the difference between expected return on the risky asset and the return on risk-free assets.

Risk-free rate   The return on an asset with no default risk. Generally measured using U.S. treasury instruments. A proxy for the pure time value of money.

Road Show   Process of pitching a new security offering and soliciting information from potential buyers. Typically involves traveling from city to city.

Round lot   Common stock trading unit of 100 shares.

S&P 500   Gauge of large cap U.S. equities market.

SEC   Securities and Exchange Commission.

SEO   Seasoned equity offering.

SML   Security market line.

Sale and lease-back   An arrangement whereby a firm sells its existing assets to a financial company which then leases them back to the firm. This is often done to generate cash.

Sales-type lease   An arrangement wherein a firm leases its own equipment.

Sarbanes-Oxley Act   Legislation enacted by the U.S. Congress to try to protect investors from corporate abuses. Requires increased disclosure and transparency from public firms.

Scenario analysis   Analysis of the effect on a project of different scenarios with each scenario involving many variable changes.

Seasoned equity offering (SEO)   A new public stock issue after the company's stock has been previously issued publically. Also called a seasoned new issue.

Secondary markets   Where already-existing securities are bought and sold on the exchanges or in the over-the-counter market.

Security market line (SML)   A straight line that shows the equilibrium relationship between systematic risk and expected rates of return.

Semistrong form efficiency   Theory that the market is efficient with respect to all publicly available information.

Seniority   The order of repayment. In the event of bankruptcy, senior debt must be repaid in full before subordinated debt receives any payment.

Sensitivity analysis   Analysis of the effect on the project when there is some change in a critical variable such as sales or costs.

Separation principle   The principle that portfolio choice can be separated into two independent tasks: (1) determination of the optimal risky portfolio, which is a purely technical problem, and (2) the personal choice of the best mix of the risky portfolio and the risk-free asset.

Serial correlation   The correlation between a variable and the lagged value of the same variable.

Shareholder   Holder of equity shares in a firm. The terms shareholders and stockholders usually refer to owners of common stock in a corporation.

Sharpe Ratio   The risk premium of an asset divided by its standard deviation.

Shelf registration   An SEC procedure that allows a firm to file a master registration statement summarizing planned financing for a two-year period, and then file short statements when the firm wishes to sell any of the approved master statement securities during that period.

Shirking   The tendency to do less work when the possible return is smaller.

Short hedge   Protecting the value of an asset held by selling a futures contract.

Short run   A period of time in which certain equipment and resources are fixed.

Short sale   Sale of a security that an investor doesn't own but has instead borrowed.

Shortage costs   Costs that fall with increases in the level of investment in current assets.

Short-term debt   An obligation having a maturity of one year or less from the date it was issued. Sometimes called unfunded debt.

Side effects   Effects of a proposed project on other parts of the firm.

Sight draft   A commercial draft demanding immediate payment.

Simple interest   Interest calculated by considering only the original principal amount.

Sinking fund   An account managed by the bond trustee for the purpose of repaying the bonds.

Smooth dividends   The propensity for a firm's dividends to display less variability than its earnings.

Sole proprietorship   A business owned by a single individual. Pays no corporate income tax but has unlimited liability for business debts and obligations.

Speculating   Extremely high-risk investing.

Speculative motive   The need to hold cash in order to be able to take advantage of future opportunities.

Spot exchange rate   Exchange rate between two currencies for immediate delivery.

Spot interest rate   Interest rate on a loan that is made today.

Spot trade   An agreement today for settlement in two days.

Stakeholder   Anyone, other than stock or bond holders, who has a potential claim on the cash flow of the firm.

Standard deviation   The square root of the variance. The standard statistical measure of the spread of a sample.

Standardized normal distribution   A normal distribution with a mean of 0 and a standard deviation of 1.

Standby fee   Amount paid to an underwriter who agrees to purchase any stock that is not subscribed to by a public investor in a rights offering.

Standby underwriting   An agreement wherein an underwriter agrees to purchase any stock that is not purchased by a public investor.

Standstill agreements   Contracts wherein the bidding firm in a takeover attempt agrees to limit its holdings in the target firm.

Stated annual interest rate   The annual interest rate without consideration of compounding. Also called the annual percentage rate (APR).

Statement of cash flows   Accounting statement that explains the change in accounting cash and equivalents for a firm over time.

Static trade-off theory of capital structure   Theory that the firm's capital structure is determined by a trade-off between the value of tax shields and the costs of financial distress.

Stock dividend   Payment of a dividend in the form of stock rather than cash. A stock dividend comes from treasury stock, increases the number of shares outstanding, and reduces the value of each share.

Stock repurchase   Occurs when a firm repurchases their own shares.

Stock split   Increases the number of outstanding shares of stock while making no change in shareholders' equity.

Stockholder   Holder of equity shares in a firm. The terms stockholder and shareholders usually refer to owners of common stock.

Stockholders' books   Set of books kept by firm management for its annual report that follows Financial Accounting Standards Board (FASB) rules. The tax books follow the IRS rules.

Stockholders' equity   The residual claims that stockholders have against a firm's assets. Calculated by subtracting total liabilities from total assets.

Stockout   Running out of inventory.

Straight voting   A shareholder may cast all of his or her votes for each candidate for the board of directors.

Straight-line depreciation   A method of depreciation wherein each year the firm depreciates a constant proportion of the initial investment less salvage value.

Strike price   Price at which an option can be exercised. Also called the exercise price.

Strong form efficiency   Theory that the market is efficient with respect to all available information, public or private.

Subordinate debt   Debt whose holders have a claim on the firm's assets only after senior debtholders' claims have been satisfied.

Subscription price   Price that existing shareholders pay for a share of stock in a rights offering.

Sunk cost   A cost that has already occurred and cannot be reversed. Such costs should be ignored when deciding whether to accept or reject a project.

Supermajority provisions   A part of a corporate charter that requires a percentage of affirmative votes greater than 50% (often 66.6%) to approve important transactions such as mergers.

Sustainable growth rate   The maximum growth rate that can be achieved with no external equity financing while maintaining a constant debt-equity ratio.

Swap   Agreement between two counterparties to exchange cash flows over time.

Synergy   When if the value of a combined firm after a merger is greater than the sum of the values of the firms pre-merger.

Syndicate   A group of investment banking companies that agree to cooperate in a joint venture to underwrite an offering of securities for resale to the public.

Syndicated loan   A loan whose funding comes from multiple participants.

Synthetic stock   A combination of buying a call, selling a put, and investing at the risk-free rate that mimics the return on the underlying stock.

Systematic risk   A risk that affects a large number of assets, each to a greater or lesser degree. Also called market risk or common risk.

T-bill   Treasury bill.

TIPS   Treasury inflation-protected securities.

Takeover   General term referring to the transfer of control of a firm from one group of shareholders to another.

Taking delivery   Refers to the buyer actually assuming possession of the asset agreed upon in a forward contract.

Target cash balance   Optimal amount of cash for a firm to hold. Considers the trade-off between the opportunity costs of holding too much cash and the trading costs of holding too little.

Target firm   A firm that is the object of a takeover by another firm.

Target payout ratio   A firm's long-run dividend-to-earnings ratio.

Targeted repurchase   The firm buys back its own stock from a potential bidder, usually at a substantial premium, to forestall a takeover attempt.

Tax books   Set of books kept by firm management for the IRS that follows IRS rules. The stockholders' books follow Financial Accounting Standards Board (FASB) rules.

Taxability premium   Extra compensation required by bondholders because of unfavorable tax treatment.

Taxable acquisition   An acquisition in which shareholders of the acquired firm will realize capital gains or losses that will be taxed.

Tax-free acquisition   An acquisition in which the selling shareholders are considered to have exchanged their old shares for new ones of equal value and in which they have experienced no capital gains or losses.

Tender offer   Public offer to buy shares of a target firm.

Term structure   Relationship between spot-interest rates and maturities.

Terms of sale   Conditions on which firm proposes to sell its goods and services for cash or credit.

Time value of money   Price or value put on time.

Times interest earned (TIE) ratio   EBIT divided by interest. Measures how well a company has its interest obligation covered.

Tombstone   An advertisement that announces a public offering of securities. It identifies the issuer, the type of security, the underwriters, and where additional information is available.

Total asset turnover ratio   Sales divided by total assets. Used to measure how effectively a firm is using its assets.

Total cash flow of the firm   Total cash inflow minus total cash outflow.

Total debt ratio   Total debt divided by total assets.

Total dollar return   The sum of dividend income and capital gain or loss on an investment.

Trade acceptance   Written demand that has been accepted by a firm to pay a given sum of money at a future date.

Trade credit   Credit granted to other firms.

Trading range   Idea that investors prefer when the price of a firm's stock falls within certain bounds. An incentive to perform stock splits.

Transactions motive   The need to hold cash that arises from normal disbursement and collection activities of the firm.

Treasury bill   Short-term, discount government debt maturing in less than one year.

Treasury bond   Long-term federal government debt obligations.

Treasury inflation-protected securities (TIPS)   U.S. government securities that promise payment in real, not nominal, terms.

Treasury stock   Shares of stock that have been issued and then repurchased by a firm.

Treasury yield curve   Plot of Treasury yields relative to maturity.

Triangular arbitrage   Performing three offsetting deals simultaneously to obtain an arbitrage profit.

Trust receipt   A device by which the borrower holds the inventory in "trust" for the lender.

Unbiased forward rate (UFR) States that the forward rate is equal to the expected spot rate.

Uncovered interest parity (UIP) States that the expected currency spot rate is a function of the current spot rate and the interest rates in the countries.

Underpricing Issuing of securities below the fair market value.

Underwriter An investment firm that buys an issue of security from the firm and resells it to the investors.

Underwriting discount Difference between the underwriter's buying price and the offering price. A fee for the service of the underwriting syndicate.

Unfunded debt Short-term debt.

Unlevered beta The sensitivity of the value of the firm's assets to the market direction. Also called asset beta.

Unlevered cash flow Cash flow available to equityholders in a firm if the firm had no debt.

Unseasoned new issue Initial public offering (IPO).

Unsystematic risk Any risk that specifically affects a single asset or a small group of assets. Also called unique, idiosyncratic, or diversifiable risk.

VC Venture capital.

Value additivity (VA) principle The value of the firm is the sum of the values of the firm's different projects, divisions, or entities.

Value portfolio Portfolio of common share stocks that have an average P/E ratio substantially less than that of the market index.

Variable cost A cost that varies directly with volume and is zero when production is zero.

Variance The average squared deviation from the mean.

Venture capital (VC) Early-stage financing of young companies seeking to grow rapidly.

Vertical acquisition Acquisition in which the acquired firm and the acquiring firm are at different steps in the same production process.

WACC Weighted average cost of capital.

Waiting period Time during which the Securities and Exchange Commission studies a firm's registration statement. During this period the firm may distribute a preliminary prospectus.

Warrant A security that gives the holder the right—but not the obligation—to buy shares of common stock directly from a company at a fixed price for a given time period.

Weak form efficiency Theory that the market is efficient with respect to historical price information.

Weighted average cost of capital (WACC) The weighted average cost of a firm's common equity, preferred stock, and debt.

White knight A friendly new bidder in a hostile takeover contest.

White squire A third party in a takeover attempt who is invited to make a significant investment in the target firm by the target firm.

Winner's curse The average investor wins—that is, gets his desired allocation of a new security issue—because those who knew better avoided the issue.

Wire transfer An electronic transfer of funds from one bank to another that eliminates the mailing and check clearing times associated with other cash-transfer methods.

Working capital management A term used to describe short-term financial management.

Work-in-progress A form of inventory. Composed of unfinished products.

YTM Yield to maturity.

Yankee bonds Foreign bonds denominated in U.S. dollars issued in the United States by foreign banks and corporations.

Yield to maturity (YTM) The discount rate that equates the present value of the interest payments and redemption value of a bond with the present price of a bond.

Zero-balance account (ZBA) A checking account in which a zero balance is maintained by a transfer of funds from a master account in an amount only large enough to cover checks presented.

Zero coupon bonds Bonds with no coupons.

Name Index

A

Agrawal, Anup, 544
Ai, Henfjie, 453
Allen, Franklin, 596
Allen, Jeffrey, 913
Altman, Edward I., 525–526, 924–925, 930–931
Andrade, Gregor, 526, 897, 906
Ang, J., 598, 670
Asquith, Paul, 594, 761

B

Banz, R. W., 388, 451
Bar-Or, Yuval, 526
Barnea, A., 759
Becher, David A., 460
Bell, Alexander Graham, 447
Benioff, Marc, 627
Beranek, W., 933
Bernanke, Ben, 120
Bernardo, Antonio, 596
Bhattacharya, S., 595
Biddle, G. C., 456
Boehmer, R., 933
Boone, Audra L., 882
Booth, J., 640
Brav, A., 602
Brigham, E. F., 758
Briloff, Abraham, 60
Bris, Arturo, 526, 927
Bruno, A. V., 619

C

Campbell, Cynthia J., 761
Caton, Gary L., 761
Chatterjee, S., 934
Chen, N., 385
Chew, Donald H., 593
Coval, Joshua, 447
Cowan, A. R., 761
Cox, John C., 772
Cutler, David M., 526–527

D

Dabora, Emil M., 450
Datta, Sudip, 907
Davydenko, Sergei A., 929
DeAngelo, Harry, 547–548, 593, 599, 603
Deangelo, Linda, 593, 599, 603
Dhillon, U. S., 934
Dimson, Elroy, 321–323, 360
Dodge, Craig, 17
Dolvin, Steven, 292, 469

E

Ebbers, Bernie, 17
Eberhart, Allan C., 933
Ederington, Louis h., 761
Ellison, Lawrence, 15, 722

F

Fama, Eugene F., 388, 401, 453, 455, 599
Fan, Joseph P. H., 545
Fisher, Irving, 260
Flath, D., 669
Franklin, Benjamin, 91
Franks, Julian R., 929
French, Kenneth R., 388, 401, 453, 599
Froot, Kenneth A., 450

G

Gilson, Stuart C., 926, 932
Grabowski, Roger J., 323
Graham, John R., 157–158, 211, 220, 398, 408, 544–546, 597, 602
Grullon, Gustavo, 590

H

Hall, Brian J., 461
Hansen, Robert S., 593, 628
Harford, Jarrad, 907
Harris, M., 760
Hartford, Jarrad, 831
Harvey, Campbell R., 157–158, 211, 220, 398, 408, 545–546, 602
Haugen, R. A., 759
Heron, R., 897
Higgins, Robert C., 75
Hong, H., 456
Hull, John C., 694, 734

I

Ibbotson, Roger G., 307–310, 315
Ikenberry, D., 458
Ingersoll, Jonathan E., 760, 772
Inselbag, I., 560
Iskandar-Datta, Mai, 907

J

Jensen, Michael C., 536, 539, 589, 889
Jordan, Bradford D., 292, 445, 449, 469

K

Kaplan, R. S., 456
Kaplan, Steven, 526, 912
Karolyi, Andrew, 17

Kaufold, H., 560
Keim, D. B., 451
Keynes, John Maynard, 449, 533, 829
Kolasinski, Adam, 450, 452
Kose, John, 596, 926, 932
Kumar, Alok, 597
Kumar, Raman, 593

L

Lai, Kam Wah, 640
Lakonishok, J., 458
Lamont, Owen, 450
Lang, Larry H. P., 539, 926, 932
Lease, Ronald, 935
Lee, I., 633–634, 636
Levine, R., 447
Lewis, M., 760
Li, Xu, 450, 452
Lie, E., 897
Liebman, Jeffrey B., 461
Lindahl, F. W., 456
Lintner, John, 361, 600
Litwak, Mark, 159
Lochhead, S., 633–634, 636
Lubben, Stephen J., 526

M

McConnell, John J., 913, 933, 935
McGrattan, E. R., 441
Majluf, N., 897
Malkiel, B. G., 439
Malmendier, Ulrike, 907
Mandelker, G., 456
Mansi, Sattar A., 831
Markowtiz, Harry, 347
Marsh, Paul, 321–323, 360
Masulis, Ronald, 900
Maxwell, William F., 831
Mazzeo, M. A., 761
Meckling, W., 536
Mehra, R., 323
Metrick, Andrew, 618
Michaely, Roni, 590, 594, 602, 913
Mikkelson, W. H., 758
Miller, Merton, 292, 433, 495, 504–505, 532, 543, 595
Miller, Thomas, 469
Mitchell, M., 897
Mitchell, Mark, 906
Modigliani, Franco, 495, 504–505, 532
Moeller, Sara, 904–905
Moonves, Leslie, 15
Moore, W. T., 761

Subject Index

Some Commonly Used Notations

AR	Abnormal return	$R_B(1 - t_C)$	After-tax cost of debt
APT	Arbitrage pricing theory	R_F	Risk-free interest rate
CAPM	Capital asset pricing model	R	Nominal interest rate
CAR	Cumulative abnormal return	r	Real interest rate
C_t	Cash flow at period t	R_S	Cost of equity
Corr(x, y) or ρ_{xy}	Correlation between x and y	$\overline{R}$ or $E(R)$	Expected returns
		R^2	R squared
Cov(x, y) or σ_{xy}	Covariance between x and y	RP	Risk premium
d	Dividend payout ratio	$S_£(t)$	Spot exchange rate between British pound and U.S. dollar at time t
Dep	Depreciation		
Div_t	Dividend payment at period t	**SML**	Security market line
e	2.71828 (base for natural logarithms)	t_c	Corporate income tax rate
E	Exercise price of option	V_L	Value of a levered firm $(V_L = B + S)$
EBIT	Earnings before interest and taxes		
EPS	Earnings per share	V_U	Value of an unlevered firm $(V_U = S)$
g	Growth rate	r_{WACC}	Weighted average cost of capital
IRR	Internal rate of return	β	Beta; the slope of the market model; a measure of risk
L_t	Lease payment in year t		
NPV	Net present value	β_{asset}	Asset beta or firm beta
P_t	Price of stock at time t	β_{equity}	Equity beta
PV	Present value	σ	Standard deviation
R_m	Return on market portfolio	σ^2	Variance
R_p	Return on portfolio P	π	Inflation rate
R_B	Cost of debt	Σ	Sum of

Some Useful Formulas

1 Present Value (Chapter 4)

The discounted value of T future cash flows

$$PV = \frac{C_1}{1 + r} + \frac{C_2}{(1 + r)^2} + \cdots + \frac{C_T}{(1 + r)^T}$$

$$= \sum_{t=1}^{T} \frac{C_t}{(1 + r)^t}$$

2 Net Present Value (Chapter 4)

Present value minus initial costs

$$NPV = PV - Cost$$

$$C_0 = -Cost$$

$$NPV = -C_0 + \sum_{t=1}^{T} \frac{C_t}{(1 + r)^t}$$

3 Perpetuity (Chapter 4)

The value of C received each year, forever

$$PV = \frac{C}{r}$$

4 Annuity (Chapter 4)

The value of C received each year for T years

$$PV = C\left[\frac{1 - \frac{1}{(1 + r)^T}}{r}\right]$$

5 Growing Perpetuity (Chapter 4)

The value of a perpetuity that grows at rate g, where the first payment is C

$$PV = \frac{C}{r - g}$$

6 Growing Annuity (Chapter 4)

The value of a T-period annuity that grows at the rate g, where the first payment is C

$$PV = C\left[\frac{1}{r - g} - \frac{1}{r - g} \times \left(\frac{1 + g}{1 + r}\right)^T\right]$$

7 Measures of Risk for Individual Assets (Chapter 11)

$$Var(R_A) = \sigma_A^2 = \text{Expected value of } (R_A - \overline{R}_A)^2$$

$$SD(R_A) = \sigma_A = \sqrt{Var(R_A)}$$

$$Cov(R_A, R_B) = \sigma_{AB} = \text{Expected value of}$$

$$\left[(R_A - \overline{R}_A)(R_B - \overline{R}_B)\right]$$

$$Corr(R_A, R_B) = \rho_{AB} = Cov(R_A R_B)/\sigma_A \sigma_B$$

8 Expected Return on a Portfolio of Two Assets (Chapter 11)

$$\overline{R}_p = X_A\overline{R}_A + X_B\overline{R}_B$$

9 Variance of a Portfolio of Two Assets (Chapter 11)

$$\sigma_p^2 = X_A^2 \times \sigma_A^2 + 2X_A X_B \times \sigma_{AB} + X_B^2 \times \sigma_B^2$$

10 Beta of a Security (Chapter 11)

$$\beta_A = \frac{Cov(R_A, R_M)}{\sigma^2(R_M)}$$

11 Capital Asset Pricing Model (Chapter 11)

$$\overline{R}_A = R_F + \beta_A \times (\overline{R}_M - R_F)$$

12 k-Factor Model (Chapter 12)

$$R_i = R_F + B_{i1}F_1 + \beta_{i2}F_2 + \cdots + \beta_{ik}F_k + \epsilon_j$$

13 Leverage and the Cost of Equity (Chapter 16)

Before tax:

$$R_S = R_0 + \frac{B}{S}(R_0 - R_B)$$

After tax:

$$R_S = R_0 + \frac{B}{S}(1 - T_C)(R_0 - R_B)$$

14 Value of the Firm under Corporate Taxes (Chapter 16)

$$V_L = V_U + t_C B$$

15 Weighted Average Cost of Capital (Chapter 16)

$$\left(\frac{S}{S + B}\right)R_S + \left(\frac{B}{S + B}\right)R_B(1 - t_c)$$

16 Equity Beta (Chapter 18)

No-tax case:

$$\beta_{Equity} = \beta_{Asset}\left(1 + \frac{Debt}{Equity}\right)$$

Corporate tax case:

$$\beta_{Equity} = \left(1 + \frac{(1 - t_C)Debt}{Equity}\right)\beta_{Unlevered\ firm}$$

17 Black-Scholes Model (Chapter 22)

$$C = SN(d_1) - Ee^{-Rt}N(d_2)$$

where $d_1 = \left[\ln(S/E) + (R + \sigma^2/2)t\right]/\sqrt{\sigma^2 t}$

$$d_2 = d_1 - \sqrt{\sigma^2 t}$$